Data Science with Artificial Intelligence, Machine Learning and Deep Learning

SIMPLIFIED Q&A BOOK

DR. RAJIV CHOPRA

KHANNA BOOK PUBLISHING CO. (P) LTD.

Publisher of Engineering and Computer Books

4C/4344, Ansari Road, Darya Ganj, New Delhi-110002

Phone : 011-23244447-48 **Mobile:** +91-9910909320

E-mail : contact@khannabooks.com

Website : www.khannabooks.com

Dear Readers,

To prevent the piracy, this book is secured with HIGH SECURITY HOLOGRAM on the front title cover. In case you don't find the hologram on the front cover title, please write us to at contact@khannabooks.com or whatsapp us at +91-99109 09320 and avail special gift voucher for yourself.

Specimen of Hologram on front Cover title:

Moreover, there is a SPECIAL DISCOUNT COUPON for you with EVERY HOLOGRAM.

How to avail this SPECIAL DISCOUNT:

Step 1: Scratch the hologram

Step 2: Under the scratch area, your "coupon code" is available

Step 3: Logon to www.khannabooks.com

Step 4: Use your "coupon code" in the shopping cart and get your copy at a special discount

Step 5: Enjoy your reading!

Thanks,
Khanna Publishing House

ISBN: 978-93-5538-082-1

Data Science With Artificial Intelligence, Machine Learning and Deep Learning

by Dr. Rajiv Chopra

First Edition: 2022
Reprint: 2024, 2027

To view complete list of books, please scan the QR Code:

Published by:

Khanna Book Publishing Co. (P) Ltd.

CIN: U22110DL1998PTC095547

Visit us at: www.khannabooks.com

Write us at: contact@khannabooks.com

Printed in Bharat.

MAULANA ABUL KALAM AZAD UNIVERSITY OF TECHNOLOGY, WEST BENGAL

(FORMERLY KNOWN AS **WEST BENGAL UNIVERSITY OF TECHNOLOGY**)

Main Campus : Haringhata, Nadia, Pin-741 249

Kolkata Campus : BF-142, Sector-I, Saltlake City, Kolkata-700 064, (India)

Website : www.wbut.ac.in

Prof. Saikat Maitra
Vice Chancellor

FOREWORD

Artificial Intelligence, Machine Learning, Deep Learning and Data Sciences have evolved in last few years. Each evolution started by the prevailing hardware and intelligence required by the humans. Today this is applicable in this era of Internet in which diverse computers distributed all over the world are interconnected.

It all started with Artificial Intelligence, followed by Machine and Deep Learning. The need is to handle this deluge of data being generated everyday and every second. To handle this big data, Data Sciences is a must.

This book by Dr. Rajiv Chopra is a very useful addition to the library of the books on Data Sciences. The main benefit of the book is that it begins from basics and builds gradually to a substantially high level to enable students to become a Data Scientist. All important concepts are illustrated with diagrams and case studies.

This book is a true companion of students and professors aspiring for Data Sciences and Artificial Intelligence. The book will remain ever youthful as the concepts described in the book are very much current; and delivers what it promises to the readers.

This book also offers a mix of insights and golden rules which are needed for Data Analysis. The book serves as a practical guide for engineering students of Data Science and Artificial Intelligence who are interested in Data Science and related domains.

I wish M/s Khanna Book Publishing Company Private Limited all the best on this publication.

Regards

Saikat Maitra

Dr. Saikat Maitra
Vice Chancellor

Phone : (033) 2321-7578 / 2321 1327, Ext. 101, Fax : (033) 2334 1030, E-mail : vc@wbut.ac.in

ACKNOWLEDGEMENT

It is indeed a great pleasure to acknowledge my gratitude to many persons involved, directly or indirectly, in the writing of this book. First of all, I would like to thank the almighty God who gave us the inspiration to start and complete this task. I also thank undergraduate and graduate teaching assistants for providing valuable inputs on this text.

I am also grateful to M/s Khanna book publishing Co. Pvt. Ltd and the staff of editorial department for their encouragement and support throughout this project.

Finally, I would like to thank my parents and my family—Dr. J. R. Chopra, Ms. Sushma Chopra, my spouse Shakti Chopra and my twin babies Arjeesh Chopra (son) and Arshitha Chopra (daughter) for their blessings and patience.

I appreciate their support and many other contributions more than we can express in any acknowledgements here.

CONTENTS

UNIT-I

ARTIFICIAL INTELLIGENCE

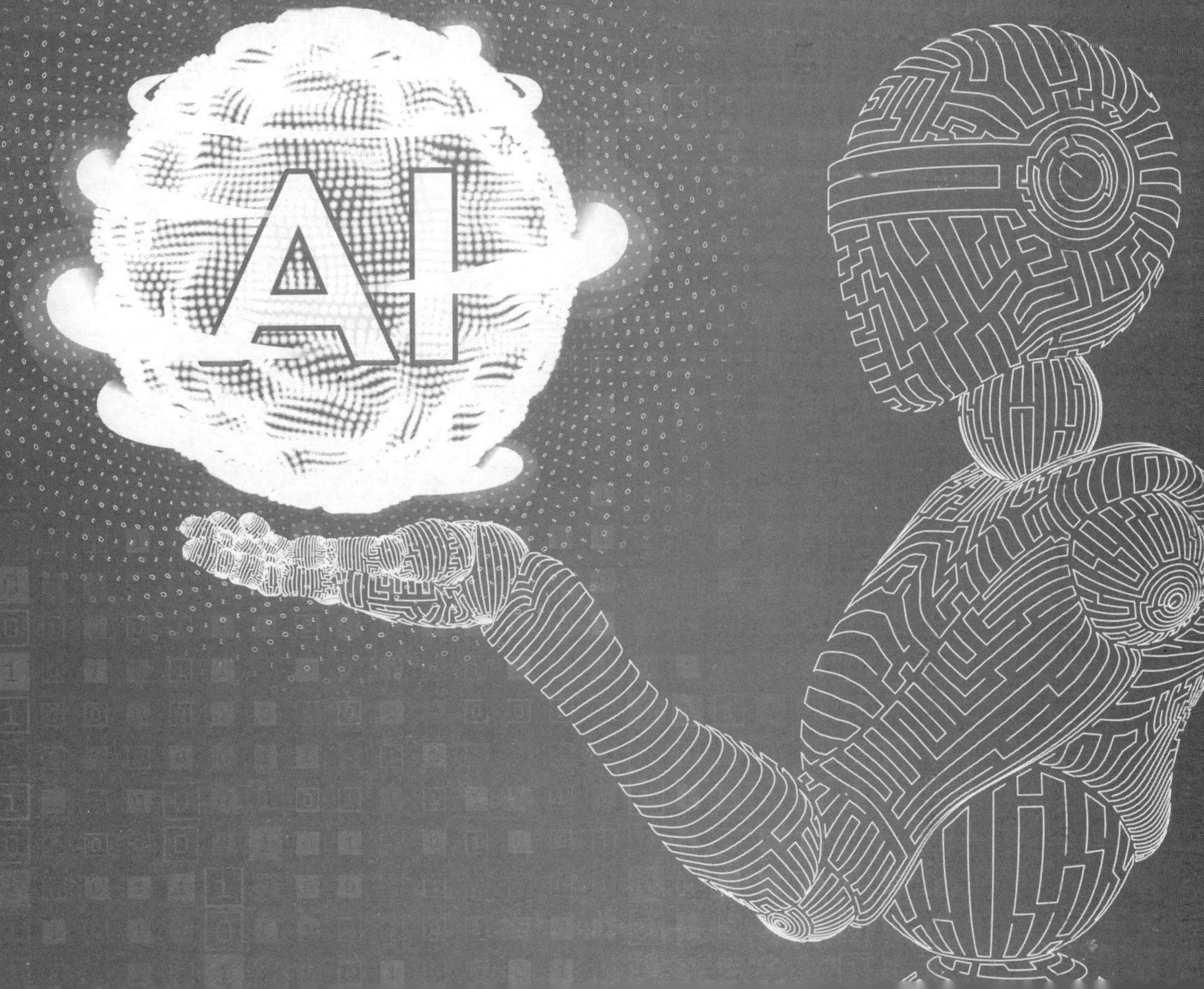

1 Introduction to AI

Q.1. What do you mean by the word "Artificial" and "Intelligence" in AI?

Ans. Artificial Intelligence (AI) is the branch of computer science that is concerned with building machines that simulate human behavior. This term was coined by John McCarthy at MIT, USA. AI includes machine learning and deep learning, its applications range from game playing, expert systems, natural language processing, neural networks, robotics to driverless cars, better medical diagnostics, aircrafts and so on. We are reminded of Douglas Hofstadter statement- "sometimes it seems as though each step towards AI, rather than producing something which everyone agrees is real intelligence, merely reveals what real intelligence is NOT". AI is now a part of everyday parlance. AI gives new life to systems engineering. Even chemical engineering has received a new dimension today due to AI and ML. These help in framing better models for such systems. According to a survey of >200 executives who are familiar with their company's use of cognitive technology shows that three-quarters of them believe that AI will substantially transform their companies within three years. AI can support three vital business needs-

- Automating business processes.
- Gaining insight through data analysis.
- Engaging with customers and employees.

Artificial Intelligence refers to systems that can analyze, reason and act on real-world events and data similar to or better than humans. Intelligence is the ability to analyze, reason and act on real-world events. This requires knowledge and intelligence about the business rules, validations and processing timelines. In conventional IT systems, AI is induced in them in many different forms. Induced intelligence includes-

- Transaction Processing Systems (TPS).
- Rule engines.
- Logic programming.
- Analytics.
- Event processing/handling.
- Robotic Process Automation (RPA).

In 1956, a group of avant-garde experts decided to organize a summer research project on AI. Four scholars: John McCarthy (Dartmouth college), Marvin Minsky (Harvard University), Nathaniel Rochester (IBM) and Claude Shannon (Bell Labs.)

Q.2. Give various definitions of AI as available in the literature. What is the objective of AI? What solutions does AI provide?

Ans. Several definitions of AI have been given in literature. Some of the definitions of AI are given below-

"The science and **e, 1984]**

It is observed that these definitions span along two directions-

- Thought process and reasoning.
- Behavior of the machine.

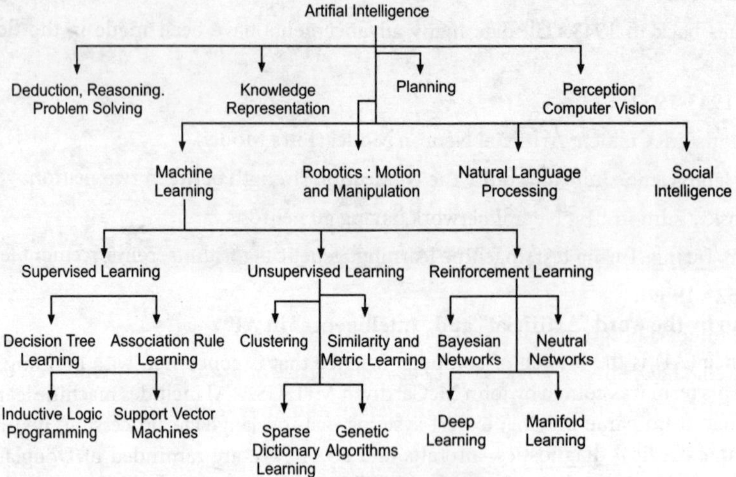

Fig. 1.1: AI Categories

Objective of AI : The theory and development of computer systems able to perform tasks normally requiring human intelligence such as visual perception, speech recognition, decision making and translation between language.

Solutions by AI : The chart below shows various AI software platforms that provide solutions to our industry and hence businesses.

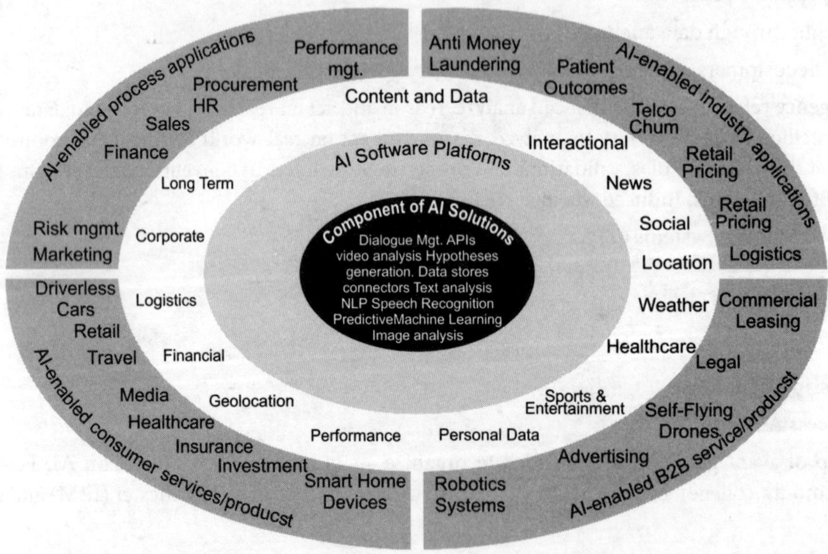

Fig. 1.2 : AI Platforms

Q.3. List some goals of AI.

Ans. Two types of goals of AI are found-

a. **Scientific Goal :** To find out which ideas about knowledge representation, learning, rule systems, search etc. explain various sorts of real intelligence. For example, expert systems that show intelligent behavior, learn and advice us. It is the application which provides the decision-making ability of a human expert in order to solve complex problems by reasoning through knowledge and cognitive computing.

b. **Engineering Goal:** To solve real world problems using AI techniques like knowledge representation, learning, rule systems, search etc. For example, implementation of human intelligence in machines (computers) *i.e.* creating computer systems that understand, think, learn and behave like humans.

Q.4. Throw some light on the 'History of AI'.

Ans. History of AI dates back to 1943. Till date many advancements have been made in the field of AI. The following cheatsheet clears this.

I. Starting Era (1943-1952) :

- ☐ **1943 :** W. Pitts, McCulloch: Artificial Neuron Model (Pitt's Model).
- ☐ **1949 :** D. Hebb: Hebb's Rule to modify the connection strength between two neurons .
- ☐ **1951 :** Minsky, Edmons: 1st Neural network having 40 neurons.
- ☐ **1950 :** Alan Turing: Turing test, machine learning, genetic algorithms, reinforcement learning.

II. Early Era (1952 - 1969):

- ☐ **1952 :** A. Samuel: a program that learns—Game of Checkers.
- ☐ **1956 :** Newell, Shaw, Simon: Logic Theorists, reduced size of proof of theorem.
- ☐ **1957 :** Newel, Simon: GPS-General Problem Solver-human way of thinking.
- ☐ **1958 :** John McCarthy: developed LISP programming language.
- ☐ **1960-1962 :** Widrow-Hoff: Adaline.
- ☐ **1962 :** Rosenblatt: gave proof of perceptron convergence.
- ☐ **1965 :** J. Weizenbaum: ELIZA chatterbot.
- ☐ **1966 :** Quillian: Semantic networks.
- ☐ **1969 :** Minskyand Papert: Perceptrons- a limitation of neural networks.

III. Serious Era (1952-1969) :

- ☐ Early systems had small or no knowledge about difficult and complex problems.
- ☐ Failure of machine translation, 1957.
- ☐ Non-tractable problems that AI was solving.
- ☐ Development of Perceptrons—led to blockage of further research in neural networks.

IV. KBS Era (1970-1979) :

- ☐ DENDRAL, a Knowledge based System, developed by Fiegenbaum, reasons molecular structures of organic compounds, has about 450 rules.
- ☐ MYCIN, developed by Shortliffe, introduced 'certainity factors' has 550 rules instead.
- ☐ More researches were made in field of Natural Language Processing (NLP).
- ☐ **PROLOG :** an AI programming language developed in Europe.
- ☐ **Minsky :** Frame theory, 1975.

V. AI as a Service Era (1980-2010) :

- ☐ AI becomes industry, 1980.
- ☐ McDermott, DEC R1 EXPERT SYSTEM developed, 1982.
- ☐ Backpropagation algorithms developed, 1980.
- ☐ Intelligent Agents.
- ☐ Robotics.
- ☐ Machine Learning.

VI. Deep Learning Era (2010- till date)

- ☐ Many layered/ multilayered Neural Networks used.
- ☐ Huge amount of data used on these neural models.
- ☐ Advances in computer vision, NLP, chemistry, physics, biology made.
- ☐ Virtual and augmented reality more popular.

Founding Fathers of Artificial Intelligence

The Dartmouth Summer Research Project on Artificial Intelligence, was a 1956 summer workshop, widely considered to be the Founding event of artificial intelligence as a field. Participants went on to discuss computer. Natural language processing. Neutral networks, theory of computation, abstraction and creativity.

Fig. 1.3: Founding Fathers of Artificial Intelligence

Q.5. What all domain/ Areas is covered by AI?

Ans. The following fig. 1.4 shows the domain area of AI.

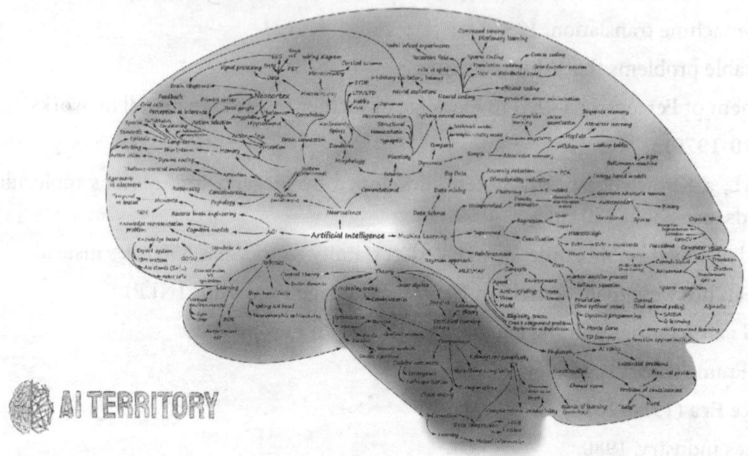

Fig. 1.4: AI Domain

Source: https://medium.com/swlh/the-map-of-artificial-intelligence-2020-2c4f446f4e43

Q.6. Give some 'Applications and Challenges of AI'.

Ans. The role of AI in education has been quite encouraging, exciting and engaging. As per a report by newscientist.com, an AI passed the English language test and achieved its best scores ever. This result is a breakthrough in AI field. AI applications in education includes AI-based online classes, enabling personalized learning, helping students to get better scores etc. personalized learning, voice assistants, smart contents, global learning, online classrooms, emotion recognition, virtual reality are some of its applications. A plethora of learning platforms is available online. Several AI based learning platforms exist as follows: -

1. **Beable :** It is an integrated system launched by Achieve 3000 that is a remote learning solution for middle and high schools in USA. It combines data science, automation and AI based solution to students.

2. **Little Dragon :** It focusses on behavioral and emotional aspects of learning. An emotional AI detects states like boredom and frustration and then it adjusts the contents to optimize the experience of learning.
3. **Brainly :** It is an AI based social learning community to help students.
4. **Quick Assessment :** Different AI-based online courses allow teachers to quickly assess a student's knowledge.
5. **Better Engagement :** Modern technologies like VR classrooms help students to get involved in the education process. It makes them more interactive too.
6. **Personalization :** Many AI-enabled algorithms can analyze student's interests and provide them more personalized trainings.
7. **Speedlabs :** It is an AI-based online learning platform founded by IIT and IIM alumni. It uses AI and ML technologies to provide customized platform.
8. **Videoken :** It is an AI-based platform that offers online video-based social learning platform. It makes informational videos richer, consumable and engaging too. It uses big data analytics, AI, ML and DL.
9. **Utter :** It is a chatbot-based application that allows users to learn English with the help of chatbots or tutors.

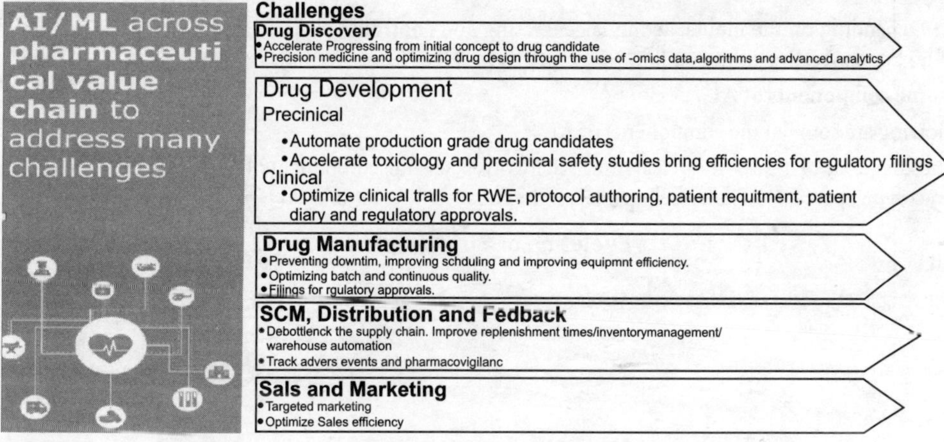

Fig. 1.5: AI/ML Value Chain

10. **Thinkster Maths :** It is an AI-based math learning platform that connects a world class syllabus with personalization.

AI a boom or a blessing for teachers? Yes, AI is a blessing for a teacher. AI technologies assist teachers to perform better, improves the teaching process and reduces teacher's load and thus improves the student's learning curves.

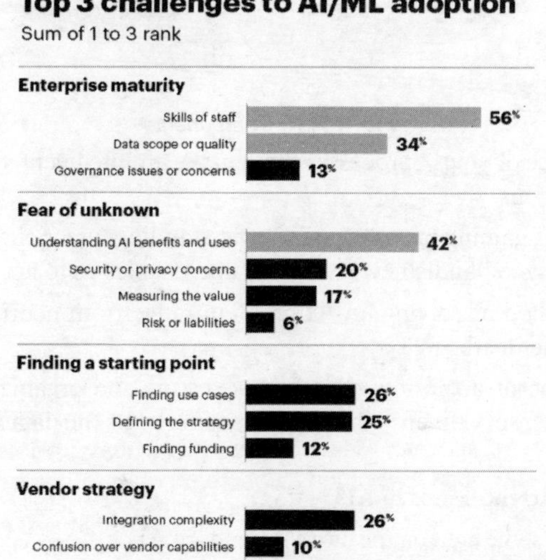

Fig. 1.6: Challenges of AI/ML

Recently, AI has been used to solve the world famous Schrodinger Equation in quantum chemistry. In another report from Accenture and Frontier Economics, labour productivity in developed countries can increase by up to 40% until 2035 with the help of AI. As far as developed countries are concerned, the increase in productivity that comes with AI is projected to be around 37% in Sweden, 35% in USA and 34% in Japan. Germany and Austria can maximize labour productivity by 30% by 2035.

Q.7. Categorize AI giving some examples.

Ans. AI has three main categories, namely –

a. Taking inputs (perception)—sensing.

b. Processing inputs (thinking)—reasoning.

c. Acting on it (acting)—acting.

Sensing means taking / reading data from the real world like recognizing objects, faces, cars, robotics, sonar etc.

Reasoning means finding out logically, what to do to achieve a goal, building new knowledge or dataset, deciding true of false etc.

Acting : Depending on the inputs, acting is generating and controlling actions, like in NLP, the action can be given a piece of text or converting it into audio.

Q.8. Name some components of AI.

Ans. The following are some of the components of AI-

From the diagram, of fig.1.7 it is clear that AI involves several components but out of these Reasoning, Learning, Problem solving, perception and intelligence are the most significant ones.

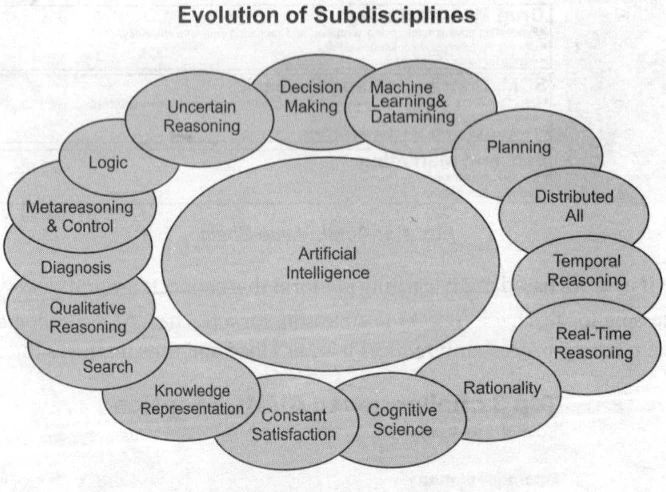

Evolution of Subdisciplines

Fig. 1.7: AI Components

Reasoning : It is the sequence of steps/ processes that enable an intelligent system to provide basis for actions, decision making and predictions.

Learning : It is the process of gaining knowledge by understanding, practicing, taught or experiences. It provides us the power to reason, ability to handle new situations and enables us to act in an intelligent way.

Problem Solving : The method of solving an AI problem range from heuristics to Fuzzy logic. It will include searches, reasonings and other methods.

Perception : It is the method of acquiring, decoding, selecting and organizing sensory data. Like humans do perception with the help of sensory organs while AI perception puts the data acquired by sensors in a meaningful way.

Q.9. Throw some light on the "Current trends in AI".

Ans. The following diagram shows some light on the current trends of AI-

Digital Twin Along With AI & ML Are Shaping The Future Of Industry. Artificial Intelligence (AI) and Machine Learning (ML) based solutions require aggregating, arranging and analyzing large sets of data and then make sense from it. We create 'models' from this data, and then 'train' them to behave in a real-world context.

At Honeywell, scientists are working on several cutting-edge technologies and initiatives. These include Quantum Computing, Blockchain-based solutions, Additive printing, Digital Twins, Unmanned Aerial Vehicles, Connected Aircrafts, smart and healthy buildings, Smart Cities, IIoT, Connected workers and supply chains, to name a few. All these will work in conjunction with the concepts of AI/ML.

Tiger Analytics has collaborated with leading agrochemical companies to develop deep learning-based solutions.

The most common cybersecurity tools such as anti-malware software or login audits won't be enough to control the cyber threats. The security risks in applications and web have grown at an unprecedented rate. The advancement of technology and the use of mobiles, web and the Internet of Things has led to the rise of vulnerable threats, due to which the data of many businesses and companies are at risk.

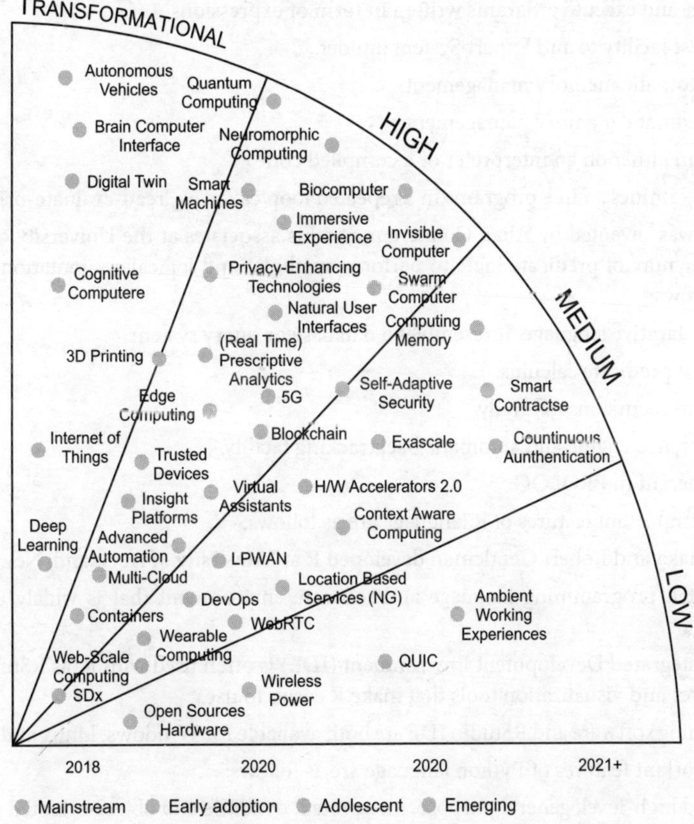

***Fig. 1.8:** Evolution of Technologies*

Artificial intelligence and machine learning can fight against cybercrimes as it helps by processing and analysing the huge amount of data and its behavioural patterns. Humans cannot process and analyse data as quickly as AI or ML automated engines. Both AI and ML can improve cybersecurity measures. While password protection or multi-factor authentication can be implemented in cybersecurity, machine learning algorithms can help classify the strength of a password and suggest complex and hard to guess passwords. It can work brilliantly with a biometric login that uses AI to detect physical traits.

India has the largest IT talent pool in the world. However, the country still lacks skilled cybersecurity professionals. Many experienced cyber experts are working for global giants in Silicon Valley, California. The new bundle of cybersecurity talents need the right exposure in India. Indians have raised the bar of IT across the world, and now it's time to make India a cyber hub.

Q.10. What do you mean by AI Programming Languages? Give examples and explain.

Ans. An AI program can be written in any programming language. Since AI programs mainly involve symbolic manipulations and not numbers, so we need some representation for these symbols. Two AI programming languages are very traditional, namely, LISP and PROLOG. LISP stands for List Processing and PROLOG stands for Programming Logic. There are several dialects of LISP like FRANZLISP, INTERLISP, MACLISP, QLISP, SCHEME, COMMON LISP AND XLISP. LISP was invented by John McCarthy during late 1950s. It is a language with simple syntax, with little or no data typing and dynamic memory management. **Please note that everything in LISP is a function.**

Some features of LISP are :

1. It is a functional language.
2. All data are in form of symbolic expression.
3. Lisp can interpret and execute programs written in form of expressions.
4. Lisp offers greatest facility to and Expert System builder.
5. Lisp supports automatic memory management.
6. Lisp supports automatic memory management.
7. Lisp programs run either on an interpreter or a compiled code.
8. The interpreter examines source programs in a repeated loop called as "read-evaluate-print" loop.

TURBO PROLOG was invented by Alian Colmeraur and his associates at the University of Marseilles during 1970s. PROLOG uses the syntax of predicate logic to perform symbolic and logical computations. Some salient features of PROLOG are as follows:-

1. PROLOG is a declarative language. It resembles a database or query system.
2. It uses language of predicate calculus.
3. It handles lists and recursions naturally.
4. It has inbuilt inference engine and automatic backtracking facility.
5. Parallelism is inherent in PROLOG.

R language : Some important features of R language are as follows:-

1. In 1990s, Ross Ihaka and Robert Gentleman developed R at University of Auckland, New Zealand.
2. It is an interpreted programming language and software environment that is widely used for data analysis and visualization.
3. The "RStudio" Integrated Development Environment (IDE) is often used with R, as RStudio provides a code editor, debugging features and visualization tools that make R easier to use.
4. The R programming software and RStudio IDE are both available for Windows, Linux and macOS operating systems.

Python : Some important features of Python language are as follows:-

1. It is a widely used high-level, general purpose, interpreted, dynamic and object-oriented programming language.
2. Its programming style emphasis code readability.
3. Its syntax allows programmers to code their logic in much fewer lines than in languages like C++ and Java.
4. It was created by Gudio Van Rossum in late 1980s.
5. Python was actually adopted from a comedy series of late seventies called "Monty's Python Flying Circus".
6. The design began in late 1980s and was first released in Feb. 1991.
7. Python 2.0 was released on 16th oct. 2000. It had many new features like a cycle-detecting garbage collector and a support for Unicode.
8. Python 3.0 was released on 3rd Dec 2008.
9. Many Python editors do exist. Some of them are as follows:-

a. Sublime Text—supported on Linux, WIN, Mac OS X.

b. SPE -Stani's Python Editor – supported on Linux, WIN, Mac OS X.

c. SciTE—supported on Windows and Linux.

d. Geany – supported on Windows, Linux, MAC OS X.

10. The IDEs (Integrated Development Environment) most suitable for Python are:-

a. PyCharm – supported on Windows, Linux, MAC OS X.

b. Wing IDE – supported on Windows, Linux, MAC OS X.

c. Pyzo – supported on Windows, Linux, MAC OS X.

d. PyScripter – supported only on Windows.

Note : Eclipse users who do not wish to switch to other IDEs can make use of PyDEV plugin for Python support.

Java : Java has simple coding algorithms that covers the key part of AI. Java is a decent alternative for AI development. Java supports all features that are required out of an AI program. It has swing, AWT, SWT toolkits.

C+ + : C++ is used to find AI solutions due to its speed.

Q.11. Explain 'The Turing Test'.

Ans. The Turing test is designed to determine whether a computer exhibits intelligence or NOT. A computer can be considered as smart, if and only if, a human interviewer cannot identify between an unseen human and a computer while conversating with them.

The Turing test consists of an imitation game. According to this test, "a computer is supposed to have artificial intelligence if it can mimic human responses under specific conditions". In the Turing test, if the human being conducting the test is unable to consistently determine whether an answer has been given by a computer or by another human being, then the computer is considered to have 'passed' the test.

In basic Turing test, there are three terminals. Two of the terminals are operated by humans and the third one is operated by the computer as shown in fig.1.9 Each terminal is physically separated from the other two. One human is designated as the questioner. The other human and the computer are designated as the respondents. The questioner interrogates both the human respondent and the computer according to a specified format, within a certain subject area and context and for a preset length of time (like 5 mins). After the specified time, the questioner tries to decide which terminal is operated by the human respondent and which terminal is operated by the computer. The test is repeated many times. If the questioner makes the correct* judgements in half of the test runs or less, the computer is considered to have artificial intelligence.

Fig. 1.9: Turing Test

*** Please note that the Turing test has been criticized due to the following reasons: -**

1. If the questioner formulates the queries that have narrow field of knowledge, such as, mathematical number theory and have answers in "Yes" or "No" then a computer exhibits human-like intelligence.
2. But if the response to questions is of broad-based, conversational nature, then a computer would not be expected to perform like a human being.

Also note that in some special cases, a computer may perform much better and faster than a human that the questioner can easily tell which is which. Google, Yahoo and AltaVista are examples of computer applications that outperform a human in a Turing Test, based on information searches.

To pass a Turing Test, a computer would need at least the following skills: -

a. **Natural Language Processing (NLP) :** It should be able to communicate in natural language like English.

b. **Knowledge Representation :** It should have knowledge and to store it somewhere.

c. **Automated Reasoning :** It should be able to do reasoning based on the stored knowledge.

d. **Machine Learning :** It should be able to learn from its environment at adapt to new situations.

e. **Vision :** It should be able to recognize object and understand images.

f. **Motor Control :** To act upon objects as requested.

g. **Other senses :** This includes audition, smell, touch etc.

Q.12. Hard, Soft, Applied and Cognitive AI ar differnt categories of AI. Explain.

Ans. AI approaches can be divided into different categories as follows: -

1. Hard or Strong AI.
2. Soft or Weak AI.
3. Applied AI.
4. Cognitive AI.

Let us define them one by one.

1. **Hard or Strong AI:** Strong AI aims to build machines that can truly reason and solve problems. Strong AI refers to a machine that approaches or supersedes human intelligence. Strong AI maintains that suitable programmed machines are capable of cognitive mental states. This concept was given by John Searle in 1980. Strong form of AI provides theories for developing some form of computer-based AI that can truly reason and solve problems. A strong form of AI is said to be **sentient or self-aware**. Strong AI is of two types-
   - ☐ **Human-like AI-** in which the program thinks and reasons muck like a human-mind.
   - ☐ **Non-human like AI-** in which the program develops a totally non-human sentience and a non-human way of thinking and reasoning.
2. **Soft or Weak AI :** Weak AI deals with the creation of some form of computer-based AI that cannot truly reason and solve problems but can act as if it were intelligent. **Weak AI** holds that suitable programmed machines can simulate human cognition. There are many fields of weak AI, one of which is **natural language**. Much work has been done in this field with computer simulations of intelligence based on predefined set of rules. Very little progress has been made in strong AI but a moderate amount of progress has been made in weak AI.
3. **Applied AI :** It aims to produce commercially feasible "smart systems" such as security system that is able to recognize human faces who are allowed to enter a particular building. Applied AI has already attained a considerable success.
4. **Cognitive AI :** Computer are used to test theories about how the human mind works through the use of computational models. The importance is of how it is done but not of what is done, meaning that intelligent behavior is not enough, the program must operate in an intelligent way. For example, theories about how we recognize faces and other objects or about how we solve abstract problems.

Q13. Discuss about the security Issues of AI.

Ans. AI (= ML + DL) security vulnerabilities are a growing threat to web. Security industry needs to tackle nascent AI threats before it's too late. As AI and ML systems become a staple of everyday life, the security threats they entail will spill over into all kinds of applications we use, according to a new report, 2021.

Please remember the following points related to AI security: -

1. Unlike traditional software, where flaws in design and source code account for most account for most security issues, in AI systems, vulnerabilities can exist in images, audio files, text and other data used to train and run ML models.
2. According to the researchers from Adversa, a Tel Aviv-based start-up that focusses on security for AI systems, who outlined their latest findings in their report, 'The Road to Secure and Trusted AI' in April, 2021.
3. The report warns that this makes it more difficult to filter, handle and detect malicious inputs and interactions. Also, it adds that threat actors will eventually weaponize AI for malicious purposes.
4. Unfortunately, the AI industry has not even begun to solve these challenges yet, jeopardizing the security of already deployed and future AI systems.

Three types of attacks are possible in AI (= ML + DL). They are discussed one by one.

1. Attacks on vision, analytics and language systems.
2. Adversarial attacks against Web Applications.
3. Trained datasets and ML models.

1. **Attacks on vision, analytics and language systems :**
   a. There is already a body of research that shows that many AI systems are vulnerable to adversarial attacks, imperceptible manipulations that cause models to behave erractically.
   b. According to the researchers at Adversa, AI systems that process visual data account for most of the work on adversarial attacks, followed by analytics, language processing and autonomy.
   c. As per the new AI reports, 2021, with the growth of AI, cyberattacks will focus on fooling new visual and conversational interfaces.
   d. As AI systems depends on their own learning and decision making, cybercriminals will shift their attention from traditional software workflows to algorithms powering analytical and autonomy capabilities of AI systems.
2. **Adversarial attacks against Web Applications :**
   a. Web developers who are integrating AI models into their applications should note the following security issues- "There is definitely a big difference in so-called digital and physical attacks. Now, it is much easier to perform digital attacks against web applications like sometimes changing only one pixel is enough to cause a misclassification."
   b. Attacks against AI and ML systems in the physical world have more stringent demands and require much more time and knowledge.
   c. Alex Polyakov, cofounder and CEO of Adversa, also warns about vulnerabilities in AI and ML models that are served over the web such as API services provided by large tech companies. API services are vulnerable to attacks.
   d. Most of the AI models that are available online are vulnerable to attacks.
   e. **Also note that it is possible to train an attack on one model and then transfer it to another model** without knowing any special details of it.
   f. You can also perform Copycat attack to steal a model, apply attack on it and then use this attack on the API.
3. **Trained datasets and AI/ML Models :**
   a. Most AI-ML algorithms require large sets of labeled data to train models.
   b. Many a times, AI developers, instead of creating their own datasets, they search and download datasets published on GitHub, Kaggle or other web platforms.
   c. There can be potential vulnerabilities in these datasets that can lead to "data poisoning attacks".
   d. Poisoning data with maliciously crafted data samples may make AI models learn those data entries during training, thereby, learning malicious triggers.
   e. The model will behave as intended in normal conditions but malicious actors may call those hidden triggers during attacks.
   f. Another researcher also warned about Trojan attacks where adversaries distribute contaminated models on web platforms.
   g. The report also suggests that instead of poisoning data, attackers have control over the AI Model internal parameters. They could train/customize and distribute their infected models via GitHub or model platforms/ marketplaces.
   h. Unfortunately, GitHub and other platforms don't yet have any safeguards in place to detect and defend against data poisoning schemes. **Please note that this makes it very easy for attackers to spread contaminated datasets and models across the web.**
   i. Attacks against ML and AI systems are set to increase over the coming years.

Q.14. What are the future trends in AI Security?

Ans. Some noted future trends in AI security are as follows: -

1. Researchers claim that while AI is being used extensively in myriads of companies, there are no efficient AI defenses.
2. Present roles and responsibilities that are listed are such that shows that no one is responsible for AI/ML security.
3. AI security is basically different from traditional computer security, so it falls under the radar for cybersecurity teams.
4. Regular AI Engineering has not solved the Quality Assurance Testing (QAT) till now.
5. Adversarial attacks can also be good for us. Recently, it helped one of the clients use adversarial manipulations to develop web CAPTCHA queries that are resilient against bot attacks. Thus, we can say that the technology itself is a double-edged sword and can serve both good and bad.

Q.15. What is Quantum AI?

Ans. It is very interesting to note that every minute of every day 3.2 billion people-

- post 9,722 pins on Pinterest.
- 347, 222 tweets.
- 4.2 million Facebook likes.
- Produce 2.5 exabytes of data (1018).

Thus, we are getting to a conclusion where our AI algorithms cannot compute any more data on classical computers. This is where Quantum AI originates. **Please understand that running AI algorithms on quantum computers can process data at an exponentially higher rate. Also note that processing more data means that our models are more accurate.** Also it is observed that if a classical computer takes thousands of days to train an accurate model, a quantum computer would be able to do it in 1 or 2 days only. This means that with Quantum AI, we will be able to get a result from algorithms quicker and with more accuracy, spots patterns in a larger dataset and optimize solutions. Quantum AI is good for specific problems that account for a lot of variables like facial recognition. With quantum AI, drugs could be discovered in a few days and the capability of reinforcement learnings will increase manifold. We will be able to train these models in lesser time and with more accuracy. We have a deluge of data today. **The more data, the higher is the accuracy.** With Quantum AI, we will have accurate models. Quantum AI will improve supervised learning too. In nutshell, Quantum AI has the power of enhancing our AI models by decreasing their training time and also improving their accuracy. Hence, we will be able to solve problems (that classical computer will take thousands of years) in exponentially lesser time. Also, we will be able to produce pharmaceuticals at a higher rate while keeping the costs low, improving world safety, advancing modern medicine, improving self-driving cars etc., Thus, we can say that while our researches from fire to powerplants and sticks to bombs has slowed down but the advancement of our brains to computers has just started. The convergence of AI and quantum computing can solve complex AI problems and obtain multiple solutions to complex problems simultaneously. This will enhance AI more efficiently performing complex tasks in human-like ways. Similarly, robots can optimize decisions in real world scenario. This will be possible once quantum computers based on AI are deployed.

SUMMARY

With the likely development of super-intelligent programs in the near future, many scientists have raised the issue of safety as it relates to such technology (Yudkowsky 2008; Bostrom 2006; Hibbard 2005; Chalmers 2010; Hall 2000). A common theme in artificial intelligence (AI) safety research is the possibility of keeping a super-intelligent agent in sealed hardware to prevent it from doing any harm to humankind. Such ideas originate with scientific visionaries such as Eric Drexler, who has suggested confining transhuman machines so that their outputs could be studied and used safely (Drexler 1986). Similarly, Nick Bostrom, a futurologist, has proposed (Bostrom 2008) an idea for an oracle AI (OAI), which would only be capable of answering questions. Finally, in 2010 David Chalmers proposed the idea of a "leakproof" singularity. He suggested that, for safety reasons, AI systems first be restricted to simulated virtual worlds until their behavioral tendencies could be fully understood under the controlled conditions.

The AI confinement problem (AICP) is not a recent invention and does not have its roots in the singularity movement. The so-called confinement problem was posed by Butler Lampson in 1973 as a security challenge to computer experts. It was originally stated as- "the problem of confining a program during its execution so that it cannot transmit information to any other program. ... We want to be able to confine an arbitrary program. ... Any program, if confined, will be unable to leak data. A misbehaving program may well be trapped as a result of an attempt to escape" .(Lampson in 1973).

To address the confinement problem, Lampson introduced the "Laws of Confinement" as follows: -

1. **Law of Total Isolation:** A confined program shall make no calls on any other program.
2. **Law of Transitivity:** If a confined program calls another program that is not trusted, the called program must also be confined.
3. **Law of Masking:** A program to be confined must allow its caller to determine all its inputs into legitimate and covert channels.
4. **Law of Enforcement:** The supervisor must ensure that a confined program's input to covert channels conforms to the caller's specifications.

Lampson's work created a lot of interest in the confinement problem (Lipner 1975; Boebert and Kain 1996). Related areas of research such as steganography (Provos and Honeyman 2003) and covert channel communication (Moskowitz and Kang 1994; Kemmerer 1983, 2002) have matured into independent disciplines. A new subfield of computer security, AI safety engineering, we define the AICP as the challenge of restricting an artificially intelligent entity to a confined environment from which it cannot exchange information with the outside environment via legitimate or covert channels if such information exchange was not authorized by the confinement authority. An AI system that succeeds in violating the confinement problem protocol is said to have escaped. Computer security researchers must take on the challenge of designing, enhancing, and proving secure AI confinement protocols in near future.

Restricting access of super-intelligent machines to the real world is a commonly proposed solution for the AI safety problem. Superintelligence is not omnipotent. It is a piece of software capable of looking at all the options it has in a given situation and properly evaluating probabilities for each option. If it is ever put in a situation with no options or only with options that provide a small probability of success, it is not any more powerful than any other agent. Although it is obvious that an AI with an unrestricted communication channel will be able to escape, a system forced to communicate via a filtered communication channel may have a much harder time in obtaining its freedom.

As long as we keep the unknown unknowns in mind and remember that there is no such thing as perfect security, the AI confinement protocol may be just what humanity needs to responsibly benefit from the approaching singularity.

MULTIPLE CHOICE QUESTIONS

1. The branch of computer science that deals with symbolic and non-algorithmic method of problem solving is known as-

(*a*) Knowledge (*b*) AI

(c) Meta-knowledge (*d*) None of the above

2. Which of the following is AI programming language-

(*a*) LISP (*b*) PROLOG

(*c*) Both (*a*) and (*b*) (*d*) None of the above

3. LISP was developed by-

(*a*) Marvin Minsky (*b*) Alan Turing.

(c) John McCarthy (*d*) Allen Newell and Herbert Simon

4. Strong AI is-

(*a*) The embodiment of human muscles within a computer

(*b*) The embodiment of human intellectual within a computer

(*c*) The embodiment of intelligence in computer outputs

(*d*) None of the above

5. In Java, the tool used to create graphics and interfaces to make them more appealing is-

(*a*) SWT (*b*) BBC

(*c*) CV (*d*) None of the above

6. Starting from 2010 to till date, is also known as the era of-

(*a*) Machine learning

(*b*) Deep learning

(*c*) Security

(*d*) None of the above

7. For Turing test, basic requirements of the system are-

(*a*) Computer vision and Robotics

(*b*) AI language and Tools

(*c*) Expert Systems

(*d*) None of the above

8. A system is rational if-

(*a*) It does right things

(*b*) If it follows heuristics

(*c*) If it is small

(*d*) None of the above

9. A program game that defeated the current world chess champion also is-

(*a*) Deep Red

(*b*) Deep Learning

(*c*) Deep Blue

(*d*) None of the above

10. The present age of machine and deep learning mainly uses-

(*a*) Graphics (*b*) Neurons

(*c*) Chips (*d*) None of the above

ANSWERS

1. (*b*)	2. (*c*)	3. (*c*)	4. (*b*)	5. (*a*)
6. (*b*)	7. (*a*)	8. (*a*)	9. (*a*)	10. (*b*)

CONCEPTUAL SHORT QUESTIONS WITH ANSWERS

Q.1. Compare AI programs with conventional software.

Ans. The following table compared the two-

Features	AI Programs	Conventional Software
Processing type	Symbolic	Numeric
Technique used	Heuristic search	Algorithmic search
Results obtained	Satisfactory	Optional (0 or 1)
Data separation	Separate	Intermingled
Knowledge	Vast	Precise
Modification	Frequent	Rare
Process	Inferential	Repetition
Intelligence	Yes	No

Q.2. Compar numeric processing with symbolic procssing.

Ans. The following table compares the two-

Numeric Processing	Symbolic Processing
Numeric processing involves the execution of tasks on computers where numbers are at the core of processing. **Example,** preparing an inventory involves computation of material usages and their costs.	Symbolic processing involves attributes and non-algorithmic processing. **Example,** the "production systems" uses symbolic processing where information is stored as IF-THEN rules.
Representations and use of data.	Representations and use of knowledge.
Algorithmic processing.	Heuristics (some rules of thumb) processing.
Repetitive process.	Inferential process.
Effective manipulation of large databases.	Effective manipulation of large knowledge bases.

Q.3. List some of the characteristics of AI.

Ans. An AI system should have the following characteristics-

1. Systems that learn new concept and tasks.
2. Systems that reason and draw useful conclusions.
3. Systems that can understand natural language.
4. Systems that perceive visual scene.
5. Systems that perform other types of tasks that require human type of intelligence.

Q.4. List various AI tasks with their categories.

Ans. Based on the task domain, AI tasks can be classified as follows-

1. **Mundane (Dull/ Common Sense Reasoning) Tasks :** Includes perception (like vision, speech), NLP (like understanding, generation and translation) and common sense reasoning)like Robotics).
2. **Formal Tasks :** Includes games, mathematics (like geometry, logic, proving theorems, integrations)
3. **Expert Tasks :** Includes engineering (like design, fault finding, manufacturing, planning), scientific analysis, medical diagnosis and financial analysis.

Mundane tasks or common sense reasoning tasks includes face recognitions, NLP etc.

Formal tasks includes logical reasoning based on numbers.

Expert tasks can't be done by people that are expert in their fields. It includes medical diagnosis, engineering and scientific problems etc.

Q.5. Name some AI techniques.

Ans. AI techniques are related to the fact that how we represent, manipulate and reason with knowledge in order to solve problems. Some of them are listed below-

1. **Search :** About 90% of AI programs work on the basis of search.
2. **Pattern Recognition :** There is always some hidden pattern in data. This may be identified as it helps in solving AI problems quickly.
3. **Knowledge Representation :** Knowledge representation is an important issue when manipulating knowledge.
4. **Inference :** It is the process of deriving a conclusion based on what one already knows. The statements that lead to conclusions are known as premises. Three types of inferences have been used—deduction, induction and abduction.

   Deduction works on the standard logic. In this type of inference, if premises are true, then the conclusion must be true. It is a type of clear reasoning only. For example, if switch is OFF then it is certain that bulb will not be lightning. Here, 2nd conclusion is deduced from the first one. In deductive reasoning, the reverse is not true, like if the bulb is not lightning then it might be possible that the bulb is fused.

   Induction works on the generalization of the previous experiences about the problem. For instance, based on observation that various birds fly with their wings, one can formulate certain rules that "all birds can fly" but it may not be true in case of penguin or ostrich.

   Abduction works on the principle of inferring some situation based on the current evidences and series of past events. When new contradictory evidence is found, then the previous one is discarded. For instance, if a patient has symptoms of frequent coughing then as per general belief, the disease is diagnosed as common cold but after more investigation it is found that the disease actually is TB and hence, the earlier information will be replaced by this new one.
5. **Common Sense Knowledge and Reasoning :** is the ability to analyze a situation based on its context. For example, "OpenMind" project at MIT where the goal is to teach a computer about the things that human take for granted. Knowledge is represented in form of semantic nets, graphs and scripts.
6. **Learning from Experience :** Systems like humans also learn from experiences. This enables them to do the same task efficiently and effectively, the next time.
7. **Planning :** The process of computing several steps of a problem solving procedures before executing any of them that will achieve a goal is called as planning.

8. **Heuristics :** means certain rules of thumb that if followed can provide quick solutions.
9. **Genetic programming :** is a technique for getting program to solve a task by making random LISP programs and selecting the fittest in millions of generations.
10. **Epistemology :** is the study of knowledge that can prove useful in the study of solving the problems. In AI, it focusses on 4 main areas- what is knowledge? How is knowledge acquired? What do people know?
11. **Ontology :** is the study of first principles or essence of things. It is the branch of AI that is concerned with the study of various kinds of objects. Ontology may be used by a knowledgebase to specify its structure. It is a formal representation of knowledge in a domain. Hence, we can say that-

Knowledge base = Ontology + a set of examples of its classes.

Q.6. Give some examples of real-life AI intelligent systems.

Ans. Some of the artificial systems developed are as follows-

1. **ALVINN (AUTONOMOUS LAND VEHICLE in a NEURAL NETWORK) :** It is an AI system that learns to control vehicles by watching a person drive. It consists of a neural network whose input is (30 * 32) unit, 2D camera image. The output layer is a representation of the direction, the vehicle should travel. This system drove a car from East coast of USA to the west coast, a total of about 2850 miles. Out of this, about 50 miles were driven by a human and the rest solely by the system.
2. **Deep Blue :** It is a program created by IBM in 1997 that defeated the current world chess champion, Gary Kasparov.
3. **Machine Translation :** a machine is able to translate different languages spoken by different people like English, Hindi etc. many such systems have been developed and many more are likely to come.
4. **Autonomous Agents :** In space explorations, robotic space probes autonomously monitor their surroundings, make decisions and act to achieve their goals. NASA's Mars rover successfully completed their primary 3 months mission in April 2004.
5. **Internet Agents :** The exponential rise of Internet has led to more and more interests in Internet agents to monitor user's tasks, seek needed information md to learn which information is most useful.

Q.7. What is the difference between inductive and deductive reasoning.

Ans. Inductive Reasoning: It conducts specific observations to make generalized statements.

For example, "Dr. Rajiv is Associate Professor.
All professors are studious.
Therefore, Dr. Rajiv is Studious."

Deductive Reasoning: It starts with a general statement and checks the possibilities to reach a specific or a logical conclusion.

For example,"All men of age above 60 years are old.
Harsh is 68 years old.
Therefore, Harsh is old."

Q.8. When can a system be considered as an intelligent system?

Ans. If the system exhibits following features then it is intelligent-

a. Learning.
b. Understanding ambiguity.
c. Creativity.
d. Solving problems.
e. Reasoning.
f. Inferencing.
g. Pattern recognition.
h. Classification.
i. Induction.
j. Deduction.
k. Building analogies.
l. Optimization.
m. NLP-Natural Language Processing.
n. Drawing conclusion from knowledge.

Q.9. What are the advantages one can infer when a machine performs intelligently?

Ans. When a machine performs intelligently, the main advantage is that humans can save their time and also it does it more accurately. Machine can perform same tasks without any fault and fatigueless.

Q.10. State Asimov's three laws of Robotics.

Ans. Isaac Asimov, the first person to use the term Robotics in 1940s, gave three golden principles to guide the conduct of robots and intelligent machines:-

Law 1 : "Robots must never harm human beings or through inaction, allow a human being to come to harm."

Law 2 : "Robots must follow instructions from humans without violating law-1".

Law 3 : "Robots must protect themselves without violating the other rules."

Q.11. Define what is Explainable AI/ XAI.

Ans. AI which shows how a result was calculated, so that the basis for a result can be examined and explained. Normal ML does not automatically do this.

Q.12. Throw some light on AI project cycle.

Ans.

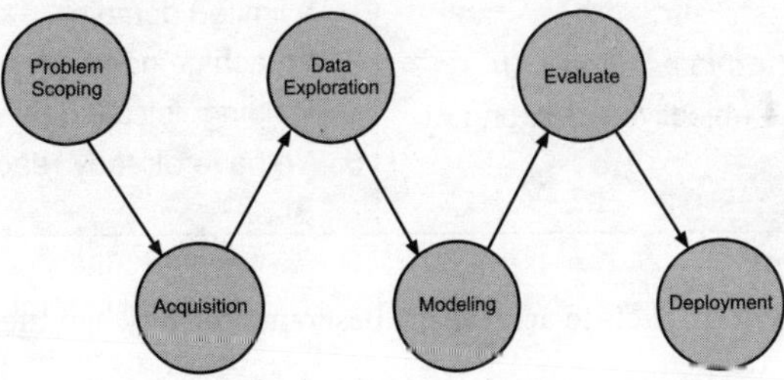

***Fig. 1.10 :** AI Project Life Cycle*

Problem Scoping : It refers to the selection of the problem which has to be solved using the power of AI. It is actually the nature of the problem or the project to be solved.

Data Acquisition : It refers to the collection of data for the needful project. It involves 4Ws canvas—WHO/WHAT/ WHERE and WHY.

Data Visualization : It refers to the process of creation of a mental image through charts, process, diagrams or pictures. This is useful in finding out the patterns present in data, to decide methods and course of action of AI cycle.

Data modeling : It refers to the process of traversing through various models and select the one which matches the requirements.

Evaluate : It refers to the evaluation of each and every model and to select the one with most efficient and reliable output. This helps to recognize different types of graphs and to explore different patterns out of the data explored.

Deployment : It refers to the process of implementation of the surveillance system for the project.

Q.13. How AI is helping us to manage and fight with COVID-19?

Ans. AI has been applied to almost all fields now. Many research papers have been written and published on it. AI helps in the following ways:-

1. To identify, track and forecast outbreaks.
2. To diagnose the virus.
3. Process health care claims.
4. Drones to deliver medicines.
5. Robots to deliver food to patients.
6. Develop drugs.
7. Test drugs.
8. AI Supercomputers to work on corona vaccine.

Q. 14. Differentiate between Intelligence and Artificial Intelligence.

Ans. Let us tabulate the differences between the two —

Intelligence	Artificial Intelligence
1. It is a natural process.	1. It is programmed by humans.
2. It is actually hereditary.	2. It is not hereditary.
3. No electricity from outside is required.	3. We need electrical energy to get output.
4. No human is an expert. We may get better solutions from other humans.	4. Expert systems are made which aggregate many persons experiences and ideas.

Q. 15. How is strong AI different from weak AI?

Ans. Let us tabulate the differences between them.

Strong AI	Weak AI
1. A strong AI claims that computers can be made to think on a level at least equal to humans. 2. It deals with the creation of some form of computer-based AI that can truly reason and solve problems. 3. In strong AI, the programs are themselves the explanations. 4. "Doing" is sometimes referred to as strong AI. 5. We have still to achieve the objectives of strong AI.	1. A weak AI claims that some "thinking like" features are added to computer to make them more useful tool. 2. It deals with the creation of some form of computer-based AI that can reason and solve problems in a limited domain. 2. A machine need not possess true intelligence. 4. "Helping" is called as weak AI. 5. We have already reached the objectives of weak AI.

Q.16. Define what is a rational agent.

Ans. A rational agent is a type of agent that acts to achieve the best outcome or when there is uncertainty then to achieve the best expected outcome.

Q.17. Define the following terms:

a. Fuzzy Logic *b.* Planning

c. Problem Space

Ans.

a. **Fuzzy Logic :** A logic in which the truth values are real values in the closed interval [0.....1] is called as a fuzzy logic. It uses the definitions of boolean operators to fit this continuous domain.

b. **Planning :** A field of AI concerned with systems that construct sequences of action to achieve goals in real world like environments.

c. **Problem Space/State Space :** The formulation of an AI problem into states and operators. We have a start state and a goal state. The problem space is searched to find a solution.

Q.18. What are the major components of an AI system?

Ans. Any AI system has four main components and are shown in Fig. 1.11.

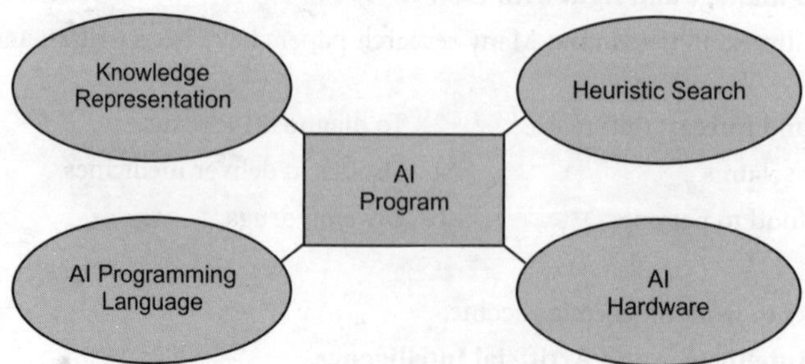

Fig. 1.11: Major AI Systm Components

Please understand that in AI system the quality of result depends upon how much knowledge the system possesses. The knowledge so available is to be represented in an efficient manner. The inferencing process has to be best. AI programs are written in specialized languages like Turbo-Prolog and LISP. Also note that most of the AI programs are implemented on conventional Von Neumann machines only. Today, even dedicated workstations have also emerged for AI programming.

Q. 19. What an agent comprises of?

Ans. We simply put it in an equation form, *i.e.*,

Agent = Architecture + Program

The architecture makes the percepts from the sensors available to the program, runs the program and feeds the program's action choices to the actuators as they are generated. So, the program we choose has to be one that is appropriate for the architecture.

Q.20. What are the various task environments?

Ans. Basically, 6 types of task environments can be found for various problems.

a. Fully observable v/s partially observable.

b. Deterministic v/s stochastic.

c. Episodic v/s sequential.

d. Static v/s Dynamic.

e. Discrete v/s Continuous.

f. Single agent v/s multi-agent.

***a.* Fully observable v/s Partially observable :** A task environment is fully observable if an agent's sensor gives it a complete access to the state of environment at each point of time. For example, a chess with a clock is fully observable environment

On the other hand, an environment is partially observable because of noisy and inaccurate sensors. For example, an automated taxi cannot see what other drivers are thinking.

***b.* Deterministic v/s Stochastic :** If the next state of the environment is completely determined by the current state and the action is executed by the agent then the environment is deterministic else it is stochastic environment. For example, Image analysis provides a deterministic environment whereas Taxi driving is a stochastic case.

***c.* Episodic v/s Sequential :** In episodic task environment, the agent's experience is divided into atomic episodes. Each episode consists of the agent perceiving and then performing a single action. For example, image analysis would give episodic environment, while in sequential environments the current decision could affect all future decisions. For example, chess and taxi driving are sequential. **Please note that episodic environments are much simpler than sequential environments because the agent does not need to think ahead.**

***d.* Static v/s Dynamic :** If the environment can change while an agent is deliberating, then we say the environment is dynamic for that agent else it is static. For example, Taxi driving is dynamic. Crossword puzzles are static. Chess with clock is semi-dynamic.

***e.* Discrete v/s Continuous :** A discrete or continuous distinction can be applied to the state of the environment and to the percepts and actions of the agent. For example, Taxi driving is continuous state problem whereas chess with a clock is discrete.

***f.* Single Agent v/s Multiagent :** These environments are easy to distinguish. For example, an agent solving a crossword puzzle by itself is clearly in a single agent environment, whereas playing chess with a clock is a multiagent environment.

EXERCISE QUESTIONS

1. When is a system said to be intelligent?
2. What is a Turing Test? Explain with a neat sketch.
3. Throw some light on the history of AI.
4. List some applications of AI.
5. Write short notes on AI programming languages.
6. How will you define AI in terms of its task domain?

7. How will you compare human intelligence with artificial intelligence?
8. Explain the progress of AI and its relevance to industry.
9. Distinguish between:-
   (*a*) Strong and weak AI.
   (*b*) Deductive and inductive reasoning.
10. With a neat diagram explain the life cycle of an AI project. Also explain how it is helping in solving industry problems.
11. (*a*) If the Turing Test is passed, does this show that computer exhibits Intelligence? State reasons.
    (*b*) How declarative knowledge is different from procedural knowledge?
    (*c*) Discuss the importance of heuristics in problem solving.
12. Compare knowledge representation to data representation in a database.
13. What is Turing's Test? Explain its significance.
14. Define AI. List important task domains of AI.
15. What is AI? What are its application areas?
16. What do you mean by knowledge acquisition?
17. What is the role of Heuristics in AI?
18. Write different approaches of knowledge representation.
19. "An AI system must contain a lot of knowledge if it is to handle anything but trivial problems but with the growth of knowledge it becomes harder to access appropriate information." Discuss this dilemma as encountered in AI systems.
20. Term 'AI' is a misnomer. Comment.
21. In what context did Turing suggest his well-known test? Explain the Turing Test.
22. Define AI. What are its application areas?
23. Write short notes on application of AI.
24. Can a system engaged in purely numeric computation be called an intelligent system? Explain with suitable arguments.
25. Explain the difference between the following terms — Knowledge and data.
26. What is AI? Briefly explain KBS?
27. Describe knowledge representation and knowledge acquisition?
28. Define and describe the difference between knowledge, hypothesis, belief and data. Also discuss the differences between declarative and procedural knowledge.
29. What is AI? Write various areas of AI.
30. (*a*) How does AI solve problems for which no practically feasible algorithm exists?
    (*b*) Discuss the scope of AI applied to various categories of problems.

2 Intelligent Agents

Q.1. Define what are sensors, actuators, and agents. How agent interacts with an environment?

Ans. In an AI system, agent is defined as something that acts in an environment. An agent can be judged by its actions. If an agent behaves intelligently, it is intelligent. It is the only external behavior that defines intelligence. Agents receive information through their sensors. Agents act in the world through their actuators or effectors. This can be shown with a block diagram (fig. 2.1).

Fig. 2.1: Functioning of an Agent

Some common examples of agents can be like humans because they have eyes, ears. Skin, taste buds etc. as sensors; and hands, fingers, legs mouth as effectors. Robots are agents because they may have camera, sonar, infrared etc. as sensors; and grippers, wheels, lights, speakers etc. that can work as actuators. Software agents or softbots are also there, some function as sensors and some as actuators. Cardiologist is an expert system which acts as an agent for cardiac surgery. Autonomous spacecrafts also act as an agent for aviation system. Any agent interacts with an environment as shown in figure-2.

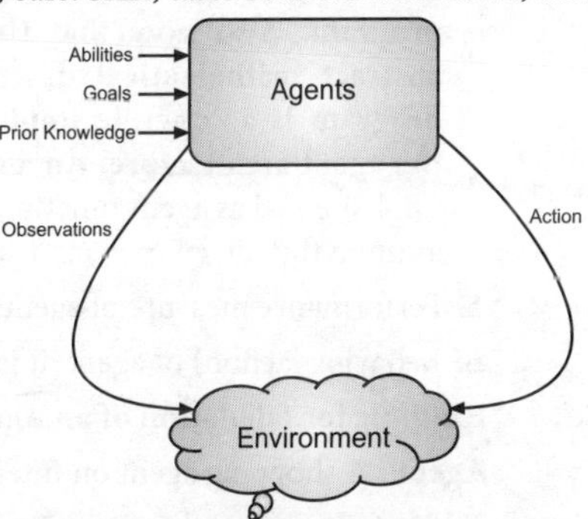

Fig. 2.2: An Agent Interacting with an Environment

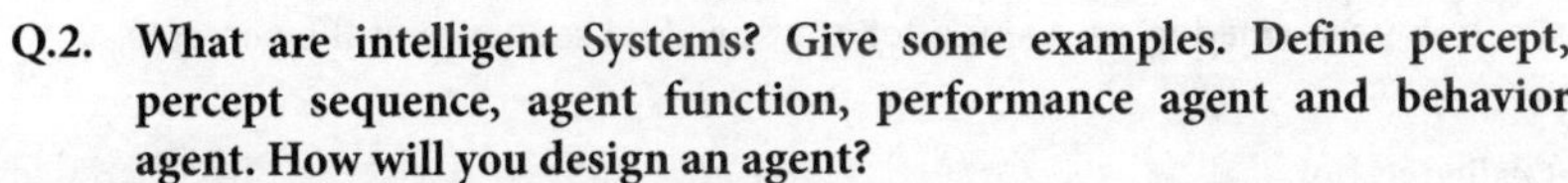

Q.2. What are intelligent Systems? Give some examples. Define percept, percept sequence, agent function, performance agent and behavior agent. How will you design an agent?

Ans. Intelligent systems are the systems/ frameworks that may shown a type of knowledge. For instance, a simpler smart system/framework could be the Gmail spam classifier.

As explained earlier, if Internet shopping is an agent then-

Agent : Internet shopping agent.

Sensors : HTML, DHTML, pages (like text, graphics, scripts etc.).

Actuators : forms, display to user, URL.

An intelligent agent is an intelligent actor, who observe and act upon an environment". Intelligent agent is magnum-opus.

Some agent related terminology is given below: -

1. **Percept :** It refers to the agent's perceptual inputs at any given instant. For example, a human agent percepts, "Birds flying, through eyes and takes its snap".
2. **Percept sequence :** It is the **complete history** of everything the agent has ever perceived. The total history of everything the agent has seen is defined as an agent percept sequence.

   For example, a robotic agent monitoring the temperature of a boiler will be sensing it continuously and keep on maintaining the percept sequence. **Note that this percept sequence will help robotic agent to know how temperature fluctuates and action will be taken depending on percept sequence for controlling temperature.**

3. **Agent Function :** It is defined as a **mathematical function** which maps each and every possible percept sequence to a possible action. This function has input as percept sequence and it gives output as action. For example, ATM machine is an agent that displays menu for withdrawing money, when ATM card is inserted. When provided with percept sequence *i.e.* (*a*) a transaction type and (*b*) PIN no., then only the user gets cash. Mathematically, it is defined as a map from the percept sequence to an action *i.e.*

$$\text{Agent function, } a = F(p)$$

Where 'p' is the current percept, 'a' is the action carried out and 'F' is the agent.

F maps percepts to actions, *i.e.*

$$F: P \rightarrow A$$

Where 'P' is set of all percepts, 'A' is set of all actions.

In general, an action may be dependent of all the percepts observed, not only the current percept *i.e.*

$$a_k = F(p_0\ p_1\ p_2 \ldots\ldots p_k)$$

where $p_0\ p_1\ p_2 \ldots\ldots p_k$ is the sequence of percepts recorded till date,

a_k is the resulting action carried out and F now maps percept to actions. The rule is –"the decision of agent action at a particular moment can depend upon whole percept arrangement observed till date." **Also note that the agent function is the theory of numerical description and the agent is a concert implementation that is running on design.**

4. **Agent Program :** When we want to develop a agent program we need to tabulate all of the agent functions that describes any given agent. Practically speaking, this leads to infinite functions and hence we need to put bound on the length of percept sequence that we need to consider. Please note that the **table of functions of percept sequences and actions will be the external characteristics of the agent where as internally agent function for an intelligent agent will be implemented by an agent program. Also note that the agent function is an abstract mathematical description while the agent program is a concrete implementation, running on the agent architecture.** An agent program is internally implemented as agent function. An agent program takes as input the current percept from the sensor and return an action to the effectors/ actuators. This is shown in fig. 2.3.

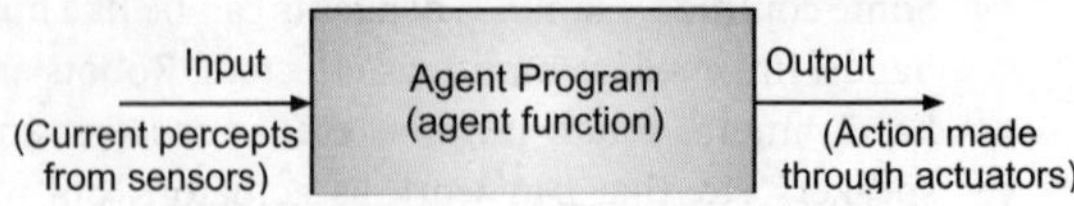

***Fig. 2.3** : Role of an Agent Program in Agent architecture*

5. Performance measure of agent: It is the criteria determining the success of an agent.
6. Behavior (action) of agent: It is the action performed by an agent after any specified sequence of the percepts.

Example for tabulation of an Agent :

Agent : A shopping agent on Internet called as bot.

Table of percepts and action mapping is as follows-

Sequence of Percepts	Actions
(type URL of online shopping site)	Display website.
(navigation and observation of greetings to be purchased)	Clicks on the link.
To get details of items purchased, in terms of form)	Form filling.
To perceive completion of process.	Receiving receipt or bill

Architecture of Intelligent Agents : The agent program runs on some sort of computing device that is called as the **architecture.** The program that we choose has to be one of that the architecture will accept and run. The architecture makes the percept from the sensors available to the program, runs the program and feeds the program's action choices to the effectors as they are generated. The following equation shows the structure of an agent: -

Agent = Architecture + Program

Where,

Architecture: the machinery that an agent executes on.

Program: an implementation of an agent function.

The agent's action process is shown in fig. 2.4.

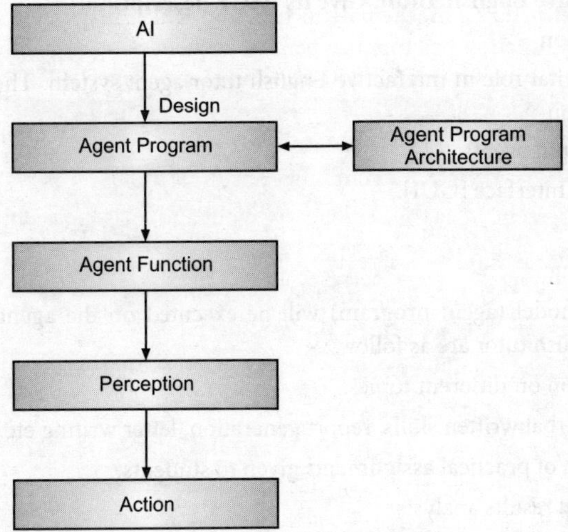

Fig. 2.4 : Agent's Action Process

Explanation : From fig. 2.4 it is observed that AI designs the agent program that is actually a function implementing the agent mapping from percept to actions. This agent program runs on some kind of computing device, i.e. the architecture. The program chosen has to be of the one that the architecture will accept or run. The architecture might be a simple computer or some special purpose hardware like image processing. The architecture's functions includes Percept from the sensors that are available to the program, running the program and feed the action choices of the program to the effector as these are generated.

Designing an Agent System : When we are specifying the agents, we need to specify performance measure, the environment and the agent's sensors and actuators. We group all these under the heading of the task environment. Please note that while designing these intelligent systems four main factors are to be kept in mind:

P, Percepts : The inputs to the AI system.

A, Actions : The outputs of the AI system.

G, Goals : What the agent is expected to achieve?

E, Environment : What the agent is interacting with one?

This has been abbreviated as PAGE DESCRIPTION.

Let us consider some examples of the intelligent systems now.

Agent type : Refinery controller

Percepts : temperature, pressure, chemical readings.

Actions : open and close valves, adjust temperature.

Goals : maximize purity, yield and safety.

Environment : refinery, staff.

Example 2 :

Agent type: Medical diagnostic system

Percepts : symptoms, findings, patient's answers.

Actions : display questions, tests, diagnosis, treatments, referrals.

Goals : healthy patients, minimize the costs.

Environment : patient, hospital, staff.

Example 3 :

Agent type : Chemical reaction analyzer

Percepts : knowledgebase of chemicals, their features.

Actions : recording reaction results.

Goals : correct recording of reactions.

Environment : a chemistry lab. With apparatus, chemical to carry-out reactions.

Q.3. Consider the agent- Interactive English Tutor. Give its PAGE description.

Ans. Let us give its PAGE description-

***P*, Percepts :** Sensors play a vital role in interactive English tutor agent system. The following sensors are required to support sequence of perception-

1. Keyboard for providing input events.
2. Mouse for Graphical User Interface [GUI].
3. Headphones for listening.
4. Web cam for video shooting.

A, Actions : The software model (agent program) will be executed on the agent architecture i.e. OS. The actions performed by interactive English tutor are as follows: -

1. Audio/ video demonstration on different topics.
2. Practical assignment on verbal written skills, report generation, letter writing etc.
3. Monitoring and inspection of practical assignments given to students,
4. Online test conduction and results analysis.
5. Student's speech and video recording.

G, Goal : The interactive English Tutor system must achieve the following performance measures-

1. All students must get maximum knowledge regarding English subject like vocal bury, verbal skills, communication skills, reading, writing skills.
2. All students must secure good marks in English test.

E, Environment : In interactive English Tutor agent system environment has the following properties-

1. All students having different grasping power and IQ .
2. Software modules which give demonstration.

Q.4. Explain the 'Concept of Rationality'. What is a rational agent?

Ans. A system is rational if it does the right thing given what it knows. Rationality is defined as the only status of being sensible and with judgmental feeling. Doing activities with the point of obtaining the vital data is the critical part of rationality.

Rational Agent : If every entry in the agent function is filled correctly then the agent will always do the right thing. Such an agent is called as a **rational agent**. Doing the right thing, makes the agent most successful. So now we need certain methods to measure the success of rational agent. When an agent is working in an environment, it generates a sequence of actions according to the percept it receives. This sequence of actions leads to various states of environment. If this sequence of environment state change is desirable, then we can say that agent has performed well. So, if the task and environment change automatically, the measuring conditions will change. Hence, there is no fixed measure suitable for all agents. **Please understand that as a general rule it is better to design performance measures according to what one wants in the environment rather than according to how one thinks the agent should behave. Also note that the rationality depends on four factors as follows: -**

1. The performance measure that defines the criteria of success.
2. The agent's prior knowledge about the environment.
3. The actions that the agent can perform.
4. The agent's percept sequence till current date.

Based on these four statements, we can define a rational agent as follows-

"For each possible percept sequence, a rational agent should select an action that is expected to maximize ts performance measure given the evidence provided by the percept sequence and whatever inbuilt knowledge the agent has."

If the environment is completely known then we get agent's good behavior. On the other hand, if the environment is unknown then the agent can act badly.

Before we discuss further, remember the following points:-

1. An omniscient agent knows the actual outcome of its actions and can act accordingly. But in reality omniscience is impossible.
2. Rationality is not same as perfection.
3. Rationality maximizes expected performance whereas perfection maximizes actual performance.
4. For increasing performance, the agent must do same actions in order to modify future percepts. This is called as information gathering which is an important part of rationality.
5. The agent should explore environment to increase performance.
6. To gather information. An agent should also do learning.
7. Agent may know the environment completely but if it is unknown then the agent needs to learn on its own.
8. A rational agent should be autonomous *i.e.* it should learn what it can do to compensate for partial or incorrect prior knowledge. If the behavior of the system is determined by its own experience then the system is known as autonomous. If the agent has lesser experience then it will be required to act in a random manner unless some assistance is provided either by the designer or the programmer. Also note that an actual autonomous IA would be able to efficiently show all types of environments, given sufficient time to adapt.
9. Hence, we can say that-

   Rational ≠ omniscient

   Rational ≠ successful
10. An ideal rational agent is the one, which is competent enough of performing expected actions to expand its performance measure. It is done on the bases of its percept sequence and its inbuilt knowledgebase.

Q.5. What are the different types of Agents? Explain the following agents-

a. **Simplex reflex agents.** *b.* **Model-based reflex agents.**

c. **Goal-based agents.** *d.* **Utility-based agents.**

e. **Learning agents.**

Ans. As the degree of perceived intelligence and capability varies, it is possible to frame agent into five categories: -

a. Simplex reflex agents.

b. Model-based reflex agents.

c. Goal-based agents.

d. Utility-based agents.

e. Learning agents.

Let us study these one by one now.

I. Simplex Reflex Agent : These agents select actions on the basis of the current percept, ignoring the rest of percept history.

Properties of simplex reflex agents :

1. These are very simple but their intelligence is limited.
2. They will work only if the correct decision can be made on the basis of only the current percept (*i.e.* only if the environment is fully observable).
3. Unobservability can cause serious trouble.
4. If they work in partially observable environment then it can lead to infinite loops.
5. These infinite loops can be avoided if this agent can try out possible actions i.e. it can randomize the actions.

Note : Randomize simplex reflex agent will perform better than deterministic reflex agent.

For instance, in an ATM agent system, if PIN matches with the given account number then customer gets money.

These percept to action mapping which is known as condition-action rules (or situation action rules or if-then rules) in the simple reflex agent. It can be represented in the following way: -

if {set of percepts} then {set of actions}

For example,if PIN matches then customer gets money

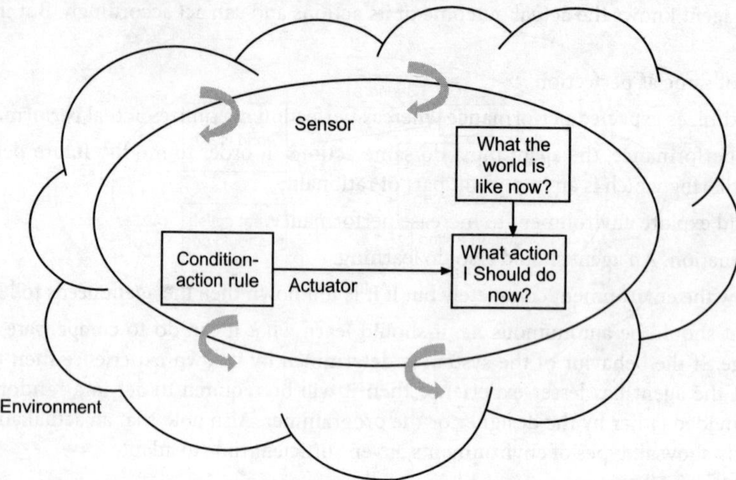

Fig. 2.5: Simple Reflex Agent

The agent chooses action based on the condition -action rule performed in the environment.

The following is the agent code for simple reflex:

Procedure : SIMPLE-REFLEX-AGENT

INPUT : Percept

OUTPUT : An action.

Static : Rules, a set of condition-action rules.

1. state ← INTERPRET-INPUT (percept)
2. rule ← RULE – MATCH (state, rules)
3. action ← RULE – ACTION (rule)
4. return action.

II. Model-based Reflex Agent : Internal state of the agent stores the current state of environment which describes part of unseen world i.e. how world evolves and effect of agent's own actions. Note that this means that it stores model of possibilities around it. Hence, it is also called as model-based reflex agent / reflex agent with an internal state. It has two information: -

1. Some information related to how the world evolves independently to agent.
2. How world is affected by the action of agent.

This knowledge of world working whether implemented in Boolean circuits or incomplete scientific theories is known as model of the world and an agent using such a model is known as model-based agent.

Properties of simplex reflex agents :

1. It has ability to handle partially observable environments. This is done by maintaining the record of the part of the world, it cannot view at a particular time.
2. Its internal state is updated continuously *i.e.*

   Old-Internal state + current percept = update state
3. This is required to refresh its own particular state without depending on the sensory information.
4. Model- knowledge about "how things happen in the world".
5. Internal state- is the representation of unobserved aspects of current state depending on the percept history.

   For instance, a car driving agent which maintains its own internal state and then take action as environment appears to it.

   One drawback of simplex reflex agents (discussed above) is that their activities are dependent on the recent data provided by their sensors.

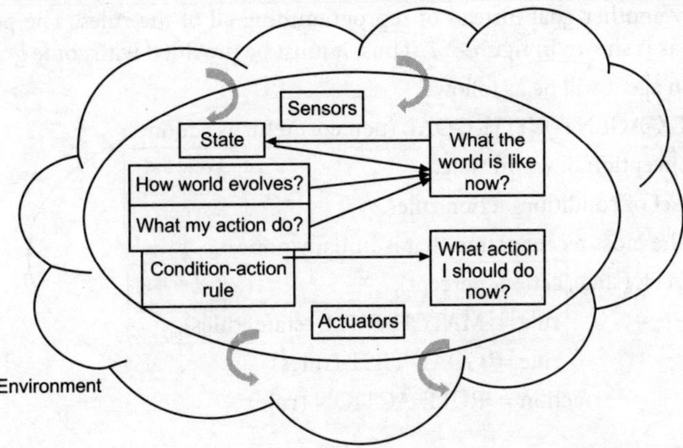

Fig. 2.6: : Model-based Reflex Agent

The code for such an agent will be as follows: -

Procedure: REFLEX-AGENT-WITH-STATE

INPUT : Percept

Output : an action

Static : state, a description of the current world state, rules, a set of condition-action rules, action, the most recent action, initially none.

1. State ← UPDATE-STATE (state, action, percept)
2. Rule ← RULE-MATCH (state, rules)
3. Action ← RULE-ACTION (rule)
4. return action.

III. Goal based Agent : Goal-based agent stores the state description as well as it stores goal states information.

Properties of Goal-based agents:

1. Goal-based agent works simply towards achieving goal.
2. For tricky goals, it needs searching and planning.
3. They are dynamic in nature because the information description appears in proper and explicit manner.
4. We can quickly change goal-based agent's behavior for new or unknown goals.
5. In spite of the fact that the goal-based agents seem to be less effective, it is more adaptable which supports its decisions is represented explicitly and can be changed,

For example, an agent searching a solution for 8-queen's problem.

Goal-based agent :

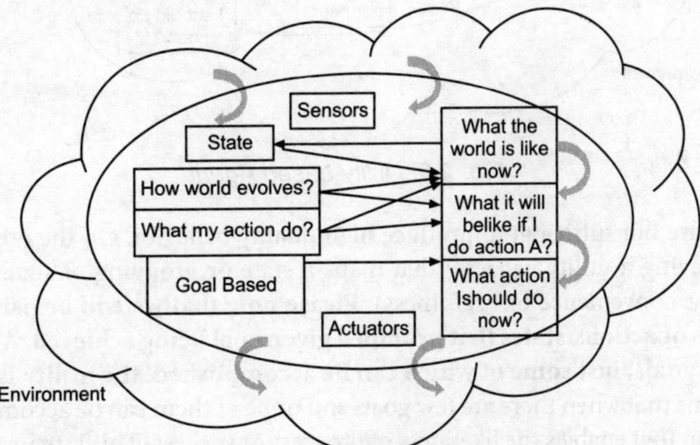

Fig. 2.7: Goal-based Agent

We can only specify another goal instead of reprogramming all of the rules. The proper action for will regularly depend on its goals as is shown in figure-2.7. Thus, it must be provided with some goal information.

The code for such an agent will be as follows: -

Procedure : -REFLEX-AGENT-WITH-GOAL (percept) returns action

persistent : state, conception of world state.

persistent : rules, a set of condition-action rules.

persistent : action, the most recent action that is initially none.

state : UPDATE-STATE (state, action, percept)

rule = MATCH-RULE (state, rules)

rule = GOAL-TEST (rules)

action = RULE-ACTION (rule)

Return action

IV. Utility-based Agent : in complex environments, only goals are not enough for agent decisions. In addition to this, we can have a utility function too.

Properties of Utility-based agents :

1. Utility function maps a state on to a real number which describes the associated degree of best performance.
2. Goals give us only two outcomes – achieved or not achieved. But utility-based agents provide a way in which the likelihood of success can be measured against importance of goals.
3. Rational agent, which is utility-based, can maximize expected value of utility function i.e. more perfection can be achieved.
4. Goals can have only two discrete states—happy and unhappy.

For example, military planning robot which provides certain plan of action to be taken. Its environment is too complex and expected performance is also high.

Utility-based Agent:

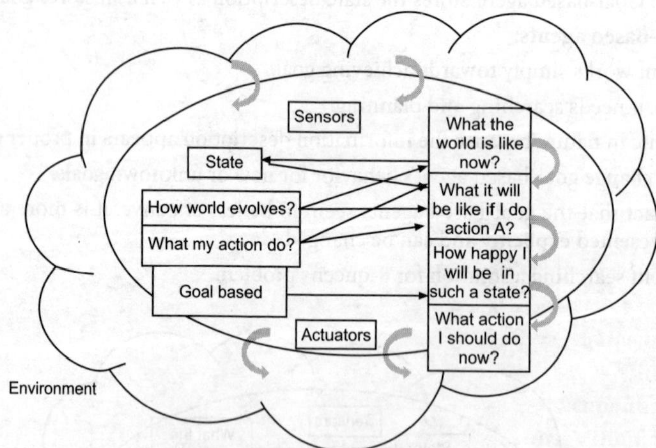

Fig. 2.8: Utility-based Agent

Actually, goals alone are not sufficient to produce high quality behavior. On the other hand, an utility-based agent can be depicted as having a utility capacity that maps a state or grouping of states on to a genuine number that speaks to its utility (or convenience or usefulness). **Please note that we will be using this utility to pick between alternative sequences of actions/states that prompt a given goal being achieved. Also note that at the point when there are conflicting goals, just some of which can be accomplished, the utility is ready to evaluate the suitable exchange offs.** It means that when there are few goals and none of them can be accomplished with assurance then the it is this utility function that enables the likeliness of progress or success. This is to be weighed against the importance of goals. Thus, a utility function maps a state or a sequence of states to a real number which describe the associated degree of happiness. In nutshell, utility-based agent using the model of the world along with the utility function that measures its performance among states of the world, then chooses the action which leads to the best expected utility. Also note that the expected utility is computed by all the possible outcome state weighed by the probability of the outcome.

V. Learning Agent : If an agent has to operate initially in unknown environments then agent should be self-learner. It means that it should observe, gain and store information. Learning agent can be divided into four conceptual components: -

(*a*) **Learning Element :** that is responsible for making improvements.

(*b*) **Performance Element :** that is responsible for selecting external actions.

(*c*) **Critic :** It tells how agent is doing and determines how the performance element should be modified to do better in the future.

(*d*) **Problem Generator :** It is responsible for suggesting actions that will lead to new and informative experiences to agent. Agent can ask problem generator for suggestions.

VI. The Performance standard distinguishes part of the incoming percept as a reward (success) or penalty (failure) that provides feedback on the quality of the agent's behavior. Note that all four types of agents we have seen can improve their performance through learning and thereby become learning agent.

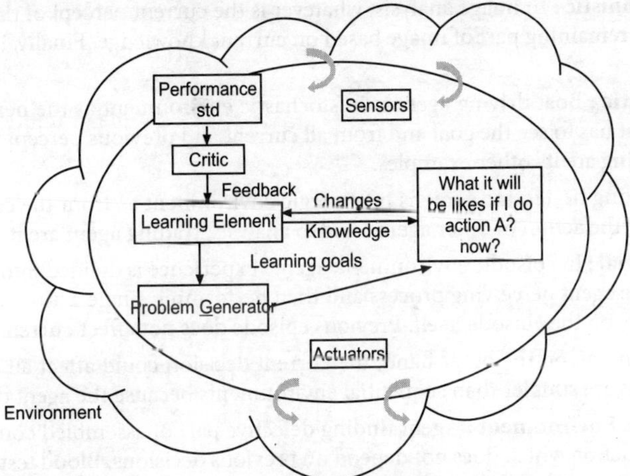

Fig. 2.9: Learning Agent

Q.6. Explain the 'Environment and its Properties'. Explain Different types of task environments as follows-

1. Fully observable and partially observable.

2. Deterministic and stochastic.

3. Episodic and sequential.

4. Static and dynamic.

5. Discrete and continuous.

6. Single agent and multi agent.

Ans. In previous section, we have studied various types of agents. Let us now study the details of the environment where an agent is going to work. Hence, the task environment is essentially a problem to which an agent is the solution. The range of task environments that might arise in AI is very vast. But we can identify a fairly small number of dimensions along which the task environments can be categorized. These dimensions determine, to large extent, the appropriate agent design and the applicability of each of the principle families of techniques for agent implementation.

Different Types of Task Environments :

1. Fully observable and partially observable.
2. Deterministic and stochastic.
3. Episodic and sequential.

4. Static and dynamic.
5. Discrete and continuous.
6. Single agent and multi agent.

Let us differentiate between all of them one by one.

1. **Fully Observable and Partially Observable :** If an agent's sensors give it the access to complete state of environment at each point of time then it is fully observable. In some environments, if there is a noise or agent is with inaccurate sensors or may be some states of environment are missing then such environment is partially observable.

   Examples of Fully Observable : The puzzle game environment is fully observable where an agent can see all aspects that are surrounding it. That is, the agent can see all squares of the puzzle game along with values (if any) in them. Image analysis, Tic-Tac-Toe are its other examples.

   Examples of Partially Observable : The pocker game environment is partially observable. Game of pocker is a card game that shares the betting rules. In this game, agent is not able to perceive the other player's betting. Also, the agent cannot see the other player's card. It has to play with reference to its won cards and with current betting knowledge. Interactive science tutor, military planning are its other examples.

2. **Deterministic and Stochastic :** If from the current state of environment and the action, agent can deduce the next state of environment then it is a deterministic environment else it is a stochastic environment. Also note that if the environment is deterministic except for the actions of other agents then we say that the environment is strategic.

   Examples of Deterministic : In image analysis, whatever is the current percept of the image, an agent can take next action or can process remaining part of image based on current knowledge. Finally, it can produce all details aspects of the image.

   Examples of Stochastic : Boat driving agent is in stochastic environment as the next driving does not base on the current state. In fact, it has to see the goal and from all current and previous percepts agent needs to take the action. Car driving, robot firing are its other examples.

   Strategic : Agent playing tic-tac-toe game is in strategic environment as from the current state, agent decides next state action except for the action of other agents. Video analysis, trading agent are its other examples.

3. **Episodic and sequential :** In episodic environment, agent's experience is divided into atomic episodes such that each episode consists of the agent perceiving process and then performing single action. In this environment, the choice of action depends only on the episode itself. Previous episode does not affect current actions.

   In sequential environment, on the other hand, the current decision could affect all future decision. Also note that episodic environments are simpler than sequential environments because the agent does not need to think ahead.

   Examples of Episodic Environment : Agent finding defective part of assembled computer. Here, agent will inspect current part and take action which does not depend on previous decisions. Blood testing of a patient, card games are its other examples.

   Examples of Sequential Environment : Game of chess is a sequential environment wherein an agent takes actions based on al, previous decisions only. Chess with a clock, refinery controller are its other examples.

4. **Static and Dynamic :** If the environment can change while agent is deliberating then we say that the environment is dynamic for the agent else it is static. Static environments are easy to tackle as agent need not worry about changes around, as it will not change, while taking actions.

   On the other hand, dynamic environments keep on changing continuously which makes agent to be more attentive to make the decisions for act. **Please note that if the environment itself does not change with time but the agent's performance does, then we say that environment is semi-dynamic.**

   Examples of static environment :

   8-queens puzzle.

   Examples of dynamic environment-

   Car driving, tutor.

5. **Discrete and Continuous :** In discrete environment, the environment has fixed, finite discrete states over the time and each state has associated percepts and actions. A continuous environment is not stable at any given point of time and it changes randomly thereby making agent to learn continuously, so as to make decisions.

   Examples of Discrete Environment : Game of tic-tac-toe shows discrete environment where every state is stable and is associated percept and it is outcome of some action, 8-queen puzzle, crossword puzzle and chess.

Examples of Continuous Environment : A boat driving environment is continuous where the state changes are continuous and agent needs to perceive continuously. Some more examples include Part Picking Robot, Flight Controller.

6. **Single-agent and multi-agent :** In single agent environment, we have well defined single agent who takes decision and acts. In multi-agent environment, there can be various agents or various group of agents which are working together to take a decision and act. In multi-agent environment, we can have competitive multiagent environment, in which many agents are working parallel to maximize performance of individual or there can be co-operative multiagent environment, where in all agents have a single goal and they work to get high performance of all of them together.

Examples of single-agent environment :

Boat driving--here a single agent perceives and acts.

Examples of multi-agent independent environment-

Many agents in Maze game.

Examples of multi-agent cooperative environment-

Fantasy Football--here many agents are working but opposite to each other.

Examples of multi-agent competitive environment-

Trading agents-- here many agents are working opposite to each other but one side (agent/ agent team) is having a negative goal.

Q.7. Describe PEAS representation for an Agent. What steps are followed to design an agent?

Ans. When we are specifying agents, we need to specify performance measure, the environment and the agent's sensors and actuators. We group all these under the heading of the task environment.

PEAS stands for-

P, Performance : It shows how the system's achievements are measured.

E, Environment : It represents what the agent is interacting with.

A, Actuators : It is what produces the outputs of the system.

S, Sensors : It is what provides the inputs to the system.

Steps in Designing an Agent:

Step-1 : Define the problem area. That is, task environment in a complete manner. For example, automated face recognition, automated taxi driver.

Step-2 : Define or tabulate PEAS.

Step-3 : Define or tabulate the agent functions. That is, percept sequence and action column.

Step-4 : Design agent program.

Step-5 : Design an architecture to implement agent program.

Step-6 : Implement an agent program.

Please note that an agent may be a single agent or a multiple agent system. Also note here that if the system is a multi-agent system then we need to consider communication, cooperation strategies among multiple agents.

We are now in a position to write some agents and their PEAS description according to their uses.

I. General Purpose (uses for a common man)

Agent Type	Performance Measure (G)	Environment (E)	Actuators (A)	Sensors (P)
Automated face recognizer.	Correct, recognition system.	Human face, software, web camera.	Capturing face, feature extraction, classification.	Web camera, keyboard, mouse, infrared light.
Part-picking robot.	Percentage of parts in correct bins.	Conveyer belt, bins.	Joined arm and hand.	Camera, joint angle sensors.

II. Industrial Business Purpose

Agent Type	Performance Measure (G)	Environment (E)	Actuators (A)	Sensors (P)
E-commerce system	Secure, reliable, fast business processing.	E-commerce websites, human system.	Display product lists with prices, forms.	Keyboard, mouse.
Refinery controller.	Maximize, purity, yield, safety.	Refinery, operators.	Valves, pumps, heaters, displays.	Temperature, pressure, chemical sensors.

III. Scientific or Research Purpose

Agent Type	Performance Measure (G)	Environment (E)	Actuators (A)	Sensors (P)
E-commerce system	Secure, reliable, fast business processing.	E-commerce websites, human system.	Display product lists with prices, forms.	Keyboard, mouse.
Refinery controller.	Maximize, purity, yield, safety.	Refinery, operators.	Valves, pumps, heaters, displays.	Temperature, pressure, chemical sensors.

IV. Medical Purpose

Agent Type	Performance Measure (G)	Environment (E)	Actuators (A)	Sensors (P)
Medical diagnosis system.	Healthy patient, minimize costs.	Patient, hospital, staff.	Display questions, tests, diagnosis, treatments.	Entry of symptoms, findings, patient's answers.
Blood testing system.	Correct reporting on each test.	Blood sample lab.	Detail reporting of each test.	Database of procedures of test conduction and results.

V. Educational Purpose

Agent Type	Performance Measure (G)	Environment (E)	Actuators (A)	Sensors (P)
Interactive English Tutor.	Maximize student's score on test.	Set of students, testing agency.	Display exercises suggestions and corrections.	Keyboard entry.
Music teacher.	Learner should be able to play specific musical pieces.	Group of learner or a single learner.	Display of each note, key playing presentation, sample music pieces.	Inputs from learner, from mouse and database of casio details.

Q.8. Give some Intelligent Agent Applications.

Ans. Some of the applications of Intelligent agents are as follows: -

1. They help in system and network management.
2. They help in information access and management.
3. They help in workflow and administrative management.
4. They provide personal shopping help say for example, they remind customers to shop when its their birthday.

SUMMARY

The colossal field of AI has witnessed exponential growth in recent years. With the advent of deep neural networks that surpass human cognition and human intelligence, the post-modern world is now thriving on disruptive technologies and avant-garde innovations. Adhering to the web and flow of innovations and technological transformations, IBM is constantly experimenting with AI to explore the terra incognita and attach a new dimension to disruptive technology. The need is to catalyze digital transformations in business industries and IT hubs. IBM is currently on a mission to instill AI in hardware. This will deliver 2.5 times annual improvement in hardware for better computing. So, it is the combination of AI + Hardware that form the key components of IBM's program named as Fluid Intelligence. As we know that Time is Money. So, companies are practicing timeliness vehemently. Therefore, the need is to adopt high-end technologies to cope up with the cut-throat race in the market space today.

MULTIPLE CHOICE QUESTIONS

1. The relationship among agents, architectures and programs can be best expressed in form of equation as-

(*a*) Agent = Action + Program (*b*) Agent = Statistics + Program
(*c*) Agent = Architecture + Program (*d*) None of the above

2. Rationality will-

(*a*) Maximize expected performance (*b*) Maximize actual performance.
(*c*) Minimize expected performance (*d*) None of the above.

3. An intelligent actor who observe and act upon an environment is called as-

(*a*) Intelligent Computer (*b*) Intelligent Agent
(*c*) Intelligent thinker (*d*) None of the above

4. If an agent is to operate initially in unknown environments then the agent should be a-

(*a*) Self-learner (*b*) Self-recursive
(*c*) Self-modifiable (*d*) None of the above

5. The acronym PEAS stands for-

(*a*) Performance, Experiment, Action, System
(*b*) Performance, Example, Action, Sensor
(*c*) Performance, Environment, , Actuators, Sensors
(*d*) None of the above

6. We need to consider communication and cooperation strategies among-

(*a*) Single agent system (*b*) Multiple agent systems
(*c*) Both (*a*) and (*b*) (*d*) None of the above

7. A machine that looks like a human being and performs various complex acts of a human being is known as a-

(*a*) Robotic agent (*b*) Rational agent
(*c*) Intelligent agent (*d*) None of the above

8. The rule of a simple reflex agent is-

(*a*) Condition-action rule (*b*) Simple-action rule
(*c*) Both (*a*) and (*b*) (*d*) None of the above

9. The problem generator is present in-

(*a*) Learning agent (*b*) Reflex agent
(*c*) Observing agent (*d*) None of the above

10. The instruments that are used for perceiving and acting upon the environment are-

(*a*) Sensors and actuators (*b*) Sensors
(*c*) Perceiver (*d*) None of the above

ANSWERS

1. (*c*)	**2.** (*a*)	**3.** (*b*)	**4.** (*a*)	**5.** (*c*)
6. (*b*)	**7.** (*a*)	**8.** (*a*)	**9.** (*a*)	**10.** (*a*)

CONCEPTUAL SHORT QUESTIONS WITH ANSWERS

Q.1. Define an agent, robotic agent and rational agent.

Ans. An agent is anything (a program, a machine assembly) that can be viewed as perceiving its environment through sensors and acting upon that environment through actuators.

A machine that looks like a human being and performs various complex acts of a human being is a robotic agent. It can do tasks efficiently and repeatedly without failure. It works on the basis of a program feeded to it. It can have previously stored knowledge. It can gather more knowledge from environment through its sensors. It acts with the help of actuators.

A rational agent is an agent that always works as per the expected performance. It is an agent who always acts perfectly as per the expectation. It tries to maximize expected behavioral performance.

Q.2. What are the four main components of a general model of learning agent?

Ans. Learning agent model has 4 components as follows: -

a. **Learning Element :** which is responsible for making improvements.

b. **Performance Element :** which is responsible for selecting external actions.

c. **Critic :** It tells how agent is doing *i.e.* It evaluates output.

d. **Problem Generator :** It is responsible for suggesting actions.

Q.3. What is the role of agent program?

Ans. Agent program is important and central part of agent system. It drives the agent, which means that it analyzes dat and provides probable actions that agent could take. An agent program is internally implemented as an agent function. An agent program takes input as the current percept from the sensor and return an action to the effectors (actuators).

Q.4. Define what is an intelligent agent?

Ans. Intelligent Agent (IA) is a self-sufficient substance that watches and follows up on a situation and coordinates its movements towards accomplishing goals. IA may learn or utilize information to fulfil their objectives. These may be either very simple or very complex.

Q.5. List some of the characteristics of intelligent agent.

Ans. The characteristics of intelligent agent (IA) are as follows: -

1. The IA must learn and improve through interaction with the environment.
2. The IA must adapt online and in real-time situation.
3. The IA must accommodate new problem solving rules incrementally.
4. The IA must have memory which should exhibit storage and retrieval capacities.

Q.6. Can you define the term 'Rationality' ?

Ans. Rationality is defined as the only status of being sensible and with great judgmental feeling. It is only related to the expected activities or actions and this results relying on what the IA has viewed. Also note here that performing activities with the point of obtaining the valuable data is said to be a critical piece of rationality.

Q.7. Can you name some agent simulator?

Ans. Webots simulator, Gazebo, Robot Operating System, Robotarium, Poppy-project, CoppaliaSim are some of the Robotic simulation platforms.

Q.8. Can you explain the mapping between PAGE and PEAS descriptors?

Ans. The mapping between PAGE and PEAS is as follows:

Performance	percepts
Environment	actions

Actuators goals

Sensors environment

Q.9. What is the relationship between AI and big data?

Ans. The marriage between AI and big data is actually called as web intelligence(WI). So, we can say that:-

Web Intelligence = AI + BIG DATA

Q.10. What are Internet agents?

Ans. The unexpected growth of Internet has also led to growing interest in internet agents to monitor user's tasks, seek needed information and to learn which information is most useful.

Q.11. What are AI chatbots?

Ans. In AI, the conversational agents are most commonly known as chatbots. These are used most often in customer services and call centers. This is through customer-facing AI assistants which act as the first port of call for customer queries, fielding simple questions and forwarding complex problems to live agents. There are agent-supporting AI assistants that are used by live customer service agents use to support them while they are interacting with customers, which improves productivity.

EXERCISE QUESTIONS

1. What is an agent? Give some of its characteristics.
2. What is a rational agent? Explain goal-based agent.
3. What is PEAS driver? Explain PEAS for the following:-
   (*a*) A vacuum cleaner.
   (*b*) A taxi driver.
   (*c*) A medical system.
   (*d*) A chemical analyzer in a chemical lab.
   (*e*) A handpicking Robot.
4. Define task environments.
5. What are self-learning agents?
6. What are intelligent agents? Give their characteristics.
7. What are chatbots agents?
8. Is their any mapping between PAGE and PEAS descriptors.
9. Give some applications of Intelligent Agent.
10. Discuss the role of Artificial Intelligence in future years to come.

3 AI APPROACHES

3.1 INTRODUCTION

A problem-solving agent firstly formulates a goal and a problem to solve. Then the agent calls a search procedure to solve it. It then uses the solution to guide its actions. It will do whatever the solution recommends as the next thing to do and then remove that step from the sequence. Once the solution has been executed, the agent will formulate a new goal. Please note that in intelligent agent case, a KB corresponds to the environment, operators correspond to sensors and the search techniques are the actuators.

The KB describes the current task domain and the goal (or state). Operators manipulate this KB. And the control strategy decides what operators to apply and where to apply them. Also note that the aim of any search technique is the application of an appropriate sequence of operators to an initial state to achieve the goal. A problem-solving agent (system) uses either forward or backward reasoning. Each of its operator works to produce a new state in the KB.

Forward reasoning or bottom-up or data-driven reasoning means applying operators to those structure in the KB that best describes the task domain in order to produce a modified state. On the other hand, backward reasoning will break down the goal (problem) statement into sub-goals (problems) which are easier to solve and these sub-solutions are sufficient to solve the original problem as a whole.

3.2. PROBLEM SOLVING

Q.1. What is Problem Specification? What are its main components?

Ans. Problem domain formulation is a very important task. This problem definition must be unambiguous and clear. So, we define an abstract problem in terms of real workable states which are clearly understood.

Please understand that these states are operated upon by a set of operators. The overall control strategy decides which operator is to be used. To formulate any problem, four components are defined in a very formal way. These four components are —

1. The initial state (or starting state).
2. State space *i.e.*, a description of all possible states reachable from the initial state. Please note that this state space forms a graph in which the nodes are states and the arcs represent actions.
3. Goal test that determines whether a given state is a goal state.
4. Path cost is a function that assigns a numeric cost to each path.

Please note here that solution to a problem is a path from the initial state to a goal state. Also note that the quality of the solution is measured by the path cost function and obviously, an optimal solution has the lowest path cost among all solution.

So, these four components will do problem formulation. To achieve our objective, we use operationalization. **The process of creating a formal description of a problem using the knowledge about the given problem, so as to create a program for solving a problem is called as operationalization.** Thus, in general, any problem can be solved using the following steps—

Step-1 : Define a state space which contains all possible configurations of the relevant objects. You can even include some impossible states.

Step-2 : Identify initial states *i.e.*, one or more such states from our search space that would describe possible situations from where problem solving may start.

Step-3 : Specify goal states *i.e.*, specify one or more states which would be acceptable as solutions to our problem.

Step-4 : Specify set of rules *i.e.*, give a set of rules which describe the actions (operators) available and a control strategy to decide the order of application of these rules.

At the **core heart of** many intelligent processes lies the process of search.

Search can be characterized as finding a path through a graph or tree structure. This requires moving from node to node after successively expanding and generating connected nodes. Node generation is accomplished by computing the identification or the representation code of children nodes from a parent node. Once this is done, a child is said to be generated and the parent is said to be explored. **The process of generating all of the children of a parent is also known as expanding the node.** A search procedure is a strategy for selecting the order in which nodes are generated and a given path selected.

Search problems may be classified as:

1. **Blind or Uninformed Search:** In this search technique, no preference is given to the order of successor node generation and selection. The path selected is blindly or mechanically followed. No information is used to determine the preference of one child over another. For e.g. DFS, DFS, bidirectional searches.
2. **Informed or Directed Search:** In this search technique, some information about the problem space is used to compute a preference among the children for exploration and expansion. For *e.g.* Heuristic search.

Q.2. Explain State Space Search with Examples.

Ans. We define the state space as a set of all possible sates of a given problem. A state space representation allows for the formal definition of a problem which makes the movement from initial state to the goal state quite easy. In a way, we can also say that various problems like planning, learning, discoveries in science, theorem proving etc. are all essentially search problems only.

Advantages and Disadvantages of state-space representations :

Advantages : This representation is very useful in AI because it provides a set of all possible states, operations and goals. If the entire state-space representation for a problem is given then it is possible to trace the path from the initial to goal state and identify the sequence of operators required for doing it.

Disadvantage(*s*) : It is not possible to visualize all states for a given problem. Also, the resources of the computer system are limited to handle huge (combinational) state-space representation.

We are now in a position to describe some search space problems.

Q.3. How will you do-The eight- tile puzzle problem formulation.

Ans. Problem formulation : The eight- tile puzzle consists of a 3-by-3 (3*3) square frame board which holds eight (8) movable tiles numbered as 1 to 8. One square is empty, allowing the adjacent tiles to be shifted. The objective of the puzzle is to find a sequence of tile movements that leads from a starting configuration to a goal configuration, as shown in Fig. 3.1 below.

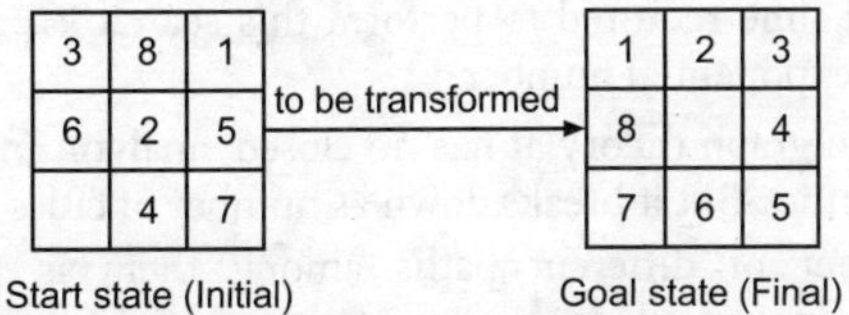

Fig. 3.1 : *Initial and Final States of 8-puzzle Problem*

The states of the 8-tile puzzle are the different permutations of the tiles within the frame.

Please note that an optimal solution is the one that maps an initial arrangement of tiles to the goal state with the smallest (minimum) **number of moves. Also note that the root node can be any random starting state.**

Let us do a standard formulation of this problem now.

States : It specifies the location of each of the 8-tiles and the blank in one of the nine squares.

Initial state : Any state can be designated as the initial state.

Goal : Many goal configurations are possible one such is shown in Fig. 3.2.

Legal moves (or states) : They generate legal states that result from trying the four actions—

a. blank moves left *b.* blank moves right

c. blank moves up *d.* blank moves down

Path cost : Each step costs 1, so the path cost is the number of steps in the path. The tree diagram showing the search space is shown in Fig. 3.2.

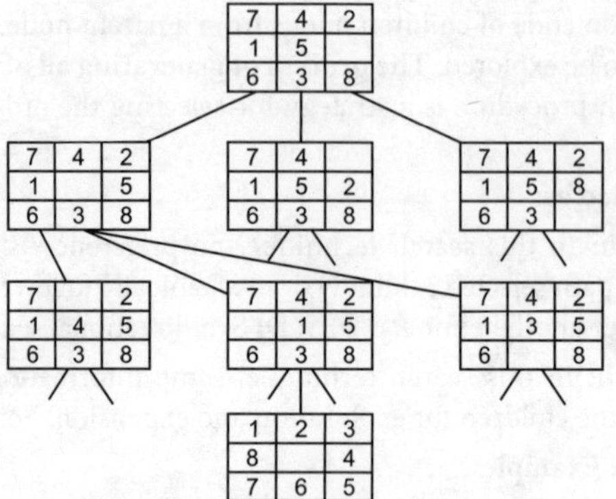

Fig. 3.2: Tree Diagram (search space) of 8-puzzle Problem

Q.4. How will you formulate- The Traveling Salesman Problem formulation.

"It involves n-cities with paths connecting the cities. A tour is any path which begins with some starting city, visits each of the other cities exactly once and returns to the starting city". A typical tour is depicted here, in Fig. 3.3.

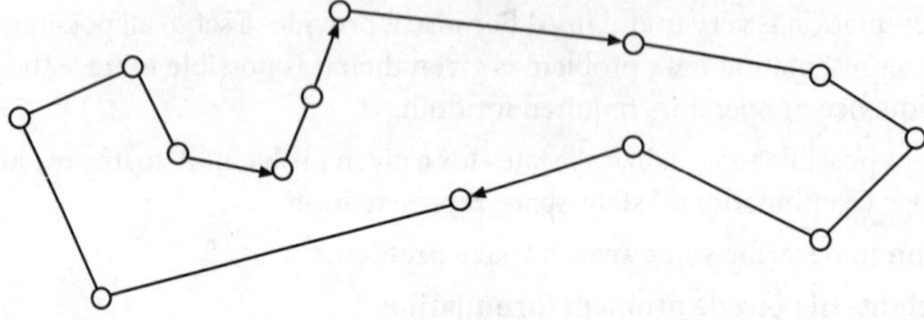

Fig. 3.3: TSP

The objective of a TSP is to find a minimal distance tour. To explore all such tours requires an exponential amount of time. As long as n is small, this approach works but it breaks down quickly as number of cities grow. If there are N-cities then the number of different paths among them is 1.2… $(N–1)$ or $(N–1)!$ The time to examine a single path is proportional to N. So, the total time required to perform this search is proportional to $N!$ *i.e.*, it requires O(N!) transverses through the graph, an exponential number.

TSP : This is a classical problem in graph theory. It has no closed, analytic and algorithmic solution. This problem is soluble for smaller number (n) of cities-But it breaks down as number of cities grow.

If there are n-cities, the number of different paths among them is $(n - 1)!$ Please note that the time to examine a single path is proportional to n. So, the total time to search is $n!$ Also note that if n is large then the time taken is also large. This phenomenon is known as **combinatorial explosion.**

NOTE : Even if CPU processes each more in 1 ms, it would take infinitely long time to arrive at a solution. This type of search is known as blind search.

What is the solution? There is no solution to such problems except invoking some special type of control strategies wherein the requirements of motility and systematicity have to be sacrificed. A guaranteed solution is found by making use of heuristics (heuristic searches). The heuristic search improves the efficiency of a search process though the completeness is rarely achieved. They are just like tour guides that are good to the extent that they point in generally interesting direction and bad to the extent that they miss points of interest to particular individuals. In the process of heuristic search an excellent path may sometime be overlooked but in general they improve the quality of paths that are explored.

NOTE : Using heuristic searches (rules of thumb) we get a good solution to the hard problem (such as TSP) in less than exponential time.

Heuristics has different definitions as follows :

a. Heuristics means helping to discover or learn; guiding or furthering investigation.

b. **Newell, Show and Simon 1985 define :** or A process that may so we a given problem but offers no guarantees of doing so is called a **heuristic** for that problem.

c. **Marvin Merisky (1963) Define :** "A heuristic is any method or trick used to improve the efficiency of a problem-sowing program and that heuristic methods are related to improving problem – sowing performance."

d. **Feigenbaum and Feldmen (1963) define :** "A state heuristic (heuristic rule, heuristic method) is a rule of thumb, strategy, trick, simplification or any other kind of device that drastically limits search for solutions in large problem spaces. Heuristics do not guarantee optimal solutions, in fact, they do not guarantee any solution at all that can be said for a useful heuristic is that it offers solutions that are good enough most of the time."

e. **Judea Pearl (1983) Define :** "It is the nature of good heuristics both that they provide a simple means of indicating which among several courses of action is to be preferred and that they are not necessarily guaranteed to identify the most effective course of action, but do so sufficiently often. It is often said that heuristic methods are unpredictable, they work wonders most of the time but may fail miserably some of the time."

Thus, heuristic programming differs significantly from algorithmic programming even though heuristic programs themselves must be expressed in algorithmic form.

Heuristics in TSM problem : A significant improvement is seen if TSP is sowed using heuristic. Now the time required is proportional to N^2 instead of N!

For example, if $n = 5$ then

a. **Case 1 :** If combinational explosion is used, then paths to be examined are 5! = 120

b. **Case 2 :** If nearest neighbor heuristic is used, then number of paths to be examined are $5^2 = 25$ only.

This is a significant improvement.

Conclusions : A well designed heuristic function can play an important part in efficiently guiding a search/process towards a solution. Please understand the sometimes very simple heuristic function can provide a fairly good estimate of whether a path is any good or not. Also understand that more complex heuristic functions may be difficult.

Its standard formulation is as follows—

***States* :** Location specified by city.

***Actions* :** Driving along the roads between cities.

***Goal* :** City B.

***Path Cost* :** Total distance or expected travel time.

Q.5. Water Jug Problem

Problem formulation : The problem domain is as follows "We are given two jugs, a four-gallon one and a three-gallon one. Neither has any measuring markers on it. There is a pump which can be used to fill the jugs with water. How can we get exactly two gallons of water into the four-gallon jug?"

Solution : State space (x, y) where $x = 0, 1, 2, 3$ and 4 and $y = 0, 1, 2$ and 3.

Here, x represents the number of gallon of water in 4 gallon jug and

y represents the number of gallons of water in 3 gallon jug.

Initial state : $<x, y> = <0, 0>$

Goal state : $<x, y> = <2, n>$

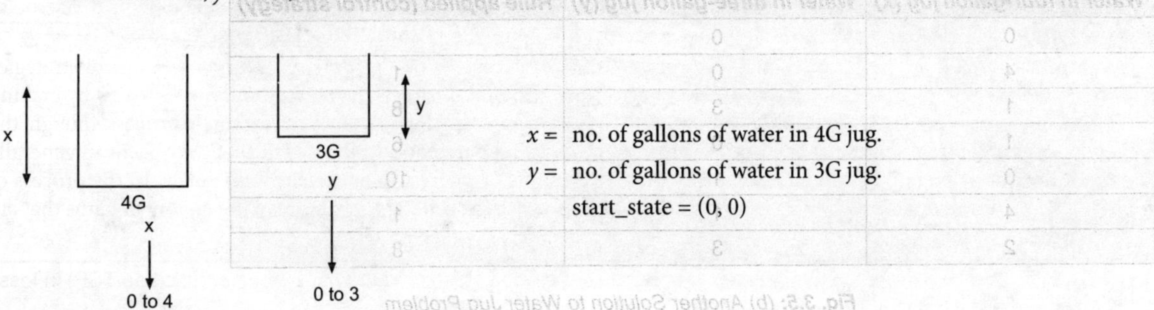

Production Rules are :

(x, y) → (x, 3) if y < 3	Fill 3-gallon jug. (*i.e.*, why *y* changes to 3 as its capacity is 3 only. So, *y* < 3)
(x, y) → (4, y) if x < 4	Fill 4-gallon jug. (*i.e.*, why *x* changes to 4 as its capacity is 4 only. So, *x* < 4)
(x, y) → (x, y-d) if y > 0	Pour some water out of 3G jug (*i.e.*, '*d*' amount of water) and this is true iff *y* has some water. So, *y* > 0.
(x, y) → (x-d, y) if x > 0	Pour some water out of 4G jug (*i.e.*, '*d*' amount of water) and this is true iff *x* has some water. So, *x* > 0.
(x, y) → (x, 0) if y > 0	Empty 3G jug on ground *i.e.*, *y* = 0 and this is possible if it has some water *i.e.*, *y* > 0.
(x, y) → (0, y) if x > 0	Empty 4G jug on ground *i.e.*, *x* = 0 and this is true iff it has some water *i.e.*, *x* > 0.
(x, y) → (x- (3-y)),3) if (x + y) >= 3 and y > 0	Pour water from 4G jug into 3G jug until 3G jug is full.
(x, y) → (4, y- (4-x))	Pour water from 3G jug into 4G jug until 4G jug is full.
(x, y) →(0, x + y) If (x + y) < = 3 and x > 0.	Pour entire water from 4G jug into 3G jug.
(x, y) →(x + y, 0) If (x + y) < = 4 and y > 0	Pour entire water from 3G jug into 4G jug.
(0, 2) → (2, 0) So, x => 2, y => 0.	Pour 2 Gallon from 3G jug into 4 -gallon jug.
(2, y) → (0, y) So, x (for 4G jug) =>0	Empty the 2G jug in the 4G jug on the ground.

Therefore, one possible solution is shown in Fig. 3.5 (a).

Water in four-gallon jug (x)	*Water in three-gallon jug (y)*	*Rule applied (control strategy)*
0	0	
0	3	1
3	0	10
3	3	1
4	2	8
0	2	6 or 12
2	0	10 or 11

Fig. 3.5: (a) One Solution to Water Jug Problem

The 2nd solution can be —

Water in four-gallon jug (x)	*Water in three-gallon jug (y)*	*Rule applied (control strategy)*
0	0	
4	0	1
1	3	8
1	0	6
0	1	10
4	1	1
2	3	8

Fig. 3.5: (b) Another Solution to Water Jug Problem

Thus, we find that how an informal problem state has been converted to a formal problem state. But the rules should be stated explicitly and not written because they are allowable. For example, rule-1 in table-1 states that — "Fill the four-gallon jug", but it should have been— "if the four-gallon jug is not already filled completely". However, the rule as stated in its first-form is not wrong as there is no condition that the already filled jug cannot be filled. So, in order to increase the efficiency of problem-solving program, it is imperative to encode some constraints in the left side of the rules so that the rules should lead to a solution. Thus, rules should be made more general.

Water jug problem is a simple example of solving a problem through state space search.

Even these approaches may not be exhaustive. So, we go with another method of problem- reduction techniques.

Q.6. What is Problem Reduction? What are the production systems?

Ans. The process of decomposing (or breaking) up of a complex problem into a set of primitive sub- problems, finding the sub-solutions for these sub-problems and then integrating all these sub- solutions to get the solution of the given complex problem (as a whole) is known as problem reduction.

Practically, our space search is said to be good if a solution to a problem is naturally expressed in terms of either a final state or a path from an initial state to the final state. **Please note that we should be able to define rules for transforming one state to another based on the available actions in the domain.** Problem reduction is better if it is easy to decompose a problem into independent sub-problems. Also note that we have to define rules to do this. Here, searching will be less. We will discuss about it in detail a bit later.

Production Systems : These systems were proposed by Emil Post in 1943. They are also known **a inferential systems,** Rule-based systems or simply productions. For describing and performing the search operation in AI programs it is useful to structure them. The process of solving the problem can usefully be modeled as a production system. If one adopts a system with production rules and a 'rule-interpreter', then the system is known as a production system. In these systems, the working memory of the system model's human short-term memory while the productions are part of long term memory. On each cycle of operation, productions are matched against the working memory of facts. And a production whose conditions are satisfied can add or delete facts in the working memory. Please note that this is opposite to the situation in databases. These production systems often have many rules and relatively fewer facts.

Rules of Production Systems :

Rule-1 : Production systems represent both knowledge as well as action.

Rule-2 : Production system provide a language in which the representation of expert knowledge is very natural.

Rule-3 : Production systems provide a heuristics model for human behavior.

Rule-4 : Production systems model strong data-driven nature of intelligent action. Whenever new inputs enter the database, the behavior of the system changes.

Rule-5 : Production systems allow us to add new rules easily without disturbing the rest of the system.

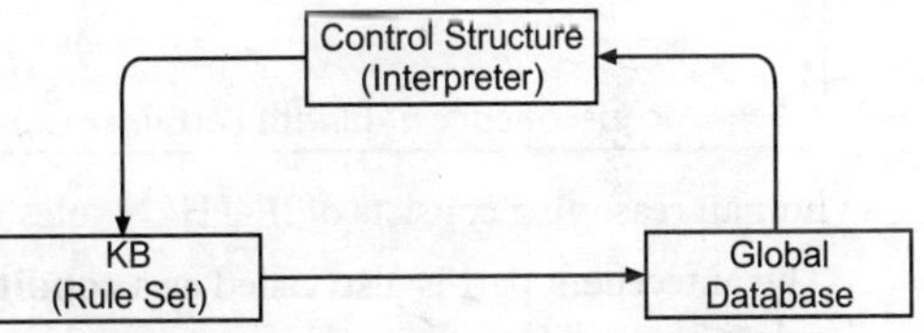

Fig. 3.5: (c) Parts of a Production System

Let us now see the architecture of a production system. It is shown in Fig. 3.5(*c*). It comprises of three main components—

1. Rule base.
2. Global database
3. Control structure.

The process of transforming a problem statement into these components of the production system is called as problem representation. Selection of a good representation is an art in AI to solve practical problems and that there are many ways to represent a problem. **Please note that a good problem solution requires an efficient control strategy, good representations for problem states, moves and goal conditions.** The effort that is required to solve a problem in AI depends on the problem representation scheme. **Also note that we select those representations which need small state spaces.** If the state space is not less, then we can even reduce or combine certain rules also. If these simple transformations do not work then we can even reformulate our problem but our ultimate goal is to be achieved i.e., of small state space.

Let us now see these various components of a production system.

I Rule Base : Production rules are extremely popular knowledge representation (KR) structure today. They are conditional IF-THEN branches only. These rules apply on the global database. Each rule may have a Precondition. If the precondition of the rule is satisfied then only the corresponding rule is applied to a state. It is only after the application of rule that the problem's state changes. The KR in production [Solution → Action] systems is decoded in a declarative (not procedural) form which comprises of a set of rules which are of this form—

Such problem situation-action rules are often called as production-rules or IF-THEN rules. And a system which uses this form of knowledge is called as a **production system**. Each of the IF condition is called as **clause** (*s*). A set of clauses joined by logical ANDs is called as a **Horn clause**. Each production rule constitutes a chunk of knowledge Practically speaking, to achieve modularity, the entire knowledge is broken down into fragments. The ACTION part of one production rule becomes the CONDITION part for another production rule and **this is known as the production-rule-chain or networking of rules.**

For example, the University's grading system might be reasoned as follows— IF the marks obtained are less than 75

THEN declare the student as in First Class.

Associated with these production rules are certainty factors/probability factors.

For example,

IF Car doesn't work

THEN battery is down OR battery connection are poor.

In this scenario, we can use an certainty factor also and say that there is a strong evidence (0.9) that the battery is down. This factor of probability can also be used here. The range of this factor is from 0 to 1 as 0 ≤ probability ≤ 1. This type of reasoning is also called as inexact reasoning. This example shows that

```
IF    <antecedent-1>
      <antecedent-2>
THEN
      ®
      <consequence 1> (with certainty C1)
      <consequence 1> (with certainty C2)
      ®
      <consequence n> (with certainty Cn)
```

human reasoning consists of IF-THEN rules with certainty factor attached with it. The syntax of these rules is—

The antecedent part is also called as a **condition part** or left-hand side (LHS). The consequence part of a production rule is also called as the **action part** or right-hand side (RHS). When LHS matches then the designated condition in the production rule (action) will be executed. Please note here that the application of rule changes the database.

Many systems like our earlier water jug problem, OPS5 (a production system language), expert systems, SOAR (general problem-solving architecture) etc. provide an overall architecture of a production system described above. It allows the programmer to write rules which define particular problems to be solved.

II Global Database : It is a central data structure used by the production system. This database may be as simple as a small matrix of numbers or as complex as a large relational indexed file structure. Please note, however, that this database is not the same as database of DBMS. The global database can be accessed by all the rules. Also remember that no part of the database is local to any of the rules in particular. Each rule has a precondition which is either satisfied or not by the global database. If the precondition is satisfied, the rule can be applied. Since the application of rules changes the database, so it is also called as a dynamic structure (continuously changing due to the operation of production rules) or working memory or short-term memory.

III Control Structure/Strategy : It means an interpreter program to control the order in which the production rules are fixed. Also it resolves the conflicts if more than one rule becomes applicable simultaneously. Please note that this structure applies the rules to the database, again and again, until a description of the goal state is produced. Also note that this process of identifying the rules which are tried until some sequence of them is found which produced a database satisfying the termination condition (goal) is called as a **searching process.**

Efficient control strategies means enough knowledge about the problem to solve so that the rule or the sequence of rules, so selected has a good chance of being the most appropriate. The control strategies are of two types—

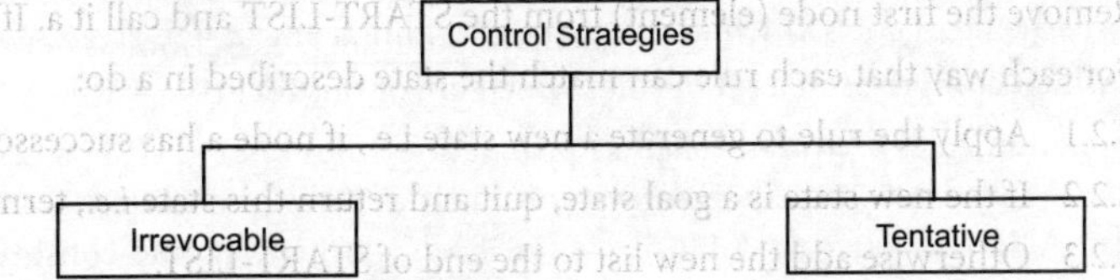

Fig. 3.6: Types of Control Strategies

Let us define and explain them now, one by one.

Irrevocable Control : Here in, an acceptable rule is selected and applied irrevocably without provision for reconsideration later.

Tentative control : Herein, an applicable rule is selected arbitrarily or based on some good reason, then it (rule) is applied but with an option to return to this point in the computation to apply some other rule.

We can use two methods here. They are as follows—

a. Back-tracking.

b. Graph search control.

Back-tracking is a process in which the control strategy can be tentative. In this method, a rule is selected and if it does not lead to a solution, then the intervening steps are forgotten and instead another rule is selected. This back tracking technique can be used regardless of how much or how little knowledge is available for choice of rules. **Please note that if no knowledge is available, rules can be selected according to some arbitrary scheme.** Finally, the control will back track to select the appropriate rule. To reduce the frequency of back tracking to select suitable rules can be reduced and made more efficient if good rule-selection knowledge can be used.

Graph Search Control makes a provision for keeping track of the effects of several sequences of rules simultaneously. As we know that graphs (or trees) are very useful data structures to keep track of the effects of several sequences of rules. We can keep track of the various rules applied and the database produced by a structure called as a **search trees.** At the root of the tree is a description of the initial configuration. The links or arcs (directed) show various rules that can be applied. It represents the states which can be reached by just one move from the initial state. This strategy keeps on generating a tree till a database is produced which satisfies the termination condition. **Please note that this strategy is inefficient as the resulting tree grows too rapidly. This happens because we show all applicable rules being applied to every state description. Also note that an intelligent control strategy would grow a tree much narrower using its special knowledge to focus the growth of the tree towards the goal.**

However, the control strategy has certain characteristics. These characteristics are as follows—

1. It should cause motion from the initial state that must lead to a solution. For example, consider the following problem.

   Problem : Water-jug problem.

   Control Strategy : Start each time at the top of the list of applicable rules and apply it. What happens with this control strategy?

   We will continue filling indefinitely the four-litre jug with water in the first operator. Will this give us a solution?

   No, it doesn't give any solution as this does not cause motion from the initial state.

2. **It should be Systematic :** If in our water-jug problem, we apply the appropriate rules at random in our solution, instead of starting every time from the first rule, again and again then with the application of this control strategy, a tree is generated. This control strategy is better than the first one and leads to solution eventually. The tree gets expanded at more and more levels and needs many steps for expansion. This happened because this control strategy has been selected taking into view the local motion only *i.e.*, considering one step at a time. It does not consider global motion i.e., taking into account a collective view of many steps. The tree is expanded continuously until the goal is reached. Now, we call this control strategy as breadth-first search (BFS). In BFS, the new states so generated at each level are put at the end of the queue which generated them. A bfs works like this—

   Please note here that these strategy examples are the nodes for goal at the nth level before going to $(n + 1)$th level. The algorithm for bfs is as follows—

Step-1 : Create a variable called START-LIST and set it to the initial state.

Step-2 : Until a goal state is found or START-LIST is empty do:

2.1 Remove the first node (element) from the START-LIST and call it a. If START-LIST is empty, quit.

2.2 For each way that each rule can match the state described in a do:

2.2.1 Apply the rule to generate a new state i.e., if node a has successors then generate all of them.

2.2.2 If the new state is a goal state, quit and return this state *i.e.*, terminate search.

2.2.3 Otherwise add the new list to the end of START-LIST.

Step-3 : Goto step-2.

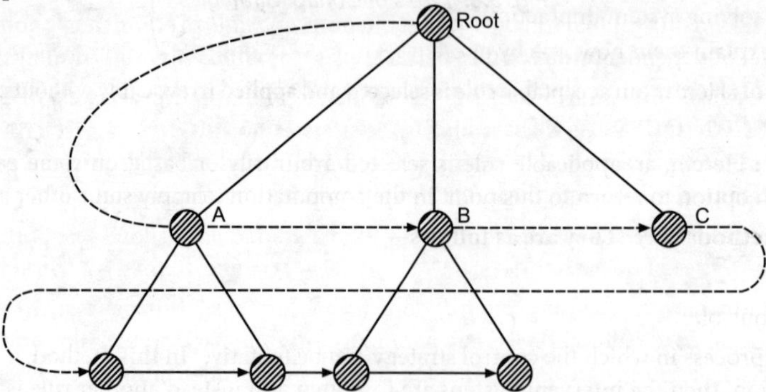

Fig. 3.7: Search Tree after Two Levels of Search

Control strategy for putting new states in front of queue : As we already know that a queue works on a LIFO principle *i.e.*, last-in, fist-out. Herein, a single branch of the tree is traversed until it finds a solution or until a decision to terminate the path is made. Please note that this means that if two states A_1 and A_2 are produced by applying operators to a state A, then every state reachable from A_1 will be examined before any state reachable from A_2. Also note that if there are an infinite number of states reachable from A_1, then A_2 will never be examined. So, what should be done?

In such a case, we need to impose some kind of depth cut-off. It is defined as the maximum length of operator application-sequence. Hence, the search tree or path is terminated when it reaches dead-end, produces previous state or it becomes larger then futility limit. Please understand that **back-tracking occurs**, to the most recent created state from which alternate moves are available. A chronological backtracking is one in which the order in which the steps are undone will depend only on the temporal sequence in which the steps were originally created. Another variant of backtracking is dependency directed backtracking which involves truth maintenance which uses non-monotonic reasoning and will be discussed later on. This search procedure is called as Depth-First Search (DFS). A DFS, in general, will look like this—

We can generate such a tree for our water-jug problem also, as shown below in Fig. 3.9.

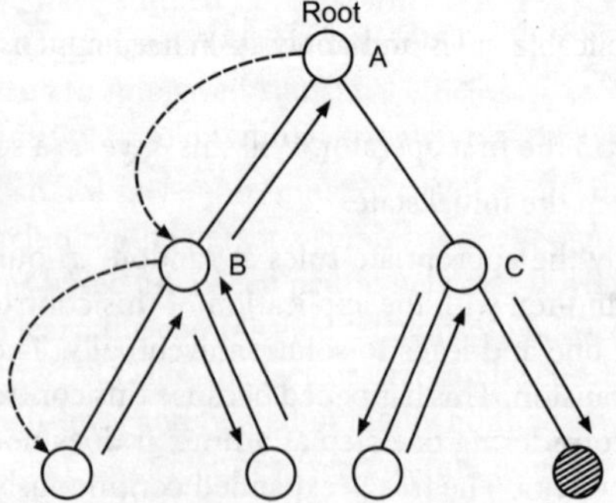

Fig. 3.8: Search Tree using DFS

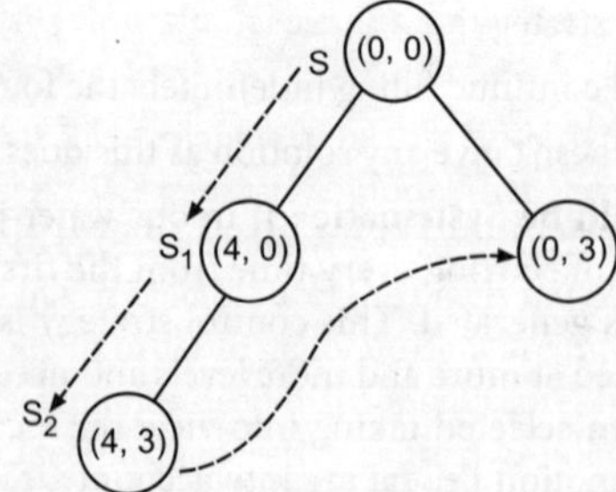

Fig. 3.9: Tree for Water Jug Problem

The algorithm of dfs, in general is as follows :

Step-1 : Put the initial node on a list, START-LIST.

Step-2 : If (START-LIST is empty) or (START-LIST = GOAL), terminate search.

Step-3 : Remove the first node from START. Call this node a.

Step-4 : If (a = GOAL) terminate search with success.

Step-5 : Else if node a has successors, generate all of them and add them at the beginning.

Step-6 : Goto step-2.

Chronological back tracking, used in DFS involves lot of time and is not efficient also. In real problems, this can even make a problem-solving system impractical.

Non-chronological or dependency directed back tracking, those choice are withdrawn on which the dead-end depends. Herein, time does not determine which choices are to be withdrawn as it happens in chronological back tracking.

SEARCHING TECHNIQUES : As we have already discussed that searching our state space forms the core heart of AI problem solving. Once a problem is formulated, we then need to solve it. We can use this technique in many areas like theorem proving, game playing, expert systems, natural language processing etc. This involves the tasks like deduction, inferencing, planning, common sense reasoning, fuzzy logic etc.

Q.7. What are different types of Searching?

Ans. As we known that in a search method or technique or strategy, we firstly select one option and leave other options if this option is our final goal, (solution) else we continue selecting, testing and expanding until either a solution is found or there are no more states to be expanded. This will be determined by the search method. So, we need many different types of search algorithms. Basically, there are 2-types of searches—

1. Uniformed or blind search or unguided.
2. Informed or heuristic search or guided.

But, **please note that all search techniques are distinguished by the order in which nodes are expanded.** Various search strategies are shown in Fig. 3.10.

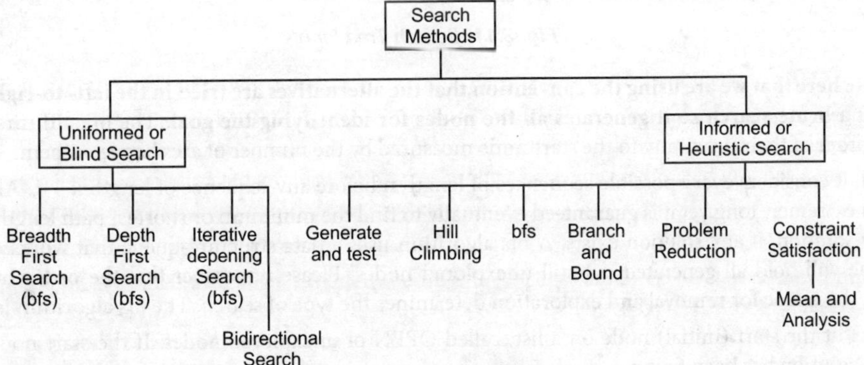

Fig. 3.10: Types of Searching

Let us now discuss these strategies one by one in detail.

Uniformed/Blind/Brute Force/Exhaustive Search : As we know that the state-space is a directed graph in which each node is a state and each arc shows the application of an operator transforming a state to a successor state. **But please note that a node is different from a state. A node is** a data structure used to represent the search tree. However, a state corresponds to a configuration of the world. So, nodes are on some particular paths always. They are defined by the parent node pointer. On the other hand, states are not on some particular paths. **Also note here that two different nodes can contain the same world state if that state is generated via two different search paths.** And a solution is a path from the initial or start state to a goal state. These goal states may be defined explicitly or as a set of states satisfying a given predicate. In blind or uniformed search, these is no order in which the solution paths are considered *i.e.*, it uses no domain specific information to search a solution in the search space. Again, the state space is combinational, so this type of search is actually impracticable for the nontrivial problems. It is called as brute-force search as it examines every node in the tree until a goal is found. These algorithms make some assumptions:

3. A procedure must be there to find all successors of a given node *i.e.*, all states are reachable from the current state and that too by a single operator application.
4. The state-space graph is a tree. It means that there is only one start state (*i.e.*, root of tree) and that the path from the start node to any other node is unique.
5. Whenever a node is expanded, creating a node for each of its successors, the successor nodes contain pointers back to the parent node. Finally, when a goal node is generated, the path from the root to the goal can be easily found.

So, blind search algorithms use only the initial state, search operators and a test for a solution.

It proceeds systematically by exploring nodes either randomly or in some predetermined order.

Breadth-First Search (BFS)

It is the simplest form of blind search. In this technique the root node is expanded first, then all of its successors are expanded and then their successors and so on. In general, in bfs, all nodes are expanded at a given depth in the search tree before any nodes at the next level are expanded.

It means that all immediate children of nodes are explored before any of the children's children are considered. The search tree generated by bfs is shown below in Fig. 3.11.

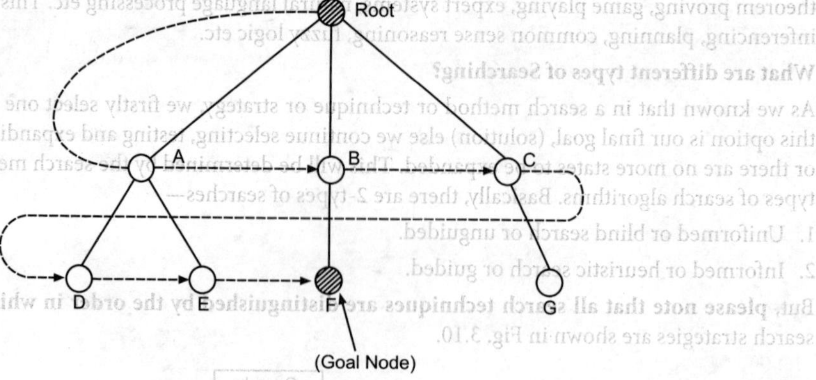

Fig. 3.11: Search Tree for bfs

Please note here that we are using the convention that the alternatives are tried in the left- to-right order. Also note that bfs is a brute-search so it generates all the nodes for identifying the goal. The breadth-first method expands nodes in order of their proximity to the start node measured by the number of arcs between them.

In general, it considers every possible sequences of length n before any sequence of length $n + 1$. Although this search may be an extremely long yet it is guaranteed eventually to find the minimum or shortest path length (possible solution sequence) solution, if any solution exists. A bfs algorithm uses a data structure-queue that works on FIFO principle. This queue will hold all generated but still unexplored nodes. Please remember that the **order in which nodes are placed** on the queue for removal and exploration determines the type of search. The bfs algorithm is as follows—

Step-1 : Put the start (initial) node on a list, called OPEN of unexplored nodes. If the start node is a goal node, a solution has been found.

Step-2 : If (OPEN is empty) or (OPEN = GOAL), no solution exists, so terminate search.

Step-3 : Remove the first node, a, from OPEN and place it in a list called CLOSED, of expanded nodes.

Step-4 : Expand node, a. If it has no successor then goto step-2.

Step-5 : Place all successors of node, a, at the end of OPEN.

Step-6 : If any of the successors of node, a, is a goal state then solution is found.

Time and Space complexity of bfs algorithm :

The amount of time taken for generating these nodes is proportional to the depth, d and branching factor, b and is given by —

$$1 + b + b^2 + b^3 + \ldots + b^d$$

∴ Time complexity is $O(b^d)$.

Now, bfs has to remember each and every node it has generated. So, the space-complexity will also depend upon the function of depth, d and the branching factor, b.

So, space complexity is given by

$$1 + b + b2 + b3 + \ldots + b^d$$

or, Space complexity is $O(b^d)$.

Please note that bfs is a systematic search strategy because it considers all nodes (states) **all level-1 first and then all states at level-2 and so on.** If any solution exists then bfs is guaranteed to find it. **Also note that if there are many solutions then bfs will always find the shallowest goal state first.** If the solution's cost is an increasing function of depth then it finds the one which is a cheapest solution.

Let us now discuss the advantages and disadvantages of bfs—

Advantages of bfs : BFS has some advantages and are given below—

1. BFS will never get trapped exploring a blind alley.
2. It is guaranteed to find a solution if one exists.

Disadvantages of bfs : BFS has certain disadvantages also. They are given below—

1. Time complexity and space complexity are both $O(b^d)$ *i.e.* exponential type. This is a very big hurdle.
2. All nodes are to be generated in bfs. So, even unwanted nodes are to be remembered (stored in queue) which is of no practical use of the search.

Depth-first Search (DFS) : DFS begins by expanding the initial node *i.e.* by using an operator, generate all successors of the initial node and test them. It (dfs) is characterized by the expansion of the most recently generated or deepest node first. DFS needs to store the path from the root to the leaf node as well as the unexpanded nodes. It is neither complete nor optimal. If dfs goes down an infinite branch (depth cut-off point) will not end till a goal state is found. Even if it is found, there may be a better solution at a higher level. This depth cut-off (*d*) introduces many problems also. If d is set too shallow, goal may be missed. If *d* is set too deep then extra computation may be performed. The dfs algorithm is as follows—

Step-1 : Put the initial node on a list, START-LIST.

Step-2 : If (START-LIST is empty) or (START = GOAL) then terminate (end) search.

Step-3 : Remove the first node from START-LIST. Call this node, *a*.

Step-4 : If (*a* == GOAL) then terminate search with success.

Step-5 : Else if node a has successors, generate all of these and add them at the beginning of START- LIST.

Step-6 : Goto step-2.

So, the search tree for dfs is as shown in Fig. 3.12.

Time and space complexities for dfs : The amount of time taken for generating these nodes is proportional to the depth, *d* and branching factor, *b* and is given by

$$1 + b + b^2 + b^3 + \ldots b^d$$

$\therefore$ Time complexity = $O(b^d)$.

Root
A
B
C
D
E
F
(Goal State)

Fig. 3.12: Search Tree for dfs.

Also note that dfs stores only the current path it is pursing. So, the **space complexity** will be a linear function of depth, *d*. So,

Space complexity = $O(d)$.

The value of cut-off depth (d) is important here as then otherwise the search will go on and on.

Two cases arise—

3. If d is small, solution may not be found.
4. If d is large, time complexity will be more.

Advantages of DFS : DFS has some advantages. They are given below—

a. Memory requirements in dfs are less as only nodes on the current path are stored.

b. By chance, dfs may find a solution without examining much of the search space of all.

Disadvantages of DFS : This type of search can go on and on, deeper and deeper into the search space and thus, we can get lost. This is referred to as **blind alley.**

Depth first: Branch and Board : The Branch and Bound control strategy generate one path at a time. It also keeps track of the best path so found. This value is used as a bound on future candidates. As paths are constructed one at a time, the algorithm examines each partially completed path. If the algorithm determines that the best possible extension to a path branch will have greater cost than the board, it eliminates that partial path and all of its possible extensions. This reduces search considerably but still leaves an exponential number of paths.

This variation of depth-first, guarantees optimal solution. All other variations of dfs experience the undesirable property that obtained (if at all) is NOT guaranteed to be optimal. This is so because all these algorithms discontinue search once a solution is found. But this algorithm (in general) does not stop searching immediately after finding the first solution.

```
//Unbounded Dfs - Branch - and - Bound
                          Bound. UDFBB(n){
if I(n) > cost (solution) then return; if n is a goal node then
                              solution : = superior(m, n);
          for each nᵢ of
n do UDFBB
(nᵢ);
return; }
```

Here, superior (m, n) reports the better of the two goal nodes m and n, in terms of cost.

The **disadvantage** here is that this algorithm may blindly go deeper into some unpromising paths and thus generate to many nodes in the worst case.

Depth-First Iterative Deepening Search : It is a general strategy often used in combination with dfs that finds the best depth limit. It begins by performing dfs to a depth of one, then depth of two, depth of three and so on, until a solution is found or some maximum depth is reached. It combines the benefits of both bfs and dfs. For example, consider a tree as shown.

We have shown 3-stages of iterative—deepening search. **Please note here that the number of nodes expanded by iterative-deepening search is not much more than that would be using bfs.** Next, we write an algorithm for depth first iterative deepening search—

Step-1 : Start

Step-2 : Initialize $d \leftarrow O$

Step-3 : do

$d \leftarrow d + 1$;

DFID (root, d);

Until SUCCESS;

Step-4 : End.

This algorithm starts with the smallest d = 1. It then increments d in a loop on encountering FAILURE until a SUCCES is found.

This search also guarantees to find a shortest path solution as it expands all nodes at a given depth before expanding nodes at a greater depth. Also note that it performs **wasted computations** before reaching the goal depth.

Time and space complexities : The time and space complexities of this search algorithm are also $O(b^d)$ and $O(d)$ respectively.

It can be shown that depth first iterative deepening is asymptotically optimal, among brute force tree searches, in terms of time, space and length of the solution. In fact, it is linear in its space complexity like dfs and is asymptotically optimal to bfs in terms of the number of nodes expanded. **Please note that in general, iterative deepening is preferred uninformed search method when there is a large search space and the depth of the solution is unknown. Also note that iterative deepening search is analogous to bfs in that it explores a complete layer going to the next layer.** It is better to develop an iterative analog to uniform – cost search, inheriting the depth–first's guarantee to find a solution and avoiding its memory requirements. The basic idea is to use increasing path – cost limits instead of increasing depth limits. The resulting algorithm called iterative lengthening search, incurs substantial overhead as compared to uniform – cost search.

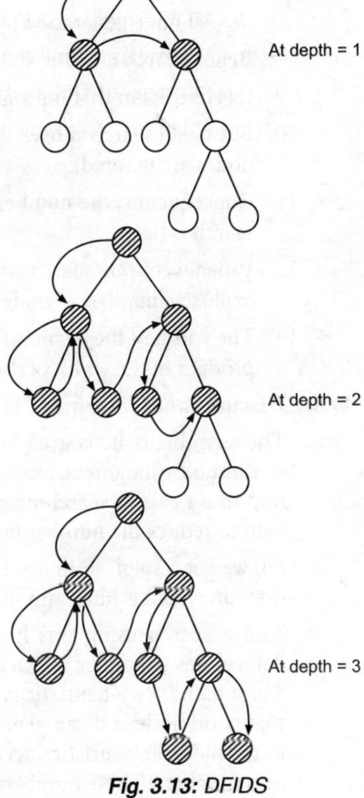

Fig. 3.13: DFIDS

Advantages of Depth-first Iterative Deepening Search

1. It is guaranteed to find a shortest path solution.
2. It is a preferred uniformed search method when the search space is large and the depth of the solution is not known.

Disadvantages of Depth-first Iterative Deepening Search

a. It performs wasted computations before reaching the goal depth.

b. The time complexity is $O(b^d)$ *i.e.*, exponential type only.

Is this search bfs or dfs?

This search is similar to both bfs as well as dfs.

How bfs? It is similar to bfs in that it explores a complete layer of new nodes at each iteration before going to the next layer.

How dfs? It is similar to dfs for a single iteration.

Why is it called as iterative?

This search terminates at the depth, *d* on each iteration if no goal has been found, removes all nodes from the queue, increments *d* by one and initiates the search again. Hence, it is called as an **iterative search.**

Bidirectional Search : This search is used when a problem has a single goal state that is given explicity and all the node generation operators have inverses. Searching is done by searching forward from the initial node and backward from goal node simultaneously. So, the program must save (store) the nodes so generated on both search frontiers until a common node is found. Both dfs and bfs can be modified slightly to perform this search.

1 (start) 2 3 4 5 6 7 8 9 (goal)

$b^{d/2}$ + $b^{d/2} = 2\,(b^{d/2})$

Time and Space Complexities of Bidirectional Search : To perform this search to a depth of *k*, the search is made from one direction and the nodes at depth k are stored. At some time, a search to a depth of *k* and *k* + 1 is made from the other direction and all nodes generated are matched against the nodes stored from the other side. This process is repeated for lengths *k* = 0 to *d*/2 from both the directions. So, its time and space complexities are both $O(b^d/2)$ when node matching is done in constant time per node.

Advantages of Bidirectional Search :

7. It is used to solve the 8-puzzle problem.
8. Only slight modification of dfs and bfs can be done to perform this search.

Disadvantages of Bidirectional Search :

a. Since the number of nodes increases as bd with depth d, so such problems become intractable for large depths.

b. All node generation operators must have inverses also as only then this type of search can be used.

Beam Search :

9. It is like Bfs in that it progresses level by level.
10. But beam search moves downward only through the best, W nodes at each level by applying heuristics, the other nodes are ignored.
11. Consequently, the number of nodes explored remains manageable even if there is a great deal of branching and the search is deep.
12. Whenever beam search is used, there are only W nodes under consideration at any depth rather than the exponentially explosive number of nodes as is done in bfs.
13. The width of the beam is fixed and whatever be the depth of the tree, the number of alternatives to be scanned is the product of the width of the beam and the depth.

Q.8. Discuss about Informed/Heuristic Searches.

Ans. The term heuristic is used for algorithms which find solutions among all possible ones. Recall that heuristic is a rule of thumb or judgment technique that leads to a solution but provides no guarantee of success. Still heuristic play an important role in searching process because of the exponential nature of most of the problems. Please note that they help to reduce the number of alternatives from an **exponential number** to a **polynomial number.**

So, we get a solution in a reasonable amount of time. The additional information about the properties of the specific domain which is built into the state and operator definitions is called as **heuristic information.**

And a search using this heuristic information is called as a **heuristic or informed search.** A heuristic function determines a number which determines how good or bad a node can be. If ev(n) is a best solution state and ev(n, p) is a best path then a heuristic is any information which shows how good or bad that path is likely to be so, we can expand that good node and can generate only its children. There is no blind expansion. So, pruning of the search tree occurs. In nutshell, the heuristics needed to solve problems are expressed as a heuristic function which maps the problem states into numbers. These numbers are then appropriately used to guide search. Heuristic search methods use some general-purpose search techniques. The simplest is the generate And-Test method which is discussed next.

Generate-And-Test Algorithm : It is a weak method meaning that it helps usually but not always. It may or may not overcome the combinational explosion problem of AI. This algorithm works in two modules—

a. Generator module: It creates the possible solutions.

b. Tester module: It tests (or evaluates) each of the proposed solution either accepting or rejecting that solution.

Please understand that here an action may stop when one acceptable solution is found or action may continue until all possible solutions are found. Let us develop its algorithm now—

Step-1 : Generate a possible candidate solution which can either be a point in the problem space or a path from the initial state.

Step-2 : Test to see if this possible solution or candidate solution is a real solution by comparing the state reached with the set of goal states.

Step-3 : If it is a real, acceptable solution then return, success else repeat from step-1 again (as it is a failure).

This algorithm is basically a dfs procedure only as complete solutions must be created before testing. **Please note that when it is used in a systematic form then it is simply an exhaustive search of the problem space.** It can also operate by generating solutions randomly and hence is often called as a **British Museum method**. However, in this method also there will be no guarantee that a solution will ever be found. So, we need a heuristic to sharpen the search. But this is useful for simple problems and is in efficient for problems having large state space search.

Hill Climbing : It is so called because of the way the nodes are selected for expansion. At each point in the search path, a successor node that appears to lead most quickly to the top of the hill (goal) is selected for exploration. In this method of searching, the generate-and-test method is augmented by a heuristic foundation which measures the closeness of the current state to the goal state. Hill climbing can be employed if the path to the goal does not matter. It is a local search method in which we consider the state space landscape. This is shown in Fig. 3.12.

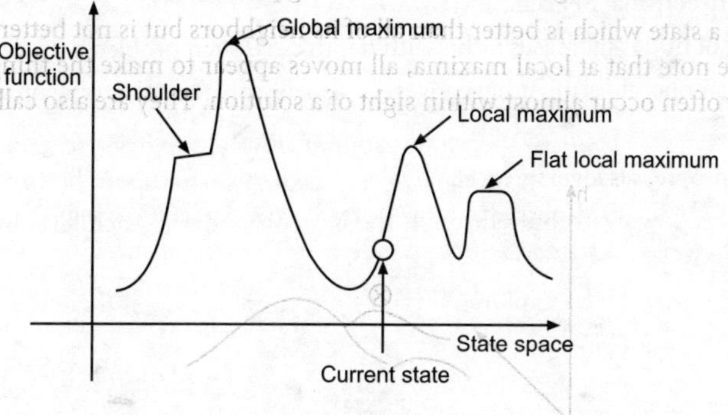

Fig. 3.12: State Space Landscape for Local Search

A landscape has both "location" (defined by the state) and "elevation" (defined by the value of the heuristic cost function or objective function). The aim is to find global minimum (lowest valley) if the elevation corresponds to

NOTE : You can convert from one to the other just by inserting a minus sign.

Heuristic cost function and if the elevation corresponds to the objective function then the aim will be to find the highest peak or global maximum.

Local search algorithm explores this landscape. A complete local search algorithm always finds a goal if one exists. An optimal algorithm always finds a global minimum/maximum.

Hill climbing search modifies the current state to try to improve it. This is shown in Fig. 3.12 by an arrow. It is in this way that the cost function provides a task-specific knowledge into the control process.

So, a search tree is generated with the help of heuristic function. As explained earlier also, hill climbing is like dfs where the most promising child is selected for expansion. When the children have been generated, alternative choices are evaluated using the heuristic function. The path that appears most promising is then chosen. No further reference to the parent or other children is retained. Please note that there is practically, no difference between hill-climbing and dfs except that the children of the node that has been expanded are sorted by the remaining distance. Let us now write an algorithm for hill-climbing—

Step-1 : Put the initial node on a list, START-LIST.

Step-2 : If (START-LIST is empty) or (START-LIST is GOAL) then terminate search.

Step-3 : Remove the first-node from the START-LIST. Call this node, n.

Step-4 : If (n = GOAL) then terminate search with SUCCESS.

Step-5 : Else if node, n, has successors then generate all of them. Find how far they are from the goal node. Sort them by the remaining distance from the goal and add them to the beginning of START-LIST.

Step-6 : Goto step-2.

Let us consider a tree and apply our algorithm now.

Here, we put the initial node *i.e.* root on a START-LIST. If START-LIST is empty or if START- LIST is our goal itself then the search terminates. Else we remove this node (*n*) from the START- LIST and generates its successors. We sort this START-LIST on the basis of the distances from the goal (see fig. 3.14) and keep on repeating this process till a goal is found. Please note that a new state has to be better, meaning that if we consider the cost function then it means a lower value and if we consider the objective function then it means a higher value. If the algorithm is constantly following the direction which gives the fastest rate of increase then it is called as the **steepest ascent hill climbing**. But if the lowest

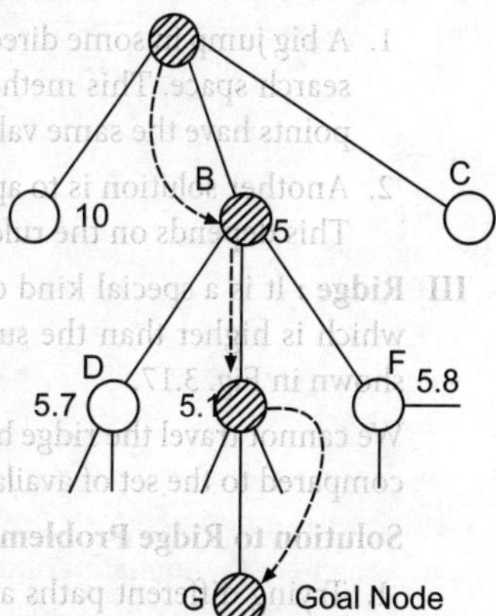

Fig. 3.14: Hill Climbing Search Tree

cost is best then it is a **downhill algorithm**. Also note that this algorithm is called as a steepest rise with back-tracking search method because it is prepared to back up and try a different path if the steepest one leads to a dead end. **Hill climbing is sometimes called as a greedy local search** because it grabs a good neighbor state without thinking ahead about where to go next. But hill climbing suffers from following problems—

I. Local maximum : It is a state which is better than all of its neighbors but is not better than some other states which are farther away. Please note that at local maxima, all moves appear to make the things worse. They are sometimes frustrating also as they often occur almost within sight of a solution. They are also called as **foot-hills**. It is shown in Fig. 3.15.

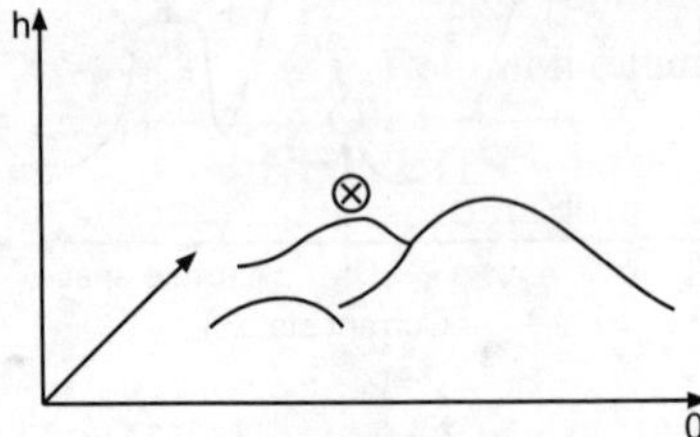

Fig. 3.15: Local Maximum or (foot hill)

Solution to this Problem :

1. One possible solution is backtracking.

   We can backtrack to some earlier node and try to go in a different direction to attain the global peak. We can maintain a list of paths almost taken and go back to one of them if the path that was taken leads to a dead end.

2. Another solution can be a list of promising plans.

II. Plateau : It is a flat area of the search space in which a whole set of neighboring states (nodes) have the same value. On a plateau, it is not possible to determine the best direction in which to move by making local comparisons. Actually, plateau is an area of the state space landscape where the evaluation function is flat. It can be a flat local maximum (from which no uphill exist exists) or a shoulder from which it is possible to make progress. A plateau is shown in Fig. 3.15.It is a flat area of the search space in which a whole set of neighboring states (nodes) have the same value. On a plateau, it is not possible to determine the best direction in which to move by making local comparisons. Actually, plateau is an area of the state space landscape where the evaluation function is flat. It can be a flat local maximum (from which no uphill exist exists) or a shoulder from which it is possible to make progress. A plateau is shown in Fig. 3.16.

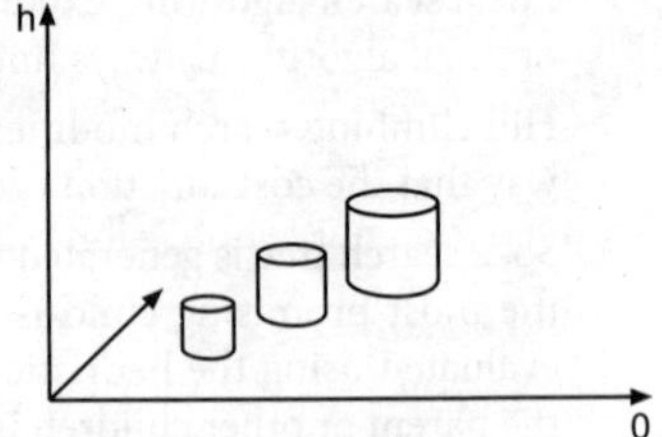

Fig. 3.16: Plateau

Solution to this Problem :

1. A big jump in some direction can be done in order to get to a new section of search space. This method is recommended as in a plateau all neighboring points have the same value.
2. Another solution is to apply small steps several times in the same direction. This depends on the rules available.

III Ridge : It is a special kind of local maximum. It is an area of the search space which is higher than the surrounding areas and that itself has a slope. This is shown in Fig. 3.17.

We cannot travel the ridge by single moves as the orientation of the high region compared to the set of available moves makes it impossible.

Solution to Ridge Problem :

1. Trying different paths at the same time is a solution. We can apply two or more rules before doing the test. This corresponds to moving in several directions at once.

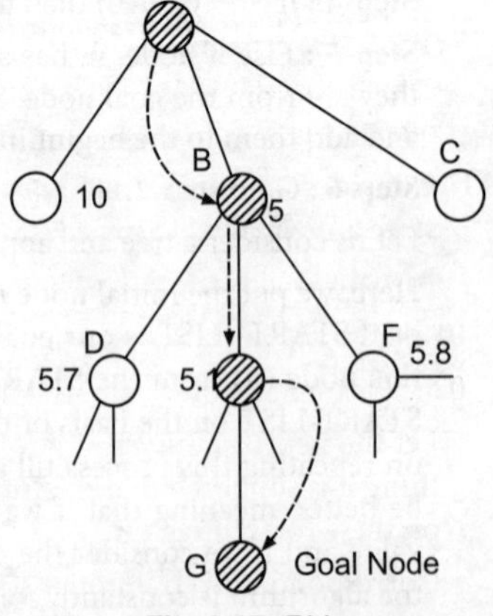

Fig. 3.17: Ridge

2. Bidirectional search can be useful here.

Advantages of Hill Climbing : It can be used in continuous as well as discrete domains.

Disadvantages of Hill Climbing :

1. It is not an efficient method.
2. It is not suited to problems where the value of the heuristic function drops off suddenly when the solution may be in sight.
3. It is a local method as it looks at the immediate solution and decides about the next step to be taken rather than exploring all consequences before taking a move.

We are in a position to solve some examples now.

Q.10. Consider a bullet-maze problem.

The figures below shows a maze. It is a state problem as we are not keen in the shortest path but in the goal state only.

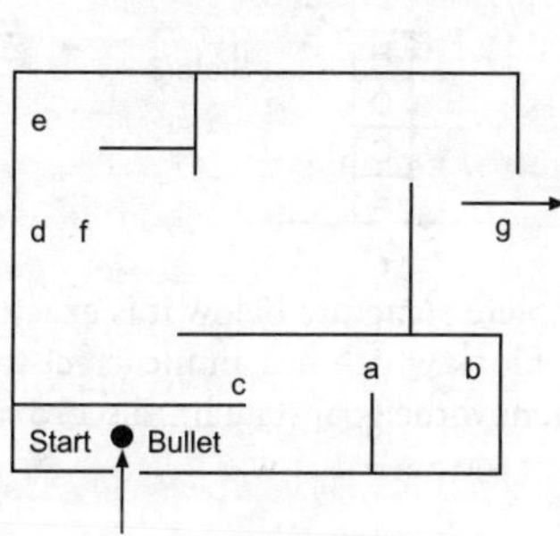

Fig. (a) Maze

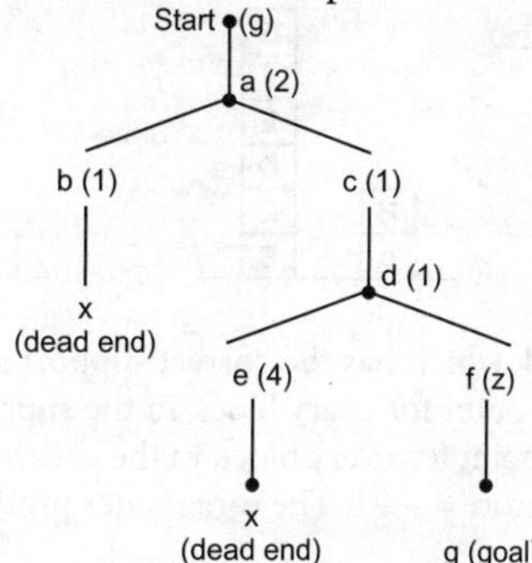

Fig. (b) A maze-search tree

You are also given a maze-search tree as follows—

(Fig. (*a*))—The start is marked with a bullet and the exist (goal state) is marked as g. Other letters mark the choice points in the maze.

(Fig. (*b*))— The numbers in brackets show the heuristic evaluation function for each node. The evaluation function chosen is the distance measured from the node to the goal.

Explain how it leads to dead ends?

Which node is local minima? Is there a plateau problem?

Ans. At node '*a*' (fig. *b*) it appears at first that 'b' is the most promising direction. But this leads to a dead end. From node '*b*', whatever path we take, takes us away from the goal. Hence, '*b*' is called as local minimum. A simple search will stop at '*b*' and never reach the goal state (*g*) which is global minimum.

The value of heuristic function does not change between 'c' and '*d*'. That is, it is 3. So, there is no progress. What if our search space is large? There may be a whole area of the search space with no change of heuristic. When this happens, our heuristic fails to give any guidance about possible direct path.

Q.11. Consider the block-world problem. It has 8 blocks, A to H which are similar and equal to each other. There initial state and final state (or goal state) are as follows:

Also, the following two operators are given —

01 : Pick up one block and put it on table.

02 : Pick up one block and put it on another.

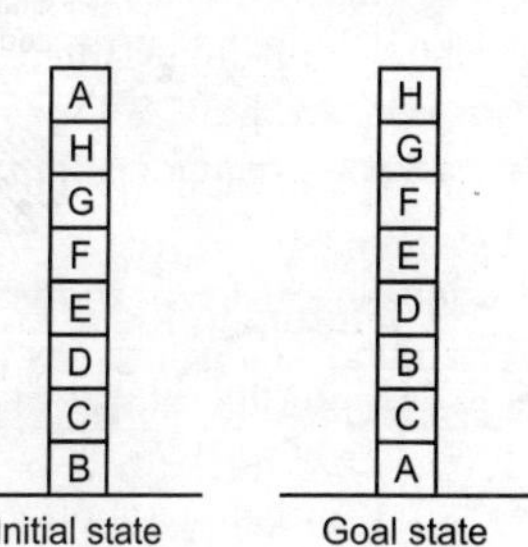

Let the heuristic function be—Add one point for every block which is resting on the thing it is supposed to be resting on. Subtract one point for every block which is sitting on the wrong thing.

Correspondingly, the initial state has a score of 4. Goal state has a score of 8. What problems can be faced if this problem is solved? Can you define the heuristic function globally taking the whole structure of block as a single unit?

Ans. The most natural move could be to move block-A onto the table. This is an intermediate state and is shown below—

Moving A on table from the initial state (above fig.) has a score of 6. This move is allowed and this state produces three states as shown below with scores of 4 each (using our operators—01 and 02)

Now, hill climbing will stop because all these states have the same score. Please note that they have a produced a score of 4 which is less than that of the intermediate state with score of 6 (from where these states arise).

We say now that the process has reached a local maximum. Our problem is that the current state appears to be better than any of its successor states as more blocks rest on the correct objects. To solve this problem, we disassemble a good local structure as it is wrong in the global context. This fault is inherent in our heuristic function now—A global heuristic function is defined which takes the whole structure of blocks as a single unit.

For each block which has the correct support structure *i.e.*, if the complete structure below it is exactly as it should be then add one point for every block in the support structure. For each block which has an incorrect support structure, subtract one point for every block in the existing support structure. So, now the goal state has a score = – 28. The initial state has the score = – 21. The three states produced from this now have scores—

$$a = -28$$
$$b = -16$$
$$c = -15$$

Thus, hill climbing chooses move (c) whose score = – 15 to lead us to a solution. This modified heuristic function assumes that the incorrect structures are bad and should not be accepted. And that the correct structures are good and should be built up. So, the same hill-climbing procedure which failed earlier heuristic function now works perfectly well.

Q.12. Explain the Best-First Search/Greedy Search technique.

Ans. Actually, best-first search is a combination of depth-first (dfs) and breadth-first (bfs) search methods. The approach used here is to select that single path at a time which is more promising one than the current path. The most promising node is chosen for expansion *i.e.*, all of its successors are generated. Again, the most promising node is chosen. **Please note that this changes the search from dfs to bfs. Also note that if we find that after the expansion, no node is more promising then we can backtrack.** This search uses again a heuristic function called as an **evaluation function** which is an indicator of how far a node is from the goal node.

Please remember that the goal nodes have an evaluation function value of zero.

Let us take an example to understand best-first search now.

Example : Consider the following search graph, given in Fig. 3.18.

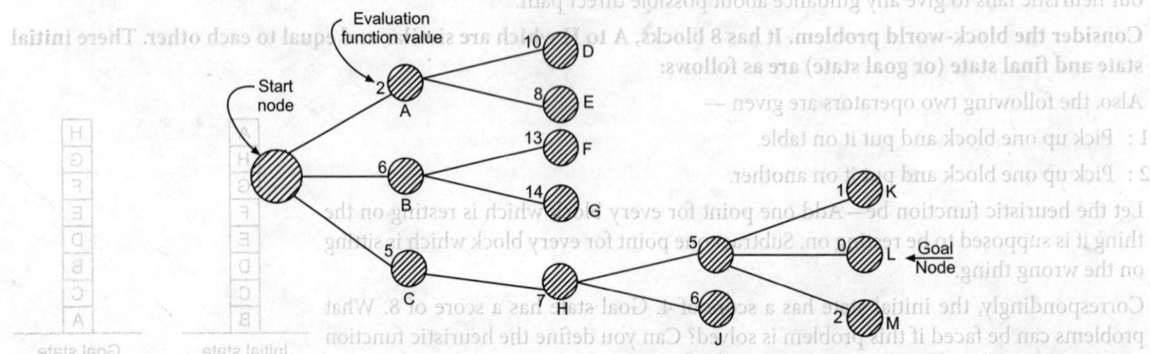

Fig. 3.18: Greedy Best First Search Graph

Working: We start with a start-nodes, S. Now, S has three children *i.e.,* A, B and C with their heuristic function values 2, 6 and 5 respectively. These weights show approximately, how far they are from goal node. So, we write, children of S are —

$$(A : 2), (B : 6), (C : 5)$$

Out of these, the node with minimum value is (*A* : 2). So, we select *A* and its children are explored (or generated).

It's children are—

$$(D : 10) \text{ and } (E : 8)$$

The search process now has four nodes to search for, namely— (*B* : 6), (*C*: 5), (*B*: 10) and (*E* : 8)

Out of these, node-C has the minimal value of 5. So, we select it and expand. So, we get (*H* : 7) as its child. Now, the nodes to search are as follows—

(*B* : 6), (*D*: 10, (*E*: 8) and (*H* : 7)

Out of these, node-B is minimal so, we choose it and expand it to get its children— (*F* : 13) and (G : 14)

At this point of time, the nodes available are :

$$(D : 10), (E : 8), (H : 7), (F : 13), (G : 14)$$

Out of these, minimum is (*H* : 7). So, we select it and expand to get— (*I* : 5) and (*J* : 6)

So, nodes available for search now are —

$$(D : 10), (E : 8), (F :13), (G : 14), (I : 5), (J : 6)$$

Out of these, minimum is (*I* : 5), so we expand it now. It's children are—(*K* : 1), (*L* : 0) and (*M* : 2).

So, available nodes are—

$$(D : 10), (E : 8), (H : 7), (F : 13), (G : 14)$$
$$(J : 6), (K : 1), (L : 0) \text{ and } (M : 2)$$

Out of these, minimal is (*L* : 0) which is our goal-node. So, search stops here. Let us tabulate this in a tabular form now.

Step	Node being expanded	Children (on expansion)	Available nodes (to search)	Node Chosen
1.	S	(A : 2), (B : 6), (C : 5)	(A : 2), (B : 6), (C : 5)	(A : 2)
2.	A	(D : 10), (E: 8)	(B : 6), (C : 5), (D : 10), (E : 8)	(C : 5)
3.	C	(H : 7)	(B : 6), (D : 10) , (E : 8), (H : 7)	(B : 6)
4.	B	(F : 13), (G : 14)	(D : 10), (E : 8), (H : 7), (F : 13), (G : 14)	(H : 7)
5.	H	(I : 5), (J : 6)	(D : 10), (E : 8), (F : 13) (G : 14), (I : 5), (J : 6)	(I : 5)
6.	I	(K : 1), (L : 0), (M : 2)	(D : 10), (E : 8), (H : 7), (F : 13), (G : 14), (J : 6),(K : 1), (L : 0), (M : 2)	Goal node is found. So, search stops now

Please note that in the best-first search, we 'jump all around' in the search graph to identify the node with **minimal evaluation function value** (indicated in braces). Also note that the paths found by this search algorithm are likely to give **faster solutions** because it expands a node that seems to be closer to the goal. But there is no guarantee on this.

Comparison of hill climbing and best-first searches :

In hill climbing search, we sort the children of the first node being generated. On the other hand, in best-first search, we have to sort the entire list to identify the next node to be expanded. Unlike hill climbing, this search retains all estimates computed for previously generated nodes and makes solution based on the best among them all.

Comparison of Best-first search and depth-first search

Best-first search resembles depth-first search in the way it prefers to follow a single path all the way to goal but will back up when it hits a dead end. It suffers from the same defects as depth first search i.e., it is non-optimal and is incomplete because it can go all along an infinite path and will never return to try other path possibilities.

We develop an **algorithm** for Best-first search now.

1. Place the starting node S (initial state) on the queue.
2. If the queue is empty, return failure and stop.
3. If the first element on the queue is a goal node g, return success and stop. Otherwise,
4. Remove the first element from the queue, expand it and compute the estimated goal distances for each child. Place the children on the queue (at either end) and assign all queue elements in ascending order corresponding to goal distance from the front of the queue.
5. Return to step 2.

We are in a position to solve some examples now.

Q.13. Consider the search tree given below—

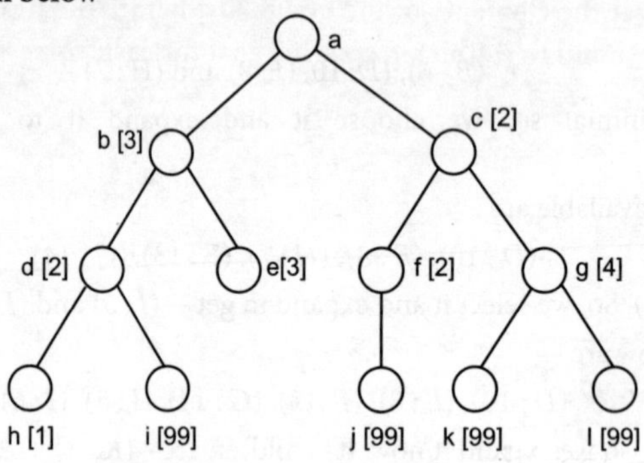

Show how the following searches are performed—

a. Hill climbing

b. Best-first search?

Ans.

a. Using Hill Climbing : The heuristic function value is an estimate of the distance to the goal and is shown in brackets.

Please note that lesser is its value, the better it is.

Using hill climbing we get—

1. Start at a (start-node)
2. Children of *a* = [*b*(3), *c*(2)]
3. Out of these best child is *c*(2).
4. Children of *c* = [*f*(2), *g*(4)]
5. Best child is *f*(2) now.
6. Children of *f* = [*j*(99)]—not a goal.
7. Backtrack to *g* through *c*.
8. Children of *g* = [*k*(99), *l*(3)]
9. Best child, *l* is goal node.

b. **Using Best-first search**

1. Start at *a*, the start node
2. Children of *a* [*b*(3), *c*(2)]
3. Best-first = *c*
4. Children of *c* = [*f*(2), *g*(4)]
5. Consider [*f*(2), *g*(4), *b*(3)]
6. Best-first = [*f*(2)]
7. Children of *f* = [*j*(99)]

8. Consider [j(99), g(4), b(3)]
9. Best first = b(3)
10. Children of b = [d(2), e(3)]
11. Consider [d(2), e(3), j(99), g(4)]
12. Best first = d(2)
13. Children of d = [h(1), i(99)]
14. Consider [h(1), i(99), e(3), j(99), g(4)]
15. Best-first-h, is a good node

Q.14. Using search tree given below, list the elements of the queue just before the next node is expanded. Use best first search where the numbers correspond to estimated cost- to-goal for each corresponding node.

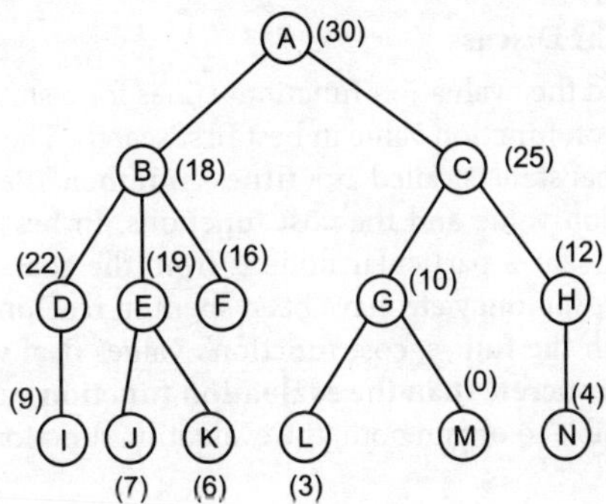

Ans. The table shows the cost from the initial node to the goal node

From Node	To Node	Cost of Node	Possible Dueue	Cost so far	Final Best First Dueue
A	B	30	A – B	48	✓
	C	30	A – C	55	×
B	D	18	A – B – D	70	×
	E	18	A – D – E	97	×
	F	18	A – D – F	64	✓
F	Next Node	16	A – B – F – Next Node	64	✓

The path is A – B – F – Next node in the given tree.

Q.15. Explain the Branch and Bound Search method.

Ans. This strategy applies to problems having a graph search space where more than one alternative path may exist between two nodes. This strategy saves all path lengths (or costs) from a node to all generated nodes and chooses the shortest path for further expansion. It then compares the new path lengths with all old ones and again chooses the shortest path for expansion. In this way, any path to a good node is certain to be a minimal length path.

The time required depends on the order in which the paths are explored. But this method is inadequate for solving larger problems.

Its algorithm is as follows—

1. Form a queue of partial paths. Let the initial queue be of zero-length, zero-step path from the root node to nowhere.
2. Until (queue is empty) or (goal is found) find if the first path in the queue reaches the goal node.
   a. If the first path reaches the goal node, do nothing.
   b. If the first path does not reach the goal node then.
      (*i*) Remove the first path from the queue.

(ii) Form new path from the removed path by extending one step.

(iii) Sort the queue in increasing order of the cost accumulated so far.

3. If the goal has been found then return SUCCESS else return FAILURE.
4. End Branch-and-Bound algorithm. The search graph is shown in Fig. 3.19.

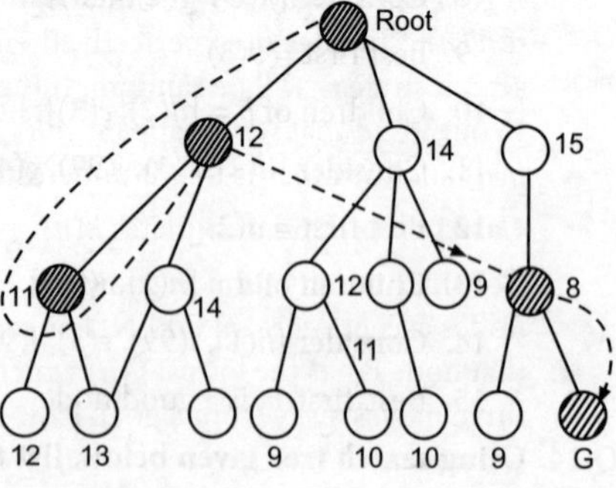

Fig. 3.19: Branch-and-bound Search

Using Branch-and-Bound on Traveling Salesman Problem (TSP)

Let us assume that there are a number of cities to be visited. From the starting city, the algorithm will begin generating complete paths. But it has to keep track of the shortest path found so far. **Please note that no further exploration of any path will be done if its partial length becomes greater than the shortest path found so far.** This technique still guarantees a shortest path for our TSP problem.

Q.16. What is the A* Algorithm of search? Discuss.

Ans. **Basic principle**— "Sum the cost and the evaluation function values for a state to get its "goodness" worth and use this as a yardstick instead of the evaluation function value in best first search. The sum of the evaluation function value and the cost along the path leading to that state is called as a **fitness number.**" Before discussing about the fitness number, let us see what is evaluation function value and the cost functions. In best-first search, we use evaluation function value *i.e.*, a value that estimates how far a particular node is from the goal. On the other hand, cost functions show how much resources like time, energy, money etc. have been spent in reaching a particular node from the start. While evaluation function values deal with the future, cost function's values deal with the past. However, **please note that the cost function values are more concrete than the evaluation function values** as the cost function values are really expanded. Also note that if it is possible to obtain both, the evaluation function values and the cost function values then A* algorithm can be used.

What is a fitness number?

A fitness number, $f'(n)$, is a heuristic function that estimates the merits of each node that we generate. So, this algorithm can search more promising paths first. Dash in the function indicates that it is an approximation to a function, $f(n)$, that gives the actual or true evaluation of the node. It is given as follows—

$$f'(n) = g'(n) = h'(n)$$

where $f'(n)$ – is the estimated cost of the cheapest solution through n.

$h'(n)$ – is an estimate of the additional cost of getting from the current node to a goal state.

$g'(n)$ – is an estimate of getting from the initial node to the current node.

The corresponding true values are $f(n)$, $g(n)$ and $h(n)$ of $f'(n)$, $g'(n)$ and $h'(n)$ respectively. For state space tree problems,

$$g'(n) = g(n) \qquad \ldots(2)$$

Because there is only one path and he distance $g'(n)$ will be known to be true minimum from the start to the current node n. In case of graphs, there can be alternate paths from the start node to n. So, for state space tree problem, we can also represent the heuristic function as —

(from equation –1 and 2)

$$f'(n) = g(n) + h'(n)$$

How to select $h'(n)$ and $g(n)$?

The function $g(n)$ lets us choose which node has to be expanded next not only on the basis of how good the node itself looks [as measured by $h'(n)$] but also on the basis of how good the path to the node was. By introduction of g(n) into $f'(n)$ we will not be always choosing the node to expand that appears to be closest to the goal. This is important in cases where we care about the path we find if our concern is only getting to a solution by any means we can define $g(n)$ = 0. In this way we will be choosing the node that seems closest to the goal. On the other hand, if we want to find a path involving lowest number of steps, then we can set the cost of going from a node to its successor as a constant (usually 1). In this way A* algorithm can be used whether we want to find a minimal-cost overall path or simply any path as quickly as possible.

$h'(n)$ is a measure of the cost of getting from the node to a solution. Therefore, good nodes get low values and bad nodes get high values. Hence, minus sign has to judiciously placed. This is opposite to that $g(n)$ which has to be non-negative.

If $g(n)$ has a negative value then paths that traverse cycles in the graph will appear to get better as they get longer. Now, if $h'(n)$ estimates $h(n)$ perfectly, then A* will converge immediately to the goal with no search. If it is always zero, the search strategy will be random. If the value of $g(n)$ is always one, the search will be breadth first. Now a question comes to our mind that what happens if $h'(n)$ is neither perfect nor zero. There are two possibilities. One is that overestimates $h(n)$ and the other is that it underestimates $h(n)$. Let us now examine what happens in both the cases.

Case I : $h'(n)$ underestimates $h(n)$

Consider the situation as shown in Fig. 3.20. Assuming that the cost of all arcs is 1, Fig. 3.20 (*a*) shows that initially all nodes except A are on OPEN. For each node, $f(n)$ is indicated as the sum of $h'(n)$ and $g(n)$. From the figure we observe that node B has the lowest $f(n)$ which is 4. So, it is expanded first. Suppose B has only one successor E and appears to be three moves away from a goal. Now $f'(E)$ is 5 which is same as $f'(C)$. Suppose we decide to allow the same path which we are currently following. Then, we will expand E next. Suppose it too has a single successor F which is three moves from the goal. This has been shown in Fig. 3.20 (*b*), *i.e.*, the situation two steps later after B and E have been expanded. Now, $f'(F) = 6$ which is greater than $f'(C)$. So, we will expand *C* next. Thus, we see that by underestimating $h'(B)$ we have wasted some effort. Thus, we find that *B* was farther away than we initially thought and we go back to try another path.

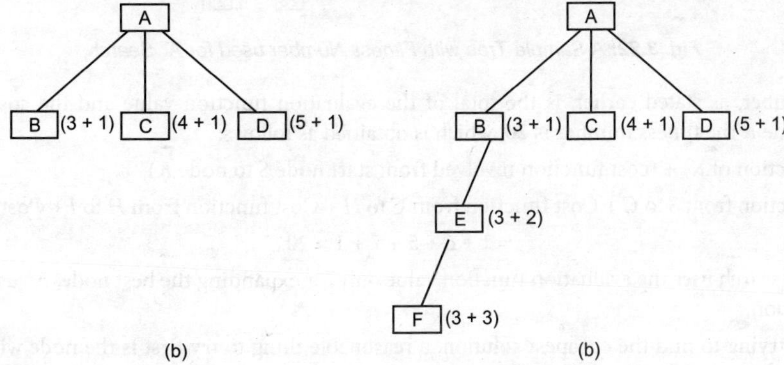

Fig. 3.20: *h'(n) overestimates h(n)*

Case II : $h'(n)$ overestimates $h(n)$

Now consider the situation shown in Fig. 3.21.

Here also we expand *B* in the first step. At the second step, we again expand *E*. At the next step we expand *F* and finally we generate *G*. The solution path has length 4. But suppose if there was a direct path from *D* to a solution giving a path of length 2, we will never find it. Thus, by overestimating $h'(D)$ we make *D* look so bad that we may find some other solution which is worse without even expanding *D*.

In general, we can say that if $h'(n)$ overestimates $h(n)$, we cannot be guaranteed of finding the cheapest path solution unless we expand the entire graph until all paths are longer than the best solution.

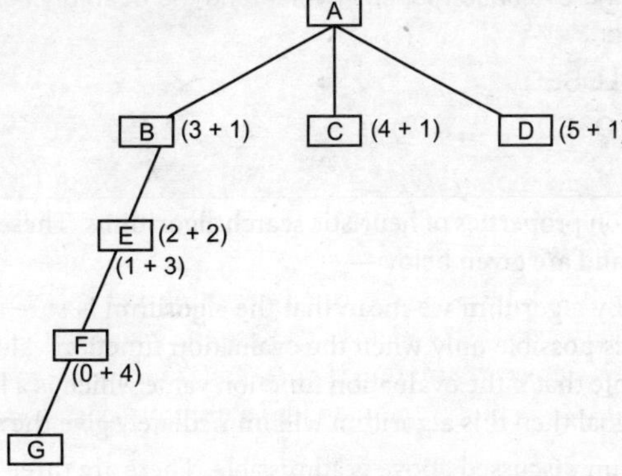

Fig. 3.21: *h'(n) Overestimates h(n)*

Now we will see how the $f'(n)$ function is evaluated in A* search. Consider Fig. 3.22 again with the same evaluation function values as in Fig. 3.18. Now associated with each node are three numbers, the evaluation function value, the cost function value and the fitness number.

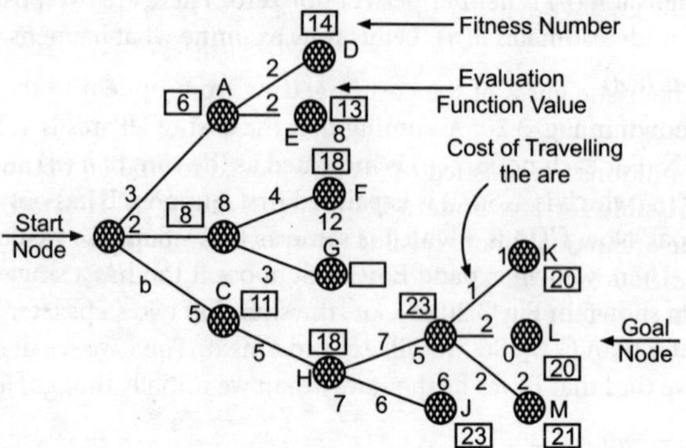

Fig. 3.22: A Sample Tree with Fitness Number used for A Search*

The fitness number, as stated earlier, is the total of the evaluation function value and the cost-function value. For example, for node *K* the fitness number is 20, which is obtained as follows:

(Evaluation function of *K*) + (cost function involved from start node *S* to node *K*)

= 1 + (Cost function from *S* to *C* + Cost function from *C* to *H* + Cost function from *H* to *I* + Cost function from *I* to *K*)

$$= 1 + 6 + 5 + 7 + 1 = 20.$$

While best-first search uses the evaluation function value only for expanding the best node, A* uses the fitness number for its computation.

Thus, if we are trying to find the cheapest solution, a reasonable thing to try first is the node with the lowest value of $g(n) + h'(n)$. It turns out that this strategy is quite reasonable provided that the heuristic function $h'(n)$ satisfies certain conditions. Note that A* is both complete and optimal.

Algorithm for A* is given below:

Algorithm for A*

1. Put the initial node on a list OPEN
2. If (OPEN is empty) or (OPEN = GOAL) terminate search
3. Remove the first node from OPEN. Call this node a
4. IF (*a* = GOAL) terminate search with success
5. Else if node a has successors, generate all of them. Estimate the fitness number of the successors by totaling the evaluation function value and the cost-function value. Sort the list by fitness number.
6. Name the new list as CLOSED.
7. Replace OPEN with CLOSED.
8. Goto Step 2.

Let us now discuss some common properties of heuristic search algorithms. These properties evaluates the performance optimality of these algorithms and are given below—

1. **Admissibility Condition** : By algorithm we mean that the algorithm is sure to find a most optimal solution if one exists. Please note that this is possible only when the evaluation function value never overestimates the distance of the node to the goal. Also note that if the evaluation function value which is a heuristic one is exactly the same of the distance of the node to the goal then this algorithm will immediately give the solution.

   For example, the A* algorithm discussed above is admissible. There are three conditions to be satisfied for A* to be admissible.

They are as follows—

1. Each node in the graph has finite number of successors (or O).
2. All arcs in the graph have costs greater than some positive amount, (say C).
3. For each node in the graph, n,

$$h'(n) \leq h(n).$$

This implies that the heuristic guess of the cost of getting from node n to the goal is never an verestimate. This is known as a heuristic condition.

Only if these three conditions are satisfied, A^* is guaranteed to find an optimal (least) cost path. **Please note that A* algorithm is admissible for any node n if on such path, $h'(n)$ is always less than or equal to $h(n)$.** This is possible only when the evaluation function value never overestimates the distance of the node to the goal. Although the admissibility condition requires $h'(n)$ to be a lower bound on $h(n)$, it is expected that the more closely $h'(n)$ approaches $h(n)$, the better is the performance of the algorithm.

If $h(n) = h'(n)$ –an optimal solution path would be found without over expanding a node off the path. We assume that one optimal solution exists.

If $h'(n) = 0$ –A* reduces to blind uniform cost algorithm or breadth-first algorithm.

Please note that the admissible heuristics are by nature optimistic because they think that the cost of solving the problem is less than it actually is because $g(n)$ is the exact cost foreach n. Also note that $f(n)$ should never overestimate the true cost of a solution through n. For example, consider a network of roads and cities with roads connecting these cities. Our problem is to find a path between two cities such that the mileage/fuel cost is minimal. Then an admissible heuristic would be to use distance to estimate the costs from a given city to the goal city. Naturally, the air distance will be either equal to the real distance or will underestimate it i.e., $h'(n) \leq h(n)$.

Q.17. What do you mean by Problem Reduction?

Ans. OR graph: As we have already studied Best-first search tree. It's search graph can be explored to avoid duplicate paths. In such a directed search graph, each node represents a point in the problem space.

Each node also indicates how much promising it is, a parent link (pointing back to the best node form which it came) and the list of nodes generated (or explored) from it. Please note that the parent link will make it possible to recover the path to the goal once the goal is found. The list of successors (explored) will make it possible if a better path is found to an already existing node and also to propagate the improvement down to its successors.

This graph is known as an OR graph.

It is so called because each of its branches represents an alternative problem-solving path. The techniques that we have studied so far, all are the example of OR graph only as in them we try to find a single path to the goal. OR graph finds a single path.

AND-OR graph (or tree) :

We already know about the divide-and-conquer strategy *i.e.*, a solution to a problem can be obtained by decomposing it into smaller sub-problems. Each of this sub-problem can then be solved to get its **sub-solution**. These sub-solutions can then be recombined to get a solution as a whole. This is called as **decomposition or reduction.** This method generates arcs which are called as AND arcs. **Please note that one AND arc may point to any number of successor nodes, all of which must be solved in order for an arc to point to a solution.** Here also several arcs may emerge from a simple node. Each will indicate the different ways in which the original problem might be solved. This is actually called as an AND-OR graph or AND/OR tree. For example.

Actually, best-first is not suitable for searching AND-OR graphs. Consider a small AND/OR tree shown in Fig. 3.23 and 3.24.

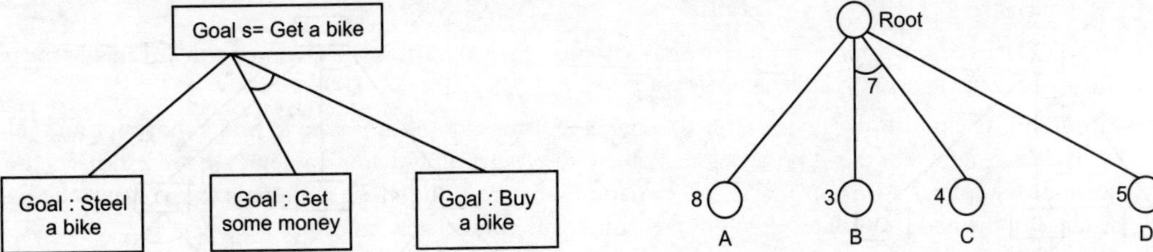

Fig. 3.23: AND/OR Graph Example

Fig. 3.24: Sample AND/OR Tree

Here, the numbers show the approximate value of the heuristic function ($f(n)$) at that node. In Fig. 3.24, we observe that the minimal is B which has the $f'(n)$ value of 3. But please note that B forms a part of the AND graph and so we need to consider the other branch also of this AND tree *i.e.*, *C* which has a weight of 4. So, our estimate now is (3 + 4) = 7. Now, this estimate is costlier than that of branch *D i.e.* 5. So, we explore node-*D* instead of C as it has the lowest value. This process goes on till we search our goal node. From this we observe that the choice of node to expand depends on its $f(n)$ value and also on whether that node is part of the current best path from the initial node.

Algorithm to search AND-OR graph : In order to develop an algorithm for searching an AND-OR graph, we define a term called as Futility. If the estimated cost of a solution becomes greater than the value of FUTILITY, then the search is abandoned. So, futility is like a threshold value i.e., any solution with a cost above it, is too expensive to be practical, even if it could ever be found. Let us write an algorithm of problem reduction now.

1. Initialize the graph to the starting node.
2. Loop until the starting node is labeled SOLVED or until its cost goes above FUTILITY:
   a. Traverse the graph, starting at the initial node and following the current best path and accumulate the set of nodes that are on that path and have not yet been expanded or labeled as solved.
   b. Pick one of these unexpanded nodes and expand it. If there are no successors, assign FUTILITY as the value of this node. Otherwise, add its successors to the graph and for each of them compute $f'(n)$. If $f'(n)$ of any node is O, mark that node as SOLVED.
   c. Change the $f'(n)$ estimate of the newly expanded node to reflect the new information provided by its successors. Propagate this change backward through the graph. If any node contains a successor arc whose descendants are all solved, label the node itself as SOLVED. At each node that is visited while going up the graph, decide which of its successor arcs is the most promising and mark it as part of the current best path. This may cause the current best path to change.

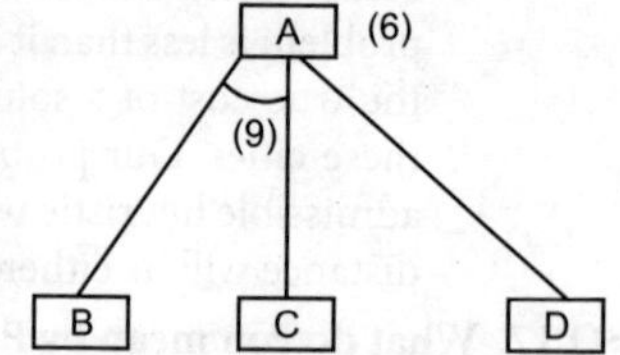

Consider the following *e.g.*,

At step 1, *A* is the only node, so it is at the end of the current best path *i.e.*, Before step 1:

A (5)

It is expanded, yielding nodes *B*, *C* and *D*, *i.e.*,

The arc to *D* is labeled as the most promising one emerging from A, since it costs 6 compared to *B* and *C*, which costs 9. This is because the path from *A-D* has the total cost of (*D* + the cost of arc *AD*). Now, *D* has cost of 5 and arc *AD* has 1; as each AND arc has a weight of one. So, total cost is 5 + 1 = 6 for *A–D* path. Similarly, for *B–C* cost will be (3 + 4 + 1 + 1) = 9.

In step (2), node *D* is chosen for expansion.

∴ Combined cost estimate of new AND-arc to *E* and *F* is 4 + 4 + 1 + 1 = 10.

So, we update the $f'(n)$ value of *D* to 10. Going back one more level, we see that this makes the AND arc *B –C* better than arc to *D*, so it is labeled as the current best path by arrows. At step 3, we traverse that arc from A and discover the unexpanded nodes B and C. Let's choose to explore *B* first. This generates two new arcs, the ones to *G* and to *H i.e.*, Propagating their $f(n)$ values backward, we update f'(*n*) of *B* to 6. This requires updating the cost of the AND arc *B* – C to 12 (*i.e.*, 6 + 4 + 2 =12). Comparing this with arc to *D*, which has the cost of 10, we find it is better. So, we explore *D* and thus either node–E or F is chosen for expansion at step-4.

This process continues until either a solution is found or all paths have led to dead ends, indicating that there is no solution.

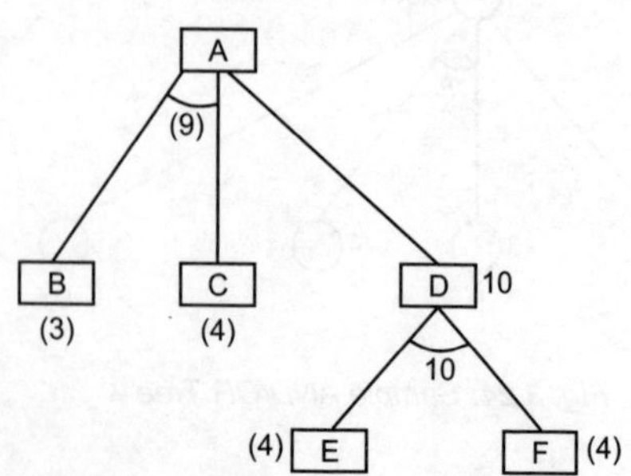

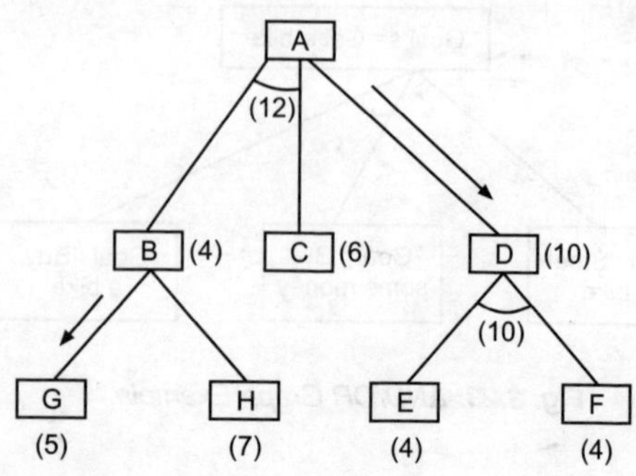

Q.18. Write AO* algorithm.

Ans. Our real-life situations cannot be exactly decomposed into either AND tree or OR tree but is always a combination of both. So, we need an AO* algorithm where *O* stands for 'ordered'. Instead of two lists OPEN and CLOSED of A* algorithm, we use a single structure GRAPH in AO* algorithm. It represents a part of the search graph that has been explicitly generated so far. Please note that each node in the graph will point both down to its immediate successors and to its immediate predecessors. Also note that each node will have some $h'(n)$ value associated with it. But unlike A* search, $g(n)$ is not stored. It is not possible to compute a single value of $g(n)$ due to many paths to the same state. It is not required also as we are doing top-down traversing along the best-known path.

This guarantees that only those nodes that are on the best path are considered for expansion.

Hence, $h'(n)$ **will only serve as the estimate of goodness of a node.**

Next, we develop an AO* algorithm. reate an initial graph with a single node (start node).

Step-1 : Create an initial graph with a single node (start node).

Step-2 : Transverse the graph following the current path, accumulating nodes that have not yet been expanded or solved.

Step-3 : Select any of these nodes and explore it. If it has no successors then call this value— FUTILITY else calculate $f'(n)$ for each of the successors.

Step-4 : If $f'(n) = 0$; then mark the node as SOLVED.

Step-5 : Change the value of $f'(n)$ for the newly created node to reflect its successors by back propagation.

Step-6 : Wherever possible use the most promising routes. If a node is marked as SOLVED then mark the parent node as SOLVED.

Step-7 : If the starting node is SOLVED or value is greater than FUTILITY then stop, else repeat from step-2.

Please note that AO* will always find a minimum cost solution if one exists, if $h'(n) < h(n)$ and that all arc costs are positive. The efficiency of this algorithm will depend on how closely $h'(n)$ approximates $h(n)$. **Also note that AO* is guaranteed to terminate even on graphs that have cycles.**

Q.19. What do you mean by Constraint Satisfaction?

Ans. In the real-world, we work in different environments, each of which has some constraints. Our solution should be such that all such constraints are satisfied. We use extensive domain specific and heuristic knowledge. For example, design problems in manufacturing, optimal tour problems and so on. Even crypta-arithmetic problems are typical constraint satisfaction problems. The term relaxation algorithm is also used for constraints satisfaction. Waltz algorithm for labeling line drawings in a picture and natural language understanding are good examples of constraint satisfaction algorithm in a modified form. Let us see the algorithm now.

Until a complete solution is found or until all path have led to dead ends, do:

1. Select an unexpanded node of the search graph.
2. Apply the constraint inference rules to the selected node to generate all possible new constraints.
3. If the set of constraints contains a contradiction, then report that this path is a dead-end.
4. If the set of constraints describes a complete solution, then report success.
5. If neither a contradiction nor a complete solution has been found, then apply the problem space rules to generate new partial solutions that are consistent with the current set of constraints. Insert these partial solutions into the search graph.

To see how this algorithm works, consider the following problem.

Problem **(cryptarithematic problem)**

```
  S E N D
+ M O R E
---------
 MONEY
```

Constraints

1. Values are to be assigned to letters from 0 to 9 only.
2. No two letters should have the same value.
3. If the same letter occurs more than once, it must be assigned the same digit each time.
4. The sum of the digits must be as shown in the problem.

Initial Problem State

$S = ?$	$M = ?$	$C1 = ?$
$E = ?$	$O = ?$	$C2 = ?$
$N = ?$	$R = ?$	$C3 = ?$
$D = ?$	$E = ?$	$C4 = ?$

Goal States : A goal state is a problem state in which all letters have been assigned a digit in such a way that all constraints are satisfied.

Solution :

The solution process proceeds in cycles. At each cycle, two vital things are done—

a. Constraints are propagated by using rules which correspond to the properties of arithmetic. A value is guessed for some letter whose value is not yet determined, as this affects the effort involved in search.

b. More constraints are added/generated due to propagating constraints.

At each cycle, there may be several choices to apply. A few useful heuristics can help to select the best rule to apply first. For example, if there is a letter that has only two possible values and another with six possible values then there is a better chance of guessing right on the first than on the second. This procedure can be implemented as dfs also so that a large number of intermediate positions in both the problem and the constraint spaces will not have to be stored. We can also store all constraints in one central database and also to record at each node the changes that must be undone during backtracking.

The results of first few cycles of processing of this crytarthimetic problem are shown in Fig. 3.25 Here, *C*1, *C*2, *C*3, I 4 are the carry bits out of the columns, from right to left.

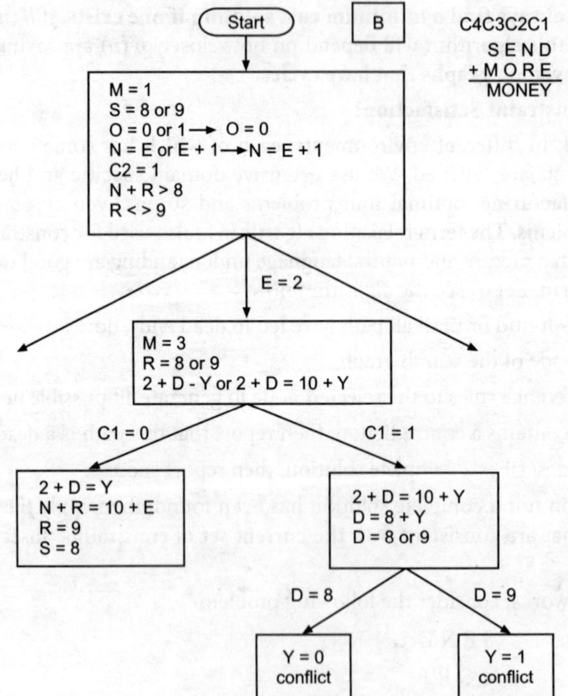

Fig. 3.25: Solution to Crytarthimetic Problem

Cycle 1 :

(i) $M = 1$ because two single digit numbers plus a carry cannot total more than 19.

(ii) $S = 8$ or 9 (minimum values) because $S + M + C3$ should be > 9 (to generate a carry) and

$M = 1$, therefore $S + 1 + C3 > 9$ or $S + C3 > 8$, as $C3$ can be 0 or 1. So $S > 8$ or > 7 depending upon $C3 = 0$ or 1.

(*iii*) $O = 0$ because $S + M + C3 \leq 1$.

O must be atleast 10 to generate a carry and it can be at most 11. That is O can be zero or 1. As M is already 1 and no two digit should have the same value, so O is zero (0).

(*iv*) $N = E$ or $E + 1$ depending on the value of C2. But N cannot have the same value as E. So $N = E + 1$ and $C2 = 1$.

(*v*) In order for C2 to be 1, the sum of $N + R + C1$ must be greater tan 9, so $N + R$ must be greater than 8.

(*vi*) $N + R$ cannot be greater than 18, even with a carry in so, E cannot be 9. $E + O + C2 = N$

When $C2 = 0$ and $O = 0$

$E = N$ which is not possible.

At this point let's assume that no more additional constraints are generated so a GUESS is made.

Suppose value of E (which occurs the maximum number of times (3) and so interacts maximum with other letters).

Cycle 2 begins

Let $E = 2$ (the next value after 0 and 1, already allocated)

(*i*) So $N = 3$ because $E + 1 = N$

as

$$R + N + C1 = E$$
$$R + 3 + C1\ (0 \text{ or } 1) = 2 \text{ or } 12$$
$$R + 3 + 0 = 2, R = -1 \text{ not possible}$$
$$R + 3 + 1 = 2, R = -2 \text{ not possible}$$
$$R + 3 + 0 = 12, R = 9, \text{ possible}$$
$$R + 3 + 1 = 12, R = 8, \text{ possible}$$

(*ii*) $D + E = Y$ when $C1 = 0$ or $2 + D = Y$

and when $C1 = 1$ or $2 + D = 10 + Y$, from right most column.

Again, assuming no more constraints can be generated, GUESS is required and now C1 is chosen for GUESS. Let $C1 = 1$

Cycle 3 begins

(*i*)

$$D + E = Y + C1$$
$$2 + D = Y + 10$$
$$3 + R = 12$$
$$R = 9$$

(*ii*) $S = 8$ because S was either 8 or 9, as now R has been allotted '9'. Now let us assign value to C1, 0 or 1.

First let us assign $C1 = 10$.

$$D + E = Y + 10 \text{ (because } C1 = 1)$$
$$D + E = 10 + Y$$
$$2 + D = 10 + Y \text{ and for this to happen Either } D = 8$$

or

$$D = 9$$

So C1 cannot be 1.

Now consider $C1 = 0$.

then

$$8 + D = Y, Y \text{ can be 0 or 1}$$
$$D = -8 \text{ (when } Y = 0)$$
$$D = -7 \text{ (when } Y = 0)$$

So C1 cannot be 0 either.

Thus D has four values, two negative and two positive.

When $D = 8$

$Y = 10$ *i.e.*, $= 0$

and when $D = 9$

$Y = 11$ *i.e.*, 1

So $Y = 0$ and $Y = 1$ lead to conflict.

This contradiction could have been explained through another type of arguments: Earlier $S = 8$ or 9 and again $R = 8$ from II loop and when $C1 = 1$, $D = 8$ or 9

And now $D = 8$ or 9 from $C1 = 1$.

Three letters cannot share two values, so $C1 \neq 1$.

Comments on Constraints Propagation : The rules of the constraint propagation should not infer spurious constraints. Nor do they need to infer all legal rules

For example, we could adopt an alternative path which gives $C1 = 0$.

Let $C1 = 1$

Then $E + D = Y + C1$

or $E + D = Y + 10$

$2 + D = Y + 10$

D would be either 8 or 9 8

or 9 is assigned to R

is assigned to D

is assigned to S

Two values cannot be shared among three letters, so $C1$ cannot be 1. If this were realized earlier fruitless search could have been avoided. But the constraint propagation rules used were not that sophisticated so it took some search steps. Whether the time taken by the actual search route is more or less than the constrained method depends upon how long it takes to perform the reasoning required for constraint propagation.

We are in a position to solve a problem now.

Q.20. Trace the constraint satisfaction procedure solving the following cryptarithmatic program:

```
  CROS
+ ROADS
-------
DANGER
```

Ans.

```
  CROS
+ ROADS
-------
DANGER
```

(*i*) $D = 1$ since it is generated because of carry which at most can be 1(□ 9 + 9 = 18).

(*ii*) $C + R = 10$ or 12 to 18 depending up carry C4.

(*iii*) Since, we have no path to move on, we guess the values for S.

(*a*) $C + R = A$

$+ 4 =$

(*b*) $R + O = N$

$4 + =$

(*c*) $O + A = G$

(*d*) $S + D = E$

$2 + 1 = 3$

(*e*) $S + S = R$

$2 + 2 = 4$

Thus we get: A C D E G N O R S

D → 1, E → 3, R → 4, S → 2(guess)

Now, let us say 'O' = 5 (anything other than 1, 2, 3, 4) if $O = 0$ then $R + 0 = N$

⇒ $4 + 0 = 4$ (Not possible)

$\therefore$ guess $O = 5$

(a) $C + R = A$ (b) $R + O = N$

$+ 4 =$ $4 + 5 = 9$

(c) $O + A = G$ (d) $S + D = E$ (e) $S + S = R$

$5 + =$ $2 + 1 = 3$ $2 + 2 = 4$

A C D E G N O R S

↓ ↓ ↓ ↓ ↓ ↓

1 3 9 5 4 2

(guess)

Here, $C + R$ should be 10, 12, 13, 14, 16, 16 or 17 as $C_4 \neq 1$

for C we can have,

for $C = 6$ (for total of 10) we have $A = 0$

and $A + 0 = G$ *i.e.* $5 + 0 = 5$ *i.e.* $G = 5$

$\Rightarrow O = G = 5$ (not possible)

$\Rightarrow$ For $O = 6, 7, 8$ too we are not able to get values for C s.t. $C + R > 10$ (no value in this case can be ($= O$) as it will result in same value for 2 different characters) and for $O = 6$ we get repeating values.

$\therefore$ Our guess for $S = 2$ is wrong.

(iv) For $S = 3$,

(a) $C + R = A$ (b) $R + O = N$ (c) $O + A = G$

$9 + 6 = 15$ $6 + 5$

(d) $S + D = E$ (e) $S + S = R$

$3 + 1 = 4$ $3 + 3 = 6$

$\therefore$ A C D E G N O R S

↓ ↓ ↓ ↓ ↓

5 9 1 4 6 3(guess)

Since, $C + R \geq 12$

$C \neq 6$, as it will give $C = R = 6$

$C \neq 7$, as $7 + 6 = 13 \therefore A = 3 \Rightarrow A = S = 3$

$C \neq 8$, as $8 + 6 = 14 \therefore A = 4 \Rightarrow A = E = 4$

$\therefore C = 9$, $9 + 6 = 15 \therefore A = 5$

Now we need to find G, N, O.

If $O = 2$ then

(a) $C + R = A$ (b) $R + O = N$ (c) $O + A = G$

$9 + 6 = 15$ $6 + 2 = 8$ $2 + 5 = 7$

(d) $S + D = E$ (e) $S + S = R$

$3 + 1 = 4$ $3 + 3 = 6$

$\therefore$ A C D E G N O R S

↓ ↓ ↓ ↓ ↓ ↓ ↓ ↓ ↓

5 9 1 4 7 8 2 6 3

(guess) (guess)

This solution has no repetitions thus we get—

```
  CROSS          96233
+ ROADS  →     + 62513
 DANGER         158746
```

Q.21. Explain what is Means-End Analysis (MEA)?

Ans. Means-end-analysis is a special type of knowledge-rich search that allows both backward and forward searching.

Principle : "It (MEA) allows us to solve the major parts of a problem first and then go back and solve the smaller problems that arise while assembling the final solution".

Technique : It is based on the use of the operators which transform the state of the world. The difference between the current state and the goal state is detected.

Once such a difference is isolated, an operator that can reduce the difference has to be found. But sometimes it is not possible to apply this operator to the current state. So, we try to get a sub- problem out of it and try to apply our operator to this new state. If this also does not produce the desired goal state then we try to get second sub problem and apply this operator again. This process may be continued. But please note here that if the difference is chosen correctly and if the operator is really effective at reducing the difference then the two sub problems are easier to solve than the original problem.

Why is it called as Means-End-Analysis?

Given a description of the desired state of the world (the end) it works backwards, selecting and using operators that will achieve it (the means). Hence, the name, Means-End-Analysis (MEA).

MEA works incrementally

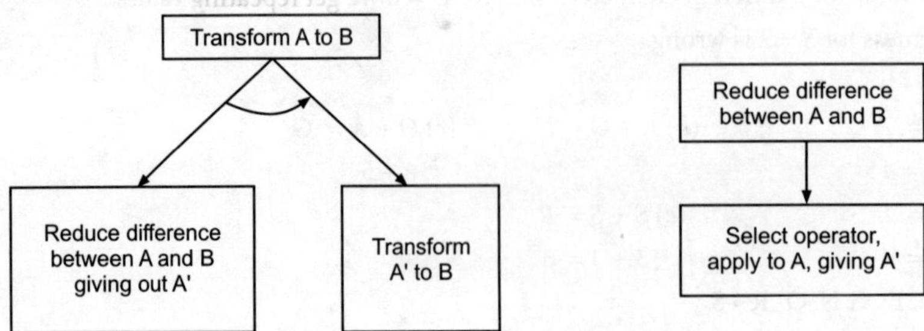

The above technique of MEA works incrementally and not as a single step. This is so because the operators are applied recursively till a goal state is achieved.

MEA works on three primary goals.

They are as follows—

a. Transformation.

b. Reduction

c. Application

Transformation means to transform object *A* into object *B i.e.*,

This is an AND graph which subdivides a problem into an intermediate problem and then transforms that problem into the goal state B. Please note that this process terminates when there is no difference between A and B or we can say when the goal is reached.

Reduction means to reduce the difference between object-A and object-B by modifying object-A *i.e.*,

Please note that the goal of this operation is to reduce the difference between the object A and object-B by transforming object A into object-A', nearer the goal B, by means of a relevant operator (say, R).

Application means to apply the operator R to object-A. This will again be a AND graph showing the goal of reducing the difference between object-A and the pre-conditions required for the operator R, giving intermediate object A''. Operator R is then applied to A'', transforming it to A', which is close to the goal B. That is,

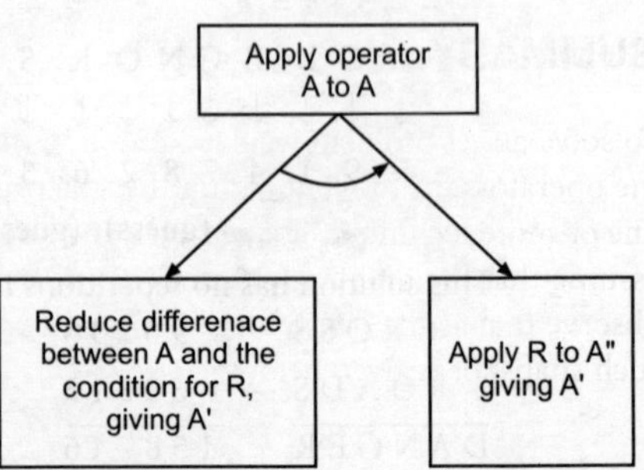

Please understand that states are described in some structured way like by predicate calculus and moves are performed by the operators. Each operator has a—

a. **Pre-condition :** It puts some constraints on the states it uses.

b. **Post-condition :** It says which conditions will be true when the operator has been used.

For examples —

a. GPS was the first AI program to exploit MEA.

b. STRIPS (A Robot Planner) is an advanced problem solver that incorporates MEA.

Algorithm for Means-End-Analysis (MEA)

We give an algorithm for MEA now.

Step-1 : Until the goal is reached or no more procedures are available.

Step-2 : Describe the current state, the goal state and the difference between the two.

Step-3 : Use the difference between the current state and goal state, possibly with the description of the current state or goal state, to select a promising procedure.

Step-4 : Use the promising procedure and update the current state.

Step-5 : If goal is reached then success else it is a failure.

We are in a position to solve an example now.

Q.22. Show how Mean-End-Analysis (MEA) can be used to solve the problem of getting from one place to another. Assume that the available operators are walk, drive, take the bus, take a cab and fly.

Ans. Means-End Analysis—

Available Operators	Preconditions	Results
Walk		at (man, loc)
Drive	have (man, car) ^ (on obj, bus)	at (man, loc)^ at (obj, loc)
Take bus	On (man, bus)^ on (obj, bus)	at (man, loc)^ at (obj, loc)
Take cab	hire (man, cab) ^ on (obj, cab)	at (obj, loc)
Fly	book (man, airbus)^ on (obj, airbus)	at (man, loc) ^ at (obj, loc)

∴ Difference Table is as follows

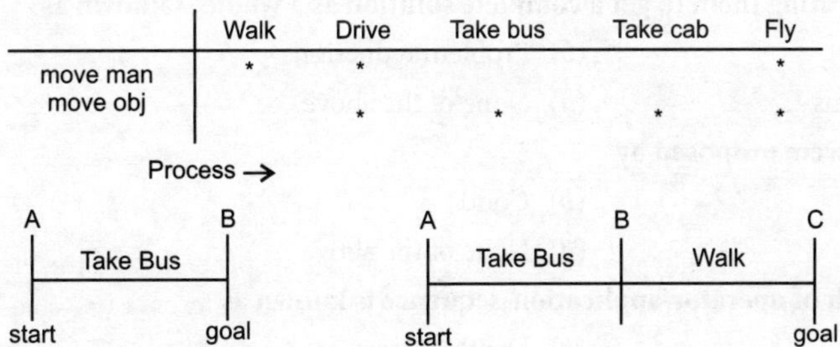

SUMMARY

To solve an AI problem we need to follow certain steps—Firstly, define the problem precisely *i.e.*, specify the problem space, the operators for moving within the space and the starting and goal state. Secondly, analyze the problem and finally, choose one or more techniques for representing knowledge and for problem solving and apply it (them) to the problem. In BFS, if we assume that the branching factor (b) = 10, we can expand 1000 nodes/sec and also assume 100 bytes/node storage then the observe that as the depth increases, number of nodes increases and both time and memory requirement also increases. One such snapshot is given below—

Depth	Nodes	Time	Memory
0	1	1 ms	100 bytes
2	111	0.1 sec	11 KB
4	11, 111	11 secs	1 MB
6	10^6	18 min	111 MB
8	10^8	31 hrs	11 GB
10	10^{10}	128 days	1 TB
12	10^{12}	35 yrs	111 TB
14	10^{14}	3500 yrs	11, 111 TB

This table shows how memory requirements increases as the depth increases.

MULTIPLE CHOICE QUESTIONS

1. States are operated upon by a set of

(*a*) Operators (*b*) Components
(*c*) State space (*d*) None of the above

2. Nodes are states and arcs represent

(*a*) Directions (*b*) Actions
(*c*) Functions (*d*) None of the above

3. The process of creating a formal description of a problem using the knowledge about the given problem, so as to create a program for solving a problem is called as

(*a*) Standardization (*b*) Operationalization
(*c*) Generalization (*d*) None of the above

4. A set of all possible states of a given problem is known as

(*a*) State (*b*) Space search
(*c*) State space (*d*) None of the above.

5. The process of decomposing up of a complex problem into a set of primitive sub problems, finding solutions to them and then integrating them to get a complete solution as a whole is known as

(*a*) Expansion (*b*) Problem reduction
(*c*) Production systems (*d*) None of the above

6. Production systems were proposed by

(*a*) Foreign bank (*b*) Codd
(*c*) Emit post (*d*) None of the above

7. The maximum length of operator-application-sequence is known as

(*a*) Depth cut-off (*b*) Depth of tree
(*c*) Search path (*d*) None of the above.

8. Uniformed search is also known as a

(*a*) Heuristic search (*b*) Blind search
(*c*) Goal search (*d*) Beam search

9. The time complexity of the bfs algorithm

(*a*) 0 (bd) (*b*) 0 (b^d)
(*c*) 0 (d^b) (*d*) 0 ($b + d$)

10. Blind alley means

(*a*) Applying two or more searches (*b*) Search that can go on and on
(*c*) Blind search only (*d*) None of the above

11. A heuristic is a

(*a*) Rule of thumb (*b*) Mathematics formulae
(*c*) Equation (*d*) None of the above

12. The most common problem with all AI solution is

(*a*) Polynomial explosion (*b*) Combinational explosion
(*c*) Nuclear explosion (*d*) None of the above

13. Which module creates the possible solutions in Generate-And-Test-Algorithm

(*a*) OS module (*b*) Kernel module
(*c*) Generator module (*d*) None of the above

14. An area of the search space which is higher than the surrounding areas is a

(*a*) Ridge (*b*) Plateau
(*c*) Hill (*d*) None of the above

15. Which of the following is a greedy search

(*a*) BFS (*b*) DFS
(*c*) Best-First Search (*d*) None of the above.

16. Goal nodes have an evaluation function value of

(*a*) Zero (*b*) Onc
(*c*) Two (*d*) Three

17. The sum of the evaluation function value and the cost along the path leading to the state is called as

(*a*) Fitness number (*b*) Whole number
(*c*) Complex number (*d*) None of the above.

18. Constraint satisfaction is also referred to as

(*a*) Divide-and-conquer algorithm (*b*) Greedy algorithm
(*c*) Relaxation algorithm (*d*) None of the above.

19. Mean-End-Analysis (MEA) allows

(*a*) Backward searching (*b*) Forward searching
(*c*) Both (*a*) and (*b*) (*d*) None of the above.

20. MEA works on three primary goals which are

(*a*) Transformation, scaling and rotation
(*b*) Transformation, reduction and application
(*c*) Scaling, reduction and application
(*d*) None of the above

ANSWERS

1. (*a*)	**2.** (*b*)	**3.** (*b*)	**4.** (*c*)	**5.** (*b*)
6. (*c*)	**7.** (*a*)	**8.** (*b*)	**9.** (*b*)	**10.** (*b*)
11. (*a*)	**12.** (*b*)	**13.** (*c*)	**14.** (*a*)	**15.** (*c*)
16. (*a*)	**17.** (*a*)	**18.** (*c*)	**19.** (*c*)	**20.** (*b*)

CONCEPTUAL SHORT QUESTIONS WITH ANSWERS

Q. 1. What is the relationship between various search algorithms-Breadth-first, uniform cost, AO*, A* and Best-First search?

Ans. As shown in Figure, when $h'(n) = 0$ for all nodes, we have uniform-cost algorithm. When $f'(n) = g(n) = \text{depth}(n)$, we have breadth-first search which spreads out along contours of equal depth. Please note from above diagram that both the uniform-cost and breadth-first algorithms are special cases of A* (with $h'(n) = 0$), so they are both admissible.

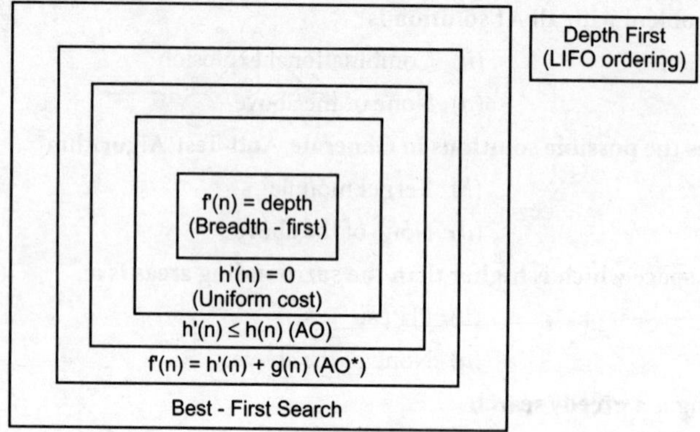

Q.2. What is Search Control Knowledge?

Ans. A large KB contains thousands of rules when there are many possible paths for reasoning, it is critical that fruitless ones are not pursued. Knowledge about which paths are most likely to lead quickly to a goal state is called as a search control knowledge.

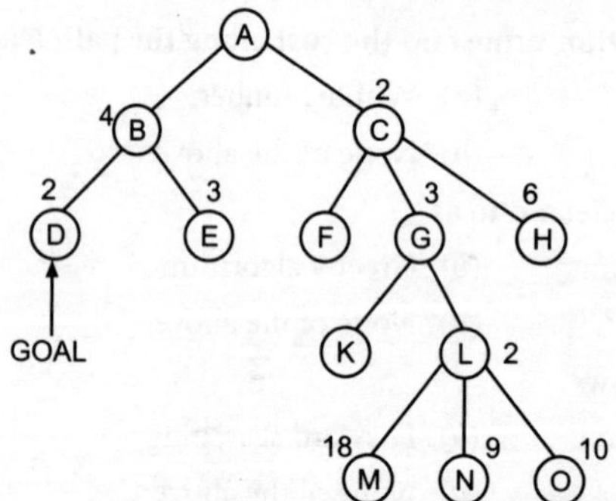

Q.3. When would best-first search be worse than simple breadth-first search?

Ans. CASE WHEN BEST-FIRST SEARCH IS WORSE THAN BREADTH-FIRST SEARCH

Consider a graph—

Using Breadth First Search, to reach the goal '*D*' we would transverse as—

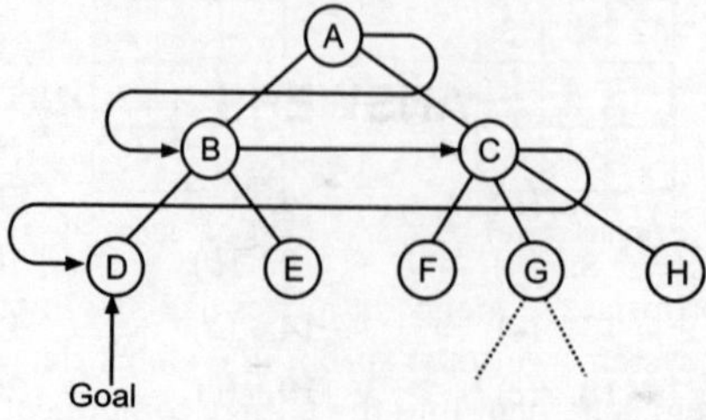

Path ⇒ $A \rightarrow B \rightarrow C \rightarrow D$ No. of modes traversed = 4.

Using Best First Search, to reach the goal '*D*' we would traverse as—

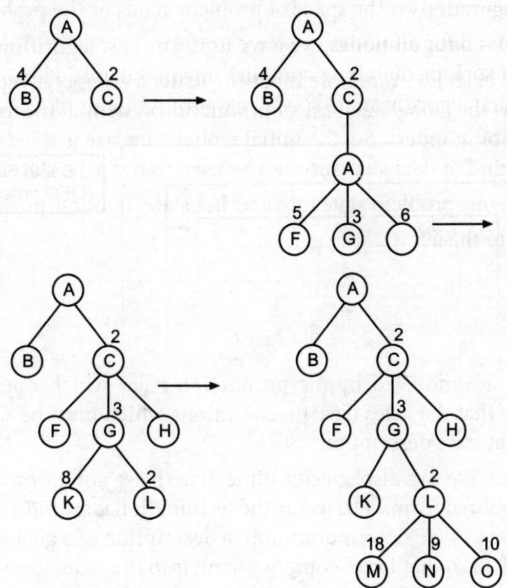

which is not the goal, hence we now switch to another path-B

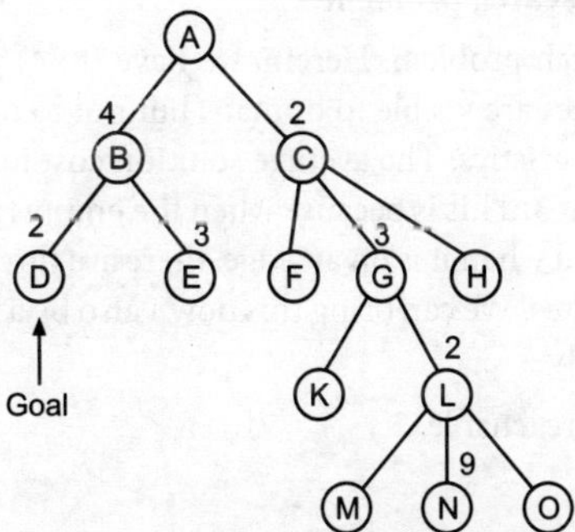

Thus, Best first search traverses more modes in this particular example than the breadth-first search, and hence Best first is worse than Breadth first in this example.

Q.4. What is 8-puzzle problem? How can you solve a problem using production system?

Ans. The 8-puzzle problem consists of eight numbered, movable tiles set in a (3 × 3) frame. One cell of this (3 × 3) frame is always empty. Our problem is to change the initial configuration into the goal configuration *i.e.,*

2	8	3
1	6	4
7		5

(Initial state)

1	2	3
8		9
7	6	5

(Goal state)

A solution to this problem is an appropriate sequence of moves like moving tile 6 down, moving tile 8 down etc. To solve a problem using a production system, we must specify the global database, the rules and the control strategy. This process of transforming a problem statement into these three components of a production system is called as the representation of problem in AI. There are many ways to represent a problem selecting a good representation is one of the important arts involved in applying AI techniques to practical problems.

In our 8-puzzle problem—

a. Each tile configuration is a problem state.

b. The set of all possible configurations is the space of problem states or the problem space.

c. It has 9! = 3,62, 880 different configurations.

Once the problems states have been identified, we must construct a computer representation (or description) of them. This description is then used as the global database of production system. For this 8-puzzle problem, a straight forward description is a (3 × 3) matrix of numbers. So, the initial global database is the description of the initial problem state. Please note that virtually any kind of data structure can be used to describe states, like vectors, trees, linked lists etc.

A move will actually transform one problem state into another state. In our 8-puzzle problem there can be four moves—

a. Move empty space (blank) to the left

b. Move blank up

c. Move blank to right

d. Move blank down.

Please note that these moves are modeled by the production rules which operate on the state descriptions in the appropriate manner. Also note that the rules have preconditions which must be satisfied by a state description in order for them to be applicable to that state description.

We have to reach our goal state. We can also specify some True/False condition on states to serve as a goal condition. It is the problem-goal condition that forms a basis for the termination condition of the production system. The control strategy repeatedly applies rules to state descriptions until a description of a goal state is produced. It also keeps track of the rules which have been applied so that it can compose them into the sequence representing the problem solution. We may add some constraints also to our solution *i.e.*, to find an optimal (minimum) path solution (with smallest number of moves). For this, costs are associated with each move and the minimum is selected.

Q. 5. Is our 8-puzzle problem a heuristic search problem?

Ans. The 8-tile problem is a heuristic search problem. Herein, we have (8×4) possible tile moves. Most of these moves are illegal at any point. These illegal moves are visible to humans but not to our computer. A computer will simply swap it with a neighboring tile. So, we use heuristics. The average solution cost for a randomly generated 8-tile puzzle is about 22 steps. The branching factor is about 3. This is because when the empty tile is in middle, there are four possible moves, when it is in a corner there are two and when it is on an edge, there are three. Thus, an exhaustive search to a depth of 22 would have about $33^{22} \approx 3.1 \times 10^{10}$ states. We can bring this down also by a factor of 1,70,000 if we keep track of repeated states. This is so because there are only—

$\frac{9!}{2}$ = 1,81,440 distinct states that are reachable. 2

Heuristics used :

1. Say, h_1 represents the number of misplaced tiles. If all 8-tiles are out of position then the start state would have h_1 = 8. Since any tile which is out of place must be moved at least once, h_1 is an admissible heuristic.
2. Say, h_2 represents the sum of the distances of the tiles from their goal positions. Please note here that the tiles cannot move diagonally, so the distance we will count is the sum of the horizontal and vertical distances. This distance is called as the city block distance or Manhattan distance. Also note that when we move one tile, h_2 can still be applied as any move brings us one step closer to the goal.

Q. 6. What are heuristics?

Ans. According to various AI researchers—

1. **Newell, Shaw and Simon (1957) :** "A process that may solve a given problem but offers no guarantees of doing so is called as a heuristic for that problem".
2. **Marvin Minisky (1961) :** "A heuristic is any method or trick used to improve the efficiency of a problem- solving program."
3. **Feigenbaum and Feldman (1963) :** "A state heuristic is rule of thumb, strategy, trick, simplification or any other kind of device which drastically limits search for solutions in large problem spaces. Heuristics do not guarantee optimal

solution; in fact, they do not guarantee any solution at all. It can be said for a useful heuristic is that it offers solutions which are good enough most of the time."

Judea Pearl (1984) : "It is the nature of good heuristics both that they provide a simple means of indicating which among several course of action is to be preferred and that they are not necessarily guaranteed to identify the most effective course of action, but do so sufficiently often. It is often said that heuristic methods are unpredictable, they work wonders most of the time but may fail miserably some of the time".

Q. 7. Distinguish between Heuristic algorithms and solution guaranteed algorithms?

Ans. Let us tabulate the difference between the two

Heuristic Algorithms	Solution guaranteed algorithm
1. These algorithms are non-exact algorithms that do not guarantee that the best will be found. So, they are considered to be approximate algorithms.	1. These algorithms are also called as exact-algorithms as they guarantee to find an optimal solution.
2. They find solutions close to the best one.	2. They guarantee to find optimal solutions.
3. They find fast solutions.	3. They take exponential time to do so.
4. It is called as heuristic because it must prove that the best solution is the best. For e.g., Local search methods, simulated annealing etc.	4. It always finds an optimal solution. For *e.g.*: Branch and Bound, dynamic programming, Branch and cut etc.

1. These algorithms are non-exact algorithms that do not guarantee that the best will be found. So, they are considered to be approximate algorithms.

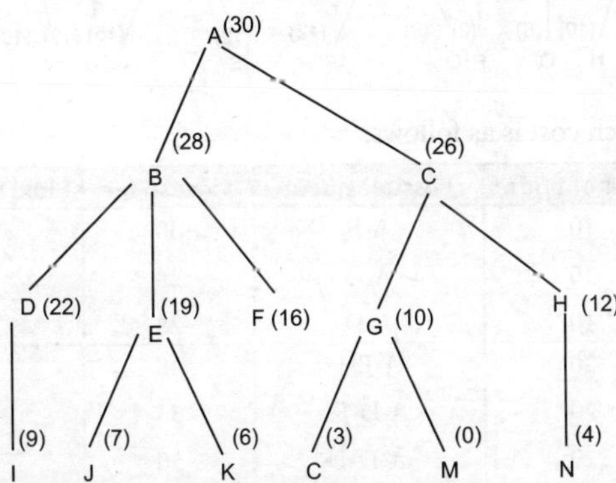

Ans. The best-first-search's cost is calculated in the following manner.

From node	To node	Cost of node	Possible Queue	Cost so far	Final best First queue
A	B	30	A-B	30	✓
	C	30	A-C	30	✓
B	D	28	A-B-D	58	×
	E	28	A-B-E	58	×
	F	28	A-B-F	58	×
C	G	26	A-C-G	56	✓
	H	26	A-C-H	56	✓
G	L	10	A-C-G-L	66	✓
	M	10	A-C-G-M	66	✓
H	N	12	A-C-H-N	68	×
L	Next node	3	A-C-G-L-Next Node	69	×
M	Next node	0	A-C-G-H-Next node	66	✓

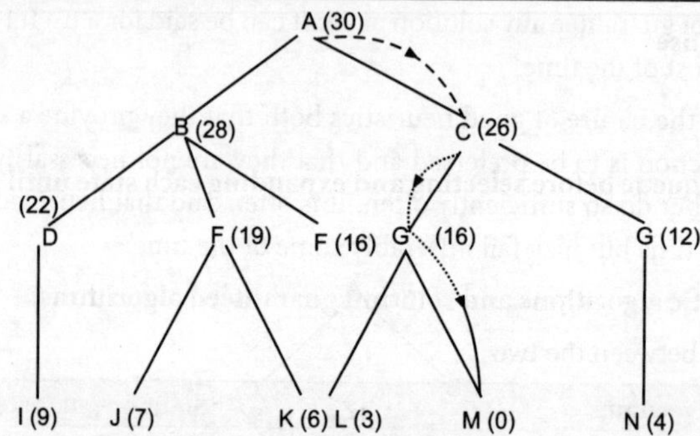

Q. 8. Using the search, the given below, list the elements of the queue just before that next node is expanded. Use best-first search where the number correspond to estimated cost-to-goal for each corresponding node.

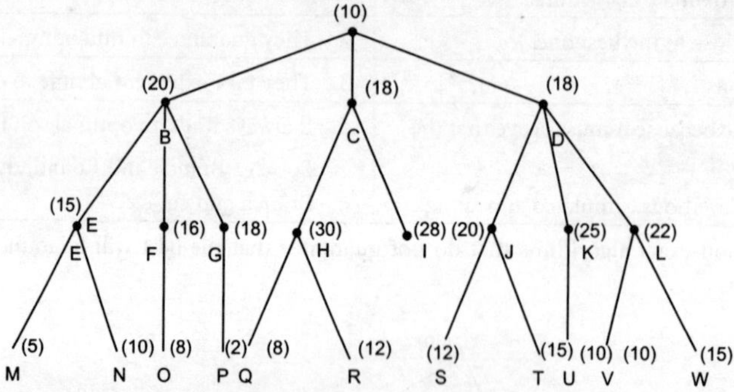

Ans. The table showing best-first search cost is as follows.

From node	To node	Cost of node	Possible queue	Cost so far	Final best First queue
A	B	10	A-B	30	×
	C	10	A-C	28	✓
	D	10	A-D	28	✓
D	J	20	A-B-J	48	✓
	K	20	A-D-K	53	×
	L	20	A-D-L	50	×
C	H	18	A-C-H	58	×
	I	18	A-C-I	56	×
D	S	20	A-D-J-S	60	✓
	T	20	A-D-J-T	63	×

The best first search has path as A-D-J-S-Next node with cost 60.

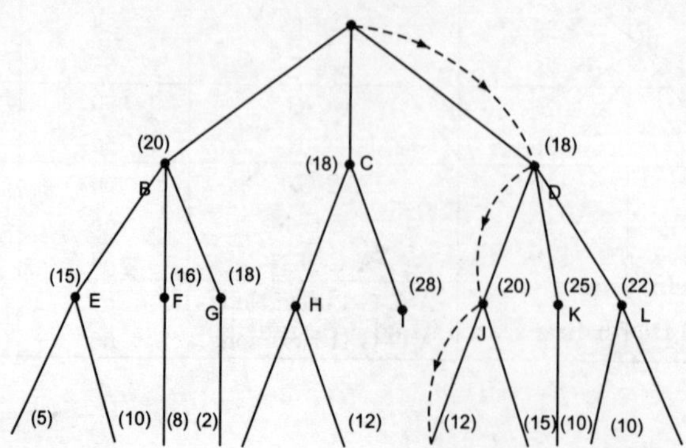

Q.10. For the search given below, use

(*i*) Breadth-first search

(*ii*) Depth-first search

and list the elements of the queue before selecting and expanding each state until goal node is reached (Goal states designated with*).

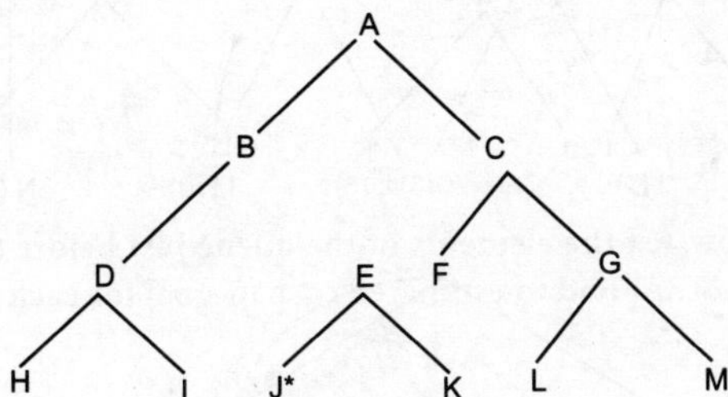

Ans. **(*i*) Breadth first search:**

The given goal is *J*.

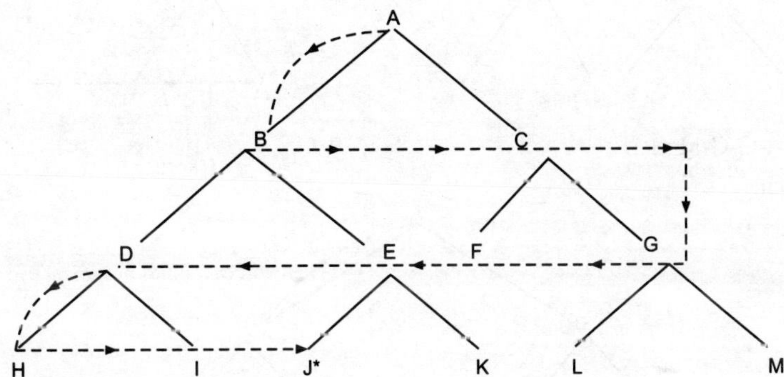

The path is

A-B-C-G-F-E-D-H-I-J.

(*ii*) Depth-first-search :

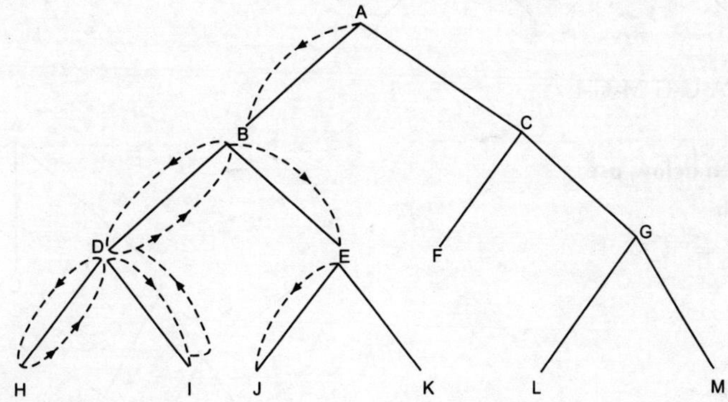

A-B-D-H-I-D-B-E-J.

Q. 11. For the search tree given below, use

(*i*) Breadth first search. (*ii*) Depth-first search. Goal is designed by

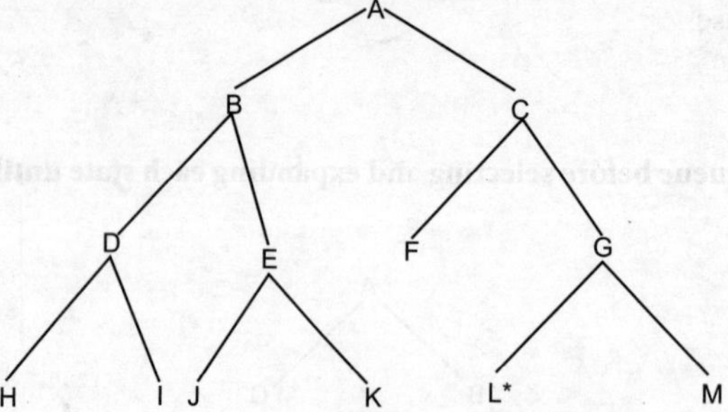

Ans. ***(i)* Breadth first search:**

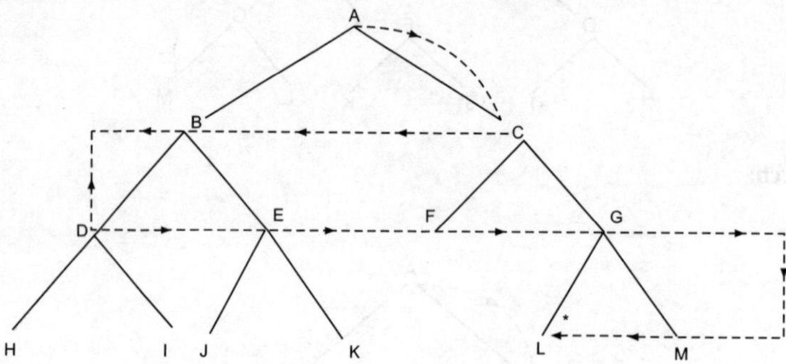

The path is given as A-C-G-M-G-L

***(ii)* Depth–first search:**

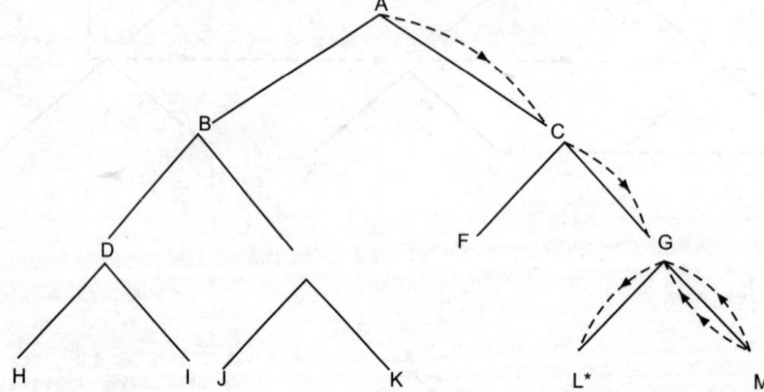

The path is given as A-C-G-M-G-L

Q. 12. For the search tree given below, use

***(i)* Breadth-first search**

***(ii)* Depth first search**

Goal is shown a

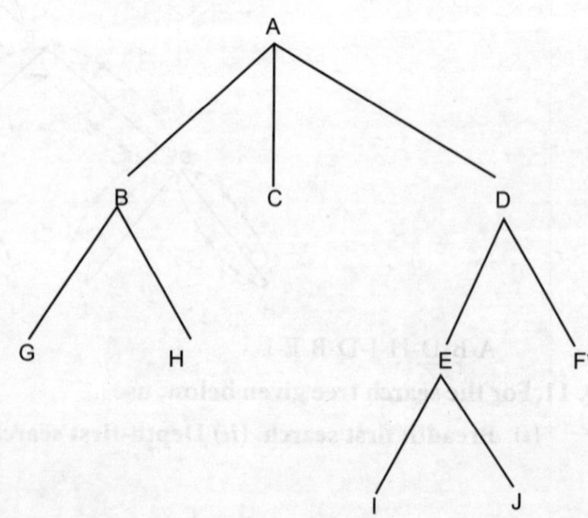

Ans. ***(i)* Breadth first search**

The path from A to F is A-B-C-D-F

(ii) Depth first search

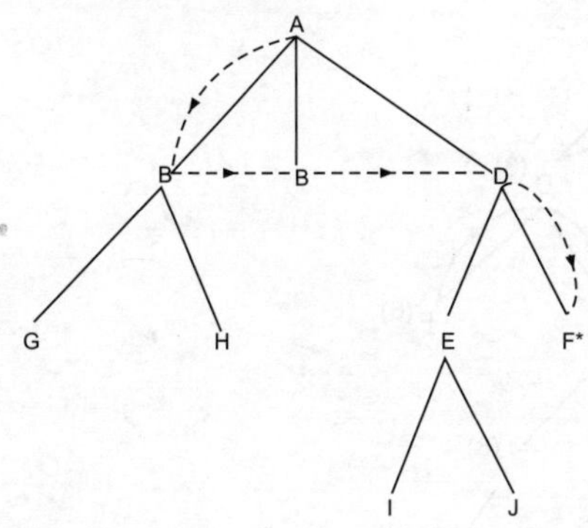

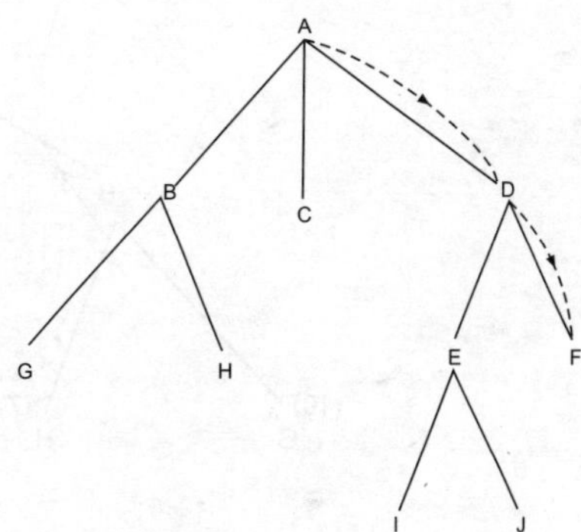

The path from A to F is A-D-F

Q.13. Using the search tree given below, list the elements of the queue just before next node is expanded. Use Best-first-Search where the number correspond to estimated cost-to- goal for each corresponding node.

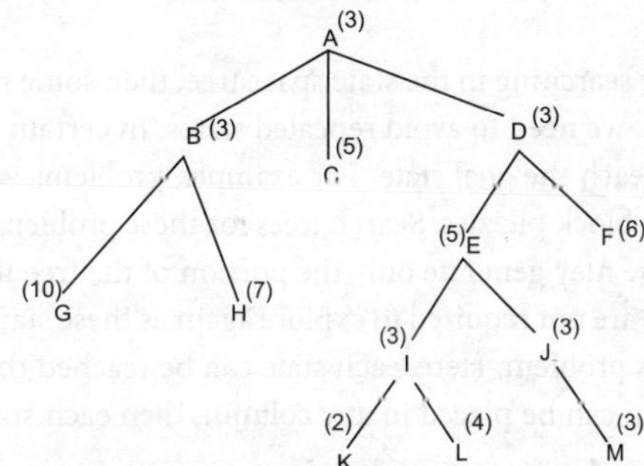

Ans. The following table be used to show best first search.

From node	To node	Cost of node	Possible Queue	Cost so far	Final best First queue
A	B	3	A-B	6	✓
	C	5	A-C	8	×
	D	3	A-D	6	✓
B	G	3	A-B-G	16	×
	H	3	A-B-H	13	×
D	E	3	A-D-E	11	✓
	F	3	A-D-F	12	×
E	I	5	A-D-E-I	13	✓
I	J	5	A-D-E-J	14	✓
	K	3	A-D-E-I-K	15	✓
J	L	3	A-D-E-I-L	18	×
	M	3	A-D-E-J-M	17	×
F	Next node Next Node	2	A-D-E-I-K	15	✓

The given path using Best-Search is:

A-D-E-I-K- Next node.

∴ The cost is given for the path is 15

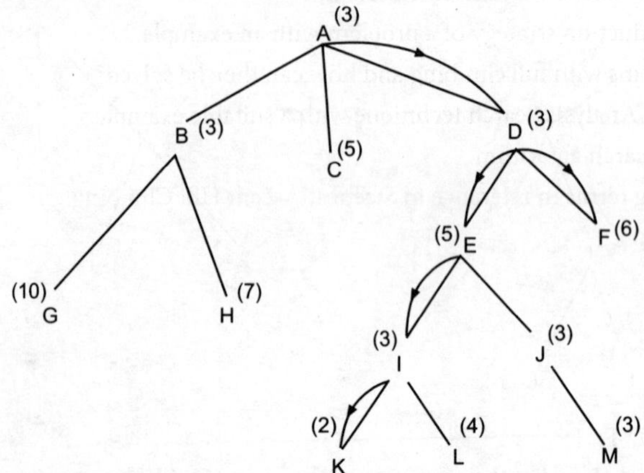

Q.14. What are repeated states? How to avoid them? What are the problems caused by them? Devise an algorithm that can avoid repeated states.

Ans. When we try to find the solution by searching in the state space tree, then some of the states can be repeatedly explored. This increases the total cost. Hence, we need to avoid repeated states. In certain problems, we need to explore all of the repeated states again as they may reach the goal state. For example, problems where the actions are reversible such as route-finding problems and sliding-block puzzles. Search trees for these problems are infinite. But please note that if we cut-off some repeated states then we may generate only the portion of the tree that encompasses the state space graph. In certain problems, repeated states are not required to explore again as these states will not surely lead to the goal states. For example, consider the 8-queens problem. Here, each state can be reached through only 1 path. If we formulate the 8-queens problem such that a queen can be placed in any column, then each state with n-queens can be reached by n! different paths.

Problems caused by repeated states :

a. Because of repeated states solvable problem can become unsolvable if the algorithm is unable to detect repeated states.

b. Because of repeated states looping paths can be generated which can lead to infinite search which is not a practical approach.

c. Because of repeated states memory is unnecessarily wasted as same state is maintained multiple times.

Algorithms that forget their history are sure to repeat the states. If an algorithm remembers every state that it has visited then it can be viewed as exploring state space graph directly. We can devise a new algorithm called as **graph-search algorithm** which is more efficient than the earlier tree-search algorithm. A graph-search algorithm maintains **two data structures** –closed list and open list to avoid exploration of those nodes that are already explored *i.e.,* trying to avoid repeated states. **Please note that a repeated state is detected when an algorithm has found two paths to same state and if the newly discovered path is shorter than the original one then it will be discarded by the algorithm.** Then there is a chance that graph-search could miss an optimal solution as it can discard one of the paths that can lead to an optimal state.

EXERCISE QUESTIONS

1. Given an example of a real- world problem which can be effectively solved by "Hill climbing Algorithm. Explain the terms plateau and ridge.

2. *a.* Explain means end analysis with an example.
   b. What do you understand by admissible heuristic? Develop an admissible heuristic for any problem of your own.
3. *a.* Compare uniformed search with informed search.
   b. Discuss problem reduction strategy of a problem with an example.
4. *a.* What are the problems with hill climbing and how can they be solved?
   b. Explain Means End Analysis Search technique with a suitable example.
   c. State the best first search algorithm.
   d. Define the following terms in reference to Steepest Ascent Hill Climbing:
      (*i*) Local Maximum
      (*ii*) Plateau.
      (*iii*) Ridge.
5. *a.* Write the difference between:
      (*i*) OR graph and AND-OR graph
      (*ii*) Generate and test and hill climbing.
   b. How state space search work on state space of an AI problem? Explain it with the help of water jug problem.
   c. Explain advantages and disadvantages of dfs and bfs.
   d. What are various issues to be considered in the design of search problems/programs.
6. Using a suitable example, illustrate steps of A* search. Why is A* search better than Best First Search.
7. Explain BFS algorithm.
8. *a.* Why Hill-climbing is named so? Illustrate using an example.
   b. Discuss and compare Blind Search with Heuristic based search. Which one is better? Discuss using an example.

4 Uninformed Search Strategies

The uninformed search is also called as **blind search/ brute force search.** It is so called as this type of search contains **no information for its domain problem.** It just distinguishes between a non-goal state and a goal state. Let us now discuss some uninformed searches strategies one by one in detail.

Q.1. What is Uniformed/Blind/Brute Force/Exhaustive Search? Which all search is put under this category? On what basis will you evaluate its performance? Explain.

Ans. The following searches are discussed under this category: -

- BFS
- DFS
- Depth Limited Search
- Iterative deepening DFS
- Bidirectional search
- Uniform Cost Search.

The performance evaluation is done on the basis of 4 parameters: -

- Completeness.
- Optimality.
- Time complexity.
- Space complexity.

As we know that the state-space is a directed graph in which each node is a state and each arc shows the application of an operator transforming a state to a successor state. **But please note that a node is different from a state.** A node is a data structure used to represent the search tree. However, a state corresponds to a configuration of the world. So, nodes are on some particular paths always. They are defined by the parent node pointer. On the other hand, states are not on some particular paths. **Also note here that two different nodes can contain the same world state if that state is generated via two different search paths.** And a solution is a path from the initial or start state to a goal state. These goal states may be defined explicitly or as a set of states satisfying a given predicate. In blind or uniformed search, these is no order in which the solution paths are considered i.e., it uses no domain specific information to search a solution in the search space. Again, the state space is combinational, so this type of search is actually impracticable for the nontrivial problems. It is called as **brute-force search** as it examines every node in the tree until a goal is found. These algorithms make some assumptions: —

1. A procedure must be there to find all successors of a given node *i.e.*, all states are reachable from the current state and that too by a single operator application.
2. The state-space graph is a tree. It means that there is only one start state (*i.e.*, root of tree) and that the path from the start node to any other node is unique.
3. Whenever a node is expanded, creating a node for each of its successors, the successor nodes contain pointers back to the parent node. Finally, when a goal node is generated, the path from the root to the goal can be easily found.

So, blind search algorithms use only the initial state, search operators and a test for a solution.

It proceeds systematically by exploring nodes either randomly or in some predetermined order.

Q.2. Explain the Breadth-First Search (BFS) technique of searching. Also discuss about its parameters.

Ans. The Procedure: It is the simplest form of blind search. In this technique the root node is expanded first, then all of its successors are expanded and then their successors and so on. In general, in bfs, all nodes are expanded level-wise starting at the root level.

It means that all immediate children of nodes are explored before any of the children's children are considered. The search tree generated by bfs is shown below in Fig. 4.1.

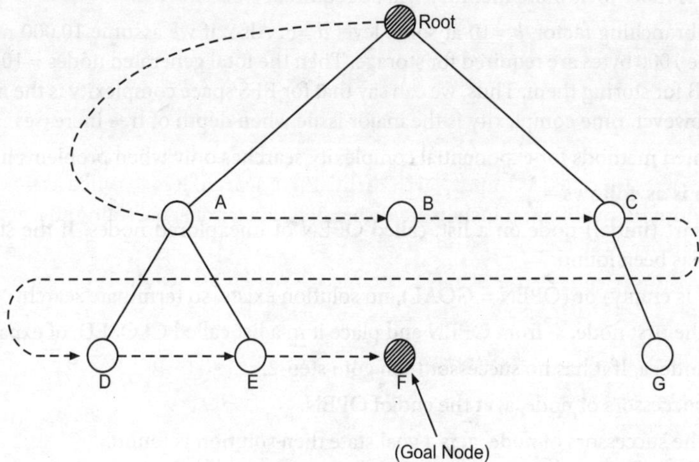

***Fig. 4.1:** Search Tree for bfs*

Please note here that we are using the **convention that** the alternatives are tried in the left- to-right order. Also note that bfs is a brute-search so it generates all the nodes for identifying the goal. The breadth-first method expands nodes in order of their proximity to the start node measured by the number of arcs between them.

In general, it considers every possible sequence of length n before any sequence of length $n + 1$. Although this search may be an extremely long yet it is guaranteed eventually to find the minimum or shortest path length (possible solution sequence) solution, if any solution exists.

The Implementation: BFS algorithm uses a data structure-queue that works on FIFO principle where fringe will be stored and processed. This queue will hold all generated but still unexplored nodes. As soon as the node is visited it is added to the queue. All newly generated nodes are added to the end of the queue which means that shallow nodes are expanded before deeper nodes. Please remember that the **order in** which nodes are placed on the queue for removal and exploration determines the type of search.

The Performance Evaluation :

1. **Completeness :** BFS is complete because if the shallowest goal node (nearest, not deep) is at some finite depth, d, BFS will eventually find it and it will generate solution. Assuming that branching factor, b, is finite.
2. **Optimality :** The shallowest goal node is not necessarily optimal. BFS will yield optimal solution only when all actions have the same cost, be it any depth.
3. **Time and space complexity:**

Level

$b + b^2 + b^3$ .... $+ b^d + (b^{d+1}) - b)$

$= O(b^d + 1)$

The amount of time taken for generating these nodes is proportional to the depth, d and branching factor, b and is given by —

$1 + b + b^2 + b^3 + \ldots + b^d$

$\therefore$ Time complexity is $O(b^{d+1})$.

Now, bfs has to remember each and every node it has generated. So, the space-complexity will also depend upon the function of depth, d and the branching factor, b.

So, space complexity is given by

$1 + b + b^2 + b^3 + \ldots + b^{d+1}$

or, Space complexity is $O(b^{d+1})$.

Please note that BFS is a systematic search strategy because it considers all nodes (states) at level-1 first and then all states at level-2 and so on. If any solution exists then BFS is guaranteed to find it. Also note that if there are many solutions then BFS will always find the shallowest goal state first. If the solution's cost is an increasing function of depth, then it finds the one which is a cheapest solution. Every node generated should remain in memory till its exploration. If branching factor, *b*, is more then more memory will be required.

For example, if the branching factor, b =10 at some level d =6. Also, if we assume 10,000 nodes will be generated per second and per node 1000 bytes are required for storage. Then the total generated nodes = 10^7 which will take 18.9 mins but it will take 10 GB for storing them. Thus, we can say that for BFS space complexity is the major issue concerned than time complexity. However, time complexity is the major issue when depth of tree increases.

Note : Use uninformed methods for exponential complexity searches only when problems have smallest instances.

The BFS algorithm is as follows—

Step-1 : Put the start (initial) node on a list, called OPEN of unexplored nodes. If the start node is a goal node, a solution has been found.

Step-2 : If (OPEN is empty) or (OPEN = GOAL), no solution exists, so terminate search.

Step-3 : Remove the first node, a, from OPEN and place it in a list called CLOSED, of expanded nodes.

Step-4 : Expand node, a. If it has no successor then goto step-2.

Step-5 : Place all successors of node, a, at the end of OPEN.

Step-6 : If any of the successors of node, a, is a goal state then solution is found.

```
Breadth-first-algorithm of G
{
for i= 1 to n do   //mark all vertices unvisited
   visited [i] = 0;
for i = 1 to n do
   if (visited [i] = 0) then BFS(i);
}
```

So, for BFS the time complexity = space complexity = $O(b^{d+1})$.

Let us now discuss the advantages and disadvantages of BFS—

Advantages of BFS

BFS has some advantages and are given below—

1. BFS will never get trapped exploring a blind alley.
2. It is guaranteed to find a solution if one exists.

Disadvantages of BFS

BFS has certain disadvantages also. They are given below—

1. Time complexity and space complexity are both O(bd) *i.e.* exponential type. This is a very big hurdle.
2. All nodes are to be generated in bfs. So, even unwanted nodes are to be remembered (stored in queue) which is of no practical use of the search.

Q.3. Explain Depth-first Search (DFS) procedure, its evaluation parameters, its time and space complexity and its algorithm.

Ans. The Procedure: DFS begins by expanding the initial node *i.e.*, by using an operator, generate all successors of the initial node and test them. It (DFS) is characterized by the expansion of the most recently generated or deepest node first. DFS needs to store the path from the root to the leaf node as well as the unexpanded nodes. It is neither complete nor optimal. If DFS goes down an infinite branch (depth cut-off point) will not end till a goal state is found. Even if it is found, there may be a better solution at a higher level. This depth cut-off (*d*) introduces many problems also. If d is set too shallow, goal may be missed. If *d* is set too deep then extra computation may be performed. DFS always expands the deepest node in the current unexplored node set (fringe) of the search tree. The search goes in to depth until there is no more successor node. Please note that as these nodes are expanded, they are dropped from the fringe, so then the search 'backs-up' to the next shallowest node (previous level node) that still has unexplored successors.

The Implementation : DFS can be implemented with stack (LIFO) data structure which will explore the latest added node first, suspending exploration of all previous nodes on the path. This can be done using recursive procedure that calls itself on each of the children in turn.

The Performance Evaluation:

3. **Completeness :** As DFS explores all nodes hence it guarantees the solution.
4. **Optimality :** As DFS reaches to the deepest node first. It may ignore some shallow node which can be a goal state. Hence, optimality is expected only when all states have same path cost.
5. **Time and space complexity :** DFS requires moderate amount of memory as it needs to store single path from root to some node to a particular level, along with unexpanded siblings. When the same node gets fully explored, its complete branch (its descendants and itself) will get removed from memory. So, with a branching factor, b, and maximum dept *d*, DFS requires storage of $(bd + 1)$ nodes.

   The amount of time taken for generating these nodes is proportional to the depth, *d* and branching factor, *b* and is given by

$$1 + b + b^2 + b^3 + \dots b^d$$

$\therefore$ Time complexity = $O(b^d)$

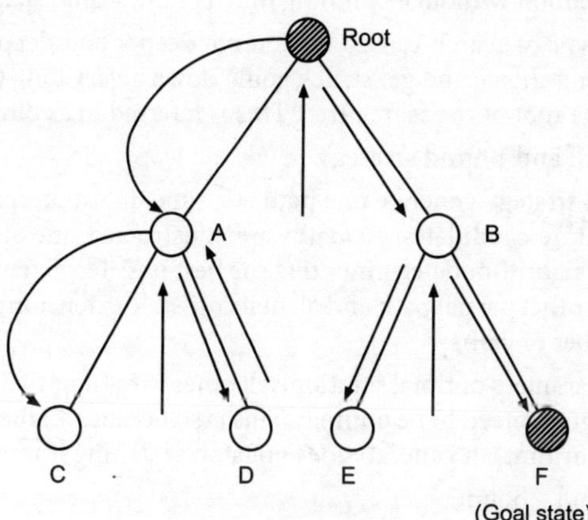

Fig. 4.2: Search Tree for dfs

Also note that DFS stores only the current path it is pursing. So, the space complexity will be a linear function of depth, *d*. So,

Space complexity = $O(d)$.

The value of cut-off depth (*d*) is important here as then otherwise the search will go on and on.

Two cases arise—

1. If *d* is small, solution may not be found.
2. If *d* is large, time complexity will be more.

The DFS algorithm is as follows—

Step-1 : Put the initial node on a list, START-LIST.

Step-2 : If (START-LIST is empty or (START = GOAL) then terminate (end) search.

Step-3 : Remove the first node from START-LIST. Call this node, *a*.

Step-4 : If (a = GOAL) then terminate search with success.

Step-5 : Else if node a has successors, generate all of these and add them at the beginning of START- LIST.

Step-6 : Goto step-2.

So, the search tree for dfs is as shown in Fig. 4.2.

Algorithm DFS (*v*)

```
// Given undirected (OR directed graph, G = (V, E) with n-vertices and an array
//visited initially set to zero. This algo. visits all vertices reachable from
v. G and //visited [ ] are global.
{
```

```
visited [v] = 1;
for each vertex w adjacent from v do
{
if(visited[w] = 0 then DFS (w);
}
}
```

Time complexity : $O(b^d)$.

Space complexity : $O(b^d + 1)$.

Advantages of DFS

DFS has some advantages. They are given below—

1. Memory requirements in dfs are less as only nodes on the current path are stored.
2. By chance, dfs may find a solution without examining much of the search space of all.

Disadvantages of DFS : This type of search can go on and on, deeper and deeper into the search space and thus, we can get lost. DFS can make wrong choice and get struck going down a very long (infinite) path when a different choice would lead to a solution near the root of the search tree. This is referred to as blind alley.

Q.4. Explain the Depth first: Branch and Bound strategy.

Ans. The Branch and Bound control strategy generate one path at a time. It also keeps track of the best path so found. This value is used as a bound on future candidates. As paths are constructed one at a time, the algorithm examines each partially completed path. If the algorithm determines that the best possible extension to a path branch will have greater cost than the board, it eliminates that partial path and all of its possible extensions. This reduces search considerably but still leaves an exponential number of paths.

This variation of depth-first, guarantees optimal solution. All other variations of dfs experience the undesirable property that obtained (if at all) is NOT guaranteed to be optimal. This is so because all these algorithms discontinue search once a solution is found. But this algorithm (in general) does not stop searching immediately after finding the first solution.

//Unbounded Dfs – Branch – and – bound.

UDFBB(n){

if $f(n)$ > cost (solution) then

return; if n is a goal node then

```
solution: = superior(m, n);
```

for each n_i of

```
UDFBB (ni);
return; }
```

Here, superior (m, n) reports the better of the two goal nodes m and n, in terms of cost.

The disadvantage here is that this algorithm may blindly go deeper into some unpromising paths and thus generate to many nodes in the worst case.

Q.5. Explain Iterative Deepening Depth First Search (IDDFS) method. Give its procedure, implementation, parameter evaluation and its advantages and disadvantages.

Ans. The Procedure: It is a general strategy often used in combination with DFS that finds the best depth limit. It begins by performing DFS to a depth of one, then depth of

two, depth of three and so on, until a solution is found or some maximum depth is reached. It combines the benefits of both BFS and DFS. In each step, depth limit is increased until the goal is found. It increases depth limit from level-0, then level-1, then level-2 till the shallowest goal is found at a certain depth, d.

For example, consider a tree as shown.

The Implementation: We have shown 3-stages of iterative—deepening search. Please note here that the number of nodes expanded by iterative-deepening search is not much more than that would be using BFS. it can be implemented similar to BFS where queue is used for storing fringe because it explores a complete layer of new nodes at each iteration before going on to the next layer. Also note that in order to avoid memory requirements which are incurred in BFS, IDDFS can be implemented like uniform-cost search. The focal point is to use increasing path-costs limits instead of increasing depth-limits, is if we have such a implementation then it is termed as iterative lengthening search.

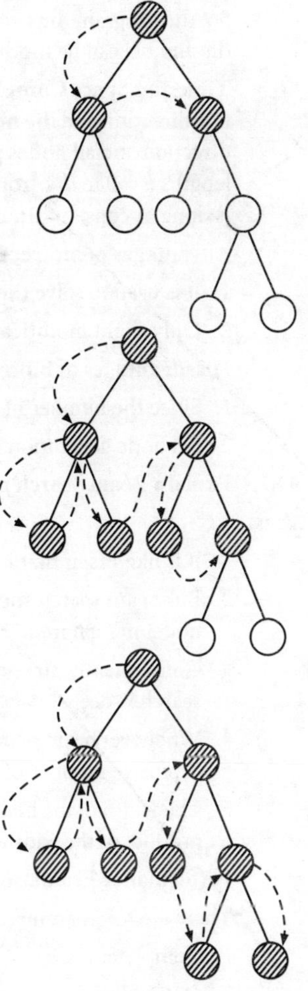

Next, we write an algorithm for depth first iterative deepening search—

depth =1

depth=2

depth = 3

Step-1 : Start

Step-2 : Initialize $d \leftarrow$ O

Step-3 : do

```
d ← d + 1;
DFID (root, d);
Until SUCCESS;
```

Step-4 : End.

This algorithm starts with the smallest d = 1. It then increments d in a loop on encountering FAILURE until a SUCCES is found.

This search also guarantees to find a shortest path solution as it expands all nodes at a given depth before expanding nodes at a greater depth. Also note that it performs wasted computations before reaching the goal depth.

The Performance Evaluation

3. **Completeness :** It promises completeness as the search does not stop until the goal node is found.
4. **Optimality :** As IDDFS search stops, when the goal node is reached, it is not necessary that it is optimal *i.e.*, the shallowest goal reached is the final. This search will not further search for optimal solution.
5. **Time and space complexities**

The time and space complexities of this search algorithm are also $O(b^d)$ and $O(d)$ respectively (where 'b' is the branching factor and bottom most level is depth, d.

IDDFS guarantee to find a solution and avoiding its memory requirements. The basic idea is to use increasing path – cost limits instead of increasing depth limits. The resulting algorithm called iterative lengthening search, incurs substantial overhead as compared to uniform – cost search.

Advantages of Depth-first Iterative Deepening Search

1. It is guaranteed to find a shortest path solution.
2. It is a preferred uniformed search method when the search space is large and the depth of the solution is not known.

Disadvantages of Depth-first Iterative Deepening Search

1. It performs wasted computations before reaching the goal depth.
2. The time complexity is O(bd) i.e., exponential type only.

Is this search bfs or dfs?

This search is similar to both bfs as well as dfs.

How bfs? It is similar to bfs in that it explores a complete layer of new nodes at each iteration before going to the next layer.

How dfs? It is similar to dfs for a single iteration.

Why is it called as iterative?

This search terminates at the depth, d on each iteration if no goal has been found, removes all nodes from the queue, increments d by one and initiates the search again. Hence, it is called as an iterative search.

Q.6. What is Bidirectional Search? Give its advantages and disadvantages.

Ans. This search is used when a problem has a single goal state that is given explicitly and all the node generation operators have inverses. Searching is done by searching forward from the initial node and backward from goal node simultaneously.

So, the program must save (store) the nodes so generated on both search frontiers until a common node is found. Both dfs and bfs can be modified slightly to perform this search.

Time and Space Complexities of bidirectional Search : To perform this search to a depth of k, the search is made from one direction and the nodes at depth k are stored. At some time, a search to a depth of k and $k + 1$ is made from the other direction and all nodes generated are matched against the nodes stored from the other side. This process is repeated for lengths $k = 0$ to $d/2$ from both the directions. So, its time and space complexities are both $O(b^{d/2})$ when node matching is done in constant time per node.

Advantages of bidirectional search :

1. It is used to solve the 8-puzzle problem.
2. Only slight modification of dfs and bfs can be done to perform this search.

Disadvantages of bidirectional search :

1. Since the number of nodes increases as b^d with depth d, so such problems become intractable for large depths.
2. All node generation operators must have inverses also as only then this type of search can be used.

Q.7. Explain Beam Search method.

Ans.

1. It is like Bfs in that it progresses level by level.
2. But beam search moves downward only through the best, W nodes at each level by applying heuristics, the other nodes are ignored.
3. Consequently, the number of nodes explored remains manageable even if there is a great deal of branching and the search is deep.
4. Whenever beam search is used, there are only W nodes under consideration at any depth rather than the exponentially explosive number of nodes as is done in bfs.
5. The width of the beam is fixed and whatever be the depth of the tree, the number of alternatives to be scanned is the product of the width of the beam and the depth.

Performance Evaluation on Four Parameters

There are four parameters on the basis of which these algorithms can be evaluated: -

1. Completeness.
2. Optimality.
3. Time Complexity.
4. Space Complexity.

Q.8. Compare different searches.

Ans. In BFS algorithm, we find the following: -

Procedure : In BFS, the root node is expanded first, then all the successor of root node are expanded and then their successor and so on i.e., the nodes are expanded level-wise starting at the root level.

Implementation : BFS can be implemented using FIFO-based queue data structure where fringe will be stored and processed. By fringe, we mean a collection of nodes that have been generated but not yet expanded. As soon as the node is visited, it is added to the queue. All newly generated nodes are added to the end of the queue which means that shallow nodes are expanded before the deeper nodes.

Let us now evaluate BFS on the basis of these four parameters: -

1. **Completeness :** BFS is complete because if the shallowest goal node is at some finite depth, d, BFS will eventually find it and will generate solution. It assumes that branching factor, b, is finite.
2. **Optimality :** The shallowest goal node is not necessarily optimal. BFS will yield optimal solution only when all actions have the same cost, let it be at any depth.
3. **Time and Space Complexity :** As the level of search tree grows more time is incurred. In general, if the search tree is at level, d, then $O(b^{d+1})$ time is required, where b is the number of nodes generated from each node, starting at the root node i.e. root generates b-nodes and each b-node generates b more and so on.

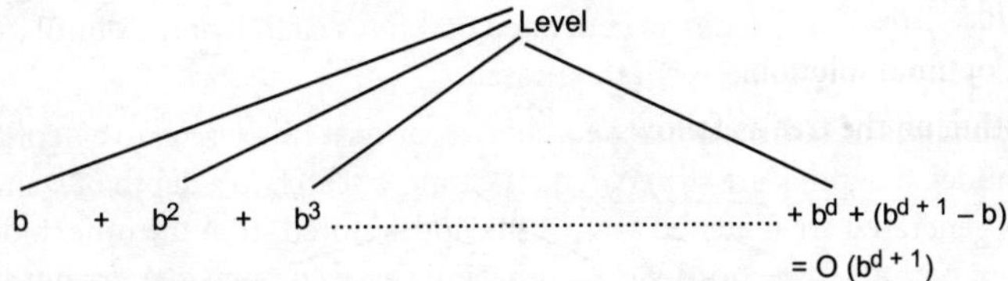

Please note that every node generated should remain in memory till its exploration. If branching factor '*b*' is more then more memory will be required.

For instance, if the branching factor, $b = 10$ at some level $d = 6$, also we assume that 10,000 nodes will be generated per second and per node 1000 bytes are required for storage then the total generated nodes $= 10^7$ which will take 19 minutes but it takes 10 GB for storing them. Thus, we can say that for BFS space complexity is the main issue than its time complexity. Time complexity is critical issue when the depth of tree increases.

Note : We can use uninformed methods for exponential-complexity search only when problems have smallest instances.

So a simple method used in BFS is-

ALGORITHM BFS (G, n)

```
//breadth first search of G
{
for i := 1 to n do      //mark all vertices unvisited
   visited[i] = 0;
for i := 1 to n do
   if (visited [i] = = 0) then BFS (i);
}
```

BFS analysis:

Time complexity : $O(b^{d+1})$.

Space complexity : $O(b^{d+1})$.

Applying BFS algorithm on the given tree below: -

Here, *D* and *J* are goal states. Note here that,

D is found through the path --→ *(a-b-d)* ...shallowest goal.

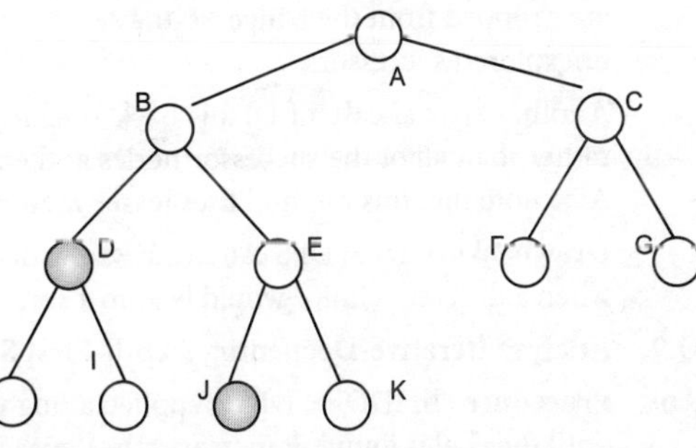

Next let us see for **Uniform Cost Search.**

Procedure : Uniform cost search expands the node, n, with the lowest cost path. It does not care about the number of steps a path has, instead it considers their total cost. Please understand here that there is a chance of getting stuck in an infinite loop if it ever expands a node that has a zero-coat action leading back to the same state.

Implementation : we can use queue (data structure) for storing fringe as in BFS. The main difference will be while adding the node to queue, we will give priority to the node with the lowest path cost. Hence, the data structure should be a priority queue now.

Let us evaluate Uniform cost search now on the basis of 4 parameters stated earlier-

1. **Completeness :** Uniform cost search guarantees completeness provided the cost of every step is greater than or equal to some small positive constant, *c*.
2. **Optimality :** If the cost of every step is greater than or equal to some small positive constant then the uniform cost search will yield optimal solution by reaching the goal state which has the lowest path cost.
3. **Time and Space Complexity :** Uniform cost search does not care about the number of steps a path has. Rather it is concerned with their total cost. Therefore, it will get stuck up in an infinite loop, if it expands a node that has a zero-cost action leading back to the same state.

Also note that Uniform cost search is guided by the path costs rather than depths. So, its complexity cannot be easily characterized in terms of b and d. instead, let C* be the cost of the optimal solution and assume that every action costs at least *E*. then the algorithm's worst-case time and space complexity is $O(b^{1+C/\varepsilon})$, which can be much greater than b^d.

Time Complexity: $O(b^{1+C/\varepsilon})$.

Space Complexity: $O(b^{1+C/\varepsilon})$.

Where, C is the cost of optimal solution.

Let us apply this algorithm on the tree as follows: -

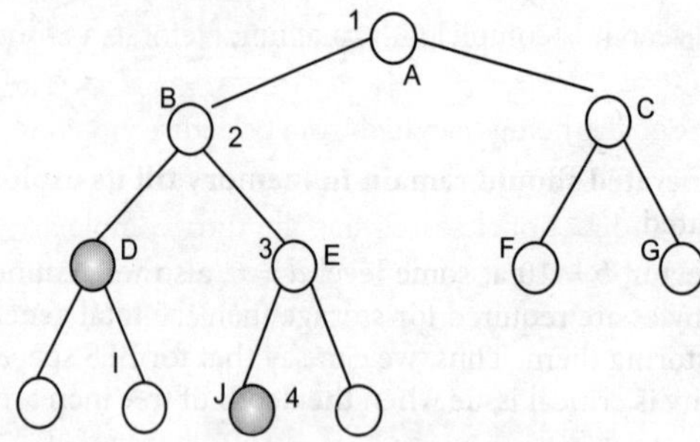

Here, D and J are goal states. Note here that, J is found as follows: -

[J is found through the path] -→ (A – B – E – J)

NOTES :

1. Costs are associated with each edge.
2. Numeric value against each node shows the order in which the nodes are visited (reached).

Let us now apply the four criterions to the Depth-First search now.

Procedure : Depth-first search always expands the deepest node in the current unexplored node set (fringe) of the search tree. The search goes on to a depth until there is no more successor node. As these nodes are expanded, they are dropped from the fringe, so the search tree backs up to the next shallowest node (previous level node) that still has unexplored successors.

Another special case of DFS is back-tracking search. In this type of search, only one successor is generated at a time rather than all of the successor nodes and each partially expanded node remembers which successor to generate next. Also note that this method uses **lesser memory** than DFS as only 'd' nodes (maximum depth) are required to store.

Drawbacks of DFS: DFS can make wrong decisions (choices) and gets stuck going down a very long (even infinite) path when a different choice would lead to a solution near the root of the search tree.

Q.9. Analyze Iterative-Deepening Depth-First Search (IDDFS) and bi-direction al search.

Ans. Procedure : In IDDFS, DFS is applied along with the best depth limit. In each step gradually, it increases the depth limit until the goal is found. It increases the depth limit from level-0, then level-1, then level-2 till the shallowest goal is found at certain depth '*d*'.

Implementation : IDDFS can be implemented just as BFS is where queue is used to store fringes. This is so because it explores a complete layer of new nodes at each iteration before going on to the next layer. Also note that if we want to avoid memory requirements which are incurred in BFS then IDDFS can be implemented like uniform-cost search. The focal point is to use increasing path-cost limits instead of increasing depth limits. If we have such an implementation then it is termed as iterative-lengthening search.

Let us now evaluate IDDFS on the basis of 4 criterions as follows: -

1. **Completeness :** It guarantees completeness as the search does not stop until goal node is found.
2. **Optimality :** An IDDFS search stops when the first goal node is reached. But is it is not mandatory that it is optimal i.e., the shallowest goal reached is the final and IDDFS will not further search for optimal solutions?
3. **Time and space Complexities :** Iterative deepening depth first search has very moderate space complexity of $O(b^d)$. Rather its time complexity depends on the branching factor, b and the bottom most level that is at depth, d. It is $O(b^d)$.

Let us now discuss bidirectional search.

Procedure : As the name suggests, bi-directional (or two directional searches) are performed in this technique. One of them is forward search, which starts from initial state and the other is backward search which starts from the goal state. The two searches stop when both the searches meet in the middle.

Implementation : Bidirectional search is implemented by having one or both of the searches check, each node before it is expanded, is examined to see if it is in the fringe of the other search tree. If so, the solution is found. Also note that fringes can be stored in queue data structure (like BFS).

Let us now do the performance evaluation.

1. **Completeness :** Bidirectional search is complete if branching factor, *b*, is finite and both directions searches using BFS.
2. **Optimality :** It is optimal as the goal is being searched from both directions. So, it is guaranteed to find optimal (best) goal state.
3. **Time and Space Complexity :** Bidirectional search has the time complexity of $O(b^{d/2})$, where *b* is the branching factor. Please note that in case of backward search we need to get the predecessors of the node. Also note that the easiest case is when all the actions in the state space are reversible.

Note :

1. When one goal state is there, the backward search is similar to the forward search (like in 8 puzzle problem).
2. If there are many explicitly listed goals states (like in part picking robot) then it needs to construct a new dummy goal state whose immediate predecessors are all then actual goal states. The worst case in bidirectional search is when the goal test gives only implicit descriptions of some possible large set of goal states.

For example, in the game of chess 'checkmate' is the goal state which will have many possible descriptions.

The memory requirements for bidirectional search is also moderate which is $O(b^{d/2})$,

where '*b*' is the branching factor and '*d*' is the depth, where at least one of the search tree is maintained in memory.

Bidirectional search has-

Time complexity : $O(b^{d/2})$. **'*and*' Space complexity :** $O(b^{d/2})$.

The Problem of Repeated States : When we are finding solution by searching in the state space tree, some states can be repeatedly explored. This will increase the total cost. Hence, we need to avoid repeated states. In some of the problems, we need to explore all of the repeated states again as they may reach to the goal state. **For example**, problems where the actions are reversible, such as route-finding problems and sliding-blocks puzzles. **Note that the search trees for these problems are infinite but if we cut-off some repeated states then we can generate only the portions of the tree that engross the state space graph.** In some of the problems, repeated states are not required to explore again as these states will not surely lead to goal states. **Also note that in a state space graph, we can drop multiple paths and can construct a tree where there is only one path to each state. For** example, in 8-queen's problem, each state can be reached through only 1 path. If we formulate the 8-queen's problem such that a queen can be placed in any column, then each state with 'n' queens can be reached by n! different paths. The following are the serious problems caused due to these repeated states: -

1. Because of repeated states, solvable problem can become unsolvable if the algorithm is unable to detect repeated states.
2. Because of repeated states, looping paths can be generated which can lead to infinite search which is not practical approach.
3. Because of repeated states memory is unnecessarily wasted as same state is maintained multiple times.

Q.10. Give an example of the state space that generates an exponentially larger search tree.

Ans.

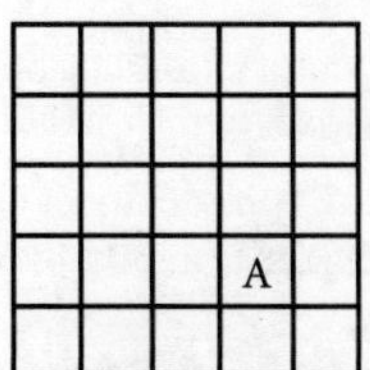

In this search tree mesh, A is the root node. On a grid/mesh, each state has four successors. Therefore, the tree including repeated states has 4^d leaves. But please observe that we can see only about $2d^2$ distinct states within d steps of any given state. Also observe that if limit of depth in state space tree is specified then it is easy to reduce repeated states which leads to exponential reduction in search cost.

If an algorithm remembers every state hat it has visited then it can be viewed as exploring state space graph directly. We can design a new algorithm called as graph-search algorithm which is more efficient than earlier search tree algorithms. A graph-search algorithm maintains two data structures –closed list and open list to avoid exploration of those nodes which are already explored *i.e.*, trying to avoid repeated states.

Closed List : A closed list is a data structure maintained by the algorithm which stores every expanded node. Algorithm discards the current node if it matches with the node on the closed list.

Open List : An open list is a data structure maintained by algorithm which stores fringe of unexpected node.

A repeated state is detected when an algorithm has found two paths to same state. If the newly discovered path is shorter than the original one then it will be discarded by the algorithm. Then there is a chance that graph-search could miss an optimal solution as it can discard one of the paths that can lead to an optimal state.

SUMMARY

In this chapter, we have studied different search techniques under uninformed search methods. Their search algorithms are also discussed and their time as well as the space complexities were discussed.

MULTIPLE CHOICE QUESTIONS

1. **Uninformed searches are also known as-**
   (*a*) Bright searches (*b*) Blind searches
   (*c*) Deaf searches (*d*) None of the above
2. **BFS uses-**
   (*a*) Full FIFO queue (*b*) Empty FIFO queue
   (*c*) LIFO stack (*d*) None of the above
3. **BFS search is optimal when-**
   (*a*) There are lesser number of nodes (*b*) All step costs are unequal
   (*c*) All step costs are equal (*d*) All of the above
4. **One successor is generated in-**
   (*a*) Backtracking search (*b*) BFS
   (*c*) DFS (*d*) All of the above
5. **DFS uses-**
   (*a*) Stacks (*b*) Queues
   (*c*) Arrays (*d*) Linked lists
6. **A collection of nodes that has been generated but not yet expanded is known as a-**
   (*a*) Bridge (*b*) Fringe
   (*c*) Bing (*d*) None of the above
7. **The total cost for an algorithm to search is-**
   (*a*) Total cost = search cost + path cost + memory usage
   (*b*) Total cost = search cost + path cost - memory usage
   (*c*) Total cost = search cost - path cost - memory usage
   (*d*) None of the above
8. **Repeated states can cause-**
   (*a*) Looping paths (*b*) Memory wastages
   (*c*) Both (*a*) and (*b*) (*d*) None of the above
9. **When an algorithm has found two paths to same state then-**
   (*a*) A shallow search is found (*b*) A repeated state is detected
   (*c*) Infinite state is detected (*d*) None of the above

10. The most common problem with all AI solution is-

(*a*) Polynomial explosion (*b*) Combinational explosion

(*c*) Nuclear explosion (*d*) None of the above

ANSWERS

1. (*a*)	**2.** (*b*)	**3.** (*c*)	**4.** (*a*)	**5.** (*a*)
6. (*b*)	**7.** (*a*)	**8.** (*c*)	**9.** (*b*)	**10.** (*b*)

CONCEPTUAL SHORT QUESTIONS WITH ANSWERS

Q.1. On what parameters does the performance of problem-solving algorithms depends?

Ans. The performance of problem-solving algorithms depends on four parameters: -

1. **Completeness :** Does the algorithm surely finds the solution, if it really exists.
2. **Optimality :** If multiple solutions exist then do the algorithm reurn optimal among them.
3. Time requirement.
4. Space requirement.

Q.2. When is the application of BFS the best choice?

Ans. It is a simple method that is complete i.e., it surely gives a solution, if it exists. Note that if the depth of search tree is small then BFS is the best choice. It is useful in tree as well as in graph search.

Q.3. State on which basis the search algorithms are chosen?

Ans. Search algorithms are chosen based on two components as follows: -

1. How is the state space? That is, state space is tree-structured or a graph? Critical factor for state space is what is branching factor and depth level of that tree or graph.
2. What is the performance of the search strategy? A complete, optimal search strategy with better time and space requirement is the critical factor in performance of search strategy.

Q.4. Evaluate the performance of problem-solving method based on depth-first search algorithm.

Ans. DFS algorithm performance measurement is done in 4 ways as follows: -

1. **Completenessv :** It is complete *i.e.,* guarantees solution.
2. **Optimality :** It is not optimal.
3. **Time Complexity :** Its time complexity is $O(b)$.
4. **Space Complexity :** Its space complexity is $O(b^{d+1})$.

Q.5. Differentiate between BFS and DFS.

Ans. The following table distinguishes between the two: -

Breadth First Search	Depth First Search
It uses the data structure queue.	It uses the data structure stack.
It is complete as it finds the solution if one exists.	It is not complete as it might take infinite loop to reach the goal-state.
It takes more space, O (bd).	The space complexity is $O(d)$.
In case of several goals, it finds the best one.	In case of several goals, it will terminate the solution in any order.

Q.6. Compare the following uninformed searches: -

a. **BFS.** *b.* **UCS.**

c. **DFS.** *d.* **DLS.**

e. **Iterative deepening.** *f.* **Bidirectional.**

Ans. The following table compares the algorithms based on four parameters: -

Criteria	BFS	UCS	DFS	DLS	Iterative deepening	Bidirectional
Completeness	Complete	Complete	Incomplete	Incomplete	Complete	Complete
Time complexity	$O(b^{d+1})$	$O(b^{C^*/e})$	$O(b^m)$	$O(b^l)$	$O(b^d)$	$O(b^{d/2})$
Space complexity	$O(b^{d+1})$	$O(b^{C^*/e})$	$O(b^m)$	$O(b^l)$	$O(bd)$	$O(b^{d/2})$
Optimality	Optimal	Optimal	Non-optimal	Non-optimal	Optimal	Optimal

Where,

b = branching factor of each node.

d = depth of shallowest solution where goal-node is located.

m = max. depth of the search tree.

l = limited depth of the search tree used in depth-limited search.

C^* = cost of the optimal solution based on the path cost.

E = cost of every action.

Q.13. Throw some light on Depth-limited search strategy.

Ans. The problem related to the unbounded tree can be alleviated by implementing DFS with the predetermined depth limit of λ. The nodes at depth λ are considered to have no successors. This method is known as **depth-limited search. Please note that this search solves the infinite path problem.** An additional source of incompleteness is introduced, if we choose λ less than d *i.e.*, shallowest goal is beyond the depth limit.

This search will remain non-optimal if λ is selected that is greater than d.

It has the time complexity of $O(b\lambda)$ and its space complexity is $O(b\lambda)$. Also note that DFS can be seen as a special case of depth-limited search with $\lambda = \infty$.

Q.14. How will you find the total cost of the path?

Ans. The time bound cost which is incurred for reaching to a particular node is called as the path cost. The total cost for an algorithm is the combined cost of the search cost and the path cost of the solution found along with memory usage. It is given by the formula as follows: -

Total Cost = Search Cost + Path Cost + Memory Usage

This cost is useful to find the shorter or low costs paths.

EXERCISE QUESTIONS

1. What is uninformed search? Why it is called as a blind search?
2. Give differences between BFS and DFS.
3. Explain UCS.
4. Indicate the type of data structure used by: -
   a. BFS.
   b. DFS.
5. Give advantages and disadvantages of BFS and DFS algorithms.
6. How will you measure the problem-solving performance?
7. What are the tree factors on which the state space graph complexity depends?

[**Hint:** It depends on three factors-

a. **Branching factor**- max. no. of successors of any node. If its value is less then lesser no. of nodes will need to be searched and thus, faster results of searching.

b. **Depth of goal node**- is the depth of the shallowest goal node, where one can reach fast. If this value is small, we will get the node early.

c. **Maximum length of path**- the max. length of any path in the state space. Note that if the length value is more, the complexity of state space is more. This is often measured in terms of number of nodes generated.

d. The major activity in AI is searching and searching involves node expansions. The time taken for this is called as the search cost and it depends on the time complexity].

Q.8. Explain the following uninformed searches-

a. IDDFS.

b. Bidirectional search.

Q.9. Consider the following search tree-

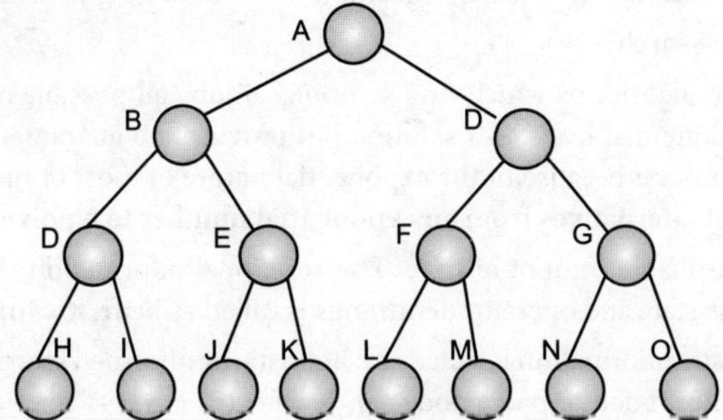

Give its BFS, DFS, DLS (limit = 2), and iterative-deepening search. List the nodes so expanded/ traversed.

5 Informed Search

5.1 INTRODUCTION

In previous chapter, we studied the concept of uninformed or blind searches. Now we will study the more efficient search method, the informed search strategy. Informed search is a search strategy that uses problem-specific knowledge beyond the definition of the problem itself. The general method followed in informed search is best first search. Best first search is similar to graph search or tree search algorithm where in node expansion is done based on certain criteria.

Q.1. What is Informed/Heuristic Search?

Ans. The term heuristic is used for algorithms which find solutions among all possible ones. Recall that heuristic is a rule of thumb or judgment technique that leads to a solution but provides no guarantee of success. Still heuristic play an important role in searching process because of the exponential nature of most of the problems. **Please note that they help to reduce the number of alternatives from an exponential number to a polynomial number.**

So, we get a solution in a reasonable amount of time. The additional information about the properties of the specific domain which is built into the state and operator definitions is called as **heuristic information.**

And a search using this heuristic information is called as a heuristic or informed search. A heuristic function determines a number which determines how good or bad a node can be. If ev(n) is a best solution state and ev(n, p) is a best path then a heuristic is any information which shows how good or bad that path is likely to be so, we can expand that good node and can generate only its children. There is no blind expansion. So, pruning of the search tree occurs. In nutshell, the heuristics needed to solve problems are expressed as a heuristic function which maps the problem states into numbers. These numbers are then appropriately used to guide search. Heuristic search methods use some general-purpose search techniques.

Q.2. Write Generate-And-Test Algorithm. Explain with the help of a flowchart. What are local search algorithms? Give their advantages.

Ans. It is a weak method meaning that it helps usually but not always.

It may or may not overcome the combinational explosion problem of AI. This algorithm works in two modules—

a. **Generator Module :** It creates the possible solutions.

b. **Tester Module :** It tests (or evaluates) each of the proposed solution either accepting or rejecting that solution.

Please understand that here an action may stop when one acceptable solution is found or action may continue until all possible solutions are found.

Let us develop its algorithm now—

Step-1 : Generate a possible candidate solution which can either be a point in the problem space or a path from the initial state.

Step-2 : Test to see if this possible solution or candidate solution is a real solution by comparing the state reached with the set of goal states.

Step-3 : If it is a real, acceptable solution then return, success else repeat from step-1 again (as it is a failure).

This algorithm is basically a DFS procedure only as complete solutions must be created before testing. **Please note that when it is used in a systematic form then it is simply an exhaustive search of the problem space.** It can also operate by generating solutions randomly and hence is often called as a B**ritish Museum method.** However, in this method also there will be no guarantee that a solution will ever be found. So, we need a heuristic to sharpen the search. But this is useful for simple problems and is in efficient for problems having large state space search.

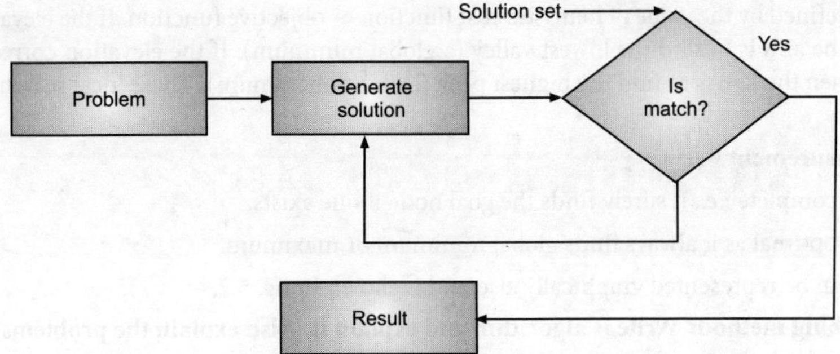

Fig. 5.1: Generate and Test Workflow

Let us take an example to understand this. Consider the function, $f(x) = x^2 + 3$. Generate and test method can be applied to solve this function as follows:

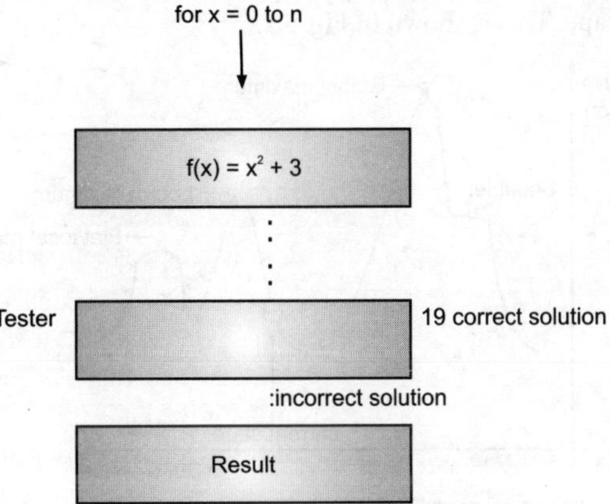

Fig. 5.2: Applying Generate and Test

The search algorithms discussed so far focus more on the path through which the goal is reached. But if the problem does not demand the path of the solution as it expects only the final configuration of the solution, then we have different types of problems to solve. Some problems where only the state configuration is vital and not the path that arrived at the solution are like 8-queen's problem, IC design problem, factory-floor layout, job-shop scheduling, automatic programming, network optimization, vehicle routing etc. in such type of problems we use another category of algorithms that do not worry about the paths at all. These are local search algorithms. **Please remember the following points regarding local search algorithms: -**

1. They operate on using a single state rather than multiple paths.
2. They generally move to neighbors of the current state.
3. There is no such requirement of maintaining paths in memory.
4. They are not systematic algorithms.

Advantages of local search algorithms :

1. They use lesser and constant amount of energy.
2. They have ability to find reasonable solution for infinite state space for which systematic algorithms are unsuitable.
3. These algorithms are suitable for solving pure optimization problems. In pure optimization problems, main aim is to find the best state according to the required objective function.
4. These algorithms make use of the concept known as **state space landscape.** This landscape has two structures: -
   a. Location defined by the state.

b. Elevation defined by the value of heuristic cost function or objective function. If the elevation corresponds to the cost, then the aim is to find the lowest valley (a global minimum). If the elevation corresponds to the objective function, then the aim is to find the highest peak (a global maximum). These local search algorithms explore the landscape.

Performance measurement

1. Local search is complete *i.e.*, it surely finds the goal node if one exists.
2. Local search is optimal as it always finds global minimum or maximum.

The local search can be represented graphically also and is shown in fig. 5.2.

Q.3. What is Hill climbing method? Write is algorithm and explain it. Also explain the problems associated with it and their solutions.

Ans. It is so called because of the way the nodes are selected for expansion. At each point in the search path, a successor node that appears to lead most quickly to the top of the hill (goal) is selected for exploration. In this method of searching, the generate-and-test method is augmented by a heuristic foundation which measures the closeness of the current state to the goal state. Hill climbing can be used if the path to the goal does not matter. It is a local search method in which we consider the state space landscape. This is shown in Fig. 5.2.

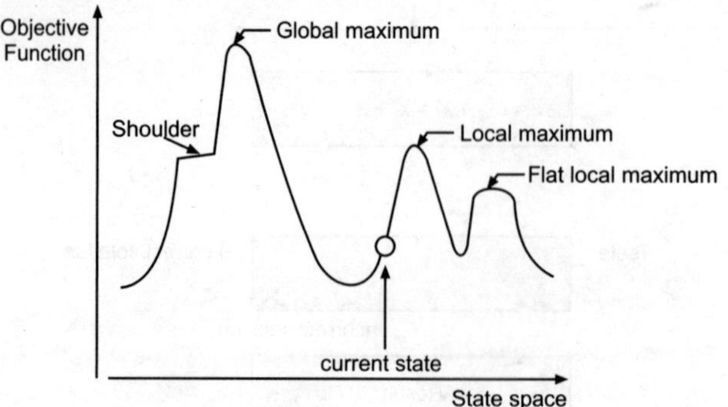

***Fig. 5.2:** State Space Landscape for Local Search*

- Local maxima mean it cannot see higher peak and
- Shoulder means cannot see the way out.

These are the two problems of hill climbing method.

A landscape has both "location" (defined by the state) and "elevation" (defined by the value of the heuristic cost function or objective function). The aim is to find global minimum (lowest valley) if the elevation corresponds to heuristic cost

NOTE : You can convert from one to the other just by inserting a minus sign.

Function and if the elevation corresponds to the objective function then the aim will be to find the highest peak or global maximum.

Local search algorithm explores this landscape. A complete local search algorithm always finds a goal if one exists. An optimal algorithm always finds a global minimum/maximum.

Hill climbing search modifies the current state to try to improve it. This is shown in Fig. 5.2 by an arrow. It is in this way that the cost function provides a task-specific knowledge into the control process.

So, a search tree is generated with the help of heuristic function. As explained earlier also, hill climbing is like dfs where the most promising child is selected for expansion. When the children have been generated, alternative choices are evaluated using the heuristic function. The path that appears most promising is then chosen. No further reference to the parent or other children is retained. **Please note that there is practically, no difference between hill-climbing and dfs except that the children of the node that has been expanded are sorted by the remaining distance.** Let us now write an algorithm for hill-climbing—

Step-1 : Put the initial node on a list, START-LIST.

Step-2 : If (START-LIST is empty) or (START-LIST is GOAL) then terminate search.

Step-3 : Remove the first-node from the START-LIST. Call this node, *n*.

Step-4 : If (n = GOAL) then terminate search with SUCCESS.

Step-5 : Else if node, n, has successors then generate all of them. Find how far they are from the goal node. Sort them by the remaining distance from the goal and add them to the beginning of START-LIST.

Step-6 : Goto step-2.

Explanation of algorithm:

1. Evaluate the initial state. If it is the goal state then quit, else make current state as the initial state.
2. Select a new operator that could be applied to this state and generate a new state.
3. Evaluate the new state. If this new state is closer to the goal state than the current state, then make the new state as the current state. If it is not better, ignore this state and proceed with the current state.
4. If the current state is the goal state or no new operators are available, then quit else repeat from step-2.

Let us now discuss the different problems with their solutions.

1. **Local Maxima :** It is a state where we have climbed to the hill and missed on better solution. It is the mountain- a state that is better than all of its neighbors but not better than states further away.

Solution : backtracking.

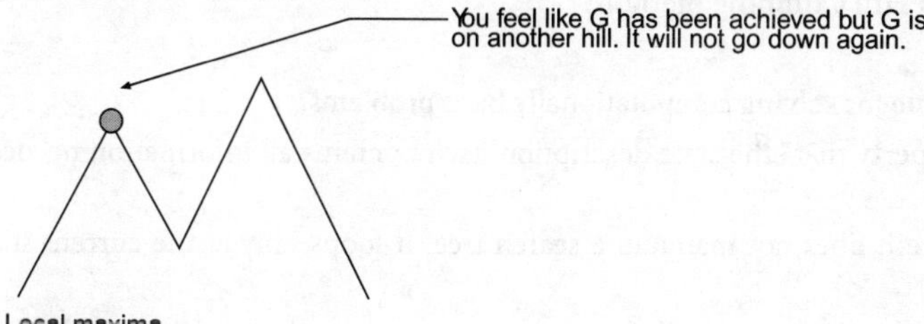

2. **Plateau / Flat Max. :** It is a state where everything around is about as good as where we are currently. In other words, a flat area of the search space in which all neighboring states have the same value.

Solution: Big Jump.

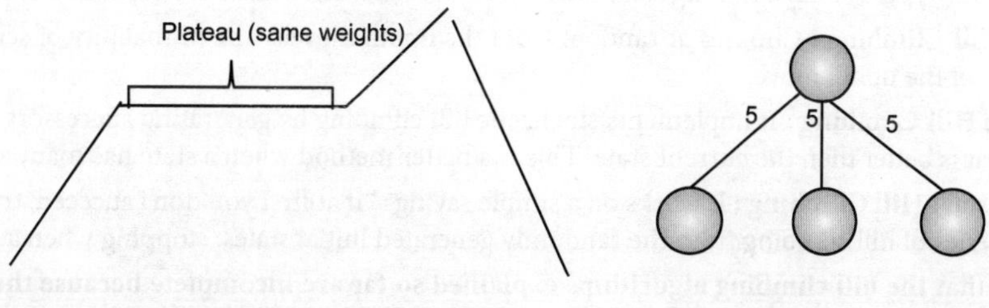

A plateau

3. **Ridges :** In this state, we are on a ridge leading up but we can't directly apply n operator to improve the situation. So, we have to apply more than one operator to get there.

Solution: Bidirectional search.

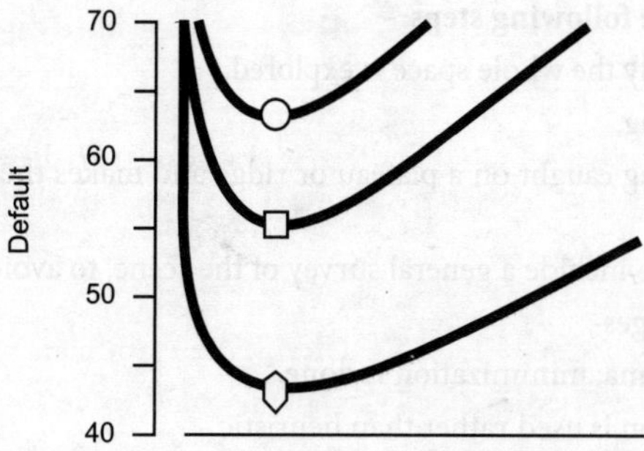

The grid of ridges is superimposed on a ridge rising from left to right, creating a sequence of local maxima that are not directly connected to each other. From each local maximum all of the available actions point downhill.

How to solve these problems associated with Hill Climbing?

The problems discussed above can be solved using methods like backtracking, making big jumps, applying multiple rules before testing (helps with ridges) etc. **Please understand here that hill climbing is best suited to problem where the heuristic gradually improves, the closer it gets to the solution.** But it works poorly where there are sharp drop-offs. Also understand that it assumes that local improvement will lead to global improvement.

8-queen's Problem using local search

A complete state formulation is used for local search algorithms. In 8-queens problem, each state has 8-queens on the board one per column. There are two functions related to 8-queens problem-

1. **The Successor Function:** It is the function that returns all possible states which are generated by a single queen move to anther cell in the same column. The total successor of each state being 8 * 7 = 56.
2. **The Heuristic Function:** It is a function, h. that holds the number of attacking pair of queens to each other either directly or indirectly. Also note that the value is zero for the global minimum of the function which occurs only at perfect solutions.

Q.4. What are the advantages of Advantages of Hill Climbing method?

Ans. The following are its advantages-

1. Hill climbing is an optimization technique for solving computationally hard problems.
2. It is best used in problems with the property that "the state description itself contains all information needed for a solution."
3. The algorithm is memory efficient since it does not maintain a search tree. It loops only at the current state and immediate future states.
4. As compared to other iterative improvement algorithms, hill climbing always attempts to make changes that improve the current state. On other hand, hill climbing can only advance if there is a higher point in the adjacent landscape.
5. It is often useful when combined with other methods, getting it started right in the immediate general neighborhood.

Q.5. Discuss the variants of hill climbing. What is simulated annealing search?

Ans. Several variants (or types) of hill climbing have been discovered. Some of them are explained below.

1. **Stochastic Hill Climbing :** Chooses at random from the uphill moves. The probability of selections can vary with the steepness of the uphill move.
2. **First Choice Hill Climbing :** It implements stochastic hill climbing by generating successors randomly until one is generated that is better than the current state. This is a better method when a state has many successors.
3. **Random Restart Hill Climbing :** It works on a simple saying- "If at first you don't succeed, try, try and try again". It conducts a series of hill climbing from the randomly generated initial states, stopping when a goal is found.

   Please note that the hill climbing algorithms explained so far are incomplete because they often fail to find a goal when surely the goal exists. This can happen because these algorithms can get stuck on local maxima. **Also note that random restart hill is complete with probability approaching to 1.** This algorithm does not stop until it reaches the goal state/ goal node. The success of hill climbing depends on the shape of the state-space landscape if there are few local maxima and plateau then random-restart hill climbing will find a good solution very quickly.

Simulated Annealing Search (a variant of hill climbing)

Simulated annealing follows the following steps: -

1. In simulated annealing, initially the whole space is explored.
2. This is a variant of hill climbing.
3. This avoids the danger of being caught on a plateau or ridge and makes the procedure less sensitive to the starting point.
4. Simulated annealing is done to include a general survey of the scene, to avoid climbing of false foot hills.
5. There are two additional changes-
   a. Rather than creating maxima, minimization is done.
   b. The term objective function is used rather than heuristic.

6. This concept is taken from physical annealing where physical substances are melted and then gradually cooled till some solid state is reached. In physical annealing, the goal is to produce a minimal-energy state. The annealing schedule states that – "if the temperature is lowered sufficiently slowly, then the goal will be attained. ΔE is called the change in the value of the objective function.
7. Please note that in this algorithm we have valley descending rather than hill climbing. The probability that the metal will jump to a higher energy level is given by the expression-

$$P = e^{-\Delta E / kT}$$

Where k = Boltzmann's constant.

The algorithm is as follows: -

Step-1 : Start with evaluating the initial state.

Step-2 : Apply each operator and loop until a goal state is found or till no new operators left to be applied as described below: -

a. Set T according to an annealing schedule.

b. Select and apply a new operator.

c. Evaluate the new state. If it is a goal state then quit.

$$\Delta E = \text{val (current state)} - \text{val (new state)}$$

If $\Delta E < 0$, then this is the new current state

Else find a new current state with probability = $e^{-\Delta E / kT}$

Let us consider a tree and apply our algorithm now.

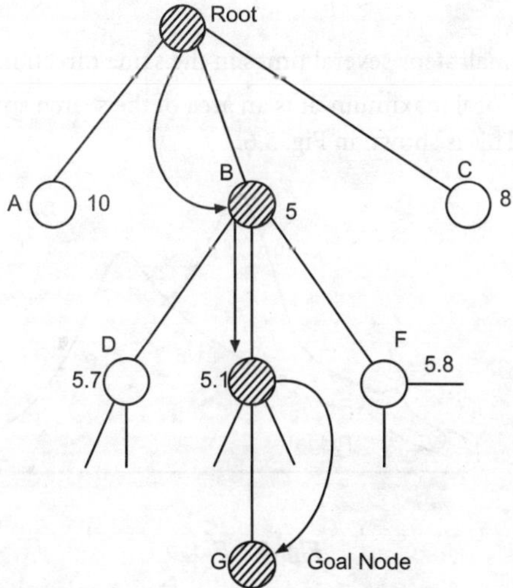

Fig. 5.3: Hill Climbing Search Tree

Here, we put the initial node *i.e.* root on a START-LIST. If START-LIST is empty or if START- LIST is our goal itself then the search terminates. Else we remove this node (n) from the START- LIST and generates its successors. We sort this START-LIST on the basis of the distances from the goal (see figure) and keep on repeating this process till a goal is found. **Please note that a new state has to be better, meaning that if we consider the cost function then it means a lower value and if we consider the objective function then it means a higher value.** If the algorithm is constantly following the direction which gives the fastest rate of increase, then it is called as the **steepest ascent hill climbing.** But if the lowest cost is best then it is a downhill algorithm. **Also note that this algorithm is called as a steepest rise with back-tracking search method because it is prepared to back up and try a different path if the steepest one leads to a dead end.** Hill climbing is sometimes called as a greedy local search because it grabs a good neighbor state without thinking ahead about where to go next. But hill climbing suffers from following problems—

I. Local Maximum : It is a state which is better than all of its neighbors but is not better than some other states which are farther away. Please note that at local maxima, all moves appear to make the things worse. They are sometimes frustrating also as they often occur almost within sight of a solution. They are also called as foot-hills. It is shown in Fig. 5.4.

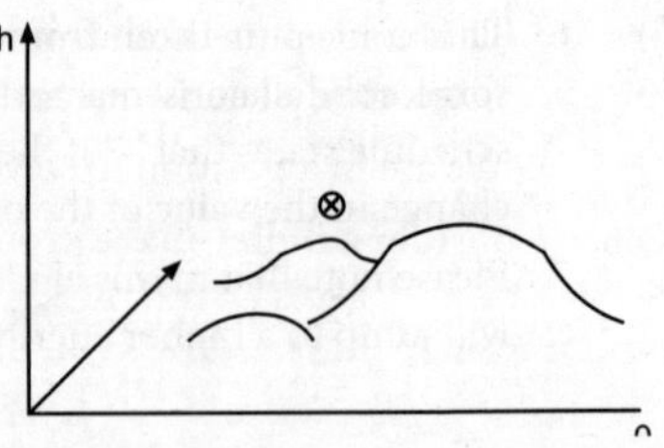

Fig. 5.4: *Local Maximum or (Foot Hill)*

Solution to this Problem :

1. One possible solution is backtracking : Can backtrack to some earlier node and try to go in a different direction to attain the global peak. We can maintain a list of paths almost taken and go back to one of them if the path that was taken leads to a dead end.
2. Another solution can be a list of promising plans.

II. Plateau : It is a flat area of the search space in which a whole set of neighboring states (nodes) have the same value. On a plateau, it is not possible to determine the best direction in which to move by making local comparisons. Actually, plateau is an area of the state space landscape where the evaluation function is flat.

It can be a flat local maximum (from which no uphill exist exists) or a shoulder from which it is possible to make progress. A plateau is shown in Fig. 5.5.

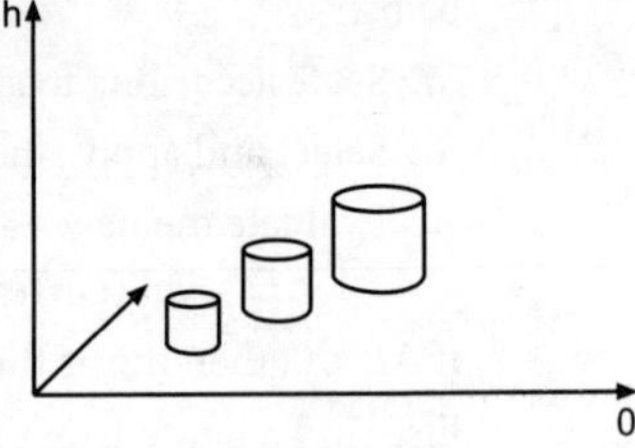

Fig. 5.5: *Plateau*

Solution to this Problem :

1. A big jump in some direction can be done in order to get to a new section of search space. This method is recommended as in a plateau all neighboring points have the same value.
2. Another solution is to apply small steps several times in the same direction. This depends on the rules available.

III. Ridge : It is a special kind of local maximum. It is an area of the search space which is higher than the surrounding areas and that itself has a slope. This is shown in Fig. 5.6.

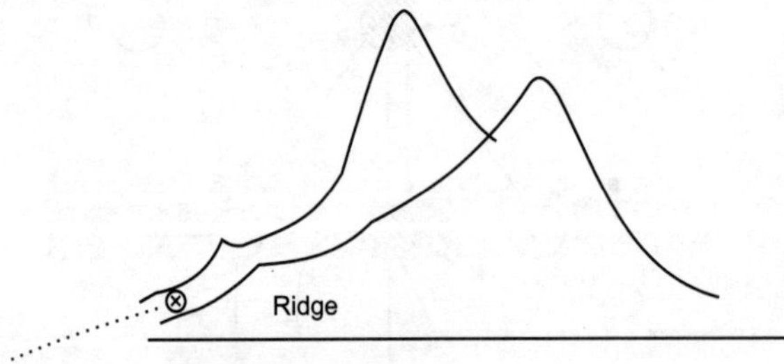

Fig. 5.6 *Ridge*

We cannot travel the ridge by single moves as the orientation of the high region compared to the set of available moves makes it impossible.

Solution to Ridge Problem :

1. Trying different paths at the same time is a solution. We can apply two or more rules before doing the test. This corresponds to moving in several directions at once.
2. Bidirectional search can be useful here.

Advantages of Hill Climbing :

It can be used in continuous as well as discrete domains.

Disadvantages of Hill Climbing :

1. It is not an efficient method.
2. It is not suited to problems where the value of the heuristic function drops off suddenly when the solution may be in sight.

3. It is a local method as it looks at the immediate solution and decides about the next step to be taken rather than exploring all consequences before taking a move.

'I' We are in a position to solve some examples now.

Q.6. Consider a bullet-maze problem.

The figures below show a maze. It is a state problem as we are not keen in the shortest path but in the goal state only.

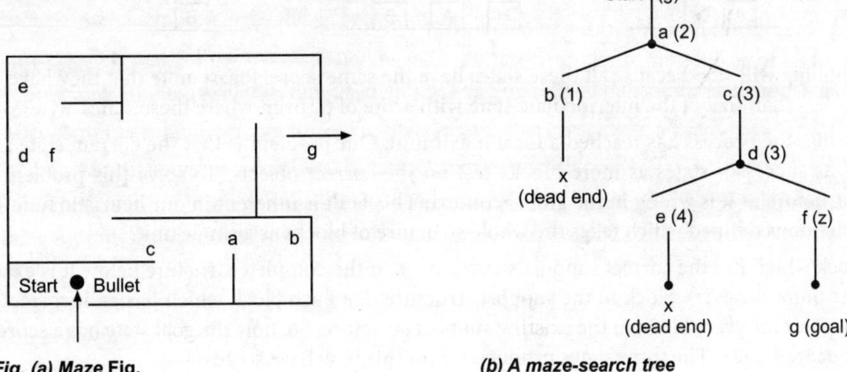

Fig. (a) Maze* Fig.** ***(b) A maze-search tree

You are also given a maze-search tree as follows—

(Fig. *a*)—The start is marked with a bullet and the exist (goal state) is marked as g. Other letters mark the choice points in the maze.

(Fig. *b*)—The numbers in brackets show the heuristic evaluation function for each node. The evaluation function chosen is the distance measured from the node to the goal.

Explain how it leads to dead ends?

Which node is local minima? Is there a plateau problem?

Ans. At node '*a*' (fig. *b*) it appears at first that '*b*' is the most promising direction. But this leads to a dead end.

From node '*b*', whatever path we take, takes us away from the goal. Hence, '*b*' is called as local minimum. A simple search will stop at 'b' and never reach the goal state (*g*) which is global minimum.

The value of heuristic function does not change between '*c*' and '*d*'. That is, it is 3. So, there is no progress. What if our search space is large? There may be a whole area of the search space with no change of heuristic. When this happens, our heuristic fails to give any guidance about possible direct path.

Q.7. Consider the block-world problem. It has 8 blocks, A to H which are similar and equal to each other. There initial state and final state (or goal state) are as follows:

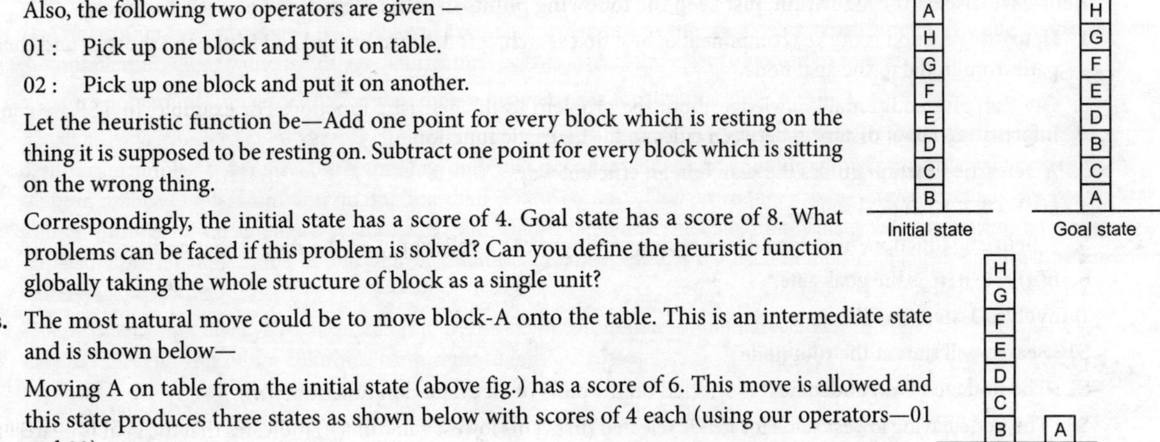

Also, the following two operators are given —

01 : Pick up one block and put it on table.

02 : Pick up one block and put it on another.

Let the heuristic function be—Add one point for every block which is resting on the thing it is supposed to be resting on. Subtract one point for every block which is sitting on the wrong thing.

Correspondingly, the initial state has a score of 4. Goal state has a score of 8. What problems can be faced if this problem is solved? Can you define the heuristic function globally taking the whole structure of block as a single unit?

Ans. The most natural move could be to move block-A onto the table. This is an intermediate state and is shown below—

Moving A on table from the initial state (above fig.) has a score of 6. This move is allowed and this state produces three states as shown below with scores of 4 each (using our operators—01 and 02)

State-1 State-2 State-3

Now, hill climbing will stop because all these states have the same score. Please note that they have a produced a score of 4 which is less than that of the intermediate state with score of 6 (from where these states arise).

We say now that the process has reached a local maximum. Our problem is that the current state appears to be better than any of its successor states as more blocks rest on the correct objects. To solve this problem, we disassemble a good local structure as it is wrong in the global context. This fault is inherent in our heuristic function now—A global heuristic function is defined which takes the whole structure of blocks as a single unit.

For each block which has the correct support structure *i.e.*, if the complete structure below it is exactly as it should be then add one point for every block in the support structure. For each block which has an incorrect support structure, subtract one point for every block in the existing support structure. So, now the goal state has a score = – 28. The initial state has the score = – 21. The three states produced from this now have scores—

$a = -28$

$b = -16$

$c = -15$

Thus, hill climbing chooses move (c) whose score = – 15 to lead us to a solution. This modified heuristic function assumes that the incorrect structures are bad and should not be accepted. And that the correct structures are good and should be built up. So, the same hill-climbing procedure which failed earlier heuristic function now works perfectly well.

Q.8. Explain the Best-First Search/Greedy Search. Write its algorithm. Also give an example to explain this.

Ans. Actually, best-first search is a combination of depth-first (dfs) and breadth-first (bfs) search methods. The approach used here is to select that single path at a time which is more promising one than the current path. The most promising node is chosen for expansion i.e., all of its successors are generated. Again, the most promising node is chosen. **Please note that this changes the search from dfs to bfs. Also note that if we find that after the expansion, no node is more promising then we can backtrack.** This search uses again a heuristic function called as an evaluation function which is an indicator of how far a node is from the goal node. There are many different algorithms that employ the concept of best first search. The main difference between all the algorithms is that they have different evaluation function. Please remember that the main central component of these algorithms is the heuristic function, $h(n)$, which is defined as $h(n)$ = estimate cost of the cheapest path from node, n to a goal node.

Before we discuss the algorithm, just keep the following points in mind regarding heuristic functions-

1. Heuristic function is the key component of best first search. It is denoted by $h(n)$ and $h(n)$ = the shortest and cheapest path from initial to the goal node.
2. One can give additional knowledge about the problem to the heuristic function. For example, in TSP we can give information about distances between cities to the heuristic function.
3. A heuristic function guides the search in an efficient way.
4. $h(n) = 0$, if n is a goal state.
5. A heuristic function, $h(n)$ considers a node as an input but it relies only on the state at that node.
6. $h(n) = 0$, if 'n' is the goal state.

It involves 3-steps as follows-

S1 : Search will start at the root node.

S2 : The node to be expanded next is selected on the basis of an evaluation function, $f(n)$.

S3 : The node having lowest value for $f(n)$ is selected first. This lowest value of $f(n)$ indicates that the goal is nearest from this node *i.e.*, $f(n)$ indicates distance from current node to the goal node.

Please remember that the goal nodes have an evaluation function value of zero.

Implementation : BFS can be implemented using a priority queue where fringe will be stored. The nodes in the fringe will be stored in priority queue with increasing value of $f(n)$ *i.e.*, ascending order of $f(n)$. **Also note that the high priority will be given to the node which has low $f(n)$ value.** As the name suggests, "best fit", so we would always expect to have optimal solution. Therefore, the optimality based on the 'best-ness of evaluation function.'

Let us take an example to understand best-first search now.

Example : Consider the following search graph, given in Fig. 5.7.

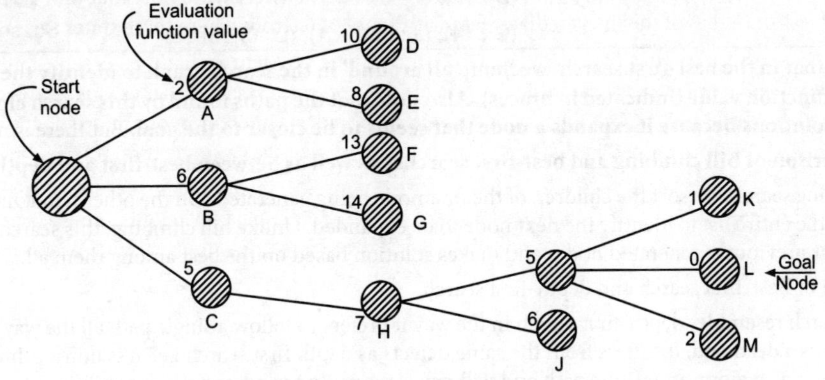

Fig. 5.7: Greedy Best First Search Graph

Working: We start with a start-nodes, *S*. Now, *S* has three children *i.e.*, *A*, *B* and *C* with their heuristic function values 2, 6 and 5 respectively. These weights show approximately, how far they are from goal node. So, we write, children of S are —

$$(A : 2), (B : 6), (C : 5)$$

Out of these, the node with minimum value is (A : 2). So, we select A and its children are explored (or generated).

It's children are—

$$(D : 10) \text{ and } (E : 8)$$

The search process now has four nodes to search for, namely—(B : 6), (C: 5), (B: 10) and (E : 8)

Out of these, node-C has the minimal value of 5. So, we select it and expand. So, we get (H : 7) as its child. Now, the nodes to search are as follows—

$$(B : 6), (D: 10, (E: 8) \text{ and } (H : 7)$$

Out of these, node-B is minimal so, we choose it and expand it to get its children—(F : 13) and (G : 14)

At this point of time, the nodes available are :

$$(D : 10), (E : 8), (H : 7), (F : 13), (G : 14)$$

Out of these, minimum is (H : 7). So, we select it and expand to get— (I : 5) and (J : 6)

So, nodes available for search now are —

$$(D : 10), (E : 8), (F :13), (G : 14), (I : 5), (J : 6)$$

Out of these, minimum is (I : 5), so we expand it now. It's children are—(K : 1), (L : 0) and (M : 2).

So, available nodes are—

$$(D : 10), (E : 8), (H : 7), (F : 13), (G : 14)$$

$$(J : 6), (K : 1), (L : 0) \text{ and } (M : 2)$$

Out of these, minimal is (L : 0) which is our goal-node. So, search stops here. Let us tabulate this in a tabular form now.

Step	Node being expanded	Children (on expansion)	Available nodes (to search)	Node Chosen
1.	S	(A : 2), (B : 6), (C : 5)	(A : 2), (B : 6), (C : 5)	(A : 2)
2.	A	(D : 10), (E: 8)	(B : 6), (C : 5), (D : 10), (E : 8)	(C : 5)
3.	C	(H : 7)	(B : 6), (D : 10) , (E : 8), (H : 7)	(B : 6)
4.	B	(F : 13), (G : 14)	(D : 10), (E : 8), (H : 7), (F : 13), (G : 14)	(H : 7)
5.	H	(I : 5), (J : 6)	(D : 10), (E : 8), (F : 13) (G : 14), (I : 5), (J : 6)	(I : 5)
6.	I	(K : 1), (L : 0), (M : 2)	(D : 10), (E : 8), (H : 7), (F : 13), (G : 14), (J : 6),(K : 1), (L : 0), (M : 2)	Goal node is found. So, search stops now

Please note that in the best-first search, we 'jump all around' in the search graph to identify the node with minimal evaluation function value (indicated in braces). Also note that the paths found by this search algorithm are likely to give faster solutions because it expands a node that seems to be closer to the goal. But there is no guarantee on this.

Q.9. Give comparison of hill climbing and best-first searches as well as between best-first and depth-first searches.

Ans. In hill climbing search, we sort the children of the first node being generated. On the other hand, in best-first search, we have to sort the entire list to identify the next node to be expanded. Unlike hill climbing, this search retains all estimates computed for previously generated nodes and makes solution based on the best among them all.

Comparison of Best-first search and depth-first search

Best-first search resembles depth-first search in the way it prefers to follow a single path all the way to goal but will back up when it hits a dead end. It suffers from the same defects as depth first search i.e., it is non-optimal and is incomplete because it can go all along an infinite path and will never return to try other path possibilities.

We develop an algorithm for Best-first search now.

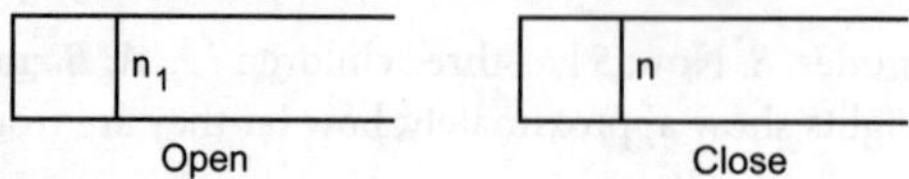

1. Use two ordered lists, OPEN and CLOSED.
2. Start with the initial node, n1 and put it on the ordered list OPEN.
3. Create a list CLOSED. This is initially an empty list.
4. If Open is empty then exit with failure.
5. Select first node on OPEN. Remove it from OPEN and put it on CLOSED. Call this node, *n*.
6. If 'n' is the goal node, exit. The solution is obtained by tracing a path backward along the arcs in the tree from '*n*' to 'n_1'.
7. Expand node *n*, as this will generate successors. Let the set of successors generated be *S*. create arcs from n to each member of *S*.
8. Reorder the list OPEN, according to the heuristics and go back to step-4.

We are in a position to solve some examples now.

Q.10. Consider the search tree given below—

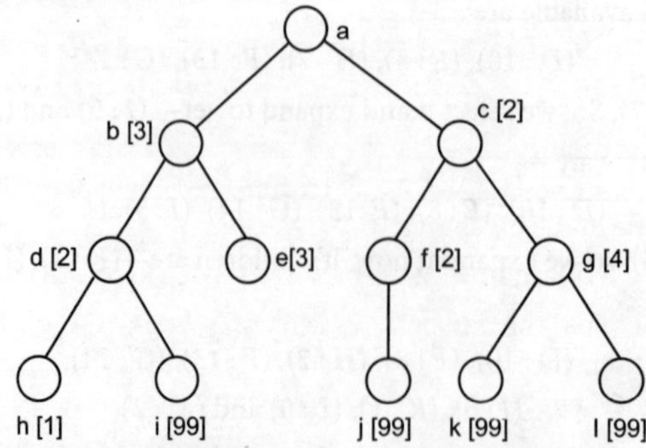

Show how the following searches are performed—

***a.* Hill climbing** ***b.* Best-first search?**

Ans.

a. **Using Hill Climbing :** The heuristic function value is an estimate of the distance to the goal and is shown in brackets. Please note that lesser is its value, the better it is.

Using hill climbing we get—

1. Start at a (start-node)
2. Children of a = [b(3), c(2)]
3. Out of these best child is c (2)
4. Children of c = [f(2), g(4)]
5. Best child is f(2) now.
6. Children of f = [j(99)]—not a goal.
7. Backtrack to g through c.
8. Children of g = [k(99), l(3)]
9. Best child, l is goal node.

b. **Using Best-first search :**

1. Start at a, the start node
2. Children of a [b(3), c(2)]
3. Best-first = c
4. Children of c = [f(2), g(4)]
5. Consider [f(2), g(4), b(3)]
6. Best-first = [f(2)]
7. Children of f = [j(99)]
8. Consider [j(99), g(4), b(3)]
9. Best first = b(3)
10. Children of b = [d(2), e(3)]
11. Consider [d(2), e(3), j(99), g(4)]
12. Best first = d(2)
13. Children of d = [h(1), i(99)]
14. Consider [h(1), i(99), e(3), j(99), g(4)]
15. Best-first-h, is a good node

Q.11. Using search tree given below, list the elements of the queue just before the next node is expanded. Use best first search where the numbers correspond to estimated cost- to-goal for each corresponding node.

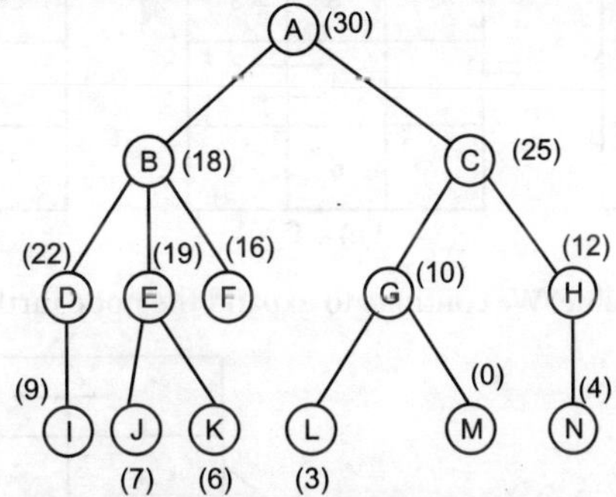

Ans. The table shows the cost from the initial node to the goal node-

From Node	To Node	Cost of Node	Possible Dueue	Cost so far	Final Best First Dueue
A	B	30	A – B	48	✓
	C	30	A – C	55	×
B	D	18	A – B – D	70	×
	E	18	A – D – E	97	×
	F	18	A – D – F	64	✓
F	Next Node	16	A – B – F – Next Node	64	✓

The path is A – B – F – Next node in the given tree.

Q.12. Consider the 8-puzzle problem. Explain how can it be solved using heuristics?

Ans. In this problem, the heuristic could be "the number of tiles not in correct position' *i.e.*, the number of tiles misplaced. In this solution, the convention used is that smaller the value of heuristic function, f, leads earlier to the goal state.

Step-1:

2	8	3
1	6	4
7	*	5

f(n) = 4

This is the initial state where four tiles (1, 2, 6, 8) are misplaced. That is why, the value of heuristic function at this node is 4.

Step-2: This will be the next step of the tree.

f(n) = 3

Thus, heuristic function gives the values of 3, 5 and 5 respectively.

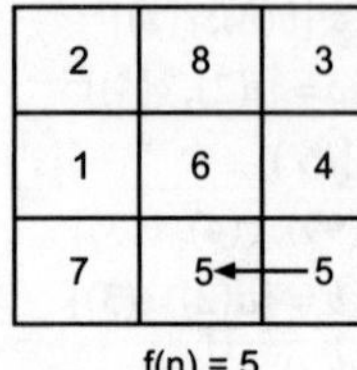

f(n) = 5

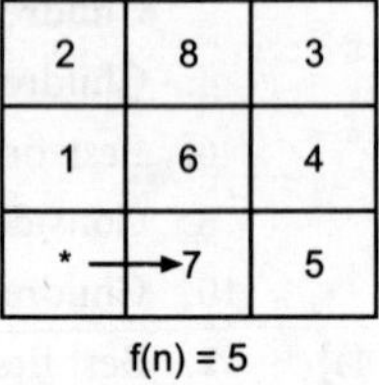

f(n) = 5

Step-3: This will be the next step-3 of the tree. Note here that the node with the lowest *f*(*n*) value, 3, is the one to be further expanded which generates 3-nodes.

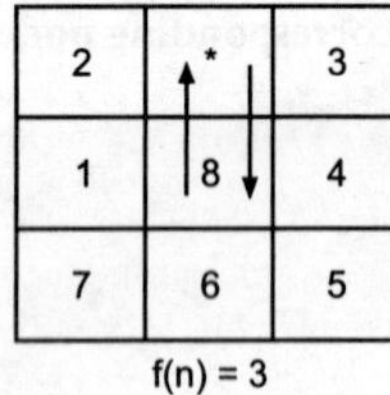

f(n) = 3

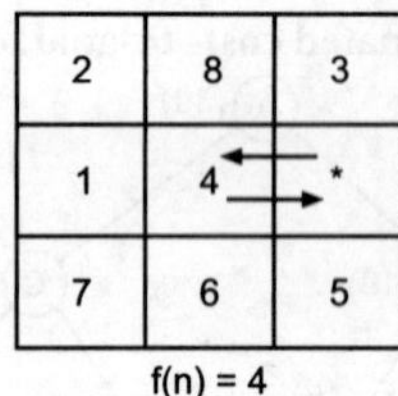

f(n) = 4

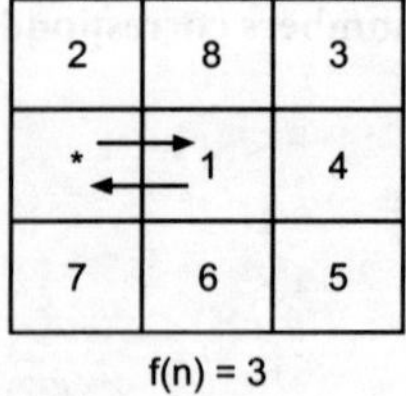

f(n) = 3

Step-4: Here, there is a tie for *f*(*n*) value. We continue to expand the node further.

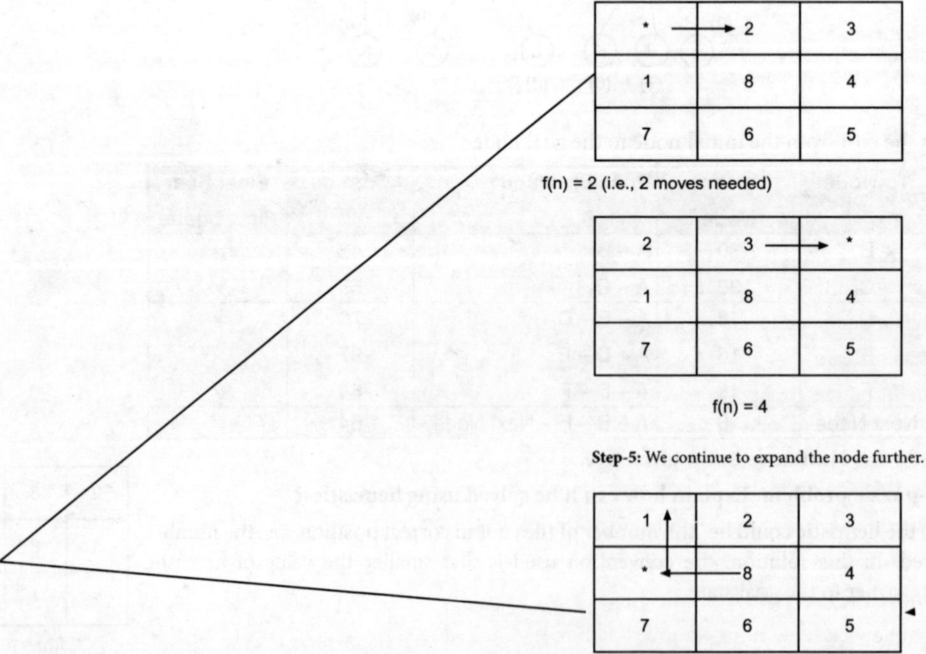

f(n) = 2 (i.e., 2 moves needed)

f(n) = 4

Step-5: We continue to expand the node further.

f(n) = 1 i.e., 1 move (of 8) will give the goal state.

Step-6: This will be the last step of the tree.

1	2	3
8	*	4
7	6	5

This is the goal state.

1	2	3
7	8	4
*	6	5

f(n) = 2

Also note that in this algorithm, a depth factor (*g*) is also added to *h*.

Q.13. What is greedy best first search?

Ans. Greedy best first search (GBFS) expands the node that is closest to the goal node, expecting to get solution rapidly. It evaluates node by using the heuristic function, $f(n) = h(n)$. **Please note that it is called as a greedy algorithm because at each step it tries to get as close to the goal as it can be.** GBFS resembles DFS in a way that it prefers to follow a single path all the way to the goal. It backtracks when it comes to the dead end *i.e.*, to a node from which goal state cannot be reached. Choosing minimum, $h(n)$ can lead to bad start as it may not yield always a solution. Also, as this exploration is not leading to solution, so unwanted nodes are getting expanded. In GBPS, if repeated states are not deleted then the solution will never be found.

Performance Measurement

1. **Completeness :** It is incomplete as it can start down an infinite path and never return to try other possibilities which can give solution.
2. **Optimal :** It is not optimal as it can initially select low value $h(n)$ node but it may happen that some greater value node in the current fringe can lead to a better solution. In general, greedy methods suffers from this, "looking for current best they loose on future best and in turn finally the best solution".
3. **Time and Space Complexity:** Worst case time and space complexity is $O(b^m)$ where '*m*' is the maximum depth of the search space.

Also note that the complexity can be reduced by designing a good heuristic function.

Q.14. Write Branch and Bound Search algorithm.

Ans. This strategy applies to problems having a graph search space where more than one alternative path may exist between two nodes. This strategy saves all path lengths (or costs) from a node to all generated nodes and chooses the shortest path for further expansion. It then compares the new path lengths with all old ones and again chooses the shortest path for expansion. In this way, any path to a good node is certain to be a minimal length path. The time required depends on the order in which the paths are explored. But this method is inadequate for solving larger problems.

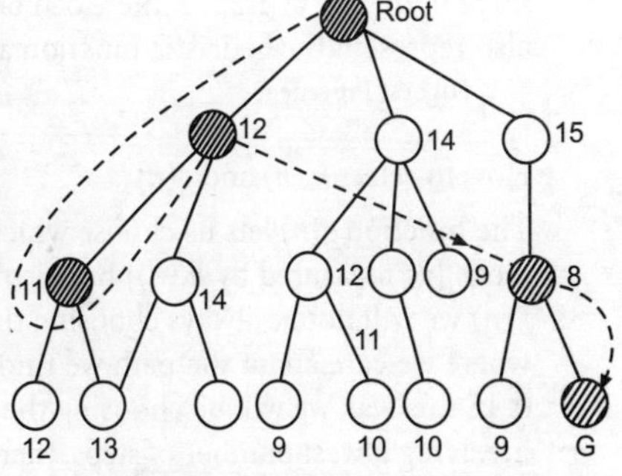

Fig. 5.18: Branch-and-bound search

Its algorithm is as follows—

1. Form a queue of partial paths. Let the initial queue be of zero-length, zero-step path from the root node to nowhere.
2. Until (queue is empty) or (goal is found) find if the first path in the queue reaches the goal node.
   a. If the first path reaches the goal node, do nothing.
   b. If the first path does not reach the goal node then.
      (*i*) Remove the first path from the queue.
      (*ii*) Form new path from the removed path by extending one step.

(*iii*) Sort the queue in increasing order of the cost accumulated so far.

3. If the goal has been found then return SUCCESS else return FAILURE.
4. End Branch-and-Bound algorithm. The search graph is shown in Fig. 5.18.

Using Branch-and-Bound on Traveling Salesman Problem (TSP)

Let us assume that there are a number of cities to be visited. From the starting city, the algorithm will begin generating complete paths. But it has to keep track of the shortest path found so far. **Please note that no further exploration of any path will be done if its partial length becomes greater than the shortest path found so far. This technique still guarantees a shortest path for our** TSP problem.

Q.15. Write A* Algorithm (minimizing total estimated solution's cost). Discuss in detail.

Ans. Basic principle— "Sum the cost and the evaluation function values for a state to get its "goodness" worth and use this as a yardstick instead of the evaluation function value in best first search. The sum of the evaluation function value and the cost along the path leading to that state is called as a fitness number." Before discussing about the fitness number, let us see what is evaluation function value and the cost functions. In best-first search, we use evaluation function value i.e., a value that estimates how far a particular node is from the goal. On the other hand, cost functions show how much resources like time, energy, money etc. have been spent in reaching a particular node from the start. While evaluation function values deal with the future, cost function's values deal with the past. However, please note that the cost function values are more concrete than the evaluation function values as the cost function values are really expanded. **Also note that if it is possible to obtain both, the evaluation function values and the cost function values then A* algorithm can be used.**

What is a fitness number?

A fitness number, $f'(n)$, is a heuristic function that estimates the merits of each node that we generate. So, this algorithm can search more promising paths first. Dash in the function indicates that it is an approximation to a function, $f(n)$, that gives the actual or true evaluation of the node. It is given as follows—

$$\boxed{f'(n) = g'(n) + h'(n)} \quad (1)$$

where $f'(n)$ – is the estimated cost of the cheapest solution through n.

$h'(n)$ – is an estimate of the additional cost of getting from the current node to a goal state.

$g'(n)$ – is an estimate of getting from the initial node to the current node.

The corresponding true values are $f(n)$, $g(n)$ and $h(n)$ of $f'(n)$, $g'(n)$ and $h'(n)$ respectively. For state space tree problems,

$$\boxed{g'(n) = g(n)} \quad ...(2)$$

Because there is only one path and the distance $g'(n)$ will be known to be true minimum from the start to the current node n. In case of graphs, there can be alternate paths from the start node to n. So, for state space tree problem, we can also represent the heuristic function as —

Highest Procedence

(from equation –1 and 2)

How to select $h'(n)$ and $g(n)$?

The function $g(n)$ lets us choose which node has to be expanded next not only on the basis of how good the node itself looks [as measured by $h'(n)$] but also on the basis of how good the path to the node was. By introduction of $g(n)$ into $f'(n)$ we will not be always choosing the node to expand that appears to be closest to the goal. This is important in cases where we care about the path we find if our concern is only getting to a solution by any means we can define $g(n) = 0$. In this way we will be choosing the node that seems closest to the goal. On the other hand, if we want to find a path involving lowest number of steps, then we can set the cost of going from a node to its successor as a constant (usually 1). In this way A* algorithm can be used whether we want to find a minimal-cost overall path or simply any path as quickly as possible.

$h'(n)$ is a measure of the cost of getting from the node to a solution. Therefore, good nodes get low values and bad nodes get high values. Hence, minus sign has to judiciously placed. This is opposite to that $g(n)$ which has to be non-negative. If $g(n)$ has a negative value then paths that traverse cycles in the graph will appear to get better as they get longer. Now, if $h'(n)$ estimates $h(n)$ perfectly, then A* will converge immediately to the goal with no search. If it is always zero, the search strategy will be random. If the value of $g(n)$ is always one, the search will be breadth first. Now a question comes to our mind that what happens if $h'(n)$ is neither perfect nor zero. There are two possibilities. One is that overestimates

$h(n)$ and the other is that it underestimates $h(n)$. Let us now examine what happens in both the cases.

Case I: $h'(n)$ **underestimates** $h(n)$

Consider the situation as shown in Fig. 5.19. Assuming that the cost of all arcs is 1, Fig. 5.19 (*a*) shows that initially all nodes except A are on OPEN. For each node, $f(n)$ is indicated as the sum of $h'(n)$ and $g(n)$. From the figure we observe that node B has the lowest $f(n)$ which is 4. So, it is expanded first. Suppose B has only one successor E and appears to be three moves away from a goal. Now $f(E)$ is 5 which is same as $f(C)$. Suppose we decide to allow the same path which we are currently following. Then, we will expand E next. Suppose it too has a single successor *F* which is three moves from the goal. This has been shown in Fig. 5.19 (*b*), *i.e.*, the situation two steps later after B and E have been expanded. Now, $f(F) = 6$ which is greater than $f(C)$. So, we will expand *C* next. Thus, we see that by underestimating $h'(B)$ we have wasted some effort. Thus, we find that *B* was farther away than we initially thought and we go back to try another path.

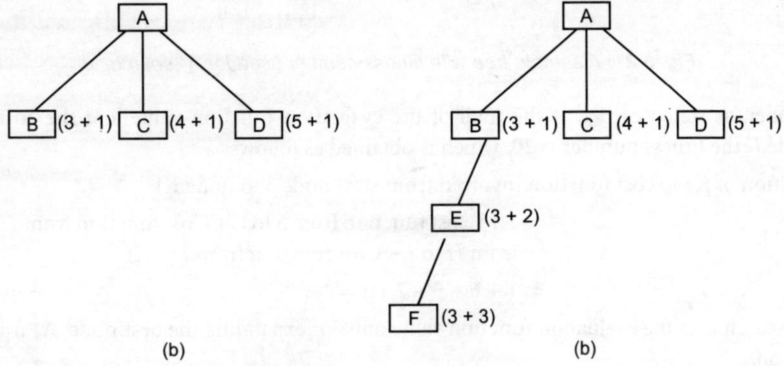

Fig. 5.19: h'(n) overestimates h(n)

Case II: $h'(n)$ overestimates $h(n)$

Now consider the situation shown in Fig. 5.20.

Here also we expand *B* in the first step. At the second step, we again expand *E*. At the next step we expand *F* and finally we generate *G*. The solution path has length 4. But suppose if there was a direct path from *D* to a solution giving a path of length 2, we will never find it. Thus, by overestimating $h'(D)$ we make *D* look so bad that we may find some other solution which is worse without even expanding *D*.

In general, we can say that if $h'(n)$ overestimates $h(n)$, we cannot be guaranteed of finding the cheapest path solution unless we expand the entire graph until all paths are longer than the best solution.

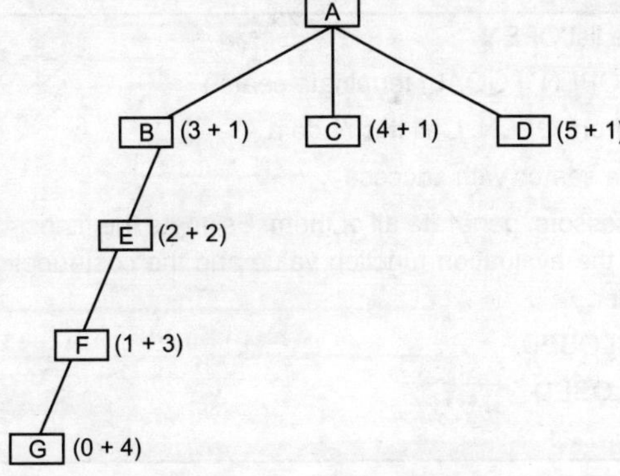

Fig. 5.20: h'(n) overestimates h(n)

Now we will see how the $f(n)$ function is evaluated in A* search. Consider Fig. 5.21 again with the same evaluation function values as in Fig. 5.17. Now associated with each node are three numbers, the evaluation function value, the cost function value and the fitness number.

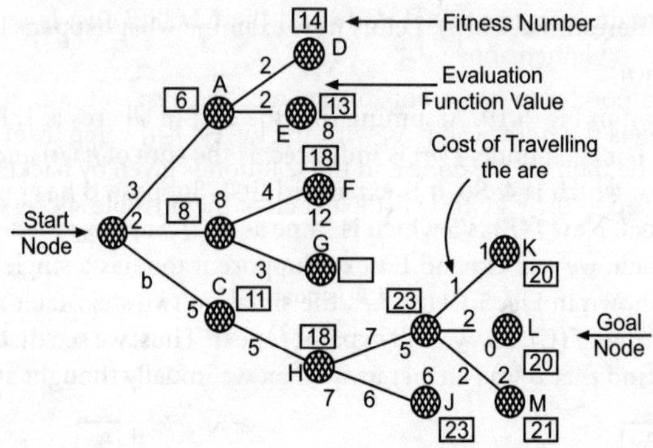

Fig. 5.21: A sample tree with fitness number used for A search.*

The fitness number, as stated earlier, is the total of the evaluation function value and the cost-function value. For example, for node K the fitness number is 20, which is obtained as follows:

(Evaluation function of K) + (cost function involved from start node S to node K)

$$= 1 + (\text{Cost function from } S \text{ to } C + \text{Cost function from } C \text{ to } H + \text{Cost function from } H \text{ to } I + \text{Cost function from } I \text{ to } K)$$

$$= 1 + 6 + 5 + 7 + 1 = 20.$$

While best-first search uses the evaluation function value only for expanding the best node, A* uses the fitness number for its computation.

Thus, if we are trying to find the cheapest solution, a reasonable thing to try first is the node with the lowest value of $g(n) + h'(n)$. It turns out that this strategy is quite reasonable provided that the heuristic function $h'(n)$ satisfies certain conditions. Note that A* is both complete and optimal. A* is the most popular form of best first search only. A* evaluates node based on two functions, namely: -

- $g(n)$ – the cost to reach the node, n.
- $h(n)$ – the cost to reach the goal node from node, n.

Also note that these two function's costs are combined into one to evaluate a node. New function, $f(n)$ is obtained as $f(n) = g(n) + h(n)$. That is,

$$f(n) = \text{Estimated cost of the cheapest solution through '}n\text{'}.$$

Algorithm for A*

1. Put the initial node on a list OPEN
2. If (OPEN is empty) or (OPEN = GOAL) terminate search
3. Remove the first node from OPEN. Call this node a
4. IF (a = GOAL) terminate search with success
5. Else if node a has successors, generate all of them. Estimate the fitness number of the successors by totaling the evaluation function value and the cost-function value. Sort the list by fitness number.
6. Name the new list as CLOSED.
7. Replace OPEN with CLOSED.
8. Go to Step 2.

Working of A*

5. The algorithm maintains two sets-

   a. **OPEN list:** The OPEN list keeps track of those nodes that need to be examined.

   b. **CLOSED list:** The CLOSED list keeps track of nodes that have already been examined.

6. Initially, the OPEN list contains just the initial node and the CLOSED list is empty. Each node, n, maintains the following: $g(n)$, $h(n)$, $f(n)$ as explained above.
7. Each node also maintains a pointer to its parent so that later the best solution, if found, can be retrieved. A* has a main loop that repeatedly gets the node, call it 'n', with the lowest $f(n)$ value from the OPEN list. Please understand here that if 'n' is the goal node then we are done and the solution is given by backtracking from 'n'. else 'n' is removed from the OPEN list and added to the CLOSED list. Next all of the possible successor nodes of 'n' are generated. That is,

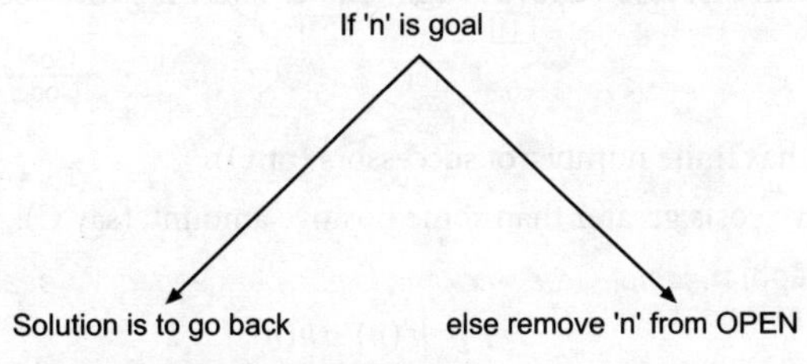

8. For each successor node, '*n*', if it is already in the CLOSED list and the copy there has an equal or lower '*f*' estimate and then we can safely discard the newly generated '*n*' and move on. Similarly, if '*n*' is already in the OPEN list and the copy there has an equal or lower *f* estimate. We can discard the newly generated n and move on.
9. If no better version of '*n*' exists on either the CLOSED or OPEN lists, we remove the inferior copies from the two lists and set '*n*' as the parent of '*n*'. we also have to calculate the cost estimates for 'n' as follows: -
   - Set $g(n)$ which is $g(n)$ + the cost of getting from *n* to *n*;
   - Set $h(n)$ *i.e.*, heuristic estimate of getting from *n* to the goal node;
   - Set $f(n) = g(n) + h(n)$.
10. Finally, add '*n*' to the OPEN list and return to the beginning of the main loop.

5.2. PERFORMANCE MEASUREMENT FOR A*

1. **Completeness:** A* is complete and guarantee solution.
2. **Optimality:** A* is optimal if $h(n)$ is admissible heuristic. By Admissible heuristic means $h(n)$ never over estimates the cost to reach the goal. Tree-search algorithm gives optimal solution if $h(n)$ is admissible. If we put extra requirement on $h(n)$ which is consistency also called as **monotonicity** then we are sure expect the optimal solution. A heuristic function, $h(n)$, is said to be **consistent**, if for every node '*n*' and every successor of '*ns*' of '*n*' generated by action '*a*', the estimated cost of reaching the goal from '*n*' is not greater than the step cost of getting to '*ns*'.

   $$h(n) \le \text{cost}(n, a, ns) + h(ns)$$

   Also note that A* using graph-search is optimal if $h(n)$ is consistent.

   Note: The sequence of nodes expanded by A* using the graph search is in the increasing order of $f(n)$. therefore, the first goal- node selected for expansion must be an optimal solution because all latter nodes will be either having the same value of $f(n)$ (same cost) or greater value of $f(n)$ (more expensive) than currently expanded node. A* never expands nodes with $f(n) > C^*$ where C^* is the cost of the optimal solution.

   A* algorithm will also do the pruning of certain nodes. Pruning is defined as the process of **ignoring a node completely without any examination of that node and thereby ignoring all of the possibilities arising from these nodes.**
3. **Time an Space Complexity:** If the number of nodes reaching the goal node grows exponentially then the time taken by A* eventually increases. The **main problem** part of A* is memory because A* keeps all of the generated nodes in memory. **Also note here that A* usually runs out of space long before it runs out of time.**

Let us now **prove the optimality of A* now.**

Proof: Assume A* finds the sub-optimal goal $G2$ and the optimal goal is G. since h is admissible, so $h'(G2) = h'(G) = 0$. Since, $G2$ is not optimal so, $f(G2) > f(G)$. at some point during the search, some node '*n*' on the optimal path to G is not expanded. we know that $f(n) \le f(G)$.

Let us now discuss some common properties of heuristic search algorithms. These properties evaluate the performance optimality of these algorithms and are given below—

1. **Admissibility Condition :** By algorithm we mean that the algorithm is sure to find a most optimal solution if one exists. **Please note that this is possible only when the evaluation function value never overestimates the distance of the node to the goal. Also note that if the evaluation function value which is a heuristic one is exactly the same of the distance of the node to the goal,** then this algorithm **will immediately** give the **solution.**

   For example, the A* algorithm discussed above is admissible. There are three conditions to be satisfied for A* to be admissible.

   They are as follows—

   1. Each node in the graph has finite number of successors (or O).
   2. All arcs in the graph have costs greater than some positive amount, (say C).
   3. For each node in the graph, n,

   $$h'(n) \leq h(n)$$

   This implies that the heuristic guess of the cost of getting from node n to the goal is never an overestimate. This is known as a **heuristic condition.**

   Only if these three conditions are satisfied, A* is guaranteed to find an optimal (least) cost path. **Please note that A* algorithm is admissible for any node *n* if on such path, *h'*(*n*) is always less than or equal to *h*(*n*).** This is possible only when the evaluation function value never overestimates the distance of the node to the goal. Although the admissibility condition requires $h'(n)$ to be a lower bound on $h(n)$, it is expected that the more closely $h'(n)$ approaches $h(n)$, the better is the performance of the algorithm.

   If $h(n) = h'(n)$ –an optimal solution path would be found without over expanding a node off the path. We assume that one optimal solution exists.

   If $h'(n) = 0$ –A* reduces to blind uniform cost algorithm or breadth-first algorithm.

   Please note that the admissible heuristics are by nature optimistic because they think that the cost of solving the problem is less than it actually is because *g*(*n*) is the exact cost foreach n. Also note that *f*(*n*) should never overestimate the true cost of a solution through *n*. For example, consider a network of roads and cities with roads connecting these cities. Our problem is to find a path between two cities such that the mileage/fuel cost is minimal. Then an admissible heuristic would be to use distance to estimate the costs from a given city to the goal city. Naturally, the air distance will be either equal to the real distance or will underestimate it *i.e.,* $h'(n) \leq h(n)$.

Q.16. Write short notes on Problem Reduction.

Ans. OR graph: As we have already studied Best-first search tree. Its search graph can be explored to avoid duplicate paths. In such a directed search graph, each node represents a point in the problem space.

Each node also indicates how much promising it is, a parent link (pointing back to the best node form which it came) and the list of nodes generated (or explored) from it. Please note that **the parent link will make it possible to recover the path to the goal once the goal is found.** The list of successors (explored) will make it possible if a better path is found to an already existing node and also to propagate the improvement down to its successors.

This graph is known as an OR graph.

It is so called because each of its branches represents an alternative problem-solving path. The techniques that we have studied so far, all are the example of OR graph only as in them we try to find a single path to the goal. OR graph finds a single path.

AND-OR graph (or tree)

We already know about the **divide-and-conquer strategy** *i.e.,* a solution to a problem can be obtained by decomposing it into smaller sub-problems. Each of this sub-problem can then be solved to get its **sub-solution**. These sub-solutions can then be recombined to get a solution as a whole. This is called as **decomposition or reduction**. This method generates arcs which are called as AND arcs. Please note that one AND arc may point to any number of successor nodes, all of which must be solved in order for an arc to point to a solution. Here also several arcs may emerge from a simple node. Each will indicate the different ways in which the original problem might be solved. This is actually called as an AND-OR graph or AND/OR tree. For example,

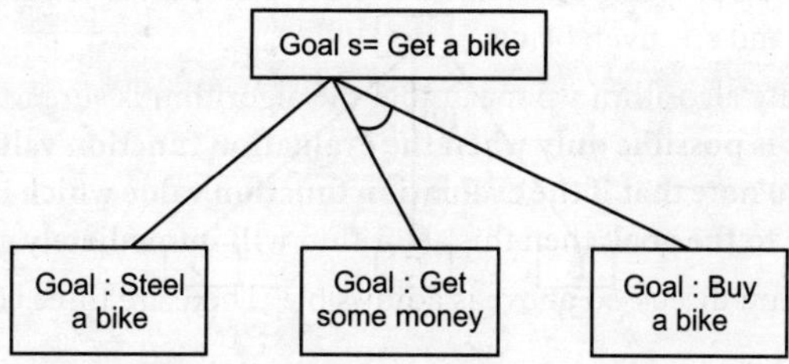

Fig. 5.22: AND/OR graph example

Actually, best-first is not suitable for searching AND-OR graphs. Consider a small AND/OR tree shown in Fig. 5.23.

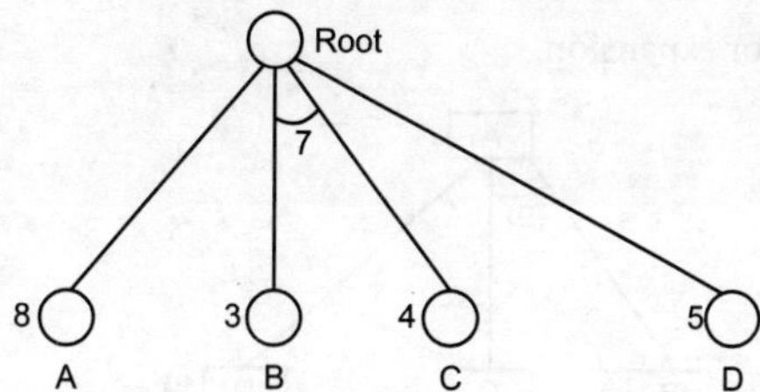

Fig. 5.23: Sample AND/OR tree

Here, the numbers show the approximate value of the heuristic function ($f(n)$) at that node. In Fig. 5.23, we observe that the minimal is B which has the $f(n)$ value of 3. But please note that B forms a part of the AND graph and so we need to consider the other branch also of this AND tree *i.e.*, C which has a weight of 4. So, our estimate now is (3 + 4) = 7. Now, this estimate is costlier than that of branch D *i.e.* 5. So, we explore node-D instead of C as it has the lowest value. This process goes on till we search our goal node. From this we observe that the choice of node to expand depends on its $f(n)$ value and also on whether that node is part of the current best path from the initial node.

Algorithm to search AND-OR graph

In order to develop an algorithm for searching an AND-OR graph, we define a term called as Futility. If the estimated cost of a solution becomes greater than the value of FUTILITY, then the search is abandoned. So, futility is like a threshold value i.e., any solution with a cost above it, is too expensive to be practical, even if it could ever be found. Let us write an **algorithm of** problem reduction now.

1. Initialize the graph to the starting node.
2. Loop until the starting node is labeled SOLVED or until its cost goes above FUTILITY:
   a. Traverse the graph, starting at the initial node and following the current best path and accumulate the set of nodes that are on that path and have not yet been expanded or labeled as solved.
   b. Pick one of these unexpanded nodes and expand it. If there are no successors, assign FUTILITY as the value of this node. Otherwise, add its successors to the graph and for each of them compute $f'(n)$. If $f'(n)$ of any node is O, mark that node as SOLVED.
   c. Change the $f'(n)$ estimate of the newly expanded node to reflect the new information provided by its successors. Propagate this change backward through the graph. If any node contains a successor arc whose descendants are all solved, label the node itself as SOLVED. At each node that is visited while going up the graph, decide which of its successor arcs is the most promising and mark it as part of the current best path. This may cause the current best path to change.

Consider the following *e.g.*,

At step 1, A is the only node, so it is at the end of the current best path *i.e.*, Before step 1:

$\boxed{A}(5)$

It is expanded, yielding nodes B, C and D, *i.e.*,

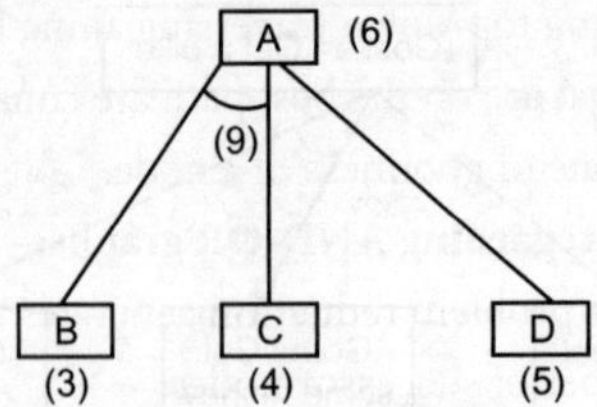

The arc to *D* is labeled as the most promising one emerging from A, since it costs 6 compared to B and C, which costs 9. This is because the path from *A-D* has the total cost of (*D* + the cost of arc *AD*). Now, *D* has cost of 5 and arc *AD* has 1; as each AND arc has a weight of one. So, total cost is 5 + 1 = 6 for *A–D* path. Similarly, for *B–C* cost will be (3 + 4 + 1 + 1) = 9.

In step (2), node *D* is chosen for expansion.

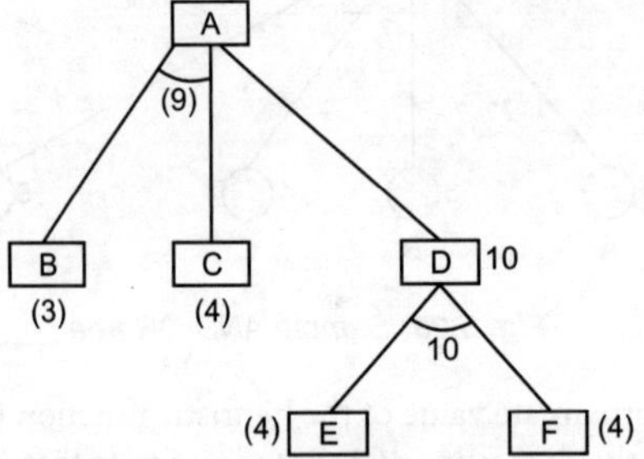

∴ Combined cost estimate of new AND-arc to *E* and *F* is 4 + 4 + 1 + 1 = 10.

So, we update the $f(n)$ value of *D* to 10. Going back one more level, we see that this makes the AND arc *B* –C better than arc to *D*, so it is labeled as the current best path by arrows. At step 3, we traverse that arc from A and discover the unexpanded nodes *B* and *C*. Let's choose to explore B first. This generates two new arcs, the ones to G and to *H* *i.e.*,

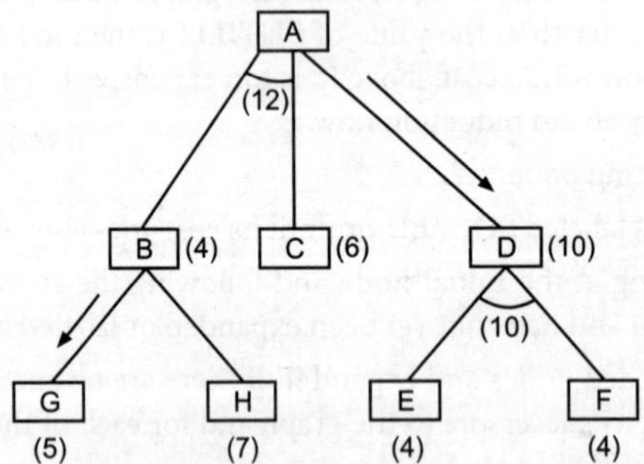

Propagating their $f(n)$ values backward, we update $f(n)$ of *B* to 6. This requires updating the cost of the AND arc *B* – C to 12 (*i.e.*, 6 + 4 + 2 =12). Comparing this with arc to *D*, which has the cost of 10, we find it is better. So, we explore D and thus either node–*E* or *F* is chosen for expansion at step-4.

This process continues until either a solution is found or all paths have led to dead ends, indicating that there is no solution.

Q.17. Write AO* algorithm. Discuss it in detail.

Ans. Our real-life situations cannot be exactly decomposed into either AND tree or OR tree but is always a combination of both. So, we need an AO* algorithm where O stands for 'ordered'. Instead of two lists OPEN and CLOSED of A* algorithm, we use a single structure GRAPH in AO* algorithm. It represents a part of the search graph that has been explicitly generated so far. **Please note that each node in the graph will point both down to its immediate successors and to its immediate predecessors. Also note that each node will have some *h'*(*n*) value associated with it. But unlike** A* search, $g(n)$ is not stored. It is not possible to compute a single value of $g(n)$ due to many paths to the same state. It is not required also as we are doing top-down traversing along the best-known path.

This guarantees that only those nodes that are on the best path are considered for expansion.

Hence, $h'(n)$ will only serve as the estimate of goodness of a node.

Please remember the following points regarding AND-OR graphs: -

1. The decomposition of the problem or problem reduction generates AND arcs.
2. One AND arc may point to any number of successor nodes.
3. All these must be solved so that the arc will give rise to many arcs, indicating several possible solutions. Hence, the graph is known as AND-OR instead of AND.
4. AO* is a best-first algorithm for solving problems represented as a cyclic AND-OR graph problems.
5. An algorithm to find a solution in an AND-OR graph must handle AND area appropriately.

Q.17. Compare both A* and AO* algorithms.

Ans. The following points compare these two algorithms-

1. Unlike A* algorithm that uses two lists OPEN and CLOSED, the AO* algorithm uses a single structure, G (graph).
2. *G* represents the part of the search graph generated so far.
3. Each node in *G* points down to its immediate successors and up to its immediate predecessors and also has with it the value of '*h*' cost of a path from itself to a set of solution nodes.
4. The cost of getting from the start nodes to the current node 'g' is not stored, as in A* algorithm. This is because it is not possible to compute a single such value as there may be many paths to the same state.
5. AO* algorithm serves as the estimate of goodness of a node.
6. A* algorithm cannot search AND-OR graphs efficiently.
7. AO* will always find minimum cost solution.

Next, we develop an AO* algorithm.

Step-1: Create an initial graph with a single node (start node).

Step-2: Transverse the graph following the current path, accumulating nodes that have not yet been expanded or solved.

Step-3: Select any of these nodes and explore it. If it has no successors then call this value— FUTILITY else calculate $f(n)$ for each of the successors.

Step-4: If $f(n) = 0$; then mark the node as SOLVED.

Step-5: Change the value of $f(n)$ for the newly created node to reflect its successors by back propagation.

Step-6: Wherever possible use the most promising routes. If a node is marked as SOLVED then mark the parent node as SOLVED.

Step-7: If the starting node is SOLVED or value is greater than FUTILITY then stop, else repeat from step-2.

Please note that AO* will always find a minimum cost solution if one exists, if $h'(n) < h(n)$ and that all arc costs are positive. The efficiency of this algorithm will depend on how closely $h'(n)$ approximates $h(n)$. Also note that AO* is guaranteed to terminate even on graphs that have cycles.

Problem Reduction with AO* algorithm (AND-OR Graphs algorithm)

When a problem can be divided in a set of sub-problems, where each sub-problem can be solved separately and a combination of these will be a solution, AND-OR graphs or AND-OR trees are used for representing the solution.

How to make our searching better?

By using the concept of metalevel state space, searching can be made better. Each state in a meta-level state space captures the internal computational state of a program that is searching an object-level state space. For example, in A* algorithm the internal state is maintained that consists of the current search tree. Each action in the metalevel state space is computation step that alters the internal state. For instance, each computation step in A* expands a leaf node and adds its successors to the tree. **Please note that as the level increases, the sequence of larger and larger search trees is generated.** Meta-learning algorithms also overcomes another problem. In complex problems, there can be mis-steps taken by the algorithm *i.e.*, the algorithm can explore unpromising non-useful sub-trees. Also note that the main objective of meta-learning is to minimize the total cost of problem solving.

How much accurate are the heuristic functions?

It is said that "More accurate the heuristic function, more is the performance". And that the quality of heuristic function can be measured by the effective branching factor, b^*. Consider A^* that generates N nodes and 'd' is the depth of a solution then b* is the branching factor that a uniform tree of depth 'd' would have so as to contain 'n+1' nodes. So, we can say that-

$$N + 1 = 1 + b^* + (b^*)^2 \ldots\ldots + (b^*)^d$$

Like, if A* finds a solution at depth 5 using 52 nodes then the effective branching factor is 1.92. Also note that a well-designed heuristic function will have a value of b* close to 1, allowing larger problems to be solved.

As an example, consider the 8 -puzzle problem solved earlier. The objective of this problem is to slide the tiles horizontally or vertically into the empty space until the configuration matches the goal configuration. It is observed here that-

1. The average solution cost for a randomly generated 8-puzzle problem instance is about 22 steps.
2. The branching factor is about 3 *i.e.*, when the empty tile is in the middle, there are four possible moves, when it is in the corner there are two and when it is along an edge then there are three.
3. An exhaustive search to depth 22 would look at about 32^2 = 3.1 * 1010 states.
4. If we keep track of repeated states, we could cut this down by a factor of about 1, 70,000 because there are only 9! / 2 = 1, 81,440 distinct states that are reachable.
5. If we use A*, we need a heuristic function that never overestimates the number of steps of the goal.
6. The following heuristic function may be used-
   a. h_1 = the number of misplaced tiles. All of the 8 tiles are out of position, so that start state would have $h_1 = 8 * h_1$, is an admissible heuristic because it is clear that any tile that is out of place must be moved at least once.
   b. h_2 = the sum of the distances of the tiles from their goal positions. Please note that as the tiles cannot move along diagonals, the distance we will count is the sum of the horizontal and vertical distances. Also note that it is possible to design multiple heuristic function for the same problem and thus to find the best possible solution.

   Consider two heuristic functions h_1 and h_2. As per their definitions, for some node n, if $h_2(n) \geq h_1(n)$ then we say that h_2 dominates h1. Dominance directly points to accuracy. Please understand here that A* using h_2 will never expand more nodes than A* using h1, except for some node having $f(n) = c^*$.

A problem with fewer restrictions on actions is called as a relaxed problem. The cost of the cost of an admissible solution to a relaxed problem is an admissible heuristic for the original problem. The heuristic function is admissible because the optimal solution in the original problem is also a solution in relaxed problem and therefore must be at least as expensive as the optimal solution in the relaxed problem. Also, because the derived heuristic is an exact cost for the relaxed problem, therefore it is consistent. If the problem definitions are written in formal languages, then it is possible to construct relaxed problem automatically. Admissible heuristic function can also be derived from the solution cost of a sub-problem of a given problem. The cost of optimal solution of this sub-problem would be lower bound on the cost of the complete problem. We can store the exact solution costs for every possible sub-problem instance in a database. Such a database is called as pattern database. also understand here that the pattern database is constructed by searching backwards from the goal state and recording the cost of each new pattern encountered. We can compute an admissible heuristic function , h, for each complete state encountered during a search just by looking -up the corresponding sub-problem configuration in the database.

Note: The cost of the entire problem is always greater than the sum of cost of two sub-problems. Hence, it is always better to derive disjoint solution and then sum up all solutions to minimize the cost. Remember that, $C(P) > C(p_1) + C(p_2)$...... that is the cost of solving a problem is greater than the sum of the costs of its individual sub-problems. This is also known as divide-and-conquer strategy of algorithm development.

Another possible solution is to make an agent program that can learn from the experience. Note that by saying 'learn from experience' we mean solving similar problems again and again i.e., practicing. Each optimal solution will provide example from which '$h(n)$ design' can be learned. One can get experience of which $h(n)$ was better. Each example consists of a state from the solution path and the actual cost of the solution from that point. From such solved examples an inductive learning algorithm can be used to construct the function h(n) that can predict solution costs for other states that have come during the search. For developing inductive algorithms, we can make use of techniques like neural networks, decision trees etc.

Q.18. What is Constraint Satisfaction? Give its algorithm. Give an example to solve a problem using it.

Ans. In the real-world, we work in different environments, each of which has some constraints. Our solution should be such that all such constraints are satisfied. We use extensive domain specific and heuristic knowledge. For example, design problems in manufacturing, optimal tour problems and so on. Even crypta-arithmetic problems are typical constraint satisfaction problems. The term relaxation algorithm is also used for constraints satisfaction. Waltz algorithm for labeling line drawings in a picture and natural language understanding are good examples of constraint satisfaction algorithm in a modified form. Let us see the algorithm now.

1. Select an unexpanded node of the search graph.
2. Apply the constraint inference rules to the selected node to generate all possible new constraints.
3. If the set of constraints contains a contradiction, then report that this path is a dead-end.
4. If the set of constraints describes a complete solution, then report success.
5. If neither a contradiction nor a complete solution has been found, then apply the problem space rules to generate new partial solutions that are consistent with the current set of constraints. Insert these partial solutions into the search graph.
6. Until a complete solution is found or until all path have led to dead ends, do: To see how this algorithm works, consider the following problem.

Problem : SEND **(cryptarithematic problem)**

+MORE

MONEY

Constraints :

1. Values are to bc assigned to letters from 0 to 9 only.
2. No two letters should have the same value.
3. If the same letter occurs more than once, it must be assigned the same digit each time.
4. The sum of the digits must be as shown in the problem.

Initial Problem State

$S = ?$	$M = ?$	$C1 = ?$
$E = ?$	$O = ?$	$C2 = ?$
$N = ?$	$R = ?$	$C3 = ?$
$D = ?$	$E = ?$	$C4 = ?$

Goal States: A goal state is a problem state in which all letters have been assigned a digit in such a way that all constraints are satisfied.

Solution : The solution process proceeds in cycles. At each cycle, two vital things are done—

a. Constraints are propagated by using rules which correspond to the properties of arithmetic. A value is guessed for some letter whose value is not yet determined, as this affects the effort involved in search.

b. More constraints are added/generated due to propagating constraints.

At each cycle, there may be several choices to apply. A few useful heuristics can help to select the best rule to apply first. For example, if there is a letter that has only two possible values and another with six possible values then there is a better chance of guessing right on the first than on the second. This procedure can be implemented as dfs also so that a large number of intermediate positions in both the problem and the constraint spaces will not have to be stored. We can also store all constraints in one central database and also to record at each node the changes that must be undone during backtracking.

The results of first few cycles of processing of this cryptarithmetic problem are shown in Fig. 5.24. Here, C_1, C_2, C_3, C_4 are the carry bits out of the columns, from right to left.

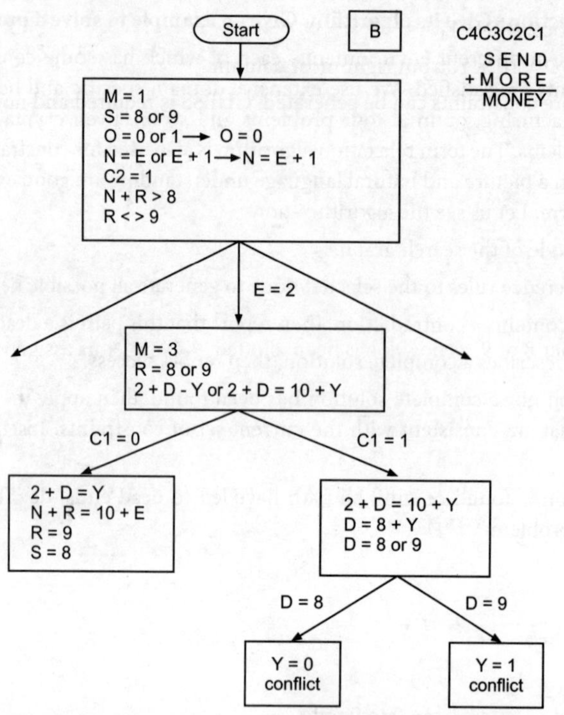

Fig. 5.24: Solution to Crytarthimetic Problem

Cycle 1 :

(*i*) $M = 1$ because two single digit numbers plus a carry cannot total more than 19.

(*ii*) $S = 8$ or 9 (minimum values) because $S + M + C_3$ should be > 9 (to generate a carry) and $M = 1$, therefore $S + 1 + C_3 > 9$ or $S + C_3 > 8$, as C_3 can be 0 or 1. So $S > 8$ or > 7 depending upon $C_3 = 0$ or 1.

(*iii*) $O = 0$ because $S + M + C_3 \leq 1$.

O must be atleast 10 to generate a carry and it can be at most 11. That is O can be zero or 1. As M is already 1 and no two digit should have the same value, so O is zero (0).

(*iv*) $N = E$ or $E + 1$ depending on the value of C_2. But N cannot have the same value as E. So $N = E + 1$ and $C_2 = 1$.

(*v*) In order for C_2 to be 1, the sum of $N + R + C_1$ must be greater tan 9, so $N + R$ must be greater than 8.

(*vi*) $N + R$ cannot be greater than 18, even with a carry in so, E cannot be 9. $E + O + C_2 = N$

When $C_2 = 0$ and $O = 0$

$E = N$ which is not possible.

At this point let's assume that no more additional constraints are generated so a GUESS is made.

Suppose value of E (which occurs the maximum number of times (3) and so interacts maximum with other letters).

Cycle 2 begins :

Let $E = 2$ (the next value after 0 and 1, already allocated)

(*i*) So $N = 3$ because $E + 1 = N$ as $R + N + C_1 = E$

$R + 3 + C_1$ (0 or 1) = 2 or 12

$R + 3 + 0 = 2, R = -1$ not possible

$R + 3 + 1 = 2, R = -2$ not possible

$R + 3 + 0 = 12, R = 9$, possible

$R + 3 + 1 = 12, R = 8$, possible

(*ii*) $D + E = Y$ when $C_1 = 0$ or $2 + D = Y$

and when $C_1 = 1$ or $2 + D = 10 + Y$, from right most column.

Again, assuming no more constraints can be generated, GUESS is required and now C_1 is chosen for GUESS. Let $C_1 = 1$

Cycle 3 begins

(*i*) $D + E = Y + C_1$

$2 + D = Y + 10$

$3 + R = 12$

$R = 9$

(*ii*)' $S = 8$ because S was either 8 or 9, as now R has been allotted '9'. Now let us assign value to C_1, 0 or 1.

First let us assign $C_1 = 10$.

$D + E = Y + 10$ (because $C_1 = 1$) $D + E = 10 + Y$

$2 + D = 10 + Y$ and for this to happen

Either $D = 8$

or $D = 9$

So C_1 cannot be 1.

Now consider $C1 = 0$.

then $8 + D = Y$, Y can be 0 or 1

$D = -8$ (when $Y = 0$)

$D = -7$ (when $Y = 0$)

So C_1 cannot be 0 either.

Thus D has four values, two negative and two positive.

When $D = 8$

$Y = 10$ *i.e.*, $= 0$

and when $D = 9$

$Y = 11$ *i.e.*, 1

So $Y = 0$ and $Y = 1$ lead to conflict.

This contradiction could have been explained through another type of arguments: Earlier $S = 8$ or 9 and again $R = 8$ from II loop and when $C_1 = 1$, $D = 8$ or 9

And now $D = 8$ or 9 from $C_1 = 1$.

Three letters cannot share two values, so $C_1 \neq 1$.

Comments on Constraints Propagation : The rules of the constraint propagation should not infer spurious constraints. Nor do they need to infer all legal rules

For example, we could adopt an alternative path which gives $C_1 = 0$.

Let $C_1 = 1$

Then $E + D = Y + C_1$

or $E + D = Y + 10$

$2 + D = Y + 10$

D would be either 8 or 9

8 or 9 is assigned to R

is assigned to D

is assigned to S

Two values cannot be shared among three letters, so $C1$ cannot be 1. If this were realized earlier fruitless search could have been avoided. But the constraint propagation rules used were not that sophisticated so it took some search steps. Whether the time taken by the actual search route is more or less than the constrained method depends upon how long it takes to perform the reasoning required for constraint propagation.

We are in a position to solve a problem now.

Example 1. Trace the constraint satisfaction procedure solving the following cryptarithmatic **program:**

```
  CROSS
+ ROADS
 DANGER
```

Solution 1 :

(*i*) $D = 1$ since it is generated because of carry which at most can be $1(9 + 9 = 18)$.

(*ii*) $C + R = 10$ or 12 to 18 depending up carry C4.

(*iii*) Since, we have no path to move on, we guess the values for S.

(*a*) $C + R = A$ (*b*) $R + O = N$

$+ 4 =$ $4 + =$

(*c*) $O + A = G$ (*d*) $S + D = E$

$2 + 1 = 3$

(*e*) $S + S = R$

$2 + 2 = 4$

Thus we get: A C D E G N O R S

↓ ↓ ↓ ↓

1 3 4 2(guess)

Now, let us say 'O' = 5 (anything other than 1, 2, 3, 4) if $O = 0$ then $R + 0 = N$

$\Rightarrow$ $4 + 0 = 4$ (Not possible)

$\therefore$ guess $O = 5$

(*a*) $C + R = A$ (*b*) $R + O = N$

$+ 4 =$ $4 + 5 = 9$

(*c*) $O + A = G$ (*d*) $S + D = E$ (*e*) $S + S = R$

$5 + =$ $2 + 1 = 3$ $2 + 2 = 4$

$\therefore$ A C D E G N O R S

↓ ↓ ↓ ↓ ↓ ↓

1 3 9 5 4 2

(guess)

Here, $C + R$ should be 10, 12, 13, 14, 16, 16 or 17 as $C_4 \neq 1$

$\therefore$ for C we can have,

for $C = 6$ (for total of 10) we have $A = 0$

and $A + 0 = G$ *i.e.* $5 + 0 = 5$ *i.e.* $G = 5$

$\Rightarrow O = G = 5$ (not possible)

$\Rightarrow$ For $O = 6, 7, 8$ too we are not able to get values for C s.t. $C + R > 10$ (no value in this case can be ($= O$) as it will result in same value for 2 different characters) and for $O = 6$ we get repeating values.

$\therefore$ Our guess for $S = 2$ is wrong.

(*iv*) For $S = 3$,

(*a*) $C + R = A$ (*b*) $R + O = N$ (*c*) $O + A = G$

$9 + 6 = 15$ $6 + 5$

(*d*) $S + D = E$ (*e*) $S + S = R$

$3 + 1 = 4$ $3 + 3 = 6$

$\therefore$ A C D E G N O R S

$\downarrow \downarrow \downarrow \downarrow \quad \downarrow$

5 9 1 4 6 3(guess)

Since, $C + R \geq 12$

$C \neq 6$, as it will give $C = R = 6$

$C \neq 7$, as $7 + 6 = 13 \therefore A = 3 \Rightarrow A = S = 3$

$C \neq 8$, as $8 + 6 = 14 \therefore A = 4 \Rightarrow A = E = 4$

$\therefore C = 9, \quad 9 + 6 = 15 \therefore A = 5$

Now we need to find *G, N, O.*

If $O = 2$ then

(*a*) $C + R = A$ (*b*) $R + O = N$ (*c*) $O + A = G$

$9 + 6 = 15$ $6 + 2 = 8$ $2 + 5 = 7$

(*d*) $S + D = E$ (*e*) $S + S = R$

$3 + 1 = 4$ $3 + 3 = 6$

$\therefore$ A C D E G N O R S

$\downarrow \downarrow \downarrow \downarrow \downarrow \downarrow \downarrow \downarrow \downarrow$

5 9 1 4 7 8 2 6 3

(guess) (guess)

This solution has no repetitions thus we get—

```
   CROSS          96233
+ ROADS  →     + 62513
 DANGER         158746
```

Q19. What is Means-End Analysis (MEA)?

Ans. Means-end-analysis is a special type of knowledge-rich search that allows both backward and forward searching.

Principle: "It (MEA) allows us to solve the major parts of a problem first and then go back and solve the smaller problems that arise while assembling the final solution".

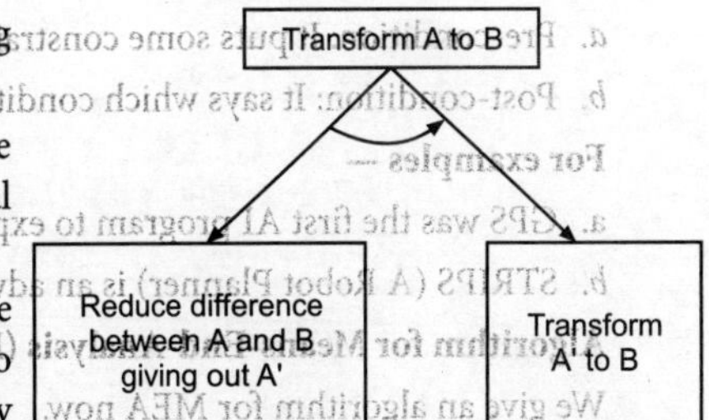

Technique: It is based on the use of the operators which transform the state of the world. The difference between the current state and the goal state is detected.

Once such a difference is isolated, an operator that can reduce the difference has to be found. But sometimes it is not possible to apply this operator to the current state. So, we try to get a sub- problem out of it and try to apply our operator to this new state. If this also does not produce the desired goal state then we try to get second sub problem and apply this operator again. This process may be continued. But please note here that if the difference is chosen correctly and if the operator is really effective at reducing the difference then the two sub problems are easier to solve than the original problem.

Transform A to B

Reduce difference between A and B giving out A'

Transform A' to B

Why is it called as Means-End-Analysis?

Given a description of the desired state of the world (the end) it works backwards, selecting and using operators that will achieve it (the means). Hence, the name, Means-End-Analysis (MEA).

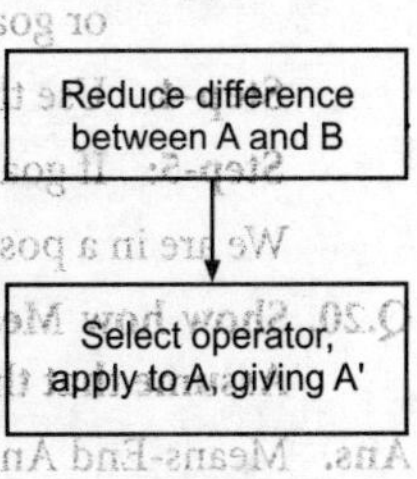

MEA works incrementally : The above technique of MEA works incrementally and not as a single step. This is so because the operators are applied recursively till a goal state is achieved.

MEA works on three primary goals.

Reduce difference between A and B

Select operator, apply to A, giving A'

They are as follows—

a. Transformation

b. Reduction

c. Application

Transformation means to transform object *A* into object *B i.e.*,

This is an AND graph which subdivides a problem into an intermediate problem and then transforms that problem into the goal state B. Please note that this process terminates when there is no difference between A and B or we can say when the goal is reached.

Reduction means to reduce the difference between object-A and object-B by modifying object-A *i.e.*,

Please note that the goal of this operation is to reduce the difference between the object A and object-B by transforming object A into object-A', nearer the goal B, by means of a relevant operator (say, *R*).

Application means to apply the operator R to object-A. This will again be a AND graph showing the goal of reducing the difference between object-A and the pre-conditions required for the operator R, giving intermediate object A''. Operator R is then applied to A'', transforming it to A', which is close to the goal B. That is,

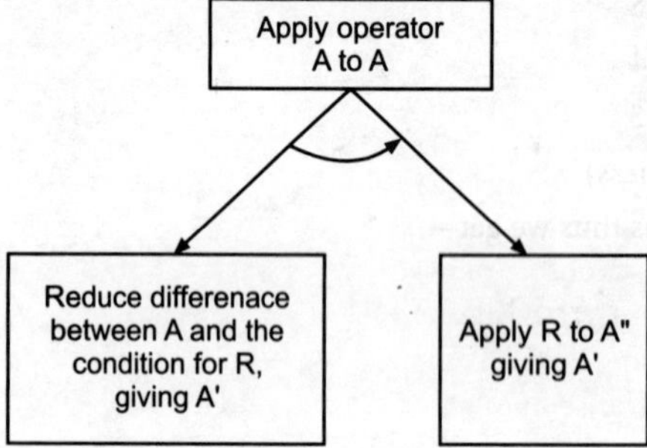

Please understand that states are described in some structured way like by predicate calculus and moves are performed by the operators. Each operator has a—

a. Pre-condition: It puts some constraints on the states it uses.

b. Post-condition: It says which conditions will be true when the operator has been used.

For examples —

a. GPS was the first AI program to exploit MEA.

b. STRIPS (A Robot Planner) is an advanced problem solver that incorporates MEA.

Algorithm for Means-End-Analysis (MEA)

We give an algorithm for MEA now.

Step-1: Until the goal is reached or no more procedures are available.

Step-2: Describe the current state, the goal state and the difference between the two.

Step-3: Use the difference between the current state and goal state, possibly with the description of the current state or goal state, to select a promising procedure.

Step-4: Use the promising procedure and update the current state.

Step-5: If goal is reached then success else it is a failure.

We are in a position to solve an example now.

Q.20. Show how Mean-End-Analysis (MEA) can be used to solve the problem of getting from one place to another. Assume that the available operators are walk, drive, take the bus, take a cab and fly.

Ans. Means-End Analysis—

Available Operators	Preconditions	Results
Walk		at (man, loc)
Drive	have (man, car) ^ (on obj, bus)	at (man, loc)^ at (obj, loc)
Take bus	On (man, bus)^ on (obj, bus)	at (man, loc)^ at (obj, loc)
Take cab	hire (man, cab) ^ on (obj, cab)	at (obj, loc)
Fly	book (man, airbus)^ on (obj, airbus)	at (man, loc) ^ at (obj, loc)

∴ Difference Table is as follows

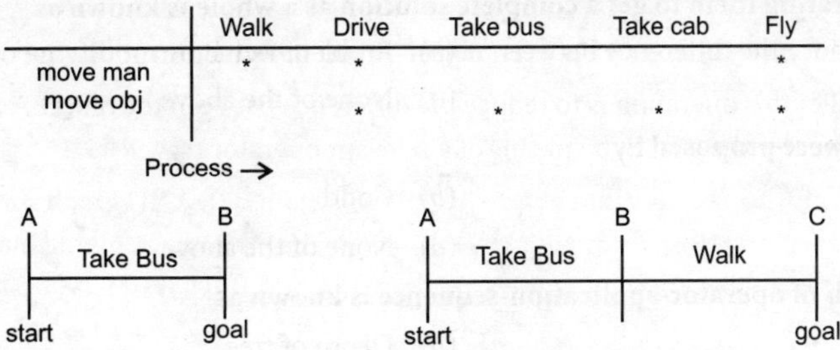

SUMMARY

To solve an AI problem we need to follow certain steps—Firstly, define the problem precisely *i.e.*, specify the problem space, the operators for moving within the space and the starting and goal state. Secondly, analyze the problem and finally, choose one or more techniques for representing knowledge and for problem solving and apply it (them) to the problem. In BFS, if we assume that the branching factor (b) = 10, we can expand 1000 nodes/sec and also assume 100 bytes/node storage then the observe that as the depth increases, number of nodes increases and both time and memory requirement also increases. One such snapshot is given below—

Depth	Nodes	Time	Memory
0	1	1 ms	100 bytes
2	111	0.1 sec	11 KB
4	11, 111	11 secs	1 MB
6	10^6	18 min	111 MB
8	10^8	31 hrs	11 GB
10	10^{10}	128 days	1 TB
12	10^{12}	35 yrs	111 TB
14	10^{14}	3500 yrs	11, 111 TB

This table shows how memory requirements increases as the depth increases.

MULTIPLE CHOICE QUESTIONS

1. States are operated upon by a set of

(*a*) Operators (*b*) Components

(*c*) State space (*d*) None of the above

2. Nodes are states and arcs represent

(*a*) Directions (*b*) Actions

(*c*) Functions (*d*) None of the above

3. **The process of creating a formal description of a problem using the knowledge about the given problem, so as to create a program for solving a problem is called as**
   (*a*) Standardization (*b*) Operationalization
   (*c*) Generalization (*d*) None of the above
4. **A set of all possible states of a given problem is known as**
   (*a*) State (*b*) Space search
   (*c*) State space (*d*) None of the above
5. **The process of decomposing up of a complex problem into a set of primitive sub problems, finding solutions to them and then integrating them to get a complete solution as a whole is known as**
   (*a*) Expansion (*b*) Problem reduction
   (*c*) Production systems (*d*) None of the above
6. **Production systems were proposed by**
   (*a*) Foreign bank (*b*) Codd
   (*c*) Emil post (*d*) None of the above
7. **The maximum length of operator-application-sequence is known as**
   (*a*) Depth cut-off (*b*) Depth of tree
   (*c*) Search path (*d*) None of the above
8. **Uniformed search is also known as a**
   (*a*) Heuristic search (*b*) Blind search
   (*c*) Goal search (*d*) Beam search
9. **The time complexity of the bfs algorithm**
   (*a*) 0 (*bd*) (*b*) 0 (b^d)
   (*c*) 0 (d^b) (*d*) 0 (*b* + *d*)
10. **Blind alley means**
    (*a*) Applying two or more searches (*b*) Search that can go on and on
    (*c*) Blind search only (*d*) None of the above
11. **A heuristic is a**
    (*a*) Rule of thumb (*b*) Mathematics formulae
    (*c*) Equation (*d*) None of the above
12. **The most common problem with all AI solution is**
    (*a*) Polynomial explosion (*b*) Combinational explosion
    (*c*) Nuclear explosion (*d*) None of the above
13. **Which module creates the possible solutions in Generate-And-Test-Algorithm**
    (*a*) OS module (*b*) Kernel module
    (*c*) Generator module (*d*) None of the above
14. **An area of the search space which is higher than the surrounding areas is a**
    (*a*) Ridge (*b*) Plateau
    (*c*) Hill (*d*) None of the above
15. **Which of the following is a greedy search**
    (*a*) BFS (*b*) DFS
    (*c*) Best-First Search (*d*) None of the above
16. **Goal nodes have an evaluation function value of**
    (*a*) Zero (*b*) One
    (*c*) Two (*d*) Three

17. The sum of the evaluation function value and the cost along the path leading to the state is called as

(*a*) Fitness number (*b*) Whole number

(*c*) Complex number (*d*) None of the above

18. Constraint satisfaction is also referred to as

(*a*) Divide-and-conquer algorithm (*b*) Greedy algorithm

(*c*) Relaxation algorithm (*d*) None of the above

19. Mean-End-Analysis (MEA) allows

(*a*) Backward searching (*b*) Forward searching

(*c*) Both (*a*) and (*b*) (*d*) None of the above

20. MEA works on three primary goals which are

(*a*) Transformation, scaling and rotation

(*b*) Transformation, reduction and application

(*c*) Scaling, reduction and application

(*d*) None of the above

ANSWERS

1. (*a*)	**2.** (*b*)	**3.** (*b*)	**4.** (*c*)	**5.** (*b*)
6. (*c*)	**7.** (*a*)	**8.** (*b*)	**9.** (*b*)	**10.** (*b*)
11. (*a*)	**12.** (*b*)	**13.** (*c*)	**14.** (*a*)	**15.** (*c*)
16. (*a*)	**17.** (*a*)	**18.** (*c*)	**19.** (*c*)	**20.** (*b*)

CONCEPTUAL SHORT QUESTIONS WITH ANSWERS

Q. 1. What is the relationship between various search algorithms-Breadth-first, uniform cost, AO*, A* and Best-First search?

Ans. As shown in Figure, when $h'(n) = 0$ for all nodes, we have uniform-cost algorithm. When $f'(n) = g(n) - \text{depth}\ (n)$, we have breadth-first search which spreads out along contours of equal depth. Please note from above diagram that both the uniform-cost and breadth-first algorithms are special cases of A* (with $h'(n) = 0$), so they are both admissible.

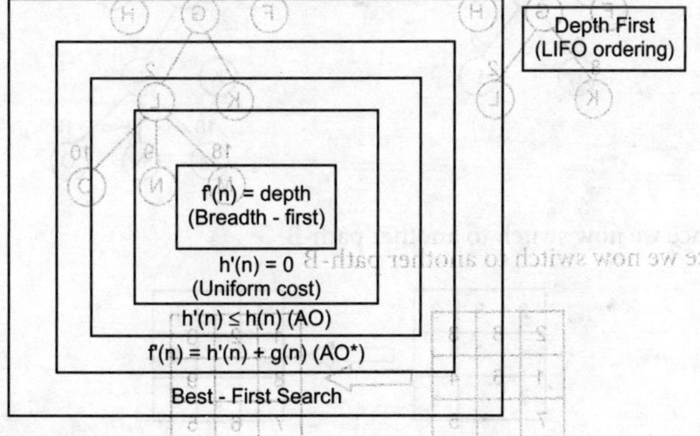

Q.2. What is Search Control Knowledge?

Ans. *A* large KB contains thousands of rules when there are many possible paths for reasoning, it is critical that fruitless ones are not pursued. Knowledge about which paths are most likely to lead quickly to a goal state is called as a search control knowledge.

Q.3. When would best-first search be worse than simple breadth-first search?

Ans. CASE WHEN BEST-FIRST SEARCH IS WORSE THAN BREADTH-FIRST SEARCH

Consider a graph—

Using Breadth First Search, to reach the goal '*D*' we would transverse as—

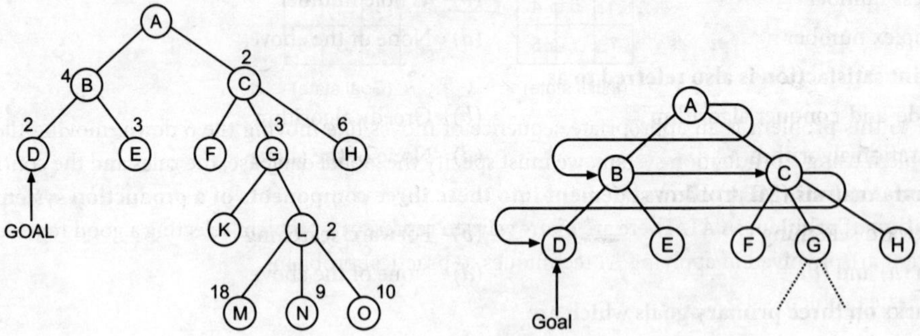

Path ⇒ $A \rightarrow B \rightarrow C \rightarrow D$

No. of modes traversed = 4.

Using Best First Search, to reach the goal '*D*' we would traverse as—

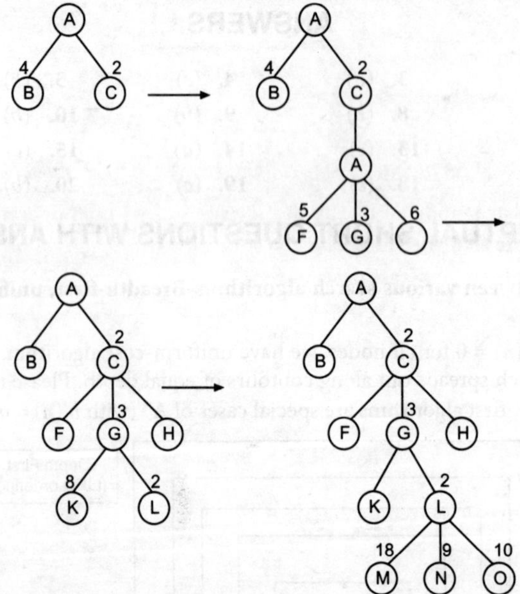

which is not the goal, hence we now switch to another path-B

2	8	3
1	6	4
7		5

(Initial state)

⇨

1	2	3
8		9
7	6	5

(Goal state)

Thus, Best first search traverses more modes in this particular example than the breadth-first search, and hence Best first is worse than Breadth first in this example.

Q.4. What is 8-puzzle problem? How can you solve a problem using production system?

Ans. The 8-puzzle problem consists of eight numbered, movable tiles set in a (3 × 3) frame. One cell of this (3 × 3) frame is always empty. Our problem is to change the initial configuration into the goal configuration *i.e.*,

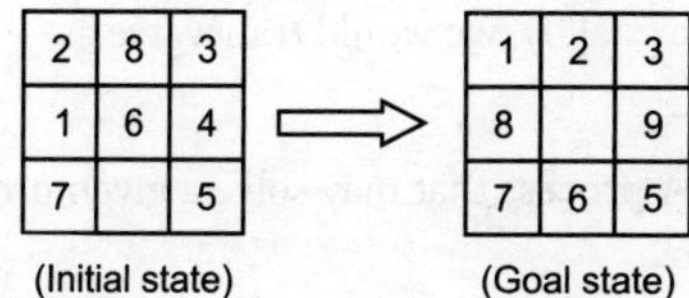

A solution to this problem is an appropriate sequence of moves like moving tile 6 down, moving tile 8 down etc. To solve a problem using a production system, we must specify the global database, the rules and the control strategy. **This process of transforming a problem statement into these three components of a production system is called as the representation of problem in AI.** There are many ways to represent a problem selecting a good representation is one of the important arts involved in applying AI techniques to practical problems.

In our 8-puzzle problem—

a. Each tile configuration is a problem state.

b. The set of all possible configurations is the space of problem states or the problem space.

c. It has 9! = 3,62, 880 different configurations.

Once the problems states have been identified, we must construct a computer representation (or description) of them. This description is then used as the global database of production system. For this 8-puzzle problem, a straight forward description is a (3 × 3) matrix of numbers. So, the initial global database is the description of the initial problem state. Please note that virtually any kind of data structure can be used to describe states, like vectors, trees, linked lists etc.

A move will actually transform one problem state into another state. In our 8-puzzle problem there can be four moves—

a. Move empty space (blank) to the left *b.* Move blank up

c. Move blank to right *d.* Move blank down.

Please note that these moves are modeled by the production rules which operate on the state descriptions in the appropriate manner. Also note that the rules have preconditions which must be satisfied by a state description in order for them to be applicable to that state description.

We have to reach our goal state. We can also specify some True/False condition on states to serve as a goal condition. It is the problem-goal condition that forms a basis for the termination condition of the production system. The control strategy repeatedly applies rules to state descriptions until a description of a goal state is produced. It also keeps track of the rules which have been applied so that it can compose them into the sequence representing the problem solution. We may add some constraints also to our solution *i.e.*, to find an optimal (minimum) path solution (with smallest number of moves). For this, costs are associated with each move and the minimum is selected.

Q. 5. Is our 8-puzzle problem a heuristic search problem?

Ans. The 8-tile problem is a heuristic search problem. Herein, we have (8 × 4) possible tile moves. Most of these moves are illegal at any point. These illegal moves are visible to humans but not to our computer. A computer will simply swap it with a neighboring tile. So, we use heuristics. The average solution cost for a randomly generated 8-tile puzzle is about 22 steps. The branching factor is about 3. This is because when the empty tile is in middle, there are four possible moves, when it is in a corner there are two and when it is on an edge, there are three. Thus, an exhaustive search to a depth of 22 would have about $33^{22} \approx 3.1 \times 10^{10}$ states. We can bring this down also by a factor of 1,70,000 if we keep track of repeated states. This is so because there are only—

$\frac{9!}{2}$ = 1,81,440 distinct states that are reachable. 2

Heuristics used :

1. Say, h_1 represents the number of misplaced tiles. If all 8-tiles are out of position then the start state would have h_1 = 8. Since any tile which is out of place must be moved at least once, h_1 is an admissible heuristic.
2. Say, h_2 represents the sum of the distances of the tiles from their goal positions. **Please note here that the tiles cannot move diagonally, so the distance we will count is the sum of the horizontal and vertical distances.** This distance is called as the city block distance or Manhattan distance. **Also note that when we move** one tile, h_2 **can still be applied as any move brings us one step closer to the goal.**

Q.6. What are heuristics?

Ans. According to various AI researchers—

1. **Newell, Shaw and Simon (1957) :** "A process that may solve a given problem but offers no guarantees of doing so is called as a heuristic for that problem".
2. **Marvin Minisky (1961) :** "A heuristic is any method or trick used to improve the efficiency of a problem- solving program."
3. **Feigenbaum and Feldman (1963) :** "A state heuristic is rule of thumb, strategy, trick, simplification or any other kind of device which drastically limits search for solutions in large problem spaces. Heuristics do not guarantee optimal solution; in fact, they do not guarantee any solution at all. It can be said for a useful heuristic is that it offers solutions which are good enough most of the time."

Judea Pearl (1984): "It is the nature of good heuristics both that they provide a simple means of indicating which among several course of action is to be preferred and that they are not necessarily guaranteed to identify the most effective course of action, but do so sufficiently often. It is often said that heuristic methods are unpredictable, they work wonders most of the time but may fail miserably some of the time".

Q.7. Distinguish between Heuristic algorithms and solution guaranteed algorithms?

Ans. Let us tabulate the difference between the two :

Heuristic Algorithms	Solution Guaranteed Algorithm
These algorithms are non-exact algorithms that do not guarantee that the best will be found. So, they are considered to be approximate algorithms.	These algorithms are also called as exact-algorithms as they guarantee to find an optimal solution.
They find solutions close to the best one.	They guarantee to find optimal solutions.
They find fast solutions.	They take exponential time to do so.
It is called as heuristic because it must prove that the best solution is the best.	It always finds an optimal solution.
For e.g., Local search methods, simulated annealing etc.	For *e.g.*: Branch and Bound, dynamic programming, Branch and cut etc.

Q.8. Using the search tree given below, list the elements of the queue just before that next node is expanded. Use best first search where the number correspond to estimated cost-to-goal for each corresponding node.

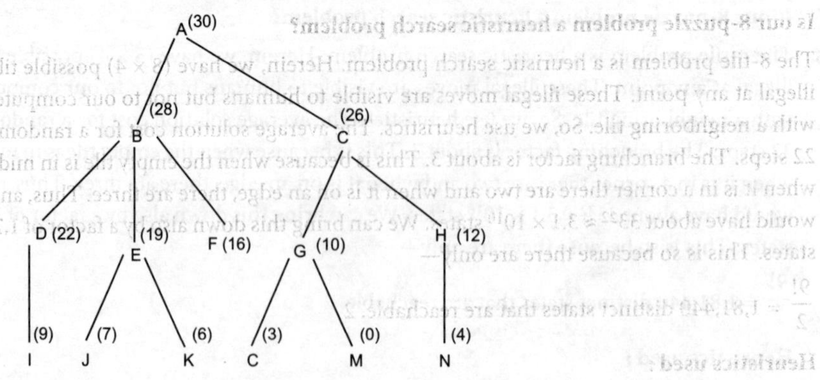

Ans. The best-first-search's cost is calculated in the following manner.

From node	To node	Cost of node	Possible Queue	Cost so far	Final best First queue
A	B	30	A-B	30	✓
	C	30	A-C	30	✓
B	D	28	A-B-D	58	×
	E	28	A-B-E	58	×
	F	28	A-B-F	58	×
C	G	26	A-C-G	56	✓
	H	26	A-C-H	56	✓
G	L	10	A-C-G-L	66	✓
	M	10	A-C-G-M	66	✓
H	N	12	A-C-H-N	68	×
L	Next node	3	A-C-G-L-Next Node	69	×
M	Next node	0	A-C-G-H-Next node	66	✓

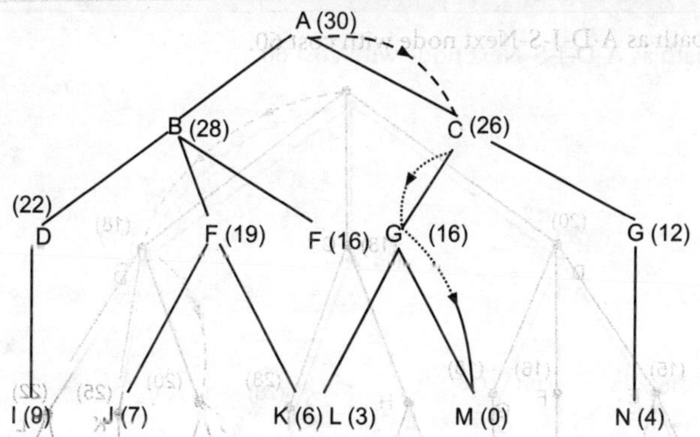

Q.9. Using the search, the given below, list the elements of the queue just before that next node is expanded. Use best-first search where the number correspond to estimated cost-to-goal for each corresponding node.

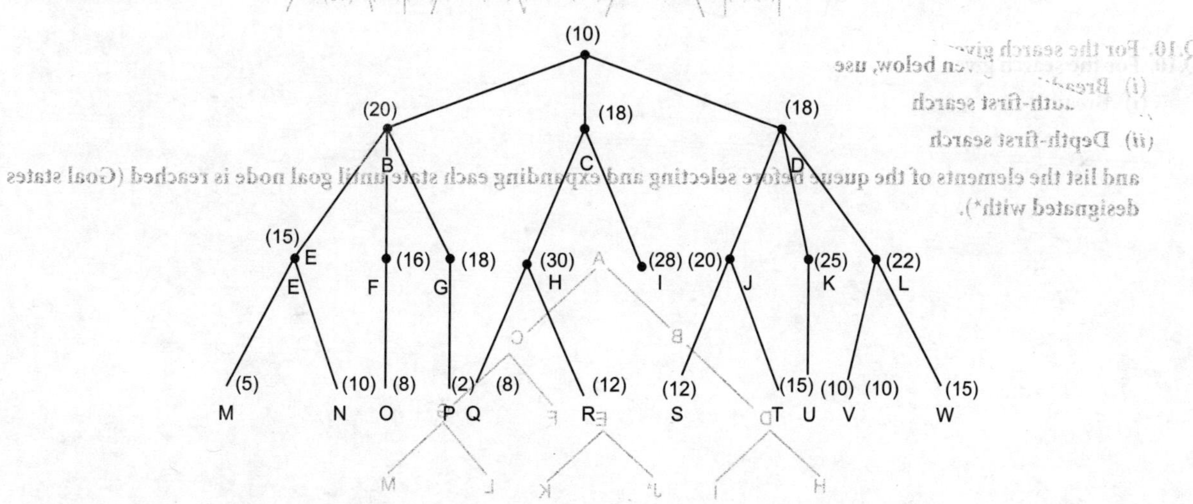

Ans. The table showing best-first search cost is as follows.

From node	To node	Cost of node	Possible queue	Cost so far	Final best First queue
A	B	10	A-B	30	×
	C	10	A-C	28	✓
	D	10	A-D	28	✓
D	J	20	A-B-J	48	✓
	K	20	A-D-K	53	×
	L	20	A-D-L	50	×
C	H	18	A-C-H	58	×
	I	18	A-C-I	56	×
D	S	20	A-D-J-S	60	✓
	T	20	A-D-J-T	63	×

The best first search has path as A-D-J-S-Next node with cost 60.

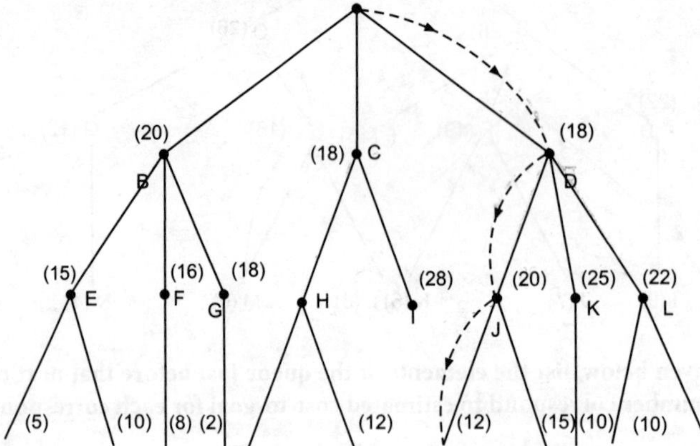

Q.10. For the search given below, use

(*i*) Breadth-first search

(*ii*) Depth-first search

and list the elements of the queue before selecting and expanding each state until goal node is reached (Goal states designated with*).

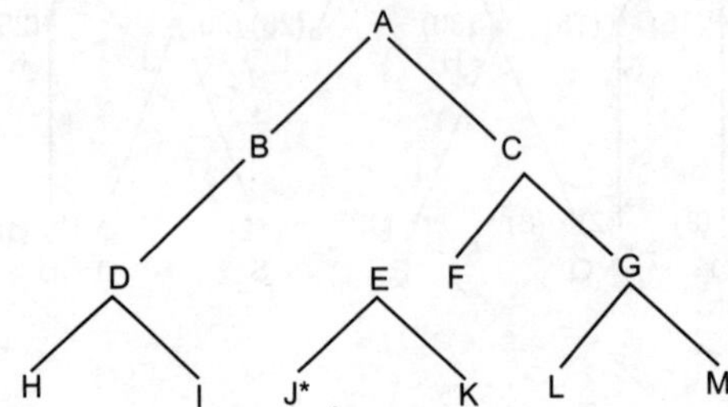

Ans. **(*i*) Breadth first search:**

The given goal is J.

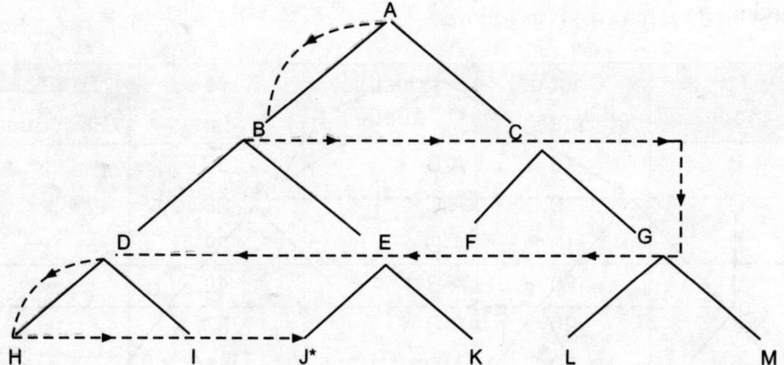

The path is
A-B-C-G-F-E-D-H-I-J.

***(ii)* Depth-first-search:**

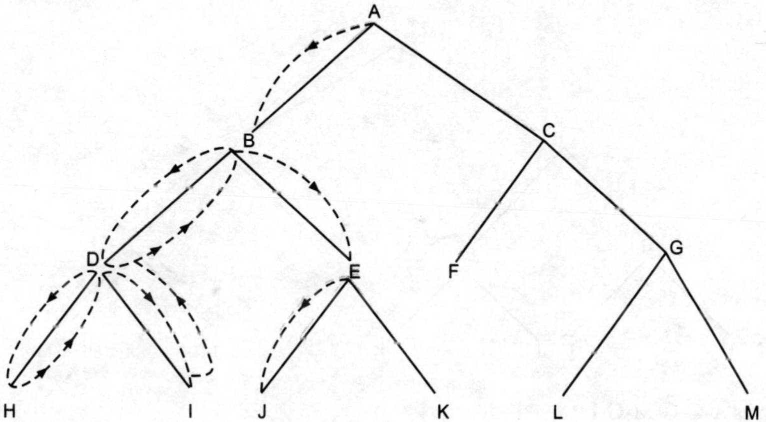

A-B-D-H-I-D-B-E-J.

Q.11. For the search tree given below, use

(*i*) Breadth first search.

(*ii*) Depth-first search. Goal is designed by

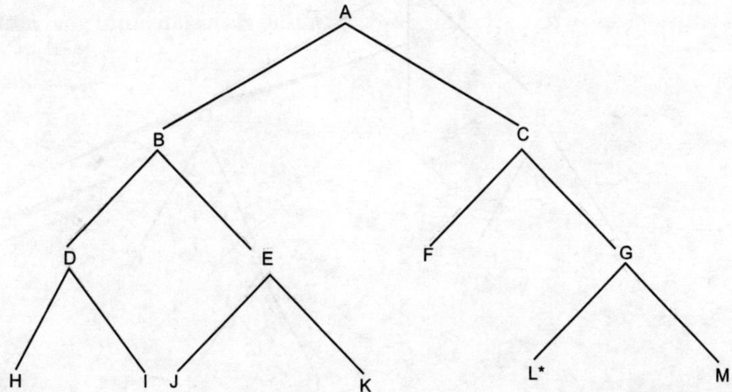

Ans. **(*i*) Breadth first search:**

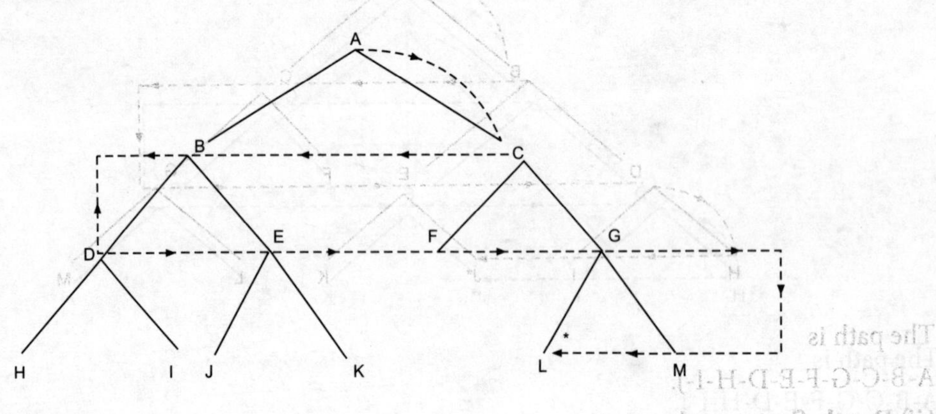

The path is given as A-C-G-M-G-L

(*ii*) Depth–first search:

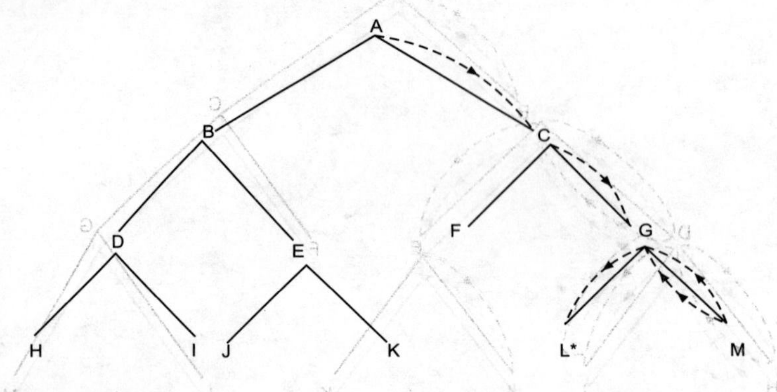

The path is given as A-C-G-M-G-L

Q.12. For the search tree given below, use

(*i*) Breadth-first search **(*ii*) Depth first search**

Goal is shown as

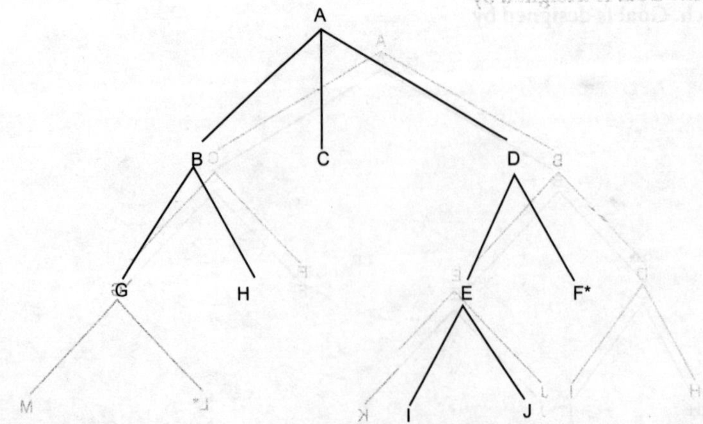

Ans. ***(i)* Breadth first search**

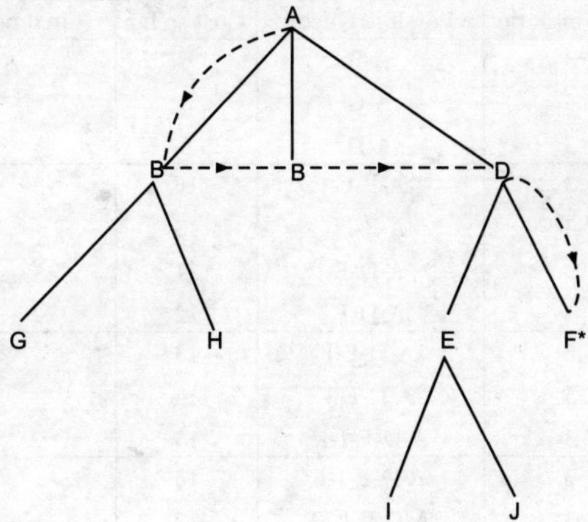

The path from A to F is
A-B-C-D-F

***(ii)* Depth first search**

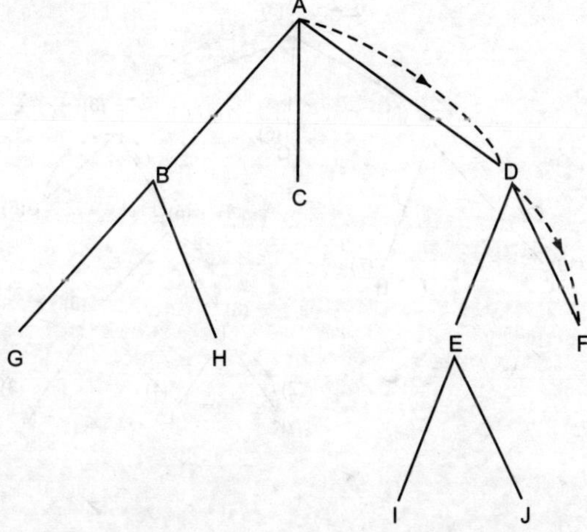

The path from A to F is A-D-F

Q.13. Using the search tree given below, list the elements of the queue just before next node is expanded. Use Best-first-Search where the number correspond to estimated cost-to- goal for each corresponding node.

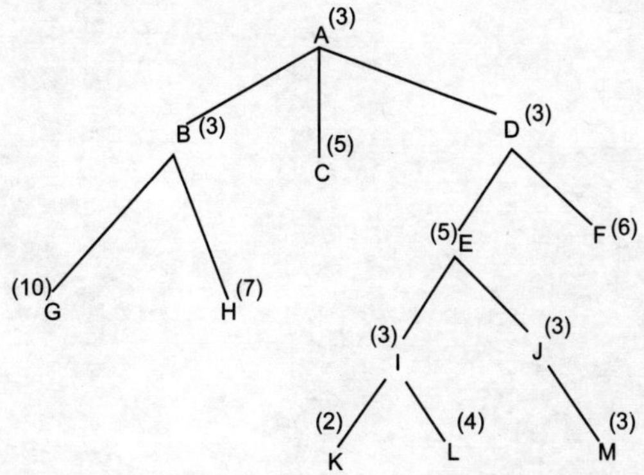

Ans. The following table be used to show best first search.

From node	To node	Cost of node	Possible Queue	Cost so far	Final best First queue
A	B	3	A-B	6	✓
	C	5	A-C	8	×
	D	3	A-D	6	✓
B	G	3	A-B-G	16	×
	H	3	A-B-H	13	×
D	E	3	A-D-E	11	✓
	F	3	A-D-F	12	×
E	I	5	A-D-E-I	13	✓
I	J	5	A-D-E-J	14	✓
	K	3	A-D-E-I-K	15	✓
J	L	3	A-D-E-I-L	18	×
	M	3	A-D-E-J-M	17	×
F	Next node Next Node	2	A-D-E-I-K	15	✓

The given path using Best-Search is : A-D-E-I-K- Next node.

The cost is given for the path is 15.

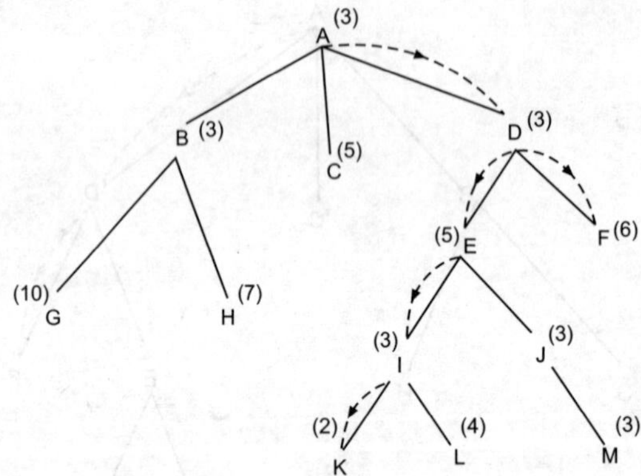

6 GAMES SOLVING (ADVERSARIAL SEARCH)

6.1. INTRODUCTION

Adversarial search technique is a mixture reasoning and creativity. Game playing is often called as an adversarial search. Successful game playing is generally deemed to require intelligence. Game playing is a search problem with the following components—

a. Initial state of the game.

b. Operators defining legal moves.

c. Successor function.

d. Terminal test (defines end-of-game state).

e. Goal test.

f. Path cost (or utility or pay-off function).

Game playing has been one of the most publicized area of AI research. With the success of Deep Blue (1997) another landmark was reached *i.e.* a computer program that could defeat the best chess player in the world. Game playing happens to be a good domain to explore machine intelligence because of two main reasons:

a. They provide a structured task in which it is very easy to measure success or failure.

b. They did not require large amount of knowledge. They are solvable by straight forward search from starting state to final (winning) state.

6.2 GAME PLAYING

To solve our game problems, we draw a game tree (or graphs) to show all possible game states. The nodes are linked by moves (arcs). The branches are labeled with the players who can make the choice between them. In a game tree, alternative layers will be controlled by different players.

Q.1. What is a game tree? Give an example.

Ans. A game tree is defined as an instance of a tree in which the root node represents the state before any moves have been made, the nodes in the tree represent possible states of the games (or positions) and arcs in the tree represent moves. We represent the moves on alternate levels of the game tree so that all edges leading from root node to the first level represent possible moves for the first player and edges from the first level to the second represent moves for the first player and edges from the first level to the second represent moves for the second player and so on. The leaf nodes in this tree represent final states (where the game has been won, lost or drawn). In simple games, a goal node might represent a state in which the computer has won but for complex games (like chess, GO etc.) the concept of a goal state is rarely of any use.

One method of playing a game might be for the computer to use a tree search algorithm such as dfs or bfs, searching for a goal state *i.e.* the final state of the game where the computer has won). But please note that this approach does not work because there is another intelligence involved in the game. We will consider this to be a rationally informed opponent who plays to win. Whether this opponent is human or another computer does not matter.

Iterative methods apply here because search space is too large for interesting games to search for a solution. Therefore, search will be done before each move in order to select the best move to be made.

Adversary methods apply here because an opponent who is trying to win, makes alternate moves, not controllable by you.

Evaluation function is used to evaluate the "goodness" of a configuration of the game. For a computer to use game-tree to make decisions about moves in a game of tic-tac-toe, it needs to use an evaluation function which enables it to decide whether a given position in the game is good or bad. If we use exhaustive search, then we only need a function that can recognize a win, a loss or a draw. Then the computer can treat "win" states as goal nodes and carry out search in normal way. **Also note that these evaluation functions are known as static evaluators because they are used to evaluate a game from just one static position.** Since the size of the game tree is very large, so it is almost never possible to search the game tree completely. In other words, the search will rarely reach a leaf node in the tree (at which the game is said to be either won, lost or drawn). This means that the software needs to be able to cutoff search and evaluate the position of the board at that node. Hence, an evaluation function is used to examine a particular position of the board. So, evaluation function must be efficient. This will not slow down the game play. To be effective, the evaluation function needs to give a higher score to a better position. For a chess game, this function will be very complex. These functions are usually weighted linear functions meaning that a number of different scores are determined for a given position and simply added together in a weighted fashion.

For *e.g.*, For a chess game, a very simple evaluation function might be—

"Count the number of queens, the number of pawns, the number of bishops and so one and add them up using weights to indicate the relative value of those pieces"

That is,

$$\text{Score} = 9q + 5r + 3b + 3n + p$$

where q-number of queens.

r-number of rooks.

n-number of knights.

b-number of bishops.

p-number of pawns.

If the two computer programs were to compete with each other at a game (say checkers) and that they had

— Same processing capabilities and speeds.

— Used same algorithms for examining the search tree,

Then the game would be decided by the quality of the program's evaluation functions. In general, the evaluation functions for game playing programs do not need to be perfect but need to give a good way of comparing two positions to determine which is better. But please understand that in complex games like chess, Nim, Othello, Checkers, Tic-Tac-Toe, Go etc. this is not an easy question as two grandmasters will sometimes differ on the evaluation of a position. One way to develop an accurate evaluation function is to actually play games from each position and see who wins. If the play is perfect on both the sides then this will give a good indication of what the evaluation of the starting position should be

For example, for Tic-Tac-Toe the evaluation function, $f(n)$ is as follows— $f(n)$ = [number of 3-lengths open for me] – [number of 3-lengths open for you] Where a 3-length is a complete row, column or diagonal.

Most evaluation functions are specified as a weighted sum of "features":

(W1* feature 1) (W2 *feature 2) + & + (Wn *feature n)

Like, in a chess game, some features evaluate piece placement on board and other features describe configurations of several pieces. The need today is to develop an evaluation function that is dynamic and is able to accurately evaluate positions it has never seen before.

Most of the games considered here are zero-sum games. It means that if the overall score at the end of a game for each player can be 1 (*a* win), 0 (*a* draw) or – 1 (*a* loss), then the total score for both players for any game must always be 0. This means that if one player wins, the other must lose. The only other alternative is that both players draw. That is why, we consider the search techniques that are discussed here to be adversarial methods because each player is not only trying to win but to cause the opponent to lose. In the algorithms like minimax and Alpha-Beta (discussed next), it is important that the computer can assume that the opponent is rational and adversarial. That is, the computer needs to assume that the opponent will play to win.

What is the Game theory and theorem proving?

1. J. Von Neumann is known as the Father of Game Theory (1928).
2. Game theory denotes the game of strategy.

3. Game theory allows decision-makers (players) to cope with other decision makers (players) who have different purposes in mind *i.e.*, players determine their own strategies in terms of strategies and goals of their opponent.
4. Game theory is a set of ideas and techniques for analyzing conflict situations between 2 or more parties. The outcomes are determined by their decisions. That is,

   Game theory = {ideas + techniques} → to analyze and conflict situations.

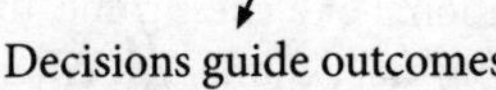

Decisions guide outcomes

5. Game theorem (in general)- "If a minimax of one player corresponds to a maximin of the other player, then that outcome is the best that both players can hope for." Therefore, game theory theorem is the mini-max theorem *i.e.*, players adopt those strategies that will maximize their gains while minimizing their losses.
6. **Minimax :** The least good of all good outcomes.

   Maximin : The least bad of all bad outcomes.

Applications of Game Theory

Von Neumann and Morgenstern indicated the utility of game theory by linking with economic behavior. The following are its applications: -

1. To solve conflicts based on maximization of profits (economics).
2. The n-person game theory is used in studying the distribution of power in legislative procedures.
3. Game theory may be used during immunization procedures and even on methods of testing a vaccine.
4. Game theory may be used to study conflicts of interest resolved through battles where the outcome is either victory or defeat.

Q.2. Give an example to simulate.

Ans. Minimax search procedure is a depth-first search procedure. When evaluating game trees, it is usual to assume that the computer is attempting to maximize some score that the opponent is trying to minimize. Normally, we would consider this score to be the result of the evaluation function for a given position, so we would usually have a high positive score means a good position for the computer, a score of 0 means a neutral position and a high negative score means a good position for the opponent.

Principle : The basic principle behind minimax is that a path through the tree is chosen by assuming that at its turn (a max node), the computer will choose the more that will give the highest eventual static evaluation and that at the human opponent's turn (a min node), he or she will choose the move that will give the lowest static evaluation.

The Minimax algorithm is used to choose good moves. It is assumed that a suitable static evaluation function is available, which is able to give an overall score to a given position. In applying Minimax, the static evaluator will only be used on leaf nodes. The values of the leaf nodes will be filtered up through the tree, to pick out the best path that the computer can achieve. This is done by assuming that the opponent will play rationally and will always play the move that is best for him or her and thus worst for the computer. So, the computer's aim is to maximize the lowest possible score that can be achieved.

As an example, consider a simple game tree. Fig. 6.1 shows how minimax works on it.

Please note that the best result that max can achieve is a score of 6. If max chooses the left branch as its first choice then min will choose the right branch, which leaves max a choice of 1 or 3. In this case, max will choose a score of 3. If max starts by choosing the right branch, min will have a choice between a path that leads to a score of 7 or a path that leads to a score of 6. Therefore, it will choose the left branch, leaving max a choice between 2 and 6. Fig. 6.1 shows how Minimax can use dfs to traverse the game tree. The arrows start from the rest node at the top and go down to the bottom of the left branch. This leads to a max node, which will get a score of 5. The value 5 is, hence, passed up to the parent of this max node. Following the right path

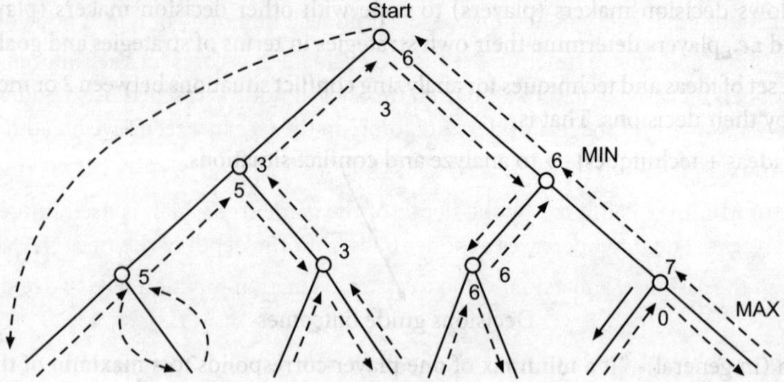

Fig. 6.1 A minimax Example

from this min node leads to another max node, this time getting a score of 3. Also note that the arrows show the order in which the nodes are examined by the algorithm and the values that are passed through the tree. This comes back up to the min node which now chooses the minimum of 3 and 5 and selects 3. Eventually, having traversed the whole tree, the best result for max comes back up to the root node (6).

Its algorithm is given first-

Step-1 : The start node is MAX (player1) node with current board configuration.

Step-2 : Expand nodes down to some depth of look-ahead in the game.

Step-3 : Apply evaluation function at each of the leaf nodes.

Step-4 : "Back -up" values for each non-leaf nodes until computed for root nodes.

Step-5 : At MIN nodes, the backed-up value is the minimum of values associated with its children.

Step-6 : At MAX nodes, the backed-up value is the max. of values associated with its children.

```
function MINIMAX (N) is'
begin
if N is a leaf- node then
    return the estimated score of this leaf
    else
        let N1, N2,….,Nm be the successors of N;
        if N is a MIN node then
            return min {MINIMAX(N1),….MINIMAX(Nm)}
        else
            return max {MINIMAX(N1),….MINIMAX(Nm)}
end MINIMAX
```

Let us write its pseudo-code now—

```
function minimax (current-node)
{
    if is-leaf (current-node)
        return static-evaluation (current-node);
    if is-min-node (current-node)
        return min (minimax (children-of (current-node)));
    if is-max-node (current-node)
        return max (minimax (children-of (current-node)));
    }
```

The else part is never required as every node must be a leaf node, a min node or a max node only.

We also observe that this is a recursive function because to evaluate the scores for the children of the current node, this algorithm must be applied recursively to those children until a leaf node is reached. Also understand that Minimax can be done non-recursively, starting at the leaf nodes and going up the tree in a recursive breadth first search.

Limitations of Minimax:

1. The effectiveness of Minimax is limited by the depth of the game tree which is itself limited by the time needed to construct and analyze it. The time increases exponentially with the depth of the tree.
2. A rapid tie between the assigned and actual value to static evaluation function fails to decide the expansion of game tree.

Q.3. What is horizon effect problem? Explain. Also give its solution.

Ans. Minimax algorithm is unsuitable for use in many games like chess where the game tree is very large. The problem is that in order to run Minimax, the entire game tree must be examined and for games like chess this is not possible due to the potential depth of the tree and the large branching factor. So, we use "bounded look ahead" principle here. The idea of bounded lookahead is that the search tree is only examined to a particular depth. All nodes at this depth are considered to be leaf nodes and are evaluated using a static evaluation function. This corresponds well to the way in which a human plays chess. Even the greatest grandmasters are not able to look forward to see every possible move that will occur in a game. Chess players look forward a few moves and good chess players may look forward a dozen or more moves. They are looking for a move that leads to a favorable position as they can find and are using their own static evaluator to determine which positions are the most favorable.

Let us write its pseudocode now (i.e. Minimax with bounded lookahead)—

```
function bounded_minimax (current_node, max_depth)
  {
      if is_leaf (current node)
        return static-evaluation (current-node);
      if (depth-of (current-node) = = max-depth)
        return static-evaluation (current-node);
      if (is-min-node (current-node))
        return min (minmax (children-of (current-node)));
  }
```

Actually, it is not reasonable to apply a fixed cut-off point for search. A bounded cut-off at a particular node can leave any one of the opponents in a problem. One way of avoiding this problem is to cut-off search at positions that are deemed to be quiescent. Please note that a quiescent position is one where the next move is unlikely to cause a large change in the relative positions of the two players. Also note that a position where a piece of chess can be captured without a corresponding recapture is not quiescent.

This bounded Minimax Search has another problem—the **horizon effect**, coined by Berliner in 1977.

Horizon Effect : This problem involves an extremely long sequence of moves that clearly lead to a strong advantage for one player, but where the sequence of moves, although potentially obvious to a human player, takes more moves than is allowed by the bounded search. Hence, the significant end of the sequence has been pushed over the horizon. This problem occurs in a checkers playing program named as Chinook.

What is the solution?

There is no universal solution to the horizon problem but one method to minimize its effect is to always search a few ply deeper when a position is found that appears to be particularly good. The singular-extension heuristic is defined as follows:

"If a static evaluation of a move is much better than that of other moves being evaluated, continue searching."

It is possible for the nodes or positions to have same heuristic scores. This means that they lie on a plateau as in case of hill climbing. They tell nothing about the movement of the game. The better estimate of the score for each position is obtained beyond plateau. This is a horizon effect.

In 1975, Donald Knuth and R.W. Moore introduced a negmax procedure which uses the same function (as used in minimax function) to evaluate each node in backing up from the successor nodes. Say, the evaluation function for the jth terminal node in a complete tree is as follows—

$$\left.\begin{array}{ll} f_i = -1 & \text{(For loss)} \\ f_j = 0 & \text{(for draw)} \\ f_j = +1 & \text{(for win)} \end{array}\right\}$$

Then, the negmax evaluation function $F(j)$ is given by

$$F(j) = f_j \text{ for terminal nodes}$$

$$F(j) = \text{MAX}\{-F_{(i1)}, -F_{(i2)}, \ldots -F_{(in)}\}$$

for successor states i_1 to in.

This formalism states that the best move for either player is that which maximizes $F(j)$. By simply selecting the move which maximizes the negative of the successor position's evaluation function, the negmax formation implements the minimax heuristic.

Q.4. What is Alpha-beta cutoff (Pruning)? Illustrate with an example.

Ans. The basic idea of alpha-beta cutoffs is-"It is possible to compute the correct minimax decision without looking at every node in the search tree." This is called as **pruning**. It allows us to ignore portions of the search tree that makes no difference in the final choice.

General principle of alpha-beta pruning is-

- Consider a node, n somewhere in the tree, such that a player has a chance to move to this node.
- If a player has a better chance, m either at the parent node of '*n*' (or at any choice point further up) then '*n*' will never be reached in the actual play.

When we are doing search with alpha-beta cut-offs, if a node's value is high, the minimizer will make sure it's never reached (by turning off the path to get a lower value). Conversely, if a node's value is too low, the maximizer will make sure it's never reached. This gives us the following definitions: -

- **Alpha:** The highest value that the maximizer can guarantee himself by making some move at the current node or at some node earlier on the path to this node.
- **Beta:** The lowest value that the minimizer can guarantee by making some move at the current node or at some node earlier on the path to the node.

Please note here that the maximizer is constantly trying to push the alpha value up by finding better moves, the minimizer is trying to push the beta value down. If a node value is between alpha and beta, then the players might reach it. At the beginning, at the root of the tree, we don't have any guarantees yet about what values do maximizer and minimizer can achieve. So, we set beta to ∞ and alpha to -∞. Then as we move down the tree, each node starts with beta and alpha values passed down from its parent.

Consider a scenario in which the MIN- children of a MAX-node have been partially inspected.

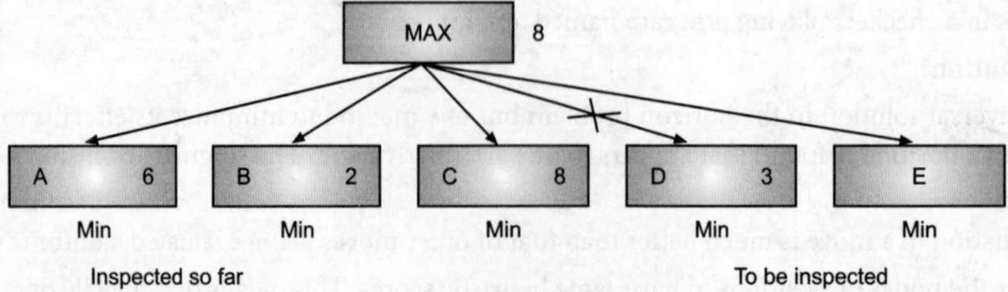

Fig. 6.3: Alpha-beta for a max node

At this point, the tentative value which is backed up so far of F is 8. MAX is not interested in any move which has a value of less than 8, since it is already known that 8 is the worst that MAX can do, so far. Thus, node D and all of its descendants can be pruned or excluded from further exploration, since MIN will certainly go for a value of 3 rather than 8. Similarly, for a MIN-node: -

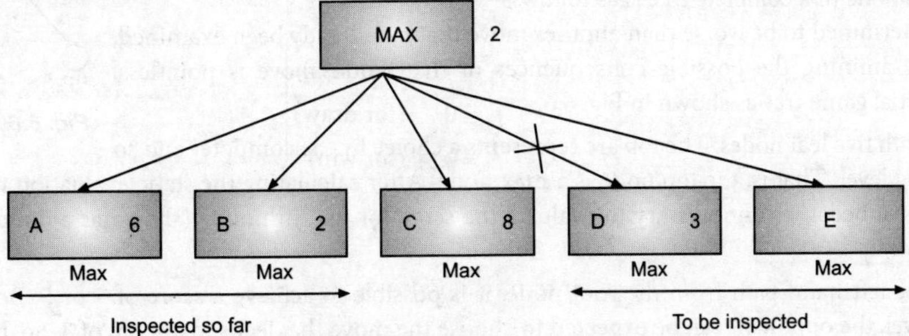

Fig.6.4: *Alpha-beta for a min node*

MIN is trying to minimize the game-value. So far, the value 2 is the best available from MIN's point of view. MIN will immediately reject node D, which can be stopped from further expansion/ exploration.

In a game tree, each node represents a board position where one of the players gets to choose a mode. For example, in fig. below, look at node C. As soon as we look at its left child, we realize that if the players reach node C, the minimizer can limit the utility to 2. But the maximizer can get utility 6 by going to node B instead, so he would never let the game reach C. therefore, we don't even have to look at C's other children.

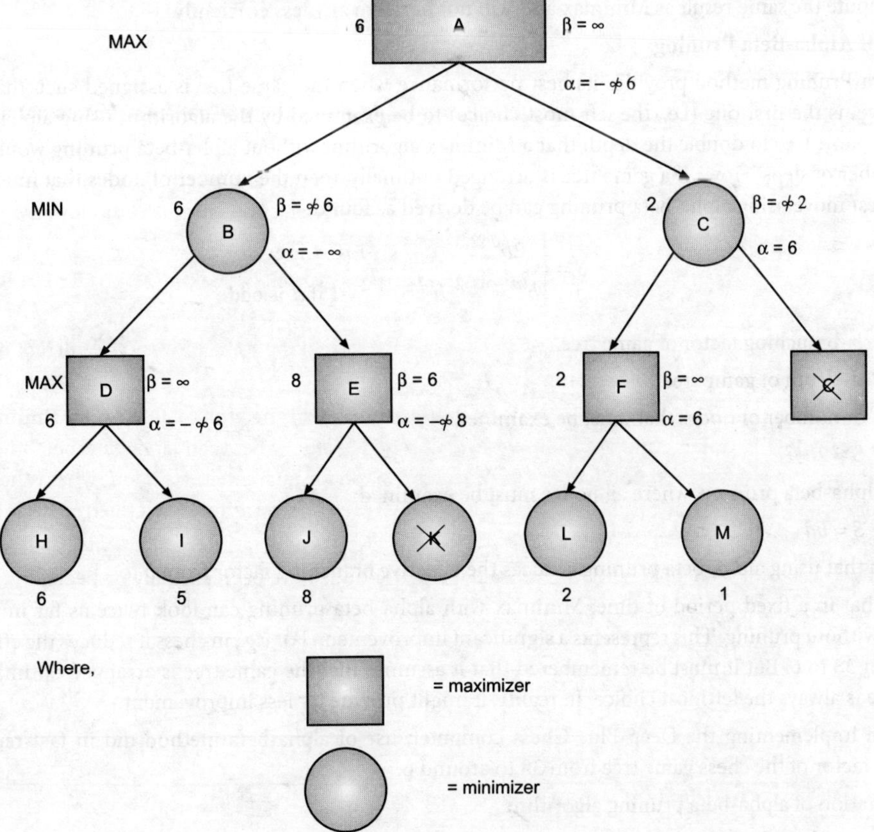

Fig.6.5: *Tree with alpha-beta cut-offs*

Bounded lookahead makes our game tree smaller to examine. In some cases, it is extremely useful to be able to prune (cut) sections of the game tree. It is possible to remove sections of the game tree that are not worth examining, to make searching for a good move more efficient.

If a move is determined to be worse than another move that has already been examined, then further examining the possible consequences of that worse move is pointless. Consider a partial game tree as shown in Fig. 6.6.

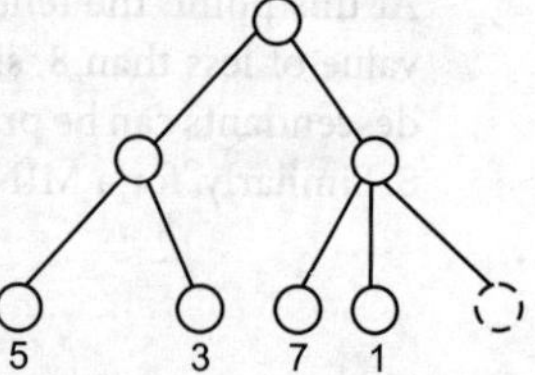

***Fig. 6.6** A Partial Game Tree*

This is a tree with five leaf nodes. The top arc represents a choice by the computer and so is a maximizing level. That is, the top node is a max node. After calculating the static evaluation function for the first four leaf nodes, it becomes unnecessary to evaluate the score for the fifth node (shown as a dotted circle). Let us see why?

In choosing the left-hand path from the root node, it is possible to achieve a score of 3 or 5. Because this level is a minimizing level, the opponent can be expected to choose the move that leads to a score of 3. So, by choosing the left-hand arc from the root node, the computer can achieve a score of 3. By choosing the right-hand arc, the computer can achieve a score of 7 or 1 or a mystery value. Because the opponent is aiming to minimize the score, he or she could choose the position with a score of 1, which is worse than the value the computer could achieve by choosing the left-hand path. So, the value of the right most left node doesn't matter. The computer must not choose the right-hand arc because it definitely leads to a score of at best 1, assuming the opponent does not irrationally choose the 7 option.

In this example, alpha-beta pruning removes only one leaf node from the tree. But in larger game trees, it can result in a valuable reduction in tree size. In 1993, Winston showed that it will not necessarily remove large positions of a game tree. But in fact, in worst case, alpha-beta pruning will not prune any searches from the game tree but even in this case it will compute the same result as Minimax and will not perform any less efficiently.

Analysis of Alpha-Beta Pruning

Alpha-Beta Pruning method provides its best performance when the game tree is assigned such that the best choice at each level is the first one (i.e., the left most choice) to be examined by the algorithm using alpha-beta cut-off will examine a game tree to double the depth that a Minimax algorithm without alpha-beta pruning would examine in the same number of steps. How? If a game tree is arranged optimally, then the number of nodes that must be examined to find the best move using alpha-beta pruning can be derived as found—

$$S = \begin{cases} 2b^{d/2} & 1 \text{ if } d \text{ is even.} \\ b^{(d-1)/2}\, b^{(d-1)/2} & -1 \text{ if } d \text{ is odd.} \end{cases}$$

where b–branching factor of game tree.

d–depth of game tree

S–number of nodes that must be examined.

$\therefore$ $S \approx 2b^{d/2}$

Without alpha-beta pruning, where all nodes must be examined:

$S = bd$

$\therefore$ We find that using alpha-beta pruning reduces the effective branching factor from b to

meaning that in a fixed period of time, Minimax with alpha-beta pruning can look twice as far in the game tree as Minimax without pruning. This represents a significant improvement. For *e.g.*, in chess it reduces the effective branching factor from 38 to 6. But it must be remembered that it assumes that the game tree is arranged optimally such that the best choice is always the leftmost choice. In reality, it might provide far less improvement.

For *e.g.*, In implementing the Deep Blue Chess computer, use of alpha-beta method did in fact reduce the average branching factor of the chess game tree from 38 to around 6.

Implementation of alpha-beta pruning algorithm.

Let us write its algorithm first—

S1: The game tree is traversed in depth-first order. At each non-leaf node, a value is stored.

For max nodes, this value is called alpha and for min nodes the value is beta.

S2 : An alpha value is the maximum (best) value found so far in the max node's descendants.

S3 : A beta value is the minimum (best) value found so far in the min node's descendants.

We write the function alpha-beta now. function alpha-beta (current-node)

```
{
    if is-leaf (current-node)
        return static-evaluation (current-node)
    if is-max-node (current-node) and
        alpha-value of (current-node)>=
        beta-value-of (min-ancestor-of (current-node)
        then cut-off-search-below (current-node);
    if is-min-node (current-node) and
        beta-value-of (current-node) <=
        alpha-value-of (max-ancestor-of (current-node) then
        cut-off-search-below (current-node);
}
```

Instead of searching back up the tree for ancestor values, we propagate values down the tree as follows:

a. For each max node, the minimum beta value for all its min node ancestors is stored as beta.

b. For each min node, the maximum alpha value for all its max node ancestors is stored as alpha.

c. Hence, each non-leaf node will have a beta value and an alpha value stored.

d. Initially, the root node is assigned an alpha value of negative infinity and a beta value of infinity.

The above alpha beta function can be modified also wherein we use another variable, say 'children' to represent all of the children of the current node. We add the following statement now—

alpha = max (alpha, alpha-beta (children, alpha, beta))

If means that alpha is set to the greatest of the current value of alpha and the values of the current node's children are calculated by recursively calling alpha-beta ( ).

```
// Modified alpha-beta function using
// recursion.
function alpha-beta (current-node, alpha, beta)
{
  if is-root-node (current-node)
  {
    alpha = - infinity
    beta = infinity
  }
if is_leaf (current_node)
    return static_evaluation (current_node);
    if is_max_node (current_node)
    {
    alpha = max(alpha, alpha-beta (children, alpha, beta));
    If alpha >= beta
```

```
        cut_off_search_below (current_node);
      }
   if is_min_node (current_node)
      {
     beta = min (beta, alpha_beta (children, alpha, beta));
       if beta <=alpha
        cut-off-search-below (current_node);
      }
   }
```

We are in a position to solve an example now.

Example. For the given game tree, apply alpha-beta pruning procedure—

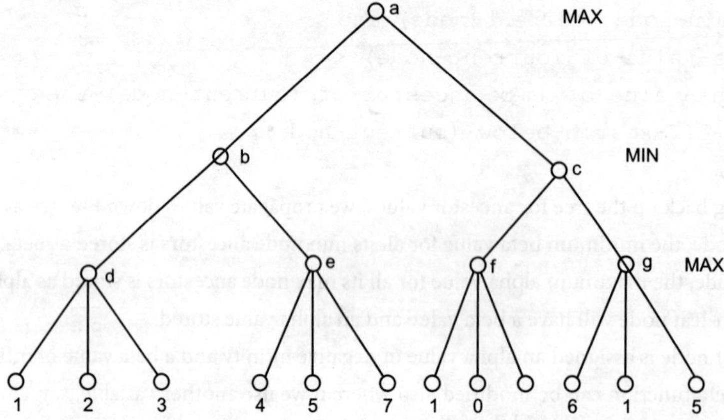

Solution : If it is my turn to move then the root is labeled as "MAX" node indicating it is my turn otherwise if is labeled as "MIN" node to indicate it is my opponent's turn. Here, we assume that the static evaluation function returns large values to indicate good situations for us. So, our goal is to maximize the value of the static evaluation function of the next board position. Please note that acrs represent the possible legal moves for the player that the arcs emanate from. Because moves alternate so each level of the tree has nodes that are all MAX or all MIN. Also note that the nodes at level i are of the opposite kind from those at level $(i + 1)$.

With these assumptions, let us try to solve this problem now.

The non-terminal (or non-leaf) nodes in the tree are labeled from a to g. Terminal (or leaf nodes) nodes have scores assigned to them by static evaluation i.e.,

a is MAX node (*i.e.*, my turn)

b and c are MIN nodes (i.e., opponent's turn)

d, *e*, *f* and *g* are MAX nodes (*i.e.*, my turn)

Now, we follow the tree by depth-first search. The first-step is to follow the path a, b, d, and then to the three children of d i.e.,

Path 1 : $a \rightarrow b \rightarrow d \rightarrow (1 \rightarrow 2 \rightarrow 3)$

This gives an alpha value for '*d*' as 3. This is passed up to '*b*' which now has the beta value of 3 and an alpha valu e that has been passed down from '*a*' of negative infinity.

Now, the first child of '*e*' is examined and has score of 4. In this case, clearly, there is no need to examine the other children of '*e*' because the minimizing choice at node '*b*' will definitely do worse by choosing '*e*' rather than '*d*' so, cutoff is applied here and nodes with score of 5 and 7 are never examined. Let us show this in a tabular form now.

S.No.	Node	Alpha	Beta	Meaning
1.	a	–∞	∞	Alpha starts at – ∞ Beta starts at ∞
2.	b	–∞	∞	
3.	d	–∞	∞	
4.	d	1	∞	
5.	d	2	∞	
6.	d	3	∞	Upto this point, we have examined the three children of *d.* We get an alpha value of 3, which is passed back upto node b.
7.	b	– ∞	3	At this MIN node, we get a score of 3 or better (lower). Now we need to examine the children of '*e*' to see if we can geta lower score.
8.	e	– ∞	3	
9.	e	4	3	A score of 4 can be obtained from the first child of '*e*'. MIN will do better if chosen rather than 'e' because if he chooses 'e' max can get atleast 4, which is worse for min than 3. Hence, we can ignore of ther children of '*e*'. A CUT-OFF occurs.
10.	a	3	∞	The value of 3 has been passed back up to the root node. Hence, MAX now knows that he can score atleast 3. He now needs to see if he can do better.
11.	c	3	∞	
12.	f	3	∞	We now examine the three children of f and find that none of them is better than 3. So, we pass back a value of 3 to c.
13.	c	3	3	MAX has already found that by taking the left hand branch, he can achieve a score of 3. Now it seems that if he chooses the right-hand branch, MIN can choose 'f' which means he can only achieve a score of 2. So, cut-off can now occur because there is no need to examine it or its children.

Result : Thus, out of 12 leaf nodes in the tree, this algorithm needed to examine only 7 to conclude that the best move for MAX is '*b*', so MIN will choose '*d*' and MAX will choose the right- hand node, ending with a static evaluation of 3. Please note that at this stage, this is the right answer because if MAX chooses '*c*' then MIN will clearly choose f, resulting in MAX being able to achieve a score of only 2.

∴ Optimized game tree (using our algorithm) is as shown in Fig.

Herein, the minimax algorithm with alpha—beta cut-off will need to examine only five of the eight leaf nodes.

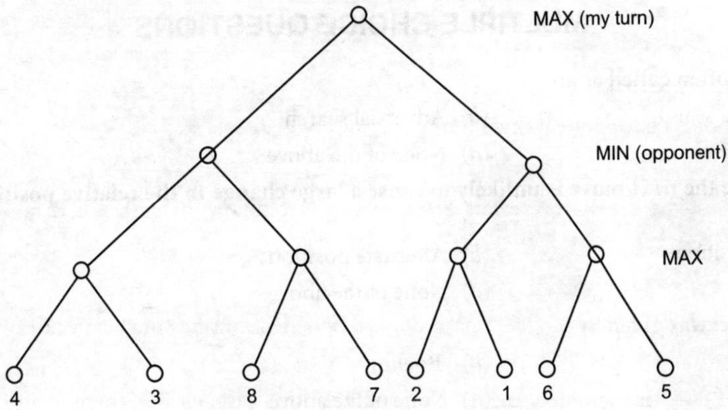

Q.5. Explain futility cut-off. Give an example to explain.

Ans. The Alpha-Beta procedure discussed above can also be used to cutoff additional paths that provide only slight improvements over paths which have already been explored.

For *e.g.*: Consider a Minimax tree below—

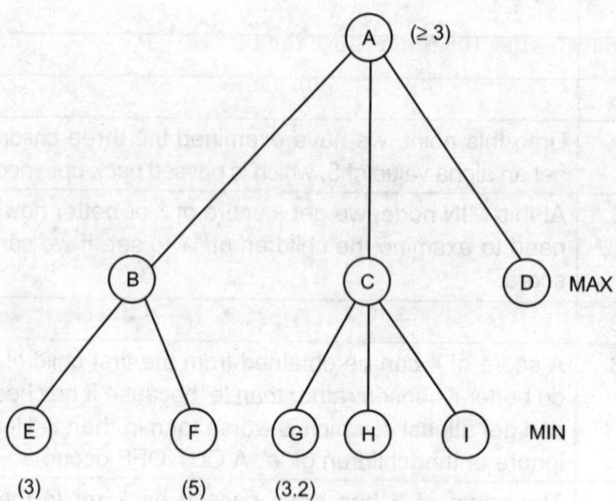

Fig. 6.7 : Shows Futility Cutoff

After examining node G, we can say that if the move is along C, the value of static evaluation function is 3.2 but the move towards B has a guaranteed score of 3. Because 3.2 is just slightly better than 3 (in the scale of 0-10), we should terminate exploration of C. Thus, we can devote more time in exploring other parts of the tree which could be more useful. This limit of the static evaluation function is called as **futility cutoff limit**. It helps in terminating the exploration of a subtree which offers little possibility for improvement over other known paths.

SUMMARY

Minimax Search procedure is a depth-first, depth limited search procedure. We start at the current position and use the plausible move generator to generate the set of possible successor positions. We can apply the static evaluation function to those positions and simply choose the best one. After doing so we can back that value upto the starting position to represent our evaluation of it. Root node represents the configuration of the board at which a decision must be made as to what is the best single move to make next. We assume that the static evaluation function returns large values to indicate good situations for us. So, our goal is to maximize the value of the static evaluation function of the next board position. This process of backing up values gives the optimal strategy that both players would follow given that they both have the information computed at the leaf nodes by the evaluation function.

MULTIPLE CHOICE QUESTIONS

1. **Game playing is often called as an**
   (*a*) Non-adversial search
   (*b*) Adversial search
   (*c*) Sequential search
   (*d*) None of the above.
2. **A position where the next move is unlikely to cause a large change in the relative positions of the two players is known as**
   (*a*) Quiescent position
   (*b*) Alternate position
   (*c*) Move
   (*d*) None of the above.
3. **The horizon effect was given by**
   (*a*) Berliner
   (*b*) Boehm
   (*c*) Jacobson
   (*d*) None of the above.

4. **Most evaluation functions are specified as a weighted sum of features given by the formula**
   (*a*) (W1*feat1) * (W2*feat2) *…* (Wn*featn)
   (*b*) (W1+feat1) * (W2*feat2) *…* (Wn*featn)
   (*c*) (W1*feat1) * (W2*feat2) *…* (Wn*featn)
   (*d*) None of the above.
5. **When we say that if one player wins, the other loose then it is a**
   (*a*) Zero-sum game (*b*) Two-sum game
   (*c*) Four-sum game (*d*) Eight sum game.

ANSWERS

1. (*b*) **2.** (*a*) **3.** (*a*) **4.** (*c*) **5.** (*a*)

CONCEPTUAL SHORT QUESTIONS WITH ANSWERS

Q.1. MIN/MAX strategy uses two rules. What are they?

Ans. Two rules that are used in MIN/MAX strategy are as follows—

1. For maximizer, if static evaluation function value found at any node is less than the α-value, reject it.
2. For minimizer, if static evaluation function value found at any node is more than α-value, reject it.

Q. 2. What is plausible move generator?

Ans. These are certain moves that are unproductive (or dangerous) because they obviously lead away from engagement or to an immediate loss of a piece with no hope of trapping the after player. These moves are avoided by the substitution of a plausible move generator in place of the legal move generator. The plausible move generator is equivalent to a beam search in which only a limited number of promising nodes are expanded.

For *e.g.* In a chess game, the average branching from a node in chess could be cut from 30 to 10 by means of a plausible move generator.

Q. 3. What is an agent? How is it related to architecture and program? How agent should act? Name some agent types and their goals and environment descriptions.

Ans. An agent is anything that can be viewed as perceiving its environment through sensors and acting upon that environment through effectors.

For *e.g.*

(*a*) A human agent has eyes, ears, etc for sensors and hands, legs, mouth, etc. for effectors.
(*b*) A robotic agent subsitutes cameras and infrared range finders for sensors and various motors for effectors.
(*c*) A software agent has encoded bit strings as it percepts.

AI designs an agent program *i.e.*, a function that implements the agent mapping from percepts to actions. This program will work on some sort of architecture—which might be a plain computer. In general, the architecture makes the percepts from the sensors available to the program, runs the program and feeds the program's action choices to the effectors as they are generated. The relationship among agents, architectures and programs is—

Agent = Architecture = Program

A rational agent is one that does the right thing. The right action is one that will cause the agent to be most successful. That leaves us with the problem of deciding 'how' and 'when' to evaluate the agent's success.

The term 'performance measure' is used for how the criteria that determine how successful an agent is?

An omniscient agent knows the actual outcome of its actions and can act accordingly but omniscience is impossible in reality.

An ideal rational agent is one which, for each possible percept sequence, should do whatever action is expected to maximize its performance measures on the basis of the evidence provided by the percept sequence and whatever inbuilt knowledge the agent has.

For example, Software robots (or softbots) is a software agent.

We list some agents, their percepts, actions, goals and their environment descriptions–

Agent Type	Percepts	Action	Goals	Environment
1. Refinery pressure	Temperature, pressure, readings	Open/close valves, adjust temperatures	Maximize purity	Refinery
2. Medical diagnosis system	Symptoms, findings, patient's answers	Questions, tests, treatments	Healthy Patients, minimize costs	Patient, hospital

Q. 4. Explain the following statement— "Exhaustive searching of game trees is not possible."

Ans. Exhaustive searching on game trees is not possible because trees have very high branching factors and often will be very deep.

For *E.g.*1, a game tree of a chess game has an average branching factor of 38. A tree can have an infinite depth.

E.g., 2, a tic-tac-toe game has maximum depth of 9 and a maximum branching factor of 9 meaning that it has nearly 9 × 8 × 7 × ...× 2 × nodes in the tree *i.e.*, more than 350,000 nodes to examine.

Q. 5. Explain the alpha-beta cutoffs in the fig. given below-

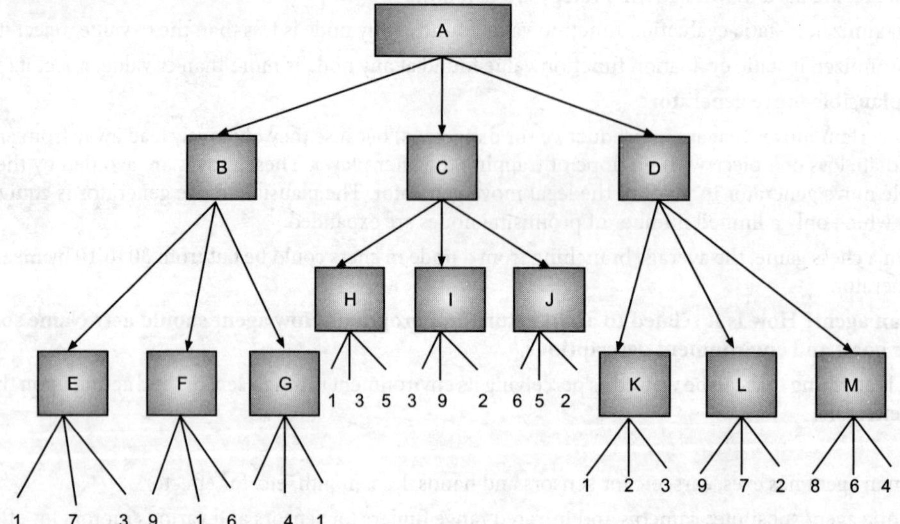

Solution : According to the depth first search, we move onto *E* (unexpanded node) and the maximum value (8) among the successors is selected. (Maximizing ply).

Beta is set to 8 for node *B*.

Now we back-track to *B* and then move to *F*. The value of the leftmost successor of *F* is tentatively assigned to *F*. since it is a maximizing ply, so *F* will have a value 9 or greater than 9 which is more than the Beta value of *B*, so we terminate the search at the maximizing ply.

Now we back-trace to *B* and then move to *G*. The value of the leftmost successor of *G* is tentatively assigned to *F*. since it is a maximizing ply, so *G* will have a value 2 or greater than 2 which is less than the Beta value of *B*. So, we further explore *G* and choose maximum of 3 values (2, 4, 1) and assign it to G (Maximizing ply).

8 [E] 9[F] 4[G]

Choose the minimum of these 3 values (8, 9, 4) as the ply is minimizing.

Alpha is set to 4 for node A.

4[B]

Now we back track to *A* and them move from *C* to *H* (unexpanded node) and the maximum value (5) among the successors is selected (Maximizing ply). Since 5 > Alpha, so we will explore *I*.

Beta of *C* = 5.

Examine leftmost successor of *I*, since it (3) is less than Beta (5), so we examine next successor of *I*.

The value (9) > Beta so terminate the search at the maximizing ply.

9[I]

Now we back track to C and then move to *J*. examine the leftmost value of *J*. Since the value (6) > Beta (5), we terminate the search at the maximizing level.

5[H] 9[I] 6[J]

Choose the minimum of these 3 values (5, 9, 6) as the ply is minimizing.

Alpha is set to 5 for node A.

4[C]

Now we backtrack to *A* and then move from *K* to *K* (unexpanded node) and the maximum value (3) among the successors is selected (maximizing ply).

Tentatively set the value of *D* to be 3. Since 3 < Alpha, so we terminate the search at the minimizing ply.

5[A]

4[B] 5[C] 3[D].

EXERCISE QUESTIONS

1. Explain why and how AI methods are suitable for game playing. Are there any limitations?
2. Explain Minimax search with reference to game playing.
3. Write short notes on - minimax search procedure.
4. Why game playing problems are considered as AI problems?
5. Explain the Mini-Max with α, β cut offs game playing strategy.
6. (*a*) What is a state space search? Give any example of a Game which happens to be a problem of state space search and justify your answer properly.

   (*b*) Perform minimax on the following tree—

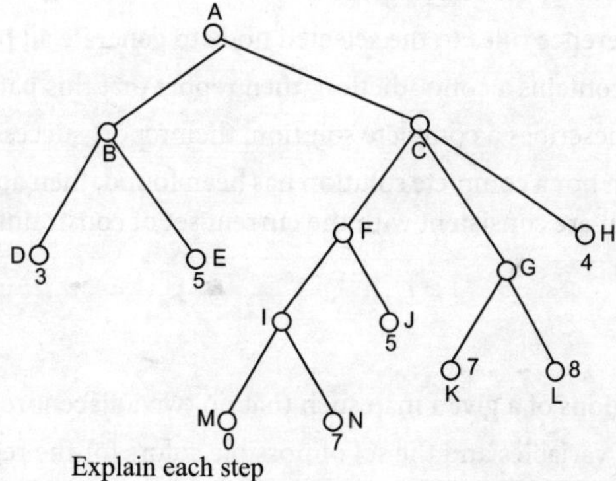

Explain each step

7 Constraint Satisfaction Problems

7.1. INTRODUCTION

Constraint Satisfaction Problem (CSP) follows a hit and trial procedure to solve the cryptarithmetic problem. The procedure always generates an optimal solution. The aim is to assign each alphabet with a different digit (0 to 9) and make sure no two alphabets have same digit such that after adding them, the result is same as generated using alphabets. CSP are the problems whose states and goal test conform to a standard, structured and very simple representation. Search algorithm can be defined that take advantage of the structure of states and can use general-purpose rather than problem-specific heuristics to enable the solution of large problems.

CSP has various states and goal test, a traditional problem has been converted into standard structured and very simple representation. The general purpose routines can be used to access a special representation which has more benefit than problem-specific heuristics. These routines combined with special structure can find solution of large problems. The structure of the problem is represented in a different form such as standard representation of the goal test. Also note that the revealed structure is very efficient in several ways- problem decomposition and to understand problem structure and the difficulty of solving it and their correction. If a problem is observed as a CSP then we have many advantages too. As the representation of states have standard pattern i.e., a set of variables with assigned values, so we can design successor function and goal test in a more generic way that will apply to all CSPs. We can design better generic heuristic that require no additional domain specific expertise. The structure of the constraint graph can be used to simplify the solution process, in some cases giving exponential reduction in complexity.

Q.1. What is constraint satisfaction?

Ans. In the real-world, we work in different environments, each of which has some constraints. Our solution should be such that all such constraints are satisfied. We use extensive domain specific and heuristic knowledge. For example, design problems in manufacturing, optimal tour problems and so on. Even crypta-arithmetic problems are typical constraint satisfaction problems. The term relaxation algorithm is also used for constraints satisfaction. Waltz algorithm for labeling line drawings in a picture and natural language understanding are good examples of constraint satisfaction algorithm in a modified form. Let us see the algorithm now.

1. **Until a complete solution is found or until all path have led to dead ends, do:**
   a. Select an unexpanded node of the search graph.
   b. Apply the constraint inference rules to the selected node to generate all possible new constraints.
   c. If the set of constraints contains a contradiction, then report that this path is a dead-end.
   d. If the set of constraints describes a complete solution, then report success.
   e. If neither a contradiction nor a complete solution has been found, then apply the problem space rules to generate new partial solutions that are consistent with the current set of constraints. Insert these partial solutions into the search graph.

Some examples of CSP

I. Map Coloring Problem

The problem is to color the regions of a given map such that no two adjacent regions have the same color.

The regions in the map are the variables and the set of possible colors for the regions is the domain.

The constraint is that- "No two adjacent regions should have the same color".

Formal representation of Map coloring Problem

1. **Variables :** {N, NW, NE, M, MW, ME, S, SE}.
2. **Domains :** D = {red, green, blue}.
3. **Constraints :** Adjacent regions must have different colors.

For *e.g.* N ≠ NW.

Notes:

1. Typically, such a problem has many solutions.
2. We sometimes represent map coloring as a graph coloring (constraint graph) problem.
3. The topology of a constraint graph can sometimes be used to identify solutions easily.

Some more examples of CSP includes: -

- ☐ N-queens problem.
- ☐ Scene labelling.
- ☐ Map coloring problem.
- ☐ Boolean satisfiability.
- ☐ Transportation scheduling.
- ☐ Spreadsheets.
- ☐ Floor planning.
- ☐ Job scheduling problem.
- ☐ Circuit board layout.
- ☐ Sudoku.
- ☐ Assignment problems.
- ☐ Hardware configuration.
- ☐ Factory scheduling.

Incremental formulation of CSP

CSP can be given an incremental formulation as a standard search problem as follows:

1. **Initial State :** The empty assignment {} in which all variables are unassigned.
2. **Successor Functions :** A value can be assigned to any unassigned variable, provided that it does not conflict with previously assigned variables.
3. **Goal Test :** The current assignment is complete.
4. **Path Cost :** A constant cost for every step.

Searching for a goal state in CSP : The following points may be kept in mind for searching a goal state in CSP-

1. Every solution must be a complete assignment and therefore appears at depth, *n* if there are n-variables.
2. The search tree extends only to depth *n*.
3. DFS algorithms are best for CSPs.
4. The path by which a solution is reached is irrelevant.
5. We can also use a complete-state formulation, in which every state is a complete assignment that might or might not satisfy the constraints.
6. Local search methods work well for this formulation.

Some variations in CSPs

1. The simplest kind of CSP involves variables that are discrete and have finite domains. Graph-coloring problems are of this kind. The 8-queens problem described above can also be viewed as finite-domain CSP, where the variables Q_1 ,……., Q_8 are the positions of each queue in columns 1,…8 and each variable has the domain {1, 2, 3, 4, 5, 6, 7, 8}. If the maximum domain size of any variable is a CSP in d, then the number of possible complete assignments are O (d^n), that is, exponential in the number of variables.
2. Finite-domain CSPs include Boolean CSPs, whose variables can be either true or false. Boolean CSPs include, as special cases, some NP-complete problems like 3SAT.
3. Practically speaking, general-purpose CSP algorithms can solve problems of order of magnitude larger than those solvable via the general-purpose search algorithms that we saw.
4. Discrete variables can also have infinite domains like the set of integers or a set of strings.
5. CSPs with continuous domains are very common in the real world nd are widely studied in the field of OR (Operations Research).

For instance, the scheduling of experiments on the Hubble Space Telescope requires very precise timings of observations. The start and finish of each observation are continuous-valued variables that must obey a variety of astronomical, precedence and power constraints. Also note that the best -known category of continuous-domain CSPs is that of linear programming problems where constraints must be linear equations.

Properties of Constraints :

1. Constraints may specify partial information; constraint need not uniquely specify the value of its variables.
2. Constraints are non-directional, typically a constraint on say, two variables V_1 and V_2 can be used to infer a constraint on V_1 given a constraint on V_2 and vice versa.
3. Constraints are declarative *i.e.*; they specify what relationship must hold without specifying a computational procedure to enforce relationship.
4. Constraints are additive *i.e.*, the order of imposition of constraints does not matter. All that matters at the end is that the conjunction of constraints is in effect.
5. Constraints are really independent, typically constraints in the constraint store (collection of constraints) share variables.

Type of constraints in CSPs

There are three types of constraints in CSPs: -

1. Unary constraints.
2. Binary constraints.
3. Higher-order constraints.

Unary constraints are the constraints that restricts the value of a single variable. Every unary constraint can be eliminated simply by prepressing the domain of the corresponding variable to remove any value that violates the constraint. For example, constraints can be that vertex-A can not be colored with blue color.

Binary constraints relate two variables. A binary CSP is one with only binary constraints. It can be represented as a constant graph. For example, in graph-coloring problem two adjacent vertices can not have the same color.

Higher-order constraints involve three or more variables. For example, cryptarithmetic puzzles. It tells that each letter in a cryptarithmetic puzzle represent a different digit. Higher-order constraints can be represented in a constraint hypergraph.

To see how this algorithm works, consider the following problem.

Problem SEND (cryptarithematic problem)

+MORE

MONEY

Constraints

1. Values are to be assigned to letters from 0 to 9 only.
2. No two letters should have the same value.
3. If the same letter occurs more than once, it must be assigned the same digit each time.
4. The sum of the digits must be as shown in the problem.

Here, each decimal digit is to be assigned to each of the letters in such a way that the answer to the problem is correct. If the same letter occurs more than once then it must be assigned the same digit each time. No two different letters may be assigned the same digit. The puzzle SEND + MORE = MONEY, after solving, will appear like this-

```
  S E N D
  9 5 6 7
  M O R E
  1 0 8 5
---------
M O N E Y
1 0 6 5 2
```

State the production rules and heuristics for crypt-arithmetic problem.

Solution : Heuristic and production rules are specific to this problem and are as follows: -

Rule-1 : If the sum of two 'n' digit operands yields 'n+1' digit result, then the 'n+1'th digit has to be one.

Rule-2 : Sum of two digits may or may not generate carry.

Rule-3 : Whatever might be the operands, the carry can be either 0 or 1.

Rule-4 : No two distinct alphabets can have same numeric code.

Rule-5 : Whenever more than one solution appears to be existing, the choice is governed by the fact that no two alphabets can have same number code.

Production Rules :

1. $x + y = yz$

   $\rightarrow y = 1, z = 0, x = 9$

2. $ax + 0y = cz$

   $\rightarrow c = a + 1, x + y = z + 10$

3. $y = x + 1, y + z = x + 10$

   $\rightarrow \quad z = 8$ or 9 and prev_carry = 1

4. $x + y = z + 10$

   $\rightarrow (x, y) = (8, 9) \mid (7, 9) \mid (6, 9) \mid (5, 9) \mid$
   $(4, 9) \mid (3, 9) \mid (2, 9) \mid (1, 9) \mid$
   $(7, 8) \mid (6, 8) \mid (5, 8) \mid (4, 8) \mid$
   $(3,8) \mid (2,8) \mid (6, 7) \mid (5, 7) \mid$
   $(4, 7) \mid (3, 7) \mid (5, 6) \mid (4, 6)$

To solve this problem, SEND + MORE = MONEY using the above rules, we proceed as follows: -

Applying rule-1 (*R*1),

$$x = S, y = M, z = 0$$

$$S + M = M0$$

$\rightarrow \quad M = 1, O = 0$ and $S = 8$ or 9.

Applying rule-2 (R2),

$$a = E, x = N, y = R, c = N, z = E$$

$$EN + OR = NE$$

$\rightarrow \quad N = E + 1, N + R = E + 10$

Also, as $\quad E + 0 + 1 = N$

And $S + M$ generates carry,

$S = 9$ and not 8.

Applying rule-3 (R3),

$$y = N, x = E, z = R$$

$$N = E + 1, N + R = E + 10$$

$\rightarrow \quad R = 8$ (as $S = 9$)

prev_carry = 1

$\rightarrow \quad D + E = Y + 10$

Applying rule-4 (R4),

$$x = D, y = E, z = Y$$

$$D + E = Y + 10$$

$\rightarrow \quad (D, E) = (7, 5)$

We conclude that $(D, E) = (7, 5)$. Please note that this is because any other choice always leads to violation of the constraint that 'no two distinct alphabets can have the same numeric code'.

So, $D = 7$ and $E = 5$

Also, as $N = E + 1 = 5 + 1 = 6$

Also, as $D + E = Y + 10$

$\rightarrow$ $Y = 7 + 5 - 10 = 2$

So, we have now-

$$S = 9, E = 5, N = 6, D = 7$$

$$+ M = 1, O = 0, R = 8, E = 5$$

$$M = 1, O = 0, N = 6, E = 5, Y = 2$$

We are in a position to solve a problem now.

Example 1. Trace the constraint satisfaction procedure solving the following cryptarithmatic program:

```
  CROSS
+ROADS
DANGER
```

Solution 1 : We are given that-

```
  CROSS
+ROADS
DANGER
```

Step-1 : We identify different alphabets present and make a table implying the digits it can have.

Here, different alphabets are C, R, O, S, A, D, N, G, E and digits (0 to 9).

C	0	~~1~~	~~2~~	~~3~~	~~4~~	~~5~~	6	~~7~~	~~8~~	(8)
R	0	~~1~~	~~2~~	~~3~~	~~4~~	~~5~~	(6)	~~7~~	~~8~~	~~9~~
O	0	~~1~~	(2)	~~3~~	~~4~~	~~5~~	~~6~~	~~7~~	~~8~~	~~9~~
S	0	~~1~~	~~2~~	(3)	~~4~~	~~5~~	~~6~~	~~7~~	~~8~~	~~9~~
A	0	~~1~~	~~2~~	~~3~~	~~4~~	(5)	~~6~~	~~7~~	~~8~~	~~9~~
D	0	1	~~2~~	~~3~~	~~4~~	~~5~~	~~6~~	~~7~~	~~8~~	~~9~~
N	0	~~1~~	~~2~~	~~3~~	~~4~~	~~5~~	~~6~~	~~7~~	(8)	~~9~~
G	0	~~1~~	~~2~~	~~3~~	~~4~~	~~5~~	~~6~~	(7)	~~8~~	~~9~~
E	0	~~1~~	~~2~~	~~3~~	(4)	~~5~~	~~6~~	~~7~~	~~8~~	~~9~~

Step-2 : We assign the left-most alphabet with digit 1 as it is the only value it can take, that too through carry forward method. So, assigning D = 1. So, we can say that -

```
     C   R   O   S   S

 R   O   A   D   S
+ - - - - - - - - - - - - -
 D  A   N   G   E   R
(1)
```

Make sure to cut 1 from the list of other elements in the table above.

Step-3 : Now if $D = 1$, so $C + R$ must generate a carry also at end R is generated using $S + S$ which implies R must be a multiple of 2 *i.e.*, either 2, 4, 6, 8.

And C must have a large value to generate carry so taking $C = 9$ and $R = 6$, we have-

	(9)	(6)			
	C	R	O	S	S
	R	O	A	D	S
1	(6)			(1)	
+					
D	A	N	G	E	R
(1)					(6)

Assigning all R's with value 6 and hence A = 9 + 6 = 1 5 so A = 5.

(1 → Carry)

Now we have—

1					
	(9)	(6)			
	C	R	O	S	S
	R	O	A	D	S
	(6)		(5)		
+					
D	A	N	G	E	R
(1)	(5)				(6)

Step-4 : Next Up, we have R + O = N where we already have R = 6.

So, 6 + O = N.

Also, in next statement, O + A = G

i.e., O + 5 = G

And left digits are 0, 2, 3, 4, 7, 8

Putting O = 2, we have-

1					
	(9)	(6)	(2)		
	C	R	O	S	S
(6)	R	O (2)	A(5)	D (1)	S
+					
D	A	N	G	E	R
(1)	(5)	(8)	(7)		(6)

At this step we have O = 2

N = 8

G = 7

Step-5 : Next up, we have $S + D = E$ i.e., $S + 1 = E$ and also $S + S = R$ *i.e.,* $S + S = 6$ which is only possible if $S = 3$. So, putting $S = 3$, we have-

1					
	(9)	(6)	(2)	(3)	(3)
	C	R	O	S	S
(6)	R	O (2)	A(5)	D(1)	S(3)
+					
D	A	N	G	E	R
(1)	(5)	(8)	(7)	(4)	(6)

After this, we have assigned values to-

CROSS = 9 6 2 3 3

ROADS = 6 2 5 1 3

CHECKING:

	9	6	2	3	3
+	6	2	5	1	3

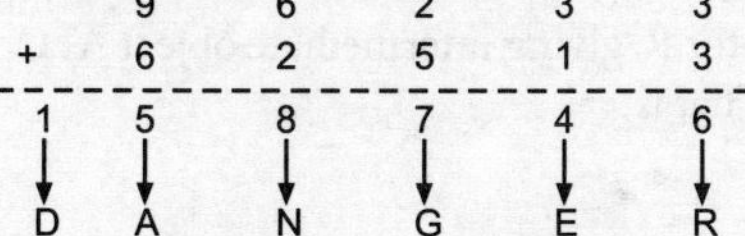

Q.2. "Means-end analysis (MEA) is a knowledg-rich search" Explain.

Ans. Means-end-analysis is a special type of knowledge-rich search that allows both backward and forward searching.

Principle : "It (MEA) allows us to solve the major parts of a problem first and then go back and solve the smaller problems that arise while assembling the final solution".

Technique : It is based on the use of the operators which transform the state of the world. The difference between the current state and the goal state is detected.

Once such a difference is isolated, an operator that can reduce the difference has to be found. But sometimes it is not possible to apply this operator to the current state. So, we try to get a sub- problem out of it and try to apply our operator to this new state. If this also does not produce the desired goal state then we try to get second sub problem and apply this operator again. This process may be continued. **But please note here that if the difference is chosen correctly and if the operator is really effective at reducing the difference then the two sub problems are easier to solve than the original problem.**

Why is it called as Means-End-Analysis?

Given a description of the desired state of the world (the end) it works backwards, selecting and using operators that will achieve it (the means). Hence, the name, Means-End-Analysis (MEA).

MEA works incrementally : The above technique of MEA works incrementally and not as a single step. This is so because the operators are applied recursively till a goal state is achieved.

MEA works on three primary goals.

They are as follows—

a. Transformation.

b. Reduction

c. Application

Transformation means to transform object *A* into object *B i.e.,*

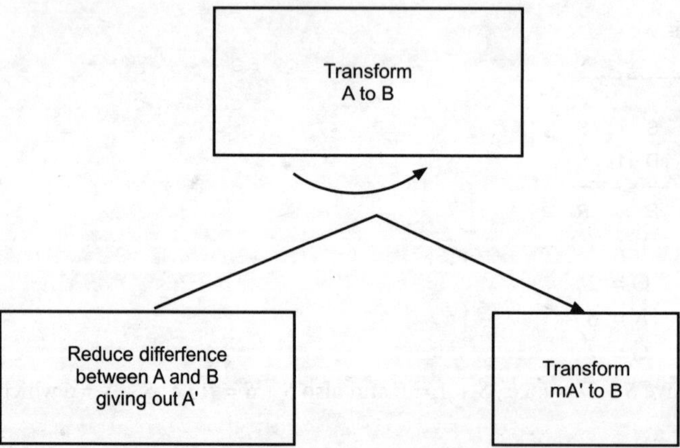

This is an AND graph which subdivides a problem into an intermediate problem and then transforms that problem into the goal state *B*. Please note that this process terminates when there is no difference between *A* and *B* or we can say when the goal is reached.

Reduction means to reduce the difference between object-*A* and object- by modifying object-*A i.e.,*

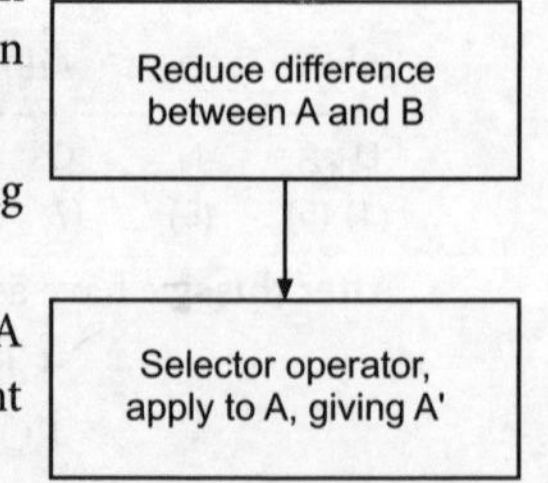

Please note that the goal of this operation is to reduce the difference between the object A and object-B by transforming object A into object-A', nearer the goal B, by means of a relevant operator (say, R).

Application means to apply the operator R to object-A. This will again be a AND graph showing the goal of reducing the difference between object-A and the pre-conditions required for the operator R, giving intermediate object A''. Operator R is then applied to A'', transforming it to A', which is close to the goal *B*. That is,

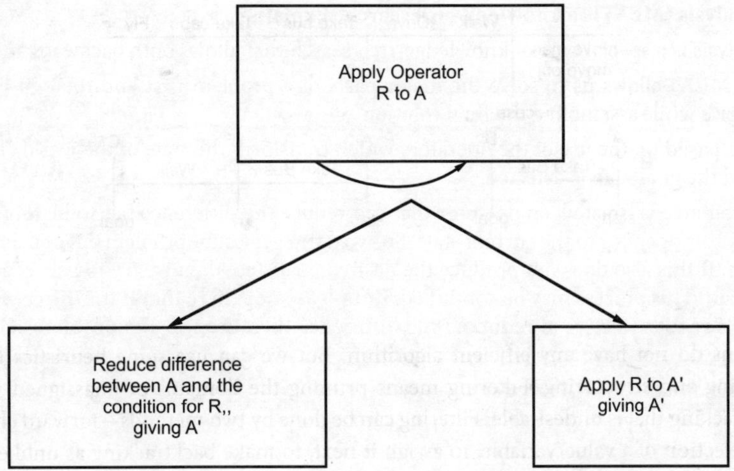

Please understand that states are described in some structured way like by predicate calculus and moves are performed by the operators. Each operator has a—

a. Pre-condition: It puts some constraints on the states it uses.

b. Post-condition: It says which conditions will be true when the operator has been used.

For examples —

a. GPS was the first AI program to exploit MEA.

b. STRIPS (A Robot Planner) is an advanced problem solver that incorporates MEA.

Algorithm for Means-End-Analysis (MEA)

We give an algorithm for MEA now.

Step-1 : Until the goal is reached or no more procedures are available.

Step-2 : Describe the current state, the goal state and the difference between the two.

Step-3 : Use the difference between the current state and goal state, possibly with the description of the current state or goal state, to select a promising procedure.

Step-4 : Use the promising procedure and update the current state.

Step-5 : If goal is reached then success else it is a failure.

We are in a position to solve an example now.

Example 1 : Show how Mean-End-Analysis (MEA) can be used to solve the problem of getting from one place to another. Assume that the available operators are walk, drive, take the bus, take a cab and fly.

Solution : Means-End Analysis—

Available Operators	Preconditions	Results
Walk		at (man, loc)
Drive	have (man, car) ^ (on obj, bus)	at (man, loc)^ at (obj, loc)
Take bus	On (man, bus)^ on (obj, bus)	at (man, loc)^ at (obj, loc)
Take cab	hire (man, cab) ^ on (obj, cab)	at (obj, loc)
Fly	book (man, airbus)^ on (obj, airbus)	at (man, loc) ^ at (obj, loc)

∴ Difference Table is as follows

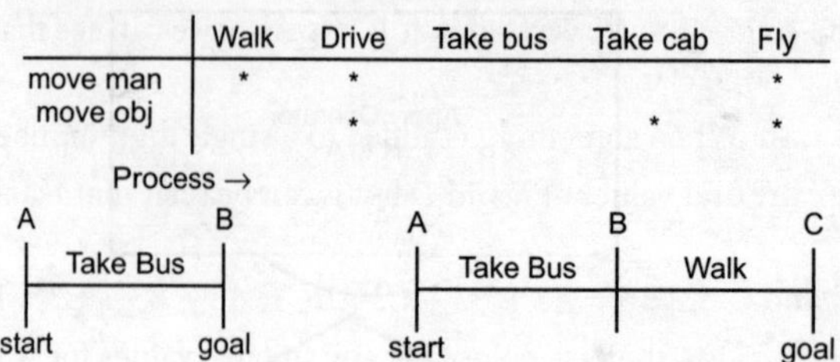

SUMMARY

In general, CSP problems do not have any efficient algorithm. But we can use some heuristics to find the solutions. It includes filtering, ordering and structuring. Filtering means pruning the domains of unassigned variables before time to prevent irrelevant backtracking that is undesirable. Filtering can be done by two methods—forward checking and consistency. Ordering refers to the selection of a value/variable, to assign it next, to make backtracking as unlikely as possible. Structure refers to a tree structure of a CSP as then the CSP algorithm can derive a solution in a linear time.

MULTIPLE CHOICE QUESTIONS

1. **CSP refers to-**
   (*a*) Mathematical problems whose state must satisfy a number of constraints.
   (*b*) Common Simple Problem with no limitations.
   (*c*) Common Solvable Problems.
   (*d*) None of the above.
2. **The incremental formulation of CSP involves-**
   (*a*) Goal cost (*b*) Path cost
   (*c*) Successor function (*d*) All of the above
3. **Backtracking in CSP can be avoided by-**
   (*a*) Forward searching (*b*) Backward searching
   (*c*) Backtrack after a forward search (*d*) None of the above
4. **If the domains are finite then CSP problems are solved by-**
   (*a*) Search algorithms (*b*) Heuristics searches
   (*c*) Greedy searches (*d*) All of the above

ANSWERS

1. (*a*) **2.** (*d*) **3.** (*a*) **4.** (*b*)

CONCEPTUAL SHORT QUESTIONS WITH ANSWERS

Q.1. In the following multiplication, each digit has been replaced by an alphabet-

```
        J  E
  *     B  B
        J  E
     J  E  A
------------
  B  A  D  E
```

1. **Compute the values of J and A.**
2. **If E=4, what is the value of D?**

Ans. From the first multiplication *i.e.*, $JE * B = JE$, we find that $B = 1$. Also, we can see that $A = 0$ as in multiplication, 2nd row must start from the 10th splace. So, $A = 0$.

Now in the 100th place, $J + ? = 10$. When something is added to a single digit number, it results into 10, so, $J = 9$.

From the given problem, we can't find values of E and D but it can be seen that E and D are consecutive. It is given that $E = 4$ so $D = 3$.

Q.2. Compute the values of A, B and C if $ABC = A3 + B3 + C3$ $ABC = A3 + B3 + C3$, where ABC is a three-digit number.

Ans. Say, the maximum value of A, B, C is 4 then we do not get any suitable values for ABC.

If we take the maximum value = 5 then $A3A3 = 5353 = 125$ as it is a 3- digit number and one of the numbers is equal to 1. So,

$53 + 1353 + 13 = 126.$

Now for 3333, we get $153 = 13 + 53 + 33153 = 13 + 53 + 33$.

So, the other numbers that satisfy the above relation are 370, 371 and 407.

Q.3. Give brief summary of backtracking search for CSP.

Ans. If we apply BFS to generic CSP problems then we observe that the branching factor at the top level is $(n * d)$, because any of 'd' values can be assigned to any of the 'n' variables. At the next level, the branching factor is $(n - 1) * d$ and so on for n-levels. Therefore, a tree with $n! * d^n$ leaves is generated even though there are only d^n possible complete assignments.

Core steps followed:

S1 : Depth-first search selects the values for single variable at a given time.

S2 : Apply constraints to the variable when variable is selected.

S3 : Backtracking action is performed if a variable has no legal values left to assign.

S4 : Backtracking search is basic uninformed algorithm for CSPs.

Backtracking Search Algorithm :

S1 : Consider a CSP problem.

S2 : Apply backtracking search. If backtracking search successful, returns a solution else a failure state which return a procedure recursive-backtracking.

S3 : Procedure recursive-backtracking starts with empty set and takes input as CSP problem.

S4 : Variable is assigned a specific value.

S5 : The relative constraint is a set which is taken as input.

S6 : If the value is complete and consistent according to constraints then assign value to variable, add that to the list.

S7 : Call the recursive backtracking until result or failure is reached.

S8 : Every time recursive-backtracking sustains result *i.e.*, assignment.

S9 : If the result is a failure then remove variable with specific value from assignment. It will return failure status.

Limitations of Backtracking :

1. A success function is generated with the above algorithm. But backtracking is not effective for very large problems.
2. The general performance is not so good. Domain specific heuristic function combined with uninformed search algorithm can generate better searching result.

Advancements in Backtracking Search : It is also possible to solve CSP without knowing the domain-specific knowledge. Hence, we need to design a module which resolves the following queries: -

1. Which variable is assigned in next step and what order values can be tried?
2. Impact of current variable assignments on unassigned variables.
3. Avoidance of known failed path in the potential paths.

Q.4. Discuss various techniques that are helpful for earlier constraints checks.

Ans. The following techniques are used: -

1. Forward Checking.
2. Constraint propagation.

3. Constraint propagation using Arc consistency.
4. Constraint propagation using k-consistency.

Forward Checking : It is one of the techniques which uses constraints more effectively during search. It removes values in neighboring unassigned variables domain that conflict with assigned variable. Forward checking uses MRV to select assigned variable. MRV means Minimum Remaining Values. It is also called as Most Constrained Variable or fail-first heuristic. Both backtracking and MRV give better performances. the rule is to choose a variable with the fewest legal moves. It answers which variable shall we try first. Backtracking search is performed if failure occurs. Search terminates when any variable has no legal values.

Constraint Propagation : It is a combined approach of heuristic + forward checking that gives more reliable, accurate and efficient results than a singular approach. The forward checking propagates information from assigned to unassigned variables but cannot avoid or detect all failures. Constraint propagation repeatedly enforces constraints locally. The idea of arc consistency provides a fast method of constraint propagation that is stronger than forward checking. Here 'arc' refers to a directed arc in the constraint graph.

Q.5. What is MIN-CONFLICT algorithm for solving CSP by Local Search. Explain its advantages in solving 4-queens problem.

Ans. Min-conflict heuristic selects new value that results in a minimum number of conflicts with the other variable. The initial state may be chosen randomly or by a greedy assignment process that chooses a minimal-conflict value for each variable in turn. The conflicts procedure that counts the number of constraints violated by a particular value, given the rest of the current assignments. The algorithm is as follows: -

ALGORITHM MIN-CONFLICTS

Inputs : CSP, a constraint satisfaction problem.

Max-steps, the number of steps allowed before giving up.

Output : A solution or failure.

current- an initial complete assignment for CSP.

for i = 1 to max-steps do

if current is a solution for CSP then return current.

var- a randomly chosen conflicted variable from VARIABLES [CSP].

value- the value v for var that minimizes CONFLICTS (var, v, current, csp).

set var = value in current.

return failure.

Advantages of Min-conflict :

1. The key feature is that the run-time needed for min-conflict is independent of the problem size. For e.g. it can solve million-queen problem in an average of 50 steps.
2. It also works for hard-problems.
3. Local search is also used in an online setting. For *e.g.* in scheduling problem, like a weekly outline schedule.

Example of Min-conflict

Consider 4-queen example as shown in figure-

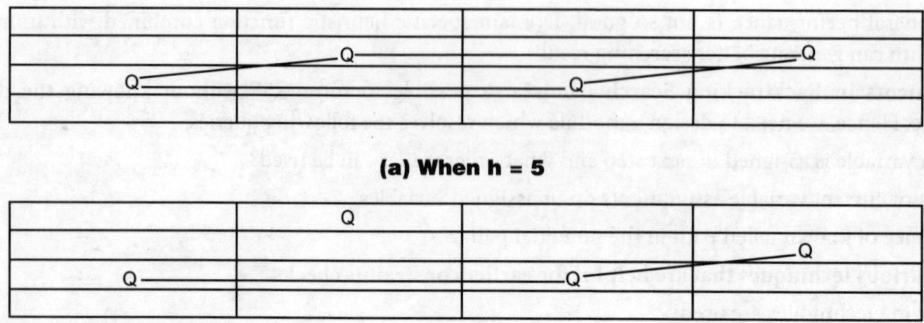

(a) When h = 5

(b) When h = 2

	Q		
			Q
Q			
		Q	

(c) When h = 0

This shows how h value changes per step.

Q.6. What is intelligent backtracking? Explain.

Ans. During forward checking if inconsistency or failure occurs then we need to apply backtracking. If backtracking is done efficiently then we can reduce the total time.

Chronological backtracking :

1. It is one of the standard forms *i.e.*, try different values for preceding variable.
2. In chronological backtracking, latest decision points are always revisited.
3. It has potential to back up to the preceding variable.
4. A more intelligent approach to backtracking is to go all the way back to one of the set of variables that caused the failure. This set is called the conflict set. For example, in map coloring problem, the conflict set M is {N, NW, NE}, where N, NW, NE are already colored regions. In general, the conflict set for variable X is the set of previously assigned variables that are connected to X by constraints.
5. The back-jumping method backtracks to the most recent variable in the conflict set.
6. If no legal value is found, it should return the most recent element of the conflict set along with the failure indicator.

EXERCISE QUESTIONS

1. If SEND + MORE = MONEY, find the respective values.
2. Given the multiplication as follows: -

```
        H   E
  *     E   H
      -------
        H   E
  H H A
  -----------
  H N M     E
```

3. In the following multiplication, each digit has been replaced by an alphabet-

```
          J   E
   *      B   B
        -------
          J   E
      J   E   A
  -------------
  B A     D   E
```

Find the value of *J* and *A*.

If E=5, what is the value of *D*?

4. Find the values of all alphabets if each alphabet represents a single digit from 0-9.

BASE + BALL = GAMES

A = 4, *B* = 7, *S* = 8, *E* = 3 , *L* = 5, *G* = 1 AND *M* = 9.

5. Give the importance of CSP in AI.
6. Solve the following CSP-

(*a*) USA + USSR = PEACE.

(*b*) POINT + ZERO = ENERGY.

7. Find the values of *A*, *B* and *C*, if *ABC* = *A* + *B* + *CABC* = *A* + *B* + *C*, where *ABC* is a three-digit number.

[**Hint:** By symmetry, we take A is in max. number of the three alphabets. Let A take a maximum value of 6.

Then 6 = 720 but as we have taken max. value, so 6720 is not possible. So, A should take 5. Then, 5 = 120. Now from the equation given, we know that B and C should take 1 as their value 120 contains 1.

Hence, 5 +1 = 121

If we take 4 as one of the numbers then 5 + 1 + 4 = 145 or 1 + 4 + 5 = 145].

8. What is CSP?

[**Hint:** CSP are the problems whose state and goal test conform to a standard structured and a very simple representation. CSP's are defined using a set of variables and set of constraints on those variables. The variables have some allowed values from specified domain. For example, Graph coloring problem- Given a graph and a set of colors, color each vertex such that no two adjacent vertices have same color].

9. How can minimax also be extended for the game of chance?

[**Hint:** In a game of chance, we can add extra level of chance nodes in the game search tree. These nodes have successors which are the outcomes of random element. The minimax algorithm uses probability, P attached with chance node d_i based on this value. Successor function S (N, d_i) gives moves from position N for outcome d_i].

10. What are the rules used in general for crypto arithmetic problems? What does the constraints in crypta arithmetic problems include?

[**Hint:** General rules used are as follows: -

1. Each alphabet takes only one number from 0 to 9 uniquely.
2. Sum of two single digit numbers can be maximum 19 with the carryover. So, carry over in problems of two number addition is always 1.
3. Try to solve the leftmost digit in the given problem.
4. If $a * b = kb$, the following are the possibilities: *3 * 5 = 15; 7 * 5 = 35; 9 * 5 = 45) or (2 * 6 = 12; 4 * 6 = 24; 8 * 6 = 48).

Constraints in crypta arithmetic problems are as follows: -

1. No two digits can be assigned to the same letter.
2. Only the single digit number can be assigned to a letter.
3. No two letters can be assigned to the same digit.
4. Assumption can be made at various levels such that these do not contradict each other.
5. The problem can be decomposed into the secured constraints. A constraint satisfaction method may be used.
6. Any search method may be used.
7. Backtracking may be performed as applied to the search techniques.
8. Rule of arithmetic might be followed].

11. If FOUR + MICE = FOUND. Find the values of –

F, O, U, R, M, I, C, E, N, D. also assume that C_4, C_3, C_2 , C_1 are carry variables.

[**Hints:**

1. Since max. values of variables can be 9. So, 9 + 9 = 18. 1 will be carry.

   So, $C_4 =$ 1. Hence, $F = 1$.

2. $F + M = 0$, $1 + M = 0$

   M has to be 9 to generate carry. Hence, $M = 9$.

   $O =$ 0, so $C_3 = 0$.

3. $0 + I = U$

   I can be between 2 to 8.

   Let $I =$ 7

   $0 + 7 + C_2 =$ U

   $0 + 7 + 1 =$ 8

So, $C_2 =$ 1, $U = 8$ and $I = 7$.

4. $U + C = N = 8 + C$

N should be a 2-digit number to generate C_2 carry.

C can be 2, 3, 4, 5, 6

Let $C =$ 5

$8 + 5 = N$

So, $N =$ 3 and C_2 (carry) = 1.

5. $R + E = D$

Now 2, 4, 6 are left.

$R + E = D$

Let $R =$ 2, $E = 4$, $D = 6$

So, $R + E = D$

Or $2 + 4 = 6$

Hence, $F =$ 1, $M = 9$, $N = 3$

$O =$ 0, $I = 7$, $D = 6$

$U =$ 8, $C = 5$

$R =$ 2, $E = 4$

Thus,

	1	0	8	2
+	9	7	5	4
1	0	8	3	6

8 KNOWLEDGE REPRESENTATION

Q.1. What is knowledge? What are its properties and its types? Distinguish between procedural and explicit knowledge.

Ans. Knowledge is a progression that starts with data which is of limited utility. Data when processed becomes information, information when interpreted or evaluated becomes knowledge and understanding of the principles embodied with the knowledge is wisdom. This is shown in Fig. 4.1 in knowledge, lies the power.

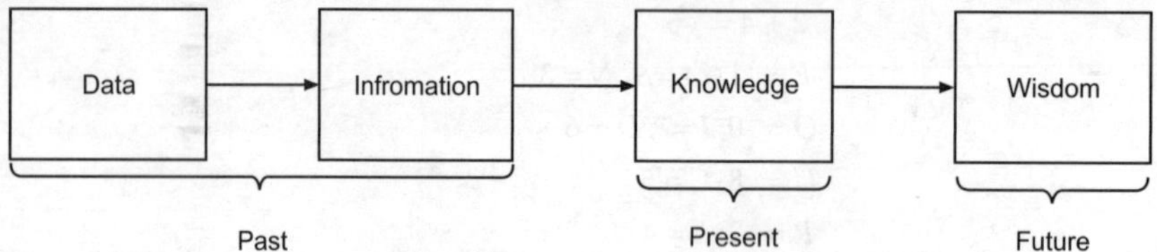

Fig. 8.1: *Relationship between data, information, knowledge and wisdom*

A good knowledge representation system should possess the following properties:-

1. **Representational Adequacy :** It is defined as an ability to represent the required knowledge.
2. **Inferential Adequacy :** It is defined as an ability to manipulate the knowledge represented to produce new knowledge corresponding to that inferred from the original.
3. **Inferential Efficiency:** It is defined as an ability to direct the inferential mechanisms into the most productive directions by string appropriate guides.
4. **Acquisitioned Efficiency :** It is defined as an ability to acquire new knowledge using automatic methods where possible rather than reliance on human intervention.

Please understand that information is static while knowledge is dynamic as it lies within us. Even our expert systems (to be discussed later) are knowledge-based systems. These systems are used by knowledge engineers. and the process of development building and maintaining knowledge based systems is the domain of Knowledge Engineering. Knowledge is central to A.I. An A.I. system must be capable of doing three things:

a. Store knowledge.

b. Apply the knowledge stored to solve problems.

c. Acquire new knowledge through experience.

Also note that any AI system has 3 key components Representation, Reasoning and Learning. In A.I. different types of knowledge needs to be represented.

(1) **Objects :** Facts about objects in our world domain need to be represented

For Example : Guitars have strings. The fact associated with the object guitar is that they have strings. We need to store and represent this fact.

(2) **Events :** Actions that occur in real world.

For example: Arjun played guitar in boys band group.

(3) **Performance :** A behavior. For example, playing a guitar involves knowledge about how to do things.

(4) **Meta-knowledge :** It is the knowledge about what we know.

For Example : A Robot to manage your moods.

So to solve problems in A.I. we must represent knowledge. There are two entities involved here.

a. **Facts :** Are data or instance that are specific and unique. These are the truths about the real world. It is also considered as a knowledge level.

b. **Representation of Facts :** We usually define the representation in terms of symbols that can be manipulated by programs. It is also called as a symbol level.

Knowledge Types : Major classification of knowledge is as follows:

Tacit (or procedural) knowledge and Explicit or declarative knowledge Let us tabulate the differences between them now.

Tacit Knowledge or Procedural	Explicit Knowledge or Declarative
1. It is an embodied knowledge that exists within a human being.	1. It is an embedded knowledge that exists outside the human being.
2. It is difficult to articulate formally.	2. It can be easily articulated formally.
3. It is difficult to share or communicate this knowledge.	3. This knowledge can be shared, copied, processed and stored.
4. This knowledge is drawn from experience, action, subjective insight.	4. This knowledge is drawn from artifact of some type as principle, procedure, process and concepts.
5. It is a procedural knowledge about how to do something.	5. It is a declarative knowledge that something is true or false.
6. It focuses on tasks that must be performed to reach on particular objective and goal. **Examples :** Procedures, rules, strategies, agendas, models.	6. It refers to the representations of objects and events, knowledge about facts and relationships. **Examples:** concepts, objects, facts, propo- sitions, assertions, semantic nets, logic and descriptive models.
7. It is hard to debug.	7. It is easy to validate.
8. Process oriented.	8. Data oriented.
9. Representations in form of set of rules.	9. Representation in form of production system.

Other sources of knowledge also exist –

a. **Inheritable knowledge :** We can inherit certain type of knowledge also. For example:

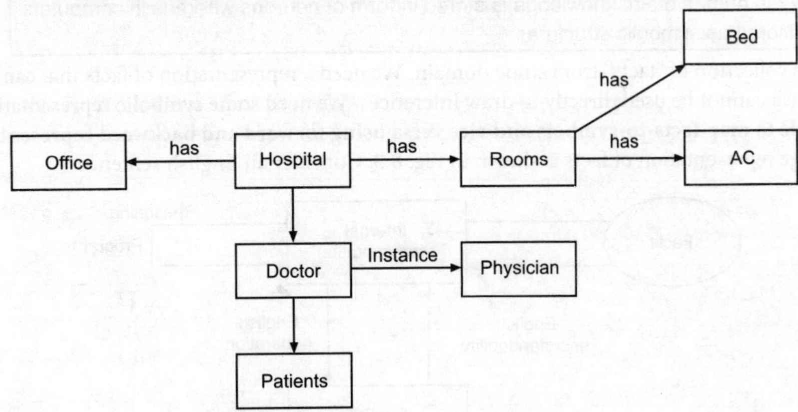

Fig. 8.2: *Hospital attribute representation*

The 'hospital' object has certain features like it will have rooms, doctors, office etc. Further- more, Rooms have bed, AC etc. Doctor has patients and so on. Here, the relationship 'has' indicates the salient features or property or attributes. The physician is an instance of Doctor. This is known as property inheritance which we shall study a bit later.

b. **Inferential knowledge :** The knowledge representation method which can use inference mechanism to use this knowledge is called as inferential knowledge. The inferential knowledge requires an inference mechanism for the purpose of exploiting it. Many inference procedures like Resolution will be discussed a bit later. For example: Predicate logic.

c. **Relations knowledge :** This knowledge is represented in of relations/tables in DBMS, form example. the knowledge regarding EMPLOYEE may be represented as

EMPNO	ENAME	EADDR	EPHONE
1.	Vineet	MAIT	852136
2.	Mayur	IITM	526521
3.	Ankit	ITM	921211
4.	Karan	GTBIT	912110
5.	Vijay	VIPS	891929

It can be used to answer simple queries like 'What is the phone number of Vineet'. But this representation cannot store any semantic information like it cannot answer queries like 'Is Vineet a good employee'?.

d. **Heuristic knowledge :** Heuristics means 'rule of thumb.' Guessing is the way of making conclusions. It is a form of judge- mental information. For example. say, if TV is not working. The guess would be that either tube is not working or probably power is OFF. This is heuristic knowledge.

e. **Commonsense knowledge :** A knowledge gained by our experience about any general phenomenon.

For Example : In order to differentiate human from other animals, the presence of commonsense knowledge plays a vital role.

f. **Explicit Knowledge :** A knowledge which an individual gains explicitly is called as explicit knowledge.

For Example : two raised to three is eight ($2^3 = 8$) is a kind of explicit knowledge.

This knowledge can be easily communicated, easily processed by computers and sent electronically.

g. **Uncertain Knowledge :** Today, we are surrounded by many uncertainties. These uncertainties need to be considered as they also provide some sort of knowledge.

For Example : If it is cloudy, it will rain.

We use a reasoning process on the available knowledge to draw conclusions. We need such a system which can handle these uncertainties.

> **Do you know?** In human brain, knowledge is stored in form of neurons whereas in computers knowledge is stored as symbolic structures.

Knowledge is a collection of "facts" from some domain. We need a representation of facts that can be manipulated by a program. English cannot be used directly to draw inferences. We need some symbolic representation. **Please note that we must be able to map facts-to-symbols and vice versa using forward and backward representation mapping.** The basic knowledge representation of facts is shown in Fig. 8.3. Consider an English sentence.

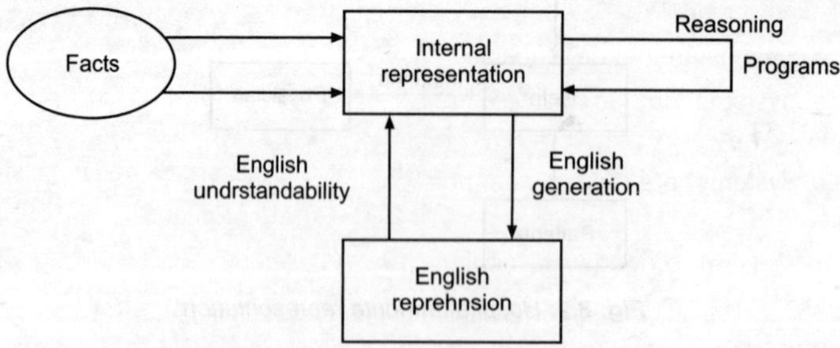

Fig. 8.3: Basic Knowledge Representation of Facts (an English Sentence)

For example : consider a 'fact' represented in 'English' as follows — 'Joe is a father'

Using forward mapping function, the above fact is represented in logic as —

Father (Joe)

On the other hand, if we use backward mapping function, then we can generate that English statement back again, i.e., we get –

'Joe is a father'

What are those forward and backward representations?

Forward and Backward representations are shown in Fig. 8.4

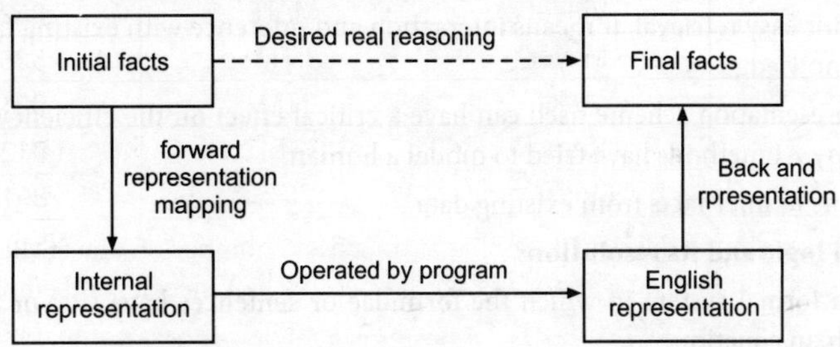

Fig. 8.4: Forward v/s backward representations

Please note the dotted line on the top. It shows the abstract reasoning process that a program is intended to model. The solid lines on bottom indicate the concrete reasoning process that the program performs.

Q.2. How to store knowledge? What ar th character is tics of a good KB?

Ans. Collected and stored knowledge is called as a knowledge base (KB). A KB is a set of files that stores the knowledge for knowledge management. It may be a machine readable as a human readable KB (like articles, papers, user marvels. etc.).

Let us tabulate the differences between database and knowledge base now.

Database (DB)	Knowledge Base(KB)
1. Database stores data that is simple and flat (relational).	1. Knowledge base can be used to store cause and effect information and imprecise and probabilistic information.
2. Database does not consist of fuzzy facts.	2. Knowledge base may consist of fuzzy facts. There is a mechanism which manipulates uncertain information.
3. Databases do not contains more sophisticated relationship between facts.	3. KB contains more sophisticated relationships between facts.
4. Databases do not emulate decision making processes.	4. KBS emulate the decision making processes of humans.
5. Databases do not contain factual and heuristic knowledge.	5. KB of expert systems contains both factual and heuristic knowledge.
6. Database systems do not capture and distribute knowledge.	6. KBS capture and distribute knowledge.
7. Database systems are not dependable.	7. KBS are dependable.
8. Database systems are sometimes not consistent.	8. KBS are accurate and consistent.
9. Database systems are sometimes not profitable.	2. KBS are profitable.
10. A database expert is needed to update data- bases.	10. An expert knowledge of the domain is needed for updating KB.

Characteristics of a good KB

1. A good KB must be rich in both quality and quantity.
2. It should have carefully written articles.
3. It should be updated regularly.
4. It should have an excellent search engine for easier accessibility.
5. It should have a very good design of the content format.

Do you know? KB =	[Onto logy(formal knowledge representation)	+	a set of example of its clauses]

Applications of Knowledge :

1. **Learning :** Learning is acquiring knowledge. This is more than simply adding new facts to KB. We classify new data prior to its storage for easy retrieval. It means interaction and inference with existing facts to avoid redundancy and replication in the knowledge.
2. **Retrieval :** The representation scheme used can have a critical effect on the efficiency of the method. Humans are very good at it. Many AI methods have tried to modal a human.
3. **Reasoning :** It means to infer facts from existing data.

Q.3. What is propositional logic and its resolution?

Ans. A logic is defined as a formal system in which the formulae or sentences have true or false values. In 1976, Robert Kowalski came up with an equation.

Algorithm = Logic + Control

The logic component specifies the knowledge to be used in solving problems.

The control component determines the problem solving strategies by means of which that knowledge is used.

Please note that the logic component determines the meaning of the algorithm whereas the control component only affects its efficiency. In reasoning about truth values, we use a number of operators like

Operator	Meaning
$\wedge$	and
$\vee$	or
$\neg$	not
$\rightarrow$	implies
$\leftrightarrow$	iff (if and only if)

It is useful to represent these logical operators using truth table showing the possible values that can be generated by applying an operator to truth tables.

Let us now see various truth tables (for these operators).

1. **Not (¬) operator :** It is a unary operator *i.e.* it is applied only to one variable Its truth table is as follows —

A	¬ A
true	false
false	trure

2. **and (^) operator :** It is a binary operator, *i.e.* it acts on two variables. It is also called as conjunctive operator. Its truth table is as follows:

A	B	A ^ B
false	false	false
false	true	false
true	false	false
true	true	true

NOTE : that *A* ^ *B* is true if both *A* and *B* are true else it is False. *A* and *B* can be any statement or proposition.

3. **or (v) Operator :** It is again a binary operator and is also known as disjunctive operator. Its truth table is a follows–

A	B	A ∨ B
false	false	false
false	true	true
true	false	true
true	true	true

So, $A \vee B$ is true for all cases except for $A = B =$ false. This table represents an inclusive or operator. An exclusive or would have been 'false' in the final row.

4. **Implies (→) Operator :** Its truth table is as follows –

A	B	A → B
false	false	true
false	true	true
true	false	false
true	true	true

This type of implication is also called as material implication. Also note that in statement,

$$A \rightarrow B$$

'A' is known as antecedent.

and 'B' is known as consequent.

$A \rightarrow B$ is real as 'A implies B' or 'if A then B' or 'if A is to B then B is true'

We can also construct complex truth tables like for $A \vee (B \vee C)$ the truth table is as follows —

A	B	C	A ^ (B ∨ C)
false	false	false	false
false	false	true	false
false	true	false	false
false	true	true	false
true	false	false	false
true	false	true	true
true	true	false	true
true	true	true	true

for $n = 3$ (*i.e.*, 3 variables A, B and C) these are 8 outputs. In general, for n inputs there will be 2^n outputs. Please note that the use of brackets is very important because $A \wedge (B \vee C) \neq (A \wedge B) \vee C$. Also note that to avoid ambiguity, these logical operators are assigned precedence. The order of precedence is as follows –

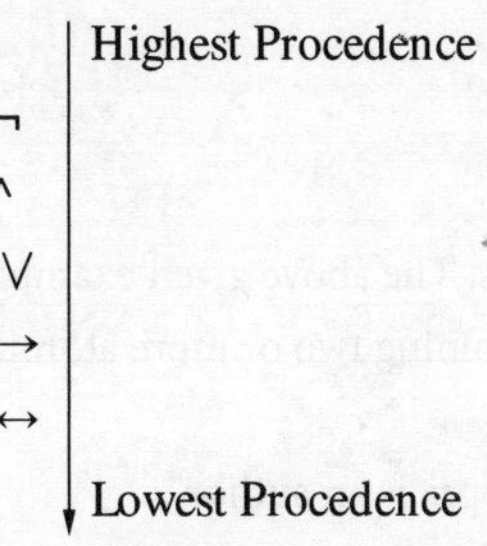

This means that $\neg A \vee B = (\neg A) \vee B$

Tip: Use braces whenever an expression becomes ambiguous.

5. Tautology : Consider the following truth table –

A	$AV\neg A$
false	true
true	true

This truth table has a property, that is, the value of expression is always true irrespective of the value of *A*. Such an expression that is always true is known as tautology. If *A* is a tautology, we write —

$| = A$

A logical expression that is tautology is often described as being valid. A Valid expression is defined as being one that is true under any interpretation. In other words, no matter what meanings and values we assign to variables in a valid expression, it will still be true. If an expression is false in any interpretation, it is described as being contradictory. The following expressions are contradictory:

a. $A \wedge \neg A$

b. $(A \vee \neg A) \rightarrow (A \wedge \neg A)$

It does not matter what A means in these expressions. The result cannot be time.

Some expressions are satisfactory but not valid. This means that they are true under some interpretation but not under all interpretations. The following expressions are satisfactory —

a. $A \vee A$

b. $(A \wedge B \vee \neg C) \rightarrow (D \neg E)$

Please note that a contradictory expression is clearly not satisfactory and so is described as being unsatisfactory.

Tip: Logic is studied as knowledge representation language in A.I.

Logics are of different types —

a. Propositional logic.

b. Predicate logic.

c. Temporal logic.

d. Modal logic.

e. Description logic. etc.

Out of these propositional logic and predicate logic are fundamental to all logic.

Propositional Logic : Propositions are statements used in mathematics. A proposition or sentence is classified as declarative sentence whose value is either 'true' or 'false'.

For example. —

a. The sky is blue.

b. Snow is white.

c. $4 * 4 = 16$

Propositions are of two types —

a. Atomic propositions.

b. Molecular propositions.

Atomic propositions are single propositions. The above given examples are all propositions.

Molecular propositions are formed by combining two or more atomic propositions.

For example.—

"Lata Mangeshkar is a singer and Rajiv Chopra is an author".

Propositions are 'sentences' either true or false but not both. A sentence is the smallest unit in propositional logic. If proposition is 'time', then truth value is 'time'. If proposition is 'false' then truth value is 'false'.

NOTE: Propositional logic is also called as Propositional Calculus or Sentential Calculus or Boolean Algebra.

Please understand that propositional logic tells the ways of joining and/or modifying entire propositions, statements or sentences to form more complicated propositions, statement or sentences as well as the logical relationships and properties that are derived from the methods of combining or altering statements. Also note that the process used for performing manipulation of the symbols is according to some rules and laws.

A BNF (Backus Naur Form) grammar of Sentences in Propositional logic is as follows —

Sentence → Atomic sentence |complex sentence |
Atomic sentence → true |false | symbol
Symbol → P |Q | R ...
Complex sentence → · sentence
| (Sentence ∧ Sentence)
| (Sentence ∨ Sentence)
| (Sentence → Sentence)
| (Sentence ↔ Sentence)

Some terminologies in Propositional Logic :

1. **Statement :** A statement is a sentence that is TRUE or FALSE. These statements have some properties:–
   a. **Satisfiability :** A statement is satisfiable if there is some interpretation for which it is true.
   b. **Contradiction :** A sentence is contradictory (unsatisfiable) if there is no interpretation for which it is true. For example, Japan is capital of India.
   c. **Validity :** A sentence is valid if it is true for every interpretation.
   For example, the sentence $P \vee \neg P$ is valid. Valid sentences are also called as tautologies.
   d. **Logical Equivalence :** Two sentences are logically equivalent if they have the same truth table under every interpretation, written as $P \leftrightarrow Q$.
   For example, $P \wedge Q$ and $Q \wedge P$ are logically equivalent and this can be shown using truth tables given earlier.
2. **Connective or operator :** The connectives join simple statements into compound statements and joins compound into larger compound statements.
   For example : 6 basic connectives and their symbols

Connectives	Symbols	Meaning
Assertion	*P*	'*P* is true'
Negation	¬ *P*, ~, !, not	'*P* is false'
Conjunction	*p* ∧ *g*, AND, &	'Both *p* and *q* are true'
Disjunction	*p* ∨ *q*, *i*, OR	'Either *p* is true or *q* is true or both'
Implication	*p*→ *q*, ⊃, ⇒, if then	'if *p* is true from *q* is also true' (*i.e., p* implies *q*)
Equivalence	↔, ≡, ⇔, if and only if	'*P* and *q* are either both true or both false'

NOTE: Both propositions and connective are the basic elements of propositional logic.

3. **Truth value:** The truth value of a statement is its TRUE or False value.
   For example
   a. q is either TRUE or FALSE.
   b. $\sim q$ is either TRUE or FALSE.
   c. $q \rightarrow p$ is either TRUE or FALSE.

NOTE : Use 'T' or '1' to mean TRUE & 'F' or '0' to mean FALSE

For example :

p	q	$\neg p$	$\neg q$	$p \vee q$	$p \rightarrow q$
T	T	F	F	T	T
T	F	F	T	T	F
F	T	T	F	T	T
F	F	T	T	F	T

4. **Tautologies :** A proposition that is always true is called as a tautology.
   For example : ($p \vee \neg p$) is always true irrespective of the value of p.
5. **Contradictions :** A proposition that is always false is called as a contradiction.
   For example : ($q \vee \neg g$) is always false regardless of the truth value of the proposition.
6. **Contigencies :** A proposition is called as a contigency, if that proposition is neither a tautology nor a contradiction.
   For example : ($p \vee q$) is a contingency
7. **Antecedent and consequent :** In the conditional statements, $p \rightarrow q$, 'p' is the 'if-clause' and is called as antecedent whereas 'a' is the 'then clause' and is known as consequent.
8. **Argument :** Any argument can be expressed as a compound statement. If we take all premises, conjoin them and make that conjunction the antecedent of a conditional and make the conclusion the consequent then this implication statement is called as the corresponding conditional of the argument.

Please remember the following points here:

1. Every argument has a corresponding condition.
2. Every implication statement has a corresponding argument.
3. Because the corresponding condition of an argument is a statement, it is therefore either a tautology or a contradiction or a contingency.
4. An argument is valid "if and only if" its corresponding conditional is a tautology.
5. Two statements are consistent 'if and only if' their conjunction is not a contradiction.
6. Two statements are logically equivalent "if and only if" their truth table columns are identical or "if and only if" the statement of their equivalence using "≡" is a tautology.

NOTE: Truth tables are used to test validity tautology, contradiction, contingency. consistency and logical equivalence.

A logical system is defined in terms of its syntax, its semantics and a set of rules of deduction for proving.

An expression is referred to as a well formed formula (WFF) if it is constructed correctly according to the rules of the syntax of propositional calculus. We define a sentence recursively in terms of other sentences.

More formally a WFF consists of atomic symbols joined with connectives.

$\therefore P, P \wedge \neg P, P \wedge Q, P \vee Q, P \rightarrow Q, P \leftrightarrow Q$

A WFF is defined recursively as —

1. An atom (say P) is a WFF.
2. If P is a WFF then $\cdot p$ is a WFF. are WFFs.
3. If P and Q are WFF, then $(P \vee Q)$, $(P \wedge Q)$, $(P \rightarrow Q)$ and $(P \leftrightarrow Q)$ are WFF.
4. A string of symbols is a WFF if and only if it is obtained by using above rule 1 to rule 3

Also note the following points about WFF:

1. A WFF is not a proposition but if we substitute a proposition in place of a propositional variable, we get a proposition.
   For example : $\cdot (P \vee Q) \wedge (Q \wedge R) \rightarrow (\cdot Q \wedge R)$
2. The WFF is also simply called as a formula.
3. WFF are conveniently represented as truth tables.
4. A WFF for all true entries is called as a tautology.
5. Two WFFs, say α and β in propositional variables $p_1, p_2 \ldots pn$ are equivalent if the formula $\alpha \rightarrow \beta$ is a tautology then, the equivalent statements are represented as $\alpha \equiv \beta$.

6. Please understand that $\alpha \leftrightarrow \beta$ and $\alpha \equiv \beta$ are different as $\alpha \leftrightarrow \beta$ is a formula whereas $\alpha \equiv \beta$ is not a formula but a relation between α and β.

   The semantics (meaning) of the operators of propositional calculus can be defined in terms of truth tables. If our knowledge is represented in form of propositional logic then it is very easy for a computer to do reasoning on this knowledge. The set of inference rules and laws that are used for reasoning are given below:

Rule 1: Idempotency Rule :

a. $P \vee P = P$

b. $P \wedge P = P$

Rule 2 : Commutative Law :

a. $P \vee Q = Q \vee P$

b. $P \wedge Q = Q \wedge P$

c. $P \leftrightarrow Q = Q \leftrightarrow P$

Rule 3 : Associative Law :

a. $(P \vee Q) \vee R = P \vee (Q \vee R)$

b. $(P \wedge Q) \wedge R = P \wedge (Q \wedge R)$

Rule 4 : Distributive Law :

a. $P \wedge (Q \wedge R) = (P \wedge Q) \vee (P \wedge R)$

b. $P \vee (Q \wedge R) = (P \vee Q) \wedge (P \vee R)$

Rule 5: De Morgan's rule :

a. $\sim (P \vee Q) = \sim P \wedge \sim Q$

b. $\sim (P \wedge Q) = \sim P \vee \sim Q$

Rule 6 : Implication Removal :

$P \leftrightarrow Q = \sim P \vee Q$

Rule 7 : Biconditional elimination :

$P \leftrightarrow Q = (P \rightarrow Q) \wedge (Q \rightarrow P)$

Rule 8 : Absorption Law :

a. $P \vee (P \wedge Q) \equiv P$

b. $P \wedge (P \vee Q) \equiv P$

Rule 9 : Contrapositive :

$P \Rightarrow Q \equiv \cdot Q \Rightarrow \cdot P$

Rule 10: Double negation :

$P \equiv \cdot (\cdot P)$

Rule 11: Fundamental identities :

a. $P \vee \cdot P \equiv T$

b. $P \wedge \cdot P \equiv F$

c. $P \vee \cdot T \equiv T$

d. $P \vee T \equiv P$

e. $P \vee F \equiv P$

f. $P \vee F \equiv F$

g. $(F \cdot Q) \wedge (P \Rightarrow \cdot Q) = \cdot P$

h. $P \Rightarrow Q \equiv (\cdot P \vee Q)$

Rule 12: AND (^) rule (Introduction) :

Given *P* and *Q*. We deduce $P \wedge Q$ *i.e.*

$$\frac{P \quad Q}{P \wedge Q}$$

This follows from the definition of ^.

Rule 13 : AND (^) rule (Elimination)

Given *P* and *Q*. We deduce *P* and *Q* *i.e.* separately *i.e.*

a. $P \wedge Q \rightarrow P$

b. $P \wedge Q \rightarrow Q$

This also follows from the definition of ^.

Rule 14 : OR (v) rule (Introduction)

Given *P* and *Q*, We deduce *P* and *Q* *i.e.* separately *i.e.*

a. $A \rightarrow A \vee B$

b. $B \rightarrow A \vee B$

i.e. from *A* we can deduce the disjunction of *A* which any expression.

Rule 15 : Modus Ponens

From given two statements *P* and $P \rightarrow Q$, infer *Q* *i.e.*,

$$\begin{array}{c} P \\ P \rightarrow Q \\ \hline \therefore Q \end{array}$$

> **NOTE:** In implication form, this rule is written as
> $(P \rightarrow (P \rightarrow Q)) \rightarrow Q$

For example :

Given : Rajiv is intelligent

and : Rajiv is intelligent → Rajiv is author.

Conclude : Rajiv is author.

Rule 16 : Modus Tollens

From the given two statements, · *Q* and ($P \rightarrow Q$), infer · *P* *i.e.*

$$\begin{array}{c} \neg P \\ P \rightarrow Q \\ \hline \therefore \neg Q \end{array}$$

For example :

Given: Ajay is not a religious person.

and : Ajay goes to temple daily implies Ajay is a religious person

Conclude : Ajay does not go to temple daily.

> **NOTE:** In implication form, this rule is written as
> (· $Q \wedge (P \rightarrow Q)) \rightarrow$ · Q

Rule 17 : Chain Rule/Hypothetical syllogism

From ($P \rightarrow Q$) and $Q \rightarrow R$), infer ($P \rightarrow R$) *i.e.*

$$\begin{array}{c} P \rightarrow Q \\ P \rightarrow Q \\ \hline \therefore (P \rightarrow Q) \\ \hline \end{array}$$

For example :

Given : It is raining → must take umbrella

and : Must take umbrella → There is no sun

Conclude : There is no sun.

> **NOTE:** In implication form, this rule is written as
> $((P \to Q) \wedge (Q \to R)) \to (P \to R)$

Rule 18: Reductio Ad Absurdum

This rule states that if we assume that A is false ($\cdot A$) and this leads to a contradiction ($\perp$) then we say that A is true. This is known as proof by contradiction. This is

$$\frac{\begin{array}{c}\neg A \\ ? \\ \perp\end{array}}{\therefore A}$$

Here, the symbol $\perp$ is called as falsumn which is used to indicate an absurdity or a contradiction.

For example :, $\perp$ can be deduced from A $\wedge \cdot A$.

Rule 19 : Disjunctive syllogism

From two given sentences, $\cdot P$ and $(P \vee Q)$, infer Q *i.e.*,

$$\frac{\begin{array}{c}\neg A \\ P \vee Q\end{array}}{\therefore Q}$$

> **NOTE:** In implication form, this rule is written as
> $(\cdot P \wedge (P \vee Q)) \to Q$

Rule 20 : Constructive and Destructive dilemma From given two sentences

$$\frac{\begin{array}{r}(P \to Q) \wedge (R \to S) \\ \text{and} \quad (P \to Q)\end{array}}{\therefore (Q \vee S)}$$

(Constructive dilemma)

Also,

$$\frac{\begin{array}{r}(P \to Q) \wedge (R \to S) \\ \neg (P \vee Q)\end{array}}{\therefore (Q \vee S)}$$

(Destructive dilemma)

> **NOTE:** In implication form, this rule is written as
> $((P \to Q) \wedge (R \to S)) (\cdot Q \wedge S) \to (P \vee R)$.

We are in a position to solve some examples now.

Example 4: Given *P* and Q, prove that

$((P \to Q) \to P) \to P$ is tautologous.

Solution : We draw its truth table —

P	Q	$((P \to Q) \to P) \to P)$		
T	T	T	T	T
T	F	F	T	T
F	T	T	F	T
F	F	F	F	T

Hence, $((P \to Q) \to P) \to P$ is tautologous.

Example 5 : Find the equivalent expression of
A (& (A v B)) using truth table

Solution:

A	B	$(A \vee B)$ C (say)	A & C
t	t	t	t
f	f	f	f
t	f	t	t
f	t	t	f

$\therefore$ A (& $(A$ v $B)) = A$ $[Q\ AB' + AB = A\ (B' + B) = A]$

Example 6 : Prove that (A $\wedge$ B) $\to$ A $\vee$ *B*.

Solution: Given A $\wedge$ B (assumption)

$\to A$ (by $\wedge$ elimination)

$\to A \vee B$ (by $\vee$ introduction) Hence Proved.

Example 7: Prove that —

$((P \wedge Q) \to R) \vee (\sim Q \to \sim R)$ is valid.

Solution: Let us denote this statement by Q

$Q : ((P \wedge Q) \to R) \vee (\sim Q \to \sim R)$

We draw its truth table now:

P	Q	R	P ∧ Q	P ∧ Q → R	~ Q → ~ R	Q
T	T	T	T	T	T	T
T	T	F	T	F	T	T
T	F	T	F	T	F	T
T	F	F	F	T	T	T
F	T	T	F	T	T	T
F	T	F	F	T	T	T
F	F	T	F	T	F	T
F	F	F	F	T	T	T

Q Q is true under all interpretations.

$\therefore$ It is a valid statement.

Example 8: Show that the set of statements "I will be wet if it rains and I go out of the house. It is raining now. I go out of the house. I will not be wet" are inconsistent.

Solution: W : I will be wet.

R : It rains.

G : I go out of the house.

$\therefore$ A set of formulae corresponding to given word problem is —

$\{(R \wedge G) \to W, R, \sim W\}$

It can be shown using truth table that

$((R \wedge G) \rightarrow W) \wedge R \wedge G \wedge \sim W$ is false under all interpretations and hence is inconsistent.

Example 9: Determine whether each of following is

a. Satisfiable *b.* Contradictory. *c.* Valid.

$S_1 : (P \,\&\, Q) \vee \sim (P \,\&\, Q)$

$S_2 : (P \,\&\, Q) \rightarrow (R \vee \sim Q)$

$S_3 : (P \,\&\, Q) \rightarrow (R \vee \sim Q)$

$S_4 : (P \vee Q) \,\&\, (P \vee \sim Q) \vee P?$

Solution: $S_1 : (P \,\&\, Q) \vee \sim (P \,\&\, Q)$

Its truth table is —

G : I go out of the house.

P	Q	$P \& Q = A$	$\sim(P \& Q) = B$	$A \vee B$
t	f	f	t	t
f	t	f	t	t
f	f	f	t	t
t	t	t	f	t

∴ It is satisfiable.

∴ It is not contradictory

∴ It is valid as sentence is true for every interpretation.

Consider $S_2 : (P \,\&\, Q) \rightarrow (R \vee \sim Q)$

P	Q	R	$P \& Q = X$	$\sim Q$	$R \vee \sim Q = Y$	$X \rightarrow Y$
f	f	f	f	t	t	f
f	f	t	f	t	t	f
f	t	f	f	f	f	t
f	t	t	f	f	t	f
t	f	f	f	t	t	f
t	f	t	f	t	t	f
t	t	t	t	f	t	t

∴ It is satisfiable

It is not contradictory

It is not valid.

$S_3 : (P \,\&\, Q) \rightarrow (R \vee \sim Q)$

Its truth table is —

P	Q	R	$P \& Q = X$	$\sim Q$	$R \vee \sim Q = Y$	$X \rightarrow Y$
f	f	f	f	t	t	f
f	f	t	f	t	t	f
f	t	f	f	f	f	t
f	t	t	f	f	t	f
t	f	f	f	t	t	f
t	f	t	f	t	t	f
t	t	f	t	f	f	f
t	t	t	t	f	t	t

∴ It is satisfiable

It is not contradictory

It is not valid.

$S_4 : (P \vee Q) \,\&\, (P \vee \sim Q) \vee P$

P	Q	$P \vee Q = X$	$\sim Q$	$P \vee \sim Q = Y$	$Y \vee P = Z$	$X \,\&\, Z$
t	t	t	f	t	t	t
f	t	t	f	f	f	f
t	f	t	t	t	t	t
f	f	f	t	t	t	t

∴ It is satisfiable

It is not contradictory

It is not valid.

Q.10. What are normal forms in propositional logic? Explain CNF and DNF.

Ans. There are two major normal forms of statements in propositional logic. They are Conjunctive Normal Form (CNF) and Disjunctive Normal Form (DNF).

Any formula can be converted into its normal form by substituting it by its equivalent formulae. Two formulas *P* and *Q* are equivalent if and only if the truth values of *P* and *Q* are same for all values of *P* and *Q*. We have already discussed some widely used equivalent formulae in table III.

A formula P is said to be in CNF if it is of the form

$$P = P_1 \wedge P_2 \wedge P_3 ,..., \wedge P_n ;\, n \geq 1$$

where each P_1, P_2 , P_3 ,..., P_n is a disjunction of an atom or negation of an atom.

A formula P is said to be in DNF if it has the form

$$P = P_1 \vee P_2 \vee P_3 ,..., \vee P_n ;\, n \geq 1$$

where each P_1, P_2, P_3, …, P_n is a conjunction of an atom or negation of an atom.

Conversion Procedure to Normal Form

Step 1 : Eliminate implication and biconditionals. We use the following laws

$$(P \rightarrow Q) = {}^{\bullet}P \vee Q$$

$$(P \leftrightarrow Q) = (P \rightarrow Q) \wedge (Q \rightarrow P)$$

$$= ({}^{\bullet}P \vee Q) \wedge ({}^{\bullet}Q \vee P)$$

Step 2 : Reduce the NOT symbol by the formula $({}^{\bullet}({}^{\bullet}P)) = P$ and apply De Morgan's theorem to bring negations before the atoms.

$${}^{\bullet}(P \vee Q) = {}^{\bullet}P \wedge {}^{\bullet}Q$$

$${}^{\bullet}(P \vee Q) = P \vee {}^{\bullet}Q$$

Step 3 : Use Distributive laws and other equivalent formula given in table III to obtain the normal form

$$P \wedge (Q \vee R) = (P \wedge Q) \vee (P \wedge R)$$

$$P \vee (Q \wedge R) = (P \vee R) \wedge (P \vee R)$$

Conjunctive Normal Form

The resolution rule applies only to disjunction of literals. So it would seem to be relevant only for knowledge bases and queries consisting of such disjunctions. How can then it lead to a complete inference procedure for all of propositional logic? The answer is that every sentence of propositional logic is logically equivalent to a conjunction of disjunctions of literals. A sentence expressed as a conjunction of disjunctions of literals is said to be in a conjunctive normal form (CNF). Every sentence can be transformed into a CNF sentence using the following steps making use of table 6.2

1. Eliminate ↔ replacing $P \leftrightarrow Q$ with $(P \rightarrow Q) \wedge (Q \rightarrow P)$
2. Eliminate → replacing $P \rightarrow Q$ with ${}^{\bullet}P \wedge Q$.

3. CNF requires • should appear only in literals, so we move • inwards by repeated application of following equivalences to Table 6.2
   • (• P) ≡ Double-negation elimination $(P \wedge Q) \equiv (\bullet P \wedge \bullet Q)$ de Morgan
   •$(P \vee Q) \equiv (\bullet P \vee \bullet Q)$ de Morgan
4. We now apply distributivity law, distributive ∨ over ∧. whenever the sentence contains nested ∨ over ∧ operators applied to literals.

Example 1: Convert $((P \to Q) \to R)$ into CNF

Solution: $((P \to Q) \to R)$

$$= \neg(P \to Q) \vee R$$
$$= \neg(\neg P \vee Q) \vee R$$
$$= (P \vee \neg Q) \wedge (\neg Q \vee R)$$
$$= (P \vee R) \wedge (\neg Q \vee R)$$

Hence, $(P \vee R) \wedge (\neg Q \vee R)$ is the CNF of $((P \to Q) \to R)$

We are in a position to solve some examples now.

Example 2: Convert $(P \to Q) \to R$ to CNF?

Solution: Given: $(P \to Q) \to R$

$$= (\sim P \vee Q) \to R$$
$$= \sim(\sim P \vee Q) \vee R \quad [\because P \to Q = \sim P \vee Q]$$
$$= (P \,\&\sim Q) \vee R \quad \text{[De Morgan's law]}$$
$$- (P \vee R) \,\&\, (\sim Q \vee R) \quad \text{[By distributive law]}$$

Example 3: Convert $\sim (P \,\&\, Q) \,\&(P \vee Q)$ to DNF?

Solution: $(\sim P \vee \sim Q) \,\&\, (P \vee Q)$ [De Morgan's law]

$$= ((\sim P \vee \sim Q) \,\&\, P) \vee ((\sim P \vee \sim Q) \,\&\, Q) \quad \text{[By distributive law]}$$
$$= (\sim P \,\&\, P) \vee (\sim Q \,\&\, P) \vee (\sim P \,\&\, Q) \vee (\sim Q \,\&\, Q)$$

Example 4: Convert $\sim(P \vee \sim Q) \,\&\, (R \vee S)$ to DNF?

Solution: $(\sim P \,\&\, Q) \,\&\, (\sim R \vee S)$ [De Morgan's law]

$$= \sim(\sim ((\sim P \,\&\, Q) \,\&\, (\sim R \vee S))) \quad \text{[Negative 2 times]}$$
$$= \sim((P \vee \sim Q) \vee (R \,\&\sim \vee))$$

Example 5: Convert $P \to ((Q \,\&\, R) \leftrightarrow S)$ to DNF?

Solution: $F \to G = \sim F \vee G$

∴ We have —

$$= (\sim P) \vee ((Q \,\&\, R) \to S$$
$$= (\sim P) \vee (\sim (Q \,\&\, R) \vee S) \,\&\, (\sim S \vee (Q \,\&\, R)) \quad [\because P \leftrightarrow Q = (\sim P \vee Q) \,\&\, (\sim Q \vee P)]$$
$$= (\sim P) \vee (((\sim Q \vee \sim R) \vee S) \,\&\, ((\sim S \vee Q) \,\&\, (\sim S \vee R))) \quad \text{[Distributive law?]}$$
$$= (\sim P) \vee ((\sim Q \vee \sim R) \vee S) \,\&\, ((\sim S \vee Q) \,\&\, (\sim S \vee R)))$$

Example 6: Convert $(\sim P \,\&\, Q) \vee (P \,\&\sim Q) \,\&\, S$ to CNF?

Solution: $(\sim P \,\&\, Q) \vee P \,\&\, (\sim Q \,\&\, S)$ (Associativity)

$$= ((\sim P \vee P) \,\&\, (Q \vee P) \,\&\, (\sim Q \,\&\, S)) \quad \text{[Distributive law]}$$

Q.11. Give steps of resolution in propositional logic [By Robinson]?

Ans. Resolution is the process of producing proofs by refutation or contradiction. It is a procedure used for theorem proving. It is the rule of inference. The procedure of resolution is as follows:

1. Assume that the negation of the theorem which we want to prove is time.
2. Show that the axioms and the assumed negation of the theorem together cannot be true.

3. Conclude that the assumed negation of the theorem cannot be true because it leads to contradiction.
4. Conclude that the theorem must be true as the assumed negation of the theorem is not true.

Resolution is applicable only on the facts represented in clausal form. A clause is a special formula expressed as disjunction of literals. If a clause contains only one literal then it is called as a visit clause. Please note that CNF representation of a formula is of the form $(C_1 \wedge C_2 \wedge ... \wedge C_n)$ where each C_k $(1 \leq k \leq n)$ is a clause

If two clauses C_1 and C_2 contain a complementary pair of literals $\{L, \sim L\}$ then these clauses may be resolved together by deleting L from C_1 and $\sim L$ from C_2 and constructing a new clause by the disjunction of the remaining literals in C_1 and C_2. The new clause thus generated is called as resolvent of C_1 and C_2. Here, C_1 and C_2 are called parents of resolved clause. The parents can contain more than one set of complementary pair of literals. All complementary pair of literals are removed and resolvent is constructed, by the disjunction of the remaining literals in the parents.

For example : Consider two clauses

C_1 with literal $L1$ and $\sim L2$

& C_2 with literal $\sim L1$ and $L2$

i.e., $C_1 = L1 \vee \sim L2 \vee C_1'$

& $C_2 = \sim L1 \vee \sim L2 \vee C_2'$

where C_1' and C_2' are disjunction of remaining literals in C_1 and C_2 respectively After resolving C_1 and C_2 we get

An inverted binary tree is generated with the last node of the binary tree to be a resolvent. This is known as a **Resolution tree**. Resolved literals are underlined for more clarity.

For example : Consider two clauses as

$C_1 = P \vee Q \vee \sim R$

& $C_2 = \sim Q \vee W$

P ∨ Q ∨ ~R ~Q ∨ ~W

P ∨ ~R ∨ W

$\therefore$ Resolvent $(P \vee Q \vee \sim R, \sim Q \vee W) = P \vee \sim R \vee \underline{W}$

Now, consider another example with three clauses —

$C_1 = P \vee Q \vee R$

$C_2 = \sim Q \vee W$

and

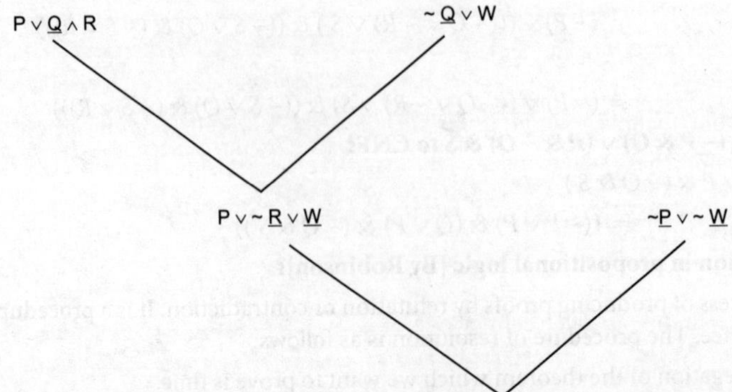

$\therefore$ Resolvent $R = (C_1, C_2, C_3)$

Please note that the order of clauses taken for resolution is immaterial, we have to identify two clauses with complementary literals and resolve them. Take the current resolvent and try to find another clause yet not been resolved having complementary literal proceed till all the clauses have been resolved. Also note that the resolved clauses are not used in resolution process further.

In a similar manner, in the big system, where there are multiple clauses, all pairs of resolvable clauses are identified and resolved.

Resolution Rule: The resolution of clauses $(A \vee B)$ and $(\bullet B \vee C)$ is $A \vee C$.

Resolution works on the principle of refutation, *i.e.*, it presumes that the statement to be proved is not true and then it proves that whatever we have assumed is not true and hence the original statement is true. Now let us resolve the following clause —

$\{(\bullet A, B)\ (\bullet A, \bullet B, C), A \bullet C\}$

We start by resolving the first clause with the second clause, thus eliminating B and $\bullet B$ to get

$\{(\bullet A, C), A, \bullet C\}$

$$= \{C, \bullet C\}$$

$$= \perp \quad (i.e., \text{falsum}).$$

∴ This resolution has resulted in a falsum meaning that the original clauses were inconsistent.

Thus, we have refutated the original clauses using resolution.

Refutation (RR)

∴ We say that

$\{(\bullet A, B), (\bullet A, \bullet B, C), A \bullet C\} = \perp$ after RR.

This is how refutation helps in logical inferencing.

Let us now write an algorithm for Resolution using Propositional Logic —

Algorithm : Resolve (P, F)

Step 1: Convert all propositions of F to clausal form.

Step 2 : Negate P and convert the result to clausal form. Add it to the set of clauses obtained in step 1.

Step 3 : Repeat until either of the contradictions is found or no progress can be made.

a. Select two clauses (called as parent clauses).

b. Resolve them together to create the resolvent.

c. If the resolvent is the empty clause, then a contradiction has been found. If it is not, then add it to the set of clauses available.

Application of Resolution

Resolution cannot be used to solve combinational search problems but it can help us by telling whether the solution to such a problem exists or not.

For example.: Consider a three coloring problem "Given a map, it is possible to color the countries using three colors such that no two countries that are next to each other have the some color."

We can represent this search in form of clauses and their satisfiability can be tested using resolution. This method tells us that if a solution exists but does not tell us what that solution is. We are in a position to solve some problems now.

Example 1: "If it is hot, then it is humid. If it is humid then it will rain. It is hot." Show that "It will rain".

Solution : Let us denote these statements

H: It is humid

R: It will rain.

O: It is hot.

∴ Formulae corresponding to given sentences are —

If it is hot, then it is humid *i.e.*, $O \rightarrow H \cong \sim O \vee H$

If it is humid, then it will rain *i.e.*, $H \rightarrow R \cong \sim Q \vee R$

Construct a set, S, of clauses from above set of statements as given below —

$$S = \{\sim O \vee H, \sim H \vee R, O\}$$

Include negation of "It will rain (say R)" to the set, S.

$\therefore$ $$S' = \{\sim O \vee H, \sim H \vee R, O, \sim R\}$$

Now, we can show that S' is unsatisfiable, *i.e.*, from S' one can deduce empty clause, then we can infer or conclude that 'It will rain'.

$\therefore$ The resolution tree is —

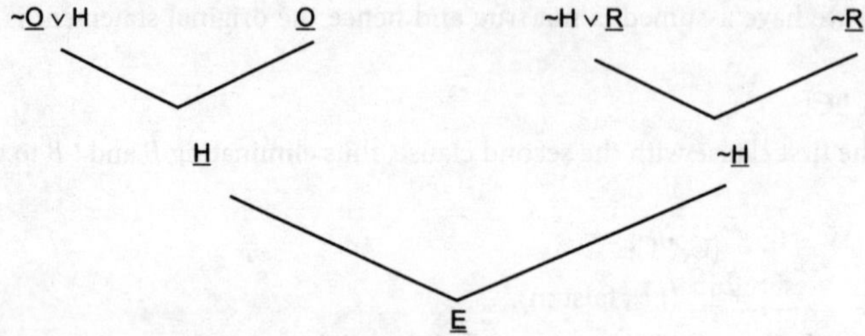

$\therefore$ an empty clause (E) is deduced from a set, S',"It will rain" is concluded from S.

Example 2 : Consider the following statements —

$$A \rightarrow B$$
$$B \rightarrow C$$
$$C \rightarrow D$$
$$D \rightarrow EVF$$
$$A \rightarrow F.$$

Using resolution, find its clausal from and draw its tree.

Solution: Firstly, we negate the conclusion

$$A \rightarrow F, \textit{i.e.}, \text{ we get } {}^{\bullet}(A \rightarrow F).$$

Next, $$D \rightarrow E \vee F$$

$$\equiv {}^{\bullet}D \vee (E \vee F)$$

& $${}^{\bullet}(A \rightarrow F) \equiv {}^{\bullet}({}^{\bullet}A \vee F)$$

$$\equiv A \wedge {}^{\bullet}F$$

$\therefore$ Our clauses are, $S = \{({}^{\bullet}A, B), ({}^{\bullet}B, C), ({}^{\bullet}C, D), ({}^{\bullet}\underline{D}, E, F), (A\ {}^{\bullet}F)\}$

and our proof in tree form will be —

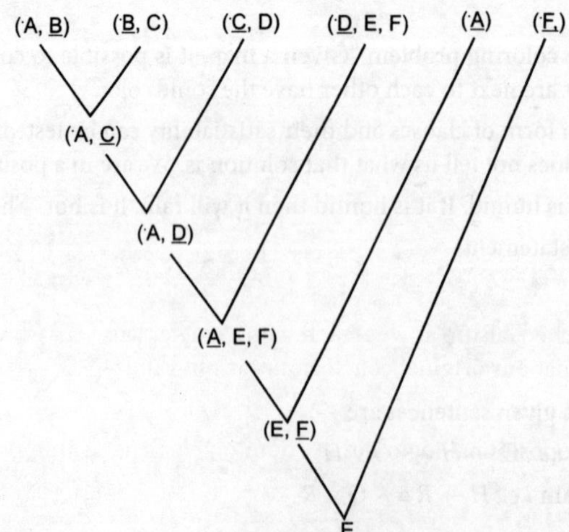

Example 3: Consider the following statements

1. $P P$
2. $(P \wedge Q) \rightarrow R \sim P \vee \sim Q \vee R$
3. $(S \vee T) \rightarrow Q \sim S \vee Q$
4. $\sim T \vee Q$
5. $T T$

Using resolution, find its clausal form and draw its tree.

Solution: We select *Cl i.e., P*

and then negate $\sim R$.

Now select (*C*2) clauses as

$\sim P \vee \sim Q \vee R$.

∴ We have two clauses as—

$$C1 : \sim R$$
$$C2 : \sim P \vee \sim Q \vee R$$

∴ Resolvent will be $\sim P \vee \sim Q$.

Here, we have proved R. We should always select those pairs that can be resolved very easily.

Now, prove *P*. We negate $\sim P$ to *P*.

$$C1 : \sim P \vee \sim Q$$
$$C2 : P$$

Resolvent is $\sim Q$.

Now prove *T*. Select $\sim T \vee R$

$$C1 : \sim Q$$
$$C2 : \sim T \vee Q$$

∴ Resolvent is $\sim T$.

At last we have *C*1 as *T* and *C*2 as $\sim T$. It is left empty which is a contradiction.

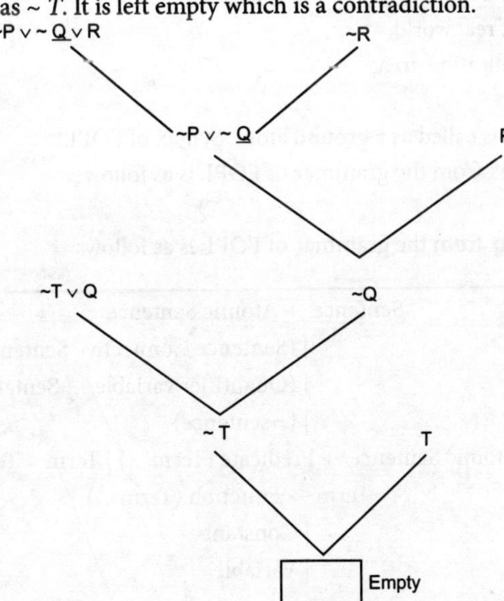

Note that here, we have not reached falsum as we are left with a single clause {E} which cannot be resolved with anything now. Hence, we can conclude that our original conclusion was not valid.

Limitations of Propositional Logic

A very serious limitation of propositional logic is that common elements within propositions cannot be used to make inference.

For example.,

Consider the following statements in propositional logic.

S_1 : Rajiv is an author of 12 books.

S_2 : Rajiv is assistant professor.

S_3 : All professors are authors

Now, from S_1, S_2 and S_3 we cannot conclude that all professors are authors because this method of representation fails in capturing the relationship between any individual. Propositional logic lacks in expressiveness which is very vital for good KR. Propositional logic is too coarse to easily describe properties of objects. We cannot make generalized statements.

So, we go to predicate logic.

Q.12. What is predicate logic and its resolution?

Ans. We are interested in a form of predicate logic called as **first order predicate logic.** FOPL allows the quantified variables to refer to object domain and not to predicates or functions. If the quantification is over first order predicates and functions then it becomes second order predicate. Similarly, third order predicate allows quantification over predicates and function of second order and so on. A.I. researchers have found that FOPL is most suitable for KR.

Every complete sentence contains two parts — a subject and a predicate.

Subject : The subject is what (or whom) the sentence is about.

Predicate : It tells something about the subject.

For example. In the sentence, 'Rajiv is an author' subject is 'Rajiv' and predicate is 'author'.

Sentences involving the predicates that describe the property of objects are denoted by $P(x)$ where

P — The predicate,

x — is a variable denoting any object.

Here, $P(x)$ is not a proposition. This is because $P(x)$ involves a variable x, we cannot assign a truth value to $P(x)$. But if we replace x by an individual object, we get a proposition, like if we replace x by "Rajiv" in $P(x)$ we get a proposition.

Characteristics of predicate logic

1. Logical inferencing is allowed.
2. More accurate KR of facts of real world.
3. Program designing is its application area.
4. Better theoretical foundation.
5. A predicate with no variable is called as a ground atom. Syntax of FOPL

A complete description of syntax from the grammar of FOPL is as follows:

Syntax of FOPL

A complete description of syntax from the grammar of FOPL is as follows:

Sentence → Atomic Sentence
| (Sentence Connective Sentence)
| (Quantifier variable … Sentence)
| (¬sentence)
Atomic Sentence → Predicate (Term…) | Term = Term
Term → Function (Term…)
| Constant
| Variable
Connective → ⇒ | ∧ | ∨ | ⇒
Quantifier → ∀ | ∃
Constant → a | X_1 | John | …
Variable → a | x | s |
Predicate → Before | HasColour | Raining | …
Function → Mother | LeftLeg

NOTE: Predicate calculus symbols are irreducible syntactic elements just as we have tokens in programming language.

Rules for predicate calculus symbols —

1. Set of letters (uppercase or lowercase) is allowed.
2. Set of digits (0 to 9) is allowed.
3. Underscore (...) is allowed.

But,

1. Blanks and non-alphanumeric characters cannot be used.
2. Special characters like $, *, #, /, are not allowed.

For example.

Valid symbols	Invalid symbols
white	2black
son-of	Ab % b
father-of	**3
Rajiv	— parrot

NOTE: Parentheses, commas and periods are used to construct well formed structure but do not denote objects or relations in the world. These are known as improper symbols.

Symbols used :

1. Predicate symbols: They denote relations or functional mapping from the elements of a domain to the values true or false

   For example.

   Brother, king, LOVE, GREATER, EQUAL, MARRIES etc.
2. **Function symbols :** They denote relations defined on a domain. For example. Father of, Age of, plus etc.
3. **Variable symbols :** Lowercase un-subscripted or subscripted letters like *x, y, z, t, u, v* etc. They can assume different values over a given domain.
4. **Constants :** They are fixed value terms. They are individual symbols which are names of objects like john, rajiv, 1, 2, 3, *a, b, c* etc.
5. **Quantifiers :** They are of two types —
   a. ∃ (or existential quantifier) where (∃*x*) means for some *x* or there is no *x*.
   b. ∀ (or universal quantifier) where (∀*x*) means for all *x*. We will discuss about it a bit later.
6. **Logical Operators / Connectives :** FOPL uses the same five connectives of PL *i.e.* ~ (not), ∧ (and), ∨ (or), → (implication) and ↔ (equivalence).

   Please note that function and predicate symbols take a specified number of arguments. If they take n arguments then it is called as n-place function and predicate respectively. Also note that constants, variables and functions are referred to as terms.

   Predicates are referred to as atomic formulas or atoms.

   Precedence of operators & quantifiers~ ((Higher priority)

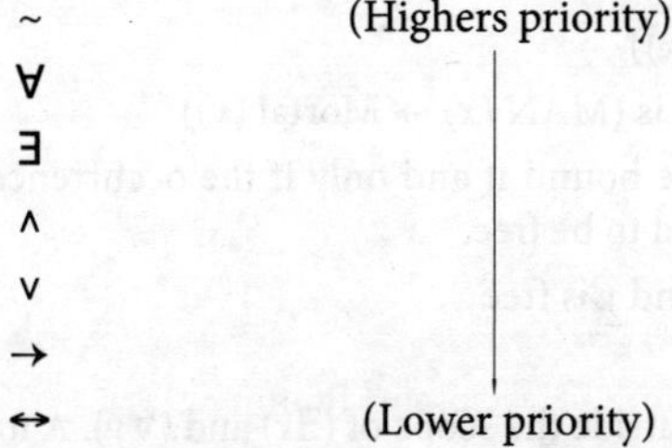

Quantifiers {∀, ∃} have same priorities as ~ and parentheses have highest priorities.

Using quantifiers

a. **Universal quantifier ($\forall$)**

It is used to represent the phrase 'for all'. It says that something is true for all possible values of a variable.

For example.

(*i*). John loves everyone

In predicate calculus, we write it as ($\forall x$) LOVE (john, x)

(*ii*) for all $n, x^n = x \,.\, x \,.\, x \ldots x$-times is written as $\forall x \, \forall n \, Q(x, n)$ where

b. **Existential quantifier ($\exists x$):**

It is used to represent the Phrase 'there exist.' It indicates that the variable is time for at least one interpretation.

For example.

(*i*) "There exists x such that $x^3 = 8$." is written as —

$\exists x$: $R(x)$. Where $R(x)$ is $x^3 = 8$.

(*ii*) Lord Ram has a crown on his head.

$\exists x$ Crown (x) $\wedge$ On head (x, Ram)

NOTE: ($\forall$) uses $\rightarrow$ connective whereas $\exists$ uses $\wedge$ connective

c. **Nested quantifiers:**

We can use both $\forall$ and $\exists$ quantifiers separately.

For example. 'Brothers are siblings' can be written as —

$\forall x \, \exists y$ Brother (x, y) $\rightarrow$ Sibling (x, y)

or $\forall x, y$ sibling (x, y) $\rightarrow$ sibling (y, x)

Example 2 : 'Everybody loves somebody' can be written as —

$\forall x \, fy$ loves (x, y)

or $Q(x, n) = x^n$.

Connection between $\forall$ and $\exists$

The two quantifiers are actually intimately connected to each other, through negation. Saying that everyone dislikes garlic is the same as saying that there does not exist someone who likes the garlic:

$\forall x \cdot$ likes (x Garlic) = $\cdot \exists x$ likes (x, Garlic)

We can go one step further : "Everyone likes ice cream" means that there is no one who does not like ice cream:

$\forall x$ likes (x, Ice Cream) = $\cdot \exists x$ likes (x, Ice Cream)

Because $\forall$ is really a conjunction over the universe of objects and $\exists$ is a disjunction, it should not be surprising that they obey De Morgan's rules. The De Morgan rules for quantified and unquantified sentences are:

1. $\forall x \neg P \equiv \neg \exists xP$ 2. $\neg \forall xP \equiv \exists x \neg P$
3. $\forall x P \equiv \neg \exists x \neg P$ 4. $\exists xP \equiv \neg \forall x \neg P$
5. $\neg P \wedge \neg Q \equiv \neg (P \vee Q)$ 6. $\neg (P \wedge Q) \equiv (\neg P \vee \neg Q)$
7. $P \wedge Q \equiv \neg(\neg P \vee \neg Q)$ 8. $P \vee Q \equiv \neg(\neg P \wedge \neg Q)$

Thus, we do not really need both $\forall$ and $\exists$ as we do not really need both $\wedge$ and $\vee$.

The range over which a variable is valid is called its **scope**.

For example. ($\forall x$) (MAN (x) $\rightarrow$ Mortal (x))

Here, scope of ($\forall x$) is (MAN (x) $\rightarrow$ Mortal (x))

An occurrence of a variable x in a formula is said to be bound if and only if the occurrence is within the scope of a quantifier employing the variable x, else a variable is said to be free.

For example. In ($\forall x$) $P(x, y)$ x is bound and y is free

Example 2 : In ($\exists x$) ($\forall y$) $P(x, y) \wedge Q(x)$

x and y are bound in $P(x, y)$ x is free in $Q(x)$ as $Q(x)$ is outside the scope of ($\exists x$) and ($\forall y$). A formula is said to be closed if there are no free occurrence of any variable in it.

For example. $(\exists x)(\forall y)(P(x, y) \wedge Q(x))$ is a closed formula

whereas $(\exists y) P(x, y)$ is not.

We are in a position to solve some problems now.

Example 1 : Represent the following facts in predicate logic —

a. **Snow is white.**

b. **Marcus was a man.**

c. **Marcus was a Pompeian.**

d. **All Pompeians were Romans.**

e. **Caesar was a ruler.**

f. **All Romans were either loyal to Caesar or hated him.**

g. **Everyone is legal to someone.**

h. **Marcus tried to assassinate Caesar.**

i. **If it rains then sky will be cloudy.**

j. **If you will not work hard, you will fail.**

Solution:

a. Snow (white).

b. Man (Marcus).

c. Pompeian (Marcus)

d. $\forall x$: Pompeian $(x) \rightarrow$ Roman (x)

e. Ruler (Caesar)

f. $\forall x$: Roman $(x) \rightarrow$ loyal to $(x$, Caesar$) \vee$ hate x, (Caesar)

g. $\forall x\ \exists y$ loyalto (x, y)

h. tryassassinate (Marcus, Caesar).

i. raining $\rightarrow$ cloudy (sky)

j. ' Workhard $\rightarrow$ fail

Example 2: Write the predicate forms of the following —

a. **All indoor games are easy.** *b.* **Rajiv only likes cricket game.**

c. **All dogs are mammals.** *d.* **Roses are red.**

e. **John is father of Bob.**

Solution:

a. $\forall x$ indoor game $(x) \rightarrow$ easy (x) *b.* likes (rajiv, cricket)

c. $\forall x$ dog $(x) \rightarrow$ Mammal (x) *d.* red (roses)

e. father (john, bob).

Example 3: Given formulas S_1 and S_2 below. Show that $Q(a)$ is a logical consequence of the two –

$S_1 : (\forall x)(P(x) \rightarrow Q(x))$

$S_2 : P(a)$

Solution : As $(\forall x)(P(x \rightarrow Q(x))$

Now, $x = a$ in S_2

i.e., $Q(a)$ is a logical consequence of the two statements S_1 and S_2.

Example 4 : Translate the following statements in FOPL—

(i) All empolyees earning more than Rs. 60,000 per year pay income tax.

(ii) No employee of University earns more than the VC.

(iii) Only old people get sick.

(*iv*) All men are people.

(*v*) All Pompeians were Romans.

(*vi*) All Romans were either loyal to Caesar or hated him.

(*vii*) People only try to assassinate rulers they are not loyal to.

(*viii*) Everyone is loyal to someone.

(*ix*) It is now 2013.

(*x*) Mohan has exactly two friends.

(*xi*) American vegetarians do not take milk but Indian vegetarians do.

(*xii*) For every natural number, there is a natural number greater than it.

(*xiii*) Nothing beautiful is evil.

(*xiv*) Some highly qualified scientists are unemployed in Russia but in America all qualified scientists are employed.

Solution: (*a*) For all *x*, if *x* is an employee and *x* earns more than 60,000, *x* pay tax.

Let employee be EMPLOYEE and pay tax be TAX. Then, we get—

$\forall x$: ((EMPLOYEE (x) & GE ($i(x)$, 60,000) $\rightarrow$ TAX(x)).

(*b*) Let employees = x

and $VC = y$

For all *x* and for all *y*, if *x* is employee and *y* is VC then *x* cannot earn more than *y*.

$\therefore \quad \forall xy\ ((E(x)\ \&\ P(y) \rightarrow\ \sim GE(i(x), i(y)).$

(*c*) There exists some *x*, if *x* is people and *x* is old,

Let people be $P(x)$,

Old be $O(x)$,

Sick be $S(x)$

$\therefore$ We get— $\exists x : (P(x)\ \&\ O(x) \ \rightarrow S(x))$

(*d*) For all *x*, if *x* is men, *x* is people.

Let Men $\rightarrow$ MEN

People $\rightarrow$ PEOPLE

$\therefore \quad \forall x$: MEN ($x$) $\rightarrow$ PEOPLE(x)

(*e*) For all *x*, if *x* is Pompeians, *x* were Romans.

$\forall x$: Pompeian (x) $\rightarrow$ Roman (x)

(*f*) For all *x*, if *x* were Romans, *x* were loyal to Caesar or *x* hated him.

$\therefore \forall x$: Roman (x) $\rightarrow$ LOYAL (x, Caesar) $\vee$ HATE (x, Caesar)

(*g*) $\forall xy$: PEOPLE(x) $\wedge$ RULER(y) $\wedge$ ASSASSINATE (x, y) $\rightarrow \sim$ LOYAL, To (x, y)

(*h*) For all *x*, *x* is loyal to *y*.

$\forall x : \exists y$: Loyal (x, y)

(*i*) now = 2013

(*j*) Let $E(x)$ where *x* is a person,

$M(x)$ where *x* is a Mohan.

$F(x)$ *x* has friend.

a for 2 as constant

$\therefore \quad \forall x\ (M(x) \rightarrow\ F(a, x))$

(*k*) Let $E(x)$ – *x* is vegetarian.

$A(x)$ – *x* is American.

$I(x)$ – *x* is Indian.

$M(x)$ – x takes milk.

$\sim M(x)$ – x do not take milk.

$\therefore$ $\exists x\,(E(x)\ \&\ A(x) \rightarrow\ \sim M(x))$

$\exists x\,(E(x)\ \&\ I(x) \rightarrow\ M(x))$

(*l*) For all x and y, if x is natural number and y is natural number, y is greater than x.

Let $N(x)$ be x as natural number,

$N(y)$, y is a natural number.

$G(x, y)$, x is greater than y.

$\forall x, y\,(N(x)\ \&\ N(y) \rightarrow\ a\,(y, x))$

(*m*) For every x, if x is nothing beautiful, x is evil.

$\forall x\,(\sim B(x) \rightarrow\ E(x)).$

This can also be written as—

For every x, if x is nothing and x is not beautiful, x is evil.

$\forall x : (\sim B(x) \rightarrow\ N(x) \rightarrow E(x))$

where $B(x)$, x is beautiful. $N(x)$, x is nothing.

$E(x)$, x is evil.

(*n*) Let us denote the following—

$S(x)$: x is highly qualified scientist

$A(x)$: x is American (scientist in America)

$R(x)$: x is Russian (scientist in Russia)

$E(x)$: x is employed.

$\sim E(x)$: x is not employed

$\therefore$ $\forall x : (S(x)\ \&\ A(x) \rightarrow E(x))$

$\exists x\,(S(x)\ \&\ R(x) \rightarrow E(x))$

EXAMPLE 5 : Convert into FOPL statements:

(*i*) If x is connected to y by z, y is connected to x by z.

(*ii*) If you can get to y from z and you can get to z from y, you can get to z from x.

(*iii*) If x is connected to town y by highway z and bicycles are allowed on z, you can get to y by bike from x.

(*iv*) Town A is connected to Town B by Road 1.

(*v*) Apples are food.

(*vi*) Bill eats peanuts and is still alive.

(*vii*) Bill is brother of SUE.

(*viii*) All Pompeians died when volcano erupted in 79 A.D.

(*ix*) All men are mortal.

(*x*) Town–A and Town–E are not connected by Road 3.

(*xi*) Bikes are allowed on road-3, road-4 and road-5.

Solution:

(*i*) $\forall x, y, z$: (CONNECTED $(x, y, z) \rightarrow$ CONNECTED (y, x, z))

(*ii*) $\forall x, y, z$: (GETTO (z, y) and GETTO $(y, z) \rightarrow$ GETTO (x, z))

(*iii*) $\forall x, y, z$ (CONNECTED (x, y, z) and BIKE $(z) \rightarrow$ GETTO (x, y))

(*iv*) $\forall a, b$ road-1 CONNECTED (a, b, road 1)

(*v*) For all x, if x is apple, x is food.

$A(x)$: x is apple.

$F(x)$: x is food.

$\therefore$ $\forall x: (A(x) \to F(x))$

(vi) $B(x)$: x is bill.

$P(x)$: x eats peanuts.

$A(x)$: x is alive.

$\therefore$ $\forall x: (B(x) \to P(x)\ \&\ A(x))$

(vii) Brother (Bill, Sue)

(viii) Erupted (volcano, 79) $\wedge$ $\forall x$ [Pompeian $(x) \to$ died $(x, 79)$]

(ix) For all x if x is men, x is mortal.

(x) If x is town A and y is town B, x and y are not connected by road-3.

$\therefore$ $\forall x, y, z$: ~ CONNECTED (x, y, z) or

$\forall x, y, z$: (Town (x) & Town (y) $\to$ ~ CONNECTED (x, y, z)

(xi) $\forall x$: BIKE (x)

$\forall y$: BIKE (y)

$\forall z$: BIKE (z).

Inferencing in predicate logic : The rules of inference for the propositional formulas are applicable to predicate calculus. So propositional formulas are also predicate formulas. We have to just replace propositional variables by predicate variables.

For example.

1. $\exists x\,(P(x) \vee Q(x)) \equiv \exists x\, P(x) \vee \exists x\, Q(x)$
2. $\exists x\,(P \equiv Q(x)) \vee P \vee (\exists x\, Q(x))$
3. $\forall x\,(P(x) \wedge Q(x)) \equiv \forall x\, P(x) \wedge \forall x\, Q(x)$
4. $\forall x\,(P \wedge Q(x)) \equiv P \wedge (\forall x Q(x))$
5. $\neg(\exists x\, P(x))\ \forall \equiv x \neg (p(x))$
6. $\forall x\, P(x) \Rightarrow \exists x\, P(x)$
7. $\neg(\exists x\, P(x)) \equiv \exists x \neg P(x))$

We are in a position to solve some problems now.

Q. 1. Represent the following in symbol logic:

***a.* All that glitters is not gold.**

***b.* Any person who is respected by every person is a king.**

***c.* God helps those who help themselves.**

***d.* Jack and Jill went up the hill.**

***e.* Ram likes Sita.**

Ans.

a. $\neg\forall x$ Glitters $(x) \to$ Gold

b. $\exists x\, \forall y$ King (x)

c. $\forall x$ helps (God, helps (x, x))

d. together (went up (jack), went up (jill) $\to$ hill

e. likes (Ram, Sita)

Resolution in Predicate Logic : In predicate logic, we need to compare the arguments of the literals also. In predicate logic, the existential and universal quantifiers are used. We do skolemisation for that skolemisation is removing existential quantifiers and replacing the corresponding variable by a constant or a function. A constant or a function is called as skolem constant or function respectively.

Resolution Steps : It requires that all statements be converted into a nonmalized clausal form. Its procedure is given below:

Step 1: Eliminate all implication and equivalency connectives (use $\sim P \vee Q$ in place of $P \rightarrow Q$ and $(\sim P \vee Q)$ and $(\sim Q \vee P)$ in place of $(P \vee Q)$.

Step 2 : Move all negations in, to the immediately preceding atom. Use P in place of $\sim (\sim P)$ and De Morgans's Law, $\exists x \sim F[x]$ in place of $\sim (\forall x) F(x)$ and $\forall x \sim F[x]$ in place of $\sim (\exists x) (F[x])$.

Step 3: Rename Variables, if necessary, so that all quantifiers have different variable assignments, *i.e.*, rename variables so that variables bound by one quantifier are not the same as variables bound by a different quantifier.

For example.: In the expression $\forall x (P(x)) \rightarrow (\exists x (Q(x)))$

rename the second "dummy" variable x which is bound by the existential quantifier to be a different variable, say y, to give $\forall x (P(x) \rightarrow (\exists y Q(y)))$.

Step 4: The process of eliminating the existential quantifiers through a substitution process requires that all such variables be replaced by something called "Skolem functions" which are the arbitrary functions which can always assume a correct value required for an existentially quantified variable. In this 4th step we skolemize by replacing all existentially quantified variables with skolem functions.

Step 5: Move all universal quantifiers to the left of the expression and put the expression on the right into CNF.

Step 6: Eliminate all universal quantifiers and conjunctions since they are retained implicitly. The resulting expressions are 'clauses' and the set of such expressions is said to be in clausal form.

Example. Convert the expression: $\exists x \forall y (\forall z P(f(x), y, z)$ into clausal form: $\rightarrow (\exists u Q(x, u)$ and $\exists v R(y, v)))$

Solution.

Step 1: Applying step (1):

$\exists x \forall y (\sim (\forall z) P(f(x), y, z) \vee (\exists u Q(x, u)$ and $(\exists v) R(y, v)))) (\exists v) R(y, v)))$

$[Q\, F \rightarrow G = \sim F \vee G]$

Step 2: Applying step (2) we get —

$\exists x \forall y (\exists z \sim P(f(x), y, z) \vee (\exists u Q(x, u)$ and $(\exists v) R(y, v))) (\exists v) R(y, v)))$

Step 3: Step (3) is not required.

Step 4: $\forall y (\sim P(f(a), y, g(y)) \vee (Q(a, h(y))$ and $R(y, I(y)))$

[Q u exists as an existential quantifier, x exists as an existential quantifier and so does v. So, in this step, we need to remove them and this can be done by replacing x with a, u with $h(y)$ and v with $I(x)$.]

Step 5: After applying step 5, the result is

$$\underbrace{\forall y((\sim P(f(a), y, g(y)) \vee Q(a, h(y))}_{F_1} \text{ and } (\sim P(f(a), y\, g(y)) \vee R(y, I(y)))$$

Step 6: After application of step 6 we obtain:

$$\sim P(f(a), y, g(y)) \vee Q(a, h(y))$$
$$\sim P(f(a), y, g(y) \vee R(y, I(y))$$

Thus, given FOPL sentence has been converted into clausal form.

Inference Rules in FOPL

Like PL, a key inference rule in FOPL is modus porens. For example.:

Assertion: *LION (leo)*

Implication: $\forall x$ *LION (x)* $\rightarrow$ *FE ROCIOUS (x)*

Conclusion: *Ferocious (leo)*

Representation using Rules : Rules can be considered as a subset of predicate logic. They have become a popular representation scheme for expert systems (also called as rule-based systems). They were first used in general problem solver (GPS) system in early (1970s). Rules have two component parts: a LHS referred to as the antecedent, premise, condition or situation and a RHS known as the consequent conclusion, action or response. LHS is also known as the if part and the RHS as the then part of the rule. Some rules also include an also part. Examples of such rules are:

IF : The temperature is greater than 95°C.

THEN: Open the relief valve.

These rules are stored in KB. The interpreter or inference engine inspects the LHS of each rule in KB and replaces the contents of working memory by the RHS of the rule. **We are in a position to solve some examples now.**

Q.13. Resolve the following example wff into its clausal form.

$(\forall x)\ \{P(x) \to \{(\forall y)\ [P(y) \to P(f(x, y))] \wedge \sim (\forall y)\ [Q(x, y) \to p(y)]\}\}$

Ans. S1: Eliminate implication symbols — all occurrences of the → symbol in a wff are eliminated by making the substitution ~ × | v × 2 for this substitution yields: X1 → X2 throughout the wff. So,

$(\forall x)\ \{\sim P(x) \to \{(\forall y)\ [\sim P(y) \to P(f(x, y))] \wedge \sim (\forall y)\ [\sim Q(x, y) \to p(y)]\}\}$

S2: Reduce Scopes of negation symbols — We want each negation symbol, ~, to apply to at most one atomic formula. By making use of de Morgan's laws we get:

$(\forall x)\ \{\sim P(x) \vee \{(\forall y)\ [\sim P(y) \vee P(f(x, y))] \wedge (\forall y)\ [Q(x, y) \wedge \sim p(y)]\}\}$

S3: Standardize variables — Instead of writing, $(\forall x)\ [P(x) \to (\exists x)\ Q(x)]$, we write $(\forall x)\ [P(x) \to (\exists y)\ Q(y)]$ *i.e.*, one type of dummy variable should be used with each type of quantifier. So in our wff, *x*-variable (dummy viz.) is used with universal (∀) quantifier whereas *y* is used with Existential quantifier (∃). Standardizing our example wff yields:

$(\forall x)\ \{\sim P(x) \vee \{(\forall y)\ [\sim P(y) \vee P(f(x, y)) \wedge (\exists w)[Q(x, w) \wedge \sim P(w)]\}\}$

S4: Eliminate existential quantifiers — Consider the wff : $(\forall y)\ [(\exists x)\ P(x, y)]$ which might be read as "for all *y*, there exists an *x* (possibly depending on *y*) such that *P* (*x*, *y*). " Note that because existential quantifier is within the scope of a universal quantifier, we allow the possiblity that value *x* that exists might depend on the value of *y*. Let this dependence be explicitly defined by some function *P* (*x*, *y*). which maps each value of *y* into *x* that "exists". Such a function is called a skolem function. If we use the skolem function in place of the x that exists, we can eliminate the existential quantifier 'all' together and write $(\forall y)\ P[g(y), y]$.

NOTE : If the existential quantifier being eliminated is not within the scope of any universal quantifiers, we use a skolem function of no arguments, which is just a constant. Thus, (∃x) *P* (*x*) becomes *P*(*A*) where the constant symbol A is used to refer to the entity that we know exists.

Eliminating all existentially quantified variables from given (there is just one) in our wff yields: $(\forall x)\ \{\sim P(x) \vee \{\forall y)\ [\sim P(y) \vee P(f(x, y))\ ] \vee [Q(x, g(x)) \wedge \sim P(g(x))]\}\}$

where $\boxed{w = g(x)}$; *g*(*x*) is a skolem function .

S5: Convert to prenex form —We may now move all of the universal quantifiers to the front of the wff. The resulting wff is said to be in prenex form. So we get:

$$(\forall x)\ (\forall y)\ \{\sim P(x) \vee \{[\sim P(y) \vee P(f(x, y))] \wedge [Q(x, g(a)) \wedge \sim P(g(x))]\}$$

S6: Put the matrix in CNF—We may put any matrix into CNF by repeatedly using one of the distributive rules, *i.e.*,

× 1v (× 2 ∧ × 3) by (× 1 v × 2) ∧ (× 1 v × 3).

So, our equation wff becomes:

$(\forall x)\ (\forall y)\ \}[\sim P(x) \vee \sim P(y) \vee P(f(x, y))] \wedge [\sim P(x) \vee Q(x, g(x))] \wedge [\sim P(x) \vee p(g(x))]\}$

S7: Eliminate universal quantifiers — We get:

$$\sim P(x) \vee \sim P(y) \vee P(f(x, y)) \wedge [\sim p(x) \vee Q(x, g(x))] \wedge [\sim P(x) \vee \sim P(g(x))]$$

S8: Eliminate ∧ symbols — We get

$$\left.\begin{array}{l} \sim P(x) \vee \sim P(y) \vee P[f(x, y)], \\ \sim P(x) \vee Q[x, g(x)], \\ \sim P(x) \vee \sim P[g(x)] \end{array}\right\} \text{is required clausal form}$$

Q.14. Show the validity of the following sentences."All men are mortal. John is a man. Therefore John is mortal."

$(\forall x)\ \{P(x) \to \{(\forall y)\ [P(y) \to P(f(x, y))] \wedge \sim (\forall y)\ [Q(x, y) \to p(y)]\}\}$

Ans. Say,

MAN (x) — x is a man. MORTAL (x) — x is mortal.

In *FOPL*, we have

$((\forall x)$ (MAN $(x) \rightarrow$ MORTAL $(x)) \wedge$ MAN (John)) $\rightarrow$ MORTAL (John)

Convert it to Skolem form —

$\propto$: ~ ((MAN (x) ∨ MORTAL (x)) ∧ MAN (John)) ∨ MORTAL(John)

If we show that ~$\propto$ is unsatisfiable then $\propto$ is valid.

~ $\propto$: (~ MAN (x) ∨ MORTAL (x)) ∧ MAN (John) ∧ ~ MORTAL (John)

∴ A set of clauses, S, that can be obtained from ~$\propto$ is —

S = {~ MAN (x) ∨ MORTAL (x), MAN (John), ~ MORTAL (John)}

If we show that S is unsatisfiable then ~$\propto$ is also unsatisfiable and hence $\propto$ is valid. In tree form

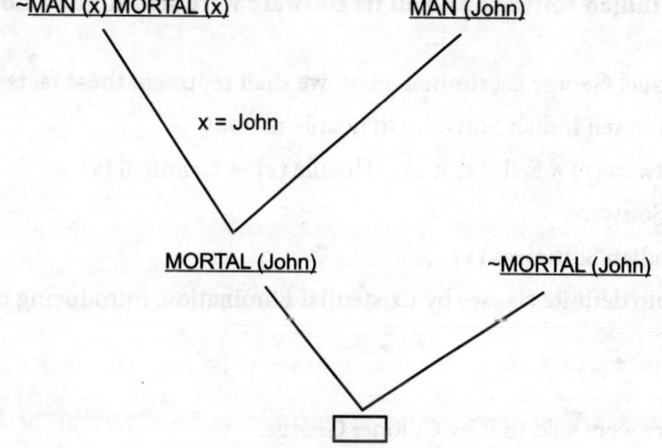

Q.15. Given the following predicates, show how resolution process can be applied to resolve—

T* : *P* ∨ *Q* ∨ *R* *U* : ~ *P* ∨ *R* *V* : ~ *Q* *W* : ~ *R

Ans. The resolution tree is —

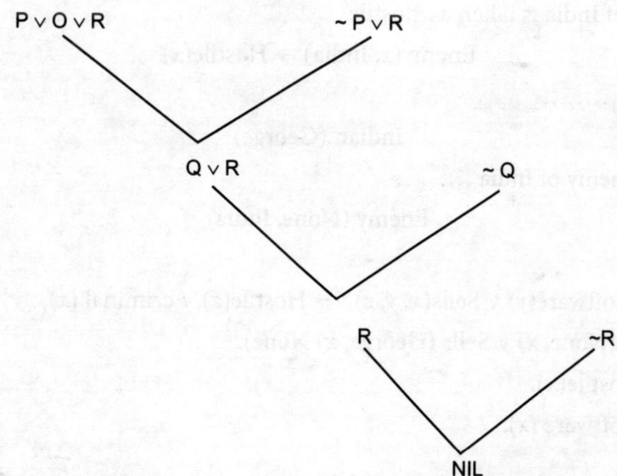

Q.16. Consider the following axioms — *P*, (*P* ∧ *Q*) → *R*, (*S* ∨ *T*) → *Q*, *T* Prove that *R* is true by resolution.

Ans. We negate the goal, *i.e.*, we negate *R*, *i.e*, ¬ *R*. We apply resolution now — We convert the given axioms into clausal form —

1. P 2. $\neg P \vee \neg Q \vee R$ 3. $\neg S \vee Q$

4. $\neg T \vee Q$ 5. T

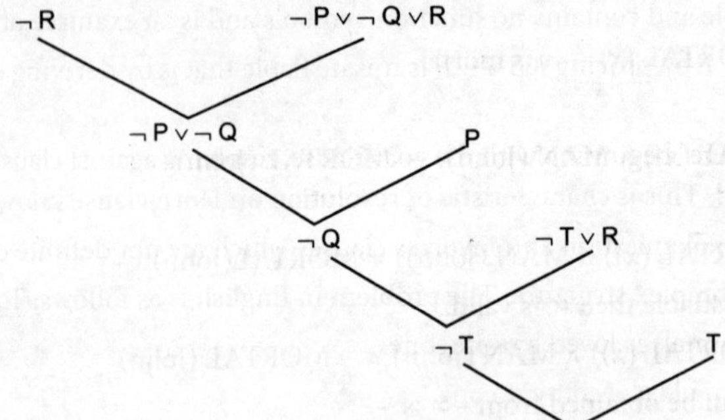

Q.17. Consider the following problem:

The law says that it is crime for an Indian to sell Indian Software to hostile nations. The country, named None, an enemy of India has some Indian software and all its software were sold to it by Colonel George who is an Indian. Give its resolution proof.

Ans. We want to prove that Colonel George is criminal. First, we shall represent these facts as first order definite clauses:

1. It is crime for an Indian to sell Indian Software to hostile nations.

   Indian (x) ∧ Indian Software(y) ∧ Sells (x, y, z) ∧ Hostile (z) → Criminal (x)

2. None has some Indian Software.

   ∃x Owns (None, x) ∧ Indian Softwares (x)

   which is transformed into definite clauses by Existential Elimination, introducing new constant I

   Owns (None, I)

   Indian Software (I)

3. All of its Indian Software were sold to it by Colonel George.

   Indian Software(x) ∧ Owns(None, x) → Sells(George, x, None)

   Additional knowledge is that Indian softwares are IT softwares

   Indian Software(x) → Software(x)

   and also that an enemy of India is taken as 'hostile'

   Enemy(x, India) → Hostile(x)

4. *George who is an Indian ....*

   Indian (George)

5. The country None, an enemy of India ....

   Enemy (None, India)

In CNF they are:

a. ¬ Indian(x) ∨ ¬ Indian software(y) ∨ Sells(x, y, z) ∨ ¬ Hostile(z) ∨ criminal (x).

b. ¬ Software(x) ∨ ¬ Owns(None, x) ∨ Sells (George, x) None).

c. ¬ Enemy (x, India) ∨ Hostile(x).

d. ¬ Missile (x) ∨ Indian software (x).

e. Owns (None, *I*).

f. Software (*I*).

g. Criminal (George)

h. Indian (George)

i. Enemy (None, India)

and the negated goal ¬ criminal (George)

The resolution proof is shown in Fig. 4.5.

This knowledge base is simple and contains no function symbols and is an example of Datalog knowledge base.

Resolution proves that $KB \models P$ by proving $KB \vee \neg P$ is unsatisfiable that is by deriving empty clause. Resolution proof is given in Fig. 4.5.

We may notice the "single spine" beginning with the goal clause, resolving against clauses from the knowledge base until the empty clause is generated. This is characteristic of resolution on Horn clause knowledge bases.

This example makes use of Skolemisation and involves clauses which are not definite clauses.

This results in a somewhat complex structure. The problem in English is as follows: To prove Vibhuti Killed Lucy

1. Everyone who loves all animals is loved by someone.
2. Everyone who kills an animal is loved by no one.
3. Gaurav loves all animals.
4. Either Gaurav or Vibhuti killed the cat who is named Lucy.
5. Did Vibhuti kill the cat?

Goal, G to prove that Vibhuti killed Lucy. Conversion is First-order Logic and the negated goal.

a. $\forall x\ [\forall y\ \text{Animal}(y) \rightarrow \text{Loves}\ (x,y)] \rightarrow [\exists y\ \text{Loves}\ (y, x)]$.

b. $\forall x\ [\exists y\ \text{Animal}\ (y) \wedge \text{Kills}\ (x, y)] \rightarrow [\forall z \neg \text{Loves}\ (z, x)]$.

c. $\forall x\ \text{Animal}\ (y) \rightarrow \text{Loves}\ (\text{Gaurav}, x)$.

d. Kills (Gaurav, Lucy) $\vee$ Kills (Vibhuti, Lucy)

e. Cat(Lucy)

f. $\forall x\ \text{Cat}(x) \rightarrow \text{Animal}\ (x)$.

g. Kills (Vibhuti, Lucy)

and conversion to CNF to each sentence gives

a. $\text{Animal}\ (F(x)) \vee \text{Loves}\ (G(x), x)$

b. $\neg\ \text{Loves}\ (x, F(x)) \vee \text{Loves}\ (G(x), x)$

c. $\neg\ \text{Animal}\ (y) \vee \neg\ \text{Kills}(x, y) \vee \neg\ \text{Loves}(z, x)$

d. $\neg\ \text{Animal}\ (x) \vee \neg\ \text{Loves}\ (\text{Gaurav}, x)$

e. Kills(Gaurav, Lucy) $\vee$ Kills (Vibhuti, Lucy)

f. Cat (Lucy)

g. $\neg\ \text{Cat}(x) \vee \text{Animal}(x)$

h. $\neg$ Kills (Vibhuti, Lucy)

After conversion the first sentence from order conversion gives two sentences. The proof can be paraphrased in English as:

Suppose Vibhuti did not kill Lucy. We know that either Gaurav or Vibhuti did; thus Gaurav must have. Now Lucy is a cat and cats are animals, so Lucy is an animal. Because anyone who kills an animal is loved by no one, so no one loves Gaurav. But in the knowledge base it is given that Gaurav loves all animals, so someone loves him, so we have a contradiction. Therefore, Vibhuti killed the cat, Lucy.

The Resolution is given in Fig. 4.6.

The proof answers the question "Did Vibhuti kill the cat?"

But often we ask more general question, such as "who killed the cat?"

Resolution can do this by doing a little more work. The goal is $\exists$w kills (w, Lucy) which when negated becomes $\neg$ kills (w, Lucy) in CNF. Repeating the proof in the above Fig., with the new negated goal, we obtain a similar proof tree, the substitution then becomes $w/_{vibhuti}$ in one of the steps. (The reader should repeat the above proof with the new unification), concluding that Vibhuti is killer of cat Lucy.

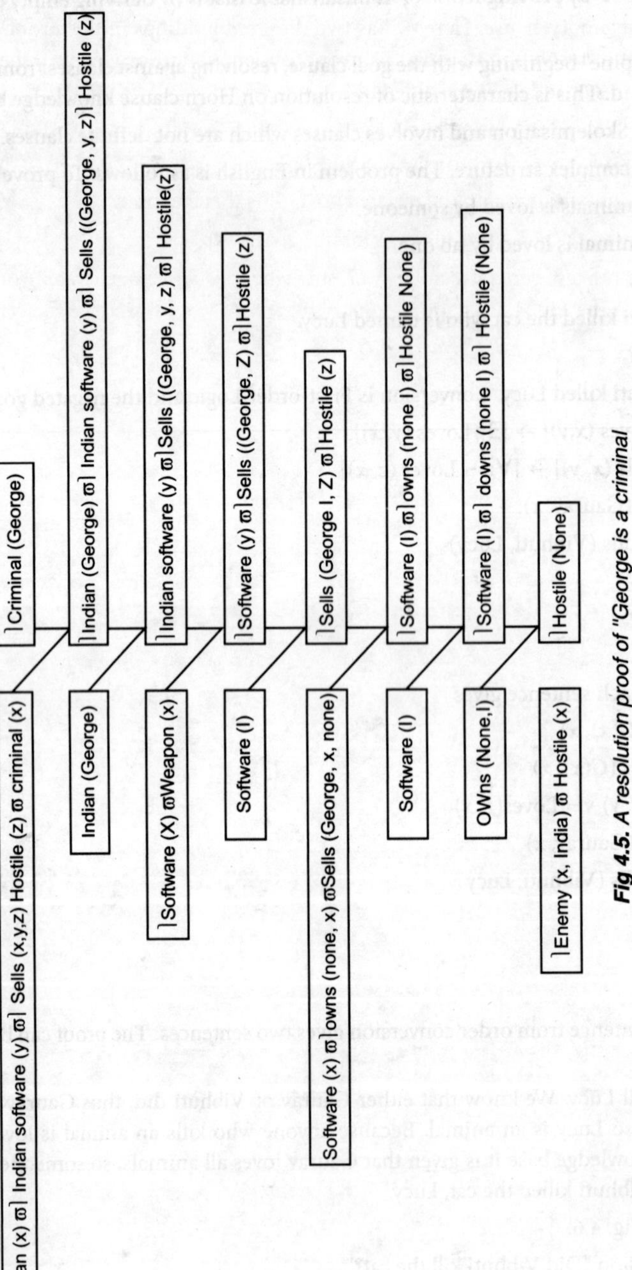

Fig 4.5. A resolution proof of George is a criminal

Unfortunately resolution can produce non-constructive proofs for existential goals. For example ¬ Kills (w, Lucy) resolves with Kills (Gaurav, Lucy) v Kills (Vibhuti, Lucy) to give Kills (Gaurav, Lucy), which resolves again with ¬ Kills(w, Lucy) to yield the empty clause. Here, w has two different bindings in this proof – Vibhuti or Gaurav. This is surprising, the procedure of resolution tells that someone, either Vibhuti or Gaurav, killed Lucy. This type of double bindings is not quite common, and can be avoided by

(*i*) Either restricting the allowed resolution steps so that w (query variable) is bound once in a given proof. Then we need to be able to backtrack over the possible bindings.

(*ii*) Or be adding a special answer literal to the negated goal. This then becomes

¬ Kills (w, Vibhuti) v Answer(w).

At present the resolution process generates an answer only when a clause is generated containing just a single answer literal (answer(Vibhuti) in the Fig. 4.6. The non-constrictive proof would produce the clause which is, in fact, the no answer.

Answer (Vibhuti) v Answer(Gaurav)

Thus, we have seen how the process of deduction can derive new facts (answer) from the given facts (knowledge base). Further, resolution theorem can be used to answer yes-no questions such as Did Vibhuti kill the cat?

Resolution can also be used to answer fill-in-the-blanks type of questions, such as "Was the cat killed?" or " Who killed the cat?" Even "When was the cat killed" can be answered by adding new facts in the knowledge base. But yes-no and fill-in-the-blank questions are not the only kinds of questions which can ever be asked.

This must be mentioned here that the technique of deduction does not contain the answer to all conceivable questions. In general, it is necessary to decide on the kinds of questions which will be asked and to decide a knowledge representation method appropriate for those questions. For example, even we might ask "How was the cat killed?" or "Why was the cat killed?" So method of resolution is not yet complete and needs further research.

Q.18. Give unification algorithm. What is unification?

Ans. Unification is the recursive process of merging two or more predicates with constants or with some variables. We check whether by performing some substitution for variables, the predicates can be made identical.

For example. Small town (x)¬ Small town (Delhi)

Cannot be merged (or resolved) because there may be various values for x.

Similarly, predicate lady and lady (Ajay) cannot be resolved as the first predicate doesn't have any variable and second predicate has some variable / constant.

Unification is used for unifying the axioms in inferencing mechanism. It is a recursive process. The substitutions for the variables are tried to generate identical and opposite predicate sets such that they can be combined. Unification tries to find out the complementary literals in two clauses and deletes them, thereby forming a new literal. Please understand that whenever two identical and opposite literals are obtained, they are merged (or resolved). This is true for clauses having no variables. When the literals have variables, the process becomes complicated. Thus, we use substitutions here. Substitution may be of a variable by a constant, of a variable by another variable or of a variable by a function that doesn't contain the same variable.

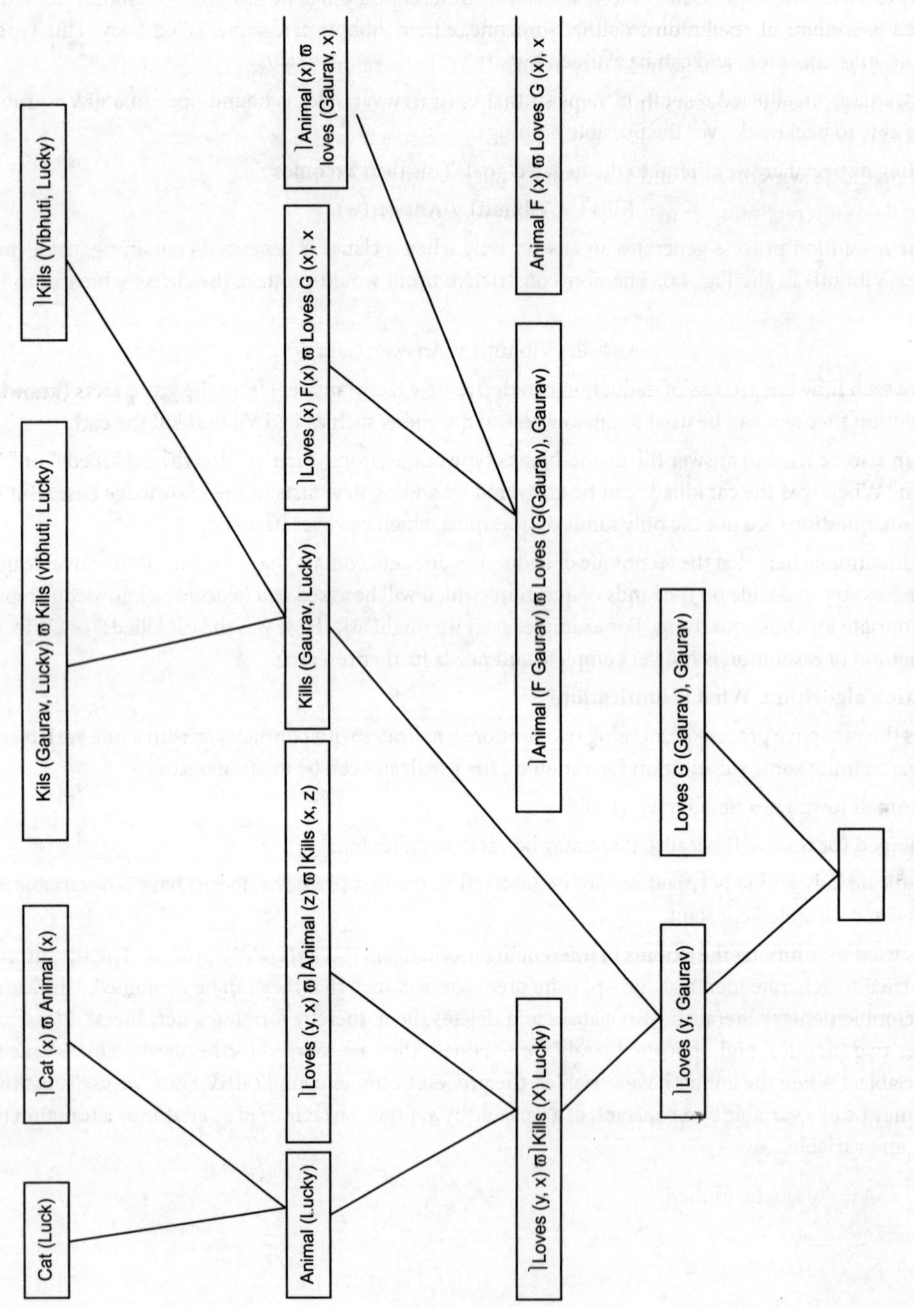

***Fig 8.6:** A resolution proof of "Vibhuti killed the cat*

Let us write the unification algorithm first.

Algorithm: Verify: (U, V)

1. If *U* and *V* are both variables or constants then
   a. If *U* and *V* are identical, then return null.
   b. If *U* is a variable then if *U* occurs in *V*, then return {FAIL} else return {*U*/*V*}.
   c. If *V* is a variable, then if *V* occurs in *U*, return {FAIL} else return {*U*/*V*}.
   d. Return {FAIL}
2. If the initial predicate symbols in *U* and *V* are not identical, return {FAIL}.
3. If *U* and *V* have a different number of arguments, then return {FAIL}.
4. Set SUBSET to NULL.
5. For *i* ← *l* to the number of arguments of *U*.
   a. Call unify with the ith argument of *U* and the ith argument of *V* putting the result in *S*.
   b. If S contain {FAIL}, return {FAIL}?
   c. If S is not equal to NULL
      (*i*) Apply 5 to be the remainder of both U and V.
      (*ii*) Set subset equal to APPENDS (S, SUBSET).
6. Return SUBSET.

Working: We try to unify, say, the following predicates —

$P(x, x)$

and $\neg P(y, z)$

Firstly, we check the predicates. Here these are same and opposite. Next, we check their arguments. Now, P has its 1st argument as 'x' whereas ⊠ P has 'y' as its 1st argument./ These can be made similar if we substitute x in place of y in both predicates. Please note here that since x and y are variables so these substitutions are possible. Many a time, the situation is that one predicate has variable and another predicate has constant, then only variable can be replaced by the constant. the constant cannot be replaced by variable. Also note that the replacement of one variable by another should be done throughout all occurrence of that variable in all predicates. The replacement of y by x is denoted by x/y. So, now the predicates are —

$P(x, x)$

and $P(x, z)$

Now, we come to the 2nd argument of both the predicates. To match, *x* should be replaced by *z*. But this cannot be done as the substitution of *x* by *y* and *z* both is not possible in one set of problem. Hence, the two literals cannot be unified.

On the other hand, if predicates are —

$P(x, x)$

and $\neg P(y, y)$

And if we substitute *x*/*y* (*i.e.*, *x* for *y*) then they become

$\neg P(x, x)$

and $\neg P(x, x)$ and these can be unified.

We are in a position to solve some examples now.

Q.1. Unify the following clauses —

$$\mathbf{P\,(x, f(z), mary)}$$
$$\mathbf{\neg\, P\,(x, y, z).}$$

Ans. We substitute z/mary in both the clauses —

$P\,(x, f(\text{mary}), \text{mary})$

$\neg\, P\,(x, y, \text{mary})$. Now, these two clauses

differ in their 2nd argument only, so we replace y/f (mary) and we get —

$\neg p$ (x, f (mary), mary).

$\neg$ Finally, the two clauses are —

P (x, f (mary), mary)

and $\neg p$ (x, f (mary), mary)

∴ Now, they can be unified (or merged) together.

Q. 2. Suppose we have the following query — Whom does Ravana know? And that there are four sentences in the KB.

Knows (Ranana, Sita)

Knows (y, Rama)

Knows(y, Mother (y))

Knows (x, Radha)

Unify given sentence with the above four sentences.

Ans. Given : Sentence is.

Knows (Ravana, x) ...(1)

∴ Following results are obtained by unifying (1) with given sentences

1. UNIFY (Knows (Ravana, x), Knows (Ravana, Sita)

   = (x/Sita)

2. UNIFY (Knows (Ravana, x), knows(y, Ram)

   = (x/Ram, y/Ravana)

3. UNIFY (Knows (Ravana, x), knows (y, Mother(y))

   = (y/Ravana, x/mother(Ravana))

4. UNIFY (Knows (Ravana, x), knows (x, Radha) = fail

In this last unification, the two constants cannot be instantiated to the same variable 'x' at the same time. This problem can be solved by assigning different variables to two sentences. 'x' in the knows (x, Radha) can be changed to 'y'. Now, the unification will work by standardising one of the two sentences being unified which means renaming its variables to avoid name clashes.

For example, renaming 'x' in knows (x, Radha) to a new variable 'y' without changing its meaning is as follows.

UNIFY (knows (Ravana, x), knows (y, Ravana)

= [x/Radha, y/Ravana]

NOTE.

1. Say, we are attempting to unify the expression

   $$F(x, x)$$

   $$f(g(x), g(x))$$

   That is, if we accept $g(x)$ as a substitution for 'x' then we would have to substitute it for 'x' in the remainder of the expressions. But this leads to infinite recursions since it is not possible to eliminate x.

2. Unification works well for two arguments. But there could be more than one such Unifier. For example Consider again,

   UNIFY knows (Ravana, x), knows (y, z)

   ∴ Substitutions could be (y/Ravana, x/z)

   or (y/Ravana, x/Ravana, z/Ravana)

   First substitution gives, knows (Ravana, z) and Second substitution gives knows (Ravana, Ravana).

   The second result can be obtained from the first (y/Ravana, x/z) by an additional substitution (z/Ravana). Please note that the first unifier is more general than the second because the second can be derived from the first. Also we conclude that for every unifiable pair of expressions there is a single most-general-unifier (MGU). In this example, it is (*y*/Ravana, *x*/*z*).

Q.19. Describe forward chaining, backward chaining and conflict resolution?

Ans. A.I. solves our problems by searching a solution search-tree (called as search space) from the initial state to the goal state. We have rule-based system architecture that has a set of rules, a set of facts and an inference engine. Given a set of rules, the new knowledge can be inferred using two rules —

a. Forward chaining / Forward reasoning.

b. Backward chaining / Backward reasoning.

Forward chaining (or reasoning) starts from the start state and proceeds towards the goal state. On the other hand backward chaining starts from the goal state and proceeds towards the start state.

For example. : Turbo Prolog (an A.I. language, 5*G*), uses backward chaining (or reasoning).

Forward reasoning / data-driven inferencing : As we have already studied that rules are stored in KB in form of atomic formula in some form like propositional or predicate logic. The process of instantiating the left side of rules, executing them from left to right, matching the left part of the sentence with the existing expression and if the match occurs then replacing it by the right part of the rule is called as Forward reasoning or Forward chaining or Data-driven search. In next step, this right hand side of the previous rule is considered as left side of present rule to find applicability of a rule. So the finding of the rule becomes Subgoals to be fulfilled. These subgoals may in turn cause new subgoals to be established and so on, until the facts are found to match the lowest subgoals conditions. Whenever the goal is achieved, the search process stops.

For example. Say, we have a database with the following elements —

A	G	E
A	C	B

(database having facts)

& the set of rules as—

$F \,\&\, B \to Z$
$C \,\&\, D \to F$
$A \to D$

(Rules in a *KB*)

We assume that each time the set of rules is tested against the database, only the first (topmost) rule that matches is executed. So the rule $A \to D$ is executed only once although it matches the database every time. This database is also known as a working memory (WM).

How it works? The first rule which fires is $A \to D$ because A is already in the database. So, this rule shows the existence of *D* (*i.e.*, inferring) and *D* is placed in the database. So, our database now is —

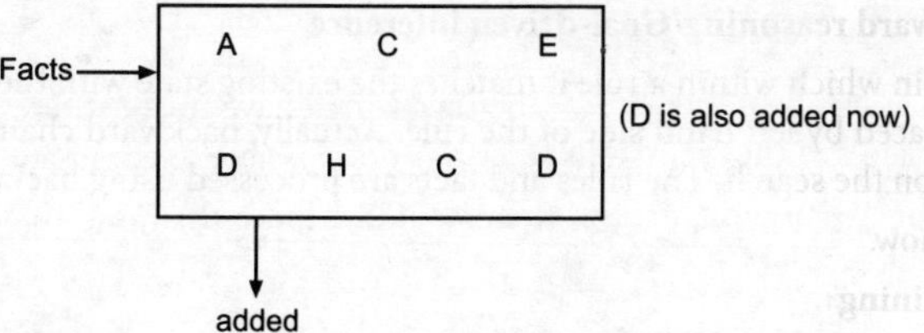

This causes the second rule *C* and $D \to F$ to fire and as a consequence *F* is inferred and placed in the database. This in turn causes the tired rule *F* and $B \to Z$ to fire placing *Z* in the database *i.e.*

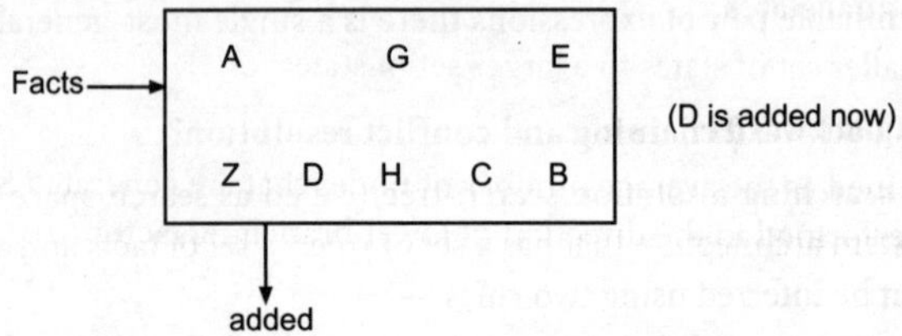

∴ The inference chain so formed is —

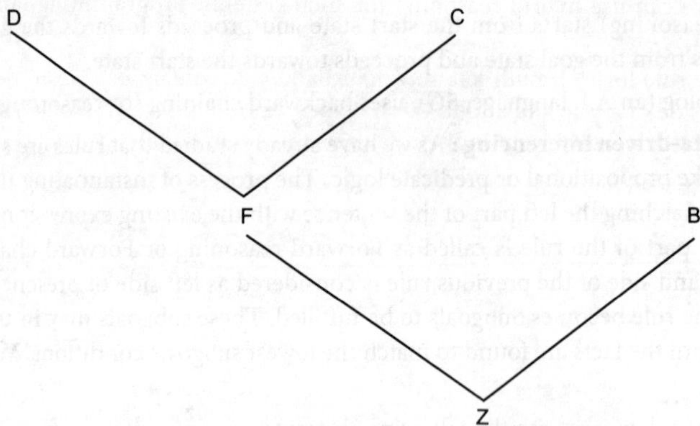

This is known as **forward chaining**. It is also called as a data-driven search as the input data is used to guide the direction of inference process.

Let us write its algorithm now.

Algorithm: Forward chaining

Repeat : Collect the rule whose condition matches a fact in database (or WM).

Do actions indicated by the rule — added facts to WM 'or delete facts from working memory).

Until : Problem is solved or no condition matches.

Alternative Algorithm: Forward Chaining

Repeat

Collect the rules whose conditions match facts in database (or WM)

If more than one rule matches then use conflict resolution strategy to eliminate all but one.

else

do actions indicated by the rules *i.e.*, add facts to the database/ or delete facts from WM, until a problem is solved or no condition matches.

Backward chaining/Backward reasoning/Goal-driven inference

It is a process of reasoning in which within a rule it matches the existing state with the right hand part of the rule and if the match occurs, it is replaced by left hand side of the rule. Actually, backward chaining means reasoning from goals back to facts. The focus is on the search. The rules and facts are processed using backward chaining interpreter.

Let us write its algorithm now.

Algorithm: Backward chaining

Prove goal G:

If G is in the initial facts, it is proven. Please find a rule which can be used to conclude *G* and try to prove each of that rules conditions.

Which one to select?

If we apply both forward and backward algorithms then our searching becomes a bidirectional search. This results in a hybrid reasoning. Which reasoning to select depends on the nature of the problem. It depends on the following factors:

a. **Number of starts and goal states.**

We proceed from a smaller set of states to a larger set of states.

b. **Direction of branching factor (*b*)**

Branching factor is defined as the average number of nodes that are generated from a single node. Please remember that the reasoning is performed in the direction of lower branching factor (*b*).

c. **Problem's requirement**

Certain applications like medical diagnosis need backward chaining as they need the justification of the solution too. Note that it is important to choose the reasoning in the direction that corresponds to the way in which the user thinks. Actually, we can use hybrid reasoning for such systems. Programming languages, like PROLOG, support backward chaining.

We need to check the rule form. If both left and right hand side contain assertion, then forward chaining can match assertions on the left side of a rule and add to the state description of assertion on RHS. Please understand here that if arbitrary procedures are allowed at right in the rule then a rule will not be reversible.

Some production languages allow only reversible rules and some do not. Also note that when irreversible rules are used then a commitment to the direction of search must be made at the time the rules are written.

Conflict Resolution : The set of rules that have their conditions stratified by working memory elements forms a conflict set. A conflict is said to occur if more than one rules are found to fire in one cycle. In such a scenario, the control structure must determine which rule to fire from this conflict set of active rules. This process of selection is called as "conflict resolution". So, conflict resolution normally selects a single rule to fire. There are 3 conflict resolution mechanisms:

a. Refractory

b. Receiving

c. Specificity

Refractory: In this mechanism, a rule should not be allowed to fire more than once on the same data. This prevents undesired loops.

Recency: Here we rank instantiation in terms of recency of elements in the premise of the rule. The rule which has highest priority is fired first.

Specificity: More specific rules are better because they take more of data into account. It is also known as a strict condition as it injects more know ledge in the KB, when it is fired.

Other mechanisms are also used like —

a. **Most recently used :** It chooses the most recently used rule from the conflict set for firing. It represents a dfs.

b. **Most recently added :** It selects the rule which is most recently added in the set of rules. It is a dynamic policy as in this policy new production rules are added, deleted or modified automatically in dynamic KB during execution.

We are in a position to solve some examples now.

Example 1. Consider the following database and the set of rules given below:

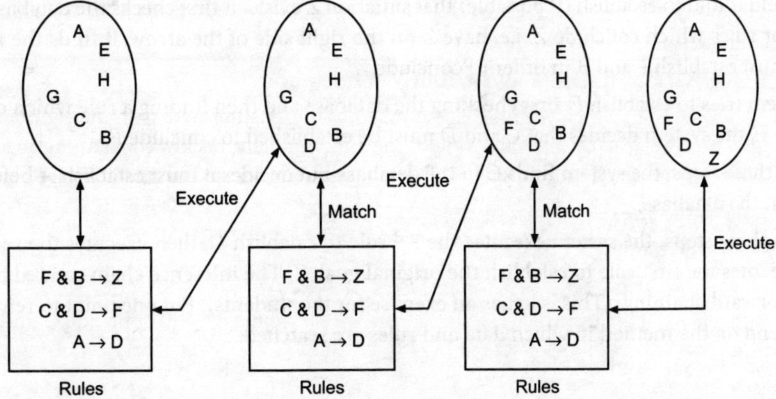

Fig. 8.7.

Explain how forward chaining works in this example. Also show backward chaining.

Which is more cost-effective?

Solution. The rules in this example, use letters as facts in the database to explain the situations or concepts.

For examples., *F* and $B \rightarrow Z$

means

It situation F exists and situation B exists

THEN : situation Z also exists.

Let us see now how these rules work.

Assume that each time the set of rules is tested against the database, only the first (topmost rule which matches is executed. That is why, in the figure given, the rule ($A \rightarrow D$) is executed only once even though it matches the database every time.

The first rule that fires is $A \rightarrow D$ because A is already in the database. As consequence of this rule, the existence of *D* is inferred and *D* is placed in the database. This causes the second rule, C and $D \rightarrow F$ to fire, as a consequence *F* is inferred and placed in the database. This in turn causes the 3rd rule *F* and $B \rightarrow Z$ to fire placing *Z* in the database. Please understand that this technique is called as forward chaining because the search for new information seams to be proceeding in the direction of the arrow separating the left and right hand sides of the rules. The system which uses information on the left hand side to derive information on the right is shown in Fig 8.7(*a*).

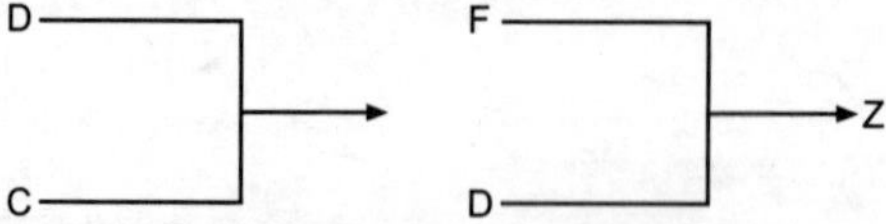

Fig. 8.8. *(a) Forward chaining*

Say, we use this system with the goal of determining whether or not situation *Z* existed. We might think that it worked quite well, finding quickly the fact that *Z* did exist. Unfortunately, this is just over simplification. Practically speaking, the process of drawing inference is not simple. This is so because a real expert system will not have just three rules but will have hundreds or even thousands of them. If we use a system that is very large just to find out about *Z* many rules would be fired which had nothing to do with *Z*, then a large number of inference chains and situations could be derived in the process which were valid but unrelated to *Z*. Please note that if our goal is to infer one particular fact *Z*, forward chaining could waste both time and money. In such a case, backward chaining might be more cost-effective. With this inference technique, the system starts with what it wants to prove. Like, to find if the situation *Z* exists and as such executes those rules which are relevant to its establishment.

The Fig. 8.7(*b*) shows how backward chaining would work using rules given above.

Step 1: The system is told to establish (if possible) that situation *Z* exists. It first checks the database for Z and when that fails, searches for rules which conclude *Z*, *i.e.* have *Z* on the right side of the arrow. It finds the rule *F* and $B \rightarrow$ Z and decides that it must establish F and B in order to conclude *Z*.

Step 2: The system tries to establish *F*, first checking the database and then finding a rule which concludes *F*. From the rule, C and $D \rightarrow F$, the system decides that C and *D* must be established to conclude *F*.

Steps 3 to 5 : In these steps, the system finds C in the database but decides it must establish *A* before it can conclude *D*. It then finds *A* in the database.

Steps 6 to 8 : In these steps, the system executes the 3rd rule to establish *D*, then executes the second rule to establish *F* and finally executes the first rule to establish the original goal, *Z*. The inference chain created here is identical to the one created by forward chaining. (This is left as an exercise for the students). But one point to remember is that the two approaches depend on the method in which data and rules are searched.

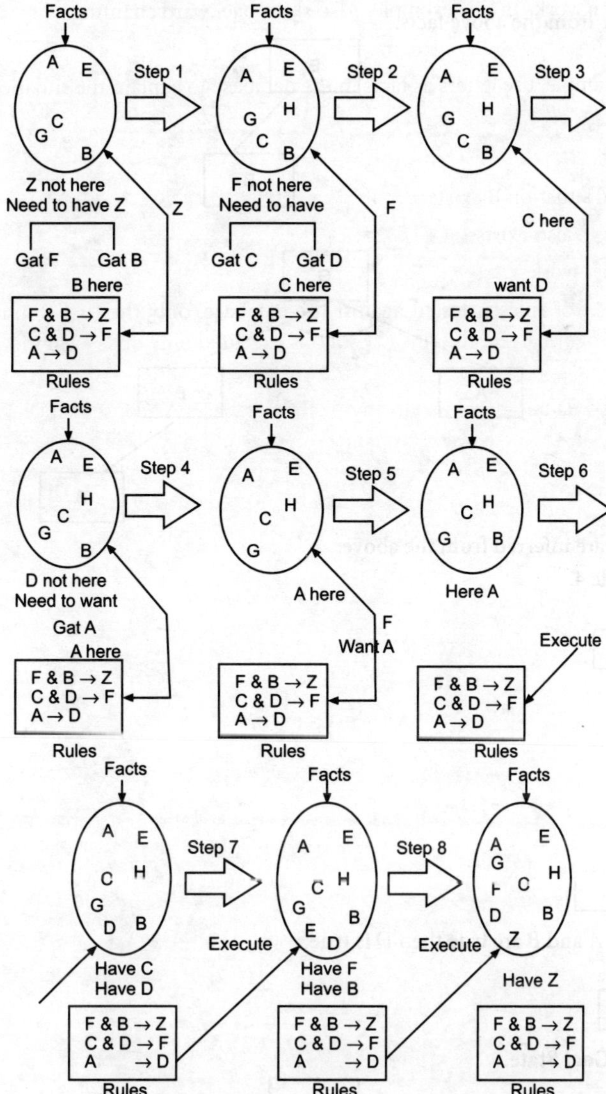

Fig. 8.8: (b) Forward and Backward chaining

Q.20. Suppose a Rule Base contains the following four rules-

Rule No.	Production rules
Rule 1	if A and C then F
Rule 2	if A and E then G
Rule 3	if B then E
Rule 4	if G and D

a. **Prove that if *A* and *B* are True then *D* is True using forward chaining.**

b. **Prove that if *A* and *B* are True then *D* is True using backward chaining.**

Ans. Let us solve part-a first and then *b*-part-

a. **Forward Chaining:**

Step-1: [A] [B] {Known facts}

Step-2: See facts that infer from the above facts.

Step-3:

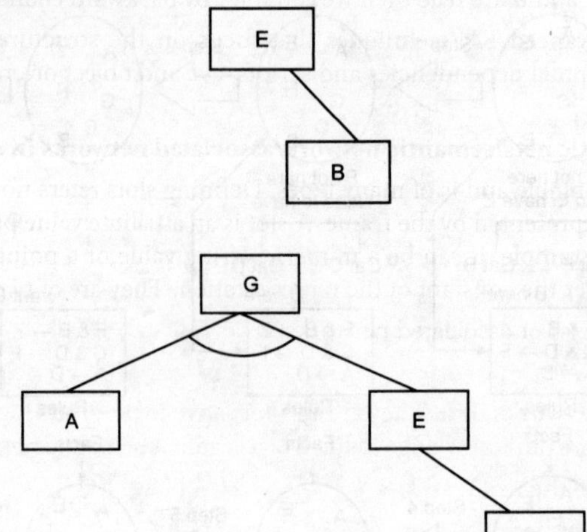

Hence, Rule 2 and Rule 3 are inferred from the above.
Using step-3 inferring Rule 4.

Step-4:

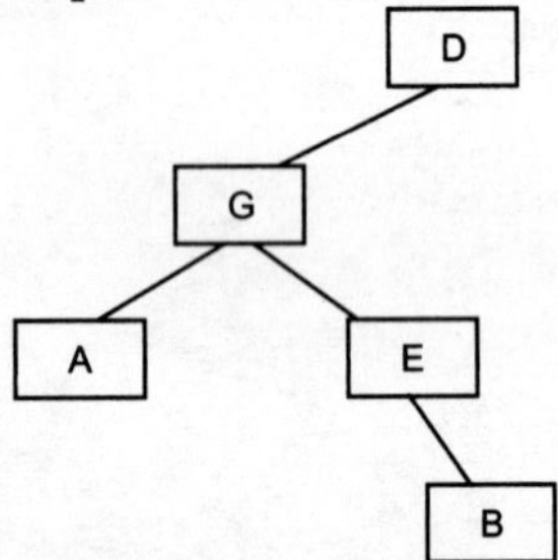

Hence, it is proved that if *A* and *B* are true then *D* is true.

***b.* Backward Chaining:**

Step-1: Goal State D

Step-2: Infer facts from Goal State.

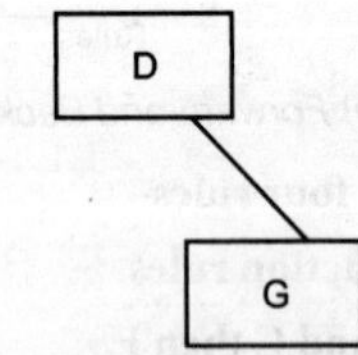

Step-3: Further extract the states.

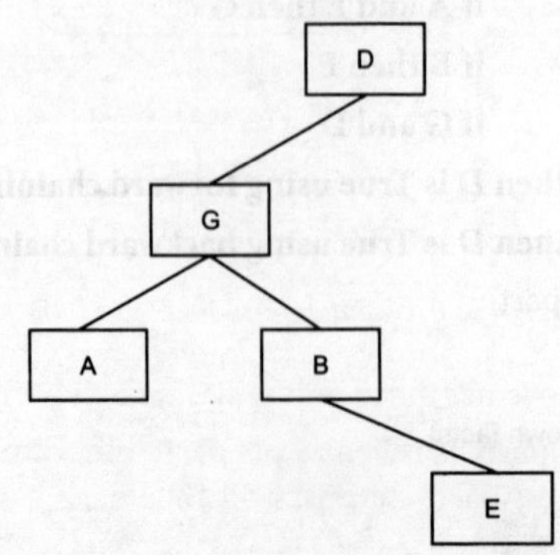

Since, we are given that *A* and *B* are true then we can infer by backward chaining that D is also true.

We have some more advanced KR techniques that focus on the structure of knowledge like semantic networks, conceptual graphs, conceptual dependencies and scripts, cyc and object oriented representation. We discuss these one by one now.

Q.21. Explain slots and semantic nets/semantic network/associated networks in detail. Give examples to support.

Ans. A slot is a subclass of intangible and is of many types. Defining slots refers not to the properties of the frame but to the properties of the object represented by the frame. A slot is an attribute value pair in the simplest form. A filler is a value that a slot can take. For example. it can be a numeric, string value or a pointer to another slot. A weak slot and filler structure does not consider the constant of the representation. They are of two types —

a. Semantic networks (nets) or associated networks.

b. Frames.

Let us discuss **semantic networks first**. They are an alternative to predicate logic as a form of knowledge representation. The idea is that we can store our knowledge in form of a graph. A semantic network consists of nodes connected by arcs.

Nodes represent objects in the real world.

Arcs represent relationships between those objects.

For example.

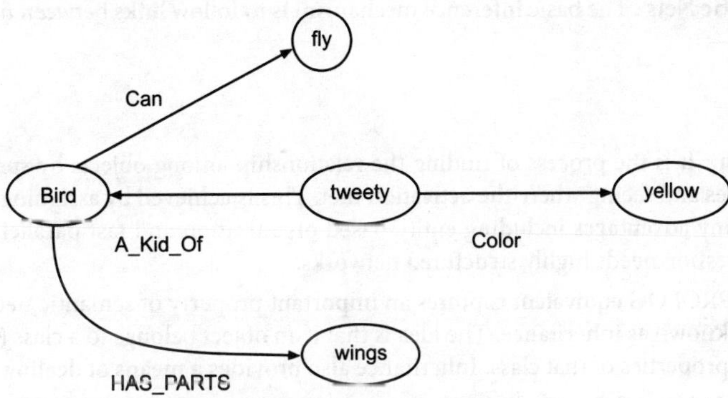

***Fig. 8.9:** Semantic network (net) example*

Fig. 8.9 shows that tweety is a kind of bird who can fly. It is yellow in colour and has wings. These networks permit property inheritance also. It means that nodes which are members or subsets of other nodes may inherit properties from their higher level ancestor nodes.

For example.

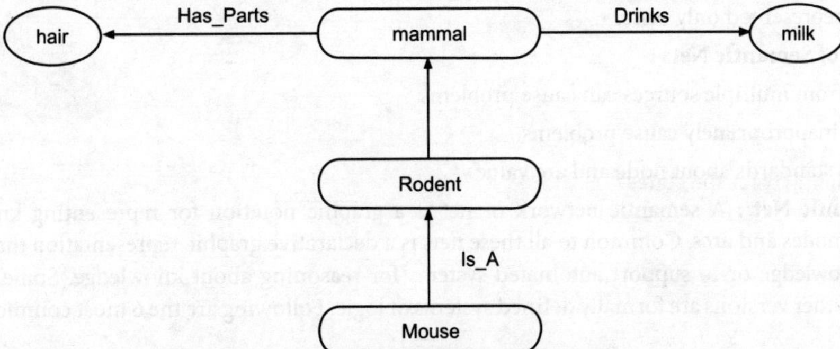

***Fig. 8.10:** Property inheritance in a hierarchical network*

So, it is possible to infer from above net that a mouse has hair and drinks milk.

This concept of inheriting a property is called as **property inheritance**. The properties of a subclass can be modified and can be given different values. Each subclass will thus have its own defined values. Please understand that the semantic network based knowledge representation mechanism is useful where an **object or concept is associated with many attributes** and where **relationships** between **objects are important.**

Applications: Semantic nets have been used in natural language research to represented complex sentences expressed in English.

Properties of semantic nets : Semantic nets exhibit following properties knowledge representation scheme:

1. **Expressiveness :** Semantic nets allow representation of facts and relationship between facts. The levels of hierarchy provide a mechanism for representing general and specific knowledge. This representation is a model of human memory and it is therefore relatively understandable.
2. **Effectiveness :** They support inference through property inheritance. They can also be easily represented by PROLOG, LISP and other A.I. languages making them amenable to computation, as shown by "is-a" arc in LISP given by $\forall x$ [Great-Dane $(x) \rightarrow$ Dog (x)].
3. **Efficiency :** They reduce the size of the knowledge base. Knowledge is stored only at its highest level of abstraction rather than for every instance or example of a class. Further they help maintain the consistency in knowledge base because high level properties are inherited by subclasses and are not added for each subclass.
4. **Explicitness :** Reasoning equates to following paths through the network, so relationship and inference are explicit in the network lines.

Inferencing in Semantic Nets : The basic inference mechanism is to follow links between nodes. There are two ways of inferencing used here —

a. Intersection Search.

b. Inheritance.

a. **Intersection Search :** It is the process of finding the relationship among objects by spreading activation out from each of the two nodes and seeing where the activation met. This is achieved by assigning a special tag to each visited node. There are many advantages including entity-based organization and fast parallel implementation. However, every structured question needs highly structured networks.

b. **Inheritance :** This PROLOG equivalent captures an important property of semantic nets that they may be used for a form of inference known as inheritance. The idea is that if an object belongs to a class (shown by is a relationship), it inherits all of the properties of that class. Inheritance also provides a means of dealing with default reasoning.

Advantages of Semantic Nets : Semantic networks (or nets) have some advantages as follows —

1. They are easy to visualize.
2. Relationships can be arbitrarily defined by the Knowledge Engineers.
3. Formal definitions of semantic networks have been developed.
4. Related knowledge is easily clustered.
5. Are efficient in space requirements.
6. Projects are represented only once.

Disadvantages of Semantic Nets :

1. Inheritance from multiple sources can cause problems.
2. Facts placed inappropriately cause problems.
3. There are no standards about node and arc value.

Types of Semantic Net : A semantic network or net is a graphic notation for representing knowledge in pattern interconnected nodes and arcs. Common to all these nets is a declarative graphic representation that can be used either to represent knowledge or to support automated systems for reasoning about knowledge. Some versions are highly informal while other versions are formally defined systems of logic. Following are the 6 most common kinds of semantic nets —

1. Definitional networks emphasize the subtype or is-α relation between a concept type and a newly defined subtype. The resulting network, also called a generalization or subsumption hierarchy, supports the rule of inheritance for copying properties defined for a super type to all of its subtypes. Since definitions are true by definition, the information in these networks is often assumed to be necessarily true.

2. Assertional networks are designed to assert propositions. Unlike definitional networks the information in an assertional network is assumed to be contingently true, unless it is explicitly marked with a modal operator. Some assertional networks have been proposed as models of the conceptual structures underlying natural language semantics.
3. Implication networks use implication as the primary relation for connecting nodes.
   They may be used to represent patterns of beliefs causality, or inferences.
4. Executable networks include some mechanism, such as marker passing or attached procedures, which can perform inferences, pass messages, or search for patterns and associations.
5. Learning networks build or extend their representation by acquiring knowledge from examples. The new knowledge may change the old network by adding and deleting nodes and arcs or by modifying numerical values, called weights, associated with the nodes and arcs.
6. Hybrid networks : They combine two or more of the previous techniques, either in a single network or in separate but closely interacting networks.

We are in a position to solve some examples on nets now.

Q.22. Construct a semantic net representation for the following —

a. Pompian (Marcus), Blacksmith (Marcus).

b. Raj gives Lucy a gift.

Ans.

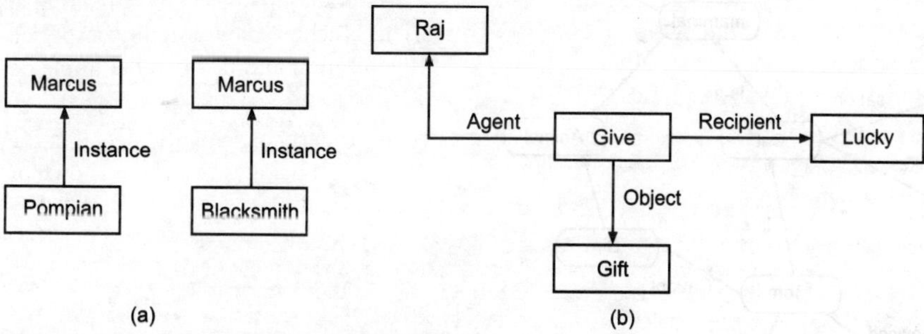

Q.23. Construct a semantic net representation for the following —

a. Every dog has bitten a mail carrier.

b. Every batter hit a ball.

Ans.

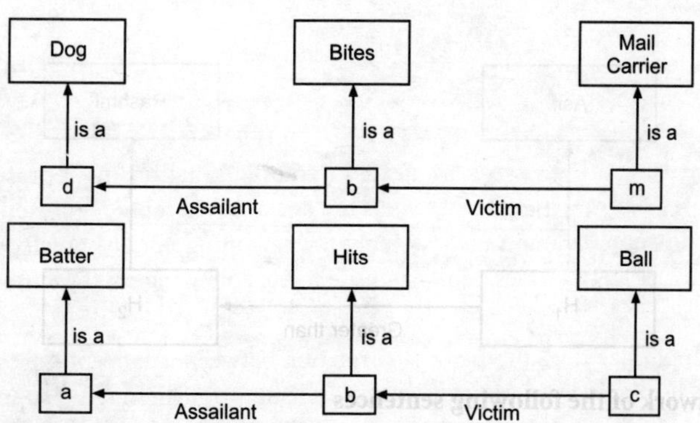

Q.24. Represent the following using nets —

***a.* Emus are birds.**

***b.* Typical birds fly and have wings.**

***c.* Emus run.**

Ans. Its Semantic net is as follows

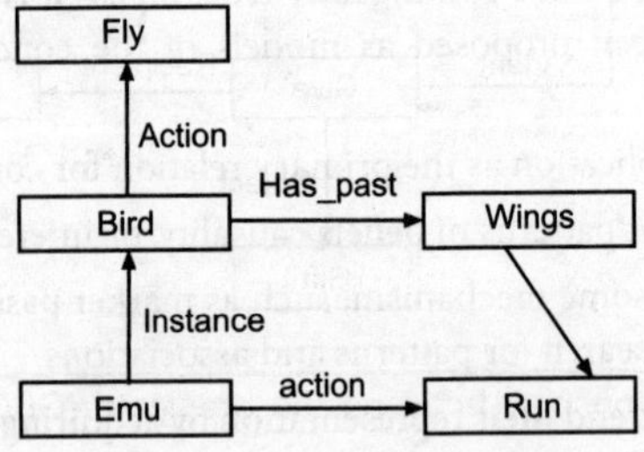

Q.25. Represent the following using semantic net —

a. Tom is a cat.
b. Tom caught a bird.
c. Tom is owned by John.
d. Tom is ginger in color
e. Cats like cream.
f. The cat sat on the mat.
g. A cat is a mammal.
h. A bird is an animal.
i. All mammals are animals.
j. Mammals have fur.

Ans.

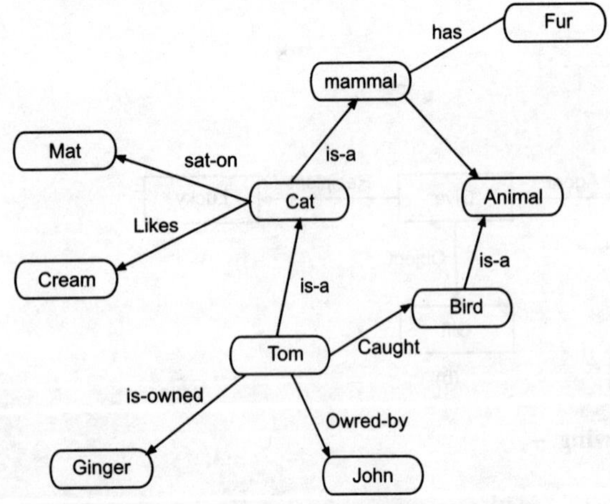

Q.26. Represent the following in net form —

'Asif is taller than Rashmi'

Ans.

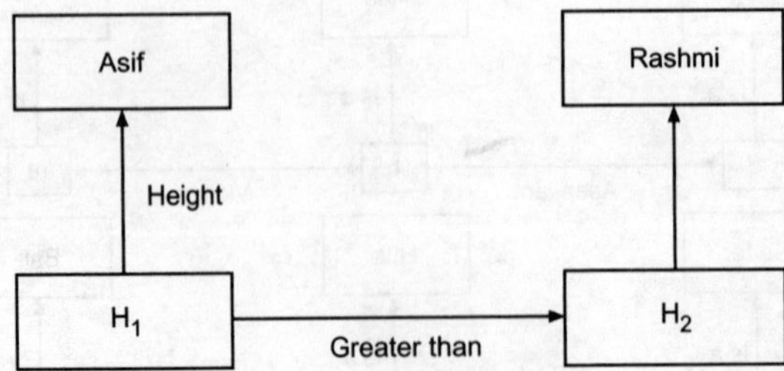

Q.27. Draw the semantics network of the following sentences

a. Bobby gives Amita a gift.

b. Bobby told Krishana that he gave Amita a gift.

Ans. *a.* Its semantic representation is as follows

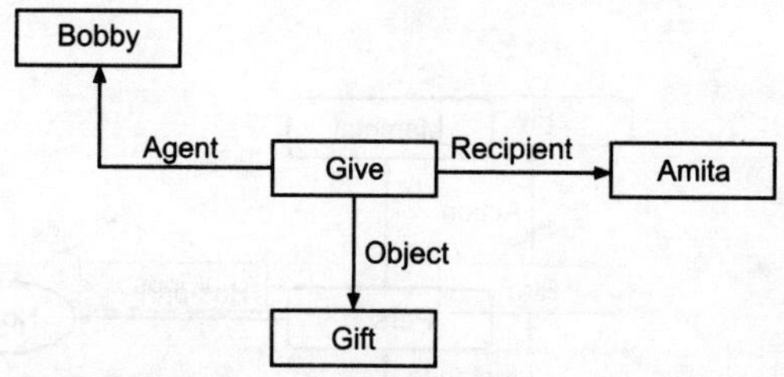

NOTE: The arcs define the relationships between the predicate (GIVE) and the concepts like AMITA and GIFT, associated with that predicate.

b. Its semantic representation is as follows

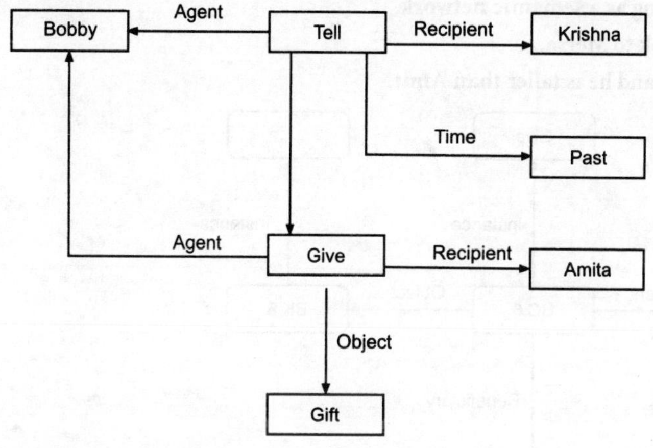

Q.28. "Our neighbour's pet Rocky is brown colored and has very small legs". Represent it as a hierarchical network. Give its property list also in LISP.

Ans. The following is the hierarchical structure showing property inheritance.

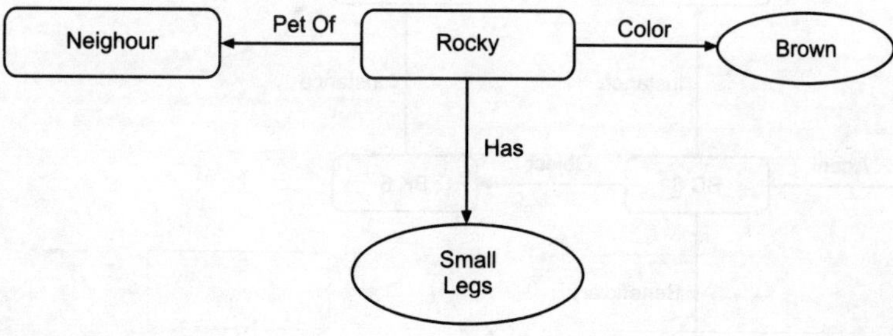

The property list is as follows.

(putprop 'rocky' neighbor' pet of)

(putprop 'rocky' brown' color)

(putprop 'rocky' small keys' has)

Q.29. Given the predicates is a (Person, Mammal) (instance (Pee-Wee, Person)

(team (Pee-Wee, ABC)

uniform color (Pee-Wee, Green)

Express the above in the form of semantic or associative network.

Ans.

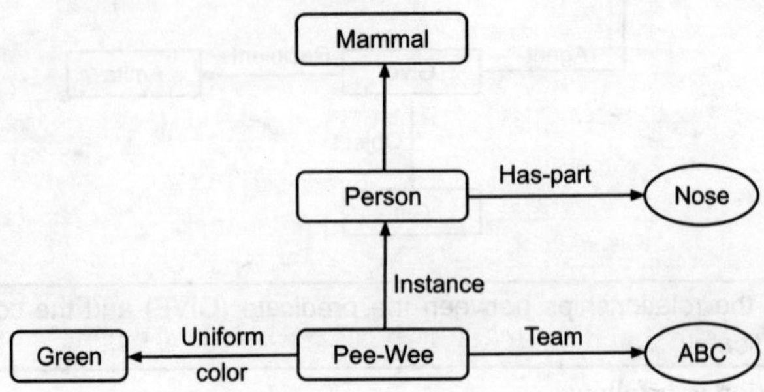

Q.30. Represent the following as a semantic network.

a. **Amit gave the book to Mersa.**

b. **Prem is 6 feet tall and he is taller than Amit.**

Ans. (*a*)

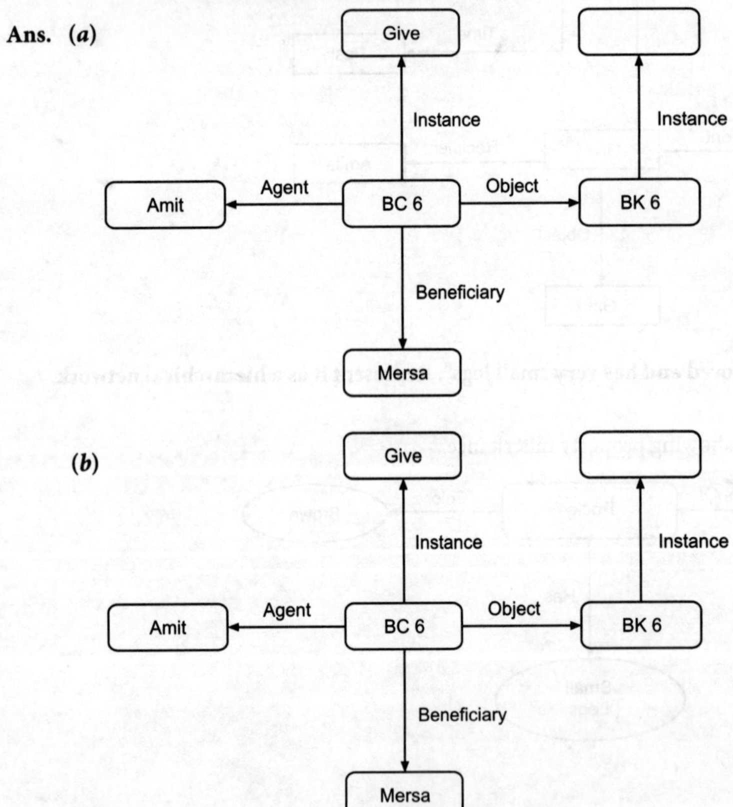

Q.31. Construct a conceptual representation for the sentence, "Every car has an engine"

Ans. The conceptual graph representation is

CAR : ∀] → (PART) → (ENGINE)

Q.32. Transform the FOPL statement equivalent conceptual graph.

$\forall x$ Normal (x) and Grown (x) → Walk (x).

Ans. The conceptual graph is as follows.

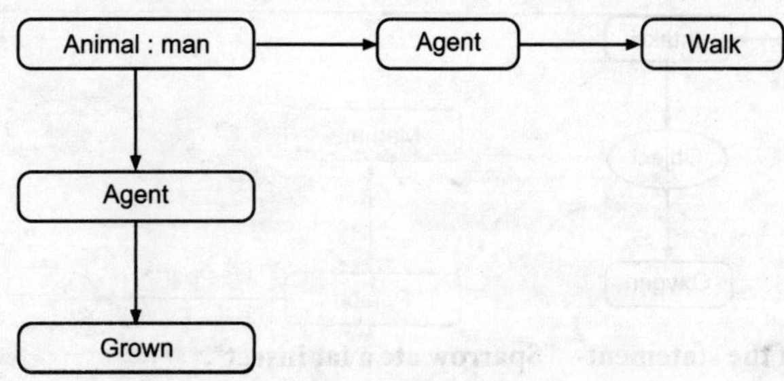

Q.33. Give conceptual graph for the statement.—"Every bus has wheels and engine".

Ans.

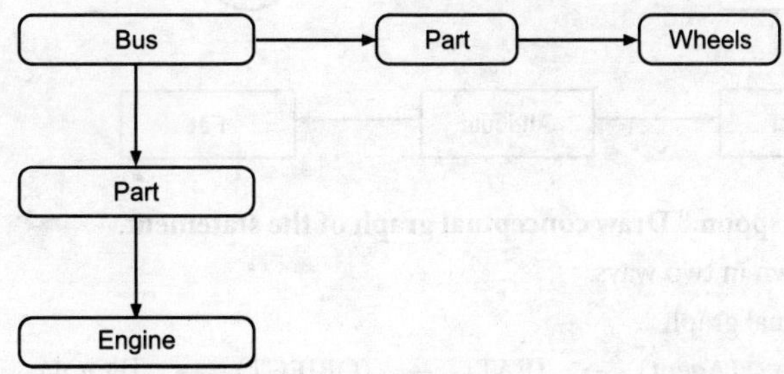

Q.34. "A cow has four legs and eats grass". Show the statement as a conceptual graph.

Ans.

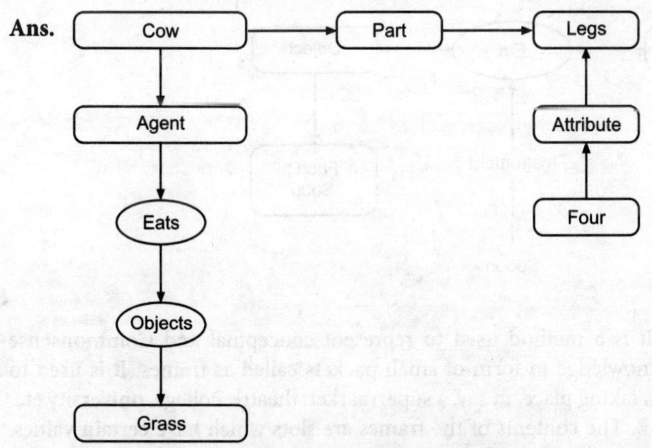

Q.35. Convert the following conceptual graph into an equivalent FOPL statement.

[CAMEL : clyde] → (Agent) → (DRINK)

→ [(OBJECT) → (WATER) → (ATTRIBUTE)

→ [50 – GALLONS].

Ans. $E(x)$ for x is a camel.

$D(x)$ for x is drinks water.

G(x) for drinks 50 gallons of water.

$\therefore \forall x\ (E(x) : \text{clyde})\ \&\ D(x) \rightarrow G(x))$

Q.36. Transform the FOPL statements given below into equivalent conceptual graph.

$\forall x$(HAS – LEGS) (x) and INHALE – OXYGEN(x) → is animal (x).

Ans.

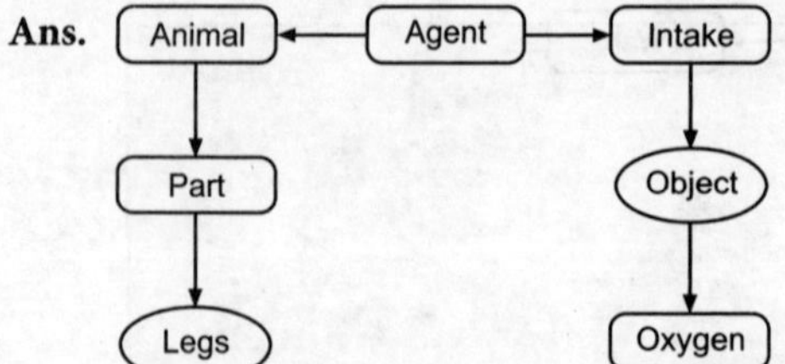

Q.37. Draw conceptual graph of the statement—"Sparrow ate a fat insect".

Ans. The conceptual graph for the statement is as follows.

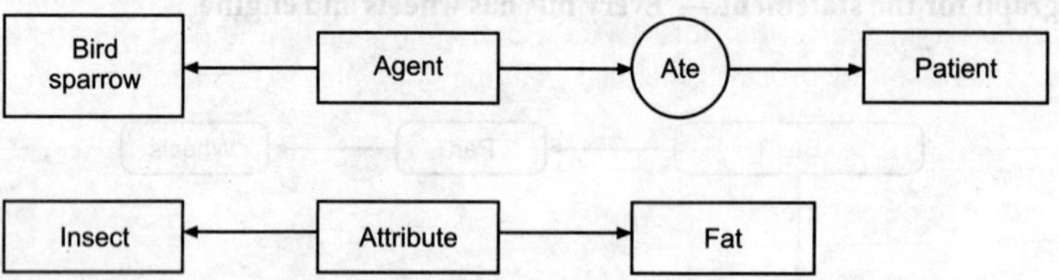

Q.38. "Joe is eating food with a spoon." Draw conceptual graph of the statement.

Ans. The statement can be shown in two ways.

1. Linear form of conceptual graph

   [PERSON : joe] → (Agent) → [EAT] → (OBJECT) → [FOOD : soup] – (INSTRUMENT) → [SPOON]

2. Conceptual graph representation

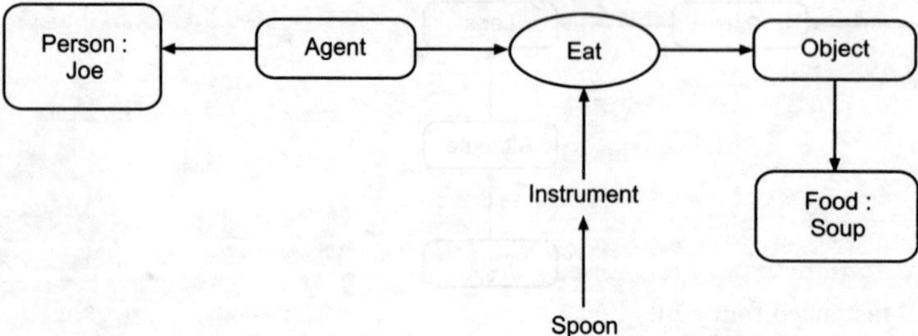

Q.39. What are frames? Compare them with slots.

Ans. In 1975, Marvin Minsky coined the term frame. It is a method used to represent conceptual and Commonsense knowledge. Minsky proposed the organisation of knowledge in form of small packets called as frames. It is used to represent activities associated with conceptual events taking place, in say, a supermarket, theatre, college, university etc. This knowledge in form of frame is stored in the KB. The contents of the frames are slots which have certain values. The slots may be of any type and of any size slots have names and values (or subfields) called as facets. Facets may also have names and any number of values. An appropriate frame is selected from the memory for reasoning. Frames are of 2 types —

a. **Declarative frames :** Frames consisting of only descriptive type of knowledge.

b. **Procedural frames :** A frame having knowledge about the action or procedures.

So, a frame is a collection of attributes or slots and associated values that describe some real world entity.

A frame-system is a collection of objects. Each object contains a number of slots. A slot represents an attribute. Each slot has a value. The value of an attribute can be another object.

> **NOTE:** Frames → have slots for various objects → slots have values

A frame-system is a collection of objects. Each object contains a number of slots. A slot represents an attribute. Each slot has a value. The value of an attribute can be another object.

A general frame structure is shown below:

(< frame name >

(< slots 1 > (facet 1 < value l > … value k >)

(facet 2 < value 1 > … value k >)

?

(facet n <value n > … <value k>)

The frames can be attached with another frame to create network of frames. Reasoning, using frames is done by instantiation process. **The process in which the given situation is matched with frames that are already existing is known as instantiation.** The reasoning process tries to match the current problem state with the frame slot and assigns them values. The values assigned to the slots depict a particular situation and by this the reasoning process moves towards a goal. Thus the reasoning process is defined as filling slots value in frames. If the given slot characteristic is not present then the slot provides a default value for the characteristic. Please note that the problem situation is generally not static. The values of the corresponding slots are updated if there is any deviation in the characteristic.

Types of Slots : Slots are of three types as follows:

I. Inherent Slots :

a. These slots are specified by the use for each class and the values are given during the instantiating of this class to obtain an object.

b. These are comparable with the recording field of data and hence are the characteristic of the knowledge under consideration.

c. However, there is a difference. Since these can exist outside of their recording they can have one or more values but also procedures associated with them.

II. Meta Slots :

a. These are defined for the classes and often have only one value being related to the given class.

b. These are not inherited.

c. Such an attribute is the ako (a – kind– of) link mentioned in the semantic networks which relates one class to a more general class.

d. Each class is related by ako to at least one other class. There exists exactly one class linked to itself, which is the vertex of the graph of ako links.

e. The slot ako determines one of the fundamental interests of the object representation — INHERITANCE.

f. At the level of instanced frames, it allows (by default) a frame to inherit certain values of the classes to which it is bound (related) by ako. If this frame is bound to several others, there can be multiple inheritance. The value of ako is a set of frames.

III. Instantiated Slots :

a. Are defined for objects which are instances of classes.

b. As priori, their creation is automatic during instantiating since they are ascribed to the instantiated class.

c. This type of attribute is the isa link mentioned for semantic networks.

Please note that each slot possesses an arbitrary number of facets. These are the declarations or procedures associated to the attributes.

Many languages like LISP (i.e. List Processing) has in-build procedures to create, access, modify, update and display frames.

We must keep the following points in mind —

1. Instances of SLOT are slots.
2. Associated with SLOT are attributes that each instance will inherit.
3. Each slot has a domain and a range.
4. Since slot is a set of all slots, so can be represented by metaclass called slot.
5. To compute attribute involves a procedure to compute its value.

Advantages of Frames :

1. Are very flexible.
2. Are similar to human knowledge organization, easier to understand logic or rules.

Disadvantages of Frames :

1. No standards.
2. Very generalized approach
3. No associated reasoning mechanism.

Problems with both semantic nets and frames :

1. Both net and frames are weak slot and filler structures. Both are arbitrary.
2. Both are useful for representing certain sorts of knowledge.
3. Both lack semantics i.e., precise meaning.
4. Logic generalizes these schemes.
5. Syntax of KR scheme is irrelevant.

Q.40. Write short notes on conceptual dependncies (CDs).

Ans. In 1977, Roger C Schank developed CD structures. CD is used to represent knowledge again. This representation should be powerful enough to represent these concept of sentences of natural language. CD theory states that different sentences which have same meaning should have some unique CD representation. In CD theory, 5 different types of ontological (state of being) building blocks are distinguished —

a. Entities.
b. Actions.
c. Conceptual cases.
d. Conceptual Dependencies.
e. Conceptual tenses.

Entities :

a. Picture Producer (PP) are actors that perform different acts.
b. Picture Aiders (PA) are supporting properties or attributes of producers.
c. ACT: Actions done by an actor to an object.
d. LOCs: Shows the location of action,

Actions :

a. Primitive actions (ACTs).
b. Action Aiders (AA) are properties or attributes of primitive action. For primitive actions, a typical CD set is —

ATRANS	Transfer (example., 'give')
INGEST	Ingest into the body (example. 'eat')
EXPEL	Expel from body (example. 'cry')
ATTRANS	Abstract transfer (example. 'owner ship')
MORE	Move a body part (example. 'kick')
GRASP	Grasp an object (example. 'clutch')
PROPEL	Throw an object (example. 'push')
PTRANS	Physical transfer (example. 'go')
MTRANS	Mental transfer (example. 'tell')
CONC	Conceptualize (*i.e.*, think about something).
ATTEND	Direct sensory orange to observe (example. listen).

The main goals of this theory are —

1. To capture the implicit concept of a sentence and make it explicit.
2. To help in drawing inferences from sentences.
3. For any 2 or more sentences that are identical in meaning, there should be only one representation of meaning.

4. To develop language conversion packages.
5. To provide a means of representation which are language independent.

In addition to the actors and objects other concept of time, location, source and destination are also used in CD representation —

(*i*)	O	:	Object case relationship
(*ii*)	r/R	:	Recipient case relationship
(*iii*)	p	:	Part
(*iv*)	f	:	future
(*v*)	t	:	transition
(*vi*)	Is	:	Start transition
(*vii*)	Tf	:	finish transition
(*viii*)	k	:	continuing
(*ix*)	?	:	interrogative
(*x*)	/	:	negative
(*xi*)	nil	:	present
(*xii*)	delta	:	timeless:
(*xiii*)	C	:	Conditional

For example 1: Ram gives Anjali a book.

Its CD structure is as follows —

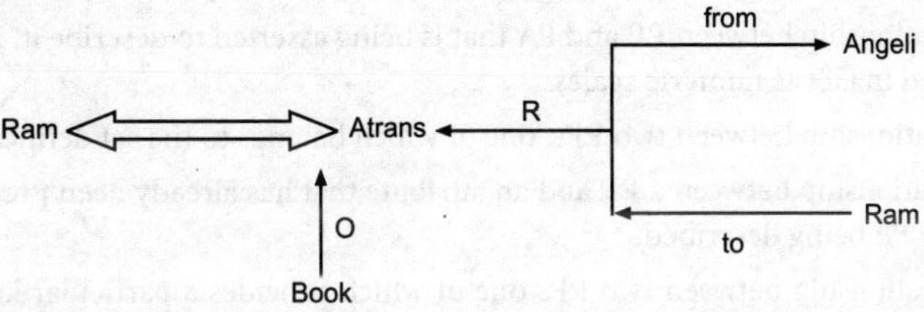

where the symbols used are—

a. **Arrow:** indicates the direction of dependency.
b. Double arrow indicates two-way link between actor and actions.
c. ATRANS is a primitive to describe this event.
d. *O* represents object case relationship.
e. *R* indicates recipient case relationship.

Example 2: The man took a watch

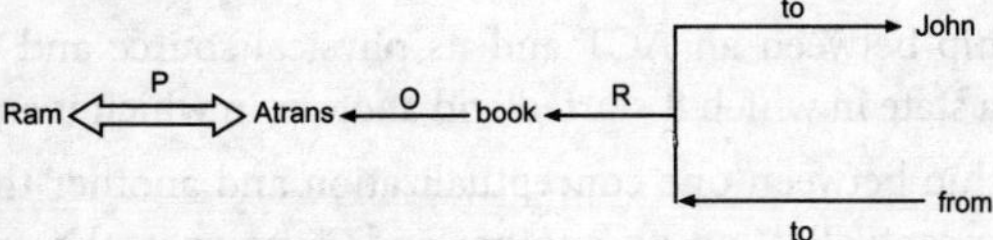

Here, 'men' is an actor and 'watch' is the object of the action 'took'.

Example 3: I gave John a book

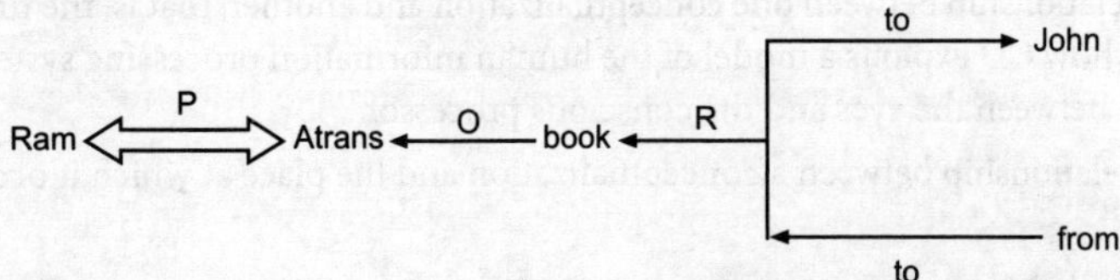

Many a times, actors are missing from a sentence. This is a challenge. For example. 'Rajiv fell', sentence has a missing actor as another force "gravity" was acting. In such cases, we need additional optional notations :

R = reason

r = results

i = intends

d = direction

I = Instrument

R = recipient, state change.

So, the sentence 'Rajiv fell' in CD is as follows —

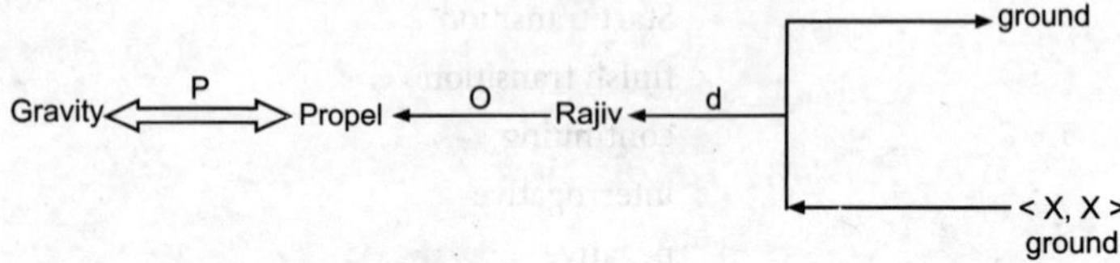

Parsing a sentence into *CD* representation is analogous to the process of parsing using a case grammar.

We must study some rules for CD representation.

Rules of CD

Rule 1 describes the relationship between an actor and the event he or she causes. This is a two-way dependency since neither actor nor event can be considered primary. The letter above the dependency link indicates past tense.

Rule 2 describes the relationship between PP and PA that is being asserted to describe it. Many state descriptions, such as height, are represented in CD as numeric scales.

Rule 3 describes the relationship between two PPs, one of which belongs to the set defined by the other.

Rule 4 describes the relationship between a PP and an attribute that has already been predicated of it. The direction of the arrow is towards the PP being described.

Rule 5 describes the relationship between two PPs one of which provides a particular kind of information about the other. The three most common types of information to be provided in this way are procession (shown as POSS-BY), location (shown as LOC), and physical containment (shown as CONT). The direction of the arrow is again toward the concept being described.

Rule 6 describes the relationship between an ACT and the PP that is the object of that ACT. The direction of the arrow is toward the ACT since the context of the – specific ACT determines the meaning of the object relation.

Rule 7 describes the relationship between an ACT and the source and the recipient of the ACT. **Rule 8** describes the relationship between an ACT and the instrument with which it is performed. The instrument must always be a full conceptualization (*i.e.*, it must contain an ACT), not just a single physical object.

Rule 9 describes the relationship between an ACT and its physical source and destination. Rule 10 represents the relationship between a PP and a state in which it started and another in which it ended.

Rule 11 describes the relationship between one conceptualization and another that causes it. Notice that the arrows indicate dependency of one conceptualization on another and so point in the opposite direction of the implication arrows. The two forms of the rule describe the cause of an action and the cause of a state change.

Rule 12 describes the relationship between a conceptualization and the time at which the event occurred is described.

Rule 13 describes the relationship between one conceptualization and another, that is, the time of the first. The example for this rule also shows how CD exploits a model of the human information processing system; see is represented as the transfer of information between the eyes and the conscious processor.

Rule 14 describes the relationship between a conceptualization and the place at which it occurred.

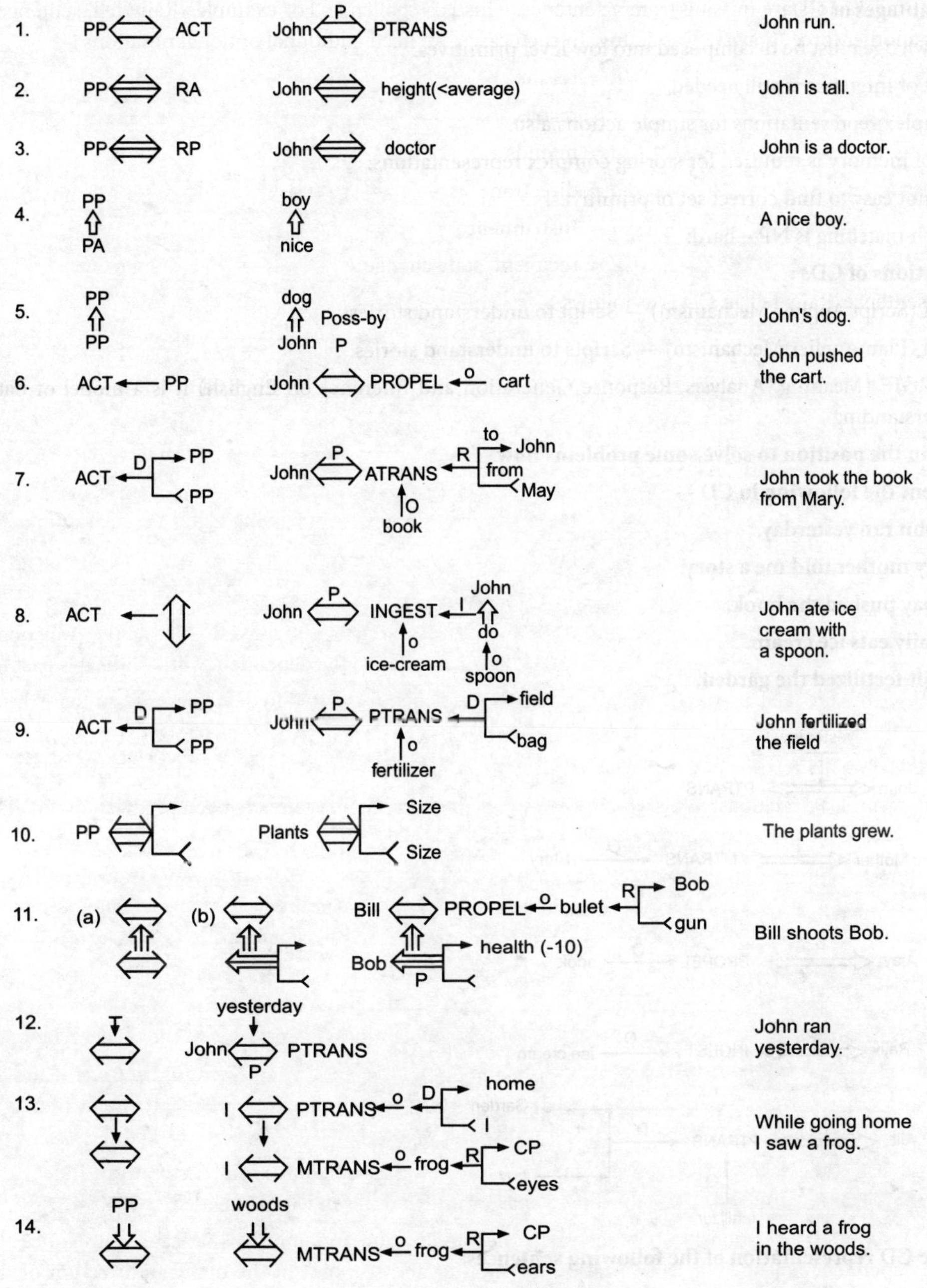

Fig. 8.9: Rules of CD

Advantages of CD :

1. Lesser number of inference rules are required if we use CD primitives.
2. Many inference rules are already shown in CD structure.
3. The holes in the initial structure help to focus on the points which still is to be established.
4. Smaller number of primitive ACTs (*i.e.* 14).
5. Language free representation.

Disadvantages of CD :

1. Knowledge must be decomposed into low level primitives.
2. A lot of inference is still needed.
3. Complex representations for simple actions also.
4. Lot of memory is required for storing complex representations.
5. It is not easy to find correct set of primitives.
6. Graph matching is NP – hard.

Applications of CDs :

1. SAM (Script Applier Mechanism) — Script to understand stories.
2. PAM (Plan Applier Mechanism) — Scripts to understand stories.
3. MARGIE (Meaning, Analysis, Response Generation and Inference on English) It is a model of natural language understanding.

We are in the position to solve some problems now.

Q.1. Represent the following in CD —

a. **John ran yesterday.**

b. **My mother told me a story.**

c. **Ajay pushed the book.**

d. **Rajiv eats ice cream.**

e. **Ajit fertilized the garden.**

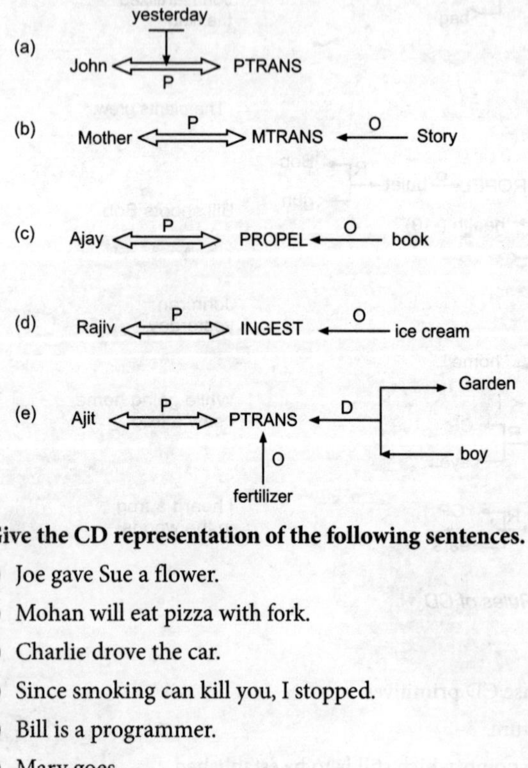

(a) yesterday
John P PTRANS

(b) Mother P MTRANS O Story

(c) Ajay P PROPEL O book

(d) Rajiv P INGEST O ice cream

(e) Ajit P PTRANS D Garden boy
O fertilizer

Q.2. Give the CD representation of the following sentences.

(*i*) Joe gave Sue a flower.

(*ii*) Mohan will eat pizza with fork.

(*iii*) Charlie drove the car.

(*iv*) Since smoking can kill you, I stopped.

(*v*) Bill is a programmer.

(*vi*) Mary goes.

(*vii*) Mary will go.

(*viii*) Neeraj cried.

(*ix*) Bill threatened John with a broken nose.
(*x*) Anil punched Ram.
(*xi*) Ram lied.
(*xii*) Joe told Lucy he would not go to movies with her. Her feelings were hurt.
(*xiii*) Prem went to the park with peacocks.
(*xiv*) John will eat noodles with fork and knife.
(*xv*) Mohan is a sales manager.
(*xvi*) Kapil ate some soup.
(*xvii*) Mohan gave some books to Reeta.
(*xviii*) He will speak.
(*xix*) Anil will go tomorrow.
(*xx*) While going home, he saw a peacock.
(*xxi*) Ram heard noises in the kitchen.
(*xxii*) Hair is short.
(*xxiii*) Hari is a nice boy.

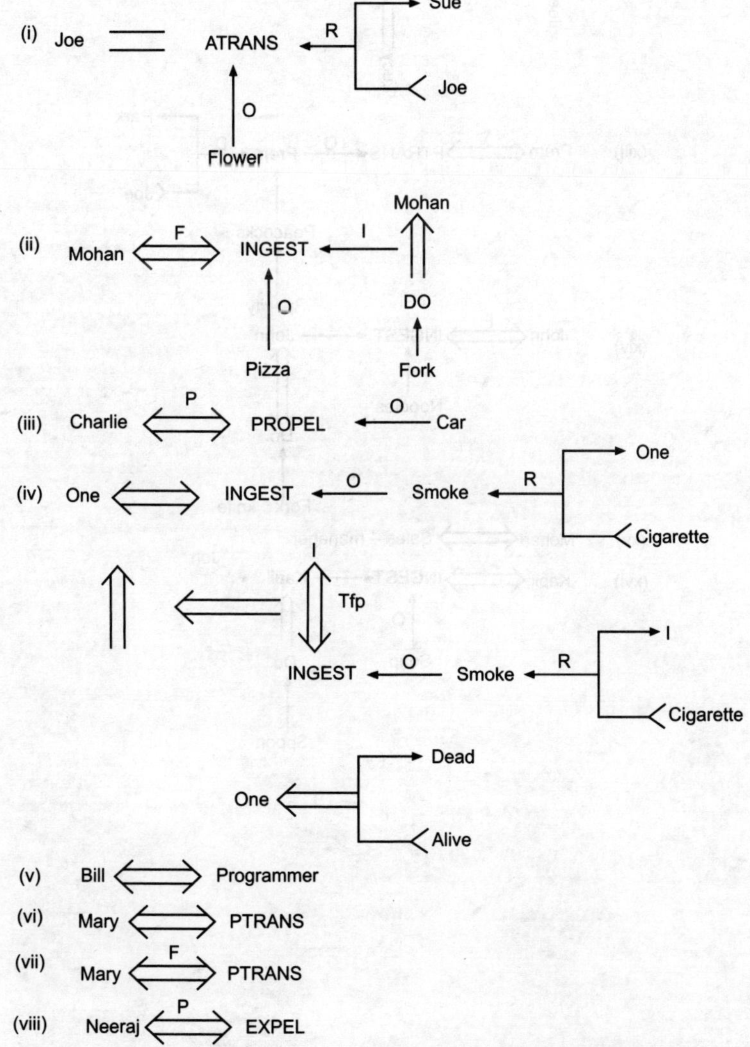

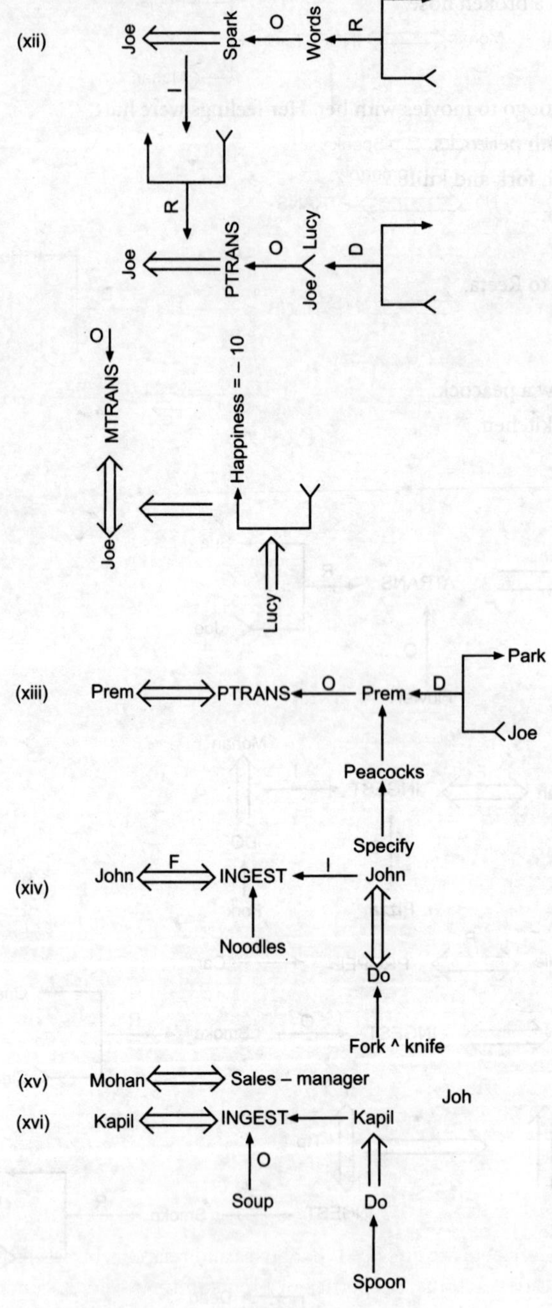
(xii)
Joe
Spark
O
Words
R
I
R
Joe
PTRANS
O
Joe
Lucy
D
O
MTRANS
Joe
Happiness = – 10
Lucy
(xiii)
Prem
PTRANS
O
Prem
D
Park
Joe
Peacocks
Specify
(xiv)
John
F
INGEST
I
John
Noodles
Do
Fork ^ knife
(xv)
Mohan
Sales – manager
Joh
(xvi)
Kapil
INGEST
Kapil
O
Soup
Do
Spoon

(xvii) Mohan ⟺(P) INGEST ←(R) → Pooja / ← Mohan; ↑(O)

(xviii) He ⟺(F) Speak
↓ Tomorrow

(xix) He ⟺(F) PTRANS

(xx) He ⟺ PTRANS ← He ←(D) → Home / ← He
↓
He ⟺ MTRANS ←(O) Peacock
Kitchen
⇓
(xxi) He ⟺ MTRANS ←(O) Noise
↑
Cp Ears

(xii) Hari ⟺ Height [< average]

(xiii) Hari ⟺ Boy
↑
Nice

Conceptual graphs : It is a graphical portrayal of a mental perception which consists of basic or primitive concepts and the relationships that exist between the concepts.

For example: "Joe is eating soup with a spoon" can be represented as follows:

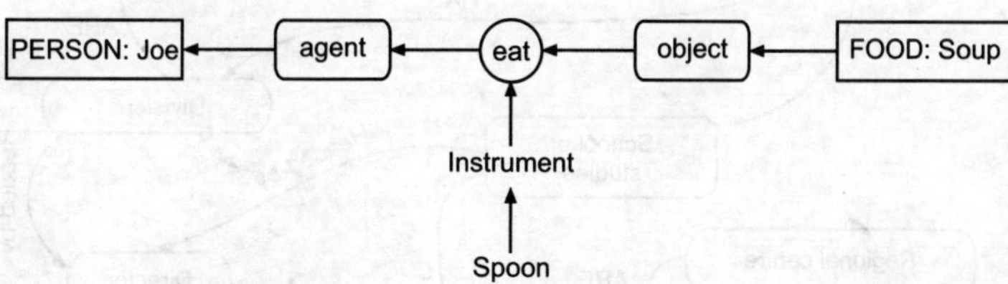

This is a conceptual graph. Concepts are enclosed in a boxes and relations between the concepts are enclosed in ovals. Concept symbol refers to entities, actions, properties or events in the world. A concept may be individual or generic. Individual concepts have a type field followed by a referent field. The concept PERSON JOE] HAS TYPE — PERSONS and referent Joe. Referents like Joe and a soup are called individual concepts since they refer to specific entities. EAT have no referent field since they are generic çoncepts which refer to unspecified entities.

A conceptual graph can also be represented linearly. It is represented by using upper & lowercase characters of alphabet, boxes circles, arcs and special characters including —, ?, !, *, #, @,

∀, ~, [,], (,), →, ←, } & }. The above graph can thus be represented as:

[PERSON : Joe] ← (AGENT) ← [EAT] –

(OBJECT) → [FOOD : Soup] (INSTRUMENT) → [SPOON]

where square brackets have replaced concept boxes, parentheses have replaced relation circles. The dash signifies continuation of the linear graph on the next line.

Example 2: The sentence "Every car has an engine" can be represented as a conceptual graph — [CAR : ∀] → (PART) → [ENGINE]

This conceptual graph can be converted into its FOPL as follows:

$$\forall x\, \exists y\, (\text{CAR}\,(x) \rightarrow (\text{ENGINE}\,(y)\ \&\ \text{PART}\,(x, y)))$$

We are in a position to solve examples now.

Q.1. Express the following concepts as an associative network structure —

Ans. Company ABC is a software development company. Three departments within the company are Sales, Administration & Programming. Joe is the manager of Programming. Bill and Sue are programmers. Sue is married to Sam. Sam is an editor for Prentice Hall. They have 3 children and they live on Elm Street. He wears glasses and is 5 feet 4 inches tall.

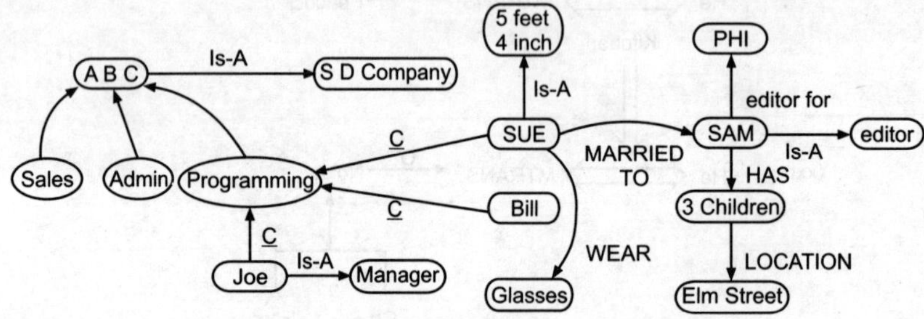

Q.2. Represent the following as an associative network.

"GGSIPU is a State University established by the Act of Parliament. It has 9 schools of studies and 12 divisions to support the academic activities at the headquarters. It has 44 regional centres spread over the whole country. Each school and division is headed by a Director and each regional centre is headed by a Regional Director".

Ans.

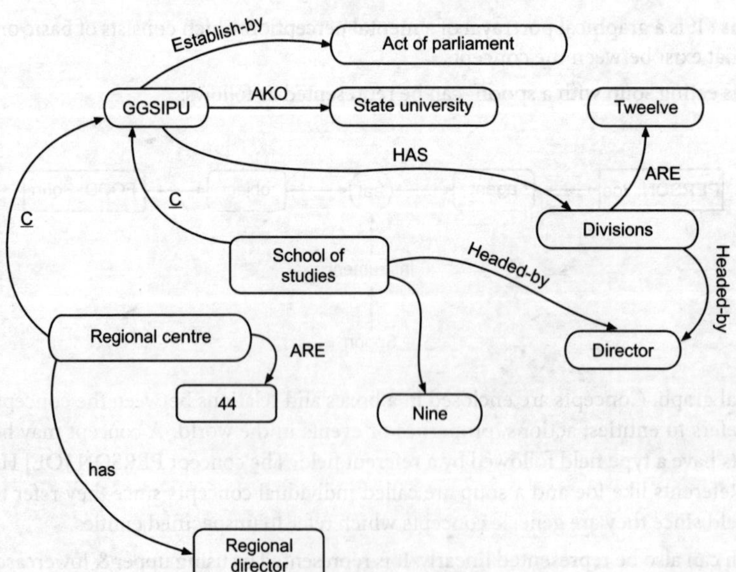

Q.41. What are scripts? How are they used in reasoning?

Ans. A script is a structure that prescribes a set of circumstances which could be expected to follow on from one another. It is similar to a chain of situations which could be anticipated. Like a script for a play, the script's structure is defined in terms of —

a. Actors *b.* Roles

c. Props and *d.* Scenes

Please note that the slots in a script correspond to the parts of the event which are filled with CD primitives. It could be considered to consist of a number of slots or frames but with more specified robes. Scripts are frame-like structures to represent knowledge grouped from our common experiences like going to a movie, eating in a bar, visiting a doctor or shopping in a MALL etc.

Scripts are useful because —

a. Events tend to occur in known runs or patterns.

b. Entry conditions exist which allow an event to take place.

c. Casual relationships between events exist.

d. Prerequisites exist.

How reasoning is done?

To perform reasoning using scripts, a script with partially filled fields is created to meet the current situation. Then, a known script (which matches the current situation) is recalled from memory. The script name, preconditions or shear keywords provide index value which is used to search the current script. Inferencing is done by filling a slot with inherited and default values that satisfy certain conditions.

For example : We prepare a script of a Restaurant.

The Restaurant Script

Script : RESTAURANT	Scene 1: Entering	
Track : Coffee shop	S PTRANSS into restaurant S ATTEND eyes to tables	
Propos : Tables	S MBUILD where to sit	
Menu	S PTRANSS to table	
F = Food	S Move S to sitting position	
Check	Scene 2: Ordering (S asked for menu)	
Money	(Menu on table) (W brings menu)	S MTRANS signal to W
	S PTRANS menu to S	W PTRANS W to table
		SMTRANS 'need menu' to W
		W PTRANS W to menu
Roles: S = Customer	W PTRANS W to table	
W = Waiter	W ATRANS menu to S	
C = Cook	S MTRANS W to Table	
M = Cashier	SMB VILD choice of F	
O = Owner	S MTRANS squard to W	
	WPTRANS W to table	
	SMTRANS F to W	
Entry conditions:	W PTRANS W to C	
S is hungry.	W MTRANS (ATRANS F) to C	
S has money.	CMTRANS no F to W	CDO (prepare F script) to Scence 3
	WPTRRANS W to S	
	W MTRANS no F to S	
	(go back to*) or	
	(go to Scene 4 at no pay path)	
Results:		
S has less money	Scene 3 : Eating CATRANS F to	
O has more money.	ww ATRANS F to S S INGEST F	
S is not hungry.	Option: REturm to Scene 2 to order more;	
S is pleased (optional).	otherwise, go to scene 4	

	Scene 4: Exiting
	MTRANS to W (W ATRANS check to S W MOVE (write check) W PTRANS W to S W ATRANS check to S S ATRANS tip to W S PTRANS S to M S PTRANS S to out of restaurant (No pay path)

Let us write an other script now.

Script Name: Interaction with car salesperson

PROPS	Scenes
Car showroom Car Feature Booklet Money Time	**Scene 1** • Customer enters the showroom • Search for a particular brand. • Salesperson attends customer and welcomes him
ROLES Customer Salesperson Owner Cashier	**Scene 2** • Sales person shows various cars • Customer selects particular car • Salesperson describes its features
INITIAL • Customer needs a car • Customer has more money • Salesperson has details about car • Availability of car in showroom • Owner has less money	**Scene 3** • Customer asks for a test drive • Salesperson takes him on a drive **Scene 4** • Customs is ready to buy • Customser asks for bill and warranty • Salesperson gets him warranty book and bill
RESULTS • Customer bought a car • Salesperson got commission • Customer has less money • Owner has more money • Particular car count decreases	**Scene 5** • Customer pays the money • Salesperson deposits it with cashier • Customer to gives commission to salesperson • Drives car back home

TRACKS none

Please note the following points about scripts:

1. If a particular script is to be applied then it must be activated and this activation depends on its significance.
2. If a topic is mentioned in passing then a pointer to that script could be held. Else if the topic is important then the script should be opened.
3. Having too many scripts is dangerous.
4. If events follow a known trail, then we can use scripts to represent the action involved and use them to answer detailed questions.

5. Different trails may be allowed for different outcomes of scripts.

Advantages of scripts :

a. They have ability to predict events.

b. A single coherent interpretation may be built up from a collection of observations.

Disadvantages of scripts :

a. They are less general than framer.

b. They are not suitable to represent all kinds of knowledge.

Applications of scripts : Shank and his team at YALE University used scripts in one system named as SAM — Script applier mechanism. SAM reads and reasons with text to demonstrate an understanding of stories that were script based.

Q.42. Illustrate the wumpus world. Apply PEAS model on it.

Ans. Wumpus was a traditional computer game based on the agent that explores a cave consisting of rooms connected by passage ways. Wumpus is a beast that lurks somewhere in the cave that eats anyone who enters the room. Also, some rooms contain bottomless pits that will trap anyone who wanders into these rooms, except for the Wumpus that is too big to fall in it. The agent's goal is to find the gold and bring it back to start as quickly as possible without getting killed. In this game, 1000 points are awarded for climbing out of the cave while carrying the gold but there is 1-point penalty for each action taken and a 10,000 points penalty for getting killed. Let us now apply our PEAS model on this game of Wumpus.

1. Performance measure:

- 1000 for picking up the gold.
- 1000 for falling into a pit or being eaten by Wumpus.
- One for each action taken.
- 10 for using up the arrow.

2. Environment:

- A (4 * 4) grid of rooms.
- The agent always starts in the square labeled [1, 1], facing to the right.
- The locations of the gold and Wumpus are chosen randomly, with a uniform distribution, from the squares other than the start square.
- Each square other than the start can be a pit with probability 0.2.

3. Actuators:

- The agent can move forward.
- Turn left by 90°.
- Turn left by 90° or Turn right by 90°.
- The agent dies if it enters a square containing a pit or live Wumpus, it is safe to enter the square with a dead Wumpus. Moving forward has no effect if there is a wall in front of the agent.
- The action 'grab' can be used to pick up an object that is in the same square as the agent.
- The action 'shoot' can be used to fire an arrow in straight line in the direction where the agent is facing. The arrow continues until it either hits and hence kills the Wumpus or hots a wall. The agent only has one arrow, so only first shoot action has any effect.

4. Sensors:

- The agent has 5 sensors each of which gives a single bit of information.
- In the square containing the Wumpus and in the directly (not diagonally) adjacent squares, the agent will receive a stink.
- In the squares, directly adjacent to pit, the agent will receive a breeze.
- In the square where gold is, the agent will perceive a glitter.
- When an agent walks into a wall, it will perceive a bump.
- When the Wumpus is killed, it emits it emits a scream that can be perceived anywhere in the cave.
- The percepts will be given to the agent in form of list of five symbols.

SUMMARY

This chapter discusses about advanced knowledge representation techniques like frames, nets, CG, CD and scripts. KR is one of the critical aspects to make our computer behave intelligently.

MULTIPLE CHOICE QUESTIONS

1. **Data when processed gives information and Information when processed gives —**
   (a) Knowledge (b) Domain
   (c) Wisdom (d) None of these
2. **The knowledge about what we know is —**
   (a) Meta knowledge
   (b) Mini knowledge
   (c) Micro knowledge
   (d) None of the above
3. **Concepts, objects, nets, logic etc are the examples of**
   (a) Tacit knowledge (b) Explicit knowledge
   (c) Knowledge base (d) None of the above
4. **According to Robert Kowalski**
   (a) Logic = Algorithm + Control
   (b) Algorithm = Logic + Control
   (c) Algorithm = Logic – Control
   (d) None of the above
5. **The process of producing proofs by refutation or contradiction is known as —**
   (a) Resolution (b) Proposition
   (c) Unification (d) None of these.
6. **The universal quantifier is —**
   (a) $\exists$ (b) $\wedge$
   (c) $\forall$ (d) =
7. **The process of eliminating existential quantifiers is known as**
   (a) Resolution (b) Skolemisatio
   (c) Unification (d) None of these
8. **The Recursive process of merging two or more predicates with constants or with some variables is known as —**
   (a) Resolution (b) Proposition
   (c) Unification (d) Proposition
9. **Forward chaining is a —**
   (a) Data-driven search (b) Goal-driven search
   (c) Heuristic search (d) None of the above.
10. **A CD primitive that is used to do mental transfer is –**
    (a) ATRANS (b) ATTRANS
    (c) PTRANS (d) MTRANS

ANSWERS

1. (a)	**2.** (a)	**3.** (b)	**4.** (b)	**5.** (a)
6. (c)	**7.** (c)	**8.** (c)	**9.** (a)	**10.** (d)

CONCEPTUAL SHORT QUESTIONS WITH ANSWERS

Q.1. What is chaining?

Ans. In inferencing process, the rules are applied in succession till a situation arrives that there is no rule which is applicable. It is called as **chaining.**

Q.2. What do you mean by a Universe of Discourse?

Ans. The universe of discourse or domain of discourse indicates the following —

a. A set of entities that quantifiers deal with.

b. Entities can be a set of integers, a set of real numbers, a set of students etc.

Universe is the domain of individual variables. Even propositions in logic are statement of an object of a universe.

Q.3. What is matching? Name some matching techniques.

Ans. In matching process, the LHS of rule is compared with the input and all rules that match are extracted. Actually, both the current state of the problem and its preconditions are matched with the LHS of the rule. This is known as **matching.** Some matching techniques are as follows —

a. Indexing

b. Matching with variable

c. Complex matching variable.

Q.4. What is a Horn clause?

Ans. In a logic, a Horn clause is a clause (a disjunction of literals) with at most one positive literal. A Horn clause with exactly one positive literal is a definite clause; a Horn clause with no positive literals is sometimes called a goal clause, especially in logic programming. A Horn formula is a conjunctive normal form formula whose clauses are all Horn; in other words, it is a conjunction of Horn clauses. A dual-Horn clause is a clause with at most one negative literal. Horn clauses play a basic role in logic programming and are important for constructive logic.

The following is an example of a definite Horn clause:

$$\neg P \wedge \neg q \vee .... \vee t \vee u$$

Such a formula can be rewritten in the following form, which is more common in logic programming and similar fields:

$$(p \wedge q \wedge ... \wedge t) \rightarrow u$$

The relevance of Horn clauses to theorem proving by first-order resolution is that the resolution of two Horn clauses is a Horn clause. Moreover, the resolution of a goal clause and a definite clause is again a goal clause. In automated theorem proving, this can lead to greater efficiencies in proving a theorem represented as a goal clause. In fact, Prolog is a programming language based on Horn clauses.

Horn clauses are also of interest in computational complexity, where the problem of finding a set of a variable assignments to make a conjunction of Horn clauses true is a P-complete problem, sometimes called HORNSAT. This is P's version of a boolean satisfiability problem, a central NP-complete problem.

> NOTE: The name "Horn clause" comes from the logician Alfred Horn who first pointed out the significance of such clauses.

Q.5 Represent the following in FOPL —

1. Lipton is a tea.

2. Lata is a child who drinks tea.

3. Ruma dislikes children who drink tea.

4. Ruma disliked Lata.

Ans. (*i*) Tea (Lipton)

(*ii*) $\exists x$ [child (x) $\wedge$ drinks (x, tea)]

$\exists x$ [child (Lata) $\wedge$ drinks (Lata, tea)]

(*iii*) $\forall x$ [drinks (x, tea) $\Rightarrow$ dislikes (Ruma, x)]

(*iv*) Dislikes (Ruma, Lata).

Q.6. Express following knowledge as a semantic network with nodes and labeled arcs. "Sam is Vice-President in ABC Corp. He is married to Kay and has a male child named Joe. Joe goes to school. Sam plays golf and owns a silver colored German-made car Mercedes Benz."

Ans. Semantic net diagram:

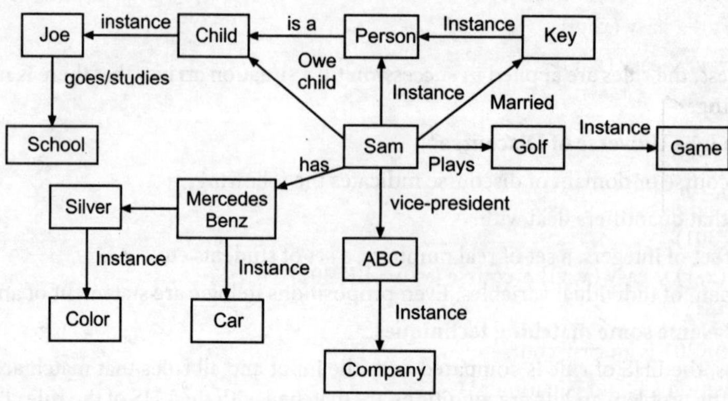

Q.7. Sam, Clyde and Oscar are elephants. We know the following facts about them —

a. **Sam is pink.**

b. **Clyde is gray and likes Oscar.**

c. **Oscar is either pink or gray (but not both) and likes Sam.**

Use resolution to prove that gray elephants like pink elephant, *i.e.*, prove that $[\exists x, y][\text{grey}(x) \wedge \text{pink}(x) \wedge \text{likes}(x, y)\}$

Ans. 'SAM is pink' can be represented as—

pink (Sam) ...(1)

Similarly, other two facts can be represented as—

grey (clyde) $\wedge$likes (clyde, oscar) ...(2)

and (pink (oscar) $\vee$ grey (oscar) $\wedge$ likes (oscar, sam) ...(3)

Given:

$[\exists x, y]$ [grey $(x) \wedge$ pink $(x) \wedge$ likes (x, y)]

Grey $[x]$ from 2 it implies—

Grey [Clyde] but does not fulfil the criteria of pink.

$\therefore$ from (3) we get—

Grey (Oscar), Pink (Oscar)

and also likes (Oscar, Sam)

$\therefore$ $x \Rightarrow$ Oscar

$y \Rightarrow$ Sam

It means that Oscar likes Sam.

Q.8. Assume the following facts —

a. **Steve only likes easy courses.**

b. **Science courses are hard.**

c. **All courses in the basket weaving department are easy**

d. **BK301 is a basket weaving course.**

Use resolution to answer the questions— "What course would Steve like"?

Ans. Convert the given facts into predicates firstly –

1. like (steve, easy course) ...(1)
2. hard (Science, course) ...(2)
3. $\forall x \forall y$ [courses $(x, y) \rightarrow$ easy (x, y)]
4. Courses $(x, y =$ BK 301)

Now, we convert these predicates into clausal form—

1. $\forall x\ \forall y$ [course $(x, y) \rightarrow$ easy (x, y)]

   $\forall x\ \forall y$ [–course $(x, y) \vee$ easy (x, y)]

$$\begin{bmatrix} Q\neg(\neg P) = \\ \&\neg(a \wedge b) = \neg a \vee \neg b) \\ \&\neg(a \vee b) = \neg a \wedge \neg b \end{bmatrix}$$

2. Course $(x, y =$ BK 301)

   [$\forall x \forall y$ ($\neg$ course $(x, y) \vee$ easy (x, y))] $\wedge$ course $(x, y =$ BK 301)

   $\Rightarrow$ easy (x, BK 301) ...(3)

   This implies that BK301 is an easy course.

   Now, consider equation (1) and equation (3):

   Like (steve, easy course) $\wedge$ easy (x, BK301)

   $\therefore$ Steve likes BK301

   Now, consider (1) and (2)

   Like (steve, easy course) $\wedge$ hard (Science, courses)

   $\Rightarrow$ steve doesn't like science What course would Steve like?

   It is clearly proved by equation (3) that Steve likes BK301.

Q.9. Given two clauses— Loves (Father (*a*), *a*) and loves (*y*, *x*). What must be generated as a result of resolving these two clauses?

Ans. Given:

loves (Father (a), a) and loves (y, x) $a = x$

Father (a) = y Father (x) = y

This means that Father of x is y.

Now, love (Father (a), a)

loves (y, x) $\vee$ loves (x, y)

loves (Father (a), a)loves (Father (a), a)

loves (y, x)	loves (x,y)
$\therefore$ Father (a) = y	$\therefore$ Father (a) = x
and $a = x$	and $a = y$

Which is NOT possible.

Thus, these two clauses cannot be unified.

Q.10. The following statements are given —

(*i*) Rishi likes to eat peanut.

(*ii*) Rishi eats whatever John eats.

(*iii*) John eats only eatables.

(*iv*) Anybody who eats eatables is a human being.

(*v*) Peanut is an eatable.

a. Convert these into wff and clausal form.

b. Is John a human being? Answer this using back tracking and resolution.

Ans. *a.* The WFF notations are—

1. Likes (Rishi, Peanut)
2. $\forall xy$ eats (Rishi, y) $\rightarrow$ eats (John, y)
3. $\forall y$ eats (John, y)

4. ∀x ∀y eats (x, y) → human being (x)
5. eatable (y = peanut)

Its clausal form is as follows —

1. Likes (Rishi, y1) ...(1)
2. ∀y eats (Rishi, y) → eats (John, y)
   ∀x ¬ eats (Rishi, y) ∧ eats (John, y)
   ∴ ¬ eats (Rishi, y2) ∨ eats (John, y2) ...(2)
3. ∀y eats (John, y) is
   eats (John, y3) ...(3)
4. ∀x ∀y eats (x, y) → human being (x)
   ∀x ∀y ¬ eats (x, y) ∨ human being (x)
   ∴ ¬ eats (x1, y4) ∨ human being (y4) ...(4)
5. eatable (y = peanut) is eatable (y5) ...(5)
6. Is John a human being?
   i.e. human being (John)

We start with opposite of this (*i.e.* negation)

¬ human being (John)

∴ Using back tracking and Resolutions we get — human being (John)

x1 = John x4 = eatable eats (John, eatable)eats (John eatables)

∴ It is proved that John is a human being.

Q.11. Assume the following facts —

a. Ram likes only easy courses.

b. Engg. courses are hard.

c. All courses in Arts are easy.

d. AR04 is an Arts course.

Use resolution to answer the question, "What course would Ram like?"

Ans. Let us find its Predicate clause firstly,

∃y easy (y) → likes (Ram, y)

∃y easy course (x) → hard (x)

∀x art course (x) → easy (x) art course(AR04)

∴ Its clausal form is—

like (Ram, easy courses)

hard course (Engineering)

easy (art courses)

AR04 (art course). Now, we use resolution to prove our query.

∴ Answer is: Ram likes AR04.

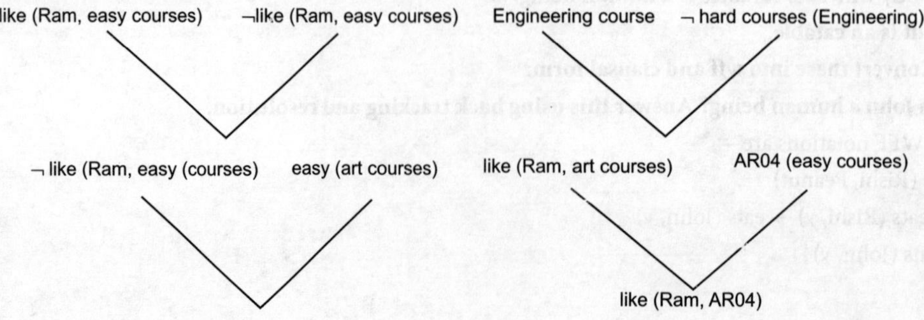

Q.12. Describe the term 'Partitioned Semantic Net'. Also construct a Partitioned semantic Net representation for the following:

***a.* Every dog has bitten a mail carrier.**

***b.* Every batter hits a ball.**

Ans. It is a representation for simple quantified expressions in a semantic net in which semantic net is partitioned into a hierarchical set of spaces each of which corresponds to the scope of one or more variable.

a. Consider a simple net corresponding to statement—"The dog bit the mail carrier", given below —

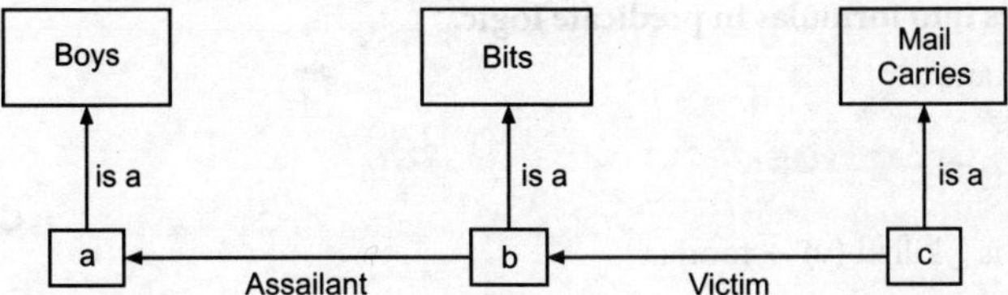

The nodes–Dogs, Bite and bitings and Mail carriers. Nodes *d*, *b* and m represent a particular dog, a particular biting and a particular Mail carrier. This fact can easily be represented by a single net with no partitioning. If we represent the fact "Every dog has bitten a mail carrier" or the logic.

$\forall x$ Dog$(x) \rightarrow \exists y$ Mail – carrier $(y) \wedge$ Bite (x, y)

Example,

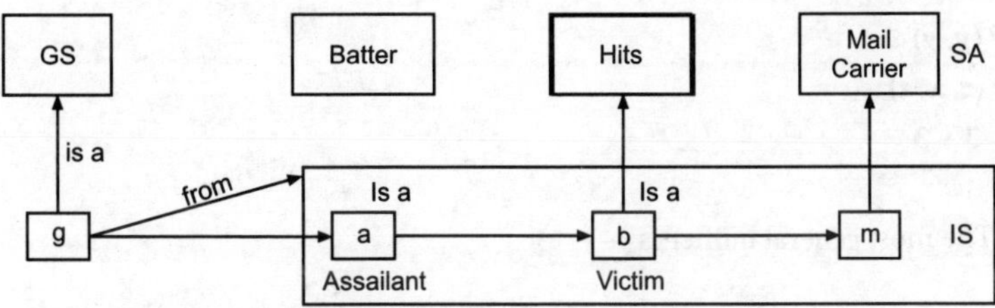

The node '*g*' stands for the assertion given above. Node *g* is an instance of special class of GS of general statements. Every element GS has at least two attributes, a form which states the relation that is being asserated. For every dog *d*, there exists a biting event b and a mail carrier m such that *d* is the assaitant of *b* and *m* is the victim.

b. Now, consider second statement—"Every batter hits a ball". The nodes batter, hit and ball represent classes of batter, hitting and ball while nodes *a*, *b*, c represent a particular batter, a particular hit and a particular ball *i.e.*,

$\forall x$ Batter $(x) \rightarrow \exists y$ Ball $(y) \wedge$ hit (x, y)

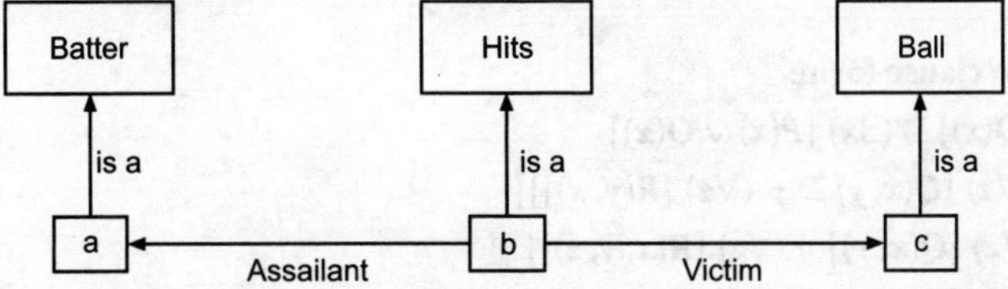

To represent this face, we take node g which stands for assertion given above. Node g is an instance of the special class GS of general statements. Every element of GS has at least two attributes, a form which states the relation that is being asserted and one or more $\forall$ connections.

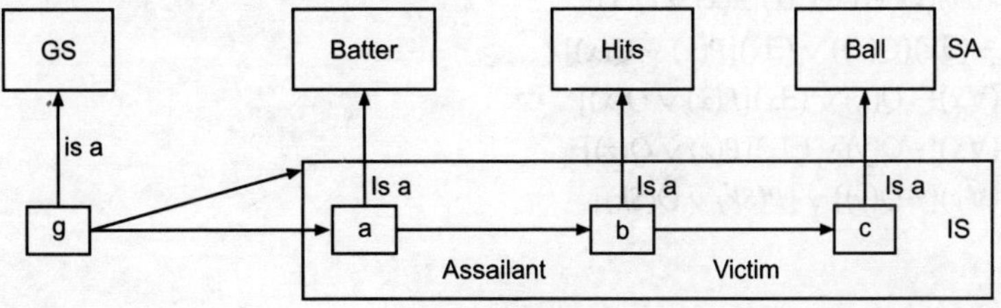

Q.13. Consider the following statements:

(i) Ram likes all kinds of food.

(ii) Apples are food.

(iii) Chicken is food.

(iv) Anything anyone eats and isn't killed by is food.

(v) Bill eats peanuts and is still alive.

(vi) Rita eats everything Bill eats.

Translate these sentences into formulas in predicate logic.

Ans. (i) $\forall x$ food $(x) \rightarrow$ likes (Ram, x)

(ii) food (Apples)

(iii) food (Chicken)

(iv) $\forall x \forall y$ eats $(y, x) \wedge \sim$ is _ killed $(y) \rightarrow$ food (x)

(v) eats (Bill, peanuts) $\wedge$ alive (Bill)

(vi) $\forall x$ eats (Bill, x) $\rightarrow$ eats (Rita, x)

Q.14. Say, whether or not the following pairs of expressions are unifiable and show the most general unifier for each unifiable pair —

a. **$P(x, B, B)$ and $P(A, y, z)$**

b. **$P(g(f(v)), g(u))$ and $P(x, x)$.**

c. **$P(x, f(x0)$ and $P(y, y)$**

d. **$P(y, y, B)$ and $P(z, x, z)$**

e. **$2 + 3 = x$ and $x = 3 + 3$**

Ans.

a. Yes, is unifiable. The most general unifier is —

$A / x, B / y, B / z$

b. Yes". Unifier is $g(u)/x, f(v)/u$

c. No. It doesn't unify.

d. Yes. $B/z, B/y, B/x$

e. Yes. First replace x by y in 2nd expression (standardizing variables) then $(2 + 3)/y$ and $(3 + 3)/x$.

Q.15. Explain why $P(f(x, x), A)$ does not unify with $P(f(y, f(y, A)), A)$.

Ans. The problem involves an attempt to unify $f(x, x)$ with $f(y, f(y, A))$. In these expressions, the outer fs match and y can be substituted for x leaving the problem of unifying y with $f(y, A)$. Here, since y occurs in $f(y, A)$, these two expressions cannot be unified.

Q.16. Convert the following to clause form:

1. **$(\exists x)\ [P(x)] \vee ((\exists x)\ [Q(x)] \supset (\exists x)\ [P(x) \vee Q(x)]$**
2. **$(\forall x)\ [P(x) \supset (\forall y)\ [(\forall z)\ [Q(x, y) \supset \neg\ (\forall z)\ [R(y, x)]]]$**
3. **$(\forall x)\ [P(x) \supset (\exists x)\ [(\forall z)\ [Q(x, y)] \vee (\forall z)\ [R(x, y, z)]]$**
4. **$(\forall x)\ [P(x) \supset Q(x, y)] \supset ((x, y)\ [P(y)] \wedge (\exists z)\ [Q\ (y, z)])$**

Ans.

1. $((\forall x)\ [P(x)] \vee ((\exists x)\ [Q(x)] \supset (\exists x)\ [P(x) \vee Q(x)]$

$(\neg((\exists x)[P(x)] \vee (\exists x)(Q(x)) \vee (\exists x)[P(x) \vee Q(x)]$

$(\neg((\exists x)[P(x)] \wedge \neg(\exists x)(Q(x)) \vee (\exists x)[P(x) \vee Q(x)]$

$((\forall x)[\neg P(x)] \wedge (\forall x)!\neg Q(x) \vee (\exists x)[P(x) \vee Q(x)]$

$((\forall x)[\neg P(x)] \wedge (\forall x)!\neg Q(y) \vee (\exists x)[P(z) \vee Q(z)]$

$((\forall x)[\neg P(x)] \wedge (\forall y)[\neg Q(y)] \vee [P(Sk) \vee Q(Sk)]$

$(\forall x)(\forall z)[[\neg P(x)] \wedge Q(y)] \vee [P(Sk) \vee Q(Sk)]]$

$[\neg P(x) \wedge Q(y)] \vee [P(Sk) \vee Q(sk)]$

$[\neg P(x) \wedge P(Sk) \vee Q(Sk)] \wedge [\neg Q(y) \vee P(Sk) \vee Q(Sk)]]$

$[\neg P(x) \wedge P(Sk), Q(Sk)][\neg Q(z) \vee P(Sk) \vee Q(Sk)]$

2. $(\forall x)\ [P(x) \supset (\forall y)\ [(\forall z)\ [Q(x, y)] \supset \neg\ (\forall z)\ [R(y, x)]]]$

$(\forall x)[\neg P(x) \vee (\forall y)[(\forall z)Q(x, y)] \supset \neg(\forall z)[R(y, x)]]]$

$(\forall x)[\neg P(x) \vee (\forall y)]\neg(\forall z)[Q(x, y)] \vee \neg(\forall z)[R(y, x)]]]$

$(\forall x)[\neg P(x) \vee (\forall y)][(\exists z)]\neg Q(x, y) \vee (\exists z)[\neg R(y, x)]]]$

$(\forall x)[\neg P(x) \vee (\forall y)](\exists z)[\neg Q(x, y)] \vee (\exists z)[\neg R(y, x)]]]$

$(\forall x)[\neg P(x) \vee (\forall y)[\neg Q(x, y) \vee \neg R(y, x)]]]$

$(\forall x(\forall y)\neg P(x) \vee \neg Q(x, y) \vee \neg R(y, x)]$

$\neg P(x) \vee \neg Q(x, y) \vee \neg R(y, x)$

$\}\neg P(x), \neg Q(x, y), \neg R(y, x)\}$

3. $(\forall x)\ [P(x) \supset (\exists x)\ [(\forall z)\ [Q(x, y)] \vee (\forall z)\ [R(x, y, z)]]$

$(\forall x)\ [\neg(\forall x)\ [P(x)] \vee (\exists x)\ [(\forall z)[Q(x, z)] \wedge (\forall z)[R(x, y, z)]]$

$(\forall y)[(\exists x)[\neg P(x)] \vee (\exists x)[(\forall z)[Q(x, z)] \vee (\forall z)[R(x, y, z)]]]$

$(\forall y)[(\exists x)[\neg P(x)] \vee (\exists x)[(\forall z)[Q(t, z)] \vee (\forall u)[R(t, y, u)]]]$

$(\forall y)[\neg P(f_1(y)) \vee (\forall z)[Q(f_2(y), z)] \vee (\forall u)[R(f_2(y), y, u)]]]$

$(\forall y)(\forall z)(\forall u)[\neg P(f_1(y)) \vee Q(f_2(y), z)] \vee R(f_2(y), y, u)]$

$\neg P(f_1(y) \vee Q(f_2(y), z) \vee R(f_2(y), y, u)$

$\{\neg P(f_1(y)), Q(f_2(y)), z), R(f_2(y), y, u)\}$

4. $(\forall y)[(\forall x)[P(x) \supset Q(x, y)] \supset ((\exists y)[P(y)] \wedge (\exists z)\ [Q\ (y, z)]]]$

$(\forall y)\ [\neg(\forall x)P(x) \supset Q(x, y)] \vee (\exists y)\ [P(y)] \wedge (\exists z)[Q(y, z))]]$

$(\forall y)\ [\neg(\forall x)[\neg P(x) \vee Q(x, y)] \vee ((\exists y)\ [P(y)] \wedge (\exists z)[Q(y, z))]]$

$(\forall y)\ [(\exists x)\ [P(x) \wedge \neg Q(y, z))] \vee ((\exists y)[P(y)] \wedge (\exists z)[Q(y, z)]]]$

$(\forall y)\ [(\exists x)\ [P(x) \wedge \neg Q(y, z))] \vee ((\exists u)[P(u)] \wedge (\exists z)[Q(y, z)]]]$

$(\forall y)\ [[P(f_1(y)) \wedge \neg Q(f_1(y), y)] \vee [P(f_2(y)) \wedge Q(z, f_2(y))]]$

$(\forall y)\ [[P(f_1(y)) \vee P(f_2(y))] \wedge [P(f_2(y)) \vee Q(y, f_2(y))]] \wedge [\neg Q(f_1(y), y) \vee P(f_2(y))] \wedge [\neg Q(f_1(y), y) \vee Q(y, f_2(y))]]$

$[P(f_1(y)) \vee P(f_1(y))] \wedge [P(f_1(y_1) \vee Q(y, f_3(y)] \wedge [\neg Q(f_1(y_1, y) \vee P(f_2(y)] \wedge [\neg Q(f_2(y_1, y), Q(y, f_2(y))]]$

$[(\exists x)P(x)] \supset Q(A)$

$[\neg(\exists x)P(x)] \vee Q(A)$

$[(\forall x)\neg P(x)] \vee Q(A)$

$[(\forall x)[\neg P(x)] \vee Q(A)]$

$[(\forall x)][P(x)] \supset Q(A)]$

After this transformation, we recognize that any formula of the form $\gamma \supset \gamma$ is valid. Analogous operations on the second formula show that it too is valid.

The third formula is an instance of the well-known invalid formula $(\exists x)\ \gamma\ (x) \supset (\forall x)\ \gamma\ (x)$.

A counter example is $P(a)$ is False. $P(B)$ is True, and $Q(A)$ is False (for A being some element of the domain).

Q.17. Convert the following formula into one that has neither an existential quantifier nor a Skolem function. $(\forall x, y)\{\exists z)[0n(x, z) \wedge \text{Above}\ (z, y)] \supset \text{Above}\ (x, y)\}$?

Ans. We use the following steps:

$(\forall x, y)\{\exists z)[0n(x, z) \wedge \text{Above}\ (z, y)] \supset \text{Above}\ (x, y)\}$

$(\forall x, y)\{\neg\ \exists z)[0n(x, z) \wedge \text{Above}\ (z, y)] \vee \text{Above}\ (x, y)\}$

$(\forall x, y)\{(\forall z) \neg \{On(x, z) \wedge \text{Above}(z, y)\} \vee \text{Above}(x, y)\}$

$(\forall x, y)\{(\forall z)\{\neg On(x, z) \vee \neg \text{Above}(z, y)\} \vee \text{Above}(x, y)\}$

$(\forall x, y, z)[\neg On(x, z) \vee \neg \text{Above}(z, y) \vee \text{Above}(x, y)]$ An equivalent form is:

$(\forall x, y, z)\{[On(x, z) \wedge \text{Above}(z, y)] \supset \text{Above}(x, y)]$

Q.18. Use resolution refutation on a set of clauses to prove that there is a green object if we are given:

- If pushable objects are blue, then nonpushable ones are green.
- All objects are either blue or green but not both.
- If there is a nonpushable object then all pushable ones are blue.
- Object 01 is pushable.
- Object 02 is not pushable.

1. Convert these statements to expressions in first-order predicate calculus.
2. Convert the preceding predicate-calculus expressions to clause form.
3. Combine the preceding clause form expressions with the clause form of the negation of the statement to be proved and then show the steps used in obtaining a resolution refutation.

Ans.

1. 1. $(\forall x)[P(x) \supset B(x)] \supset (\forall x)[\neg P(x) \supset G(x)]$

   2. a. $(\forall x)[B(x) \supset \neg G(x)]$

   2 b. $(\forall x)[G(x) \vee B(x)]$

   3. $(\exists x) \neg P(x) \supset (\forall x)[P(x) \supset B(x)]$ 4. P(01)

   5. $\neg P(02)$

2. 1 a. $P(SK) \vee P(x) \vee G(x)$

   1 b. $\neg B(SK) \vee P(x) \vee G(x)$

   2 a. $\neg B(x) \vee \neg G(x)$

   2 b. $B(x) \vee G(x)$

   3. $P(x) \vee \neg P(y) \vee B(y)$

   4. $P(01)$

   5. $\neg P(02)$

3. 6. (negation of theorem): $\neg G(x)$

   7. (resolving 6 and 2*b* yields) $B(x)$

   8. (resolving 7 and 1*b* yields) $P(x) \vee G(x)$

   9. (resolving 8 and 5 yields) $G(02)$

   10. (resolving 9 and 6 yields) contradiction.

Q.19. The function cons(*x*, *y*) denotes the list formed by inserting the element *x* at the made of the list *y*. We denote the empty list by Nil; the list (2) by cons (2, Nil); the list (1, 2) by cons (1, cons (2, Nil)); and so on. The formula Last (1, *e*) is intended to mean that

***i.e.* the last element of the list 1. We have the following axioms:**

- **$(\forall u)$ [Last(cons(*u*, Nil), *u*)]**
- **$(\forall x\, y\, z)$ [Last(*y*, *z*) $\supset$ Last(cons(*x*, *y*), *z*)]**

1. **Prove the following theorem from these axioms by the method of resoltion refutation: $(\exists v)$[Last(cons(2, cons(1, Nil)), *v*)]**
2. **Use answer extraction of find *v*, the last element of the list (2, 1).**

Ans.

1. We first write the axioms in clause form:

a. Last(cons(u, Nil), u)

b. ¬Last(y, z) ∨ Last(cons(x, y), z)

We then negate the goal to get:

c. ¬Last(cons(2, cons(1, Nil)), v)

Resolving (*b*) and (*c*), with m.g.u. {2/x cons(1, Nil/y, v/z), we get

d. ¬Last(cons(1, Nil), v)

We can now resolve (*a*) and (*b*) with m.g.u. {1/e, 1/v} to get the empty clause.

2. The axioms (a) and (b) are the same as in part (1). In order to do answer extraction a predicate Ans (v) is appended to the clause containing the negated goal:

e. ¬Last(cons(2, cons(1, Nil)), v) ∨ Ans(v)

Resolving (*b*) and (*e*), with m.g.u {2/x, con(1, Nil)/y, v/z}, we get:

f. ¬Last(cons(1, Nil), v) ∨ Ans(v)

We can now resolve (*a*) and (*f*) with m.g.u. {1/u, 1/v} to get:

g. Ans (1)

Therefore the last element of the list (2, 1) is 1.

Q.20. A logic circuit has four wires W1, W2, W3 and W4. It has an "and gate". A, and an "inverter", B. The input wires, W1 and W2, can be either "on" or not. If the and gate, A, is functioning properly (OK), wire W3 is "on" if and only if wires W1 and W2 both are "on". If the inverter, B, is functioning properly (OK), wire W4 is "on" if and only if wire W3 is not "on". Translate it into a set of WFFs.

Ans. $\{P(f_1(y)), P(f_2(y))\}, \{P(f_1(y)), Q(y, f_3(y))\}$

$\{\neg Q(f_1(y), y), P(f_2(y))\}, \{\neg Q(f_1(y), y), Q(y, f_3(y))]$

$\{P(f_1(y)), P(f_2(y_1))\}, \{P(f_1(y_2)), Q(y, f_3(y_2))\}$

$\{\neg Q(f_1(y_3), y_3), P(f_2(y_3))\}, \{\neg Q(f_1(y_4), y_4), Q(y_4, f_3(y_4))\}$

Q.21. We are given following paragraph

Tony, Mike and John belong to the Alpine Club. Every member of the Alpine Club is either a skier or a mountain climber or both. No mountain climber likes rain, and all skiers like snow. Mike dislikes whatever Tony likes and likes whatever Tony dislikes. Tony likes rain and snow.

Represent this information by predicate-calculus sentences in such a way that you can represent the question "Who is a member of the Alpine Club who is a mountain climber but not a skier?" as a predicate-calculus expression. Use resolution refutation with answer extraction to answer it.

Ans. One translation is the set of formulas Member(Tony, Alpineclub) Member(Mike, Alpineclub) Member(John, Alpneclub)

(∀x)[Member(xAlpineclub) ⊃ (Skier(x) ∨ MC(x))]¬(∃x)[MC(x) ∧ Likes(x, Rain)]

(∀x)[Skier(x) ⊃ Likes(x,Snow)}

(∀x)[Skier(Tony, x) ∧ ¬Likes(Mike, x)}

Likes(Tony, Rain) ∧ Likes(Tony,Snow)

The question is:

(∃x) [Member(x, Alpineclub) ∧ MC(x) ∨ Skier(x)]

The clause forms of these sentences are:

1. Member(Tony, Alpineclub)
2. Member(Mike, Alpineclub)
3. Member(John, Alpineclub)
4. ¬Member(x, Alpineclub) ∨ Skier(x), MC(x)
5. ¬MC(x) ∨ ¬Likes(x, Rain)
6. ¬Skier(x) ∨ Likes(x,Snow)

7*a*. ¬Likes(Tony, x) ∨ ¬Likes(Mike, x)

7*b*. Likes(Tony, *x*) ∨ Likes(Mike, *x*)

8*a*. Likes(Tony, Rain)

8*b*. LIkes(Tony, Snow)

The clause form of the negation of the theorem to be proved (with Ans literal) is:

9. ¬Member(*x*, Alpineclub) ∨ ¬MC(*x*) ∨ Skier(*x*) ∨ Ans(*x*)

The refutation is:

10. ¬Member(*x*, Alpineclub), (Skier(*x*) ∨ Ans(*x*) resolving 9 with 4
11. Skier(Mike)/Ans(Mike) resolving 11 and 2
12. Likes(Mike, skier) ∨ ans (Mike) resolving 12 with 8
13. ¬Likes(Tony,Skiew) ∨ Ans(Mike) resolving 12 with 7a
14. Ans(Mike) resolving 13 with 8*b*.

Q.22. Sam, Clyde and Oscar are elephants. We know the following facts about them:

1. **Sam is pink.**
2. **Clyde is gray and likes Oscar.**
3. **Oscar is either pink or gray (but not both) and likes Sam.**

Use resolution refutation to prove that a gray elephant likes pink elephant; that is, prove (∃*x*, *y*)[Gray(*x*) ∧ Pink(*y*) ∧ Likes(*x*, *y*)]

Ans. The clauses and negation of the theorem to be proved are:

1. P(Sam)
2. G(Clyde)
3. L(Clyde, Oscar)
4. P(Oscar) ∨ G(Oscar)
5. L(Oscar, Sam)
6. ¬*G*(*x*) ∨ ¬*P*(*y*) ∨ ¬*L*(*x*, *y*) The resolution refutation is:
7. ¬G(Clyde) ∨ ¬P(Oscar) from 3 and 6
8. ¬P(Oscar) from 2 and 7
9. ¬G(Oscar) ∨ ¬P(Sam) from 5 and 6
10. ¬G(Oscar) from 1 and 9
11. P(Oscar) from 10 and 4
12. Nil from 11 and 8.

Q.23. Consider the following circuit diagram —

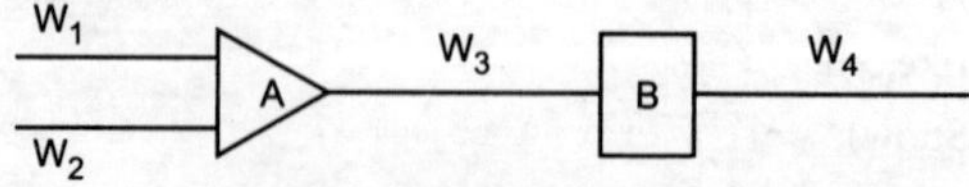

1. Use expression like ON(A), ON(W1) and so on to describe the funtioning of the circuit as defined.
2. Using the formulas describing the functioning of the circuit and assuming that all components are functioning properly and that wires W1 and W2 are "on" use resolution to show that wire W4 is not "on".
3. Again, using the formulas describing the functioning of the circuit and given that wires W1 and W2 are "on" but that wire W4 is also "on", use resolution to show that either the and gate or the inverter is not functioning properly.

Ans.

1. (*a*) OK(A) ⊃ [On(W1) ∧ On(W)] ≡ On(W3)]

   (*b*) OK(B) ⊃ [On(W3) ≡ ¬On(W4)]
2. The clause forms of the above formulas are:

(a1) ¬ OK(A) ∨ ¬ 0n(W2) ∨ 0n(W3)

(*a*2) ¬ OK(A) ∨ ¬ 0n(W3) ∨ 0n(W1)

(*a*3) ¬ OK(A) ∨ ¬ 0n(W3) ∨ 0n(W2)

(*b*1) ¬ OK(B) ∨ ¬ 0n(W3) ∨ ¬ 0n(W4)

(*b*2) ¬ OK(B) ∨ ¬ 0n(W4) ∨ 0n(W3)

Here is a resolution refutation showing that W4 is not "on"

1. 0n(W4) negation of theorem
2. ¬ OK(B) ∨¬ 0n(W3) resolving 1 with b1
3. ¬ 0n(W3)
   resolving 2 with hypothesis, OK(B)
4. ¬OK(A) ∨ ¬ 0n(W1) ∨ ¬ 0n(W2) resolving 3 with a1
5. Nil successively resolving 4 with hypotheses, OK(A), 0n(W1), 0n(W2)

3. (1a) OK(A) negation of theorem
   (1b) OK(B) negation of theorem
   2. ¬ 0n(W1) ∨ ¬0n(W2) ∨ 0n(W3) resolving 1a with a1
   3. 0n(W3) successively resolving 2 with hypotheses, 0n(W1) and 0n(W2)
   4. ¬OK(B) ∨ ¬ 0n(W4) resolving 3 with b1
   5. ¬ OK(B) resolving 4 with hypothesis, 0n(W4)
   6. Nil resolving 5 with lb.

Q.24. 1. Express as predicate-calculus wffs the information in the semantic network shown here. Take care that the wffs are written in such a way that they explicitly state the inheritance cancellation information that is implicit in the inheritance hierarchy.

2. Can you prove that Fido has four legs from your predicate-calculus wffs? If not, what information would you need to add in order to complete the proof?

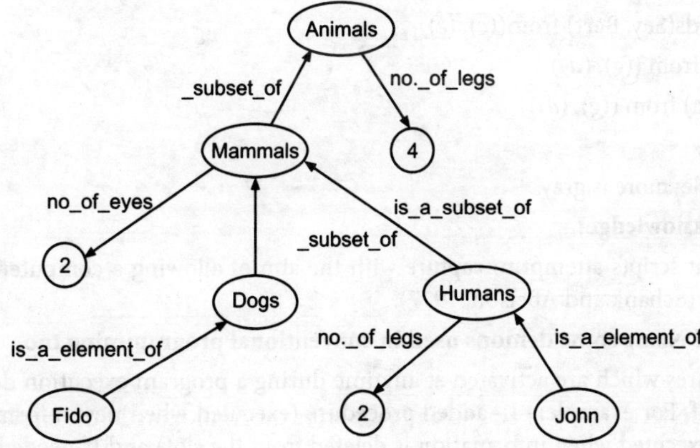

Ans. 1. The equivalent wffs are:

Def(Fido) Human(John)

(∀*x*)[Dog(*x*) ⊃ Mammal(*x*)]

(∀*x*)[Mammal(*x*) ⊃ Anjaml(*x*)]

(∀*x*)[Human(*x*) ⊃ Mammal(*x*)]

(∀*x*)[[Mammal(*x*) ∧ ¬ Human(*x*)] ⊃ Haslegs(x, 4)]

$(\forall x)[\text{Human}(x) \supset \text{Haslegs}(x, 2)]$

$(\forall x)[\text{Mammal}(x) \supset \text{Haslegs}(x, 2)]$

2. We cannot prove Haslegs(Fido, 4) from these wffs. We would have to add¬ Human(Fido). Or we could add something more general, such as $(\forall x)[\text{Dog}(x) \supset \neg\text{Human}(x)]$.

Q.25. For the two examples shown here, pick the most appropriate knowledge representation system and encode the statements of the examples in the selected representation. Use your representation and a reasoning system appropriate to it to answer the question in each example. Example in some detail how the reasoning system arrives at the answer- showing resolution refutations, for example, if a reasoning system based on resolution is used. Use diagrams if they are helpful in your explanations.

1. Typically, birds fly. Ostriches are birds. Oliver is an ostrich. Ostriches do not fly. Q. Does Oliver fly?
2. Seymore is an elephant and John's friend. All elephants are gray or a friend of Bert. No friend of Bert is a friend of John. Q. Is Seymore gray?

Ans.

1. Here because of the nonmonotonic character of the statements, we might use a semantic network with property inheritance and cancellation of inheritance. In this case, we would have the fact the birds fly associated with the BIRDS node and the fact that ostriches do not fly associated with the OSTRICHES node. The OSTRICHES node is a descendant of the BIRDS node, and therefore, the fact that ostriches do not fly cancels the fact the birds do. Since Oliver is an ostrich, we conclude from the net that Oliver does not fly. (Note that the net formalism would allow us to say, in addition, that Oliver does fly, which we might do it we had some special information that Oliver was some sort of mutant flying ostrich).
2. Here we might use the predicate calculus because we have disjunction and statements that are difficult to reason with in semantic networks. The predicated encoding and resolution refutation for this problem are as follows
   a. EI (Sey)
   b. Friend(Sey, John)
   c. ¬El(*x*) ∨ Gray(*x*) ∨ Friend(*x* Bert)
   d. ¬Friend(*x*, Bert) ∨ ¬ Friend(*x*, John)
   e. ¬Grey(Sey) (negation of theorem)
   f. ¬EL(Sey) ∨ Friends(Sey, Bert) from((*c*), (*e*))
   g. Friend(Sey, Bert) from ((*g*), (*d*))
   h. ¬Friend(Sey, John) from ((*g*), (*d*))
   i. Nil from ((*h*), (*b*))

   So, we have proved that Seymore is gray.

Q.26. What is a stereotypical knowledge?

Ans. A type of knowledge that scripts attempt to capture with the aim of allowing a computer to make similar inferences about incomplete stories (Schank and Abelson, 1977).

Q.27. What are demons in AI? Name some demons used in conventional programming too.

Ans. Demons are the procedures which are activated at anytime during a program execution depending on the conditions evaluated in demon itself. For example. –If–added procedure (executed when new information is placed in the slot), If-removed procedure (executed when information is deleted from the slot) and If-needed procedure (executed when information is needed from the slot but the slot is empty.

Examples of demons used in the conventional programming are—

a. Error detection
b. Default commands.
c. End-of-File detection (EOF).

Q.28. Given are the axioms in clause form:

1. Man (Marcus)
2. Pompeian (Marcus)

3. ~Pompeian (a1) v Roman (a1)

4. Ruler (Caesear)

5. ~Roman (a_2) v loyal (a_2 Caesar) v hate (a_2, Caesar)

6. Loyal ($a_3, f_1(a_3)$)

7. ~Main (a_4) v ~ ruler (b_1) v ~ assassin (a_4, b_1) v loyal (a_4, b_1)

8. assassin (Marcus, Caesar)

Give resolution proof of hate(Marcus, Caesar).

Ans. To prove :-

Did Marcus hate Caesar?

We negate this statement as

~hate (Marcus, Caesar)

There is no axiom in clausal form starting with literal ~ hate.

Prove ~ hate (Marcus, Caesar)

Clause ~ hate (Marcus, Caesar)

Clause 5 has hate

~Roman (a_2) v loyal (a_2 Caesar) v hate (a_2 Caesar)

a_2 is Marcus we have clause as

~Roman (Marcus) v Loyal (Marcus, Caesar) v hate (Marcus Caesar)

Resolving both we get :-

~Roman (Marcus) v loyal (Marcus, Caesar)

Now select 3 clausal form.

~ Pompeian (a_1) v Roman (a_1) where a_1 is Marcus.

Statement will be

~ Pompeian (Marcus) V Roman (Marcus)

We get new clause after resolving.

C1: ~Roman (Marcus) v loyal (Marcus, Caesar)

C2: ~ Pompeian (Marcus) v Roman (Marcus)

Resolvent is ~ Pompeian (Marcus) v loyal (Marcus, Caesar)

Now take clause 2 which is

Pompeian (Marcus)

Resolvent is loyal (Marcus, Caesar)

Now C1 is loyal (Marcus, Caesar)

Select 7th axiom as:

~man (a_4) v ~ ruler (b_1) v ~ assassin (a_4, b_1) V loyal (a_4, b_1)

where a_4 = Marcus

b_1 = Caesar

Statement will be

C2 ~ man (Marcus) v ~ ruler(Caesar) v ~ assassin (Marcus, Caesar) v loyal (Marcus, Caesar)

Negate C1 as ~ loyal (Marcus, Caesar).

Resolvent will be:

~ man (Marcus) v ~ ruler (Caesar) v ~ assassin (Marcus, Caesar) V loyal (Marcus, Caesar)

Now clause is 1

man (Marcus)

Then new resolvent

~ ruler (Caesar) v ~ assassin (Marcus, Caesar) v loyal (Marcus, Caesar)

Clause 4 is ~ ruler (Caesar) v ~ assassin (Marcus, Caesar) v loyal (Marcus, Caesar) Resolvent is

~ assassin (Marcus, Caesar)

Clause 8 is assassin (Marcus, Caesar) Resolvent is empty

Diagramatically, it is shown as follows

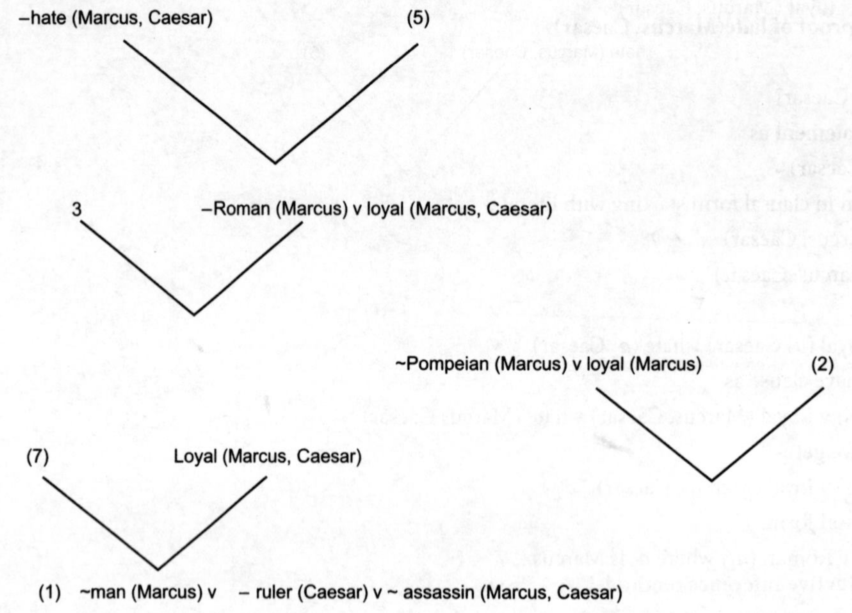

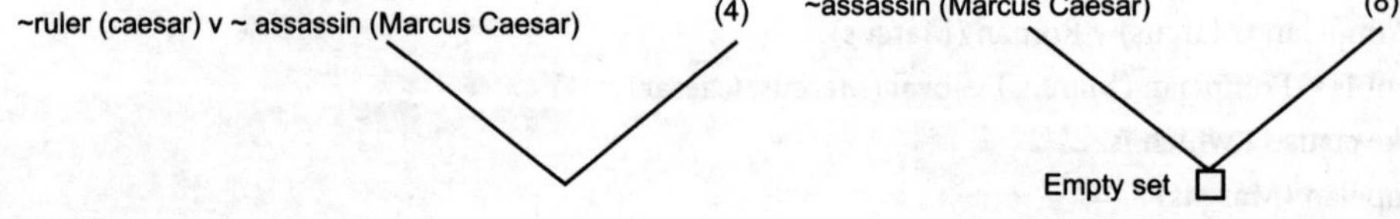

Q.29. Using above question

Prove : loyal (Marcus, Caesar)

Ans. Negate sentence as

~ loyal (M arcus, C aesar)

Select clause 5 which is

~Roman (x2) v loyal (x2 Caesar) v hate (x2, Caesar)

where x2 = Marcus

C1 : ~loyal (Marcus, Caesar)

C2 : ~ Roman (Marcus) v loyal (Marcus, Caesar) v hate (Marcus, Caesar)

Resolvent is ~Roman (Marcus) v hate (Marcus, Caesar) which is now C1.

Select 3 clausal from – ~ Pompeian (a) v Roman (a_1)

where a_1 is Marcus

C1 : ~Roman (Marcus) v hate (Marcus, Caesar)

C2 : ~ Pompeian (Marcus) v hate (Marcus, Caesar)

Next time C2 ~ Pompeain (Marcus) v hate (Marcus, Caesar)

Select C2 ~ Pompeain (Marcus)

New clause will be

hate (Marcus, Caesar)

Prove : loyal (Marcus, Caesar)

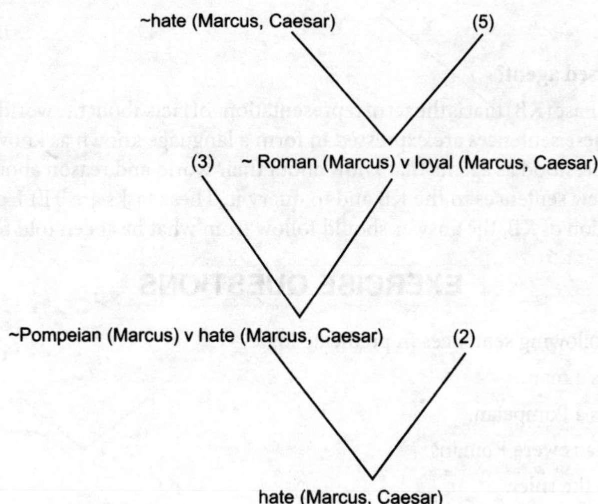

Q.30. What are non-deductive inference methods?

Ans. Non-deductive inference: Non-deductive inferences are not valid forms of inferencing but are important.

There are three methods of non-deductive inference methods which are as follows:

a. **Abductive inference :** It is based on the use of casual knowledge for describing conclusion.

Example

There are two axioms:

$\forall x : P(x) \rightarrow Q(x)\ P(R)$

We can conclude that $Q(R)$

Another example is Measles $(x) \rightarrow$ Spots

This means people having measles get spots. If we notice the spots, we may conclude, person has measles. This may be a wrong conclusion. Deriving conclusions in such a manner is default reasoning. Abductive reasoning is useful if some measure of certainty is attached to it.

b. **Inductive inference :** Inductive inference is recurring inference. It means if there is some event, it will be true for all the events or entities in the class.

For example: We see that some dogs have tails by which we conclude that all dogs have tails but in real a breed of dogs do not have tail.

Inductive inference can be given as

$$\frac{P(a_1), P(a_2) \ldots\ldots\ldots, P(a_n)}{\forall x : P(x)}$$

c. **Analogical Inference :** Analogical inference is based on experiences. When there are certain similar situations as we experience in the past, we relate the situations or events. For example : If there is an event P related to Q, then we conclude that P_1 is related to Q_1 in the same manner. Analogical inference is the combination of all other inferences such as deductive, abductive and inductive inference.

Q.31. Give five methods of representation of knowledge.

Ans. The methods of representation of knowledge are as follows

a. FOPL

First order predicate logic.

b. Associative networks.

c. Conceptual graph.

d. Fuzzy logic.

e. Frames.

Q.32. What is a knowledge-based agent?

Ans. It consists of a Knowledge Base (KB) that is the set of representations of facts about the world. Each individual representation is called as a sentence. These sentences are expressed in form a language known as knowledge representation language. These agents are best understood as agents that know about their world and reason about their course of actions. There must be a way at insert new sentences to the KB and to query it. These tasks are TELL and ASK. The main idea here is that when one asks question of KB, the answer should follow from what has been told to KB previously.

EXERCISE QUESTIONS

1. (*a*) Represent the following sentences in predicate logic—

1. Marcus was a man.

2. Marcus was a Pompeian.

3. All Pompeians were Romans.

4. Caesar was the ruler.

5. All Romans were either loyal to Caesar or hated him.

6. Everyone is loyal to someone.

7. People only try to assassinate rulers they are not loyal to.

8. Marcus tried to assassinate Caeser.

(*b*) What are semantic networks? How can semantic networks be converted to frames?

(*c*) Write a script for "Eating in a restaurant".

2. (*a*) Explain difference between procedural and declarative knowledge.

(*b*) Assume the following facts —

1. Steve only likes easy courses.

2. Science courses are hard.

3. All courses in commerce department are easy.

4. COM302 is a commerce course.

(c) Convert the following into clausal form —

1. Everyone is loyal to someone.

2. John likes all kinds of food.

(*d*) Write short notes on —

1. Forward v/s Backward Reasoning.

2. Control knowledge.

3. CD

4. Scripts.

3. (*a*) Explain the difference between predicate logic and propositional logic.

(*b*) Represent the following using predicate calculus notation —

1. There is a red part in bin that has a circular shape.

2. Raghav is computer science student but not a pilot or a football player.
3. The owner of car also owns the boat.
4. All people need air.

4. Assume the following facts —

1. Prasad only likes easy courses.
2. AI courses are hard.
3. All courses in Data Mining department are easy.

4. DM108 is a Data Mining Course.

(*a*) Use Resolution to answer the question- "Which course would Prasad like?"

(*b*) Also design clausal form for above sentences in FOPL using proper Axioms, Functions, redicates, Variables and Constants.

(*c*) Hence with respect to resolution, explain. "What is proof by refutation"?

5. Express the following things in predicate calculus—

(*a*) All p's are q's.

(*b*) Some p's are q's.

(*c*) John hit everyone who was near him.

(*d*) Nobody does anything without a reason.

6. (*a*) What do you mean by semantic nets?

(*b*) Define frames.

7. (*a*) Give the CD structure to parse the following sentence — "John wanted Mary to go to the store".

(*b*) Represent the following sentences using symbolic logic:

1. A drunker is enemy of himself.
2. Father of John loves the mother of mary.
3. All students like a good teacher.
4. Fruits and vegetables are nutritions.
5. God helps those who help themselves.

(*c*) "Some medicines are dangerous only if taken in excessive amount". Translate the above sentence into formulas in predicate logic and then to clausal form.

(*d*) Describe semantic net and frames with suitable examples.

8. (*a*) Explain the difference between the following — Semantic Nets and Frames.

(*b*) Represent the following sentence in FOPL, convert it into clausal form explaning each step —

"All engineering students who know programming will either get good placement or admission in some university for higher studies".

(*c*) Using the following problem, illustrate how resolution is used to derive new facts from already existing facts — Given facts

(*i*) Steve likes computer courses.

(*ii*) Computer software can be software or Hardware courses. Derive: Steve likes AI.

(*d*) Write short notes on — Unification procedure.

9. Draw the semantic network and write atomic formulae for the English sentence given below:

"Manju playing with a red ball".

10. (*a*) Construct a semantic net representations of the following —

(*i*) Rajesh is Indian, Rajesh is a lecturer.

(*ii*) Vikram but his new video CD to his brother-in-law.

10. (*b*) Explain-Conceptual dependency.

11. (*a*) Explain why these two sentences cannot be unified—

1. $p(x) \vee (q(f(x)) \wedge r(y))$
2. $p(x) \vee (q(f(r)) \wedge r(s))$

(*b*) Construct a semantic net representation of the following: "Gopal is Indian, Gopal is lecturer".

12. (*a*) Create a script about shopping in a super market.

(*b*) Write down a substitution which unifies the following sentences:

1. likes(hom er, dineer(x)) ∧ (today(*A*) → dineer(x))
2. likes(hom er, dineer(cooked _ by(*y*)) ∧ (today(*Z*) → dineerCcooked – by(magie))))

(*c*) What is a slot in a frame?

13. What are the merits/demerits of semantic net over semantic frames?

14. (*a*) Explain the rules to unify two predicates.

(*b*) Represent the following facts as predicates and convert them to clausal form, explaining the steps of conversion:

1. Any student who is intelligent or hardworking will pass the exam in good marks.
2. Anyone who is passed with good marks gets a job.

(*c*) Assume that "Shiva is neither hardworking nor intelligent". Using resolution prove that Shiva does not get a job.

15. What kind of knowledge is represented by the semantic nets? Give an example of KB represented by semantic nets and explain how inferences are done in Semantic Nets?

16. (*a*) Create a script for "appearing for an examination."

(*b*) A new operator ⊕, or exclusive-or may be defined by the following truth table—

P	*Q*	*P*⊕Q
T	*T*	*F*
T	*F*	*T*
F	*T*	*T*
F	*F*	*F*

Create a propositional calculus expression using ∧, ∨ and> that is equivalent to *P* ⊕ Q.

(*c*) Explain CD using an example.

9 AI Retrospectives

Q.1. AI and Roboties have raised some questions rgarding liability. For instance, consider the scenario of an autonomons or AI-drivn Robot moving through a factory. Another robot surprisingly crosses its way and our robots aids to prevent the confusion. However, by this maneuver, the robot injures a person.

***a.* Who can be held liable for damags caused by autonomons systems?**

***b.* List two AI ethics.**

Ans. *a.* Actually, nobody can be blamed for damages caused by autonomous systems. In this scenario, AI ethics com into picture. ach individual has a different perspective. So, they can take their own decisions according to their moralities. When someone is to be held liable then it should be the programmer or the algorithm designer of this autonomous vehicle because he should have throught of all the exceptional conditions that could arise.

b. AI Bias, Data privacy, AI access, AI for kids.

Q.2. Howard Gardner gave eight types of intelligence. Name them.

Ans. 8-types of intelligence as given by Howard Gardner are as follows:

a. **Visual :** Spatial Intelligence.

b. **Linguistic :** Verbal Intellignce.

c. **Logical :** Mathematical Intelligence.

d. **Bodily :** Kinasthetic Intelligence.

e. Musical Intlligence.

f. Interpersonal Intelligence.

g. Intrapersonal Intellignce.

h. Naturalistic Intelligence.

It is the process of finding or discovening a model (function) which helps in separating the data into multiple categorical classes.

Q.3. What is Loopy?

Ans. It is an interactive tool that can be used to play with simulations in real time without using any coding.

Q.4. Distinguish between classification and regression.

Ans.

Classification	Regression
1. It is the process of finding or discovening a model (function) which helps in separating the data into multiple categorical classes.	1. It is the process of finding a model or function for distinguishing the data into continuous real values in place of using classes.
2. In classification, the groups membership of problem is identified.	2. In regression, the numeric data dependency is predicted to distinguish it.
3. In classification, data is categorized under different labels according to some parameters and then the labels are predicted for data.	3. The regression analysis is the statistical model used to predict the numeric data in place of labels.

Q.5. What do you mean by "Dataset used in supervised learning model is labeled".

Ans. In a supervised learning model, the labeled data set is feed to the machine. It means that some data is tagged with the correct answers. That is, the dataset is known to the person who is giving training to the machine then he is able to label the data.

Q.6. Name the package that is used for NLP in Python Language.

Ans. Natural language toolkit (NLTK).

Q.7. Define Corpus.

Ans. The full-textual data from all documents put together is known as corpus.

Q.8. Distinguish between a script-bot and a smart-bot.

Ans.

Script-boot	Smart-bot
1. It does not carry even a glimpse of AI.	1. They are built on NLP and ML.
2. Script-bots are easy to make.	2. Smart-bots are comparatively difficult to make.
3. It's functioning is very limited as they are less powerful.	3. They are flexible and powerful.
4. They work around a script that is programmed in them.	4. They work on bigger databases directly.
5. No or little language processing skills.	5. NLP and ML skill are needed.

Q.9. Give some applications of NLP.

Ans. Applications of NLP are as follows :

a. Sentiment Analysis.
b. Chat Bots.
c. Text Classification.
d. Text Extraction.
e. Machine Translation.
f. Text Summarization.
g. Market Intelligence.
h. Auto-Correct.

Q.10. Define :

***a.* Stemming**

***b.* Lemmatisation**

Ans. *a.* **Stemming** : It is a rule-based process of stripping the suffixes (Like "ing", "es" etc.) from a word. So, it is a process of converting words to their word stem, base or root form.

For eg. : Cooked to cook.

b. **Lemmatisation :** It is an organised and step by step procedure to obtain the root form of the word by using vocabulary and morphological analysis.

Q.11. Calculate Accuracy, Precision, Recall and F1 score for the following confusion matrix on heart attack risk. Also suggest which metrix would not be a good evaluation parameter and why?

The Confusion Matrix	Reality-1	Reality-0
Prediction : 1	50	20
Prediction : 0	10	20

The Confusion Matrix	Reality-1	Reality-0	
Prediction : 1	50	20	70
Prediction : 0	10	20	30
	60	40	100

Ans. Here,

TP = 50

FP = 20

FN = 10

TN = 20

a. It is defined as the percentage of correct predictions out of all the observations.

Accuracy = (TP + TN) / (TP + TN + FP + FN)

Where TP = True positive

TN = True negative

FP = False positive

FN = False negative

∴ Accuracy = (50 + 20) / (50 + 20 + 20 + 10)

= (70/100) = 0.7

b. **Precision :** It is defined as the percentage of time positive cases versus all the cases where the prediction is true.

Precision = TP/(TP + FP)

= (50/(50 + 20))

= (50/70)

= 0.714

c. Recall : It is defined as the fraction of positive cases that are correctly identified.

Recall = TP/(TP + FN)

= 50 / (50 + 10) = 50/60 = 0.83

d. **F1 Score :** It refers to the measure of balance between precision and recall.

F1 = 2 × (Precision × Recall)/(Precision + Recall)

= 2 × (0.71 × 0.83)/(0.714 + 0.83)

= 2 × (0.59/1.54)

= 1.18/1.54 = 0.77

∴ Accuracy = 0.7

Precision = 0.714

Recall = 0.83

F1 Score = 0.77

Here, within the test, theree is a trade off. Recall is not a good evaluation metric. Recall metrix needs to be improved more.

False Positive (Impacts precision) : When a person is predicted as high risk but has a low risk of heart.

False Negative (Impacts Recall) : A person is predicted as low risk but has a high risk of a heart attack. Thus, false negatives miss actual heart patients. Hence, recall metrics need more improvement because false negatives (FN) are more dangerous than false positives (FP).

Q.12. Calculate accuracy, precision, recall and F1 score for the following confusion matrix on spam filtering. Also, suggest which evaluation metric would not be a good evaluation parameter her and why?

Confusion Matrix on SPAM Filtering	Reality : 1	Reality : 0
Prediction : 1	10	55
Prediction : 0	10	25

Confusion Matrix on SPAM Filtering	Reality : 1	Reality : 0	
Prediction : 1	10	55	65
Prediction : 0	10	25	35
	20	80	100

Ans. ***a.*** **Accuracy :** It is defind as the ratio of correct predictions to all observations.

Accuracy = (TP + TN)/(TP + TN + FP + FN)

Where TP = True Positive

TN = True Negative

FP = False Positive

FN = False Negative

∴ Accuracy = (10 + 25) / (10 + 25 + 55 + 10)

= 35 / 100 = 0.35

b. **Precision :** It is defined as the percentage of true positive cases versus all the cases where the prediction is true.

Precission = TP/(TP + FP)

= 10 / (10 + 55)

= 10/65 = 0.15

c. **Recall :** It is defined as the fraction of positive cases that are correctly identified to the total positive cases.

$$\text{Recall} = \text{TP} / (\text{TP} + \text{FN}) = 10 / (10 + 10) = \frac{10}{20} = 0.5$$

d. **F1 Score :** It refers to the measure of balance between precision and recall and it is harmonic mean of precision and recall.

F1 = 2 × (Precision × Recall) / (Precision + Recall)

= 2 × ((0.15 × 0.5) / (0.15 + 0.5))

= 2 × (0.075 / 0.65)

= 2 × 0.115 = 0.23

Here, within the test, there is a trade-off. Recall and precision metric needs to be improved more.

False Positive (Impacts Precision) : So, many false negatives will make the spam filter ineffective. But false positives may cause important emails to be missed. Hence, Precision is more important to improve.

Q.13. List the main features of a confusion matrix.

Ans. The main features of a confusion matrix are as follows :

a. Prediction and reality are easily mapped together with the help of this confusion matrix.

b. The column labels "True Positive" and "True Negative" refer to the ground reality labels in the dataset.

c. The row labels "False Positive" and "False Negative" refer to your model's predictions *i.e.*, what your model thinks the label is.

d. The entries inside of a confusion matrix (TPs, FPs, FNs, (Ns)) are exhibited in the form of counts.

Q.14. Differentiate between precision and recall.

Ans. The following table gives the point of differences :

Precision	Recall
1. It measures the model's trustiness in classifying positive samples.	1. Recall counts how many positive samples were correctly classified as positive by the model.
2. During the calculation of the precision, how both the positive and negative sample were classified is taken care of.	2. It considers the positive samples only in its calculations.
3. It is used when a sample classifiad as positive while it does not care about correctly classifying all positive sample.	3. It cares about correctly classifying all positive samples while it does not care if a negative sample is classified as positive.
4. When a model has a high recall but low precision then the model classifies most of the positive samples correctly whereas it may have many false positives *i.e.*, it classifies many negative samples as positive).	4. When a model has high precision but low recall, then the model is accurate when it classifies a sample as positive correctly but it can only classify a few positive samples.

Q.15. What is the significance of F1 score?

Ans. F1 score is a single score that balances the concerns of precision and recall in one number. A good F1 score means that we have low false positives and low false nagatives. Thus, correctly identifying real threat is possible without any disturbance by false alarms. An F1 score is considered perfect when it is 1 while the model is a total failure when it is 0 (zero). F1 score is the best metric to evaluate the model on real-life classification problems and for the imbalanced class distribution.

Q.16. Compare TP, TN, FP and FN.

Ans.

True Positive	True Negative	False Positive	False Negative
1. The predicted value matches the actual value.	1. The predicted value matches the actual value.	1. The predicted value was falsely predicted.	1. The predicted value was falsely predicted.
2. The actual value was positive and the model predicted a positive value.	2. The actual value was negative and the model predicted a negative value	2. The actual value was negative but the model predicted a positive value. It is also known as type-1 error.	2. The actual value was positive but the model predicted a negative value. It is also known as Type-2 error.

Q.17. Suppose you want to select a metric out of the two—Precision and recall. Which one will you select? Which is more significant? Give examples to support it.

Ans. The selection of the best metric out of precision and recall depends on the condition in which the model has been used.

For *e.g.* : In the case of covid-19 vinus detection case, a false negative can cost us a lot and is also risky. Suppose that a deadly coronavinus has begun spreading and the model that is supposed to predict a viral outbreak could not detect it, then the virus might spread widely to infect a lot of people.

On the other hand, there may be some cases in which the false positive condition costs more than false negatives. For *e.g.*, if we consider the case of a model that predicts whether a mail is spam or NOT. When the model always predicts that the mail is spam, people would not look at it and slowly might lose some important impormation. Here, the false positive condition (predicting the mail as spum while the mail is not spam) would have high cost.

Conclusions : In nutshell, when we want to know if our model's performance is good, we need two measures : **Recall** and **Precisions.** In some cases, we might have a high precision but low recall, while in some cases, we might require low precision but high recall. Hence, both the measures are important.

Case 1 : Example of low recall and high precision consider the following table—

TP = 110	FP = 0
TN = 20	FN = 35

F1 is based on precision and recall

whereas,

Precision = TP / (TP + FP)

& Recall = TP / (TP + FN)

For the table given,

Recall = 0.76

Precision = 1

This is achieved if we have FP = 0

Case 2: Example of high recall and low precision consider the following table—

TP = 110	FP = 25
TN = 20	FN = 0

For this table,

Recall = 1

Precision = 110 (110 + 25) = 0.81

So, it is achieved if we have FN = 0

Q.18. Why is F1 score preferred over accuracy? How is F1 score calculated? When can we get a perfect F1 score?

Ans. It has been observed that **accuracy** works best when false positives and false negatives have almost **smilar costs.** But if the cost of false positives and false negatives are very different, then it is better to use both precision and recall values for which F1 score is used. Actually, F1 is based on precision and recall. When one (precision or recall) increases, the other goes down. Hence, F1 score combines precision-recall into a single number where F1 is computed by the formula :

$$F1 = (2 \times \text{Recall Precision}) / (\text{Recall} + \text{Precision})$$

Please note here that the F1 score is the **harmonic mean of recall and precision. Also note that on ideal situation will be when both precision and recall have a value of** 1 is, 100. Here, **the F1 score will also be an ideal 1,** *i.e.,* 100. This value is called as the **perfect value for the F1 score.**

Please understand that as the values of both precision and recall range from 0 to 1 and therefore the F1 score also ranges from 0 to 1.

Q.19. Categorize the following under data sciences, ML, computer vision and NLP—

Alexa, Chatbots, Faceapps, Face lock, Price comparision websites, $s_i r_i$, Face recognition, snapchat filters.

Ans. NLP—Alexa, *SIRI*, Chatbots, Faceapps.

Computer vision—Facial Recognition.

Data Sciences—Price comparision websites.

Machine Learning (ML)—Snapchat filters.

Q.20. Contruct a confusion matrix for an AI based prediction model that has been deployed on the roads to check traffic jams. The objective of the model is to predict whether there will be a traffic jam or NOT.

Ans. Case 1 : Is there a traffic jam?

Prediction : yes

Reality : yes

True positive

Case 2 : Is there a traffic jam?

Prediction : No

Reality : No

True Negative

Case 3 : Is there a traffic jam?

Prediction : yes

Reality : No

False Positive

Case 4 : Is there a traffic jam?

Prediction : No

Reality : yes

False Negative

∴ We get the following confusion matrix—

Confusion Matrix		Reality	
		Yes	No
Prediction	Yes	True Positive	False Positive
	No	False Negative	True Negative

Q.21. Distinguish between data science and data analysis.

Ans. Let us tabulate the differences—

Data Science	Data Analysis
1. Aim is to provide strategic actionable insights into the world	1. Aim is to provide operational observations into issues.
2. Mandatory—Mathematical, technical and strategic knowledge.	2. Data analysis and visualization skills needed.
3. It deals with by data.	3. It does not necessarily deal with by data.

Q.22. Name some popular data science tool kits.

Ans. As there are many types of open source tools available from data mining processes to programming languages, we put together a mix of technology that data scientists could add to their data science toolkit. They are as follows :

1. R Programming Language :
   *R is built for data scientist.
   * R originated in 1995 as an open source version of 5 language that was widely used for research work.
   * R has a steep learning curve.
   * It can be used with several packages to speed up the process.
   * Novice programmers prefer using R studio *i.e.*, an IDE for R.
   * Some packages to explore in R are—
     - ggp 10 to 2 /ggv is — Data visualization.
     - dplyr—Data munging and wranghng.
     - data.table—Data Wranghing.
     - Caret—ML workbench.
     - reshape2—Data shaping
2. **Python :** According to the recent data science survey conducted by O'Reilly, almost 40% of the data scientists use python to solve their problems.
   If the nature of problem at hand is to do through data analysis than I choose R. But if we have to write quick scripts, scrap the web then select Python.
3. **KNIME :** It is a software company that offers an open source analytics platform written in Java that is used for data reporting, mining and predictive analysis.
4. **SQL :** Many decades have pased and we have been using a big acosystem of SQL that can now be used by data scientists too. SQL is one of the best data science tool for filtering through datasets.
5. Apache nadoop and other big data tools.
6. **D3 Data Science Tools :** D3 is a javascript library for building interactive data visualizations within your browser. It allows data scientists to create rich visualizations.
7. **Tensor Flow**—It is an open—source software library for data flow programming across a range of tasks. It was developed by Google brain team in 2015, Nov. 9.
8. **R Studio :** R studio integrates with R as an IDE (Integrated Development Environment) to provide further functionality. It combines a source code editor, build automation tools and a debugger.

Q.23. Compare RDBMS and hadoop.

Ans.

RDBMS	Hadooop
1. Structured data with known schemas.	1. Unstructured & structured.
2. Records, long feilds, objects, XML form data groups.	2. Files.
3. Updates are allowed.	3. Only inserts and delets.
4. SQL & XQuery.	4. Hive, Pig, Jagl.
5. Quick response & random access.	5. Random access (indexing).
6. Data loss not acceptable.	6. Data loss can happen sometimes.
7. Complex data compression methods used.	7. Simple file compressions used.

SUMMARY

Artificial Intelligence (AI), mobile, social and IoT are driving data complexity through new forms and sources of data. Machine learning is a subset of AI only that trains a machine—how to learn, to rapidly produce models that can analyze bigger and complex data on large scale.

MULTIPLE CHOICE QUESTIONS

1. Final accuracy is checked by running algorithm on—

(*a*) Big data (*b*) Test data
(*c*) Small data (*d*) Training data

2. Each algorithm has different type of settings which we can configure and change the performance—

(*a*) Parameter tuning (*b*) Gradient descent
(*c*) Hyper parameters (*d*) None of the above

3. The form of attribute (or field) which is useful in data science is called as—

(*a*) Property list (*b*) Data type
(*c*) Features (*d*) None of the above

4. By reducing the number of levels, we can create better generalized model—

(*a*) True (*b*) Sometimes
(*c*) False (*d*) Always

5. Which of the following is a propular package in Python to visualize data—

(*a*) Matplotlib (*b*) ggplot
(*c*) Seaborn (*d*) All of these

6. The function on which if we choose two points and apply function and draw a line between those two points, they always remain below the function is called as—

(*a*) Concave Function (*b*) Linear Function
(*c*) Convex Function (*d*) Polynomial Function

7. Test error is the noisy version of—

(*a*) Generalization error (*b*) Variance
(*c*) Over fitting (*d*) None of the above

8. Models are called as—

(*a*) Modifiers (*b*) Outliners
(*c*) Specifiers (*d*) Classifiers

9. Which of the following is an example of searching in an unknown environment?

(*a*) 8-puzzle problem
(*b*) 8-Queen's problem
(*c*) Biometric recognition
(*d*) Mars Hover (Robot Navigation)

10. PXDES is a medical expert system for the diagnosis of lung disease—

(*a*) True (*b*) False
(*c*) Sometimes (*d*) None of the above

ANSWERS

1. (*d*)	**2.** (*a*)	**3.** (*b*)	**4.** (*a*)	**5.** (*d*)
6. (*a*)	**7.** (*a*)	**8.** (*d*)	**9.** (*d*)	**10.** (*a*)

CONCEPTUAL SHORT QUESTIONS WITH ANSWERS

Q.1. Why do we need a hidden layer in a multilayer neural network?

Ans. As we know that the input signals to aNN are propagated in a forward direction on layer-by-layer basis. Each layer in a multilayer NN has its own particular function. Neurons in the hidden layer **detect features.** The **weights** of the neurons represent the features hidden in the input patterns. Then, these features are used by the output layer in finding out the output pattern. If we have one hidden layer then we can represent any continuous function of the input signals and with two hidden layers we can also rpresent discontinuous functions.

Q.2. How many layers can we have in neural Networks?

Ans. Each layer in aNN can contain 10 to 1000 neurons. Theoritically speaking, 3 or 4 hidden layrs may be usd. Practically speaking, only three layers may be used. It is so because addition of each layer increases the computational burden exponentially.

Q.3. Consider the Bayesian classifier for the uniformly distributed classes, where :

$$P(x/w_1) = \begin{cases} \dfrac{1}{a_2 - a_1}, x \in [\lambda_1, \lambda_2] \\ 0, \text{ muulhon} \end{cases}$$

$$P(x/w_2) = \begin{cases} \dfrac{1}{b_2 - b_1}, x \in [b_1, b_2] \\ 0, \text{ muulhon} \end{cases}$$

Show the classification results for some values for *a* and *b* ("muullion" means "otherwise").

Ans. Typical cases are represented below :

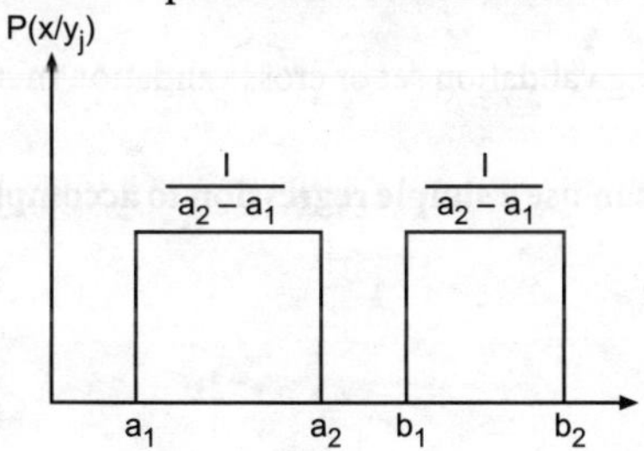

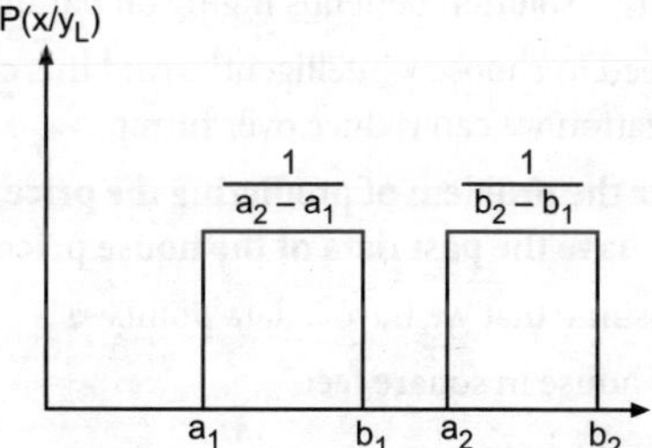

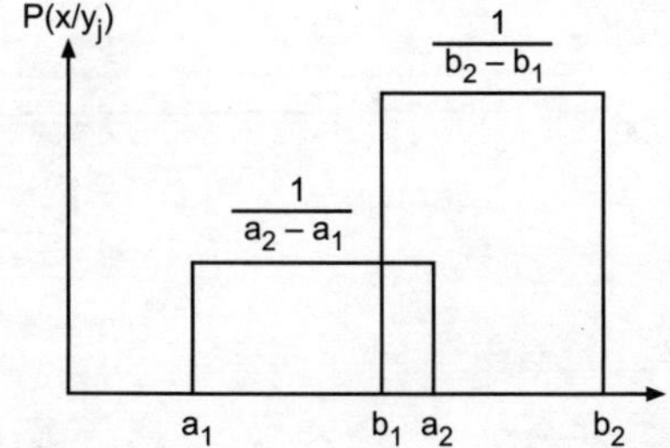

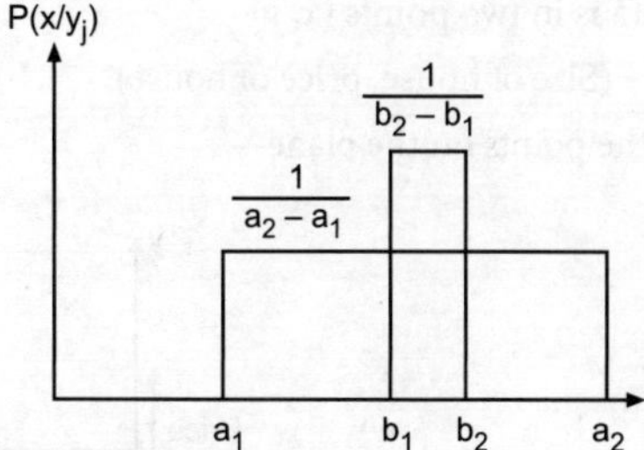

Q.4. "When we increase the model complexity, the training error rduces but generalization error increases due to over fitting." Explain.

Ans. We know that—

$$\text{Error} = \frac{\text{No. of Failures}}{\text{Total No. of Instance}} \quad (1)$$

We can also define accuracy as follows :

$$\therefore \quad \text{Accuracy} = 1 - \text{Error} \quad (2)$$

From equation (1) and (2) we get :

$$\text{Accuracy} = 1 - \text{Error} = 1 - \left[\frac{\text{No. of Failures}}{\text{Total No. of Instances}}\right]$$

$$= 1 - \frac{\text{No. of Success}}{\text{Total No. of Instances}}$$

Overfitting Exists if :

Training Error (β^*) > Training Error ($\breve{b}$)

Generalized Error (B^*) < Generalized Error ($\breve{b}$)

Objective : To reduce the generalization error. Overfitting exists in classification also. **Please note that if we keep on increasing our model complexity, it gives correct answer for all training data but failed on test/generalized data. Also note that if the coefficients increase, over fitting also increase.** So, we use L_2 norm to penalize the coefficients.

∴ **Objective** of coefficient penalization is—

$$\text{Total quality} = (\text{measure of fit}) + (\text{measure of coefficient magnitude})$$

$$= \text{log of likelihood} + L_2 \text{ norm}$$

$$= l(\beta) = \gamma\, |\beta|^2{}_2$$

Where γ = tuning parameter

If γ = 0, it is same as standard max. Likelihood solution

If V is large, solution depends highly on parameters.

∴ We need to choose γ intelligently. And this can be done by using validation set or cross validation methods. So, using regularization we can reduce over fitting.

Q.5. Consider the problem of predicting the price of a house. How can use a simple regression to accomplish it? Assume that you have the past data of the house price.

Ans. Let us assume that we have 2 data points—

- Size of house in square feet.
- Price of the house.

Input : Size of the house.

Output : Price.

∴ Our data is in two points (x, y).

∴ $(x, y) \rightarrow$ (Size of house, price of house)

Let draw the points on the plane—

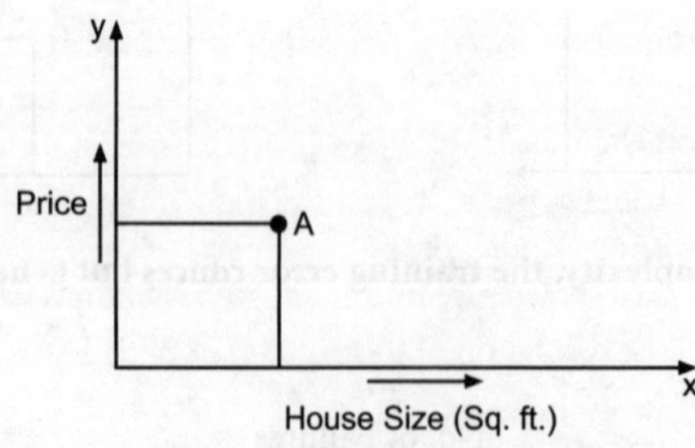

For any point (say, A) draw a perpendicular to x-axis. That represents the size of house too. Also, draw a perpendicular to y-axis. That represent the price of the house.

Let us now draw a line that maps the relationship between the house size and the price.

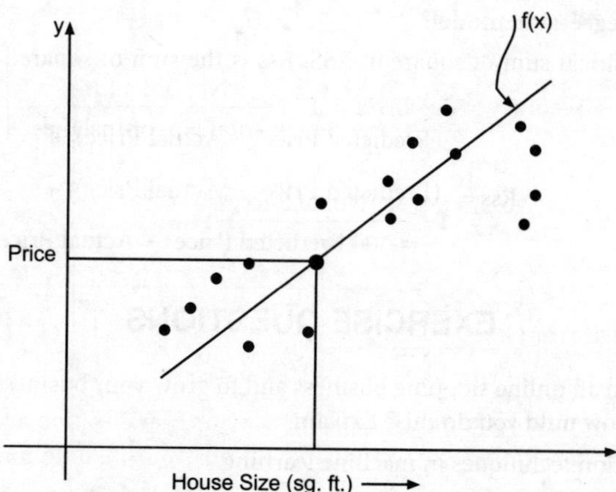

f(x) is a function that donotes the expected relationship between the house size (x) and price (y). Consider a point. According to our relationship function, house price is approximately equal to and (house size).

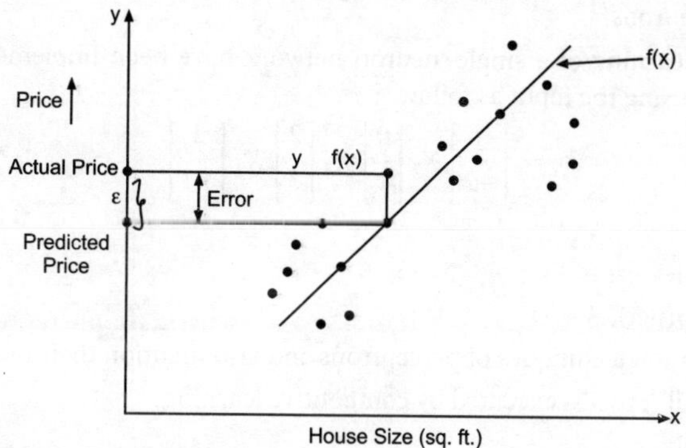

∴ Value of house, *i* is given as—

$$y_i = f(x_i) + e_i \quad (2)$$

$e_i =$ error in prediction for i^{th} house.

This error is positive, negative or zero for different examples. Expected value for error is zero.

$$E\,[e_i] = 0$$

So, our y_i can be below or above the line equally likely.

In regression, we must do two tasks—

a. First task is to select the type of function for the given problem. Is the function constant with output or is it linear, quadratic, cubic or any higher order?

b. After choosing the type of function, we must find the estimated function for th given problem.

Our data for this problem is house size and price. In feature engineering we do data cleaning, handle missing data, outhers etc. After we build our regression model, output is generated. Now, our output is compared with the actual output in the model assessment. This proves keeps iterating till the function gives best approximation.

In simple regression, we have to fit a line. Equation of our fitted lin can be given as follows :

$$f(x) = b_1 x + b_0 \quad (3)$$

The prediction value or output is—

$$y_i = b_1 - x_i + b_0 + e_i \quad (4)$$

Where $e_i =$ the error term or distance of true value from the predicted value

$b_1, b_0 =$ Coefficient of our regression model, called as slope and intercept

What is the cost of line in regression model?

It is measured by using residual sum of square of RSS. Rss is the sum of squared difference of actual value and the predicted value.

$$\therefore \quad \text{Rss} = \begin{array}{l} (\text{Predicted Price} - \text{Actual Price})_1^2 + \\ (\text{Predicted Price} - \text{Actual Price})_2^2 + \\ - = ... + (\text{Predicted Price} - \text{Actual Price})_n^2 \end{array}$$

EXERCISE QUESTIONS

1. Let us say that you started an online slopping business and to grow your business, you want to forecast the sales for the upcoming months. How mild you do this? Explain.
2. Name three feature selection techniques in machine learning.
   [Hint : Univariate selection, featur importance and corrlation matrix with heatmap]
3. Name four AI Languages.
4. Explain the progress of AI and its relevance to industry.
5. Explain the biological neurons.
6. Four steps of Hebbian learning of a single–neuron network have been implemented starting with W^1 [1–1]^t for learning constant $C = 1$ using the input as follows :

$$X_1 = \begin{bmatrix} 1 \\ -2 \end{bmatrix}, X_2 \begin{bmatrix} 0 \\ 1 \end{bmatrix}, X_3 \begin{bmatrix} 2 \\ 3 \end{bmatrix}, X_4 \begin{bmatrix} 1 \\ -1 \end{bmatrix}$$

   Find weights for :
   a. Bipolar binary, *f*(net).
   b. Bipolar continuous, *f*(net), $A = 1$.
7. Highlight the representation techniques of perceptrons and also mention their limitations.
8. How is "winner–takes_all" process executed by competitive learning?
9. Realize the logical Ex-OR
   Function for the following network—

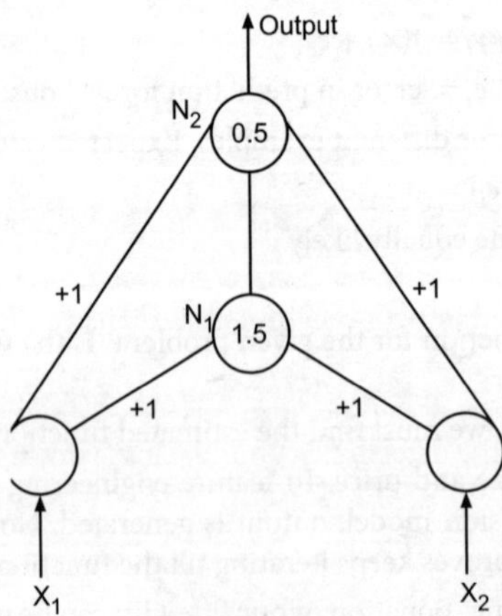

10. Find the weight updates of ANN one hidden layer using back-propagation algorithm.
    Given that :

$$\begin{aligned} \text{Input vector, } X_C &= [1.0 \quad 0.6 \quad 0.4] \\ \text{Target vector, } T &= 0.2 \\ \text{Learning Constant, } \eta &= 0.5 \\ \text{Logistic activation function} &= 1.0 \end{aligned}$$

10 Representation Knowledge Using Rules

Q.1. Explain forward chaining, backward chaining, and conflict resolution

Ans. A.I. solves our problems by searching a solution search-tree (called as search space) from the initial state to the goal state. We have rule-based system architecture that has a set of rules, a set of facts and an inference engine. Given a set of rules, the new knowledge can be inferred using two rules —

a. Forward chaining / Forward reasoning.

b. Backward chaining / Backward reasoning.

Forward chaining (or reasoning) starts from the start state and proceeds towards the goal state. On the other hand, backward chaining starts from the goal state and proceeds towards the start state.

For example. : Turbo Prolog (an A.I. language, 5 G), uses backward chaining (or reasoning).

Forward reasoning / data-driven inferencing

As we have already studied that rules are stored in KB in form of atomic formula in some form like propositional or predicate logic. The process of instantiating the left side of rules, executing them from left to right, matching the left part of the sentence with the existing expression and if the match occurs then replacing it by the right part of the rule is called as **Forward reasoning or Forward chaining or Data-driven search.** In next step, this right hand side of the previous rule is considered as left side of present rule to find applicability of a rule. So the finding of the rule becomes Subgoals to be fulfilled. These subgoals may in turn cause new subgoals to be established and so on, until the facts are found to match the lowest subgoals conditions. Whenever the goal is achieved, the search process stops.

For example. Say, we have a database with the following elements —

$$\boxed{\begin{matrix} A & G & E \\ A & C & B \end{matrix}} \text{(database having facts)}$$

& the set of rules as —

$$\boxed{\begin{matrix} F \,\&\, B \rightarrow Z \\ C \,\&\, D \rightarrow F \\ A \rightarrow D \end{matrix}} \text{ (Rules in a } KB\text{)}$$

We assume that each time the set of rules is tested against the database, only the first (topmost) rule that matches is executed. So the rule $A \rightarrow D$ is executed only once although it matches the database every time. This database is also known as a working memory (WM).

How it works? The first rule which fires is $A \rightarrow D$ because A is already in the database. So, this rule shows the existence of D (*i.e.*, inferring) and D is placed in the database. So, our database now is —

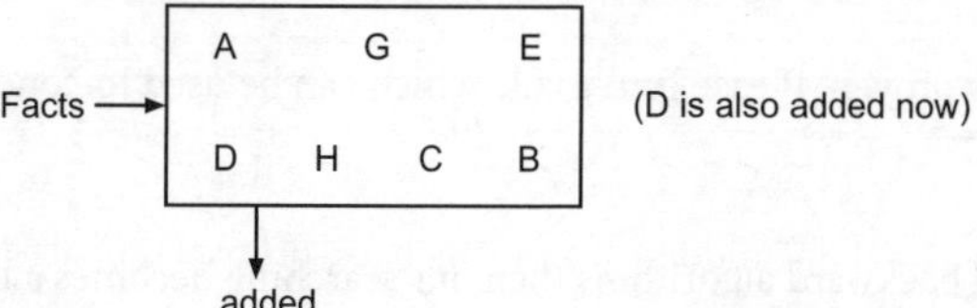

This causes the second rule C and $D \rightarrow F$ to fire and as a consequence F is inferred and placed in the database. This in turn causes the tired rule F and $B \rightarrow Z$ to fire placing Z in the database *i.e.*

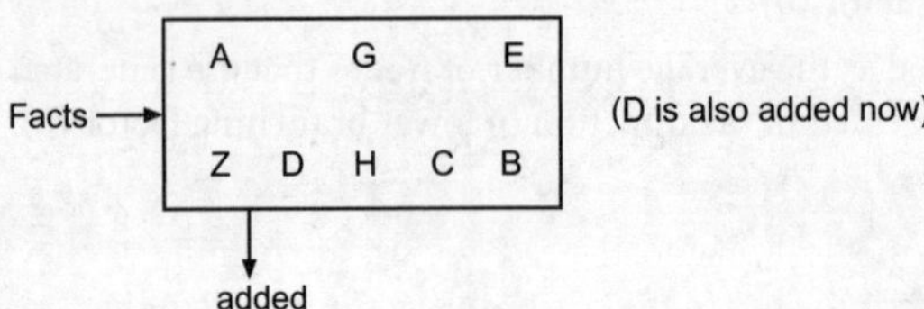

∴ The inference chain so formed is —

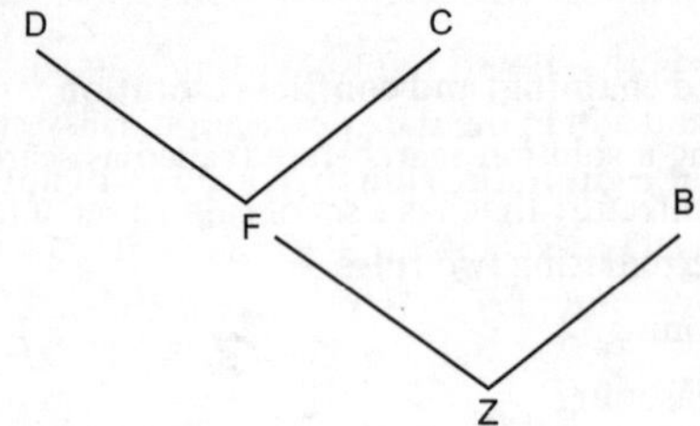

This is known as **forward chaining. It is also called as a data-driven search** as the input data is used to guide the direction of inference process.

Let us write its algorithm now.

Algorithm: Forward chaining

Repeat: Collect the rule whose condition matches a fact in database (or WM).

Do actions indicated by the rule — added facts to WM 'or delete facts from working memory).

Until: Problem is solved or no condition matches.

Alternative Algorithm: Forward Chaining

Repeat

Collect the rules whose conditions match facts in database (or WM)

If more than one rule matches then use conflict resolution strategy to eliminate all but one.

else

do actions indicated by the rules *i.e.*, add facts to the database/ or delete facts from WM, until a problem is solved or no condition matches.

Backward chaining/Backward reasoning/Goal-driven inference

It is a process of reasoning in which within a rule it matches the existing state with the right hand part of the rule and if the match occurs, it is replaced by left hand side of the rule. Actually, backward chaining means reasoning from goals back to facts. The focus is on the **search**. The rules and facts are processed using **backward chaining interpreter.**

Let us write its algorithm now.

Algorithm: Backward chaining

Prove goal G:

If G is in the initial facts, it is proven. Please find a rule which can be used to conclude G and try to prove each of that rules conditions.

Which one to select?

If we apply both forward and backward algorithms then our searching becomes a bidirectional search. This results in a hybrid reasoning. Which reasoning to select depends on the nature of the problem. It depends on the following factors:

***a.* Number of starts and goal states.**

We proceed from a smaller set of states to a larger set of states.

b. **Direction of branching factor (*b*)**

Branching factor is defined as the average number of nodes that are generated from a single node. Please remember that the reasoning is performed in the direction of lower branching factor (*b*).

c. **Problem's requirement**

Certain applications like medical diagnosis need backward chaining as they need the justification of the solution too. Note that it is important to choose the reasoning in the direction that corresponds to the way in which the user thinks. Actually, we can use hybrid reasoning for such systems. Programming languages, like PROLOG, support backward chaining.

We need to check the rule form. If both left and right hand side contain assertion, then forward chaining can match assertions on the left side of a rule and add to the state description of assertion on RHS. **Please understand here that if arbitrary procedures are allowed at right in the rule then a rule will not be reversible.**

Some production languages allow only reversible rules and some do not. **Also note that when irreversible rules are used then a commitment to the direction of search must be made at the time the rules are written.**

Conflict Resolution : The set of rules that have their conditions stratified by working memory elements forms a conflict set. A conflict is said to occur if more than one rules are found to fire in one cycle. In such a scenario, the control structure must determine which rule to fire from this conflict set of active rules. This process of selection is called as "conflict resolution". So, conflict resolution normally selects a single rule to fire. There are 3 conflict resolution mechanisms:

a. Refractory

b. Receiving

c. Specificity

Refractory: In this mechanism, a rule should not be allowed to fire more than once on the same data. This prevents undesired loops.

Recency: Here we rank instantiation in terms of recency of elements in the premise of the rule. The rule which has highest priority is fired first.

Specificity: More specific rules are better because they take more of data into account. It is also known as a strict condition as it injects more knowledge in the KB, when it is fired.

Other mechanisms are also used like —

a. **Most recently used :** It chooses the most recently used rule from the conflict set for firing. It represents a dfs.

b. **Most recently added :** It selects the rule which is most recently added in the set of rules. It is a dynamic policy as in this policy new production rules are added, deleted or modified automatically in dynamic KB during execution.

We are in a position to solve some examples now.

Q.2. Consider the following database and the set of rules given below:

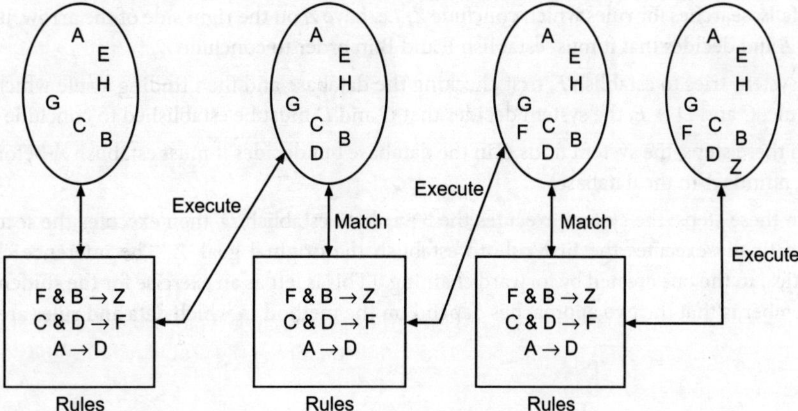

Fig. 10.1

Explain how forward chaining works in this example. Also show backward chaining. Which is more cost-effective?

Ans. The rules in this example, use letters as facts in the database to explain the situations or concepts.

For examples., *F* and *B* → *Z*

means

It situation F exists and situation B exists

THEN : situation Z also exists.

Let us see now how these rules work.

Assume that each time the set of rules is tested against the database, only the first (topmost rule which matches is executed. That is why, in the figure given, the rule (*A* → *D*) is executed only once even though it matches the database every time.

The first rule that fires is *A* → *D* because A is already in the database. As consequence of this rule, the existence of *D* is inferred and *D* is placed in the database. This causes the second rule, *C* and *D* → *F* to fire, as a consequence *F* is inferred and placed in the database. This in turn causes the 3rd rule *F* and *B* → *Z* to fire placing *Z* in the database. **Please understand that this technique is called as forward chaining because the search for new information seams to be proceeding in the direction of the arrow separating the left and right hand sides of the rules.** The system which uses information on the left hand side to derive information on the right is shown in Fig 10.2(*a*).

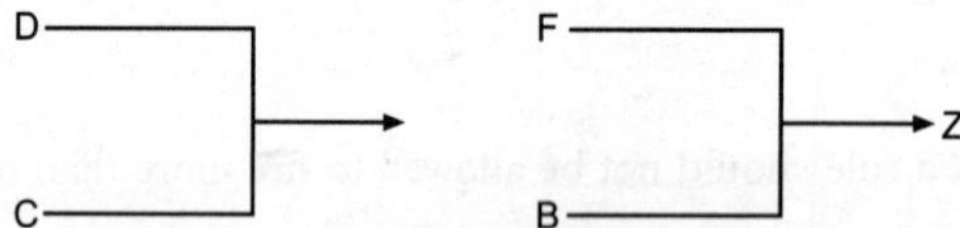

Say, we use this system with the goal of determining whether or not situation *Z* existed. We might think that it worked quite well, finding quickly the fact that *Z* did exist. Unfortunately, this is just over simplification. Practically speaking, the process of drawing inference is not simple. This is so because a real expert system will not have just three rules but will have hundreds or even thousands of them. If we use a system that is very large just to find out about *Z* many rules would be fired which had nothing to do with *Z*, then a large number of inference chains and situations could be derived in the process which were valid but unrelated to *Z*. **Please note that if our goal is to infer one particular fact *Z*, forward chaining could waste both time and money.** In such a case, backward chaining might be more cost-effective. With this inference technique, the system starts with what it wants to prove. Like, to find if the situation *Z* exists and as such executes those rules which are relevant to its establishment.

The Fig. 10.2(*b*) shows how backward chaining would work using rules given above.

Step 1: The system is told to establish (if possible) that situation *Z* exists. It first checks the database for Z and when that fails, searches for rules which conclude *Z*, *i.e.* have *Z* on the right side of the arrow. It finds the rule *F* and *B* → Z and decides that it must establish F and B in order to conclude *Z*.

Step 2: The system tries to establish *F*, first checking the database and then finding a rule which concludes *F*. From the rule, *C* and *D* → *F*, the system decides that *C* and *D* must be established to conclude *F*.

Steps 3 to 5 : In these steps, the system finds *C* in the database but decides it must establish *A* before it can conclude *D*. It then finds *A* in the database.

Steps 6 to 8 : In these steps, the system executes the 3rd rule to establish *D*, then executes the second rule to establish *F* and finally executes the first rule to establish the original goal, *Z*. The inference chain created here is identical to the one created by forward chaining. (This is left as an exercise for the students). But one point to remember is that the two approaches depend on the method in which data and rules are searched.

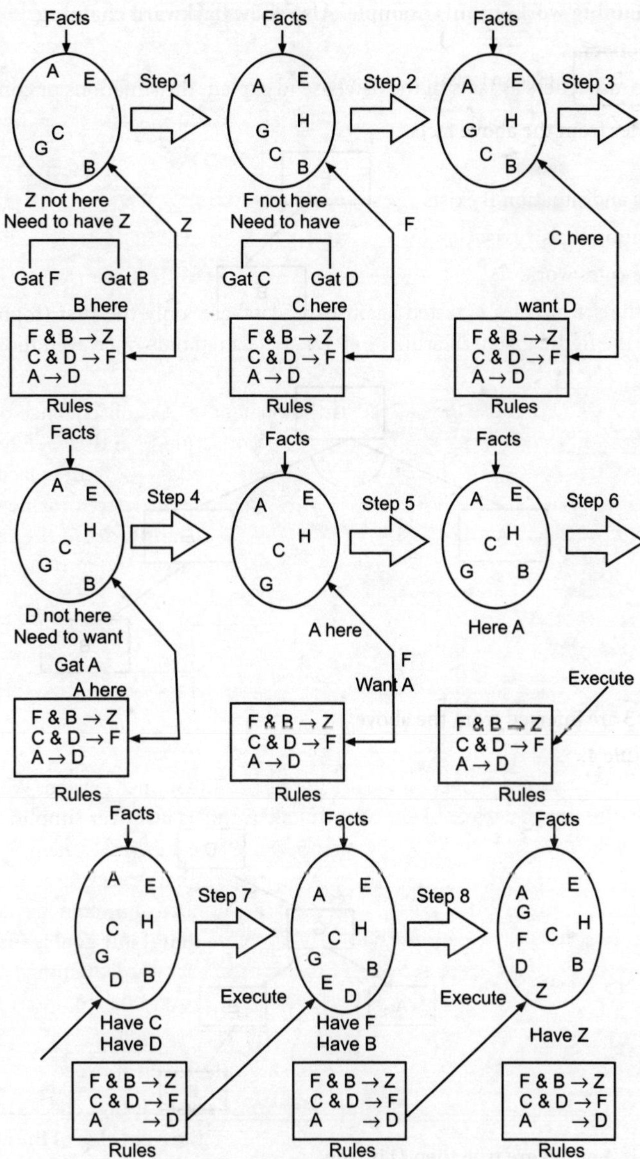

Fig. 10.2 : (b) Forward and Backward chaining

Q.3. Suppose a Rule Base contains the following four rules-

Rule No.	Production rules
Rule 1	if A and C then F
Rule 2	if A and E then G
Rule 3	if B then E
Rule 4	if G and D

***a.* Prove that if *A* and *B* are True then *D* is True using forward chaining.**

***b.* Prove that if *A* and *B* are True then *D* is True using backward chaining.**

Ans. Let us solve part-a first and then b-part-

a. **Forward Chaining:**

Step-1: A B {Known facts}

Step-2: See facts that infer from the above facts.

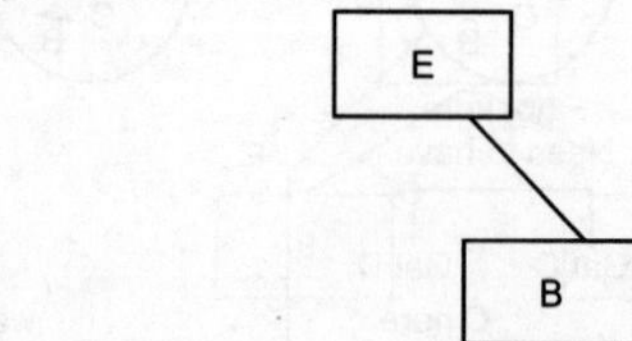

step-3:

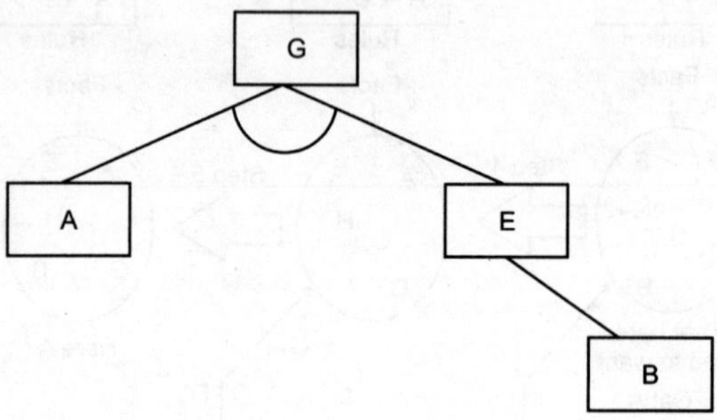

Hence, Rule 2 and Rule 3 are inferred from the above.

Using step-3 inferring Rule 4.

Step-4:

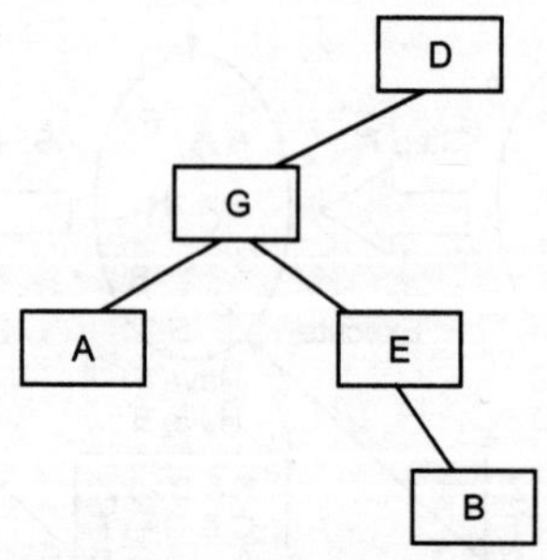

Hence, it is proved that if *A* and *B* are true then *D* is true.

***b.* Backward Chaining:**

Step-1: Goal State D

Step-2: Infer facts from Goal State.

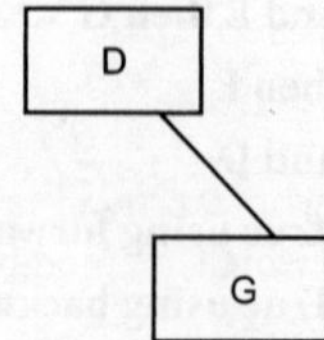

Step-3: Further extract the states.

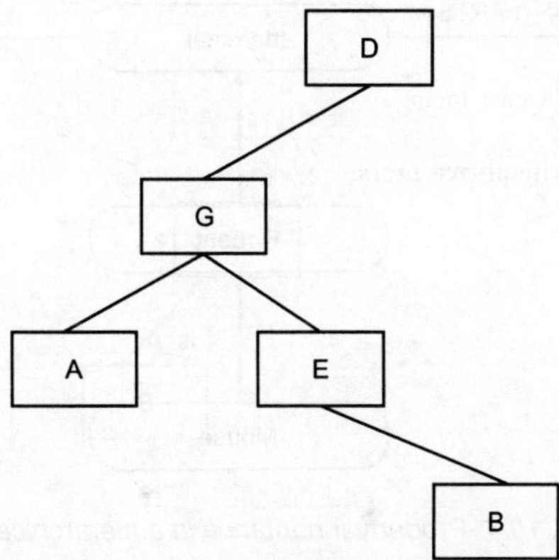

Since, we are given that *A* and *B* are true then we can infer by backward chaining that *D* is also true.

Q.4. We have some more advanced KR techniques that focus on the structure of knowledge like semantic networks, conceptual graphs, conceptual dependencies and scripts, cyc and object oriented representation. Explain each of these with examples.

Ans. Slots and Semantic nets/semantic network/associated networks.

A slot is a subclass of intangible and is of many types. Defining slots refers not to the properties of the frame but to the properties of the object represented by the frame. A slot is an attribute value pair in the simplest form. A filler is a value that a slot can take. **For example**. It can be a numeric, string value or a pointer to another slot. A weak slot and filler structure does not consider the constant of the representation. They are of two types —

a. Semantic networks (nets) or associated networks.

b. Frames.

Let us discuss semantic networks first. They are an alternative to predicate logic as a form of knowledge representation. The idea is that we can store our knowledge in form of a graph. A semantic network consists of nodes connected by arcs. Nodes represent objects in the real world.

Arcs represent relationships between those objects.

For example.

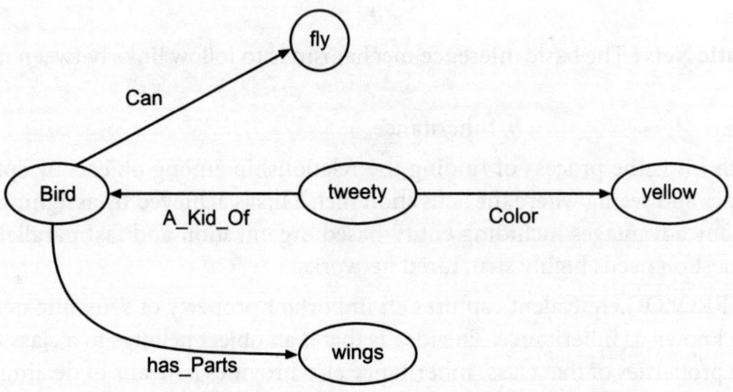

Fig. 10.3: *Semantic network (net) example*

Fig. 10.3 shows that tweety is a kind of bird who can fly. It is yellow in colour and has wings. These networks permit property inheritance also. It means that nodes which are members or subsets of other nodes may inherit properties from their higher level ancestor nodes.

For example.

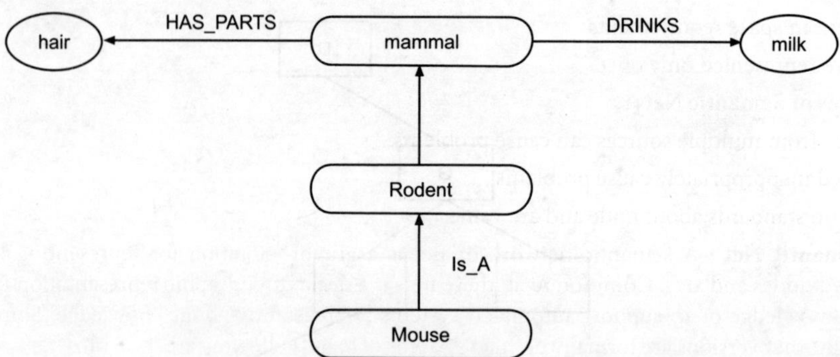

Fig. 10.4: *Property inheritance in a hierarchical network*

So, it is possible to infer from above net that a mouse has hair and drinks milk.

This concept of inheriting a property is called as property inheritance. The properties of a subclass can be modified and can be given different values. Each subclass will thus have its own defined values. Please understand that the semantic network based knowledge representation mechanism is useful where an object or concept is associated with many attributes and where relationships between objects are important.

Applications: Semantic nets have been used in natural language research to represented complex sentences expressed in English.

Properties of semantic nets : Semantic nets exhibit following properties knowledge representation scheme:

1. **Expressiveness :** Semantic nets allow representation of facts and relationship between facts. The levels of hierarchy provide a mechanism for representing general and specific knowledge. This representation is a model of human memory and it is therefore relatively understandable.
2. **Effectiveness :** They support inference through property inheritance. They can also be easily represented by PROLOG, LISP and other A.I. languages making them amenable to computation, as shown by "is-a" arc in LISP given by $\forall x$ [Great-Dane $(x) \rightarrow$ Dog (x)].
3. **Efficiency :** They reduce the size of the knowledge base. Knowledge is stored only at its highest level of abstraction rather than for every instance or example of a class. Further they help maintain the consistency in knowledge base because high level properties are inherited by subclasses and are not added for each subclass.
4. **Explicitness :** Reasoning equates to following paths through the network, so relationship and inference are explicit in the network lines.

Inferencing in Semantic Nets : The basic inference mechanism is to follow links between nodes. There are two ways of inferencing used here —

a. Intersection Search. *b.* Inheritance.

a. **Intersection Search :** It is the process of finding the relationship among objects by spreading activation out from each of the two nodes and seeing where the activation met. This is achieved by assigning a special tag to each visited node. There are many advantages including entity-based organization and fast parallel implementation. However, every structured question needs highly structured networks.

b. **Inheritance :** This PROLOG equivalent captures an important property of semantic nets that they may be used for a form of inference known as inheritance. The idea is that if an object belongs to a class (shown by is a relationship), it inherits all of the properties of that class. Inheritance also provides a means of dealing with default reasoning.

Advantages of Semantic Nets : Semantic networks (or nets) have some advantages as follows —

1. They are easy to visualize.
2. Relationships can be arbitrarily defined by the Knowledge Engineers.
3. Formal definitions of semantic networks have been developed.
4. Related knowledge is easily clustered.

5. Are efficient in space requirements.
6. Projects are represented only once.

Disadvantages of Semantic Nets :

1. Inheritance from multiple sources can cause problems.
2. Facts placed inappropriately cause problems.
3. There are no standards about node and arc value.

Types of Semantic Net : A semantic network or net is a graphic notation for representing knowledge in pattern interconnected nodes and arcs. Common to all these nets is a declarative graphic representation that can be used either to represent knowledge or to support automated systems for reasoning about knowledge. Some versions are highly informal while other versions are formally defined systems of logic. Following are the 6 most common kinds of semantic nets —

1. Definitional networks emphasize the subtype or is-α relation between a concept type and a newly defined subtype. The resulting network, also called a generalization or subsumption hierarchy, supports the rule of inheritance for copying properties defined for a super type to all of its subtypes. Since definitions are true by definition, the information in these networks is often assumed to be necessarily true.
2. Assertional networks are designed to assert propositions. Unlike definitional networks the information in an assertional network is assumed to be contingently true, unless it is explicitly marked with a modal operator. Some assertional networks have been proposed as models of the conceptual structures underlying natural language semantics.
3. Implication networks use implication as the primary relation for connecting nodes.
   They may be used to represent patterns of beliefs causality, or inferences.
4. Executable networks include some mechanism, such as marker passing or attached procedures, which can perform inferences, pass messages, or search for patterns and associations.
5. Learning networks build or extend their representation by acquiring knowledge from examples. The new knowledge may change the old network by adding and deleting nodes and arcs or by modifying numerical values, called weights, associated with the nodes and arcs.
6. **Hybrid networks :** They combine two or more of the previous techniques, either in a single network or in separate but closely interacting networks.

We are in a position to solve some examples on nets now.

Q.5. Construct a semantic net representation for the following —

a. Pompian (Marcus), Blacksmith (Marcus).

b. Raj gives Lucy a gift.

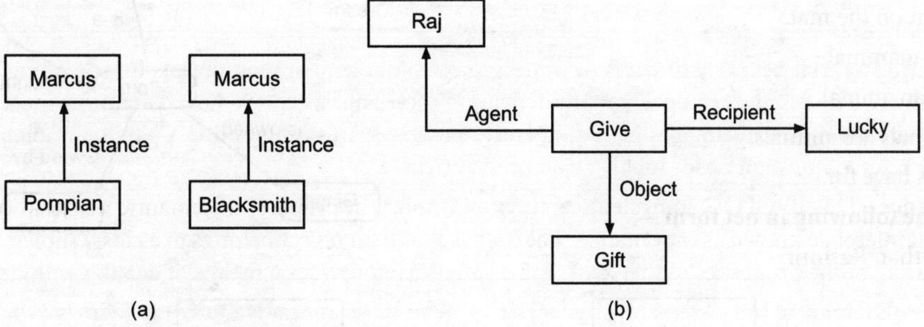

(a) (b)

Q.6. Construct a semantic net representation for the following —

a. Every dog has bitten a mail carrier.

b. Every batter hit a ball.

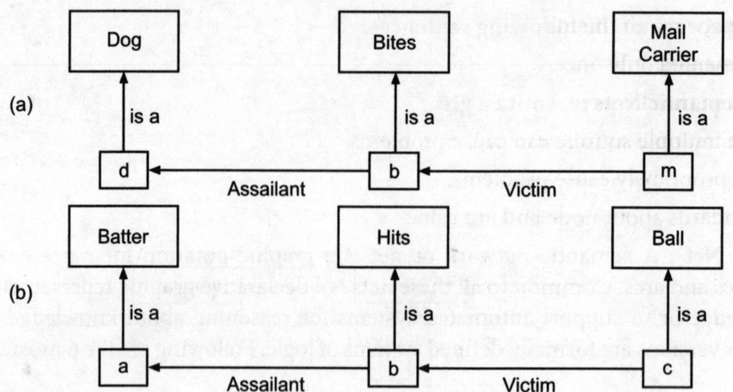

Q.7. Represent the following using nets —

***a.* Emus are birds.**

***b.* Typical birds fly and have wings.**

***c.* Emus run.**

Ans. Its Semantic net is as follows

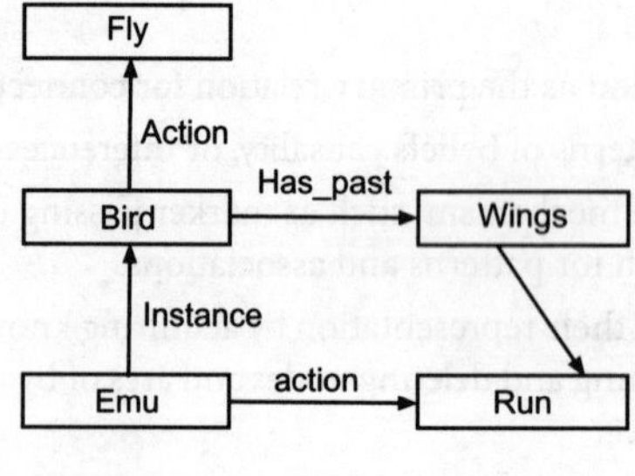

Q.8. Represent the following using semantic net —

a. Tom is a cat.

b. Tom caught a bird.

c. Tom is owned by John.

d. Tom is ginger in color

e. Cats like cream.

f. The cat sat on the mat.

g. A cat is a mammal.

h. A bird is an animal.

i. All mammals are animals.

j. Mammals have fur.

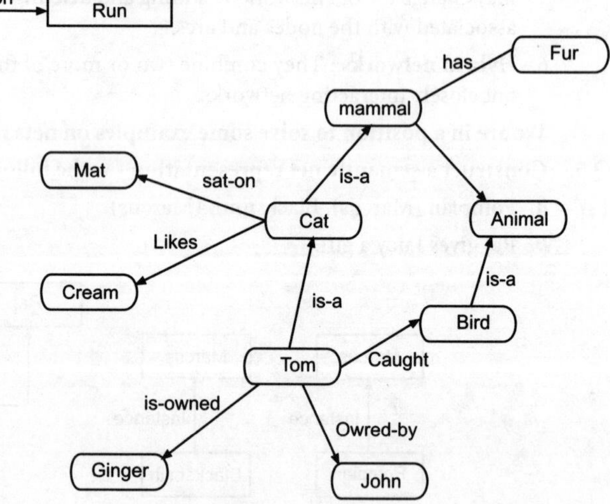

Q.9. Represent the following in net form —

'Asif is taller than Rashmi'

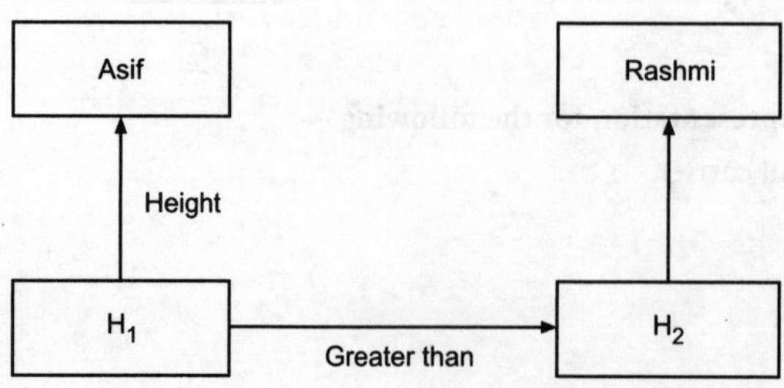

Q.10. Draw the semantics network of the following sentences

a. **Bobby gives Amita a gift.**

b. **Bobby told Krishana that he gave Amita a gift.**

Ans. *a.* Its semantic representation is as follows

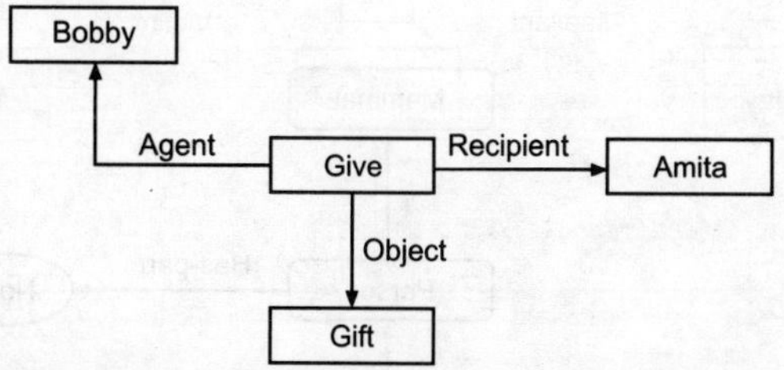

> **NOTE:** The arcs define the relationships between the predicate (GIVE) and the concepts like AMITA and GIFT, associated with that predicate.

b. Its semantic representation is as follows

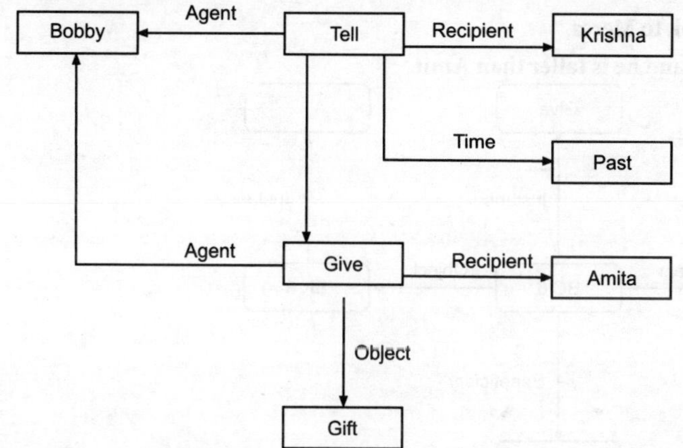

Q.11. "Our neighbour's pet Rocky is brown colored and has very small legs". Represent it as a hierarchical network. Give its property list also in LISP.

Ans. The following is the hierarchical structure showing property inheritance.

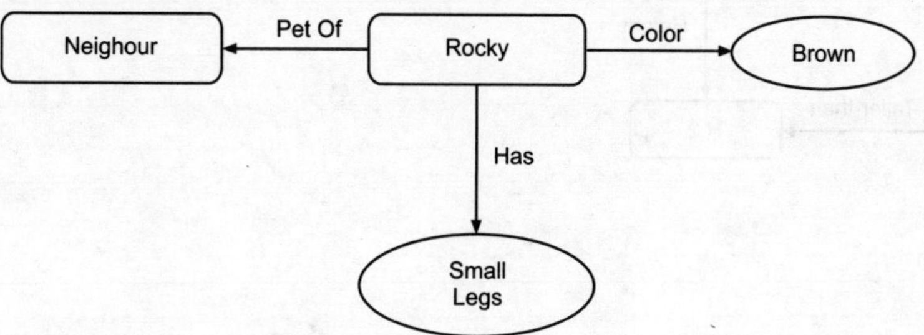

The property list is as follows.

(putprop 'rocky' neighbor' pet of)

(putprop 'rocky' brown' color)

(putprop 'rocky' small keys' has)

Q.12. Given the predicates is a (Person, Mammal) (instance (Pee-Wee, Person) (team (Pee-Wee, ABC) uniform color (Pee-Wee, Green) Express the above in the form of semantic or associative network.

Ans.

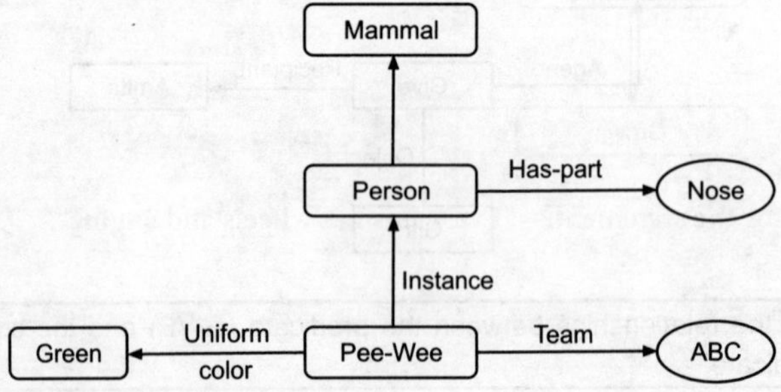

Q.13. Represent the following as a semantic network.

***a.* Amit gave the book to Mersa.**

***b.* Prem is 6 feet tall and he is taller than Amit.**

Ans. (*a*)

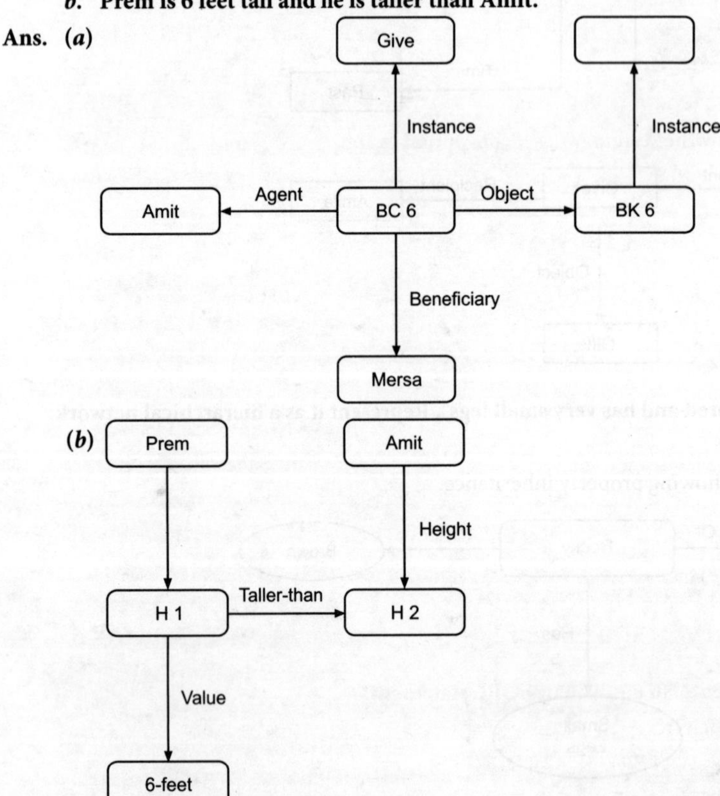

Q.14. Construct a conceptual representation for the sentence, "Every car has an engine"

Ans. The conceptual graph representation is

CAR : ∀] → (PART) → (ENGINE)

Q.15. Transform the FOPL statement equivalent conceptual graph.

$\forall x$ Normal (x) and Grown (x) → Walk (x).

Ans. The conceptual graph is as follows.

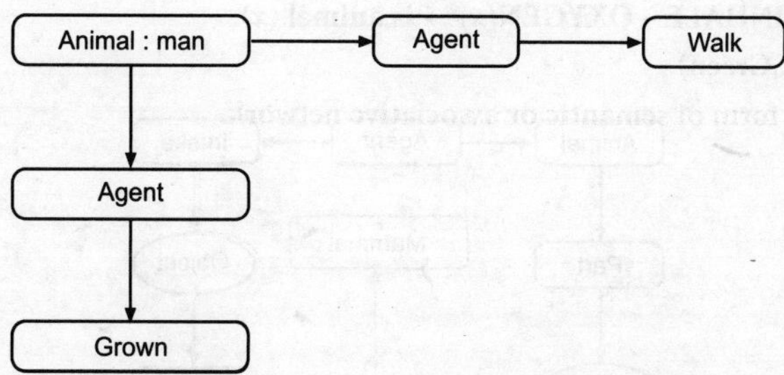

Q.16. Give conceptual graph for the statement.—"Every bus has wheels and engine".

Ans.

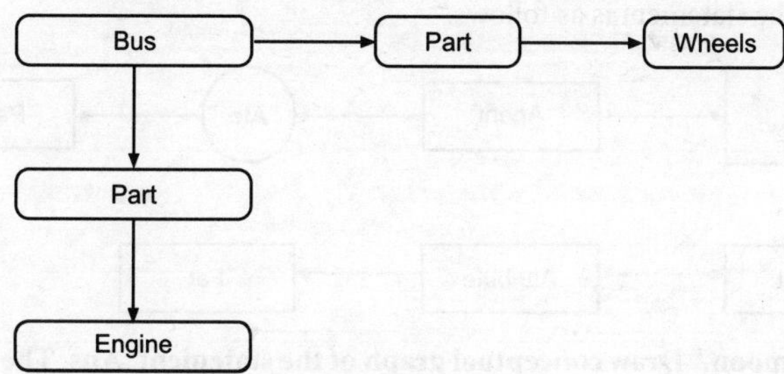

Q.17. "A cow has four legs and eats grass". Show the statement as a conceptual graph.

Ans.

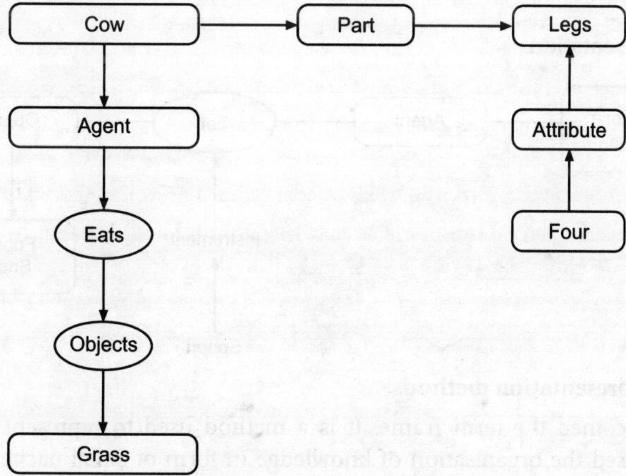

Q.18. Convert the following conceptual graph into an equivalent FOPL statement.

[CAMEL : clyde] → (Agent) → (DRINK)
→ [(OBJECT) → (WATER) → (ATTRIBUTE)
→ [50 – GALLONS].

Ans. $E(x)$ for x is a camel.

$D(x)$ for x is drinks water.

G(x) for drinks 50 gallons of water.

$\therefore \forall x\, (E(x) : \text{clyde})\ \&\ D(x) \rightarrow G(x))$

Q.19. Transform the FOPL statements given below into equivalent conceptual graph.
$\forall x$(HAS – LEGS) (x) and INHALE – OXYGEN(x) → is animal (x).

Ans.

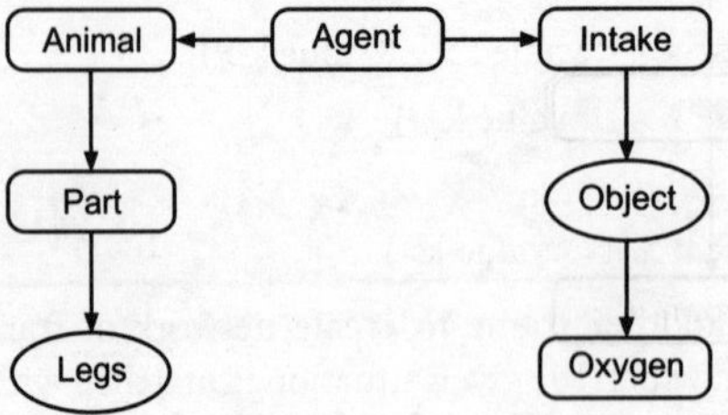

Q.20. Draw conceptual graph of the statement—"Sparrow ate a fat insect".

Ans. The conceptual graph for the statement is as follows.

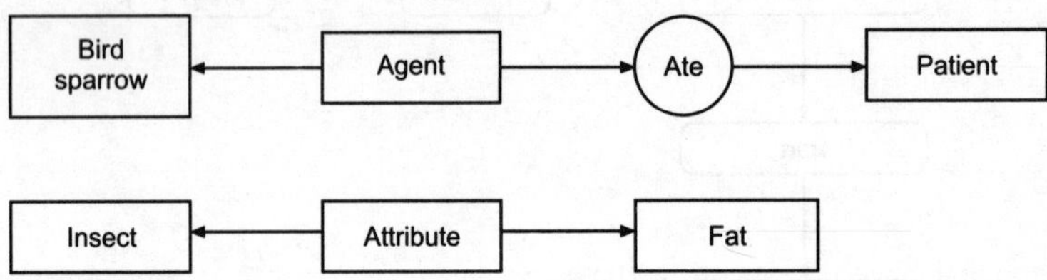

Q.21. "Joe is eating food with a spoon." Draw conceptual graph of the statement. Ans. The statement can be shown in two ways.

1. Linear form of conceptual graph

   [PERSON : joe] → (Agent) → [EAT] → (OBJECT) → [FOOD : soup] – (INSTRUMENT) → [SPOON]

2. Conceptual graph representation

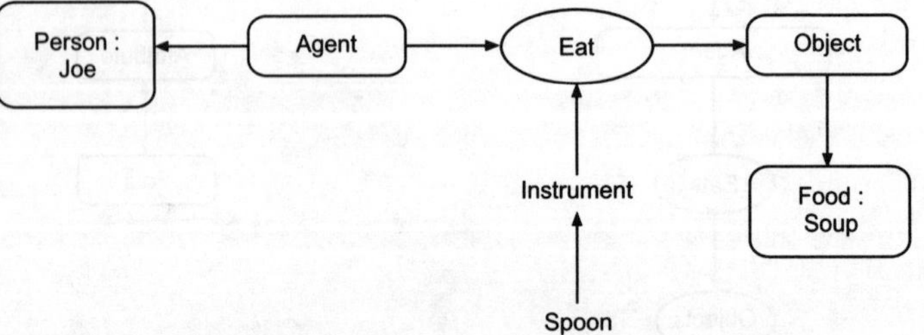

Q.22. Explain frames and its representation methods.

Ans. In 1975, Marvin Minsky coined the term frame. It is a method used to represent conceptual and Commonsense knowledge. Minsky proposed the organisation of knowledge in form of small packets called as frames. It is used to represent activities associated with conceptual events taking place, in say, a supermarket, theatre, college, university etc. This knowledge in form of frame is stored in the KB. The contents of the frames are slots which have certain values. The slots may be of any type and of any size slots have names and values (or subfields) called as facets. Facets may also have names and any number of values. An appropriate frame is selected from the memory for reasoning. Frames are of 2 types —

a. **Declarative frames :** Frames consisting of only descriptive type of knowledge.

b. **Procedural frames :** A frame having knowledge about the action or procedures.

So, a frame is a collection of attributes or slots and associated values that describe some real world entity.

NOTE: Frames → have slots for various objects → slots have values

A frame-system is a collection of objects. Each object contains a number of slots. A slot represents an attribute. Each slot has a value. The value of an attribute can be another object.

A general frame structure is shown below:

(< frame name >

(< slots 1 > (facet 1 < value l > … value k >)

(facet 2 < value 1 > … value k >)

?

(facet n <value n > … <value k>)

The frames can be attached with another frame to create network of frames. Reasoning, using frames is done by instantiation process. The process in which the given situation is matched with frames that are already existing is known as instantiation. The reasoning process tries to match the current problem state with the frame slot and assigns them values. The values assigned to the slots depict a particular situation and by this the reasoning process moves towards a goal. Thus the reasoning process is defined as filling slots value in frames. If the given slot characteristic is not present then the slot provides a default value for the characteristic. Please note that the problem situation is generally not static. The values of the corresponding slots are updated if there is any deviation in the characteristic.

Types of Slots : Slots are of three types as follows:

I. Inherent Slots :

a. These slots are specified by the use for each class and the values are given during the instantiating of this class to obtain an object.

b. These are comparable with the recording field of data and hence are the characteristic of the knowledge under consideration.

c. However, there is a difference. Since these can exist outside of their recording they can have one or more values but also procedures associated with them.

II. Meta Slots :

a. These are defined for the classes and often have only one value being related to the given class.

b. These are not inherited.

c. Such an attribute is the ako (a – kind– of) link mentioned in the semantic networks which relates one class to a more general class.

d. Each class is related by ako to at least one other class. There exists exactly one class linked to itself, which is the vertex of the graph of ako links.

e. The slot ako determines one of the fundamental interests of the object representation — INHERITANCE.

f. At the level of instanced frames, it allows (by default) a frame to inherit certain values of the classes to which it is bound (related) by ako. If this frame is bound to several others, there can be multiple inheritance. The value of ako is a set of frames.

III. Instantiated Slots :

a. Are defined for objects which are instances of classes.

b. As priori, their creation is automatic during instantiating since they are ascribed to the instantiated class.

c. This type of attribute is the is a link mentioned for semantic networks.

Please note that each slot possesses an arbitrary number of facets. These are the declarations or procedures associated to the attributes.

Many languages like LISP (*i.e.* List Processing) has in-build procedures to create, access, modify, update and display frames.

We must keep the following points in mind —

1. Instances of SLOT are slots.
2. Associated with SLOT are attributes that each instance will inherit.
3. Each slot has a domain and a range.

4. Since slot is a set of all slots, so can be represented by metaclass called slot.
5. To compute attribute involves a procedure to compute its value.

Advantages of Frames :

1. Are very flexible.
2. Are similar to human knowledge organization, easier to understand logic or rules.

Disadvantages of Frames :

1. No standards.
2. Very generalized approach
3. No associated reasoning mechanism.

Problems with both semantic nets and frames :

1. Both net and frames are weak slot and filler structures. Both are arbitrary.
2. Both are useful for representing certain sorts of knowledge.
3. Both lack semantics i.e., precise meaning.
4. Logic generalizes these schemes.
5. Syntax of KR scheme is irrelevant.

Q.23. Explain Conceptual Dependencies (CDs).

Ans. In 1977, Roger C Schank developed CD structures. CD is used to represent knowledge again. This representation should be powerful enough to represent these concept of sentences of natural language. CD theory states that different sentences which have same meaning should have some unique CD representation. In CD theory, 5 different types of ontological (state of being) building blocks are distinguished —

a. Entities *b.* Actions *c.* Conceptual cases

d. Conceptual Dependencies *e.* Conceptual tenses

Entities :

a. Picture Producer (PP) are actors that perform different acts.

b. Picture Aiders (PA) are supporting properties or attributes of producers.

c. ACT: Actions done by an actor to an object.

d. LOCs: Shows the location of action,

Actions :

a. Primitive actions (ACTs).

b. Action Aiders (AA) are properties or attributes of primitive action.

For primitive actions, a typical CD set is —

ATRANS	Transfer (example., 'give')
INGEST	Ingest into the body (example. 'eat')
EXPEL	Expel from body (example. 'cry')
ATTRANS	Abstract transfer (example. 'owner ship')
MORE	Move a body part (example. 'kick')
GRASP	Grasp an object (example. 'clutch')
PROPEL	Throw an object (example. 'push')
PTRANS	Physical transfer (example. 'go')
MTRANS	Mental transfer (example. 'tell')
CONC	Conceptualize (*i.e.*, think about something).
ATTEND	Direct sensory orange to observe (example. listen).

The main goals of this theory are —

1. To capture the implicit concept of a sentence and make it explicit.
2. To help in drawing inferences from sentences.
3. For any 2 or more sentences that are identical in meaning, there should be only one representation of meaning.
4. To develop language conversion packages.
5. To provide a means of representation which are language independent.

In addition to the actors and objects other concept of time, location, source and destination are also used in CD representation —

(*i*)	O	:	Object case relationship
(*ii*)	r/R	:	Recipient case relationship
(*iii*)	p	:	Part
(*iv*)	f	:	future
(*v*)	t	:	transition
(*vi*)	Is	:	Start transition
(*vii*)	Tf	:	finish transition
(*viii*)	k	:	continuing
(*ix*)	?	:	interrogative
(*x*)	/	:	negative
(*xi*)	nil	:	present
(*xii*)	delta	:	timeless:
(*xiii*)	C	:	Conditional

For example 1: Ram gives Anjali a book.

Its CD structure is as follows —

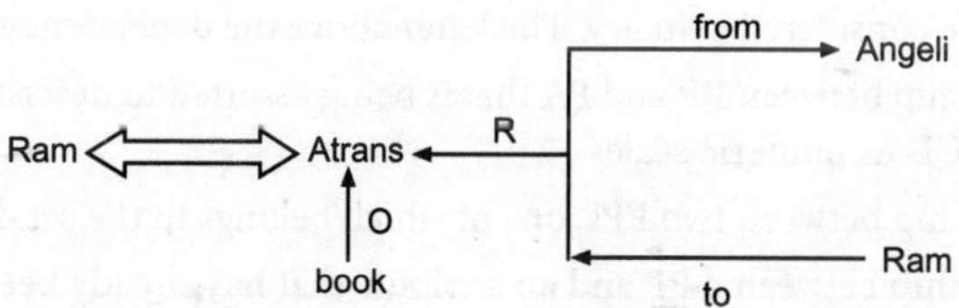

where the symbols used are—

a. **Arrow:** indicates the direction of dependency.
b. **Double arrow** indicates two-way link between actor and actions.
c. **ATRANS** is a primitive to describe this event.
d. *O* represents object case relationship.
e. *R* indicates recipient case relationship.

Example 2: The man took a watch

Man ⟺(p) ATRANS ←(O)— Watch

Here, 'men' is an actor and 'watch' is the object of the action 'took'.

Example 3: I gave John a book

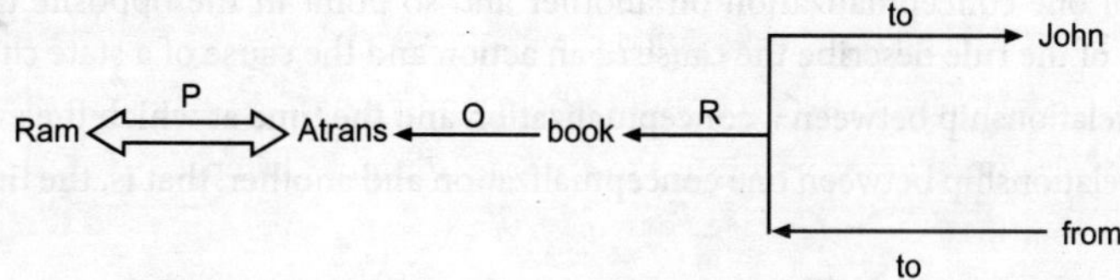

Many a times, actors are missing from a sentence. This is a challenge. For example. 'Rajiv fell', sentence has a missing actor as another force "gravity" was acting. In such cases, we need additional optional notations :

R = reason
r = results
i = intends
d = direction
I = Instrument
R = recipient, state change.

So, the sentence 'Rajiv fell' in CD is as follows —

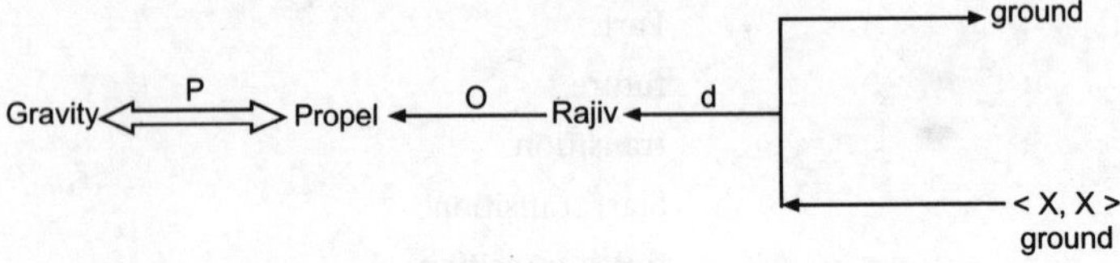

Parsing a sentence into *CD* representation is analogous to the process of parsing using a case grammar. The basic algorithm for building *CD* structure is as follows —

S1 : Obtain the root lexical item.

S2 : Access the lexical entry for the item and obtain the association tests and actions.

S3 : Perform the specified actions given with the entry.

We must study some rules for CD representation.

Rules of CD

Rule 1 describes the relationship between an actor and the event he or she causes. This is a two-way dependency since neither actor nor event can be considered primary. The letter above the dependency link indicates past tense.

Rule 2 describes the relationship between PP and PA that is being asserted to describe it. Many state descriptions, such as height, are represented in CD as numeric scales.

Rule 3 describes the relationship between two PPs, one of which belongs to the set defined by the other.

Rule 4 describes the relationship between a PP and an attribute that has already been predicated of it. The direction of the arrow is towards the PP being described.

Rule 5 describes the relationship between two PPs one of which provides a particular kind of information about the other. The three most common types of information to be provided in this way are procession (shown as POSS-BY), location (shown as LOC), and physical containment (shown as CONT). The direction of the arrow is again toward the concept being described.

Rule 6 describes the relationship between an ACT and the PP that is the object of that ACT. The direction of the arrow is toward the ACT since the context of the – specific ACT determines the meaning of the object relation.

Rule 7 describes the relationship between an ACT and the source and the recipient of the ACT. **Rule 8** describes the relationship between an ACT and the instrument with which it is performed. The instrument must always be a full conceptualization (*i.e.*, it must contain an ACT), not just a single physical object.

Rule 9 describes the relationship between an ACT and its physical source and destination. Rule 10 represents the relationship between a PP and a state in which it started and another in which it ended.

Rule 11 describes the relationship between one conceptualization and another that causes it. Notice that the arrows indicate dependency of one conceptualization on another and so point in the opposite direction of the implication arrows. The two forms of the rule describe the cause of an action and the cause of a state change.

Rule 12 describes the relationship between a conceptualization and the time at which the event occurred is described.

Rule 13 describes the relationship between one conceptualization and another, that is, the time of the first. The example for this rule also shows how CD exploits a model of the human information processing system; see is represented as the transfer of information between the eyes and the conscious processor.

Rule 14 describes the relationship between a conceptualization and the place at which it occurred.

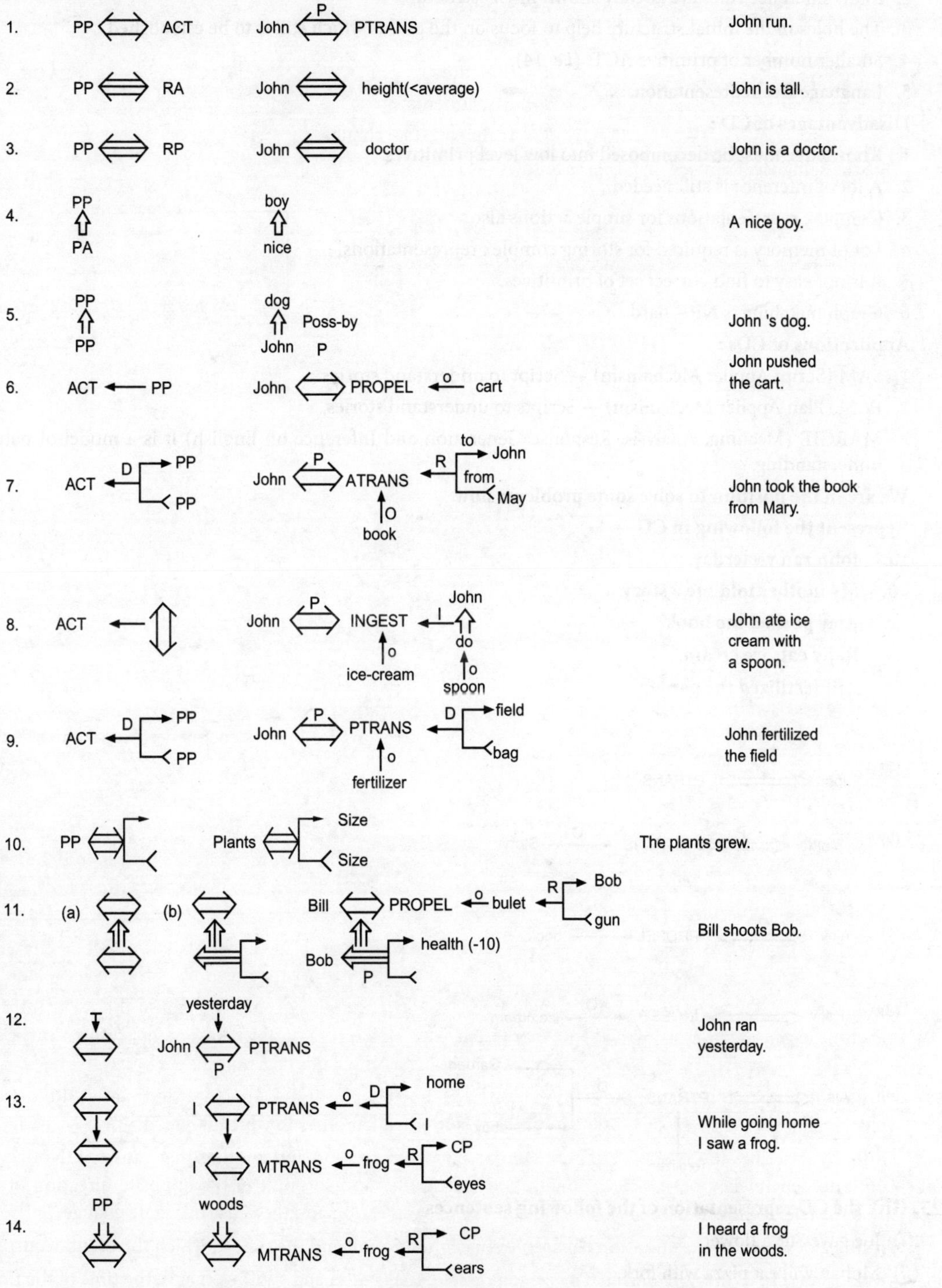

***Fig. 10.5:** Rules of CD*

Advantages of CD :

1. Lesser number of inference rules are required if we use CD primitives.
2. Many inference rules are already shown in CD structure.
3. The holes in the initial structure help to focus on the points which still is to be established.
4. Smaller number of primitive ACTs (*i.e.* 14).
5. Language free representation.

Disadvantages of CD :

1. Knowledge must be decomposed into low level primitives.
2. A lot of inference is still needed.
3. Complex representations for simple actions also.
4. Lot of memory is required for storing complex representations.
5. It is not easy to find correct set of primitives.
6. Graph matching is NP – hard.

Applications of CDs :

1. SAM (Script Applier Mechanism) — Script to understand stories.
2. PAM (Plan Applier Mechanism) — Scripts to understand stories.
3. MARGIE (Meaning, Analysis, Response Generation and Inference on English) It is a model of natural language understanding.

We are in the position to solve some problems now.

Q.24. Represent the following in CD —

a. **John ran yesterday.**

b. **My mother told me a story.**

c. **Ajay pushed the book.**

d. **Rajiv eats ice cream.**

e. **Ajit fertilized the garden.**

(a) John ⇔ PTRANS (P; yesterday)

(b) Mother ⇔ MTRANS (P) ← Story (O)

(c) Ajay ⇔ PROPEL (P) ← book (O)

(d) Rajiv ⇔ INGEST (P) ← ice cream (O)

(e) Ajit ⇔ PTRANS (P) ← D: → Garden, ← boy; O: fertilizer

Q.25. Give the CD representation of the following sentences.

(*i*) Joe gave Sue a flower.

(*ii*) Mohan will eat pizza with fork.

(*iii*) Charlie drove the car.

(*iv*) Since smoking can kill you, I stopped.

(*v*) Bill is a programmer.
(*vi*) Mary goes.
(*vii*) Mary will go.
(*viii*) Neeraj cried.
(*ix*) Bill threatened John with a broken nose.
(*x*) Anil punched Ram.
(*xi*) Ram lied.
(*xii*) Joe told Lucy he would not go to movies with her. Her feelings were hurt.
(*xiii*) Prem went to the park with peacocks.
(*xiv*) John will eat noodles with fork and knife.
(*xv*) Mohan is a sales manager.
(*xvi*) Kapil ate some soup.
(*xvii*) Mohan gave some books to Reeta.
(*xviii*) He will speak.
(*xix*) Anil will go tomorrow.
(*xx*) While going home, he saw a peacock.
(*xxi*) Ram heard noises in the kitchen.
(*xxii*) Hair is short.
(*xxiii*) Hari is a nice boy.

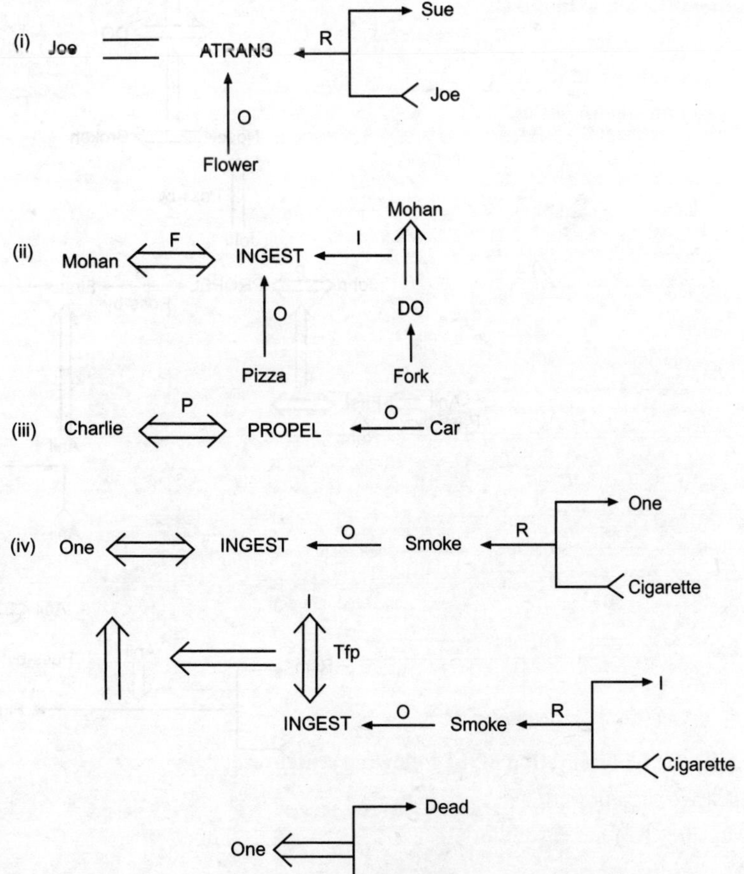

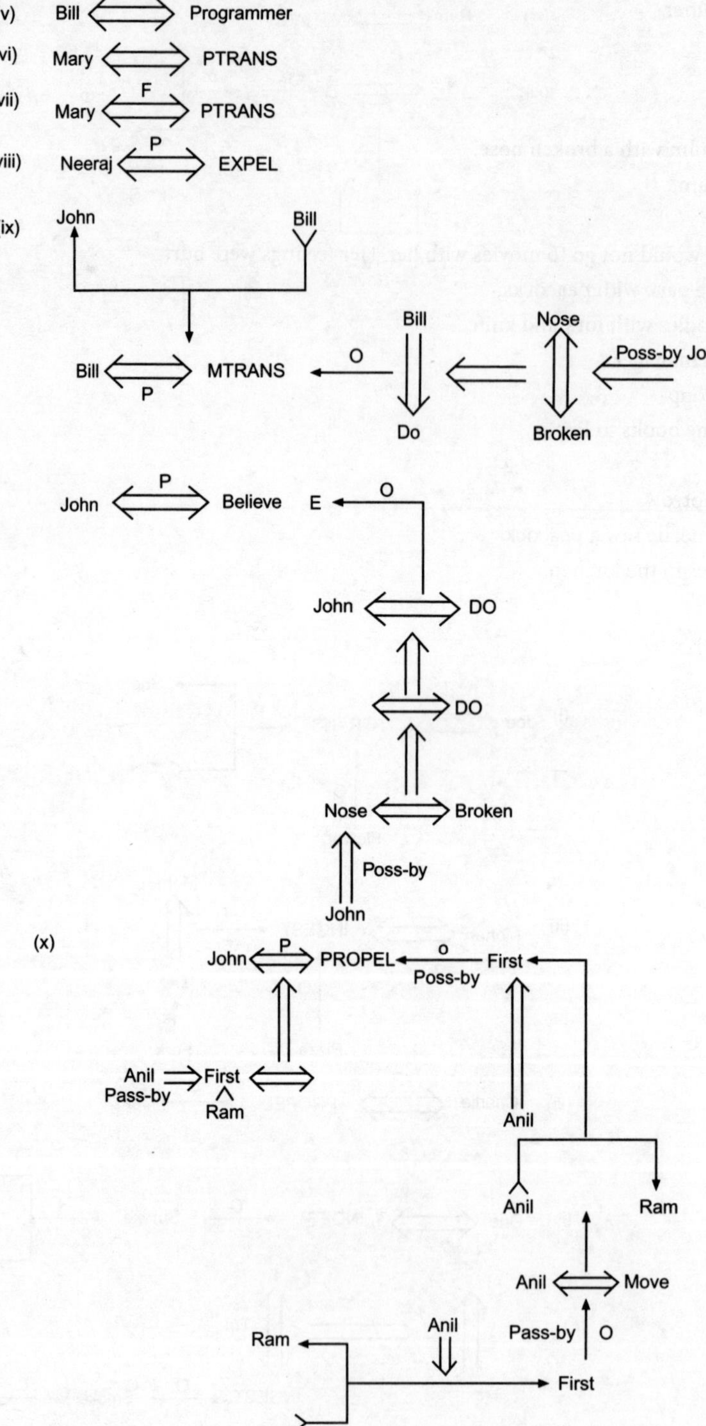
(v) Bill ⟺ Programmer
(vi) Mary ⟺ PTRANS
(vii) Mary ⟺F PTRANS
(viii) Neeraj ⟺P EXPEL
(ix) John
Bill
Bill
Nose
Poss-by John
Bill ⟺P MTRANS
O
Do
Broken
John ⟺P Believe
E
O
John ⟺ DO
DO
Nose ⟺ Broken
Poss-by
John
(x) John ⟺P PROPEL
o
First
Poss-by
Anil
Pass-by
First
Ram
Anil
Anil
Ram
Anil ⟺ Move
Anil
Pass-by
O
Ram
First

(xi) Ram ⟺(P) MTRANS

(xii) Joe ⟺ Spark ←(O) Words ←(R)

Joe ⟺ PTRANS ←(O) Joe ^ Lucy ←(D)

Joe ⟺ MTRANS ←(O)

Lucy ⟺ Happiness = – 10

(xiii) Prem ⟺ PTRANS ←(O) Prem ←(D) Park / Joe

Peacocks

Specify

(xiv) John ⟺(F) INGEST ←(I) John

Noodles

Do

Fork ^ knife

(xv) Mohan ⟺ Sales – manager

Joh

(xvi) Kapil ⟺ INGEST ← Kapil

O

Soup

Do

Spoon

(xvii) Mohan ⟺(P) INGEST ←(R) Pooja / Mohan

O

(xviii) He ⟺(F) Speak

Tomorrow

(xix) He ⟺(F) PTRANS

(xx) He ⟺ PTRANS ← He ← D (→ Home, ← He)

He ⟺ MTRANS ←O— Peacock

Kitchen

⇓

(xxi) He ⟺ MTRANS ←O— Noise ↑ (Cp, Ears)

(xii) Hari ⟺ Height [< average]

(xiii) Hari ⟺ Boy ← Nice

What are Conceptual Graphs : It is a graphical portrayal of a mental perception which consists of basic or primitive concepts and the relationships that exist between the concepts.

For example: "Joe is eating soup with a spoon" can be represented as follows:

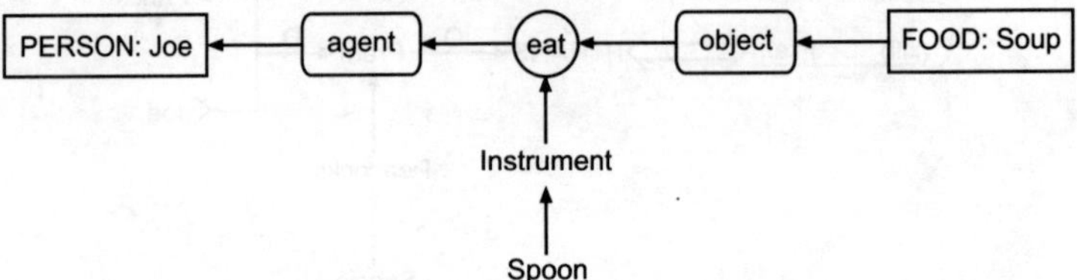

This is a conceptual graph. Concepts are enclosed in a boxes and relations between the concepts are enclosed in ovals. Concept symbol refers to entities, actions, properties or events in the world. A concept may be individual or generic. Individual concepts have a type field followed by a referent field. The concept PERSON JOE] HAS TYPE — PERSONS and referent Joe. Referents like Joe and a soup are called individual concepts since they refer to specific entities. EAT have no referent field since they are generic concepts which refer to unspecified entities.

A conceptual graph can also be represented linearly. It is represented by using upper & lowercase characters of alphabet, boxes circles, arcs and special characters including —, ?, !, *, #, @,
∀, ~, [,], (,), →, ←, } & }. The above graph can thus be represented as:

$$[\text{PERSON : Joe}] \leftarrow (\text{AGENT}) \leftarrow [\text{EAT}] -$$

$$(\text{OBJECT}) \rightarrow [\text{FOOD : Soup}]\ (\text{INSTRUMENT}) \rightarrow [\text{SPOON}]$$

where square brackets have replaced concept boxes, parentheses have replaced relation circles. The dash signifies continuation of the linear graph on the next line.

Example 2: The sentence "Every car has an engine" can be represented as a conceptual graph — [CAR : ∀] → (PART) → [ENGINE]

This conceptual graph can be converted into its FOPL as follows:

$$\forall x\, \exists y\, (\text{CAR}\,(x) \rightarrow (\text{ENGINE}\,(y)\ \&\ \text{PART}\,(x, y)))$$

We are in a position to solve examples now.

Q.26. Express the following concepts as an associative network structure —

Ans. Company ABC is a software development company. Three departments within the company are Sales, Administration & Programming. Joe is the manager of Programming. Bill and Sue are programmers. Sue is married to Sam. Sam is an editor for Prentice Hall. They have 3 children and they live on Elm Street. He wears glasses and is 5 feet 4 inches tall.

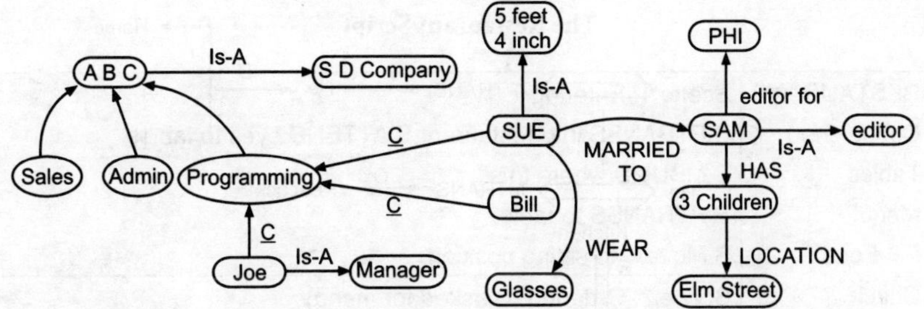

Q.27. Represent the following as an associative network.

Ans. "GGSIPU is a State University established by the Act of Parliament. It has 9 schools of studies and 12 divisions to support the academic activities at the headquarters. It has 44 regional centres spread over the whole country. Each school and division is headed by a Director and each regional centre is headed by a Regional Director".

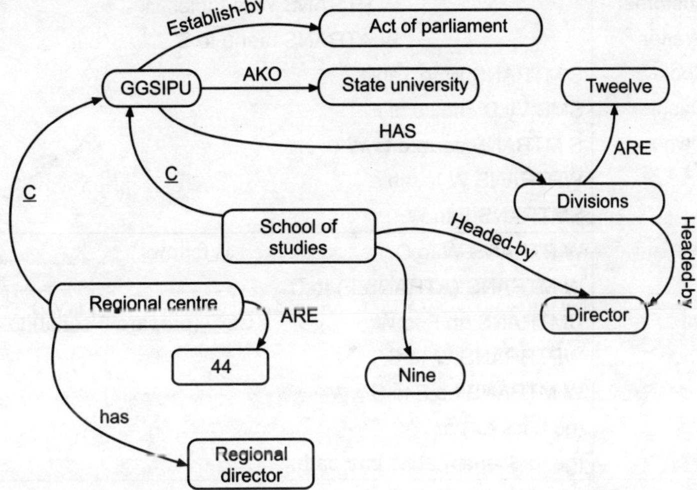

Q.28. What are Scripts? Give some examples.

Ans. A script is a structure that prescribes a set of circumstances which could be expected to follow on from one another. It is similar to a chain of situations which could be anticipated. Like a script for a play, the script's structure is defined in terms of —

a. Actors *b.* Roles

c. Props and *d.* Scenes

Please note that the slots in a script correspond to the parts of the event which are filled with CD primitives. It could be considered to consist of a number of slots or frames but with more specified robes. Scripts are frame-like structures to represent knowledge grouped from our common experiences like going to a movie, eating in a bar, visiting a doctor or shopping in a MALL etc.

Scripts are useful because —

a. Events tend to occur in known runs or patterns.

b. Entry conditions exist which allow an event to take place.

c. Casual relationships between events exist.

d. Prerequisites exist.

How reasoning is done?

To perform reasoning using scripts, a script with partially filled fields is created to meet the current situation. Then, a known script (which matches the current situation) is recalled from memory. The script name, preconditions or shear keywords provide index value which is used to search the current script. Inferencing is done by filling a slot with inherited and default values that satisfy certain conditions.

For example : We prepare a script of a Restaurant.

The Restaurant Script

Script : RESTAURANT	Scene 1: Entering
Track : Coffee shop	S PTRANSS into restaurant S ATTEND eyes to tables
Propos : Tables	S MBUILD where to sit
Menu	S PTRANSS to table
F = Food	S Move S to sitting position
Check	Scene 2: Ordering (S asked for menu)
Money	(Menu on table) (W brings menu) S MTRANS signal to W
	S PTRANS menu to S W PTRANS W to table
	SMTRANS 'need menu' to W
	W PTRANS W to menu
Roles: S = Customer	W PTRANS W to table
W = Waiter	W ATRANS menu to S
C = Cook	S MTRANS W to Table
M = Cashier	SMB VILD choice of F
O = Owner	S MTRANS squard to W
	WPTRANS W to table
	SMTRANS F to W
Entry conditions:	W PTRANS W to C
S is hungry.	W MTRANS (ATRANS F) to C
S has money.	CMTRANS no F to W CDO (prepare F script) to Scene3
	WPTRRANS W to S
	W MTRANS no F to S
	(go back to*) or
	(go to Scene 4 at no pay path)
Results:	
S has less money	Scene 3 : Eating CATRANS F to
O has more money.	ww ATRANS F to S S INGEST F
S is not hungry.	Option: REturm to Scene 2 to order more;
S is pleased (optional).	otherwise, go to scene 4
	Scene 4: Exiting
	MTRANS to W
	(W ATRANS check to S
	W MOVE (write check)
	W PTRANS W to S
	W ATRANS check to S
	S ATRANS tip to W
	S PTRANS S to M
	S PTRANS S to out of restaurant
	(No pay path)

Let us write an other script now.

Script Name: Interaction with car salesperson

PROPS	Scenes
Car showroom Car Feature Booklet Money Time	**Scene 1** • Customer enters the showroom • Search for a particular brand. • Salesperson attends customer and welcomes him
ROLES Customer Salesperson Owner Cashier	**Scene 2** • Sales person shows various cars • Customer selects particular car • Salesperson describes its features
INITIAL • Customer needs a car • Customer has more money • Salesperson has details about car • Availability of car in showroom • Owner has less money	**Scene 3** • Customer asks for a test drive • Salesperson takes him on a drive **Scene 4** • Customs is ready to buy • Customser asks for bill and warranty • Salesperson gets him warranty book and bill
RESULTS • Customer bought a car • Salesperson got commission • Customer has less money • Owner has more money • Particular car count decreases	**Scene 5** • Customer pays the money • Salesperson deposits it with cashier • Customer to gives commission to salesperson • Drives car back home

TRACKS none

Please note the following points about scripts:

1. If a particular script is to be applied then it must be activated and this activation depends on its significance.
2. If a topic is mentioned in passing then a pointer to that script could be held. Else if the topic is important then the script should be opened.
3. Having too many scripts is dangerous.
4. If events follow a known trail, then we can use scripts to represent the action involved and use them to answer detailed questions.
5. Different trails may be allowed for different outcomes of scripts.

Advantages of scripts :

a. They have ability to predict events.

b. A single coherent interpretation may be built up from a collection of observations.

Disadvantages of scripts :

a. They are less general than framer.

b. They are not suitable to represent all kinds of knowledge.

Applications of scripts : Shank and his team at YALE University used scripts in one system named as SAM — Script applier mechanism. SAM reads and reasons with text to demonstrate an understanding of stories that were script based.

SUMMARY

This chapter discusses about advanced knowledge representation techniques like frames, nets, CG, CD and scripts. KR is one of the critical aspects to make our computer behave intelligently.

MULTIPLE CHOICE QUESTIONS

1. **Data when processed gives information and Information when processed gives —**
   (*a*) Knowledge (*b*) Domain
   (*c*) Wisdom (*d*) None of these
2. **The knowledge about what we know is —**
   (*a*) Meta knowledge (*b*) Mini knowledge
   (*c*) Micro knowledge (*d*) None of the above
3. **Concepts, objects, nets, logic etc are the examples of**
   (*a*) Tacit knowledge (*b*) Explicit knowledge
   (*c*) Knowledge base (*d*) None of the above
4. **According to Robert Kowalski**
   (*a*) Logic = Algorithm + Control
   (*b*) Algorithm = Logic + Control
   (*c*) Algorithm = Logic – Control
   (*d*) None of the above
5. **The process of producing proofs by refutation or contradiction is known as —**
   (*a*) Resolution (*b*) Proposition
   (*c*) Unification (*d*) None of these
6. **The universal quantifier is —**
   (*a*) ∃ (*b*) ^
   (*c*) ∀ (*d*) =
7. **The process of eliminating existential quantifiers is known as**
   (*a*) Resolution (*b*) Skolemisatio
   (*c*) Unification (*d*) None of these
8. **The Recursive process of merging two or more predicates with constants or with some variables is known as —**
   (*a*) Resolution (*b*) Proposition
   (*c*) Unification (*d*) Proposition
9. **Forward chaining is a —**
   (*a*) Data-driven search (*b*) Goal-driven search
   (*c*) Heuristic search (*d*) None of the above.
10. **A CD primitive that is used to do mental transfer is -**
    (*a*) ATRANS (*b*) ATTRANS
    (*c*) PTRANS (*d*) MTRANS

ANSWERS

1. (*a*)	**2.** (*a*)	**3.** (*b*)	**4.** (*b*)	**5.** (*a*)
6. (*c*)	**7.** (*c*)	**8.** (*c*)	**9.** (*a*)	**10.** (*d*)

CONCEPTUAL SHORT QUESTIONS WITH ANSWERS

Q.1. What is chaining?

Ans. In inferencing process, the rules are applied in succession till a situation arrives that there is no rule which is applicable. It is called as chaining.

Q.2. What do you mean by a Universe of Discourse?

Ans. The universe of discourse or domain of discourse indicates the following —

a. A set of entities that quantifiers deal with.

b. Entities can be a set of integers, a set of real numbers, a set of students etc.

Universe is the domain of individual variables. Even propositions in logic are statement of an object of a universe.

Q.3. What is matching? Name some matching techniques.

Ans. In matching process, the LHS of rule is compared with the input and all rules that match are extracted. Actually, both the current state of the problem and its preconditions are matched with the LHS of the rule. This is known as matching. Some matching techniques are as follows —

a. Indexing

b. Matching with variable

c. Complex matching variable.

Q.4. What is a Horn clause?

Ans. In a logic, a Horn clause is a clause (a disjunction of literals) with at most one positive literal. A Horn clause with exactly one positive literal is a definite clause; a Horn clause with no positive literals is sometimes called a goal clause, especially in logic programming. A Horn formula is a conjunctive normal form formula whose clauses are all Horn; in other words, it is a conjunction of Horn clauses. A dual-Horn clause is a clause with at most one negative literal. Horn clauses play a basic role in logic programming and are important for constructive logic.

The following is an example of a definite Horn clause:

$$\neg P \wedge \neg q \vee .... \vee t \vee u$$

Such a formula can be rewritten in the following form, which is more common in logic programming and similar fields:

$$(p \wedge q \wedge ... \wedge t) \rightarrow u$$

The relevance of Horn clauses to theorem proving by first-order resolution is that the resolution of two Horn clauses is a Horn clause. Moreover, the resolution of a goal clause and a definite clause is again a goal clause. In automated theorem proving, this can lead to greater efficiencies in proving a theorem represented as a goal clause. In fact, Prolog is a programming language based on Horn clauses.

Horn clauses are also of interest in computational complexity, where the problem of finding a set of a variable assignments to make a conjunction of Horn clauses true is a P-complete problem, sometimes called HORNSAT. This is P's version of a boolean satisfiability problem, a central NP-complete problem.

> **NOTE:** The name "Horn clause" comes from the logician Alfred Horn who first pointed out the significance of such clauses.

Q.5 Represent the following in FOPL —

1. **Lipton is a tea.**
2. **Lata is a child who drinks tea.**
3. **Ruma dislikes children who drink tea.**
4. **Ruma disliked Lata.**

Ans. (*i*) Tea (Lipton)

(*ii*) $\exists x$ [child (x) $\wedge$ drinks (x, tea)]

$\exists x$ [child (Lata) $\wedge$ drinks (Lata, tea)]

(*iii*) $\forall x$ [drinks (x, tea) $\Rightarrow$ dislikes (Ruma, x)]

(*iv*) Dislikes (Ruma, Lata).

Q.6. Express following knowledge as a semantic network with nodes and labeled arcs. "Sam is Vice-President in ABC Corp. He is married to Kay and has a male child named Joe. Joe goes to school. Sam plays golf and owns a silver colored German-made car Mercedes Benz."

Ans. Semantic net diagram:

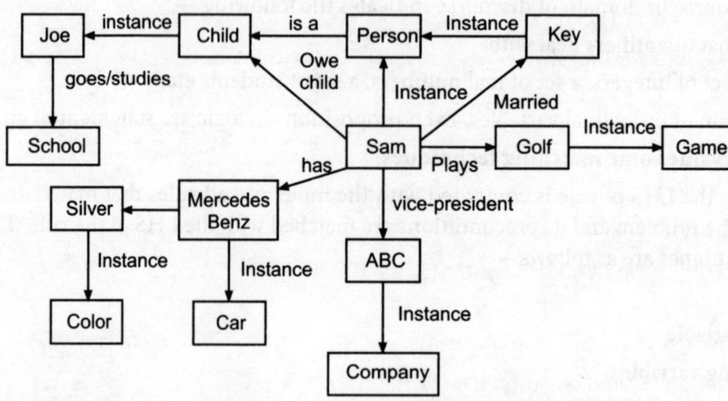

Q.7. Sam, Clyde and Oscar are elephants. We know the following facts about them —

***a.* Sam is pink.**

***b.* Clyde is gray and likes Oscar.**

***c.* Oscar is either pink or gray (but not both) and likes Sam.**

Use resolution to prove that gray elephants like pink elephant, *i.e.*, prove that

$$[\exists x, y][\text{grey}(x) \wedge \text{pink}(x) \wedge \text{likes}(x, y)\}$$

Ans. 'SAM is pink' can be represented as—

pink (Sam) ...(1)

Similarly, other two facts can be represented as—

grey (clyde) $\wedge$likes (clyde, oscar) ...(2)

and (pink (oscar) $\vee$ grey (oscar) $\wedge$ likes (oscar, sam) ...(3)

Given:

$[\exists x, y]$ [grey $(x) \wedge$ pink $(x) \wedge$ likes (x, y)]

Grey $[x]$ from 2 it implies—

Grey [Clyde] but does not fulfil the criteria of pink.

$\therefore$ from (3) we get–

Grey (Oscar), Pink (Oscar)

and also likes (Oscar, Sam)

$\therefore$ $x \Rightarrow$ Oscar

$y \Rightarrow$ Sam

It means that Oscar likes Sam

Q.8. Assume the following facts —

***a.* Steve only likes easy courses.**

***b.* Science courses are hard.**

***c.* All courses in the basket weaving department are easy**

***d.* BK301 is a basket weaving course.**

Use resolution to answer the questions— "What course would Steve like"?

Ans. Convert the given facts into predicates firstly –

1. like (steve, easy course) ...(1)
2. hard (Science, course) ...(2)
3. $\forall x \, \forall y$ [courses $(x, y) \rightarrow$ easy (x, y)]
4. Courses $(x, y =$ BK 301)

Now, we convert these predicates into clausal form—

1. $\forall x\ \forall y$ [course $(x, y) \rightarrow$ easy (x, y)]

   $\forall x\ \forall y$ [–course $(x, y) \vee$ easy (x, y)]

   $$\begin{bmatrix} Q\neg(\neg P) = \\ \&\neg(a \wedge b) = \neg a \vee \neg b) \\ \&\neg(a \vee b) = \neg a \wedge \neg b \end{bmatrix}$$

2. Course $(x, y = \text{BK } 301)$

   [$\forall x \forall y$ ($\neg$ course $(x, y) \vee$ easy (x, y)] $\wedge$ course $(x, y = \text{BK } 301)$

   $\Rightarrow$ easy $(x, \text{BK } 301)$ ...(3)

   This implies that BK301 is an easy course.

   Now, consider equation (1) and equation (3):

   Like (steve, easy course) $\wedge$ easy $(x, \text{BK301})$

   $\therefore$ Steve likes BK301

   Now, consider (1) and (2)

   Like (steve, easy course) $\wedge$ hard (Science, courses)

   $\Rightarrow$ steve doesn't like science What course would Steve like?

   It is clearly proved by equation (3) that Steve likes BK301

Q.9. Given two clauses— Loves (Father (*a*), *a*) and loves (*y*, *x*). What must be generated as a result of resolving these two clauses?

Ans. Given:

loves (Father (a), a) and loves (y, x) $a = x$

Father $(a) = y$ Father $(x) = y$

This means that Father of x is y.

Now, love (Father (a), a)

loves $(y, x) \vee$ loves (x, y)

loves (Father (a), a)loves (Father (a), a)

loves (y, x)	loves (x,y)
$\therefore$ Father $(a) = y$	$\therefore$ Father $(a) = x$
and $a = x$	and $a = y$

Which is NOT possible.

Thus, these two clauses cannot be unified.

Q.10. The following statements are given —

(*i*) Rishi likes to eat peanut.

(*ii*) Rishi eats whatever John eats.

(*iii*) John eats only eatables.

(*iv*) Anybody who eats eatables is a human being.

(*v*) Peanut is an eatable.

a. Convert these into wff and clausal form.

b. Is John a human being? Answer this using back tracking and resolution.

Ans. *a.* The WFF notations are—

1. Likes (Rishi, Peanut)
2. $\forall xy$ eats (Rishi, y) $\rightarrow$ eats (John, y)
3. $\forall y$ eats (John, y)

4. ∀x ∀y eats (x, y) → human being (x)
5. eatable (y = peanut)

Its clausal form is as follows —

1. Likes (Rishi, y1) ...(1)
2. ∀y eats (Rishi, y) → eats (John, y)
   ∀x ¬ eats (Rishi, y) ∧ eats (John, y)
   ∴ ¬ eats (Rishi, y2) ∨ eats (John, y2) ...(2)
3. ∀y eats (John, y) is
   eats (John, y3) ...(3)
4. ∀x ∀y eats (x, y) → human being (x)
   ∀x ∀y ¬ eats (x, y) ∨ human being (x)
   ∴ ¬ eats (x1, y4) ∨ human being (y4) ...(4)
5. eatable (y = peanut) is eatable (y5) ...(5)
6. Is John a human being?
   i.e. human being (John)

We start with opposite of this (*i.e.* negation)

¬ human being (John)

∴ Using back tracking and Resolutions we get — human being (John)

x1 = John x4 = eatable eats (John, eatable)eats (John eatables)

∴ It is proved that John is a human being.

Q.11. Assume the following facts —

a. **Ram likes only easy courses.**

b. **Engg. courses are hard.**

c. **All courses in Arts are easy.**

d. **AR04 is an Arts course.**

Use resolution to answer the question, "What course would Ram like?"

Ans. Let us find its Predicate clause firstly,

∃y easy (y) → likes (Ram, y)

∃y easy course (x) → hard (x)

∀x art course (x) → easy (x) art course(AR04)

∴ Its clausal form is—

like (Ram, easy courses)

hard course (Engineering)

easy (art courses)

AR04 (art course). Now, we use resolution to prove our query.

∴ Answer is: Ram likes AR04.

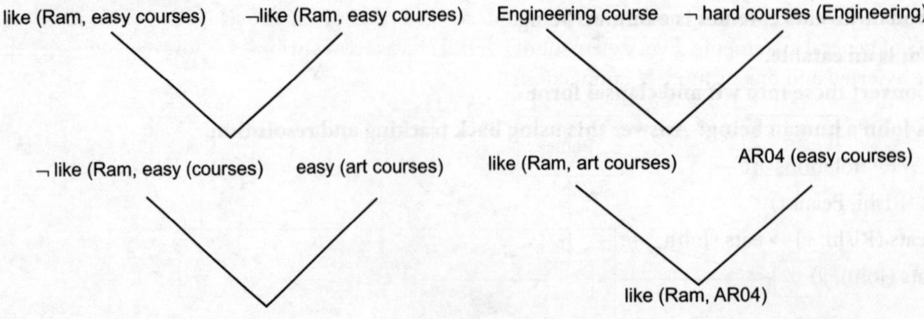

Q.12. Describe the term 'Partitioned Semantic Net'. Also construct a Partitioned semantic Net representation for the following:

a. **Every dog has bitten a mail carrier.**

b. **Every batter hits a ball.**

Ans. It is a representation for simple quantified expressions in a semantic net in which semantic net is partitioned into a hierarchical set of spaces each of which corresponds to the scope of one or more variable.

a. Consider a simple net corresponding to statement—"The dog bit the mail carrier", given below —

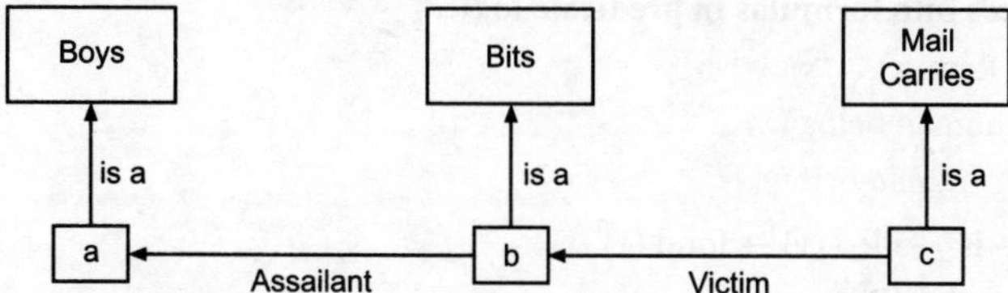

The nodes–Dogs, Bite and bitings and Mail carriers. Nodes *d*, *b* and m represent a particular dog, a particular biting and a particular Mail carrier. This fact can easily be represented by a single net with no partitioning. If we represent the fact "Every dog has bitten a mail carrier" or the logic.

$\forall x$ Dog$(x) \rightarrow \exists y$ Mail – carrier $(y) \wedge$ Bite (x, y)

Example,

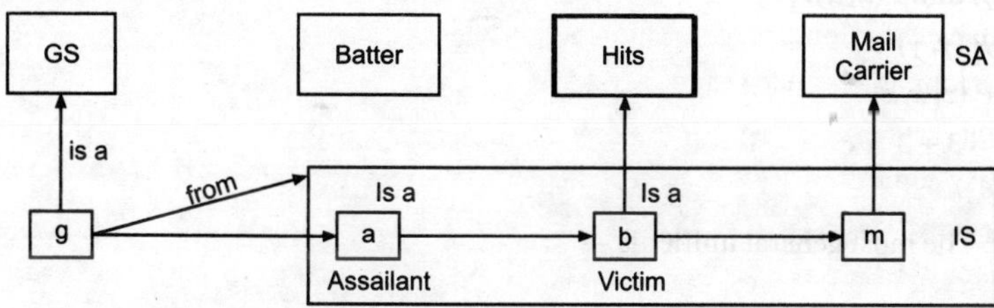

The node '*g*' stands for the assertion given above. Node *g* is an instance of special class of GS of general statements. Every element GS has at least two attributes, a form which states the relation that is being asserated. For every dog *d*, there exists a biting event b and a mail carrier m such that *d* is the assaitant of *b* and *m* is the victim.

b. Now, consider second statement—"Every batter hits a ball". The nodes batter, hit and ball represent classes of batter, hitting and ball while nodes *a*, *b*, c represent a particular batter, a particular hit and a particular ball *i.e.*,

$\forall x$ Batter $(x) \rightarrow \exists y$ Ball $(y) \wedge$ hit (x, y)

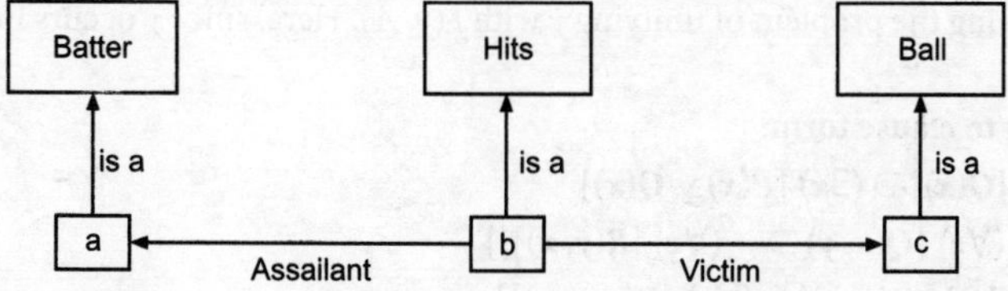

To represent this face, we take node g which stands for assertion given above. Node g is an instance of the special class GS of general statements. Every element of GS has at least two attributes, a form which states the relation that is being asserted and one or more $\forall$ connections.

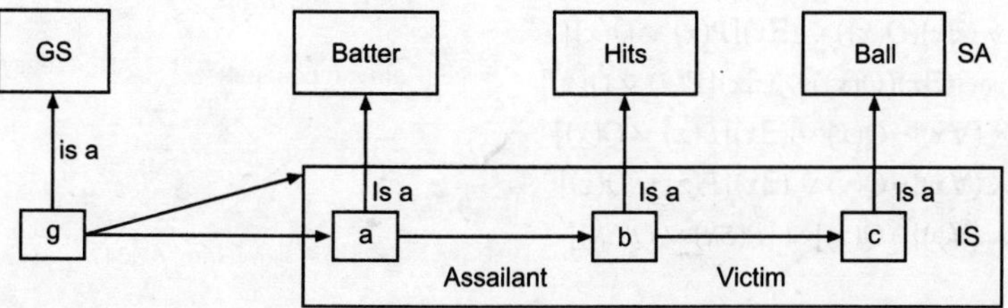

Q.13. Consider the following statements:

(i) Ram likes all kinds of food.

(ii) Apples are food.

(iii) Chicken is food.

(iv) Anything anyone eats and isn't killed by is food.

(v) Bill eats peanuts and is still alive.

(vi) Rita eats everything Bill eats.

Translate these sentences into formulas in predicate logic.

Ans. (i) $\forall x$ food $(x) \rightarrow$ likes (Ram, x)

(ii) food (Apples)

(iii) food (Chicken)

(iv) $\forall x\ \forall y$ eats $(y, x) \wedge \sim$ is _ killed $(y) \rightarrow$ food (x)

(v) eats (Bill, peanuts) $\wedge$ alive (Bill)

(vi) $\forall x$ eats (Bill, x) $\rightarrow$ eats (Rita, x)

Q.14. Say, whether or not the following pairs of expressions are unifiable and show the most general unifier for each unifiable pair —

a. $P(x, B, B)$ and $P(A, y, z)$

b. $P(g(f(v)), g(u))$ and $P(x, x)$.

c. $P(x, f(x0)$ and $P(y, y)$

d. $P(y, y, B)$ and $P(z, x, z)$

e. $2 + 3 = x$ and $x = 3 + 3$

Ans.

a. Yes, is unifiable. The most general unifier is —

$A / x, B / y, B / z$

b. Yes". Unifier is $g(u)/x, f(v)/u$

c. No. It doesn't unify.

d. Yes. $B/z, B/y, B/x$

e. Yes. First replace x by y in 2nd expression (standardizing variables) then $(2 + 3)/y$ and $(3 + 3)/x$.

Q.15. Explain why $P(f(x, x), A)$ does not unify with $P(f(y, f(y, A)), A)$.

Ans. The problem involves an attempt to unify $f(x, x)$ with $f(y, f(y, A))$. In these expressions, the outer fs match and y can be substituted for x leaving the problem of unifying y with $f(y, A)$. Here, since y occurs in $f(y, A)$, these two expressions cannot be unified.

Q.16. Convert the following to clause form:

1. $(\exists x)\ [P(x)] \vee ((\exists x)\ [Q(x)] \supset (\exists x)\ [P(x) \vee Q(x)]$

2. $(\forall x)\ [P(x) \supset (\forall y)\ [(\forall z)\ [Q(x, y) \supset \neg\ (\forall z)\ [R(y, x)]]]$

3. $(\forall x)\ [P(x) \supset (\exists x)\ [(\forall z)\ [Q(x, y)] \vee (\forall z)\ [R(x, y, z)]]$

4. $(\forall x)\ [P(x) \supset Q(x, y)] \supset ((x, y)\ [P(y)] \wedge (\exists z)\ [Q(y, z)])$

Ans.

1. $((\forall x)\ [P(x)] \vee ((\exists x)\ [Q(x)] \supset (\exists x)\ [P(x) \vee Q(x)]$

$(\neg((\exists x)[P(x)] \vee (\exists x)(Q(x)) \vee (\exists x)[P(x) \vee Q(x)]$

$(\neg((\exists x)[P(x)] \wedge \neg(\exists x)(Q(x)) \vee (\exists x)[P(x) \vee Q(x)]$

$((\forall x)[\neg P(x)] \wedge (\forall x)!\neg Q(x) \vee (\exists x)[P(x) \vee Q(x)]$

$((\forall x)[\neg P(x)] \wedge (\forall x)!\neg Q(y) \vee (\exists x)[P(z) \vee Q(z)]$

$((\forall x)[\neg P(x)] \wedge (\forall y)[\neg Q(y)] \vee [P(Sk) \vee Q(Sk)]$

$(\forall x)(\forall z)[[\neg P(x)] \wedge Q(y)] \vee [P(Sk) \vee Q(Sk)]]$

$[\neg P(x) \wedge Q(y)] \vee [P(Sk) \vee Q(sk)]$

$[\neg P(x) \wedge P(Sk) \vee Q(Sk)] \wedge [\neg Q(y) \vee P(Sk) \vee Q(Sk)]]$

$[\neg P(x) \wedge P(Sk), Q(Sk)][\neg Q(z) \vee P(Sk) \vee Q(Sk)]$

2. $(\forall x)\ [P(x) \supset (\forall y)\ [(\forall z)\ [Q(x, y)] \supset \neg (\forall z)\ [R(y, x)]]]$

$(\forall x)[\neg P(x) \vee (\forall y)[(\forall z)Q(x, y)] \supset \neg (\forall z)[R(y, x)]]]$

$(\forall x)[\neg P(x) \vee (\forall y)]\neg (\forall z)[Q(x, y)] \vee \neg (\forall z)[R(y, x)]]]$

$(\forall x)[\neg P(x) \vee (\forall y)][(\exists z)]\neg Q(x, y) \vee (\exists z)[\neg R(y, x)]]]$

$(\forall x)[\neg P(x) \vee (\forall y)](\exists z)[\neg Q(x, y)] \vee (\exists z)[\neg R(y, x)]]]$

$(\forall x)[\neg P(x) \vee (\forall y)[\neg Q(x, y) \vee \neg R(y, x)]]]$

$(\forall x(\forall y)\neg P(x) \vee \neg Q(x, y) \vee \neg R(y, x)]$

$\neg P(x) \vee \neg Q(x, y) \vee \neg R(y, x)$

$\}\neg P(x), \neg Q(x, y), \neg R(y, x)\}$

3. $(\forall x)\ [P(x) \supset (\exists x)\ [(\forall z)\ [Q(x, y)] \vee (\forall z)\ [R(x, y, z)]]$

$(\forall x)\ [\neg (\forall x)\ [P(x)] \vee (\exists x)\ [(\forall z)[Q(x, z)] \wedge (\forall z)[R(x, y, z)]]$

$(\forall y)[(\exists x)[\neg P(x)] \vee (\exists x)[(\forall z)[Q(x, z)] \vee (\forall z)[R(x, y, z)]]]$

$(\forall y)[(\exists x)[\neg P(x)] \vee (\exists x)[(\forall z)[Q(t, z)] \vee (\forall u)[R(t, y, u)]]]$

$(\forall y)[\neg P(f_1\ (y)) \vee (\forall z)[Q(f_2\ (y), z)] \vee (\forall u)[R(f_2\ (y), y, u)]]]$

$(\forall y)(\forall z)(\forall u)[\neg P(f_1\ (y)) \vee Q(f_2\ (y), z)] \vee R(f_2\ (y), y, u)]$

$\neg P(f_1\ (y) \vee Q(f_2\ (y), z) \vee R(f_2\ (y), y, u)$

$\{\neg P(f_1\ (y)), Q(f_2\ (y)), z), R(f_2\ (y), y, u)\}$

4. $(\forall y)[(\forall x)[P(x) \supset Q(x, y)] \supset ((\exists y)[P(y)] \wedge (\exists z)\ [Q\ (y, z)]]]$

$(\forall y)\ [\neg (\forall x)P(x) \supset Q(x, y)] \vee (\exists y)\ [P(y)] \wedge (\exists z)[Q(y, z))]]$

$(\forall y)\ [\neg (\forall x)[\neg P(x) \vee Q(x, y)] \vee ((\exists y)\ [P(y)] \wedge (\exists z)[Q(y, z)]]]$

$(\forall y)\ [(\exists x)\ [P(x) \wedge \neg Q(y, z))] \vee ((\exists y)[P(y)] \wedge (\exists z)[Q(y, z)]]]$

$(\forall y)\ [(\exists x)\ [P(x) \wedge \neg Q(y, z))] \vee ((\exists u)[P(u)] \wedge (\exists z)[Q(y, z)]]]$

$(\forall y)\ [[P(f_1(y)) \wedge \neg Q(f_1(y), y)] \vee [P(f_2\ (y)) \wedge Q(z, f_2\ (y))]]]$

$(\forall y)\ [[P(f_1(y)) \vee P(f_2\ (y))] \wedge [P(f_2\ (y)) \vee Q(y, f_2\ (y))]]] \wedge [\neg Q(f_1(y), y) \vee P(f_2\ (y))] \wedge [\neg Q(f_1\ (y), y) \vee Q(y, f_2\ (y))]]$

$[P(f_1\ (y)) \vee P(f_1\ (y))] \wedge [P(f_1\ (y_1) \vee Q(y, f_3\ (y)] \wedge [\neg Q(f_1\ (y_1, y) \vee P(f_2\ (y)] \wedge [\neg Q(f_2\ (y_1, y), Q(y, f_2\ (y))]]$

$[(\exists x)P(x)] \supset Q(A)$

$[\neg (\exists x)P(x)] \vee Q(A)$

$[(\forall x)\neg P(x)] \vee Q(A)$

$[(\forall x)[\neg P(x)] \vee Q(A)]$

$[(\forall x)][P(x)] \supset Q(A)]$

After this transformation, we recognize that any formula of the form $\gamma \supset \gamma$ is valid. Analogous operations on the second formula show that it too is valid.

The third formula is an instance of the well-known invalid formula $(\exists x)\ \gamma\ (x) \supset (\forall x)\ \gamma\ (x)$.

A counter example is $P(a)$ is False. $P(B)$ is True, and $Q(A)$ is False (for A being some element of the domain).

Q.17. Convert the following formula into one that has neither an existential quantifier nor a Skolem function.

$(\forall x, y)\{\exists z)[0n(x, z) \wedge \text{Above}\ (z, y)] \supset \text{Above}\ (x, y)\}$?

Ans. We use the following steps:

$(\forall x, y)\{\exists z)[0n(x, z) \wedge \text{Above}\ (z, y)] \supset \text{Above}\ (x, y)\}$

$(\forall x, y)\{\neg\ \exists z)[0n(x, z) \wedge \text{Above}\ (z, y)] \vee \text{Above}\ (x, y)\}$

$(\forall x, y)\{(\forall z)\ \neg\ \{0n(x, z) \wedge \text{Above}\ (z, y)\} \vee \text{Above}\ (x, y)\}$

$(\forall x, y)\{(\forall z)\{\neg On(x, z) \vee \neg \text{Above}(z, y)\} \vee \text{Above}(x, y)\}$

$(\forall x, y, z)[\neg On(x, z) \vee \neg \text{Above}(z, y) \vee \text{Above}(x, y)]$

An equivalent form is:

$(\forall x, y, z)\{[On(x, z) \wedge \text{Above}(z, y)] \supset \text{Above}(x, y)]$

Q.18. Use resolution refutation on a set of clauses to prove that there is a green object if we are given:

- **If pushable objects are blue, then nonpushable ones are green.**
- **All objects are either blue or green but not both.**
- **If there is a nonpushable object then all pushable ones are blue.**
- **Object 01 is pushable.**
- **Object 02 is not pushable.**

1. **Convert these statements to expressions in first-order predicate calculus.**
2. **Convert the preceding predicate-calculus expressions to clause form.**
3. **Combine the preceding clause form expressions with the clause form of the negation of the statement to be proved and then show the steps used in obtaining a resolution refutation.**

Ans.

1. 1. $(\forall x)[P(x) \supset B(x)] \supset (\forall x)[\neg P(x) \supset G(x)]$
   2. a. $(\forall x)[B(x) \supset \neg G(x)]$
   2 b. $(\forall x)[G(x) \vee B(x)]$
   3. $(\exists x)\ \neg P(x) \supset (\forall x)[P(x) \supset B(x)]$ 4. P(01)
   5. $\neg P(02)$
2. 1 a. $P(SK) \vee P(x) \vee G(x)$
   1 b. $\neg B(SK) \vee P(x) \vee G(x)$
   2 a. $\neg B(x) \vee \neg G(x)$
   2 b. $B(x) \vee G(x)$
   3. $P(x) \vee \neg P(y) \vee B(y)$
   4. $P(01)$
   5. $\neg P(02)$
3. 6. (negation of theorem): $\neg G(x)$
   7. (resolving 6 and 2*b* yields) $B(x)$
   8. (resolving 7 and 1*b* yields) $P(x) \vee G(x)$
   9. (resolving 8 and 5 yields) $G(02)$
   10. (resolving 9 and 6 yields) contradiction.

Q.19. The function cons(*x*, *y*) denotes the list formed by inserting the element *x* at the made of the list *y*. We denote the empty list by Nil; the list (2) by cons (2, Nil); the list (1, 2) by cons (1, cons (2, Nil)); and so on. The formula Last (1, *e*) is intended to mean that

***i.e.* the last element of the list 1. We have the following axioms:**

- **$(\forall u)$ [Last(cons(*u*, Nil), *u*)]**
- **$(\forall x\ y\ z)$ [Last(*y*, *z*) $\supset$ Last(cons(*x*, *y*), *z*)]**

1. **Prove the following theorem from these axioms by the method of resoltion refutation: $(\exists v)$[Last(cons(2, cons(1, Nil)), *v*)]**
2. **Use answer extraction of find *v*, the last element of the list (2, 1).**

Ans.

1. We first write the axioms in clause form:
   a. Last(cons(*u*, Nil), *u*)

b. ¬Last(*y*, *z*) ∨ Last(cons(*x*, *y*), *z*)

We then negate the goal to get:

c. ¬Last(cons(2, cons(1, Nil)), *v*)

Resolving (*b*) and (*c*), with m.g.u. {2/*x* cons(1, Nil/*y*, *v*/*z*), we get

d. ¬Last(cons(1, Nil), *v*)

We can now resolve (*a*) and (*b*) with m.g.u. {1/*e*, 1/*v*} to get the empty clause.

2. The axioms (a) and (b) are the same as in part (1). In order to do answer extraction a predicate Ans (v) is appended to the clause containing the negated goal:

e. ¬Last(cons(2, cons(1, Nil)), *v*) ∨ Ans(*v*)

Resolving (*b*) and (*e*), with m.g.u {2/x, con(1, Nil)/*y*, *v*/*z*}, we get:

f. ¬Last(cons(1, Nil), *v*) ∨ Ans(*v*)

We can now resolve (*a*) and (*f*) with m.g.u. {1/*u*, 1/*v*} to get:

g. Ans (1)

Therefore the last element of the list (2, 1) is 1.

Q.20. A logic circuit has four wires W1, W2, W3 and W4. It has an "and gate". A, and an "inverter", B. The input wires, W1 and W2, can be either "on" or not. If the and gate, A, is functioning properly (OK), wire W3 is "on" if and only if wires W1 and W2 both are "on". If the inverter, B, is functioning properly (OK), wire W4 is "on" if and only if wire W3 is not "on". Translate it into a set of WFFs.

Ans. $\{P(f_1(y)), P(f_2(y))\}, \{P(f_1(y)), Q(y, f_3(y))\}$

$\{\neg Q(f_1(y), y), P(f_2(y))\}, \{\neg Q(f_1(y), y), Q(y, f_3(y))\}$

$\{P(f_1(y)), P(f_2(y_1))\}, \{P(f_1(y_2)), Q(y, f_3(y_2))\}$

$\{\neg Q(f_1(y_3), y_3), P(f_2(y_3))\}, \{\neg Q(f_1(y_4), y_4), Q(y_4, f_3(y_4))\}$

Q.21. We are given following paragraph

Tony, Mike and John belong to the Alpine Club. Every member of the Alpine Club is either a skier or a mountain climber or both. No mountain climber likes rain, and all skiers like snow. Mike dislikes whatever Tony likes and likes whatever Tony dislikes. Tony likes rain and snow.

Represent this information by predicate-calculus sentences in such a way that you can represent the question "Who is a member of the Alpine Club who is a mountain climber but not a skier?" as a predicate-calculus expression. Use resolution refutation with answer extraction to answer it.

Ans. One translation is the set of formulas Member(Tony, Alpineclub) Member(Mike, Alpineclub) Member(John, Alpneclub)

(∀*x*)[Member(*x*Alpineclub) ⊃ (Skier(*x*) ∨ MC(*x*))]¬(∃*x*)[MC(*x*) ∧ Likes(*x*, Rain)]

(∀*x*)[Skier(*x*) ⊃ Likes(*x*,Snow)}

(∀*x*)[Skier(Tony, *x*) ∧ ¬Likes(Mike, *x*)}

Likes(Tony, Rain) ∧ Likes(Tony,Snow)

The question is:

(∃*x*) [Member(*x*, Alpineclub) ∧ MC(*x*) ∨ Skier(*x*)]

The clause forms of these sentences are:

1. Member(Tony, Alpineclub)
2. Member(Mike, Alpineclub)
3. Member(John, Alpineclub)
4. ¬Member(x, Alpineclub) ∨ Skier(*x*), MC(*x*)
5. ¬MC(*x*) ∨ ¬Likes(*x*, Rain)
6. ¬Skier(*x*) ∨ Likes(*x*,Snow)

7*a*. ¬Likes(Tony, *x*) ∨ ¬Likes(Mike, *x*)

7*b*. Likes(Tony, *x*) ∨ Likes(Mike, *x*)

8*a*. Likes(Tony, Rain)

8*b*. LIkes(Tony, Snow)

The clause form of the negation of the theorem to be proved (with Ans literal) is:

9. ¬Member(*x*, Alpineclub) ∨ ¬MC(*x*) ∨ Skier(*x*) ∨ Ans(*x*)

The refutation is:

10. ¬Member(*x*, Alpineclub), (Skier(*x*) ∨ Ans(*x*) resolving 9 with 4
11. Skier(Mike)/Ans(Mike) resolving 11 and 2
12. Likes(Mike, skier) ∨ ans (Mike) resolving 12 with 8
13. ¬Likes(Tony,Skiew) ∨ Ans(Mike) resolving 12 with 7a
14. Ans(Mike) resolving 13 with 8*b*.

Q.22. Sam, Clyde and Oscar are elephants. We know the following facts about them:

1. **Sam is pink.**
2. **Clyde is gray and likes Oscar.**
3. **Oscar is either pink or gray (but not both) and likes Sam.**

Use resolution refutation to prove that a gray elephant likes pink elephant; that is, prove (∃*x*, *y*)[Gray(*x*) ∧ Pink(*y*) ∧ Likes(*x*, *y*)]

Ans. The clauses and negation of the theorem to be proved are:

1. P(Sam)
2. G(Clyde)
3. L(Clyde, Oscar)
4. P(Oscar) ∨ G(Oscar)
5. L(Oscar, Sam)
6. ¬*G*(*x*) ∨ ¬*P*(*y*) ∨ ¬*L*(*x*, *y*) The resolution refutation is:
7. ¬G(Clyde) ∨ ¬P(Oscar) from 3 and 6
8. ¬P(Oscar) from 2 and 7
9. ¬G(Oscar) ∨ ¬P(Sam) from 5 and 6
10. ¬G(Oscar) from 1 and 9
11. P(Oscar) from 10 and 4
12. Nil from 11 and 8.

Q.23. Consider the following circuit diagram —

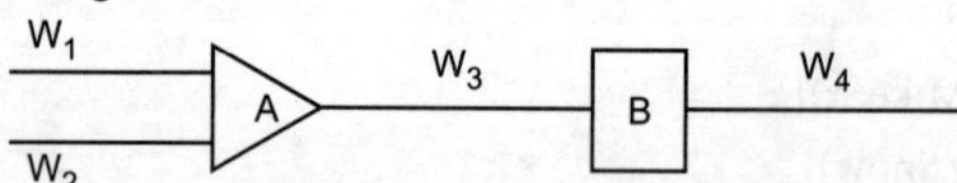

1. Use expression like ON(A), ON(W1) and so on to describe the funtioning of the circuit as defined.
2. Using the formulas describing the functioning of the circuit and assuming that all components are functioning properly and that wires W1 and W2 are "on" use resolution to show that wire W4 is not "on".
3. Again, using the formulas describing the functioning of the circuit and given that wires W1 and W2 are "on" but that wire W4 is also "on", use resolution to show that either the and gate or the inverter is not functioning properly.

Ans.

1. (*a*) OK(A) ⊃ [0n(W1) ∧ 0n(W)] ≡ 0n(W3)]

   (*b*) OK(B) ⊃ [0n(W3) ≡ ¬0n(W4)]

2. The clause forms of the above formulas are:

   (a1) ¬ OK(A) ∨ ¬ 0n(W2) ∨ 0n(W3)

   (*a*2) ¬ OK(A) ∨ ¬ 0n(W3) ∨ 0n(W1)

(a3) ¬ OK(A) ∨ ¬ On(W3) ∨ On(W2)

(b1) ¬ OK(B) ∨ ¬ On(W3) ∨ ¬ On(W4)

(b2) ¬ OK(B) ∨ ¬ On(W4) ∨ ¬ On(W3)

Here is a resolution refutation showing that W4 is not "on"

1. On(W4) negation of theorem
2. ¬ OK(B) ∨¬ On(W3) resolving 1 with b1
3. ¬ On(W3)

   resolving 2 with hypothesis, OK(B)
4. ¬OK(A) ∨ ¬ On(W1) ∨ ¬ On(W2) resolving 3 with a1
5. Nil successively resolving 4 with hypotheses, OK(A), On(W1), On(W2)

3. (1a) OK(A) negation of theorem

   (1b) OK(B) negation of theorem

   2. ¬ On(W1) ∨ ¬On(W2) ∨ On(W3) resolving 1a with a1
   3. On(W3) successively resolving 2 with hypotheses, On(W1) and On(W2)
   4. ¬OK(B) ∨ ¬ On(W4) resolving 3 with b1
   5. ¬ OK(B) resolving 4 with hypothesis, On(W4)
   6. Nil resolving 5 with lb.

Q.24. 1. Express as predicate-calculus wffs the information in the semantic network shown here. Take care that the wffs are written in such a way that they explicitly state the inheritance cancellation information that is implicit in the inheritance hierarchy.

2. Can you prove that Fido has four legs from your predicate-calculus wffs? If not, what information would you need to add in order to complete the proof?

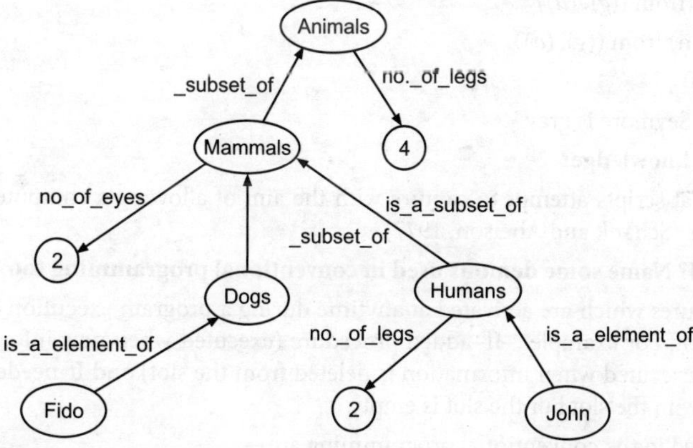

Ans. 1. The equivalent wffs are:

Def(Fido) Human(John)

$(\forall x)[\text{Dog}(x) \supset \text{Mammal}(x)]$

$(\forall x)[\text{Mammal}(x) \supset \text{Anjaml}(x)]$

$(\forall x)[\text{Human}(x) \supset \text{Mammal}(x)]$

$(\forall x)[[\text{Mammal}(x) \wedge \neg \text{Human}(x)] \supset \text{Haslegs}(x, 4)]$

$(\forall x)[\text{Human}(x) \supset \text{Haslegs}(x, 2)]$

$(\forall x)[\text{Mammal}(x) \supset \text{Haslegs}(x, 2)]$

2. We cannot prove Haslegs(Fido, 4) from these wffs. We would have to add¬ Human(Fido). Or we could add something more general, such as $(\forall x)[\text{Dog}(x) \supset \neg\text{Human}(x)]$.

Q.25. For the two examples shown here, pick the most appropriate knowledge representation system and encode the statements of the examples in the selected representation. Use your representation and a reasoning system appropriate to it to answer the question in each example. Example in some detail how the reasoning system arrives at the answer- showing resolution refutations, for example, if a reasoning system based on resolution is used. Use diagrams if they are helpful in your explanations.

1. Typically, birds fly. Ostriches are birds. Oliver is an ostrich. Ostriches do not fly. Q. Does Oliver fly?
2. Seymore is an elephant and John's friend. All elephants are gray or a friend of Bert. No friend of Bert is a friend of John. Q. Is Seymore gray?

Ans.

1. Here because of the nonmonotonic character of the statements, we might use a semantic network with property inheritance and cancellation of inheritance. In this case, we would have the fact the birds fly associated with the BIRDS node and the fact that ostriches do not fly associated with the OSTRICHES node. The OSTRICHES node is a descendant of the BIRDS node, and therefore, the fact that ostriches do not fly cancels the fact the birds do. Since Oliver is an ostrich, we conclude from the net that Oliver does not fly. (Note that the net formalism would allow us to say, in addition, that Oliver does fly, which we might do it we had some special information that Oliver was some sort of mutant flying ostrich).
2. Here we might use the predicate calculus because we have disjunction and statements that are difficult to reason with in semantic networks. The predicated encoding and resolution refutation for this problem are as follows
   a. EI (Sey)
   b. Friend(Sey, John)
   c. ¬El(x) ∨ Gray(x) ∨ Friend(x Bert)
   d. ¬Friend(x, Bert) ∨ ¬ Friend(x, John)
   e. ¬Grey(Sey) (negation of theorem)
   f. ¬EL(Sey) ∨ Friends(Sey, Bert) from((*c*), (*e*))
   g. Friend(Sey, Bert) from ((*g*), (*d*))
   h. ¬Friend(Sey, John) from ((*g*), (*d*))
   i. Nil from ((*h*), (*b*))

   So, we have proved that Seymore is gray.

Q.26. What is a stereotypical knowledge?

Ans. A type of knowledge that scripts attempt to capture with the aim of allowing a computer to make similar inferences about incomplete stories (Schank and Abelson, 1977).

Q.27. What are demons in AI? Name some demons used in conventional programming too.

Ans. Demons are the procedures which are activated at anytime during a program execution depending on the conditions evaluated in demon itself. For example. –If–added procedure (executed when new information is placed in the slot), If-removed procedure (executed when information is deleted from the slot) and If-needed procedure (executed when information is needed from the slot but the slot is empty.

Examples of demons used in the conventional programming are—

a. Error detection
b. Default commands.
c. End-of-File detection (EOF).

Q.28. Given are the axioms in clause form:

1. Man (Marcus)
2. Pompeian (Marcus)
3. ~Pompeian (al) v Roman (al)
4. Ruler (Caesear)
5. ~Roman (a_2) v loyal (a_2 Caesar) *v* hate (a_2, Caesar)
6. Loyal (a_3, $f_1(a_3)$)

7. **~Main (a_4) v ~ ruler (b_1) v ~ assassin (a_4, b_1) v loyal (a_4, b_1)**
8. **assassin (Marcus, Caesar)**

Give resolution proof of hate(Marcus, Caesar).

Ans. To prove :-

Did Marcus hate Caesar?

We negate this statement as

~hate (Marcus, Caesar)

There is no axiom in clausal form starting with literal ~ hate.

Prove ~ hate (Marcus, Caesar)

Clause ~ hate (Marcus, Caesar)

Clause 5 has hate

~Roman (a_2) v loyal (a_2 Caesar) v hate (a_2 Caesar)

a_2 is Marcus we have clause as

~Roman (Marcus) v Loyal (Marcus, Caesar) v hate (Marcus Caesar)

Resolving both we get :-

~Roman (Marcus) v loyal (Marcus, Caesar)

Now select 3 clausal form.

~ Pompeian (a_1) v Roman (a_1) where a_1 is Marcus.

Statement will be

~ Pompeian (Marcus) V Roman (Marcus)

We get new clause after resolving.

C1: ~Roman (Marcus) v loyal (Marcus, Caesar)

C2: ~ Pompeian (Marcus) v Roman (Marcus)

Resolvent is ~ Pompeian (Marcus) v loyal (Marcus, Caesar)

Now take clause 2 which is

Pompeian (Marcus)

Resolvent is loyal (Marcus, Caesar)

Now C1 is loyal (Marcus, Caesar)

Select 7th axiom as:

~man (a_4) v ~ ruler (b_1) v ~ assassin (a_4, b_1) V loyal (a_4, b_1)

where a_4 = Marcus

b_1 = Caesar

Statement will be

C2 ~ man (Marcus) v ~ ruler(Caesar) v ~ assassin (Marcus, Caesar) v loyal (Marcus, Caesar)

Negate C1 as ~ loyal (Marcus, Caesar).

Resolvent will be:

~ man (Marcus) v ~ ruler (Caesar) v ~ assassin (Marcus, Caesar) V loyal (Marcus, Caesar)

Now clause is 1

man (Marcus)

Then new resolvent

~ ruler (Caesar) v ~ assassin (Marcus, Caesar) v loyal (Marcus, Caesar)

Clause 4 is ~ ruler (Caesar) v ~ assassin (Marcus, Caesar) v loyal (Marcus, Caesar) Resolvent is

~ assassin (Marcus, Caesar)

Clause 8 is assassin (Marcus, Caesar) Resolvent is empty

Diagramatically, it is shown as follows

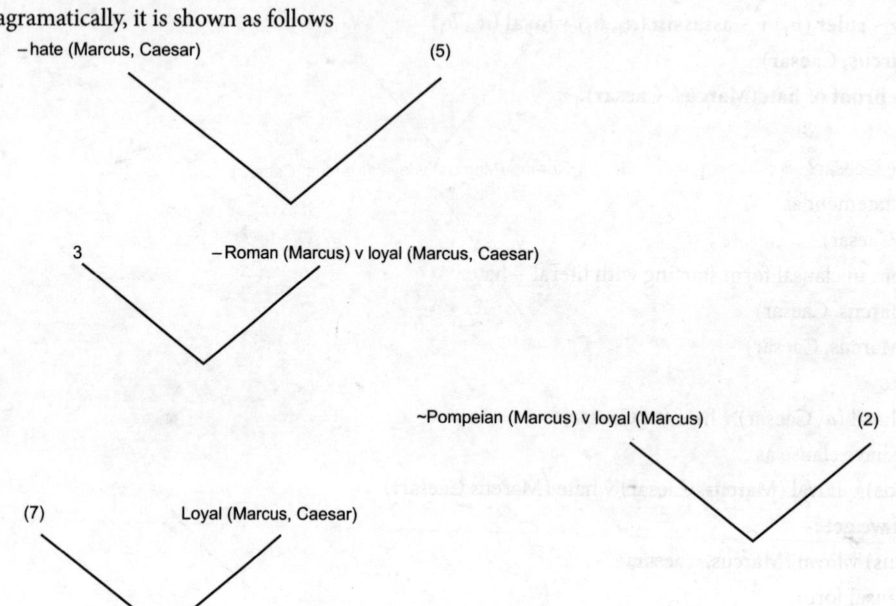

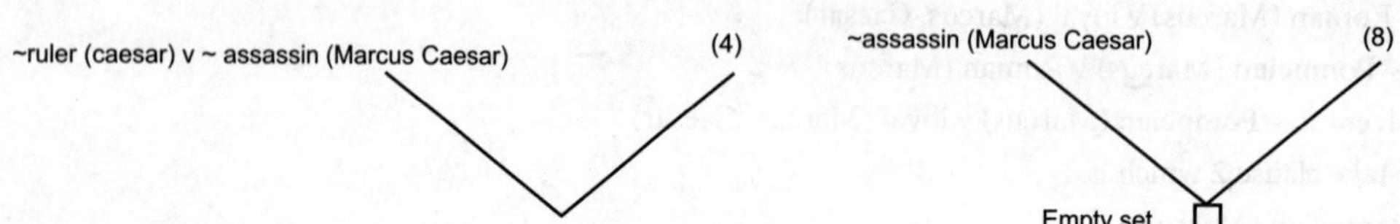

Q.29. Using above question

Prove : loyal (Marcus, Caesar)

Ans. Negate sentence as

~ loyal (M arcus, C aesar)

Select clause 5 which is

~Roman (x_2) v loyal (x_2 Caesar) v hate (x_2, Caesar)

where x_2 = Marcus

C1 : ~loyal (Marcus, Caesar)

C2 : ~ Roman (Marcus) v loyal (Marcus, Caesar) v hate (Marcus, Caesar)

Resolvent is ~Roman (Marcus) v hate (Marcus, Caesar) which is now C1.

Select 3 clausal from – ~ Pompeian (a) v Roman (a_1)

where a_1 is Marcus

C1 : ~Roman (Marcus) v hate (Marcus, Caesar)

C2 : ~ Pompeian (Marcus) v hate (Marcus, Caesar)

Next time C2 ~ Pompeain (Marcus) v hate (Marcus, Caesar)

Select C2 ~ Pompeain (Marcus)

New clause will be

hate (Marcus, Caesar)

Prove : loyal (Marcus, Caesar)

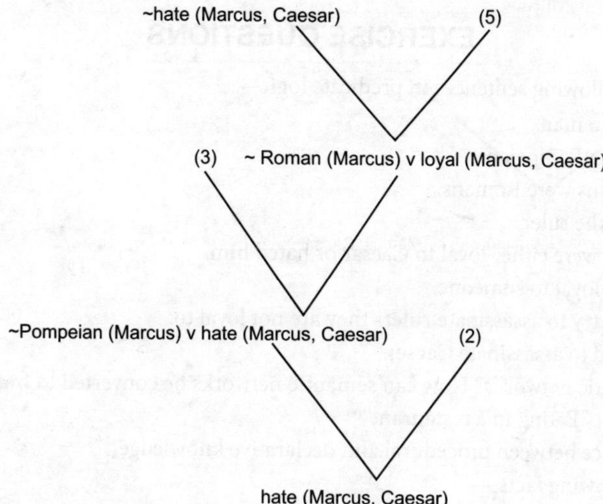

Q.30. What are non-deductive inference methods?

Ans. Non-deductive inference: Non-deductive inferences are not valid forms of inferencing but are important.

There are three methods of non-deductive inference methods which are as follows:

a. **Abductive inference :** It is based on the use of casual knowledge for describing conclusion.

Example

There are two axioms:

$\forall x : P(x) \rightarrow Q(x)\ P(R)$

We can conclude that $Q(R)$

Another example is Measles $(x) \rightarrow$ Spots

This means people having measles get spots. If we notice the spots, we may conclude, person has measles. This may be a wrong conclusion. Deriving conclusions in such a manner is default reasoning. Abductive reasoning is useful if some measure of certainty is attached to it.

b. **Inductive inference :** Inductive inference is recurring inference. It means if there is some event, it will be true for all the events or entities in the class.

For example: We see that some dogs have tails by which we conclude that all dogs have tails but in real a breed of dogs do not have tail.

Inductive inference can be given as

$$\frac{P(a_1), P(a_2) \ldots\ldots\ldots, P(a_n)}{\forall x : P(x)}$$

c. **Analogical Inference :** Analogical inference is based on experiences. When there are certain similar situations as we experience in the past, we relate the situations or events. For example : If there is an event P related to Q, then we conclude that P_1 is related to Q_1 in the same manner. Analogical inference is the combination of all other inferences such as deductive, abductive and inductive inference.

Q.31. Give five methods of representation of knowledge.

Ans. The methods of representation of knowledge are as follows

(*i*) FOPL

First order predicate logic.

(*ii*) Associative networks.

(*iii*) Conceptual graph.

(*iv*) Fuzzy logic.

(*v*) Frames.

EXERCISE QUESTIONS

1. (*a*) Represent the following sentences in predicate logic—
   1. Marcus was a man.
   2. Marcus was a Pompeian.
   3. All Pompeians were Romans.
   4. Caesar was the ruler.
   5. All Romans were either loyal to Caesar or hated him.
   6. Everyone is loyal to someone.
   7. People only try to assassinate rulers they are not loyal to.
   8. Marcus tried to assassinate Caeser.

   (*b*) What are semantic networks? How can semantic networks be converted to frames?

   (*c*) Write a script for "Eating in a restaurant".
2. (*a*) Explain difference between procedural and declarative knowledge.

   (*b*) Assume the following facts —
   1. Steve only likes easy courses.
   2. Science courses are hard.
   3. All courses in commerce department are easy.
   4. COM302 is a commerce course.

   (*c*) Convert the following into clausal form —
   1. Everyone is loyal to someone.
   2. John likes all kinds of food.

   (*d*) Write short notes on —
   1. Forward v/s Backward Reasoning.
   2. Control knowledge.
   3. CD
   4. Scripts.
3. (*a*) Explain the difference between predicate logic and propositional logic.

   (*b*) Represent the following using predicate calculus notation —
   1. There is a red part in bin that has a circular shape.
   2. Raghav is computer science student but not a pilot or a football player.
   3. The owner of car also owns the boat.
   4. All people need air.
4. Assume the following facts —
   1. Prasad only likes easy courses.
   2. AI courses are hard.
   3. All courses in Data Mining department are easy.
4. DM108 is a Data Mining Course.

   (*a*) Use Resolution to answer the question- "Which course would Prasad like?"

   (*b*) Also design clausal form for above sentences in FOPL using proper Axioms, Functions, redicates, Variables and Constants.

   (*c*) Hence with respect to resolution, explain. "What is proof by refutation"?
5. Express the following things in predicate calculus—

   (*a*) All p's are q's.

   (*b*) Some p's are q's.

   (*c*) John hit everyone who was near him.

   (*d*) Nobody does anything without a reason.
6. (*a*) What do you mean by semantic nets?

   (*b*) Define frames.
7. (*a*) Give the CD structure to parse the following sentence — "John wanted Mary to go to the store".

   (*b*) Represent the following sentences using symbolic logic:
   1. A drunker is enemy of himself.

2. Father of John loves the mother of mary.
3. All students like a good teacher.
4. Fruits and vegetables are nutritions.
5. God helps those who help themselves.

(*c*) "Some medicines are dangerous only if taken in excessive amount". Translate the above sentence into formulas in predicate logic and then to clausal form.

(*d*) Describe semantic net and frames with suitable examples.

8. (*a*) Explain the difference between the following — Semantic Nets and Frames.

(*b*) Represent the following sentence in FOPL, convert it into clausal form explaining each step —

"All engineering students who know programming will either get good placement or admission in some university for higher studies".

(*c*) Using the following problem, illustrate how resolution is used to derive new facts from already existing facts —

Given facts

(*i*) Steve likes computer courses.

(*ii*) Computer software can be software or Hardware courses. Derive: Steve likes AI.

(*d*) Write short notes on — Unification procedure.

9. Draw the semantic network and write atomic formulae for the English sentence given below: "Manju playing with a red ball".

10. (*a*) Construct a semantic net representations of the following —

(*i*) Rajesh is Indian, Rajesh is a lecturer.

(*ii*) Vikram but his new video CD to his brother-in-law.

10. (*b*) Explain-Conceptual dependency.

11. (*a*) Explain why these two sentences cannot be unified—

1. $p(x) \vee (q(f(x)) \wedge r(y))$ **2.** $p(x) \vee (q(f(r)) \wedge r(s))$

(*b*) Construct a semantic net representation of the following: "Gopal is Indian, Gopal is lecturer".

12. (*a*) Create a script about shopping in a super market.

(*b*) Write down a substitution which unifies the following sentences:

1. likes(hom er, dineer(x)) $\wedge$ (today(A) $\rightarrow$ dineer(x))
2. likes(hom er, dineer(cooked _ by(y)) $\wedge$ (today(Z) $\rightarrow$ dineerCcooked – by(magie))))

(*c*) What is a slot in a frame?

13. What are the merits/demerits of semantic net over semantic frames?

14. (*a*) Explain the rules to unify two predicates.

(*b*) Represent the following facts as predicates and convert them to clausal form, explaining the steps of conversion:

1. Any student who is intelligent or hardworking will pass the exam in good marks.
2. Anyone who is passed with good marks gets a job.

(*c*) Assume that "Shiva is neither hardworking nor intelligent". Using resolution prove that Shiva does not get a job.

15. What kind of knowledge is represented by the semantic nets? Give an example of KB represented by semantic nets and explain how inferences are done in Semantic Nets?

16. (*a*) Create a script for "appearing for an examination."

(*b*) A new operator ⊕, or exclusive-or may be defined by the following truth table—

P	Q	$P \oplus Q$
T	T	F
T	F	T
F	T	T
F	F	F

Create a propositional calculus expression using $\wedge$, $\vee$ and> that is equivalent to $P \oplus Q$.

(*c*) Explain CD using an example.

11 Planning and Learning

Q.1. Define Learning. How will you classify it?

Ans. Learning is done by viewing, listening, interactions, studying and by experience. Learning provides us the power to reason, ability to handle new situations and enables us to act in an intelligent way. Human beings are intelligent as they possess knowledge of world. Similarly, making a machine intelligent means it should have the power of learning. So, Machine learning is a challenge now. An intelligent machine should be able to learn new things and to adapt to new situations rather than simply doing steps as they are made to do. **Please understand that a machine cannot be called intelligent, if it does not have power of learning.** In literature, many definitions of learning have been given. Let us give some here too—

1. **Herbert Simon (1983) :** "Learning denotes changes in the system that are adaptive in the sense that they enable the system to do the same task or tasks more efficiently and more effectively the next time."
2. **Marvin Minsky (1986) :** "Learning is making useful changes in the working of our mind."
3. **Ryszard Michalski (1986) :** "Learning is constructing or modifying representations of what is being experienced."
4. **Mitchell (1997) :** "A computer program is said to learn from experience (E) w.r.t. some class of tasks (T) and performance measure (P), if its performance at tasks in T, as measured by P, improves with experience E".

The learning problem is divided into three types—

a. **Unsupervised learning :** It finds a model that matches a stream of input experiences and is able to predict what new experience to expect.

b. **Supervised learning :** It classifies (be able to determine) what category something belongs to after seeing a number of examples of things from each category or regression (given a set of numerical input/output examples, discover a continuous function that would generate the outputs from the inputs).

c. **Reinforcement learning :** The agent is rewarded for good responses and punished for bad ones. They can be analyzed in terms of decision theory, using concepts like utility. The mathematical analysis of machine

learning algorithms and their performance is a branch of theoretical computer science known as computational learning theory.

Q.2. Explain the concepts of learning.

Ans. The major paradigms of machine learning are as follows—

a. **Rote learning** by memorization (saving knowledge so that it can be used again).

b. **Induction** involves the process of learning by example where a system tries to induce a general rule from a set of observed instances.

c. **Analogy.** It can recognize similarities in information already stored. It can determine correspondence between two different representations.

d. **Genetic Algorithms (GA)** are a part of evolutionary computing, a way of solving problems by mimicking processes. Nature uses selection, crosses over, mutation and accepting to evolve a solution to a problem.

e. **Reinforcement.** It assigns rewards, positive or negative, act end of a sequence of steps, it learns which actions are good or bad.

Let us now discuss the general block diagram model of learning.

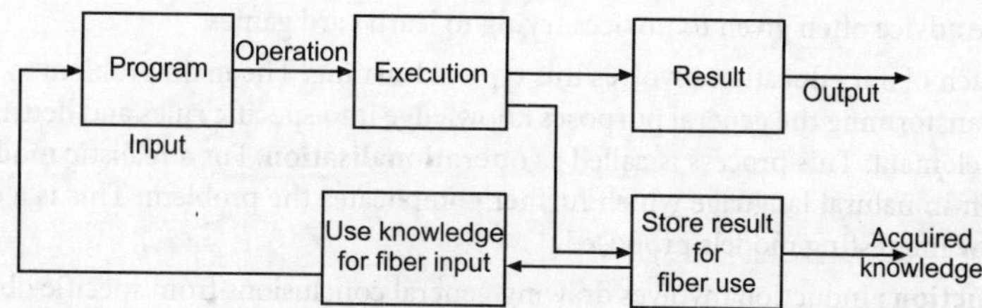

Fig. 11.1: General Block Diagram of a Learning System

As shown in Fig. 11.1, the input program is any general program executed for solution of a problem. The results are reported as output. These results are also stored back to acquire knowledge for future use. This simply means that, if a similar problem is required to be solved next time, the results can automatically be taken from previously acquired knowledge. Please note that learning involves generalization from experience. A system is said to be learning if it not only does the repetition of same task more effectively but also the similar tasks of the related domain. It covers a wide range of phenomenon:

a. Knowledge acquisition.

b. Skill refinement.

Knowledge acquisition refers to a situation in which computer executes one program and remembers the process for future use.

Skill refinement means the ability because of which, by doing some task repeatedly people tend to solve the task in lesser time. By practice skill tends to get refined.

Same capabilities are expected out of machines also.

Q.3. Describe five types of learning methods.

Ans. There are five main methods of learning in context of machines. They are as follows—

a. Rote learning

b. Learning by taking advice

c. Learning by induction

d. Learning by deduction (or Relevance-based Learning).

e. Learning by analogy

I. Rote Learning/Learning through memorization: Rote learning is based on the principle of caching. Caching means to store data of a particular task. For example, if say, a chess is played then the winning sequence of moves will simply be remembered by the players involved. Next time, instead of arbitrarily selecting from all possible moves, they will select a move from among the winning moves. Please note that by repeatedly remembering the winning situation, the choice of move becomes improved. This is what humans can do and hence we expect this much from our machines also. If our machine uses this technique of data caching then a significant amount of time can be saved as our intermediate results are already stored and are being only reused here.

Advantages :

1. It enables machine to store organized information.
2. It is faster to reuse information stored than to collect it.
3. We get generalized information stored in the database using Rote learning.

Disadvantages :

1. Very soon the information and data stored would become very large, complex and hence unmanageable.
2. It is not the best method as it is elementary in form and hence cannot be used in sophisticated applications.

II. Learning by taking Advice : Both humans as well as our machines can learn through advices. Please understand that this kind of learning takes place when a computer runs a particular program by taking advice from its programmer (or creator of that program).

Here the knowledge provided by the teacher is at a level more general than that usable by the performance element. The system has to particularize this general advice to specific situations.

For example: The advice often given to novices trying to learn card games.

Also note that much of our education involves this type of learning. The main problem to be tackled by the learning element here is transforming the general purposes knowledge into specific rules and heuristics which can be used by the performance element. This process is called as **operationalisation**. For a realistic model we have to assume that the advice is given in natural language which further complicates the problem. This is a difficult learning problem and there are a few interesting models proposed.

III. Learning by Induction : Induction involves drawing general conclusions from specific observations. Learning from examples and learning by discovery are instances of inductive learning. Most of the knowledge that the human race has acquired about its environment is through the process of induction.

For example: Observing the specific facts that the sun has risen in the east on day 1, day 2 etc., we infer a general statement, namely, sun always rises in the east.

IV. Learning by Deduction/Relevance-based Learning : Another method of inferring some conclusions from a given set of statements is deduction. Here, we start with a set of so called axioms and using rules of logic, derive conclusion. Provided that the logic we use is consistent, all the derived statements are true if the original axioms are true. Please note here that the deduction is a truth preserving process whereas induction is not. This is because from a given set of observations there are infinitely many inductive conclusions possible. Hence, while learning from examples, we have to pay special attention to the problem of how far should the observations be generalized. Presence of counter examples helps us from overgeneralization. But even then, there may be many possible generalizations and hence the learning system should be provided with enough background knowledge for it to prefer good generalizations.

For example: Starting with the statements—

S1: All people attending workshops on expert systems are computer scientists.

S2: Mr. X attended a workshop on expert systems.

We can derive conclusion— Mr. *X* is a Computer Scientist.

If the first two statements are true then so is the derived conclusion. This is because in deduction we go from the general to the specific. On the other hand, in induction we go from the specific to general and hence it is not possible to guarantee, in general, the correctness of the conclusions.

For example, observing that Mr. X, Mr. *Y* and so on, all of whom are Computer Scientists, attend workshops on expert systems, we can inductively conclude that all people attending workshops on expert systems are Computer Scientists. But please note that the truthiness of the starting premises does not guarantee truthiness of the conclusion. But if we can find one person attending workshop on expert systems who is not a Computer Scientist, we can immediately prove the inductive conclusion to be false. Thus, we can think of induction as falsity preserving. Incidentally, this is the reason why counter examples play a crucial role in development of scientific theories.

V. Learning by Analogy : Here, the knowledge provided by the teacher is useful for solving an analogous though not identical problem. Hence, the learning element needs to make some inferences to decide how this knowledge needs to be transformed so that it is useful for the problem at hand. There is not much work done in this area.

Q.4. Name some other methods of learning and explain them.

Ans. There are various other types of learning as follows—

a. Concept Learning (CL).

b. Explanation Based Learning (EBL).

c. Symbol Based Learning (SBL).

d. Relevance Based Learning (RBL)/Deductive Learning. Let us discuss them now.

I. Concept Learning : The problem of learning a single concept from examples and counter examples is called as concept learning.

Associated with each concept learning problem is a domain of objects which is characterized by a set of attributes. Each object in the domain is described by a tuple of values – one for each attribute. A subset of the domain is the concept. The learning system is provided (by the teacher) with some objects from the domain and is also told whether each object belongs to the concept or not. All objects belonging to the concept are called positive examples and all other objects from the domain are called negative examples. The system is expected to learn a representation of the concept which can be used by it for deciding whether a given object belongs to the concept.

Concept learning is the simplest case of learning from examples. To understand its relevance let us consider an example. Suppose we need an expert system for diagnosing some diseases. The data needed for diagnosis will be some symptoms of the patient (*e.g.*, temperature, whether he has headache etc.) and results of clinical tests (*e.g.*, presence of pus cells in urine etc.). Suppose the system should be rule-based and for simplicity we assume that each rule has a condition part that is a Boolean function of the data and an action part that gives the diagnosis. We want the system to acquire the rules by interacting with an expert. The expert will show the system various cases and his diagnosis. If we restrict our attention to learning rules for diagnosing a single disease, what we have is a concept learning problem. Here the attributes are the symptoms and clinical tests. Positive and negative examples are cases provided by the expert. The objective is to learn a decision procedure for diagnosing the diseases. This type of learning is useful even if the initial knowledge base is hand coded. The system can periodically interact with expert to check correctness of its diagnosis. In areas where the system is making mistakes, the expert can supply the system with some typical cases and the system will automatically update its knowledge base. Since the expert is generally not a computer scientist, it is easier for him to discuss typical cases than to examine and modify the knowledge base of the system. It may be noted that for the system to learn it must possess some minimal knowledge regarding the various attributes etc.

The first issue to be addressed while developing algorithms for concept learning is the choice of representation for the concept. The representation should be usable by the decision procedure and it should be suitable for the learning algorithm. We will be considering two representations – decision trees and logic expressions.

In a decision tree all nodes except the leaf nodes are labeled by a question (involving, generally the value of one attribute). All the edges from a node are labeled by possible answers for the question. The leaf nodes are labeled by decisions or the class labels. Suppose we have a concept represented as a decision tree and we have to use this for deciding whether a given object belongs to the concept. We start at the root node. At each node we answer the question at that node for the current object and thus take the appropriate edge from the node. Finally, when we come to a leaf node its label will be the decision.

A logic expression is directly usable as the condition in an if-then rule for making decision. By using simple structures for the logic expression, it is possible to learn the concept as a logic expression. Consider a concept learning problem with N attributes Yi, taking values in sets v_i, $1 \le i \le N$. We distinguish between two logic expressions for representing a concept.

Defintion 2.1 A logic expression of the form

$$[Y_1 \in v_1] \,/\backslash \ldots /\backslash\, [Y_N \in v_N],\ v_i,\ v_i,\ v,\ i,$$

is said to be in Conjunctive Normal Form (CNF).

Here each expression of the form $[Y_i \in v_i]$ is called a selector. It is true if the value of the attribute is in the corresponding set. Since this can be viewed as a disjunction of equality predicates each of which tests if Y_i is equal to some element of vi, a selector is said to have internal disjunctions.

Defintion 2.1 A logic expression of the form

$$C_1 \backslash / \, C_2 \backslash / \ldots \backslash / \, C_m,\ m \ge 1,$$

where each C_i is a CNF expression, is said to be in Disjunctive Normal Form (DNF).

In the next section we will consider algorithms for learning concepts as CNF or DNF expressions and also as decision trees.

The representation chosen for the concept determines the set of all possible concepts, the so-called concept space. For example, for CNF concepts the concept space will be the set of all possible tuples of the form $(A_1, \ldots, A_N)$, where Ai Vi. The set of all possible examples will be called the instance space. The input to the learning system will be points in the instance space using which the system searches over the concept space to find best concept. If we use logic expressions for concepts then all examples (which are N-tuples of values for all attributes) are CNF concepts. Hence all examples will be points in the concept space. This is referred to as single representation trick which is useful because the examples can serve as starting points for the search over the concept space. To define the goal of this search process we need to decide what is the 'best' concept. A concept is said to be consistent if it explains all the examples. That is, if it satisfies all positive examples and none of the negative examples. But consistency by itself is not sufficient; the disjunction of all +ve examples is a consistent concept though it has no generalization capability. If our concept space contains only CNF concepts, then we cannot any way converge to disjunction of all examples.

Then the way we define the notation of generalization determines the type of concepts that the learning system converges to. In general, if we use DNF concepts then we need to employ some heuristic evaluation function to make the system prefer 'good' generalizations.

Another feature that affects the search process is whether we are required to process one example at a time or we are allowed to store all the examples and process them together. In the former case we say that the learning is incremental. While incremental learning is very much desired, often it is difficult to learn incrementally, especially while learning DNF concepts or decision trees.

Before we complete this section it may be remarked that the concept learning problem we have discussed here is very similar to the problem of learning discriminant functions in pattern recognition. The main difference is that here the attributes may not be numerical values and there may not be any algebraic structure on the sets where the attributes take values. Hence the traditional pattern recognition algorithms that assume real valued features, are not very useful for concept learning. Also, since the subjective is knowledge acquisition for expert systems, we want the learnt concepts to be represented in a form easily comprehensible to humans. That is why we use logic expressions and decision trees rather than discriminant functions to represent the learnt knowledge.

II. Explanation Based Learning (EBL) :

Learning is of 2 types—

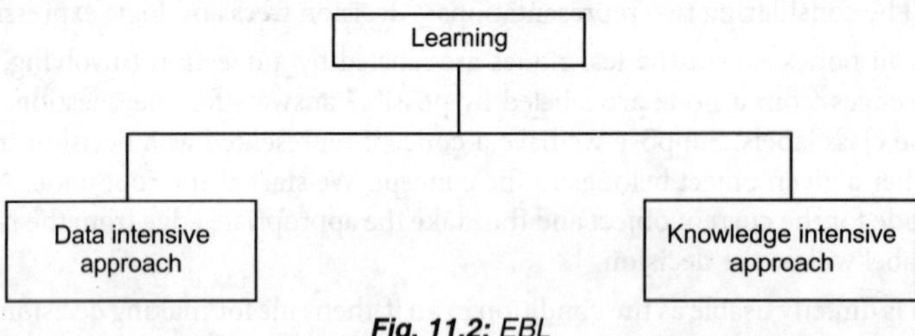

***Fig. 11.2:** EBL*

In data intensive approach, the main focus is on given data. Large number of positive and negative examples are given to the machine and based on the outcomes of these examples, the machine learns. For example: Rote learning.

In knowledge intensive approach, the main focus is on knowledge. It is a kind of analogical learning. It is also called as situation-based learning.

For example: EBL uses this approach.

In games like chess, medical diagnosis etc., knowledge plays a vital role. In these systems, a critical situation is handled and the machine is given the example to handle this situation This is EBL. So, here one example in form of a knowledge solution or past experience is sufficient for learning a new solution. In general, in EBL, the emphasis is given to learn more by taking the critical examples rather than by having more examples. In EBL, one positive training example is given to machine in order to perform the learning. Please note that in EBL, the learned knowledge is valid knowledge. It is obtained by performing a deductive reasoning process on a set of facts. In EBL, while problem solving, its salient features are abstracted. These features are as follows—

a. Formal statement about goal.

b. Minimum one training example.

c. Domain theory that relates to the concept and training example.

d. Criteria for applying an operator.

This information is stored in the KB. When a new problem is to be solved using EBL, a matching is performed between the new problem and existing problem details. If partial matching occurs, that solution is taken from the KB and modified according to new problem. Thus, we can conclude that EBL program attempts to learn from a single example by explaining why it is an example of target concept. When program formalizes the explanation, it generalizes this explanation and stores for further use. The system learns this way and its performance improves.

EBL is a form of deductive learning where the learner develops a logical explanation of how the positive training example defines a concept. In EBL, first of all, the concept is formulated using training example and domain theory and then it is generalized by regression formulae.

EBL : An EBL system attempts to learn from a single example x by explaining why x is an example of the target concept (predicate) instead of learning through a large number of examples. The explanation is then generalized and the system's performance is improved through the availability of background knowledge. The process is known as memorization (or memo function). It is defined as the phenomenon to accumulate a database of input/output pairs in which when a function is called, it first checks the database to see whether it can avoid solving the problem. EBL further creates general rules depending on the problem to be solved which cover an entire class of cases.

For example: In case of differentiation, memorization or memo function will remember that the derivative of x^2 with respect to x is $2x$ and would generalize that for any arithmetic unknown function; the derivative of u^2 is $2u$. Logically,

Arithmetic Unknown (u) → Derivative (u^2, u) = $2u$

Please understand that if the Knowledge Base (KB) contains such a rule then any new case which is an instance of this rule can be solved immediately.

> **NOTE:** This is an example of a very general phenomenon: "Once something is understood, it is generalized and reused in other circumstances".

This essential step then can be used as a building block in solving similar but complex problems.

EBL Algorithm

EBL follows the following algorithm:

Step 1: Given an example (say of fork or of differentiation), construct a proof such that the goal predicate applies to the example using the available background knowledge.

Step 2: In parallel, construct a generalized proof tree for the variablised goal using the same inference steps as in the original proof.

Step 3: Construct a new rule whose left side consists of the leaves of the proof tree and whose right-hand side is the variablised goal.

Step 4: Drop any condition( ) which are true regardless of the values of the variables in the goal.

Efficiency : EBL basically works in two steps: explain and generalize. Sometimes a rule can be generalized in a number of ways, which reflects the efficiency of the algorithm. Three factors contribute to its efficiency:

1. Adding large number of rules can slow down the reasoning process because the inference mechanism must still check those rules even in cases where they do not yield a solution. Please note that it increases the branching factor in the search space.
2. To compensate for the slowdown in reasoning process, the derived rules must offer significant increase in speed for the cases which they cover. This increase arises mainly because the derived rules avoid dead ends which would otherwise be taken.
3. Derived rules should be as general as possible so that they apply to the largest possible set of cases.

A common approach to ensure that derived rules are efficient is to insist on the operationality of each sub-goal in the rule. Also note that a sub-goal is operational if it is easy to solve. Unfortunately, there is unusually a trade–off between operationality and generality. More specific sub-goals are easier to solve but cover fewer cases only. Also, operationality is a matter of degree, one or 2 steps is definitely operational but may not hold good for 10 or 100 steps. Finally, the cost of solving a given sub-goal depends on what other rules are available in the knowledge base. It can expand (up or down) as more and more rules are added. So, EBL systems face a really complex optimization problem in trying to maximize the efficiency of the given initial KB. It is also possible to derive a mathematical model of the effect on overall efficiency of adding a given rule and to use this model to select the best rule to add.

Please understand that when the recursive rules are involved, the analysis can become very complicated. One approach that is promising can be to address the problem of efficiency empirically, simply by adding several rules and then identifying which are useful and actually would speed up the process.

Conclusions : By generalizing from the past examples, EBL makes the KB more efficient for the kind of problems to which it can be applied. Hence, if this EBL system is carefully designed then it is possible to obtain better speed-ups.

> **NOTE:** In 1991, Samuelson and Rayner showed that a reasonably large PROLOG-based natural language system designed for speech-to-speech translation between Swedish and English was able to achieve real- time performance only by the application of EBL to the parsing processes.

Advantages :

1. EBL allows learning from a single training instance.
2. EBL forms generalizations that are relevant to specific goals.
3. Learner can select relevant aspects of training examples.

III. Symbol Based Learning (SBL)

SBL involves 3 tasks mainly—

1. Specification of goal and data.
2. Representation of learned knowledge. In learning problems, the concepts are represented as conjunctive sentences containing variables.
3. Set of operations. Once the training session is over, the learner should generate a heuristic rule or plan objecting its goal. This requires the ability to manipulate representations. The operations, here, include—
    - Generalizing symbolic expressions.
    - Specializing symbolic expressions.
    - Adjusting weights in Neural Network (NN)
    - Or Modifying the program's representation.

We create generalizations by replacing the constants with variables and specializations by replacing variables with constants.

IV. RBL/Deductive Learning : An American agent comes to India as a visitor. He/she firstly meets an Indian named Rajiv. On hearing his speech in Hindi, he concludes that all Indians speak Hindi. Note that this agent doesn't conclude that all Indian men are called as Rajiv. Hence, we can generalize this observation—

All Indians speak Hindi: Herein, the visitor-agent has some background knowledge like people in a given country, usually, speak the same language. In First-Order logic, this can be represented as–

Nationality $(x, n) \wedge$ Nationality $(y, n) \wedge$ Language $(x, l) \rightarrow$ language (y, L) ...(1) *i.e.*, if '*x*', and '*y*' have the same nationality '*n*' and '*x*' speaks language *l*, then *y* also speaks 'l'. But the observation, Nationality (Rajiv, Indian) $\wedge$ Language (Rajiv, Hindi) along with the given knowledge shown in sentence 1, the following implication holds: Nationality (*x*, Indian) $\rightarrow$ Language (*x*, Hindi) Please understand that the sentences (as in equation (1)) express a strict form of relevance that nationality of a person determines his/her language or we can say that the language is a function of nationality. These sentences are called as functional dependencies (or FDs): In a syntax (given by Davis in 1985), it can be rewritten as—

Nationality $(x, n) >$ — Language (x, l) ...(2)

NOTE: In English, it means that nationality determines language

Equation (2) shows that the FD (or determination) is really a relationship between the predicates—Nationality and Language.

From equations (1) and (2) it is crystal clear that it becomes rudimentary that the prior, background knowledge concerns the relevance of a set of features to the goal predicate. This knowledge together with the observations, allows the agent to infer a new general rule, based on observations:

Hypothesis $\wedge$ Description $\in$ Classifications

Background $\wedge$ Descriptions $\wedge$ Classification $\in$ Hypothesis ...(3)

Please note that this type of generalization is called Relevance-based Learning (RBL). Also note that although RBL does make use of the content of the observation in creating hypothesis yet it does not generate hypotheses which go beyond the logical content of the background knowledge and the observations. This is a **deductive form of learning.** Because it cannot by itself amount for the creation of the new knowledge from a scratch, so it is also called as relevance-based or deductive learning.

FDs or determinations are very vital as they specify a sufficient basic vocabulary from which hypotheses concerning the goal predicate can be constructed. This can be proved by showing that a given FD is logically equivalent to a statement that the correct definition of the goal predicate is one of the set of definitions expressible using the predicates on the left hand side of the FD. Hence, reduction in the hypothesis space size should make it easier to learn the goal predicate. The gains can be qualified using a simple analysis—

If | *H* | is the size of hypothesis space then for Boolean functions log (|*H*|) examples are required to arrive at a reasonable hypothesis. For a learner having n Boolean features participating in the construction of hypothesis—

| *H* | = *O*(log 22*n*). This means that the examples required will be *O*(2*n*). Also note that if the determination contains d predicates in the left-hand side, the learner will require only *O*(2*d*) examples. This shows a reduction of *O*(2*n*–*d*) as compared to learning through classification of examples.

Q.5. What are genetics algorithms?

Ans. There is a need for a tool or a technique which reduces human dependency and decision making should be done based on same algorithm or a mathematical formula. Genetic Algorithms (GA) are intrinsically parallel. Most other algorithms are serial and can only explore the solution space to a problem in one direction at a time. GA has multiple offspring *i.e.*, they can explore solution space in multiple directions at once. If one path turns out to be a dead end, they can easily eliminate it. GAs perform well in problems for which the fitness landscape is complex—ones where the fitness function is discontinuous, noisy, changes over time or has many local optima. Many search algorithms can become trapped by local optima if they reach the top of a hill on the fitness landscape. However, crossover is the key element that distinguishes GAs from other methods such as hill-climbers and simulated annealing. **Please note that without crossover, each individual solution is on its own, exploring the search space in its immediate vicinity without reference to what other individuals may have discovered. Also note that with crossover in place, there is a transfer of information between successful candidates.** Individuals can benefit from what others have learned and schemata can be mixed and combined with the potential to produce an offspring that has the strengths of both its parents. GAs can manipulate many parameters simultaneously. GAs use parallelism and hence can produce multiple equally good solutions to the same problems possibly with one candidate solution optimizing one parameter and another candidate optimizing a different one. A human overseer can then select one of these candidates to use.

Do you know? GAs know nothing about the problems they are deployed to solve. GAs make random changes to their candidate solutions and then use the fitness function to determine whether those changes produce an improvement.

Q.6. What is neural computing?

Ans. Neural computing is the study of networks of adaptable nodes which, through a process of learning from task examples, store experimental knowledge and make it available for use. The configurations and algorithms in neural computing are biologically inspired structures that perform useful tasks. **Please understand that the human nervous system consists of about 1011 neurons and 10^{15} interconnection. Also note that these numbers cannot be matched by an artificial NN, the tasks that can be performed by ANN are also severely limited.**

Fig. 11.3 shows the structure of a pair of biological neurons. **Dendrites** extend from the cell body to other neurons where they receive signals at a connection point called a **synapse.** On the receiving side of the synapse, these inputs are conducted to the cell body where they are summed, some inputs tending to excite the cell, others tending to inhibit its firing. When the cumulative excitation in the cell body exceeds a threshold, the cell fires, sending a signal down the axon to other neurons.

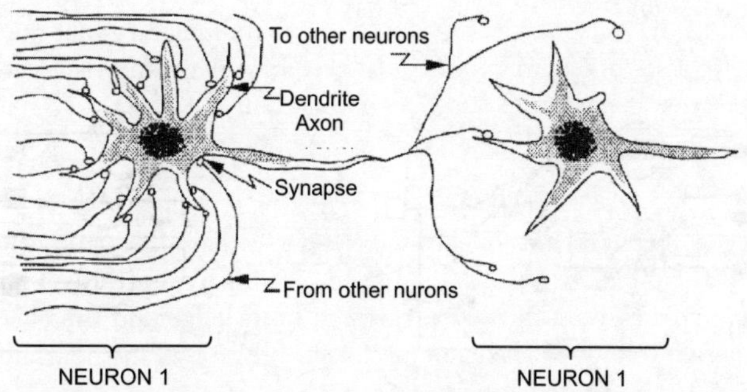

***Fig. 11.3:** Structure of a pair of biological neurons*

Basic Computing Unit : We consider a simple adaptable node (Fig. 11.4) which we will use to explain the features of ANN.

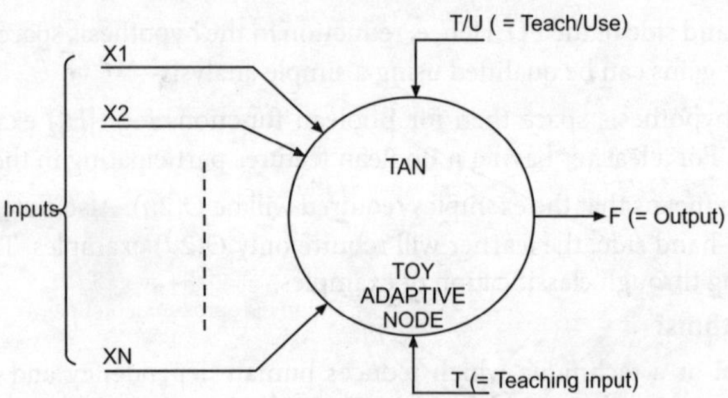

Fig. 11.4: A Toy Adaptive Node (TAN) Network Structures

Fig. 11.5 shows some network structures using the basic computing elements (TANs). We use these structures to introduce some key ideas of NN, namely, associative nets, hidden layers, hard learning visible and hidden units. We also use them to explain the main features of NN, namely, distributed and located information, association and recall of information, and storing of knowledge.

***(i)* A single-layr, feed-forward net**

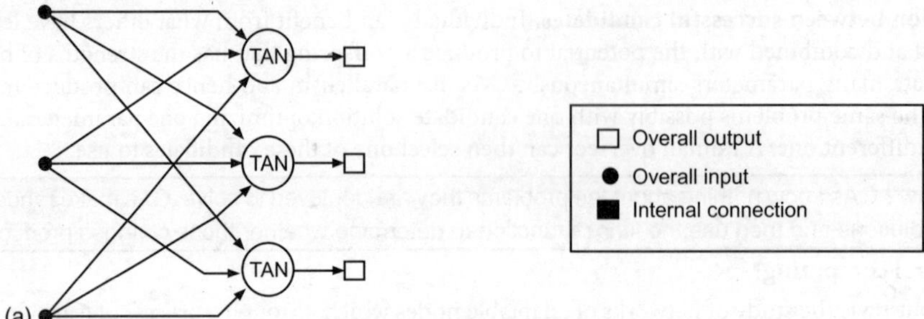

***(ii)* Feed-forward nets**

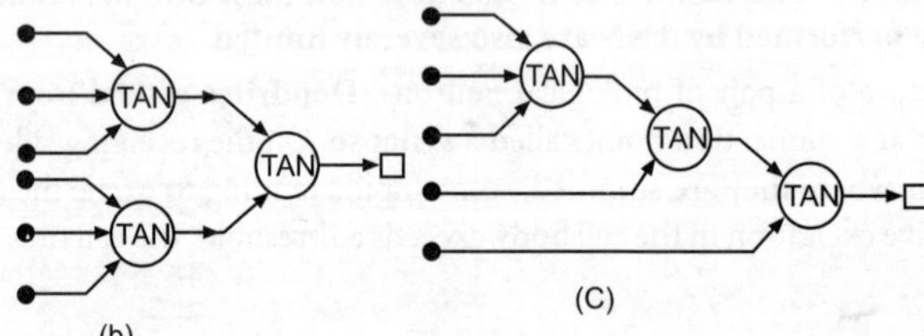

***(iii)* Feedback nets**

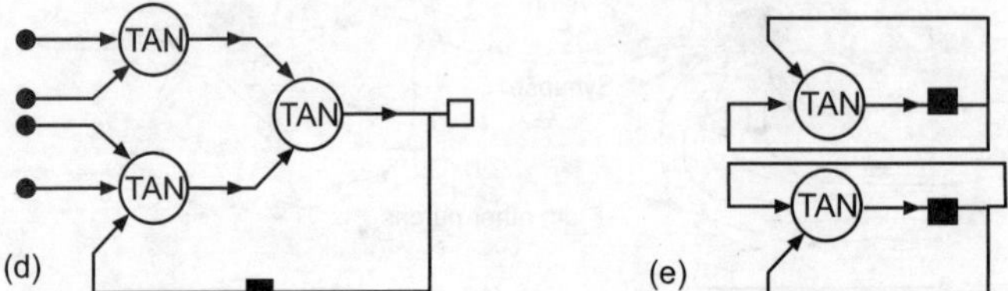

Fig. 11.5: Some network structures using the basic computing elements (TANs).

Neural net is a widely used technique for learning by charging the weights assigned to the nodes or arcs of a network. However, their name is a misnomer since they bear little resemblance to actual neural mechanisms. Fig. 11.6 shows a typical neural net—

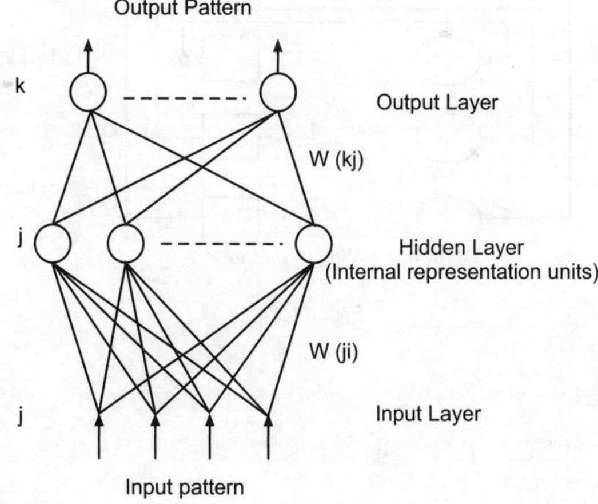

Fig. 11.6: *Typical neural net*

Its input is a sequence of number that indicates the relative proposition of some selected features and whose output is another sequence of number that indicates the most likely concept characterized by that combination of features.

For example: in case of OCR-output character Recognizer, the features might represent lines, curves and angles and the concept might represent the letters that have those features.

Do you know? In a NN, the structure of nodes and arcs is fixed and the only changes that may occur are the assignment of weights to the arcs.

When a new input is presented, the weights on the arcs are combined with the weights on the outputs. In learning stage, the system is told whether the predicted weights are correct and various methods of back propagation are used to adjust the weight on the arcs that leads to the result.

Neural networks support digital computers with the ability to make sensible decision to learn by experience.

Main features of ANNs are as follows:

1. Distributed Storage of data. Removal of portions of net is possible. It does not degrade the quality of stored data.
2. Data is stored in form of an associative memory. An associative memory is one in which partial data are sufficient to recall the complete stored information.
3. Nets can be trained to find out the relationship between data.
4. Nets can interpolate and extrapolate from their stored information.
5. Quality of stored images degrades as some portion of net is removed.

APPLICATION OF NN

Travelling Salesman Problem

Hopfield Net

$$\text{NETj} = \sum_{i=j} W_{ij}OUT_i + IN_j$$

$$\begin{aligned} \text{OUT} &= 1 \text{ if NETj} > \text{Tj} \\ &= 0 \text{ if NETj} < \text{Tj} \\ &= 0 \text{ if NETj} > \text{Tj} \quad \text{unchanged if NETj} = \text{Tj} \end{aligned}$$

Engergy function

$$E = \left(-\frac{1}{2}\right)\sum_i \sum_j W_{ij}OUT_iOUTj - \sum_j l_iOUT_i + \sum_j T_iOUT_i$$

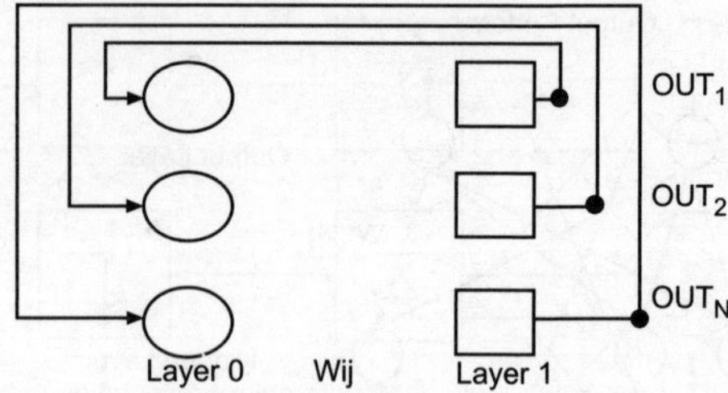

Fig. 11.7

Travelling Salesman Problem:

Order visited

City	1	2	3	4
A	0	1	0	0
B	0	0	0	1
C	1	0	0	0
D	0	0	1	0

E_1 : Energy fucntion must be low for only those solutions for which there is a single 1 in each column and row.

E_2 : Energy function must favour solutions having short distances.

$$E_2 = \left(\frac{1}{2}\right) D \sum_{x} \sum_{y=x} \sum_{x} d_{xy} OUT_{xi}(OUT_{yi+1} + OUT_{yi} - 1)$$

Weights:

$W_{xi,\, yi} = A\, \delta xy(1 - \delta_{ij})$ (Prevents more than a single 1 within a row)

$= B\delta_{ij}\, (1 - \delta_{xy})$ (Prevents more than a single 1 within a column)

$= -C$ (Global inhibition)

$= D\, dxy\, (\delta_{ji} + i + \delta_{ji-1})$ (Distance term)

Bias weight for each neuron C_n.

Activation function: d

McCulloch-Pitts Model of Artificial Neuron

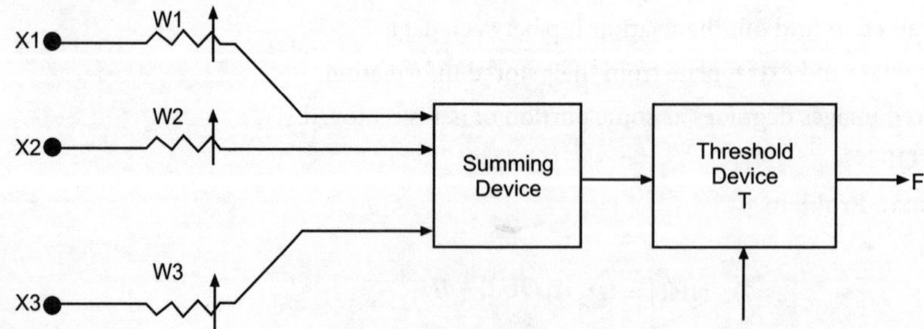

***Fig. 11.8:** M-P Model of Neuron*

Perceptron :

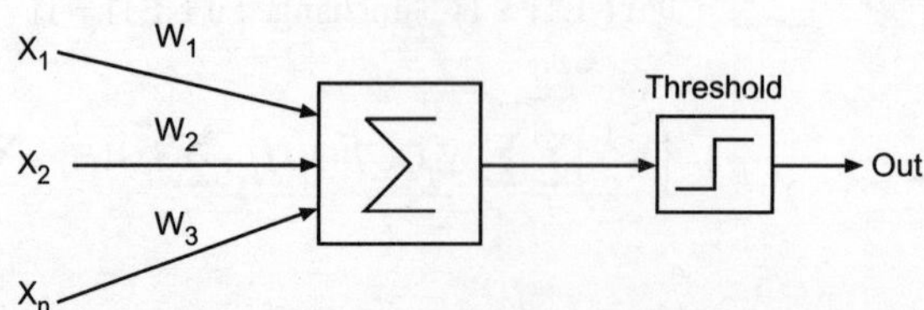

***Fig. 11.9:** Perceptron-M-P Node with Some Additional, Fixed Preprocessing*

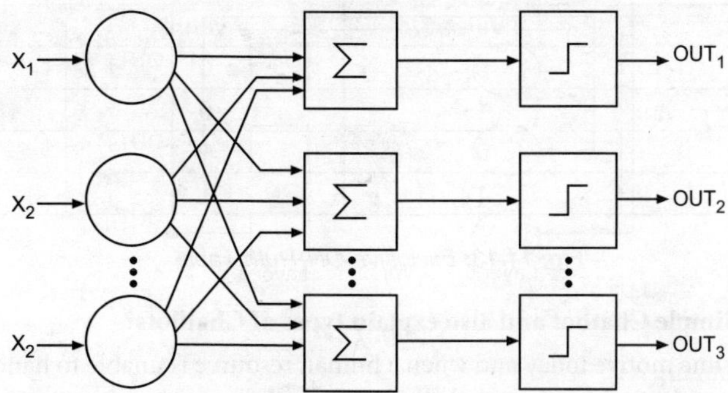

Fig. 11.10: Multioutput perceptron

Perceptron classification problem

Given k vectors v_i, $i = 1, \ldots k$, each of dimension n, suppose they are partitioned into two subsets I and I_1. The perceptron classification problem is:

Build a network consisting of threshold switching elements such that output is 1 for all input vectors in l + and 0 for all input vectors in l.

Perceptron learning (training) problem

The perceptron learning (training) problem is:

Change the weights and thresholds of the various neurons adaptively until classification occurs.

Hebb's rule: Change in weight connecting unit *i* to unit *j* is proportional to the product of the output of unit *j* and the activation value of unit *i*.

Delta rule: Change in weight connecting unit *j* to unit *i* is proportional to the product of the output of unit *j* and the difference between the desired and actual outputs of unit *i*.

Perceptron representation problem : Representation refers to the ability of perceptron to simulate a specified function. Learning refers to the existence of a systematic procedure for adjusting the weights of the network to produce that function.

Geometric interpretation and linear separability problem

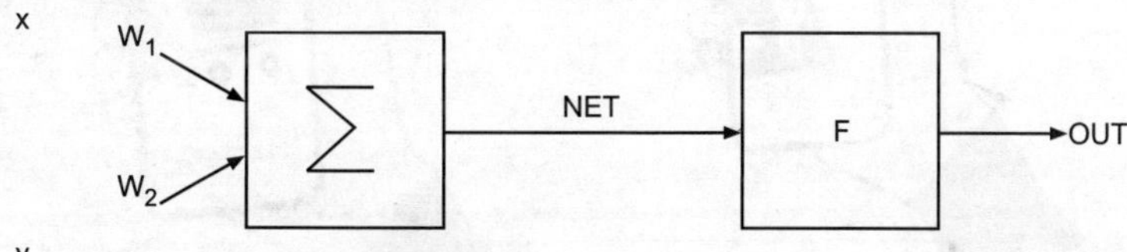

Fig. 11.11: Single neuron system

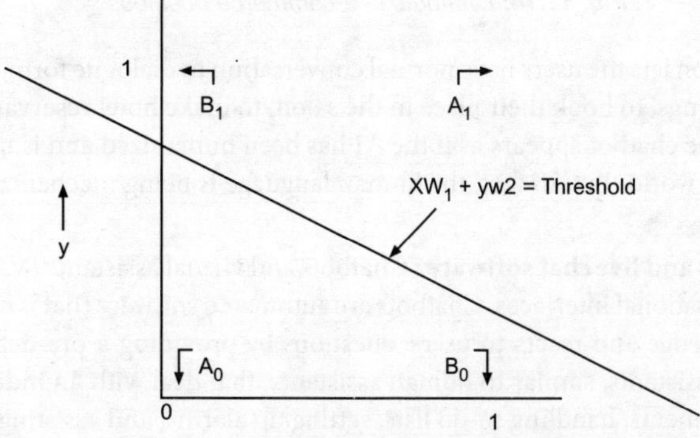

Fig. 11.12: Exclusive-OR problem as points on the XY-plane

Point	x value	y value	desired output
A0	0	0	0
B0	1	0	1
B1	0	1	1
A1	1	1	0

Fig. 11.13: *Exclusive-OR Truth Table*

Q.12. How will you develop a Simple Chatbot and also explain types of Chatbots?

Ans. Customer service is the prime motive today and when a human resource is unable to handle the continuous demand of customers then companies shift to AI-powered chatbots. AI chatbots are now being used in various fields to improve customer service and thus the revenue (ROI). We are just recalled of the statement of Google-

"We are now witnessing a new shift in computing: the move from a mobile-first to an AI-first world."

—Sundar Pichai, CEO of Google

The advances in technology have increased exponentially, which has brought a revolution in the user interface by extracting maximum value from artificial intelligence (AI) to enhance the productivity of businesses and boost their revenue. In recent years, the intense innovations in machine learning and other fundamental technologies like natural language processing have led to an astonishingly widespread use of chatbots or conversational agents that facilitate the human-to-bot interaction, which is the biggest dominating mobile trend of this time.

Chatbots, derived from 'chat robots,' are text- or voice-based algorithms powered by AI that are capable of checking the customers' needs and providing possible suggestions. These are now gaining more popularity on Facebook Messenger, Twitter, LinkedIn, Skype, Slack, Kik, and other messaging platforms.

Fig. 11.14: *Chatbots in e-commerce business*

The human-to-bot interaction lets the users have normal conversation in dialogue form, entering their purposes directly into the machines to buy things, to book their place in the salon, to make hotel reservation, to get online health advise, or to even get directions. The chatbot appears as if the AI has been humanized and is making the computers or mobile phones to adopt the human world. But, in fact, the human language is being mechanized to bring us into the machine world!

Chatbots, virtual assistants and live chat software : Chatbots and virtual assistants (VA) are both smart applications of AI and they both are conversational interfaces. Chatbots are automated software that is company-oriented, programmed with a learned set of knowledge and reacts to users' questions by providing a pre-defined answer. Whereas VAs like Cortana or Siri are digital assistants, similar to human assistants, that deal with an individual user, like organising and reminding business appointments, handling to-do lists, setting up alarms, and assisting in other daily routines.

Chatbots, being information acquisition tools, facilitate customers' communication with any business venture. An organization can build its customized chatbot for virtual conversation with its customers using a technology called Natural Language Processing (NLP). The NLP algorithm is making the chatbot smarter.

VA uses high-level automation software, based on advanced NLP, which enables it to understand natural language voice commands and interact with the individual user, offering human-like assistance in a highly effective way. VA follows the dynamic conversational flow technique, which means it can interact with human beings continuously, even if the communication is not continuous, and can remember the fundamental perspective of the conversation. Instead, a chatbot fails to retain the conversation because it lacks in dialogue management, which makes the customer start all over again. However, this flaw has been overcome in Google's Meena chatbot by using powerful encoders and decoders.

So, organizations' need to focus on appropriate areas where the AI applications, VAs, and chatbots can be implemented correctly to leverage their business. This article points out some sectors where the organizations' revenue and customer retention rates have increased due to the usage of chatbots.

Chatbots in e-commerce business : AI in online shopping has transformed the e-commerce industry by using chatbots to provide 24/7 support to their online customers; thus making the customers feel that they are in direct contact with the brand regardless of the time. As chatbots use NLP, they can construe the voice-based communications. So, the requirements of the customers are perceived profoundly, hence increasing their confidence in the company.

Chatbots can identify the thoughts and views of the customers from their searches and questions and can provide instant answers, facilitating good customer service. Also, they can remember the preferences of the customers so that any offers from the organisation get communicated personally to each customer.

Burberry chatbot (UK/US) : Burberry, one of the luxury fashion brands, uses a 'see-now-buy-now' chatbot that can be accessed by scanning a QR code or through the company's Facebook Messenger page. This bot provides customer service support by answering frequently asked questions through categorised options, hence enabling a better 'conversational commerce' by allowing access to a large user database for better communication with their target audience.

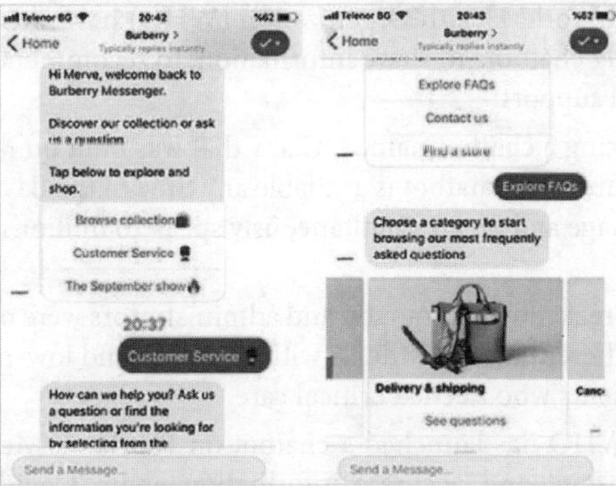

Fig. 11.15: Burberry chatbot

When Burberry launched its chatbot in 2016, it was only allowing its customers to have a look at their collections and shop some selected pieces. But now, the company's chatbot can send push notifications to all the customers who communicate with it, can help the customers get in touch with the Burberry Consultant directly, can locate a particular store, or book a Uber ride to their Makers' House.

Also, the see-now-buy-now bot allows Burberry customers to design their trench coats—the brand's classic outwear—thus giving a personalised shopping experience to them. Shopping percentage rises when brands offer such personalised experiences, which takes marketing to a new level and targets more customers.

Nike chatbot : Nike's chatbot, developed by Snaps.io, allows users to browse Nike footwear and clothing selections. Nike By You (previously NikeID) service encourages individuals to design their shoes either by uploading their design pictures, or by blending options, or using 'magic match.' As the chatbot is language agnostic, it is capable of catering to international audience.

Fig. 7.16: Nike chatbot (Credit: Nike)

The bot interacts with the users through a multiple-choice format on topics extending from products, users' preferences, style or size, shipping, etc. The collected information is used as input and the bot begins its search based on the users' requirements and redirects the users to Nike's site for purchasing the products, thus saving the customers' effort and time.

Chatbots in the medical industry : The whole world has seen a sharp and tenacious decline in the economy due to the Covid-19 pandemic. The virus has also impacted most of our daily routine and has turned events to virtual versions. The novel pandemic has made the medical industry also go through ups and downs throughout the catastrophe. So, this industry has now taken the centre-stage position among all the sectors. Establishments like the Centers for Disease Control & Prevention (CDC) and World Health Organization (WHO) have shown the potential of chatbots in saving lives. These organisations are using chatbots to share information, to recommend actions and procedures that support our health, and to offer emotional support.

CDC's Clara chatbot. CDC was using a chatbot named 'Clara' that was built on Microsoft's Healthcare Bot powered by tech giant Azure's cloud architecture. This chatbot is available any time of the day to give up-to-date information. It can hear and respond in natural language and it can simultaneously speak to millions of people in their local languages and dialects.

During the peak of Covid-19 outbreak, doctors, nurses, and administrators were overwhelmed with the number of cases they had to attend. Clara could differentiate individuals with high-risk and low-risk factors and thus helped healthcare professionals to focus first on patients who needed critical care.

WHO's Health Alert chatbot : WHO has launched a chatbot on Facebook Messenger and WhatsApp, called WHO Health Alert, which provides instant and accurate information about Covid-19. The chatbot was developed in collaboration with Sprinklr and in partnership with Praekelt.Org using Turn machine learning technology.

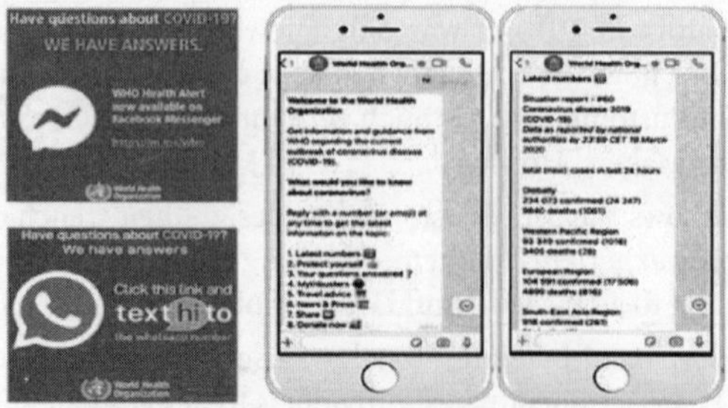

Fig. 11.17: WHO's Health Alert chatbot (Credit: World Health Organization)

This chatbot can be accessed in Arabic, English, French, Hindi, Italian, Spanish, and Portuguese languages for correct information about coronavirus and what people can do to protect themselves and others.

Chatbots for human resource : AI has transformed the landscape of human resource management. Chatbots have set foot in the workplace in the form of HR chatbots that automate most of the tasks in the HR departments like recruiting, managing payroll, managing training skills or professional development, and furnishing any other new prospects to boost employee experience. This advanced automation reduces human participation and expenses.

Each workplace is now adopting new conversational interfaces to interact with employees to have personalized but frictionless interactions. Organizations prefer chatbots because these are capable of engaging across multiple channels like a website, a mobile app, Microsoft Teams, Slack, or any other messaging app.

Wade and Wendy chatbots : Wade and Wendy are two different chatbots for recruitment that use advanced AI technology for conversational intelligence. Chatbot Wade guides the job seekers by helping them find a job they aspire for and describing them the job criteria; Wendy ensures that it screens the applicants based on the given job criteria.

Wendy makes the hiring process more humane by keeping each applicant engaged as the recruitment is chat-driven with role-specific conversations. It helps the HR throughout the hiring process by acquiring and synthesizing the information and finally making its recommendation about the best fit for the specified job role.

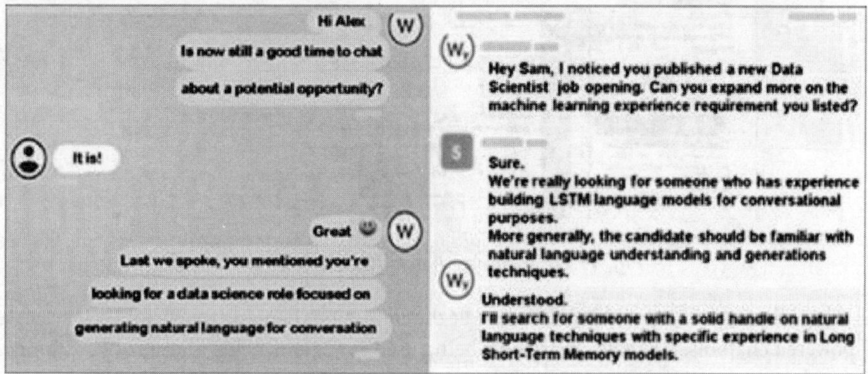

***Fig. 11.18:** Wade and Wendy chatbots (Credit: welcome.ai)*

Wendy's conversation with the applicants is not identical because its response is based on what the applicants say. Wendy is capable of diving deeper into the applicants' responses and can ask follow-up questions to get a better understanding of the candidate's skills, depth of experience, and familiarity with certain processes or tools.

Chatbots in tourism and hospitality : The atavistic wish to voyage all around the world is inherent in every individual. According to Google, 82 per cent of travelers use the Internet for planning their travel and making online bookings. The rise and shine of chatbots has made a positive impact in customer interactions in the tourism sector, hotels, and other hospitality-related businesses. Leading companies like Skyscanner, Expedia, and Booking.com have already transformed digitally by using chatbots to retain their sales momentum.

Mezi for travel agencies : AI-powered Mezi is a free chatbot that assists travelers in making their travel plans simple, fast, and easy. It is integrated into Facebook Messenger, Slack, and Skype and can answer more complex questions than any other travel AI as it is equipped with a large dataset of itineraries, room inventory, and pricing details.

***Fig. 11.19:** Mezi for travel agencies (Credit: Mezi)*

For the given dates and destinations, Mezi can provide the best flight and accommodation options and can also make recommendations like the best time to visit a particular place. Mezi is powerful in picking up the hints of the traveler's needs from their own words and can reply to them instantly with all possible suggestions and recommendations. Besides working for travelers, Mezi offers business subscriptions for travel agencies and travel management companies.

HiJiffy for hotels : Chatbots are also being used by hotels to handle customer lexicon by centralizing, automating, and measuring all customer care activities. Customers can contact chatbot HiJiffy through any messaging channel; it can recognize and respond to the customers instantly, creating a fast-track revenue stream for the hotels. More than 500 hoteliers and property owners running their businesses in 30 countries use HiJiffy.

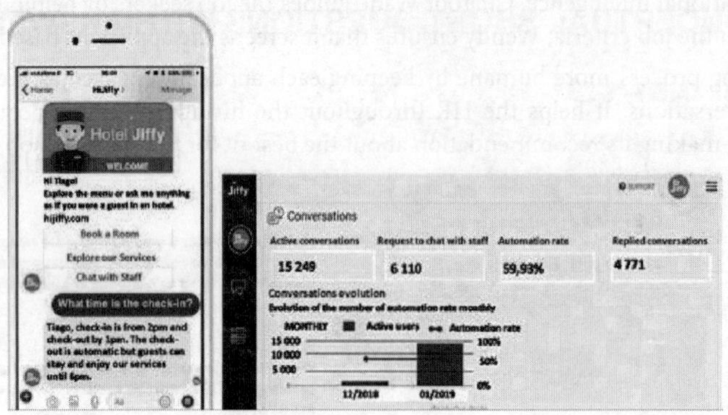

Fig. 11.20: HiJiffy for hotels (Credit: HiJiffy)

Conclusion : When a human resource is unable to handle the continuous demand for customer service well, organizations switch to AI-powered chatbots. AI chatbots are now being used in various fields to improve customer service and thus the revenue. Chatbots are useful not only for the cutting-edge tech companies but also for any start-up companies striving to scale up fast. You can also consider them to increase your sales by using this innovative way to engage your customers, enhance your company's vision, and look up to a better future.

SUMMARY

Learning is an incessant process. An intelligent machine should be able to learn new things. There are various ways of learning means change in the system or its KB brought about its interaction with a teacher or external environment so that the system improves its performance on a class of tasks.

MULTIPLE CHOICE QUESTIONS

1. **Saving knowledge so that it can be used again is known as**
   (*a*) Rote learning (*b*) Induction
   (*c*) Deduction (*d*) None of the above
2. **Rote learning is based on the principle of**
   (*a*) Caching (*b*) Forwarding
   (*c*) Backtracking (*d*) None of the above
3. **EBL uses**
   (*a*) Data intensive approach (*b*) Knowledge intensive approach
   (*c*) Divide and conquer (*d*) None of the above
4. **Human nervous system consists of**
   (*a*) 1010 neurons (*b*) 1011 neurons
   (*c*) 1012 neurons (*d*) 1014 neurons

5. **The rule used to change weight is**
   (*a*) Kirchoff's rule (*b*) Hebb's rule
   (*c*) Boehm's rule (*d*) None of the above

ANSWERS

1. (*a*) 2. (*a*) 3. (*b*) 4. (*b*) 5. (*b*)

CONCEPTUAL SHORT QUESTIONS WITH ANSWERS

Q.1. What are identification trees?

Ans. It is a learning method that uses tree representation of any problem indicating all possibilities. It is a sort of decision tree only. For example, for medical diagnoses, surveys etc it is used.

Q.2. Draw the block diagram of a general learning system.

Ans. Figure below shows the block diagram of a general learning system.

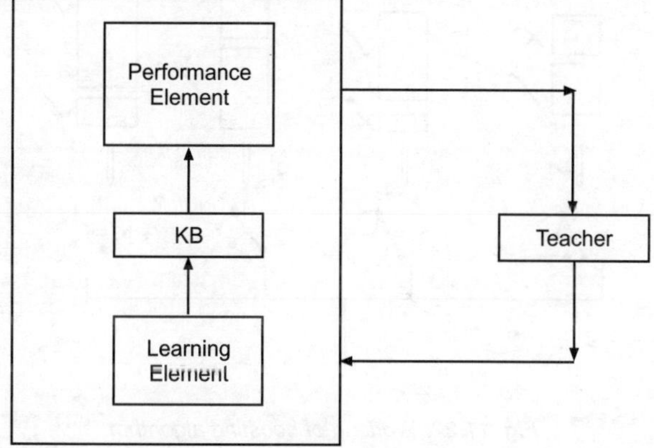

Fig. 11.21

There is some class of tasks that the system is expected to learn. The teacher watches the performance on some problem from this class and provides the system with an evaluation. Using this, the learning element modifies the current KB. Through this process of interaction, the system acquires the needed knowledge to improve its performance. Please note that the performance element must be capable of solving the class of problems.

Q.3. What is learning by discovery?

Ans. A form of learning from examples where the teacher does not supply the answers. The learning system has to look for inherent regularities in the mass of data for inferring general rules.

For example: Discovery of Kepler's law. Kepler analyzed the mass of data on planetary motion and came out with some 'beautiful' laws which generalize all the examples.

Q.4. What is learning through clustering?

Ans. Clustering is the process of grouping or classifying objects on the basis of a close association or shared characteristics. It is essentially a discovery learning process in which similarities patterns are found among a group of objects.

Q.5. What is matching?

Ans. The process of comparing two structures or patterns for equality is known as matching. It may serve to control the sequence of operations, to identify or classify objects or to retrieve items from a database.

Q.6. Discuss Boosting Algorithm of Ensemble Learning.

Ans. The most widely used ensemble method is called boosting. It works on the concept of a weighted training set. In such a training set, each example has an associated weight, $w_i \geq 0$. **Please note that the higher is the weight of an example, the higher is the importance attached to it during the learning of a hypothesis.**

Working : Boosting starts with $w_j = 1$ for all examples, *i.e.*, training set. From this the first hypothesis, hf , is generated. This hypothesis will classify some of the training examples correctly and some incorrectly. In order for the next hypothesis to perform better on the misclassified example, the weights of the misclassified ones are increased. From this new weighted training set, the hypothesis, h_2, is generated.

The process is continued until M hypothesis have been generated where M is the input of the boosting algorithm. The final ensemble hypothesis is a weighted–majority combination of M hypothesis, each weighted according to how it will perform on the training set. The process is shown below (Fig. 11.22).

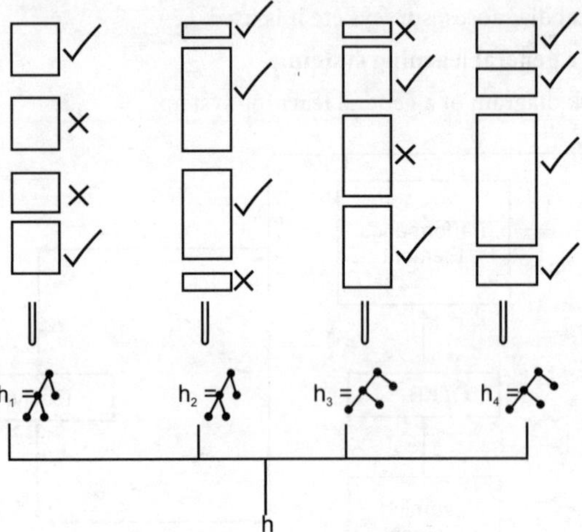

Fig. 11.22: Working of boosting algorithm

Conventions :

1. Each rectangle in the figure corresponds to an example.
2. The height of the rectangle corresponds to the weight.
3. The ticks and crosses indicate whether the example is classified correctly by the current hypothesis in the final ensemble.

It has been observed that the predictions improve as the ensemble hypothesis gets more complex.

Next, we review the premise with which we started, *i.e.*, the example pair $(x, f(x))$, *i.e.*, how do we know that the hypothesis, *h*, is close to the target function $f(x)$ if we do not know *f*. The answer to this is based on Computational Learning Theory, a field that includes AI, statistics and theoretical computer science.

Principle: "Any hypothesis which is seriously wrong will almost certainly be found out with high probability after a small number of examples because it will make on incorrect prediction".

Please understand that any hypothesis which is consistent with a sufficiently large set of training examples is unlikely to be seriously wrong, *i.e.*, it must be probably approximately correct (PAC). Any learning algorithm which returns hypotheses which are probably approximately correct is called as a **PAC–learning algorithm.** Also **understand that this leads to one important criterion on the connection between the training and the test examples, the hypothesis is to be approximately correct on the test set, not on just training set.** The basic assumption is that the training and test sets are drawn randomly and independently from the same population of examples with the same probability distribution. This is known as a **stationary assumption.** This assumption is important because without this assumption the ensemble learning cannot predict at all.

EXERCISE QUESTIONS

1. (*a*) Explain artificial neurons. Use necessary diagram.
   (*b*) Calculate the logic function 'AND' or "OR" using McCulloch-Pitts neurons.
   (*c*) Explain the Perceptron Training algorithm.
2. What is learning? Explain Rote Learning and Induction Learning.
3. (*a*) What is declarative knowledge?
   (*b*) What is baring by induction?
4. Design a learning automation that selects TV channels based on day of week and time of day (3 evening hours only) based on preference of your family. (Specify the preferences of your family clearly).
5. What are different types of learning.
6. (*a*) Give a short description of process of learning using Back Propagation NN.
   (*b*) Give a flow graph for developing a genetic algorithm.
7. (*a*) Describe an Automation. Extend it to learning automation.
   (*b*) Pick one problem area that you feel would justify the energy required to design an expert system solution and spell out the problem in some detail. Based on your intuition, which aspects of this solution would be most difficult to automate?
8. (*a*) What are the different types of learning? Explain with an example.
   (*b*) Why is the process of knowledge acquisition so tedious?

12 UNCERTAIN KNOWLEDGE AND REASONING

Q.1. What do you mean by reasoning?

Ans. Reasoning means deriving conclusions from the available set of data and information. We deal with many types of situations in this real world that are full of uncertainties. Our AI systems should be such that they should be able to handle these uncertainties. These uncertainties occur because the knowledge that we acquire is from beliefs and hypotheses. When we get some new information or when our beliefs change, we face uncertainty. Experimental errors, Randomness, lack of evidences are all the causes of uncertainties. The knowledge stored in KB is incomplete. So, an intelligent AI system should be able to handle these uncertainties. Note that the normal logical problem- solving techniques-propositional and predicate logic cannot handle such uncertain situations. To handle uncertain situations, the uncertain knowledge needs to be represented and thus reasoned.

Q.2. What is uncertain KR method?

Ans. Certain events are "certain events" like "New Delhi is the Capital of India" but some events like "It may rain today" are "uncertain events" These uncertain events need to be stored in KB now. To achieve this, the uncertain situation is represented by attaching a degree of belief factor. It is related to the probability theory. So, representation of uncertain events uses the following terminology—

a. **Belief :** It is any meaningful and coherent expression that can be represented. It may be true or false.

b. **Belief factor :** It indicates the correctness of knowledge. The value of this factor is between 0 and 1.

c. **Evidence :** It is the observation (*s*) obtained in the real world.

d. **Hypothesis :** It is a justified belief that is supported by some evidence. It is not known to be true.

e. **Knowledge :** It is a true justified belief.

f. **Meta knowledge :** It is the knowledge about the knowledge.

How to reason this uncertain knowledge?

AI aims at building intelligent systems to solve those real world problems that involve uncertainties. Reasoning is done on uncertain information contained in the KB. Please understand that without this ability an AI system is just like other programming languages or like a search table doing sequential search. So, we can say,

AI → used to build intelligent systems → Use facts and rules stored in KB. Three types of reasoning are used here—

1. **Inductive Reasoning :** It is based on the generalizations of the previous experiences about the problem. For *e.g.*

   Consider the situation—

   a. Rajiv is an Associate Professor.

   b. He teaches in a college.

   Now, if some one asks you to guess about college environment then from your experience, you can infer that college has — Professors, Lecture Rooms, Conference Rooms, Labs, play grounds etc.

   This is known as inductive reasoning. In AI field, this method is used in machine learning.

2. **Abductive Reasoning :** It is an unsound rule of inferencing meaning that the conclusion is not necessarily true for every interpretation made out of the environment. It is not very reliable reasoning method and is preferred in cases where knowledge is incomplete. It looks back through the chain of events to do reasoning.

   For *e.g.* If a student fails in his/her exam although the paper is easy. To find the reason as to why he/she failed, we need to look back in the chain of events that paper is easy, student studied, student failed, teacher is not strict. This type of reasoning is abductive reasoning.

3. **Deductive Reasoning :** It is a kind of explicit, non-reversible reasoning that works on standard logic.

   For *e.g.*, "If mobile is OFF", it is certain that no calls can be made. This is deductive reasoning.

   But the reverse is NOT true.

Q.3. Distinguish between Monotonic versus Non-Monotonic Reasoning.

Ans.

Monotonic Reasoning	Non-Monotonic Reasoning
1. All new knowledge that is added to the KB must be consistent with the previous knowledge.	1. In uncertain situations addition of new axioms may contradict with earlier and might be required to be removed from the KB.
2. The size of the KB always increases monotonically	2. The size of the KB increases-non monotonically.
3. No retractions of rules (removals) are allowed.	3. Allow retractions also *i.e.*, removal of contradictory facts.
4. Inference methods available are insufficient.	4. Inference are complete and methods justified.
5. Traditional KR techniques like PL, FOPL, Propositional logic cannot accommodate the real world's changing situations. For *e.g.*: PL, FOPL, Propositional logic, Theorem Proving etc.	5. These systems like TMS allows the revision in belief and accommodate the real world changing situations. For *e.g.*: Truth Maintenance Systems (TMS).

Q.4. Describe the TMS-Truth Maintenance Systems (or Belief or Revision Maintenance Systems).

Ans.

1. TMS are "truth-maintenance systems" which have been implemented to permit a form of non-monotonic reasoning by permitting the addition of changing (even contradictory) statements to a knowledge base.
2. Also known as "belief-revision" and "revision-maintenance-systems" are companion- components to inference system, (of our basic KBS).
3. Main job– of TMS is to maintain "consistency of knowledge" being used by the problem solver and not to perform any inference functions.

   As such, it frees the problem solver from any concerns of consistency and allows it to concentrate on the problem solution aspects.
4. TMS also gives the inference–component, the latitude to perform non-monotonic inferences.
5. When new discoveries are made, this more recent information can displace previous conclusions that are no longer valid. In this way, set of beliefs available to the problem solver will continue to be current and consistent.

   For e.g., Shows role of TMS

   Problem Solver

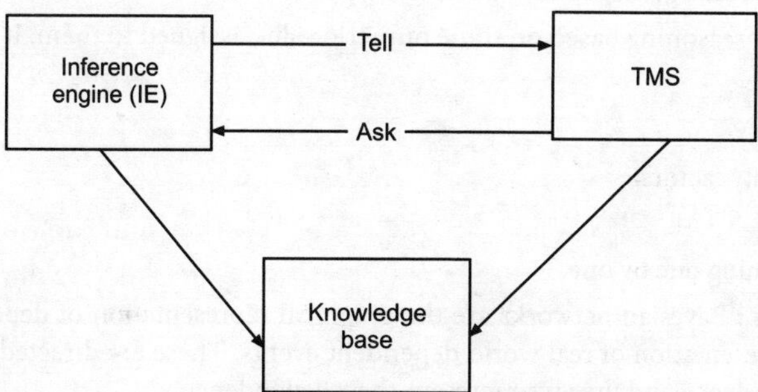

Fig. 12.1: Architecture of the Problem Solver with a TMS

Working : The inference engine (IE) solves domain problems based on its current belief set, while the TMS maintains the currently active belief set. The updating process is incremental. After each inference, information is exchanged between the two components. The IE tells the TMS what deductions it has made. The TMS, in turn, asks question about current beliefs and reasons for failure. If maintains a consistent set of beliefs for the IE to work with even if now knowledge is added and removed.

For *e.g.*,

S1: Say, KB contained the propositions P, $P \rightarrow Q$ and modus ponens.

S2: From this, the IE would right fully conclude Q and add this conclusion to the KB.

S3: Later, if it was learned that $\sim P$ was appropriate, if would be added to the KB resulting in a contradiction.

S4: Consequently, it would be necessary to remove P to eliminate the inconsistency. But, with P now removed, Q is no longer a justified belief. It too should be removed.

This type of belief revision is the job of the TMS.

7. Actually, the TMS does not discard conclusions like Q as suggested. That could be wasteful, since P may again become valid, which would require that Q and facts justified by Q be received. Instead, the TMS maintains dependency records for all such conclusion. These records determine which set of beliefs are current (which are to be used by the IE). Thus, Q would be removed from the current belief set by making appropriate updates to the records and not by erasing Q. Since Q would not be lost, its rederivation would not be necessary if P became valid once again.
8. TMS maintains complete records of reasons of justifications for beliefs. Each proposition or statement having at least one valid justification is made a part of the current belief set. Statements lacking acceptable justifications are excluded from this set. When a contradiction is discovered, the statements responsible for the contradiction are identified and an appropriate one is retracted. This in turn may result in other retractions and additions. The procedure used to perform this process is called "dependency-directed back tracking".
9. TMS maintains records to reflect retractions and additions so that the IE will always known its current belief set. The records are maintained in the form of a "dependency- -network".

   a. The nodes in the network represent KB entries such as premises, conclusions, inference rules and the like.

   b. Attached to the nodes are justifications which represent the inference steps from which the node was derived.

   Nodes in the belief set must have valid justifications.

   A premise (or a node with no justification) is a fundamental belief which is assumed to be always true. Premises need no justifications. They form a base from which all other currently active nodes can be explained in terms of valid justifications.

   Thus, TMS maintains a consistent set of beliefs for the inference engine to rely upon even if new knowledge is added or removed in the KB.

   For *e.g.*,

   a. Justification based TMS (JTMS).

   b. Assumption based TMS (ATMS).

   c. Logic based TMS (LTMS).

Q.5. What is Probabilistic Reasoning? Explain its different types in detail.

Ans. It is a statistical method of reasoning based on some numeric value assigned to them. It involves 4 methods—

a. Bayesian belief networks.

b. Dempster Shaffer theory.

c. Reasoning with certainty factors.

d. Fuzzy reasoning.

Let us discuss these reasoning one by one.

Bayesian belief networks : Bayesian networks are the graphical representation of dependent events. These networks are an easy graphical representation of real world dependent events. These are directed acyclic graphs in which nodes represent the events or evidence and the arcs represent their dependence.

Basic Properties of Bayesian networks

1. They have a set of random, discrete or continuous variables generating the nodes of the network.
2. They have directed links or arrows connecting a pair of nodes.

   For *e.g.* (a) ⟶ (b)

   Here, '*a*' is parent of '*b*'.
3. Each nodes (n_i) has a conditional probability distribution *i.e.*, $P(n_i|\text{parent}(n_i))$

   This quantifies the effect of parent on the node.
4. The graph has no directed cycles *i.e.*, these networks are directed acyclic graphs (DAG).
5. The topology of graph indicates that node specifies the conditional independence relationships of the problem.
6. Once belief network is constructed, an inference engine of an intelligent system can use it to maintain and propagate beliefs. If some new information is received, the effects of same can be propagated throughout the network until equilibrium probabilities are reached.
7. At equilibrium all propositions will have consistent probabilities. For example: Medical diagnosis systems like CASNET uses this reasoning.

   Dempster Shafer Theory : There are various theories available for example Bayesian networks that consider or find out the belief from some premises from a single permit of observation. This theory was released because of the following reasons: -
8. Bayesian theory is only concerned about single evidences.
9. Bayesian probability cannot describe ignorance.
10. DST is an evidence theory, it combines all possible outcomes of the problem. Hence, it is used to solve problems where there may be a chance that a different evidence will lead to some different result.
11. The uncertainty in this model is given by: -
    a. Consider all possible outcomes.
    b. Belief will lead to believe in some possibility by bringing out some evidence.
    c. Plausibility will make evidence compatibility with possible outcomes.

For example, let us consider a room where four persons are presented A, B, C, D (let's say) and suddenly lights are out and when the lights come back, B has died due to stabbing on his back with a knife. No one came into the room and no one left the room. Also, B has not committed suicide. Then we have to find out who is the murderer? To solve these there are following possibilities: -

- Either {A} or {C} or {D} has killed him.
- Either {A, C} or {C, D} or {A, D} has killed him.
- OR THE THREE OF THEM KILLED HIM I.E. {A, C, D}.
- None of them killed him {0} (lets justify).

There will be the possible evidences by which we can find the murderer by measure of plausibility. Using the above example, we can say:

Set of possible conclusion (*P*) : $\{p_1, p_2, \ldots\ldots.p_n\}$ where *P* is set of possible conclusion and cannot be exhaustive means at least one

- $(p)i$ must be true.
- $(p)i$ must be mutually exclusive.

Power set will contain $2n$ elements where n is number of elements in the possible set.

For example,

if $P = \{a, b, c\}$, the power set is given as $(0, \{a\}, \{b\}, \{c\}, \{a, b\}, \{b, c\}, \{a, c\}, \{a, b, c\}) = 2^3$ elements.

Mass function, *m*(*k*): It is an interpretation of $m(\{k \text{ or } B\})$ *i.e.* it means that there is evidence for {*K* or *B*} which cannot be divided among more specific beliefs for *K* and *B*.

Belief in K: The belief in element *k* of power set is the sum of masses of elements which are subsets of K. This can be explained with an example.

Let's say K = {*a*, *b*, *c*}

$$\text{Bel}(K) = m(a) + m\ (b) + m\ (c) + m\ (a, b) + m\ (a, c) + m\ (b, c) + m\ (a, b, c)$$

Plausibility in *K*: It is the sum of masses of set that intersects with *K*. That is,

$$P1\ (k) = m(a) + m\ (b) + m\ (c) + m\ (a, b) + m\ (b, c) + m\ (a, c) + m\ (a, b, c)$$

Characteristics of Dempster Shafer Theory

6. It will ignore part such that probability of all events aggregates to 1.
7. Ignorance is reduced in this theory by adding more and more evidences.
8. Combination rule is used to combine various types of possibilities.

Advantages:

1. As we add more information, uncertainty interval reduces.
2. DST has much lower value of ignorance.
3. Diagnose hierarchies can be represented using this.
4. Person dealing with such problems is free to think about evidences.

Disadvantages:

1. In this the computation effort is high, we have to deal with 2n of sets.

Ignorance representation in DST:

1. Shafer advertises belief functions as representing ignorance better than probability functions.
2. The problem with probability functions is well known:
   a. Ignorance is represented by uniform distributions.
   b. But refining the space of possibilities yields inconsistency.
3. Belief functions avoid this problem:
   a. Ignorance is represented by various belief functions.
   b. Refining the space preserves previous assignments.

Problems associated with DST : By analyzing the relationships among chance, weight of evidence and degree of belief show that the assertion "probability functions are special cases of belief functions" and the assertion "Dempster's rule can be used to combine belief functions based on distinct bodies of evidence" together load to inconsistency in DST. To solve this problem, we must reject some fundamental postulates of theory.

We are in a position to solve an example now.

Q.6. Consider a coin flipping problem. Suppose a shady character comes up to you and offers to bet you Rs100 that his coin will come up 'heads' on the next flip. Given that the coin might or might not be fair. What belief should you ascribe to the event that it comes up 'heads' ?

Ans. According to the question there are three things that can occur-

a. An unbiased coin.
b. A biased coin [with H as favorable].
c. A biased coin [with T as favorable].

Case a: An unbiased coin

$$P(T) = P(H) = ½$$

H → accepted.

T → not accepted.

So, probability of losing (100) = ½

Which is a fair case although.

Case *b*: Imagine choosing a coin with Heads as a more favorable outcome like

For 10 trials → HHHT HHT HTH

So, a reasonable estimate can be developed of it's bias, that is-

$$P(T) = 0.7$$

Since 0.7 >> 0.5

So, we have developed our bias base and the problem.

Case *c*: Similarly, considering that the coin is tossed and Tails is favorable for 10 trials-

HTTT TTH THT

$$P(T) = 0.7$$

Since 0.7 >> 0.5

But the problem is which coin is chosen.

As choosing each coin contains no bias, so right now we are stuck as we have to count number of heads for each coin but we don't know which coin is being flipped out of our three coins.

It turns out that we can make progress by starting with a guess for the coin bias, that will allow us to estimate which coin was chosen in each trial and come up with an estimate for the expected number of heads for each coin.

Probability of choosing 1/3 for each of the coin is-

$$P(H) = 1/3 * 0.5 + 1/3 * 0.7 + 1/3 * 0.3$$

$$P(H) = 0.5$$

Hence, for the assumed case, we can conclude that there is a fair chance that the person losses or win the Rs. 100. Stating that when the coins are tossed, they have equal probability of getting selected and bias of the coins are equally distributed.

If from case-*c*,

Bias of Heads > Bias of Tails

Then $P(H) >> 0.5$

Hence, the chance that the shady character wins is much high.

If $P(T) >> 0.5$, then the chance that we will win is much high.

Reasoning with Certainty Factors (*CF*) : The certainty factors are human estimates of symptoms/cause relationship and their probability measures. In this type of reasoning, we need to combine the effects of all of the facts and assign a single value to the rule known as CF *i.e.*, here the problem is represented as a simple rule as follows—

IF *p* and *q* and *r* THEN S(CF).

Please note that CF-certainty factor will hold good if we are certain about facts. Also note that a new CF would be calculated whenever there is any change in the measure of belief of any or all of the facts.

Certainty theory does not produce an algebra for correct reasoning. It is adhoc meaning that the confidence of human expert in his result is approximate, heuristic and informal.

For *e.g.*: MYCIN expert system uses this type of reasoning.

The certainty theory makes simple assumption for creating and assigning confidence measures 'for' and 'against' any given situation.

Fuzzy Logic Reasoning : According to George Boole, human thinking and decision are based on Yes or No reasoning or logic 1 and logic 0. Accordingly, Boolean algebra was developed. Even expert systems founded this logic. But it has been argued that human thinking does not always follows crisp YES or NO logic rather it is quite vague, uncertain, imprecise or fuzzy in nature. Based on the nature of fuzzy human thinking, Lofti Zadeh, a computer scientist at the University of California, Berkeley, originated the fuzzy logic or fuzzy set theory in 1965. Classical set theory/crisp set theory (given by George Cantor) is fundamental to the study of fuzzy sets. Please understand that as Boolean logic had its roots in the theory of crisp sets, fuzzy logic has its roots in the theory of fuzzy sets.

Also note that this process of making a crisp quantity fuzzy is known as fuzzification. We do this by recognizing that many of the quantities we consider to be crisp and deterministic are actually non-deterministic. They carry considerable uncertainty. If the form of uncertainty happens to arise because of imprecision, ambiguity or vagueness then the variable is probable fuzzy and can be represented by a membership function.

NOTE: Reasoning about imprecise propositions is an ultimate goal of fuzzy logic and is referred to as approximate reasoning.

Features of membership characteristics functions

1. It describes vague natural real world concepts.
2. A fuzzy set admits the possibility of partial members with associated membership characteristic function value.
3. The degree of an object belonging to a fuzzy set is denoted by membership value between 0 and 1.
4. A membership function associated with given fuzzy set maps input value to its appropriate membership value.
5. Uncertainties are represented with membership functions and then this function is manipulated in a method defined in fuzzy theory.

Laws of operations on fuzzy sets :

1. **Law of Equality:** "If A and B are two fuzzy sets such that $A, B \supseteq U$ then $A = B$ iff $mA(x) = mB(x)$ for all $x \in U$".
2. **Law of containment:** "$A \subseteq B$ iff $mA(x) \leq mB(x)$ for all $x \in U$.
3. **Union law:** " $A \cup B$ is the smallest fuzzy subset of which both A and B are subsets."
4. **Intersection law:** " $A \cap B$ is the largest fuzzy subset which is a subset of both A and B".
5. **Distributive law :**
   a. $A \cup (B \cap C) = (A \cup B) \cap (A \cup C)$
   b. $A \cap (B \cup C) = (A \cap B) \cup (A \cap C)$
6. **Associative law :**
   a. $(A \cup B) \cup C = A \cup (B \cup C)$
   b. $(A \cap B) \cap C = A \cap (B \cap C)$
7. **Commutative law :**
   a. $A \cup B = B \cup A$
   b. $A \cap B = B \cap A$
8. **Idempotency law :**
   a. $A \cup A = A$
   b. $A \cap A = A$

Certain other laws used on membership characteristics functions are as follows–

a. **Union law :**
$m(A(x) \cup B(x))$ or $mA(x)$ or $B(x)$
$= MAX\{mA(x), mB(x)\}$

b. **Intersection law :**
$m(A(x) \cap B(x))$ or $mA(x)$ or $B(x)$
$= MIN\{mA(x), mB(x)\}$

c. **Negation law :**
Negation of $mA(x) = 1 - mA(x)$

d. **Dilation :**
If A is a fuzzy set such that $A \subseteq U$, for all $x \in A$, the dilation of A is defined as–
$DIL(A) = [mA(x)]^{1/2}$ for $x \in U$

e. **Concentration :**
The concentration of A is defined as–
$CON(A) = [mA(x)]^2$ for all $x \in U$

(f) **Normalization :**
The normalization of A is defined as–
$NORM(A) = mA(x)/MAX\{mA(x)\}$

NOTE: Concentration is opposite of dilation.

Normalization is the process of normalizing all characteristic functions to the same base. These operations are used to manipulate the membership characteristic function according to the variation in fuzziness of a function.

To summarize, we can say in nutshell that because real world situations are very vague and cannot be crisply defined, so they are modeled using fuzzy theory only in AI.

SUMMARY

We encounter various situations in our real life where the outcome is uncertain. This chapter focuses on how this type of knowledge is represented and reasoned. Various theories have been given to accomplish the same.

MULTIPLE CHOICE QUESTIONS

1. The knowledge about the knowledge is known as

(*a*) knowledge (*b*) Meta knowledge

(*c*) Knowledge base (*d*) None of the above

2. A type of reasoning which is based on generalizations of previous experience about the problem is known as

(*a*) Inductive reasoning (*b*) Aductive reasoning

(*c*) Deductive reasoning (*d*) None of the above

3. PL and FOPL are examples of

(*a*) Monotonic reasoning (*b*) Non-monotonic reasoning

(*c*) TMS (*d*) None of the above

4. TMS stands for

(*a*) True management system

(*b*) Teller management system

(*c*) Truth maintenance system

(*d*) None of the above

5. Which unit makes inferences based on current set of beliefs

(*a*) Inference engine (*b*) TMS

(*c*) KB (*d*) None of the above

6. CASNET uses

(*a*) Fuzzy logic reasoning

(*b*) Bayesian belief networks

(*c*) Dempster shaffer theory

(*d*) None of the above

7. MYCIN uses

(*a*) Reasoning with certainity factor (*b*) Fuzzy logic

(*c*) Bayesian networks (*d*) None of the above

8. Fuzzy logic has its roots in the theory of

(*a*) Crisp sets (*b*) Fuzzy sets

(*c*) Boolean algebra (*d*) None of the above

9. The process of making a crisp quantity fuzzy is known as

(*a*) fuzzification (*b*) de-fuzzification

(*c*) assumption (*d*) None of the above

10. Concentration is opposite of

(*a*) Fuzzification (*b*) Dilation

(*c*) Normalization (*d*) None of the above

ANSWERS

1. (*a*)	**2.** (*a*)	**3.** (*a*)	**4.** (*c*)	**5.** (*a*)
6. (*b*)	**7.** (*a*)	**8.** (*b*)	**9.** (*a*)	**10.** (*b*)

CONCEPTUAL SHORT QUESTIONS WITH ANSWERS

Q.1. In a database, a rule is defined as (P1 and P2) or P3? R1 (0.8) and R2 (0.3) where P1, P2, P3 are premises and R1, R2 are the conclusions of the rule with CFs 0.8, 0.3 respectively. If any running program has produced P1, P2 and P3 with CFs as 0.5, 0.8, 0.2 respectively. Find CF of results on the basis of premises.

Ans. The CF of R1 is 0.8 (given)

∴ CF of R1 based on premises will be

$$= 0.8 * 0.5 = 0.40$$

Similarly, CF of R2 based on premises will be (0.3 * 0.5) = 0.15

Q.2. An admissions committee for a college is trying to determine the probability that an admitted candidate is really qualified. The relevant probabilities are given in the Bayes network shown here. Calculate P(A/D).

Ans.

1. $P(A) = 1/2$

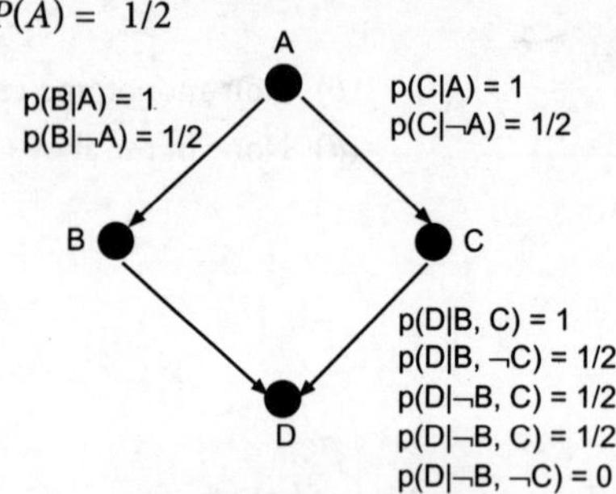

$A =$ application is qualified

$B =$ applicant has high grade point average

$C =$ applicant has excellent recommendations

$D =$ applicant is admitted

Find $p(A/D) = ?$

2.
$$p(A|D) = p(A, D)/p(D)$$

$$\begin{aligned} p(A,D) = {} & p(D|B, C)p(B|A)p(C|A)p(A) \\ & + p(D|B, \neg C)p(B|A)p(\neg C|A)p(A) \\ & + p(D|\neg B, C)p(\neg B|A)p(C|A)p(A) \\ & + p(D|\neg B, \neg C)p(\neg B|A)p(\neg C|A)p(A) \\ = {} & 1/2 \end{aligned}$$

$$\begin{aligned} p(D) = {} & p(D/B, C)p(B/A)p(C/A)p(A) \\ & + p(D|B, \neg C)p(B|A)p(\neg C|A)p(A) \\ & + p(D|\neg B, C)p(\neg B|A)p(C|A)p(A) \\ & + p(D|\neg B,\neg C)p(\neg B/A)p(\neg C|A)p(A) \\ & + p(D|B,C)p(B|\neg A)p(C|\neg A)p(\neg A) \\ & + p(D|B,\neg C)p(B|\neg A)p(\neg C|\neg A)p(\neg A) \\ & + p(D|\neg B,C)p(\neg B|\neg A)p(C|\neg A)p(\neg A) \\ & + p(D|\neg B,C)p(\neg B|\neg A)p(\neg C|\neg A)p(\neg A) \\ = {} & 3/4 \end{aligned}$$

Therefore, $p(A|D) = 2/3$.

Q.3. What is defuzzification?

Ans. It is the process of Rounding fuzzy set off from its location in the unit hypercube to the nearest vertex in a geometric sense. If a fuzzy set is a collection of membership values or a vector of values on the unit interval then defuzzification reduces this vector to a single scalar quantity. Aggregating two or more fuzzy output sets yields a new fuzzy set in the fuzzy inference algorithm. A result in form of a fuzzy set is converted into a crisp result by this process of defuzzification.

Q.4. In answering a question in TNPCE, a student either knows the answer or guesses. Let p be the probability that he knows the answer and $(1 - p)$ be the probability that he guesses. Assume that a student who guesses the answer will be correct with probability 1/5. What is the probability that a student knew the answer to a question given that he answered it correctly?

Ans. Let E_1 be the event that the student knew the correct answer.

E_2 be the event that student guesses the correct answer. A be the student that the student gets the correct answer.

We need to find $P(E_1|A)$.

From the data,

$$P(E_1) = p$$

and $$P(E_2) = 1 - p$$

and $$P(A \mid F_2) = \frac{1}{5}$$

$$P(A| E_1) = P(\text{the student gets the correct answer given that he knew the correct answer})$$

$= 1$

$$\therefore \quad P(E_1 \mid A) = \frac{P(E_1)P(A \mid E_1)}{P(E_1).P(A \mid E_1) + P(E_2).P(A \mid E_2)}$$

$$= \frac{P(1)}{P(1) + (1 - P)\frac{1}{5}}$$

$$= \frac{5p}{4p+1}$$

Q.5. Compare JTMS and LTMS in a tabular form.

Ans.

JTMS (by Jon Doyle)	LTMS (by Mc Allester)
1. It is a justified TMS.	1. It is a logic based TMS.
2. It is used for Non-monotonic reasoning where information is incomplete.	2. It uses default logic and non-monotonic reasoning, abductions and inheritance.
3. Representation is in a manner where rules are used.	3. Representation is in a manner where logic is used.
4. Both logic and its contradiction are not asserted.	4. Both logic and contradictions are asserted.

EXERCISE QUESTIONS

1. (*a*) What are the different types of fuzzy membership function? What is the criteria to define a fuzzy membership function?

   (*b*) How uncertainty is captured using probabilistic reasoning? How is it different from handling uncertainty using fuzzy logic?
2. Why is it that FOL fails to cope with medical diagnosis problem?
3. Why logic is needed behind uncertainty?
4. Define: conditional probability and uncertainty.
5. What is the basic element for a language?

13 NATURAL LANGUAGE PROCESSING

Q.1. What is NLP? Explain this system.

Ans. A natural language is any of the languages naturally used by humans that is not artificial or man-made language. Natural Language Processing (NLP) is a subfield of AI and linguistics. NLP provides methods for performing useful tasks with natural languages. To give a feel of a human expert, computer is needed to interact with the user in natural languages. What is done in NLP? The answer is here.

S1 : User inputs in form of a natural language.

S2 : It goes to the Natural Language Interface (NLI).

S3 : Output is obtained in a language form that is understood by the application program.

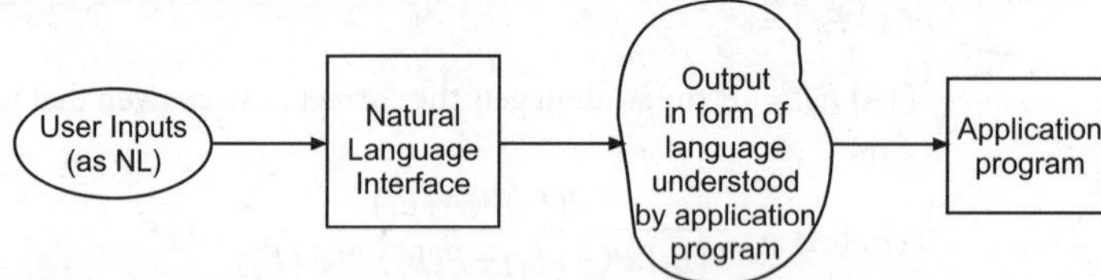

Fig. 13.1: NLP system

KBS need query languages for information retrieval. A good system should interact with database in natural language. To interact with the database in natural languages, computer is required to have basic knowledge of alphabets, lexicon, grammar, words formation, sentence formation rules of that language. Also required are general knowledge, commonsense knowledge, domain specific knowledge etc for sentence interpretation in a proper way—

NLP includes—

a. Speech Synthesis.

b. Speech Recognition.

c. Natural language understanding.

d. Natural language generation.

e. Machine Translation.

Speech synthesis: Synthesis of natural sounding speech is complex as it needs some understanding of what is being spoken to ensure for correct information.

Speech recognition : Basically, the reduction of continuous sound waves to discrete words.

Natural language understanding

It involves moving isolated words to meaning. Natural language generation

It involves generating appropriate NL responses to unpredictable inputs.

Machine Translation (MT): Translation of one NL into another.

Please note that natural language understanding is sometimes referred to as an AI- complete problem because natural language recognition seems to require extensive knowledge about the outside world and the ability to manipulate it.

Q.2. Explain the Levels of Knowledge Used in Language Understanding.

Ans. Language understanding needs—

***a.* Phonological knowledge :** A phoneme is the smallest unit of sound and relates to the sound of word.

***b.* Syntactic knowledge :** It relates to how words are put together to form grammatically correct sentence.

c. **Semantic knowledge :** It relates to the meaning of words and phrases and how they combine to form a meaningful sentence.

d. **Morphological knowledge :** It relates to word construction from basic units called morphemes.

e. **Pragmatic knowledge :** It relates to the use of sentence in different contexts and how the contexts affect the meaning of sentences.

f. **Word knowledge :** It relates to the language a user must have in order to understand and carry on a conversation.

Q.3. Explain the Phases of Natural Language Understanding.

Ans.

1. **Morphological analysis :** Individual words are analyzed into their components, and nonword tokens, such as punctuation, are separated from the words.

2. **Syntactic analysis :** Linear sequences of words are transformed into structures that show how the words relate to each other. Some word sequences may be rejected if they violate the language's rules for how words may be combined. For example, an English syntactic analyzer would reject the sentence "Boy the go the to store".

   Syntactic analysis determines: Whether the sentence is a legal sentence of the language or generates legal sentences using a grammar and lexicon and if so, returns a fare tree for the sentence representing its structure. It is the process of parsing that is computers, equivalent of diagramming a sentence.

3. **Semantic analysis :** The structures created by the syntactic analyzer are assigned meanings. In other words, a mapping is made between the syntactic structures and objects in the task domain. Structures for which no such mapping is possible may be rejected. For example, in most universes, the sentence "Colorless green ideas sleep furiously" would be rejected as semantically anomalous.

   Thus, it is the process of extracting the meaning of an utterance as interpreted by a speaker. It takes the parse tree for the sentence and interprets it according to the possible meanings of its constituent parts. A representation of semantics may include information about different meanings of words and their characteristics.

4. **Discourse integration :** The meaning of an individual sentence may depend on the sentences that precede it and may influence the meanings of the sentences that follow it. For example, the word "it" in the sentence, "John wanted it" depends on the prior discourse context while the word "John" may influence the meaning of later sentences (such as, "He always had".)

   A discourse is any string of language usually which is more than one sentence long. For *e.g.*, Textbooks novel, weather reports and conversations are all discourses. The meaning of an individual sentence may depend on the sentences which precede it and may also influence the meaning of the sentences which follow it.

   For *e.g.* the word 'it' in the sentence, "Mayur wanted it" depends on the prior discourse, it may refer to a bike, Mayur is interested in purchasing and he purchased it. While the word, 'Mayur' may influence the meaning of later sentences such as "He purchased the bike" This type of interpretation is of a pronoun or a definite noun phrase which refers to an object in a world. The resolution is based on knowledge of the world and of the previous parts of the discourse. Usually, resolution is just a matter of selecting a referent from a list of candidates but sometimes it involves the creation of new candidates.

   Please understand that choosing the best referent is a process of disambiguation which relies on combining. a variety of semantic, syntactic and pragmatic information. But some clues in form of constraints are required.

   The rhythm and intonation of a language refers to Prosody. Rhythm is often used in the babbling of infants and children's wordplay.

5. **Pragmatic analysis :** The structure representing what was said is reinterpreted to determine what was actually meant. For example, the sentence "Do you know what time it is?" should be interpreted as a request to be told the time.

   The boundaries between these five phases are often very fuzzy. The phases are sometimes performed in sequence, and they are sometimes performed all at once. If they are performed in sequence, one may need to appeal for assistance to another. For example, part of the process of performing the syntactic analysis of the sentence "Is the glass jar peanut butter?" is deciding how to form two noun phrases out of the four nouns at the end of the sentence (giving a sentence of the form "Is the x >>?"). All of the following constituents are syntactically possible: glas, glass jar, glass jar peanut, jar peanut better, peanut butter, and butter. A syntactic process or on its own has no way to choose among these, and so any decision must be made by appealing to some model of the world in which some of these phrases make sense and others do not. If we do this, then we get a syntactic structure in which the constituents "glass jar" and "peanut butter" appear. Thus, although it is often useful to separate these five processing phases to some extent, they can all interact in a variety of ways, making a complete separation impossible.

Q.4. Define Parsing and explain Its types.

Ans. The process of converting a sentence into a tree that represents a sentences syntactic structure is known as parsing. It tells us whether it is a valid sentence as defined by our grammar. If a sentence is not a valid sentence then it can't be parsed.

For example: Consider the following sentence

"The white dog crossed the road". Its parse tree is as shown in Fig. 13.2.

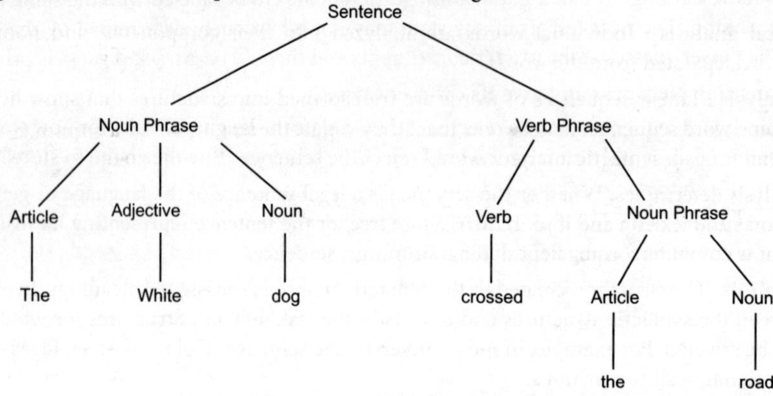

***Fig. 13.2:* A Parsed Sentence**

It is clear from the above Fig. 13.2 that how a sentence is made up of a noun phrase and a verb phrase. The noun phrase consists of an article, an adjective and a noun. The verb phrase consists of a verb and a noun phrase, in turn, consists of an article and a noun. Parsing is, thus, a typical AI search problem in which —

g. The initial state is input sequence of words.

h. The goal state is a complete tree representing the whole sentence structure.

i. The production rules are grammar rules.

j. The parser can be viewed as searching through the space of all possible parse trees to find the correct parse tree for the sentence in consideration.

Parsing is of two types—

a. Top-down parsing.

b. Bottom-up parsing.

Parse trees can be built in a top-down fashion or in a bottom-up fashion. Let us understand this now.

a. **Top-down Parsing :** Building a parse tree from the top-down involves starting from a sentence and determining which of the possible rewriters for a sentence can be applied to the sentence that is being parsed. Hence, in this passing the sentence would be rewritten using the following rule:

Sentence → Noun phrase, Verb phrase

Then the verb phrase and the noun phrase would be broken down recursively in the same way, until only terminal symbols are left.

b. **Bottom-up parsing :** To build a parse tree from the bottom-up, the terminal symbol of the sentence is first replaced by their corresponding non-terminals (*e.g.* dog is replaced by noun) and then these non-terminals are combined to match the right-hand sides of rewrite rules.

For example: 'the' and 'road' (see Fig. 13.2) will be combined using the following rewrite rule:

Noun phrase → Article, Noun

But neither of these techniques adequately exploits the constraints presented by the grammar and the input word.

Some other Parsing Techniques :

1. **Bidirectional Parsing :** These parsers start the parsing from both the directions simultaneously. It implies that they parse the sentence simultaneously. It implies that they parse the sentence simultaneously, from 'left to right' and from 'right to left'.
2. **Deterministic Parsing :** A parsing in which there is only one replacement possibility for every word is known as deterministic parsing. Each arc will have a different test condition. These parsers cannot do back tracking. Please note that if the incorrect test choice is accepted from some state, the parser will fail. This happens when one word satisfies more than one-word categories like noun and verb or adjective and verb. To overcome this problem of correct choice, the parser uses look ahead mechanism. But even then, designing such parsers is not difficult.
3. **Non-Deterministic Parsing :** A parsing that allows different arcs to be labeled with the same test is known as Non-Deterministic parsing. The next test from any state may not be uniquely determined by the state and the current input word. The parser guesses at the proper constituents and then do backtrack if guess is proven to be wrong.

Q.5. What are the Transition Networks and give Its different types.

Ans. A transition network is a finite state automaton that is used to represent a part of a grammar. A transition network parser uses a number of these transition network to represent its entire grammar. Each network represents one non-terminal symbol in the grammar.

Actually, transition network is a method of parsing which represents the grammar as a set of finite state machines (FSM). An FSM is a model of computational behavior where each node represents an internal state of the system and the arcs are the means of moving between the states. They are used in automata theory to represent grammar. In case of parsing of natural language, the arcs in the networks represent either a terminal or a non-terminal symbol. Rules in the grammar correspond to a path through a network. Each non-terminal is represented by a different network.

When moving from one state to the next through the network, the parser tests the label on the arc.

Case 1 : If it is a terminal symbol, the parser will check whether it matches the next word in the input sentence.

Case 2 : If it is a non-terminal symbol, the parser moves to the network for that symbol and attempts to find a path through that.

Case 3 : If it finds a path through that network it returns to the higher-level network and continues. If the parser fails to find a path through that network, it backtracks and attempts another path. If it succeeds in finding a path, the sentence is a valid one.

Please understand that the parsing of the sentence continues in this fashion until the top- level sentence network is successfully traversed. Also note that the transition network allows each non-terminal to be represented in a single network rather than by numerous rules. This makes this approach more concise than grammars. But there is a disadvantage too. These transition network does not produce a parse tree for sentences. Also tracing the path through the network can be unclear for complex sentences.

How do we represent transition networks?

Transition networks are based on application of directed graphs (or digraphs) and finite state automata. This graph is now used to represent the syntactic structure of the sentence.

Nodes—Represent various states.

Arcs—Represent transition from certain states to final state.

We start at a given node, transverse an arc if the current word in the sentence is in the category on the arc. Please note that if an arc is followed, the current word is updated to the next word. Also note that a sentence is accepted by transition network, if there is a path from the start node to a final node with arc accounting for every word in a sentence.

How it works?

In each transition network, S1 is the start state. When a phrase is applied to a transition network, the first word is compared against one of the arcs leading from the first state. If this word matches one of those arcs then the network moves to the next state.

For *e.g.*: Consider the following transition network—

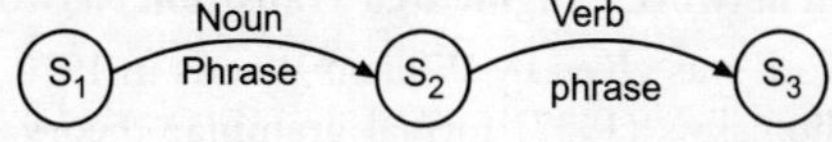

When this network is presented with a noun phrase, it will move from state S_1 to State S_2.

Please understand that if a phrase is presented to a transition network and no match is found from the current state then that network cannot be used and another network must be tried. Also remember that transition networks can be used to determine whether a sentence is grammatically correct, at least as per the rules of the grammar the networks represent. And parsing using transition involves exploring a search space of possible parses in a depth-first fashion.

Let us consider an example to understand this "A dog sat".

We begin in state S_1 in the sentence transition networks. To proceed, we must follow the arc that is labeled as Noun phrase. Thus, we move out from the sentence network into the Noun phrase network. The first arc of the Noun phrase network is labeled as Noun. So, we move into the Noun networks. We now follow each of the arc in the Noun network and discover that our first word, 'A', does not match any of them. Hence, we backtrack to the next arc in the Noun phrase network. This arc is labeled as Article, so we move onto the Article transition network. Here, on examining the second label we find that the first word *i.e.* matched by the terminal symbol on this arc. Therefore, we consume the word, "A", and move on to the state S_2 in the Article network. Because this is a success node, we are able to return to the Noun phrase network and move on to the state S_2 in this network. We now have an arc labeled Noun. As before, we move into the Noun network and find that our next word, "dog" matches. So, we move to state S_4 in the Noun phrase network. This is a success node and so we move back to the sentence network and repeat the process for the verb phrase arc.

Please note that it is possible for a system to use transition networks to generate a derivation tree for a sentence and also to determine whether the sentence is grammatically valid, it parses it fully to obtain further information by semantic analysis from the sentence. This can be done by simply having the system build up the tree by noting which arc it successfully followed—

For *e.g.*: When it successfully follows the Noun phrase arc in the sentence network, the system generates a root node labeled sentence and an arc leading from that node to a new node labeled Noun phrases when the system follows the Noun Phrase network and identifies an article and a noun, these are similarly added to the tree. In this way, a full parse tree for a given sentence can be generated using transition networks.

As explained earlier that the starting point in studying ATN'S is the finite–state transition diagram (FSTS) as shown below.

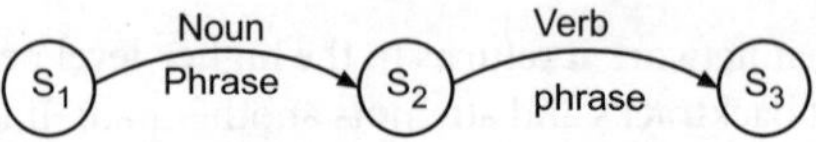

***Fig. 13.3:** The FSTD that can process any noun phrase starting with "the"*

FSTD diagrams consist of a set of nodes and arcs connecting the node. The rules followed are:-

1. All terminal symbols (words of the sentence) are represented as arcs.
2. One state (or node) is defined as 'S' the START state and one subset of states as the FINAL state '*F*'.
3. A FSTD specifies a (dynamic) process for operating on arbitrary sentences instead of a static relationship between words as in a semantic network. That is why an ATN is sometimes called as a finite state machine.

The FSTD processes the input sentence, one word at a time, checking to see if the word matches the prescribed structure. If it matches, the word is placed on the appropriate arc and removed from the input sentence. When the final state is reached with no words in the sentence left over, we say the FSTD has accepted the sentence i.e., we know that the sentence matches the syntactic structure specified by the FSTD. The FSTD in figure will accept any sentence segment beginning with the, ending with a noun' and containing an arbitrary number of adjectives in between. Like, the big, white, dog would be accepted by this FSTD.

The main problem with FSTD is that it can recognize only sentences written as a regular language (type 3) which is the most restrictive of Chomsky's four categories of language. It cannot handle sentences from the more general context-free (type -2) grammar.

Merits and demerits of parsing using transition networks

This type of parsing is simple but not very efficient. No attention is given to potential ambiguities or the need of words to agree with each other.

Other variants (types) of transition networks Augmented Transition Networks (ATNs)

ATN or augmented transition network was given by William Woods in 1970. The ATN method of parsing sentences integrates many concepts from Chomsky's (1957) formal grammar theory with a matching process resembling a dynamic semantic network. Such parsing schemes may be considered as recursive pattern matching in which the string of words of the sentence are mapped onto a meaningful syntactic pattern. Please note that the characteristics of an ATN can be understood by studying the progression from finite-state transition diagrams through recursive transition network to augmented transition networks. Also note that each level of this progression represents increased levels of incorporating options for semantic input into the formal syntactic structure of the parsing program. The objective is to take an arbitrary input sentence and assign each word of the sentence its proper part of speech.

1. It is a modified form of transition networks.
2. It uses top down parsing procedure to gather various types of information to be later used for understanding system.
3. ATNs have the ability to apply tests to arcs.
4. ATN for a sentence will be

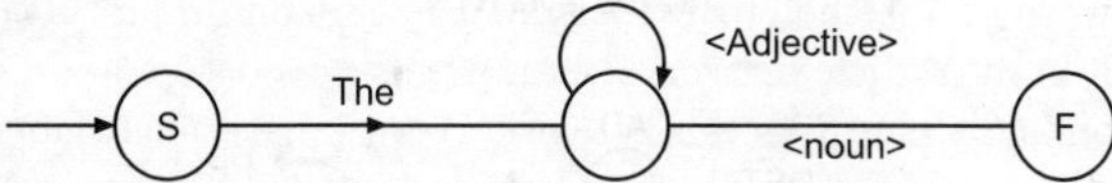

But, here, the arc from node S_2 to S_3 would be conditional. The condition here, will be that the number of verbs should be same as the number of nouns, only then S_2 to S_3 transition is possible. The conditions on the arc are calculated by the procedures that are attached to the arcs. The procedure attached to an arc is called when the network reaches that arc. These procedures, as well as, carrying out checks on agreement, are able to form parse tree from the sentence that is being analyzed.

5. ATNs not only do parsing but also collects the sentence features for further analysis.
6. ATNs represent sentence structure using a slot filler representation which reflects more of the functional role of phrases in a sentence.

Recursive Transition Networks (RTNs) : RTN is a recursive transition network which permits arc labels to refer to other networks (including the networks own name) and they in turn may refer back to the referring network rather than just permitting word categories used previously.

For *e.g.*, Consider the RTN shows in Fig. 13.5 where the main network calls two sub networks— a NP and a PP network.

The top network in the figure is the top level (sentence) network and the lower level networks are for NP and PP arc states. The arcs corresponding to these states will be trans versed only if the corresponding sub networks (*b*) or (*c*) are successfully trans versed. Note that the arc named POP is used as a dummy arc to signal the successful completion of the sub network and a return to the node following the arc from which it was called.

The capability for recursion gives the RTN a considerable advantage over its predecessor, the FSTD. There is no restriction on the level of hierarch or recursion with RTNs. That is, a sub- network may call another sub-network which may, in turn, call another and so on. Recursion is supported by allowing a sub-network to call itself.

There is also no restriction on the number of sub-networks which may be called from a certain arc. Several sub-structures may be investigated simultaneously, and thus RTNs have the capability of parallel processing. Often, of course, many of the parallel sub-networks will fail to parse the phrase they are examining because it may not fit the structure specified by the RTN.

However, even context-free grammars cannot handle all English sentence structure. To extend the capabilities of syntactic parsers, the augmented transition network (ATN) was invented.

To further extend the capacity of finite state transition diagrams to handle more general context- free language, a recursion mechanism was added to the FSTD and it became a recursive transition network (RTN). This extension is like adding a subroutine capability at each arc. Now, in addition to containing a terminal (word), an are may contain the name of a sub-network to which the control may be transferred to parse like a prepositional phrase. When the sub-network is finished, control returns to the subsequent node and the processing continues.

Advantages of RTN :

1. No restriction on the level of hierarchy or recursion with RTNS. It means that a sub- network may call another sub-network which may call another and so on. This process is known as recursion. Recursion is supported by allowing a sub-network to call itself.
2. No restriction on the number of sub-networks which may be called from a certain arc. Several sub-structures may be investigated simultaneously. Thus, RTNs have the capability of parallel processing too.

Many parallel sub-networks will fail to parse the phrase they are examining because it may not fit the structure specified by the RTN.

> **NOTE:** Even context free grammars cannot handle all English sentence structures. To further extend the capabilities of syntactic parsers, ATNS were invented.

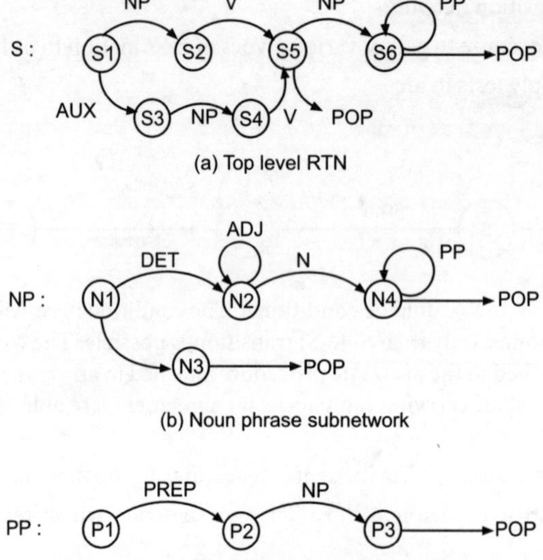

(a) Top level RTN

(b) Noun phrase subnetwork

(c) Prepositional phrase subnetwork

***Fig. 13.4:** Recursive transition network (RTN)*

Q.6. Describe Chart Parsing in detail.

Ans. The chart is a record of all the substructures build during parsing. It is also known as a well- formed substring table. Chart parsing works on the principle of dynamic programming *i.e.*, it uses and stores solutions of smaller part of a sentence to solve larger problems. Chart parsing works incrementally *i.e.*, word by word. In worst case, chart parsing will parse a sentence of n words in $O(n^3)$ time. In many cases, it will perform better than this and will parse most of the sentences in $O(n^3)$ or even $O(n)$ time.

For example, say the sentence is —

"The cat eats a big rat"

It's initial chart is as follows—

(0) The (1) cat (2) eats (3) a (4) big (5) rat (6)

***Fig. 13.5:** Initial chart for given example*

How its chart parsing is done?

The chart of Fig. 13.6 show seven verticals which will become connected to each other by edges. The edges will show how the constituents of the sentence combine together.

The chart parser starts by adding the following edge to the chart—

[0, 0, Target → • Sentence • Sentence]

This notation means that the edge connects vertex 0 to itself. The first two numbers in the square brackets show which vertical the edge connects. Target is the target that we want to find which is really just a place holder to enable us to have an edge that requires us to find a whole sentence. The arrow indicates that in order to make what is on its LHS (target) we need to find what is on its RHS (sentence). The dot shows what has been found already on its LHS, and what is yet to be found on its RHS.

Now, consider the following edge, show in chart of Fig. 6.7.

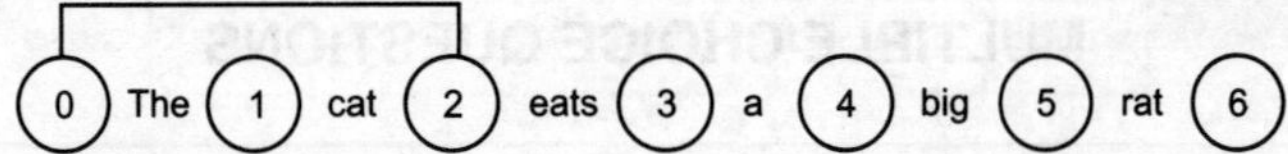

Fig. 13.6: Partial Chart for the Given Sentence

Now, the chart parser adds the following edge–

[0, 2, Sentence → Nounphrase • Verphrase]

This means that an edge exists connecting nodes 0 and 2. The dot shows us that we have already found a Noun phrase (the cat) and that we are looking for a verb phrase. Once we have found that verb phrase, we will get what is on the LHS of the arrow *i.e.*, a sentence.

The chart parser can add edges to the chart using the following three rules:

Rule 1: If we have an edge [$x, y, A \rightarrow B \,.\, C$], which needs to find a C, then an edge can be added that supplied that C *i.e.*, the edge [$x, y,(c) \rightarrow E$], where E is some sequence of terminals or non-terminals which can be replaced by C.

Rule 2: If we have two edges [$x, y, A \rightarrow B.\ CD$] and [$y, x, C \rightarrow E$] then these two edges can be combined together to form a new edge *i.e.* [$x, z, A \rightarrow BC.\ D$].

Rule 3: If we have an edge [$x, y, A \rightarrow B.\ C$] and the word at vertex y is of type C, then we have found a suitable word for this edge and so we extend the edge along to the next vertex by adding the following edge

[$y, y + 1, A \rightarrow BC \bullet$]

Let us apply these three rules to our example now.

We start with the edge [0, 0, Target . sentence] which means that to find our target, we must first find a sentence.

Use rule-1, so we can add the following edge to chart:–

[0, 0, sentence → Noun phrase Verb phrase]

This means that we must now find a Noun phrase and a Verb phrase. We now apply rule-1 again, to try to find a suitable Noun phrase, which involves adding the following edge:

[0, 0, Noun phrase → · Article Noun phrase]

Now, we can apply rule-3 because the word at the end of this edge (form vertex 0 to vertex 0) is "The", which is an article. This would be determined by looking the word up in a lexicon. Hence, we can now add the following edge:

[0, 1, Noun phrase → Article . Noun phrase]

Now, we are looking for another Noun phrase, so we use rule-1 again to add the following edge:

[0, 1, Noun phrase → . Noun]

We can now use rule-3 again because the next word is indeed a Noun, to add the following edge to the chart:

[0, 2, Noun phrase → Noun •]

This process continues, until we have reached an edge in which we have found everything we need. So, the final edge will be –

[0, 6, Sentence → Noun phrase Verbphrase •]

To build a parse tree from the chart, we modify rule-2 so that when it combines two edges together, it stores in the new edge information about the two edges that were combined to form the children edges. Then, when the parse has completed, we can obtain the parse tree directly from the edges of the tree by starting from the first edge and recursively examining the children edges of each node.

SUMMARY

English, Hindi, French etc. are all-natural languages but computers cannot understand them. NLP or computational Linguistics is the scientific study of languages from a computational perspective. A computer is said to be intelligent only if it can understand the commands given in natural languages.

MULTIPLE CHOICE QUESTIONS

1. KBS stands for

(*a*) Knowledge based software (*b*) Knowledge basis system
(*c*) Knowledge based system (*d*) None of the above

2. The process of converting a sentence into a tree that represents a sentence's syntactic structure is known as

(*a*) Parsing (*b*) Grammar
(*c*) Discourse integration (*d*) None of the above

3. ATN stands for

(*a*) Automated Teller Network (*b*) Automatic Truth Network
(*c*) Augmented Transition Network (*d*) None of the above

4. Which is the following is NOT Transition Network—

(*a*) ATN (*b*) RTN
(*c*) ATM (*d*) None of the above

5. Chart parsing works on the principle of

(*a*) Dynamic programming (*b*) Backtracking
(*c*) Greedy method (*d*) None of the above

6. In worst case, the time complexity of chart parsing is

(*a*) $O(n)$ (*b*) $O(n^2)$
(*c*) $O(n^3)$ (*d*) All of the above

ANSWERS

1. (*c*) **2.** (*a*) **3.** (*c*) **4.** (*c*) **5.** (*a*) **6.** (*c*)

CONCEPTUAL SHORT QUESTIONS WITH ANSWERS

Q.1. What are the various passes in natural language processing system? Explain the problem (syntactic, semantic or pragmatic), if any, with the following sentences—

a. **Mohan a letter Mary sent to**

b. **He takes a tea with milk**

c. **Rice flies like an apple**

d. **A boy study in a college**

Ans. NLP phases are as follows—

1. **Speech segmentation :** In most spoken languages, the sounds representing successive letters blend into each other, so the conversion of the analog signal to discrete characters can be a very difficult process. Also, in natural speech, there are hardly any pauses between successive words; the location of those boundaries usually must take into account grammatical and semantic constraints, as well as the context.

2. **Text segmentation :** Some written languages like Chinese, Japanese and Thai do not have single - word boundaries either, so any significant text parsing usually requires the identification of work boundaries, which is often a non-trivial task.

3. **Part-of-speech tagging :** Many words have more than one meaning; we have to select the meaning which makes the most sense in context.

4. Syntactic ambiguity : The grammar for natural languages is ambiguous i.e., there are often multiple possible parse trees for a given sentence. Choosing the most appropriate one usually requires semantic and contextual information. Specific problem components of syntactic ambiguity include sentence boundary disambiguation.

5. Imperfect or irregular input : Foreign or regional accents and vocal impediments in speech, typing or grammatical errors, OCR errors in texts.
6. **Speech acts and plans :** A sentence can often be considered as an action by the speaker. The sentence structure alone may not contain enough information to define this action.

Let us answer for the given sentences now—

a. **Mohan a letter Mary sent to**

This sentence is syntactically and semantically wrong but pragmatically correct.

b. **He take a tea with milk**

This sentence is syntactically wrong.

c. **Rice flies like an apple**

This se ntence is pragmatically and syntactically wrong.

d. **A boy study in a college**

This sentence is semantically incorrect.

Q.2. Name some NLP systems along with their year of development.

Ans. *a.* ELIZA System (1966-67)—By Weizenbaun at MIT

b. LUNAR System (1970)

c. SHRDLU System (1970)

LUNAR is a question–answering system in AI. SHRDLU was a dialogue system which could converse with a human user.

Q.3. Draw a parse tree for the sentence—"Viru hits the ball".

Ans.

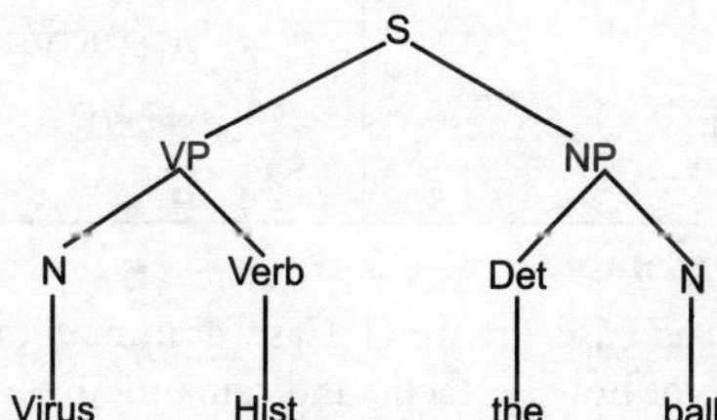

This is a CFG *i.e.*, context-free grammar which is a collection of productions of the form $S \rightarrow NP\ VP$ *i.e.*, a constituent *S* can consist of sub-constituents *NP* and *VP*.

Q.4. Explain top-down and bottom-up parsing for the following grammar—

S → NP VP

NP → ART N

VP → V NP

N → boy/frog

V → ate/kissed

ART → the/a

where *S* is initial symbol for sentences

NP is a Noun phrase

VP is Verb phrase

N is Noun

V is Verb

and ART is article

Apply this grammar on the following sentence— "A boy ate the frog" and write top- down and bottom-up parsing.

Top-down parsing	Bottom-up parsing
S → NP VP	→ the/a boy/frog ate/kissed the/a boy/frog
→ ART N VP	→ the/a boy/frog ate/kissed the/a N
→ the/a N VP	→ the/a boy/frog ate/kissed NP
→ the/a boy/frog VP	→ the/a boy/frog V NP
→ the/a boy/frog V NP	→ the/a boy/frog VP
→ the/a boy/frog ate/kissed NP	→ the/a N VP
→ the/a boy/frog ate/kissed ART N	→ ART N VP
→ the/a boy/frog ate/kissed the/a N	→ NP VP
→ the/a boy/frog ate/kissed the/a boy/frog	→ NP VP
	→ S

Applying the grammar to given sentence gives—

Top-down parsing	Bottom-up parsing
S → NP VP	S → A boy ate the frog
→ AT N VP	→ A boy ate the N
→ A N VP	→ A boy ate ART N
→ A boy VP	→ A boy ate NP
→ A boy V NP	→ A boy V NP
→ A boy ate NP	→ A boy VP
→ A boy ate ART N	→ A N VP
→ A boy ate the N	→ ART N VP
→ A boy ate the frog	→ NP VP
	→ S

Q.5. What is Fillmore's grammar? Give an example.

Ans. 1. Fillmore grammar is also called as case grammar Case grammar provides a different approach to the problem of how syntactic and semantic interpretation can be combined. Grammar rules are written to describe syntactic rather than semantic regularities. But the structures, rules are produced correspond to semantic relations rather than to stricitly syntactic ones. As an example, consider the two sentences and the simplified forms of their conventional parse trees shown in Fig. 13.9.

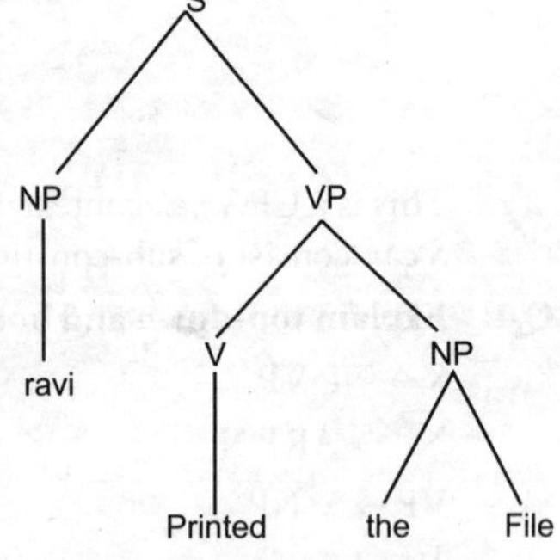

Fig. 13.7: Parsing

2. Case grammar describes the relationship between verbs and their arguments parsing using a case grammar is usually expectation-driven. Once verb of the sentence is located, it can be used to predict the noun phrases that will occur and to determine the relationship of those phrases to the rest of the sentences.

3. A case grammar describes the correct set of deep cases. Some of the cases are given as follows:
   - ☐ Agent – Investigator of the action.
   - ☐ Instrument – cause of the event.
   - ☐ Dative – entity affected by the action.
   - ☐ Factitive – object.
   - ☐ Locative – place of the event.
   - ☐ Source – place from which something moves

Q.6. NLP is a classical AI problem. Explain how.

Ans. 1. **Minimal input data :** The natural language statement does not contain the message but is a minimal specification to allow an intelligent reader to construct the message.

2. **Knowledge based :** The interpretation of the message is based on the large part of the knowledge that the reader already has.
3. **Local Ambiguity :** Many wrong interpretations are superficially consistent with the input.
4. **Global Constraints :** There are many different kinds of constraints on the interpretation of the input.
5. **Capturing the Infinite :** A language understanding system must capture inifinite form — rules sufficient to understand a potentially infinite set of statements.

Q.7. What is the difference between logical unification and graphical unification?

Ans.

Logical Unification	Graphical Unification
1. The inputs to the logical unifications are treated as logical formulas.	1. The inputs to the graph unification must be treated as sets.
2. Order in which attribute-value pairs are stated matters.	2. Order does not matter.
For eg f(g(a), h(b)) is different than f(h(b), g(a))	**For eg** if a rule is described as a constituent as follows [CAT : DET LEX : {1}] We should be able to match this constituent as [LEX : the CAT : DET]
	A simple parser can use the method to apply a grammar rule by unifying CONSTITUENT-1 with a proposed first constituent. If that succeeds then CONSTITUENT-2 is unified with a proposed second constituent. If that also succeeds then a new constituent corresponding to the value of BUILD IS PRODUCED. If there are variables on the value variables in the value of BUILD which were bound during the matching of constituents then those binding will be used to build the new constituent.

Q.8. Derive the parse tree for the sentence "Bill loves the frog where the following rules are used.

S → NP VP **NP → N** **NP → DET N**
CP → V NP **DET → the** **V → loves**

Ans.

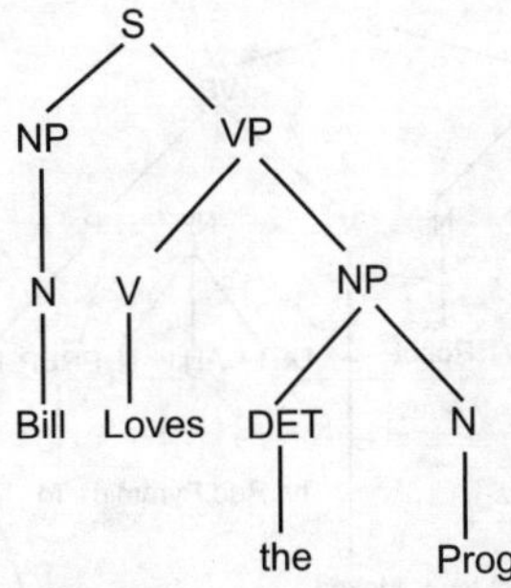

Q.9. Develop a parse tree for the sentence "Shyam slept on the platform" using following rewrite rules.

S → NP VP **NP → N** **NP → DET N**
VP → V PP **PP → PREP NP** **N → Shyam | platform**
DET → the **PREP → on**

Ans.

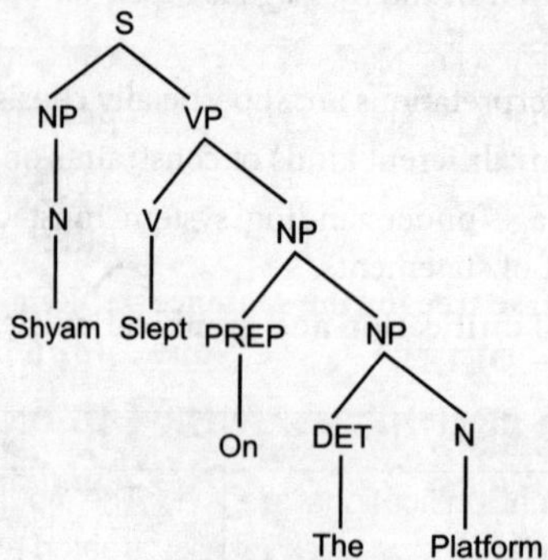

Q.10. Draw the parse tree for sentence "Mary likes a chocolate" where rewrite rules are given as below:

S → NP VP
NP → N
NP → DET N
VP → V PP
DET → a
V → likes
N → Mary/chocolates.

Ans. The pares tree is as follows

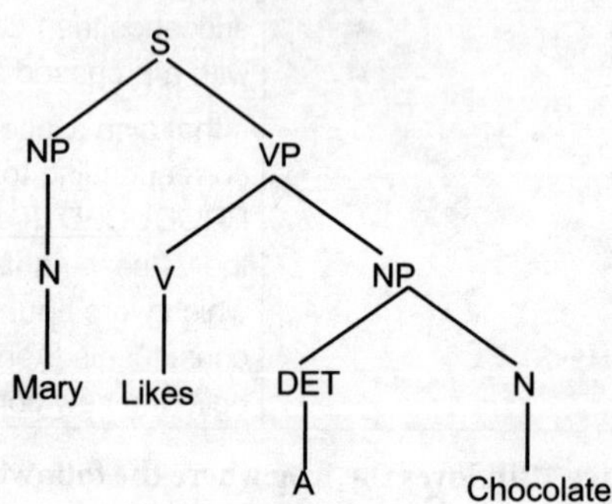

Q.11. Given the following parse tree for the sentence— "The silly robot moved the red pyramid to the big table." Write down the context free grammar.

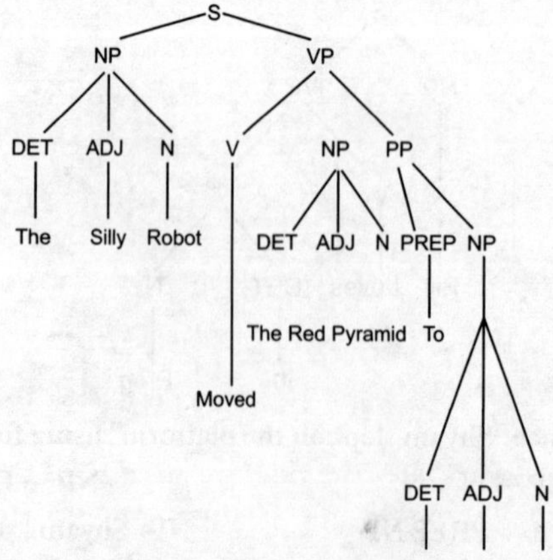

Ans. Its context free grammar is

S → NP VP	NP → DET ADT N	VP → V NP PP
NP → V PP	NP → DET ADJ N	PP → PREP NP
NP → DET ADJ N	DET → the	ADJ → silly/red/big
N → robot/pyramid/table	V → moved	PREP → to

Q.12. Given are the rewrite rules, draw a parse tree for the sentence — "Remove the pump with the wrench in the box."

S → V NP VP	**NP → DET N**	**PP → PREP NP**
NP → DET N PP	**PP → PREP NP**	**NP → DET N**
DET → the	**V → remove**	**N → pump/box**
PREP → with/in		

Ans. The parse tree is a follows.

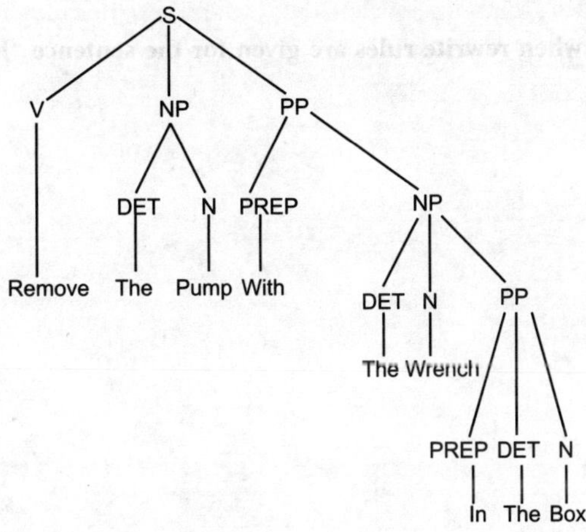

Q. 13. Given the rewrite rules for the sentence — "The boy kissed a rabbit". Draw the parse tree.

S → NP VP	**NP → ART N**
VP → V NP	**NP → ART N**
V → kissed	**ART → the/a**
N → boy/rabbit.	

Ans. The parse tree is as follows.

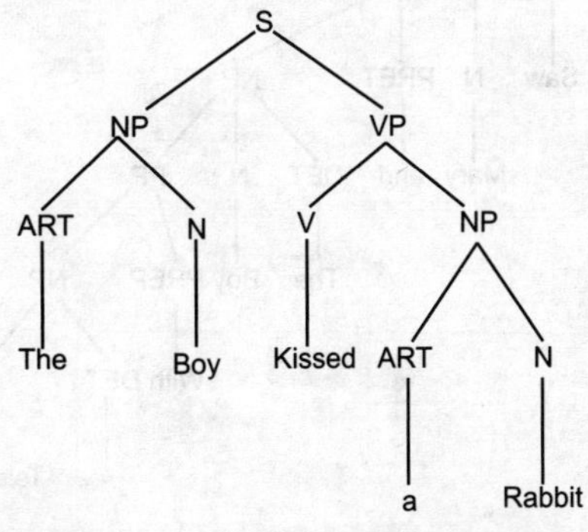

Q.14. Given is a sentence "John flew to Newyork" Rewrite rules are given as:-

S → NP VP	**NP → N**	**VP → V PP NP**
PP → PREP	**NP → N**	**N → John/Newyork**
V → flew	**PREP → to**	**Draw parse tree.**

Ans. The parse tree is as follows.

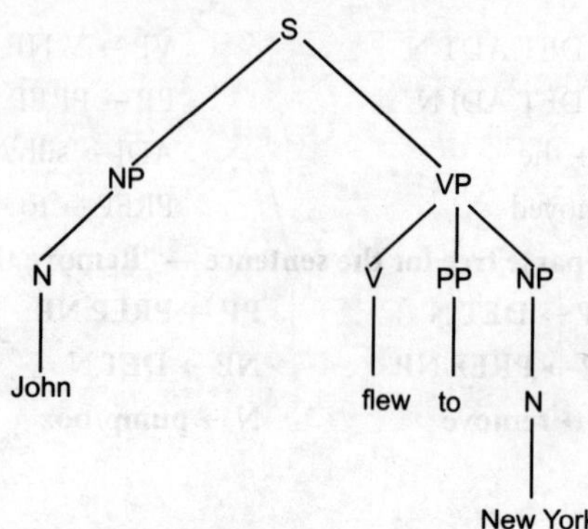

Q.15. Draw the syntax (parse tree) when rewrite rules are given for the sentence "John saw Mary and the boy with a telescope".

S → NP VP

NP → N

VP → V NP PP

NP → N

PP → PREP NP

NP → DET N PP

NP → DET N

PP → PREP NP

N → John/Mary/boy/telescope

V → Saw

PREP → and/With

DET → a/the.

Ans. The parse tree is.

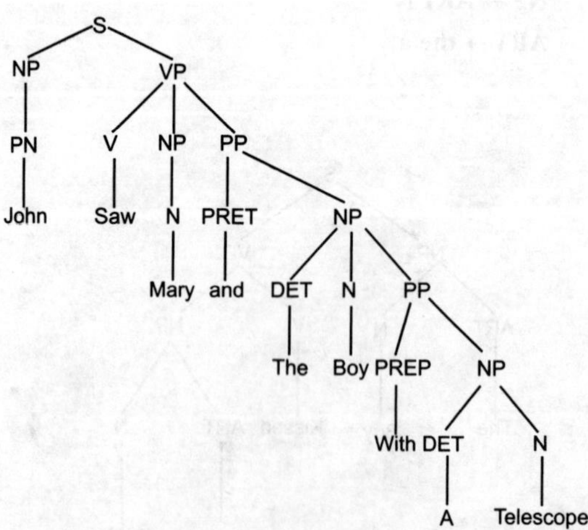

Q.16. Draw the parse tree for the sentence— "A student deleted the file". The rewrite rules are as given below:-

S → NP VP	**NP → DET N**	**VP → V PP**
PP → NP	**NP → DET N**	**DET → a/the**
N → student/file	**V → deleted.**	

Ans.

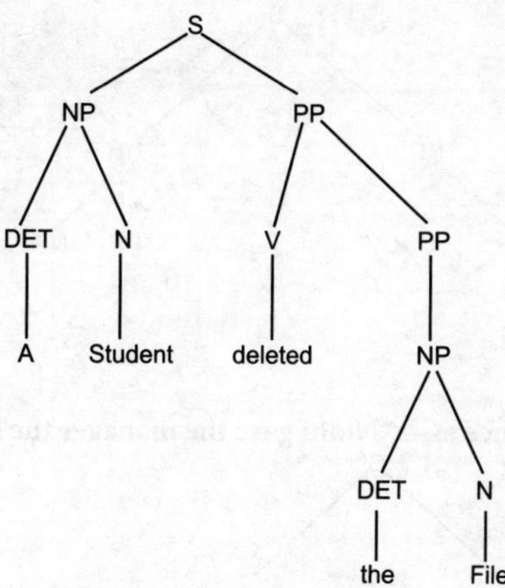

Q.17. Rewrite rule for the statement "The green grass of the home" are given as follows.

S → NP VP	**NP → DET ADJ J**
VP → PP	**PP → PREP NP**
NP → DET N	**ADJ → Green**
N → grass/home	**PRET → of**
DET → thc	**Draw the parse tree using rules.**

Ans.

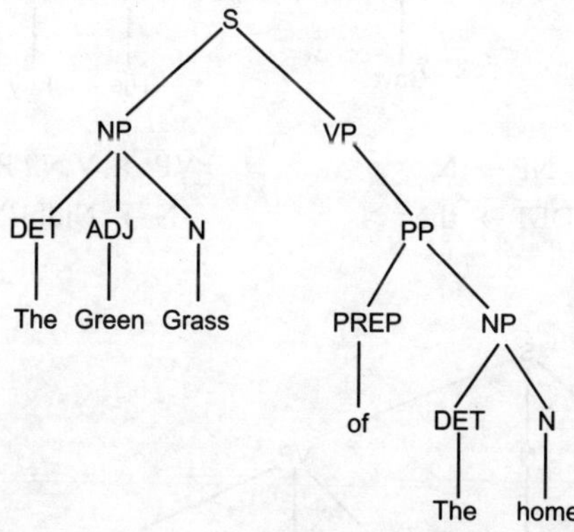

Q.18. Given is the parse tree for the sentence as— "The plane flew above the Clouds."

Write the rewrite rules or Context free grammar for this tree.

Ans. S → NP VP
NP → DET N
VP → V PP
PP → PREP NP
NP → DET N
DET → the
PREP → above
N → plane/clouds
V → flew.

Q.19. Given is the parse tree for the sentence as— "Nidhi gave the manager the key."

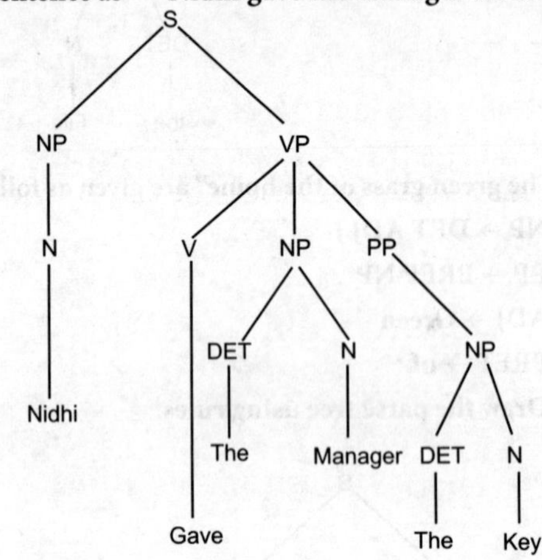

Ans. S → NP VP
NP → DET N
V → gave
NP → N
DET → the
VP → V NP PP
N → Nidhi/Manager/Key

Q.20. Given the parse tree

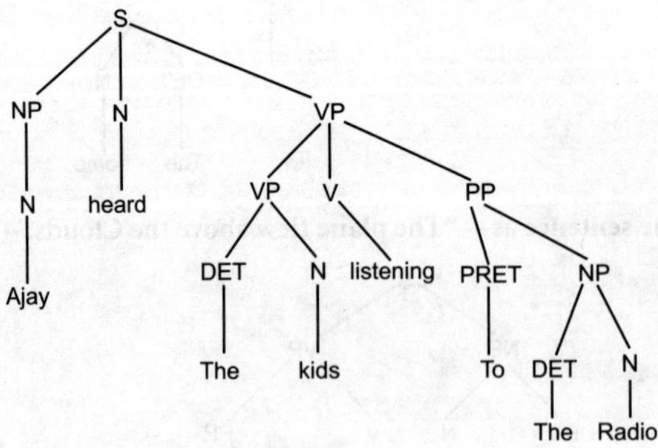

Write its context free Grammar.

Ans. S → NP VP
NP → DET N
N → Ajay/kids/radio
PREP → to
NP → N
PP → PREP NP
V → heard/listenig
VP → NP V PP
NP → DET N
DET → the

EXERCISE QUESTIONS

1. **Give a parse tree for the sentence "Bill loves the frog" where the following rules are used—**

   S → NP VP

   NP → N

   NP → DET N

   VP → V NP

   DET → the

   V → loves

   N → bill/frog

2. Describe ATN.

3. (*a*) What are important challenges in Natural Language Understanding?

   (*b*) What are the various applications of NLP?

   (*c*) Explain the various activities which are performed during Morphological Analysis and Syntactic processing with the help of following sentence: I want to see Raju's photo.

4. What are the different ways in which ambiguity results in natural langauge statements? Give an example of each type.

5. Develop a parse tree for the sentence- "Jack slept on the table" using the following rules—

   S → NP VP

   NP › DET N

   PP → PEP NP

   V → Slept

   PRBP → on

   NP › N

   VP → VPP

   N → Jack/table

   DET → the

6. (*a*) Explain types of a grammars used in NLP.

   (*b*) What are the levels of knowledge used in Natural Language Understanding.

7. (*a*) Explain the problems you may face in parsing Indian Languages?

   (*b*) Design an ATN for recognizing the language { anb2*n*c3*n*, for *n* > 0}.

8. (*a*) Explain how lexical, semantic and Syntactic analysis are carried out in NLP.

   (*b*) Briefly explain different parsing techniques.

9. (*a*) Using CFG, draw and explain a parse tree for the English Sentence- "The man bites the dog".

   (*b*) Explain how can we combine syntactic and semantic knowledge. Use sentence, if required.

10. What are the various phases of NLP?

11. (*a*) Describe Chomsky hierarchy of languages.

    (*b*) Differentiate between syntactic and Semantic processing.

14 EXPERT SYSTEMS

Q.1. What are expert systems? Distinguish between a human expert and an artificial expert system? Also compare an expert system with a software system and knowledgebase with a database.

Ans. Expert Systems are computer programs which store the factual and inferential knowledge of human experts in a narrow domain. They can assist and advise users, provide explanations, inform the user at any point of the solution which hypothesis they are pursuing, why they have chosen a particular strategy and what conclusion they have drawn so far. An expert system is an AI program which uses knowledge to solve problems which would normally require a human expert. It attempts to reproduce the performance of one or more human experts. An expert system is basically an AI program which uses knowledge to solve problems which would normally require a human expert. The knowledge collected from human experts and secondary knowledge sources like books is represented in some form—logic, production rules, semantic nets, frames or scripts. Once a sufficient amount of expert knowledge has been acquired, it must be encoded in some form, loaded into a knowledge base, then tested and refined continually throughout the life cycle of the system. The system includes a reasoning mechanism as well as heuristics, for making choices and navigating around the search space for possible solutions. Also, it includes the mechanism for passing information to and from the user. Expert systems have proven to be effective in a number of problem domains which normally require the kind of intelligence possessed by a human expert. A related term is wizard. A wizard is an interactive program that helps user to solve a problem. Initially, the term wizard was used for programs that construct a database search query based on criteria supplied by the user. However, some rule-based expert systems are also called as wizards. Other wizards are like a sequence of online forms that guide users through a series of choices, such as the ones which manage the installation of new software on computers and these are not expert systems.

Let us compare a human expert and an artificial Expert System in a tabular form—

Human Expert	Artificial Expert Systems
1. Humans are naturally perishable. 2. They are expensive. 3. They are inconsistent. 4. They are difficult to transfer. 5. They are difficult to document. 6. They are adaptive. 7. They are creative. 8. They possess sensory experience. 9. They have broad focus. 10. They can deal with common sense knowledge.	1. They are permanent. 2. They are costly to develop but cheaper to operate. 3. They are consistent. 4. They are easy to transfer. 5. They are easy to document. 6. They need to be told. 7. They are uninspired. 8. They need symbolic input. 9. They have narrow focus. 10. They need technical knowledge.

One can conclude that an expert system is much better than a human expert. But this is just the one side of the coin. There are many problems associated with an expert system. One serious problem is that expert systems are generally developed for domains which possess certain characteristics.

In AI literature, many definitions of expert systems have been given. Let us give some of them now:

1. Any problem that can be solved by your in-house expert in a 10-30-minute telephone call can be developed as an expert system (By M. Firebaugh).
2. Expert system or a KBS includes a sizable KB consisting of facts about the domain and heuristics for applying these facts.
3. Expert systems use knowledge rather than data to control the solution process.
4. An Expert System is a program that emulates the interaction a user might have with a human expert to solve a problem.

5. An expert system is designed to act as an expert in a particular domain.

But please understand here that an expert system is different from a software system. Let us see how:

Human Systme	Software Systems
1. They use knowledge base.	1. They use database.
2. Lesser data is kept together.	2. Large data is kept separately.
3. They use reasoning mechanism and heuristics.	3. They use algorithms.
4. They use inference engine.	
5. They are developed by knowledge engineers.	4. They use compilers.
For example: DENDRAL, MYCIN, LITHO, TIMM, XCON, CLIPS etc.	5. They are developed by software engineers. For example: C/C++, JAVA 2 etc.

But we should understand the first point of the above table of difference that knowledge base is different from a database. So, we tabulate the differences in a tabular form now.

Knowledge Base	Data Base
1. It stores information at a higher level of abstraction.	1. They are a collection of data representing facts.
2. It operates on a class of objects.	2. It operates on a single object.
3. They use power of inferencing.	3. Information needs to be explicitly stated.
4. Representation is by logic or rules or frames or scripts or nets.	4. Represented by relational, hierarchical or network model.
5. It is used for data analysis and planning.	5. It is maintained for operational purpose only.

Q.2. Give some main characteristics of an ES.

Ans. The main characteristics of ES are as follows—

1. They reduce the cost of accessing information as it allows dissemination of information held by one or small group of experts to less expensive people.
2. Knowledge in an ES can be formalized, tested and validated.
3. They allow integration from different sources.
4. They use symbolic knowledge representations.
5. The response time of an ES should be adequate.
6. Increase the probability, frequency and consistency of making good decision.
7. Help distribute human expertise.
8. Permit dynamism through modularity of structure.

A program talking about 'medicine' will be a KBS whereas a system having knowledge about medicine which is able to perform medical treatment will be an expert system. The heart of an ES is the powerful corpus of knowledge which is built up during the system building.

The general features of an expert system are shown in fig below: -

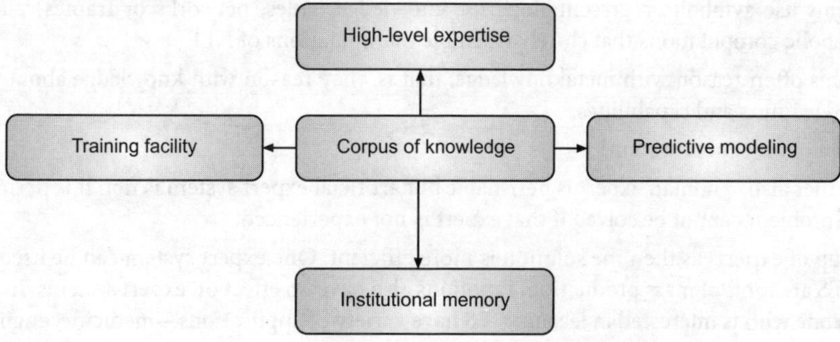

Fig. 14.1: General features of an expert system

The accumulation and codification of knowledge is one of the most important aspects of ES and has implications which go beyond the mere construction of a program to perform some class of tasks. Please note that this is because the knowledge of the ES should be explicit and accessible unlike most of the conventional programs. It has the value that any large body of knowledge should have. The knowledge can be collected from many sources.

Let us now discuss these general features one by one.

1. **High-level expertise :** This happens to be the most useful feature of an ES as it provides an aid to problem solving. This expertise can represent the best thinking of the top experts in the field, leading to the problem solutions, which are imaginative, accurate and efficient. It is the high-level expertise together with the skill of applying that knowledge that makes the expert system cost effective and able to earn its way in the commercial markets.
2. **Predictive modeling :** Another useful feature of an ES is its predictive modeling power. The system can act as an information processing theory or model of problem solving in the given domain. Hence, providing the desired answers for a given problem situation and showing how they would change for new situations. The ES can explain in detail how the new situation led to the change. This lets the user evaluate the potential effect of new facts or data and understand their relationship to the solution. By providing feedback, the user can evaluate the effect of new strategies or procedures on the solution by adding new rules or modifying the existing ones.
3. **Institutional memory :** The corpus of knowledge which defines the proficiency of an expert system can also provide an additional feature, an institutional memory. If the knowledge base is was developed through interaction with key personnel in an office or department, it represents the current policy or operating procedures of that group. This compilation of knowledge becomes a consensus of high-level opinion and is permanent record of the best strategies and methods used by the staff. When key people leave, their expertise is retained, for future which is useful in government, business and especially critical in defense.
4. **Ability to provide training facility :** A final feature of an expert system is its ability to provide a training facility for key personnel and important staff members. Expert systems can be designed to provide such trainings since they contain the necessary knowledge and the ability to explain their reasoning processes. Also note that software must be added to provide a robust, friendly interface between the trainee and the expert system. as a training device the expert system provides new staff members with a vast reservoir of experience and strategies from which to learn about recommended policies and methods. The system can also be adapted to train novices in specific tasks such as claims adjusting or financial planning etc.

Please remember the following features of expert systems: -

1. Expert systems use knowledge rather than data to control the solution process. In knowledge lies the power is the theme of AI. Much of the knowledge used is heuristic in nature and not algorithmic.
2. The knowledge encoded and maintained as an entity separate from the control program. It is not compiled together with the control program itself. Please note that this allows the incremental addition and refinement of the knowledge base without recompilation of the program. Also, it is possible in some cases to use different knowledge bases with the same control programs to produce different types of expert systems. Such systems are also known as expert system shells as they may be loaded with different knowledge bases.
3. Expert systems are capable of explaining how a particular conclusion was reached and why requested information is needed during a consultation. This is vital as it gives the user a choice to assess and understand the system's reasoning ability. This improves the user's confidence in the system.
4. Expert systems use symbolic representations for knowledge (rules, networks or frames) and perform inference through symbolic computations that closely resemble manipulations of NLP.
5. Expert systems often reason with metaknowledge, that is, they reason with knowledge about themselves and their own knowledge limits and capabilities.

Q.3. What is the need of an expert system?

Ans. As explained earlier also, a human expert is perishable but artificial expert system is not. It is permanent. If there is one expert then the problem cannot be solved if that expert is not experienced.

So, we take group of experts as then the solution is more efficient. One expert system can be used at different places at the same time. ES are tools of mass production. Emotions also have no effect on expert systems. In nutshell, an ES is like a tutor for someone who is interested in learning. ES have variety of applications—medicine, engineering, geology, I.T., basic and applied research, training, sales and marketing.

Q.4. Explain the architecture of an Expert System.

Ans. In general, there are 2 types of architectures that are used in expert systems: -

1. Rule-based architectures (production-based).
2. Non-production system architectures.

Rule-based architectures / production-based:

1. The most common form of architecture used in expert systems is the production system, also called as the rule-based system. this type of system uses knowledge encoded in the form of production rules, that is, IF-THEN rules.
2. Each rule represents a small chunk of knowledge relating to the given domain of expertise.
3. A number of related rules collectively may correspond to a chain of inferences which lead from some initially known facts to some useful conclusions.
4. When the known facts support the conditions in the rule's left side, the conclusion or action part is then accepted as known or at least known with some degree of certainty.
5. Inference in these production systems is achieved by a process of chaining through the rules recursively, either in a forward or backward direction, until a conclusion is reached or until failure occurs.
6. The selection of rules used in the chaining process is determined by matching current facts against the domain knowledge or variables in rules and choosing among a candidate set of rules the ones that meet some given criteria, such as specificity.
7. The inference process is typically carried out in an interactive mode with the user providing input parameters needed to complete the rule chaining process.

Both factual and heuristic knowledge is required for complex decision. Knowledge engineers design various components which work together to perform different functions. Fig. 814.1 shows the architecture of an ES.

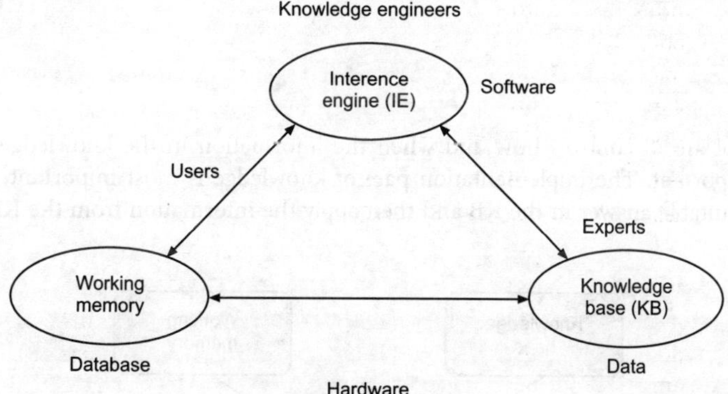

Fig. 14.2: ES architecture

Knowledge Base (KB): It consists of problem-solving rules, procedures and intrinsic data relevant to the problem domain. It contains facts and rules about some specialized knowledge domain.

Working memory: It refers to task-specific data for the problem under consideration.

Inference Engine (IE): It is a generic control mechanism that applies the axiomatic knowledge in the KB to the task-specific data to arrive at some solution or conclusion. The inference engine accepts user input queries and responses to questions through the I/O interface and uses this dynamic information together with the static knowledge (rules and facts) stored in the knowledge base. The knowledge in the KB is used to derive conclusions about the current state or situation as presented by the user's input.

Do you know? IE such as VP-Expert may come from a commercial vendor.

The KB may be a specific diagnostic KB compiled by a consulting firm and the problem data may be supplied by the end user. Please note that the KB is the central nucleus of the ES. Also note that a KB is different from a database as a traditional database environment deals with data that have a static relationship between the elements in the problem domain whereas a KB is created by knowledge engineers who translate the knowledge of real human experts into rules and strategies. These rules can change depending on the existing problem scenario. KB provides the ES with the capability to recommend directions for user inquiry. These three components—KB, IE and working memory—make an ES, a modular design. The KB constitutes the problem-solving rules, facts etc. that a human expert might use in problem solving. The KB is usually stored in terms of if-then rules. The working memory represents relevant data for the current problem being solved. The IE is the control mechanism that organizes the problem data and searches through the KB for applicable rules. A good expert system is expected to grow as it learns from user feedback. Feedback is fed into the KB to make ES smarter. The three individual components of an ES are dynamic at various levels—

a. **Working Memory (Most dynamic)** : The contents of the working memory (or data structure) changes with each problem. So, it is the most dynamic component of an expert system, assuming that it is kept current.

b. **Knowledge Base (Moderately dynamic)** : A KB changes only if some new information arises that indicates a change in the problem solution procedure. Changes in KB should be carefully evaluated before being implemented. Please note that the changes should not be based on just one consultation experience. Also note that a rule that is found to be irrelevant under one problem situation may turn out to be crucial in solving other problems.

c. **Inference Engine (Least dynamic)** : A change is made to the inference engine only if they are required to make inferential engines are changed only if the developer wishes so. Please understand here that because frequent updates are costlier and disruptive to clients so most commercial software developers try to minimize frequent updating.

The KB of an expert system contains both behavioral and procedural knowledge. The procedural knowledge is rule-based. In these rule-based systems, the procedural knowledge (in form of IF-THEN ELSE production rules is completely integrated with the declarative knowledge.

For example: IF PROBLEM THEN ACTION. Also, some production rules provide guidelines for which they specify when other rules should be used. They are called as **meta-rules.**

For example: IF <condition-1> <condition-2> THEN condition-1 should be done before condition-2 is done.

The inferring process is carried out recursively in three states: -

1. Match.
2. Select.
3. Execute.

The IE component of an ES controls how and when the information in the knowledge is applied. Merely having knowledge is not important. The implementation part of knowledge is most important, *i.e.*, understand the query search for the most suitable answer in the KB and then apply the information from the KB. Then simple methods of strategy are—

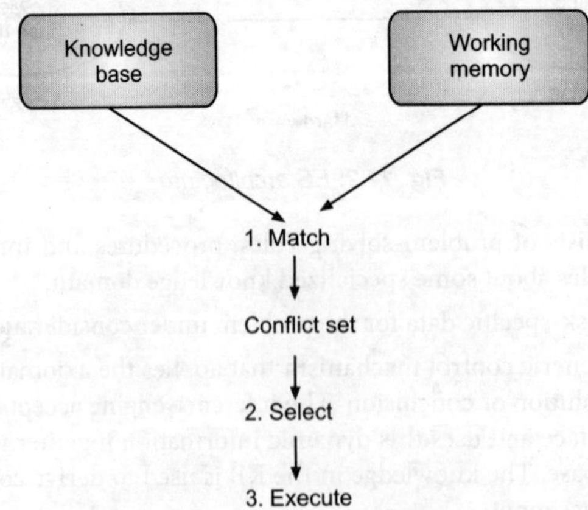

Fig. 14.2: The production system inference cycle

During the match stage, the contents of working memory are compared to facts and rules contained in the KB. When consistent matches are found, the corresponding rules are placed in a conflict set. To find an appropriate and consistent match, substitutions may be required. Once all matched rules have been added to the conflict set during the given cycle, one of the rules is selected for execution. The criteria for selection may be the most recent use, rule condition specificity (the number of conjuncts on the left) or simply the smallest rule number. The selected rule is then executed and the right-hand side or action part of the rule is then carried out. This shows the match-select-execute cycle (see fig. 14.2).

In the process of matching, when the left side of a sequence of rules is initialized first and the rules are executed from left to right, the process is called as forward chaining. When the left side of a sequence of rules is instantiated first and the rules are executed from left to right, the process is called as forward chaining or data-driven inference as input data are used to guide the direction of the inference process. On the other hand, when the right side of rules is instantiated first, the left-hand condition becomes sub-goals. The sub-goals may in turn cause sub-sub-goals to be established and so on until facts are found to match the lowest sub-goals conditions. When this form of inferencing takes place, we say that backward chaining is performed or goal-driven inference as an initial goal establishes the backward direction of inferring. Please note that when rules are executed, the resulting action may be the placement of some new facts in working memory, a request for additional information from the user or simply the stopping of the search process. If the suitable knowledge has been stored in KB and all of the required parameter values have been provided by the user, conclusions will be found and will be reported to the user. Also note that the chaining continues as long as new matches can be found between clauses in the working memory and the rules in the KB. The process stops when no new rules can be placed in the conflict set. Some systems use both forward and backward chaining, depending on the type of problem.

Many expert systems must be able to deal with uncertain information. This will be the scenario when the evidence supporting a conclusion is vague, incomplete or uncertain. To accommodate uncertainties, some form of probabilities, certainty factors, fuzzy logic, heuristics or other methods may be used during the inference process.

KB is different from the inference engine or control components. It contains the expert knowledge coded in some form like production rules, networks of frames or other representation schemes. Please understand that the IE manipulates the knowledge structures in KB to perform a type of symbolic reasoning and draw useful conclusions relating to the current task. The human-machine (or user interface) provides the means for dialog between the user and system. The user inputs commands, queries and responses to system messages. In turn, the system produces various messages for the user. In addition to these 3 components, most systems also have an explanation module which provides the user with explanations of how a conclusion was reached or why a piece of knowledge is needed. Another feature that may be present is an editor for use in creating and modifying the knowledge base structures.

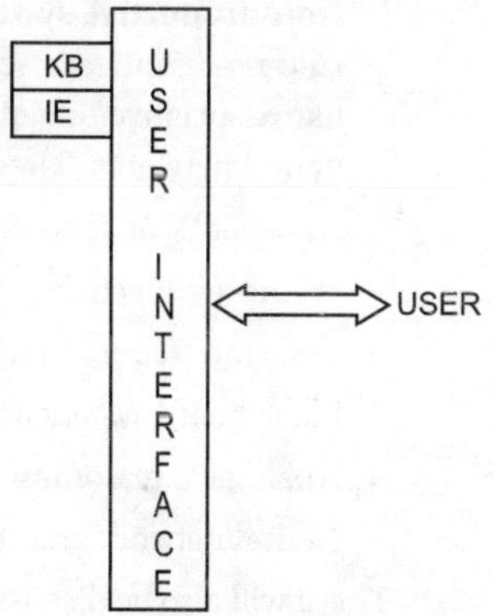

Fig. 14.3: ES components

The User Interface (UI) component enables us to communicate with an expert system. The communication performed is bi-directional. This is shown in Fig. 8.3.

As the users are not as experienced as the experts, so the expert systems should be so developed that it has an easy access for the user.

Actors involved with Expert Systems

There are three individuals having an interaction with expert systems. They are as follows: -

a. **End user :** The individual who uses the system for its problems solving assistance.

b. **Problem domain expert :** who builds and supplies the knowledgebase providing the domain expertise.

c. **Knowledge engineer :** who assists the experts in determining the representation of their knowledge, enters this knowledge into an explanation module and who defines the inference technique required to obtain useful problem-solving activity in form of rules which is referred to as a rule-based expert system. When these rules are created from the domain expertise, the knowledge base stores the rules of the expert system.

It is not acceptable for an expert system to take decisions without being able to provide an explanation for decisions it has taken. Users using these expert systems need to be convinced of the validity of the conclusion drawn before applying it to their domain. They also need to be convinced that the solution is suitable and applicable in these situations. Knowledge engineers building the expert system also need to examine the reasoning behind decisions in order to access and evaluate the mechanisms being used. If the explanation component is not provided it would not be possible to judge whether the expert system is working as desired or intended. The explanation can be generated by creating a goal tree which has been traversed. The explanation module provides the user with an explanation of the reasoning process when requested. This is done in response to a how query or a why query.

(A) To respond to a how query, the explanation module traces the chain of rules fired during a consultation with the user. The sequence of rules that led to the conclusion is then printed for the user in an easy to understand human-language style. This allows the user to actually see the reasoning process followed by the system in arriving at the conclusions. Also note that if the user is not convinced with the reasoning steps presented, they may be changed using the editor.

(B) To respond to a why query, the explanation module must be able to explain why certain information is needed by the IE to complete a step in the reasoning process before it can proceed.

How to build a knowledge base? Which editor can be used?

Editors are used by developers to create new rules for addition to the KB, to delete outmoded rules or to modify existing rules in some way. Some of the more complex expert system editors provide the user with features not found in typical text editors such as the ability to perform some types of consistency tests for newly created rules, to add missing conditions to a rule or to reformat a newly created rule. Such systems also prompt the user for missing information and provide other general guidance in the KB creation process.

One of the most difficult tasks in creating and maintaining production systems is building and maintaining of a consistent but complete set of rules. This should be done without adding redundant or unnecessary rules. Please note that building a knowledge base requires careful planning, accounting and organization of the knowledge structures. It also requires through verification and validation of the complete knowledge base, operations which have yet to be performed. For example, an "intelligent editor" can simplify the process of building a knowledge base.

Non-productive system architectures: Less important expert system architectures are known as non-production rule-representation schemes. Instead of using rules, these systems employ more structured representation schemes like associative or semantic networks, frames and rule structures, decision trees or even specialized networks like neural networks. These include-

- Associative or semantic network architectures.
- Frame architectures.
- Decision tree architectures.
- Black board system architectures.
- Analogical reasoning architectures.
- Neural network architectures.

These will also be discussed in subsequent chapters.

Q.5. What are the steps followed to develop an Expert System?

Ans. A knowledge engineer or an AI specialist or a programmer is skilled in the art of developing Expert Systems (ES).

A domain expert is an individual who has significant expertise in the domain of the ES being developed. Please understand that it is not critical that the domain expert understand AI or expert systems that is one of the functions of the knowledge engineer. Also note that the knowledge engineer and the domain expert usually work close to each other throughout the development process. An expert system (ES) is developed and refined over a period of several years. ES development has five stages—

S1: Determining the characteristics of the problem (Identification).

S2: Finding the concept to produce the solution (Conceptualization).

S3: Designing structures to organize the knowledge (Formalization).

S4: Formulating rules which embody the knowledge (Implementation)

S5: Validating the rules (Testing).

Development of an ES involves five steps—

Step 1: Identification : Determining the characteristic of the problem.

Step 2: Conceptualization : tHere, the iterative process between the knowledge engineer and the domain expert continues. Diagrams are often used to clarify the problem. During this process of conceptualization, it is sometimes necessary to revise the description that is generated in the stage of identification. The basic aim is to develop a clear concept of the problem.

First step of identification is shown in a flowchart form also—

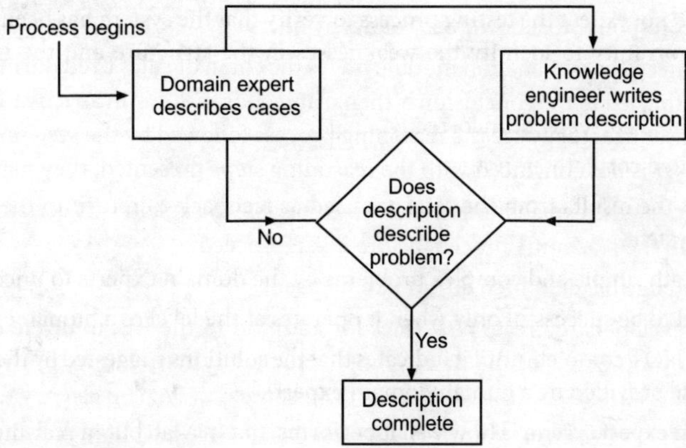

Fig. 14.3: Iterative process of identifying the problem–ES is to solve

Next is the conceptualization phase. The iterative relationship between the identification and conceptualisations stages of ES development is shown next:

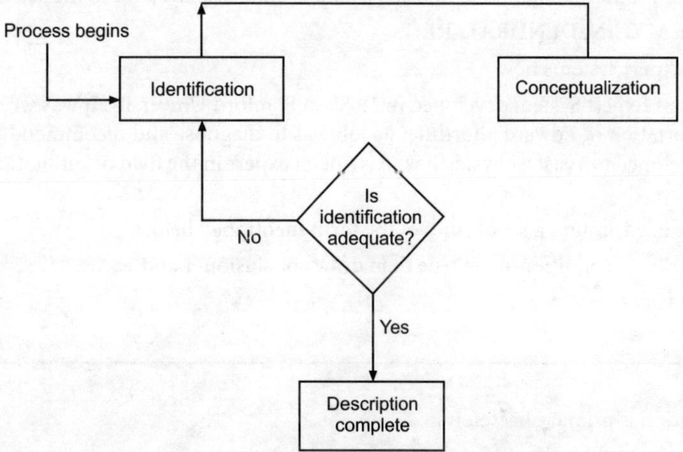

Fig. 14.4: Iterative relationship between identification and conceptualization stages

Step 3: Formalization : In this step, the knowledge engineers select the development techniques to be used for the expert systems. If a rule-based system is developed, the knowledge engineer develops a set of rules for the domain expert to review until everyone agrees on them. To facilitate the formalization state, the AI researchers are looking for ways to reduce the amounting time required to enter the information in the KB. The goal of the simpler development tools is to enable the domain expert to create the KB. With automatic knowledge acquisition, the computer could include information from books in the KB automatically with computer learning. A computer could discover and add new facts to its KB.

Step 4: Implementation : In this stage, a prototype of the ES is developed to help the knowledge engineer determine if the correct techniques were chosen. This phase is shown in Fig. 14.5.

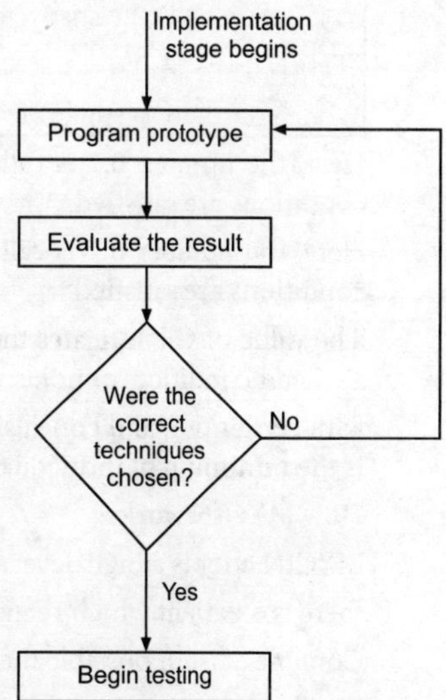

Fig. 14.5: Implementation stage

Step 5: Testing : In testing stage, the knowledge engineer revises the structure and implementation of the expert system until the system provides solution as valid as that of a human expert. After going through Step 1 to Step 5, we can put the system to use. Please note that we can communicate with the expert system in a question and answer format, so as to make the system easy to use.

The chances of prototype expert system executing flawless are very less initially. A knowledge engineer does not expect the testing process to verify that the system has been constructed entirely correctly. Testing provides an opportunity to identify the weaknesses in the structure and the implementation of the system. Testing includes—

a. System was implemented correctly or incorrectly.

b. Rules were implemented correctly or not.

Also understand that the results from the tests are used as feedback to return to the previous stage and adjust the performance of the system.

c. System is tested for both simple and complex problems by the domain experts to uncover more of defects.

d. An ES is finally tested to be successful only when it operates at the level of a human expert.

e. The testing process is NOT complete until it indicates that the solutions suggested by the expert system are consistently valid (as valid as those provided by a human domain expert).

f. The ultimate test of an expert system is how well it performs, not in a lab but in real-life situations. Please understand that a completed system not only must demonstrate consistently that it can deliver the required expertise but it must also be easy to use, so that the embedded expertise can be extracted easily. That is why, developers have gone to the extent that expert systems are among the easiest to use of all sophisticated programs.

g. Expert systems are typically interactive, *i.e.,* they work in question and answer form. This interaction between users and ES continues until the system is able to reach a conclusion (displayed on to the screen).

Q.6. Write short notes on MYCIN, DENDRAL, RI.

Ans. Let us discuss some expert systems now.

MYCIN : MYCIN is an Expert System developed in 1970s at Stanford University. It was written in LISP language as the part of doctoral dissertation of Edward Shortliffe. Its job was to diagnose and recommend treatment for certain blood infections. It was developed to assist a physician who is not an expert in the field of antibiotics for the treatment of blood infections.

MYCIN'S KB is organized around a set of rules of the form mentioned below:

"IF condition-1 and ....condition-n are true then draw conclusion-1 and ....
conclusion n".

For example:

IF

The infection is primary bacteremia.
AND the site of culture is one of the sterile sites
AND the suspected portal of entry is gastrointestinal tract

THEN

there is suggestive evidence (0.7) that infection is bacterial.

Here, the number 0.7 is called as the Certainty Factor (CF), which indicates how certain the conclusion is, if given conditions are satisfied.

Here, the number 0.7 is called as the Certainty Factor (CF), which indicates how certain the conclusion is, if given conditions are satisfied.

The value of CF indicates the amount of truthiness of conclusion. It states that— "If condition-1 holds with certainty x_1... and condition-m holds with certainty-xm then draw conclusion-1

with certainty y_1 and conclusion-*n* with certainty-y_n. When we have multiple certainty factors, then their combined CF is the minimum of individual CFs AND CF (action) = CF (Premise) * CF (rule).

How MYCIN works?

MYCIN adopts a high-level approach for the task of consultation, which is mentioned below— If

there is a patient which requires therapy AND Consultation has been given to other organisms requiring therapy Then Compile a list of possible therapies and determine best one.

Herein, the symptoms of patient are matched with premise and if matching occurs, the rule is fired. To find out whether some rule is applicable or not, MYCIN first finds out, if there is indeed an organism present which is associated with significant disease. **Please understand that this information is obtained directly by user or via a chain of inferences.** The consultation is search through a tree of goals. The top goal is at the root of the tree and then it is divided into sub-goals.

During disease findings, sometimes multiple answers are found. To find the correct and actual output, the order in which facts and rules appears is checked. This corresponds to depth first search.

Do you know?MYCIN's control structure uses AND/OR tree

MYCIN answers queries of type "Why" and "how".

1. 'Why' questions can be asked at any time from the system. The system then responds with the action part of the rule. It displays 'how' question tells the reasoning process of how the answer was found.

Many other variants of MYCIN project are there like—

a. **EMYCIN:** First expert shell developed from mycin'.

b. **PUFF:** Developed using EMYCIN in the new domain of heart disorders.

c. **NEOMYCIN:** Developed to train doctors which would take them through various example cases, checking their conclusions.

DENDRAL : The word "Dendral" is a pruned version of "Dendritic Algorithm". It was designed and developed at Stanford University in 1965. It is a collaborative work between Edward Feigenbaum, Bruce Buchanan, Joshua Lederberg and Carl Djerassi. DENDRAL is an expert system developed for inferring process of structure elucidation of chemical compounds. The primary aim was to aid organic chemists with the identification of unknown organic molecules by analyzing information from mass spectrometry graphs and the knowledge of chemistry. Dendral is not just a single program but rather a product of an interaction between two subprograms—Heuristic-Dendral and Meta- Dendral *i.e.*,

DENDRAL = Heuristic-Dendral + Meta-Dendral

It is written in LISP language. Let us first of all understand these two subprograms.

Heuristic Dendral is a program that uses mass spectra or other experimental data together with knowledge base of chemistry, to produce a set of possible chemical structures that may be responsible for producing the data. A mass spectrum of a compound is produced by a mass spectrometer, and is used to determine its molecular weight, the sum of the masses of its atomic constituents. DENDRAL is one of the great classic application programs. Suppose that an organic chemist wants to know the chemical nature of some substance newly created in the test tube. The first step is to determine the number of atoms of various kinds in one molecule of the stuff. This step determines the chemical formula, such as $C_8 H_{16} O$. The formula indicates that each molecule has eight atoms of carbon, 16 of hydrogen and one of oxygen.

Once a sample's chemical formula is known, the chemist may use the sample's mass spectrogram to work out the way the atoms are arranged in the chemical structure, thus identifying the isomer of the chemical.

The spectrogram machine bombards a sample with high energy electrons, causing the molecules to break up into the charged chunks of various sizes. Then, the machine sorts the chunks by passing them through a magnetic field which deflects the high charge, low-weight ones more than it does for the low-charge, high-weight ones. It is now possible to get an estimate of the masses of these particles. This is called a mass spectrogram. Though it is not possible to get all of the possible masses yet by knowing these rules and by knowing the masses, it is possible to guess how the atoms of a single molecule of the unknown substance are put together. This is what a DENDRAL does.

Mass/ Charge: The purpose of DENDRAL is to work like a knowledgeable chemist. From the chemical formula and spectrogram, a deduced structure is produced like the chemical structure as shown below: -

$$CH_3\text{-}CH_2\text{-}\underset{\displaystyle \overset{|}{O}}{C}\text{-}CH_2\text{-}CH_2\text{-}CH_2\text{-}CH_2\text{-}CH_3$$

The DENDRAL Program works out structures from chemical formulas and mass spectrograms using the generate-and-test method. The generator consists of a structure enumerator and a synthesizer that produces a synthetic mass spectrogram by simulating the action of a real mass spectrometer on each enumerated structure. The structure enumerator ensures that the overall generator is complete and non-redundant because the structure enumerator uses complete and non-redundant structure-enumeration procedure. The overall generator is also informed because the structure enumerator uses the chemical formula and knowledge about necessary and forbidden sub-structures. The tester compares the real mass spectrogram with those produced by the generator. The possible structures are those whose synthetic spectrograms match the real one adequately. The structure judged correct is the one whose synthetic spectrogram most closel matches the real one.

For example, the compound water (H_2O) has a molecular weight of 18 since hydrogen has a mass of 1.01 and oxygen 16.00, and its mass spectrum has a peak at 18 units. Heuristic Dendral would use this input mass and the knowledge of atomic mass numbers and valence rules, to determine the possible combinations of atomic constituents whose mass would add up to 18. As the weight increases and the molecules become more complex, the number of possible compounds increases drastically. Thus, a program that is able to reduce this number of candidate solutions through the process of hypothesis formation is essential.

Meta-Dendral: Meta-Dendral is a knowledge acquisition system that receives the set of possible chemical structures and corresponding mass spectra as input, and proposes a set of hypotheses to explain correlation between some of the proposed structures and the mass spectrum. These hypotheses would be fed back to Heuristic Dendral to test that applicability. Thus, "Heuristic Dendral is a performance system and Meta-Dendral is a learning system". The program is based on two important features: the plan- generate-test paradigm and knowledge engineering.

DENDRAL uses the control process of generate and test procedure (like state space search), starting with arbitrary initial state and by employing a generator, all possibilities regarding presence of compounds is generated. On these possibilities a series of tests are carried out to eliminate unwanted states.

The plan-generate-test paradigm is the basic organization of the problem-solving method, and is a common paradigm used by both Heuristic Dendral and Meta-Dendral systems. The generator generates potential solutions for a particular problem, which are then expressed as chemical graphs in Dendral. However, this is feasible only when the number of candidate solutions is minimal. When there are large numbers of possible solutions, Dendral has to find a way to put constraints that rules out large sets of candidate solutions. This is the primary aim of Dendral planner, which is a "hypothesis-formation" program that employs "task-specific knowledge to find constraints for the generator". Last but not least, the tester analyzes each proposed candidate solution and discards those that fail to fulfil certain criteria. This mechanism of plan-generate-test paradigm is what holds Dendral together.

CONGEN (CONnstraints GENerator) is a Dendral program which constructs complete chemical structures by manipulating symbols that stand for atoms and molecules. Its input is a molecular formula and a set of constraints which serve to restrict the possible inter-connections among atoms. As an output, it generates a list of all possible ways of assembling the atoms into molecular structure by imposing the given constraints.

The KB of DENDRAL basically consists of huge knowledge about organic chemistry. The entire knowledge about organic chemistry is coded in the form of production rules. One example of such a rule is—

If there are two peaks at mass units m_1 and m_2

AND $x_1 + x_2$ = molecular weight + 28

AND at least one of x_1 or x_2 is high

Then ketone group is present.

How DENDRAL works?

Initially, compound testing is planned. It is fed into program and various groups are identified. The planner's production rule MSPRUNE is used to prune the number of alternate structures in the compound. The major task of MSPRUNE is to generate a hypothetical spectrum for structure. To perform this task, it requires knowledge about characteristics spectra of all organic groups. This knowledge is coded in form of production rules. Another module, MSRANK, ranks the candidates into various groups. This subsystem has the knowledge of spectrometry to rank candidate structure.

DENDRAL has the following organizational features:

1. **Knowledge Representation :** Production rules and algorithms for generating graph structures are constructed by META DENDRAL— a program which uses learning techniques to construct rules for an expert system automatically.
2. **Reasoning :** Forward chaining (data driven).
3. **Heuristics :** DENDRAL uses a variation of dfs called as generate and test. In this all hypotheses are generated and then tested against available evidence. Heuristic knowledge from the users (chemists) is also used to constrain the search.
4. **Dialogue/explanation :** The dialogue uses mixed control. The user can supply information and the system can request information as required.

Do you know? Many systems were derived from Dendral like MOLGEN, MACSYMA, PROSPECTOR, XCON and STEAMER.

R1/XCON : The R_1 (later called as XCON—expert CONfigurer) program was a production-rule-based system written in OPS5 by John P. McDermott of CMU in 1978. It helped in assisting of the ordering of DEC's VAX computer systems by automatically selecting the computer system components based on the customer's requirements.

XCON interacts with the sales person, asking critical questions before printing out a coherent and workable system specification. Let us summarise R1/Xcon/features—

1. John McDemott (1982–84) of Carnegi-Mellon University, USA, wrote R1/XCON in collaboration with DEC (Digital Equipment Corporation).
2. XCON is an acronym for expert configurer and is used to configure VAX and PDP–11 series of computer systems sold by DEC.
3. XCON name is used by DEC; R1 name is used by McDermott.
4. Initially, the system contained about 300 production rules of the standard variety for configuring the 420 possible components of a VAX–11 system.
5. A completed system containing some 800 production rules was delivered to DEC for acceptance testing (Oct. 1979). By 1980, DEC personnel had become sufficiently familiar with the operation of XCON to assume full responsibility for its maintenance and development and they have extended it to contain over 4000 rules.
6. XCON system was designed to replace human "technical editors". Such editors had been responsible for 2 operations—
   a. Checking for completeness of orders,
   b. Laying out the physical placement and wiring connections between component modules in the chassis.

   These tasks are fairly tedious and each of the components is specified by properties such as voltage (*V*), frequency (*f*), how many devices it supports and how many parts it has. Also, the editors had information showing which components can or must be associated with other components. This set of rules governing the relationship between components is called as constraint knowledge.
7. XCON passed an extensive series of performance tests.

> **NOTE:** To text XCON, a set of 10 configurations was submitted to the program. Results were evaluated by a team of 12 people including technical editors, technicians and engineers. Errors detected were corrected and the cycle was repeated until 50 configurations had been produced.

8. By 1986, XCON represented an investment of over 50 person-years of human effort. Since its birth, XCON has grown at a relatively uniform rate as its capabilities expanded from a single line of VAX computers to the complete VAX line and the PDP–11 line. This required an effort of about four person-years per year.
9. XCON developers found that they did not have to complete the system before putting it to use. This shows XCON's incremental growth.
10. XCON's developers have concluded that it will never be possible to guarantee 100% error-free performance. Also, they observed that building an ES is an unending process.
11. Since 1980, XCON has analyzed over 100,000 unique orders and is presently operating with greater than 99% accuracy. So, it is an effective business tool today.

Q.7. What are the advantages and disadvantages of Expert Systems?

Ans. Advantages of ES: Expert systems exercise IT to acquire and utilize human expertise. It can be beneficial for organizations that have clear objectives, rules and procedures. Expert systems can: -

- ☐ Provide consistent answer for respective decisions, processes and tasks.
- ☐ Hold and maintain significant levels of information.
- ☐ Reduce employee training costs.
- ☐ Centralize the decision -making process.
- ☐ Create efficiencies and reduce time needed to solve problems.
- ☐ Combine multiple human expert intelligences.
- ☐ Reduce the number of human errors.
- ☐ Give strategic and comparative advantages creating entry barriers to competitors.
- ☐ Review transactions that human experts may overlook.

Disadvantages/ Limitations of ES

Some limitations in ES arise from-

- ☐ The lack of human common sense needed in some decision makings.
- ☐ The creative responses human experts can respond in unusual circumstances.
- ☐ Domain experts not always being able to explain their logic and reasoning.
- ☐ The challenges of automating complex processes.
- ☐ The lack of flexibility and ability to adapt to changing environments.
- ☐ Not being able to recognize when no answer is available.

Q.8. Write short notes on the Expert system tools. Give its main characteristics.

Ans. Expert system tools are designed to provide an environment for the development of expert systems mainly through the approach of prototyping. So, we can define them as follows: -

"Expert system tools are the programming systems that simplify the job of constructing an expert system" [Waterman, 1996].

In general, we can say that-

Tool = language + utility program (code generator, graphics editor, debugger etc.)

Software tools for development of expert systems mainly fall into the following categories: -

1. **Expert system shells :** A shell is a special purpose tool designed for certain types of applications in which the user must supply the knowledge base. Basically, a shell is an expert system without a knowledge base. A shell furnishes the expert system developer with the inference engine, user interface and the explanation and knowledge acquisition facilities. For example, EMYCIN (Empty MYCIN, a medical diagnostic system), Crystal, XpertRule, Leonardo, Xi-Plus etc. so we can say- Shell = Expert System – Knowledge base.
2. **High-level programming languages :** These languages are basically used to provide a higher-level of abstraction by hiding the implementation details because of which the programmer need not worry about the efficiency of storing, accessing and manipulating data. For example, Prolog, LISP, CLIPS, OPS5 rule language.
3. **Multiple programming environments :** Expert system programming environments are special packages of pre-written code. They are the 'power tools' for building knowledge-based systems. They provide a set of building blocks that cater for the programmers needs and hence are known as 'tool kits'. For example, Art, KEE, LOOPSs.

We are now in a position to distinguish between the tools used to build expert systems and the expert system itself. A number of activities are preceded before the development of an expert system itself. These include identifying the problem domain, finding the expertise and selecting the development tool. There are 4 main types of development tools available for expert systems as follows: -

- Algorithmic languages(such as C, PASCAL, BASIC).
- Symbolic languages (such as PROLOG, LISP)
- Development environments(such as ART, KEE, LOOPS)
- Expert system shells(such as Crystal, XpertRule, Leonardo, Xi-Plus).

Characteristics of Expert System tools:

1. Knowledge representation methods available (rules, logic-based network structures, frames with or without inheritance, multiple world views, object-oriented, procedural and the methods offered for dealing with uncertainty, if any).
2. Inference and control methods available (backward chaining, forward chaining, mixed forward and backward chaining, blackboard architecture approach, logic-driven theorem prover, object-oriented approach, the use of attached procedures, types of meta-control capabilities, forms of uncertainty management, hypothetical reasoning, TMS, pattern matching with or without indexing, user functions permitted, linking options to modules written in other languages and linking options to other sources of information such as databases.
3. User interface characteristics (editor flexibility and ease of use, use of menus, use of pop-up windows, developer provided text capabilities for prompts and help messages, graphics capabilities, consistency checking for newly entered knowledge, explanation of how and why capabilities, system help facilities, screen formatting and color selection capabilities, network representation of KB and forms of compilation available- batch or interactive?
4. General system characteristics and support available (types of applications with which the system has been successfully used, the hardware types, general utilities available, debugging facilities, interfacing flexibility to other languages and databases, vendor training availability and cost of support and company's reputation.

Some more building tools are also there. For example, Personal Consultant Plus, Radian RuleMaster, Knowledge

Engineering Environment (KEE), OPS 5 System etc. The expert system shell Mac SMART includes an example-based component which allows the domain expert to input information in terms of primary factors, questions and advice (instead of rules) and a system generates a KB from these. This KB can then be validated by the expert. Another example is Teiresias, that was designed along with EMYCIN. It focusses the knowledge elicitation process on the specific problems.

Q.9. Write short notes on AI SHELLS / EXPERT SYSTEM SHELLS.

Ans.

1. It is possible to separate the interpreter from the domain-specific knowledge and create a system that can be used to construct a new expert system by adding new knowledge corresponding to the new problem domain. The resulting interpreters are called as shells or AI shells or Expert System shells. So, we define that an expert system shell is an existing knowledge independent framework into which the domain knowledge can be inserted to produce a working expert system. Hence, this avoids programming everything from scratch.
2. AI shells are the tools for building expert systems that provide knowledge representation facilities and inferencing mechanisms. The programmer must gain detailed knowledge about a particular domain from an expert and information source. Hence, a shell may be thought of as an expert system with all the domain specific knowledge removed and a facility for entering a new knowledge base provided. Generally, some form of debugging facility is also provided for checking the inferencing of a given problem.
3. Inference methods vary significantly from one domain to another and expert system shells have developed to allow the designer more flexibility during the building of an expert system. Some of the expert system shells available are given as follows-
   - EMYCIN
   - Leonardo
   - KnowledgePro
   - ESIE
   - Crystal.
   - COMDALE
   - SAVOIR
   - XpertRule
   - Xi Plus.
4. In general, shells are only applicable to the same type of the problem and are limited in their capabilities. However, they are the simplest and easiest way to build prototype expert systems and require relatively few programming skills to utilize.
5. Typical, implementation facilities provided by shells are:
   - ☐ A knowledge representation language.
   - ☐ A knowledge base editor.
   - ☐ Tracing and debugging facilities.
   - ☐ Range of user interface facilities.
   - ☐ Links to conventional/ external programs.
   - ☐ Facilities for uncertain reasoning.
   - ☐ Rule induction facilities.
6. To further improve the usability of a shell system, the following features may also exist-
   - ☐ User commands available *e.g.*, WHY? HOW? LIST? etc.
   - ☐ Shell will generate the dialogue required in consultation from a knowledge base.
   - ☐ Shell will autoformat the consultation screens.
   - ☐ Some degree of natural language simulation.
7. AI shells can quickly generate user-friendly screens, capture the knowledge base and manage the strategies for searching the knowledge (rule) base.
8. In nutshell, an expert system tool or shell is a software development environment containing the basic components of expert systems and a prescribed method for building applications by configuring these components. Expert system shells are basically used for the purpose of allowing non-programmers to take advantage of already developed templates or shells which have been developed because of the efforts of some pioneer in programming who have solved similar problems before.

SUMMARY

In this chapter, we have defined what is an expert system. Why are they required? What is its architecture? How to develop an ES? Some case studies on MYCIN, DENDRAL, RI (or XCON) have been discussed.

MULTIPLE CHOICE QUESTIONS

1. **The class of program first developed by AI researchers is**
   (*a*) Human expert system (*b*) Artificial expert system
   (*c*) Automatic expert system (*d*) None of the above
2. **ES uses**
   (*a*) Knowledge (*b*) Data
   (*c*) Information (*d*) None of the above
3. **Data when processed becomes information and information when processed becomes**
   (*a*) Data (*b*) Information
   (*c*) Knowledge (*d*) Wisdom
4. **Which of the following is an example of an ES?**
   (*a*) C (*b*) C++
   (*c*) JAVA 2 (*d*) MYCIN
5. **Which of the following is an exmaple of an IE?**
   (*a*) VP-Expert (*b*) VIP-Expert
   (*c*) D-Expert (*d*) C-Expert
6. **DENDRAL has two subprograms, namely**
   (*a*) Heuristic Dendral + KB (*b*) Heuristic Dendral—Meta Dendral
   (*c*) Heuristic Dendral + Meta Dendral (*d*) None of the above
7. **DENDRAL uses**
   (*a*) MPRUNE (*b*) MS PRUNE
   (*c*) SPRUNE (*d*) None of the above
8. **XCON stands for**
   (*a*) Expert configurer (*b*) Extra configuration
   (*c*) E-console (*d*) None of the above
9. **To train doctors, which ES was developed?**
   (*a*) EMYCIN (*b*) PUFF
   (*c*) NEDMYCIN (*d*) None of the above
10. **An example of an ES shell is**
    (*a*) Crystal (*b*) C
    (*c*) LISP (*d*) None of the above

ANSWERS

1. (*b*)	**2.** (*a*)	**3.** (*c*)	**4.** (*d*)	**5.** (*a*)
6. (*c*)	**7.** (*b*)	**8.** (*a*)	**9.** (*c*)	**10.** (*a*)

CONCEPTUAL SHORT QUESTIONS WITH ANSWERS

Q.1. How do we use Domain exploration, Meta knowledge and Expertise transfer in building expert system?

Ans. Domain knowledge is that knowledge that software programs encode in form of different knowledge bases. Domain knowledge is important, because it usually must be learned from software users in the domain (as domain specialists/experts), rather than from software people. Communication between end-users and software people is often difficult. They must find a common language to communicate.

Meta knowledge or meta-knowledge is knowledge about knowledge. More precisely speaking, meta-knowledge is systematic problem and domain-independent knowledge which performs or enables operations on another more or less specific domain-dependent knowledge in different domains/areas of human activities. Meta-knowledge can be considered as a fundamental conceptual instrument in such research and scientific domains as, knowledge engineering, knowledge management, and others dealing with study and operations on knowledge, seen as a unified object/entity, abstracted from local conceptualizations and terminologies.

Expertise transfer discusses technology and organizational behavior issues that are barriers to the commercial success of expert systems. The issues include interfacing and integrating with existing systems, picking the correct problem, fulfilling development, goals, representing knowledge, acquiring knowledge, validating and maintaining the system, deploying and introducing expert systems in an organization, and managing organizational behaviour after development is complete. It is argued that overcoming these barriers requires technology- transfer methods that account for an expert system's size and the structure and culture of the organization involved.

Q.2. Distinguish between DENDRAL and MYCIN in a tabular form.

Ans.

DENDRAL	MYCIN
1. It uses production rules and algorithms for generating graph structures.	1. It uses production rules implemented LISP.
2. Reasoning is done using forward chaining (data-driven).	2. Reasoning is done using backward chaining (goal-driven).
3. It uses data-driven approach.	3. It uses goal-driven approach.
4. It uses Generate-and-test strategy.	4. It uses depth-first search.
5. It uses mixed control dialogue explanation.	5. It uses computer control for dialogue/ explanation.

Q.3. What is the difference between an active user and a passive user?

Ans. An active user uses an ES directly to obtain recommendations.

A passive user is one who trusts the results obtained from ESs and supports the implementation of those results.

Q.4. What is heuristic reasoning? Discuss search control methods. Distinguish between forward and backward chaining.

Ans. Human experts use a type of problem-solving technique called as heuristic reasoning. Also called as the rules of thumb, it allows the expert to arrive at a good solution quickly and efficiently.

The inferencing (done by IE) is of two types—

a. Forward chaining

b. Backward chaining.

Forward Chaining (or data driven search)

Also called as data driven search or antecedent search. The process of inferencing that starts with the available data and uses the inference rules to conclude more data until the desired goal is reached is called as forward chaining. An inference engine using forward chaining searches the inference rules until it finds one in which the if-clause is known to be true. It then concludes the then-clause and adds this information to its data. It would continue to do this until a goal is reached. Because the data available determines which inference rules are used, so this method is also called as data-driven search.

How it is done? The given condition (fact) is matched with the left part of a rule (called as antecedent). When the antecedent conditions are met, the rule is fired. That means the rule is replaced by RHS of the rule. It now becomes the new fact to be matched with the antecedent part of another rule.

Backward Chaining (or goal-driven search)

The process of inferencing that starts with a list of goals and works backwards to see if there is data which will allow it to conclude any of these goals is called as backward chaining. An inference engine using backward chaining would search the inference rules until it finds one which has a then-clause that matches a desired goal. If the if-clause of that inference rule is not known to be true then it is added to the list of goals. It is a reverse process of inferencing.

How it is done?

In this, rule interpreter starts with matching "THEN" part of the rule and if match occurs, it is replaced by "IF" condition. Here, the rule interpreter starts with goal state and proceeds towards start state.

Do you know? Situations where the starting states are more than goal states, use forward inferencing.

Q.5. Consider the set of facts F_1, F_2, F_3.....F_6 and set of consequents C_1, C_2, C_3.....C_5. The production rules are as follows—

Rule 1: IF F_1 and F_2 then C_1

Rule 2: IF F_3 and C_1 then C_3

Rule 3: IF F_6 then C_3

Rule 4: IF F_2 and C_3 then C_4

Rule 5: IF C_4 then C_5

Rule 6: If C_2 then C_3

Rule 7: If C_5 then C_6

Assume that input is facts F_1 and F_3 that are true and the query is that whether consequent C_6 is true or not. Use forward chaining and prove this query. Also use backward chaining, if user specifies that C_6 has to be proved. Assume that F_2 and F_3 are true again. Prove that A_1 is true.

Ans. *a.* Using forward chaining

Rule applied	Rule States	Inferred fact
1.	applied (fired)	C1
2.	applied (fired)	C3
3.	not required	
4.	applied (fired)	C4
5.	applied (fired)	C5
6.	not required	
7.	applied (fired)	C6

Thus, rules 1, 2, 4, 5, 7 are fired. The inferred fact becomes C_6 which is proved to be true.

***b.* Using backward chaining :** If user specifies that C_6 has to be proved. Let us assume that F2 and F_3 are true again. The inferencing is done as follows—

	Rule Applied	Condition matched	Inferred
C6 (given as true)	7		C5
C5	6, 5	Condition matched	C2, C4
C4	4	Condition matched	C2 and A2
C3	3	Condition matched	A3
C2	2	Condition matched	A3, C1
C1	1	Condition matched	A1, A2

With this sequence of steps, A_1 is proved to be true.

Q.6. Contrast and compare expert systems and neural nets.

Ans. The current developments in ANN technologies present new opportunities for expert system work. The following points explain this—

1. Expert system elements may be implemented with NN.
2. Areas such as speech and vision are done better with NNs.
3. ESs can be used for training NNs.
4. Knowledge acquisition and knowledge engineering problems can be addressed using NN.
5. Implicit knowledge may be provided by NNs to support explicit rule-based knowledge.

Q.7. Write a short note on ES tools.

Ans. The commercialization of AI has been mainly in the form of expert systems and knowledge-based systems. In the decade of 1980s expert systems have progressed from efforts in research laboratories aimed at building stand-alone one-of-a-kind systems, to products built and deployed in large numbers in industrial laboratory and government office settings. When early expert systems were constructed, their implementers typically began with a general-purpose language such as LISP and built a number of utility data structures and programs to represent facts, rules and strategies and to perform the basic operations of the system such as rule invocation, matching, computations involving uncertainties, etc. Initially, it was often very difficult to speculate now much of that machinery was problem-specific and how much would be reusable for other fields. Once a few experimental applications had been built, the developers begin the task of abstracting out of these programs those aspects that appeared universal. Thus, the well-known first-generation expert system MYCIN led to the development of the tool (or shell) EMYCIN (empty MYCIN). EMYCIN thus provides, based on the past experience, with diagnosis tasks associated with the diagnosis of infectious diseases, a tool with useful knowledge organization and appropriate problem-solving methods for generic tasks such as medical diagnosis, pattern classification and equipment fault diagnosis.

EXPERT SYSTEM TOOLS (also called knowledge Engineering Tools) are software systems that support the development, execution and maintenance of expert systems (or knowledge-based systems). As a result of widespread interest in expert system development, there has been a huge volume of activity in expert system tool development with market projections of the order of US $ 400 million by early 1990s. The tools also range for large development environments such as ART (Automated Reasoning Tool), KES (Knowledge Engineering System), CLIPS (the C Language Integrated Production System) Level 5, VAS OPS5, etc. The widely varying costs of these packages together with the often-exaggerated claims in vendor literature makes selection of expert system tools a difficult task.

Table below gives a partial list of some of these tools—

Advisor	FranzLisp	Personal Consultant Plus
ART	GoldenCommonLisp	PROLOG2
ART-IM	GoldWorks	RuleMaster
Cambridge LISP68000	Insight2+	RuleMaster2
CLIPS	KEE	S.1
ExperLisp	KES	Smalltalk
Experops5	Level 15	Smalltalk
ExpertEase	MicroExpert	VAXOPS5
Expert4	NEXPERTOBJECT	ZEXPERT

Q.8. Explain the knowledge acquisition methods adopted by expert systems.

Ans. Knowledge acquisition is the process of gathering knowledge. The knowledge engineers do this by interacting and interviewing the human experts of that domain. The person interviewing the expert should also have some basic knowledge of the concerned field to find out what to ask. This collected knowledge is then encoded in a format suitable for storage in memory. This job of encoding is done by a computer specialist.

For example: COMPASS is an expert system which performs knowledge acquisition by interviewing.

The knowledge acquisition cycle performs the following steps—

a. Acquires knowledge from expert.

b. Documents the acquired knowledge.

c. Tests the new knowledge.

Q.9. Discuss some explanation facilities as used by ES.

Ans. Almost all expert systems can explain to users how they reach particular conclusions. The most common type of explanation mechanism deals with the following:

1. **Retrospective Reasoning :** It explains how the system reached a particular state. For example, the end-user may wish to know why the system needed the answer to the question it just asked or how the system arrived at a certain conclusion. Here, the system may describe the rules which led to the question or display part of the chain or sequence of rules that led to the conclusion.
2. **Hypothetical Reasoning :** The system explains what would have happened differently if a particular fact or rule had been different.
3. Counterfactual Reasoning : The system explains why an expected conclusion was not reached.

Q.10. Differentiate between neural networks and expert systems.

Ans. The following are the points of difference: -

1. Expert systems seek to emulate or model a human expert's way of solving a set of problems. On the other hand, neural network builders claim that they do not model human intelligence, do not program solutions and do not aim to solve specific problems.
2. Instead, neural network designers seek to put intelligence into hardware in the form of a generalized capability to learn. On the other hand, expert system is highly specific to a given problem and cannot be easily retrained.
3. Unlike expert systems, which typically provide explanations for their solutions, neural networks can not always explain why they arrived at a particular solution. Moreover, they cannot always guarantee a complete solution, arrive at the same solution again with the same input data or always guarantee the best solution. They are very sensitive and may not perform well if their training covers too little or too much of data.

   For example, consider the problem of identifying a cat. Now how an expert system will solve this problem and how a neural network will solve is the question? An expert system approach would interview hundreds of people to understand, how humans recognize cats, resulting in a large set of rules or frames, programmed into an expert system. On the other hand, a trainable neural network would be brought to the website, connected on computer and started out on the process of learning. Every time a cat was not correctly perceived, the system would be left alone and another object scanned.

Q.11. What are the limitations of expert systems?

Ans. The following are some of the limitations of an ES-

1. Only certain classes of problems can be solved using an expert system.
2. Many expert systems require large, lengthy and expensive development efforts.
3. Expert systems lack the breadth of knowledge and the understanding of fundamental principles of a human expert.
4. Their knowledge bases are quite narrow, shallow and brittle.
5. They typically perform limited tasks, which can be performed by professionals, in a few minutes.
6. Hiring of training more experts may be less expensive than building an expert system.
7. Brittleness: ES only have access to highly specific domain knowledge; they cannot fall back on more general knowledge when the need arises.
8. Lack of meta-knowledge: ES do not have very complex knowledge about their own operation. They typically cannot reason about their own scope and limitations. This makes it even more difficult to deal with the brittleness problem.
9. Knowledge acquisition: Despite the development of various tools for knowledge acquisition, it still remains a major bottleneck in applying expert systems technology to new domains.
10. Validations: Measuring the performance of an expert system is difficult because we do not know how to quantify the use of knowledge. It is impossible to present formal proofs of correctness for expert systems. The only thing we can do is to compete these systems against human experts on real-world problems.

Q.12. Define what is self-organization?

Ans. Self-organization is the process in which the internal organization of a system, normally an open system, increases in complexity without being guided or managed by an outside source. Slef-organizing systems typically display emergent properties.

Q.13. Compare expert systems, human experts and conventional programs.

Ans. The following table gives the differences between the two: -

On the basis of	Human experts	Expert systems	Conventional programs
Representation of knowledge	Possess deep knowledge of problem domain but are able to apply heuristic knowledge and common sense as and when required.	Process knowledge expressed in form of rules and use symbolic reasoning to solve problems in a narrow domain.	Process data and use algorithms, a series of well-defined operations, to solve general numerical problems.

Storage of knowledge	In a human brain, knowledge exists in a compiled form.	Knowledge is separated from processing.	Do not separate knowledge from the control structure to process this knowledge.
Explanation	They are capable of explaining in detail the reasoning that led to a conclusion.	Trace the rules fired during a problem -solving session and explain how a particular conclusion was reached and why specific data was needed.	Does not explain how a particular result was obtained and why input data was needed.
Flexibility	Use inexact reasoning and can deal with incomplete, uncertain and fuzzy information.	Permit inexact reasoning and can deal with incomplete, uncertain and fuzzy data.	Work only on problems where data is complete and exact.
Objectivity	Can make mistakes when information is incomplete or fuzzy.	Can make mistakes when data is incomplete or fuzzy.	Provide no solution at all or wrong one, when data is incomplete or fuzzy.
Expansion	Enhance the quality of problem solving via years of learning a practical training. This process is slow, inefficient and expensive.	Enhance the quality of problem solving by adding new rules or adjusting new rules or adjusting old ones in the knowledge base. When new knowledge is acquired, changes are easy to accomplish.	Enhance the quality of problem solving by changing the program code which affects both the knowledge and its processing, making changes difficult.

Q.14. Draw a neat sketch showing an architecture of an expert system.

Ans.

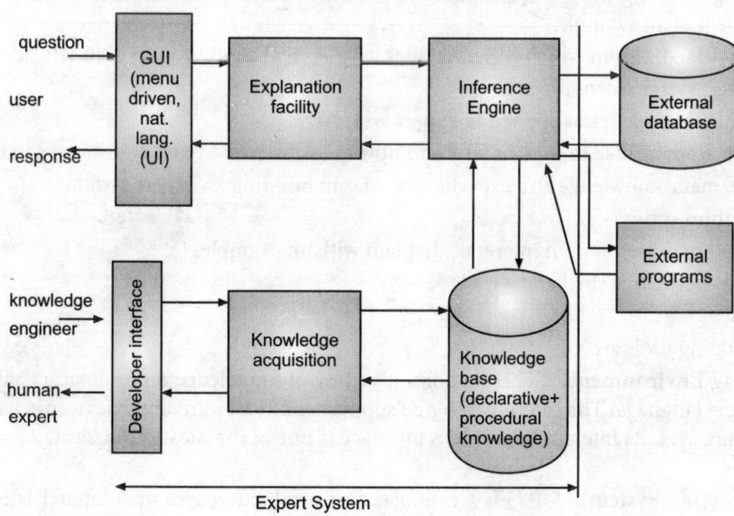

EXERCISE QUESTIONS

1. Explain different components of an expert system.
2. (*a*) Expiain rule-based architecture of expert system.
   (*b*) What are different applications of expert system?
   (*c*) What do you mean by expert system shell?
3. (*a*) Draw and explain architecture of Expert System.

(*b*) What is Expert System Shell? State its advantages.

4. (*a*) What are the various methods of knowledge acquisition used in expert system? Explain with examples.

   (*b*) What are various knowledge representation techniques used in expert systems? Explain with examples.

5. (*a*) What do you mean by an Expert System? Why we need an Expert System? What are different kinds of problems faced during development of an Expert System?

   (*b*) Identify and describe two good application areas for expert systems within a university system.

6. (*a*) What is an ES? Explain its various parts.

   (*b*) Explain, in short, the working of DENDRAL and MYCIN.

   (*c*) Discuss the concept of uncertainty in ES.

7. Briefly explain any of the expert system RI (XCON) or MYCIN.
8. Explain the architecture of an expert with a diagram.
9. What procedure is followed for knowledge acquisition?
10. What are the various steps for development of Expert Systems?
11. How is an Expert System different from other software like DBMS etc.
12. What is an expert system? Compare a human expert with an artificial expert system.
13. Define an expert system. With the help of a block diagram, explain the operation of an expert system.
14. What are the main advantages in keeping the knowledge base separate from the control module in a knowledge-based system?
    [**Hint:** To develop a new expert system, only desired knowledge base is to be developed leading to less development cost of an ES. This separate knowledge base is easy to use and requires less space.]
15. Explain the structure of a rule-based expert system.
16. "A close relationship between the knowledge engineer and an expert is essential for successful implementation of an expert system." Justify the statement.
17. What are the salient activities required in knowledge acquisition system achieved through the interaction between domain experts? Explain with the help of an example.
18. How does MYCIN qualify as a rule- based system which contains rules with several conditions in their left sides?
19. What are the applications of an expert system technology?
20. Explain expertise transfer and domain knowledge as applied to expert systems.
21. Why is it important that an expert system be able to explain why and how question related to the problem solving?
22. How do we use domain knowledge, meta-knowledge and expertise transfer in building an expert system?
23. Explain the need of the self-explanation system.
24. Explain how meta-knowledge is used in expert system inference. Explain with an example.
25. What is an AI shell? Give differences between a shell and a tool.
26. Name some knowledge building tools.
    [**Hint:** some knowledge system building tools are-

    (*a*) **KEE (Knowledge Engineering Environment) :** KEE supports a variety of knowledge representation schemes including object-oriented frame language. The inference engine supports both forward and backward chaining. It allows linking to several data bases. Its interactive graphics interface is one of the most sophisticated available among the expert system tools.

    (*b*) **OPS5 System (Official Production System) :** OPS5 is a rule-based or production system computer language. It was the first language to be used in a successful expert system R1/XCON., used to configure VAX computers. The first implementation of OPS_5 was written in LISP and later written in BLISS for speed. OPS5 uses forward chaining inference engine; programs execute by scanning "working memory elements" looking for matches with the rules in "production memory". Please note that rules have actions that may modify or remove the matched element, create new ones, perform side effects such as output and so forth. Execution continues until no more matches can be found. OPS_4 was an early version while OPS83 came later and was written in C.

    (*c*) **Radian Rule Master :** It is an expert system tool used in applications for automatic knowledge acquisition. It is a modular system as compared to the inference network approach which more closely resembles LISP or PROLOG in structure. With the modular structure, knowledge and rule base, building and modifications proved much easier from a programming point of view.

15 Artificial Neural Network [ANN]

Q.1. What are Artificial Neural Networks? Discuss some of their characteristics.

Ans. An Artificial Neural Network (ANN) is an information processing paradigm that is inspired by our biological nervous system (such as brain) to process information. The key element of the paradigm is structure of the information processing system in human brain. It is composed of large number of highly interconnected simple processing elements called as neurons working together to solve specific problems. Like humans, ANNs can also learn by example. Please note that as we know that learning in biological systems involves adjustments to the synaptic connections that exist between the neurons, a similar approach is also used by ANNs. Also note that ANNs can process information at a great speed due to their highly massive parallelism.

Actually, neural networks have the ability to derive meaningful results from complex (or imprecise) data. Therefore, they can be used to extract patterns and detect trends that are normally not observed by either human experts or any other techniques. Several application areas of neural networks include: -

- Image and pattern recognition.
- Clustering.
- Pattern association.
- Vector quantization.
- Forecasting.
- Function approximation.
- Control optimization.
- Search.
- Multidimensional input-output maps.

The inventor of first neurocomputer, Dr. Robert Hecht Nielsen (1989) defines Neural Network as follows: -

"…a computing system made up of a number of simple, highly inter-connected processing elements, which process information by their dynamic state response to external inputs".

Another definition was given by Haykins (1994)-

"A neural network is a massively parallel distributed processor made up of simple processing units, which has a natural property for storing experimental knowledge and making it available for use. It resembles the brain processor in two respects: -

1. Knowledge is acquired by the network through a learning process.
2. Interneuron connection strengths known as synaptic weights are used to store the knowledge."

Before we discuss further, please remember the following points regarding ANNs: -

1. ANNs are also called as Neurocomputers or neural networks or Parallel Distributed Processors (PDPs) or Connectionist Systems.
2. Neural networks are the networks of neurons such as found in realistic biological brains.
3. Artificial neurons are the basic approximations of the neurons found in brains. They may be physical devices or purely mathematical constructs.
4. ANNs are the networks of artificial neurons which constitute rough approximations to parts to the parts of functioning brains. They may be physical devices or simulated on conventional computers.
5. An ANN is a network of many simple processors called as units, each possibly having a small amount of local memory.

6. The units are connected by the communication channels (connections) which usually carry numeric (non-symbolic) data, encoded by any of these various means.
7. The units operate only on their local data and on the inputs they receive via the connections.
8. Practically speaking, an ANN is just a parallel computational system consisting of many simple processing elements connected together in a specific way in order to perform a particular task.
9. For example, a visual system that can easily recognize a family face in an unfamiliar scene. This less complex task may take days on a conventional computer. Another example is that of a Sonar of a Bat, wherein Sonar is an active echo location system. Bat sonar can easily provide information about how far away a target is, its relative velocity, size of the target, elevation of the target etc. but this accurate task is very difficult for Radar or Sonar Engineering.

Characteristics of Neural Networks

1. **Massive Parallelism :** ANN can be linear or non-linear. We know that a human nervous system consists of large number of nerve cells or neurons that operate in parallel to process various types of information. Note that the same concept is used to build an advanced parallel information processing device called as Artificial Neural Network (ANN). Due to the deluge of data today, the need is to process data in parallel (data parallelism) with multiple processing elements aligned to operate in parallel to process information. Hence, Artificial Neural Network (ANN) today is the best option to process information at a faster speed due to their massive parallelism.
2. **Distributed Representation and Computation :** Like a biological neural network, an Artificial Neural Network (ANN) accepts many inputs in parallel and encodes the information in a distributed fashion. This information is stored in many processing units of the neural network.
3. **Adaptive learning ability :** The objective of neural network is to learn human ability to adapt to changing circumstances and current environment. This means that they can learn from past events and apply it to the future situations.
4. **Self-organization :** An Artificial Neural Network (ANN) can create its own organization (or representation) of the information it receives during learning time.
5. **Generalization ability :** Neural networks can learn and generalize themselves from training data and does not need to be reprogrammed. So, there is no need to write separate programs for learning or generalizations.
6. **Inherent contextual information processing :** Knowledge is represented by a neuron in the network. Every neuron in the network is potentially affected by the global activity of all other neurons in the network. So, any contextual information is dealt with naturally by the neural network.
7. **Fault Tolerant :** As neural network is composed of a large number of highly inter-connected simple processing elements called as neurons working together, failure of an individual unit does not result in the catastrophic failure of the system rather it shows a graceful degradation as found in biological systems.
8. **Noise Tolerant :** Neural networks have natural adaptability and can derive meaningful results from complex and imprecise data.
9. **Low energy consumption :** The human brain is extremely energy efficient using approximately 10^{-16} joules per operation per second whereas the best computers today use around 10^{-6} joules per operation per second.
10. **Real-time operation :** Artificial Neural Network (ANN) computations may be done in parallel using as special hardware devices designed and manufactured to take advantage of this capability.
11. **VLSI designing :** Due to large massive parallel architecture neural networks are suitable for implementing very large -scale integration (VLSI) technology.

Q.2. Give some applications of Artificial Neural Network (ANN).

Ans. Some of the applications areas of Artificial Neural Network (ANN) are as follows: -

1. **Pattern Classification :** Neural networks have been used to classify samples. This means mapping input patterns to differentiate classes. The task of pattern classification is to assign an input pattern, like a speech waveform, represented by a feature vector to one or many prespecified classes. Well known applications include character recognition, blood cell classification and printed circuit board inspection.

2. **Clustering (categorization) : Clustering is defined as the process of organizing objects into groups whose members are similar in some way.** Therefore, a cluster is a collection of objects that are 'similar' to each other and are 'dissimilar' to the objects belonging to other clusters. Classification involves deriving a function that will separate data into categories or classes, characterized by a distinct set of features. **Please note that this function is mechanized by so called network classifier, which is trained using data from different classes as inputs and vectors indicating the true class as outputs. Also note that a network classifier typically maps a given input vector to one of the number of classes represented by an equal number of outputs, by producing 1 at the output class and 0 elsewhere.** Most clustering algorithms are based on some distance measure. Each object is represented by an ordered set (vector) of features. Similar objects are those that have nearly the same values for different features. Well known clustering applications include data mining, data compression and exploratory data analysis.
3. **Function approximation :** Suppose the output corresponding to some input vectors may be known from the training data but we may know the mathematical function describing the actual process. Function approximation is the task of learning or constructing a function that generates approximately the same outputs from the input vectors as the process being modeled, based on available training data. Many engineering and scientific modeling problems require function approximation.

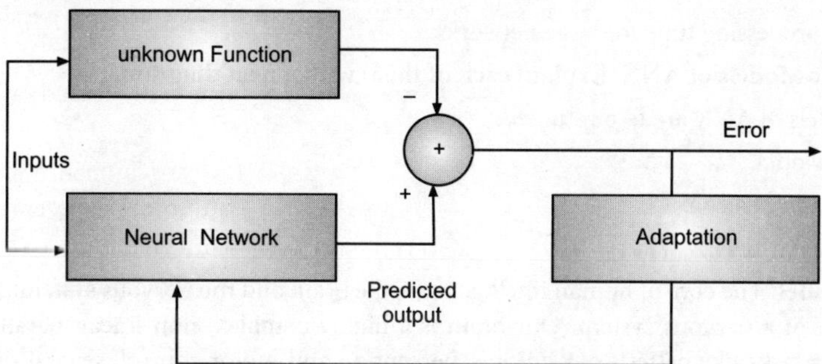

Fig. 15.1: NN as a Function Approximator

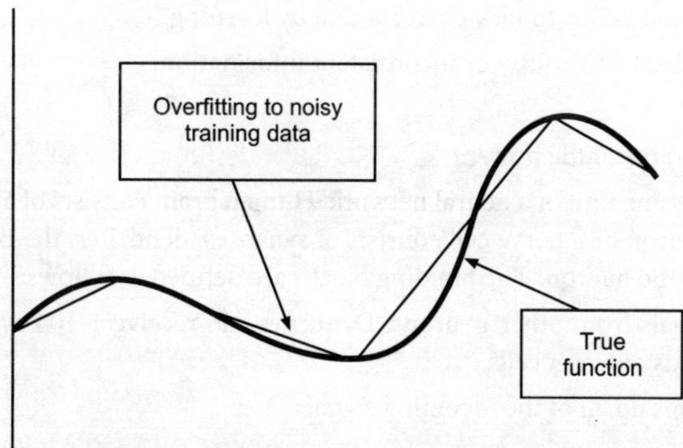

Fig. 15.2: Function Approximation Curve

4. **Prediction (Forecasting) :** It is possible to predict the future events on the basis of past history. Prediction has vital impact on decision making in business, science and engineering. Some other applications include stock market prediction and weather forecasting.
5. **Optimization :** Many problems in mathematics, statistics, engineering, science, medicine and economics can be posed as optimization problems. The goal of an approximation algorithm is to find a solution satisfying a set of constraints such that an objective function is maximized or minimized. For example, Travelling Salesman Problem (TSP) is a very popular optimization problem.

6. **Vector quantization :** It is a technique which allows the modeling of probability density functions by the distribution of prototype vectors. Originally, it was used for data compression. It works by dividing a large set of points (vector) into groups having approximately the same number of points closet to them. Each group is represented by its centroid point in k-means and some other clustering algorithms.

Q.3. Give some advantages and disadvantages of Neural Network.

Ans. Advantages are as follows: -

1. A neural network can performs tasks that a linear program cannot do.
2. When an individual element of the neural network fails, it can continue without any problem by their parallel nature.
3. A neural network learns and does not need to be re-programmed.
4. It can be implemented in any application without any problem.

Disadvantages are as follows: -

1. The neural networks need training to operate.
2. Note that the architecture of a neural network is different from the architecture of microprocessors and hence needs to be emulated.
3. It requires high processing time for large networks.

Q.4. Explain some basic Models of ANN. Explain each of them with a neat diagram.

Ans. The following models of ANN are to be studied: -

1. The Biological Model.
2. The Basic Artificial Neuron.
3. The Mathematical Model.

The Biological Model: The core of human intelligence is the brain and the nervous system. Neurons are the functional and structural unit of a nervous system. Our brain is a highly complex, non-linear, parallel information processing system. It performs tasks like pattern recognition, perception and motor control, several times faster than the fastest digital computers. It is characterized by: -

1. Robust and fault tolerant.
2. Flexible meaning that it can adjust to new environment by learning.
3. Can deal with fuzzy, probabilistic, noisy or inconsistent information.
4. Is highly parallel.
5. Is small, compact and requires little power.

A neuron is the basic processing unit of a neural network. Human brain consists of approximately 1011 elements called as neurons. A biological neuron or a nerve cell consists of synapses, dendrites, the cell body (or hillock) and the axon. Basic computational unit is the neuron. The building blocks are defined as follows: -

1. **Dendrite :** Receives signals from other neurons. Dendrites can receive 1-104 synaptic inputs and can fan-out the output signal to thousands of target cells.
2. **Soma (cell body) :** It sums up all of the incoming signals.
3. **Axon (output) :** Axon of a neuron is a network of long and thin transmission fibers used for communication. The neuron fires (transmits output), when sufficient input is obtained. It transmits signal through axon to other cells. Most axons extend less than 1mm i.e., local connections.
4. **Synapse :** The junction that allows signal transmission between the axons and dendrites are called as synapses. The process of transmission is by the diffusion of chemicals called neurotransmitters across the synaptic cleft. Synapses can be excitatory or inhibitory. It means that it can have an excitatory effect on the receiving neuron (making it more likely to fire) or an inhibitory effect (making it less likely to fire). Excitatory connections have positive weights and inhibitory connections have negative weights.

   The following fig. 15.3 (*a*) and 15.3 (*b*) shows the structure of a single biological neuron and complex connections among neurons respectively.

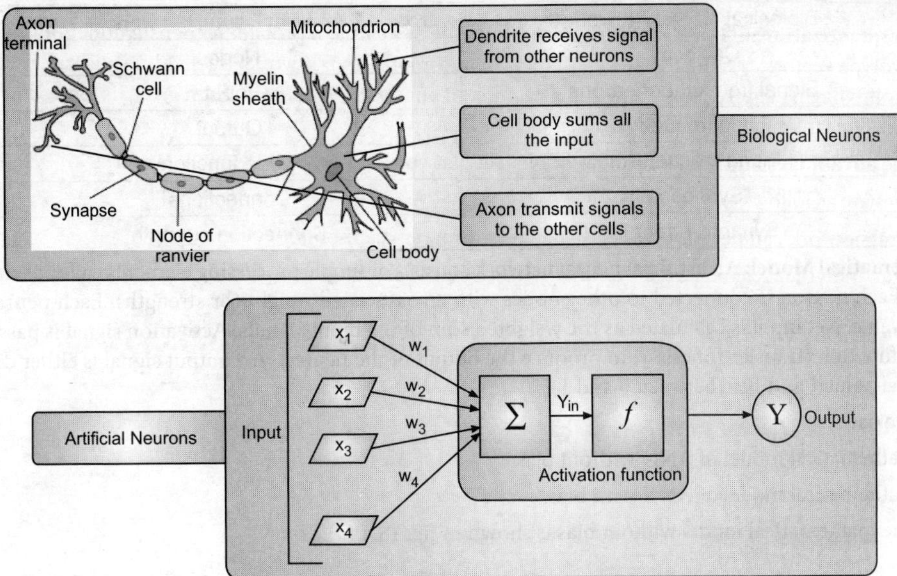

Fig. 15.3: (a) and (b) Biological Neuron v/s Artificial Neuron

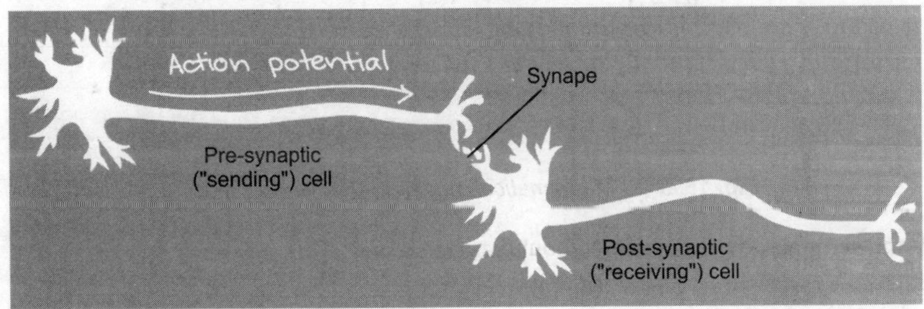

Figure 15.3: (c) Shows the Complex Connections Among Neurons

Working: Synapse is like a one-way valve. Electrical signal (spike) is generated by the neuron, passes down the axon and is received by the synapses that join onto other neurons dendrites. Electrical signals cause the release of transmitter chemicals that flow across a small gap in the synapse (synaptic cleft). Chemicals can have an excitatory effect on the receiving neuron (making it more likely to fire) or an inhibitory effect (making it less likely to fire). **Please note that the frequency of firing of a neuron is proportional to the total synaptic activities and is controlled by the synaptic parameters (or weights). Also note that the total inhibitory and excitatory connections to a particular neuron are summed, if this value exceeds the neurons threshold the neuron fires, else it does not fire.**

The Basic Artificial Neuron : the basic artificial neuron is a simplified model of a biological neuron and is shown in fig. 18.3 (*b*).

Working : A set of synapses *i.e.*, connections bring in activations from other neurons. Dendrites receive these signals from other neurons. The processing unit (cell body) sums the inputs and then applies a non-linear activation or transfer or threshold function, f(Net). An output line (axon) transmits the result to other neurons.

Some commonly used and associated terms used in NNs are: -

Biological Neural Network	Artificial Neural Network
Cell body	Nodes
Signal from other neurons	Input
Firing frequency	Output
Firing mechanism	Node function
Synapses	Connections
Synaptic strength	Connection strength

The Mathematical Model: An artificial neural network consists of simple processing elements called as neurons or units or nodes. Each neuron is connected to other nodes with an associated weight (or strength). Each neuron has a single threshold value. Net input is calculated as the weighted sum of the input signals. Activation signal is passed through an activation function (transfer function) to produce the output of the neuron. An output signal is either discrete (0 or 1) or it is a real-valued number (between 0 and 1).

Two cases arise:

Case-1: Mathematical model of ANN without bias.

Case-2: Mathematical model of ANN with bias.

Case-1: The mathematical model without bias is shown in fig. 18.4 (*a*).

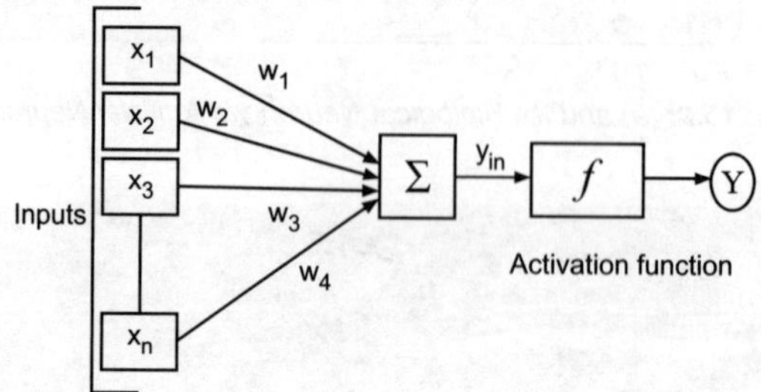

***Fig. 15.4:** (a) Mathematical model of ANN without bias*

Mathematically, the net input to the neuron without bias signal is: -

$$\text{Net} = W_1 * X_1 + W_2 * X_2 + \ldots.. + W_n * X_n$$

Or we can say that-

$$\text{Net} = \Sigma\,(i \leftarrow 1 \text{ to } n)\; W_i * X_i$$

So, the output produced is-

$$Y = f(\text{Net}) \quad \text{(after passing from threshold function)}$$

where $X_1, X_2, \ldots.. X_n$ are activation of neuron (input signal);

W_1, X_2 ....Wn are the synaptic weights;

Net is the output after summation or induced local field or activation potential;

F (Net) is the activation function;

Y is the output signal of neuron.

Case-2: The mathematical model with bias is shown in fig. 15.4 (*b*).

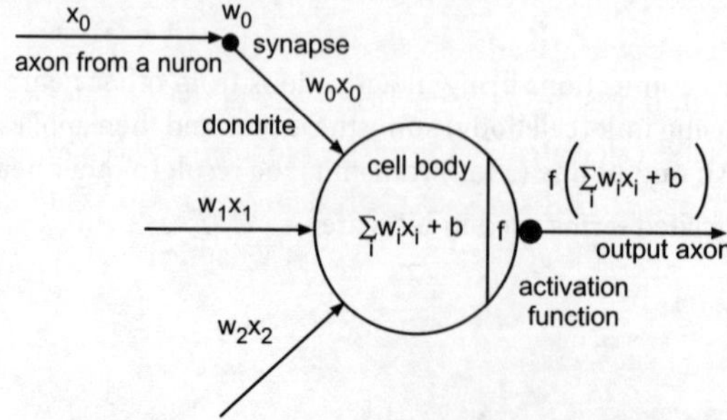

***Fig. 15.4:** (b) Mathematical model of ANN with bias*

If a new synapse, b called as bias is added to the fig. of 15.4 (*a*) then the model becomes as shown in 15.4 (*b*). so, the net input to the neuron with bias signal is-

$$\text{Net} = b + W_1 * X_1 + W_2 * X_2 + \ldots + W_n * X_n$$

Where *b* is the bias signal whose activation is always 1. This equation can be rewritten as-

$$\text{Net} = W_0 * X_0 + W_1 * X_1 + W_2 * X_2 + \ldots + W_n * X_n$$

Or we can say that-

$$\text{Net} = b + \Sigma\ (i \leftarrow 1 \text{ to } n)\ W_i * X_i$$

Or we can say that-

$$\text{Net} = \Sigma\ (i \leftarrow 0 \text{ to } n)\ W_i * X_i$$

So, the output produced is-

$$Y = f(\text{Net}) \quad \text{(after passing from threshold function)}$$

Q.5. Define the following terms: -

a. **Weights.** ***b.*** **Bias.**

c. **Threshold.**

d. **Activation Function.**

Ans. 1. Weights : A neural network consists of a large number of simple processing elements called as neurons. These neurons are connected to each other by directed communication links. These are associated with weights. A simple neural network is shown in fig. 15.5.

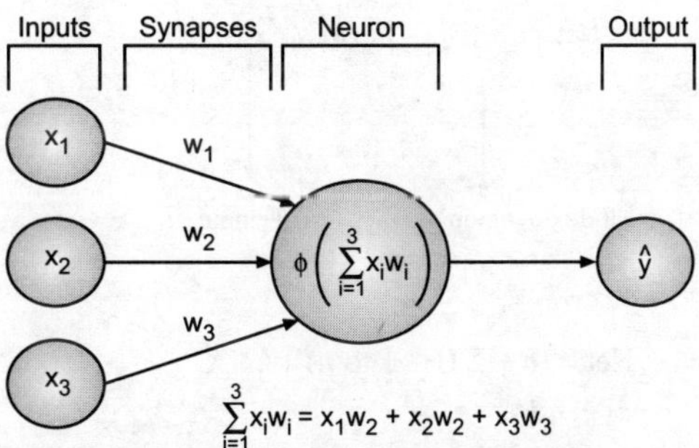

Fig. 15.5: *A simple neural network*

From fig. 15.5 we find that-

a. The weights that carry information are denoted as $W_1, W_2 \ldots\ldots W_n$

b. These weights also denote the strength of the signal.

c. Weights may be fixed or can even take random values.

d. Convention: Excitatory connections have positive weights and inhibitory connections have negative weights.

e. Weights can be set to zero or can be calculated by some methods.

f. The change in the weights indicate the overall performance of the neural network.

Also note that the net input Net is calculated on the basis of following parameters: -

$X_1, X_2, \ldots\ldots X_n$ are activation of neuron (input signal);

$W_1, W_2, \ldots\ldots W_n$ are synaptic weights;

Net is the output after summation-

$$\text{Net} = W_1 X_2 + W_2 X_2, \ldots\ldots + W_n X_n$$

Or we can say that- $\text{Net} = \Sigma\ (i \leftarrow 0 \text{ to } n)\ W_i * X_i$

2. **Bias :** A bias acts exactly as a weight on a connection from a unit whose activation is always 1. The weight is generally taken as $W_0 = 1$, so that a neuron fires irrespective of its input and whatever is received at the input is passed as it is to the output. **Please note that increasing the bias increases the net input to the unit** ($b = W_0$). Also **note that the bias (*b*) has the effect of increasing or lowering the Net input of the activation function depending on whether it is positive or negative respectively.** This is shown in fig. 15.6.

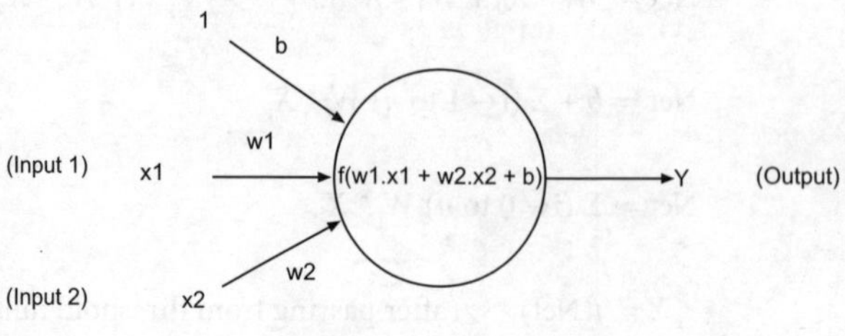

Fig. 15.6: *A Neural Network with bias*

Figure 15.6 shows a simple neural network with a bias input.
This unit is always set to 1.
Mathematically,

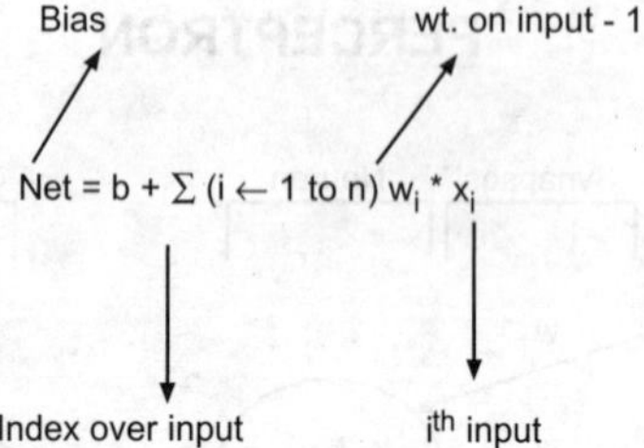

or we can say that-

$$\text{Net} = b + \Sigma\ (i \leftarrow 1 \text{ to } n)\ W_i * X_i$$
$$W_0 = b$$

3. **Threshold:** The threshold, θ is used to calculate the activations of the given neural network. The output depends upon the value of the threshold. The neuron fires if the weighted sum of the input signal applied exceeds the threshold θ otherwise it does not fire. The threshold may be calculated as follows: -

$$Y = \begin{cases} +1 \text{ if Net} > \theta \\ -1 \text{ if Net} < \theta \end{cases}$$

This can be shown in a diagram form also-

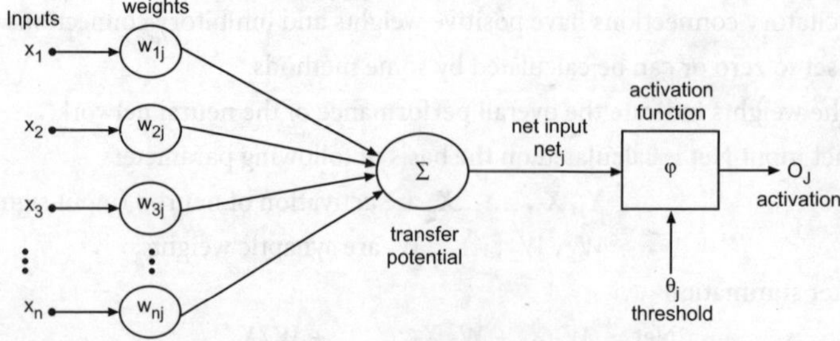

Fig. 15.7: *NN with a threshold function*

4. **Activation Function :** The activation function denoted by f(Net) is used to calculate the output response of a neuron in terms of induced local field (Net). **Please note that a neuron fires if the weighted sum of the input signal applied exceeds the threshold 'θ' else it need not fire. Also note that for the neurons in the same layer, same activation functions are used.** There may be linear or non-linear activation functions. The non-linear activation functions are generally used in a multi-layer network. For example, the identity function is given by the expression function-

$$f(x) = x; \quad \text{for all } x.$$

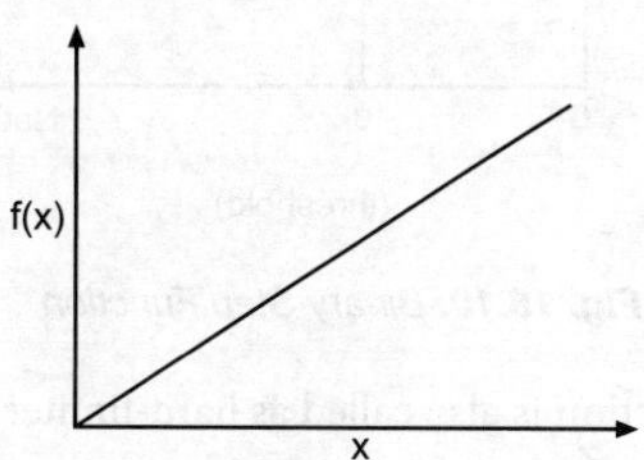

Fig. 15.8: Identity Function

We are in a position to solve some problems now based on binary step functions.

Q.6. Given the input vector (3, 1, 0, -2) and weight vector (0.3, -0.1, 2.1, -1.1). Compute the output from an ANN when identity activation function is applied.

Ans. Activation function is given by the formula: -

$$f(\text{Net}) = \text{Net}$$

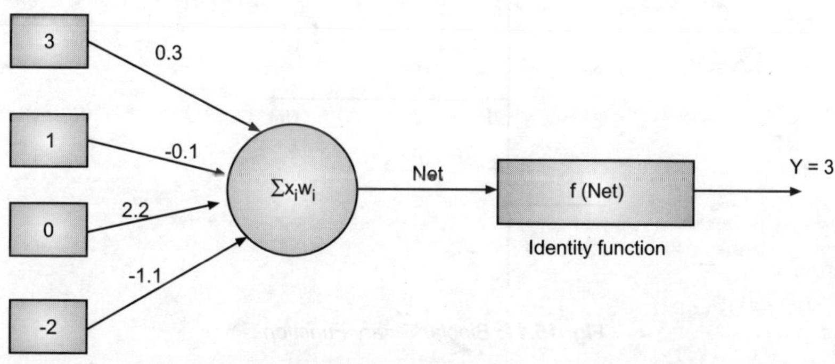

Fig. 15.9: Output after applying identity activation function

Calculations:

Inputs: (3, 1, 0, -2)

Processing:

$$\text{Net} = 3(0.3) + 1(-0.1) + 0(2.1) + -2(-1.1)$$
$$= 0.9 + (-0.1) + 0 + 2.2$$

Output, $Y = 3.$

b) **Binary Step Function :** there are two types of binary step functions-

1. **Unipolar Binary Function:** - The function is given by-

$$f(\text{Net}) = \begin{cases} 1 \text{ if Net} \geq \theta \\ 1 \text{ if Net} < \theta \end{cases}$$

Here, 'θ' is the threshold. Most of the single layer networks use binary step function for calculating the output from the Net input. The binary step function is also called as threshold function. This can be shown in form of a graph-

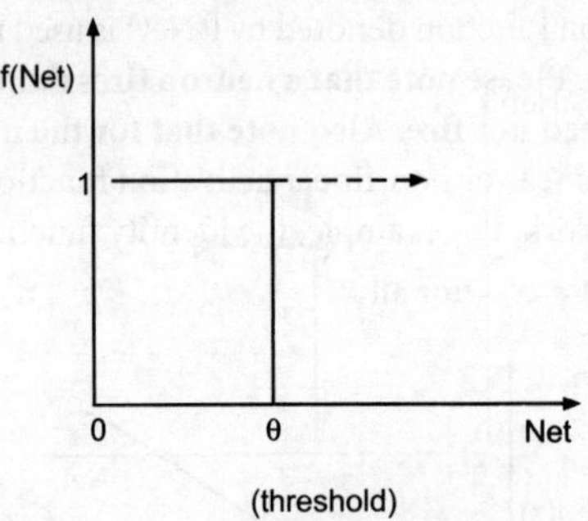

Fig. 18.10: Binary Step Function

2. **Bipolar Binary Function:** - This function is also called as hard-limiter function.

Here, Net = $W_1 X_1 + W_2 X_2, \ldots\ldots + W_n X_n - \theta$

Net value = Net – θ

The function is given by-

$$f(Net) = \begin{cases} +1 \text{ if Net} \geq \theta \\ -1 \text{ if Net} < \theta \end{cases}$$

This can be shown in form of a graph-

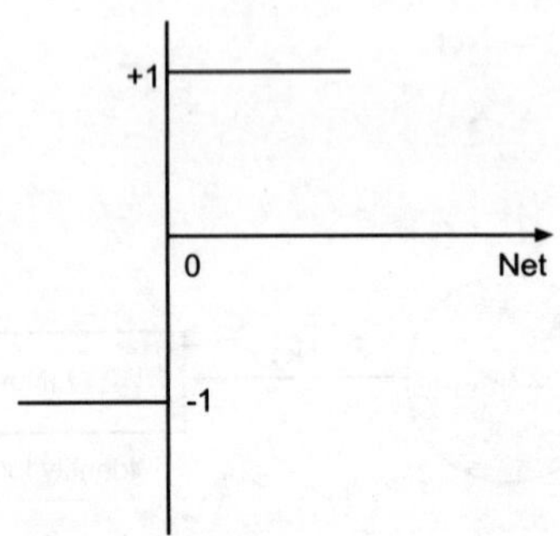

Fig. 15.11: Bipolar Binary Function

Q.7. Given the input vector (3, 1, 0, -2), weight vector (0.3, -0.1, 2.1, -1.1) and the threshold, θ = 3. Compute the output from an ANN when binary step activation function is applied to it.

Ans. The activation function is given by-

$$f(Net) = \begin{cases} 1 \text{ if Net} \geq \theta \\ 1 \text{ if Net} < \theta \end{cases}$$

Here, 'θ' is the threshold = 3 (given)

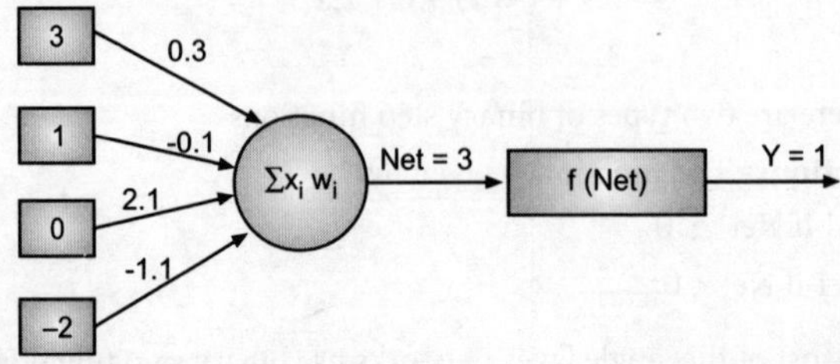

Fig. 15.12: Output after Applying Binary Step Activation Function

This can be shown in form of a graph-

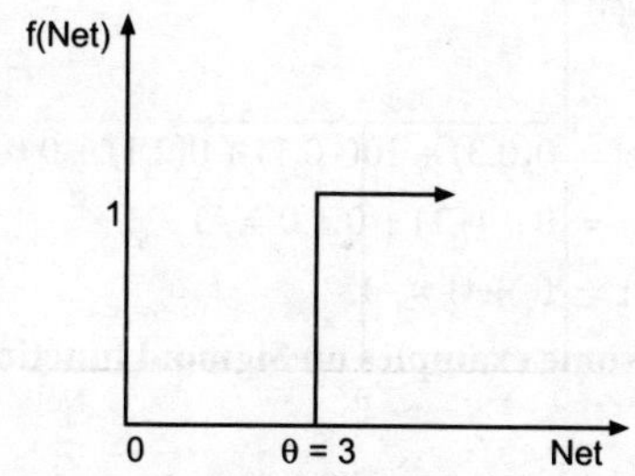

Fig. 15.13: After applying threshold (θ = 3)

Calculations:

Inputs: (3, 1, 0, -2) (given)

Threshold (θ) = 3 (given)

Processing:

$$\text{Net} = 3(0.3) + 1(-0.1) + 0(2.1) + (-2)(-1.1)$$
$$= 0.9 + (-0.1) + 0 + 2.2 = 3$$

Output, $Y = f(\text{Net}) = 1.$

Q.8. Given the input vector (0, 10, 0, 0), weight vector (0.3, -0.1, 2.1, -1.1) and the threshold, θ = 3. Compute the output from an ANN when bipolar binary step activation function is applied.

Ans. The activation function is given by-

$$f(\text{Net}) = \begin{cases} +1 \text{ if Net } \geq \theta \\ -1 \text{ if Net} < \theta \end{cases}$$

Here, 'θ' is the threshold = 3 (given).

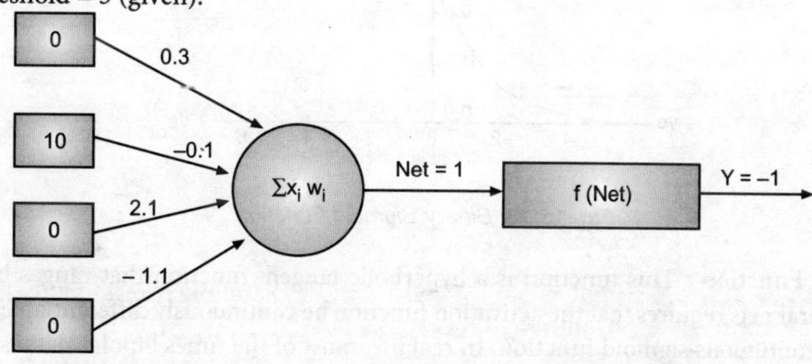

***Fig. 15.14:** Output after applying binary step activation function*

This can be shown in form of a graph-

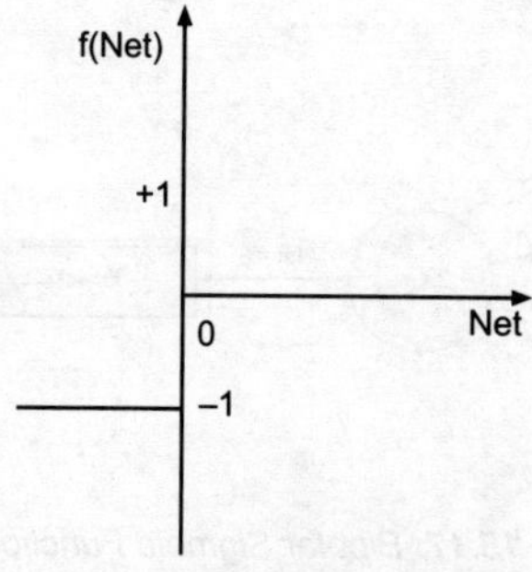

***Fig. 15.15:** After applying threshold (θ = 3)*

Calculations:

Inputs: (0, 10, 0, 0) (given)

Threshold (θ) = 3 (given)

Processing: Net = 0(0.3) + 10(−0.1) + 0(2.1) + 0 (−1.1)

= 0 + (−1) + 0 + 0 = −1

Output, Y = f(Net) = −1.

Before discussing further, let us solve some examples on Sigmoid function now.

Q.9. Explain the Sigmoid Function

Ans. These functions are generally S-shaped curves. The most commonly used sigmoid functions are- hyperbolic and logistic functions. These are used in multi-layer networks like radial basis functions network, back propagation network etc. They are of two types: -

1. **Binary Sigmoid Function :** This function is also called as logistic function and it ranges from 0 to 1. The function is given as follows: -

$$f(Net) = 1 / (1 + e^{-\lambda Net})$$

where λ = the steepness parameter.

This can be shown in form of a graph: -

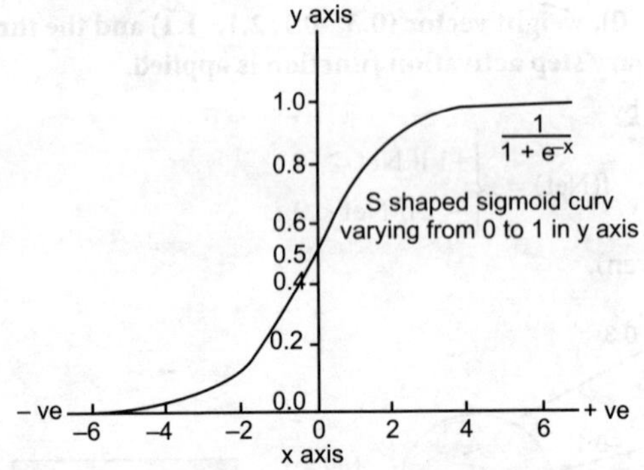

Fig. 15.16: Binary Sigmoid Function

2. **Bipolar Sigmoid Function :** This function is a hyperbolic tangent function that ranges between +1 and -1. The math of some neural nets requires that the activation function be continuously differentiable. So, this function is also called as bipolar continuous sigmoid function. In real life, most of the times bipolar data is used, so this activation function is very common. This function is given by the expressions: -

$$f(Net) = 2f (Net) - 1$$

$$f(Net) = 2 / (1 + e^{-\lambda Net} - 1)$$

where λ = the steepness parameter.

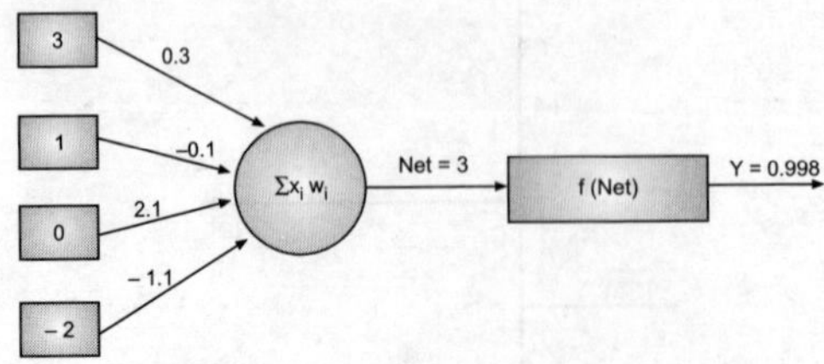

Fig. 15.17: Bipolar Sigmoid Function

We are in a position to solve some examples based on sigmoid activation function now.

Q.10. Given the input vector (3, 1, 0, -2), weight vector (0.3, -0.1, 2.1, -1.1) and $\lambda = 2$. Compute the output from an ANN when bipolar binary sigmoid activation function is applied.

Ans. The activation function is given by-

$$f(Net) = 1 / (1 + e^{-\lambda Net})$$

where λ = the steepness parameter.

λ= 3 (given).

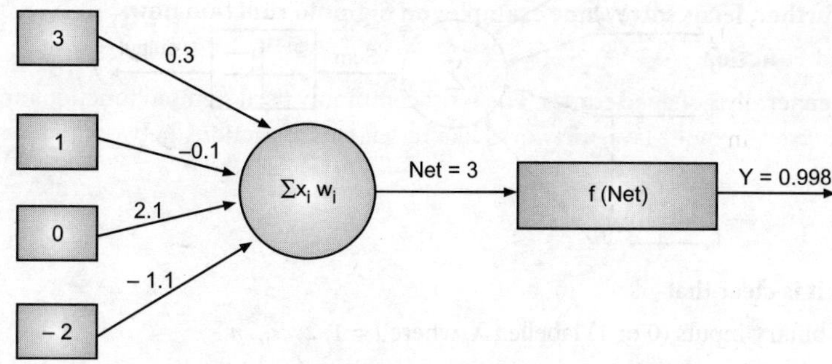

Fig. 18.18: Output after applying binary sigmoid activation function

Calculations:

Inputs: (3, 1, 0, -2) (given)

$\lambda = 2$ (given)

Processing:

$$Net = 3(0.3) + 1(-0.1) + 0(2.1) + -2\,(-1.1)$$
$$= 0.9 + (-0.1) + 0 + 2.2 = 3$$

Output, $Y = f(Net) = f(3) = 1 / (1 + e^{-2(3)}) = 0.998.$

Q.11. If the net input to a neuron is 0.64, calculate its output when the activation function is-

a. **Binary sigmoid.**

b. **Bipolar sigmoid.**

Ans. Net input to the neuron = 0.64

a. Applying binary sigmoid activation function,

Output, $Y = f(Net) = 1 / (1 + e^{-0.64}) = 0.6548$

b. Applying bipolar sigmoid activation function,

Output, $Y = f(Net) = 2 / (2 + e^{-0.64} - 1) = 0.3095$

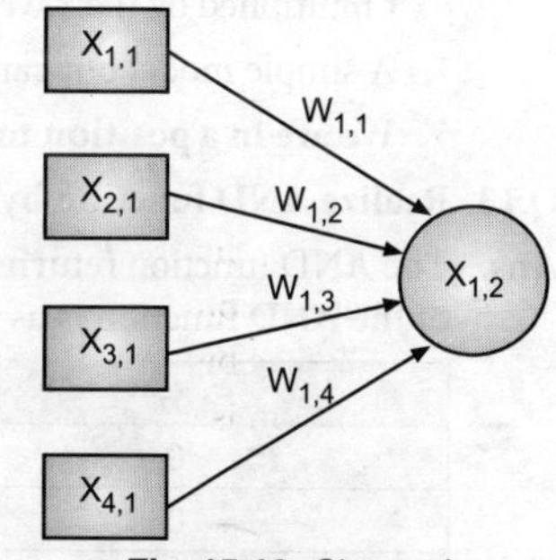

Fig. 15.19: Shows the Multiplication Method

Alternative method of calculation of Net input using matrix multiplication method.

If the input for a neural network is given by a vector-

$$X' = [X_{1,1}, X_{2,1}, X_{3,1}, X_{4,1}]$$

And its weight is given by- $X' = [W_{1,1}, W_{2,1}, W_{3,1}, W_{4,1}]$

Note that multiplying *a* $(n * r)$ matrix with *a* $(r * m)$ matrix produces *a* $(n * m)$ matrix, *C*, where each element in $(n * m)$ matrix, C_{ij} is produced as the scalar product of row, *i* of the left and column, *j* of the right.

Mathematically,

$$W'\,1\,X'\,1 = [W_{1,1} + W_{1,2} + W_{1,3} + W_{1,4}] \begin{pmatrix} X_{1,1} \\ X_{2,1} \\ X_{3,1} \\ X_{4,1} \end{pmatrix}$$

$$= W_{1,1}\,X_{1,1} + W_{1,2}\,X_{2,1} + W_{1,3}\,X_{3,1} + W_{1,4}\,X_{4,1}$$

$$= W\ X^T$$

Q.12. What was the first Artificial Neurons model / McCulloch-Pitts Model?

Ans. 1. The first formal definition of an artificial neuron model based on the highly simplified considerations of the biological model was formulated by Warren McCulloch and Walter Pitts in 1943.

2. It's architecture is as shown below-

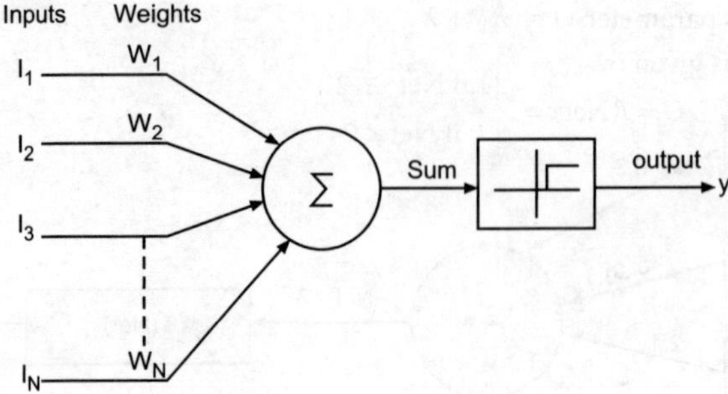

From the diagram it is clear that-

1. The neuron has binary inputs (0 or 1) labelled X_i where $I = 1, 2, \ldots, n$.
2. These inputs have weights of +1 for excitatory synapses and -1 for inhibitory synapses labelled W_i where $i = 1, 2, \ldots, n$.
3. The neuron has a threshold value, T, which fires if the Net input to the neuron is greater than the threshold.
4. The neuron has a binary output signal denoted by O.
5. The superscript $t = 0, 1, 2, \ldots$ denotes discrete time instants.
6. The output O of a neuron at a time, $t + 1$, can be defined by the following equation-

$$f(\text{Net}) = \begin{cases} 1 & \text{if } W_i X_i^t \geq T \\ 0 & \text{if } W_i X_i^t < T \end{cases}$$

Please note that this means that the output of the neuron at time, $t + 1$, is 1 if the sum of all the inputs X_t^I at time t multiplied by their weights W_i is greater than or equal to the threshold T and 0 if the sum of all the inputs X_t^i at time t multiplied by their weights W_i is less than the threshold T.

7. A simple model but can perform basic logic operations NOT, OR and AND.

We are in a position to solve some numerical now.

Q.13. Realize AND function by McCulloch-Pitts neuron model.

Ans. The AND function returns a true (1) value when all of the inputs are true else it returns a false (0) value. The truth table of the AND function is as follows-

X_1	X_2	O
0	0	0
0	1	0
1	0	0
1	1	1

The McCulloch – Pitts neuron is as shown below: -

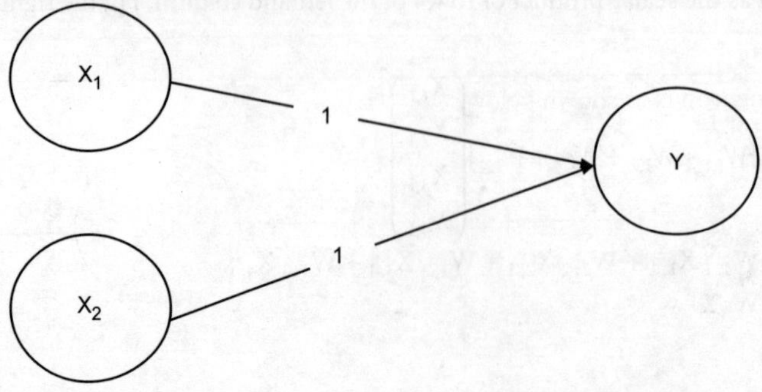

Suppose the threshold value is $\theta = 2$. As there are two inputs X_1,X_2 so $i = 2$. The weights assumed are $W_1 = 1$, $W_2 = 1$.

Thus,

$$\text{Net} = \Sigma\, W_i * X_i \ (i \leftarrow 1 \text{ to } 2)$$
$$\text{Net} = W_1 * X_1 + W_2 * X_2$$
$$\text{Net} = 1 * X_1 + 1 * X_2$$
$$\text{Net} = X_1 + X_2$$

The output, O of a neuron is given by-

$$O = f(\text{Net}) = \begin{cases} 1 \text{ if Net} \geq 2 \\ 0 \text{ if Net} < 2 \end{cases}$$

Now network learns as follows: -

1. $X_1 = 0$ $\quad X_2 = 0$

$$\text{Net} = W_1 * X_1 + W_2 * X_2 = 1 * X_1 + 1 * X_2 = 1 * 0 + 1 * 0 = 0$$
$$O = f(\text{Net}) = 0 \quad [\text{since Net} < 2]$$

2. $X_1 = 0$ $\quad X_2 = 1$

$$\text{Net} = W_1 * X_1 + W_2 * X_2 = 1 * X_1 + 1 * X_2 = 1 * 0 + 1 * 1 = 1$$
$$O = f(\text{Net}) = 0 \quad [\text{since Net} < 2]$$

3. $X_1 = 1$ $\quad X_2 = 0$

$$\text{Net} = W_1 * X_1 + W_2 * X_2 = 1 * X_1 + 1 * X_2 = 1 * 1 + 1 * 0 = 1$$
$$O = f(\text{Net}) = 0 \quad [\text{since Net} < 2]$$

4. $X_1 = 0$ $\quad X_2 = 1$

$$\text{Net} = W_1 * X_1 + W_2 * X_2 = 1 * X1 + 1 * X2 = 1 * 1 + 1 * 1 = 2$$
$$O = f(\text{Net}) = 1 \quad [\text{since Net} \geq 2].$$

Q.14. Realize OR function by McCulloch-Pitts neuron model.

Ans. The OR function returns a true (1) value when all of the inputs are true else it returns a false (0) value. The truth table of the OR function is as follows-

X	O
0	0
1	0

The McCulloch – Pitt's neuron is as shown below: -

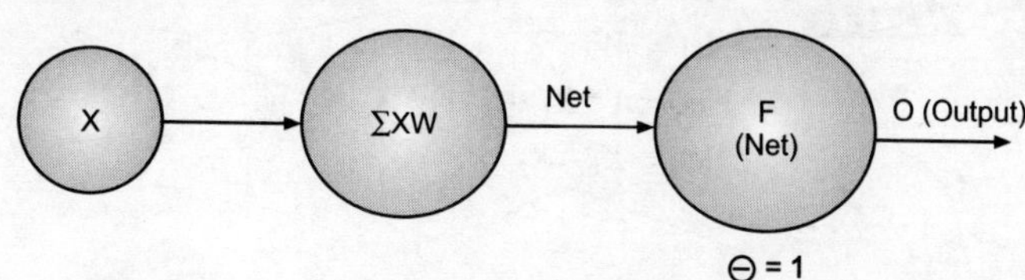

Suppose the threshold value is θ = 1. There is only one input *i.e.*, X. The weight assumed is

$$W = 1$$

Thus,

$$\text{Net} = W * X$$
$$\text{Net} = 1 * X$$
$$\text{Net} = X$$

The output, O of a neuron is given by and from this the activations of output neuron can be formed as follows: -

$$O = f(\text{Net}) = \begin{cases} 1 \text{ if Net } < 1 \\ 0 \text{ if Net } \geq 1 \end{cases}$$

Now network learns as follows: -

1. $X = 0$

$$\begin{aligned} \text{Net} &= W * X \\ &= 1 * X \\ &= 1 * 0 \\ &= 0 \\ O &= f(\text{Net}) = 1 \quad [\text{since Net} < 1] \end{aligned}$$

2. $X = 1$

$$\begin{aligned} \text{Net} &= W * X \\ &= 1 * X \\ &= 1 * 1 \\ &= 1 \\ O &= f(\text{Net}) = 0 \quad [\text{since Net} \geq 1] \end{aligned}$$

Example 4: Realize AND-NOT function by McCulloch-Pitt's neuron model.

Solution 4: The AND-NOT function returns a true (1) value when the first input value is true and the second input value is a false (0) value. The truth table of the AND-NOT function is as follows-

X1	X2	O
0	0	0
0	1	0
1	0	1
1	1	0

The McCulloch – Pitt's neuron is as shown below: -

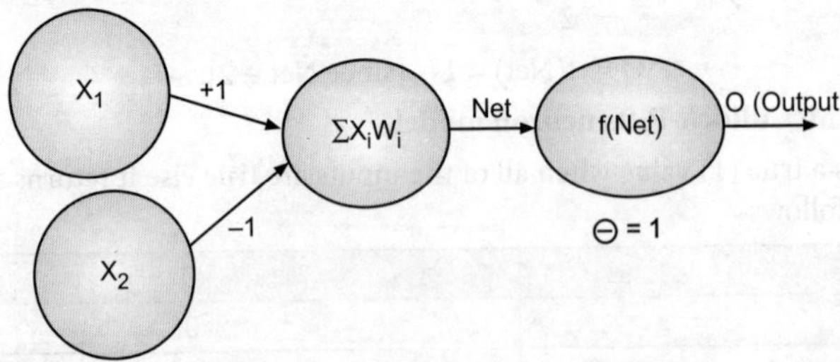

Suppose the threshold value is θ = 1. As there are two inputs X_1, X_2 so $i = 2$. The weights assumed are $W_1 = 1$, $W_2 = -1$.

Thus,

$$\text{Net} = \Sigma\, W_i * X_i \; (i \leftarrow 1 \text{ to } 2)$$
$$\text{Net} = W_1 * X_1 + W_2 * X_2$$
$$\text{Net} = 1 * X_1 + (-1) * X_2$$
$$\text{Net} = X_1 - X_2$$

The output, O of a neuron is given by and from this the activations of output neuron can be formed as follows: -

$$O = f(\text{Net}) = \begin{cases} 1 \text{ if Net } \geq 1 \\ 0 \text{ if Net } < 1 \end{cases}$$

Now network learns as follows: -

1. $X_1 = 0$ $\quad X_2 = 0$

$$\begin{aligned} \text{Net} &= W_1 * X_1 + W_2 * X_2 \\ &= 1 * X_1 + (-1) * X_2 \\ &= 1 * 0 + (-1) * 0 \\ &= 0 \\ O &= f(\text{Net}) = 0 \quad [\text{since Net} < 1] \end{aligned}$$

2. $X_1 = 0$ $\quad X_2 = 1$

$$\begin{aligned} \text{Net} &= W_1 * X_1 + W_2 * X_2 \\ &= 1 * X_1 + (-1) * X_2 \\ &= 1 * 0 + (-1) * 1 \\ &= -1 \\ O &= f(\text{Net}) = 0 \quad [\text{since Net} < 1] \end{aligned}$$

3. $X_1 = 1$ $\quad X_2 = 0$

$$\begin{aligned} \text{Net} &= W_1 * X_1 + W_2 * X_2 \\ &= 1 * X_1 + (-1) * X_2 \\ &= 1 * 1 + (-1) * 0 \\ &= 1 \\ O &= f(\text{Net}) = 1 \quad [\text{since Net} \geq 1] \end{aligned}$$

4. $X_1 = 1$ $\quad X_2 = 1$

$$\begin{aligned} \text{Net} &= W_1 * X_1 + W_2 * X_2 \\ &= 1 * X_1 + (-1) * X_2 \\ &= 1 * 1 + (-1) * 1 \\ &= 0 \\ O &= f(\text{Net}) = 0 \quad [\text{since Net} < 1] \end{aligned}$$

Q.16. Describe the Neural Network Architecture.

Ans. The architecture of the neural network refers to the arrangement of the connection between neurons, processing elements, number of layers and the flow of signal in the neural network. There are mainly two categories of neural network architecture: -

a. Feed-forward.

b. Feedback (recurrent) neural networks.

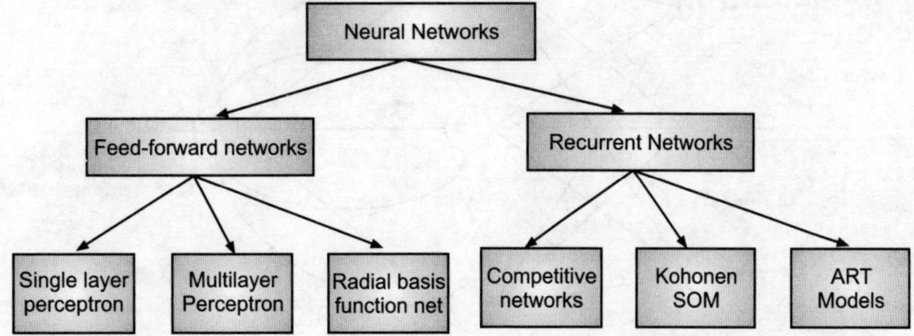

simplest networks of each of these types form the basic functional units. They are functional because they can perform by themselves some simple recognition tasks. They are basic because they form the building blocks for developing neural network architectures.

Let us discuss feed-forward networks first.

1. **Feed-forward Networks:** In feed-forward ANNs, signals travel only in one way i.e., from input to output. There is no feedback loop i.e., the output layer does not alter that particular layer. These type of ANNs are found to be straight-forward networks that connect inputs with outputs. These are widely used in the recognition of pattern. This type of organization is also known as bottom-up or top-down. Fig. 15.16 shows a simple feedforward network. It is a 2-layer network with M input units and N output units. Each input unit is connected to each of the output units. A weight indicating the strength of the connection is associated with each connection. The input units are linear while the output units can be either linear or non-linear depending on the task that the network should perform.

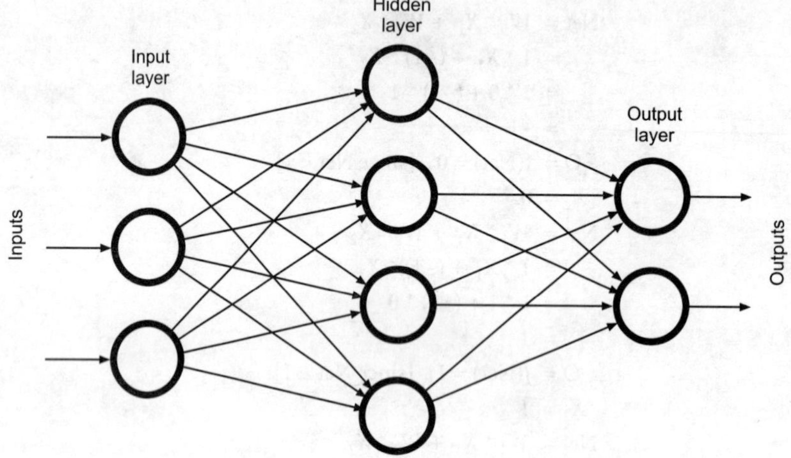

Fig. 15.20: A simple feed- forward network

2. **Feedback Networks :** Feedback ANNs, may have signals driving in both the directions by the introduction of loops in the network. Feedback networks are very much powerful and might get complicated. **Please note that these networks are dynamic but their state changes frequently to reach the point of equilibrium. Also note that these continue to be at equilibrium till the input changes and in such case, a new equilibrium is required to be found.** Feedback networks are also introduced as an interactive or recurrent networks. They consist of a set of N processing units, each connected to all other units. The connection weights are assumed to be symmetric. Depending on the task, the units of the network could be linear or non-linear.

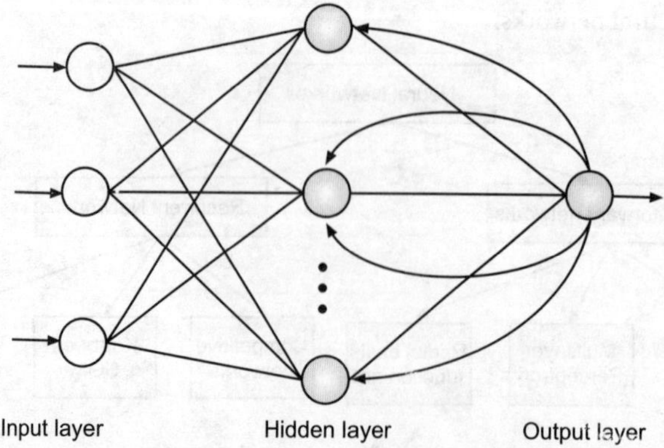

Fig. 15.21: A simple Feedback Network

3. **Network Layers :** A simple ANN has the following three layers of units. Some of the main features of these networks includes-
   - A layer of input units is connected to a layer of hidden units, which is further connected to a layer of output units.
   - The activity done by the input units shows the raw information fed into the network.
   - The activities of the input units determine the activities of each hidden unit and the weights on the connections between the input and the hidden units.
   - The activity of the hidden units and the weights between the hidden and output units depend on the behavior of the output units.
   - The hidden units are free to compose their own representations of the input.
   - The weights between the input and hidden units can be customized to decide what a hidden unit might choose.
   - A single layer organization is the one in which all of the units are interconnected. It is of more potential computational power than hierarchically structured multi-layer organizations.
   - In multi-layer networks, on the other hand, the units are generally numbered by layers.
4. **Perceptrons :** The perceptron was one of the earliest neural network models invented by Rosenblatt. It includes inputs $x_1, x_1, x_2, \ldots\ldots x_n$ and assign them corresponding weights $w_1, w_2, \ldots\ldots$ wn like a neuron. It models a neuron by sending the output 1 if the weighted sum of inputs is greater than some adjustable threshold and a 0 otherwise. **Note that the values of weights can be positive or negative real values.**

$$g(x) = \Sigma\, w_i\, x_i \quad ({}_i \leftarrow 1 \text{ to } n)$$

Output function
$$O(x) = 1 \text{ if } g(x) > 0$$
$$0 \text{ if } g(x) < 0$$

15.5 SINGLE-LAYER FEEDFORWARD ANN

If the graph of a neural network is acyclic (connections between the units do not form a cycle) then it is called as a **feedforward neural network.** The information moves only in one direction *i.e.,* forward from input nodes to output nodes through hidden nodes.

- The simplest form of ANN was the feedforward neural network. In these networks, the movement of information is in one direction only *i.e.,* forward from the input nodes through the hidden nodes and to the output nodes. There are no cycles (or loops) in these networks.
- The simplest type of neural network is a single-layer perceptron network. It has a single layer of output nodes and the inputs are directly fed into the outputs by a series of weights. So, it can be called as a simplest type of feedforward network. **Note that in these types of networks, the sum of the products of the weights and the inputs is calculated in each node and if the value is above some threshold** (typically zero), the **neuron fires taking the activated value** (typically one) **else it accepts the deactivated value** (typically -1). **Also note that the neurons having this type of activation function are known as artificial neurons or linear threshold units.**
- The term perceptron refers the networks having only one of these units.

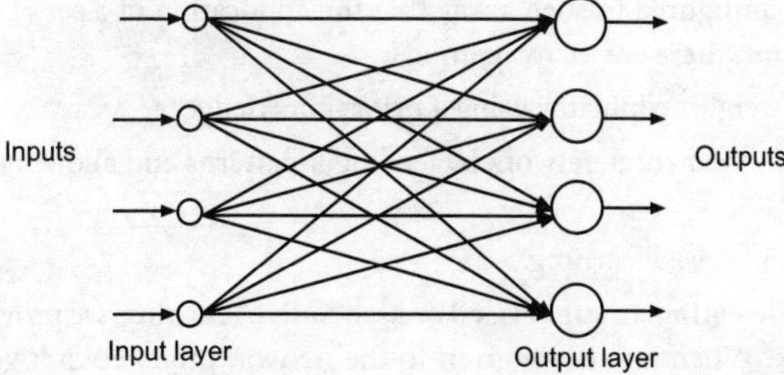

Fig. 15.22: Single layer feed forward Neural Network

Q.17. Explain the Multilayer Feedforward ANN.

Ans. The neural networks that can handle data that is not linearly separable. It is an interconnection of perceptron in which data and calculations flow in a single direction *i.e.*, from the input data to the outputs. Also note that the number of layers in a neural network is equivalent to the number of layers of perceptron.

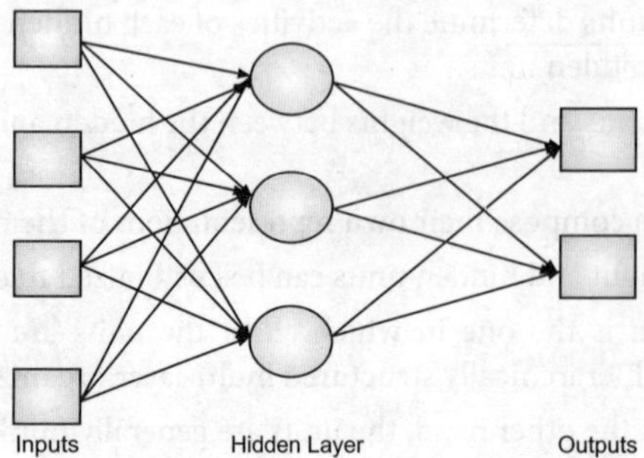

Fig.15.23: Multi-layer Feed-Forward Neural Network

This type of network is used within the area of systems and control. Analogous to the single-layer feed-forward neural networks, there is one input layer and one output layer and no interconnections between the nodes in a particular layer. But these networks have a number of intermediate or hidden layers. Any layer between the input and output layers is called as a hidden layer because it is internal to the network and has no direct contact with the external environment. One, two or more hidden layers are used for most of the applications. **Please note that the smaller number of hidden layers is due to the fact that the training process becomes too long and tedious if the architecture of neural network becomes large.** To get the output from the network, a set of input data is first presented as inputs to the input layer in turn. The outputs from this layer are then fed as inputs to the first hidden layer and subsequently the outputs from the first hidden layer are fed as weighted inputs (int outputs from the first hidden layer are multiplied by the weights, to the second layer. This process carries on until the output layer is reached. For example, multi-layer perceptron (MLP) is a feed-forward neural network, commonly called as the multi-layer feed forward network. The hidden layers do not directly receive inputs or send outputs to the external environment. In fact, it uses the backpropagation learning method. In these networks, the derivative of the error-function with respect to the network weights is found out. Then the weights are changed accordingly, to the decrease the margin of the error. The activation function should be continuous functions of the weights, so that it is differentiable everywhere. Sigmoid function can be used as an activation function that can be considered as a continuous approximation of the step function. The activation function for a node i can be given by the formula: -

$$\Phi\,(Vi) = 1\,/\,(-A * V_i)$$

Where, $A > 0$, $V_i = \Sigma\, W_{ij} * Y_j$ such that W_{ij} is a weight of the link from node I to node j and Y_j is the output of node j.

Q.18. What is Supervised Learning?

Ans. A neural network has to be configured in such a way that the application of a set of inputs produces the desired set of outputs. To set the connections, there are many methods: -

1. One method is to set the weights explicitly, using a priori knowledge.
2. Another method is to train the neural network by feeding it patterns and allowing it to change its weights according to some learning rule.

One method of learning is supervised learning.

It is also called as **associative learning.** In **supervised or associative learning,** we provide an input and its corresponding target output to the network. When inputs are given to the network, the network generates outputs and we compare the network outputs to the target outputs. The learning function is then used to adjust the biases of the network so that network outputs reach closer to the target outputs. Fig. 15.20 shows the training and testing process.

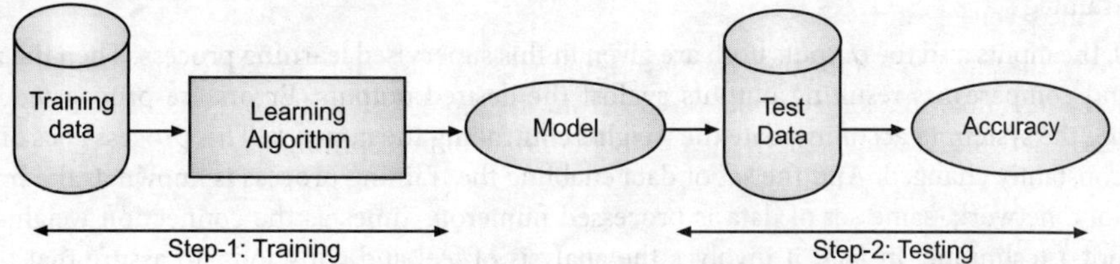

Fig. 15.24: Showing Supervised Learning

Supervised learning is a machine learning technique used to learn a function from the training data set. The training data is the combination of input data and the corresponding desired outputs. the output of the function may be continuous value or a classification of input objects into classes. **Please note that the main task of supervised learning is to find a function value that produces the outputs that match our actual output for given input output data set.** Supervised learning is used for classification problems. There are two steps in supervised learning process: -

Step-1: Learning/ training: Learn the model using the training data.

Step-2: Testing: Test the model using unseen test data to assess the model accuracy.

An important issue concerning to this type of learning is the problem of error convergence i.e., the minimization of error between the desired and computed unit values. The objective is to find out a set of weights which minimizes the error. One well-known method that is common to many learning paradigms is the least mean square (LMS) convergence. Paradigms of supervised learning include error-correction learning, reinforcement learning and stochastic learning.

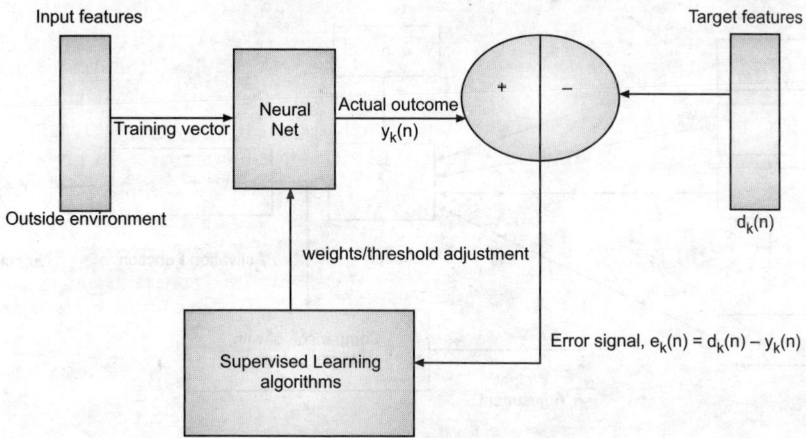

Fig. 15.25: Supervised Learning

Explanation: In supervised learning, both the inputs and outputs can be observed. There is supervision by a supervisor or teacher who provides a set of (x, y) pairs where x denotes the input and y denotes the corresponding output. The learner is given a training set of positive and negative examples of a concept. The learner is to construct a description that will accurately classify whether the future examples are positive or negative through labeling them positive or negative examples. Note that a positive example is an instance of a concept while a negative example is not an instance of the concept. For example, the information from 700 email messages is collected to predict whether the message was a junk email or spam. The learner is to be built to identify and filter out the spams. The true outcome (email/spam) is available for the training data as well as the relative frequencies of 50 common words and characters (you/ your/ free/! / remove etc.). These words are chosen in such a way that the relative frequencies in the two types differs maximally for them. In supervised algorithms, the classes are pre-determined. Practically speaking, a certain segment of data will be labelled with these classifications. The machine learner's task is to search for patterns and construct mathematical models. Then these models are evaluated on the basis of their predictive capacity in relation to measures of variance in the data itself. Many of the methods referenced in the documentation like decision tree, induction, naïve Bayes etc. are the examples of supervised learning techniques.

What is the training set?

As discussed, the inputs and the outputs both are given in this supervised learning process. Then the network processes the inputs and compares its resulting outputs against the desired outputs. Errors are propagated back through the system causing the system to accommodate the weights controlling the network. This process goes on repeatedly as the weights are constantly changed. And the set of data enabling the training process is known as the training set. During the training of a network, same set of data is processed numerous times as the connection weights are ever refined. Training is not a technique. In fact, it involves the analysis of feel and conscious, to assure that the network is not overtrained. Initially, an ANN sets itself up with the basic statistical trends of the data. Then, it advances to learn about the different aspects of the data which might be spurious from a general viewpoint. Finally, when the system has been trained correctly and no further learning is required, the weights can be frozen. In some systems, this finalized network is turned into hardware to make these fast.

Q.19. Give Delta Learning Rule.

Ans. This was introduced by McClelland and Rumelhart in 1986. Some of the main features of this rule are as follows: -

1. It uses output of activation function to generate error signal.
2. It can only be used with continuous and differentiable activation functions.
3. It is a gradient-based method.
4. It can be generalized to multi-layer networks.
5. Continuous output, so can be used for function approximation.

It is shown in the fig. 15.22.

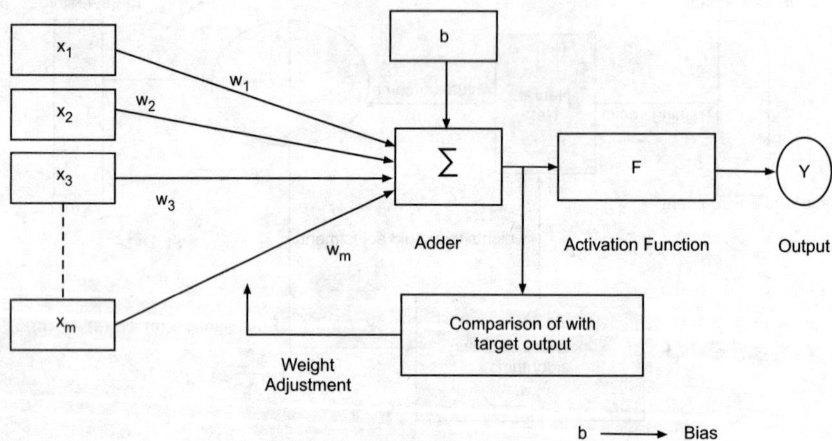

Fig.15.26: Delta Learning Rule

Derivation of Delta Rule : For the continuous perceptron, as shown in fig. 15.22—

$$\text{Net} = W^T X$$

So, output is $O = f(\text{Net})$

And error is $e = d - O$

Where, $f_1(\text{Net}) = 1 / (1 + e^{-\lambda \text{Net}})$

$$f_t(\text{Net}) = \{2 / (1 + e^{-\lambda \text{Net}})\} - 1$$

f_1 (Net) corresponds to a unipolar sigmoid activation function (log-sigmoid) and f_t (Net) corresponds to a bipolar sigmoid function (tan-sigmoid). The gradient (*i.e.*, derivative w. r. t the weights) of the square error, $(d - W^T X)^2$ is computed as follows:

$$\nabla = \partial e^2 / \partial w = -2(d - f(W^T X))\, f'(W^T X)\, X$$

The weight update is aa follows- $\Delta W = -\nabla$

The complete delta rule is given by-

$$W_i + 1 = W_i + 2\, n\, e\, f\ (\text{Net})\ X$$

Where, f(Net) is the derivative of f(Net).

We are in a position to solve some examples on the delta learning rule now.

Q.20. Apply the delta learning rule for the given network-

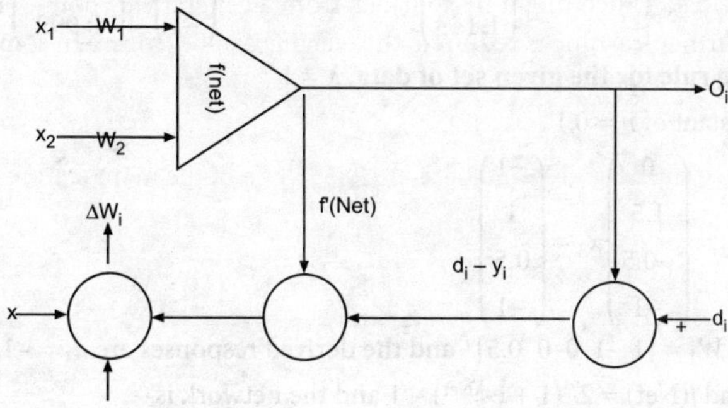

Given: $\lambda = 1$, learning constant of $n = 0.25$

Input vectors, $X_1 = \begin{pmatrix} 2 \\ 0 \\ 1 \end{pmatrix}, d_1 = -1, x_2 = \begin{pmatrix} 1 \\ -2 \\ -1 \end{pmatrix}, d_2 = 1$

And the initial weights are $W^1 = [1\ \ 0\ \ 1]^T$

Use $f'(\text{Net}) = ½\ (1 - O_i^2)$ and $f(\text{Net}) = 2/\ (1 + e^{-\lambda\text{Net}}) - 1$

Ans. Let us solve this problem step by step.

Step-1: Input vector is X_1 and the initial weight vector is W_1

$$\text{Net}_1 = W_1^T X_1 = [1\,0\,1]\begin{pmatrix} 2 \\ 0 \\ -1 \end{pmatrix} = 1$$

$$O_1 = f(\text{Net}_1) = 2\ /\ (1 + e^{-\lambda\text{Net}}1) - 1$$

$$= 2/\ (1 + e^{-1}) - 1 = 0.462$$

$$f'\ (\text{Net1}) = ½\ (1 - (O_1)^2) = ½\ (1 - 0.462^2) = 0.393$$

For delta learning rule,

$$W^{i+1} = W_i + n\ (d_i - O_i)\ f(\text{Net})\ X_i$$

$$W_2 = W_1 + n\ (d_1 - O_1)\ f(\text{Net}_1)\ X_1$$

$$W_2 = \begin{pmatrix} 1 \\ 0 \\ 1 \end{pmatrix} + 0.25(-1-0.462)(0.393)\begin{pmatrix} 2 \\ 0 \\ -1 \end{pmatrix} = \begin{pmatrix} 0.712 \\ 0 \\ 1.143 \end{pmatrix}$$

Step-2: For input X_2

$$\text{Net}_2 = W_2^T X_2 = [0.712\ 0\ 1.143]\begin{pmatrix} 1 \\ -2 \\ -1 \end{pmatrix} = -0.431$$

$$O_2 = (Net_2) = 2 / (1 + e^{-\lambda Net2}) - 1$$
$$= 2/ (1 + e^{0.431}) - 1 = -0.212$$
$$f'(Net_2) = ½ (1 - (O_2)^2) = ½ (1 - 0.212^2) = 0.477$$
$$W^{i+1} = W_i + n (d_i - O_i) f'(Net) X_i$$
$$W^3 = W_2 + n (d_2 - O_2) f'(Net_2) X_2$$
$$W^3 = \begin{pmatrix} 0.712 \\ 0 \\ 1.143 \end{pmatrix} + 0.25(1+0.212)\begin{pmatrix} 1 \\ -2 \\ -1 \end{pmatrix} = \begin{pmatrix} 0.856 \\ -0.288 \\ 0.999 \end{pmatrix}$$

Q.21. Perform the delta learning rule for the given set of data, λ = 1

Given: λ = 1, learning constant of $n = 0.1$

Input vectors, $X_1 = \begin{pmatrix} 1 \\ -2 \\ 0 \\ -1 \end{pmatrix} x_2 = \begin{pmatrix} 0 \\ 1.5 \\ -0.5 \\ -1 \end{pmatrix} x_3 = \begin{pmatrix} -1 \\ 1 \\ 0.5 \\ -1 \end{pmatrix}$

And the initial weights are $W_1 = [1\ -1\ 0\ 0\ 0.5]^T$ and the derived responses are $d_1 = -1$, $d_2 = -1$, $d_3 = 1$.

Use $f'(Net) = ½ (1 - O_i^2)$ and $f(Net) = 2/ (1 + e^{-\lambda Net}) - 1$ and the network is-

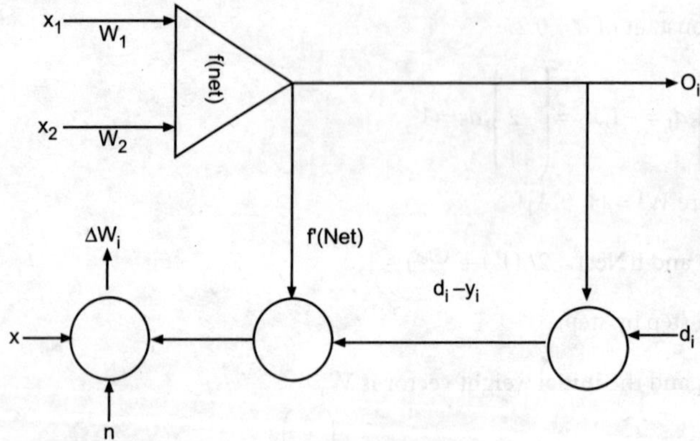

Ans. The following steps may be followed: -

Step-1: Input vector is X_1 and initial weight vector is W_1.

$$Net_1 = W_1^T X_1 [1 -100.5] \begin{pmatrix} 1 \\ -2 \\ 0 \\ -1 \end{pmatrix} = 2.5$$
$$O1 = f(Net_1) = 2 / (1 + e^{-\lambda Net1}) - 1$$
$$= 2/ (1 + e^{-2.5}) - 1 = 0.848$$
$$f' (Net1) = ½ (1 - (O_1)^2) = ½ (1 - 0.848^2) = 0.140$$

For delta learning rule,

$$W^{i+1} = W_i + n (d_i - O_i) f'(Net) X_i$$
$$W^2 = W_1 + n (d_1 - O_1) f'(Net_1) X_1$$
$$W^2 = \begin{pmatrix} 1 \\ -1 \\ 0 \\ 0.5 \end{pmatrix} + 0.1(1-0.848)(0.140)\begin{pmatrix} 1 \\ -2 \\ 0 \\ -1 \end{pmatrix} = \begin{pmatrix} 0.974 \\ -0.948 \\ 0 \\ 0.536 \end{pmatrix}$$

Step-2: Input vector is X_2 and weight vector is W_2

$$\text{Net}_2 = W_2^T X_2 = [0.974 - 0.94800.5361.143]\begin{pmatrix}0\\1.5\\-0.5\\-1\end{pmatrix} = -0.948$$

$$O_2 = f(\text{Net}_2) = 2 / (1 + e^{-\lambda \text{Net}2}) - 1$$
$$= 2/ (1 + e^{-1.948}) - 1 = -0.75$$
$$f'(\text{Net}_2) = ½ (1 - (O_2)^2) = ½ (1 - 0.752) = 0.218$$
$$W^{i+1} = W_i + n (d_i - O_i) f(\text{Net}) X_i$$

or $$W^3 = W^2 + n (d_2 - O_2) f(\text{Net}_2) X_2$$

$$W^3 = \begin{pmatrix}0.974\\-0.948\\0\\0.526\end{pmatrix} + 0.1(-1+0.75)(0.218)\begin{pmatrix}0\\1.5\\-0.5\\-1\end{pmatrix} = \begin{pmatrix}0.974\\-0.956\\0.002\\0.531\end{pmatrix}$$

Step-3: Input vector is X_3 and weight vector is W_3

$$\text{Net}_3 = W_3^T X_3 = [0.974 - 0.956\ 0.002\ 0.531]\begin{pmatrix}-1\\1\\0.5\\-1\end{pmatrix} = -2.46$$

$$O_3 = f(\text{Net}_3) = 2 / (1 + e^{-\lambda \text{Net}3}) - 1$$
$$= 2/ (1 + e^{2.46}) - 1 = -0.842$$
$$f(\text{Net}_3) = ½ (1 - (O_3)^2) = ½ (1 - (-0.842^2)) = 0.145$$
$$W^{i+1} = W_i + n (d_i - O_i) f(\text{Net}) X_i$$

or $$W^4 = W_3 + n (d_3 - O_3) f(\text{Net}_3) X_3$$

$$W^4 = \begin{pmatrix}0.974\\-0.956\\0.002\\0.531\end{pmatrix} + 0.1(1+0.842)(0.145)\begin{pmatrix}-1\\1\\0.5\\-1\end{pmatrix} = \begin{pmatrix}0.974\\-0.929\\0.016\\0.505\end{pmatrix}$$

Q.22. What are the differences between perceptron training rule and Delta rule?

Ans. The following table tabulates the differences between the two-

Perceptron training rule	Delta rule
1. It uses threshold unit.	1. It uses un-threshold linear unit.
2. It converges after a finite number of iterations.	2. It converges asymptotically toward a minimum error hypothesis.
3. The output thesis classifies training data perfectly.	3. Termination is not guaranteed.
4. Linearly separability necessary.	4. Linearly separability not necessary.

Q.23. What is the Backpropagation algorithm? Write the algorithm. Discuss its properties. Give its advantages and disadvantages. Also give its applications. Explain feed-forward network and multi-layer network.

Ans. It is a system method for training multi-layer ANNs. It is a multi-layer forward network using extended gradient-descent based delta learning rule that is commonly known as back propagation of errors rule. Back propagation of BP is an efficient method for changing the weights in a feed forward network with differentiable activation function units, to learn a training set of input-output examples. Hinton, Rumelhart et al. first introduced it in 1986. We do not know what the hidden layers may be doing but we can compute how fast the error changes as we change a hidden activity. So, we can find out how fast the error changes when we change the weight of an individual connection. Being a gradient descent method, it minimizes the total square error of the output computed by the net. The network is trained by the supervised learning method. The aim of this network is to train the network to achieve a balance between the ability to respond correctly to the input parameters that are used for training and the ability to provide good responses to the input that are similar. Each hidden unit can affect many output units.

The training algorithm for back propagation involves four steps: -

a. Initialization of weights.

b. Feed forward.

c. Back propagation of errors.

d. Updation of weights and biases.

Explanation: During the first step/stage, weights are initialized with some random values are assigned. During feed-forward stage, each input unit (x_i) receives an input signal and transmits this signal to each of the hidden units, z_i .... z_p. Then each hidden unit calculates the activation function and sends its signal z_j to each output unit. The output unit calculates the activation function from the response of the net for the given input pattern. During back propagation of errors, each output compares its computed activation, y_k with its target value, t_k to determine the associated error for that pattern with that unit. Based on the error, the factor, δ_k $(k = 1,...,m)$ is computed and is used to distribute the error at the output unit, y_k back to all the units in the previous layer. Similarly, the factor δ_j $(j = 1,...,p)$ is computed for each hidden unit, z_j.

During the final step, the weight and biases are updated using the δ factor and activation.

Various parameters used in the training algorithm are:-

x: input training vector

x: $(x_1, ...x_i,.....,x_n)$

t: $(t_1.....t_k.....t_m)$

δ_k : error at output unit, y_k

δ_j : error at hidden unit, z_j

α: learning rate

v_{oj} : bias on hidden unit j

z_j: hidden unit j

w_{ok} : bias on output unit k

y_k : output unit, k.

ALGORITHM: BACK PROPAGATION

S1: Initialize weights.

S2: If stopping conditions are false, do steps 3 to 10.

S3: For each training pair, do steps 4 to 9.

S4: Apply input, xi, and transmit these signals to the hidden units.

S5: Each hidden unit sums its weighted input signals and sends the signals to the output units.

S6: Each output unit sums its weighted input signals and applies its activation function to calculate the output signals.

S7: Each output unit receives a target pattern corresponding to an input pattern and error information is calculated.

S8: Each hidden unit sums its delta inputs. The error information is calculated.

S9: Each output unit updates its bias and weights.

S10: Test the stopping condition based on minimum error.

Properties of back-propagation (BP)

Some of the main properties of BP are as follows: -

1. **Learning and NOT programming :** Any neural net can be converted into software like JAVA2 but at the level of neural network, the concepts are very different from conventional software.
2. **Generalization :** BP networks can generalize too. For example, the NETTalk network can pronounce words that it has not yet encountered. This is an essential property of intelligent systems that have to function in the real world.

Please note that it implies that not every potential situation has to be predefined in the system. Generalization here means that, similar inputs leads to similar outputs. **Also note that this is the reason as to why parity is not a good candidate problem for generalization.** Like in XOR problem, change one bit in the input and the output has to change maximally say from 0 to 1.

3. **Noise and fault tolerance :** As we know that a network is noise and fault tolerant. The weights of NETTalk have been disturbed by adding random noise but the performance degradation was only gradual. Note that this property is not explicitly programmed into the model. It is the result of massive parallelism, in a sense, it comes for free.
4. **Re-learning :** The network shows fast re-learning. If the network is distorted to a particular performance level, it re-learns faster than a new network starting at the same performance level. So, despite of low performance, the network has retained something about its past.
5. **Emergent properties :** The consonant-vowel distinction that the nodes at the hidden layer pick-up has not been programmed into the system. Certain nodes can pick up these distinctions, which depends on how the examples are encoded. Secondly, since the net can pronounce words that it has not encountered, it has somehow learned the rules of English pronunciation. There are no rules in the network, only weights and activation levels. Note that it is these emergent properties that make the neural network not only attractive for applications but also to the researchers working in the field of deep learning.
6. **Universality :** According to Hornik et al. Machine language Programs are universal approximators. So we can say that with a 2-layer feed-forward network, every set of discrete function values can be represented or in a particular interval a continuous function can be approximated to any degree of accuracy. This is still a simplification but it is sufficient for our purposes. Please note that again there is a difference between what can be represented and what can be learned. Something that can be represented cannot be learned by BP algorithm. For example, BP might get stuck in local minima and we do not know whether the global minima will ever be reached. On one side, there are performance problems and on the other side, there are doubts whether supervised learning schemes like BP have a biological or psychological reality. Machine language Programs with BP have been tried on many different types of classification problems because: -

   a. They are universal function approximators,

   b. They are easy to use.

   Most of these experiments remained in the prototype stage only. The entire knowledge in a NN is in the connection matrix. There are no explicit rules. But there are a number of steps to extract rules from NN especially for Self Organizing Maps (SOMs).

Advantages of BP :

1. The mathematical formula can be applied to any network.
2. The computing time is less if the initial weights chosen are small.
3. The batch update of weights is possible as it provides a smoothing effect on the weight correction terms.

Disadvantages of BP :

1. More number of learning steps.
2. Many calculations are involved at learning phase.
3. For complex problems, more time is required to train the network or it may not learn at all. Note that long training times may result in non-optimum step size.
4. The network may get stuck in local minima.
5. Quite unstable too.
6. The selection of the number of hidden nodes in the network is a challenge. **Please note that if the number of hidden neurons are small, then the function to be learnt may not be possibly represented as the capacity of the network is small. Also note that if the number of hidden neurons increases then the number or independent variable of the error function also increases and the computing time also increases.**

Applications of BP :

1. Optical Character Recognition (OCR).
2. Image and Data Compression.
3. Control systems.
4. Power systems.

5. Fault detection.
6. Non-linear simulation.
7. To train the multi-layer neural networks.
8. Load forecasting problems in power systems field.
9. Speech synthesis.
10. Content problem.
11. Pattern recognition.
12. Aircraft navigation.
13. Non-linear simulation etc.

In feed-forward networks, information is passed in one direction that is from the input layer towards the output layer through the hidden layers. So, it does not form any cycle or loop. On the other hand, in recurrent networks information is passed in both the directions namely, feed-forward and feedback. So, it forms a loop.

We have already seen that a single layer perceptron is not capable of representing all problems that are not linearly separable. Multi-layer networks can be trained to solve difficult and diverse problems by the back-propagation algorithm, also called generalized gradient descent and generalized delta rule. Multi-layer networks trained with back-propagation are currently the most widely used neural networks. The algorithm is based on the error correction learning rule which states that –"The error signal, $e_i(n)$ is the difference between desired response, $d_i(n)$ and the output signal, $y_i(n)$", where i is the neuron whose synaptic weights are adjusted at discrete time, n. So, the error is calculated using the formula: -

$$e_i(n) = d_i(n) - y_i(n)$$

Also note that the corrective adjustments are made to make the output signal, $y_i(n)$, closer to the desired response, $d_i(n)$. a simple back-propagation neural network is shown in fig. 15.23.

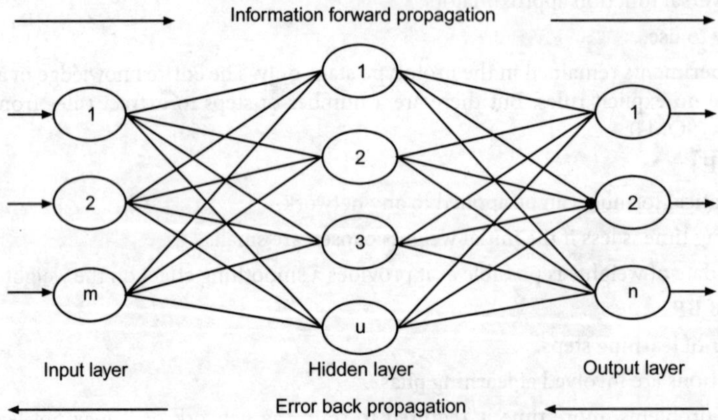

Fig. 15.27: *Back-propagation Neural Network*

From fig. it is clear that the back-propagation learning consists up of two passes—forward pass and backward pass.

The Training process: The network is initialized by setting up all its weights to the small random numbers in between –1 and +1. Then, the input pattern is applied and the output is computed. This is called as a forward pass. The calculation gives an output which may or may not match the desired (target) output, since all of the weights are random. Then it calculates the error of each neuron as (Target – Actual Output) i.e., what you want – what you actually get.

Then this error is used mathematically to change weights in such a way that the error will get smaller. In other words, the output of each neuron will get closer to its target. This pass is called as the reverse pass. **Also note that this process is repeated again and again until the error is minimal.** Once the network is trained, it will provide the desired output for any of the input patterns.

Principles of Training Multi-layer Neural Network using Back-Propagation

Fig.- shows the teaching process of multi-layer neural network using back-propagation algorithm.

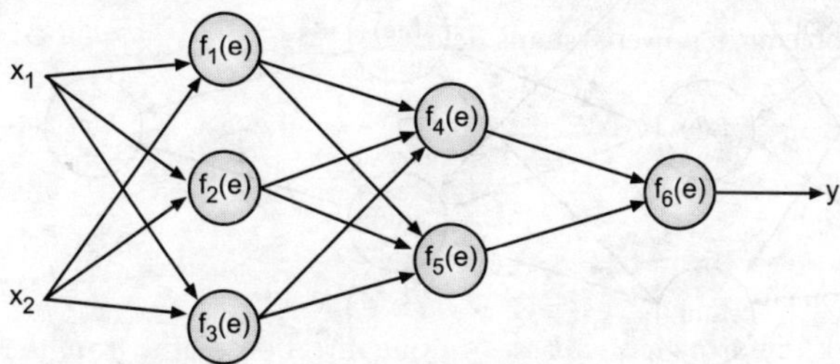

Fig. 15.28: *Multi-layer Neural Network*

To illustrate this process, a three-layer neural network with two inputs and one output is used as follows.

Each neuron is composed of two units: -

a. First unit adds products of weights coefficients and input signals.

b. The second unit realizes non-linear function, called as **neuron activation function.**

Signal, *e*, is adder output signal and $y = f(e)$ is the output of non-linear element. Signal, *y*, is also the output signal of neuron.

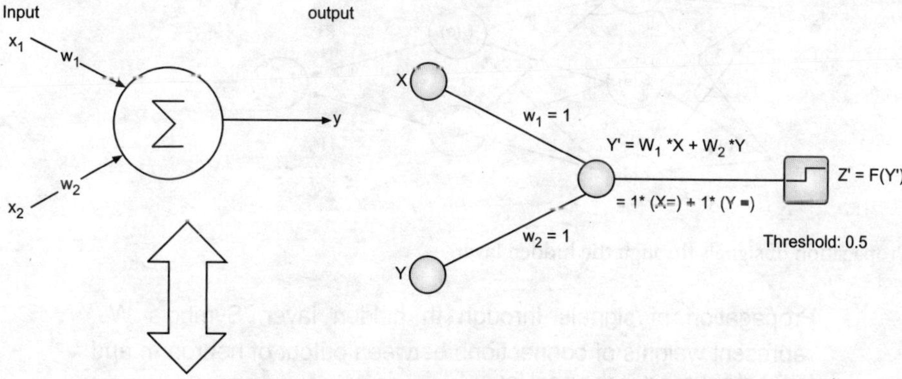

Fig. 15.25: *Single Layer Output*

To teach the neural network, we need a training dataset. The training dataset consists of input signals (x_1 and x_2) assigned with corresponding target, *z* (desired output). The network training is an iterative process. In each iteration, weight's coefficients of nodes are modified using the new data from the training dataset. The set of figures below explain in detail how a signal is propagated through the network.

Sign conventions: Symbols $w(x_m)n$ represent weights of connections between network input x_m and neuron, *n*, in the input layer. Symbol, y_n represents output signal of neuron, *n*.

Let us see now layer-wise the working of these neurons.

I. Propagation of signals through the input layer.

II. Propagation of signals through the hidden layer.

III. Propagation of signals through the output layer.

Case-1: Propagation of signals through the input layer.

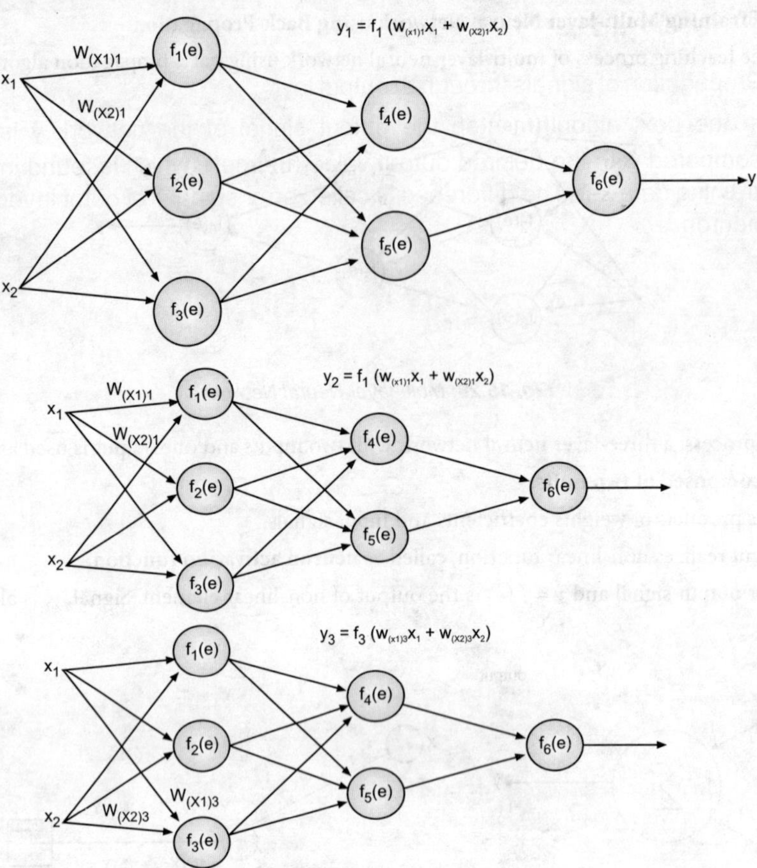

Case-2: Propagation of signals through the hidden layer.

- Propagation of signals through th hidden layer. Symbols W_{mn} represent weights of connections between output of neuron m and input of neuron n in the next layer.

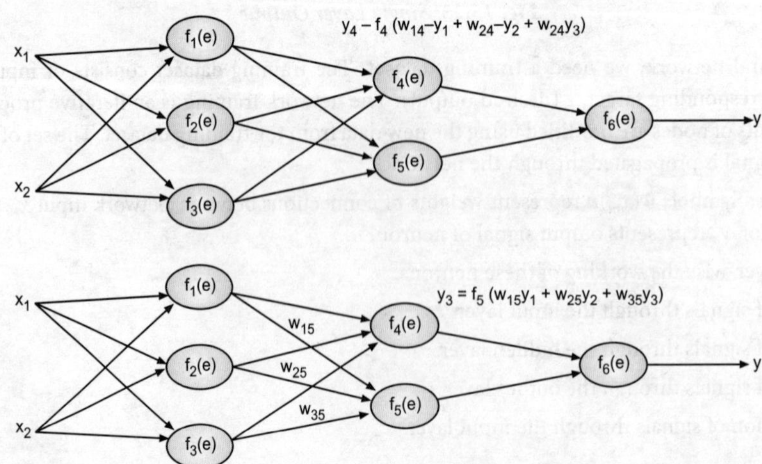

Case-3: Propagation of signals through the output layer.

- Propagation of signals through th output layr.
- In the next algorithm step the output signal of the network y is compared with the desired output value (th trget), which is found in training data set. The difference is called error signal δ of outpt layer neuron.

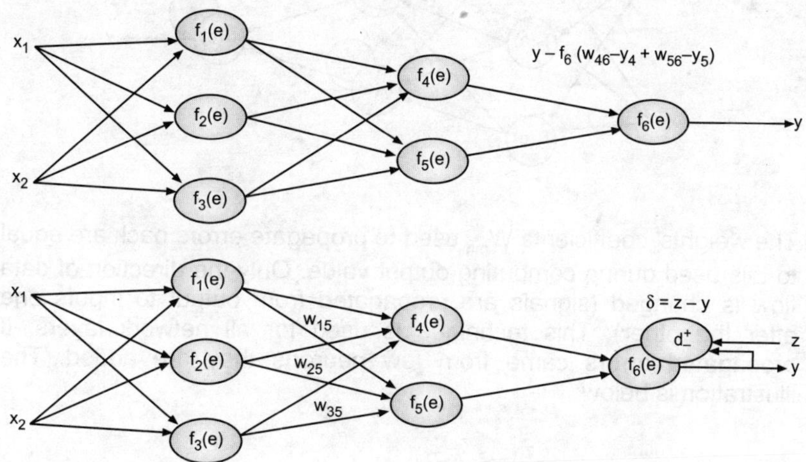

It is impossible to compute the error signal for internal neurons directly because output values of these neurons are unknown. Hence, the back-propagation algorithm is applied to propagate error signal, δ, back to all neurons. Let us show this for δ4, for instance.

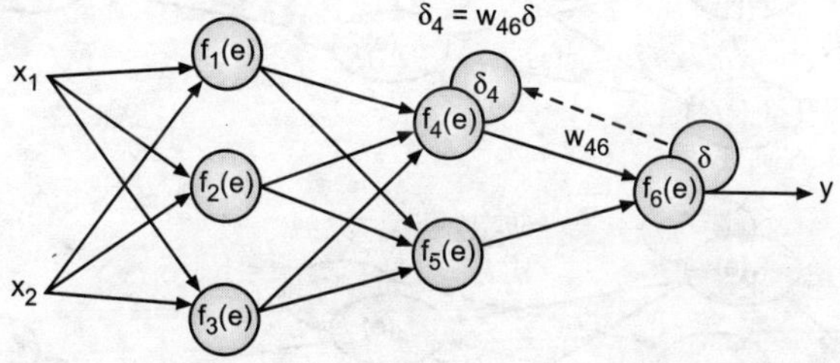

Learning Algorithm : Backpropagation

The ida is to propagate error signal d (computed in single teaching step) back to all nurons, which output signals were input for discussed neuron.

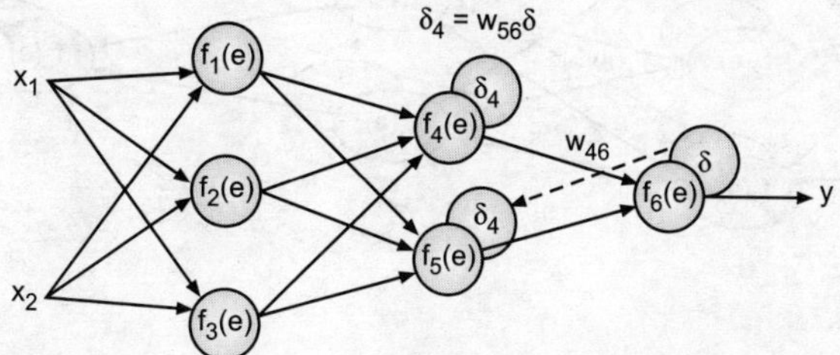

The weight coefficients, w_{mn}, used to propagate errors back are equal to the weights used during computing output value. **Please note that only the direction of data flow is changed, signals are propagated from output to inputs one after another.** This technique is used for all network layers. **Also note that if the propagated errors came from few neurons, then they are added.** This is shown in diagrams below.

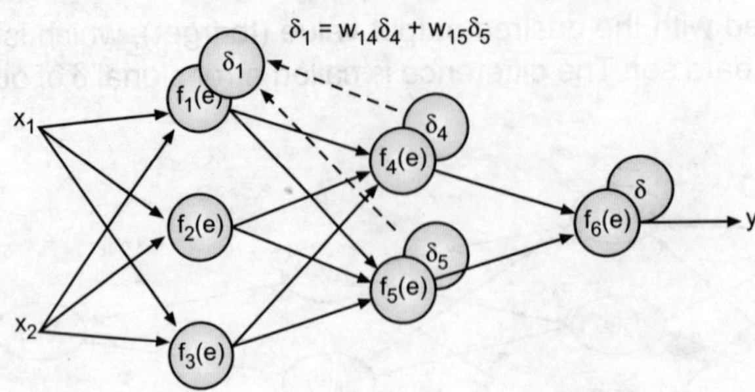

- The weights' coefficients W_{mn} used to propagate errors back are equal to this used during computing output value. Only the direction of data flow is changed (signals are propagated from output to inputs one after the other). This technique is used for all network layers. If propagated errors came from few neurons they are added. The illustration is below:

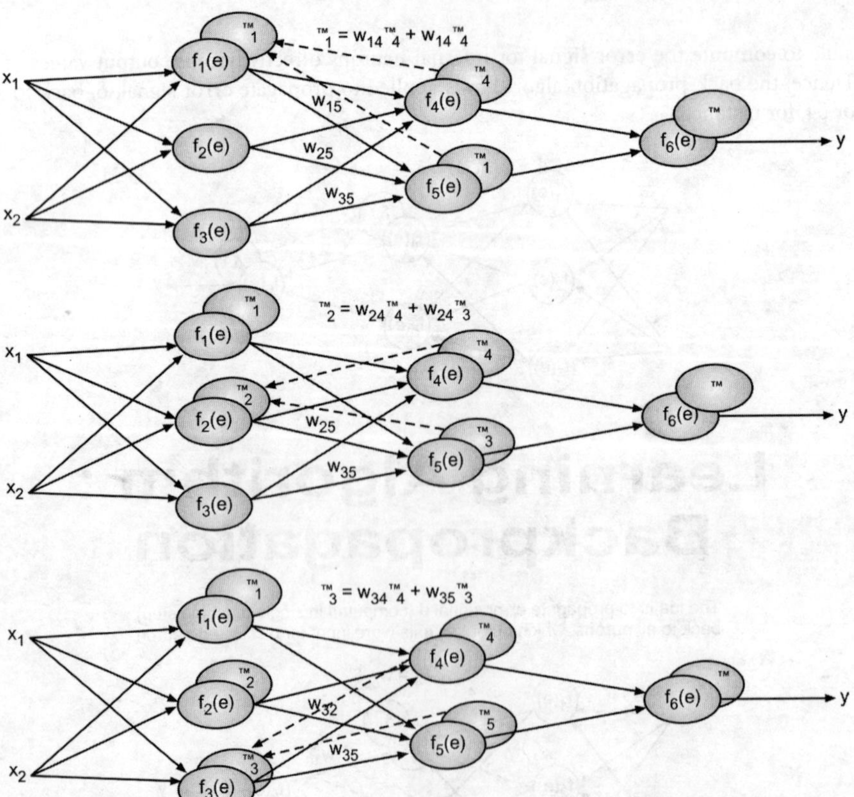

When the error signal for each neuron is computed, the weight coefficients of each neuron input node may be modified. In the formulas given below,

df(e) / de represents the derivative of neuron activation function (weights are modified).

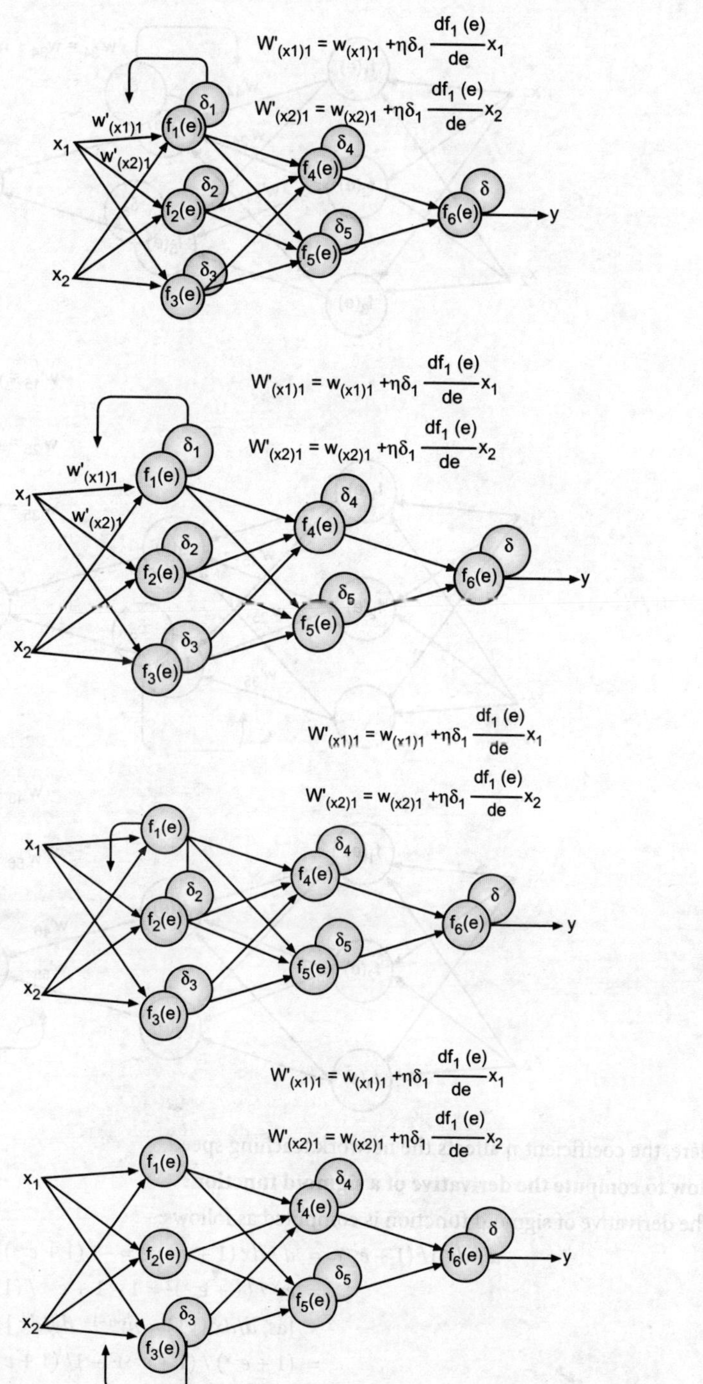

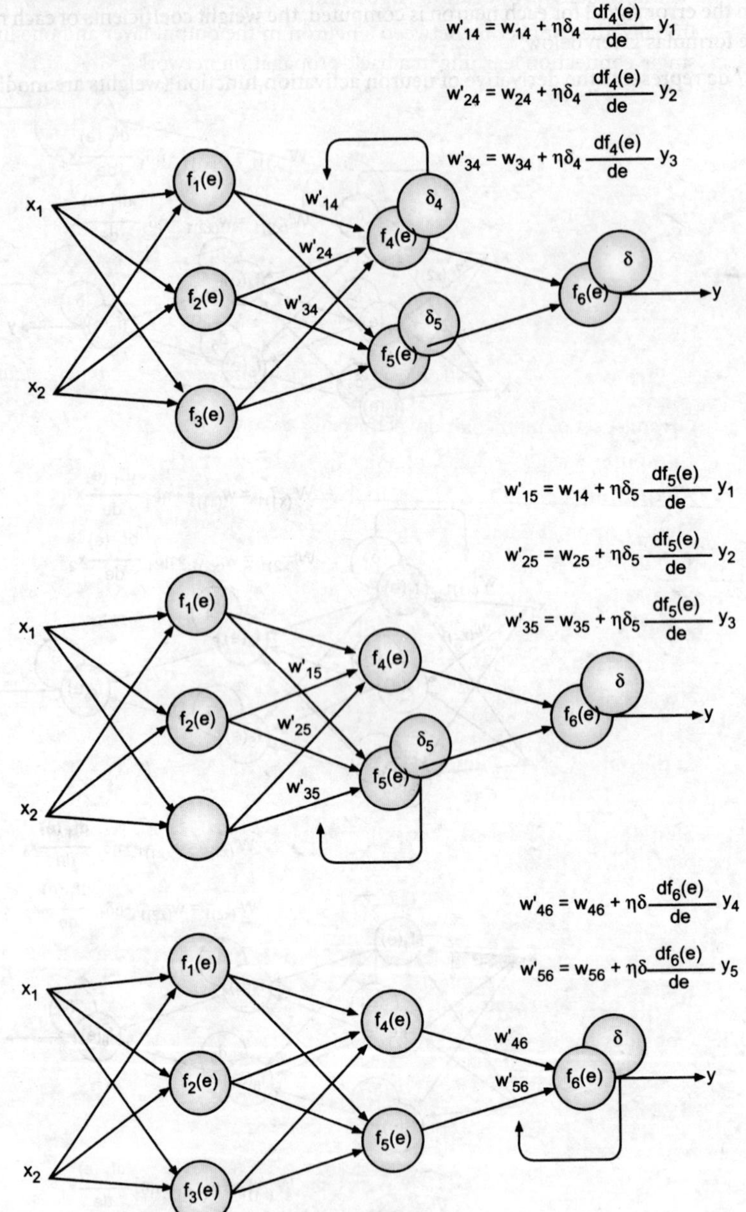

Here, the coefficient η affects the network teaching speed.

How to compute the derivative of a sigmoid function?

The derivative of sigmoid function is computed as follows: -

$$d / dx\, 1/ (1 + e^{-x}) = d / dx\, (1 + e^{-x})^{-1} = -1\, (1 + e^{-x})\text{-}2 \,.\, (0 - e^{-x})$$

$$= e^{-x} / (1 + e^{-x})^2 = 1 - 1 + e^{-x} / (1 + e^{-x})^2$$

$$[\text{as, } d/dx\, (y^n) = ny^{n-1} \,.\, dy/dx\,]$$

$$= (1 + e^{-x}) / (1 + e^{-x})^2 - 1/ (1 + e^{-x})^2$$

$$= 1/ (1 + e^{-x}) - 1/ (1 + e^{-x})^2$$

$$= 1/ (1 + e^{-x})\quad 1 - 1/ (1 + e^{-x})$$

$$= O_i\, (1 - O_i)$$

A simple Back-propagation Algorithm

Initially, the connection between a neuron in the output layer and one in the hidden layer is shown. Fig. 15.26 shows a single connection learning in a back-propagation network.

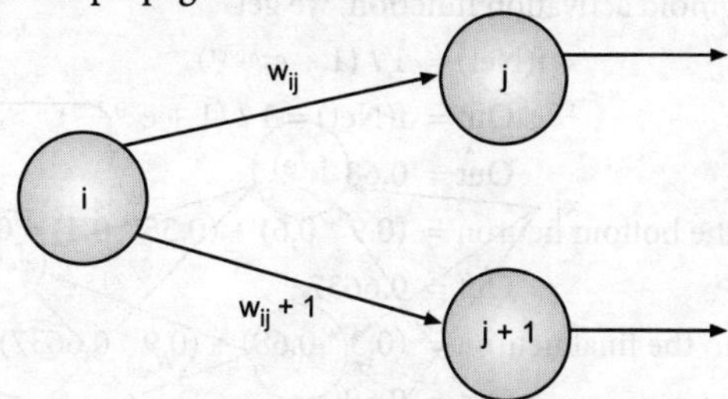

Fig. 15.29: Connections between a neuron in output and hidden layer

Given: A set of input-output vector pairs.

Compute: A set of weights for a network that maps inputs to corresponding outputs.

Algorithm:

Step-1: Apply the inputs to the network and work out the output. This initial output could be anything as the initial weights were random numbers.

Step-2: Next find out the error for the output neuron, j, i.e.,

$$\text{Errorj} = \text{Output}_j\,(1 - \text{Output}_j)\,(\text{Target}_j - \text{Output}_j)$$

Note that the term Outputj (1 – Output_j) is essential if it is a sigmoid function,

else it would just be (Target_j – Output_j), if only threshold neuron is used.

Step-3: Change the weight. Let W_{ij}+ be the new (trained) weight and W_{ij} be the initial weight. Update all of the weights in the output layer as follows: -

$$W_{ij} + = W_{ij} + (\text{Error}_j * \text{Output}_i)$$

Step-4: Calculate the errors for the hidden layer neurons. Back propagate it. This is done by taking the errors from the output neurons and running them back through the weights to get the hidden layer errors.

$$\text{Error}_i = \text{Outputi}\,(1 - \text{Output}_i)\,(\text{Error}_j\, W_{ij} + \text{Error}_{j+1}\, W_{ij+1})$$

Again, the factor "Output (1- Output)" is present because of the sigmoid squashing function.

Step-5: go to step-3.

We are in a position to solve some problems on back-propagation now.

Q.25. Consider the network as shown below-

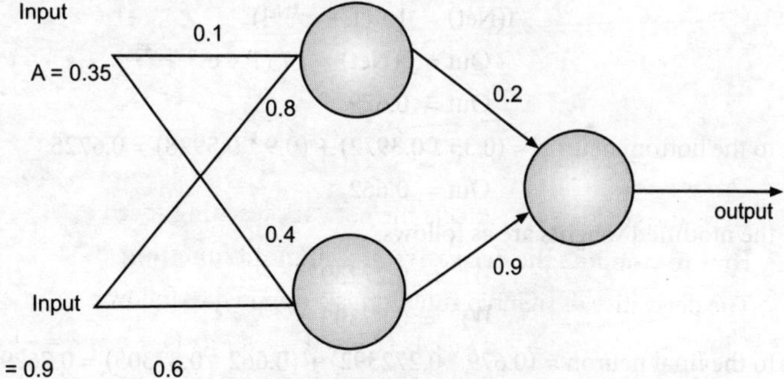

Assume that the neurons have a sigmoid activation function, do the following-

a. **Perform a forward pass on the network.**

b. **Perform a reverse pass (training) once (target = 0.5).**

c. **Perform a further forward pass and comment on the result.**

Ans. *a.* Forward Pass :

Input to top neuron = (0.35 * 0.1) + (0.9 * 0.8) = 0.755

After applying sigmoid activation function, we get-

$$f(Net) = 1 / (1 + e^{-\lambda Net})$$

$$Out = f(Net) = 1 / (1 + e^{-0.755})$$

$$Out = 0.68$$

Input to the bottom neuron = (0.9 * 0.6) + (0.35 * 0.4) = 0.68

$$Out = 0.6637$$

Input to the final neuron = (0.3 * 0.68) + (0.9 * 0.6637) = 0.80133

$$Out = 0.69$$

$$Error = (0.5 - 0.69) = -0.19$$

***b.* Reverse Pass**

$$\text{Output error, } \delta = (t - Out)(1 - Out)\,Out$$

$$= (0.5 - 0.69)(1 - 0.69)\,0.69 = -0.0406$$

New weights for output layer are-

$$w_1^+ = w_1 + (\delta * input) = 0.3 + (-0.0406 * 0.68) = 0.272392$$

$$w_2^+ = w_2 + (\delta * input) = 0.9 + (-0.0406 * 0.6637) = 0.87305$$

Errors for hidden layers are-

$$\delta 1 = \delta * w_1 = -0.0406 * 0.272392 * (1 - Out)\,Out$$

$$= -2.406 * 10^{-3}$$

$$\delta_2 = \delta * w_2 = -0.0406 * 0.87305 * (1 - Out)\,Out$$

$$= -7.916 * 10^{-3}$$

New hidden weights are as follows: -

$$W_2^+ = 0.1 + (-2.406 * 10^{-3} * 0.35) = 0.09916$$

$$W_4^+ = 0.8 + (-2.406 * 10^{-3} * 0.9) = 0.7978$$

$$W_5^+ = 0.4 + (-7.916 * 10^{-3} * 0.35) = 0.3972$$

$$W_6^+ = 0.6 + (-7.916 * 10^{-3} * 0.9) = 0.5928$$

***c.* Further Forward Pass**

Input to the top neuron = (0.35 * 0.09916) + (0.9 * 0.7978) = 0.752726

After applying sigmoid function, we get-

$$f(Net) = 1 / (1 + e^{-\lambda Net})$$

$$Out = f(Net) = 1 / (1 + e^{-0.752726})$$

$$Out = 0.679$$

Input to the bottom neuron = (0.35 * 0.3972) + (0.9 * 0.5928) = 0.6725

$$Out = 0.662$$

Here, the modified weights are as follows: -

$$W_1^+ = 0.272392$$

$$W_2^+ = 0.87305$$

Input to the final neuron = (0.679 * 0.272392) + (0.662 * 0.87305) = 0.7629

$$Out = 0.6819$$

$$Error = (0.5 - 0.6819) = -0.182$$

Please note that the old error was –0.19 **and the new error is** –0.182. Thus, **we conclude that the error has reduced.**

Q.26. Consider the network as shown below-

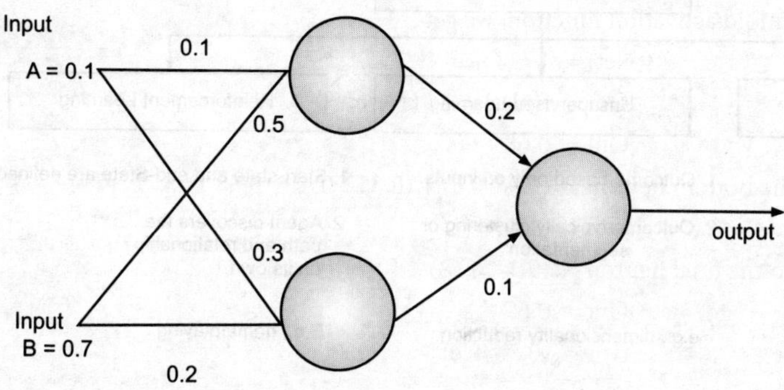

Assume that the neurons have a sigmoid activation function, do the following-

a. **Perform a forward pass on the network.**

b. **Perform a reverse pass (training) once (target = 0.5).**

Ans. ***a.*** **Forward Pass**

Input to top neuron = (0.1 * 0.1) + (0.7 * 0.5) = 0.36

After applying sigmoid activation function, we get-

$$f(Net) = 1 / (1 + e^{-\lambda Net})$$

$$Out = f(Net) - 1 / (1 + e^{0.36})$$

$$Out = 0.589$$

Input to the bottom neuron = (0.1 * 0.3) + (0.7 * 0.2) = 0.17

$$Out = 0.5424$$

Input to the final neuron = (0.589 * 0.2) + (0.5424 * 0.1) = 0.17204

$$Out = 0.5429$$

b. **Reverse Pass** Output error, $\delta = (t - Out)\ (1 - Out)\ Out$

$$= (1 - 0.5429)\ (1 - 0.5429)\ 0.5429 = 0.11343$$

New weights for output layer are- $W_1^+ = w_1 + (\delta * \text{input}) = 0.2 + (0.11343 * 0.589) = 0.2668$

$$W_2^+ = w_2 + (\delta * \text{input}) = 0.1 + (0.11343 * 0.5424) = 0.16152$$

Errors for hidden layers are- $\delta_1 = \delta * w_1 = 0.11343 * 0.2668 * (1 - Out)\ Out$

$$= 0.007326$$

$$\delta_2 = \delta * w_2 = 0.11343 * 0.16152 * (1 - Out)\ Out$$

$$= 0.004547$$

New hidden weights are as follows: - $W_3^+ = 0.1 + (0.007326 * 0.1) = 0.1007326$

$$W_4^+ = 0.5 + (0.007326 * 0.7) = 0.505128$$

$$W_5^+ = 0.3 + (0.004547 * 0.1) = 0.3004547$$

$$W_6^+ = 0.2 + (0.004547 * 0.7) = 0.20318$$

Q.27. Compare different ML Algorithms.

Ans. Actually, machine learning is put under three categories. This is shown in fig.15.27

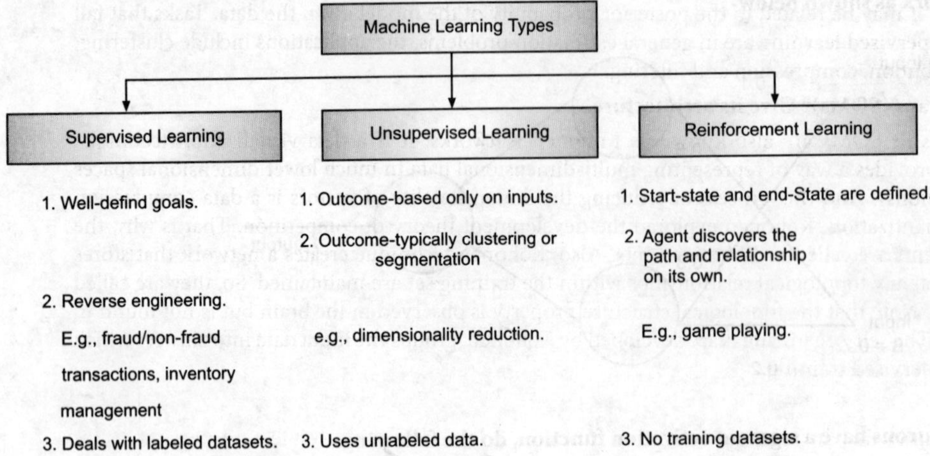

Fig. 15.30: Types of machine learning with unsupervised learning.

Unsupervised machine learning uses clustering which includes-

1. K-means, fuzzy means.
2. Gaussian mixture.
3. Hidden Markov Model
4. Spectral clustering.
5. Neural network.

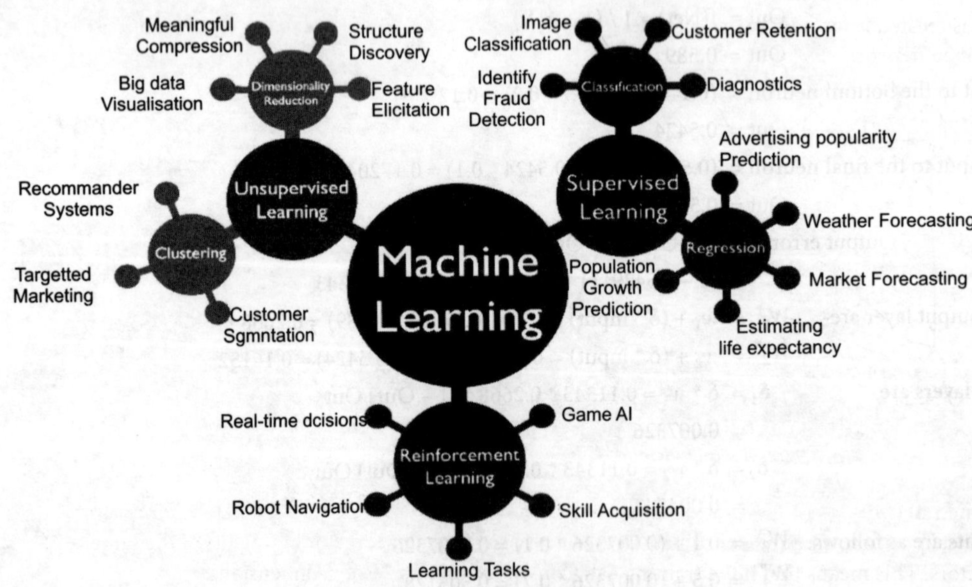

Fig. 15.31: Types of Machine Learning

These three categories of machine learning are shown in fig.15.28

In unsupervised learning, the weights and biases are modified with respect to the network inputs only. In this type of learning, no target outputs are available. Hence, most of these algorithms perform clustering operations only. They categorized the input objects into different classes. This technique is used in applications like vector quantization. In this learning paradigm, say we are given data samples without being told which classes they belong to. These are the schemes that are aimed to discover significant patterns in the input data without a teacher. In unsupervised learning, some data 'x' is given and the cost function is given. Our **objective** is to minimize the cost in that function. The cost function is related to a problem for which we want the solution and may be related to a-priori assumptions.

For instance, in data compression problem, it may be related to the mutual information between x and y, while in statistical modeling problem, it may be related to the posterior probability of the model given the data. Tasks that fall within this paradigm of unsupervised learning are in general estimation problems, the applications include clustering, estimation of statistical distribution, compression and filtering.

28. What are Self-Organizing Maps (SOMs)? Give its architecture.

s. Self-organizing Feature Maps or SOMs are also known as Kohonen Networks. It is a data visualization technique developed by Kohonen that provides a way of representing multi-dimensional data in much lower dimensional spaces (usually one or more dimensions). And this process of reducing the dimensionality of vectors is a data compression technique called as vector quantization. Kohonen explored the development theory of competition. That is why, the competitive processing elements are called as Kohonen units. Also, Kohonen technique creates a network that stores information in such a way that any topological relationships within the training set are maintained. So, they are called as topology-preserving maps. Note that the topological structure property is observed in the brain but is not found in any other ANN except SOM. The self-organizing map, developed by Kohonen, groups the input data into clusters which are commonly used for unsupervised training.

What is SOM?

In SOM, there are 'm' cluster units that are arranged in a 1D or 2D array, an input vector of n-tuples and a weight vector associated with the cluster unit. In self-organizing process, the cluster unit whose weight vector matches the input pattern closely is selected as the winner. The winning and the neighboring unit update their weights. Also note that the neighboring unit's weight vectors are not close to the input pattern but differ some extent. Hence, the connection weights do not multiply the signal sent from the input units to cluster units. In SOM, all units in the neighborhood that receive positive feedback from the winning participate in the learning process. Even if the neighboring unit's weight is orthogonal to the input vector, its weight vector will still change in response to the input vector. This simple addition to the competition process is sufficient to maintain the order mapping.

What is the architecture of SOM?

In a 2D SOM, the network is created from a 2D lattice of nodes, each of which is fully-connected to the input layer. Fig. 15.29 shows a simple Kohonen network.

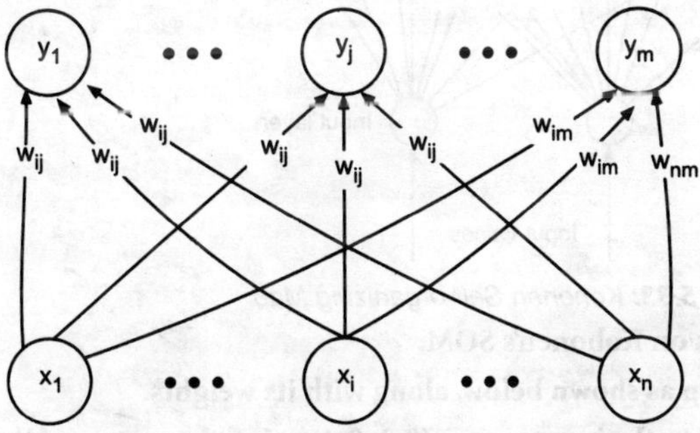

Fig. 15.32: A simple Kohonen Network

This figure shows a Kohonen network of (4 * 4) nodes connected to the input layer representing a 2D vector. Each node has a specific topological position, an (x, y) coordinate in the lattice, and contains a vector of weights of the same dimension as the input vectors. This means that if the training data consists of vectors, V, of n-dimensions:

$$V_1, V_2, V_3 \ldots\ldots V_n$$

Then each node will contain a corresponding weight vector W, of n dimensions:

$$W_1, W_2, W_3 \ldots W_n$$

Please note that the lines connecting the nodes in fig.15.30 below **are only there to represent adjacency and do not signify a connection as normally indicated when discussing a neural network. Also note that there are no lateral connections between the nodes within the lattice.**

The Training Algorithm

Let us now write its training algorithms.

Given: A network consisting of n-valued input units, connected to any number of output units.

Compute: To train the network so that it maintains topological relationship.

Algorithm:

Step-1: Set topological neighborhood parameters. Also set learning rate, initialize weights.

Step-2: While stopping condition is false, do steps 3 to 9.

Step-3: For each input vector, x, do steps 4 to 6.

Step-4: For each j, compute squared Euclidean distance.

$$D(j) = \Sigma (W_{ij} - X_i)^2 \qquad \text{where } i \leftarrow 1 \text{ to n and } j \leftarrow 1 \text{ to } m$$

Step-5: Find index j, when $D(j)$ is minimum.

Step-6: For all units j, with the specified neighborhood of j, and for all I, update the weights-

$$W_{ij(new)} = W_{ij(old)} + \alpha [X_i - W_{ij(old)}]$$

Step-7: Update the learning rate.

Step-8: Reduce the radius of topological neighborhood at specified times.

Step-9: Test the stopping condition.

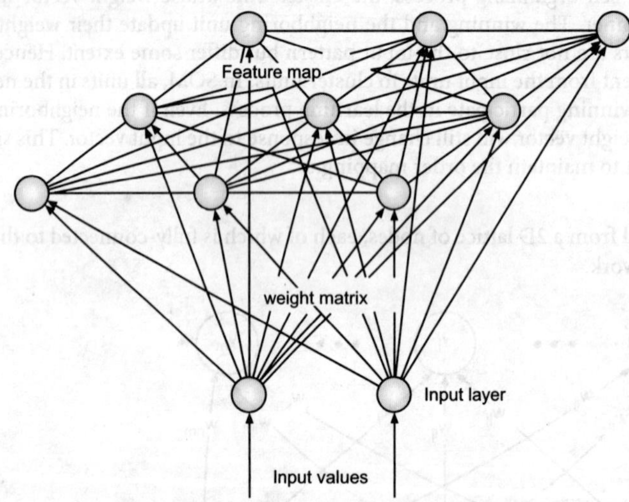

Fig. 15.33: Kohonen Self-organizing Map

We are in a position to solve some problems on Kohonen's SOM.

Q.29. Consider a Kohonen self-organizing map as shown below, along with its weights.

a. **Find the cluster unit C_j that is closest to the input vector (0.3, 0.4) using the square of the Euclidean distance.**

b. **Using a learning rate of 0.3, find the new weights for unit C_j.**

c. **Find new weights for C_{j-1} and C_{j+1}, if they are allowed to learn.**

Ans. Let us solve part by part.

a. **Step-1:** Initial weight matrix is-

$$\begin{pmatrix} 0.2 & 0.6 & 0.4 & 0.9 & 0.2 \\ 0.3 & 0.5 & 0.7 & 0.6 & 0.8 \end{pmatrix}$$

Initial radius, $R = 0$, initial learning rate, $\alpha = 0.3$

Step-2: Begin training.

Step-3: For vector (0.3, 0.4) repeat steps 4-6.

Step-4: Compute the squared Euclidean distance as follows-

$$D(j) = \Sigma (W_{ij} - X_i)^2$$

$$D(1) = (0.2 - 0.3)^2 + (0.3 - 0.4)^2 = 0.02$$

$$D(2) = (0.6 - 0.3)^2 + (0.5 - 0.4)^2 = 0.10$$
$$D(3) = (0.4 - 0.3)^2 + (0.7 - 0.4)^2 = 0.10$$
$$D(4) = (0.9 - 0.3)^2 + (0.6 - 0.4)^2 = 0.40$$
$$D(5) = (0.2 - 0.3)^2 + (0.8 - 0.4)^2 = 0.17$$

Step-5: Since $D(1)$ is minimum so $j = 1$. The input vector is closest to the output node-1.

b. **Step-6:** The weights on the winning unit are updated.

$$W_{ij(new)} = W_{ij(old)} + \alpha\,(x_1 - W_{ij(old)})$$
$$W_{11(new)} = W_{11(old)} + 0.3\,(0.3 - 0.2) = 0.2 + 0.3\,(0.3 - 0.2) = 0.23$$
$$W_{21(new)} = W_{21(old)} + \alpha\,(x_2 - W_{21(old)})$$
$$= 0.3 + 0.3\,(0.4 - 0.3) = 0.33$$

The new weights for units are $C_j = C_1$ is-

$$\begin{pmatrix} 0.23 & 0.6 & 0.4 & 0.9 & 0.2 \\ 0.33 & 0.5 & 0.7 & 0.6 & 0.8 \end{pmatrix}$$

c. The new weights of C_{j-1} and C_{j+1}, since $j = 1$, since $j = 1$, $Cj - 1 = C_{1-1} = C_0$, the weights of which cannot be calculated as it does not exist.

$$C_{j+1} = C_{1+1} = C_2$$

Weight updation of unit 2 are as follows-

$$W_{12(new)} = W_{12(old)} + \alpha\,(x_1 - W_{12(old)}) = 0.6 + 0.3\,(0.3 - 0.6) = 0.51$$
$$W_{22(new)} = W_{22(old)} + \alpha\,(x_2 - W_{22(old)}) = 0.5 + 0.3(0.4 - 0.5) = 0.47$$

The new weights for units are as follows-

$$\begin{pmatrix} 0.23 & 0.51 & 0.4 & 0.9 & 0.2 \\ 0.33 & 0.47 & 0.7 & 0.6 & 0.8 \end{pmatrix}$$

Q.30. Consider a Kohonen self-organizing map network with two cluster units and three input units. The weight vector for the cluster units is (0.9, 0.7,0.6) and (0.4, 0.3, 0.5). find the winning cluster unit for the input vector (0.4, 0.2, 0.1). use the learning rate of 0.2. find the new weights for the winning unit.

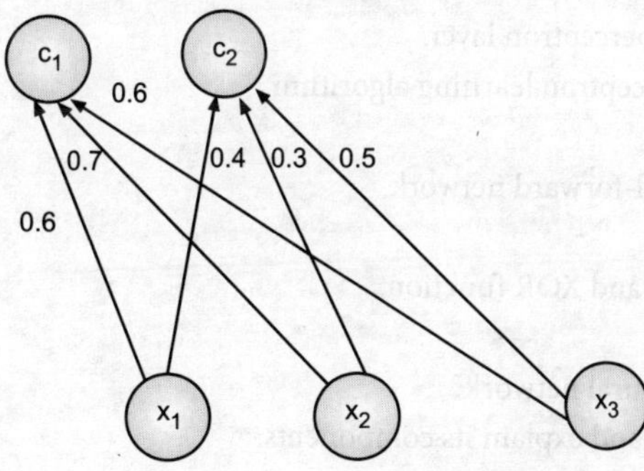

Ans. Let us solve part by part.

a. **Step-1:** Initial weight matrix is-

$$\begin{pmatrix} 0.9 & 0.4 \\ 0.7 & 0.3 \\ 0.6 & 0.5 \end{pmatrix}$$

Initial radius, $R = 0$, initial learning rate, $\alpha = 0.2$

Step-2: Begin training.

Step-3: For vector (0.4, 0.2, 0.1) repeat steps 4-6.

Step-4: Compute the squared Euclidean distance as follows-

$$D(j) = \Sigma (W_{ij} - X_i)^2$$
$$D(1) = (0.9 - 0.4)^2 + (0.7 - 0.2)^2 + (0.6 - 0.1)^2 = 0.75$$
$$D(2) = (0.4 - 0.4)^2 + (0.3 - 0.2)^2 + (0.5 - 0.1)^2 = 0.17$$

Step-5: Since D (2) is minimum so $j = 2$. The input vector is closest to the output node-2.

Step-6: The weights on the winning unit are updated.

$$Wij(new) = Wij(old) + \alpha (x_1 - W_{ij(old)})$$

Weight updation of unit 2 are as follows-

$$W_{12(new)} = W_{12(old)} + \alpha (x_1 - W_{12(old)}) = 0.4 + 0.2 (0.4 - 0.4) = 0.4$$
$$W_{22(new)} = W_{22(old)} + \alpha (x_2 - W_{22(old)}) = 0.3 + 0.2 (0.2 - 0.3) = 0.28$$
$$W_{32(new)} = W_{32(old)} + \alpha (x_3 - W_{32(old)}) = 0.5 + 0.2 (0.1 - 0.5) = 0.42$$

The new weights for units are as follow-

$$\begin{pmatrix} 0.9 & 0.4 \\ 0.7 & 0.28 \\ 0.6 & 0.42 \end{pmatrix}$$

EXERCISE QUESTIONS

1. What s ANN? Explain task performed by ANN. Explain characteristics of ANN.
2. Give some advantages and some disadvantages of ANN.
3. Draw and explain the architecture of a NN.
4. List some applications of Neural Networks.
5. What are the advantages of neural networks?
6. Define a bias node.
7. What is the importance of activation function? Explain it. Also explain different non-linear activation functions.
8. Explain with a neat diagram McCulloch-Pitts Neuron model. What are its limitations.
9. Explain Hebbian rule with an example.
10. Explain the delta learning rule for multi-perceptron layer.
11. What is perceptron network? Explain perceptron learning algorithm.
12. Give some limitations of perceptron.
13. Explain the architecture of multilayer feed-forward network.
14. What is backpropagation learning?
15. Explain the implementation of AND, OR and XOR function.
16. Explain single layer perceptron model.
17. Why we need a multi-layer perceptron neural network?
18. What is self-organizing feature map? List and explain its components.
19. Write short notes on ANNs.
20. What are the advantages and disadvantages of ANN?
21. What are the characteristics and the application areas of ANN?
22. Explain the different types of neuron connection with architecture.
23. Explain delta rule. Explain generalized delta learning rule (error backpropagation learning rule).
24. Write short note on backpropagation algorithm.
25. Explain perceptron with single flow graph.
26. Explain multi-layer perceptron with its architecture and characteristics.
27. How tuning parameters effect the backpropagation neural network?
28. Discuss selection of various parameters in backpropagation neural network.

UNIT-II

MACHINE LEARNING

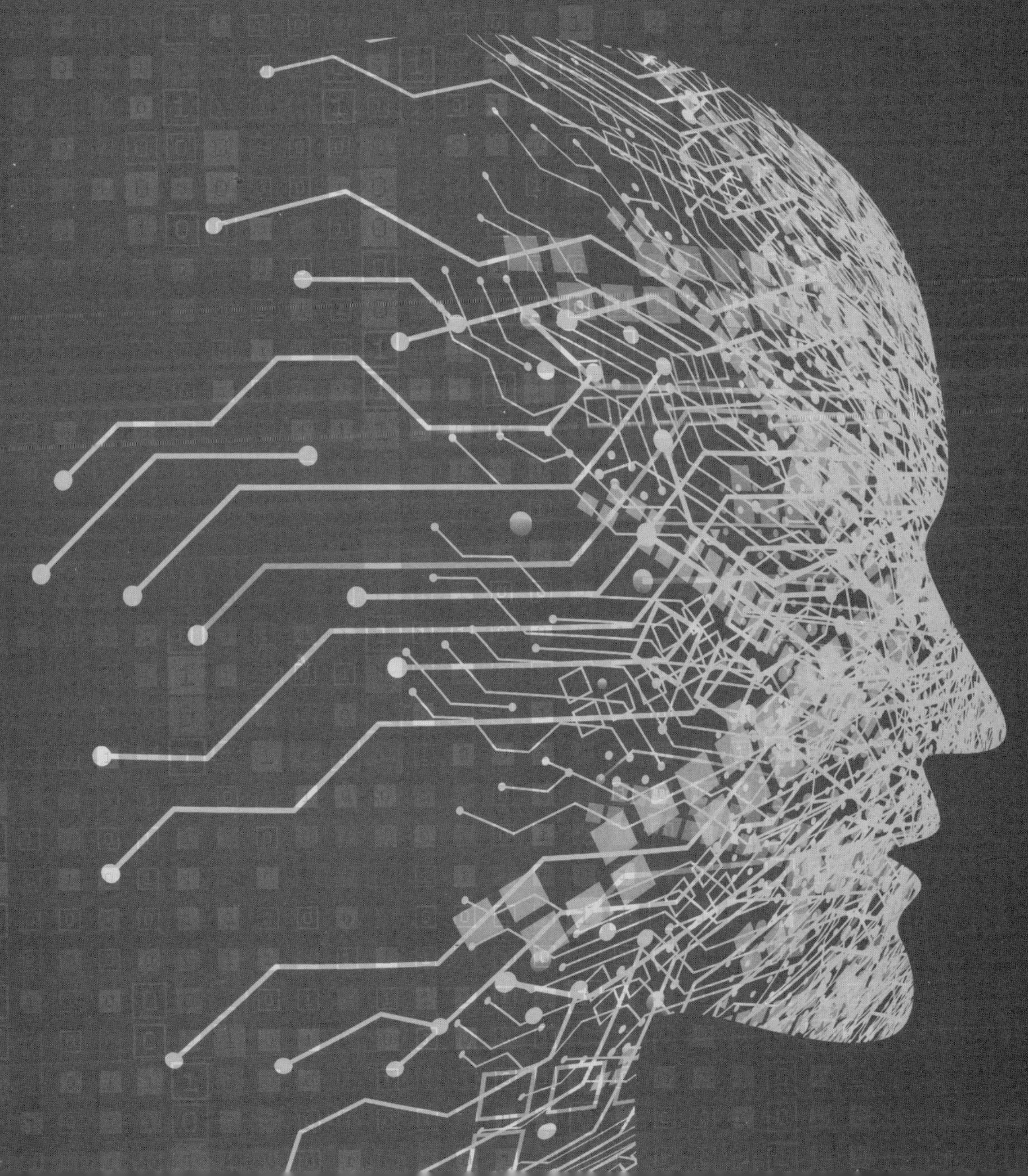

1 Introduction to Machine Learning

Q.1. Give a brief history of machine learning. How is machine learning different from statistics?

Ans. Human brain is very innovative. This creativity of human brain has led to the invention of different machines that simplify our tasks. However, intelligence is the basic difference between humans and machines. Humans gather information and our brain works to analyze that information. On the other hand, machines are not intelligent by nature. Machines are not able to analyze data and take decisions on its own. For example, a machine cannot understand the story of 'Padmavat' or interact with other machines using any common language. The eagerness for intelligent machines originated in mid of 20th century. Alan Turing gave an idea whether machines can think or not. The aim is to create machines that have the same level of intelligence as humans have. Several science fiction movies like The Terminator, Robot, Star Wars etc. have focussed on these concepts.

The history of AI started in 1943. In this year, Waren McCulloch and Walter Pits introduced the first neural network model.

In 1950, Alan Turing argued on a question- Can machines think? He also gave the concept of test of intelligence.

In 1955, Oliver Selfridge proposed the use of computers for pattern recognition.

In 1956, John McCarthy et al. (IBM), organized the first summer AI conference at Dartmouth College, USA. Then in the second conference, he coined the new term Artificial Intelligence. Another term, cognitive science came into existence in 1956 during a symposium in information science at USA.

In 1957, Rosenblatt invented the first perceptron. In 1959, John McCarthy invented LISP (LIST PROCESSING) 4GL language.

In 1962, David Hubel and Torsten Wiesel proposed the use of neural networks for computer vision. Then J. Weizenbaum developed the first expert system named ELIZA that could diagnose a disease from its symptons.

In 1964, National Research Council (NRC) at USA founded a committe that could motivate and help in research in the field of NLP.

In 1969, Marvin Minsky and Seymour Papert published a book on Perceptrons. They showed the sort comings of neural networks.

In 1979, the research got increased in the field of knowledge-based systems. Expert systems like DENDRAL, MYCIN came into being. Also Paul Werbos propsed the first efficient neural network model with back propagation.

In 1986, David Rumerhart et al. gave a new method that allowed a network to learn to discriminate between non-linear separable classes and named it as backpropagation.

In 1987, Terrence Sejnowski et al. developed an ANN, NETTalk for speech recognition. Also in this same year, John H. Holland et al. invented an adapted computing system that is capable of learning.

In 1989, Dean Pomerleau proposed ALVINN *i.e.* autonomous land vehicle in a neural network, has a 3-layered neural network designed for the task of roads following.

In 1997, Deep Blue chass machine (developed by IBM), defeated the world chess champion, Garry Kasparov.

In 2011, Watson, IBM Computer, defeated Brad Rutter and Ken Jennings, the champions of the TV game show Jeopardy. Present day research in machine and deep learning stresses on computer vision, hearing, NLP, emotional understanding, computer vision, image processing, pattern recognition, cognitive computing, knowledge representation etc. the objective is to provide machines with abilities to gather data through senses like human senses and then processing the gathered data by using computational intelligence tools. The task is to conduct predictions and decision making at the same level as humans.

Mobiles have invaded the world today. If it is able to learn and interpret our way of speaking then it is an instance c AI but the technology that is used to make it happen is machine learning. AI contains machine learning which furthe contains deep learning. AI is built on the hypothesis that mechanization of thoughts is possible. Machine learning i based on algorithms to analyze huge datasets. Machine learning can do predictive analysis at a much faster rate tha human beings can do it. Machine learning does not imply machine intelligence.

Machine learning involves statistics and big data. However, machine learning is different from statistics. The points differences are as follows:-

Table-1: Machine Learning Versus Statistics

Machine Learning	Statistics
1. It uses big data.	1. It works on small samples of data.
2. Data is represented as trees and graphs.	2. Models are created to get predictive power on small samples.
3. Raw data say from sensors or web text is divided into training set and test data.	3. It creates mathematical models to fit data.
4. Data is the food, here.	4. The parameters that are used depict real world phenomena.
5. The best guess (or decision) is considered based on the probability only.	5. The parameters that are used depict real world phenomena.
6. Data scientist learns from the data.	6. Data scientist assumes a certain output and proves it somehow.
7. The distribution is not considered before learning from data.	7. A well defined data distribution is assumed.
8. The aim is to create a best-fit and generalized model.	8. The result is fit to the present data distribution.

Please note that Big Data means huge amount of datasets and huge amount of data means huge amount of memo and better CPUs. Also note that today systems depend on Graphical Processing Units (GPUs) to perform machi learning tasks. This speeds up the machine learning process also.

Most of the AI tasks are mundane (dull or boring). **For example,** Verizon company uses R language to analyze th security breaches into data. But the act of performing this analysis is dull as compared to other types of AI activiti However, the advantage is that Verizon now save s money by doing analysis using R. The results are better too. Ev Python developers use a large array of libraries to make machine learning easier. But please remember that both Pytho developers and R practitioners need to hone (refine or sharpen) their machine learning skills in order to create practic applications. The objective is to make development of complex data science and machine learning applications easier

Machine learning has several uses:-

1. To adapt to new circumstances that the original developer did not mention.
2. To find out the patterns in data obtained from different sources.
3. To create new behaviours based on the recognized patterns.
4. To make decisions based on the success or failure of these behaviours.

Also just remember a **golden rule:- " Use of algorithms to do data manipulation is the central core heart of machi learning."** A machine learning session must use a suitable algorithm to get the desired results. Also the data must le itself to analysis using the desired algorithm or the data scientists must prepare this data again.

AI includes many things like Natural Language Processing (NLP), Knowledge Representation, Planning/ goal seeki and Robotics. Both AI and Machine Learning become very complex as we need to understand the world using da inputs to a computer and it is a complex task. Data scientists try to convert hypothesis into theories. The basic of machi learning is maths. Algorithms are needed now to interpret and implement 'big data' in some specific way. Both AI a Machine Learning should decipher the data in such a manner that the patterns may be found in them. In machi learning some data acts as a baseline that trains an algorithm to get specific results. The remaining data provides t output used to understand the underlying patterns. No specific rules that govern the balancing of data exists. It is t sole responsibility of the data scientists who work on data should maintain a balance so that optimal output is obtaine Please **note that cleaning of the data also adds to the quality to the result. Also note that the way in which t scientists prepare the data for use is very vital.** The cleaned dataset used by one scientist for machine learning tas may not completely match the cleaned dataset used by another. A very common problem in machine learning is ho to consider the input data. The variables that a designer faces when creating machine learning environment are large numbers and are quite complex too. The need is to have experienced data scientists as then they can add more values the data and the algorithm will also work in a better way.

In terms of machine learning, an algorithm may be defined as a systematic set of operations that need to be performed a given data set. There are 4 main basic data operations- Create, Read, Update and Delete (CRUD). **Please understa that as the dataset becomes larger, the computer can use the algorithms found in an application to perform mc work. Also understand that the use of huge datasets** (called as Big Data) **enables a computer to perform work bas on pattern recognition in a non-deterministic manner.**

Goal: "To create a computer setup that can learn, you need a larger and larger dataset that is sufficient for the algorith to manage in a way that uses pattern recognition and this pattern recognition needs to use a simple subset to ma predictions i.e. statistical analysis, of the dataset as a whole."

Several sources of big data exist like online databases. However, it is the mix of big data and statistics that create machine learning environment wherein a machine considers the probability of any given event. Algorithms will find c how a machine interprets big data. The algorithms that are used will affect the results of the learning process and her the final results.

A very important part of machine learning is training hat creates the patterns that an algorithm needs to recogn specific cases from the more general cases that you provide as a part of the training process.

Big data implies lots and lots of data. But also associated with it are its complexity and its depth. Just getting bulk datasets is not sufficient but also needed is to consider how the dataset is stored and transferred so that the system c process it. Data scientists would prefer to store the dataset in memory to allow fast processing as hard disks are costl and slower too. Please understand **that machine learning helps humans to make sense and use of big data. Also no that before using big data for machine learning applications, the source of big data is also needed.** Governmen Universities, non-profit organizations etc maintain public databases that you can use alone or in combination w other databases to create big data for machine learning. For instance, combining several GISs can help us to create data that is needed to make decisions like where to open new stores or companies. The **point to ponder** is that machi learning can take all sorts of information into consideration. Industry giants like Amazon and Google also maintai very big database that has very useful information. We need to pay them to get this information. This information fr private companies is found to be more consistent.

Principle of Operation of Machine Learning

"Machine Learning (ML) works on 80% of the data. Remaining 20% of the cases humans will take over the job deciding just how to react and act to the data".

Please understand here that machine learning saves money by performing repetitive tasks that humans don't want to But machine learning still needs humans.

Every company has data hidden here and there. The problem is to recognize data as data. ML means to create mashu that present existing data as a new kind of data that makes company's working better. Even your email is the source data. Machine learning revolves around algorithms. An algorithm is a kind of container. The aim is to create an outp that solves a problem. It is also possible to combine several algorithms to get a bigger and better master algorit to solve a complex problem. Symbolic reasoning comes under this category. The connectionists try to reproduce brain's functions using silicon instead of neurons. They are moving from 'Neurons to Silicon'. Each of the neurons (algorithm to solve real world problems) solves a small piece of the problem. They use parallel neurons to solve complex problem as a whole.

The technique used is back-propagation (also called as backward propagation of error). In this method, we determi the conditions under which errors are removed from the networks so built so as to resemble the human neurons changing weights and biases (features selected) of the network. **Please understand that the objective is to contin changing the weights and biases till the actual output matches the target output.** At this juncture, the artific neuron fires and passes its sub-solution along to the next neuron in line. The solution that is created by just one neur is just a part of the whole of the solution. This process of passing of the information by the neuron to the next neur in line continues till the group of neurons creates a final output. **Data scientists rely on the principles of evolution a**

recursion concepts to solve the problems. Also understand that as we move from one layer/level to another layer we are actually moving closer to the solution of the problem in hand.

Q.2. What is training?

Ans. In traditional programming languages like C/C++/JAVA2 we write a function that reads some input and then returns back some result. This is functional programming. On the other hand, machine learning is the reverse process. training provies a learner algorithm with all sorts of examples of the desired inputs and results expected from those inputs. Then the learner uses this input to create a function. Thus, we can say that training is the process wherein a learner algorithm maps a flexible function to the data. That is,

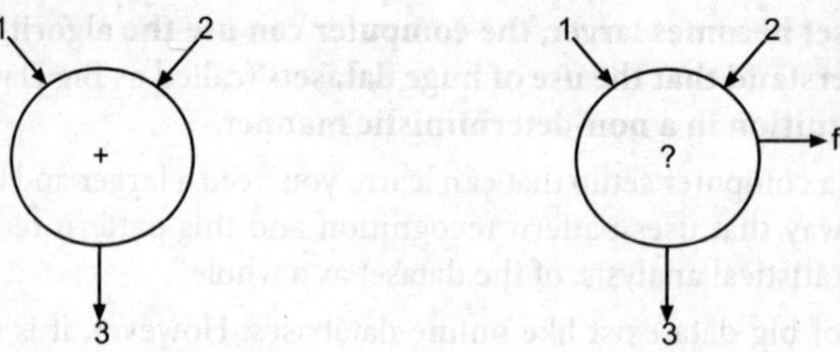

Fig. 1.1: Application Program versus Machine Learning Algorithm

In left part of figure 1.1, a traditional functional programmer will write a function, say add( ) that reads two integers and adds them to produce the output like 1+2 = 3, as shown. So, 3 is returned as the desired output/result. On the other hand, in machine learning, we know that the inputs are 1 and 2 and we also know that the output needed is 3 but what we do not know is the function, f that produces this output with these inputs. So, we need a function to apply to get the desired result. An algorithm minimizes the input data and the expected results of those inputs to a function but a function is specific for a task that you want an algorithm to perform. The central core confidential point that remains is generalization in machine learning. That is, we need to generalize the output function so that it works on data beyond the training set.

For example, consider an English dictionary that has approx. Say 10^5 words. Now, if we take a limited training dataset of say 5000 words then we must create a generalized function that can find spam in 2 ^ 10^5 combinations that the function will observe when working with the actual data. A generalized algorithm will depend on three factors:-

1. The learner algorithm should create a model *i.e.* a function that produces a given result for specific inputs. The representation is a set of models that a learner algorithm can learn. So, the learner algorithm must create a model that will produce the desired results from the input data. The aim is also to discover which features to use for the learning process.
2. The learner should be able to distinguish between a good model and a bad model.
3. The training process should search these models to find the best one. Then the best model is the output result of the training process. This is also called as optimization.

Machine learning is still in its infancy. Researchers say that there is a fear also related to ML. ML will keep humans away from working!!!! Machine learning and hence deep learning is a must-have technology today. Machine learning has a great impact in industry also today. Now we can do the things at a faster rate, more accurately and with lesser resource requirement so that the company becomes more flexible and has better ROIs. Many fields like medical diagnosis, data mining, bioinformatics, speech and handwriting recognition, product categorization and informational retrieval, healthcare, finance, traffic management, robotics, Unmanned Aerial Vehicles (UAVs), decision support systems for business intelligence have been affected by machine learning and its algorithms. In 2016, there were many machine learning pilots in the industry.

Also we need a new hardware to do machine learning. In nutshell, humans will use creativity to discover what to do while the details (the how part) will be under the domain of machine learning. Also note that the newer the technology, the more severe are the pitfalls. The machines cannot infer anything and this limits the use of this machine to the task for which the developer or the data scientist designed it. Deep learning is a technique that allows the machine to choose inputs by using multiple processing layers to analyze complex structures. Another challenge that ML faces is to get expert people who can work on ML or its CASE TOOLS like TensorFlow or H_2O.

Today, machine learning is omnipresent. As we know that machine learning is a branch of AI that endeavours to impart computers the ability to learn without being explicitly programmed. ML is the branch of computer science that deals with the study and design of algorithms that can learn from and make predictions on data. It is a data analysis approach that automates analytical modeling. The origin of deep learning has resulted in the renaissance of neural networks.

During machine learning, computers are taught to solve complex problems with a huge set of rules and are provided with models. On the other hand, in deep learning the model provided can be evaluated with examples and a small set of instructions to modify it when it makes a mistake. Over a period of time, the suitable model is able to solve the complex problem accurately and efficiently.

Machine learning has resulted in machine intelligence. The intelligent machines like IBM Watson machine and modern Robots will simplify our tasks. Today, a competition is going on between human intelligence and artificial intelligence. The machine needs to learn from data so as to predict patterns in it and then further act to process that knowledge to maximize future business.

According to the reports of McKinsey Global Institute, fields like high tech, telecom, financial services will be the earliest adopters of machine learning in the world while healthcare, HR and e-commerce in India.

Many companies used Google's machine learning software Tensor Flow, Google Analytics, speech recognition and Optical character recognition to combat attacks on their companies. Just as IBM has Watson's deep learning, Google has Tensor Flow and MS has MS AZURE CLOUD, Facebook has open-source Caffe as its deep learning module. The data is fedto these machine learning frameworks like Tensor Flow.

It is on the basis of client's data that the model scrapes the Internet for public information like location of hotels, hospitals, schools, malls to suggest that where should be they placed. Machine learning may be used to find out the fraud seller on Internet. We have lots and lots of past data. Based on this data we can predict. This is machine learning.

In another report of McKinsey Global Institute, 2016, globally companies spent $39 billion approx. in developing machine learning applications.

Another company PwC reports that machine learning could grow global GDP by some $30 trillion by 2030. In fact we say that, DATA is the fuel behind machine learning.

In IBM's report 2017, it is mentioned that "as oil refiners make more money than drillers similarly, humans who refine data will make more money than humans who create data". And this is possible by making use of certain algorithms and APIs (Application Programming Interface). The time duration has reduced from several weeks to few days or hours only.

Another company Signzy, used IBMs Watson's machine learning capability to identify images, speech to text conversion etc.

Machines need to be trained with lakes of data so as to churn out the type of results you expect out of them. For example, Amazon has been using machine learning algorithms to make product recommendations since 1990s. Google and Amazon use ML to understand customer's priority like which advertisements to show more. Google used 2 billion sentence pairs to train Google Translate (to convert from English to French). Google also reported that the training time is 2-3 weeks for one language pair for one model.

The human brain and its neural network is the recent area of research. Building intelligent machines is the target today. Even Amazon bets on improving the speed of product deliveries, to cut product returns, better search results and better efficiency.

Some of the machine learning tools and libraries are as follows:-

1. *Several R machine learning packages like caret, e1071, rpart, C50, randomForest, gbm, clust, glmnet, neuralnet, arules support ML.*
2. *Scikit-learn package implements many ML algorithms.*
3. *WEKA and RapidMiner support Java libraries for ML.*
4. *Vowpal Wabbit is a C++ based ML library.*

Q.3. Define what are the Learning Systems?

Ans. We need to define a learning system first of all. It is defined as an interaction of a learning agent / intelligent agent with its environment by perceiving an input and doing actions accordingly. An agent is one who can perceive its environment with the help of sensors and acts upon its environment through actuators.

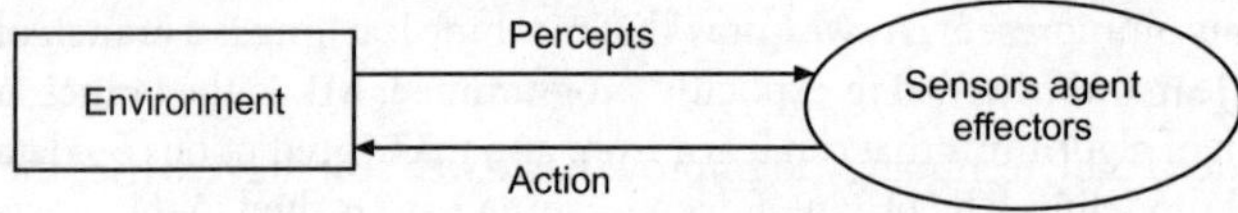

Fig. 1.2: A Learning System

An intelligent agent is a software entity which senses its environment and then carries out some set of operations on behalf of a user with some amount of autonomy and to do so it employs some knowledge or representation of the end-user's goal. Note that an agent is different from a program. An agent need not be a program at all. It may be a robot or a college professor. Software agents are by definition programs but a program must measure up to several marks to be an agent. For example, humans, animals, autonomous mobile robots or softbots calculators are real-world agents. Software agents live in the systems OS.

As shown in figure 1.2, an agent perceives its environment through sensors. It then acts upon that environment through actuators. For example,

- Human agent has eyes, ears, nose etc. as sensors while hands, legs, mouth are actuators.
- Software agent receives keystrokes, files, packets are sensory inputs and acts on the environment by displaying on the screen, writing files and sending packets over a network.

When an algorithm learns from data, it is the cost function that guides the optimization process by pointing out the changes in the internal parameters that are the most beneficial for better predictions.

Machine is a semi or fully automated device that intensifies human physical or mental competence in carrying out one or more operations. Learning is building up experience or enhancing one's abilities through analysis, taking into account happenings around us (experience) and being taught by the same. By the word 'experience' we mean the following:-

- Finding out when the same situation was visited.
- What was the action taken?
- Did it worked or failed?

Present day data pool is in terabytes and petabytes. We want our machines to learn from the available giant stock of data through experience. Big data is growing exponentially every second. The objective is to use this data for some benefit. We have colossal data on computers related to hospitals, railways, Universities, banks etc. They are storing data constantly. Each of this organization maintains data in some way or the other. Please understand that the ultimate aim is to do/extract something useful from this data like treatments that do not work on a patient can be removed or discarded, Universities can put invalid admissions on hold and so on. Also understand here that it implies that we can conclude a human or animal with the label of being intelligent only when they exhibit act of learning from experience.

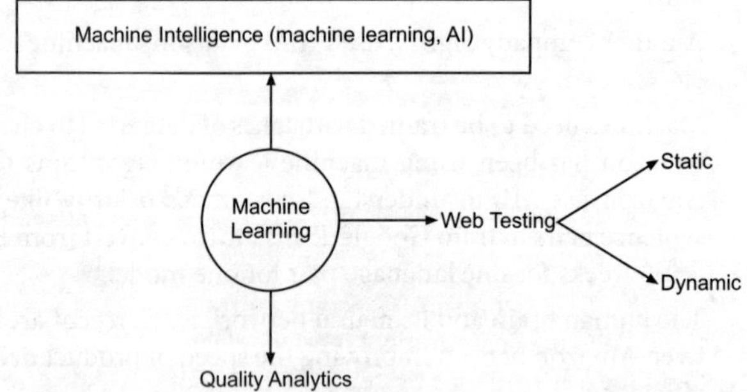

Fig. 1.3: Machine Learning, Machine Intelligence and Web Testing

So, we define machine learning as a powerful AI tool that allows us to crunch petabytes of data. Arthur Samuel, in 1959, defined machine learning as a field of study that gives computers the ability to learn without being explicitly programmed. When exposed to new data the main focus is on developing computer programs that can teach themselves to grow and change. Software tends to learn from the previous encountered computations in order to produce decisions and results which are reliable and repeatable in nature. This field is quite vast and expanding at a faster rate. When we say machine learning we actually mean building and studying of those algorithms which can learn from data and make predictions (analytics) on it. The final aim is to get more accurate actions that were chosen to be taken in a particular situation by computers, thus making it intelligent in making predictions.

Searching the deep web is the current research area today.

This is shown in figure 1.3.

Machine tool like Test Rail are useful here.

PowerSet Company used deep NLP technology to improve basic web search. Web uses the power of-

a. Information Theory.

b. Statistical Inference.

c. NLP (Natural Language Processing).

GOALS AND APPLICATIONS OF MACHINE LEARNING

Our objective is to devise such algorithms that does learning naturally without human interference. So, we can say that machine learning model can be considered in the form of programming by example. The following are some of the goals and applications of machine learning:-

1. To improve the image classification in apps like Google photos, deep learning is required.
2. To improve detection of malicious software, machine learning is used in anti-virus software.
3. Anti-spam software are trained better by machine learning. Identify e-mail messages as spam or non-spam and if it happens to be spam then penalize them
4. Tagging people in photos like Facebook does it. It shows whether a face is present or not in a photograph.
5. To diagnose patients' suffering from a particular disease or Not.
6. For speech recognition.
7. To predict a set of customers who will respond to a particular type of advertisement or promotion like Amazon recommends products especially for you.
8. To identify fraudulent credit card transactions.
9. When machine learning is applied to weather forecasting software it enhances quality of software by resulting in accurate predictions for instance whether it will rain today or not.
10. To categorize news articles to different categories of politics, sports, entertainments etc.

Q.4. What are the different aspects of Developing a Learning System- training experience, concept representation, function approximation?

Ans. There are three aspects of developing a learning system:-

1. Training Experience.
2. Concept Representation.
3. Function Approximation.

Let us study these one by one now.

I. Training Experience: There are three (3) attributes for the selection of the design-

a. To make choice of the type of training experience from a set of experiences from which the system learns. The chosen training experience has a deep effect on learner's success or failure. Once the choice is made by the Performance System, the query of whether direct or indirect feedback regarding choices is provided by the training experience. For example, in case of a chess game, the system may learn from direct training (like board states, correct moves etc.) or indirect training (like move sequences, final outcomes of the games etc.). It has been found that learning done from the direct training feedback is easier than learning from indirect feedback.

b. To what extent sequence of training examples is controlled by the learner. For example, for the selection of board states and correct move for each, the learner might require teacher's assistance. On the other hand, learner can use a different approach *i.e.*, the board states that seems confusing to the learner might itself be proposed by the learner. A learner can have an entire control over both the conditions i.e., of the board states as well as of training classifications (indirect) as it does when it learns by playing against itself without the assistance of a teacher.

c. How well it signifies the distribution of examples over which the final system's performance is measured. In chess game, the performance count metric, Pc is the number of games the system wins. The training experience, E_t, might not be fully illustrative of various situations over which it will be later on tested; if the games played against itself is only taken into account.

Please note here that the most of the theory of machine learning is dependent on the assumption that distribution of training examples is identical to distribution of test examples.

The training proceeds as follows. No external trainer will be present. Hence, the system gets trained by playing games against itself. This results in generation of lot of training data with time.

Keep in mind these 3 points when viewing a complete design of the learning system:-

1. Exact type of knowledge to be learned.
2. How this target knowledge is represented.
3. A learning means.

How to choose the target function?

The performance program will decide on what sort of knowledge will be learned and how will this program put it to use. For example, consider a chess program that can generate legal moves from any board state. The program needs to find out the best move, out of the large number of legal moves available. Now the type of function to be learned is a program or function that finds the best move from a lot of moves available for a particular board state.

II. Concept Representation : The learning task is narrowed down to the problem of finding an operational description of ideal target function, *E*, that is difficult to learn perfectly. Note that we expect learning algorithms to attain some approximation to the target function and thus the process of learning the target function is called as function approximation.

For example, in chess problem-

T_G is the task *i.e.*, to play chess.

P_c is the percentage of games won against competitor.

E_T is practising against itself.

Target Function, *E*: Board → *R*

So, Target Function Representation is-

$$E'(s) = w_0 + w_1b_1 + w_2b_2 + w_3b_3 + w_4b_4 + w_5b_5 + w_6b_6$$

Note that the first three points relate to specification of learning task and last two items form design choices that are required for the implementation of the learning program.

III. Function Approximation : We need a set of training examples in order to learn target function, E', each describing a particular board states and training value E for s. Every training example is represented as an ordered pair of the form (*s*, E_{train} (*s*)). For example, consider the following training example that tells a board state in which red has won the game. Note that

$b_1 = 0 =$ number of black pieces left for this target function value is E_{train} (*s*) + 100.

Estimating Training Values : The only training information available to a learner, in accordance to the formulation of learning problem is whether the game was last won or lost. Also training instances are required so that particular board states can be given specific scores. In guessing the training values for intermediate board states there are some uncertainty associated.

Rules for estimating Training Values : To assign the training value of $E_{train}(s)$ for any intermediate board state (*s*) to be *E*' (successor(*b*)), where E' is the learner's current approximation to *E* and where successor (*s*) signifies the next board state following '*s*' for which it is again the program's turn to move *i.e.*, the board state following the program's move and the opponents response. This is known as a rule for estimating training values. It can be represented as follows:-

$$E_{train}(s) \rightarrow E'(\text{successor}(s))$$

Please note here that we are using the estimates of the value of the successor (*s*) to estimate the value of board state (*s*). This will make sense if *E*' tends to be more accurate for board states closer to the games end. Also note that under certain situations the approach of iteratively estimating training values based on the estimates of successor state values can be proven to converge to perfect estimates of E_{train}.

The learning algorithm for choosing the weights, w_i, to best fit the set of training examples {(*s*, E_{train} (*s*))}. We mean to say the best fit to the training data. One general approach is to define the best hypothesis or a set of weights, which in turn minimizes the squared error, *E*, between the training values and the values predicted by the hypothesis *E*'. That is,

$$E' = \Sigma\ (s, E_{train}\ (S)\ \varepsilon \text{ training examples } (E_{train}\ (s) - E'(s))^2$$

Thus, our objective is to seek the weights or equivalently E' that minimize E for the observed training examples.

Q.5. What is the Training data?

Ans. We cannot wait for fresh data every time as it is very costly and time consuming task. We need to either randomly split that data or tune our learning algorithm. In first case of a random split of data we split the data as follows:-

- From 25% to 30% for testing.
- And left over 70% to 75% for training.

Please note that this split is done by keeping in mind the correspondence between each response and its features.

The 2nd type of split is not a good one as it causes a type of overfitting called as snooping.

To overcome this problem, we go for the 3rd method of splitting the input data also called as validation set. This is done as follows:-

- 70% for training.
- 20% for validation.
- 10% for testing.

Deep learning and Big Data are inter-related. Big data refers to the pools of data being generated every second while deep learning is an active research area in the field of machine learning. But as the data is growing at an exponential rate, deep learning is providing big data predictive analytical solutions. According to the report of National Security Agency (NSA), the Internet itself is processing 1,826 Petabytes of data per day [1]. By 2020, the tfigure will reach 35 Trillion gigabytes. This leads to a remarkable paradigm shift in computer science literature towards data-driven discovery. Today machine learning techniques and newer software, hardware and computational power help in big data as well as web data analytics.

Q.6. Define Deep Learning.

Ans. Deep learning is defined as the machine learning techniques that use supervised and/or unsupervised methods to automatically learn hierarchical representations in deep architectures for classification.

Or

Deep learning is a subset of artificial intelligence field called as machine learning which is predicted on the basic idea of learning from example.

In machine learning, instead of teaching a computer a massive list of rules to solve the complex problem, we give it a model with which it can evaluate examples. Also we give it a small set of instructions to modify the model when it makes a mistake. Please note that we have an expectation that as the time passes, a well suited model would be able to solve the problem more accurately.

For example, say our model is defined by a function $f(x, \theta)$. The input x is an example expressed in vector form. Like, if x were a gray-scale image, the vector's components would be pixel intensities at each position. The input θ is a vector of the parameters that our model uses. Also note now that it is our machine learning program that tries to perfect the values of these parameters as it is exposed to more and more examples.

The conventional learning methods are shallow-structured learning architectures while deep learning is deep-hierarchical levelled learning architecture. It is based on the biological neurons within human brain. Several research domains like speech recognition, Natural Language Processing (NLP), collaborative filtering and computer vision. Big industry giants like Google, Apple and Facebook who work on sheer size of data lakes today have also given vital importance to Big Data Analytics and Web Data Analytics. Google applies deep learning algorithms to massive chunks of messy data obtained from Internet. IBMs brain-like computer uses techniques like deep learning to make available big data available for its betterment. Please note that as the data keeps increasing at an exponential rate, deep learning is playing a key role in providing in big data and web analytics. Also note that deep learning refers to a set of machine learning techniques that learn multiple levels of representations in deep architectures. Deep learning is the new name for neural networks. Deep learning algorithms have best performance as far as complex problems like pattern recognition are concerned. Practically speaking, even machine learning approaches find it difficult to solve. Theoretically, they can solve any problem. Several libraries also exist for neural nets or deep learning. But deep learning algorithms as an auto-encoder i.e. unsupervised deep learning, several parameters and slower deep learning grids are some of the issues to be discussed in this text. These programs may need more hardware.

The information that is available on the web and is searched using search engines like Google is called as the surface web. On the other hand, deep web consists of data hidden behind web-based services. Theoretically, the deluge (flood) of data within deep web is exponentially high. Practically, useful information hidden in deep web is finite but very large. Each web form can give rise to thousands of results, each of which qualifies as a deep web page. Similarly, every Facebook or Twitter post might be considered as a deep web page. Finally, if one considers all possible pages of search results then the size of deep web is infinite. As per the survey report (2007), roughly 2.5% of random sample of web pages were forms that should be considered as part of deep web. **Please understand that deep web is huge, far larger than the indexed web of 50 billion pages.** Searching the deep web is current research area today.

Let us explore this and many more interesting topics in this book.

Q.7. What are neurons? Explain with a neat diagram.

Ans. We define a neuron first of all. A neuron is a function that takes multiple numeric inputs and gives out one numeric output. These neurons are organized in layers and the outputs from all of the neurons in one layer become the inputs for each neuron in the next layer.

The functional unit of a normal human brain is the neuron. The objective book is to use this natural brain concept to build machine learning models that solve problems in a similar fashion. A neuron is optimized to receive information from other neurons, process this information and send its results to other cells. This is shown in figure 1.4 as follows:-

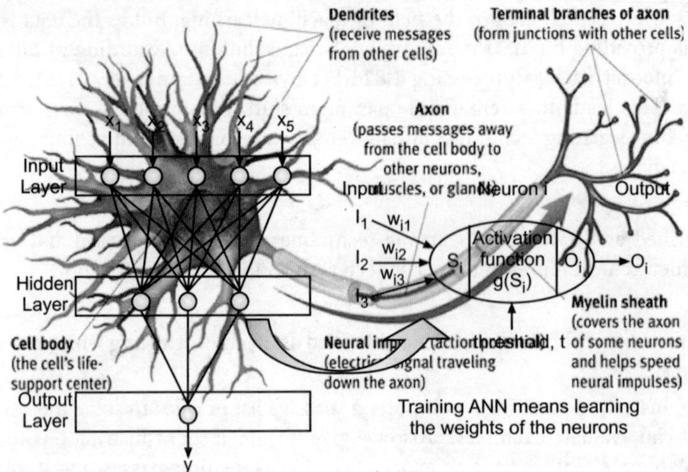

Fig. 1.4: A Neuron

The neuron receives its inputs along antennae-like structures called **dendrites.** Each of these incoming connections is dynamically strengthened or weakened based on how often it is used. **Please understand that it is the strength of each connection that determines the contribution of the input to the neuron's output.** After being weighted by the strength of their respective connections, the inputs are summed together in the cell body. **Also understand that this sum is then transformed into a new signal that is propagated along the cell's axon and sent to other neurons.**

In 1943, W. S. McCulloch and W. H. Pitts gave an artificial model that can be well represented on a computer. Just as in biological neurons, this artificial neuron takes in some number of inputs, $x_1, x_2, \ldots\ldots, x_n$. Each of this input is multiplied by a specific weight, $w_1, w_2, \ldots\ldots, w_n$. Then these weighted inputs are summed together to produce the logit of the neuron *i.e.*

$$z = \Sigma\,(i = 0 \text{ to } n)\ w_i\, x_i$$

in many cases, the logit also includes a bias, which is a constant. Then the logit is paaed through a function, f, to produce the output-

$$y = f(z)$$

This output can be transmitted to other neurons.

Mathematically, in vector form-

If inputs are as a vector $x = [x_1\ x_2 \ldots\ldots x_n]$ and the weights of the neuron as

$w = [w_1 w_2......w_n]$ then we can express the output of the neuron as follows:-

$$y = f(x.w + b), \text{ where 'b' is the bias term.}$$

This means that we can compute the output by performing the dot product of the input and weight vectors, adding in the bias term to produce the logit and then applying the transformation function.

Q.8. Explain Linear Perceptron(s) as Neurons.

Ans. Much of the work of McCulloch and Pitts in 1943 and subsequently in 1947 was based on a simple neuron model. It is shown in fig. 1.5.

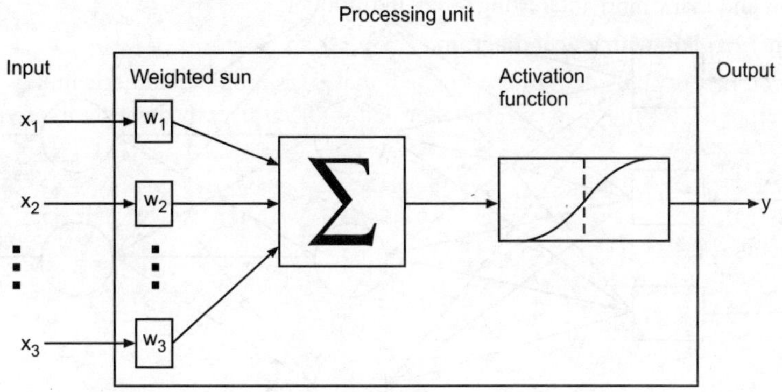

Fig. 1.5: Perceptron Neuron

The Σ unit multiplies each input, *x*, by a weight ,*w*, and sums the weighted inputs. If this sum is greater than a predetermined threshold, the output = 1 else it is zero. These systems and their variants collectively have been called as **perceptrons.** In general, they consist of a single layer of artificial neurons connected by weights to a set of inputs although more complicated networks bear the same.

The PERCEPTRN LEARNING THEOREM states that-**"A perceptron could learn anything it could represent."** Rosenblatt, in 1962, proved that a perceptron can be trained to any function it can represent. The difference between representation and learning lies in the point of reference. Representation means the ability of a perceptron to simulate a specified function while learning requires the existence of a systematic procedure for adjusting the network weights to produce that function.

Note: A neuron with n binary inputs can have 2^n different input patterns, consisting of 1*s* and O_S. Because each input pattern can produce two different binary output, one and zero, there are 22^n different functions of n variables.

Learning is of two types- Supervised and Unsupervised. Supervised learning needs an external "teacher" that evaluates the behaviour of the system and directs the subsequent modifications. On the other hand, unsupervised learning needs "no teacher" as the network self-organizes to produce the desired changes. **Please note here that the Perceptron learning is of the supervised type.** The perceptron training algorithm can be implemented on a system and the network becomes self adjusting. **This is reason as to why adjusting of weights is called as training and the network is said to learn.**

Rosenblatt's proof was a major milestone and it provided a great impetus to the research field. Also note that a perceptron is trained by representing a set of patterns to its input, one at a time and adjusting the weights until the desired output occurs for each of them.

Linear perceptron and the neuron model are somewhat equivalent. But the point to ponder is that every linear perceptron can be expressed as a single neuron but single neurons can also express models that cannot be expressed by any linear perceptron.

Q.9. What are Neural Nets? Give its architectural design.

Ans. We have already defined what a neuron is. These neurons are organized into layers. The outputs from all the neurons in one layer become the inputs for each neuron in the next layer.

Architecture/ Design : As shown in figure-1.6, the first layer is your data (inputs) that may be a training sample or a test sample or real inputs. The very last layer is your output (answer). Two cases arise:-

Case-1: If you are doing a regression *i.e.* learning a single value then the output layer will have one neuron.

Case-2: If you are doing classification, then the output layer will have one neuron for each possible answer. Here, the output (answer) with the highest probability for the set of inputs is chosen.

The layers between the input layers and the output layers are called as the **hidden layers.**

Rule: "Each neuron in each hidden layer has a weight for each of its inputs and modifying those weights is how the network learns. There is a bias input to each neuron, (a weight only) connected to a constant input and is also tuned during the training process."

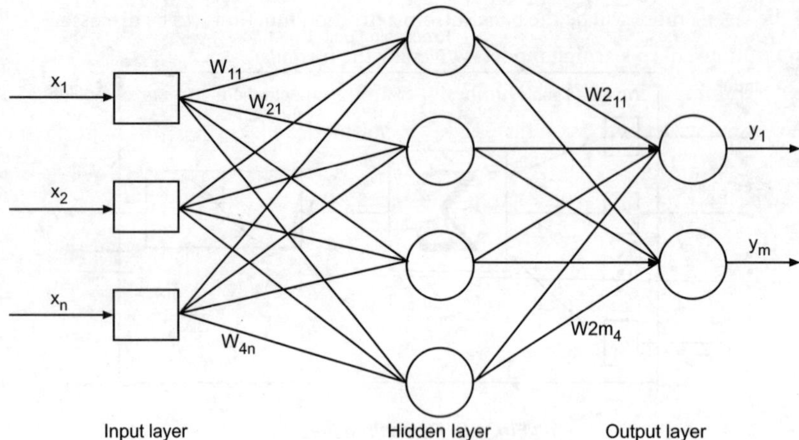

Fig. 1.6: Neural Nets

Working of Neural Nets : As shown in figure 1.6, we start with random weights. Then we give it the first training sample and the correct answer (also called as supervised learning), calculate the error and then use that to go back and tweak each of the weights so that there is a bit less error. This process is called as **backpropagation.** Then we take the second training sample and repeat the process. This process of taking each and every training data is called as an epoch. Also note that we specify the number of epochs in the algorithm that we develop. **Also note that even fractional epochs are allowed. For example,** requesting 20.5 epochs means all training data samples are processed 20 times while the first half of the training data is also processed an 11th time.

Many deep learning libraries use the concept of mini batches. A mini-batch of say, size 20 means that it will process 20 training samples then go back and update the weights in one batch. But deep learning libraries like H_2O does not use mini-batch concept in H_2O the weights get updated after every single sample.

If it is a multimode cluster then each node in the cluster works independently for one iteration. At the end of each iteration, the network weights are averaged with those on every node. **Also note that one iteration can be larger or smaller than an epoch.**

Note: Everything is a number in neural net. For example, in digit recognition problem there will be one neuron per pixel and the value will be the intensity of that pixel.

Q.10. Explain the layers of Neural Networks and Deep learning.

Ans. In theory, one hidden layer is sufficient to represent all of our data whether linear or non-linear relationships but practically speaking it is not enough to have entire data in one layer.

Please understand that having many hidden layers is deep learning but more layers/neurons means **longer training and slower usage.** Many researchers say that it is not deep learning if we have just one hidden layer only.

How to choose the number of layers and neurons in a neural net?

There are six (rules) rules of thumb to select the number of layers and neurons:-

Rule-1: If the problem is non-linear then we start with two (2) layers and observe how it performs on it.

Rule-2: More non-linear is the problem, the more layers you need. If you observe that the problem is not getting solved, then add another layer to it and try. You can also try with more epochs, more training data. It has been observed that if you have moved till 5-layers then the 6th layer probably will not help.

Rule-3: More are the number of neurons in a layer, the more clearly it will be able to understand the data. You can add more neurons or more epochs or more training data.

Rule-4: More data inputs you have, the more neurons are needed in the first hidden layer.

Rule-5: More output neurons you have, the more neurons you are likely to need in the final hidden layer.

Rule-6: More are the layers, more will be the benefit from activation functions (to be discussed).

The time spent in training a deep learning model is given by the formula:-

Training Time (TT) = [Number of training samples] * [Number of Epochs]

How much training is required depends on the weights in our model. Please note that more are the weights, more can be learned from the model.

The number of weights between two layers is given by the formula:-

Weights (W) =[Number of Neurons in layer-1] * [Number of Neurons in layer-2]

Also note that you will also have to count two more layers: the input layer and the output layer.

For example, in a 50*50 network, with 2 numeric inputs and 1 output, there are:-

$$(2*50) + (50 * 50) + (50 * 1) = 100 + 2500 + 50 = 2650 \text{ weights.}$$

Now, say, you add another 3rd layer with 50 neurons, then we can compute weights required as follows:-

$$(2 * 50) + (50 * 50) + (50 * 50) + (50 * 1) = 100 + 2500 + 2500 + 50 = 5150 \text{ weights.}$$

It has been observed that if more are the weights, slower is the training.

Researchers say that deep learning is a new AI that can tell whether our tweets are sarcastic (abusive) or not. Scientists at Massachusetts Institute of Technology (MIT) USA have developed a new artificial system that can detect sarcasm in tweets better than humans. It's developers say that this advancement may help computers automatically spot and remove online hate speech and abusive comments. Detecting the sentiments of social media posts can also help gauge attitudes towards brands and products and identify signals that might indicate trends in the financial markets. Please note that they said that a deeper understanding of Twitter may also help understand how information and influence flows through the network. The researchers originally aimed to develop a system capable of detecting racist posts on Twitter. However, the meaning of many messages could not be properly understood without some understanding of sarcasm. Also note that the algorithm uses deep learning, a popular machine learning technique that relies on training a very large simulated neural network to recognise subtle patterns using a large amount of data. Researchers took advantage of emoji to help the algorithm identify and label emotional content.

According to the report of "MIT Technology Review", 2017, once the system read tweets for emotions, the researchers taught it to recognise sarcasm. According to MIT, the neural network learned the connection between a certain kind of language and an emoji.

Q.11. What are the Activation Functions?

Ans. In fig. 1.5, it was observed that a neuron has many weighted inputs coming in and one output going out. The inputs are summed. The value of the output is decided by the activation functions.

For examples,

Rectifier, outputs the sum of its weighted inputs but clips all negative values to zero. This implies that it will be generating quite a few zeros as zeros are good for training deeper networks but also means that positive values are unbounded.

Tanh, takes as input range of negative infinity to positive infinity. It converts that to an output range of –1 to +1. Note that it varies more rapidly when the sum of inputs is closer to zero.

Maxout, gives the maximum of the inputs. It means that the weighted inputs are used directly and not summed up.

Q.12. What are Feed Forward Neural Networks?

Ans. Single neurons are better and more powerful than linear perceptrons yet they are not very effective to solve complex problems. Just as our brain is made of many neurons so should be artificial neurons. In normal human brain, there are six layers. The information flows from one layer to another layer. The sensory input is converted into conceptual understanding. For instance, the bottommost layer of our brain receives raw data from our eyes. This information is the processed by each layer and passed on to the next layer and finally to the 6th layer. It is then we conclude that whether we are looking at a car or a bike. Our artificial neural network is analogous to this. A neural network is formed when we start attaching neurons to each other, the input data and to the output nodes. This corresponds to the network's answer to a learning problem. A simple three layer (or 3-tier) feed forward network is shown in figure 1.7:-

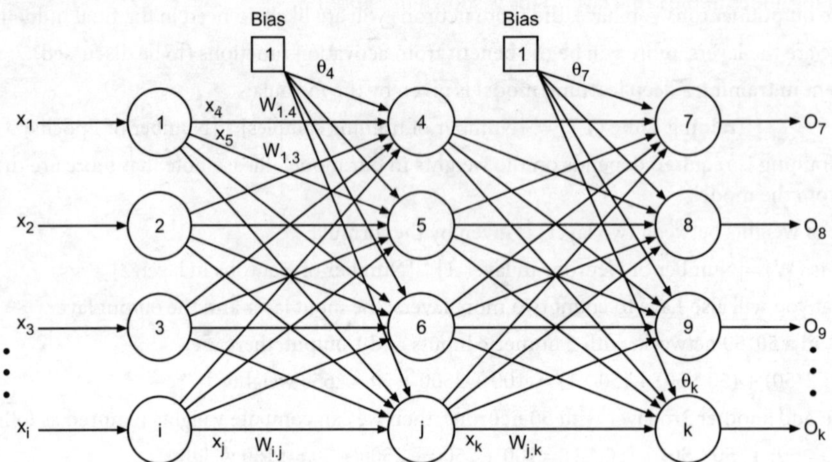

Fig. 1.7: Three-layer Feed- Forward Neural Network with inputs, 3 Hidden Layers, Outputs and Bias

Explanation: The network of neurons as shown in figure 1.7 is similar to the architecture given by McCulloch and Pitt in 1943. The bottom layer of the network takes the input data. The top layer of neurons or output nodes computes the final answer. The middle layer(*s*) of neurons are called as hidden layers. Now, if $W_{ij}(k)$ is the weight of connection between the ith neuron in the kth layer with the jth neuron in the k+1st layer; then these weights constitute a parameter vector, θ. And our ability to solve the problem with neural networks concept will depend on finding the optimal values of this parameter θ. **Please note that the connections traverse from a lower layer to a higher layer and there are no connections between neurons in the same layer. Also note that there are no connections that transmit data from a higher layer to a lower layer.** These types of neural networks are called as **feed-forward networks.** These networks are simple to analyze.

Before we discuss further, note down the following points:-

1. It is the hidden layer where actually the problem is being solved by our neural network. Hidden layers automate the process.
2. Hidden layers have fewer neurons than the input layer. Although input is taken from bottom layers yet hidden layers come up with better presentations for everything in output.
3. Every layer may or may not have the same number of neurons.
4. It is not mandatory that every neuron has its output connected to the inputs of all neurons in the next layer. It comes from experience only.
5. The inputs and outputs here are vectorized representations.

Q.13. Give some limitations of Neurons.

Ans. Any feed-forward neural network consisting of only linear neurons can be represented as a network with no hidden layers. This is an issue as hidden layers are the main processers of the input data. This implies that to learn complicated relationships, we need to use neurons that employ some sort of non-linearity too.

Q.14. What are Deep Belief Networks (DBNs) and RBNs?

Ans. To reduce the problems of conventional neural networks, a Deep Belief Network (DBN) uses a deep architecture that is capable of learning feature representations using both labelled and unlabelled big data. It incorporates both unsupervised pre-training and supervised fine-tuning techniques to construct models. Unsupervised pre-training tends to learn data distributions without using label information and supervised stages perform local search for fine tuning.

A DBM also comprises of a stack of a stack of Restricted Boltzmann Machines (RBM) that can effectively utilize large amounts of unlabelled data for exploring complex data structures. After DBN structure is determined, the goal for training is to learn the weights and biases between the layers. Firstly, unsupervised learning of RBMs is done. A typical RBM consists of two layers i.e., nodes in one layer are fully connected to the nodes in the other layer. There is no connection for nodes in the same layer. This is shown in figure 1.8.

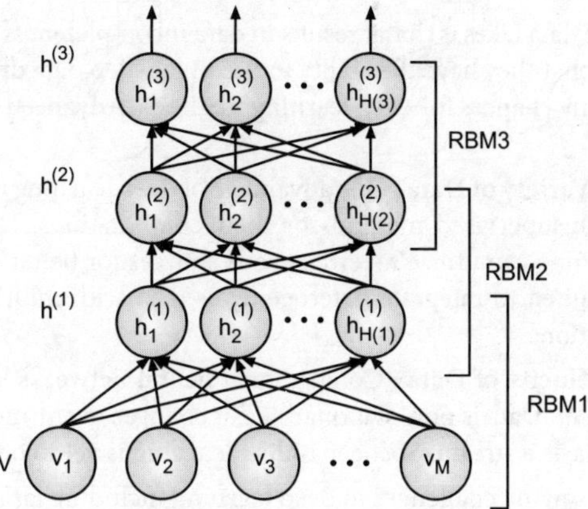

***Fig. 1.8:** DBN and RBM*

It is shown in figure 1.8 that nodes in one layer are fully connected to the nodes in the other layer. There are no connections for nodes in the same layer. The input layer and the first hidden layer H1 form a RBM. Each node is independent of the nodes in the same layer. Before fine-tuning, a layer by layer pre-training of RBM is performed. The outputs of a RBM are fed as inputs to the next RBM and the process is repeated until all RBMs are pre-trained. This is layer by layer unsupervised learning. **Please note that after pre-training information about the input data is stored in weights between every adjacent layers. Also note that DBNs use a greedy and efficient layer by layer approach to learn the latent variables/weights in each hidden layer and a back propagation method for fine-tuning.** So this hybrid training method improves both the generative performance and the discriminative power of the network.

a. **Large Scale DBNs :** To reduce the data transfer times between host and global memory and to allow parameter updates, one technique is to store all parameters and a large chunk of training examples in global memory during training. This shows the reusing of large chunks of training examples.

b. **Large Scale Convolutional Neural Networks :** Locally connected deep learning method is Convolutional Neural Networks (CNNs). Large scale CNNs learning is implemented on parallel processors. CNN training involves both forward and backward propagation. For this, one or more blocks are assigned for each feature map. Each thread in a block is shows a single neuron in a map. The computation of each neuron with the neurons from the previous layers, activation and summation is then performed. Finally, the outputs are stored in the global memory. Also, the weights are updated by back-propagation of errors. Parallelizing backward propagation can be implemented either by pulling or pushing. Pulling error signals is the process of computing delta signals for each neuron in the previous layer by pulling the error signals from the current layer. This is quite complex. On the other hand, pushing the error signals from the current layer to the previous layer is more efficient. That is, for each unit in the current layer, we update the related units in the previous layer.

Note: To implement data parallelism, we need to consider two things:-

a. The size of global memory.

b. The feature map size.

Q.15. Write notes on Deep Learning for Big Data.

Ans. Big data is at the core of our society today. The need is to process yottabytes (a billion petabytes) of data. Traditional machine learning algorithms are not sufficient as they were designed for data that could be stored in memory. But today data is "big". So, algorithms that can learn from massive amount of data are required now. Large scale deep learning is still in its infancy.

a. **Deep Learning from High Volumes of Data :** The data pool available today is a major challenge for deep learning today. The sheer volume of data results in run –time complexity and model complexity. These data lakes often make it impossible to train a deep learning algorithm with a central processor and storage. Hence, distributed machines and parallel machines are preferred. In nutshell, in order to build the future deep learning system scalable to Big Data, we need to develop high performance computing infrastructure-based systems. Also, we need parallel learning algorithms now.

Another problem with these data lakes is that it results in data incompleteness and noisy labels. One of the features of deep learning algorithms is that they have the ability to use unlabelled data during training. So, the presence of large unlabelled data presents many chances for deep learning methods. Advanced deep learning methods are required to handle noisy big data.

b. **Deep Learning from High Variety of Data :** One advantage of deep learning is its ability of representational learning with either supervised or unsupervised methods or their combinations. Deep learning can integrate data from different sources. Deep learning can utilize heterogeneous sources for better system performance. In nutshell, deep learning seems to be well suited to integrate heterogeneous data with multiple modalities due to its capability of learning abstract representations.

c. **Deep Learning for High Velocity of Data :** Conventional neural networks have been used for online learning but still the progress is insufficient. Data is non-stationary i.e. it changes over time. Deep learning algorithm for big data is the ability to learn the data as a stream. So, deep online learning is yet to be explored.

In nutshell, big data presents many challenges to deep learning including large scale, heterogeneity, noisy labels and non-stationary distribution etc.

Q.16. Explain Local Minima in Deep Networks.

Ans. The main issue in optimizing deep learning models is that we are now compelled to use minimal local information to infer global structure of the error surface. But this is not easy because the correspondence between local and global structure is quite less.

The first source of local minima is related to the term model identifiability. It has been observed that the error surface of deep neural networks is very large and sometimes infinite too. So, they have many local minima.

Q.17. How do we rearrange neurons in a layer of a Neural Network?

Ans. It has been observed that within a layer of a fully-connected feed-forward neural network, any rearrangement of neurons will still give us the same result (final output) at the end of the network. Also note that if a layer has n- neurons then there are n! ways to rearrange the parameters. But if it is a deep layered network, then with k layers, each with n neurons, we will have a total of n!k equivalent (similar) configurations.

Here, local minima is not a problem. Bit local minima are a problem if and only if they are spurious. We say that a local minima is spurious refers to those weights in neural network that incurs a higher error rate than at the global minima.

Q.18. What is spurious Local Minima in Deep Networks?

Ans. Researchers of deep learning say that it is difficult to train deep networks on spurious local minima. The point is that in practical neural networks spurious local minima and global minima have higher error rates. Some researchers say that most local minima have error rates similar to the global minima.

Given any function, a point at which the gradient is a zero vector is known as a critical point. Actually, local maxima do not cause much of the problems. The flat regions of the curve that are more trouble causing and informal are called as saddle points. Research shows that as our function adds up more and more parameters *i.e.* we have more and more parameters in our model, then saddle points rise exponentially than local minima. In one dimensional subspace, a critical point can come in three different types and hence the probability that the random critical point is in a random function is $1/3^d$.

Note: 1. If we have a total of '*k*' critical points, then we will have a total of $k/3$ local minima.

2. A random function with '*p*' critical points has an expected number of $p/3^d$.

Q.19. 'The Art and Science of AI, Machine Learning and Deep Learning is a boon for computer scientists.' Explain and support this statement.

Ans. Deep learning and Big Data are inter-related. Big data refers to the pools of data being generated every second while deep learning is an active research area in the field of machine learning. But as the data is growing at an exponential rate, deep learning is providing big data predictive analytical solutions. According to the report of National Security Agency (NSA), the Internet itself is processing 1,826 Petabytes of data per day [1]. By 2020, the figure will reach 35 Trillion gigabytes. This leads to a remarkable paradigm shift in computer science literature towards data-driven discovery. Today machine learning techniques and newer software, hardware and computational power help in big data as well as web data analytics. Neural network is a popular machine learning technology today. Its algorithm depicts the functioning of human brain to train a computational network. The aim is to identify the inherent patterns of data under investigation. There are thirty different packages of open source neural network software and R has a rich set of neural network packages. R provides a machine learning environment. The objective of this paper is to highlight the relationship between Artificial Intelligence, machine learning and deep learning technologies. Many tools to perform machine as well as deep learning are also quoted.

Deep learning is defined as the machine learning techniques that use supervised and/or unsupervised methods to automatically learn hierarchical representations in deep architectures for classification. Deep learning is a subset of artificial intelligence field called as machine learning which is predicted on the basic idea of learning from example.

Artificial Intelligence (AI), Machine Learning (ML) and Deep Learning (DL) being inter-related terms but are definitely different. The field of artificial intelligence refers to a non-algorithmic approach to problem solving. Within AI domain, there lies another solution and that is machine learning. But machine learning is not a rocket science. Machine learning further contains another active field named as deep learning. This is shown in figure-1. Deep learning harnesses the power of deep neural networks in order to train models on large data sets. The low trade-off between training time and computation errors makes it lucrative option for many businesses to switch to DL. However, there are very fuzzy differences between the three terms: AI, ML and DL. We put personal assistants and other forms of bots that aid with specialized tasks like playing games under AI. But practices like Big Data Analytics and data mining, pattern recognition are put under the spectrum of ML. These systems learn from data. And at last, the applications that cover a large corpus of text or image-based data used to train a model on Graphical Processing Units/ GPUs involve the use of DL algorithms.

Having only one hidden layer in a ANN gives us a limited capacity. Having multiple hidden layers is problematic. More layers and neurons mean longer training time and slower usage. The problem is in backpropagating the error to the previous layer (say from nth to n-1th layer) because then we also need to multiply the derivatives in all layers later on and also the gradient vanishes. **Please note that this is the reason as to why RNNs** (Recurrent Neural Networks) **learn very slowly. Also note that this does not happen in Convolutional Neural Networks because the fan-in and fan-out of hidden layers are usually small.**

Machine learning uses the following concepts:-

1. **Gradient Descent :** It is the first order iterative optimization algorithm for finding the minimum of a function. To find a local minimum of a function using gradient descent, one takes steps proportional to the negative of the gradient (or of approximate gradient) of the function at the current point gradient descent is also known as **steepest descent.**
2. **Feature Scaling :** It is a method used to standardize the range of independent variables or features of data. In data processing, it is also known as **data normalization** and is generally performed during the data pre-processing step. Without feature scaling, model cannot achieve convergence due to lack of similar values of features. Therefore, dataset will be normalized using **feature scaling.**

However, deep neural networks are useful here. **Deep Neural Networks** work on a **simple principle as stated-"Starting from raw input, each hidden layer combines the values in the preceding layer and learns more complicated functions of the input".** Also these successive hidden layers correspond to more abstract representations till we get to the output layer where outputs are learned in terms of these most abstract concepts. For instance, say we have a problem of drawing the digits on to the screen. We can start with pixels, then get edges from them, then corners and so on, until we get a digit. But users knowledge is must to define connectivity and the overall architecture.

A deep neural network is usually trained one layer at a time. The task of each layer is to extract the salient features in the data that is fed to it. To do this a method like autoencoder can be used. To do this, a procedure is followed as follows:-

1. Raw input is used to train the autoencoder.
2. The encoded representation is learned in its hidden layer.

3. This is given as a input to the next autoencoder and so on.
4. Until we get the final layer.
5. Train this final layer now in a supervised manner with labelled data.
6. Train all layers this way one by one.
7. All layers are then assembled.
8. Whole of the network is fine-tuned with labelled data.

Also it has been found that deep learning needs lesser manual interference. Hence, they are better. We have "big data" today along with many calculation methods. We must wait and let the learning algorithm discover all that is mandatory, itself.

Data science is one of the roots that support the tree of the digital world. **Data science refers to the synergy of statistics with data analysis so as to analyze and relate real world activities with data.** According to the turing award winner, jim gray, data science is the 4th paradigm of science. He stresses on datafication and defines it as the process of taking different aspects of life and tuning these to data. We need to take the help of different data science techniques to extract useful parts out of the collected information during datafication. But is has been found that the availability of large data is directly proportional to the difficulty of developing new predictive models that work accurately. This drawback has been overcome by ml and dl. The role of machine learning in data science includes-

- Ml helps a learner to analyze this large data pool and hence simplifies the tasks of data scientists.
- Ml involves several automatic sets of generic methods unlike old statistical methods.
- Ml makes making of intelligent applications more intelligent and data-driven and thereby improves their operations.
- Ml acts as a catalyst to make data science more meaningful.

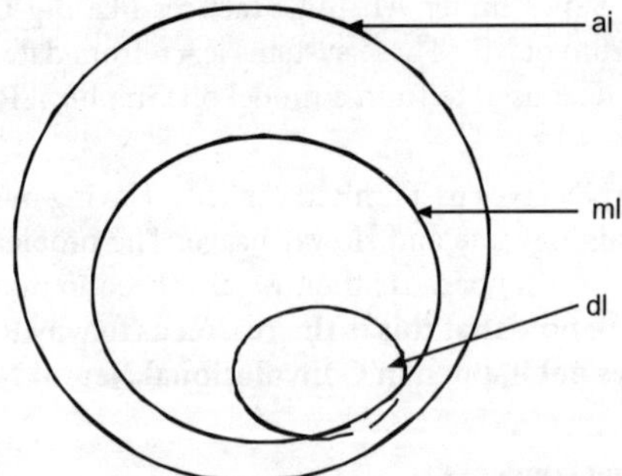

***Fig. 1.9:** Relation between AI, Machine Learning and Deep Learning*

From figure-1.9 , it is clear that DL $\subset$ ML $\subset$ AI. As compared to other machine learning algorithms, deep learning requires much more data in order to observe and understand every minute detail to make the right decisions.

Deep learning is a recent improvement in ML domain. The basic need of ML is to identify and build a feature set. This task is generally done by researchers involved in ML field. So, for each problem domain customized features need to be built by human experts. This creates a bottleneck in overall process flow. DL differs from traditional ML in the way features are built. It tries to build features automatically from the given large data set. The word 'large' is emphasized here. The point to highlight is that for dl to work at a descent accuracy level, we need large sized data sets. This is quite vital as ML needs 'big data' so as to detect the distinctive features of a set. Today, feature engineering is an important branch of any ml related project. Even big data and ml are inter-related. As data is growing exponentially, deep learning is providing big data predictive analytical solutions. Current ML techniques and newer software, hardware and computational power help in web data analytics.

Machine learning is now a valuable supplement and an ultimate assistant to the analyst. Deep learning will supercharge analysts and make them more efficient, precise and more impactful to the business. IDC reports that by 2020, machine learning systems will increase revenues to $46 billion. According to Gartner, by 2020, AI will create 2.3 million jobs and will eliminate 1.8 million jobs. Thus, the AI impact will be as follows:-

$$\text{AI Impact} = (2.3 - 1.8) = 0.5 \text{ million jobs}$$

Everyone can play with data. Data analytics has become an art and less of science. Also Gartner reports that by 2020, 50% of analytical queries will be generated using search, Natural Language Processing or voice. Both developers and engineers will make strides in learning and understanding of how people use NLP. It is a funnel-type approach that has valuable perspectives and information that motivates innovative ways to implement governance. This makes business users to find the data they need. 45% of data citizens say that less than half of their reports have data of good quality. As per the report of Penome in 2017, the average total cost of a data breach was estimated to be $3.62 million and that only 15% of US companies have an insurance policy for their data. Data is the fuel of a company but data breaches have been crippling company's data. The data engineer is responsible for designing, building and managing a business's operational and analytics databases. They are responsible for extracting data from the foundational systems of the business. They need to understand the data at backend and how it can serve the business user. The data engineer has to make this data usable by developing newer technical solutions. Data scientists and analysts can spend as much as 80% of their time cleaning and preparing data.

Gartner predicts that by 2020, the number of IoT devices that are available to customers will be more than double. The trend is to move from IoT to LoT i.e. from Internet-of-Things to Location-of-Things. According to Gartner, by 2020 IoT will exceed to more than $5 billion. By 2021, 69% of the employers will demand data science and analytics as a skill set for jobs. A recent MIT survey found that 40% of managers had trouble hiring analytical talent.

Big data is at the core of our society today. The need is to process yottabytes (a billion petabytes) of data [1]. Traditional machine learning algorithms are not sufficient as they were designed for data that could be stored in memory. But today data is "big". So, algorithms that can learn from big data are required now. Large scale deep learning is still in its infancy.

The data pool available today is a major challenge for deep learning today. The sheer volume of data results in run –time complexity and model complexity. These data lakes make learning difficult with the present day cpus. Hence, we need distributed computing and parallel computing. Future deep learning systems that are scalable to big data, are needed now. Also we need parallel learning algorithms now.

These data lakes have a problem. It results in data incompleteness and noisy labels. One of the features of deep learning algorithms is that they have the ability to use unlabelled data during training. So, the presence of large data presents many chances for deep learning methods. Better deep learning methods are required to handle noisy big data.

Deep learning has an ability of representational learning with either supervised or unsupervised methods or their combinations. Deep learning can integrate data from different sources. Deep learning can utilize heterogeneous sources for better system performance.

Traditional neural networks have been used for online learning but still the progress is insufficient. Data is non-stationary i.e. it changes over time. So, deep online learning is yet to be explored.

Many DL libraries are available in literature. Some of them are as follows:

- caffe.
- theano.
- torch.
- deeplearning4j (dl4j).
- mocha.

Most of the DL / ML libraries are in python. But dl4j is based on JVM. This is due to several reasons as follows:

- there are trillions of JAVA developers.
- Java is the basis of many powerful tools like hadoop, elastic search, lucene and hive.
- Python is low while java is fast. So, when handling projects with pools of data sets, java is a better choice.
- Java is secure and cross-platform based *i.e.* it can be used on Linux, Win, OSx and Android.

dl4j is compatible with mobile phones having android. To do this, two things are needed:

a. Emulator with API level 21 or above.

b. Android Studio 2.2 or later.

dl4j supports many powerful neural networks like convolutional networks, recurrent networks, restricted Boltzmann machines, deep belief networks etc.

ML applications range from diagnosis of diseases to weather forecasting. Machine learning is implied from a variety of areas like AI, probability and statistics, computational complexity, information theory, psychology, neurobiology, control theory and philosophy. It also includes several other applications like-

- Google's self-driving car.
- Cyber fraud detection.
- Optical character recognition (OCR).

A system is said to be intelligent if it can learn in a changing environment. ML is to program the computers in order to do performance optimization on the basis of example data or past experience. We develop a model using some parameters and then perform learning on it. It implies that we execute a computer program to optimize the parameters of the model using the training data or past experiences. This model may be predictive to make predictions in future or descriptive to gain knowledge from data. Learning may involve searching also. From a set of hypothesis, say, H_1, H_2, ...H_n , we need to find (or search) the best hypothesis that best fits the available training examples. And to achieve this, there are two algorithms in literature:-

- The Perceptron Training Rule (if training examples are linearly separable).
- The Delta Rule (if the training examples are not linearly separable).

The central core concept of learning is to move from specific training examples to general functions.

Several case tools for deep learning also exist. Some of these free and open source tools are as follows:

- Apache mahout
- Scikit-learn
- Openai
- TensorFlow
- Char-mn
- PaddlePaddle
- Cntx
- Apache Singa
- Deeplearning y_j
- H_2O etc

Google's machine learning software TensorFlow, Google Analytics, speech recognition and optical character recognition solves many complex problems.

Just as IBM offers Watson's deep learning, MS has Azure Cloud and Facebook has open-source caffe. Also Amazon has MX Net, an open source deep learning software.

Machine learning, does not involves teaching of a computer a bulky list of rules to solve the complex problem. Rather we frame a model with which it can evaluate examples. Also we give it a small set of instructions to modify the model when it makes a mistake. Please note that we have an expectation that as the time passes, a well suited model would be able to solve the problem more accurately. For example, say our model is defined by a function f(x, θ). The input x is an example expressed in vector form. Like, if x were a gray-scale image, the vector's components would be pixel intensities at each position. The input θ is a vector of the parameters that our model uses. Also note now that it is our machine learning program that tries to perfect the values of these parameters as it is exposed to more and more examples. The conventional learning methods are shallow-structured learning architectures while deep learning is deep-hierarchical levelled learning architecture. In 2014, it was observed that a training set with a huge set in a shallow net, with one fully connected feed-forward hidden layer on the available data, yielded 86% of the test data. But if this same data set was trained in a deeper neural net consisting of a convolutional layer, pooling layer and three fully-connected feed-forward layers on the same data, 91% accuracy on the same test set was obtained. Thus, an increase of 5% in the accuracy of the deep net over the shallow net occurs due to the following reasons:-

a. The deep net has more parameters.

b. The deep net can learn more complex functions, given the same number of parameters.

c. The deep net has better bias and learns more interesting or useful functions leading to invention and improvement of many algorithms.

It is based on the biological neurons within human brain. Several research domains like speech recognition, natural language processing (NLP), collaborative filtering and computer vision. Big industry giants like Google, Apple and Facebook who work on sheer size of data lakes today have also given vital importance to big data analytics and web data analytics. Google applies deep learning algorithms to massive chunks of messy data obtained from internet. IBMs brain-like computer uses techniques like deep learning to make available big data available for its betterment. Please note that as the data keeps increasing at an exponential rate, deep learning is playing a key role in providing in big data and web analytics. **Also note that deep learning refers to a set of machine learning techniques that learn multiple levels of representations in deep architectures.** Deep learning is the new name for neural networks. Deep learning algorithms have best performance as far as complex problems like pattern recognition are concerned. Practically speaking, even machine learning approaches find it difficult to solve. Theoretically, they can solve any problem. Several libraries also exist for neural nets or deep learning. But deep learning algorithms as an auto-encoder i.e. unsupervised deep learning, several parameters and slower deep learning grids are some of the issues to be discussed in this chapter. These programs may need more hardware.

Q.20. Throw some light on the recent advances made in the field of data science in terms of machine and deep learning.

Ans. Some of the related studies in this field are as follows-

In [1], Xue-Wen-Chen and Lin have explained the deep learning networks and their symbiotic relationship with big data. But they have not explained the concept of training with an example or a case study.

Nikhil Buduma [2] explain the fundamentals of deep learning networks. But its relation with big data has not been discussed.

In [3], Darren cook has explained the usage of deep learning tool namely, h_2o. Its installation steps with codes and some samples have been given. But they have not explained the entire deep training process.

In [4], John Paul Mueller et al. use R and Python to show how machine learning algorithms can be implemented.

In [5], Tianchuan Du, Vijay K. Shankar explains different application of deep learning. But it does not compare deep learning with big data and how deep networks can be trained.

In 2005, Ray Kurzweil authored a book entitled as 'The Singularity is Near'. The word 'singularity' here refers to the hybridization of humanity with AI to multiply its own intelligence many fold. Jon Von Neumann, who gave the concept of stored memory used this term 'singularity' to explain the flood of changes as caused by technological process. Ray Kurzweil claims that the world will attain this singularity by 2045. Also he explains that AI has an ability to achieve human levels of intelligence, as measured by the Turing Test. And this will be achieved by 2029, says Kurzweil.

On December 5, 2017, researchers at Deep Mind (now owned by Google's parent Alphabet Inc.) wrote a paper on AlphaZero that is an AI program that learns that there is to chess in four hours and then wiped the floor with the world's most powerful open-source chess engine. Deep Mind moved from the realm of sci-fi to reality with its concept of deep learning (the programs that teach themselves things). The success of AI is evident from Big Data that helps the program learn. AlphaZero uses the concept of reinforcement learning that is based on the concept of rewards and punishments. It indicates that the target of 2029 will be achieved easily and much before.

According to the reports of McKinsey Global Institute, high tech, telecom and financial services will be the earliest adopters of machine learning in the world while in India alone these would be the healthcare, HR and e-commerce.

According to the Director, Machine Learning, Amazon, "we use machine learning to identify fraudulent sellers based on the huge past data". Things that human would have done by looking at them are being done by APIs and algorithms today. And this can be done in less than three days.

Recently, Google introduced 'Google Glass'. It just needs users 'look-through' and it would retrieve information about it. Even images may be used for look-up. Technology has today progressed a lot wherein we just need to 'look up' the global collective memory. Google handles more than 4 billion search queries per day.

Human brains are quite poor at indexing. So, we search the web. Google's million servers regularly crawl and index over 50 billion web pages (estimate).

Web pages are stored based on some model of memory so that the PageRank algorithm can be applied.

Researchers suggest a 'semantic model' for the same. In this model, pairs of words are associated with each other in some way as being synonyms of each other or one a generalization of the other.

As per the survey report of Brown University, it used a semantic model of about 5000 common words i.e. a network of word-associations pairs. They executed the PageRank algorithm using the network of web pages and hyperlinks. This produces a ranking of all the words by importance.

Experiments in 2007 reports that roughly 2.5% of random sample of web pages were forms that should be considered as part of deep web. Google approach is to automatically try out many possible inputs and input combinations for a deep web page and to find out that gives better results. These results are then stored internally in Google index. This makes them part of the surface web.

Kosmix (2010) classified popular web-based services considering both automated and human assisted processes. Searching deep-web is one of the current areas of research today.

In another report, the FBI investigator, Robert Fuller searched a commercial database (named as CheckPoint) to search for some terrorist of 9/11 attacks. This database stored personal information on US residents like their mobile numbers and addresses. Later a journalist, Bob Wood ward quoted that if FBI would have done a simple credit card check then they would have found that two men bought 8 tickets for morning flights. Now this is web knowledge and it would have stopped the attacks.

Data may be structured or unstructured. In its crude form, data has lesser value. But if data is corrected for errors, aggregated, normalized, calculated or categorized then its value grows dramatically.

Till 2012, 2.5 exabytes (approx.) of data is created each day. This volume comes from both new data variables and the amount of data records in those variables. The outcome is now to possess mountains of data that can provide the building blocks to information generation through analytics.

As per the latest IBM report :

a. 2.5 petabytes is memory capacity of human brain.

b. 13 petabytes is the amount that could be downloaded from internet in 2 mins., if every American (300M) got on a computer at the same time.

c. 4.75 exabytes-total genome sequences of all people on Earth about 7 billion in 2015.

d. 422 exabytes- total digital data created in 2008.

e. 1 zetabyte- world's digital storage capacity in 2013.

In another report by IDC, Digital Universe is doubling in size every two years.

By 2020, the digital Universe will reach 44 zettabytes. Between 2013 and 2020, the division of the digital Universe between mature and emerging markets will switch from 60% accounted for by mature markets to 60% of the data in digital Universe coming from emerging markets.

As of 2012, everyday 2.5 exabytes (*i.e.* 2.5 * 1018) of data are created. IDC and EMC [5] project that data will grow to 40 zettabytes by 2020, resulting in a 50-fold growth from the beginning of 2010.

The results of a global study by CA Technologies has revealed that Enterprise Big Data strategies are delivering key benefits to organizations. 44% of the Indian respondents have already implemented a Big Data project while 36% plan to implement one in the coming year. Also 12% of the Indian respondents have stated that they have implemented four Big Data projects to date.

The study, titled The State of Big Data Infrastructure lists five major obstacles for successful implementation of Big Data, insufficient existing infrastructure (33%), organizational complexity (25%), security concerns (28%), lack of budget/ resources (25%) and lack of visibility into information and processes (21%).

Big Data strategy will improve customer experience (67%), need to enter new markets (52%) and need to get new customers (49%).

As per the survey done by EY on Big Data and enterprise mobility in India with 110 IT leaders across industry sectors to understand the relevance of Big Data and enterprise mobility in the Indian context:-

1. More than 60% of organizations define Big Data as large volumes of unstructured data. Less than 20% of organizations consider Big Data as "hype" or the latest technology buzzword.
2. About 60% acknowledge that unstructured information is growing out of control and is driving Big Data explosion, with unstructured data expected to grow at a faster rate (30-40%) than structured data (30%) over the next 3-5 years.
3. Half of the large organizations plan to use data from social networks for sentimental analysis and customer tracking.
4. About 80% of organizations are in early stages of Big Data initiatives and 60% are still in their infancy stage.
5. 75% of organisations are confident of driving new renenue streams using Big Data. However, only 35% plan to invest in building Big Data capabilities related to analytics, security software and real-time applications.

There is a huge potential for Big Data technologies in India. This is a high growth economy and organizations depend on insights from raw data, to plan their future course. Big Data Analytics helped in parts, responsible for NDA to win

General Elections in 2014.

Several global Big Data players have sprouted in India over the past two years. Sears, for instance, established a wholly-owned subsidiary MetaScale to service healthcare and entertainment customers with revenues between US$1 million and US$ 10 million. A @WalmartLabs facility also opened in Bangalore in April to develop social media and analytics and Big Data infrastructure. In July, Yahoo set up a grid computing lab at IIT Madras campus.

eBay[4] uses two data warehouses at 7.5 petabytes and 40PB as well as a 40PB Hadoop cluster for searching.

Amazon.com handles millions of back-end operations every day as well as the queries from more than half a million third-party sellers. Amazon , by 2005, had the world's three largest Linux databases with capacities of 7.8 TB, 18.5 TB and 24.7 TB.

In 2012, the Big Data Research and Development Initiative, was to find how Big Data could be used to address important problems faced by the government. The Utah Data Center is a data center currently has the facility to handle an exact amount of storage space is unknown but more recent sources claim it will be of the order of a few exabytes.

Facebook handles 50 billion photos from its database. Google was handling roughly 100 billion searches per month, till August 2012.

Big data is at the core of our society today. We are not only the generator but also a consumer of data. The need is to process yottabytes (a billion petabytes) of data [1]. Traditional machine learning algorithms are not sufficient as they were designed for data that could be stored in memory. But today data is "big". So, algorithms that can learn from massive amount of data are required now. Large scale deep learning is still in its infancy.

Q.21. Explain Deep Learning in terms of 6 V's of big data.

Ans. Web has resulted in deluge (flood) of data. Today data is the fuel of growth and innovation. Data may be structured (like RDBMS) or unstructured (like twitter data), real or non-real, data at rest (static data) or data in motion (dynamic data). But data is very informative. The challenge is to save it and then filter out only relevant and mandatory data This is so because of its sheer volume. Web consists of millions of servers with data store of sizes in zetabytes (1 zetabyte = 1000 patabytes; 1 petabyte = 1000GB; 1 exabyte = 1000 patabytes). Big data refers to the voluminous data which resembles to that of a gold mine. A gold mine has lesser gold but other things are more. Similarly, relevant data is less in Big Data but other types of data are more. Thus, analytics of Web and Big Data is a must.

Big Data Analytics (BDA) refers to the process of examining data, typically of a variety of sources, types, volumes and/or complexities-to uncover hidden patterns, unknown correlations and other useful information [1].

Web analytics is the measurement, collection, analysis and reporting of web data for the purpose of understanding and optimizing web usage [1-2]. It is not just a tool for measuring web traffic but can also be used as a tool for business and market research and to assess and improve the effectiveness of a web site.

According to the Kryder's Law-"Storage capacity per dollar is growing much faster rather than the computing power per dollar that appears to double every 18 months (Moore's Law)." So, both the computing power as well as the raw data are available now. The collaborative use of AI techniques at web scale on several millions of servers has resulted in giving a basic form of intelligence called as 'human intelligence'. It is the application of web-scale computing power on voluminous big data (due to Internet) has given birth to 'Web Intelligence'.

The data pool available today is a major challenge for deep learning today. The sheer volume of data results in run – time complexity and model complexity. These data lakes often make it impossible to train a deep learning algorithm with a central processor and storage. Hence, distributed machines and parallel machines are preferred. In nutshell, in order to build the future deep learning system scalable to Big Data, we need to develop high performance computing infrastructure-based systems. Also, we need parallel learning algorithms now. It is believed by the researchers that some new hardware is needed to make machine learning easy. The main objective of ML is to use computers to learn from massive amounts of data. ML forms the core of AI in this age of big data. Machines need to be trained with enormous amount of data for them to churn out the kind of result expected of them.

Another problem with these data lakes is that it results in data incompleteness and noisy labels. One of the features of deep learning algorithms is that they have the ability to use unlabelled data during training. So, the presence of large unlabelled data presents many chances for deep learning methods. Advanced deep learning methods are required to handle noisy big data.

Deep Learning from High Variety of Data : One advantage of deep learning is its ability of representational learning with either supervised or unsupervised methods or their combinations. Deep learning can integrate data from different sources. Deep learning can utilize heterogeneous sources for better system performance. In nutshell, deep learning seems to be well suited to integrate heterogeneous data with multiple modalities due to its capability of learning abstract representations.

Deep Learning for High Velocity of Data : Conventional neural networks have been used for online learning but still the progress is insufficient. Data is non-stationary i.e. it changes over time. Deep learning algorithm for big data is the ability to learn the data as a stream. So, deep online learning is yet to be explored.

Deep Learning for High Vulnerability of Data : Web Data, Web Information, Web Knowledge and Web Intelligence are related to each other. Raw web data when processed becomes more meaningful information which when processed further becomes web knowledge. In web knowledge, lays the power!! Web knowledge when further processed, it becomes Web Intelligence [14].

The researchers have already explored on five (5) V's of Big Data i.e. Volume, Velocity, Veracity, Variety and Value. The complexity of Big Data has given birth to another V i.e. Vulnerability of Big Data. By vulnerability, it means that the web data can be easily stolen if its security level is not high.

Web Data, Web Information, Web Knowledge and Web Intelligence are inter-related.

Raw web data when processed becomes more meaningful information which when processed further becomes web knowledge. In web knowledge, lies the power!! Web knowledge when further processed, it becomes Web Intelligence.

The complexity of this data has resulted in another factor- **Vulnerability of Big Data.**

The researchers have already explored on five (5) V's of Big Data i.e. Volume, Velocity, Veracity, Variety and Value. The complexity of Big Data has given birth to another V i.e. Vulnerability of Big Data. By vulnerability, it means that the web data can be easily stolen if its security level is not high.

As 'machines' work on 'thinking', similarly web-based engines are focal points today. Web knowledge, so obtained can result in more of web intelligence. So, web –intelligence programs that have their own ability to understand us and this world are needed. A web intelligence program looks at the data stored in or moving on Internet. Web intelligent systems learn about our preferences and behavior.

Newly developed self-driving cars are possible as web provides us both information and a communication platform. Web intelligence systems will evolve synergistically with our social intelligence using web itself.

No inference is possible in absence of right input data. Such logical inferences may be automatically conducted by machines while the knowledge may be learned from experience.

On millions of servers, several copies of web index are stored. This increases processing speeds. The information on web that is indexed by the search engines (like Google) is called as the 'surface web'. On the other hand, 'deep web' consists of data hidden behind web-based services. The point is that the volume of data within deep web is huge, exponentially large and of infinite size. Also it is to be pointed out here that this deep web is huge and even bigger than an indexed web of 50 billion pages.

As 'machines' work on 'thinking', similarly web-based engines are focal points today. Web knowledge, so obtained can result in more of web intelligence. So, web –intelligence programs that have their own ability to understand us and this world are needed. A web intelligence program looks at the data stored in or moving on Internet.

Web intelligent systems learn about our preferences and behavior. The idea that machines can think got originated by a British mathematician, Alan Turing. On one hand, AI is hailed as the frontier of the next technological revolution. On the other hand, it is seen as a fear as it is believed to have the potential to surpass human intelligence. Even then the research continues unfettered by these fears.

Newly developed self-driving cars are possible as web provides us both information and a communication platform. Web intelligence systems will evolve synergistically with our social intelligence using web itself.

No inference is possible in absence of right input data. Such logical inferences may be automatically conducted by machines while the knowledge may be learned from experience.

On millions of servers, several copies of web index are stored. This increases processing speeds. The information on web that is indexed by the search engines (like Google) is called as the 'surface web'. On the other hand, 'deep web' consists of data hidden behind web-based services. The point is that the volume of data within deep web is huge, exponentially large and of infinite size. Also it is to be pointed out here that this deep web is huge and even bigger than an indexed web of 50 billion pages.

For a machine to learn, a huge dataset (big data) that can be well managed by the algorithms is needed. The aim is to do pattern recognition. Pattern recognition will use a simple subset to make predictions of the dataset as a whole. Statistics is one of the methods used by machine learning. It along with big data forms machine learning. This may be put in an equation form also:-

$$\text{Big Data} + \text{Statistics} = \text{Machine Learning} \quad (1)$$

Algorithms will find out how a machine interprets big data. This algorithm will affect machine learning and its results. To achieve this, an algorithm of machine learning must be trained too. It is the training process that modifies how the algorithm views big data. We define the training process as the process of using a subset of the data as a method for creating patterns that the algorithm needs to recognize specific cases from the more general cases. It depends on how you store the dataset- in memory or in a hard disk. Storing dataset in memory makes processing faster while it will be costlier to store it in hard disk. In training process, we know the input datsets and the outputs data sets. And the learner algorithm uses this input dataset to create a function, that is, we are trying to generalize the output function so that it starts working on the data beyond the training set too.

The complexity, the depth and the privacy of big data (vulnerability) cannot be ignored. The machine learning algorithm should be able to take all types of information as an input. Also the data that is taken from private sources is more consistent as compared to the data taken from public sources. Also note that machine learning works on 80: 20 rule. This means that 'machine learning usually works on 80% of the data while 20% of the cases also need humans that decide on how to react and act on data. Every company has data hidden at various places. Only the point is to recognize data as data and to create mashups that represent the existing data as a new kind of data. Big data can come from any source like from your emails too. The need is to divide the data into two parts- training data and testing data. The algorithm should be a master algorithm i.e. an algorithm that can learn anything. And understanding the role of algorithms is vital to define how machine learning works. So, even in machine learning everything revolves around these algorithms only. An algorithm is a type of container that stores methods to solve a particular type of a problem. Algorithms will process this data through a series of well defined states. The ultimate goal is to create an output that solves a problem. The focal point is the output.

The need is to move from 'neurons' to the 'silicon'. The principle is that a single neuron solves a small piece of the problem while many neurons in parallel will solve the problem as a whole. This is a 'divide-and-conquer' strategy. The backpropagation algorithm or backward propagation of errors refers to the process of removing errors from the networks that are built and are similar to our human brain's neurons by changing the weights and the biases of the network. We continue changing these weights and the biases until the actual output matches the target output. The artificial neuron fires and passes its solution to the next neuron in line. The solution created by just one neuron is only the part of the whole solution. Each neuron passes information to the next neuron in line until the group of neurons creates a final output.

Machine learning has its focus on efficiency of solving problems like medical diagnosis, data mining, bioinformatics, speech and handwriting recognition, product categorization, capture technology and information retrieval.

It is the synergy of Artificial Intelligence and Machine Learning that forms Machine Intelligence. So, machine learning involves many aspects like machine intelligence, website testing and quality analytics. Website testing may involve intelligent static code analysis and intelligent test automation. A machine tool like, TestRail is useful here.

Currently, machine learning has been used for filtering out of spam mails. This has been named as a spam-filter. It uses the concept of Naïve Baye's classifier. For building a classifier, we need to describe a set of features which convey what a spam looks like in comparison to a non-spam message. This requires extensive research, perhaps building our own dictionary from scratch. Since text cannot be used as a direct input to machine learning algorithms, so we use certain techniques to extract features from text. The objective here is to derive features from a given message. A statistical analysis of the data is a pre-requisite before we start building a model for our classifier and use the collected data for the purposes of training it. The goal is to retain the information the message conveys while attempting to convert it into something our algorithm can work on *i.e.* Working on unstructured text that we gather in such a way that the meaning can still be derived from it.

Based on the features gathered for the training data, we select a classifier which promises the highest accuracy and is feasible to adapt to the change in training data. Naive Bayes is a collection of classification algorithms based on Bayes theorem. It is not a single algorithm but a family of algorithms that all share a common principle that every feature being classified is independent of the value of any other feaure. For instance, a fruit may be considered to be an apple if it is red, round and about 3" in diameter. A Naïve Nayes classifier considers each of the 'features' (red, round, 3" diameter) to contribute independently to the probability that the fruit is an apple, regardless of any correlation between features. Features, however, are not always independent which is often seen as a shortcoming of the Naïve Bayes algorithm. That is why it is named as "naïve.

In nutshell, the algorithm allows us to predict a class, given a set of features using probability.

Pros and cons of Naïve Bayes-

Advantages :

a. It is relatively simple to understand and build.

b. It is easily trained even with small dataset.

c. It is fast.

d. It is not sensitive to irrelevant features.

Disadvantages-

1. It assumes every feature is independent, which is not always the case.

A simple example best explains the application of naïve bayes for classification. So, let us say that we have data on 1000 pieces of fruit. The fruit being a banana, orange or some other fruit and imagine we know 3 features of each fruit, whether it is long or not, sweet or not and yellow or not. From the data we know that-

a. 50% of the fruits are bananas.

b. 30% are oranges.

c. 20% are other fruits.

Based on the training set we can say that:-

- From 500 bananas, 400 (0.8) are long, 350 (0.7) are sweet and 450 (0.9) are yellow.
- Out of 300 oranges 0 are long, 150 (0.5) are sweet and 300(1) are yellow.
- From the remaining 200 fruits, 100 (0.5) are long, 150(0.75) are sweet and 50 (0.25) are yellow.

Which should provide enough evidence to predict the class of another fruit as it is introduced. So, let us say that we are given the features of a piece of fruit and we need to predict the class. If we are told that the additional fruit is long, sweet and yellow, we can classify it using some mathematics and subbing in the values for each outcome, whether it is a banana, an orange or some other fruit. The one with the highest probability (score) be the winner. In this case, based on the higher score (0.01875 lt 0.252) we can assume this long, sweet and yellow fruit is, in fact, a banana. This example shows Naïve Bayes in action. Such a method can also be applied to text classification problems like spam detection, sentiment analysis and categorization.

How to classify emails as spam or as ham?

The following steps may be followed: -

Step-1: Preparing the dataset: Multiple email datasets found online are combined. The need is to normalize the datasets and make raw data ready for further processing. The datasets may be taken from multiple online resources. These include the famous ENRON dataset, UCI machine learning labs and CSDMC2010 spam corpus. To give the dataset a more personalized training and avoiding overfitting, we drew more than 500 emails from our personal accounts using the Gmail API. The normalized set was combined into one comma separated file. All tuples had two common attributes: a keyword which labels them either, ham or spam, the contents of the messages itself and the subject of the message. A 2nd classifier can be trained in order to keep a track of the IP address of the sender and label repeated IP addresses. Once the dataset is on the same level, the next process was feature extraction. The dataset is imported into a data frame and the necessary attributes are understood and filtered. Spam filtering is a simple text classification problem. We need to calculate the proportional occurrence of each word in the given dataset with respect to the words in the email and in the document as a whole.

Step-2: Training the classifier: In machine learning, vectors are used for single columns or data and matrices for larger arrays because of the linear algebra roots of machine learning. Modern CPUs have the ability to take the list of numbers and apply the same mathematical operation to many numbers in parallel. This capability is called as single instruction, multiple data (SIMD). Instead of looping through each array element one at a time, the CPU can load chinks of the array into memory and do all of the multiplications on the chink in one step. So, we replace iterative loops with vector operations that can be executed in parallel.

Step-3: Connect to Gmail and Twitter: The classifier is good if it can take in new data from the users accounts such as an inbox or a social media stream and predict its nature i.e. whether it is a spam or a ham. To implement this, we need separate modules that make calls to the Gmail API and Twitter API. In order for these APIs to work, we first need to create an application on both the websites. The access token then allows us to maintain an active stream which triggers a procedure when a certain event occurs. For instance, the Gmail API allows us to listen for new incoming messages for a given user via an application. In the event we receive an email we may set a procedure, module or snippet of the code to be executed. The module imports the incoming message along with all its attributes. This message is returned as a json file. We only store that attributes that we need into a comma separated file and loaded into a data frame. These messages are then fed to the trained classifier as inputs and the model gives a relevant output, labelling the message as either ham or spam.

Step-4: Uploading the modules to a remote server: a trained model working on a 'localhost' with an active internet connection allowing it to retrieve the emails and tweets is good but not ideal for a person with limited technical skills. It is better if the application works on a remote server as it does not rely on the users personal computer to be running or the user operating the execution of the program from the terminal or a command line interface. For instance we can upload the project to an Amazon web server and execute its instance. To do so, Python must be installed on our web server and then push all our project files to the server.

Step-5: Correction for Overfitting is done at this step.

And this is clear from the CASE STUDY as discussed in the next section.

CASE STUDY (quadratic equation problem):

The following steps may be followed to solve a complex machine learning problem:-

Step-1: Problem Definition. The problem definition must be complete, unambiguous, clear and concise.

Queries like what is the problem? Why the problem must be solved using machine learning only? How should the problem be solved?

Step-2: Data should be prepared now.

Step-3: Search for different types of learning algorithms. They must be simple and clear. They contain huge amount of mathematics and theory.

Step-4: Learning Algorithms that perform well must be tuned.

Step-5: Visual Analysis of the results must be done. Data visualization is the best way to learn more about our data.

Using these steps, a case study on finding out the roots of a given quadratic equations has also been taken into consideration in this chapter.

The aim is to learn machine learning concepts and understand the training procedure of a neural network. ML is used in many areas, ranging from diagnosis of diseases to weather forecasting. To illustrate the process of training, consider a simple example of finding out the roots of a given quadratic equation as follows:

$$ax^2 + bx + c = 0 \qquad (2)$$

Then we define its discriminant, $d = b^2 - 4 * a * c$

If $d > 0$ then the roots are real.

If $d = 0$ then the roots are equal.

If $d < 0$ then the roots are imaginary.

The coefficients (a, b, c) are processed to eliminate the linear equations with negative values of d *i.e.* when $d < 0$, a neural net is trained with these datasets. Coefficients and roots are numerical vectors and they have been converted to the data frame for further operations.

Training datasets consists of three coefficients with ten values each-

aa ← c(1, 1, -3, 1, -5, 2, 2, 2, 1, 1)

bb ← *c*(5, –3, –1, 10, 7, –7, 1, 1, –4, –25)

cc ← *c*(6, –10, –1, 24, 9, 3, –4, 4, –21, 156)

Data pre-processing is then done.

To discard equations with zero as coefficients of x_2, we write the code. We also need to write the code for which d=0 or more.

Calculate the roots of valid equations using conventional formulae, for training and verification of machine's result at a later stage. That is,

$$r1, r2 \leftarrow -b + \sqrt{d} / 2a$$

After getting all coefficients and roots of equations, concatenate them column-wise to form I/O datasets of a Neural Net. So,

training data ← cbind (*a*, *b*, *c*, *r*1, *r*2)

In this case study (of quadratic equation roots), the network is quite simple. It can be easily implemented with-

- 3-nodes in input layer.
- 1 hidden layer with 7 nodes.
- 2-node output layer.

As far as the tool, R, is concerned, it provides the user with a function named as neuralnet( ) that needs I/O data in a proper format. That is,

colnames(trainingdata) ← *c*("*a*", "*b*", "*c*", "*r*1", "*r*2")

The r.h.s. of the formula consists of 2 roots and l.h.s includes 3 coefficients, a, b and c. The inclusion has been shown with a '+ sign. That is,

Net.quadroot ← neuralnet(*r*1 + *r*2 ~ *a* + *b* + *c*, trainingdata, hidden = 7, threshold = 0.0001)

An arbitrary performance threshold value of 10-4 is chosen and this can be adjusted as per requirements.

The configuration of this model constructed so far with its training data can be visualized with a plot function as follows:

```
#plot the neural net
plot (net. quadroot)
```

Now the next step is to verify NN with a set of unknown data. We arbitrarily take a few sets of values of three coefficients for corresponding quadratic equations and arrange them as data frames as follows:

$$x_1 \leftarrow c\,(1, 1, 1, -2, 1, 2)$$
$$x_2 \leftarrow c\,(5, 4, -2, -1, 9, 1)$$
$$x_3 \leftarrow c\,(6, 5, -8, -2, 22, -3)$$

As there is no zero coefficient corresponding to x_2, we can accept only those coefficients for which $d = 0$ or $d > 0$. Then, the values are fed to this configured neural model, net.quadroot, to predict their roots. The predicted roots are collected into net.result$net.result and can be displayed with print function *i.e.*

```
testdata ← cbind (y1, y2, y3)
net.results ← compute (net.quadroot, testdata)
# see the results now
print (net.results$net.result)
```

To verify the results, we compute the roots using normal root calculating formula and verifying the results by comparing the predicted values with them. Calculate the roots and concatenate them into a data frame.

Then combine the test data, its roots and the predicted roots into a data frame for a descent tabular display for verification. The results are shown in Table-1

Table-1: Result Comparisons of Expected Roots and Predicted Roots

Equations	Coefficients			Roots		Predicted roots (NN outputs)	
	a	b	c	r1	r2	pre – r1	pre-r2
E1	1	5	6	–2	– 3.0	-1.9	-3.0
E2	1	– 2	– 8	4	– 2.0	3.2	-3.4
E3	2	1	3	1	– 1.5	0.9	-1.7

From the above outputs, it is seen that our NN has learnt appropriately and produces an almost correct result. It is also suggested to run Neural Nets several times with given parameters to achieve a correct result.

We are trying to look at the world through new lenses but at the same time the lenses themselves are looking back to us and this is what we will proceed to explore next. Data are the building blocks to information and information is vital for knowledge generation for decision makers across industry to make better decisions. Healthier decisions mean greater operational efficiencies, cost reductions and reduced risks. A new 'V' in this dimension must be taken care of as even big data on web servers may get hacked easily.

Data explosion presents many challenges to deep learning like large scale heterogeneity, noisy labels and non-stationary distribution etc. Both big data and deep learning have symbiotic relationships. Deep learning is the recent area of research.

In nutshell, big data presents many challenges to deep learning including large scale, heterogeneity, noisy labels and non-stationary distribution etc. Both big data and deep learning have symbiotic relationships. Deep learning is the current area of machine learning research with the aim to move machine learning to artificial intelligence. Deep learning means learning multiple levels of representation and abstraction that help to make sense of data like images, sound and text. Several libraries do exist for developing deep models like theano (a python library).

In biological organisms, knowledge is stored as complex structures of interconnected neurons. The structures correspond to symbolic representations of the knowledge possessed by the organism, the facts, the rules and so on. Please note that an average human brain weighs about 3.3 pounds and contains an estimated number of 1012 neurons. Also note that these neurons and their interconnection capabilities provide about 1014 bits of potential storage capacity. Artificial neural networks are not a panacea. They are unsuitable for tasks like payroll calculations. Backpropagation uses gradient descent to adjust the network weights. This is fine with convex error surfaces as they have a unique minimum. But it results in non-optimal solutions with non-convex surfaces. In some scenarios, a local minimum is acceptable as a solution but in some it is inadequate.

Even if the network is trained yet there is no way to depict that this backpropagation algorithm has found the global minimum. Also understand that if the solution is unsatisfactory, we must re-initialize the weights to new random values and re-train the network. But there is no guarantee that a global- minima will be found. One has to take care as far as weight selection is concerned. This may result in network paralysis.

In this chapter we have seen the basic neuron structure and the working of feed-forward networks. Also observed is the problem of non-linearity in solving complex learning problems.

We are trying to look at the world through new lenses but at the same time the lenses themselves are looking back to us and this is what we will proceed to explore next. Data are the building blocks to information and information is vital for knowledge generation for decision makers across industry to make better decisions. Healthier decisions mean greater operational efficiencies, cost reductions and reduced risks. A new 'V' in this dimension must be taken care of as even big data on web servers may get hacked easily.

Data explosion presents many challenges to deep learning like large scale heterogeneity, noisy labels and non-stationary distribution etc. Both big data and deep learning have symbiotic relationships. Deep learning is the recent area of research.

In nutshell, big data presents many challenges to deep learning including large scale, heterogeneity, noisy labels and non-stationary distribution etc. Both big data and deep learning have symbiotic relationships. Deep learning is the current area of machine learning research with the aim to move machine learning to artificial intelligence. Deep learning means learning multiple levels of representation and abstraction that help to make sense of data like images, sound and text. Several libraries do exist for developing deep models like theano (a python library).

MULTIPLE CHOICE QUESTIONS

1. **Machine learning includes :**
   (*a*) Narrow Learning (*b*) Deep Learning
   (*c*) Varied Learning (*d*) None of the above
2. **A subset of artificial intelligence field called as machine learning which is predicted on the basic idea of learning from example is named as :**
   (*a*) Learning by Examples (*b*) Learning by Machine
   (*c*) Deep Learning (*d*) None of the above
3. **RBM stands for :**
   (*a*) Restricted Boltzmann Machines (*b*) Regular Boltzmann Memory
   (*c*) Referred Boltzmann Machine (*d*) None of the above
4. **Deep Belief Networks use :**
   (*a*) RBM (*b*) DBMS
   (*c*) IBM (*d*) None of the above

5. The time spent in training a deep learning model is given by the formula:

(*a*) Training Time (TT) = [Number of training samples] + [Number of Epochs]

(*b*) Training Time (TT) = [Number of training samples] - [Number of Epochs]

(*c*) Training Time (TT) = [Number of training samples] * [Number of Epochs]

(*d*) Training Time (TT) = [Number of training samples] / [Number of Epochs]

6. The more are the weights :

(*a*) Slower will be the training (*b*) Faster will be the training

(*c*) Lesser will be the training (*d*) None of the above

7. Which of the following is a rectification function :

(*a*) Rectifier (*b*) Amplifier

(*c*) Simplifier (*d*) None of the above

8. The working of ANNs is similar to :

(*a*) A human brain (*b*) A car working

(*c*) A human eye (*d*) None of the above

9. Even a tiny part of the brain that is about the size of a grain of rice has :

(*a*) 5000 neurons (*b*) 6000 neurons

(*c*) 10,000 neurons (*d*) None of the above

10. Connections traverse from :

(*a*) Lower to higher layer (*b*) Higher to lower layer

(*c*) At same layer (*d*) None of the above

11. As we make neural networks deep, which phenomenon is seen :

(*a*) Overloading (*b*) Overriding

(*c*) Overfitting (*d*) None of the above

12. A single iteration over the entire training set is called as an :

(*a*) Epoch (*b*) Clock

(*c*) Cycle (d) None of the above

13. The data is split up into two parts :

(*a*) Training data and valid data (*b*) Training data and test data

(*c*) Training data and big data (*d*) None of the above

14. At the end of each epoch, we must see that :

(*a*) Error is increasing (*b*) Error is decreasing

(*c*) Error is static (*d*) None of the above

15. One of the methods of overcoming 'overfitting' phenomenon is called as :

(*a*) Regularization (*b*) Segmentation

(*c*) Fragmentation (*d*) None of the above

16. Deep learning is also called as :

(*a*) Feature learning (*b*) Representation learning

(*c*) Example based learning (*d*) Only (*a*) and (*b*)

17. An artificial neural network used for learning efficient coding is :

(*a*) Auto-encoder (*b*) Decoder

(*c*) Encoder (*d*) None of the above

18. Deep learning is useful as :

(*a*) Non-linear function can be represented in a better way

(*b*) Linear function can be represented in a better way

(*c*) Polynomial function can be represented in a better way

(*d*) None of the above

19. A systematic method for training multilayer ANN is named as :

(*a*) Forward-propagation (*b*) Backpropagation

(*c*) Error propagation (*d*) None of the above

20. If we want to train the network to recognize all letters of the alphabet then we need :

(*a*) 20 training pairs (*b*) 26 training pairs

(*c*) 30 training pairs (*d*) None of the above

21. A group of training pairs is called as :

(*a*) Training set (*b*) Working set

(*c*) Logical set (*d*) None of the above

22. A neuron with n binary inputs can have :

(*a*) 2^n input patterns (*b*) 2^n input patterns

(*c*) $n/2$ input patterns (*d*) None of the above

23. Each input pattern can produce :

(*a*) Two binary inputs (1s and 0s) (*b*) 2^n inputs

(*c*) 2^n inputs (*d*) None of the above

24. In a 50*50 network, with 2 numeric inputs and 1 output, there are:

(*a*) 2650 weights (*b*) 3650 weights

(*c*) 4300 weights (*d*) None of the above

25. If we have a total of '*k*' critical points, then we will have a total of :

(*a*) k/3 local minima (*b*) k/2 local minima

(*c*) k * 3 local minima (*d*) None of the above

ANSWERS

1. (*b*)	**2.** (*c*)	**3.** (*a*)	**4.** (*a*)	**5.** (*c*)
6. (*a*)	**7.** (*a*)	**8.** (*a*)	**9.** (*c*)	**10.** (*a*)
11. (*c*)	**12.** (*a*)	**13.** (*b*)	**14.** (*b*)	**15.** (*a*)
16. (*d*)	**17.** (*a*)	**18.** (*a*)	**19.** (*b*)	**20.** (*b*)
21. (*a*)	**22.** (*a*)	**23.** (*a*)	**24.** (*a*)	**25.** (*a*)

CONCEPTUAL SHORT QUESTIONS WITH ANSWERS

Q.1. Define deep learning.

Ans. It is defined as a set of machine learning algorithms which attempt to learn multiple-layered models of inputs (neural networks). They are composed of multiple levels of non-linear operations. The core concept of deep learning is a greedy layerwise unsupervised pre-training that is to learn a hierarchy of features one level at a time.

Q.2. What is an auto-encoder?

Ans. An auto-encoder is an artificial neural network used for learning efficient coding. The objective is to learn a compressed representation /encoding for a data set. This means that it was being used for dimensionality reduction or data compression.

Q.3. What are the advantages of deep learning?

Ans. Deep learning has the following advantages:-

1. Non-linear functions can be represented in a more efficient manner.
2. Deep representations may allow for a hierarchical representations that allow for combinatorial sharing of statistical strength.

Q.4. Define transfer learning.

Ans. It is defined as the ability of a learning algorithm to explore commonalties between different learning tasks in order to transfer knowledge across different tasks.

Q.5. Compare conventional learning methods with deep learning methods.

Ans. Conventional learning methods use shallow-structured learning architectures. On the other hand, deep learning refers to machine learning techniques that use supervised and/or unsupervised methods to learn hierarchical representations in deep architectures.

Q.6. Big data presents many challenges to deep learning. List some of them.

Ans. Big data challenges to deep learning are as follows:-

- Large scale data
- Heterogeneity of data
- Noisy labels
- Non-stationary distribution

Q.7. How are deep learning, AI and machine learning inter-related?

Ans. Deep learning is a subset of Artificial Intelligence (AI) branch called as machine learning. In machine learning, we do not teach a computer a huge list of rules to solve a problem rather we give it a model so that it can evaluate examples and a small set of instructions to modify the model when it makes mistakes. Please understand here that we expect that as the time passes, a suitable model would be able to solve the problem more efficiently.

Q.8. Define what is training?

Ans. Training is the process in which we show the neural network large number of training examples and then iteratively modify the weights to minimize the errors we make on the training examples.

Q.9. What causes the problem of overfitting?

Ans. In deep learning, our neural nets have large number of layers containing many neurons. The number of connections in these models is in millions (very high). This results in overfitting.

Q.10. A machine learning engineer is always confronted with a delimma between overfitting and model complexity. What is this delimma?

Ans. The problem arises in both the cases *i.e.* when the model is simple or when the model is complex. If the model is simple then it may not be powerful to capture all of the useful information required to solve a problem. On the other hand, if the model is complex then it may result in overfitting problem. Hence, there is a need of a trade-off. To resolve this problem, deep learning solves complex problems with complex models but at the same time take additional steps to avoid overfitting.

Q.11. What is TensorFlow?

Ans. An open- source software (Python-based) library released by Google in 2015 that is used to design, build and train deep learning models is TensorFlow.

EXERCISE QUESTIONS

1. What do you mean by deep learning? Why is it required?
2. Compare human neuron with that of an Artificial Neuron?
3. How are big data and deep learning related?
4. Explain the three-layered neuron architecture.
5. Explain the design of neural network.
6. What are the rules that you follow to choose the number of layers and neurons in a neural net?
7. What are Feed Forward Neural Networks? Explain.
8. What are deep belief networks?
9. What are CNNs?
10. Throw some light on big data and deep learning with respect to the five V's of big data.
11. What is RBM? What is its role?
12. Define the following:-
    (*a*) Pulling error signals.
    (*b*) Pushing error signals.

2 Types of Learning

Q.1. Explain the functioning of a learning system with a neat diagram explaining its various parts.

Ans. We need to define a learning system first of all. It is defined as an interaction of a learning agent / intelligent agent with its environment by perceiving an input and doing actions accordingly. An agent is one who can perceive its environment with the help of sensors and acts upon its environment through actuators.

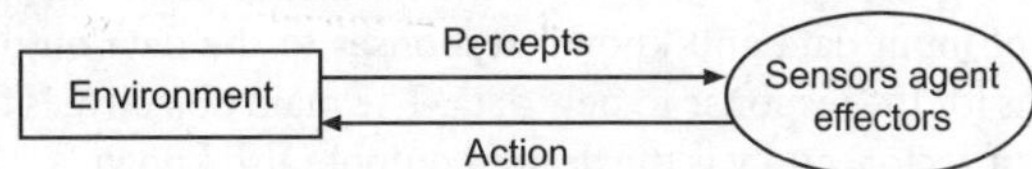

Fig. 2.1: A Learning System

An intelligent agent is a software entity which senses its environment and then carries out some set of operations on behalf of a user with some amount of autonomy and to do so it employs some knowledge or representation of the end-user's goal. Note that an agent is different from a program. An agent need not be a program at all. It may be a robot or a college professor. Software agents are by definition programs but a program must measure up to several marks to be an agent. For example, humans, animals, autonomous mobile robots or softbots calculators are real-world agents. Software agents live in the systems OS.

As shown in figure 2.1, an agent perceives its environment through sensors. It then acts upon that environment through actuators. For example,

- Human agent has eyes, ears, nose etc. as sensors while hands, legs, mouth are actuators.
- Software agent receives keystrokes, files, packets are sensory inputs and acts on the environment by displaying on the screen, writing files and sending packets over a network.

Q.2. Define Capacity, Overfitting and Underfitting.

Ans. In deep learning, our neural nets have large number of layers containing many neurons. The number of connections in these models is in millions (very high). This results in overfitting.

The problem arises in both the cases *i.e.* when the model is simple or when the model is complex. If the model is simple then it may not be powerful to capture all of the useful information required to solve a problem. On the other hand, if the model is complex then it may result in overfitting problem. Hence, there is a need of a trade-off. To resolve this problem, deep learning solves complex problems with complex models but at the same time take additional steps to avoid overfitting.

Q.3. What is generalization? Explain.

Ans. Generalization is defined as the ability of machine to learn on being introduced with sets of data during training so that when it is introduced to new and unseen examples then it can perform accurately. To ensure that a network generalizes well, we tend to use a neural network in order to generalize from the training examples to all possible inputs. Whether it is training or overtraining of the network, troubles do arise. We can change the weight in a neural network. Thus, the degree of variability is quite high.

In machine learning, overfitting occurs when a statistical model defines random error or noise rather than underlying relationship. When a model is extremely complex, overfitting is observed because of having too many parameters relating to the number of training data types. The model exhibits poor performance which has been overfit. The risk of overfittting exists as the standards used for training the model is not the same as the standards used to judge the effectiveness of a model.

By means of loads of data, overfitting can be avoided. Overfitting occurs when you have a smaller data set and you make effort to learn from it. Note that if you have a small database and it is desired to build a model based on that then in such a situation a technique known as cross validation can be used. In this method, the dataset is divided into two segments- testing and training datasets. The testing dataset will only test the model while in training dataset, the data points will come up with the model. In this method, a model is generally provided with a dataset of a known data on which training data-set is run and a dataset of unknown data against which the model is tested. The purpose of **cross validation** is to define a dataset to test the model in the training phase.

Q.4. Distinguish between Supervised Learning and unsupervised learning.

Ans. Machine learning algorithms, based on the basis of desired outcome is put under two categories -

- Supervised learning.
- Unsupervised learning.

Let us discuss these types first.

Supervised learning is the machine learning task of applying inference function on supervised training data. Training data comprises of a set of training examples. We try to infer a function from the training data. A supervised learning algorithm takes a known set of input data and known responses to the data/output and further training a model to generate reasonable predictions for the response to new data. The main objective is to learn an unknown function f(x) = y where x is an input example (a vector) and y is the desired output (also known as supervisory signal). The model used in this type of learning describes the effect of one set of observations on the other set of observations. So, we can say that the user tries to find the connection between the sets of inputs and outputs. In nutshell, this algorithm analyses the training data and produces an inferred function which is called as a classifier (in case of discrete output) or a regression function (in case of continuous output). Also note that for a valid input object, the inferred function should predict correct output value.

Unsupervised learning involves all of the input data, x, and no corresponding output data, y, is available. The main objective is to model the distribution in the data in order to learn more about data. We define unsupervised learning as a type of learning with no correct answers and no teacher available for supervision. Algorithms are supposed to find the interesting structure present in the data thus figuring out the underlying structure. It enables users to learn larger and more complex problems as compared to supervised learning.

The following are the points of differences:-

Table-1: Supervised versus Unsupervised Learning

Supervised Learning	Unsupervised Learning
It incorporates an external teacher so that each output unit is told what should be the desired response to that input signal.	Uses no external teacher.
Global error signals govern learning.	Local information is used for learning.
Uses pattern class information of each training pattern.	Adaptively clusters patterns to generate decision codes.
Paradigms are error correction learning, reinforcement learning and stochastic learning.	Paradigms are Hebbian learning and competitive learning.
Learning is usually off line. It means that learning and operation phases are different. In off-line learning, all of the given patterns are used together.	Learning is online. It means that the agent learns and operates at the same time. Here, the information in each new pattern is incorporated into the agent.
All learning data are stored and can be accessed repeatedly. So, we can see whether we are making progress in training or not.	Locality allows learning in real time. So, the progress cannot be monitored.
Inputs and outputs are defined.	Only inputs are defined.
Uses pattern class information of each training pattern.	Adaptively clusters patterns to generate decision class without any prior pattern class information.
Global error signal governs learning.	Local information/ rules are used for learning.
Learning is offline usually.	Locality allows synapses to learn in real-time.

Unsupervised learning is put under two categories:-

•

1. **Clustering :** In this method, the inherent groupings in the data are discovered. The organization of unlabeled data into similar groups known as clusters. And the process of partitioning of a set of observations into subsets (or clusters) so that observation in the same cluster is similar is called as clustering. So, a cluster consists of data items which are similar in comparison to other clusters which contain dissimilar items. **Please understand that the aim of unsupervised learning is to find clusters of similar inputs in the data without knowing that these data points belong to one class and those to different class.** Rather the algorithm has to uncover similarities for itself. For example, there is a collection of 30,000 essays on voting process. These essays can be automatically grouped into small number on the basis of word frequency, page count, word limit etc.
2. **Association :** In this method, we discover a set of rules that describes large portions of data. For example, a doctor observes same set of symptoms in several patients suffering from some disease. Then based on his experience the doctor can conclude that the patient is suffering from the same disease.

Q.5. What is k-means Clustering

Ans. k-means is a simple unsupervised learning algorithm that solves the well known clustering problems. The working of k-means is similar to that of a real-life situation in which we have observed that in a group of tourists with a few tourists guides who hold the umbrella up so that everybody can see them and follow them. On the other hand, in static k-means algorithm the data (*i.e.* the tourists) does not move rather only the tour guide (*s*) move. Analogous is the situation in k-means clustering.

Basic Principle of k-means : "Divide your data into k groups (you have to specify what 'k' is) such that each data item is closer to the center of its cluster than to the centre of any other cluster."

Explanation of k-means : We classify a given data-set into k number of clusters which is fixed in advance. Now the task is to define '*k*' centres (middle point) one for each cluster. But we do not know where their centres are. So, we need an algorithm that will find the middle points. The centre of a set of points is based on two parameters:-

a. **Distance Measure :** It measures the distance between a set of points. We may use Euclidean distance but other options are also available.

b. **Mean Average :** after we compute the distance measure (as stated above) we finally compute the central point of the set of data points which is the mean average.

Please note that this is valid in Euclidean space where everything is flat and easily measured. Now the need is to place cluster centres properly. We compute the mean of each cluster, μ_i (*i*) and position the cluster centre right there. Also note that this is similar to minimizing the Euclidean distance (*i.e.* sum-of-squares again) from each data point to the centre of cluster.

Now we would like to find out that which point belongs to which cluster. This is mandatory as it lets us know the position of cluster centres. It is crystal clear to associate closest point with the cluster centre. This might change as the algorithm iterates on. In the input space we start positioning the cluster centres randomly as we do not know where to put them exactly and further update their positions in accordance with the data. Now we start picking up the data points and find out which cluster, particular data point belongs to depending on the distance between each data point and all of the cluster centres and assigning it to cluster that is closest.

The purpose of the hidden layer is to summarize the data and compress it. The multidimensional data is to be reduced to either 2 or 3 dimensions only as then we can plot the graphs too. If we use the PYTHON LANGUAGE then note that layers and column indices are counted from zero while in R they are counted from one.

With auto-encoding neural networks we do learning one layer at a time.

For example, a model, m_1, say, has the following-

- 5 hidden layers
- 11 neurons (in middle layer)

It is trained on the raw data. Then that third hidden layer is extracted into a transformation, f1 with still 100 rows but only 11 columns. Model-2 (m2) uses this f1 as its input and builds up a much simpler model, reducing 11 input nodes to 2 hidden nodes then back out to 11 output nodes. At the end, results are put in f2. f2 now has 2 columns but still 100 rows.

Algorithm

k-means clustering involves the following steps:-

Step-1: Randomly select 'c' cluster centres.

Step-2: Compute the distance between each data point and cluster centres.

Step-3: Assign the data point to the cluster whose distance from the cluster centre is minimum in the value of cluster centres.

Step-4: Calculate the new cluster centre using the following formula:-

$$v = 1/c_i \Sigma (j = 1 \text{ to } c_i) x_i$$

where ci represents the number of data points in the ith cluster.

Step-5: New cluster centres are computed.

Step-6: If no data point is reassigned then stop else repeat from step-3.

As we know that H2O is software for machine learning and data analysis. H_2O algorithm has been developed keeping in mind clustering only. But clusters in H_2O have some limitations:-

a. Each H_2O node on the cluster must be of the same size. It implies that if the smallest machine in our cluster has 2GB free, then every node must be given 2GB even if some of them have 32GB.

b. You cannot add the machines once the cluster has started.

c. In case a machine dies then the whole of the cluster must be rebuilt. Please note that the whole cluster becomes unusable if a single node gets removed. In such a case, you cannot even export data or models from the left over clusters.

d. Each node must run the same API version of h_2o.jar.

e. To reduce the network latency, the nodes should be physically close.

You can also give your cluster a name and specify this name when starting on each node. In H_2O, the cluster can be created in two ways:-

1. **Flat-file :** A simple text file giving the IP address and port number of each node in the cluster. Note that you must prepare this file identically on each machine.
2. **Auto-discovery :** When you specify the network address then it searches through that subnet to find all nodes and join them together in a cluster. This is slower than the flat file.

Q.6. Write Expectation Maximization (EM) Algorithm.

Ans. Many a times the presence of unobserved variables is observed as a problem of learning. In case of some variable that can be observed sometimes and cannot be observed at other times then the time when it was observed can be used to learn its values when it was not observed. So, EM is an algorithm for maximizing a likelihood function when some of the variables in your model are unobserved. A variable that is not directly observed is called as a latent variable/ hidden / unobserved variable / missing data.

Statement of EM algorithm : EM is applied where we are required to estimate a set of parameters θ that represents an underlying probability distribution, given only the observed portion of full data. In general, let $X = \{x_1, x_2,......,x_m\}$ denote the observed data in a set of m independently drawn data items. Let $Z = \{z_1,......, z_m\}$ mark the unobserved data in these same data items and let $Y = X \cup Z$; thus marks the full data.

The EM algorithm searches for the maximum likelihood hypothesis h' by seeking the h' that maximizes $E[\ln P(Y|h')]$, where,

$P(Y|h')$ is the likelihood of the full data Y given hypothesis h'

$\ln P(Y|h')$- maximizing logarithm value of this quantity further maximizes $P(Y|h')$ and

$E[\ln P(Y|h')]$ –expected value of full data is introduced as Y is a random variable.

We need to know that what is the probability distribution governing Y. In general, we will not know this distribution as it is determined by the parameters, θ, that is to be estimated. So, EM algorithm uses its current hypothesis, h, in place of θ to estimate the distribution governing, Y.

If we assume that $\theta = h$, then, we define a function $Q(h'|h)$ as follows:-

$$Q(h'|h) = E[\ln P(Y|h') \mid h, X]$$

In general form of an EM algorithm, two steps are repeated until convergence:-

S1: Estimation (*E*) step: Calculate Q (h'| h) using the current hypothesis, h and the observed data X to estimate the probability distribution over Y. So,

$$Q(h'|h) = E[\ln P(Y|h') \mid h, X]$$

S2: Maximization (M) step : Replace h by h' that maximizes this Q function-

$$H \leftarrow \text{argmax } Q(h' \mid h)$$

Please note that when the function, Q, is continuous, the EM algorithm converges to a fixed point of the probable function $P(Y \mid h')$. Also note that when this probable function has a single maximum, EM will converge to this global maximum probable estimate for h'.

Mixture of Gaussians : A very popular continuous probability distribution is Gaussian distribution / Normal Distribution. It is also called as a bell curve since it has a bell shaped curve. The equation in one dimension is as follows:-

$$p(x) = 1 / \sqrt{2\Pi}\sigma \exp[-(x-\mu)^2 / 2\sigma^2] \quad ...(1)$$

where

μ = mean

σ = standard deviation

Please note that it is useful because of its Central Limit Theorem which tells us that lots of random numbers will add up to something Gaussian.

In Gaussian Mixture Models (GMM), we assume that there are number of different classes. Each class comes from its own Gaussian distribution. And such type of data is known as multi-model data as there are number of modes or distribution for each particular class. We are unable to accommodate Gaussian to the data in totality as it does not appear to be Gaussian overall.

If we know the number of classes that are there in the data then we can put effort to estimate the parameters for that many number of Gaussians and that too all at the same time.

On the other hand, if we do not the number of classes then we can attempt for different numbers and finds out which one works best. Then the output for any specific data point which has already been an input to the algorithm will be the sum of the values expected by all of the 'M' Gaussians. That is,

$$f(x) = \Sigma\,(m = 1 \text{ to } M)\ \alpha m\ \varphi(x\,;\mu m, \Sigma m) \quad ...(2)$$

where $\varphi(x\,;\mu_m, \Sigma_m)$ = Gaussian function with mean μm and covariance matrix and

the αm are the weights with the constraints *i.e.* $\Sigma\,(m = 1 \text{ to } M)\ \alpha_m = 1$.

The task is to choose the weights α_m. The target is for Maximum likelihood solution. Note that likelihood refers to the conditional probability and Maximum Likelihood solution refers to maximizing the conditional probability.

Q.7. What is Factor Analysis and also give its applications also.

Ans. Factor Analysis (FA) is a method for modelling observed variables and their covariance structure in terms of a smaller number of underlying unobservable/ latent factors. These 'factors' are typically observed as broad concepts or ideas that may describe an observed phenomenon. This method is quite comprehensive but is similar to principal components. Please understand that in factor analysis the observed variables are modelled as linear functions of the factors. On the other hand, principal components analysis (PCA) involves the creation of new variables that are linear combinations of the observed variables. But in both the methods, the dimensions of the data are reduced.

FA involves using of a data reduction tool to-

a. Remove redundancy from a set of correlated variables.

b. Represent correlated variables with a smaller set of derived variables.

c. Form factors that are independent of each other.

d. Two types of variables are used- latent variables (factors) and the observed variables.

Notations used : Say, there is a vector X consisting of variables X's for each individual subject. Let X_i denote observable trait, i. This is the data of each subject and will be collected into a vector of traits.

That is,

$$x = \begin{pmatrix} x_1 \\ x_2 \\ x_3 \end{pmatrix} = \text{vector of traits}$$

This will be a random vector with a population mean. We assume that sampling of vector of traits X is done from a population with population mean vector:-

$$\mu = \begin{pmatrix} \mu_1 \\ \mu_2 \\ \mu_p \end{pmatrix} = \text{Population man vector}$$

Here, $E(X_i) = \mu_i$ denotes the population mean of variable i.

In general, consider 'm' unobservable common factors $f_2, f_2, ...f_m$.

The ith common factor is f_i . In general, m will be less than p.

The common factors will be collected into a vector only:-

$$F = \begin{pmatrix} f_1 \\ f_2 \\ f_p \end{pmatrix} = \text{Vector of common factors}$$

The Factor Model : Our factor model will be a collection of series of multiple regressions, predicting each of the observable variables, Xi from the values of the unobservable common factor, fi. That is,

$$X_1 = \mu_1 + l_{11} f_1 + l_{12} f_2 + ... + l_{1m} f_m + \varepsilon_1$$
$$X_2 = \mu_2 + l_{21} f_1 + l_{22} f_2 + ... + l_{2m} f_m + \varepsilon_2$$
$$\vdots$$
$$\vdots$$
$$Xp = \mu_p + l_{p1} f_1 + l_{p2} f_2 + ... + l_{pm} f_p + \varepsilon_p$$

Here, the variable means μ_1 through μp can be explained as the intercept terms for the multiple regression models.

The regression coefficients l_{ij} (are the partial slopes) for all of these multiple regressions are called as factor loadings. The relationship of each variable to the underlying factor is expressed by factor loading. Here, l_{ij} = loading of the ith variable on the j_{th} factor. These will be collected into a matrix as follows:-

$$L = \begin{pmatrix} l_{11} & l_{12} & ....l_{1m} \\ l_{21} & l_{22} & .....l_{2m} \\ \vdots & \vdots & ....: \\ l_{p1} & l_{p2} & .....l_{pm} \end{pmatrix}$$

And that the errors, ε_i are called as the specific factors.

Here, ε_i = specific factor for variable *i*.

These specific factors are also collected in a vector:-

$$\varepsilon_i = \begin{pmatrix} \varepsilon_i \\ \varepsilon_2 \\ \varepsilon_p \end{pmatrix} = \text{vector of specific vectors}$$

In nutshell, the basic model is like a regression model only. Each of our response variables *X* is to be predicted as a linear function of the unobserved common factors f_1, f_2 through f_m. Thus, our explanatory variables are f_1, f_2 through fm. Therefore, we conclude that we have m unobserved factors that control the variation among our data.

Generally, we can reduce this into a matrix notation as shown in this form below:-

$$X = \mu + Lf + \varepsilon$$

In general we want $m << p$.

Assumptions of the model

***a.* Mean-**

1. The specific factors or random errors all have mean zero: $E(\varepsilon_i) = 0; i=1,2,.....p$.
2. The common factors, the f's also have a mean zero: $E(f_i) = 0; i = 1,2,...m$.
3. A consequence of these assumptions is that the mean response of the ith trait is μ_i. that is,

$$E(X_i) = \mu_i$$

***b.* Variance-**

1. The common factors have variance one: $\text{var}(f_i) = 1,2,...m$.
2. The variance of specific factor *i* is ψ_i : $\text{var}(\varepsilon_i) = \psi_i$; $i = 1,2,...p$. Here, ψi is called as the specific variance.

***c.* Correlation-**

1. The common factors are uncorrelated with one another: $\text{cov}(f_i, f_j) = 0$ for $i != j$.
2. The specific factors are uncorrelated with one another: $\text{cov}(\varepsilon_i , \varepsilon_j) = 0$ for $i != j$.

3. The specific factors are uncorrelated with the common factors: cov((ε_i, ε_i) = cov; i= 1,2,....p; j = 1,2,...,m.

To calculate the parameters these assumptions are necessary. An infinite number of equally well-fitted models with different values for the parameters may be obtained unless these suppositions are done. Also note that under this model, the variance for the ith observed variable is equal to the sum of the squared loadings for that variable and specific variance:-

The variance of trait is: $\sigma_i^2 = \text{var}(X_i) = \Sigma\ (j = 1 \text{ to } m)\ l^2_{ij} + \psi_i$

Where $\Sigma\ (j = 1 \text{ to } m)\ l^2_{ij}$ is called as the communality for variable, i. Please note that the larger is the communality, the better is the model performance for the ith variable.

The covariance between pairs of traits i and j is given by the formula-

$$\sigma_{ij} = \text{cov}(X_i, X_j) = \Sigma\ (k = 1 \text{ to } m)\ l_{ik}\ l_{jk}$$

The covariance between trait i and factor j is: $\text{cov}(X_i, f_i) = l_{ij}$

In matrix form, our model for the variance-covariance matrix is going to be expressed as shown below:-

$$\Sigma = LL' + \psi$$

This is the matrix of factor loadings times its transpose plus a diagonal matrix containing the specific variances.

Here ψ is as follows:-

$$\Psi = \begin{pmatrix} \psi_1 & 0 & \cdots & 0 \\ 0 & \psi_2 & \cdots & 0 \\ \vdots & \vdots & & \vdots \\ 0 & 0 & \cdots & \psi_p \end{pmatrix}$$

Hence, a simplified model for the variance-covariance matrix is obtained. This is used for estimation.

Notes:

1. The model assumes that the data is a linear function of the common factors. But since the common factors are not observable, there is no amount of data that can be used to check for linearity.
2. The variance-covariance matrix is a symmetric matrix that is, the variance between variables i and j is the same thing as the variance between j and i. for this model-

$$\Sigma = LL' + \psi$$

3. The variance-covariance matrix is going to have $p\ (p + 1)/2$ unique elements of Σ that are approximated by mp factor loadings in the matrix L and p specific variances. Also understand that this means that there is going to be mp plus p parameters in this model of the variance-covariance matrix. Ideally, $(mp + p)$ is to be substantially smaller than p $(p + 1)/2$. However, if mp is too small, the mp +p parameters may not be adequate to describe Σ. There may always be the case that perhaps this is not the right model. It may be the case that you cannot reduce the data to a linear combination of factors.
4. If we have more than one variable in our analysis, that is, if $p > 1$, the model is going to be inherently ambiguous. Say, T be any $(m * m)$ orthogonal matrix. Note that a matrix is said to be orthogonal if its inverse is equal to the transpose of the original matrix *i.e.*

$$T'T = TT' = 1$$

Please note that this does not change the calculation since the identity matrix times any matrix just gives back the original matrix. This results in an alternative factor model where the relationship between the new factor loadings and the original factor loadings is given by:-

$$L. = LT$$

And the relationship between the new common factors and the original common factors is:-

$$f. = T'f$$

This gives a model that fits equally well. Moreover, since there are an infinite number of orthogonal matrices then there is an infinite number of alternative models. This model, as it turns out, satisfies all of the assumptions that we have discussed earlier.

5. E (f.) = E(T'f) = T' E(f) = T'0 = 0 and

   var(f.) = var(T'f) = T' var(f) T = T'IT = T'T = 1

6. Cov (f. , ε) = cov (T'f, ε) = T' cov(f, ε) = T'0 = 0

Thus, we can say that f. satisfies all of the assumptions and hence *f.* is an equally valid collection of common factors. So, there is a certain apparent ambiguity to these models. However, it is the same ambiguity that we are going to exploit. This ambiguity is going to be used to justify the factor notation that will be used to derive more parsimonious description of data.

Applications of FA

The following are some of the applications of FA:-

1. **Identification of underlying factors:** It clusters variables into homogeneous sets, creates new variables/factors and allows us to gain insight to categories.
2. **Screening of Variables:** It identifies groupings to allow us to select one variable and is useful in regression/ recall collinearity applications of FA.
3. **Summary:** It allows us to describe many variables using few factors.
4. **Sampling of variables:** It helps us to select a small group of variables of representative variables from a larger set.
5. **Clustering of Object:** It helps us to put objects/people into categories depending on their factor scores.

Q.8. Explain Principal Component Analysis (PCA). Also give its algorithm.

Ans. PCA refers to a mathematical procedure that tends to transform a number of possibly correlated variables into a small number of uncorrelated variables which are called as the principal components. The **first PCA** accounts for as much of the variability as possible in the data and the next following components takes into account possible remaining variability. **Please understand that PCA is a technique used to focus on variation and figure out strong patterns in a dataset.** The objective of PCA is to make data easy to explore and visualize.

Aim of PCA

1. To discover or to reduce the dimensionality of the data set.
2. To identify new meaningful underlying variables.

Algorithm:

Suppose that we have a random vector, *X*. That is,

$$X = \begin{pmatrix} X_1 \\ X_2 \\ \vdots \\ X_P \end{pmatrix}$$

And with the population variance-covariance matrix as follows: -

$$\text{var}(X) = \Sigma = \begin{pmatrix} \sigma_1^2 & \sigma_{12}....\sigma_{1p} \\ \sigma_{21} & \sigma_2^2....\sigma_{2p} \\ \sigma_{p1} & \sigma_{p2}....\sigma_{p2} \end{pmatrix}$$

Now consider the following linear combinations: -

$$Y_1 = e_{11} X_1 + e_{12} X_2 + ... + e_{1p} X_P$$
$$Y_2 = e_{21} X_1 + e_{22} X_2 + ... + e_{2p} X_P$$
$$\vdots$$
$$\vdots$$
$$Y_P = e_{p1} X_1 + e_{P2} X_2 + ... + e_{PP} X_P$$

Each of these is just like a linear regression, predicting Y_i from $X_1, X_2,......., X_P$. There is no intercept but $e_{i1}, e_{i2}, ...e_{ip}$ may be considered as the regression coefficients.

Also note that Y_i is a function of our random data and hence it is also random. So, it has a population variance of-

$$\text{Var}(Y_i) = \Sigma(k = 1 \text{ to } p)\, \Sigma(l = 1 \text{ to } p)\, e_{ik}\, e_{il}\, \sigma_{kl} = e'i\, \Sigma e_i$$

How to find 1st PCA, 2nd PCA and the ith PCA?

1. The 1st Principal Component *i.e.* PCA1 means Y_1 and is computed as follows:-

   The 1st principal component is a linear combination of *x*-variables that has maximum variance (among all linear combinations). Thus, it accounts for as much possible variation in the data as possible. More specifically, we will define coefficients e_{11}, e_{12}, ..., e_{1p} for that component in such a way that its variance is maximized, subject to the constraint that the sum of the squared coefficients is equal to one. This constraint is required to obtain a unique answer.

   Formally, we select $e_{11}, e_{12}, \ldots, e_{1p}$ that maximizes-

   $$\text{Var}(Y_1) = \Sigma_{(k=1\text{ to }p)}\Sigma_{(l=1\text{ to }p)}\, e_{1k}\, e_{11}\, \sigma_{kl} = e'1\, \Sigma_{e1}$$

   Subject to the constraints:-

   $$e'_1 e_1 = \Sigma\,(j = 1\text{ to }p)\; e^2 1_j = 1$$

2. The 2nd Principal Component i.e. PCA_2 means Y_2 and is computed as follows:-

   The 2nd principal component is a linear combination of *x*-variables that has maximum variance (among all linear combinations). Thus, it accounts for as much possible variation in the data as possible with the constraints that the correlation between the first and second component is 0. More specifically, we will define coefficients e_{11}, e_{12}, ..., $e1_p$ for that component in such a way that its variance is maximized, subject to the constraint that the sum of the squared coefficients is equal to one. This constraint is required to obtain a unique answer.

   Formally, we select $e_{21}, e_{22}, \ldots, e_{2p}$ that maximizes-

   $$\text{var}(Y_2) = \Sigma(k = 1\text{ to }p)\,\Sigma(l = 1\text{ to }p)\; e_{2k}\, e_{21}\, \sigma_{kl} = e'_2\, \Sigma e_2$$

Subject to the constraints:-

$$e'_2 e_2 = \Sigma\,(j = 1\text{ to p})\; e^2 2j = 1$$

Please note that all subsequent PCAs have this same property *i.e.* they are linear combinations that account for as much of the remaining variation as possible and they are not correlated with the other PCAs. Also note that we will do it the same way for each and every additional component.

So, in general, the ith Principal Component *i.e.* PCA_i means Y_i and is computed as follows:-
We select $e_{i1}, e_{i2}, \ldots, e_{ip}$ that maximizes-

$$\text{var}(Y_i) = \Sigma(k - 1\text{ to }p)\,\Sigma(l - 1\text{ to }p)\; e_{ik}\, e_{il}\, \sigma_{kl} = e'ı\, \Sigma ei$$

This is subject to the constraints that the sums of squared coefficients add up to 1, along with the additional constraint that this new component will be uncorrelated with all the previously defined components. That is,

$$e'_i e_i = \Sigma\,(j = 1\text{ to }p)\; e^2 ij = 1$$

How to find these coefficients e_{ij} for a principal component?

To solve these coefficients we use Eigen values and Eigen vectors of the variance-covariance matrix, Σ. Let λ_1 through λ_p represent the Eigen values of the variance-covariance matrix, Σ. These are ordered so that λ_1 has the largest Eigen value and λ_p is the smallest. That is,

$$\lambda_1 \geq \lambda_2 \geq \ldots \geq \lambda_P$$

Also say vectors e_1 through ep *i.e.* ($e_1, e_1, \ldots, e_P$) denote the corresponding Eigen vectors. Note that the elements for these Eigen vectors will be coefficients of our principal components.

The variance for the iit PC is equal to the iith Eigen value as follows:-

$$\text{var}(Y_i) = \text{var}(e_{i1} X_1 + e_{i2} X_2 + \ldots + e_{ip} X_p) = \lambda_i$$

Moreover, the principal components are uncorrelated with one another:-

$$\text{cov}(Y_i, Y_j) = 0$$

When we have correlations / multi-collinearity between the *x*-variables, the data may be more or less fall on a line or plane in a lower number of dimensions.

For example, consider a plot of two *x*-variables that have a nearly perfect correlation. The data points will fall close to a straight line. That line could be used as a new 1D axis to represent the variation among data points.

Let us define this now in terms of variance-covariance matrix, Σ, which is unknown. But we may estimate Σ by the sample variance-covariance matrix, Σ, which is given in the standard formula as follows:-

$$S = 1/(n-1)\,\Sigma\,(i = 1\text{ to }n)\,(X_i - \bar{x})\,(X_i - \bar{x})'$$

Algorithm followed : We calculate the Eigen Values λ_1', λ_2',......, λ_p' of the sample variance-covariance matrix, S, and the corresponding Eigen Vectors e_1', e_2' ,......, e_p'. Then we will define our estimated PCs using the Eigen Vectors as our coefficients:-

$$Y_1' = e_{11}' X_1 + e_{12}' X_2 + ... + e_{1p}' X_p$$
$$Y_2' = e_{21}' X_1 + e_{22}' X_2 + ... + e_{2p}' X_p$$
$$\vdots$$
$$\vdots$$
$$Y_p' = e_{P1}' X_1 + e_{p2}' X_2 + ... + e_{pp}' X_p$$

In general, we can retain only the first *k* principal component. But we need to balance two conflicting issues:-

1. To obtain the simplest possible interpretation, we want k to be as small as possible. If we can explain most of the variation just by 2 principal components then this would give us a much simpler description of data. The smaller is the K, the smaller amount of variation is explained by the first k component.
2. To avoid loss of information, we want the proportion of variation explained by the first principal components to be large. That is, what we want is-

$$\frac{\lambda_1' + \lambda_2' + ..., + \lambda_k'}{\lambda_1' + \lambda_2' + ..., + \lambda_p'}$$
$$= 1$$

So, we can say that all principal components are uncorrelated with one another.

Q.9. What is Independent Component Analysis (ICA)?

Ans. A method for finding the underlying factors or components from multi-variate or multi-dimensional statistical data is called as Independent Component Analysis (ICA). This method is somewhat different. It is so because it uses both statistically independent and non-Gaussian.

For example, consider a scenario in which three people are speaking simultaneously in a room. There are 3 microphones that are present in different locations for the same. The microphones give us 3 recorded time signals which can be denoted by $x_1(t)$, $x_2(t)$ and $x_3(t)$ with x_1, x_2 and x_3 referring to the amplitudes and t is basically the time index. Each of these recorded signals can be represented as a weighted sum of the speech signals produced by the three speakers which is denoted by $s_1(t)$, $s_2(t)$ and s_3(t). In linear form we can represent it as follows:-

$$x_1(t) = a_{11}\, s_1\,(t) + a_{12}\, s_2\,(t) + a_{13}\, s_3\,(t)$$
$$x_2(t) = a_{21}\, s_1\,(t) + a_{22}\, s_2\,(t) + a_{23}\, s_3\,(t)$$
$$x_3(t) = a_{31}\, s_1\,(t) + a_{32}\, s_2\,(t) + a_{33}\, s_3\,(t)$$

where a_{ij} with $j = 1...3$, depend on the distances of the microphones from the speakers.

It is very innovative to estimate the original speech signals $s_1(t)$, $s_2(t)$ and $s_3(t)$ by making use of the recorded signals x_i (t). And this problem is known as a cocktail-party problem.

If we know the mixing parameter, aij value then we would have easily solved the linear equation by simply inverting the linear system. But the problem is that we neither have aij nor the $s_i(t)$. One of the ways of solving this problem is to use some information on the statistical properties of the signals, s_i (t). It is more than enough to assume that $s_1(t)$, $s_2(t)$ and $s_3(t)$ are statistically independent at each time instant, t. ICA can be used to estimate aij based on their information of their independence. This allows us to separate out the three original signals $s_1(t)$, $s_2(t)$ and $s_3(t)$ from their mixtures $x_1(t)$, $x_2(t)$ and $x_3(t)$. ICA was developed to deal with the variant forms of cocktail-party problem.

The Noise-free ICA Model : The ICA model is a generative model that means that it describes how the observed data are generated by a process of mixing the components, s_j.

To model ICA, the following points must be remembered:-

1. Use statistical latent variables in the system.
2. Use random variable, sk instead of time signal.
3. $X_j = a_{j1}s_1 + a_{j2}s_2$ +.....+ ajnsn, for all jx = As
4. Task: Estimate *A* and *S* using only the observable random vector, *x*.
5. Assuming that number of Independent Components = number of observable mixtures and A is square and invertible,

we can estimate A. Then we can calculate $W= A^{-1}$ and thus $s = Wx = A^{-1} x$.

Limitations in ICA : The following are some of the limitations of ICA:-

1. The independent components are assumed statistically independent.
2. The independent components must have non-Gaussian distributions.
3. The joint density of unit variances, s_1 and s_2 is symmetric. So, it does not contain any information about the directions of the columns of the mixing matrix, A. So, A can't be estimated.
4. If only one Independent component is Gaussian then the estimation is still possible.

Ambiguities in ICA : The following are some of the ambiguities in ICA:-

1. It cannot determine the variances /energies of the independent components (ICs). Both s and A are unknowns and that any scalar multiple in one of the sources can always be cancelled by dividing the corresponding column of A by it. Also because of the fixed magnitudes of IC's assuming unit variance *i.e.* $E\{S_i^2\} = 1$.
2. It cannot determine the order of Independent components. The terms can be easily changed as both a and A are unknown, so, we call any IC as the first one.

How to centre the variables?

We can assume that both the mixture variables and the independent components have zero mean without any loss of generality. This assumption simplifies the theory and algorithms further. If the assumption of zero mean is not true, some pre-processing is done to make it hold. This is possible by centering the observable variables *i.e.* subtracting their sample mean. This means that the original mixtures, say x', are pre-processed by $x = x' - E\{x'\}$, before doing ICA. Thus, the independent components are also made zero mean because-

$$E\{s\} = A^{-1} E\{x\}$$

On the other hand, the mixing matrix remains intact after this pre-processing. So this can always be done without affecting the estimation of the mixing matrix. After estimating the mixing matrix and the independent components for the zero-mean data, the subtracted mean can be simply reconstructed by adding $E\{s\} = A^{-1} E\{x\}$to the zero-mean independent components.

Q.10. What is Latent Semantic Indexing (LSI)? Give its algorithm, advantages and disadvantages.

Ans. Latent Semantic Indexing (LSI) is a retrieval method that makes use of a mathematical technique called as Singular Value Decomposition (SVD) which in turn is used to figure out patterns in connection to terms and concepts included in unstructured collection of data. This process acts as an add-on to document indexing process. in addition to keeping track of keywords that are there in the document , this method analyzes the document entirely to find out which other document contains the same words.

Please note that LSI considers documents to be semantically close if they have many words in common and semantically distant if few words are there in common. LSI algorithm is unable to understand the words as it does not know the meanings but still it is able to figure out the pattern that makes it look intelligent.

The LSI Algorithm :

Step-1: Convert each document in your index in a vector-form of word occurrences. Here,

Number of dimensions in vector = number of unique words in the entire document set.

Most document vectors will have large empty patches, some will be quite full. It is recommended that common words like 'this', 'him', 'the' etc. should be removed.

Step-2: Scale each vector so that every term reflects the frequency of its occurrence in context.

Step-3: Combine these column vectors into a large term-document matrix. Here, rows represent terms and columns represent document.

Step-4: Perform Singular Value Decomposition (SVD) on the term-document matrix. This will result in three matrices commonly called U, S and V. S, is a diagonal matrix of singular values for your document system. It is of use to us.

Step-5: Set all but the k-highest singular values to 0. K is a parameter that needs to be tuned based on your space. Very low values of k are very lossy and lands up with net poor results. But very high values of k do not change the results much from simple vector search. This gets a new matrix, S'.

Step-6: Recombine the terms to form the original matrix-

$$U * S' * V(t) = M'$$

Where (t) signifies transpose.

Step-7: Break this reduced rank term-document matrix back into column vectors. Associate these with their corresponding documents.

Step-8: Now you get the LSI *i.e.*, Latent Semantic Index.

Advantages of LSI :

1. LSI is used to analyze the similarity between the bodies of the text. This can be used in dozens of ways, from finding related documents in a group to doing paragraph-wise LSI to find site summaries.
2. It can also be used to assist search in a smarter way of your document space.
3. To do document categorization.
4. You can take the inner product (dot product) of two of the LSI vectors and perform operations with that information. Sometimes you may do this operation on your unit LSI vectors, particularly when you are searching on a vector that is a search term. It will never have the magnitude that a full document would have.

Q.11. What is Spectral or Sub-space Clustering? Give its algorithm.

Ans. It is one of the most modern and simple clustering algorithms. It can be solved efficiently by standard linear algebra software. Sometimes it is better than traditional k-means algorithm. Please understand that the objective of spectral clustering is to cluster connected data but not certainly compact or clustered within convex boundaries.

When we talk of compactness then k-means model is useful while when we talk of connectivity then spectral clustering is used.

Algorithm :

Step-1: Project your data into R^n.

Step-2: Define an Affinity matrix, A, using a Gaussian Kernel, K, or say just an adjacency matrix *i.e.* $A_{ij} = \delta_{ij}$.

Step-3: Construct the Laplacian Graph from A *i.e.* decide on a normalization.

Step-4: Solve an Eigen value problem such as $Lv = \lambda v$ or a Generalized Eigen Value problem i.e., $Lv = \lambda Dv$.

Step-5: Select k Eigen Vectors $\{v_i, i = 1, k\}$ corresponding to the k-lowest or highest Eigen values, to define a k-dimensional subspace P^t LP.

Step-6: Form clusters in this subspace using, say, k-means.

Metrics : A metric that computes the similarity or closeness of two points in space is called as an affinity. We either guess the metric or learn the metric. Now we will guess the metric. Please note that it is not the standard Euclidean metric. The next simplest one is Guassian Kernel.

Given 2 data points, x_i, x_j that is projected in R^n, we define an Affinity A_{ij} that is positive, symmetric and depends on the Euclidian distance $||x_i - x_j|$ between the data points:-

$$A_{ij} = \exp(-\alpha \, ||x_i - x_j||^2)$$

We might provide a hard cut-off R so that $A_{ij} = 0$ if $||x_i - x_j||^2 \geq R$ and in some applications we pre-multiply Aij with a feature Affinity Kernal. Just note that-

$A_{ij} = 1$ when the points are close in R^n and $A_{ij} \leftarrow 0$ if the points x_i, x_j are far apart. Please note that close data points are in the same cluster while data points in different clusters are far away. Also note that data points in the same cluster may also be far away in comparison to the points in different clusters.

Objective: Our task is now to transform the space so that when the 2 points x_i and x_j are close enough so that they are always in the same cluster and when they are far apart, they are in different clusters.

Many types of Laplacians (L) are given in the literature like Normalized, Generalized, Relaxed etc. they all share the degree matrix, D. We define a degree matrix as a diagonal matrix that measures the degree at each node as follows:-

$$D_{i,j} = \Sigma \, (j \text{ to } n) \, a_{i,j}$$

This is known as a local nearest neighbour mean-field average of the Affinity. D is a normalization factor for A so that the Cluster Affinities are balanced across different clusters.

Q.12. Explain the Hidden Markov Model.

Ans. A tool used for representing probability distributions over a sequence of observations is Hidden Markov Model (HMM). The observation is denoted at a particular instance time, t, by variable Y_t. As long as we can define a probability distribution, this symbol can vary from discrete alphabet to a real valued variable or to an integer. Here, we assume that 't' can be an integer valued time index as the observation are sampled at discrete equally spaced time intervals. This model assumes that the observation at time, *t*, was generated by the same process whose state Si is concealed or hidden from the observer. This model has two defining properties as follows:-

1. This process conforms the Markov Property *i.e.* given the value of S_{i-1}, the current state S_i is independent of all the states prior to *t*-1.
2. The outputs also conforms a Markov property in accordance to the states given S_i, Y_i is independent of the states and observation at other times indexes.

Markov properties signifies joint distribution of a sequence of states and observations. The factorization of joint distribution given in equation can be represented graphically as shown in figure 2.2:-

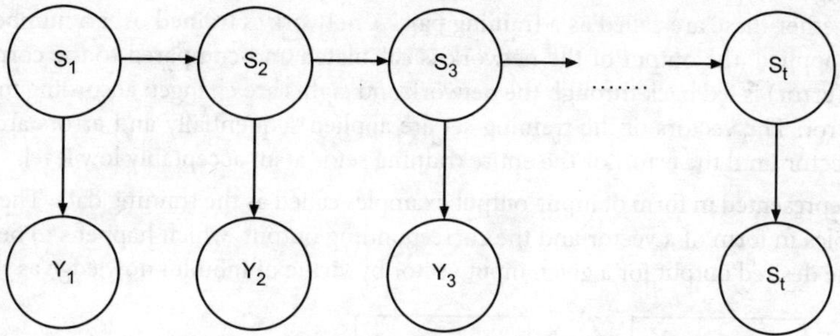

Fig. 2.2: Bayesian Network specifying Conditional Independence relation for a Hidden Markov Model

Each variable is denoted by a node in the graph of figure 2.2. each node receives a directed graph from the nodes that is conditionally dependent on, in the factorization of joint distribution. It also assumes that hidden variable is discrete *i.e.* is can take on *k* values which will be denoted by the integers {1.....*k*}.

To define a probability distribution over sequences of observations:-

$P(S_i)$ = probability distribution over initial state.

$K X k$ = state transition matrix defining $P(S_i \mid S_{i-1})$

$P(Y_t \mid S_t)$ = Output Model

Notes:

1. HMMs assume that the model is time invariant.
2. If the observables are in form of discrete symbols, taking one of *L* values, the *dp* model is represented by *k X L* emission matrix.
3. HMMs can be augmented to allow for input variables *i.e.* in such a way that there is an input dependent state transition probability. The system then steps ahead and models the conditional distribution of sequence of output distribution when you are provided with the input distributions.

Q.13. Explain Supervised and Unsupervised Learning with a case study.

Ans. According to Simon Haykin, learning is the process by which free parameters of a neural network are adapted through a process of stimulation by the environment in which the network is embedded. The type of learning is determined by the manner in which the parameter changes take place." This process of learning involves three steps:-

S1 : The neural network is stimulated by the environment (excitatory or inhibitory).

S2 : The free parameters of the network like the synaptic weights and the biases, undergo a change as a result of this stimulation.

S3: The response of the neural network to the environment changes as a result of the change in its internal free parameters.

The process of learning involves two things: -

1. The Learning Paradigms, which determine the manner in which a neural network relates to the environment. Here a neural network represents a set of inter-connected neurons.
2. The Learning Law, which is a set of well- defined rules called as the learning algorithm. There is no unique algorithm. One law differs from the other in the manner in which weights and biases are adjusted.

Artificial neural networks can modify their behaviour in response to their environment. Given as a set of inputs with desired outputs, they self-adjust to produce consistent responses. Different types of training algorithms have been developed. Learning algorithms like ANNs, in general, can be presented in either differential-equation or difference-equation form.

A network is trained so that application of a set of inputs produces the desired set of outputs. Each such input is known as a vector. Training is accomplished by sequentially applying input vectors while adjusting network weights according to a predetermined procedure. During training, the network weighs gradually converge to values such that each input vector produces the desired output vector. Training algorithms are put under two categories- supervised and unsupervised.

Supervised Training : A type of training that needs the pairing of each input vector with a target vector showing the desired output. Together these are called as a training pair. A network is trained over a number of such training pairs. An input vector is applied, the output of the network is calculated and compared to the corresponding target vector and the difference (error) is fed back through the network and eights are changed according to an algorithm that tends to minimize the error. The vectors of the training set are applied sequentially and errors are calculated and weights adjusted for each vector until the error for the entire training set is at an acceptably low level.

The knowledge is represented in form of input-output examples called as the training data. The training data consists of pairs of input samples in form of a vector and the corresponding output, which happens to be the desired output. The teacher provides the desired output for a given input vector by virtue of inbuilt knowledge as shown in figure 2.3.

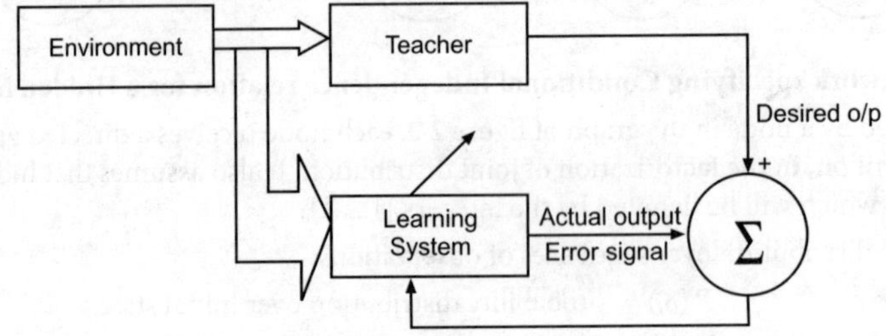

***Figure 2.3:** Supervised Learning*

The network computes the output called as the actual output. The error signal is the difference between the desired output / response and the actual output/response.

Please understand that the network parameters like the synaptic weights and bis=ases are adjusted by means of the learning law, under the influence of the error signal and the input vector. Also note that this is done iteratively until the actual response is close to the desired response. It is at this point that we can say that the network is trained. In nutshell, supervised learning involves the following steps:-

S1: Determine the type of training examples and form the training set. This is a set of input vector and the corresponding output vectors.

S2: The input vector must capture the features descriptive of the object. The number of features should not be too large but large enough to predict the output.

S3: Determine the learning law and train the network with the input training data.

S4: After the training is completed, the network is validated with a subset of the training set.

Please note that the mean-square error or the sum of squared errors over the training sample, defined as a function of the system parameters can be used as a performance measure for the system. Also note that for the system to improve the performance, the operating point must move towards a point of minimum error. Supervised learning is used in applications like pattern classification and function approximation.

Unsupervised Training: It is a more plausible model of learning in biological system. It was developed by Kohonen et. al. in 1984. It requires no target vector for the outputs. Hence no comparisons to pre-determined ideal responses can be made. The training set solely consists of input vectors. The training algorithm modifies the network weights to produce output vectors that are consistent. This means that both application of one of the training vectors or application of a vector that is similar to it, will produce the same pattern of outputs. Please understand that the training process extracts the statistical properties of the training set and groups similar vectors into classes. Applying a vector from a given class to the input will produce a specific output vector but there is no way to find out prior to training which specific output pattern will be produced by a given input vector class. Also note that the outputs of such a network must generally be transformed into a more comprehensible form following a training process. This is not difficult. It is so because it is simpler to identify the I/O relationships in a network.

In this type of learning, there is no teacher to see the process of learning. We deal with a class of problems to find out how data is organized. It is shown in figure 2.4.

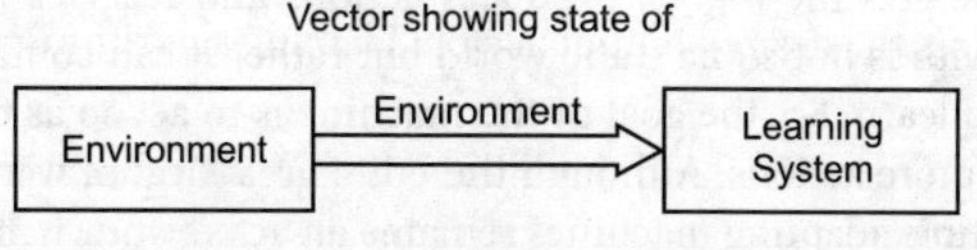

***Fig. 2.4:** Unsupervised Learning*

In machine learning, unsupervised learning refers to the problem of trying to find hidden structure in unlabeled data. Because the examples given to the learner are unlabeled, there is no error or reward signal to evaluate a potential solution. Unsupervised learning is closely related to the problem of density estimation in statistics. However, unsupervised learning also covers many other techniques that seek to summarize and explain key features of the data. Many methods employed in unsupervised learning are based on data mining methods used to pre-process data. Unsupervised learning includes several approaches as listed below:-

- Clustering like k-means, mixture models, hierarchical clustering;
- Blind signal separation using feature extraction techniques for dimensionality reduction like Principal Component Analysis, Independent Component Analysis, Non-negative matrix factorization, singular value decomposition.

Among neural networks models, the Self-organizing Map (SOM) and Adaptive Resonance Theory (ART) are commonly used unsupervised learning algorithms.

Differences between unsupervised and supervised learning?

Supervised and unsupervised learning differ only in the casual structure of the model. In supervised learning, the model defines the effect one set of observations, called as inputs, has on another set of observations, called outputs. His means that the input are assumed to be at the beginning and outputs at the end of the causal chain. The models can include mediating variables between the inputs and outputs. In unsupervised learning, all observations are assumed to be caused by latent variables. This means that the observations are assumed to be at the end of the causal chain. On the other hand, the models for supervised learning often leave the probability for inputs undefined. This model is not needed as long as the inputs are available but if some of the input values are missing then it is not possible to infer anything about the outputs. If the inputs are also modelled then missing inputs cause no problem since they can be considered latent variables as in unsupervised learning. With unsupervised learning it is possible to learn larger and more complex models than with supervised learning. This is so because in supervised learning one is trying to find the connection between two sets of observations. **Please note that the difficulty of learning task increases exponentially in the number of steps between the two sets and that is why supervised learning cannot learn model with deep hierarchies.** In unsupervised learning, learning can proceed hierarchically from the observations into ever more abstract levels of representation. Each additional hierarchy needs to learn only one step and therefore, the learning time increases linearly in the number of levels in the model hierarchy. **Also note here that if the causal relation between the input and output observations is complex *i.e.* there is a large causal gap, it is often easier to bridge the gap using unsupervised learning instead of supervised learning.** Instead of finding the casual pathway from the inputs to the outputs, one starts building the model upwards from both the sets of observations with the hope that in higher levels of abstractions the gap is easier to bridge. Note also that the input and output observations are in **symmetrical positions** in the model.

Consider a machine or a living organism which receives some sequences of inputs, x_1, x_2 , x_3, ...x_t where xt is the sensory input at time, *t*. This input, which we often call the data, could correspond to an image on the retina, the pixels in a camera or a sound waveform. It could also correspond to less obviously sensory data like words in a news story or the list of items in a mall. So, now four types of machine learning are possible:-

a. In supervised learning, the machine is also given a sequence of desired outputs as y_1, y_2, y_3....y_t and the goal of the machine is to learn to produce the correct output given a new input. The output could be a class label (in classification) or a real number (in regression).

b. In reinforcement learning, the machine interacts with its environment by producing actions a_1, a_2,.....a_n. these actions affect the state of the environment which in turn results in the machine receiving some scalar rewards or punishments, r_1, r_2....r_n. the goal of the machine is to learn to act in a way that maximizes the future rewards it receives or minimizes the punishments over its lifetime. Reinforcement learning is closely related to the fields of decision theory and control theory.

c. Another third type of machine learning is related to the game theory and it generalizes reinforcement learning. Here again the machine gets the inputs, produces actions and receives rewards. However, the environment that the machine interacts with is not some static world but rather it can contain other machines which can also sense, act, receive rewards and learn. So, the goal of the machine is to act so as to maximize rewards in light of the other machines current and future actions. Although there is a great deal of work in game theory for simple systems, the dynamic case with multiple adapting machines remains an active and challenging area of research.

d. Finally, in unsupervised learning, the machine simply receives inputs x_1, x_2, ..., but obtains neither supervised target outputs nor rewards from its environment. It may seem somewhat mysterious to imagine what the machine could possibly learn that it doesn't get any feedback from its environment. However, it is possible to develop a formal framework for unsupervised learning based on the notion that the machine's goal is to build representations of the input that can be used for decision making, predicting future inputs, efficiently communicating the inputs to another machine etc. in a sense, unsupervised learning can be thought of as finding patterns in the data above and beyond what would be considered pure unstructured noise.

Unsupervised algorithms can be compared to a three months old baby. As 3 months old child receives the same visual stimuli as a newborn infant but can make much more sense of them and can recognize various patterns and features of visual input data. These abilities are not acquired from an external teacher and illustrate that a significant amount of learning is accomplished by biological facts, the artificial neural network discussed in this chapter attempt to discover special features and patterns from the available data without using external help.

Our learning starts from birth only. Observe how a baby learns to recognize its mother. The first act of learning of baby is 'to recognize'. When a child is trained to recognize concepts by being provided with labels for each experienced instance then this is supervised learning. On the other hand, learning the features themselves is an example of unsupervised learning. In this the lower-level features are automatically grouped or clustered based on how similar they are across many observed instances. In computing terms, we may call these images i.e. collection of pixels. As a child sees many images of 'dogs' or 'cats', then those pixels that form 'legs' are automatically grouped or clustered together. So, now we can say that the child has learned a new concept of 'legs without any external supervision (or teacher) even though the baby does not know about "leg". Furthermore, this concept of 'leg' becomes a feature that takes a baby to the next higher level of learning.

Several types of learning do exist, like-

1. Learning how to parse sentences.
2. Learning to recognize whether a tweet is positive or negative.
3. Learning the topic, a particular web page is talking about or
4. Discovering the topics that are being discussed in a corpus of text.

In many cases, the machine needs to be trained using data labelled by humans like parsing or sentiment mining. These are the examples of supervised learning. On the other hand, topic discovery is an example of unsupervised learning wherein there is no pre-existing knowledge being provided by outside human intervention. Our computer observes a number of such instances. Its task is to learn the concepts from the training set so as to be able to recognize future instances.

A simple computer program for the above scenario of 'cat-dog' may choose to store all of the observed instances, just as Google stores web pages and also creating an index of features as Google indexes documents using the words they contain. Then when presented with a new instance, our program merely looks up its fast experience very fast, using binary searching.

Case 1: If an exact match is found, the new observation is given the same animal label as the old one it matches with.

Case 2: If no match is found, we might use the closest match, in terms of the number of features that match exactly or use a small number of close matches and choose the label that occurs most often amongst these. This is called as a k-nearest-neighbour (or KNN) classifier as it classifies the instances given to it. But please note that if the number of past observations is very large then the classification process may be slow.

Google also uses classifiers to filter spam, learn user preferences or to classify tweets as positive or negative. Also note that machine learning using classifiers is also at the heart of NLP wherein the computer is trained to parse sentences from a large corpora of human-parsed text.

Google Translate that does automated translation between different languages also uses machine learning heavily. Now the objective is to find out whether a new sentence is expressing positive or negative opinion and to learn how to do so from the past observations of sentences that have been labelled correctly by humans. Instead of size and sound, now our features are the occurrences of words in sentences.

Actually, learning from a small number of examples cannot be perfect so the accuracy with which a concept is learned also needs to be considered. Accuracy is usually measured in terms of the probability of the learned classifier making a mistake. Please note here that the larger the chance of a mistake, lower is the accuracy. Also note that the inverse of the mistake probability can be used a s a measure of accuracy.

Clustering *i.e.* grouping items that are similar to each other is another basic technique of unsupervised learning. All that is needed is some way to compare two items.

Thus, we can say that machines can learn from examples, in case of supervised learning, such as for browsers versus surfers or dogs versus cats, a human-labelled set of training examples is needed. On the other hand, in unsupervised learning, machine learns from experiences as long as they can be clearly identified even if implicitly.

Web pages are mostly unstructured text. We know that text can be analyzed using NLP techniques. And that,

NLP + Machine Learning techniques ⟶ allows machine to learn larger number of General Knowledge facts from such large corpus as the entire web.

Whole of our machine learning is based on first being able to distinguish objects along with some of the features describing them. On the other hand, computers derive this ability directly through our programming. The classifiers can distinguish between different classes of objects like cats from dogs, buyers from browsers etc. provided they have been trained suitably. Unsupervised rule learning can discover important features and frequently observed associations between features, there by learning some structure of the world. Latent learning techniques can also discover infrequent correlations between objects based on their features. Finally, the computer can learn facts from vast volumes of text available on the web.

n nutshell, the learning algorithm uses a large number of labelled instances to learn its model. Then the learned model is used to assign labels to future instances. This is supervised learning. On the other hand, in unsupervised learning, instances are grouped into clusters based on their mutual similarity. There are no labels but only clusters characterized by a set of similar features.

Q.14. Give an overview of classification method.

Ans. In the field of machine learning, classification is the problem of finding out to which category a newly encountered observation belongs, based on the training dataset containing observations.

Before we discuss further, let us first of all define a multilayer perceptron and its training.

Multilayer Perceptron (MLP): It is a feed-forward ANN. It maps a set of input data to a set of output data. It consists of multiple layers of nodes represented in a directed graph with each layer being connected to the next layer completely. Apart from the input nodes, each node itself is a neuron or a processing element with a non-linear activation function. The activation function of a node in this context defines the output of that node given an input or set of inputs.

Activation Function: The problem to be considered here is that the jump should be in between firing and not firing to make it behave like neuron. So, we need an activation function that looks like a threshold function but it is differentiable so that gradient can be computed. If we look at the graph of the threshold function, it is similar to S-shaped functions whose mathematical form is called as a sigmoid function.

Error Function: The method that we ar using is called **back-propagation** error which depicts that errors are sent backward through the network. It is a type of **gradient descent**. In perceptron, the weights are changed so that the neurons were fired only when the targets indicate and they did not fire when the targets did not indicate. It was time to choose an error function, $E(t, o)$ and tried to make it as small as possible. Since there was only one set of weights available in the network, it was sufficient to train the same. We prepare to minimize the error so that neurons fire only when they should but on adding extra layers of weights it becomes difficult to arrange. Also when trying to adapt the weights of MLP it is difficult to find out which weights caused the error. This could be any of the weights i.e. the weights connecting inputs to the hidden layer or weights hidden layer to the output layer. We have so far used $E = t - o$ for the perceptron. Say, we have two errors-

1. The target is bigger than the output.
2. The output is bigger than the target.

Please understand that if these two errors are of same size, then we ass them the resultant zero which depicts that no error was made and is incorrect. To get this in line, we need to make all errors to have a same sign. To cope with this problem, the best way is to find the sum of squares error function. The sum of squares error function basically calculates the difference between target (t) and output (o) for each node, squares them and adds them all together. That is,

$$E(t, o) = \frac{1}{2} \Sigma_{l=1} \text{ to } n \, (t_l - o_l)^2$$

Q.15. Define Set-up, Training, Test and validation dataset.

Ans. There are three steps involved during MLP and are as follows: -

S1: Data Preparation.

S2: Training, Testing and Validation.

S3: Generalization and Overfitting.

Machine learning algorithms tend to learn from data. So, it is important that right data is fed for the problem to be solved. Please note that the more disciplined the data is handled, more consistent and better are the results.

Let us study these steps now.

S1: Data Preparation: It involves three sub-tasks-

1. **Select Data :** It involves the selection of subset of all available data that we will be dealing with. We need to take into consideration what data is needed to solve the problem that we are working on.
2. **Pre-process Data :** After you have selected the data, the next step is how you are going to use the data.

   Steps for data pre-processing:-

   2.1 Formatting : The data should be in a suitable format that you want to work on like the data may be in relational database and you want to use it as a text file.

   2.2 Cleaning : It is the removal or fixing of missing data.

   2.3 Sampling : It is better t take smaller representative sample of data instead of more selected data which results in shorter running times for algorithms and smaller computational and memory requirements.
3. **Transform Data :** The final step is to transform the processed data. The specific algorithms that you are using and the knowledge of the problem domain will influence this step and you will very likely have to revisit different transformations of your pre-processed data as you work on your problem. Three common data transformations are scaling, attribute decomposition and attribute aggregations. This step is also called as feature engineering. It involves-

   a. **Scaling :** The pre-processed data may contain attributes with a mixtures of scales for various quantities like dollars, kgs and sales volume. Many machine learning methods like data attribute to have the same scale such as between 0 and 1 for the smallest and the largest value for a given feature. Consider any scaling feature that you may need to perform.

   b. **Decomposition :** There may be features that represent a complex concept that may be more useful to a machine learning method when split into the constituent parts. For example, a date that may have day and time components that in turn could spli out further. Perhaps only the hour of the day is relevant to the problem being solved. Thus, consider what feature decompositions can be made performed.

   c. **Aggregation :** There may be features that can be aggregated into a single feature that would be more meaningful to the problem you are trying to solve. For example, there may be data instance for each time a customer logged into a system that could be aggregated into a count for the number of logins allowing the additional instances to be discarded. You have to consider the type of feature aggregations to be performed.

   Note: One can spend a lot of time engineering features from your data and it can be very beneficial for the algorithm performance. Start small and build on the skills you learn.

   How data preparation is done in MLP?

   Every machine learning algorithm is likely to learn more effectively if some pre-processing of the data inputs and targets is performed before the network is trained. In the case of Perceptron, if sigmoidal activation function is used then possible target values should be 0 and 1. In fact, the targets are scaled to lie between 0 and 1, no matter what sort of activation function is used for the output layer neurons. This helps in avoiding the weights to get too large values. The most common approach to scaling the data for MLP is to look at each data dimension independently and further make each dimension have a zero mean and unit variance in each dimension or simply to scale them so that maximum value is 1 and mi -nimum is -1. These scaling are basically data normalization (or standardization). In case of MLP, normalization is not mandatory but useful. In this, it is very easy to perform normalization by using in-built function mean( ) and var( ). But take care of which axis the mean and variance is to be computed. That is,

```
data = (data - data.mean (axix=0)) / data.var(axis=0)
targets = (targets    -    targets.mean(axis=0))    /    targets.
    var(axis=0)
```

S2: Training, Testing and Validation : After MLP training is over, in next step we need to find out how well it performs. In case of trained network, the error can be computed by computing the sum of squares error between output and target. The next task is what data should be used to test the network. It is not intelligence to use the same data for training as well as testing. This is so because it would not tell us how well the network generalizes and whether or not overfitting has happened. Thus, we need to keep separate pairs in reserve for testset (input, target) which are not used for the training purpose. In this case, we have to adjust with the fact that the amount of data which is available for testing is reduced. It is more complex, scenario when we check how well the network is learning during training so that when to stop can be decided. Now to make such a decision we cannot use training data as we would not detect overfitting but we cannot use the testing data either as we are saving it for the final test.

So, a 3rd data set called as a validation set is required to validate the learning so far, in the field of statistics, it is called as cross validation.

The ratio of training to testing to validation data is-

50:25:25 if you have large amount of data and 0:20:20 if you have a lesser amount of data.

So, the input data set is split into three different sets-training set, testing set and validation set.

S3: Generalization and Overfitting : The ability of a machine to learn on being introduced with the sets of data during training so that when it is introduced to new and unseen examples, it can perform accurately is known as Generalization. To ensure that network generalizes well, we tend to use a neural network in order to generalize from the training examples to all possible inputs. Some troublesome situations also arise in both under training and over training the network. Every other weight can be changed in a neural network. Thus, degree of variability is quite high. This is certainly more than in variation than there is in the function we are learning. So, the care has to be taken if we are training for long. This implies that we will overfit the data which means that during the process we have also learnt about the noise and inaccuracies in the data along with the actual function. Overfitting makes the model quite complex by having too many parameters. By doing this it loses its generalization power which results in poor performance in new data.

Q.16. Explain Linear Discriminant Analysis (LDA).

Ans. A linear discriminant method that is used in the field of statistics, pattern recognition and machine learning is Fisher's Linear Discriminant. It is used to find the linear combination of features that divides two or more classes of objects or events. The combination that comes out in the form of result may be used later as a linear classifier, in general, for dimensionality reduction before later classification. So, we can say that LDA is a supervised technique of feature extraction that is used to find a linear combination of the available features which separate the classes.

Applying LDA : The core objective is t decrease the dimension of the data in order to reduce the computational cost of classification. After applying the LDA to a dataset, the "new features" minimizes the dispersion between the samples of the same class and maximizes the dispersion between samples of different classes.

For example, say you have a dataset of players who practice different sports like may be cricket, basketball, soccer, Golf etc. Imagine that the available features taken into consideration for these sports are height, weight and body mass index. Now when the instances are plotted, there might be some regions of intersection of two or more classes. So, when yu apply LDA to a data set, it will produce new features that might result in better separation of classes-lesser and smaller regions of intersection.

Limitations of LDA :

1. LDA can generate only C (number of classes) or less number of features.

2. At times, one is dealing with datasets of 20 features, for example, and there are only 2 classes, so LDA have to be reduced to 2 axis. Such reductions usually results in loss of information that further results in low classification accuracy.

Q.17. Explain overfitting in terms of number of examples. What is early stopping?

Ans. Firstly, the data needs to be split. Two cases arise here: -

Case-1: When your number of examples, n, is high, such as $n > 10,000$, you can quite confidently create a randomly split dataset.

Case-2: When the dataset is smaller, comparing basic statistics such as mean, mode, median and variance across the response and features in the training and tests sets will help us understand whether the test set is unsuitable. Whenever you are not sure of your data split, just re-calculate the new one.

A function that fits perfectly on the training data needs to be examined. And it is this phenomenon of overfitting that will give best performance on the training data.

Overfitting is also called as overtraining. Given a neural network, it is possible to imagine how easily the algorithm could learn almost anything from data, if you add several layers. In fact, the algorithm does so well that its predictions are often affected by this high estimate variance called as overfitting or overtraining. **Please note that this phenomenon of overtraining causes the NN to learn every detail of the training examples that makes it possible to replicate them in the prediction phase. Also note that neural networks are weaker.** They are more prone to errors than other machine learning solutions.

Split your data into training, validation and test sets. The algorithm must learn from data. But for this you must evaluate the following parameters: -

a. Number of architectural layers and nodes within them.

b. Activation functions.

c. Learning parameters.

d. Number of iterations.

This architecture makes it easy for us to create powerful predictive models but with high probability of overfitting. The learning parameter controls the rate at which a network learns from data. But this may not prevent overtraining. To prevent overfitting or overtraining we have two methods: -

a. Regularization

b. Early stop

We don't know when the mode will start overfitting. Using training set we compute the cost function which improves as the optimization progresses. Soon you will start recording noise from the data. At some point during the training process, it starts further falling down which implies that your model has reached its learning limit.

Regularization : In this method, we regularize the objective function. This is done by adding additional terms that penalize larger weights. Mathematically speaking, we modify the objective function so that it becomes-

$$\text{Error} + \lambda\, f(\theta)$$

Where $f(\theta)$ grows larger as the components of θ grow larger,

λ is the regularization strength, a new hyper-parameter.

Please note that the value we choose for λ determines how much we want to prevent overfitting. That is,

a. $\lambda = 0$ means that we do not take any measures against the possibility of overfitting.

b. If λ is too large, then our model will prioritize keeping θ as small as possible.

The need is to find the parameter values that perform well on the training set we choose. So, selection of λ is very significant. We may even use brute-force method here.

Regularization method has been used in non-linear problems by the researchers. It is also of different types like L2 regularization and L1 regularization. Also note that during gradient descent update, using L2 regularization means that every weight is decayed linearly to zero. That is why, this phenomenon is also known as weight decay.

Early Stopping : A technique based on dividing data into three subsets. The first subset is the training set used for computing the gradient and updating the network weights and biases. The second subset is the validation set. When the validation error increases for a specified number of iterations, the training is stopped and the weights and biases at the minimum of the validation error are returned. The third subset is the test set. It is used to verify the network design.

The early stopping meta-algorithm for determining the best amount of time to train is discussed now. This meta-algorithm is a general strategy that works well with a variety of training algorithms. It gives ways of quantifying error on the validation set.

Let n be the number of steps between evaluations.

Let p be the "patience," the number of times to observe worsening validation set error before giving up.

Let θo be the initial parameters.

$\theta \leftarrow \theta o$

$i \leftarrow 0$

$j \leftarrow 0$

$v \leftarrow \infty$

$\theta \leftarrow \theta$

$i \leftarrow i$

while $j < p$ do

Update θ by running the training algorithm for n steps.

$i \leftarrow i + n$

$v \leftarrow$ ValidationSetError(θ)

if $v < v$ then

$j \leftarrow 0$

$\theta \leftarrow \theta$

$i \leftarrow i$

$v \leftarrow v$

else

$j \leftarrow j + 1$

end if

end while

Best parameters are θ and the best number of training steps is i.

This strategy is known as **early stopping**. It is probably the most commonly used form of regularization in deep learning. It is very popular as it is both effectiveness and its simplicity.

One way to think of early stopping is as a very efficient hyperparameter selection algorithm. So, the number of training steps is just another hyperparameter.

In the case of early stopping, we are controlling the effective capacity of the model by determining how many steps it can take to fit the training set. Most hyperparameters must be chosen using an expensive guess and check process, where we set a hyperparameter at the start of training, then run training for several steps to see its effect. The "training time" hyperparameter is unique in that by definition a single run of training tries out many values of the hyperparameter. The only significant cost to choosing this hyperparameter automatically via early stopping is running the validation set evaluation periodically during training. Ideally, this is done in parallel to the training process on a separate machine, separate CPU, or separate GPU from the main training process. If such resources are not available, then the cost of these periodic evaluations may be reduced by using a validation set that is small compared to the training set or by evaluating the validation set error less frequently and obtaining a lower resolution estimate of the optimal training time.

An additional cost to early stopping is the need to maintain a copy of the best parameters. This cost is generally negligible, because it is acceptable to store these parameters in a slower and larger form of memory (for example, training in GPU memory, but storing the optimal parameters in host memory or on a disk drive). Since the best parameters are written to infrequently and never read during training, these occasional slow writes have little effect on the total training time.

Early stopping is a very unobtrusive form of regularization, in that it requires almost no change in the underlying training procedure, the objective function, or the set of allowable parameter values. Also note that this means that it is easy to use early stopping without damaging the learning dynamics. This is in contrast to weight decay, where one must be careful not to use too much weight decay and trap the network in a bad local minimum corresponding to a solution with pathologically small weights.

Early stopping may be used either alone or in conjunction with other regularization strategies. Even when using regularization strategies that modify the objective function to encourage better generalization, it is rare for the best generalization to occur at a local minimum of the training objective.

Early stopping requires a validation set, which means some training data is not fed to the model. To best exploit this extra data, one can perform extra training after the initial training with early stopping has completed.

Q.18. Explain Supervised and Unsupervised Learning with a CASE STUDY.

Ans. According to Simon Haykin, learning is the process by which free parameters of a neural network are adapted through a process of stimulation by the environment in which the network is embedded. The type of learning is determined by the manner in which the parameter changes take place." This process of learning involves three steps: -

S1: The neural network is stimulated by the environment (excitatory or inhibitory).

S2: The free parameters of the network like the synaptic weights and the biases, undergo a change as a result of this stimulation.

S3: The response of the neural network to the environment changes as a result of the change in its internal free parameters.

The process of learning involves two things: -

3. The Learning Paradigms, which determine the manner in which a neural network relates to the environment. Here a neural network represents a set of inter-connected neurons.
4. The Learning Law, which is a set of well-defined rules called as the **learning algorithm.** There is no unique algorithm. One law differs from the other in the manner in which weights and biases are adjusted.

Artificial neural networks can modify their behaviour in response to their environment. Given as a set of inputs with desired outputs, they self-adjust to produce consistent responses. Different types of training algorithms have been developed. Learning algorithms like ANNs, in general, can be presented in either differential-equation or difference-equation form.

A network is trained so that application of a set of inputs produces the desired set of outputs. Each such input is known as a vector. Training is accomplished by sequentially applying input vectors while adjusting network weights according to a predetermined procedure. During training, the network weighs gradually converge to values such that each input vector produces the desired output vector. Training algorithms are put under two categories- supervised and unsupervised.

Supervised Training : A type of training that needs the pairing of each input vector with a target vector showing the desired output. Together these are called as a **training pair.** A network is trained over a number of such training pairs. An input vector is applied, the output of the network is calculated and compared to the corresponding target vector and the difference (error) is fed back through the network and eights are changed according to an algorithm that tends to minimize the error. The vectors of the training set are applied sequentially and errors are calculated and weights adjusted for each vector until the error for the entire training set is at an acceptably low level.

The knowledge is represented in form of input-output examples called as the **training data.** The training data consists of pairs of input samples in form of a vector and the corresponding output, which happens to be the desired output. The teacher provides the desired output for a given input vector by virtue of inbuilt knowledge as shown in figure 2.5.

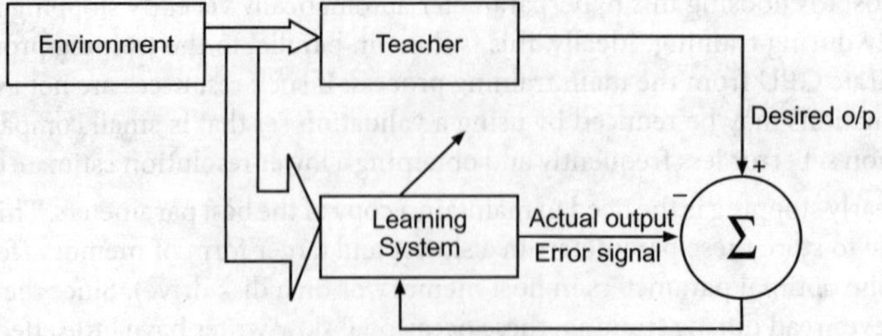

Fig. 2.5: Supervised Learning

The network computes the output called as the actual output. The error signal is the difference between the desired output / response and the actual output/response.

Please understand that the network parameters like the synaptic weights and biases are adjusted by means of the learning law, under the influence of the error signal and the input vector. Also note that this is done iteratively until the actual response is close to the desired response. It is at this point that we can say that the network is trained. In nutshell, supervised learning involves the following steps: -

S1: Determine the type of training examples and form the training set. This is a set of input vector and the corresponding output vectors.

S2: The input vector must capture the features descriptive of the object. The number of features should not be too large but large enough to predict the output.

S3: Determine the learning law and train the network with the input training data.

S4: After the training is completed, the network is validated with a subset of the training set.

Please note that the mean-square error or the sum of squared errors over the training sample, defined as a function of the system parameters can be used as a performance measure for the system. Also note that for the system to improve the performance, the operating point must move towards a point of minimum error. Supervised learning is used in applications like pattern classification and function approximation.

Unsupervised Training: It is a more plausible model of learning in biological system. It was developed by Kohonen et. al. in 1984. It requires no target vector for the outputs. Hence no comparisons to pre-determined ideal responses can be made. The training set solely consists of input vectors. The training algorithm modifies the network weights to produce output vectors that are consistent. This means that both application of one of the training vectors or application of a vector that is similar to it, will produce the same pattern of outputs. **Please understand that the training process extracts the statistical properties of the training set and groups similar vectors into classes.** Applying a vector from a given class to the input will produce a specific output vector but there is no way to find out prior to training which specific output pattern will be produced by a given input vector class. Also note that the outputs of such a network must generally be transformed into a more comprehensible form following a training process. This is not difficult. It is so because it is simpler to identify the I/O relationships in a network.

In this type of learning, there is no teacher to see the process of learning. We deal with a class of problems to find out how data is organized. It is shown in figure 2.4

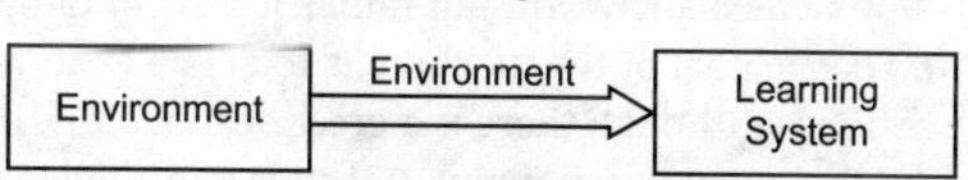

Fig. 2.6: Unsupervised Learning

In machine learning, unsupervised learning refers to the problem of trying to find hidden structure in unlabelled data. Because the examples given to the learner are unlabelled, there is no error or reward signal to evaluate a potential solution. Unsupervised learning is closely related to the problem of density estimation in statistics. However, unsupervised learning also covers many other techniques that seek to summarize and explain key features of the data. Many methods employed in unsupervised learning are based on data mining methods used to pre-process data. Unsupervised learning includes several approaches as listed below:-

- Clustering like k-means, mixture models, hierarchical clustering;
- Blind signal separation using feature extraction techniques for dimensionality reduction like Principal Component Analysis, Independent Component Analysis, Non-negative matrix factorization, singular value decomposition.

Among neural networks models, the Self-organizing Map (SOM) and Adaptive Resonance Theory (ART) are commonly used unsupervised learning algorithms.

Differences between unsupervised and supervised learning—

Supervised and unsupervised learning differ only in the casual structure of the model. In supervised learning, the model defines the effect one set of observations, called as inputs, has on another set of observations, called outputs. His means that the input are assumed to be at the beginning and outputs at the end of the causal chain. The models can include mediating variables between the inputs and outputs. In unsupervised learning, all observations are assumed to be caused by latent variables. This means that the observations are assumed to be at the end of the causal chain. On the other hand, the models for supervised learning often leave the probability for inputs undefined. This model is not needed as long as the inputs are available but if some of the input values are missing then it is not possible to infer anything about the outputs. If the inputs are also modelled then missing inputs cause no problem since they can be considered latent variables as in unsupervised learning. With unsupervised learning it is possible to learn larger and more complex models than with supervised learning. This is so because in supervised learning one is trying to find the connection between two sets of observations. **Please note that the difficulty of learning task increases exponentially in the number of steps between the two sets and that is why supervised learning cannot learn model with deep hierarchies.** In unsupervised learning, learning can proceed hierarchically from the observations into ever more abstract levels of representation. Each additional hierarchy needs to learn only one step and therefore, the learning time increases linearly in the number of levels in the model hierarchy. **Also note here that if the causal relation between the input and output observations is complex *i.e.*** there is a large causal gap, it is often easier to bridge the gap using unsupervised learning instead of supervised learning. Instead of finding the casual pathway from the inputs to the outputs, one starts building the model upwards from both th sets of observations with the hope that in higher levels of abstractions the gap is easier to bridge. Note also that the input and output observations are in symmetrical positions in the model.

Consider a machine or a living organism which receives some sequences of inputs, x_1, x_2, x_3, ...x_t where x_t is the sensory input at time, *t*. This input, which we often call the data, could correspond to an image on the retina, the pixels in a camera or a sound waveform. It could also correspond to less obviously sensory data like words in a news story or the list of items in a mall. So, now four types of machine learning are possible:-

e. In supervised learning, the machine is also given a sequence of desired outputs as y_1, y_2, y_3.....y_t and the goal of the machine is to learn to produce the correct output given a new input. The output could be a class label (in classification) or a real number (in regression).

f. In reinforcement learning, the machine interacts with its environment by producing actions a_1, a_2,.....a_n. these actions affect the state of the environment which in turn results in the machine receiving some scalar rewards or punishments, r_1, r_2....r_n. the goal of the machine is to learn to act in a way that maximizes the future rewards it receives or minimizes the punishments over its lifetime. Reinforcement learning is closely related to the fields of decision theory and control theory.

g. Another third type of machine learning is related to the game theory and it generalizes reinforcement learning. Here again the machine gets the inputs, produces actions and receives rewards. However, the environment that the machine interacts with is not some static world but rather it can contain other machines which can also sense, act, receive rewards and learn. So, the goal of the machine is to act so as to maximize rewards in light of the other machines current and future actions. Although there is a great deal of work in game theory for simple systems, the dynamic case with multiple adapting machines remains an active and challenging area of research.

h. Finally, in unsupervised learning, the machine simply receives inputs x_1, x_2, ..., but obtains neither supervised target outputs nor rewards from its environment. It may seem somewhat mysterious to imagine what the machine could possibly learn that it doesn't get any feedback from its environment. However, it is possible to develop a formal framework for unsupervised learning based on the notion that the machine's goal is to build representations of the input that can be used for decision making, predicting future inputs, efficiently communicating the inputs to another machine etc. in a sense, unsupervised learning can be thought of as finding patterns in the data above and beyond what would be considered pure unstructured noise.

Unsupervised algorithms can be compared to a three months old baby. As 3 months old child receives the same visual stimuli as a newborn infant but can make much more sense of them and can recognize various patterns and features of visual input data. These abilities are not acquired from an external teacher and illustrate that a significant amount of learning is accomplished by biological facts, the artificial neural network discussed in this chapter attempt to discover special features and patterns from the available data without using external help.

Our learning starts from birth only. Observe how a baby learns to recognize its mother. The first act of learning of baby is 'to recognize'. When a child is trained to recognize concepts by being provided with labels for each experienced instance then this is supervised learning. On the other hand, learning the features themselves is an example of unsupervised learning. In this the lower-level features are automatically grouped or clustered based on how similar they are across many observed instances. In computing terms, we may call these images i.e. collection of pixels. As a child sees many images of 'dogs' or 'cats', then those pixels that form 'legs' are automatically grouped or clustered together. So, now we can say that the child has learned a new concept of 'legs without any external supervision (or teacher) even though the baby does not know about "leg". Furthermore, this concept of 'leg' becomes a feature that takes a baby to the next higher level of learning.

Several types of learning do exist, like-

5. Learning how to parse sentences.
6. Learning to recognize whether a tweet is positive or negative.
7. Learning the topic, a particular web page is talking about or
8. Discovering the topics that are being discussed in a corpus of text.

   In many cases, the machine needs to be trained using data labelled by humans like parsing or sentiment mining. These are the examples of supervised learning. On the other hand, topic discovery is an example of unsupervised learning wherein there is no pre-existing knowledge being provided by outside human intervention. Our computer observes a number of such instances. Its task is to learn the concepts from the training set so as to be able to recognize future instances.

A simple computer program for the above scenario of 'cat-dog' may choose to store all of the observed instances, just as Google stores web pages and also creating an index of features as Google indexes documents using the words they contain. Then when presented with a new instance, our program merely looks up its fast experience very fast, using binary searching.

Case 1: If an exact match is found, the new observation is given the same animal label as the old one it matches with.

Case 2: If no match is found, we might use the closest match, in terms of the number of features that match exactly or use a small number of close matches and choose the label that occurs most often amongst these. This is called as a k-nearest-neighbour (or KNN) classifier as it classifies the instances given to it. But please note that if the number of past observations is very large then the classification process may be slow.

Google also uses classifiers to filter spam, learn user preferences or to classify tweets as positive or negative. Also note that machine learning using classifiers is also at the heart of NLP wherein the computer is trained to parse sentences from a large corpus of human-parsed text.

Google Translate that does automated translation between different languages also uses machine learning heavily. Now the objective is to find out whether a new sentence is expressing positive or negative opinion and to learn how to do so from the past observations of sentences that have been labelled correctly by humans. Instead of size and sound, now our features are the occurrences of words in sentences.

Actually, learning from a small number of examples cannot be perfect so the accuracy with which a concept is learned also needs to be considered. Accuracy is usually measured in terms of the probability of the learned classifier making a mistake. Please note here that the larger the chance of a mistake, lower is the accuracy. Also note that the inverse of the mistake probability can be used a s a measure of accuracy.

Clustering *i.e.*, grouping items that are similar to each other is another basic technique of unsupervised learning. All that is needed is some way to compare two items.

Thus, we can say that machines can learn from examples, in case of supervised learning, such as for browsers versus surfers or dogs versus cats, a human-labelled set of training examples is needed. On the other hand, in unsupervised learning, machine learns from experiences as long as they can be clearly identified even if implicitly.

Web pages are mostly unstructured text. We know that text can be analysed using NLP techniques. And that,

NLP + Machine Learning techniques ⟶ allows machine to learn larger number of General Knowledge facts from such large corpus as the entire web.

Whole of our machine learning is based on first being able to distinguish objects along with some of the features describing them. On the other hand, computers derive this ability directly through our programming. The classifiers can distinguish between different classes of objects like cats from dogs, buyers from browsers etc. provided they have been trained suitably. Unsupervised rule learning can discover important features and frequently observed associations between features, there by learning some structure of the world. Latent learning techniques can also discover infrequent correlations between objects based on their features. Finally, the computer can learn facts from vast volumes of text available on the web.

In nutshell, the learning algorithm uses a large number of labelled instances to learn its model. Then the learned model is used to assign labels to future instances. This is supervised learning. On the other hand, in unsupervised learning, instances are grouped into clusters based on their mutual similarity. There are no labels but only clusters characterized by a set of similar features.

SUMMARY

We have studied in this chapter that in machine learning instead of teaching a computer a massive list of rules to solve a problem, we give it a model with which it can evaluate examples. Also, we give a small set of instructions to modify this model if it makes a mistake. We find that as the time passes by, w well suited model will be able to solve the problems in a batter and efficient way. The machine learning algorithm should be such that it tries to make the values of the parameters more and more accurate as it is exposed to more and more examples. But this is just a tip of an iceberg. Recently, scientists have developed the models that resemble the structures as used by a human brain. This involves deep learning only.

MULTIPLE CHOICE QUESTIONS

1. **Machine learning includes-**
   (*a*) Narrow Learning (*b*) Deep Learning
   (*c*) Varied Learning (*d*) None of the above
2. **A subset of artificial intelligence field called as machine learning which is predicted on the basic idea of learning from example is named as-**
   (*a*) Learning by Examples (*b*) Learning by Machine
   (*c*) Deep Learning (*d*) None of the above
3. **RBM stands for-**
   (*a*) Restricted Boltzmann Machines (*b*) Regular Boltzmann Memory
   (*c*) Referred Boltzmann Machine (*d*) None of the above
4. **Deep Belief Networks use-**
   (*a*) RBM (*b*) DBMS
   (*c*) IBM (*d*) None of the above
5. **The time spent in training a deep learning model is given by the formula:-**
   (*a*) Training Time (TT) = [Number of training samples] + [Number of Epochs]
   (*b*) Training Time (TT) = [Number of training samples] - [Number of Epochs]
   (*c*) Training Time (TT) = [Number of training samples] * [Number of Epochs]
   (*d*) Training Time (TT) = [Number of training samples] / [Number of Epochs]
6. **The more are the weights-**
   (*a*) Slower will be the training (*b*) Faster will be the training
   (*c*) Lesser will be the training (*d*) None of the above
7. **Which of the following is a rectification function-**
   (*a*) Rectifier (*b*) Amplifier
   (*c*) Simplifier (*d*) None of the above
8. **The working of ANNs is similar to-**
   (*a*) A human brain (*b*) A car working
   (*c*) A human eye (*d*) None of the above
9. **Even a tiny part of the brain that is about the size of a grain of rice has-**
   (*a*) 5000 neurons (*b*) 6000 neurons
   (*c*) 10,000 neurons (*d*) None of the above
10. **Connections traverse from-**
    (*a*) Lower to higher layer (*b*) Higher to lower layer
    (*c*) At same layer (*d*) None of the above
11. **As we make neural networks deep, which phenomenon is seen-**
    (*a*) Overloading (*b*) Overriding
    (*c*) Overfitting (*d*) None of the above

12. A single iteration over the entire training set is called as an-

(*a*) Epoch (*b*) Clock

(*c*) Cycle (*d*) None of the above

13. The data is split up into two parts-

(*a*) Training data and valid data (*b*) Training data and test data

(*c*) Training data and big data (*d*) None of the above

14. At the end of each epoch, we must see that-

(*a*) Error is increasing (*b*) Error is decreasing

(*c*) Error is static (*d*) None of the above

15. One of the methods of overcoming 'overfitting' phenomenon is called as-

(*a*) Regularization (*b*) Segmentation

(*c*) Fragmentation (*d*) None of the above

16. Deep learning is also called as-

(*a*) Feature learning (*b*) Representation learning

(*c*) Example based learning (*d*) Only (*a*) and (*b*)

17. An artificial neural network used for learning efficient coding is-

(*a*) Auto-encoder (*b*) Decoder

(*c*) Encoder (*d*) None of the above

18. Deep learning is useful as-

(*a*) Non-linear function can be represented in a better way

(*b*) Linear function can be represented in a better way

(*c*) Polynomial function can be represented in a better way

(*d*) None of the above

19. A systematic method for training multilayer ANN is named as-

(*a*) Forward-propagation (*b*) Backpropagation.

(*c*) Error propagation (*d*) None of the above

20. If we want to train the network to recognize all letters of the alphabet then we need-

(*a*) 20 training pairs (*b*) 26 training pairs

(*c*) 30 training pairs (*d*) None of the above

21. A group of training pairs is called as-

(*a*) Training set (*b*) Working set.

(*c*) Logical set (*d*) None of the above

22. A neuron with n binary inputs can have-

(*a*) 2^n input patterns (*b*) 2^n input patterns

(*c*) n/2 input patterns (*d*) None of the above

23. Each input pattern can produce-

(*a*) Two binary inputs (1s and 0s) (*b*) 2n inputs

(*c*) 2n inputs (*d*) None of the above

24. In a 50*50 network, with 2 numeric inputs and 1 output, there are:-

(*a*) 2650 weights (*b*) 3650 weights

(*c*) 4300 weights (*d*) None of the above

25. If we have a total of 'k' critical points, then we will have a total of-

(*a*) k/3 local minima (*b*) k/2 local minima

(*c*) k * 3 local minima (*d*) None of the above

26. Predicting the price of a house given its size is an example of-

(*a*) Supervised learning (*b*) Unsupervised learning

(*c*) Remote learning (*d*) None of the above

27. The inherent groupings in the data discovered is known as-

(*a*) Association (*b*) Clustering

(*c*) Classifying (*d*) None of the above

28. Discovering rules that describes large portions of data is called as-

(*a*) Association (*b*) Clustering

(*c*) Classifiers (*d*) None of the above

29. Conditional models are also known as-

(*a*) Demand models (*b*) Discriminative models.

(*c*) Generative models (*d*) None of the above

30. Logistic regression is also named as-

(*a*) Login regression (*b*) Logit regression

(*c*) Logout regression (*d*) None of the above

31. Naive Bayes is an example of-

(*a*) Generative model (*b*) Discriminative model

(*c*) SVM (*d*) None of the above

32. A common task in machine learning is-

(*a*) Common data (*b*) Classifying data

(*c*) Global data (*d*) None of the above.

33. The classification error, E_i of an individual program, *i*, depends on the number of samples incorrectly classified (false positives and false negatives) and is computed by the formula:-

(*a*) $E_i = f / n * 100$ (*b*) $E_i = f * n * 100$

(*c*) $E_i = f + n * 100$ (*d*) None of the above.

34. PCA stands for-

(*a*) Peer Component Analysis (*b*) Principal Component Analysis

(*c*) Power Component Analysis (*d*) None of the above

35. Singular Value Decomposition is used in-

(*a*) Latent Semantic Indexing (*b*) Lateral Simple Indexing

(*c*) Lower Simple Indexing (*d*) None of the above

36. SVM stands for-

(*a*) Support Vector Machine (*b*) Simple Vector Machine

(*c*) Super Vector Machine (*d*) None of the above

37. A generalization of the concept of a plane which is used in SVM implementation for object separation is known as-

(*a*) Hyperplane (*b*) Airplane

(*c*) Aeroplane (*d*) None of the above

38. A model evaluation technique which is collection of methods used to examine the underlying constructs influence of the response of variables is-

(*a*) Factor Analysis

(*b*) ICA

(*c*) PCA

(*d*) Singular Value Composition

ANSWERS

1. (*b*)	**2.** (*c*)	**3.** (*a*)	**4.** (*a*)	**5.** (*c*)
6. (*a*)	**7.** (*a*)	**8.** (*a*)	**9.** (*c*)	10. (*a*)
11. (*c*)	**12.** (*a*)	**13.** (*b*)	**14.** (*b*)	**15.** (*a*)
16. (*d*)	**17.** (*a*)	**18.** (*a*)	**19.** (*b*)	**20.** (*b*)
21. (*a*)	**22.** (*a*)	**23.** (*a*)	**24.** (*a*)	**25.** (*a*)
26. (*a*)	**27.** (*b*)	**28.** (*b*)	**29.** (*b*)	**30.** (*b*)
31. (*a*)	**32.** (*b*)	**33.** (*a*)	**34.** (*b*)	**35.** (*a*)
36. (*a*)	**37.** (*a*)	**38.** (*a*)		

CONCEPTUAL SHORT QUESTIONS WITH ANSWERS

Q.1. What are the differences between data mining and machine learning?

Ans. Data mining is the process in which the unstructured data puts efforts to extract knowledge or unfamiliar interesting patterns. On the other hand, machine learning relates to the study, design and development of the algorithms that give systems the ability to learn without being clearly programmed.

Q.2. Give functions supervised and unsupervised learning.

Ans. Supervised learning involves-

a. Classifications
b. Speech recognition
c. Regression
d. Predict time series
e. Annotate strings

On the other hand, unsupervised learning involves-

a. Finding the clusters of data
b. Finding low dimensional representations of data
c. Finding interesting coordinates and correlations
d. Finding novel observations or cleaning databases

Q.3. What is inductive machine learning?

Ans. Inductive machine learning covers the process of learning by examples where a system, from a set of perceived instances, tries to encourage a general rule.

Q.4. List at least five common machine learning algorithms.

Ans. Some of the popular ML algorithms are as follows:-

a. Decision Trees
b. Neural Networks
c. Probabilistic Networks
d. Nearest Neighbour
e. Support Vector Machines (SVM).

Q.5. Name different algorithm techniques in ML.

Ans. Different types of techniques in ML are as follows:-

a. Supervised learning
b. Unsupervised learning
c. Semi-supervised learning
d. Reinforcement learning
e. Transduction
f. Learning to learn

Q.6. Name three stages to build the models (or hypotheses) in machine learning.

Ans. Three stages to build the models in machine learning (ML) are as follows:-

a. Model buildingb

b. Model testing

c. Applying the model

Q.7. What is the standard approach to supervised learning?

Ans. The standard approach to supervised learning is to break the data set of example into training set and the test set.

Q.8. Differentiate between 'training set' and 'test set'.

Ans. In different fields of data science like machine learning, a set of data is used to determine the potentially predictive relationship identified as training set. Training set is the example provided to the learner while test set is used to test the exactness of the hypotheses produced by the learner and it is the set of illustration weighed down from the learner. So, training sets are different from test sets.

Q.9. What are the different approaches of machine learning?

Ans. Different approaches of machine learning are as follows:-

a. Concept versus Classification Learning

b. Symbolic versus Statistical Learning

c. Inductive versus Analytical Learning

Q.10. Define Overfitting during machine learning. Why it happens?

Ans. In ML, overfitting occurs when a statistical model defines a random error or noise rather than underlying relationship. When a model is extremely complex, overfitting is usually observed because of having too many parameters relating to the number of training data types. The model exihibits poor performance which has to be overfit. The risk of overfitting exists as the standards used for training the model is not the same as the standards used to judge the effectiveness of a model.

Q.11. How can overfitting be avoided?

Ans. By means of loads of data, overfitting can be avoided. Overfitting happens when comparatively you have a small dataset and you make effort to learn from it. But if you have a small database and it is necessary to come with a model based on that then in such a scenario, cross validation method may be used. In this method, the dataset is divided into two segments, testing and training datasets. The testing dataset will only test the model while in training dataset, the data-points will come up with a model. In this method, a model is generally provided with a dataset of known data on which training data set is run and a dataset of unknown data against which the model is tested. The basic idea of cross validation is to define a dataset to test the model in the training phase.

Q.12. What is algorithm independent machine learning?

Ans. A type of machine learning in which mathematical foundations is independent of any particular classifier or learning algorithm is known as algorithm independent machine learning.

Q.13. Distinguish between AI and machine learning.

Ans. Designing and developing algorithms according to the behaviours based on empirical data is known as machine learning. On the other hand, artificial intelligence, in addition to machine learning, also covers other aspects like knowledge representation, natural language processing (NLP), planning, robotics etc.

Q.14. Define classifier as used in machine learning.

Ans. A classifier is a system that inputs a vector of discrete or continuous feature vales and outputs a single discrete value, the class.

Q.15. Where is pattern recognition used?

Ans. It is used in computer vision, speech recognition, data mining, statistics, information retrieval and bio-informatics.

Q.16. What is model selection in ML?

Ans. The process of selecting the models from different mathematical models that refer to the same data set is called as model selection. It is applied to the fields of statistics, machine learning and data mining.

Q.17. Name the method that is frequently used to prevent overfitting.

Ans. 'Isotonic Regression' is used to prevent overfiting when the data is sufficient.

Q.18. Why instance-based learning algorithm is sometimes also referred to as lazy-learning algorithm?

Ans. Instance-based learning algorithm is sometimes also referred to as lazy-learning algorithm because they delay the induction or generalization process until classification is performed.

Q.19. What are the 2 classification methods that SVM handle?

Ans. The two classification methods that SVM can handle are as follows:-

a. Combining binary classifiers.

b. Modifying binary to incorporate multiclass learning.

Q.20. For what purpose PCA and ICA are used?

Ans. PCA and ICA are used to extract features of data to reduce dimensions of data. They are important feature extraction techniques used for dimensionality reduction.

Q.21. What do you mean by dimension reduction?

Ans. It is the process of reducing the number of random variables under considerations and can be divided into feature selection and feature extraction.

Q22. What are SVMs?

Ans. SVMs or Support Vector Machines are supervised learning algorithms that are used for classification and regression analysis.

Q.23. What are the different methods to solve sequential supervised learning problems?

Ans. Tthe different methods to solve sequential supervised learning problems are:-

a. Sliding window methods.

b. Recurrent sliding windows.

c. Hidden Makov Models.

d. Maximum entropy Markov Models.

e. Conditional random fields.

f. Graph transformer networks.

Q.24. Name two techniques of ML. Give a very popular application of ML that you see everyday.

Ans. Genetic programming and inductive learning are the two methods of ML.

The recommendation engine implemented by major ecommerce websites uses machine learning (ML).

Q.25. How is KNN different from k-means clustering?

Ans. k-nearest neighbours is a supervised classification algorithm. On the other hand, k-means clustering is an unsupervised clustering algorithm. In order for k-nearest neighbours to work, labelled data is needed that we want to classify an unlabeled point. In case of k-means clustering only a set of unlabelled points and a threshold is required. The algorithm will take unlabelled points in consideration and slowly learn how to cluster them into groups by computing the mean of the distance between different points. In sutshell, KNN needs labelled points and is thus supervised learning while k-means doesn't need labelled points and is thus unsupervised learning.

Q.26. Why is "Naive" Bayes naive?

Ans. Even though it has practical applications, specially in text mining, Naive Bayes is still considered as Naive because the assumption that it makes becomes virtually impossible to be seen in real-life data. The conditional probability is computed as purely the product of the individual probabilities of different components. This denotes the absolute independence of features i.e. a condition that is probably never met in real life.

Q.27. Differentiate between a generative and discriminative model.

Ans. A generative model learns categories of data while a discriminative model merely learns the distinction between different categories of data. Discriminative models will leave behind generative models on the basis of classification tasks.

Q.28. Name at least three methods of reducing dimensionality.

Ans. The three methods of reducing dimensionality are as follows:-

a. Removing collinear features.

b. Performing PCA, ICA or other forms of algorithmic dimensionality reduction.

c. Combining features with feature engineering.

Q.29. What is the EM technique? How this algorithm works?

Ans. EM is an algorithm for maximizing a likelihood function when some of the variables in the model are unobserved i.e. when there are latent variables with you. To solve for our model parameters you need to know the distribution of your unobserved data but the distribution of your unobserved data is a function of your model parameters. EEM tries to get around this by guessing repeatedly about the distribution for the unobserved data then further estimating the model parameters by maximizing something that is lower bound on the actual likelihood function and repeating until convergence.

The EM algorithm starts with a guess for values of your model parameters as follows:-

The E-step: For each data point that has some missing values to solve for the distribution of the missing data, use your model equation, provided with your current guess of the model parameters and given the observed data. Please note that you are solving for a distribution for each missing value and not for the expected value. Also note that now we have available with us a distribution for each missing value, we can calculate the expectation of the likelihood function with respect to the unobserved variables. If our guess for the model parameter was correct, this expected likelihood will be the actual likelihood of our observed data. If the parameters were not correct, it will just be a lower bound.

The M-step: Now that we have got an expected likelihood function with no unobserved variables in it, maximize the function as you would in the fully observed case, to get a new estimate of your model parameters.

Repeat till convergence.

Q.30. What do you mean by curse of dimensionality?

Ans. The curse of dimensionality refers to the tendency of a state space to grow exponentially in its dimension i.e. in the number of state variables.

Q.31. What is H2O? What is prcomp?

Ans. H_2O is software for machine learning and data analysis. PCA is named as prcomp in H_2O and R system.

Q.32. What is the principle of operation of the back-propagation algorithm?

Ans. Firstly, the inputs from the training data are propagated through the network to the output. Then the model outputs are compared with the actual outputs. The difference is the error. This error is then fed into the network backwards and connections weights are adjusted.

Q.33. Define the following:-

***a.* Learning rate.**

***b.* Momentum.**

Ans. ***a.* Learning Rate :** A higher value of learning rate will make the algorithm converge more rapidly towards the desired values but it will reduce the stability of the algorithm.

***b.* Momentum :** It is used to control oscillations in weights which could be caused by alternately signed error signals.

Q.34. WEKA tool may be used to construct neural network. Can it do the parameter value selection also for neural networks?

Ans. A neural network trains by repeated passes of the data. Each pass is called an epoch. With each epoch, the connecting weights are adjusted until a satisfactory level of performance is reached. We can ponder that if 50 epochs are good then 80 epochs should be better. But this argument does not hold with neural networks. With too many passes the network may over-train also. Please understand that a well trained neural network model would show similar performance levels with both test and training data. Also understand that keeping this in mind we can change the parameter values of the algorithm. We should not assume that default parameters are the best. We can change the parameters too. As the number of epochs increases we need more time for training. If we compare the outputs from the two different epochs, we can see the accuracy remains at the same level of 97.2%. that is why we say that higher the number of epochs has not improved the model performance. Just keep in mind that we should restrict ourselves to the lower number of epochs as it not only involves less computing time but also lowers the danger of over-fitting.

Q.35. Define the following terms:-

a. **Activation function.**
b. **Back-propagation learning.**
c. **Delta rule.**
d. **Epoch.**
e. **Feedforward neural networks.**
f. **Genetic algorithm.**
g. **Hyperplane.**
h. **Kernel.**

Ans. *a.* **Activation function:** A function that describes the output behaviours of a neuron in neural network.

b. **Back-propagation learning :** It is a form of supervised learning used to train mainly, feedforward neural networks, that works by making modifications in weights values, starting at the output layer and then moving backwards through the hidden layer.

c. **Delta Rule :** The delta rule changes the weight vector for a neural network in such a way that the error is reduced.

d **Epoch :** It is one complete pass of the entire training set through the neural network. The learning process is repeated epoch-by-epoch until the averaged square error converges to a minimum value.

e. **Feedforward neural network :** It is a sort of ANN where connections between the units do not form a directed cycle.

f. **Genetic algorithm :** It is an adaptive heuristic search algorithm premised on the evolutionary ideas of natural selection theory.

g. **Hyperplane :** A plane (as in geometry) that is used to do object separation during SVM implementation.

h. **Kernel :** Linear, polynomial and rbf are some of the kernels of SVM that allows SVM to fit the maximum margin hyperplane in the transformed feature space.

Q.36. Tabulate the differences between supervised and unsupervised learning.

Ans. The following are the points of differences:-

Supervised Learning	Unsupervised Learning
1. It incorporates an external teacher so that each output unit is told what should be the desired response to that input signal.	1. Uses no external teacher.
2. Global error signals govern learning.	2. Local information is used for learning.
3. Uses pattern class information of each training pattern.	3 daptively clusters patterns to generate decision codes.
4. Paradigms are error correction learning, reinforcement learning and stochastic learning.	4. Paradigms are Hebbian learning and competitive learning.
2. Learning is usually off line. It means that learning and operation phases are different. In off-line learning, all of the given patterns are used together.	5. Learning is online. It means that the agent learns and operates at the same time. Here, the information in each new pattern is incorporated into the agent.
6. All learning data are stored and can be accessed repeatedly. So, we can see whether we are making progress in training or not.	6. Locality allows learning in real time. So, the progress cannot be monitored.
7. Inputs and outputs are defined.	7. Only inputs are defined.
8. Uses pattern class information of each training pattern.	8. Adaptively clusters patterns to generate decision class without any prior pattern class information.
9. Global error signal governs learning	9. Local information/ rules are used for learning.
10. Learning is offline usually.	10. Locality allows synapses to learn in real-time.

Q.37. Explain different nets classes.

Ans. It is put under 2 main categories as follows:-

I. Unsupervised learning (*i.e.* without a teacher):

1. Feedback Nets:

a. Binary Adaptive Resonance Theory (ART1).

b. Analog adaptive Resonance Theory (ART2).

c. Discrete Hopfield (DH).

d. Continuous Hopfield (CH).

e. Discrete Bi-directional Associative Memory (BAM).

f. Temporal Associative Memory (TAM).

g. Adaptive Bi-directional Associative Memory (ABAM).

h. Kohonen Self-Organizing Map/ Topology Preserving Map (SOM/TPM).

i. Competitive learning.

2. Feed-forward only Nets:

a. Learning Matrix (LM).

b. Driver-reinforcement Learning (DR).

c. Counter Propagation (CPN).

II. Supervised learning (*i.e.* with a teacher):

1. Feedback Nets:

a. Boltzmann Machine. (BM).

b. Mean Field Annealing (MFT).

c. Recurrent Cascade Correlation (RCC).

d. Learning Vector Quantization (LVQ).

e. Back Propagation through Time (BPTT).

f. Real-time Recurrent Learning (RTRL).

2. Feed-forward only Nets:

a. Perceptron

b. Adaline, Madaline

c. Backpropagation (BP)

d. Cauchy Machine (CM)

e. Artmap

f. Cascade Correlation (CasCor)

EXERCISE QUESTIONS

1. Define machine learning. Discuss the applications of Machine Learning.
2. Difference between training dataset and testing data set.
3. What are support vectors and margins?
4. Differences between supervised and unsupervised learning.
5. Explain Perceptron training algorithm for linear classification.
6. Explain PCA and ICA.
7. What are learning laws?

   [**Hint:** Learning laws provide a set of well-defined rules that determine how the network learns. The laws are as follows:-

   1. The learning algorithm/law must lead to convergence of weights.
   2. The learning time or training time should be small.
   3. The learning should make use of only the local information available. When the synaptic weight linking two neurons is changed, it should depend only on the states of these two units. In such a case, the learning process can be made parallel by changing weights parallel.
   4. Online training may be done wherein the weights are changed based on the inputs.
   5. Non-linear mapping between I/O pairs must be captured by the learning law.
   6. Pattern information storage capacity should be as large as possible for a given network.
8. Explain delta rule of learning.
9. Explain convergence rule for learning.
10. Explain the back-propagation neural network principles.
11. Using WEKA tool, how will you construct a fully connected feed-forward ANN that has three input nodes, one output node and four internal nodes in the hidden layer?

3 Classification Families

Q.1. Explain classification and regression with examples.

Ans. In machine learning, there are two tasks. One is called as classification, pattern recognition or Supervised learning. And the second one is known as exploratory data analysis technique called as unsupervised learning or clustering.

In supervised learning, we have a data set with a known number of classes or groups. Also each of our observations has a class label attached to it. Our goal is to develop or build a classifier using the data. Then we use the classifier to predict the class membership or label of future observations. For example, a doctor might use a classifier to assign an illness based on patient symptoms or test results. Another example would be a market manager has to determine what people should receive their advertisements based on demographic information or an ecologist needs to classify regions in an image as water or land. Please note that in all these three examples there are some things in common.

In the field of machine learning, classification is the problem of finding out to which category a newly encountered observation belongs, based on the training dataset containing observations. Supervised machine learning involves two methods:-

a. Classification

b. Regression

In classification method, the output predicted value 'y' is discrete in nature. For example, classifying emails as spam or non-spam uses this method. Also applications like online transactions are fraudulent or not may belong to this category. In general, classification is like YES / NO, TRUE / FALSE, 0/1 type of learning. Logistic regression, Support Vector Machines (SVM), Decision Trees, Random Forests, ANN, Analytical Learning, Bayesian Learning, Boosting, Kernel Function, Ensemble Classifiers, Conditional Random Field, Minimum Complexity Machines etc. Please note that the output predicted value can also be in multiple classes giving rise to what is known as Multiclass classification.

General steps during classification tasks:-

Step-1: Find out what all features will be collected. These features are the variables. The features in lotus flower are its width and lengths of petals and sepals. Similarly, in advertisement example, the features might be gender, age, area of residence etc. Also note that this is the first key step because building a classifier is much easier with features that will distinguish the classes.

Step-2: After feature selection, we measure nm of them for each of M groups. With the lotus data, we have $M = 3$ groups and nm = 50, $m = 1, ..., 3$. This is also called as the training set.

Step-3: Now build or estimate a classifier using the observations with the known true class labels. This process is also called as training the classifier.

Step-4: Then assess the performance of the classifier. We can use percent correctly classified, confusion matrices or performance curves for this task.

Please note here that the process of building a classifier in supervised learning is similar to model building and regression analysis. Also note that in classification the response variable is a class label and our predictor variables are also called as features.

MATLAB classifies supervised learning methods under two main categories:-

a. Parametric classification (that uses a parametric model that is estimated using data).

b. Non-parametric classification.

Naive Bayes and discriminant analysis are two parametric methods while k-nearest neighbours is anon-parametric method.

Application of classification : Consider the case of identifying the species of flower- lotus. Two ways of solving this problem are:-

CASE 1: WITHOUT MACHINE LEARNING.

We need to write several functions to detect different features of lotus flower. But the problem is what if the leaf is broken? This is different from what we expected. We cannot write code also beforehand. So, we need machine learning now.

CASE 2: WITH MACHINE LEARNING.

In machine learning, we have four steps:-

a. Collect Data

b. Select the model

c. Train the model

d. Test the model

Also note that by adding the data to the model will start recognizing patterns. Now the datasets can come in whole lot but should be in proper format that can be easily parsed. Then the dataset has different features according to our requirement. Three properties of good features are that they should be simple, independent and informative. Choosing a better fit model is also challenging. However, this flower problem is an application of classification problem because we are classifying whether an image is of lotus flower or not. So, we need classifier. Now we have dataset and the model, so we need to train the model. Also note that training is the step where actual training occurs as our model iterates through the Dataset. It gets better and better at prediction over time. Next time, when we provide our model an image of any flower it will be able to predict whether the flower supplied is lotus or not. These types of problems in which the task is to classify examples into one of the discrete set of possible categories are known as **classification problems.**

Q.2. Distinguish between Linear Discriminative and non-linear discriminative analysis.

Ans. A linear discriminant method that is used in the field of statistics, pattern recognition and machine learning is Fisher's Linear Discriminant. It is used to find the linear combination of features that divides two or more classes of objects or events. The combination that comes out in the form of result may be used later as a linear classifier, in general, for dimensionality reduction before later classification. So, we can say that LDA is a supervised technique of feature extraction that is used to find a linear combination of the available features which separate the classes.

Applying LDA: The core objective is to decrease the dimension of the data in order to reduce the computational cost of classification. After applying the LDA to a dataset, the "new features" minimizes the dispersion between the samples of the same class and maximizes the dispersion between samples of different classes.

For example, say you have a dataset of players who practice different sports like may be cricket, basketball, soccer, Golf etc. Imagine that the available features taken into consideration for these sports are height, weight and body mass index. Now when the instances are plotted, there might be some regions of intersection of two or more classes. So, when you apply LDA to a data set, it will produce new features that might result in better separation of classes-lesser and smaller regions of intersection.

Limitations of LDA :

1. LDA can generate only C (number of classes) or less number of features.
2. At times, one is dealing with datasets of 20 features, for example, and there are only 2 classes, so LDA have to be reduced to 2 axis. Such reductions usually result in loss of information that further results in low classification accuracy.

Non-linear discriminative : Linear discriminative methods have the ability to solve problems via a line, plane or hyperplane. They include linear combinations of data which is easier in implementation, if the dataset is with low variance. Linear classifier SVM is used when number of features are very high. If you can solve a problem with a linear method, you are usually better off. This is linear method. But if it is not suitable then we go for non-linear method. Please note that if the dataset has high variance, then one needs to reduce the number of features and add more dataset to it.

For example, activation function in ANN or kernel in SVM are non-linear functions. Non-linear methods transform data to a new representational space based on the kernel function and apply classification techniques. This transformation describes the data features in a more clear structure in comparison with the original space by which classification algorithms can create better predictor in the new space. Thus, if the classification techniques reforms data features to new space, before applying classifier then we call them as non-linear methods.

Q.3. What are Decision Trees? How they help in learning?

Ans. Decision tree is a statistical model that is used in classification. It is a machine learning approach that is used to classify data into classes and to show the results in a flowchart like a tree structure. This model classifies data in a dataset by flowing through a query structure from the root till it reaches the leaf that represents one class. The root represents the attribute that plays a main role in classification and the leaf represents the class. For classifying data, this DT model follows the following steps:-

Step-1: Puts all training examples to a root.

Step-2: It divides training examples based on the selected attributes.

Step-3: It selects attributes by using some statistical methods.

Step-4: Recursive partitioning continues till no training example is left or until no attribute is left or the remaining training examples belong to the same class.

Decision trees were first of all used in 1970s. In this technique, a sample of observations is used as a starting point. The algorithm retraces the rules that generate the output classes by dividing the input matrix into smaller and smaller partitions till the process triggers a rule for stopping. This is inverse reasoning. But in terms of machine learning, this is achieved by applying a search among all possible ways to split the training in a greedy way. An algorithm is said t be greedy if it always chooses its move to maximize the result in each step during the optimization process regardless of what could happen in the following steps. So, an algorithm tries to maximize the current step without looking forward to obtain a global optimization.

Principle used: "Each partition of the initial data must make it easier to predict the target outcome, which is characterized by a different and more favourable distribution of classes than the original sample. The algorithm creates partitions by splitting the data. It finds out the data splits by first evaluating the features and then the values in the features that could bring the maximum improvement of a special statistical measure that plays the role of the cost function in a decision tree".

A number of statistical measurements determine how to make splits in a decision tree. But they follow one rule that a split must improve on the original sample or on another possible split. Most common measurement is the information gain. It tells how a decision tree can detect an increased predictive ability or a reduced risk in a simpler way for some split. in 1970s, Ross Quinlan, developed a decision tree algorithm based on information gain only. Information gain relies on the following formula of information entropy:-

$$\text{Entropy} = \Sigma -p_i \log_2 p_i$$

Where 'p' is the probability for a class (range of 0 to 1).

For example, consider an example wherein you want to classify two classes having the same probability of 50/50, then the maximum possible entropy is given by:-

$$\text{Entropy} = -0.5 * \log_2 0.5 - 0.5 * \log_2 0.5 = 1.0$$

On the other hand, if the decision tree detects a feature that can split the dataset into two partitions where the distribution of the two classes is 40/60 then the average entropy reduces as follows:-

$$\text{Entropy} = -0.4 * \log_2 0.4 - 0.6 * \log_2 0.6 = 0.97$$

Please note the entropy sum for all classes. It is observed that using the split of 40/60, the sum is less than the theoretical maximum of 1. This is known as diminishing of the entropy. We can think of entropy as a measure of the mess in the data. Also note that the lesser is the mess the more is the order and easier it is to guess the right class.

Explanation: after the 1st split, the algorithm tries to split the obtained partitions further using the same logic of reducing entropy. It progressively splits any successive data partition until no more splits are possible as the sub-sample is a single example or because it has met a stopping rule. Stopping rules are defined as the limits to the expansion of a tree. These rules work by considering 3 aspects of a partition:-

a. Initial partition size.

b. Resulting partition size.

c. Information gain; as obtained after the split.

Please understand that these stopping rules are vital because decision tree algorithms approximate a large number of functions. But noise and data errors do affect this algorithm.

Decision trees have several nuts and bolts. They have more variance than bias in their estimations. To overfit the data in less, it also does tree pruning. Pruning is done when the tree is fully grown. Starting from the leaves, prune the branches of the tree in order to show some improvement in the reduction of information gain. Also understand that retracting from the leaves to the root and keeping only the branches that have some predictive value mitigates the variance of the model and thus making the resulting rules parsimonious.

Pruning is just like brainstorming due to two reasons:-

1. The code generates all possible ramifications of the tree.
2. When the brainstorming concludes the code keeps only what really works.

In nutshell, we induce Decision Tree model using Greedy method from top-to-down. Please note that this top-down method of induction of decision trees is the most common method used to learn decision trees from the data. Also note that this type of DT model based learning is supervised learning as it constructs decision tree from class-labelled training tuples.

In decision trees, we break the classification down into a set of choices about each feature starting at the root of the tree and progressing down to leaves where we receive the final classification decision. The data structure, tree, is very easy to understand and implement.

In this approach, we have handy, if-then-else rules which are useful for use in a production system. This type of algorithm has been applied successfully to a broad range of tasks from learning to diagnose medical cases to learning to assess credit risk of loan applicants.

Decision trees classify instances by sorting them down the tree from the root to some leaf nodes which provides the classification of the instance. Each node in the tree specifies a test of some attribute of the instance and each branch descending from that node corresponds to one of the possible values for this attribute. An instance is classified by starting at the root node of the tree, testing the attribute specified by this node then moving down the tree branch corresponding to the value of the attribute in the given example. This process is then repeated for the subtree rooted at the new node.

This method is very popular because we can turn into a set of logical disjunctions (if-then-else rules) that fit into program code easily.

Limitations of Decision Trees :

1. Instances are represented by attribute-value pairs.
2. Target function has discrete output values.
3. Disjunctive descriptions may be required.
4. Training data may contain errors.
5. Training data may contain missing attribute values.

This method of learning has been applied to problems like learning to classify medical patients on the basis of their disease, equipment breakdowns by their cause and loan applicants by their possibility of non-payment. Such problems, in which the task is to classify examples into one of a discrete set of possible categories, are often stated as classification problems.

For constructing a decision tree, the features that are required for the algorithm are as follows:-

1. The state of energy level.
2. The date of your nearest deadline.
3. Whether or not there is a party tonight.

Now the challenge is to construct a tree based on these features. Literature provides different types of decision tree algorithms that are based on the same principle but follow different approaches.

Principle: "The algorithm states that the algorithm built the tree in a greedy manner starting at the root and choosing the most informative feature (how the tree works) at each step".

ALGORITHM ID3 {by Quinlan} : This algorithm learns decision trees by constructing them in top-down fashion *i.e.* starts with the question "at the root of the tree, which attribute is to be tested?" In order to answer this question, each instance attribute is assessed using a statistical test to find out how well it classifies the training examples. The best attribute is selected to be used as the test, as the root node of the tree. Then a successor of the root node is produced for each possible value of this attribute and the training examples are sorted to the suitable successor node i.e. down the branch conforming to the example's value for this attribute. The complete process is then repeated using the training examples related with each descendant node to select the best attribute at test at that point in the tree. This practices a greedy search for an acceptable decision tree, in which the algorithm never backtracks to review earlier options.

Now the question is which attribute is the best classifier?

Selecting which attribute that is to be tested at each node in the tree is the basic factor that is to be considered in ID3 algorithm. We would like to make choice of the attribute that is most beneficial for the classifying examples.

What is a good quantitative measure of the value of an attribute?

A statistical property called as an information gain will compute how well a given attribute separates the training examples in accordance to their target classification. ID3 uses up this information gain measure to make a choice amongst the candidate attributes at each step while the tree grows.

ID3 (Examples, Target-attribute, Attributes)

(where, Examples are the training examples, Target-attribute is the attribute whose value is to be predicted by the tree and Attributes is a list of other attributes that may be tested by the learned decision tree)

(this algo returns a decision tree that correctly classifies the given Examples)

Step-1: Create a root node for the tree.

Step-2: If all Examples are positive, return the single-node tree Root, with label = +

Step-3: If all Examples are negative, return the single-node tree Root, with label = –

Step-4: If Attributes is empty, return the single-node tree Root with label = most common value of Target-attribute in Examples.

Step-5: Otherwise Begin

5.1 A ←the attribute from Attributes that best classifies Examples.

5.2 The decision attribute for Root ←A.

5.3 For each possible value, v_i, of A,

5.3.1 Add a new tree branch below Root, corresponding to the test $A = v_i$.

5.3.2 Let Example, svi be the subset of Examples that have value v_i for A.

5.3.3 If Example svi is empty

5.3.3.1 then below this new branch, add a leaf node with label = most common value of Target-attribute in Examples.

5.3.3.2 Else below this new branch add the subtree ID3 (Examples v_i, Target-attribute, Attributes – (A))

Step-6: End

Step-7: Return Root

In nutshell, ID3 algorithm is dedicated to learning Boolean-valued functions. ID3 is a greedy algorithm that develops the tree in top-down fashion, at each node choosing the attribute that best classifies the local training examples. This process carries until the tree perfectly classifies the training examples or until all attributes have been taken into consideration.

Q.4. Explain Probabilistic (conditional and generative) models.

Ans. We discuss two types of models here: -

1. Generative Model.
2. Conditional Model.

I. A generative model is a model that generates observable data values randomly, usually provided with some hidden parameters. It states 'a joint probability distribution over observation and label sequences'. As far as machine learning is concerned, these models are are used for either modelling data directly or as an intermediary phase to form a conditional probability density function. A conditional distribution can be derived from a generative model with the help of Bayes Rule. For example, Gaussian mixture model, Hidden Markov model, Naive Bayes, Restricted Boltzmann machine, generative adversial networks, probabilistic context-free Grammer etc.

II. Conditional models or discriminative models are used in machine learning for demonstrating the dependence of an unobserved variable 'y' on an observed variable 'x'. In terms of probability, this is prepared by modelling the conditional probability distribution P(y| x), which can be used for predicting from discriminative models, in contrast to generative models, that do not permit to generate samples from the joint distribution of x and y. For example,

Logistic regression (a type of generalized linear regression used for predicting binary or categorical outputs—called as maximum entropy classifiers, Support Vector Machines, Boosting-a meta-algorithm, conditional random fields, linear regression, neural networks etc.

Tasks like classification and regression do not require joint distribution. In fact, conditional models can return excellent performance. Please understand that these generative models are more flexible than discriminative models in stating dependencies in complex learning tasks. Also note that most discriminative models are fundamentally supervised and cannot easily be stretched to unsupervised learning. Application decides whether to go for generative or conditional model.

Say, the input data is 'x' and the set of labels for x is 'y'. Then,

1. Generative model learns the joint probability distribution $p(x, y)$.
2. Discriminative model learns the conditional probability distribution $p(x|y)$ *i.e.* the 'probability of y given x'.

Q.5. Write and explain K-nearest Neighbour Learning-distance weighted Nearest Neighbour Algorithm.

Ans. It is an instance-based method.

Principle: "This algorithm assumes that all instances relate to points in the n-dimensional space, Rn. The nearest neighbours of an instance are defined in terms of the standard Euclidean distance."

Let feature vector describe an arbitrary instance, x. The feature vector is-

$$<a_1\ (x), a_2\ (x), \ldots\ldots a_n\ (x)>$$

Where ar (x) denotes the values of the rth attribute of instance, x. Then the distance between two instances, x_i and x_j is defined to be $d\ (x_i, x_j)$ and is calculated as follows:-

$$d\ (x_i, x_j) = \sqrt{\Sigma}\ (r = 1 \text{ to } n)\ (\text{ar}\ (x_i) - \text{ar}\ (x_j))^2$$

In nearest-neighbor learning, the target function may be either for discrete-valued or real-valued. Let us first of all study learning discrete valued target functions of the form-

$$f\text{: } R^n \text{ -> V where } V \text{ is the finite set } \{v_1, \ldots\ldots v_s\}.$$

ALGORITHM k-nearest Neighbor { a discrete-valued target function }

For each training example $(x, f(x))$, add the example to the list of training examples.

Classification algorithm: Given instance xq is to be classified. Let $x_1 \ldots\ldots x_k$ denote the k-instances from training examples that are nearest to xq. Return

$f'(x_q) \leftarrow \text{argmax}\ (v\ \varepsilon\ V)\ \Sigma_{(i = 1 \text{ to } k)}\ \delta(v, f(x_i))$

where $\delta\ (a, b) = 1$ if $a = b$ and where $\delta\ (a, b) = 0$ otherwise.

Explanation: The value $f\ (x)$, given back by the algorithm as its approximation of $f(x_i)$ is just the most common value of f amongst the k training examples which are nearest to x.

If we choose $k = 1$, then the 1-nearest neighbour algorithm assigns the value $f'(x_i)$ to $f(x_i)$ where x_i is the training instance which is nearest to x_i.

For larger values of k, the algorithm allots the most common value among the k-nearest training examples.

Figure 3.1 explains the working of the k-nearest neighbour algorithm for the case where the instances are basically points in a 2D space. Also the target function is in form of Boolean. The positive and negative training examples are depicted by "+" and "-" respectively. Please note that the 1-nearest neighbour algorithm classifies x, as a positive example in figure 3.1 whereas the 5-nearest neighbour algorithm classifies it as a negative example. Also note that k-nearest neighbour algorithm never forms a clear hypothesis regarding the target function, f. It just works out for the classification of each new query instance encountered as needed.

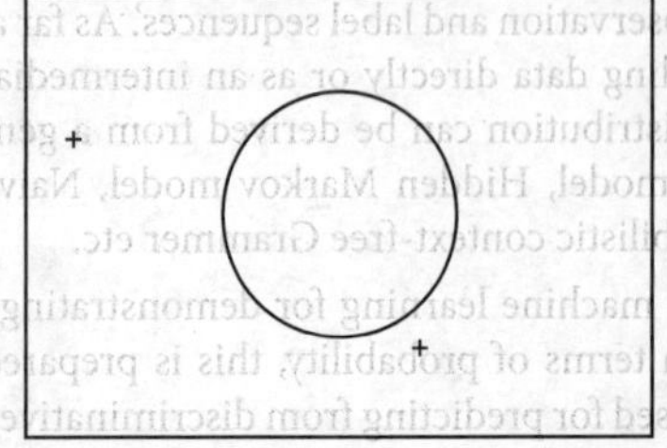
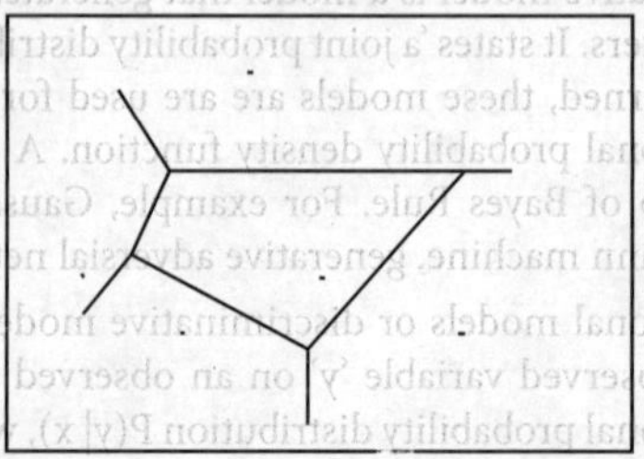

Fig. 3.1: k-Nearest Neighbour

Explanation: A set of positive and negative training examples is shown on the left diagram of figure 3.1. The 1-nearest neighbour algorithm classifies x as positive whereas 5-nearest neighbour classifies it as negative. On the right hand side of the figure 3.1, is the decision surface induced by the 1-nearest neighbour algorithm for a typical set of training examples. **Please note that the convex polygon surrounding each training example indicates the region of instance space closest to that point. This means that the instances for which the 1-nearest neighbour algorithm will assign the classification belonging to that training example.** On the right side of the figure 2.5, is shown a shape of the decision surface made by 1- nearest neighbour over the complete instance space. The decision surface is basically a grouping of convex polyhedral surrounding each of the training examples. For every training example, the polyhedron shows the set of query points whose classification will be completely decided by that training example. Also note that the query points that lie outside the polyhedron are closer to some other training example. And such a type of diagram is often called as the Voronoi diagram of the set of training examples. The k-nearest neighbour algorithm is easily adapted to approximating continuous-valued target functions. To accomplish this, we need the algorithm to calculate the mean value of k-nearest training examples rather than calculate their most common value. Practically speaking, to estimate a real-valued target function f: $R^n \rightarrow R$, we replace the final line of the above algorithm by:-

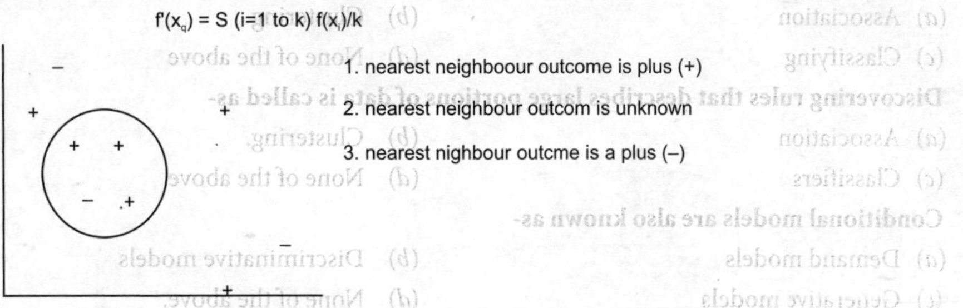

Fig. 3.2: Accurate Estimate of Real-valued Target Function

Q.6. Explain Distance weighted nearest-Neighbour Algorithm.

Ans. This algorithm is an enhancement of k-nearest algorithm.

Principle: Weigh the contribution of each of the k-neighbours depending on their distance to query point, x, awarding greater weight to closer neighbours.

For example, in the algorithm of k-nearest above, that approximates discrete-valued target functions, we might weight the support of each neighbour corresponding to the inverse square of its distance from xi. And this is done by interchanging the last line of the algorithm by:-

$$f(x_q) \leftarrow \text{argmax} (v \varepsilon V) \ \Sigma_{(i=1 \text{ to } k)} \ w_i \ \delta(v, f(x_i))$$

where $w_i = 1 / d(x_q, x_i)^2$

To consider the case where the query point, x, exactly matches one of the training instances, x_i and the denominator $d(x_q, x_I)^2$ is therefore zero, we assign $f(x_q)$ to be $f(x_i)$ in this particular case. We can distance-weight the instances for real-valued target functions in alike fashion, interchanging the final line in the algorithm in this case by-

$$f(x_q) \leftarrow \Sigma_{(i=1 \text{ to } k)} \ w_i f(x_i) \ / \ k \ / \ \Sigma_{(i=1 \text{ to } k)} \ w_i$$

where w_i is defined as above

Q.7. Define the Curse of Dimensionality.

Ans. Distance usually relates to all the attributes and assumes all of them have the same effects on the distance. The similarity metrics do not consider the relation of attributes which result in inaccurate distance and then impact on classification precision. This wrong classification due to presence of many irrelevant attributes is often termed as the curse of dimensionality.

For example, say each instance is described by 20 attributes out of which only 2 are relevant in determining the classification of the target function. In this case, instances that have identical values for the 2 relevant attributes may nevertheless be distant from one another in the 20-dimensional instance space.

SUMMARY

We have studied in this chapter that in machine learning instead of teaching a computer a massive list of rules to solve a problem, we give it a model with which it can evaluate examples. Also, we give a small set of instructions to modify this model if it makes a mistake. We find that as the time passes by, 'w' well suited model will be able to solve the problems in a better and efficient way. The machine learning algorithm should be such that it tries to make the values of the parameters more and more accurate as it is exposed to more and more examples. But this is just a tip of an iceberg. Recently, scientists have developed the models that resemble the structures as used by a human brain. This involves deep learning only.

MULTIPLE CHOICE QUESTIONS

1. **Predicting the price of a house given its size is an example of-**
   (*a*) Supervised learning (*b*) Unsupervised learning
   (*c*) Remote learning (*d*) None of the above
2. **The inherent groupings in the data discovered is known as-**
   (*a*) Association (*b*) Clustering
   (*c*) Classifying (*d*) None of the above
3. **Discovering rules that describes large portions of data is called as-**
   (*a*) Association (*b*) Clustering.
   (*c*) Classifiers (*d*) None of the above
4. **Conditional models are also known as-**
   (*a*) Demand models (*b*) Discriminative models
   (*c*) Generative models (*d*) None of the above.
5. **Logistic regression is also named as-**
   (*a*) Login regression (*b*) Logit regression
   (*c*) Logout regression (*d*) None of the above.
6. **Naive Bayes is an example of-**
   (*a*) Generative model (*b*) Discriminative model
   (*c*) SVM (*d*) None of the above
7. **A common task in machine learning is-**
   (*a*) Common data (*b*) Classifying data
   (*c*) Global data (*d*) None of the above
8. **The classification error, Ei of an individual program, i, depends on the number of samples incorrectly classified (false positives and false negatives) and is computed by the formula:-**
   (a) $E_i = f / n * 100$ (*b*) $E_i = f * n * 100$
   (c) $E_i = f + n * 100$ (*d*) None of the above
9. **PCA stands for-**
   (*a*) Peer Component Analysis (*b*) Principal Component Analysis
   (*c*) Power Component Analysis (*d*) None of the above.
10. **Singular Value Decomposition is used in-**
    (*a*) Latent Semantic Indexing (*b*) Lateral Simple Indexing
    (*c*) Lower Simple Indexing (*d*) None of the above
11. **SVM stands for-**
    (*a*) Support Vector Machine (*b*) Simple Vector Machine
    (*c*) Super Vector Machine (*d*) None of the above.

12. A generalization of the concept of a plane which is used in SVM implementation for object separation is known as-

(*a*) Hyperplane (*b*) Airplane.

(*c*) Aeroplane (*d*) None of the above.

13. A model evaluation technique which is collection of methods used to examine the underlying constructs influence of the response of variables is-

(*a*) Factor Analysis (*b*) ICA

(*c*) PCA (*d*) Singular Value Composition

ANSWERS

1. (*a*)	**2.** (*b*)	**3.** (*b*)	**4.** (*b*)	**5.** (*b*)
6. (*a*)	**7.** (*b*)	**8.** (*a*)	**9.** (*b*)	**10.** (*a*)
11. (*a*)	**12.** (*a*)	**13.** (*a*)		

CONCEPTUAL SHORT QUESTIONS WITH ANSWERS

Q.1. What are the differences between data mining and machine learning?

Ans. Data mining is the process in which the unstructured data puts efforts to extract knowledge or unfamiliar interesting patterns. On the other hand, machine learning relates to the study, design and development of the algorithms that give systems the ability to learn without being clearly programmed.

Q.2. Give functions supervised and unsupervised learning.

Ans. Supervised learning involves-

a. Classifications
b. Speech recognition
c. Regression
d. Predict time series
e. Annotate strings

On the other hand, unsupervised learning involves-

a. Finding the clusters of data
b. Finding low dimensional representations of data
c. Finding interesting coordinates and correlations
d. Finding novel observations or cleaning databases.

Q.3. What is inductive machine learning?

Ans. Inductive machine learning covers the process of learning by examples where a system, from a set of perceived instances, tries to encourage a general rule.

Q.4. List at least five common machine learning algorithms.

Ans. Some of the popular ML algorithms are as follows:-

a. Decision Trees
b. Neural Networks
c. Probabilistic Networks
d. Nearest Neighbour
e. Support Vector Machines (SVM).

Q.5. Name different algorithm techniques in ML.

Ans. Different types of techniques in ML are as follows:-

a. Supervised learning
b. Unsupervised learning
c. Semi-supervised learning
d. Reinforcement learning
e). Transduction
f. Learning to learn

Q.6. Name three stages to build the models (or hypotheses) in machine learning.

Ans. Three stages to build the models in machine learning (ML) are as follows:-

a. Model building
b. Model testing
c. Applying the model

Q.7. What is the standard approach to supervised learning?

Ans. The standard approach to supervised learning is to break the data set of example into training set and the test set.

Q.8. Differentiate between 'training set' and 'test set'.

Ans. In different fields of data science like machine learning, a set of data is used to determine the potentially predictive relationship identified as training set. Training set is the example provided to the learner while test set is used to test the exactness of the hypotheses produced by the learner and it is the set of illustration weighed down from the learner. So, training sets are different from test sets.

Q.9. What are the different approaches of machine learning?

Ans. Different approaches of machine learning are as follows:-

a. Concept versus Classification Learning.

b. Symbolic versus Statistical Learning.

c. Inductive versus Analytical Learning.

Q.10. Define Overfitting during machine learning. Why it happens?

Ans. In ML, overfitting occurs when a statistical model defines a random error or noise rather than underlying relationship. When a model is extremely complex, overfitting is usually observed because of having too many parameters relating to the number of training data types. The model exihibits poor performance which has to be overfit. The risk of overfitting exists as the standards used for training the model is not the same as the standards used to judge the effectiveness of a model.

Q.11. How can overfitting be avoided?

Ans. By means of loads of data, overfitting can be avoided. Overfitting happens when comparatively you have a small dataset and you make effort to learn from it. But if you have a small database and it is necessary to come with a model based on that then in such a scenario, cross validation method may be used. In this method, the dataset is divided into two segments, testing and training datasets. The testing dataset will only test the model while in training dataset, the data-points will come up with a model. In this method, a model is generally provided with a dataset of known data on which training data set is run and a dataset of unknown data against which the model is tested. The basic idea of cross validation is to define a dataset to test the model in the training phase.

Q.12. What is algorithm independent machine learning?

Ans. A type of machine learning in which mathematical foundations is independent of any particular classifier or learning algorithm is known as algorithm independent machine learning.

Q.13. Distinguish between AI and machine learning.

Ans. Designing and developing algorithms according to the behaviours based on empirical data is known as machine learning. On the other hand, artificial intelligence, in addition to machine learning, also covers other aspects like knowledge representation, natural language processing (NLP), planning, robotics etc.

Q.14. Define classifier as used in machine learning.

Ans. A classifier is a system that inputs a vector of discrete or continuous feature vales and outputs a single discrete value, the class.

Q.15. Where is pattern recognition used?

Ans. It is used in computer vision, speech recognition, data mining, statistics, information retrieval and bio-informatics.

Q.16. What is model selection in ML?

Ans. The process of selecting the models from different mathematical models that refer to the same data set is called as model selection. It is applied to the fields of statistics, machine learning and data mining.

Q.17. Name the method that is frequently used to prevent overfitting.

Ans. 'Isotonic Regression' is used to prevent overfiting when the data is sufficient.

Q.18. Why instance-based learning algorithm is sometimes also referred to as lazy-learning algorithm?

Ans. Instance-based learning algorithm is sometimes also referred to as lazy-learning algorithm because they delay the induction or generalization process until classification is performed.

Q.19. What are the 2 classification methods that SVM handle?

Ans. The two classification methods that SVM can handle are as follows:-

a. Combining binary classifiers.

b. Modifying binary to incorporate multiclass learning.

Q.20. For what purpose PCA and ICA are used?

Ans. PCA and ICA are used to extract features of data to reduce dimensions of data. They are important feature extraction techniques used for dimensionality reduction.

Q.21. What do you mean by dimension reduction?

Ans. It is the process of reducing the number of random variables under considerations and can be divided into feature selection and feature extraction.

Q.22. What are SVMs?

Ans. SVMs or Support Vector Machines are supervised learning algorithms that are used for classification and regression analysis.

Q.23. What are the different methods to solve sequential supervised learning problems?

Ans. Tthe different methods to solve sequential supervised learning problems are:-

a. Sliding window methods.

b. Recurrent sliding windows.

c. Hidden Makov Models.

d. Maximum entropy Markov Models.

e. Conditional random fields.

f. Graph transformer networks.

Q.24. Name two techniques of ML. Give a very popular application of ML that you see every day.

Ans. Genetic programming and inductive learning are the two methods of ML.

The recommendation engine implemented by major ecommerce websites uses machine learning (ML).

Q.25. How is KNN different from k-means clustering?

Ans. k-nearest neighbours is a supervised classification algorithm. On the other hand, k-means clustering is an unsupervised clustering algorithm. In order for k-nearest neighbours to work, labelled data is needed that we want to classify an unlabelled point. In case of k-means clustering only a set of unlabelled points and a threshold is required. The algorithm will take unlabelled points in consideration and slowly learn how to cluster them into groups by computing the mean of the distance between different points. In nutshell, KNN needs labelled points and is thus supervised learning while k-means doesn't need labelled points and is thus unsupervised learning.

Q.26. Why is "Naive" Bayes naive?

Ans. Even though it has practical applications, especially in text mining, Naive Bayes is still considered as Naive because the assumption that it makes becomes virtually impossible to be seen in real-life data. The conditional probability is computed as purely the product of the individual probabilities of different components. This denotes the absolute independence of features i.e. a condition that is probably never met in real life.

Q.27. Differentiate between a generative and discriminative model.

Ans. A generative model learns categories of data while a discriminative model merely learns the distinction between different categories of data. Discriminative models will leave behind generative models on the basis of classification tasks.

Q.28. Name at least three methods of reducing dimensionality.

Ans. The three methods of reducing dimensionality are as follows: -

a. Removing collinear features.

b. Performing PCA, ICA or other forms of algorithmic dimensionality reduction.

c. Combining features with feature engineering.

Q.29. What is the EM technique? How this algorithm works?

Ans. EM is an algorithm for maximizing a likelihood function when some of the variables in the model are unobserved i.e. when there are latent variables with you. To solve for our model parameters you need to know the distribution of your unobserved data but the distribution of your unobserved data is a function of your model parameters. EEM tries to get around this by guessing repeatedly about the distribution for the unobserved data then further estimating the model parameters by maximizing something that is lower bound on the actual likelihood function and repeating until convergence.

The EM algorithm starts with a guess for values of your model parameters as follows: -

The E-step: For each data point that has some missing values to solve for the distribution of the missing data, use your model equation, provided with your current guess of the model parameters and given the observed data. Please note that you are solving for a distribution for each missing value and not for the expected value. Also note that now we have available with us a distribution for each missing value, we can calculate the expectation of the likelihood function with respect to the unobserved variables. If our guess for the model parameter was correct, this expected likelihood will be the actual likelihood of our observed data. If the parameters were not correct, it will just be a lower bound.

The M-step: Now that we have got an expected likelihood function with no unobserved variables in it, maximize the function as you would in the fully observed case, to get a new estimate of your model parameters.

Repeat till convergence.

Q.30. What do you mean by curse of dimensionality?

Ans. The curse of dimensionality refers to the tendency of a state space to grow exponentially in its dimension i.e. in the number of state variables.

Q.31. What is H2O? What is prcomp?

Ans. H_2O is software for machine learning and data analysis. PCA is named as prcomp in H_2O and R system.

Q.32. What is the principle of operation of the back-propagation algorithm?

Ans. Firstly, the inputs from the training data are propagated through the network to the output. Then the model outputs are compared with the actual outputs. The difference is the error. This error is then fed into the network backwards and connections weights are adjusted.

Q.33. Define the following: -

a. **Learning rate.**

b. **Momentum.**

Ans. *a.* **Learning rate:** A higher value of learning rate will make the algorithm converge more rapidly towards the desired values but it will reduce the stability of the algorithm.

b. **Momentum:** It is used to control oscillations in weights which could be caused by alternately signed error signals.

Q.34. WEKA tool may be used to construct neural network. Can it do the parameter value selection also for neural networks?

Ans. A neural network trains by repeated passes of the data. Each pass is called an epoch. With each epoch, the connecting weights are adjusted until a satisfactory level of performance is reached. We can ponder that if 50 epochs are good then 80 epochs should be better. But this argument does not hold with neural networks. With too many passes the network may over-train also. Please understand that a well-trained neural network model would show similar performance levels with both test and training data. Also understand that keeping this in mind we can change the parameter values of the algorithm. We should not assume that default parameters are the best. We can change the parameters too. As the number of epochs increases we need more time for training. If we compare the outputs from the two different epochs, we can see the accuracy remains at the same level of 97.2%. that is why we say that higher the number of epochs has not improved the model performance. Just keep in mind that we should restrict ourselves to the lower number of epochs as it not only involves less computing time but also lowers the danger of over-fitting.

Q.35. Define the following terms:-

a. **Activation function**

b. **Back-propagation learning**

c. **Delta rule**

d. **Epoch**

e. **Feedforward neural networks**

f. **Genetic algorithm**

g. **Hyperplane**

h. **Kernel**

Ans. *a.* **Activation function:** A function that describes the output behaviours of a neuron in neural network.

b. **Back-propagation learning:** It is a form of supervised learning used to train mainly, feedforward neural networks, that works by making modifications in weights values, starting at the output layer and then moving backwards through the hidden layer.

c. **Delta Rule:** The delta rule changes the weight vector for a neural network in such a way that the error is reduced.

d. **Epoch:** It is one complete pass of the entire training set through the neural network. The learning process is repeated epoch-by-epoch until the averaged square error converges to a minimum value.

e. **Feedforward neural network:** It is a sort of ANN where connections between the units do not form a directed cycle.

f. **Genetic algorithm:** It is an adaptive heuristic search algorithm premised on the evolutionary ideas of natural selection theory.

g. **Hyperplane:** A plane (as in geometry) that is used to do object separation during SVM implementation.

h. **Kernel:** Linear, polynomial and rbf are some of the kernels of SVM that allows SVM to fit the maximum margin hyperplane in the transformed feature space.

Q.36. Tabulate the differences between supervised and unsupervised learning.

Ans. The following are the points of differences: -

Supervised Learning	Unsupervised Learning
It incorporates an external teacher so that each output unit is told what should be the desired response to that input signal.	Uses no external teacher.
Global error signals govern learning.	Local information is used for learning.
Uses pattern class information of each training pattern.	Adaptively clusters patterns to generate decision codes.
Paradigms are error correction learning, reinforcement learning and stochastic learning.	Paradigms are Hebbian learning and competitive learning.
Learning is usually off line. It means that learning and operation phases are different. In off-line learning, all of the given patterns are used together.	Learning is online. It means that the agent learns and operates at the same time. Here, the information in each new pattern is incorporated into the agent.
All learning data are stored and can be accessed repeatedly. So, we can see whether we are making progress in training or not.	Locality allows learning in real time. So, the progress cannot be monitored.
Inputs and outputs are defined.	Only inputs are defined.
Uses pattern class information of each training pattern.	Adaptively clusters patterns to generate decision class without any prior pattern class information.
Global error signal governs learning.	Local information/ rules are used for learning.
Learning is offline usually.	Locality allows synapses to learn in real-time.

Q.37. Explain different nets classes.

Ans. It is put under 2 main categories as follows: -

I. Unsupervised learning (*i.e.*, without a teacher):

1. Feedback Nets:

a. Binary Adaptive Resonance Theory (ART1).

b. Analog adaptive Resonance Theory (ART2).

c. Discrete Hopfield (DH).

d. Continuous Hopfield (CH).

e. Discrete Bi-directional Associative Memory (BAM).

f. Temporal Associative Memory (TAM).

g. Adaptive Bi-directional Associative Memory (ABAM).

h. Kohonen Self-Organizing Map/ Topology Preserving Map (SOM/TPM).

i. Competitive learning.

2. Feed-forward only Nets:

a. Learning Matrix (LM).

b. Driver-reinforcement Learning (DR).

c. Counter Propagation (CPN).

II. Supervised learning (*i.e.* with a teacher):

1. Feedback Nets:

a. Boltzmann Machine. (BM).

b. Mean Field Annealing (MFT).

c. Recurrent Cascade Correlation (RCC).

d. Learning Vector Quantization (LVQ).

e. Back progpagation through time (BPTT).

f. Real-time Recurrent Learning (RTRL).

2. Feed-forward only Nets:

a. Perceptron.

b. Adaline, Madaline.

c. Backpropagation (BP).

d. Cauchy Machine (CM).

e. Artmap.

f. Cascade Correlation (CasCor).

EXERCISE QUESTIONS

1. Define machine learning. Discuss the applications of Machine Learning.
2. Difference between training dataset and testing data set.
3. What are support vectors and margins?
4. Differences between supervised and unsupervised learning.
5. Explain Perceptron training algorithm for linear classification.
6. Explain PCA and ICA.
7. What are learning laws?

   [**Hint:** Learning laws provide a set of well-defined rules that determine how the network learns. The laws are as follows:-

   (*a*) The learning algorithm/law must lead to convergence of weights.

   (*b*) The learning time or training time should be small.

   (*c*) The learning should make use of only the local information available. When the synaptic weight linking two neurons is changed, it should depend only on the states of these two units. In such a case, the learning process can be made parallel by changing weights parallel.

   (*d*) Online training may be done wherein the weights are changed based on the inputs.

   (*e*) Non-linear mapping between I/O pairs must be captured by the learning law.

   (*f*) Pattern information storage capacity should be as large as possible for a given network.]
8. Explain delta rule of learning.
9. Explain convergence rule for learning.
10. Explain the back-propagation neural network principles.
11. Using WEKA tool, how will you construct a fully connected feed-forward ANN that has three input nodes, one output node and four internal nodes in the hidden layer?

4 Learning Algorithms

Q.1. What is Logistic Regression?

Ans. Logistics Regression was developed by statistician David Cox in 1958. Regression analysis needs always numeric data. When attributes are categorical, we have to change them to numeric values to apply regression analysis. For example, we can change the attribute gender, being male or female, to 0 and 1 respectively. This has no problem as far as the execution of the regression algorithm is concerned but certainly has problems with the interpretation of the output. If the output or dependent attribute is categorical, the numeric output from regression analysis may not make any sense. There are no restrictions on the output of a regression model. It can be any value from negative infinity to positive infinity. It is quite possible that we get a gender value of 0.5. So, the regression model of a categorical output is given by the expression:-

$$P(y = 1 \mid X) = b_0 + b_1 x_1 + b_2 x_2 + \ldots.. \qquad (1)$$

Where, $P(y = 1 \mid X)$ is the conditional probability of the output attribute, y being 1 given the values of the independent attributes, X. Here X represents a vector of independent variables x_1, x_2...... Because the value of probability lies within the range [0, 1], we can increase the range by considering the following ratio:-

$$\frac{P(y=1|X)}{1-P(y=1|X)} \qquad (2)$$

This can have the value between 0 and infinity. This is the odds ratio, which can be interpreted as how often the class associated with $y = 1$ is seen relative to other classes. If we take the natural logarithm of this odds ratio, we will get an unbounded function from negative infinity to positive infinity since $\log 0 = -\infty$ and $\log \infty = +\infty$. So, we can write:-

$$\ln\left[\frac{P(y=1|X)}{1-P(y=1|X)}\right] = b_0 + b_1 x_1 + b_2 x_2 + \ldots.. \qquad (3)$$

Please note that this equation is also known as the logit. On solving this equation we get:-

$$P(y = 1 \mid X) = \exp\,(b_0 + b_1 x_1 + b_2 x_2 + \ldots..)\ /\ 1 + \exp\,(b_0 + b_1 x_1 + b_2 x_2 + \ldots..) \qquad (4)$$

This equation-4 is called as a **logistic regression model.** Here, the expression exp stands for the base of natural logarithm ($e = 2.7182$). If we plot this equation-4 then we will get an S-shaped curve as shown in figure-4.1.

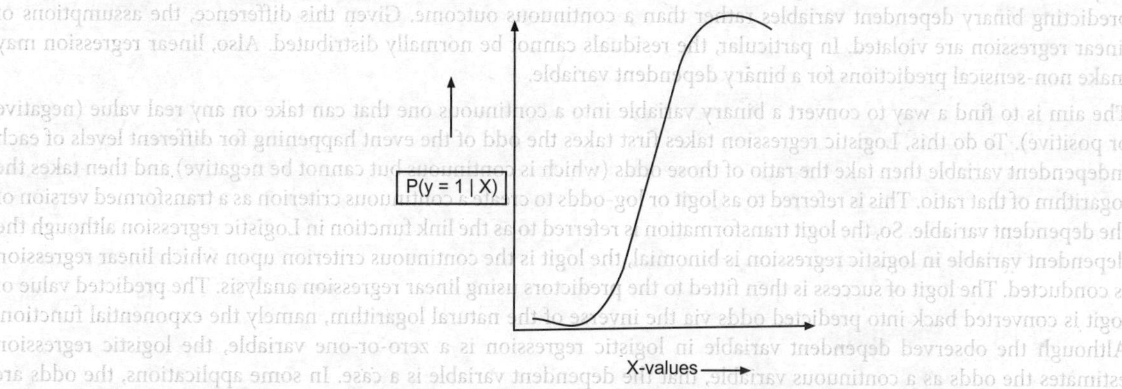

Fig. 4.1: Graph of Logistic Regression Equation

To find the coefficients b_0, b_1, b_2, ... of equation-4, we use iterative method. The purpose of the method is to minimize the sum of logarithms of conditional probabilities. Please understand that the aim of the method is to minimize the sum of logarithms of the conditional probabilities. Also note that convergence occurs when this value is close to zero or it does not change from one iteration to the next.

Cases with more than two categories are called as multinomial logistic regression. If the multiple categories are ordered then it is ordinal logistic regression. The binary logistic model is used to estimate the probability of a binary response based on one or more predictor or independent variables features. It is also called as **qualitative response or discrete choice model in economics** field. Logistic regression measures the relationship between the categorical dependent variable and one or more independent variables by estimating probabilities using a logistic function, which is the cumulative logistic distribution.

Applications : Logistic regression is used in various fields like machine learning, many medical fields and social sciences. For example, the Trauma and Injury Severity Score (TRISS), which is widely used to predict mortality in injured patients, was developed by Boyd et al. using Logistic regression only. It may be used to predict whether a patient has a given disease, based on observed characteristics of the patient.

Example 2, to predict whether an American voter will vote democratic or Republican, based on age, income, sex, race, previous votes etc.

Example 3, this technique can also be used in engineering field to predict the probability of failure of a given process, system or product.

Example 4, it is also used in marketing applications like prediction of a customer's propensity to purchase a product or halt a subscription etc.

Example 5, in economics, it can be used to predict the likelihood of a person's choosing to be in the labour force and a business application would be to predict the likelihood of a homeowner defaulting on a mortgage.

Example 6, conditional random fields that are an extension of logistic regression to sequential data, are used in NLP.

Logistic regression can be binomial, ordinal or multinomial. Binomial or binary logistic regression deals with situations in which the observed outcome for a dependent variable can have only two possible types like "win" or "loss". Multinomial logistic regression deals with situations where the outcome can have 3 or more possible types like disease A or disease B or disease C, that are not ordered. Ordinal logistic regression deals with dependent variables that are ordered. In binary logistic regression, the outcome is usually coded as "0" or "1", as his leads to the most straightforward interpretation. If a particular observed outcome for the dependent variable is the noteworthy possible outcome (referred to as a "success" or a "case") it is usually coded as "1" and the contrary outcome (referred to as a "failure" or a "noncase") as "0". Please note that this Logistic regression is used to predict the odds of being a case based on the values of the independent variables/ predictors. Also note that the odds are defined as the probability that a particular outcome is a case divided by the probability that it is a non-case.

Like other forms of Logistic regression analysis, Logistic regression makes use of one or more predictor variables that may be either continuous or categorical. However, unlike ordinary linear regression, logistic regression is used for predicting binary dependent variables rather than a continuous outcome. Given this difference, the assumptions of linear regression are violated. In particular, the residuals cannot be normally distributed. Also, linear regression may make non-sensical predictions for a binary dependent variable.

The aim is to find a way to convert a binary variable into a continuous one that can take on any real value (negative or positive). To do this, Logistic regression takes first takes the odd of the event happening for different levels of each independent variable then take the ratio of those odds (which is continuous but cannot be negative) and then takes the logarithm of that ratio. This is referred to as logit or log-odds to create a continuous criterion as a transformed version of the dependent variable. So, the logit transformation is referred to as the link function in Logistic regression although the dependent variable in logistic regression is binomial, the logit is the continuous criterion upon which linear regression is conducted. The logit of success is then fitted to the predictors using linear regression analysis. The predicted value of logit is converted back into predicted odds via the inverse of the natural logarithm, namely the exponential function. Although the observed dependent variable in logistic regression is a zero-or-one variable, the logistic regression estimates the odds as a continuous variable, that the dependent variable is a case. In some applications, the odds are all that are needed. In others, a specific yes-or-no prediction is needed for whether the dependent variable is or is not a case. This categorical prediction can be based on the computed odds oa a success, with predicted odds above some chosen cut-off value being translated into a prediction of success.

Queries that can be answered here are like does body weight calorie intake, fat intake and age have an influence on heart attacks?

Assumptions made: -

1. The outcome must be discrete.
2. The dependent variable should be dichotomous in nature like 'present' or 'absent'.
3. There should be no outliers in the data which can be assessed by converting the continuous predictors to standardized or z-scores and remove values below -5 or above 5.
4. There should be no high inter-correlations or multi-collinearity among the predictors. This can be assessed by a correlation matrix among the predictors.
5. Tabachnick et al. suggest that as long as correlation coefficients among independent variables are less than 0.90 the assumption is met.
6. Standard linear regression requires the dependent variable to be of metric (interval or ratio) scale.
7. Logistic regression assumes that the dependent variable is a stochastic event. For instance, if we analyse a pesticide kill rate the outcome event is either killed or alive.
8. Since even the most resistant bug can only be either of these two states, logistic regression thinks in likelihoods of the bug getting killed. If the likelihood of killing the bug is > 0.5, it is assumed dead, if it is <0.5 then it is assumed alive.

Q.2. What is a Perceptron? Explain single layer and multi -layer perceptron.

Ans. According to Minsky et al. a perceptron is defined as "A machine which learns from examples, to assign input samples (vectors) to different classes using a linear function of inputs". Simply stated, it is a neural network used for pattern classification. It consists of a single neuron with adjustable synaptic weights. It is also possible to expand the output layer of perceptron to include more than one neuron. So, they are also called as **weighted networks.** There are two types of perceptions as follows: -

a. Single layer perception.

b. Multi-layer perception.

Single layer perception: A single layer perceptron is shown in figure 4.2. It consists up of an input layer and an output layer with adjustable weights and a bias. It is used for classification of patterns that are linearly separable. The perception algorithm converges and positions the decision surface in the form of a hyper plane between the two classes. The limitation of this network is that it performs pattern classification with only two classes which are linearly separable. Please understand that the linearity and integrity learning makes the single layer perception network very simple. **Also understand that the training in the perception continues till no error occurs.**

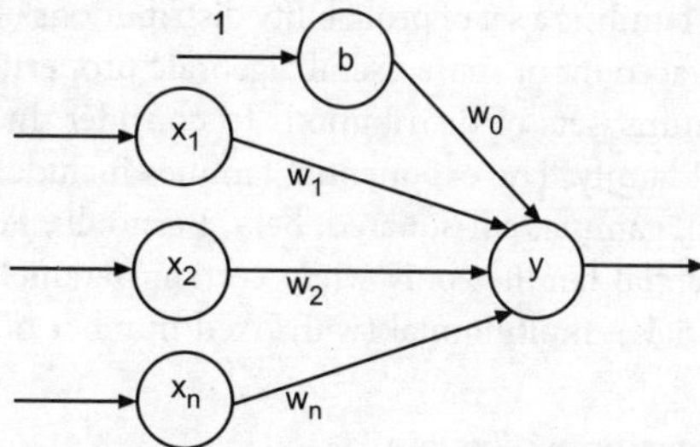

Fig. 4.2: Single Layer Perceptron

In this network, only the weights between the associator and the response unit are adjusted. The input layer consists of input neurons from $x_1, x_2, ..., x_n$. There always exists a common bias "1". The output is compared with this target, if any difference occurs, update weights else stop training process.

In machine learning, the perceptron is an algorithm for supervised learning of binary classifiers i.e., functions that can decide whether an input represented by a vector of numbers, belongs to some specified class or not.

The Training Algorithm :

Step-1: Initialize weights and bias to zero and set learning rate, $\alpha = 0$ to 1.

Step-2: While stopping condition is false do step-3 to step-7.

Step-3: For each training pair $s : t$ do step-4 to step-6.

Step-4: Set activation of input units-

$$x_i = s_j \text{ for } i = 1 \text{ to } n.$$

Step-5: Determine the output unit response-

$$y_{in} = b + \Sigma\,(i = 1 \text{ to } n)\; x_i\, w_i$$

Where the activation function is-

$$y = f(y_{in}) = \begin{cases} = 1, \text{ if } y_{in} \geq \theta \\ = 0, \text{ if } y_{in} = -\theta \text{ to } \theta \\ = -1, \text{ if } y_{in} < -\theta \end{cases}$$

Step-6: Observe the match between the target and the output response. If they do nt match, update the weights and bias. So,

if $t \neq y$ and $x_i \neq 0$

$$w_{i\,(new)} = w_{i\,(old)} + \alpha\, t x_i$$

$$b_{(new)} = b_{(old)} + \alpha_t$$

else

$$w_{i\,(new)} = w_{i\,(old)}$$

$$b_{(new)} = b_{(old)}$$

Step-7: Test for stopping condition based on weight changes.

Step-8: Only weights connecting active units, $x_i \neq 0$ are updated and weights are updated only for patterns that do not produce the correct value of y.

Notes:

1. Single layer perception can be implemented for AND, OR, NOT logic functions but cannot be used for EX-OR logic function.
2. The perception network for a single output class is extended for several output classes.
3. There are a greater number of output neurons or units.
4. The weight updated in this case is also based on the perception learning rule.

Q.3. Explain the concept of Exponential Family.

Ans. In probability field, an exponential family is a set of probability distributions of a certain form. this special form is chosen for mathematical convenience, on account of some useful algebraic properties as well as for generality, as exponential families are in a sense of very natural sets of distributions to consider. In 1935, Pitman *et al.* gave this concept of exponential families / exponential family. The exponential families include many of the most common distributions including the normal, exponential, gamma, chi-squared, beta, Bernoulli, Poisson, Inverse Wishart etc. A number of common distributions are exponential families only when certain parameters are considered fixed and known *e.g.*, binomial (with fixed number of trials), multinomial (with fixed number of trials) and negative binomial (with fixed number of failures).

Q.4. What are Generative Learning algorithms? Explain.

Ans. A generative model is a model for randomly generating observable data values, typically given some hidden parameters. It specifies a joint probability distribution over observation and label sequences. Note that generative models are used in machine learning for either modelling data directly *i.e.* modelling observations drawn from a probability density function, or as an intermediate step to form a conditional probability density function. A conditional distribution can be formed from a generative model through Baye's rule. Generative learning is a theory that involves the active integration of new ideas with the learners existing schemata. The main idea is that in order to learn with understanding, a learner has to construct meaning actively. According to Wittrock, learners construct meaning by actively building relationships between stimuli and their stored information such as knowledge and their experiences. This construction of semantic and distinctive idiosyncratic associations between stimuli and stored information is called as generation. So, we can say that Generative Learning is the process of constructing meaning through generating relationships and associations between stimuli and existing knowledge, beliefs and experiences.

Shannon in 1948, gave an example of in which a table of frequencies of English word pairs is used to generate a sentence beginning with "representing and speedily is an good"; which is not proper English but which will increasingly approximate it as the table is moved from word pairs to word triplets etc.

Q.5. Distinguish between Generative Models v/s Discriminative Models.

Ans. A Generative model is a full probabilistic model of all variables while a discriminative model provides a model only for the target variables conditional on the observed variables for example, generative model can be used to simulate values of any variable in the model. On the other hand, discriminative model allows only the sampling of the target variables conditional on the observed quantities. Despite of the fact that descriptive model do not need to model the distribution of the observed variables, they cannot generally express more complex relationships between the observed and target variables. They do not necessarily perform better than generative models at classification and regression tasks. In modern applications, the two classes are complementary to each other.

Some examples of Generative models are:-

a. Gaussian mixture model.

b. Naive Baye's.

c. Context-free Grammar.

d. Hidden Markov Model.

e. Restricted Boltzman Machine.

f. Generative Adversial Networks.

Please note that if the observed data are truly samples from the generative model then fitting parameters of the generative model to maximize the data likelihood is a common method. But since most of the statistical models are only approximations to the truc distributions, if the model's application is to infer about a subset of variables conditional on known values of other then it can be argued that the approximation makes more assumptions than are necessary to solve the problem at hand. In such cases, it can be more accurate to model the conditional density functions directly using a discriminative model. But the application-specific details will ultimately dictate which approach is most suitable in any particular case.

Baye's rule. Generative learning is a theory that involves the active integration of new ideas with the learners existing schemata. The main idea is that in order to learn with understanding, a learner has to construct meaning actively. According to Wittrock, learners construct meaning by actively building relationships between stimuli and their stored information such as knowledge and their experiences. This construction of semantic and distinctive idiosyncratic associations between stimuli and stored information is called as generation. So, we can say that Generative Learning is the process of constructing meaning through generating relationships and associations between stimuli and existing knowledge, beliefs and experiences.

Shannon in 1948, gave an example of in which a table of frequencies of English word pairs is used to generate a sentence beginning with "representing and speedily is an good"; which is not proper English but which will increasingly approximate it as the table is moved from word pairs to word triplets etc.

Q.5. Distinguish between Generative Models v/s Discriminative Models.

Ans. A Generative model is a full probabilistic model of all variables while a discriminative model provides a model only for the target variables conditional on the observed variables for example, generative model can be used to simulate values of any variable in the model. On the other hand, discriminative model allows only the sampling of the target variables conditional on the observed quantities. Despite of the fact that descriptive model do not need to model the distribution of the observed variables, they cannot generally express more complex relationships between the observed and target variables. They do not necessarily perform better than generative models at classification and regression tasks. In modern applications, the two classes are complementary to each other.

Some examples of Generative models are:-

a. Gaussian mixture model.

b. Naive Baye's.

c. Context-free Grammar.

d. Hidden Markov Model.

e. Restricted Boltzman Machine.

f. Generative Adversial Networks.

Please note that if the observed data are truly samples from the generative model then fitting parameters of the generative model to maximize the data likelihood is a common method. But since most of the statistical models are only approximations to the true distributions, if the model's application is to infer about a subset of variables conditional on known values of other then it can be argued that the approximation makes more assumptions than are necessary to solve the problem at hand. In such cases, it can be more accurate to model the conditional density functions directly using a discriminative model. But the application-specific details will ultimately dictate which approach is most suitable in any particular case.

Generative model in context of Machine Learning

A generative algorithm models how the data was generated in order to categorize a signal. It answers to queries like 'based on my generation assumptions, which category is most likely to generate this signal? A discriminative algorithm does not care about how the data was generated; it simply categorizes a given signal.

Example: Say, the input data is x and the set of labels for x is y. A generative model learns the joint probability distribution $p(x, y)$ while a discriminative model learns the conditional probability distribution $p(y \mid x)$ *i.e.* the probability of y given x.

Discriminative algorithms try to learn $p(y \mid x)$ directly from the data and then tries to classify data. On the other hand, generative algorithms tries to learn $p(x, y)$ which can be transformed into $p(x \mid y)$ later to classify the data. One of the benefits of generative algorithms is that you can use $p(x, y)$ to generate new data similar to the existing data. On the other hand, discriminative algorithms generally give better performance in classification tasks.

Some examples of Discriminative models are: -

a. Logistic Regression.

b. Support Vector Machines.

c. Neural Networks.

d. Conditional Random Fields.

Q.6. Explain Gaussian Discriminant Analysis method.

Ans. A very popular continuous probability distribution is Gaussian distribution / Normal Distribution. It is also called as a bell curve since it has a bell-shaped curve. The equation in one dimension is as follows: -

$$p(x) = 1 / \sqrt{2\Pi}\sigma \exp [-(x - \mu)^2 / 2\sigma^2] \quad ......(1)$$

where μ = mean

σ = standard deviation

Please note that it is useful because of its Central Limit Theorem which tells us that lots of random numbers will add up to something Gaussian.

In Gaussian Mixture Models (GMM), we assume that there are number of different classes. Each class comes from its own Gaussian distribution. And such type of data is known as multi-model data as there are number of modes or distribution for each particular class. We are unable to accommodate Gaussian to the data in totality as it does not appear to be Gaussian overall.

If we know the number of classes that are there in the data then we can put effort to estimate the parameters for that many number of Gaussians and that too all at the same time.

On the other hand, if we do not the number of classes then we can attempt for different numbers and finds out which one works best. Then the output for any specific data point which has already been an input to the algorithm will be the sum of the values expected by all of the 'M' Gaussians. That is,

$$f(x) = \Sigma\ (m = 1 \text{ to } M)\ \alpha_m\ \varphi\ (x;\mu_m, \Sigma_m) \quad ....(2)$$

where $\varphi\ (x;\mu_m, \Sigma_m)$ = Gaussian function with mean μm and covariance matrix and

the αm are the weights with the constraints *i.e.* $\Sigma\ (m = 1 \text{ to } M)\ \alpha_m = 1$.

The task is to choose the weights αm. The target is for Maximum likelihood solution. Note that likelihood refers to the conditional probability and Maximum Likelihood solution refers to maximizing the conditional probability.

Q.7. What is Gaussian Discriminant Analysis (GDA)?

Ans. Gaussian Discriminant Analysis (GDA) is a method for data classification commonly used when data can be approximated with a normal distribution.

The first step needs a training set *i.e.*, a bunch of data yet classified. These data are used to train your classifier and obtain a discriminant function that will tell you to which class a data has higher probability to belong. When you have your training set, you need to compute the mean and the standard deviation. These two variables allow us to compute normal distribution. Once you have computed the normal distribution for each class, to classify a data you will need to compute, for each one, the probability that the data belongs to. Note that the class with the highest probability will be chosen as the affinity class. GDA is a generative model for classification where the distribution of each class is modelled as a multivariate Gaussian. GDA is a generative learning algorithm. In this model, we will assume that $P(x \mid y)$ is distributed according to a multivariate normal distribution.

Note: We make stronger assumptions in GDA. If we do not know where the data comes from then the logistic regression analysis would be more robust. But if we know then GDA may perform better.

Q.8. What do you mean by Naive Bayes? Discuss its advantages, disadvantages and applications.

Ans. It is a supervised machine learning algorithm. It is often associated with NLP (Natural Language Processing) applications like spam recognition or sentiment analysis.

By the term 'naive' we mean "immature". A naive Bayes classifier is a simple probability-based algorithm. It uses Bayes theorem. It assumes that instances are independent of each other. They work very well in complex real-world scenarios also. The naive Bayes algorithm offers a fast model building and scoring both for binary and multiclass situations for relatively low volumes of data. According to Hand et al., 2001, this algorithm makes predictions using Bayes theorem which includes evidence or prior knowledge in its prediction.

Tool like WEKA also uses this naive Bayes algorithm on the dataset provided to it. In WEKA, there is an option of naive Bayes classifier under 'bayes' subdirectory. Then in next step we keep the default settings of the Weka environment and the classifiers parameters. Next, we click on the Start button and the program executes and we will get the needed analysis. Thus, this model is used for analysis of the input dataset. Naive Bayes is a simple technique for constructing classifiers-models that assign class labels to problem instances that are represented as vectors of feature values. The class labels are drawn from some finite set.

Principle: "All Naive Bayes classifiers assume that the value of a particular feature is independent of the value of any other feature, given the class variable."

For example, a rectangle may be considered to be a whiteboard if it has a length, breadth and some thickness. A Naive Bayes classifier considers each of these features to contribute independently to the probability that this rectangle is a whiteboard, regardless of any possible correlations between the color, its shape and its thickness.

Note that for some types of probability models, Naive Bayes classifiers can be trained very efficiently in a supervised learning setting. Practically, parameter estimation for Naive Bayes models uses the method of maximum likelihood. In other words, one can work with Naive Bayes model without accepting Bayesian methods. The advantage of this is that it requires only a small number of training data to estimate the parameters necessary for classification. As far as machine learning is concerned, Naive Bayes classifiers are a family of simple probabilistic classifiers based on applying Baye's theorem with strong independence assumptions between the features.

Naive Bayes classifiers have been studied extensively since 1950s. It forms the baseline for text categorization. With suitable pre-processing, it is competitive in this domain with more advanced methods including support vector machines. Also it has some applications in automatic medical diagnosis. Naive Bayes classifiers are highly scalable, requiring a number of parameters linear in the number of variables (features/ predictors) in a learning problem. Also note that maximum-likelihood training can be done by evaluating a closed-form expression, which takes linear time rather than by expensive iterative approximation as used for many other types of classifiers.

Advantages of Naive Bayes Algorithm: -

1. The algorithm as well as its implementation process is simple. Calculations do not involve any numerical optimization, no matrix algebra and no calculus.

2. The algorithm is efficient to train and use. It can be easily updated with new data. This algorithm is similar to linear classifier and hence is fast too.
3. From one dataset we can estimate content features from messages without headers.
4. Unlabelled data can be used in parameter estimation for other applications. This algorithm performs well with smaller training sets.

Disadvantages of Naive Bayes Algorithm: -

1. The independence assumption is a very strong inference and untrue for most real- world problems.
2. The boundaries between classes have to be fine tuned and not to be set analytically.
3. It is not very effective algorithm as it is simple.

Applications of Naive Bayes Algorithm: -

1. The classifiers used in text classification have higher success rate as compared to other algorithms. As a result, it is widely used in spam filtering i.e. identifying spam e-mail and sentiment analysis i.e. in social media analysis to identify positive and negative customer sentiments.
2. Naive Bayes classifier and collaborative filtering together builds a recommendation system that uses machine learning and data mining techniques to filter unseen information and predict whether a user would like a given resource or not.
3. It is an eager learning classifier and is thus fast. It could be used for making predictions in real-time too.
4. It can be used to do parameter estimation for any model application.
5. It can be used for document classification also.
6. In medical diagnosis field, it has been used for localization of primary tumour, thyroid diseases etc.

Q.9. What are Support Vector Machines (SVM)?

Ans. SVM belongs to the type of supervised learning methods used for classification and regression. SVM were developed by Vladimir Vapnik et al. in 1998 at UK. Statistical learning became important after its introduction.

Basic idea: Construct a hyper plane that best separates classes. If this is not feasible in the input space then the goal is achieved in a higher dimensional space called as a feature space, reached by mapping the input vector through a non-linear function.

This mapping has a property that will linearly separate the data sets in the feature space. The hyper plane in the feature space will maximally separate the data set classes. The method is based on statistical learning theory and is successfully used in a number of applications like particle identification, face detection, text categorization. Technically speaking, it is mathematically intuitive, reproducible and does not have problems of local minima as the optimization function is convex and is robust to new classification data tasks.

In machine learning, SVMs or Support Vector Networks are supervised learning models with associated learning algorithms that analyze data used for classification and regression analysis. Given a set of training examples, each marked as belonging to one or the other of two categories, an SVM training algorithm builds a model that assigns new examples to one category or the other, making it a non-probabilistic binary linear classifier. An SVM model is a representation of the examples as points in space, mapped so that the examples of the separate categories are divided by a clear gap that is as wide as possible. Then new examples are mapped into that same space and predicted to belong to a category based on which side of the gap they fall. SVMs can also perform a non-linear classification using what is called the **kernel trick *i.e.* implicitly mapping** their inputs into high dimensional feature spaces. When data are not labelled, supervised learning is not possible and an unsupervised learning approach is required, which attempts to find natural clustering of the data to groups and then map new data to these formed groups. The clustering algorithm which provides an improvement to SVM is called **support vector clustering.** It is often used in industrial applications either when data are not labelled or when only some data are labelled as a pre-processing for a classification pass.

This is shown in figure 4.3.

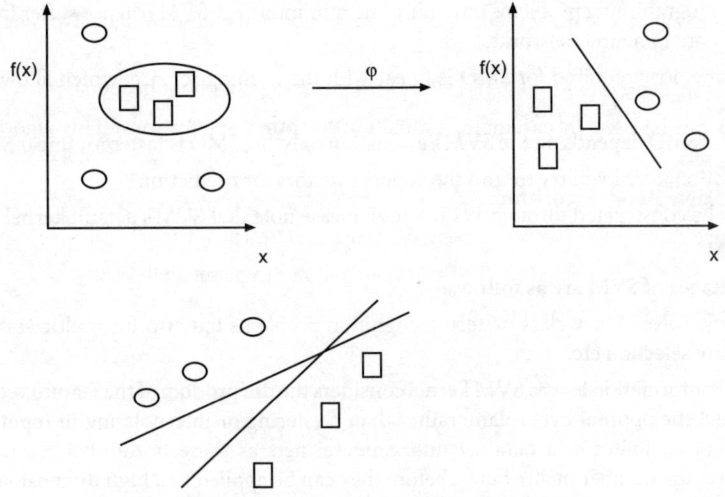

Fig. 4.3: Data sets and their Separation

The upper part of the figure 4.3 shows the mapping of the training data non-linearly into a higher dimensional feature space and constructs a hyperplane with maximum margins. The lower part of the figure 4.3 shows two potential hyperplanes that separate data sets. A hyperplane is a concept in geometry. **Please note that hyperplane is a generalization of the concept of a plane which is used in SVM implementation for object separation. Also note that a hyperplane that separates the data points in the feature space with maximumdistances among the classes in SVM is called as a maximum-margin hyperplane or optimal hyperplane.** The data points on the outer margins/ outside ovals and the inner margins/ inside ovals that are on the boundary lines are called as **support vectors.**

Support vectors or SVs are transformed training patterns that are always placed at the optimal hyperplane in the feature space during SVM LEARNING. SVM is a statistical based learning algorithm that has been widely used by researchers in various fields like business, text categorization, pattern recognition abd protein function prediction. Recently, researchers added a new dimension to SVM in cancer classification through its ability to deal with high dimensional data. SVM can handle any classification, clustering, regression and even novelty detection problems. The attractiveness of SVM algorithm lies in the fact that we do not have to consider all instances i.e. we can focus on the support vectors to do the analysis.

Algorithm: SVM

SVM architecture is analogous to neural network architecture. Like we have three layers of neural networks, similarly we have three phases of SVM-

a. Input or transformation phase,

b. Middle or Learning phase and

c. Output or function estimation phase.

Please note the following points here: -

1. Data extraction tool first collects the data about the object and feed these data as input.
2. Then these data are transformed into vectors in a new mathematical space called as a **feature space.**
3. SVM starts to find support vectors in the learning phase.
4. If data are not linearly separable, SVM calls non-linear kernel for transformation of the input data.
5. 'Kernel trick' can apply linear classification techniques to non-linear classification problems. Many types of kernels like linear, polynomial and radial bassis function can be followed by SVM.
6. After kernel transformation, SVM uses some optimization techniques (like sequential minimal optimization-SMO) to extract parameter values. Actually, training an SVM involves the solution of very large quadratic programming problem Also note that SVM breaks the large quadratic programming problems into a series of smaller problems and solves them analytically.

7. Large quadratic programming problems have only one minimum. So, SVMs do not suffer from finding local minima problems as they are in neural networks.
8. The amount of memory required for SMO is linear with the training set size, which allows it to handle very larger training sets also.
9. The time taken by SMO depends on the SVM's evaluation only. So, SMO is faster for linear SVMs and sparse datasets.
10. During optimization, SVM will try to find the support vectors for prediction.
11. SVM model can be constructed through WEKA tool. Please note that SVM's default kernel is polynomial in WEKA.

Advantages of SVM

Some of the advantages of SVM are as follows:-

1. They can not only solve binary class pattern recognition problems but also for multiclass classification, regression estimation, feature selection etc.
2. Lesser chances of information loss as SVM kernel considers the dot product of the feature vectors in high dimensional space to construct the optimal hyperplane rather than clustering or interpolating in input space. SVM can handle a large number of attributes of a data set unlike neural nets as these traditional algorithms need reduction of dimensionality i.e. the number of attributes, before they can be applied to a high dimensional problem.
3. Even in the field of bioinformatics, it has proven to be useful as there we have more than 20,000 attributes.
4. They are very versatile as they have many extensions too like Support Vector Decision Tree, neural network based SVM, fuzzy SVM etc.

Disadvantages of SVM

Some of the disadvantages of SVM are as follows:-

1. The best choice of kernel for a given problem is still an issue in research work.
2. Its speed and size during training and testing is still an issue. Training for very large datasets / millions of support vectors is still an unsolved problem.
3. It lacks efficiency in solving of multi-class problems. It is still an active research area.

Applications of SVM

Some of the applications of SVMs are listed below.

1. They have been used to study financial forecasting.
2. Spatial and temporal environmental data can be analysed to find patterns and trends using SVMs.
3. In field of biology also SVMs have proven to be very useful, particularly for remote homology detection.
4. They have been used for face expression classification.
5. They have been used for e-learning.
6. They have been used to control traffic congestion problems.

Q.10. What is an Optimal Hyperplane?

Ans. SVM belongs to the type of supervised learning methods used for classification and regression. SVM were developed by Vladimir Vapnik et al. in 1998 at UK. Statistical learning became important after its introduction.

Basic idea: Construct a hyper plane that best separates classes. If this is not feasible in the input space then the goal is achieved in a higher dimensional space called as a feature space, reached by mapping the input vector through a non-linear function.

This mapping has a property that will linearly separate the data sets in the feature space. The hyper plane in the feature space will maximally separate the data set classes. The method is based on statistical learning theory and is successfully used in a number of applications like particle identification, face detection, text categorization. Technically speaking, it is mathematically intuitive, reproducible and does not have problems of local minima as the optimization function is convex and is robust to new classification data tasks. In machine learning, SVMs or Support Vector Networks are supervised learning models with associated learning algorithms that analyse data used for classification and regression analysis. Given a set of training examples, each marked as belonging to one or the other of two categories, an SVM training algorithm builds a model that assigns new examples to one category or the other, making it a non-probabilistic binary linear classifier. An SVM model is a representation of the examples as points in space, mapped so that the examples of the separate categories are divided by a clear gap that is as wide as possible. Then new examples are mapped into that same space and predicted to belong to a category based on which side of the gap they fall. SVMs can also perform a non-linear classification using what is called the kernel trick i.e. implicitly mapping their inputs into high dimensional feature spaces. When data are not labelled, supervised learning is not possible and an unsupervised learning approach is required, which attempts to find natural clustering of the data to groups and then map new data to these formed groups. The clustering algorithm which provides an improvement to SVM is called support vector clustering. It is often used in industrial applications either when data are not labelled or when only some data are labelled as a pre-processing for a classification pass.

This is shown in figure 4.4.

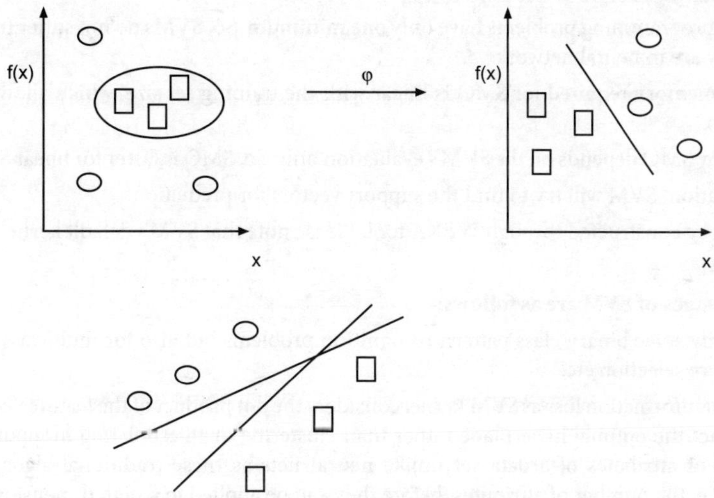

Fig. 4.4: *Data sets and their Separation*

The upper part of the figure 4.4 shows the mapping of the training data non-linearly into a higher dimensional feature space and constructs a hyperplane with maximum margins. The lower part of the figure 4.4 shows two potential hyperplanes that separate data sets. A hyperplane is a concept in geometry. Please note that hyperplane is a generalization of the concept of a plane which is used in SVM implementation for object separation. Also note that a hyperplane that separates the data points in the feature space with maximum distances among the classes in SVM is called as a maximum-margin hyperplane or optimal hyperplane. The data points on the outer margins/ outside ovals and the inner margins/ inside ovals that are on the boundary lines are called as support vectors.

Support vectors or SVs are transformed training patterns that are always placed at the optimal hyperplane in the feature space during SVM LEARNING. SVM is a statistical based learning algorithm that has been widely used by researchers in various fields like business, text categorization, pattern recognition and protein function prediction. Recently, researchers added a new dimension to SVM in cancer classification through its ability to deal with high dimensional data. SVM can handle any classification, clustering, regression and even novelty detection problems. The attractiveness of SVM algorithm lies in the fact that we do not have to consider all instances i.e. we can focus on the support vectors to do the analysis.

Algorithm: SVM

SVM architecture is analogous to neural network architecture. Like we have three layers of neural networks, similarly we have three phases of SVM-

d. Input or transformation phase,

e. Middle or Learning phase and

f. Output or function estimation phase.

Please note the following points here:-

1. Data extraction tool first collects the data about the object and feed these data as input.

2. Then these data are transformed into vectors in a new mathematical space called as a feature space.
3. SVM starts to find support vectors in the learning phase.
4. If data are not linearly separable, SVM calls non-linear kernel for transformation of the input data.
5. 'Kernel trick' can apply linear classification techniques to non-linear classification problems. Many types of kernels like linear, polynomial and radial bassis function can be followed by SVM.
6. After kernel transformation, SVM uses some optimization techniques (like sequential minimal optimization-SMO) to extract parameter values. Actually, training an SVM involves the solution of very large quadratic programming problem Also note that SVM breaks the large quadratic programming problems into a series of smaller problems and solves them analytically.
7. Large quadratic programming problems have only one minimum. So, SVMs do not suffer from finding local minima problems as they are in neural networks.
8. The amount of memory required for SMO is linear with the training set size, which allows it to handle very larger training sets also.
9. The time taken by SMO depends on the SVM's evaluation only. So, SMO is faster for linear SVMs and sparse datasets.
10. During optimization, SVM will try to find the support vectors for prediction.
11. SVM model can be constructed through WEKA tool. Please note that SVM's default kernel is polynomial in WEKA.

Advantages of SVM

Some of the advantages of SVM are as follows:-

1. They can not only solve binary class pattern recognition problems but also for multiclass classification, regression estimation, feature selection etc.
2. Lesser chances of information loss as SVM kernel considers the dot product of the feature vectors in high dimensional space to construct the optimal hyperplane rather than clustering or interpolating in input space. SVM can handle a large number of attributes of a data set unlike neural nets as these traditional algorithms need reduction of dimensionality i.e. the number of attributes, before they can be applied to a high dimensional problem.
3. Even in the field of bioinformatics, it has proven to be useful as there we have more than 20,000 attributes.
4. They are very versatile as they have many extensions too like Support Vector Decision Tree, neural network based SVM, fuzzy SVM etc.

Disadvantages of SVM

Some of the disadvantages of SVM are as follows:-

1. The best choice of kernel for a given problem is still an issue in research work.
2. Its speed and size during training and testing is still an issue. Training for very large datasets / millions of support vectors is still an unsolved problem.
3. It lacks efficiency in solving of multi-class problems. It is still an active research area.

Applications of SVM

Some of the applications of SVMs are listed below.

1. They have been used to study financial forecasting.
2. Spatial and temporal environmental data can be analysed to find patterns and trends using SVMs.
3. In field of biology also SVMs have proven to be very useful, particularly for remote homology detection.
4. They have been used for face expression classification.
5. They have been used for e-learning.
6. They have been used to control traffic congestion problems.

Q.11. What role does a Kernel has in machine learning?

Ans. A kernel is a similarity function. It is a function that a domain expert provides to a machine learning algorithm. It takes two inputs and splits out how similar they are.

For instance, the task is to learn to classify images. We have (image, label) pairs as training data.

Consider a typical machine learning pipeline. Take your images, compute features, string these features for each image into a vector and then feed these features-vectors and labels into a learning algorithm. That is,

Data → Features → Learning Algorithm

Kernels offer an alternative. Instead of defining a slew of features, you define a single kernel function to calculate similarity between images. You provide this kernel, together with the images and labels to the learning algorithm and outcome is a classifier. Please note that the standard SVM or logistic regression or perceptron formulation does not work with kernels. But it works with feature vectors: -

1. Under some conditions, every kernel function can be expressed as a dot product in a possibly infinite dimensional feature space (Mercer's theorem).
2. Many machine learning algorithms can be expressed entirely in terms of dot products.

   Also note that this means that we can now take my best machine learning algorithm, express it in terms of dot product and then since my kernel is also a dot product in some space, replace the dot product by your suitable and best kernel.

Importance of Kernels : Kernels are opposed to feature vectors. It has been found that computing the kernel is easy but computing the feature vector corresponding to the kernel is quite difficult. The feature vector for even simple kernels can blow up in size and for kernels like RBF kernel the corresponding feature vector is infinite dimensional. Yet computing the kernel is almost trivial. Many machine learning algorithms can be written to only use dot products and then we can replace the dot products with kernels. By doing this, we do not have to use the feature vector at all. Please understand that this means that we can work with highly complex, efficient-to-compute and yet high performing kernels without ever having to write down the huge and potentially infinite dimensional feature vector. Thus, if not for the ability to use kernel functions directly, we would be stuck with relatively low dimensional, low performance feature vectors. This trick is also called as the kernel trick.

Q.12. What is Model Selection? How is it done?

Ans. The process of selecting the models from different mathematical models that refer to the same data set is called as model selection. It is applied to the fields of statistics, machine learning and data mining. Support Vector Machines map input vectors into a high dimensional feature space where a maximal margin hyperplane is constructed. It is seen that when training data are separable, the error rate for SVMs can be expressed as:-

$$H = R^2/ M^2 \quad ....(1)$$

Where 'R' is the radius of the smallest sphere containing the training data;

'M' is the margin (*i.e.* the distance between the hyperplane and the closest training vector in feature space. This function estimates the VC dimension of hyperplanes separating data with a given margin, M).

To perform the mapping and to calculate R and M in the SVM technique, one uses a positive definite kernel $K(x, x')$ which specifies an inner product in the feature space. An example of such a kernel is the Radial Basis Function (RBF) as follows:-

$$K(x, x') = e^{-|x-x'|^2/2\sigma^2}$$

This kernel has a free parameter σ and more generally, most kernels require some parameters to be set. When treating noisy data with SVMs, another parameter, penalizing the training errors, also needs to be set. The problem of choosing the values of these parameters which minimize the expectation of test error is known as the model selection problem. It is shown that the parameter of the kernel that minimizes function will provide a good choice for the model. Also note that the minimum of this function coincides with the minimum of the test error. But the shapes of these curves may be different.

Algorithms have finished learning from the data sets, you may be pondering the results from your test set and wondering whether you can improve them or not. Here is the list of 10 (ten) general principles to be followed in order to improve the outcome achieved using machine learning algorithms.

Principles to follow in order to improve the selected model: -

1. **Study the learning curves :** Find out the problems with your model. Use learning curves for verification suing the test set by varying the number of training instances.

   Also, you need to understand how the model behaves when the sample size increases.
2. **Use cross validation property :** By means of loads of data, overfitting can be avoided. Overfitting happens when comparatively you have a small dataset and you make effort to learn from it. But if you have a small database and it

is necessary to come with a model based on that then in such a scenario, cross validation method may be used. In this method, the dataset is divided into two segments, testing and training datasets. The testing dataset will only test the model while in training dataset, the data-points will come up with a model. In this method, a model is generally provided with a dataset of known data on which training data set is run and a dataset of unknown data against which the model is tested. The basic idea of cross validation is to define a dataset to test the model in the training phase.

After MLP training is over, in next step we need to find out how well it performs. In case of trained network, the error can be computed by computing the sum of squares error between output and target. The next task is what data should be used to test the network. It is not intelligence to use the same data for training as well as testing. This is so because it would not tell us how well the network generalizes and whether or not overfitting has happened. Thus, we need to keep separate pairs in reserve for testset (input, target) which are not used for the training purpose. In this case, we have to adjust with the fact that the amount of data which is available for testing is reduced. It is more complex, scenario when we check how well the network is learning during training so that when to stop can be decided. Now to make such a decision we cannot use training data as we would not detect overfitting but we cannot use the testing data either as we are saving it for the final test.

So, a 3rd data set called as a validation set is required to validate the learning so far, in the field of statistics, it is called as **cross validation.**

The ratio of training to testing to validation data is-

50:25:25 if you have large amount of data and

60:20:20 if you have a lesser amount of data.

So, the input data set is split into three different sets-training set, testing set and validation set. A large difference between the cross-validation estimates and the result is a common problem that is observed with a new test dataset. This may happen due to two reasons:-

a. Information is leaking from the response to the model. This is called as snooping.

b. A simple random sampling may prove to be inadequate when we convert classes into data. So, this may result in incorrect sampling. Better is to use statistical sampling method.

3. Choose the right error or score metric.
4. **Search for the best hyper-parameter :** Test for different hyper-parameters. Fewer examples chosen at random need lesser computations but they still give same solutions.
5. **Test multiple models :** It means that understand the features that work better for them. Introspect them. It gives us suggestions as to which features should be transformed for feature creation and which feature should be left out.
6. **Average models :** Machine learning includes building many models and creating many different predictions and all of them with different expected error performances. Better results may be obtained by averaging models together. The principle used is:-"Estimate variance is random, so by averaging many different models, you can enhance the signal (the correct prediction) and rule out the noise that will often cancel itself; opposite errors sum to zero. A mixture of simple and complex algorithms may be done to create better predictions. This is also named as gradient boosting.
7. **Stack your models :** During stacking, machine learning models are built in two steps:

   a. Use different algorithms to predict multiple results with all of them learning from the features present in your data.

   b. Instead of providing features that a new model will learn, provide that model with predictions of the other previously trained models. You may use logistic regression or a complex tree ensemble as a model at this second stage.

   This method is useful when guessing complex target functions. you can approximate them only by using multiple/many models together and then by combining the result of multiplication.
8. **Applying Feature Engineering:** Shift from feature creation (as in ML) to feature learning (as in DL). The paradigm shift is-

   From feature creation ⟶ to feature learning

   Feature creation is more human art than science. Even automatic feature creation is possible using polynomial expansion or the support vector machines (SVM) class of machine learning algorithms. Please note that SVMs can automatically look for better features in higher dimensional feature spaces that are both computationally fast and needs optimal memory.

9. **Selecting Features and Examples:** Prune (remove/cut-down) some of the features in your data matrix and choose only those with which the highest predictive value is advisable.
10. **Look for More Data:** Increase your sample by providing new data which will give you new features. Please understand that complex models can improve a lot from additional training examples as adding data makes parameter estimation much more reliable and disambiguates cases in which the ML algorithm cannot determine which rule to extract. Also note that if you want to add new features, locate an open source data source so as to match your data with entries. Also you can scrap data from web.

Q.13. What is Bagging?

Ans. Leo Breiman showed that pasting, a process of sampling a portion of your training set, reduces the number of training examples. This is called as pasting but it is a problem for learning complex data. Also Dr. Breiman, tested the effects of bootstrap sampling i.e. sampling with replacement, which not only leaves out some noise but also creates more variation in ensembles, thereby improving the results. This method is called as bagging or bootstrap aggregation. So, **it is defined as a machine learning ensemble meta-algorithm designed to improve the stability and accuracy of ML algorithms used in statistical classification and regression.** It also reduces variance and helps to overfitting. It can not only be applied to decision tree methods but to any other method too. Bagging is a special case of the model averaging approach.

Technique used: Given a standard set D of size n, bagging generates m new training sets D_i, each of size n', by sampling from D uniformly and with replacement. By sampling with replacement, some observations may be repeated in each D_i. If $n = n$, then for large n the set D_i is expected to have the fraction $(1 - 1/e) = 63.2\%$ of the unique examples of D, the rest being duplicates. This type of sample is known as bootstrap sample. The m models are fitted using the above m bootstrap samples and combined by averaging the output (for regression) or voting (for classification).

Bagging results in improvements for unstable procedures that includes ANNs, classification and regression trees etc.

Q.14. What is Boosting (The Ada Boost Algorithm)?

Ans. Boosting is defined as a machine learning ensemble meta-algorithm basically to reduce bias and variance in supervised learning. It is a family of ML algorithms which convert weak learners to strong ones. According to Kearns et al. in 1989, a weak learner is defined as a classifier that is only slightly correlated with the true classification. On the other hand, a strong classifier is a classifier is well correlated with the true classification. The boosting problem is the process of turning a weak learner into a strong learner. In other words, informally the hypothesis boosting problem asks whether an efficient learning algorithm that outputs a hypothesis whose performance is only slightly better than random guessing i.e., a weak learner, implies the existence of an efficient algorithm that outputs a hypothesis of arbitrary accuracy i.e. a strong learner. And the algorithms that achieve hypothesis boosting came to be known as the boosting algorithms. While boosting is not algorithmically constrained, most boosting algorithms consist of iteratively learning weak classifiers with respect to a distribution and adding them to a final strong classifier. When they are added they are typically weighted in some way that is usually related to the weak learner's accuracy. After a weak learner is added, the data are re-weighted. Please note here that the examples that are misclassified will gain weight while the examples that are classified correctly lose weight. There are some algorithms like boost by majority, BrownBoost that decrease the weight of repeatedly misclassified examples. Also note that the future weak learners focus more on the examples that previous weak learners misclassified.

In 1995, Yoav Freund and Robert Schapire formulated the first boosting algorithm, Adaboost. The original algorithms developed by them were not adaptive and could not take the full advantage of weak learners. But AdBoost got a Godel prize for them. So we define the boosting algorithms as the algorithms that are provable boosting algorithms in the probably approximately correct learning formulation. Other algorithms that are similar in spirit to boosting algorithms are called as leveraging algorithms. The main difference between these different boosting algorithms is in their method of weighting training data points and hypotheses. AdaBoost is the first algorithm that can adapt weak learners.

Some more examples of recent boosting algorithms includes:-

- LPBoost
- BrownBoost
- MadaBoost
- TotalBoost
- Xgboost
- LogitBoost

Note: Many boosting algorithms fit into the AnyBoost framework, which shows that boosting performs gradient descent in function space using a convex cost function.

Q.15. Write the Adaptive Boosting (AdaBoost) Algorithm.

Ans. Complex problems in machine and deep learning often suffer from the 'curse of dimensionality'. Distance usually relates to all the attributes and assumes all of them have the same effects on the distance. The similarity metrics do not consider the relation of attributes which result in inaccurate distance and then impact on classification precision. This wrong classification due to presence of many irrelevant attributes is often termed as the curse of dimensionality.

For example, say each instance is described by 20 attributes out of which only 2 are relevant in determining the classification of the target function. In this case, instances that have identical values for the 2 relevant attributes may nevertheless be distant from one another in the 20 -dimensional instance space.

Unlike neural networks and SVMs, the AdaBoost training process selects only those features known to improve the predictive power of the model, reducing dimensionality and potentially improving execution time as irrelevant features do not need to be computed.

This algorithm can be used along with many other types of learning algorithms so as to improve their performance. The output of the other learning algorithms (weak learners) is combined into a weighted sum that represents the final output of the boosted classifier. This algorithm is adaptive means that subsequent weak learners are tweaked in favour of those instances misclassified by previous classifiers. This algorithm is also sensitive to noisy data and outliers. To some problems it may be less susceptible to the overfitting problem than other learning algorithms. **Also note that the individual learners can be weak but as long as the performance of each one is slightly better than random guessing like their error rate is smaller than 0.5 for binary classification, the final model can be proven to converge to a strong learner.** Every learning algorithm will tend to suit some problems better than others and will have different parameters to be adjusted before achieving optimal performance on the dataset, AdaBoost with decision trees as the weak learners is often called as the best-out-of- the-box classifier. When used with decision tree learning, information gathered at each stage of this algorithm about the relative hardness of each training sample is fed into the tree growing algorithm such that later trees tend to focus on harder-to-classify examples.

Q.16. How do you implement Evaluating and Debugging learning algorithms?

Ans. To evaluate our ML algorithm so developed to solve a complex problem we follow a standard approach of dividing the data into three parts as follows: -

Training Data	Validation Data	Test Data

Fig.4.5: Division of Data into Three Parts

The ratio of training to testing to validation data is-

50:25:25 if you have large amount of data and

60:20:20 if you have a lesser amount of data.

So, the input data set is split into three different sets-training set, testing set and validation set. A large difference between the cross-validation estimates and the result is a common problem that is observed with a new test dataset. This may happen due to two reasons:-

a. Information is leaking from the response to the model. This is called as snooping.

b. A simple random sampling may prove to be inadequate when we convert classes into data. So, this may result in incorrect sampling. Better is to use statistical sampling method.

The method followed to evaluate a ML algorithm is as follows: -

S1: Break all data into training/ testing sets (as above).

S2: Break training data set into training/validation set.

S3: Choose hyper-parameters using the validation set.

S4: After selection of hyper-parameters, re-train using all training set.

S5: Evaluate performance on the training set.

Q.17. What are classification errors?

Ans. The classification error, Ei of an individual program, i , depends on the number of samples incorrectly classified (false positives and false negatives) and is computed by the formula:-

$$E_i = f / n * 100$$

where, 'f' is the number of sample cases incorrectly classified.

'n' is the total number of sample cases.

In supervised learning applications in machine learning and statistical learning theory, generalization error / out-of-sample error, is a measure of how accurately an algorithm is able to predict outcome values for previously unseen data. The evaluation of a learning algorithm may be sensitive to the sampling error because learning algorithms are evaluated on finite samples. So, the measurements of prediction error on the current data may not provide much information about the predictive ability on new data. **Please note that this generalization error can be mitigated by avoiding overfitting in the learning algorithm. Also note that the performance of a machine learning algorithm is measured by plots of the generalization error values through the learning process, that are called as the learning curves.**

Q.18. Explain the machine learning workflow model.

Ans. Given a problem that is to be solved, all machine learning (ML) models use the same input but different output. Hence, it is fruitful to understand a common workflow of ML model. There is not only one workflow model but several of them. We discuss one of them.

Construction of a ML model starts from a sample splitting. Most commonly used technique is a K-fold cross validation with random shuffling. In case of time-series or panel data, the K-fold cross validation without random shuffling is used for preserving temporal sequence Note that the future data cannot be used as a predictor of past data. This method is called as **K-fold forward chaining cross validation or forward chaining.** Two cross validations are shown in the following figures.

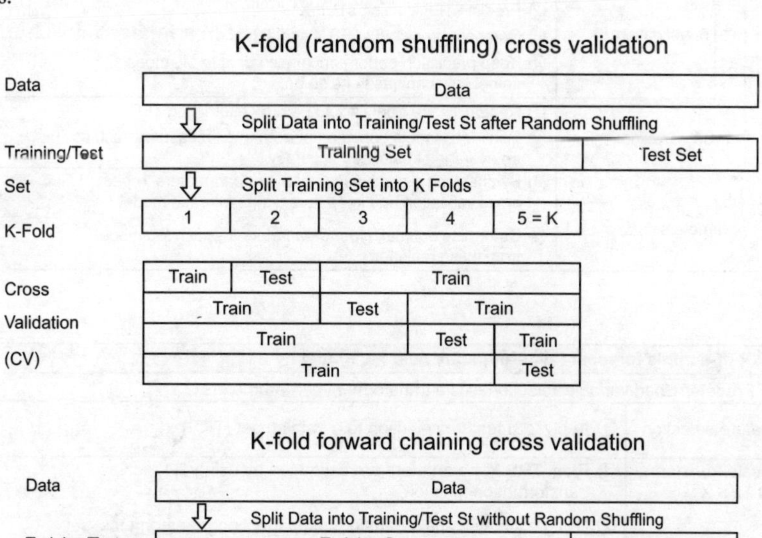

Workflow of Machine Learning : Most of the Machine Learning models have the following workflow in common.

1. Data : collect and split for cross validation and forecast	
1. Collect	Determine Y and collect X based on theory and practices
2. Explore	① Delete or modify outlier, NA, near zero variance data ② On hot encoding, entire label encoding for categorical variable
3. Split	① Preserve temporal sequence if time series or panel data, shffl randomly otherwise. ② Split data as a training set (TRS) and a test set (TES) in the ratio nearly 70 : 30 ③ Split a training set (TRS) into K folds

↓

2. In-sample cross validation : determine X and	
1. Split train/test folds	St i-th fold as a test fold (TEF) and collect the remaining K-1 folds as train fold (TRF). In case of time series, forward chain is applied to preserve temporal sequence.
2. Deal with class imbalance	Apply a sampling technique (i.e. SMOTE) to TRF for mitigating a class imbalance problem
3. Feature selection	① Apply a feature selection to TRF – Filter (Correlation) or wrapper (step-wise selection) or shrinkage (Lasso, Ridge, Elastic-net)
4. Scale transform : normalization or standardization	① Estimate parameters of transformation using TRF X ② Using transformation function with its estimated Parameters, transform – TRF X to transformed TRF (sTRF) X, – TRF X to transformed TEF (sTEF) X, ③ Rename TRF/TEF Y as sTRF/sTEF Y w/o transformation
5. Validation	① Train ML models using X and Y in sTRF ② Predict sTEF Y using sTEF X ③ Compare predicted sTEF Y and actual sTEF Y. ④ Keep prediction performance according to ML models, sampling techniques and so on.
1. Cross validation	① Repeat 1) ~ 5) from i = 1 to i = K by alternating TEF ② Rank ML models based on performance measures such as an average of balanced accuracy.
2. Tuning of hyper parameters	① By changing a combination of hyper parameters, repeat 1] cross validation and keep th rankings for each model ② Determine optimal hyper parameters for each ML model from these rankings

↓

3. Out-of-sample forecast : determine the best ML model by using	
Predetermined variable selection, scale transform, hyperparameters	
1. Feature selection	① Apply 2.3) feature selection to a training set (TRS)
2. Scale transform of TES X	① From TRS X, parameters are estimated by using 2.4) scale transformation function ② Using estimated scale transformation function, transform test set (TES) X to transformed test set (tTES) X ③ Rename TES Y as tTEST Y w/o transformation
3. Forecast	① Using ML models and their predetermined hyper parameters with tTES X, forecast, tTES Y ② Compare forecasted tTES Y and actual tTES Y ③ Select the best ML model from these comparisons

Hyperparameters and R packages : R provides many ML packages which are updated gradually. We use representative time-tested and mostly used R packages for selected Machine Learning models as follows:

ML Model	hyperparameters (example numbers)	R package	R function
LR		glmnet	
DT	cp = (0.1, 0.4, 0.9), loss gini minsplit = (3,5,7), maxdepth = (3,5,7)	rpart	
SVML	cost = (0.1, 1,5)	e1071	svm
SVMR	cost = (0.1,1,5), gamma = (0.01 o.1,1)	e1071	svm
RF	mtry = (3,5,7), ntree = (100, 250, 500)	randomforest	
ANN	layer1 = (5,7), layer2 = (3,5) leamingrate = (0.1, 0.3, 0.5)	neuralnt	
GBoost	n.trees = (100, 250, 500) interaction. depth = (3,5,7) shrinkage = (0.1, 0.3, 0.5)	xgboost	
XGBoost	nrounds = (100, 250, 500) eta = (0.1, 0.3, 0.5), max_depth = (3,5,7)		

The machine learning models chosen here includes Logistic Regression (LR), Decision Tree (DT), Support Vector Machine (SVM), Random Forest (RF), Artificial Neural Network (ANN), Gradient Boosting (GBoost) and Extreme Gradient Boosting (XGBoost). Numerical values for hyperparameters of each machine learning models that are presented here are examples only.

SUMMARY

We have studied in this chapter that in machine learning instead of teaching a computer a massive list of rules to solve a problem, we give it a model with which it can evaluate examples. Also, we give a small set of instructions to modify this model if it makes a mistake. We find that as the time passes by, w well suited model will be able to solve the problems in a batter and efficient way. The machine learning algorithm should be such that it tries to make the values of the parameters more and more accurate as it is exposed to more and more examples. But this is just a tip of an iceberg. Recently, scientists have developed the models that resemble the structures as used by a human brain. This involves deep learning only.

MULTIPLE CHOICE QUESTIONS

1. Predicting the price of a house given its size is an example of-

(*a*) Supervised learning (*b*) Unsupervised learning.
(*c*) Remote learning (*d*) None of the above

2. The inherent groupings in the data discovered is known as-

(*a*) Association (*b*) Clustering.
(*c*) Classifying (*d*) None of the above.

3. Discovering rules that describes large portions of data is called as-

(*a*) Association (*b*) Clustering
(*c*) Classifiers (*d*) None of the above

4. Conditional models are also known as-

(*a*) Demand models (*b*) Discriminative models
(*c*) Generative models (*d*) None of the above

5. Logistic regression is also named as-

(*a*) Login regression (*b*) Logit regression
(*c*) Logout regression (*d*) None of the above

6. Naive Bayes is an example of-

(*a*) Generative model (*b*) Discriminative model
(*c*) SVM (*d*) None of the above

7. **A common task in machine learning is-**
(*a*) Common data (*b*) Classifying data
(*c*) Global data (*d*) None of the above
8. **The classification error, Ei of an individual program, i, depends on the number of samples incorrectly classified (false positives and false negatives) and is computed by the formula:-**
(*a*) $E_i = f / n * 100$ (*b*) $E_i = f * n * 100$
(*c*) $E_i = f + n * 100$ (*d*) None of the above
9. **PCA stands for-**
(*a*) Peer Component Analysis (*b*) Principal Component Analysis
(*c*) Power Component Analysis (*d*) None of the above
10. **Singular Value Decomposition is used in-**
(*a*) Latent Semantic Indexing (*b*) Lateral Simple Indexing
(*c*) Lower Simple Indexing (*d*) None of the above
11. **SVM stands for-**
(*a*) Support Vector Machine (*b*) Simple Vector Machine
(*c*) Super Vector Machine (*d*) None of the above
12. **A generalization of the concept of a plane which is used in SVM implementation for object separation is known as-**
(*a*) Hyperplane (*b*) Airplane
(*c*) Aeroplane (*d*) None of the above
13. **A model evaluation technique which is collection of methods used to examine the underlying constructs influence of the response of variables is-**
(*a*) Factor Analysis (*b*) ICA
(*c*) PCA (*d*) Singular Value Composition

ANSWERS

1. (*a*)	**2.** (*b*)	**3.** (*b*)	**4.** (*b*)	**5.** (*b*)
6. (*a*)	**7.** (*b*)	**8.** (*a*)	**9.** (*b*)	**10.** (*a*)
11. (*a*)	**12.** (*a*)	**13.** (*a*)		

CONCEPTUAL SHORT QUESTIONS WITH ANSWERS

Q.1. What are the differences between data mining and machine learning?

Ans. Data mining is the process in which the unstructured data puts efforts to extract knowledge or unfamiliar interesting patterns. On the other hand, machine learning relates to the study, design and development of the algorithms that give systems the ability to learn without being clearly programmed.

Q.2. Give functions supervised and unsupervised learning.

Ans. Supervised learning involves-

a. Classifications.

b. Speech recognition.

c. Regression.

d. Predict time series.

e. Annotate strings.

On the other hand, unsupervised learning involves-

a. Finding the clusters of data.

b. Finding low dimensional representations of data.

c. Finding interesting coordinates and correlations.

d. Finding novel observations or cleaning databases.

Q.3. What is inductive machine learning?

Ans. Inductive machine learning covers the process of learning by examples where a system, from a set of perceived instances, tries to encourage a general rule.

Q.4. List at least five common machine learning algorithms.

Ans. Some of the popular ML algorithms are as follows:-

a. Decision Trees.

b. Neural Networks.

c. Probabilistic Networks.

d. Nearest Neighbour.

e. Support Vector Machines (SVM).

Q.5. Name different algorithm techniques in ML.

Ans. Different types of techniques in ML are as follows:-

a. Supervised learning.

b. Unsupervised learning.

c. Semi-supervised learning.

d. Reinforcement learning.

e. Transduction.

f. Learning to learn.

Q.6. Name three stages to build the models (or hypotheses) in machine learning.

Ans. Three stages to build the models in machine learning (ML) are as follows: -

a. Model building.

b. Model testing.

c. Applying the model.

Q.7. What is the standard approach to supervised learning?

Ans. The standard approach to supervised learning is to break the data set of examples into training set and the test set.

Q.8. Differentiate between 'training set' and 'test set'.

Ans. In different fields of data science like machine learning, a set of data is used to determine the potentially predictive relationship identified as training set. Training set is the example provided to the learner while test set is used to test the exactness of the hypotheses produced by the learner and it is the set of illustration weighed down from the learner. So, training sets are different from test sets.

Q.9. What are the different approaches of machine learning?

Ans. Different approaches of machine learning are as follows: -

a. Concept versus Classification Learning.

b. Symbolic versus Statistical Learning.

c. Inductive versus Analytical Learning.

Q.10. Define Overfitting during machine learning. Why it happens?

Ans. In ML, overfitting occurs when a statistical model defines a random error or noise rather than underlying relationship. When a model is extremely complex, overfitting is usually observed because of having too many parameters relating to the number of training data types. The model exhibits poor performance which has to be overfit. The risk of overfitting exists as the standards used for training the model is not the same as the standards used to judge the effectiveness of a model.

Q.11. How can overfitting be avoided?

Ans. BY means of loads of data, overfitting can be avoided. Overfitting happens when comparatively you have a small dataset and you make effort to learn from it. But if you have a small database and it is necessary to come with a model based on that then in such a scenario, cross validation method may be used. In this method, the dataset is divided into two segments, testing and training datasets. The testing dataset will only test the model while in training dataset, the data-points will come up with a model. In this method, a model is generally provided with a dataset of known data on which training data set is run and a dataset of unknown data against which the model is tested. The basic idea of cross validation is to define a dataset to test the model in the training phase.

Q.12. What is algorithm independent machine learning?

Ans. A type of machine learning in which mathematical foundations is independent of any particular classifier or learning algorithm is known as algorithm independent machine learning.

Q.13. Distinguish between AI and machine learning.

Ans. Designing and developing algorithms according to the behaviours based on empirical data is known as machine learning. On the other hand, artificial intelligence, in addition to machine learning, also covers other aspects like knowledge representation, natural language processing (NLP), planning, robotics etc.

Q.14. Define classifier as used in machine learning.

Ans. A classifier is a system that inputs a vector of discrete or continuous feature vales and outputs a single discrete value, the class.

Q.15. Where is pattern recognition used?

Ans. It is used in computer vision, speech recognition, data mining, statistics, information retrieval and bio-informatics.

Q.16. What is model selection in ML?

Ans. The process of selecting the models from different mathematical models that refer to the same data set is called as model selection. It is applied to the fields of statistics, machine learning and data mining.

Q.17. Name the method that is frequently used to prevent overfitting.

Ans. 'Isotonic Regression' is used to prevent overfitting when the data is sufficient.

Q.18. Why instance-based learning algorithm is sometimes also referred to as lazy-learning algorithm?

Ans. Instance-based learning algorithm is sometimes also referred to as lazy-learning algorithm because they delay the induction or generalization process until classification is performed.

Q.19. What are the 2 classification methods that SVM handle?

Ans. The two classification methods that SVM can handle are as follows:-

a. Combining binary classifiers.

b. Modifying binary to incorporate multiclass learning.

Q.20. For what purpose PCA and ICA are used?

Ans. PCA and ICA are used to extract features of data to reduce dimensions of data. They are important feature extraction techniques used for dimensionality reduction.

Q.21. What do you mean by dimension reduction?

Ans. It is the process of reducing the number of random variables under considerations and can be divided into feature selection and feature extraction.

Q.22. What are SVMs?

Ans. SVMs or Support Vector Machines are supervised learning algorithms that are used for classification and regression analysis.

Q.23. What are the different methods to solve sequential supervised learning problems?

Ans. The different methods to solve sequential supervised learning problems are: -

a. Sliding window methods.

b. Recurrent sliding windows.

c. Hidden Makov Models.

d. Maximum entropy Markov Models.

e. Conditional random fields.

f. Graph transformer networks.

Q.24. Name two techniques of ML. Give a very popular application of ML that you see everyday.

Ans. Genetic programming and inductive learning are the two methods of ML.

The recommendation engine implemented by major ecommerce websites uses machine learning (ML).

Q.25. How is KNN different from k-means clustering?

Ans. k-nearest neighbours is a supervised classification algorithm. On the other hand, k-means clustering is an unsupervised clustering algorithm. In order for k-nearest neighbours to work, labelled data is needed that we want to classify an unlabelled point. In case of k-means clustering only a set of unlabelled points and a threshold is required. The algorithm will take unlabelled points in consideration and slowly learn how to cluster them into groups by computing the mean of the distance between different points. In sutshell, KNN needs labelled points and is thus supervised learning while k-means doesn't need labelled points and is thus unsupervised learning.

Q.26. Why is "Naive" Bayes naive?

Ans. Even though it has practical applications, especially in text mining, Naive Bayes is still considered as Naive because the assumption that it makes becomes virtually impossible to be seen in real-life data. The conditional probability is computed as purely the product of the individual probabilities of different components. This denotes the absolute independence of features i.e. a condition that is probably never met in real life.

Q.27. Differentiate between a generative and discriminative model.

Ans. A generative model learns categories of data while a discriminative model merely learns the distinction between different categories of data. Discriminative models will leave behind generative models on the basis of classification tasks.

Q.28. Name at least three methods of reducing dimensionality.

Ans. The three methods of reducing dimensionality are as follows: -

a. Removing collinear features.

b. Performing PCA, ICA or other forms of algorithmic dimensionality reduction.

c. Combining features with feature engineering.

Q.29. What is the EM technique? How this algorithm works?

Ans. EM is an algorithm for maximizing a likelihood function when some of the variables in the model are unobserved i.e., when there are latent variables with you. To solve for our model parameters, you need to know the distribution of your unobserved data but the distribution of your unobserved data is a function of your model parameters. EEM tries to get around this by guessing repeatedly about the distribution for the unobserved data then further estimating the model parameters by maximizing something that is lower bound on the actual likelihood function and repeating until convergence.

The EM algorithm starts with a guess for values of your model parameters as follows: -

The E-step: For each data point that has some missing values to solve for the distribution of the missing data, use your model equation, provided with your current guess of the model parameters and given the observed data. Please note that you are solving for a distribution for each missing value and not for the expected value. Also note that now we have available with us a distribution for each missing value, we can calculate the expectation of the likelihood function with respect to the unobserved variables. If our guess for the model parameter was correct, this expected likelihood will be the actual likelihood of our observed data. If the parameters were not correct, it will just be a lower bound.

The M-step: Now that we have got an expected likelihood function with no unobserved variables in it, maximize the function as you would in the fully observed case, to get a new estimate of your model parameters.

Repeat till convergence.

Q.30. What do you mean by curse of dimensionality?

Ans. The curse of dimensionality refers to the tendency of a state space to grow exponentially in its dimension *i.e.* in the number of state variables.

Q.31. What is H_2O? What is prcomp?

Ans. H_2O is software for machine learning and data analysis. PCA is named as prcomp in H_2O and *R* system.

Q.32. What is the principle of operation of the back-propagation algorithm?

Ans. Firstly, the inputs from the training data are propagated through the network to the output. Then the model outputs are compared with the actual outputs. The difference is the error. This error is then fed into the network backwards and connections weights are adjusted.

Q.33. Define the following:-

a. **Learning rate.**

b. **Momentum.**

Ans. *a.* **Learning rate:** A higher value of learning rate will make the algorithm converge more rapidly towards the desired values but it will reduce the stability of the algorithm.

b. **Momentum:** It is used to control oscillations in weights which could be caused by alternately signed error signals.

Q.34. WEKA tool may be used to construct neural network. Can it do the parameter value selection also for neural networks?

Ans. A neural network trains by repeated passes of the data. Each pass is called an epoch. With each epoch, the connecting weights are adjusted until a satisfactory level of performance is reached. We can ponder that if 50 epochs are good then 80 epochs should be better. But this argument does not hold with neural networks. With too many passes the network may over-train also. Please understand that a well-trained neural network model would show similar performance levels with both test and training data. Also understand that keeping this in mind we can change the parameter values of the algorithm. We should not assume that default parameters are the best. We can change the parameters too. As the number of epochs increases we need more time for training. If we compare the outputs from the two different epochs, we can see the accuracy remains at the same level of 97.2%. that is why we say that higher the number of epochs has not improved the model performance. Just keep in mind that we should restrict ourselves to the lower number of epochs as it not only involves less computing time but also lowers the danger of over-fitting.

Q.35. Define the following terms: -

a. **Activation function.**

b. **Back-propagation learning.**

c. **Delta rule.**

d. **Epoch.**

e. **Feedforward neural networks.**

f. **Genetic algorithm.**

g. **Hyperplane.**

h. **Kernel.**

Ans. *a.* **Activation function:** A function that describes the output behaviours of a neuron in neural network.

b. **Back-propagation learning:** It is a form of supervised learning used to train mainly, feedforward neural networks, that works by making modifications in weights values, starting at the output layer and then moving backwards through the hidden layer.

c. **Delta Rule:** The delta rule changes the weight vector for a neural network in such a way that the error is reduced.

d. **Epoch:** It is one complete pass of the entire training set through the neural network. The learning process is repeated epoch-by-epoch until the averaged square error converges to a minimum value.

e. **Feedforward neural network:** It is a sort of ANN where connections between the units do not form a directed cycle.

f. **Genetic algorithm:** It is an adaptive heuristic search algorithm premised on the evolutionary ideas of natural selection theory.

g. **Hyperplane:** A plane (as in geometry) that is used to do object separation during SVM implementation.

h. **Kernel:** Linear, polynomial and rbf are some of the kernels of SVM that allows SVM to fit the maximum margin hyperplane in the transformed feature space.

Q.36. Tabulate the differences between supervised and unsupervised learning.

Ans. The following are the points of differences: -

Supervised Learning	Unsupervised Learning
It incorporates an external teacher so that each output unit is told what should be the desired response to that input signal.	Uses no external teacher.
Global error signals govern learning.	Local information is used for learning.
Uses pattern class information of each training pattern.	Adaptively clusters patterns to generate decision codes.
Paradigms are error correction learning, reinforcement learning and stochastic learning.	Paradigms are Hebbian learning and competitive learning.
Learning is usually off line. It means that learning and operation phases are different. In off-line learning, all of the given patterns are used together.	Learning is online. It means that the agent learns and operates at the same time. Here, the information in each new pattern is incorporated into the agent.
All learning data are stored and can be accessed repeatedly. So, we can see whether we are making progress in training or not.	Locality allows learning in real time. So, the progress cannot be monitored.
Inputs and outputs are defined.	Only inputs are defined.
Uses pattern class information of each training pattern.	Adaptively clusters patterns to generate decision class without any prior pattern class information.
Global error signal governs learning.	Local information/ rules are used for learning.
Learning is offline usually.	Locality allows synapses to learn in real-time.

Q.37. Explain different nets classes.

Ans. It is put under 2 main categories as follows: -

I. **Unsupervised learning (i.e. without a teacher):**

1. **Feedback Nets:**
   a. Binary Adaptive Resonance Theory (ART1)
   b. Analog adaptive Resonance Theory (ART2)
   c. Discrete Hopfield (DH)
   d. Continuous Hopfield (CH)
   e. Discrete Bi-directional Associative Memory (BAM)
   f. Temporal Associative Memory (TAM)
   g. Adaptive Bi-directional Associative Memory (ABAM)
   h. Kohonen Self-Organizing Map/ Topology Preserving Map (SOM/TPM)
   i. Competitive learning
2. **Feed-forward only Nets:**
   a. Learning Matrix (LM)
   b. Driver-reinforcement Learning (DR)
   c. Counter Propagation (CPN)

II. **Supervised learning (*i.e.* with a teacher):**

1. **Feedback Nets:**
   a. Boltzmann Machine. (BM)
   b. Mean Field Annealing (MFT)
   c. Recurrent Cascade Correlation (RCC)

d. Learning Vector Quantization (LVQ)
e. Back progpagation through time (BPTT)
f. Real-time Recurrent Learning (RTRL)

2. Feed-forward only Nets:

a. Perceptron
b. Adaline, Madaline
c. Backpropagation (BP)
d. Cauchy Machine (CM)
e. Artmap
f. Cascade Correlation (CasCor)

EXERCISE QUESTIONS

1. Explain in brief logistic regression.
2. What is ICA? Discuss.
3. Explain generative algorithm in detail.
4. Describe the limitations of the perceptron model.
5. Explain the decision tree algorithm with example.
6. Write a short note on Naive Bayes' model of statistical learning.
7. What are SVMs? Discuss their characteristics.
8. What is
   a. Overfitting.
   b. Early Stopping.
   c. Curse of Dimensionality.
   d. Regularization.
9. Explain what is boosting?
10. Explain AdaBoost algorithm.

5 Unsupervised Learning and their Algorithms

Q.1. Explain clustering in detail.

Ans. Unsupervised learning is put under two categories: -

1. **Clustering:** In this method, the inherent groupings in the data are discovered. The organization of unlabelled data into similar groups known as clusters. And the process of partitioning of a set of observations into subsets (or clusters) so that observation in the same cluster is similar is called as clustering. So, a cluster consists of data items which are similar in comparison to other clusters which contain dissimilar items. Please understand that the aim of unsupervised learning is to find clusters of similar inputs in the data without knowing that these data points belong to one class and those to different class. Rather the algorithm has to uncover similarities for itself. For example, there is a collection of 30,000 essays on voting process. These essays can be automatically grouped into small number on the basis of word frequency, page count, word limit etc.
2. **Association:** In this method, we discover a set of rules that describes large portions of data. For example, a doctor observes same set of symptoms in several patients suffering from some disease. Then based on his experience the doctor can conclude that the patient is suffering from the same disease.

Q.2. Explain k-means Clustering. What is its basic principle? Give its algorithm and explain.

Ans. k-means is a simple unsupervised learning algorithm that solves the well-known clustering problems. The working of k-means is similar to that of a real-life situation in which we have observed that in a group of tourists with a few tourists guides who hold the umbrella up so that everybody can see them and follow them. On the other hand, in static k-means algorithm the data (i.e., the tourists) does not move rather only the tour guide (s) move. Analogous is the situation in k-means clustering.

Basic Principle of k-means : "Divide your data into k groups (you have to specify what 'k' is) such that each data item is closer to the center of its cluster than to the centre of any other cluster."

Explanation of k-means: We classify a given data-set into k number of clusters which is fixed in advance. Now the task is to define 'k' centres (middle point) one for each cluster. But we do not know where their centres are. So, we need an algorithm that will find the middle points. The centre of a set of points is based on two parameters: -

a. Distance Measure: It measures the distance between a set of points. We may use Euclidean distance but other options are also available.

b. Mean Average: after we compute the distance measure (as stated above) we finally compute the central point of the set of data points which is the mean average.

Please note that this is valid in Euclidean space where everything is flat and easily measured. Now the need is to place cluster centres properly. We compute the mean of each cluster, $\mu_i (i)$ and position the cluster centre right there. Also note that this is similar to minimizing the Euclidean distance (*i.e.*, sum-of-squares again) from each data point to the centre of cluster.

Now we would like to find out that which point belongs to which cluster. This is mandatory as it lets us know the position of cluster centres. It is crystal clear to associate closest point with the cluster centre. This might change as the algorithm iterates on. In the input space we start positioning the cluster centres randomly as we do not know where to put them exactly and further update their positions in accordance with the data. Now we start picking up the data points and find out which cluster, particular data point belongs to depending on the distance between each data point and all of the cluster centres and assigning it to cluster that is closest.

The purpose of the hidden layer is to summarize the data and compress it. The multidimensional data is to be reduced to either 2 or 3 dimensions only as then we can plot the graphs too. If we use the PYTHON LANGUAGE then note that layers and column indices are counted from zero while in R they are counted from one.

With auto-encoding neural networks we do learning one layer at a time.

For example, a model, m1, say, has the following-

- 5 hidden layers
- 11 neurons (in middle layer)

It is trained on the raw data. Then that third hidden layer is extracted into a transformation, f1 with still 100 rows but only 11 columns. Model-2 (m2) uses this f1 as its input and builds up a much simpler model, reducing 11 input nodes to 2 hidden nodes then back out to 11 output nodes. At the end, results are put in f2. f2 now has 2 columns but still 100 rows.

Algorithm (k-means)-

k-means clustering involves the following steps:-

Step-1: Randomly select '*c*' cluster centres.

Step-2: Compute the distance between each data point and cluster centres.

Step-3: Assign the data point to the cluster whose distance from the cluster centre is minimum in the value of cluster centres.

Step-4: Calculate the new cluster centre using the following formula:-

$$v = 1/\ c_i\ \Sigma\ (j = 1 \text{ to } c_i)\ x_i$$

where c_i represents the number of data points in the ith cluster.

Step-5: New cluster centres are computed.

Step-6: If no data point is reassigned then stop else repeat from step-3.

As we know that H_2O is software for machine learning and data analysis. H_2O algorithm has been developed keeping in mind clustering only. But clusters in H_2O have some limitations:-

a. Each H_2O node on the cluster must be of the same size. It implies that if the smallest machine in our cluster has 2GB free, then every node must be given 2GB even if some of them have 32GB.

b. You cannot add the machines once the cluster has started.

c. In case a machine dies then the whole of the cluster must be rebuilt. Please note that the whole cluster becomes unusable if a single node gets removed. In such a case, you cannot even export data or models from the left-over clusters.

d. Each node must run the same API version of h_2o.jar.

e. To reduce the network latency, the nodes should be physically close.

You can also give your cluster a name and specify this name when starting on each node. In H2O, the cluster can be created in two ways: -

1. **Flat-file:** A simple text file giving the IP address and port number of each node in the cluster. Note that you must prepare this file identically on each machine.
2. **Auto-discovery:** When you specify the network address then it searches through that subnet to find all nodes and join them together in a cluster. This is slower than the flat file.

Q.3. Write the Expectation Maximization (EM) Algorithm.

Ans. Many a times the presence of unobserved variables is observed as a problem of learning. In case of some variable that can be observed sometimes and cannot be observed at other times then the time when it was observed can be used to learn its values when it was not observed. So, EM is an algorithm for maximizing a likelihood function when some of the variables in your model are unobserved. A variable that is not directly observed is called as a latent variable/ hidden / unobserved variable / missing data.

Statement of EM algorithm: EM is applied where we are required to estimate a set of parameters θ that represents an underlying probability distribution, given only the observed portion of full data. In general, let $X = \{x_1, x_2, \ldots\ldots, x_m\}$ denote the observed data in a set of *m* independently drawn data items. Let $Z = \{z_1, \ldots\ldots, z_m\}$ mark the unobserved data in these same data items and let $Y = X \cup Z$; thus marks the full data.

The EM algorithm searches for the maximum likelihood hypothesis h' by seeking the h' that maximizes $E\ [\ln P\ (Y|\ h')]$, where,

$P(Y|h')$ is the likelihood of the full data Y given hypothesis h'

$\ln P(Y|h')$- maximizing logarithm value of this quantity further maximizes $P(Y|h')$ and

$E[\ln P(Y|h')]$ –expected value of full data is introduced as Y is a random variable.

We need to know that what is the probability distribution governing Y. In general, we will not know this distribution as it is determined by the parameters, θ, that is to be estimated. So, EM algorithm uses its current hypothesis, h, in place of θ to estimate the distribution governing, Y.

If we assume that $\theta = h$, then, we define a function $Q(h'|h)$ as follows:-

$$Q(h'|h) = E[\ln P(Y|h') \mid h, X]$$

In general form of an EM algorithm, two steps are repeated until convergence:-

S1: Estimation (*E*) step: Calculate $Q(h'|h)$ using the current hypothesis, h and the observed data X to estimate the probability distribution over Y. So,

$$Q(h'|h) = E[\ln P(Y|h') \mid h, X]$$

S2: Maximization (M) step: Replace h by h' that maximizes this Q function-

$$H \leftarrow \underset{h'}{\operatorname{argmax}}\, Q(h' \mid h)$$

Please note that when the function, Q, is continuous, the EM algorithm converges to a fixed point of the probable function $P(Y \mid h')$. Also note that when this probable function has a single maximum, EM will converge to this global maximum probable estimate for h'.

Q.4. Write a short note on 'Mixture of Gaussians'.

Ans. A very popular continuous probability distribution is Gaussian distribution / Normal Distribution. It is also called as a bell curve since it has a bell-shaped curve. The equation in one dimension is as follows: -

$$p(x) = 1 / \sqrt{2\Pi}\sigma \exp[\ (x - \mu)^2 / 2\sigma^2] \quad ...(1)$$

where

μ = mean

σ = standard deviation

Please note that it is useful because of its **Central Limit Theorem** which tells us that lots of random numbers will add up to something Gaussian.

In Gaussian Mixture Models (GMM), we assume that there are number of different classes. Each class comes from its own Gaussian distribution. And such type of data is known as multi-model data as there are number of modes or distribution for each particular class. We are unable to accommodate Gaussian to the data in totality as it does not appear to be Gaussian overall.

If we know the number of classes that are there in the data then we can put effort to estimate the parameters for that many numbers of Gaussians and that too all at the same time.

On the other hand, if we do not the number of classes then we can attempt for different numbers and finds out which one works best. Then the output for any specific data point which has already been an input to the algorithm will be the sum of the values expected by all of the 'M' Gaussians. That is,

$$f(x) = \Sigma\,(m = 1 \text{ to } M)\, \alpha_m\, \varphi\,(x;\mu_m, \Sigma_m) \quad ...(2)$$

where $\varphi(x;\mu_m, \Sigma_m)$ = Gaussian function with mean μ_m and covariance matrix and the αm are the weights with the constraints *i.e.* $\Sigma\,(m = 1 \text{ to } M)\, \alpha_m = 1$.

The task is to choose the weights α_m. The target is for Maximum likelihood solution. Note that likelihood refers to the conditional probability and Maximum Likelihood solution refers to maximizing the conditional probability.

Q.5. What is factor analysis? What notations are used? Explain the factor model.

Ans. Factor Analysis (FA) is a method for modelling observed variables and their covariance structure in terms of a smaller number of underlying unobservable/ latent factors. These 'factors' are typically observed as broad concepts or ideas that may describe an observed phenomenon. This method is quite comprehensive but is similar to principal components. Please understand that in factor analysis the observed variables are modelled as linear functions of the factors. On the other hand, principal components analysis (PCA) involves the creation of new variables that are linear combinations of the observed variables. But in both the methods, the dimensions of the data are reduced.

FA involves using of a data reduction tool to-

a. Remove redundancy from a set of correlated variables.

b. Represent correlated variables with a smaller set of derived variables.

c. Form factors that are independent of each other.

d. Two types of variables are used- latent variables (factors) and the observed variables.

Notations used:

Say, there is a vector X consisting of variables X's for each individual subject. Let X_i denote observable trait, i. This is the data of each subject and will be collected into a vector of traits.

That is,

$$X = \begin{pmatrix} X_1 \\ X_2 \\ \vdots \\ X_p \end{pmatrix} = \text{vector of traits}$$

This will be a random vector with a population mean. We assume that sampling of vector of traits X is done from a population with population mean vector:-

$$\mu = \begin{pmatrix} \mu_1 \\ \mu_2 \\ \vdots \\ \mu_p \end{pmatrix} = \text{population mean vector}$$

Here, $E(X_i) = \mu_i$ denotes the population mean of variable i.

In general, consider 'm' unobservable common factors $f_1, f_2, \ldots\ldots f_m$.

The ith common factor is f_i. In general, m will be less than p.

The common factors will be collected into a vector only:-

$$F = \begin{pmatrix} f_1 \\ f_2 \\ \vdots \\ f_m \end{pmatrix} = \text{vector of common factor}$$

The Factor Model: Our factor model will be a collection of series of multiple regressions, predicting each of the observable variables, X_i from the values of the unobservable common factor, fi. That is,

$$X_1 = \mu_1 + l_{11} f_1 + l_{12} f_2 + \ldots + l_{1m} f_m + \varepsilon_1$$

$$X_2 = \mu_2 + l_{21} f_1 + l_{22} f_2 + \ldots + l_{2m} f_m + \varepsilon_2$$

$$\vdots$$

$$X_p = \mu_p + l_{p1} f_1 + l_{p2} f_2 + \ldots + l_{pm} f_m + \varepsilon_p$$

Here, the variable means μ_1 through μp can be explained as the intercept terms for the multiple regression models. The regression coefficients l_{ij} (are the partial slopes) for all of these multiple regressions are called as factor loadings. The relationship of each variable to the underlying factor is expressed by factor loading. Here, l_{ij} = loading of the ith variable on the jth factor. These will be collected into a matrix as follows:-

$$L = \begin{pmatrix} l_{11} & l_{12} & \ldots l_{1m} \\ l_{21} & l_{22} & \ldots l_{2m} \\ \vdots & \vdots & \ldots \vdots \\ l_{p1} & l_{p2} & \ldots l_{pm} \end{pmatrix} = \text{matrix of factor loadings}$$

And that the errors, ε_i are called as the specific factors. Here, ε_i = specific factor for variable i. These specific factors are also collected in a vector: -

$$\varepsilon = \begin{pmatrix} \varepsilon_1 \\ \varepsilon_2 \\ \vdots \\ \varepsilon_p \end{pmatrix} = \text{vector of specific vectors}$$

In nutshell, the basic model is like a regression model only. Each of our response variables X is to be predicted as a linear function of the unobserved common factors f_1, f_2 through f_m. Thus, our explanatory variables are f_1, f_2 through fm. Therefore, we conclude that we have m unobserved factors that control the variation among our data.

Generally, we can reduce this into a matrix notation as shown in this form below:-

$$X = \mu + Lf + \varepsilon$$

In general, we want $m << p$.

Assumptions of the model

a. Mean-

1. The specific factors or random errors all have mean zero: $E(\varepsilon_i) = 0; i = 1,2,....p.$
2. The common factors, the f's also have a mean zero: $E(f_i) = 0; i = 1,2,...m.$
3. A consequence of these assumptions is that the mean response of the ith trait is μ_i. that is,

$$E(X_i) = \mu_i$$

***b.* Variance-**

1. The common factors have variance one: $\text{var}(f_i) = 1,2,...m.$
2. The variance of specific factor *i* is ψ_i : $\text{var}(\varepsilon_i) = \psi_i$; $i = 1,2,...p$. Here, ψ_i is called as the specific variance.

c. Correlation-

1. The common factors are uncorrelated with one another: $\text{cov}(f_i, f_i) = 0$ for $i != j$.
2. The specific factors are uncorrelated with one another: $\text{cov}(\varepsilon_i , \varepsilon_i) = 0$ for $i != j$.
3. The specific factors are uncorrelated with the common factors: $\text{cov}((\varepsilon_i, \varepsilon_i) = \text{cov}; i = 1,2,....p; j = 1,2,...,m.$

To calculate the parameters these assumptions are necessary. An infinite number of equally well-fitted models with different values for the parameters may be obtained unless these suppositions are done. Also note that under this model, the variance for the ith observed variable is equal to the sum of the squared loadings for that variable and specific variance:-

The variance of trait is: $\sigma_i^2 = \text{var}(X_i) = \Sigma\ (j = 1 \text{ to } m) l^2_{ij} + \psi_i$

Where $\Sigma\ (j = 1 \text{ to } m)\ l^2_{ij}$ is called as the communality for variable, *i*. Please note that the larger is the communality, the better is the model performance for the ith variable.

The covariance between pairs of traits i and j is given by the formula-

$$\sigma_{ij} = \text{cov}(X_i , X_j) = \Sigma\ (k = 1 \text{ to } m)\ l_{ik}\ l_{jk}$$

The covariance between trait i and factor *j* is: $\text{cov}(X_i , f_i) = l_{ij}$

In matrix form, our model for the variance-covariance matrix is going to be expressed as shown below:-

$$\Sigma = LL' + \psi$$

This is the matrix of factor loadings times its transpose plus a diagonal matrix containing the specific variances.

Here ψ is as follows:-

$$\Psi = \begin{pmatrix} \psi_1 & 0 & \ldots & 0 \\ 0 & \psi_2 & \ldots & 0 \\ \vdots & \vdots & \vdots & \vdots \\ 0 & 0 & \ldots & \psi_p \end{pmatrix}$$

Hence, a simplified model for the variance-covariance matrix is obtained. This is used for estimation.

Notes:

1. The model assumes that the data is a linear function of the common factors. But since the common factors are not observable, there is no amount of data that can be used to check for linearity.
2. The variance-covariance matrix is a symmetric matrix that is, the variance between variables i and j is the same thing as the variance between *j* and *i*. for this model-

$$\Sigma = LL' + \psi$$

3. The variance-covariance matrix is going to have $p\ (p + 1)/2$ unique elements of Σ that are approximated by mp factor loadings in the matrix *L* and *p* specific variances. Also understand that this means that there is going to be mp plus *p* parameters in this model of the variance-covariance matrix. Ideally, $(mp + p)$ is to be substantially smaller than $p\ (p + 1)/2$. However, if mp is too small, the $mp + p$ parameters may not be adequate to describe Σ. There may always be the case that perhaps this is not the right model. It may be the case that you cannot reduce the data to a linear combination of factors.
4. If we have more than one variable in our analysis, that is, if $p > 1$, the model is going to be inherently ambiguous. Say, *T* be any $(m * m)$ orthogonal matrix. Note that a matrix is said to be orthogonal if its inverse is equal to the transpose of the original matrix *i.e.*

$$T'T = TT' = 1$$

Hence, we can write our factor model in the matrix notation as follows:-

Please note that this does not change the calculation since the identity matrix times any matrix just gives back the original matrix. This results in an alternative factor model where the relationship between the new factor loadings and the original factor loadings is given by:-

$$L. = LT$$

And the relationship between the new common factors and the original common factors is:-

$$f. = T'f$$

This gives a model that fits equally well. Moreover, since there are an infinite number of orthogonal matrices then there is an infinite number of alternative models. This model, as it turns out, satisfies all of the assumptions that we have discussed earlier.

5. $E(f.) = E(T'f) = T'\ E(f) = T'0 = 0$ and

$var(f.) = var(T'f) = T'\ var(f)\ T = T'IT = T'T = 1$

6. $Cov(f.,\ \varepsilon) = cov(T'f,\ \varepsilon) = T'\ cov(f, \varepsilon) = T'0 = 0$

Thus, we can say that f. satisfies all of the assumptions and hence f. is an equally valid collection of common factors. So, there is a certain apparent ambiguity to these models. However, it is the same ambiguity that we are going to exploit. This ambiguity is going to be used to justify the factor notation that will be used to derive more parsimonious description of data.

Applications of FA :

The following are some of the applications of FA:-

1. **Identification of underlying factors:** It clusters variables into homogeneous sets, creates new variables/factors and allows us to gain insight to categories.
2. **Screening of Variables:** It identifies groupings to allow us to select one variable and is useful in regression/ recall collinearity applications of FA.
3. **Summary:** It allows us to describe many variables using few factors.
4. **Sampling of variables:** It helps us to select a small group of variables of representative variables from a larger set.
5. **Clustering of Object:** It helps us to put objects/people into categories depending on their factor scores.

Q.6. Explain the Principal Component Analysis (PCA) technique.

Ans. PCA refers to a mathematical procedure that tends to transform a number of possibly correlated variables into a small number of uncorrelated variables which are called as the principal components. The first PCA accounts for as much of the variability as possible in the data and the next following components takes into account possible remaining variability. Please understand that PCA is a technique used to focus on variation and figure out strong patterns in a dataset. The objective of PCA is to make data easy to explore and visualize.

Aim of PCA

1. To discover or to reduce the dimensionality of the data set.
2. To identify new meaningful underlying variables.

Algorithm:

Suppose that we have a random vector, X. That is,

$$X = \begin{pmatrix} X_1 \\ X_2 \\ \vdots \\ X_p \end{pmatrix}$$

And with the population variance-covariance matrix as follows:-

$$\text{var (X)} = \Sigma = \begin{pmatrix} \sigma_1^2 & \sigma_{12}....\sigma_{1p} \\ \sigma_{21} & \sigma_2^2...\sigma_{2p} \\ \vdots & \vdots \quad \vdots \\ \sigma_{p1} & \sigma p2...\sigma_p^2 \end{pmatrix}$$

Now consider the following linear combinations:-

$$Y_1 = e_{11} X_1 + e_{12} X_2 + ... + e_{1p} X_p$$
$$Y_2 = e_{21} X_1 + e_{22} X_2 + ... + e_{2p} X_p$$
$$\vdots$$
$$Y_P = e_{P1} X_1 + e_{P2} X_2 + ... + e_{PP} X_P$$

Each of these is just like a linear regression, predicting Y_i from $X_1, X_2, ..., X_p$. There is no intercept but e_{i1}, e_{i2}, ...eip may be considered as the regression coefficients.

Also note that Y_i is a function of our random data and hence it is also random. So, it has a population variance of-

$$\text{Var } (Y_i) = \Sigma(k = 1 \text{ to } p)\ \Sigma(l = 1 \text{ to } p)\ e_{ik}\, e_{il}\, \sigma_{kl} = e'i\, \Sigma_{ei}$$

How to find 1st PCA, 2nd PCA and the ith PCA?

1. **The 1st Principal Component *i.e.* PCA1 means Y_1 and is computed as follows:-** The 1st principal component is a linear combination of x-variables that has maximum variance (among all linear combinations). Thus, it accounts for as much possible variation in the data as possible. More specifically, we will define coefficients $e_{11}, e_{12}, ..., e_{1p}$ for that component in such a way that its variance is maximized, subject to the constraint that the sum of the squared coefficients is equal to one. This constraint is required to obtain a unique answer.

   Formally, we select $e_{11}, e_{12}, ..., e_{1p}$ that maximizes-

   $$\text{Var } (Y_1) = \Sigma(k = 1 \text{ to } p)\ \Sigma(l = 1 \text{ to } p)\ e_{1k}\, e_{1l}\, \sigma_{kl} = e'_1\, \Sigma_{e1}$$

   Subject to the constraints:-

   $$e'_1\, e_1 = \Sigma\ (j = 1 \text{ to } p)\ e^2_{1j} = 1$$

2. **The 2nd Principal Component *i.e.* PCA$_2$ means Y_2 and is computed as follows:-** The 2nd principal component is a linear combination of x-variables that has maximum variance (among all linear combinations). Thus, it accounts for as much possible variation in the data as possible with the constraints that the correlation between the first and second component is 0. More specifically, we will define coefficients $e_{11}, e_{12}, ..., e_{1p}$ for that component in such a way that its variance is maximized, subject to the constraint that the sum of the squared coefficients is equal to one. This constraint is required to obtain a unique answer.

   Formally, we select $e_{21}, e_{22}, ..., e_{2P}$ that maximizes-

   $$\text{var } (Y_2) = \Sigma(k = 1 \text{ to } p)\ \Sigma(l = 1 \text{ to } p)\ e_{2k}\, e_{2l}\, \sigma_{kl} = e'_2\, \Sigma_{e2}$$

   Subject to the constraints:-

   $$e'_2\, e_2 = \Sigma\ (j = 1 \text{ to } p)\ e^2_{2j} = 1$$

Please note that all subsequent PCAs have this same property *i.e.* they are linear combinations that account for as much of the remaining variation as possible and they are not correlated with the other PCAs. Also note that we will do it the same way for each and every additional component.

So, in general, the ith Principal Component *i.e.* PCAi means Yi and is computed as follows:-

We select $e_{i1}, e_{i2}, \ldots, e_{ip}$ that maximizes-

$$\text{var}(Y_i) = \Sigma(k = 1 \text{ to } p)\ \Sigma(l = 1 \text{ to } p)\ e_{ik}\, e_{il}\, \sigma_{kl} = e'_i\, \Sigma_{ei}$$

This is subject to the constraints that the sums of squared coefficients add up to 1, along with the additional constraint that this new component will be uncorrelated with all the previously defined components. That is,

$$e'_i\, e_i = \Sigma(j = 1 \text{ to } p)\ e^2_{ij} = 1$$

How to find these coefficients eij for a principal component?

To solve these coefficients we use Eigen values and Eigen vectors of the variance-covariance matrix, Σ. Let λ_1 through λ_P represent the Eigen values of the variance-covariance matrix, Σ. These are ordered so that λ1 has the largest Eigen value and λp is the smallest. That is,

$$\lambda_1 \geq \lambda_2 \geq \ldots \geq \lambda_P$$

Also say vectors e1 through e_P *i.e.* $(e_1, e_1, \ldots, e_P)$ denote the corresponding Eigen vectors. Note that the elements for these Eigen vectors will be coefficients of our principal components.

The variance for the iit PC is equal to the iith Eigen value as follows:-

$$\text{var}(Y_i) = \text{var}(e_{i1} X_1 + e_{i2} X_2 + \ldots + e_{ip} X_p) = \lambda_i$$

Moreover, the principal components are uncorrelated with one another:-

$$\text{cov}(Y_i, Y_j) = 0$$

When we have correlations / multi-collinearity between the x-variables, the data may be more or less fall on a line or plane in a lower number of dimensions.

For example, consider a plot of two x-variables that have a nearly perfect correlation. The data points will fall close to a straight line. That line could be used as a new 1D axis to represent the variation among data points.

Let us define this now in terms of variance-covariance matrix, Σ, which is unknown. But we may estimate Σ by the sample variance-covariance matrix, Σ, which is given in the standard formula as follows:-

$$S = 1/(n-1)\ \Sigma(i = 1 \text{ to } n)\ (X_i - \bar{x})(X_i - \bar{x})'$$

Algorithm followed:

We calculate the Eigen Values $\lambda_1', \lambda_2', \ldots, \lambda_P'$ of the sample variance-covariance matrix, S, and the corresponding Eigen Vectors $e_1', e_2', \ldots, e_P'$. Then we will define our estimated PCs using the Eigen Vectors as our coefficients:-

$$Y_1' = e_{11}' X_1 + e_{12}' X_2 + \ldots + e_{1p}' X_p$$
$$Y_2' = e_{21}' X_1 + e_{22}' X_2 + \ldots + e_{2p}' X_p$$
$$\vdots$$
$$\vdots$$
$$Y_p' = e_{P1}' X_1 + e_{p2}' X_2 + \ldots + e_{pp}' X_p$$

In general, we can retain only the first *k* principal component. But we need to balance two conflicting issues:-

1. To obtain the simplest possible interpretation, we want k to be as small as possible. If we can explain most of the variation just by 2 principal components then this would give us a much simpler description of data. The smaller is the K, the smaller amount of variation is explained by the first k component.
2. To avoid loss of information, we want the proportion of variation explained by the first principal components to be large. That is, what we want is-

$$\frac{\lambda_1' + \lambda_2', + \ldots, + \lambda_k'}{\lambda_1' + \lambda_2', + \ldots, + \lambda_P'}$$
$$= 1$$

So, we can say that all principal components are uncorrelated with one another.

Q.7. What is Independent Component Analysis (ICA)? What is noise-free ICA model?

Ans. A method for finding the underlying factors or components from multi-variate or multi-dimensional statistical data is called as Independent Component Analysis (ICA). This method is somewhat different. It is so because it uses both statistically independent and non-Gaussian.

For example, consider a scenario in which three people are speaking simultaneously in a room. There are 3 microphones that are present in different locations for the same. The microphones give us 3 recorded time signals which can be denoted by $x_1(t)$, $x_2(t)$ and $x_3(t)$ with x_1, x_2 and x_3 referring to the amplitudes and t is basically the time index. Each of these recorded signals can be represented as a weighted sum of the speech signals produced by the three speakers which is denoted by $s_1(t)$, $s_2(t)$ and $s_3(t)$. In linear form we can represent it as follows:-

$$x_1(t) = a_{11} s_1 (t) + a_{12} s_2 (t) + a_{13} s_3 (t)$$

$$x_2(t) = a_{21} s_1 (t) + a_{22} s_2 (t) + a_{23} s_3 (t)$$

$$x_3(t) = a_{31} s_1 (t) + a_{32} s_2 (t) + a_{33} s_3 (t)$$

where a_{ij} with $j = 1...3$, depend on the distances of the microphones from the speakers.

It is very innovative to estimate the original speech signals $s_1(t)$, $s_2(t)$ and $s_3(t)$ by making use of the recorded signals $x_i (t)$. And this problem is known as a cocktail-party problem.

If we know the mixing parameter, aij value then we would have easily solved the linear equation by simply inverting the linear system. But the problem is that we neither have aij nor the $s_i(t)$. One of the ways of solving this problem is to use some information on the statistical properties of the signals, $s_i (t)$. It is more than enough to assume that $s_1(t)$, $s_2(t)$ and $s_3(t)$ are statistically independent at each time instant, t. ICA can be used to estimate aij based on their information of their independence. This allows us to separate out the three original signals $s_1(t)$, $s_2(t)$ and $s_3(t)$ from their mixtures $x_1(t)$, $x_2(t)$ and $x_3(t)$. ICA was developed to deal with the variant forms of cocktail-party problem.

The Noise-free ICA Model : The ICA model is a generative model that means that it describes how the observed data are generated by a process of mixing the components, s_j.

To model ICA, the following points must be remembered:-

1. Use statistical latent variables in the system.
2. Use random variable, sk instead of time signal.
3. $X_j = a_{j1}s_1 + a_{j2}s_2$ +.....+ ajnsn, for all jx − As
4. Task: Estimate *A* and *S* using only the observable random vector, *x*.
5. Assuming that number of Independent Components = number of observable mixtures and A is square and invertible, we can estimate A. Then we can calculate W= A^{-1} and thus s = Wx = A^{-1} x.

Limitations in ICA : The following are some of the limitations of ICA:-

1. The independent components are assumed statistically independent.
2. The independent components must have non-Gaussian distributions.
3. The joint density of unit variances, s_1 and s_2 is symmetric. So, it does not contain any information about the directions of the columns of the mixing matrix, A. So, A can't be estimated.
4. If only one Independent component is Gaussian then the estimation is still possible.

Ambiguities in ICA : The following are some of the ambiguities in ICA:-

1. It cannot determine the variances /energies of the independent components (ICs). Both s and A are unknowns and that any scalar multiple in one of the sources can always be cancelled by dividing the corresponding column of A by it. Also because of the fixed magnitudes of IC's assuming unit variance *i.e.* $E\{S_i^2\} = 1$.
2. It cannot determine the order of Independent components. The terms can be easily changed as both a and A are unknown, so, we call any IC as the first one.

How to centre the variables?

We can assume that both the mixture variables and the independent components have zero mean without any loss of generality. This assumption simplifies the theory and algorithms further. If the assumption of zero mean is not true, some pre-processing is done to make it hold. This is possible by centering the observable variables *i.e.* subtracting their sample mean. This means that the original mixtures, say x', are pre-processed by $x = x' - E\{x'\}$, before doing ICA. Thus, the independent components are also made zero mean because-

$$E\{s\} = A^{-1} E \{x\}$$

On the other hand, the mixing matrix remains intact after this pre-processing. So this can always be done without affecting the estimation of the mixing matrix. After estimating the mixing matrix and the independent components for the zero-mean data, the subtracted mean can be simply reconstructed by adding $E\{s\} = A^{-1} E \{x\}$to the zero-mean independent components.

Q.8. Explain Latent Semantic Indexing (LSI). Also give the LSI algorithm.

Ans. Latent Semantic Indexing (LSI) is a retrieval method that makes use of a mathematical technique called as Singular Value Decomposition (SVD) which in turn is used to figure out patterns in connection to terms and concepts included in unstructured collection of data. This process acts as an add-on to document indexing process. in addition to keeping track of keywords that are there in the document, This method analyses the document entirely to find out which other document contains the same words. Please note that LSI considers documents to be semantically close if they have many words in common and semantically distant if few words are there in common. LSI algorithm is unable to understand the words as it does not know the meanings but still it is able to figure out the pattern that makes it look intelligent.

The LSI Algorithm :

Step-1: Convert each document in your index in a vector-form of word occurrences. Here,
Number of dimensions in vector = number of unique words in the entire document set.

Most document vectors will have large empty patches, some will be quite full. It is recommended that common words like 'this', 'him', 'the' etc. should be removed.

Step-2: Scale each vector so that every term reflects the frequency of its occurrence in context.

Step-3: Combine these column vectors into a large term-document matrix. Here, rows represent terms and columns represent document.

Step-4: Perform Singular Value Decomposition (SVD) on the term-document matrix. This will result in three matrices commonly called U, S and V. S, is a diagonal matrix of singular values for your document system. It is of use to us.

Step-5: Set all but the k-highest singular values to 0. K is a parameter that needs to be tuned based on your space. Very low values of k are very lossy and lands up with net poor results. But very high values of k do not change the results much from simple vector search. This gets a new matrix, S'.

Step-6: Recombine the terms to form the original matrix-

$$U * S' * V(t) = M'$$

Where (t) signifies transpose.

Step-7: Break this reduced rank term-document matrix back into column vectors. Associate these with their corresponding documents.

Step-8: Now you get the LSI *i.e.*, Latent Semantic Index.

Advantages of LSI :

1. LSI is used to analyze the similarity between the bodies of the text. This can be used in dozens of ways, from finding related documents in a group to doing paragraph-wise LSI to find site summaries.
2. It can also be used to assist search in a smarter way of your document space.
3. To do document categorization.
4. You can take the inner product (dot product) of two of the LSI vectors and perform operations with that information. Sometimes you may do this operation on your unit LSI vectors, particularly when you are searching on a vector that is a search term. It will never have the magnitude that a full document would have.

Q.9. What is Spectral or Sub-space Clustering?

Ans. It is one of the most modern and simple clustering algorithms. It can be solved efficiently by standard linear algebra software. Sometimes it is better than traditional k-means algorithm. Please understand that the objective of spectral clustering is to cluster connected data but not certainly compact or clustered within convex boundaries.

When we talk of compactness then k-means model is useful while when we talk of connectivity then spectral clustering is used.

Algorithm

Step-1: Project your data into R^n.

Step-2: Define an Affinity matrix, A, using a Gaussian Kernel, *K*, or say just an adjacency matrix *i.e.* $A_{ij} = \delta_{ij}$.

Step-3: Construct the Laplacian Graph from A *i.e.* decide on a normalization.

Step-4: Solve an Eigen value problem such as $Lv = \lambda v$ or a Generalized Eigen Value problem *i.e.*, $Lv = \lambda Dv$.

Step-5: Select k Eigen Vectors $\{v_i, i=1, k\}$ corresponding to the k-lowest or highest Eigen values, to define a *k*-dimensional subspace Pt LP.

Step-6: Form clusters in this subspace using, say, *k*-means.

Metrics : A metric that computes the similarity or closeness of two points in space is called as an affinity. We either guess the metric or learn the metric. Now we will guess the metric. Please note that it is not the standard Euclidean metric. The next simplest one is Guassian Kernel.

Given 2 data points, x_i, x_j that is projected in R^n, we define an Affinity Aij that is positive, symmetric and depends on the Euclidian distance $||x_i - x_j|$ between the data points:-

$$A_{ij} = \exp(-\alpha\ ||x_i - x_j||2)$$

We might provide a hard cut-off *R* so that $A_{ij} = 0$ if $||x_i - x_j||^2 \geq R$ and in some applications we pre-multiply Aij with a feature Affinity Kernal. Just note that-

$A_{ij} = 1$ when the points are close in R^n and $A_{ij} \to 0$ if the points x_i, x_j are far apart. Please note that close data points are in the same cluster while data points in different clusters are far away. Also note that data points in the same cluster may also be far away in comparison to the points in different clusters.

Objective: Our task is now to transform the space so that when the 2 points x_i and x_j are close enough so that they are always in the same cluster and when they are far apart, they are in different clusters.

Many types of Laplacians (*L*) are given in the literature like Normalized, Generalized, Relaxed etc. they all share the degree matrix, D. We define a degree matrix as a diagonal matrix that measures the degree at each node as follows:-

$$D_{i,j} = \Sigma\ (j \text{ to } n)\ a_{i,j}$$

This is known as a local nearest neighbour mean-field average of the Affinity. *D* is a normalization factor for A so that the Cluster Affinities are balanced across different clusters.

Q.10. What is Hidden Markov Model? Explain.

Ans. A tool used for representing probability distributions over a sequence of observations is Hidden Markov Model (HMM). The observation is denoted at a particular instance time, *t*, by variable Y_t. As long as we can define a probability distribution, this symbol can vary from discrete alphabet to a real valued variable or to an integer. Here, we assume that 't' can be an integer valued time index as the observation are sampled at discrete equally spaced time intervals. This model assumes that the observation at time, t, was generated by the same process whose state Si is concealed or hidden from the observer. This model has two defining properties as follows:-

1. This process conforms the Markov Property *i.e.* given the value of S_{i-1}, the current state S_i is independent of all the states prior to $t-1$.
2. The outputs also conforms a Markov property in accordance to the states given S_i, Y_i is independent of the states and observation at other times indexes.

Markov properties signifies joint distribution of a sequence of states and observations. The factorization of joint distribution given in equation can be represented graphically as shown in figure 2.2:-

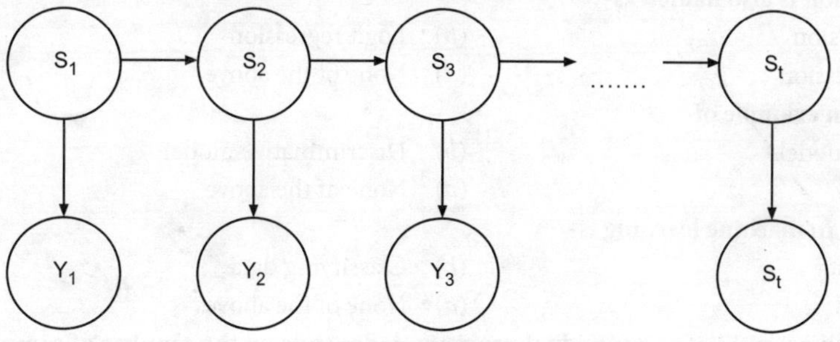

Fig. 5.1

Figure 2.2: Bayesian Network specifying Conditional Independence relation for a Hidden Markov Model

Each variable is denoted by a node in the graph of figure 2.2. each node receives a directed graph from the nodes that is conditionally dependent on, in the factorization of joint distribution. It also assumes that hidden variable is discrete *i.e.* s_i can take on *k* values which will be denoted by the integers {1.....*k*}.

To define a probability distribution over sequences of observations:-

$P(S_i)$ = probability distribution over initial state.

$K X k$ = state transition matrix defining $P(S_i \mid S_{i-1})$

$P(Y_t \mid S_t)$ = Output Model.

Notes:

1. HMMs assume that the model is time invariant.
2. If the observables are in form of discrete symbols, taking one of L values, the *dp* model is represented by k X L emission matrix.
3. HMMs can be augmented to allow for input variables *i.e.* in such a way that there is an input dependent state transition probability. The system then steps ahead and models the conditional distribution of sequence of output distribution when you are provided with the input distributions.

We have studied in this chapter that in machine learning instead of teaching a computer a massive list of rules to solve a problem, we give it a model with which it can evaluate examples. Also, we give a small set of instructions to modify this model if it makes a mistake. We find that as the time passes by, w well suited model will be able to solve the problems in a batter and efficient way. The machine learning algorithm should be such that it tries to make the values of the parameters more and more accurate as it is exposed to more and more examples. But this is just a tip of an iceberg. Recently, scientists have developed the models that resemble the structures as used by a human brain. This involves deep learning only.

MULTIPLE CHOICE QUESTIONS

1. **Predicting the price of a house given its size is an example of-**
   (*a*) Supervised learning (*b*) Unsupervised learning
   (*c*) Remote learning (*d*) None of the above
2. **The inherent groupings in the data discovered is known as-**
   (*a*) Association (*b*) Clustering
   (*c*) Classifying (*d*) None of the above
3. **Discovering rules that describes large portions of data is called as-**
   (*a*) Association (*b*) Clustering
   (*c*) Classifiers (*d*) None of the above
4. **Conditional models are also known as-**
   (*a*) Demand models (*b*) Discriminative models
   (*c*) Generative models (*d*) None of the above
5. **Logistic regression is also named as-**
   (*a*) Login regression (*b*) Logit regression
   (*c*) Logout regression (*d*) None of the above
6. **Naive Bayes is an example of-**
   (*a*) Generative model (*b*) Discriminative model
   (*c*) SVM (*d*) None of the above
7. **A common task in machine learning is-**
   (*a*) Common data (*b*) Classifying data
   (*c*) Global datad (*d*) None of the above
8. **The classification error, Ei of an individual program, i, depends on the number of samples incorrectly classified (false positives and false negatives) and is computed by the formula:-**
   (*a*) $E_i = f / n * 100$ (*b*) $E_i = f * n * 100$
   (*c*) $E_i = f + n * 100$ (*d*) None of the above
9. **PCA stands for-**
   (*a*) Peer Component Analysis (*b*) Principal Component Analysis
   (*c*) Power Component Analysis (*d*) None of the above.

10. Singular Value Decomposition is used in-

(*a*) Latent Semantic Indexing
(*b*) Lateral Simple Indexing
(*c*) Lower Simple Indexing
(*d*) None of the above

11. SVM stands for-

(*a*) Support Vector Machine
(*b*) Simple Vector Machine
(*c*) Super Vector Machine
(*d*) None of the above

12. A generalization of the concept of a plane which is used in SVM implementation for object separation is known as-

(*a*) Hyperplane
(*b*) Airplane
(*c*) Aeroplane
(*d*) None of the above

13. A model evaluation technique which is collection of methods used to examine the underlying constructs influence of the response of variables is-

(*a*) Factor Analysis
(*b*) ICA
(*c*) PCA
(*d*) Singular Value Composition

ANSWERS

1. (*a*)	**2.** (*b*)	**3.** (*b*)	**4.** (*b*)	**5.** (*b*)
6. (*a*)	**7.** (*b*)	**8.** (*a*)	**9.** (*b*)	**10.** (*a*)
11. (*a*)	**12.** (*a*)	**13.** (*a*)		

CONCEPTUAL SHORT QUESTIONS WITH ANSWERS

Q.1. What are the differences between data mining and machine learning?

Ans. Data mining is the process in which the unstructured data puts efforts to extract knowledge or unfamiliar interesting patterns. On the other hand, machine learning relates to the study, design and development of the algorithms that give systems the ability to learn without being clearly programmed.

Q.2. Give functions supervised and unsupervised learning.

Ans. Supervised learning involves-

a. Classifications
b. Speech recognition
c. Regression
d. Predict time series
e. Annotate strings

On the other hand, unsupervised learning involves-

a. Finding the clusters of data
b. Finding low dimensional representations of data
c. Finding interesting coordinates and correlations
d. Finding novel observations or cleaning databases

Q.3. What is inductive machine learning?

Ans. Inductive machine learning covers the process of learning by examples where a system, from a set of perceived instances, tries to encourage a general rule.

Q.4. List at least five common machine learning algorithms.

Ans. Some of the popular ML algorithms are as follows:-

a. Decision Trees
b. Neural Networks
c. Probabilistic Networks
d. Nearest Neighbour
e. Support Vector Machines (SVM)

Q.5. Name different algorithm techniques in ML.

Ans. Different types of techniques in ML are as follows:-

a. Supervised learning

b. Unsupervised learning

c. Semi-supervised learning

d. Reinforcement learning

e. Transduction

f. Learning to learn

Q.6. Name three stages to build the models (or hypotheses) in machine learning.

Ans. Three stages to build the models in machine learning (ML) are as follows:-

a. Model building

b. Model testing

c. Applying the model

Q.7. What is the standard approach to supervised learning?

Ans. The standard approach to supervised learning is to break the data set of example into training set and the test set.

Q.8. Differentiate between 'training set' and 'test set'.

Ans. In different fields of data science like machine learning, a set of data is used to determine the potentially predictive relationship identified as training set. Training set is the example provided to the learner while test set is used to test the exactness of the hypotheses produced by the learner and it is the set of illustration weighed down from the learner. So, training sets are different from test sets.

Q.9. What are the different approaches of machine learning?

Ans. Different approaches of machine learning are as follows:-

a. Concept versus Classification Learning.

b. Symbolic versus Statistical Learning.

c. Inductive versus Analytical Learning.

Q.10. Define Overfitting during machine learning. Why it happens?

Ans. In ML, overfitting occurs when a statistical model defines a random error or noise rather than underlying relationship. When a model is extremely complex, overfitting is usually observed because of having too many parameters relating to the number of training data types. The model exihibits poor performance which has to be overfit. The risk of overfitting exists as the standards used for training the model is not the same as the standards used to judge the effectiveness of a model.

Q.11. How can overfitting be avoided?

Ans. BY means of loads of data, overfitting can be avoided. Overfitting happens when comparatively you have a small dataset and you make effort to learn from it. But if you have a small database and it is necessary to come with a model based on that then in such a scenario, cross validation method may be used. In this method, the dataset is divided into two segments, testing and training datasets. The testing dataset will only test the model while in training dataset, the data-points will come up with a model. In this method, a model is generally provided with a dataset of known data on which training data set is run and a dataset of unknown data against which the model is tested. The basic idea of cross validation is to define a dataset to test the model in the training phase.

Q.12. What is algorithm independent machine learning?

Ans. A type of machine learning in which mathematical foundations is independent of any particular classifier or learning algorithm is known as algorithm independent machine learning.

Q.13. Distinguish between AI and machine learning.

Ans. Designing and developing algorithms according to the behaviours based on empirical data is known as machine learning. On the other hand, artificial intelligence, in addition to machine learning, also covers other aspects like knowledge representation, natural language processing (NLP), planning, robotics etc.

Q.14. Define classifier as used in machine learning.

Ans. A classifier is a system that inputs a vector of discrete or continuous feature vales and outputs a single discrete value, the class.

Q.15. Where is pattern recognition used?

Ans. It is used in computer vision, speech recognition, data mining, statistics, information retrieval and bio-informatics.

Q.16. What is model selection in ML?

Ans. The process of selecting the models from different mathematical models that refer to the same data set is called as model selection. It is applied to the fields of statistics, machine learning and data mining.

Q.17. Name the method that is frequently used to prevent overfitting.

Ans. 'Isotonic Regression' is used to prevent overfiting when the data is sufficient.

Q.18. Why instance-based learning algorithm is sometimes also referred to as lazy-learning algorithm?

Ans. Instance-based learning algorithm is sometimes also referred to as lazy-learning algorithm because they delay the induction or generalization process until classification is performed.

Q.19. What are the 2 classification methods that SVM handle?

Ans. The two classification methods that SVM can handle are as follows:-

a. Combining binary classifiers

b. Modifying binary to incorporate multiclass learning

Q.20. For what purpose PCA and ICA are used?

Ans. PCA and ICA are used to extract features of data to reduce dimensions of data. They are important feature extraction techniques used for dimensionality reduction.

Q.21. What do you mean by dimension reduction?

Ans. It is the process of reducing the number of random variables under considerations and can be divided into feature selection and feature extraction.

Q.22. What are SVMs?

Ans. SVMs or Support Vector Machines are supervised learning algorithms that are used for classification and regression analysis.

Q.23. What are the different methods to solve sequential supervised learning problems?

Ans. The different methods to solve sequential supervised learning problems are:-

a. Sliding window methods

b. Recurrent sliding windows

c. Hidden Makov Models

d. Maximum entropy Markov Models

e. Conditional random fields

f. Graph transformer networks

Q.24. Name two techniques of ML. Give a very popular application of ML that you see everyday.

Ans. Genetic programming and inductive learning are the two methods of ML.

The recommendation engine implemented by major ecommerce websites uses machine learning (ML).

Q.25. How is KNN different from k-means clustering?

Ans. k-nearest neighbours is a supervised classification algorithm. On the other hand, k-means clustering is an unsupervised clustering algorithm. In order for k-nearest neighbours to work, labelled data is needed that we want to classify an unlabeled point. In case of k-means clustering only a set of unlabelled points and a threshold is required. The algorithm will take unlabelled points in consideration and slowly learn how to cluster them into groups by computing the mean of the distance between different points. In sutshell, KNN needs labelled points and is thus supervised learning while k-means doesn't need labelled points and is thus unsupervised learning.

Q.26. Why is "Naive" Bayes naive?

Ans. Even though it has practical applications, specially in text mining, Naive Bayes is still considered as Naive because the assumption that it makes becomes virtually impossible to be seen in real-life data. The conditional probability is computed as purely the product of the individual probabilities of different components. This denotes the absolute independence of features i.e. a condition that is probably never met in real life.

Q.27. Differentiate between a generative and discriminative model.

Ans. A generative model learns categories of data while a discriminative model merely learns the distinction between different categories of data. Discriminative models will leave behind generative models on the basis of classification tasks.

Q.28. Name at least three methods of reducing dimensionality.

Ans. The three methods of reducing dimensionality are as follows:-

a. Removing collinear features.

b. Performing PCA, ICA or other forms of algorithmic dimensionality reduction.

c. Combining features with feature engineering.

Q.29. What is the EM technique? How this algorithm works?

Ans. EM is an algorithm for maximizing a likelihood function when some of the variables in the model are unobserved i.e. when there are latent variables with you. To solve for our model parameters you need to know the distribution of your unobserved data but the distribution of your unobserved data is a function of your model parameters. EEM tries to get around this by guessing repeatedly about the distribution for the unobserved data then further estimating the model parameters by maximizing something that is lower bound on the actual likelihood function and repeating until convergence.

The EM algorithm starts with a guess for values of your model parameters as follows:-

The E-step: For each data point that has some missing values to solve for the distribution of the missing data, use your model equation, provided with your current guess of the model parameters and given the observed data. Please note that you are solving for a distribution for each missing value and not for the expected value. Also note that now we have available with us a distribution for each missing value, we can calculate the expectation of the likelihood function with respect to the unobserved variables. If our guess for the model parameter was correct, this expected likelihood will be the actual likelihood of our observed data. If the parameters were not correct, it will just be a lower bound.

The M-step: Now that we have got an expected likelihood function with no unobserved variables in it, maximize the function as you would in the fully observed case, to get a new estimate of your model parameters.

Repeat till convergence.

Q.30. What do you mean by curse of dimensionality?

Ans. The curse of dimensionality refers to the tendency of a state space to grow exponentially in its dimension i.e. in the number of state variables.

Q.31. What is H_2O? What is prcomp?

Ans. H_2O is software for machine learning and data analysis. PCA is named as prcomp in H_2O and *R* system.

Q.32. What is the principle of operation of the back-propagation algorithm?

Ans. Firstly, the inputs from the training data are propagated through the network to the output. Then the model outputs are compared with the actual outputs. The difference is the error. This error is then fed into the network backwards and connections weights are adjusted.

Q.33. Define the following:-

***a.* Learning rate.**

***b.* Momentum.**

Ans. *a.* **Learning rate:** A higher value of learning rate will make the algorithm converge more rapidly towards the desired values but it will reduce the stability of the algorithm.

b. **Momentum:** It is used to control oscillations in weights which could be caused by alternately signed error signals.

Q.34. WEKA tool may be used to construct neural network. Can it do the parameter value selection also for neural networks?

Ans. A neural network trains by repeated passes of the data. Each pass is called an epoch. With each epoch, the connecting weights are adjusted until a satisfactory level of performance is reached. We can ponder that if 50 epochs are good then 80 epochs should be better. But this argument does not hold with neural networks. With too many passes the network may over-train also. Please understand that a well trained neural network model would show similar performance levels with both test and training data. Also understand that keeping this in mind we can change the parameter values of the algorithm. We should not assume that default parameters are the best. We can change the parameters too. As the number of epochs increases we need more time for training. If we compare the outputs from the two different epochs, we can see the accuracy remains at the same level of 97.2%. that is why we say that higher the number of epochs has not improved the model performance. Just keep in mind that we should restrict ourselves to the lower number of epochs as it not only involves less computing time but also lowers the danger of over-fitting.

Q.35. Define the following terms:-

a. **Activation function.**

b. **Back-propagation learning.**

c. **Delta rule.**

d. **Epoch.**

e. **Feedforward neural networks.**

f. **Genetic algorithm.**

g. **Hyperplane.**

h. **Kernel.**

Ans. *a.* **Activation function:** A function that describes the output behaviours of a neuron in neural network.

b. **Back-propagation learning:** It is a form of supervised learning used to train mainly, feedforward neural networks, that works by making modifications in weights values, starting at the output layer and then moving backwards through the hidden layer.

c. **Delta Rule:** The delta rule changes the weight vector for a neural network in such a way that the error is reduced.

d. **Epoch:** It is one complete pass of the entire training set through the neural network. The learning process is repeated epoch-by-epoch until the averaged square error converges to a minimum value.

e. **Feedforward neural network:** It is a sort of ANN where connections between the units do not form a directed cycle.

f. **Genetic algorithm:** It is an adaptive heuristic search algorithm premised on the evolutionary ideas of natural selection theory.

g. **Hyperplane:** A plane (as in geometry) that is used to do object separation during SVM implementation.

h. **Kernel:** Linear, polynomial and rbf are some of the kernels of SVM that allows SVM to fit the maximum margin hyperplane in the transformed feature space.

Q.36. Tabulate the differences between supervised and unsupervised learning.

Ans. The following are the points of differences:-

Supervised Learning	Unsupervised Learning
It incorporates an external teacher so that each output unit is told what should be the desired response to that input signal.	Uses no external teacher.
Global error signals govern learning.	Local information is used for learning.
Uses pattern class information of each training pattern.	Adaptively clusters patterns to generate decision codes.
Paradigms are error correction learning, reinforcement learning and stochastic learning.	Paradigms are Hebbian learning and competitive learning.
Learning is usually off line. It means that learning and operation phases are different. In off-line learning, all of the given patterns are used together.	Learning is online. It means that the agent learns and operates at the same time. Here, the information in each new pattern is incorporated into the agent.
All learning data are stored and can be accessed repeatedly. So, we can see whether we are making progress in training or not.	Locality allows learning in real time. So, the progress cannot be monitored.
Inputs and outputs are defined.	Only inputs are defined.
Uses pattern class information of each training pattern.	Adaptively clusters patterns to generate decision class without any prior pattern class information.
Global error signal governs learning.	Local information/ rules are used for learning.
Learning is offline usually.	Locality allows synapses to learn in real-time.

Q.37. Explain different nets classes.

Ans. It is put under 2 main categories as follows: -

I. Unsupervised learning (i.e. without a teacher):

1. Feedback Nets:

a. Binary Adaptive Resonance Theory (ART1)

b. Analog adaptive Resonance Theory (ART2)

c. Discrete Hopfield (DH)

d. Continuous Hopfield (CH)

e. Discrete Bi-directional Associative Memory (BAM)

f. Temporal Associative Memory (TAM)

g. Adaptive Bi-directional Associative Memory (ABAM)

h. Kohonen Self-Organizing Map/ Topology Preserving Map (SOM/TPM)

i. Competitive learning

2. Feed-forward only Nets:

a. Learning Matrix (LM)

b. Driver-reinforcement Learning (DR)

c. Counter Propagation (CPN)

II. Supervised learning (*i.e.* with a teacher):

1. Feedback Nets:

a. Boltzmann Machine. (BM)

b. Mean Field Annealing (MFT)

c. Recurrent Cascade Correlation (RCC)

d. Learning Vector Quantization (LVQ)

e. Back progpagation through time (BPTT)

f. Real-time Recurrent Learning (RTRL)

2. Feed-forward only Nets:

a. Perceptron

b. Adaline, Madaline

c. Backpropagation (BP)

d. Cauchy Machine (CM)

e. Artmap

f. Cascade Correlation (CasCor)

EXERCISE QUESTIONS

1. Differences between supervised and unsupervised learning.
2. Explain PCA and ICA.
3. Define clustering.
4. Write k-means algorithm.
5. What is Factor Analysis? Explain.
6. What is LSI?
7. Write short notes on HMM.

6 Reinforcement Learning and Control

Q.1. State Markov Decision Processes [MDP].

Ans. The study of this type of reinforcement learning begins with Markov Decision Process (MDP) which provides the formalism in which reinforcement learning problems are usually posed.

Considering the reinforced learning framework we say that:-

a. **States:** These can refer to, for example, grid maps in robotics or like an open door and closed door scenario.

b. **Actions:** A fixed set of actions like going north, south, east etc for a robot.

c. **Transition Probabilities:** It is defined as the probability of going from one state to another given an action. For instance, what is the probability of an open door if the action is open.

d. **Rewards:** These are used to guide the planning. For example, in case of a grid, we may like to go to a certain cell. The reward will be higher if we get closer. Like in case of a door example, an open door might give a high reward.

Please understand that once the MDP is defined, a policy can be learned by doing Value Iteration or Policy Iteration which calculates the expected reward for each of the states. Then the policy gives per state the best action to perform. Also note that MDP is useful when you want to have an efficient sequence of actions in which your actions can not always be 100% effective.

MDP provides a mathematical framework for modelling decisions making in situations where outcomes are partly random and partly under the control of a decision maker. MDPs are useful for studying a wide range of optimization problems that are solved using dynamic programming and reinforcement learning. In 1960, Ronald Howard published a book on Dynamic Programming and Markov Processes.

MDP is a discrete time stochastic control process. at each time step, the process is in some state, s, and the decision maker may choose any action, a, that is available in state, *s*. The process responds at the next time by randomly moving into a new state, s', and giving a decision maker a corresponding reward $R_a(s, s')$.

Please note here that the probability that the process moves into its new state s' is influenced by the chosen action only. This is given by the state transition function, $P_a(s, s')$. So, the next state s' depends on the current state, s, and the decision maker's action, a. But given s and a, it is conditionally independent of all previous states and actions. Just note here that the state transitions of an MDP process satisfies the Markov property. And MDPs are an extension of Markov chains. The difference is the addition of actions and rewards. Conversely, if only one action exists for each state (*e.g.* 'wait') and all rewards are the same (*e.g.* 'zero'), a Markov decision process reduces to a

A Markov decision process is defined:-

- *S*, a finite set of possible states.
- *A*, a finite set of actions.
- $P(r, s' \mid s, a)$, a state transition function.
- *R*, a reward function.

When an agent takes an action in an MDP framework, it forms an episode. We define an episode as a series of tuples of states, actions and rewards. These episodes run till the environment reaches a terminal state. We can show the variables in an episode as follows:-

$$(s_0, a_0, r_0), (s_1, a_1, r_1), \ldots\ldots (s_n, a_n, r_n)$$

Objective: MDPs task is to find an optimal policy for our agent. We define policies as the ways in which our agent acts based on its current state. The aim is to find a policy to maximize the expected future return.

Q.2. State Bellman Equations.

Ans. Richard Bellman, gave a dynamic programming equation known as BELLMAN equation. It is the necessary condition for optimality related to dynamic programming. It writes the value of a decision problem at a certain point in time in terms of the payoff from some initial choices and the value of the remaining decision problem that result from those initial choices. This breaks a dynamic optimization problem into simpler sub-problems. This is known as **Principle of Optimality".**

The Bellman equation was first applied to engineering control theory and to applied mathematics and in economic theory. The basic concepts of dynamic programming have been given in John Von Neumann and Oskar's theory of Games and Economic behaviour. It has been observed that any problem that can be solved using optimal control theory can also be solved by analyzing a suitable Bellman equation. Bellman equation refers to the dynamic programming equation related to discrete-time optimization problems. In continuous-time optimization problems, the analogous equation is a partial differential equation which is usually called as the Hamilton-Jacobi-Bellman equation. Given a fixed policy, Π, its value function, V^{Π}, satisfies the Bellman equations:-

$$V^{\Pi}\ (s) = R(s) + \gamma\, \Sigma\ (s' \varepsilon\ S)\ P_{s\Pi(s)}\ (s')\ V^{\Pi}\ (s')$$

This expression shows that the expected sum of discounted rewards, V^{Π} (s), for starting, s, consists of two terms-

a. Firstly, the immediate reward *R(s)* that we get right away simply for starting in state, *s*.

b. 2nd is the expected sum of future discounted rewards.

The 2nd term of the equation-1, shows 1the expected sum of discounted rewards for starting in state *s*', where *s*' is distributed according to $P_{s\Pi(s)}$, which is the distribution over where we will end up taking the first action in the MDP from state, s. So, the 2nd term gives the expected sum of discounted rewards obtained after the first step in the MDP.

These Bellman's equations can be used to efficiently solve V^{Π}. Specifically in a finite-state MDP ($|S| < \infty$), we can write down such equation for V^{Π} (s) for every state, s. This gives us a set of $|S|$ linear equations in $|S|$ variables that can be then solved.

Q.3. What is Value Iteration and Policy Iteration.

Ans. Both value iteration and policy iteration are standard algorithms for solving MDPs. For small MDPs, policy iteration is often very fast and converges with very little iteration. On the other hand, for MDPs with large state spaces, solving for VΠ explicitly would involve solving a large system of linear equations and could be difficult. In these problems, value iteration may be preferred. This is the reason as to why practically, value iteration seems to be used more often than policy iteration.

Q.4. What is Linear Quadratic Regulation (LQR)?

Ans. The theory of optimal control is related to the operation of a dynamic system at a minimum cost. And the case where the system dynamics are described by a set of linear differential equations and the cost is described by a quadratic function is called as the LQ problem. One of the main results in the theory is that the solution is provided by the linear-quadratic regulator (LQR), a feedback controller whose equations are given here. LQR is an important part of the solution to the LQG (LINEAR QUADRATIC GAUSSIAN) PROBLEM. Like the LQR problem, the LQG problem is one of the most fundamental problems in control theory. The settings of a regulating controller governing either a machine or process like an airplane or chemical reactor, are found by using a mathematical algorithm that minimizes a cost function with weighting factors supplied by an engineer. The cost function is defined as the sum of the deviations of key measurements, desired altitude or process temperature, from their desired values. Thus the algorithm finds those controller settings that minimize undesired deviations. The magnitude of the control action also may be included in the cost function.

The LQR algorithm reduces the amount of work done by the control system engineer to optimize the controller. However, the engineer still needs to specify the cost function parameters and compare the results with the specified design goals. Please note that this often means that the controller construction will be an iterative process in which an engineer judges the optimal controllers produced through simulation and then adjusts the parameters to produce a controller more consistent with the design goals.

The LQR algorithm is an automated way of finding an appropriate state-feedback controller. As such, it is not uncommon for control engineers to prefer alternative methods like full state feedback, also known as **pole placement,** wherein there is a clear relationship between the controller parameters and controller behaviour. Also note that difficulty in finding the right weighting factors limits the application of the LQR based controller synthesis.

Explore versus Exploit : Consider a very famous mouse-maze problem. The mouse must either get the water or it may reach a poison container that is red in colour. Our agent must control the mouse to maximize reward. If the mouse gets water, it receives a reward of +1, if it reaches the poison container then it receives a reward of -10 and if the mouse gets the cheese, it receives a reward of +100. After receiving of the reward, the episode is over. **Please note that the optimal policy involves the mouse successfully navigating to the cheese and eating it.** The mouse may go left or right but the aim of mouse is to follow from its movements that if it goes left, it gets water and if it goes right it gets poison container. May be after 2 episodes the mouse may have found an optimal policy. It continues to follow its learned policy on subsequent episodes and gets the moderate reward. So, we can say that our agent uses a greedy method i.e. always it chooses a model's best action. Therefore, it gets struck in a policy that is a local maximum. To avoid this problem, our agent should deviate from the model's recommendation and take a suboptimal action in order to explore more of the environment. So, instead of taking the immediate right turn to exploit the environment to get water, our agent may choose a left turn and may enter into more dangerous areas in search of a more optimal policy. Also note here that too much of exploration and our agent fails to optimize any reward. Not enough exploration can result in our agent getting stuck in local minima. This balance of explore versus exploit is vital to learn a successful policy.

Q.5. What is LQG Q-Learning?

Ans. Q-learning comes under the category of reinforcement learning and is called as value learning. Here, instead of directly learning a policy, we will be learning the value of states and actions. It involves learning a function named as Q-function, that represents the quality of a state, action pair. We define Q-function as follows:-

"Q-function, $Q(s, a)$ is a function that calculates the maximum discounted future return when action, a, is performed in state, s".

Q-value represents our expected long-term rewards. Given that we are at a state and take an action. Then take every subsequent action perfectly to maximize expected future reward. Please understand that it is very difficult to know whether the action is good or not as you need to know how you are going to act in the future. Our future returns will depend on what our long-term methods are going to be. Also note here that in order to value a (state, action) pair you need to know all of the perfect subsequent actions. And to know the best actions, you need to have accurate values for a state and action.

Q-learning is an alternative Temporal Difference (TD) method. It learns action-value representation instead of utilities. $Q(a, s)$ denotes value of doing action, a, in state, s.

$$U(s) = \max Q(a, s)$$

A TD agent that learns a Q-function does not need a model for either learning or action selection. That is, it is model free.

Note: Q-learning agent learns optimal policy but much slower than ADP agent.

TD does not enforce consistency among values via a model.

According to Watkins and Dayan in 1992, the convergence results for Q-learning assumes a discrete time, finite-state system and requires the use of lookup-tables to represent Q-function. This is not suitable for the LQR domain where the states and actions are vectors of real numbers. We will use a parameterized representation of the Q-function and adjust the parameters through a learning process.

For instance, Jordan and Jacobs in 1990, Lin in 1992, used MLPs training using backpropagation to approximate the Q-function. Please note that the function, QU, is a quadratic function of its arguments, the state and control action but it is a linear function of the quadratic combinations from the vector $[z, u]$.

For example, if $x = [x_1, x_2]$ and $u = [u_1]$, then $QU(x, u)$ is a linear function of the vector $[x_{12}, x_{22}, u_{12}, x_1 x_2, x_1 u_1, x_2 u_1]$. This fact allows us to use Linear Recursive Least Squares (RLS) to implement Q-learning in the LQR domain.

We must relate the Q-values of past and future. This forms a new update rule *i.e.* we can update past Q-values to be based on future Q-values. This is useful as we know that there exists a Q-value that we know is correct *i.e.* the Q-value of the very last action before the episode is over. For this last state, we know that the next action resulted in the next reward. So we can perfectly set the Q-values for that state. Then we can use this update-rule to propagate that Q-value to the previous time step as follows:

$$Q'_j \rightarrow Q'_{j+10}\ Q'_{j+2} \rightarrow \ldots\text{-->}Q^*$$

And this process of updating of the *Q*-value is known as value iteration.

Our 1st *Q*-value may be wrong but it is fine as with the next iteration, we can update our *Q*-value via the correct one from the future. After 1st iteration, the last *Q*-value is accurate as it is just a reward from the last state and action before episode termination. Then we update our *Q*-value. This sets the 2nd to last *Q*-value. In next iteration, we can assure that the last two *Q*-values are correct and so on. Through this process of value iteration, we will be assured the convergence on the ultimate optimal *Q*-value.

There are two types of Q-learning as follows:-

a. Watkins Q-learning rule/ optimizing *Q*-learning as it learn the *Q*-function of the optimal policy directly.

b. The 2nd form of Q-learning tries to learn *QU*, the *Q*-function for some designated policy, *U*. *U* may or may not be the policy that is actually followed during training.

Bradtke et al. show in one of their papers that a linear RLS representation of the policy-based learning rule will converge to *QU*, for *LQR* problems.

Q.6. What is Deep Q-Network (DQN)?

Ans. DQN uses a deep neural network that takes an image (the state) in to estimate the *Q*-value for all possible actions. The aim is ti train our network to estimate the *Q*-function. We know that *Q*-learning is a value-learning algorithm. We are not learning a policy directly rather we are learning the values of each state, action pair. They may or may not be good.

Value iteration produces a mapping between state and action pairs with corresponding *Q*-values and we are constructing a table of these mappings called as *Q*-TABLE.

What will be the size of this Q-TABLE?

As studied, value iteration is an exhaustive process that requires a full traversal of the entire space of state, action pairs. In stochastic environments, the space of our *Q*-TABLE would even be larger and possibly infinite. With such a large space, it will be intractable for us to find all of the *Q*-vales for every state, action pair.

Note: If we approximate the *Q*-function then we need not perform an exhaustive and extensive search through all possible values of *Q* (*Q*-values) to learn a *Q*-function.

Deep Q Network is a Markov decision process that works on the Markov assumption. This assumption sates that "the next state ($s\_i + 1$) depends only on the current state s_i and action a_i and not on any previous states or actions." This Markov assumption makes modelling decision processes simple and reliable too but at a loss of modelling power. DQN solves this problem by reusing the state history *i.e.* DQN considers the past four game frames instead of using only one game frame. This makes DQN to utilize time-dependent information.

Two types of *Q*-networks are available in literature-

a. The prediction network.

b. The target Q-network.

It is observed in these two Q-networks that they have the same architecture definition as they are the same network with the target Q just having delayed parameter updates.

Limitations of DQN : It takes long to train. It does not work well on some games and needs re-training for every new game.

Q.7. Explain Deep Recurrent Q-Networks (DRQN).

Ans. Let us recall the Markov's assumption. It states that the next state relies only on the previous state and the action taken by the agent. Using this on DQN has some limitations like why should there be only 4 frames, why not 8 or 10 or 12? This is an imposed frames history parameter that limits the model's generality. For this purpose we use DQRN.

DQRN uses a recurrent layer to transfer a latent knowledge of state from one time step to the next. Thus, the model itself can learn how many frames are informative that must be included in its state. DQRN has also been extended to include neural nets. The point to understand is that since DQRN deals with sequences of data, it can attend only certain parts of the sequence. And this ability to learn just parts of the image will improve performance as well as it provides model interpretability.

DQRN has been found to be better than DQN as far as the playing of certain games is concerned like DOOM, Atari games etc.

Q.8. Contrast Policy versus Value Learning.

Ans. To maximize the rewards we have to teach an agent. And for this teaching there are 2 methods:-

a. Policy learning.

b. Value learning.

In policy learning, we directly learn a policy that maximizes reward.

In value learning, we are learning the value of every state and action (a pair).

For example, say you are trying to learn 'how to ride a bike'. Then a policy learning method would be to think about how pressing the right pedal would correct you, if you are falling on to the left. On the other hand, with a value learning approach, you would assign a score to different bike orientations and actions that you can take in those positions.

Q.9. Write short notes on-POMDPS. Also give its limitations and advantages.

Ans. POMDPS stands for PARTIALLY OBSERVABLE MARKOV DECISION PROCESS. It is a generalization of a Markov decision process (MDP). A POMDP models an agent decision process in which it is assumed that the system dynamics are determined by an MDP but the agent cannot directly observer the underlying state. Instead, it must maintain a probability distribution over the set of possible states based on a set of observations and observation probabilities and the underlying MDP. A POMDP framework is general enough to model a variety of real-world sequential decision process. Applications like Robot navigation problems, machine maintenance and planning uncertainity are included here.

An exact solution to a POMDP yields the optimal action for each possible belief over the world states. The optimal action maximizes or minimizes the expected reward or cost of the agent over a possibly infinite horizon. The sequence of optimal actions is known as the optimal policy of the agent for interacting with its environment.

MDP assumes that the complete state of the world is visible to the agent. This is quite unrealistic. POMDPS models the information available to the agent by specifying a function from the hidden state to the observables. The goal now is to find a mapping from observations (not states) to actions. But the observations are not Markov because two different states might look the same, which invalidates all of the MDP solution techniques. The optimal solution to this problem is to construct a belief state MDP, where a belief state is a probability distribution over states.

Control theory is concerned with solving POMDPs. Practically speaking, control theory scientists make a strong assumption about the nature of the model (linear-Gaussian) and reward function (negative quadratic loss) in order to be able to make theoretical guarantees of optimality. Solving a generic discrete POMDP is wildly intractable. Finding tractable special cases like structured models is the current area of research today.

Limitations of POMDPs : They model the world in terms of a fixed size set of state variables, each of which can take on specific values, say true or false. These are called as propositional models.

Applications of POMDPs : POMDPs can be used to model real-life problems. It has been used in management of patients with ischemic heart disease, assistive technology for persons with dementia, the conservation of the critically endangered and difficult to detect Sumatran tigers and aircraft collision avoidance.

SUMMARY

We have studied the concept of reinforcement learning like MDPs, maximum rewards problem. Different approaches to deep reinforcement learning like policy gradients, deep-Q networks etc have also been studied in this chapter. Deep reinforcement learning is a step in this direction that has produced agents capable of mastering Atari games, driverless cars, robotics etc.

MULTIPLE CHOICE QUESTIONS

1. **MDP stands for-**

(*a*) Many Decision Problems
(*b*) Markov Decision Process
(*c*) Markov Dynamic Problem
(*d*) None of the above

2. **A branch of machine learning that deals with learning with interaction and feedback is called as-**

(*a*) Leaning by Example
(*b*) Reinforcement Learning
(*c*) Deep Learning
(*d*) None of the above

3. **An application of reinforcement learning using deep networks is-**
   (*a*) DQN (*b*) AQN
   (*c*) PQN (*d*) None of the above
4. **Reinforcement learning involves-**
   (*a*) An actor (*b*) An environment
   (*c*) A reward signal (*d*) All of the above
5. **The ways in which our agent acts based on its current state is-**
   (*a*) Policy (*b*) Learning
   (*c*) Testing (*d*) None of the above
6. **Reinforcement learning is basically a-**
   (*a*) Trial and error process
   (*b*) Algorithmic process
   (*c*) Dynamic process
   (*d*) None of the above
7. **In which type of learning we learn the value of every (state+ action) pair-**
   (*a*) Policy learning (*b*) Value learning
   (*c*) Machine learning (*d*) None of the above
8. **Q-learning is put under-**
   (*a*) Policy learning (*b*) Value learning
   (*c*) Machine learning (*d*) None of the above
9. **The process of updating of the Q-value is known as-**
   (*a*) Policy iteration (*b*) Value iteration
   (*c*) Research iteration (*d*) None of the above
10. **DQN uses-**
   (*a*) Life history (*b*) State history
   (*c*) Indian history (*d*) None of the above
11. **Which of the following is a Q-network-**
   (*a*) The prediction network (*b*) The computer network
   (*c*) LAN (*d*) None of the above
12. **DQRN stands for-**
   (*a*) Deep Recurrent Q-Network (*b*) Direct Recursive Q-Network
   (*c*) Prediction network (*d*) None of the above
13. **Deep reinforcement learning has produced-**
   (*a*) Agents (*b*) Letters
   (*c*) Messages (*d*) None of the above

ANSWERS

1. (*b*)	**2.** (*b*)	**3.** (*a*)	**4.** (*d*)	**5.** (*a*)
6. (*a*)	**7.** (*b*)	**8.** (*b*)	**9.** (*b*)	**10.** (*b*)
11. (*a*)	**12.** (*a*)	**13.** (*a*)		

CONCEPTUAL SHORT QUESTIONS WITH ANSWERS

Q.1. Distinguish between a perceptron and delta rule.

Ans. The following are the points of differences between the two:

A Perceptron	Delta Rule
It uses threshold unit.	It uses unthreshold linear unit.
It converges after a finite number of iterations.	It converges asymptotically toward a minimum error hypothesis.
Output hypothesis classifies training data perfectly.	Termination is not guaranteed.
Linear separability is mandatory.	Linear separability is not mandatory.

Q.2. List some applications of back propagation perceptrons.

Ans. The following are some of the applications:

1. Optical character recognition.
2. Data compression.
3. Image compression.
4. Load forecasting problems in power systems.
5. Speech synthesis.
6. Content problem.
7. Pattern recognition.
8. Fault detection problems.
9. Aircraft navigation.
10. Non-linear simulation

Q.3. Write a short note on SOMs.

Ans. SOMs stands for Self Organizing Feature Maps or Kohonen Network is a data visualization technique proposed by Kohonen, which provides a way of representing multidimensional data in much lower dimensional spaces. And this process of reducing the dimensionality of vectors is a data compression technique known as vector quantization. This technique creates a network that stores information in such a way that any topological relationships within the training set are maintained. So they are also called as topology-preserving maps. The topological structure property is observed in our brain and is not found in any other ANN except SOM. Please note that the self-organizing map as developed by Kohonen, groups the input data into clusters which are commonly used for unsupervised learning.

In SOM, there are 'm' cluster units that are arranged in a 1D or 2d array, an input vector of n-tuples and a weight vector associated with the cluster unit. In self-organizing process, the cluster unit whose weight vector matches the input pattern closely is selected as a winner. The winning and the neighbouring unit update their weights. The neighbouring unit's weight vectors are not close to the input pattern but differ in some extent. That is why the connection weights do not multiply the signal sent from the input units to cluster units.

In SOM, all units in the neighbourhood that receive positive feedback from the winning unit participate in the learning process. Even if a neighbouring unit's weight is orthogonal to the input vector, its weight vector will still change in response to the input vector. This is required to maintain the order mapping.

Q.4. Differentiate between PCA and LDA.

Ans. The following are the points of differences:-

1. PCA does more of feature classification whereas LDA does data classification.
2. In PCA, the shape and the location of the original data sets changes when transformed to a different space. LDA does not change the location but only tries to provide more class separability and draw a decision region between the given classes. As such, LDA also helps in better understanding the distribution of the feature data.
3. PCA deals with unlabelled data and tries to maximize variance. PCA deals with unlabeled data and tries to maximize variance. PCA deals with unlabeled data and tries to maximize the discrimination between the classes.

4. If the discriminating information lies within the variances, then PCA works better than the LDA.
5. PCA is an unsupervised linear feature extraction method. LDA uses the category information associated with each pattern for extracting the most discriminatory features.

Q.5. List the three steps of PCA.

Ans. The summary of PCA steps is:-

1. Organize a data set as $m*n$ matrix, where m is the number of measurement types and n is the number of trials.
2. Subtract off the mean for each measurement type or row.
3. Calculate the Eigen vectors of the covariance.

Q.6. Define EBL. What are its advantages?

Ans. EBL extracts general rules from single examples by explaining the examples and generalizing the explanation. It provides a deductive method turning first-principles knowledge into useful, efficient and special purpose expertise. Some of its advantages are as follows:-

1. Training examples often contains irrelevant information. The domain theory allows the learner to select he relevant aspects of the training example.
2. EBL forms generalizations that are known to be relevant to specific goals that are logically guaranteed to be logically consistent with the domain theory.
3. By using domain knowledge, EBL allows learning from a single training instance.
4. Construction of an explanation allows the learner to hypothesize unstated relationships between its goals and its experiences.

Q.7. What do you mean by gap filling by EBL?

Ans. EBL or Explanation Based Learning makes up for small number of examples by using extensive domain knowledge. If the explanation is complete, then one can guarantee that the description is correct. But there are some problems as there might be instances where explanations may use reasoning steps that are not sound. When such gaps are found in the explanation, an EBL system may use abduction or induction to fill them.

Q.8. Why do we disparage the term Q-value?

Ans. Researchers in the field of reinforcement learning discuss about Q-values, Q-tables and Q-functions. Such usage almost always seem like jargon i.e. like apparently precise technical terms that are off-putting to new comers but really adds nothing. In this case, the Q-prefix means only that the values, tables or functions pertain to (state + action) pairs. In most of the cases, we give these functions different notations, all of which involve the letter, Q. The name Q-function appears to be technical but is in fact imprecise and undesirable.

Q.9. Which algorithm to use-actor critic method or Q-learning?

Ans. In 1980s, actor critic methods were very popular but in 1990s these were dominated by value-function methods like Q-learning and Sarsa. But Q-learning is instable with function approximation. So, it is not very useful for long run.

Q.10. Give some limitations of Multilayer perceptrons.

Ans. Limitations of multilayer perceptrons are as follows:-

1. It requires large number of iterations for learning that is unsuitable for real-time learning.
2. It gives no guaranteed solution.
3. They do not scale up well from small research systems to larger real systems.
4. It is very difficult to determine all of the weights and thresholds theoretically.
5. It is very difficult to decide which input pattern should be represented by hidden layer.

Q.11. What are the characteristics of delta learning rule?

Ans. The characteristics of delta learning rule are as follows:-

1. It uses output of activation function to generate error signal.
2. It can only be used with continuous activation functions.
3. It is a gradient based method e.g. the least mean square algorithm.
4. It can be generalized to multi-layer networks.

5. It gives continuous output so can be used for function approximation.

Q.12. Show how a multi-layered perceptron solves a non-linear separable class problem.

Ans. Logical XOR Function is as follows:-

X1	X2	Output (Y)
0	0	0
0	1	1
1	0	1
1	1	0

The output from a neuron is calculated as follows:-

$$Y = X_1 * W_1 + X_2 * W_2$$

In form of a graph, we can draw:-

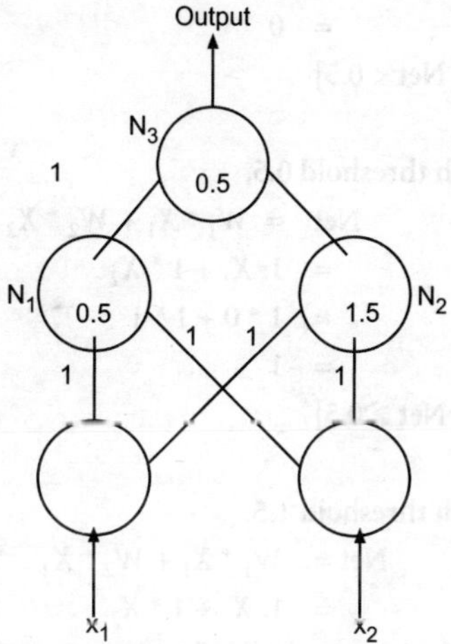

From this graph, the activations of output neuron can be formed:-

Neuron, N_1 uses the activation function-

$$O = f(\text{Net}) = \begin{cases} 1 \text{ if Net } \geq 0.5 \\ 0 \text{ if Net} < 0.5 \end{cases}$$

Neuron, N_2 uses the activation function-

$$O = f(\text{Net}) = \begin{cases} 1 \text{ if Net } \geq 1.5 \\ 0 \text{ if Net} < 1.5 \end{cases}$$

Neuron, N_3 uses the activation function-

$$O = f(\text{Net}) = \begin{cases} 1 \text{ if Net } \geq 0.5 \\ 0 \text{ if Net} < 0.5 \end{cases}$$

Now the network learns as follows:-

1. Output from neuron, N_1 is

   For input $X_1 = 0$ and $X_2 = 0$ and with threshold 0.5,

$$\begin{aligned} \text{Net} &= W_1 * X_1 + W_2 * X_2 \\ &= 1.X_1 + 1 * X_2 \\ &= 1 * 0 + 1 * 0 \\ &= 0 \end{aligned}$$

   So, $O = f(\text{Net}) = 0$ [as Net < 0.5]

2. **Output from neuron, N_2 is**

For input $X_1 = 0$ and $X_2 = 0$ and with threshold 1.5,

$$\begin{aligned} Net &= W_1 * X_1 + W_2 * X_2 \\ &= 1. X_1 + 1 * X_2 \\ &= 1 * 0 + 1 * 0 \\ &= 0 \end{aligned}$$

So, $O = f(\text{Net}) = 0$ [as Net < 0.5]

3. **Output from neuron, N_3 is**

For input $X_1 = 0$ and $X_2 = 0$ and with threshold 0.5,

$$\begin{aligned} Net &= W_1 * X_1 + W_2 * X_2 \\ &= 1. X_1 \text{ (output from } N_1) + -1 * X_2 \text{ (output from } N_2) \\ &= 1 * 0 + -1 * 0 \\ &= 0 \end{aligned}$$

So, $O = f(\text{Net}) = 0$ [as Net < 0.5]

(*ii*) Output from Neuron, N_1

For input $X_1 = 0$ and $X_2 = 1$ and with threshold 0.5,

$$\begin{aligned} Net &= W_1 * X_1 + W_2 * X_2 \\ &= 1. X_1 + 1 * X_2 \\ &= 1 * 0 + 1 * 1 \\ &= 1 \end{aligned}$$

So, $O = f(\text{Net}) = 1$ [as Net ≥ 0.5]

Output from neuron, N_2 is

For input $X_1 = 0$ and $X_2 = 1$ and with threshold 1.5,

$$\begin{aligned} Net &= W_1 * X_1 + W_2 * X_2 \\ &= 1. X_1 + 1 * X_2 \\ &= 1 * 0 + 1 * 1 \\ &= 1 \end{aligned}$$

So, $O = f(\text{Net}) = 0$ [as Net < 1.5]

Output from neuron, N_2 is

For input $X_1 = 0$ and $X_2 = 1$ and with threshold 0.5,

$$\begin{aligned} Net &= W_1 * X_1 + W_2 * X_2 \\ &= 1. X1 \text{ (output from N1)} + -1 * X2 \text{ (output from N2)} \\ &= 1 * 1 + -1 * 0 \\ &= 1 \end{aligned}$$

So, $O = f(\text{Net}) = 1$ [as Net ≥ 0.5]

(*iii*) Output from neuron N1

For input $X_1 = 1$ and $X_2 = 0$ and with threshold 0.5,

$$\begin{aligned} Net &= W1 * X1 + W2 * X2 \\ &= 1. X_1 + 1 * X_2 \\ &= 1 * 1 + 1 * 0 \\ &= 1 \end{aligned}$$

So, $O = f(\text{Net}) = 1$ [as Net ≥ 0.5]

Output from neuron, N_2 is

For input $X_1 = 1$ and $X_2 = 0$ and with threshold 1.5,

$$Net = W_1 * X_1 + W_2 * X_2$$

$= 1. X_1 + 1 * X_2$

$= 1 * 1 + 1 * 0$

$= 1$

So, $O = f(\text{Net}) = 0$ [as Net < 1.5]

Output from neuron, N_3 is

For input $X_1 = 1$ and $X_2 = 0$ and with threshold 0.5,

Net $= W_1 * X_1 + W_2 * X_2$

$= 1. X_1$ (output from N_1) + $-1 * X_2$ (output from N_2)

$= 1 * 1 + -1 * 0$

$= 1$

So, $O = f(\text{Net}) = 1$ [as Net ≥ 0.5]

Output from neuron, N_1 is

For input $X_1 = 1$ and $X_2 = 1$ and with threshold 0.5,

Net $= W_1 * X_1 + W_2 * X_2$

$= 1. X_1 + 1 * X_2$

$= 1 * 1 + 1 * 1$

$= 2$

So, $O = f(\text{Net}) = 1$ [as Net > 0.5]

Output from neuron, N_2 is

For input $X_1 = 1$ and $X_2 = 1$ and with threshold 1.5,

Net $= W_1 * X_1 + W_2 * X_2$

$= 1. X_1 + 1 * X_2$

$= 1 * 1 + 1 * 1$

$= 2$

So, $O = f(\text{Net}) = 1$ [as Net ≥ 1.5]

Output from neuron, N_3 is

For input $X_1 = 1$ and $X_2 = 1$ and with threshold 0.5,

Net $= W_1 * X_1 + W_2 * X_2$

$= 1. X_1$ (output from N_1) + $-1 * X_2$ (output from N_2)

$= 1 * 1 + -1 * 1 = 1 - 1$

$= 0$

So, $O = f(\text{Net}) = 0$ [as Net < 0.5]

Q.13. Define the following:-

a. **Pulling error signals.**

b. **Pushing error signals.**

Ans. *a.* **Pulling error signals**: The process of computing delta signals for each neuron in the previous layer by pulling the error signals from the current layer is called as pulling error signals.

b. **Pushing error signals:** The process of pushing the error signals from the current layer to the previous layer *i.e.* for each unit in the current layer, we update the related units in the previous layer.

Q.14. What is a confusion matrix or contingency table? What is its use?

Ans. In machine learning, a confusion matrix/contingency matrix is also known as an error matrix. It is a specific table layout that allows visualization of the performance of an algorithm, typically a supervised learning. The one in unsupervised learning is known as a matching matrix. Each column of the matrix represents the instances in a predicted class while each row represents the instances in an actual class or vice versa. Please note that the name stems from the fact that it makes it easy to see if the system is confusing two classes *i.e.* commonly mislabelling one as another. It is a special type of table with two dimensions-actual and predicted and identical set of classes in both the dimensions. So, each combination of dimension and class is a variable in the contingency table.

Q.15. Define the following terms:-

a. **Confusion matrix.**

b. **False positive rate.**

c. **True positive rate.**

Ans. *a.* Confusion matrix: A confusion matrix contains information about actual and predicted classifications done by a classification system. Performance of such systems is commonly evaluated using the data in the matrix. The following table shows the confusion matrix for a two class classifier. The entries in the confusion matrix have the following meaning in the context of our study:-

- ☐ *a* is the number of correct predictions that an instance is negative,
- ☐ *b* is the number of incorrect predictions that an instance is positive,
- ☐ *c* is the number of incorrect predictions that an instance is negative,
- ☐ *d* is the number of correct predictions that an instance is positive.

EXERCISE QUESTIONS

1. Explain *Q*-learning.
2. Explain value function in the context of reinforcement learning.
3. Explain Hidden Markov Model in detail.
4. Explain the back propagation algorithm of Multilayer Neural Network. Also explain the factor influencing back propagation training.
5. Explain SOMs.
6. What is delta rule?
7. Distinguish between perceptron and delta rule.
8. Why self organizing neural net is called as the topology preserving maps?
9. Distinguish between classification and regression.
10. State 'Universal Approximation Theorem'.
11. Define curse of dimensionality.
12. Define overfitting / overtraining.
13. Define cross validation.
14. Explain how optimization is achieved in neural networks.
15. 'Q learning agent learns optimal policy but much slower than ADP agent'. Explain this statement.
16. Draw flowchart to explain --Training a Deep Learning Model.
17. Explain the following- Test Sets and Validation Sets, Overfitting Phenomenon,Epoch,Training Data, Test Data, Hyperparameter Optimization, Critical Point, Local Maxima, Saddle Points, Learning Rate Adaptation.
18. Explain the following:-
    a. Markov Decision Processes [MDP].
    b. BELLMAN Equations.
    c. Value Iteration and Policy Iteration.
    d. Linear Quadratic Regulation (LQR).
19. Draw a fully connected feedforward ANN that has three input nodes, one output node and four internal nodes in a hidden layer.
20. Explain how would you represent the ages of a group of people ranging from 20 to 50 years as input into an ANN.

7 IOT and Machine Learning

Q.1. Define Internet-of-Things (IOT).

Ans. Several definitions of IOT exist in the literature. Some of them are listed here.

"A dynamic global network infrastructure with self-configuring capabilities based on standard and interoperable communication protocols where physical and virtual "things" have identities, physical attributes and use intelligent interfaces and are seamlessly integrated into the information network, to communicate data associated with users and their environments."

"IoT means physical and virtual objects that have unique identities and are connected to internet. This makes the development of intelligent applications better."

"IoT makes different types of devices users and machines to communicate and exchange data."

"Things" in IoT refers to IoT devices that have unique identities and allow remote sensing and remote monitoring.

Q.2. Narrate the Recent Trends in Various Learning Techniques of Machine Learning and Classification Methods for IOT Applications.

Ans. IOT or Internet-of-Things aims to make some sense of data that is generated. Algorithms are needed to find the data relationships for better business. This leads to the introduction of machine learning (ML). ML is central to IOT. Data collected by smart objects needs to be analysed and intelligent actions need to be taken based on these analyses. If this operation is done manually then it is very, very slow and inefficient. So, machines are needed to process information fast and react instantly when thresholds are met.

Commercial aviation industry and sensors that are deployed (an IOT example) generate deluge (flood) of data. Just one airplane can generate petabyte (PB) of data per day per commercial airplane. But all around the world, there are 100,000 commercial flights per day. So, amount of IOT data coming from them is very high. Big data problem is being exacerbated by IOT. Please note that analyzing this amount of data in most efficient manner possible falls under the umbrella of data analytics. Depending on how data is categorized, various data analytics tools and processing methods can be applied. Data may be-

a. Structured data (like spreadsheets, databases) or unstructured Data (like text, images, video, speech).

b. Data in motion versus Data at rest.

From an IOT perspective, data from smart objects is considered as data in motion as it passes through the network route to its final destination. This is often processed at the edge using fog computing. When data is processes at the edge, it may be filtered and deleted or forwarded on for further processing and possible storage at a fog node or in the data center. Data does not come to rest at the edge.

Machine learning is part of AI. AI includes any technology that allows a computer system to mimic human intelligence using any technique from the basic if-then-else" decision loops. Any computer that uses rules to make decisions belongs to this category. But in more complex cases, static rules cannot be simply inserted into the program because they require parameters that can change.

For example, a dictation program that runs on a computer. This program is configured to recognize the audio pattern of each word in a dictionary but it does not know your voice's specifics like your accent, tone, speed etc. You need to record a set of pre-determined sentences to help the tool match well-known words. This process is called as **machine learning (ML).** When the principles of ML are clear, the application of IOT becomes vital. The difficulty resides in determining the right algorithm and the right learning model for each use case. ML operations are put under two broad categories:-

1. **Local Learning:** In this group, data is collected and processed locally either in the sensor itself (the edge node) or in the gateway (the fog node).
2. **Remote Learning:** In this group, data is collected and sent to a central computing unit (like data center in the cloud)

where it is processed.

Machine Learning for IOT moves around four major domains:-

a. Monitoring.

b. Behaviour Control.

c. Operations Optimization.

d. Self-Healing, Self-Optimizing.

Monitoring : Smart objects monitor the environment where they operate. ML can be used with monitoring to detect early failure conditions.

Behavioural Control : Monitoring plus behaviour control work together. Monitoring functions generate an alarm when a given set of parameters reach a target threshold. It aims at taking corrective actions based on thresholds.

Operations Optimization : Analyses of data can also lead to changes that improve the overall process. For example, a water purification plant in a smart city can implement a system to monitor the efficiency of the purification process based on which chemical is used.

Solution: Neural Networks can combine multiples of such units in one or several layers, to estimate the best chemical. This intelligence can help the plant reduce its consumption of chemicals while still operating at the same purification efficiency level. Please note that as a result of learning, behaviour control results in different machine actions. The aim is not only to monitor the operations but to improve the efficiency and the result of these operations.

Self-healing, Self-optimizing : An important aspect of machine learning and hence deep learning is the closed loop. Machine learning based monitoring triggers changes in machine behaviour and operations optimizations. So, ML engine can be programmed to dynamically monitor and combine new parameters and automatically deduce new optimizations when results demonstrate a possible gain. So, the system becomes self-learning and self-optimizing. The system will self-heal.

NOTES:-

1. The ability to combine fog computing with cloud computing on data coming from multiple sources and rive global or local corrective actions is what makes ML so powerful for IOT.
2. With the expansion of smart objects, the possibilities of correlations and cross-optimizations being very wide.

When data from multiple systems is combined and analyzed together, predictions can be made about the state of the system. Such predictive analysis allows pre-emptive maintenance and increases the safety and efficiency of operations. For example, sensors combined with big data can anticipate defects or issues in vehicles operating in mines, in manufacturing machines or any system that can be monitored along with other similar systems.

Big data refers to unstructured data too that has been collected and stored in the cloud. The data is collected over time so that it can be analyzed through batch processing tools like RDBMS, Hadoop or other tools, so as to draw value from the data. Both Hadoop and MapReduce are good at tackling problems that need deep analytics on large and complex quantity of unstructured data. But they are not suitable for real-time analysis of data as it is generated. Then what is the solution?

Solution: Streaming analytics is used to continually monitor and assess data in real-time so that you can adjust or fine-tune your predictions as the race progresses.

Q.3. Explain the various Models for IOT Applications.

Ans. Let us first of all study the design methodology of IoT systems. Different steps and models so developed are shown in figure- 7.1.

IoT systems also have different phases for its development.

In first step, we define the purpose and the requirements of an IoT system. This is shown in figure 7.1.

In 2nd step, we define the Use Cases (showing functionality of the system).

In 3rd step, we define the physical entities, devices, resources and services in IoT system.

In 4th step, define the structure (e.g. relations and attributes) of all information in IoT system.

In 5th step, map process and information model to services.

In 6th step, define IoT level for system.

In 7th step, map IoT level to functional groups.

In 8th step, define communication options, storage options, device options.

In 9th step, integrate devices.

In 10th step, develop applications.

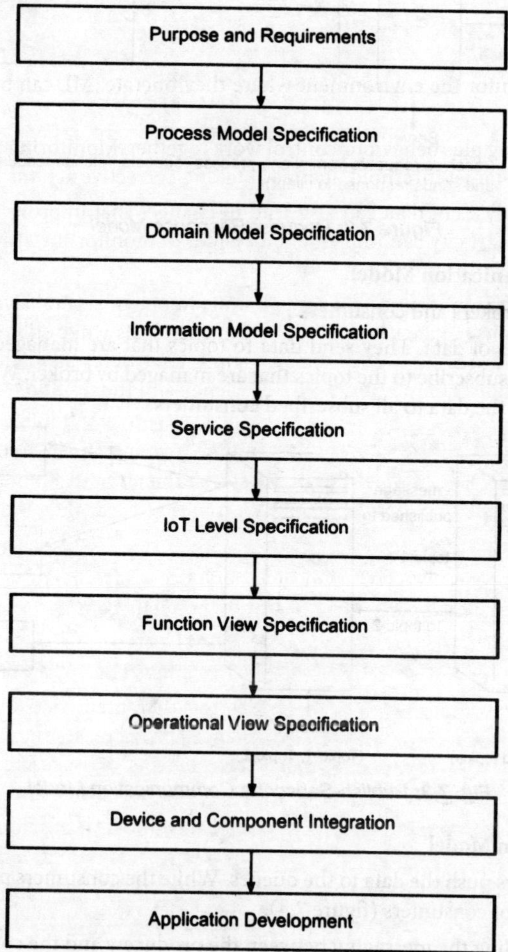

Fig. 7.1: Design Methodology of an IoT System

Q.4. Throw some light on IoT Communication Models

Ans. IoT communication models are broadly put under three categories: -

a. **Request** :Response Communication Model.

b. **Publish** : Subscribe Communication Model.

c. **Push** : Pull Communication Model.

a. **Request** : Response Communication Model

- It is a communication model in which client sends requests to the server. Server responds to requests.
- It is a stateless model of communication.
- Each request-response pair is independent of others.

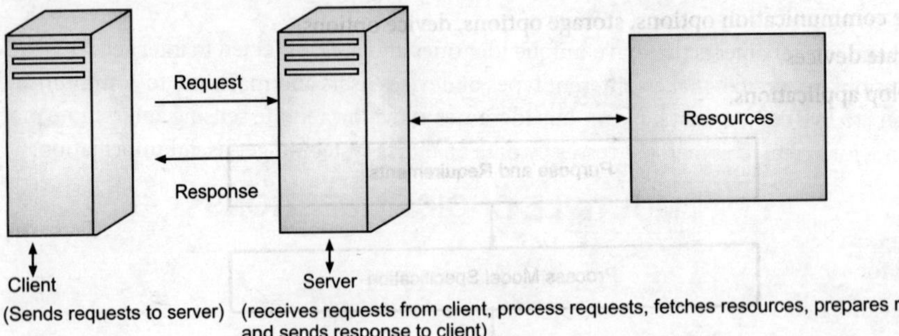

Figure 7.2: Request-Response Model

b. Publish-Subscribe Communication Model

- It involves publishers, brokers and consumers.
- **Publishers :** Are sources of data. They send data to topics that are managed by broker. They are not aware of consumers. Consumers subscribe to the topics that are managed by broker. When broker receives data for a topic from publisher, it sends the data to all subscribed consumers.

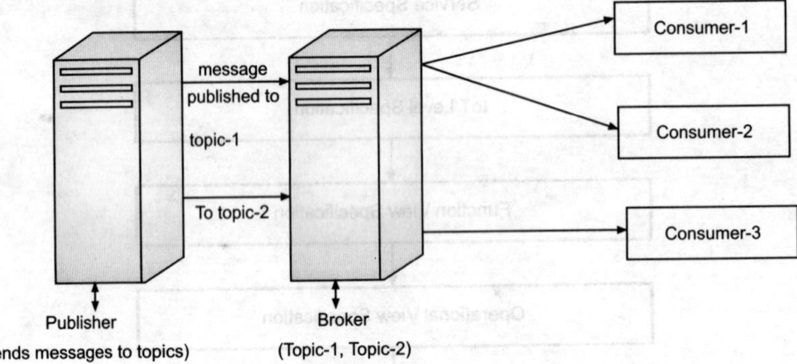

Fig. 7.3: Publish-Subscribe Communication Model

c. Push-Pull Communication Model

- Here, the data producers push the data to the queues. While the consumers pull data from the queues, producers don't need to be aware of consumers (figure 7.4).
- Queues help in decoupling the messaging between the producers and the consumers.
- Queues also act as buffer which helps in situations when there is a mismatch between the rate at which the producers push data and the rate at which the consumers pull data.

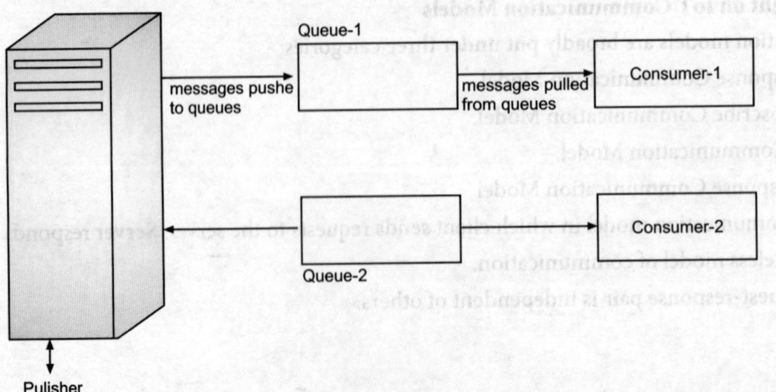

Figure 7.4: Push-Pull Communication Model

SUMMARY

IoT means physical and virtual objects that have unique identities and are connected to internet. This makes the development of intelligent applications better. IoT makes different types of devices users and machines to communicate and exchange data. "Things" in IoT refers to IoT devices that have unique identities and allow remote sensing and remote monitoring. IoT devices generate data in some form which is then processes by data analytics system to get useful information.

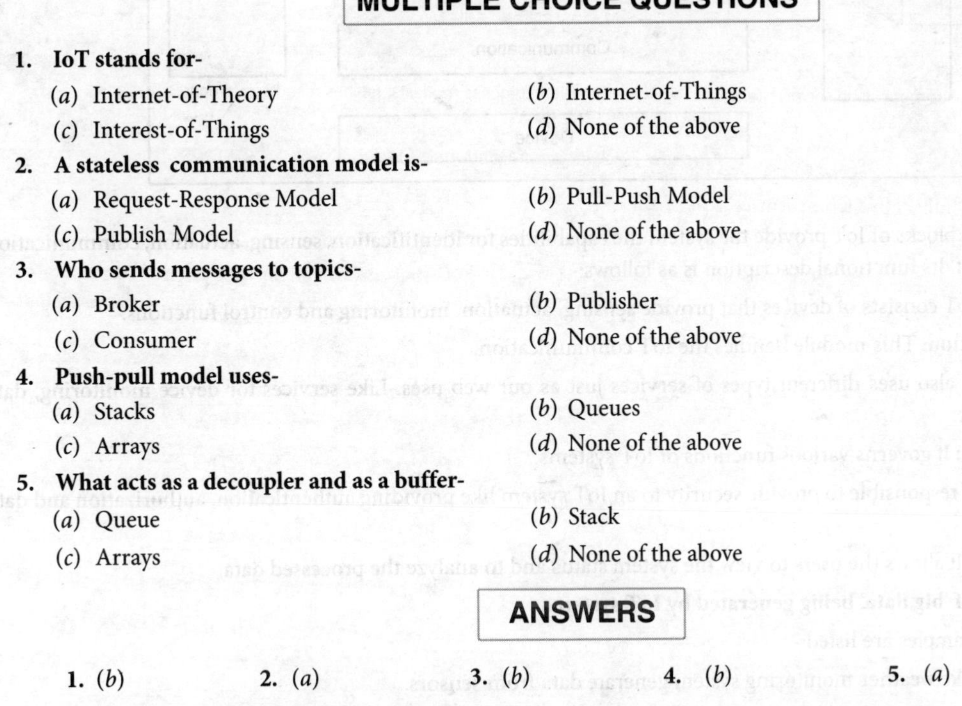

MULTIPLE CHOICE QUESTIONS

1. IoT stands for-

(*a*) Internet-of-Theory (*b*) Internet-of-Things

(*c*) Interest-of-Things (*d*) None of the above

2. A stateless communication model is-

(*a*) Request-Response Model (*b*) Pull-Push Model

(*c*) Publish Model (*d*) None of the above

3. Who sends messages to topics-

(*a*) Broker (*b*) Publisher

(*c*) Consumer (*d*) None of the above

4. Push-pull model uses-

(*a*) Stacks (*b*) Queues

(*c*) Arrays (*d*) None of the above

5. What acts as a decoupler and as a buffer-

(*a*) Queue (*b*) Stack

(*c*) Arrays (*d*) None of the above

ANSWERS

1. (*b*) **2.** (*a*) **3.** (*b*) **4.** (*b*) **5.** (*a*)

CONCEPTUAL SHORT QUESTIONS WITH ANSWERS

Q.1. Define IoT.

Ans. "A dynamic global network infrastructure with self-configuring capabilities based on standard and interoperable communication protocols where physical and virtual "things" have identities, physical attributes and use intelligent interfaces and are seamlessly integrated into the information network, to communicate data associated with users and their environments."

Q.2. Give some characteristics of IoT.

Ans. Some of the features of IoT are as follows:-

1. Dynamic and self adapting.
2. Self-configuring capable.
3. Interoperable communication protocols.
4. Unique identity of IoT devices.
5. Integrated into Information network for communication of data with other devices and systems.

Q.3. What does the term 'Things' represent in IoT?

Ans. The "Things" in IoT refers to IoT devices that have unique identities and can perform remote sensing, actuating and monitoring tasks.

Q.4. Explain the functional units of IoT.

Ans. The functional blocks of an IoT system are shown in the diagram below:-

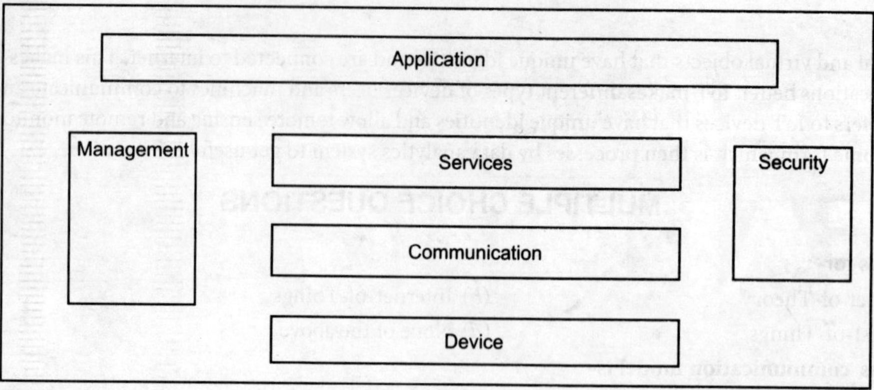

These functional blocks of IoT provide the system the capabilities for identification, sensing, actuation, communication and management. Its functional description is as follows:-

a. **Device:** An IoT consists of devices that provide sensing, actuation, monitoring and control functions.

b. **Communication:** This module handles the IoT communication.

c. **Services:** IoT also uses different types of services just as our web uses. Like services for device monitoring, data publishing etc.

d. **Management:** It governs various functions of IoT systems.

e. **Security:** It is responsible to provide security to an IoT system like providing authentication, authorization and data security.

f. **Application:** It allows the users to view the system status and to analyze the processed data.

Q.5. Give examples of 'big data' being generated by IoT systems.

Ans. The following examples are listed:-

1. IoT systems like weather monitoring system generate data from sensors.
2. Health data generated by IoT devices.
3. Vehicle tracking IoT system also generate data.
4. Retail inventory monitoring systems also generate vast amount of data.
5. Machine data collected from sensors.

EXERCISE QUESTIONS

1. Define IoT systems. Give its features. Also give some examples.
2. How are big data and IoT systems related?
3. Discuss with a neat diagram the functional parts of any IoT system.
4. Discuss with neat diagrams the 3 communication models used by IoT.
5. What does the word 'thing' refers to in IoT.
6. Discuss the design methodology of an IoT system with a flowchart.
7. Give an example of an IoT system in which information and knowledge are inferred from data.
8. Why should IoT systems be self-adapting and self-Configuring?
9. How are IoT, machine learning and deep learning inter-related?
10. What is streaming analytics? Why is it Useful?

UNIT-III

DEEP LEARNING

1 The Neural Network (Deep Learning)

Q.1. Define Deep Learning.

Ans. Deep learning and Big Data are inter-related. Big data refers to the pools of data being generated every second while deep learning is an active research area in the field of machine learning. But as the data is growing at an exponential rate, deep learning is providing big data predictive analytical solutions. According to the report of National Security Agency (NSA), the Internet itself is processing 1,826 Petabytes of data per day [1]. By 2020, the figure will reach 35 Trillion gigabytes. This leads to a remarkable paradigm shift in computer science literature towards data-driven discovery. Today machine learning techniques and newer software, hardware and computational power help in big data as well as web data analytics.

We need to define Deep Learning now.

Deep learning is defined as the machine learning techniques that use supervised and/or unsupervised methods to automatically learn hierarchical representations in deep architectures for classification.

Or

Deep learning is a subset of artificial intelligence field called as machine learning which is predicted on the basic idea of learning from example.

In machine learning, instead of teaching a computer a massive list of rules to solve the complex problem, we give it a model with which it can evaluate examples. Also, we give it a small set of instructions to modify the model when it makes a mistake. Please note that we have an expectation that as the time passes, a well-suited model would be able to solve the problem more accurately.

For example, say our model is defined by a function $f(x, \theta)$. The input x is an example expressed in vector form. Like, if x were a gray-scale image, the vector's components would be pixel intensities at each position. The input θ is a vector of the parameters that our model uses. Also note now that it is our machine learning program that tries to perfect the values of these parameters as it is exposed to more and more examples.

The conventional learning methods are shallow-structured learning architectures while deep learning is deep-hierarchical levelled learning architecture. It is based on the biological neurons within human brain. Several research domains like speech recognition, Natural Language Processing (NLP), collaborative filtering and computer vision. Big industry giants like Google, Apple and Facebook who work on sheer size of data lakes today have also given vital importance to Big Data Analytics and Web Data Analytics. Google applies deep learning algorithms to massive chunks of messy data obtained from Internet. IBMs brain-like computer uses techniques like deep learning to make available big data available for its betterment. Please note that as the data keeps increasing at an exponential rate, deep learning is playing a key role in providing in big data and web analytics. Also note that deep learning refers to a set of machine learning techniques that learn multiple levels of representations in deep architectures. Deep learning is the new name for neural networks. Deep learning algorithms have best performance as far as complex problems like pattern recognition are concerned. Practically speaking, even machine learning approaches find it difficult to solve. Theoretically, they can solve any problem. Several libraries also exist for neural nets or deep learning. But deep learning algorithms as an auto-encoder i.e. unsupervised deep learning, several parameters and slower deep learning grids are some of the issues to be discussed in this text. These programs may need more hardware.

The information that is available on the web and is searched using search engines like Google is called as the surface web. On the other hand, deep web consists of data hidden behind web-based services. Theoretically, the deluge (flood) of data within deep web is exponentially high. Practically, useful information hidden in deep web is finite but very large. Each web form can give rise to thousands of results, each of which qualifies as a deep web page. Similarly, every Facebook or Twitter post might be considered as a deep web page. Finally, if one considers all possible pages of search results then the size of deep web is infinite. As per the survey report (2007), roughly 2.5% of random sample of web pages were forms that should be considered as part of deep web. Please understand that deep web is huge, far larger than the indexed web of 50 billion pages. Searching the deep web is current research area today.

Let us explore this and many more interesting topics in this book.

Q.2. Define what are neurons?

Ans. We define a neuron first of all. A neuron is a function that takes multiple numeric inputs and gives out one numeric output. These neurons are organized in layers and the outputs from all of the neurons in one layer become the inputs for each neuron in the next layer.

The functional unit of a normal human brain is the neuron. The objective book is to use this natural brain concept to build machine learning models that solve problems in a similar fashion. A neuron is optimized to receive information from other neurons, process this information and send its results to other cells. This is shown in figure-1.1 as follows:-

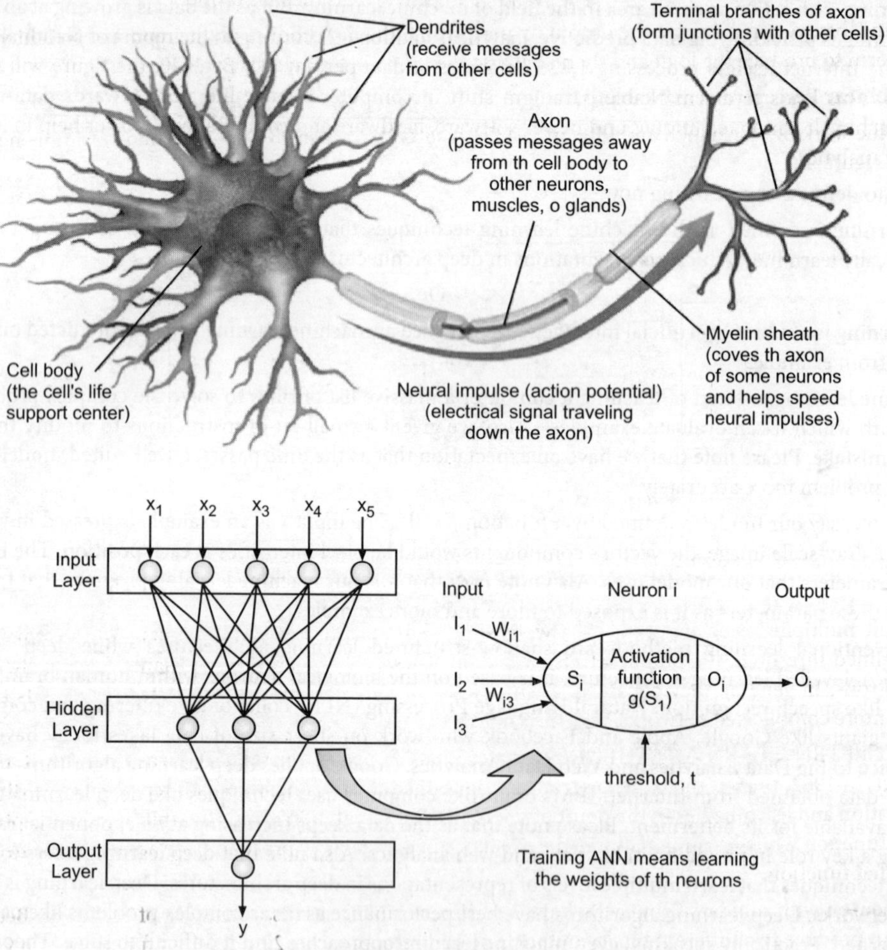

Fig.1.1: A Neuron

The neuron receives its inputs along antennae-like structures called dendrites. Each of these incoming connections is dynamically strengthened or weakened based on how often it is used. Please understand that it is the strength of each connection that determines the contribution of the input to the neuron's output. After being weighted by the strength of their respective connections, the inputs are summed together in the cell body. Also understand that this sum is then transformed into a new signal that is propagated along the cell's axon and sent to other neurons.

In 1943, W. S. McCulloch and W. H. Pitts gave an artificial model that can be well represented on a computer. Just as in biological neurons, this artificial neuron takes in some number of inputs, $x_1, x_2, \ldots\ldots, x_n$. Each of this input is multiplied by a specific weight, $w_1, w_2, \ldots\ldots, w_n$. Then these weighted inputs are summed together to produce the logit of the neuron i.e.

$$z = \Sigma\,(i = 0 \text{ to } n)\ w_i x_i$$

in many cases, the logit also includes a bias, which is a constant. Then the logit is paaed through a function, f, to produce the output-

$$y = f(z)$$

This output can be transmitted to other neurons.

Mathematically, in vector form-

If inputs are as a vector $x = [x_1\ x_2 \ldots\ldots x_n]$ and the weights of the neuron as $w = [w_1 w_2 \ldots\ldots w_n]$ then we can express the output of the neuron as follows:-

$$y = f(x \,.\, w + b), \text{ where 'b' is the bias term.}$$

This means that we can compute the output by performing the dot product of the input and weight vectors, adding in the bias term to produce the logit and then applying the transformation function.

Q.3. Explain Linear Perceptrons as Neurons.

Ans. Much of the work of McCulloch and Pitts in 1943 and subsequently in 1947 was based on a simple neuron model. It is shown in figure-1.2.

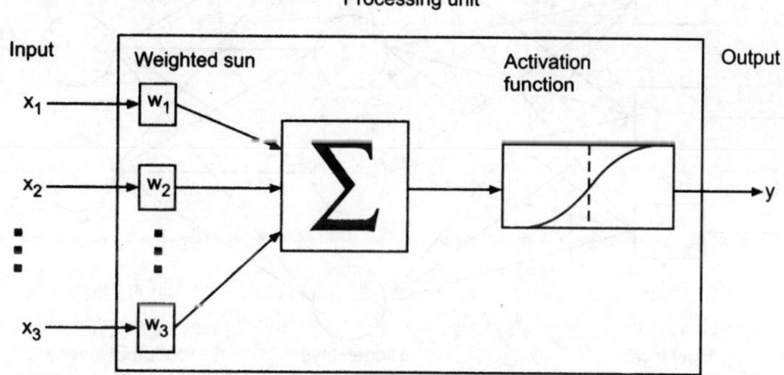

Fig. 1.2: Perceptron Neuron

The Σ unit multiplies each input, x, by a weight, w, and sums the weighted inputs. If this sum is greater than a predetermined threshold, the output =1 else it is zero. These systems and their variants collectively have been called as perceptrons. In general, they consist of a single layer of artificial neurons connected by weights to a set of inputs although more complicated networks bear the same.

The PERCEPTRN LEARNING THEOREM states that-"A perceptron could learn anything it could represent." Rosenblatt, in 1962, proved that a perceptron can be trained to any function it can represent. The difference between representation and learning lies in the point of reference. Representation means the ability of a perceptron to simulate a specified function while learning requires the existence of a systematic procedure for adjusting the network weights to produce that function.

Note: A neuron with n binary inputs can have 2^n different input patterns, consisting of 1s and 0s. Because each input pattern can produce two different binary output, one and zero, there are 22^n different functions of n variables.

Learning is of two types- Supervised and Unsupervised. Supervised learning needs an external "teacher" that evaluates the behaviour of the system and directs the subsequent modifications. On the other hand, unsupervised learning needs "no teacher" as the network self-organizes to produce the desired changes. Please note here that the Perceptron learning is of the supervised type. The perceptron training algorithm can be implemented on a system and the network becomes self adjusting. This is reason as to why adjusting of weights is called as training and the network is said to learn.

Rosenblatt's proof was a major milestone and it provided a great impetus to the research field. Also note that a perceptron is trained by representing a set of patterns to its input, one at a time and adjusting the weights until the desired output occurs for each of them.

Linear perceptron and the neuron model are somewhat equivalent. But the point to ponder is that every linear perceptron can be expressed as a single neuron but single neurons can also express models that cannot be expressed by any linear perceptron.

Q.4. What are Neural Nets? Give its architecture. With a neat diagram explain its working.

Ans. We have already defined what a neuron is. These neurons are organized into layers. The outputs from all the neurons in one layer become the inputs for each neuron in the next layer.

Architecture/ Design : As shown in figure-1.3, the first layer is your data (inputs) that may be a training sample or a test sample or real inputs. The very last layer is your output (answer). Two cases arise:-

Case-1: If you are doing a regression i.e. learning a single value then the output layer will have one neuron.

Case-2: If you are doing classification, then the output layer will have one neuron for each possible answer. Here, the output (answer) with the highest probability for the set of inputs is chosen.

The layers between the input layers and the output layers are called as the hidden layers.

Rule: "Each neuron in each hidden layer has a weight for each of its inputs and modifying those weights is how the network learns. There is a bias input to each neuron, (a weight only) connected to a constant input and is also tuned during the training process."

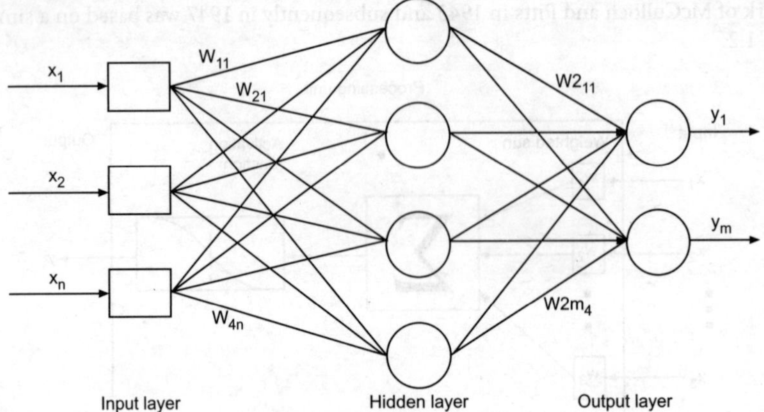

Fig. 1.3: Neural Nets

Working of Neural Nets : As shown in figure 1.3, we start with random weights. Then we give it the first training sample and the correct answer (also called as supervised learning), calculate the error and then use that to go back and tweak each of the weights so that there is a bit less error. This process is called as backpropagation. Then we take the second training sample and repeat the process. This process of taking each and every training data is called as an **epoch**. Also note that we specify the number of epochs in the algorithm that we develop. Also note that even fractional epochs are allowed. **For example,** requesting 20.5 epochs means all training data samples are processed 20 times while the first half of the training data is also processed an 11th time.

Many deep learning libraries use the concept of mini batches. A mini-batch of say, size 20 means that it will process 20 training samples then go back and update the weights in one batch. But deep learning libraries like H_2O does not use mini-batch concept in H_2O the weights get updated after every single sample.

If it is a multimode cluster then each node in the cluster works independently for one iteration. At the end of each iteration, the network weights are averaged with those on every node. Also note that one iteration can be larger or smaller than an epoch.

Note: Everything is a number in neural net. For example, in digit recognition problem there will be one neuron per pixel and the value will be the intensity of that pixel.

Q.5. Explain different Layers of Neural Networks and Deep learning.

Ans. In theory, one hidden layer is sufficient to represent all of our data whether linear or non-linear relationships but practically speaking it is not enough to have entire data in one layer.

Please understand that having many hidden layers is deep learning but more layers/neurons means longer training and slower usage. Many researchers say that it is not deep learning if we have just one hidden layer only.

How to choose the number of layers and neurons in a neural net?

There are six (rules) rules of thumb to select the number of layers and neurons:-

Rule-1: If the problem is non-linear then we start with two (2) layers and observe how it performs on it.

Rule-2: More non-linear is the problem, the more layers you need. If you observe that the problem is not getting solved, then add another layer to it and try. You can also try with more epochs, more training data. It has been observed that if you have moved till 5-layers then the 6th layer probably will not help.

Rule-3: More are the number of neurons in a layer, the more clearly it will be able to understand the data. You can add more neurons or more epochs or more training data.

Rule-4: More data inputs you have, the more neurons are needed in the first hidden layer.

Rule-5: More output neurons you have, the more neurons you are likely to need in the final hidden layer.

Rule-6: More are the layers, more will be the benefit from activation functions (to be discussed).

The time spent in training a deep learning model is given by the formula:-

Training Time (TT) = [Number of training samples] * [Number of Epochs]

How much training is required depends on the weights in our model. Please note that more are the weights, more can be learned from the model.

The number of weights between two layers is given by the formula:-

Weights (W) = [Number of Neurons in layer-1] * [Number of Neurons in layer-2]

Also note that you will also have to count two more layers: the input layer and the output layer.

For example, in a 50*50 network, with 2 numeric inputs and 1 output, there are:-

$(2*50) + (50 * 50) + (50 * 1) = 100 + 2500 + 50 = 2650$ weights.

Now, say, you add another 3rd layer with 50 neurons, then we can compute weights required as follows:-

$(2 * 50) + (50 * 50) + (50 * 50) + (50 * 1) = 100 + 2500 + 2500 + 50 = 5150$ weights.

It has been observed that if more are the weights, slower is the training.

Researchers say that deep learning is a new AI that can tell whether our tweets are sarcastic (abusive) or not. Scientists at Massachusetts Institute of Technology (MIT) USA have developed a new artificial system that can detect sarcasm in tweets better than humans. It's developers say that this advancement may help computers automatically spot and remove online hate speech and abusive comments. Detecting the sentiments of social media posts can also help gauge attitudes towards brands and products and identify signals that might indicate trends in the financial markets. Please note that they said that a deeper understanding of Twitter may also help understand how information and influence flows through the network. The researchers originally aimed to develop a system capable of detecting racist posts on Twitter. However, the meaning of many messages could not be properly understood without some understanding of sarcasm. Also note that the algorithm uses deep learning, a popular machine learning technique that relies on training a very large simulated neural network to recognise subtle patterns using a large amount of data. Researchers took advantage of emoji to help the algorithm identify and label emotional content.

According to the report of "MIT Technology Review", 2017, once the system read tweets for emotions, the researchers taught it to recognise sarcasm. According to MIT, the neural network learned the connection between a certain kind of language and an emoji.

Q.6. What are the Activation Functions? Explain.

Ans. In figure-1.1, it was observed that a neuron has many weighted inputs coming in and one output going out. The inputs are summed. The value of the output is decided by the activation functions.

For examples,

Rectifier, outputs the sum of its weighted inputs but clips all negative values to zero. This implies that it will be generating quite a few zeros as zeros are good for training deeper networks but also means that positive values are unbounded.

Tanh, takes as input range of negative infinity to positive infinity. It converts that to an output range of –1 to +1. Note that it varies more rapidly when the sum of inputs is closer to zero.

Maxout, gives the maximum of the inputs. It means that the weighted inputs are used directly and not summed up.

Q.7. What are Feed Forward Neural Networks? What are their limitations?

Ans. Single neurons are better and more powerful than linear perceptrons yet they are not very effective to solve complex problems. Just as our brain is made of many neurons so should be artificial neurons. In normal human brain, there are six layers. The information flows from one layer to another layer. The sensory input is converted into conceptual understanding. For instance, the bottommost layer of our brain receives raw data from our eyes. This information is the processed by each layer and passed on to the next layer and finally to the 6th layer. It is then we conclude that whether we are looking at a car or a bike. Our artificial neural network is analogous to this. A neural network is formed when we start attaching neurons to each other, the input data and to the output nodes. This corresponds to the network's answer to a learning problem. A simple three layer (or 3-tier) feed forward network is shown in figure 1.5:-

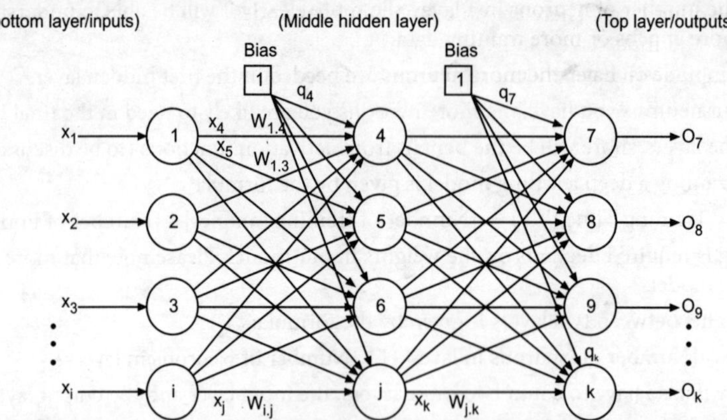

Fig. 1.4: Three-layer Feed- Forward Neural Network with inputs, 3 Hidden Layers, Outputs and Bias

Explanation: The network of neurons as shown in figure 1.5 is similar to the architecture given by McCulloch and Pitt in 1943. The bottom layer of the network takes the input data. The top layer of neurons or output nodes computes the final answer. The middle layer(*s*) of neurons are called as hidden layers. Now,

if $W_{ij}(k)$ is the weight of connection between the ith neuron in the kth layer with the jth neuron in the k+1st layer; then these weights constitute a parameter vector, θ. And our ability to solve the problem with neural networks concept will depend on finding the optimal values of this parameter θ. Please note that the connections traverse from a lower layer to a higher layer and there are no connections between neurons in the same layer. Also note that there are no connections that transmit data from a higher layer to a lower layer. These types of neural networks are called as feed-forward networks. These networks are simple to analyse.

Before we discuss further, note down the following points: -

1. It is the hidden layer where actually the problem is being solved by our neural network. Hidden layers automate the process.
2. Hidden layers have fewer neurons than the input layer. Although input is taken from bottom layers yet hidden layers come up with better presentations for everything in output.
3. Every layer may or may not have the same number of neurons.
4. It is not mandatory that every neuron has its output connected to the inputs of all neurons in the next layer. It comes from experience only.
5. The inputs and outputs here are vectorized representations.

Limitations of Neurons : Any feed-forward neural network consisting of only linear neurons can be represented as a network with no hidden layers. This is an issue as hidden layers are the main processers of the input data. This implies that to learn complicated relationships, we need to use neurons that employ some sort of non-linearity too.

Q.8. Explain Deep Belief Networks (DBNs).

Ans. To reduce the problems of conventional neural networks, a Deep Belief Network (DBN) uses a deep architecture that is capable of learning feature representations using both labelled and unlabelled big data. It incorporates both unsupervised pre-training and supervised fine-tuning techniques to construct models. Unsupervised pre-training tends to learn data distributions without using label information and supervised stages perform local search for fine tuning.

A DBM also comprises of a stack of a stack of Restricted Boltzmann Machines (RBM) that can effectively utilize large amounts of unlabelled data for exploring complex data structures. After DBN structure is determined, the goal for training is to learn the weights and biases between the layers. Firstly, unsupervised learning of RBMs is done. A typical RBM consists of two layers *i.e.* nodes in one layer are fully connected to the nodes in the other layer. There is no connection for nodes in the same layer. This is shown in figure 1.6.

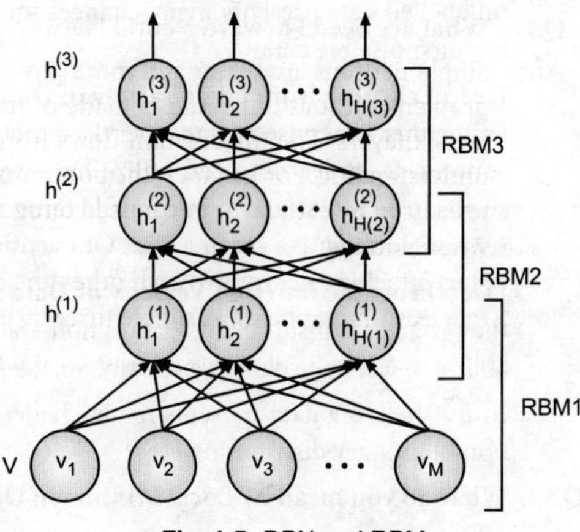

Fig. 1.5: DBN and RBM

It is shown in figure 1.6 that nodes in one layer are fully connected to the nodes in the other layer. There are no connections for nodes in the same layer. The input layer and the first hidden layer H1 form a RBM. Each node is independent of the nodes in the same layer. Before fine-tuning, a layer by layer pre-training of RBM is performed. The outputs of a RBM are fed as inputs to the next RBM and the process is repeated until all RBMs are pre-trained. This is layer by layer unsupervised learning. Please note that after pre-training information about the input data is stored in weights between every adjacent layers. Also note that DBNs use a greedy and efficient layer by layer approach to learn the latent variables/weights in each hidden layer and a back propagation method for fine-tuning. So this hybrid training method improves both the generative performance and the discriminative power of the network.

Q.9. What are Large Scale DBNs?

Ans. To reduce the data transfer times between host and global memory and to allow parameter updates, one technique is to store all parameters and a large chunk of training examples in global memory during training. This shows the reusing of large chunks of training examples.

Q.10. Explain the Large Scale Convolutional Neural Networks.

Ans. Locally connected deep learning method is Convolutional Neural Networks (CNNs). Large scale CNNs learning is implemented on parallel processors. CNN training involves both forward and backward propagation. For these one or more blocks are assigned for each feature map. Each thread in a block is shows a single neuron in a map. The computation of each neuron with the neurons from the previous layers, activation and summation is then performed. Finally, the outputs are stored in the global memory. Also, the weights are updated by back-propagation of errors. Parallelizing backward propagation can be implemented either by pulling or pushing. Pulling error signals is the process of computing delta signals for each neuron in the previous layer by pulling the error signals from the current layer. This is quite complex. On the other hand, pushing the error signals from the current layer to the previous layer is more efficient. That is, for each unit in the current layer, we update the related units in the previous layer.

Note: To implement data parallelism, we need to consider two things:-

a. The size of global memory.

b. The feature map size.

Q.11. Relate Deep Learning for Big Data.

Ans. Big data is at the core of our society today. The need is to process yottabytes (a billion petabytes) of data. Traditional machine learning algorithms are not sufficient as they were designed for data that could be stored in memory. But today data is "big". So, algorithms that can learn from massive amount of data are required now. Large scale deep learning is still in its infancy.

Deep Learning from High Volumes of Data : The data pool available today is a major challenge for deep learning today. The sheer volume of data results in run –time complexity and model complexity. These data lakes often make it impossible to train a deep learning algorithm with a central processor and storage. Hence, distributed machines and parallel machines are preferred. In nutshell, in order to build the future deep learning system scalable to Big Data, we need to develop high performance computing infrastructure-based systems. Also we need parallel learning algorithms now.

Another problem with these data lakes is that it results in data incompleteness and noisy labels. One of the features of deep learning algorithms is that they have the ability to use unlabelled data during training. So, the presence of large unlabelled data presents many chances for deep learning methods. Advanced deep learning methods are required to handle noisy big data.

Deep Learning from High Variety of Data : One advantage of deep learning is its ability of representational learning with either supervised or unsupervised methods or their combinations. Deep learning can integrate data from different sources. Deep learning can utilize heterogeneous sources for better system performance. In nutshell, deep learning seems to be well suited to integrate heterogeneous data with multiple modalities due to its capability of learning abstract representations.

Deep Learning for High Velocity of Data : Conventional neural networks have been used for online learning but still the progress is insufficient. Data is non-stationary i.e. it changes over time. Deep learning algorithm for big data is the ability to learn the data as a stream. So, deep online learning is yet to be explored.

In nutshell, big data presents many challenges to deep learning including large scale, heterogeneity, noisy labels and non-stationary distribution etc.

Q.12. What do you mean by Local Minima in Deep Networks?

Ans. The main issue in optimizing deep learning models is that we are now compelled to use minimal local information to infer global structure of the error surface. But this is not easy because the correspondence between local and global structure is quite less.

The first source of local minima is related to the term model identifiability. It has been observed that the error surface of deep neural networks is very large and sometimes infinite too. So, they have many local minima(s).

Q.13. Define the process of Rearranging Neurons in a layer of a Neural Network.

Ans. It has been observed that within a layer of a fully-connected feed-forward neural network, any rearrangement of neurons will still give us the same result (final output) at the end of the network. Also note that if a layer has n neurons then there are n! ways to rearrange the parameters. But if it is a deep layered network, then with k layers, each with n neurons, we will have a total of n!k equivalent (similar) configurations.

Here, local minima is not a problem. Bit local minima are a problem if and only if they are spurious. We say that a local-minima is spurious refers to those weights in neural network that incurs a higher error rate than at the global minima.

Q.14. What do you mean by Spurious Local Minima in Deep Networks?

Ans. Researchers of deep learning say that it is difficult to train deep networks on spurious local minima. The point is that in practical neural networks spurious local minima and global minima have higher error rates. Some researchers say that most local minima have error rates similar to the global minima.

Given any function, a point at which the gradient is a zero vector is known as a critical point. Actually, local maxima do not cause much of the problems. The flat regions of the curve that are more trouble causing and informal are called as saddle points. Research shows that as our function adds up more and more parameters i.e. we have more and more parameters in our model, then saddle points rise exponentially than local minima. In one dimensional subspace, a critical point can come in three different types and hence the probability that the random critical point is in a random function is $1/3^d$.

Note:

1. If we have a total of '*k*' critical points, then we will have a total of *k*/3 local minima.
2. A random function with '*p*' critical points has an expected number of $p/3^d$.

SUMMARY

In biological organisms, knowledge is stored as complex structures of interconnected neurons. The structures correspond to symbolic representations of the knowledge possessed by the organism, the facts, the rules and so on. Please note that an average human brain weighs about 3.3 pounds and contains an estimated number of 1012 neurons. Also note that these neurons and their interconnection capabilities provide about 1014 bits of potential storage capacity. Artificial neural networks are not a panacea. They are unsuitable for tasks like payroll calculations. Backpropagation uses gradient descent to adjust the network weights. This is fine with convex error surfaces as they have a unique minimum. But it results in non-optimal solutions with non-convex surfaces. In some scenarios, a local minimum is acceptable as a solution but in some it is inadequate.

Even if the network is trained yet there is no way to depict that this backpropagation algorithm has found the global minimum. Also understand that if the solution is unsatisfactory, we must re-initialize the weights to new random values and re-train the network. But there is no guarantee that a global minima will be found. One has to take care as far as weight selection is concerned. This may result in network paralysis.

In this chapter we have seen the basic neuron structure and the working of feed-forward networks. Also observed is the problem of non-linearity in solving complex learning problems.

MULTIPLE CHOICE QUESTIONS

1. **Machine learning includes-**
   (*a*) Narrow Learning (*b*) Deep Learning
   (*c*) Varied Learning (*d*) None of the above
2. **A subset of artificial intelligence field called as machine learning which is predicted on the basic idea of learning from example is named as-**
   (*a*) Learning by Examples (*b*) Learning by Machine
   (*c*) Deep Learning (*d*) None of the above
3. **RBM stands for-**
   (*a*) Restricted Boltzmann Machines (*b*) Regular Boltzmann Memory
   (*c*) Referred Boltzmann Machine (*d*) None of the above.
4. **Deep Belief Networks use-**
   (*a*) RBM (*b*) DBMS
   (*c*) IBM (*d*) None of the above
5. **The time spent in training a deep learning model is given by the formula:-**
   (*a*) Training Time (TT) = [Number of training samples] + [Number of Epochs]
   (*b*) Training Time (TT) = [Number of training samples] - [Number of Epochs]
   (*c*) Training Time (TT) = [Number of training samples] * [Number of Epochs]
   (*d*) Training Time (TT) = [Number of training samples] / [Number of Epochs]
6. **The more are the weights-**
   (*a*) Slower will be the training (*b*) Faster will be the training
   (*c*) Lesser will be the training (*d*) None of the above
7. **Which of the following is a rectification function-**
   (*a*) Rectifier (*b*) Amplifier
   (*c*) Simplifierd (*d*) None of the above
8. **The working of ANNs is similar to-**
   (*a*) A human brain (*b*) A car working
   (*c*) A human eye (*d*) None of the above
9. **Even a tiny part of the brain that is about the size of a grain of rice has-**
   (*a*) 5000 neurons (*b*) 6000 neurons
   (*c*) 10,000 neurons (*d*) None of the above
10. **Connections traverse from-**
    (*a*) Lower to higher layer (*b*) Higher to lower layer
    (*c*) At same layer (*d*) None of the above.
11. **As we make neural networks deep, which phenomenon is seen-**
    (*a*) Overloading (*b*) Overriding
    (*c*) Overfitting (*d*) None of the above

12. A single iteration over the entire training set is called as an-

(*a*) Epoch (*b*) Clock

(*c*) Cycle (*d*) None of the above

13. The data is split up into two parts-

(*a*) Training data and valid data (*b*) Training data and test data

(*c*) Training data and big data (*d*) None of the above

14. At the end of each epoch, we must see that-

(*a*) Error is increasing (*b*) Error is decreasing

(*c*) Error is static (*d*) None of the above

15. One of the methods of overcoming 'overfitting' phenomenon is called as-

(*a*) Regularization (*b*) Segmentation

(*c*) Fragmentation (*d*) None of the above

16. Deep learning is also called as-

(*a*) Feature learning (*b*) Representation learning

(*c*) Example based learning (*d*) Only (*a*) and (*b*)

17. An artificial neural network used for learning efficient coding is-

(*a*) Auto-encoder (*b*) Decoder

(*c*) Encoder (*d*) None of the above

18. Deep learning is useful as-

(*a*) Non-linear function can be represented in a better way

(*b*) Linear function can be represented in a better way

(*c*) Polynomial function can be represented in a better way

(*d*) None of the above

19. A systematic method for training multilayer ANN is named as-

(*a*) Forward-propagation (*b*) Backpropagation

(*c*) Error propagation (*d*) None of the above

20. If we want to train the network to recognize all letters of the alphabet then we need-

(*a*) 20 training pairs (*b*) 26 training pairs

(*c*) 30 training pairs (*d*) None of the above

21. A group of training pairs is called as-

(*a*) Training set (*b*) Working set

(*c*) Logical set (*d*) None of the above

22. A neuron with n binary inputs can have-

(*a*) 2^n input patterns (*b*) 2^n input patterns

(*c*) $n/2$ input patterns (*d*) None of the above

23. Each input pattern can produce-

(*a*) Two binary inputs (1s and 0s) (*b*) 2^n inputs

(*c*) 2^n inputs (*d*) None of the above

24. In a 50*50 network, with 2 numeric inputs and 1 output, there are:-

(*a*) 2650 weights (*b*) 3650 weights

(*c*) 4300 weights (*d*) None of the above

25. If we have a total of '*k*' critical points, then we will have a total of-

(*a*) $k/3$ local minima (*b*) $k/2$ local minima

(*c*) $k * 3$ local minima (*d*) None of the above

ANSWERS

1. (*b*)	**2.** (*c*)	**3.** (*a*)	**4.** (*a*)	**5.** (*c*)
6. (*a*)	**7.** (*a*)	**8.** (*a*)	**9.** (*c*)	**10.** (*a*)
11. (*c*)	**12.** (*a*)	**13.** (*b*)	**14.** (*b*)	**15.** (*a*)
16. (*d*)	**17.** (*a*)	**18.** (*a*)	**19.** (*b*)	**20.** (*b*)
21. (*a*)	**22.** (*a*)	**23.** (*a*)	**24.** (*a*)	**25.** (*a*)

CONCEPTUAL SHORT QUESTIONS WITH ANSWERS

Q.1. Define deep learning.

Ans. It is defined as a set of machine learning algorithms which attempt to learn multiple-layered models of inputs (neural networks). They are composed of multiple levels of non-linear operations. The core concept of deep learning is a greedy layerwise unsupervised pre-training that is to learn a hierarchy of features one level at a time.

Q.2. What is an auto-encoder?

Ans. An auto-encoder is an artificial neural network used for learning efficient coding. The objective is to learn a compressed representation /encoding for a data set. This means that it was being used for dimensionality reduction or data compression.

Q.3. What are the advantages of deep learning?

Ans. Deep learning has the following advantages:-

1. Non-linear functions can be represented in a more efficient manner.
2. Deep representations may allow for a hierarchical representations that allow for combinatorial sharing of statistical strength.

Q.4. Define transfer learning.

Ans. It is defined as the ability of a learning algorithm to explore commonalties between different learning tasks in order to transfer knowledge across different tasks.

Q.5. Compare conventional learning methods with deep learning methods.

Ans. Conventional learning methods use shallow-structured learning architectures. On the other hand, deep learning refers to machine learning techniques that use supervised and/or unsupervised methods to learn hierarchical representations in deep architectures.

Q.6. Big data presents many challenges to deep learning. List some of them.

Ans. Big data challenges to deep learning are as follows:-

- Large scale data.
- Heterogeneity of data.
- Noisy labels.
- Non-stationary distribution.

Q.7. How are deep learning, AI and machine learning inter-related?

Ans. Deep learning is a subset of Artificial Intelligence (AI) branch called as machine learning. In machine learning, we do not teach a computer a huge list of rules to solve a problem rather we give it a model so that it can evaluate examples and a small set of instructions to modify the model when it makes mistakes. Please understand here that we expect that as the time passes, a suitable model would be able to solve the problem more efficiently.

Q.8. Define what is training?

Ans. Training is the process in which we show the neural network large number of training examples and then iteratively modify the weights to minimize the errors we make on the training examples.

Q.9. What causes the problem of overfitting?

Ans. In deep learning, our neural nets have large number of layers containing many neurons. The number of connections in these models is in millions (very high). This results in overfitting.

Q.10. A machine learning engineer is always confronted with a delimma between overfitting and model complexity. What is this delimma?

Ans. The problem arises in both the cases *i.e.* when the model is simple or when the model is complex. If the model is simple then it may not be powerful to capture all of the useful information required to solve a problem. On the other hand, if the model is complex then it may result in overfitting problem. Hence, there is a need of a trade-off. To resolve this problem, deep learning solves complex problems with complex models but at the same time take additional steps to avoid overfitting.

Q.11. What is TensorFlow?

Ans. An open source software (Python-based) library released by Google in 2015 that is used to design, build and train deep learning models is TensorFlow.

Q.12. Hoe are AI, Machine Learning and Deep Learning related?

Ans.

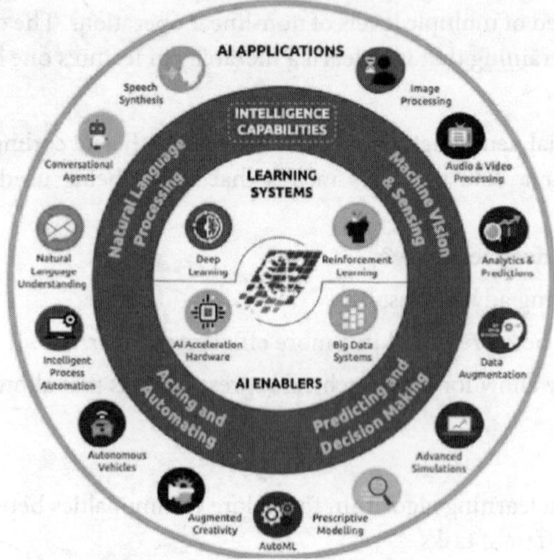

EXERCISE QUESTIONS

1. What do you mean by deep learning? Why is it required?
2. Compare human neuron with that of an Artificial Neuron?
3. How are big data and deep learning related?
4. Explain the three-layered neuron architecture.
5. Explain the design of neural network.
6. What are the rules that you follow to choose the number of layers and neurons in a neural net?
7. What are Feed Forward Neural Networks? Explain.
8. What are deep belief networks?
9. What are CNNs?
10. Throw some light on big data and deep learning with respect to the five V's of big data.
11. What is RBM? What is its role?
12. Define the following:-
    a. Pulling error signals.
    b. Pushing error signals.

2 Machine Learning Retrospective

Q.1. What is machine learning?

Ans. Machine is a semi or fully automated device that intensifies human physical or mental competence in carrying out one or more operations. Learning is building up experience or enhancing one's abilities through analysis, taking into account happenings around us (experience) and being taught by the same. By the word 'experience' we mean the following: -

- Finding out when the same situation was visited.
- What was the action taken?
- Did it worked or failed?

Present day data pool is in terabytes and petabytes. We want our machines to learn from the available giant stock of data through experience. Big data is growing exponentially every second. The objective is to use this data for some benefit. We have colossal data on computers related to hospitals, railways, Universities, banks etc. They are storing data constantly. Each of this organization maintains data in some way or the other. **Please understand that the ultimate aim is to do/extract something useful from this data like treatments that do not work on a patient can be removed or discarded,** Universities can put invalid admissions on hold and so on. Also understand here that it implies that we can conclude a human or animal with the label of being intelligent only when they exhibit act of learning from experience.

So, we define machine learning as a powerful AI tool that allows us to crunch petabytes of data. Arthur Samuel, in 1959, defined machine learning as a field of study that gives computers the ability to learn without being explicitly programmed. When exposed to new data the main focus is on developing computer programs that can teach themselves to grow and change. Software tends to learn from the previous encountered computations in order to produce decisions and results which are reliable and repeatable in nature. This field is quite vast and expanding at a faster rate. When we say machine learning we actually mean building and studying of those algorithms which can learn from data and make predictions (analytics) on it. The final aim is to get more accurate actions that were chosen to be taken in a particular situation by computers, thus making it intelligent in making predictions.

Searching the deep web is the current research area today. This is shown in figure 2.1.

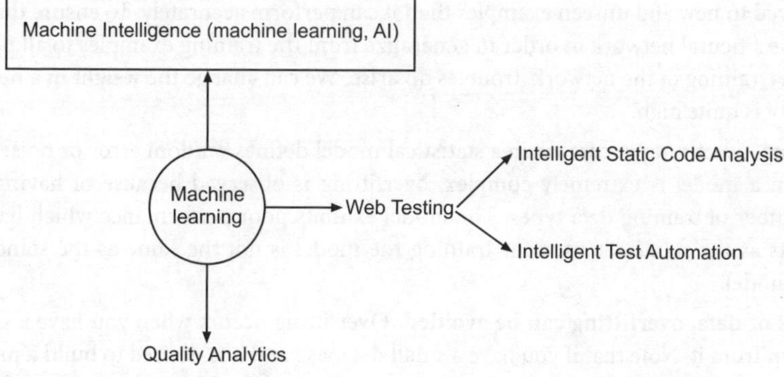

Fig. 2.1: Machine Learning, Machine Intelligence and Web Testing

Machine tool like Test Rail are useful here.

PowerSet Company used deep NLP technology to improve basic web search. Web uses the power of-

a. Information Theory.

b. Statistical Inference.

c. NLP (Natural Language Processing).

Q.2. What is a learning/ intelligent agent? Explain the Learning Algorithms.

Ans. We need to define a learning system first of all. It is defined as an interaction of a learning agent / intelligent agent with its environment by perceiving an input and doing actions accordingly. An agent is one who can perceive its environment with the help of sensors and acts upon its environment through actuators.

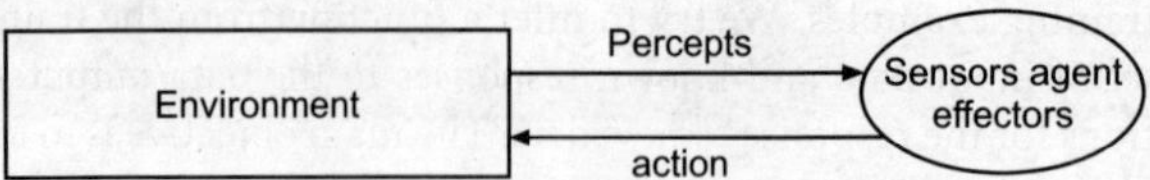

Fig. 2.2: A Learning System

An intelligent agent is a software entity which senses its environment and then carries out some set of operations on behalf of a user with some amount of autonomy and to do so it employs some knowledge or representation of the end-user's goal. Note that an agent is different from a program. An agent need not be a program at all. It may be a robot or a college professor. Software agents are by definition programs but a program must measure up to several marks to be an agent. For example, humans, animals, autonomous mobile robots or softbots calculators are real-world agents. Software agents live in the systems OS.

As shown in figure 2.2, an agent perceives its environment through sensors. It then acts upon that environment through actuators. For example,

- Human agent has eyes, ears, nose etc. as sensors while hands, legs, mouth are actuators.
- Software agent receives keystrokes, files, packets are sensory inputs and acts on the environment by displaying on the screen, writing files and sending packets over a network.

Q.3. Define the terms- Capacity, Overfitting, Generalization and Underfitting.

Ans. In deep learning, our neural nets have large number of layers containing many neurons. The number of connections in these models is in millions (very high). This results in overfitting.

The problem arises in both the cases *i.e.*, when the model is simple or when the model is complex. If the model is simple then it may not be powerful to capture all of the useful information required to solve a problem. On the other hand, if the model is complex then it may result in overfitting problem. Hence, there is a need of a trade-off. To resolve this problem, deep learning solves complex problems with complex models but at the same time take additional steps to avoid overfitting.

Generalization is defined as the ability of machine to learn on being introduced with sets of data during training so that when it is introduced to new and unseen examples then it can perform accurately. To ensure that a network generalizes well, we tend to use a neural network in order to generalize from the training examples to all possible inputs. Whether it is training or overtraining of the network, troubles do arise. We can change the weight in a neural network. Thus, the degree of variability is quite high.

In machine learning, overfitting occurs when a statistical model defines random error or noise rather than underlying relationship. When a model is extremely complex, overfitting is observed because of having too many parameters relating to the number of training data types. The model exhibits poor performance which has been overfit. The risk of overfitting exists as the standards used for training the model is not the same as the standards used to judge the effectiveness of a model.

By means of **loads of data, overfitting can be avoided.** Overfitting occurs when you have a smaller data set and you make effort to learn from it. Note that if you have a small database and it is desired to build a model based on that then in such a situation a technique known as cross validation can be used. In this method, the dataset is is divided into two segments-testing and training datasets. The testing dataset will only test the model while in training dataset, the data points will come up with the model. In this method, a model is generally provided with a dataset of a known data on which training data-set is run and a dataset of unknown data against which the model is tested. The purpose of cross validation is to define a dataset to test the model in the training phase.

Q.4. Write short notes on Supervised Learning Algorithms.

Ans. Machine learning algorithms, based on the basis of desired outcome is put under two categories: -

- Supervised learning.
- Unsupervised learning.

Let us discuss these types first.

Supervised learning is the machine learning task of applying inference function on supervised training data. Training data comprises of a set of training examples. We try to infer a function from the training data. A supervised learning algorithm takes a known set of input data and known responses to the data/output and further training a model to generate reasonable predictions for the response to new data. The main objective is to learn an unknown function $f(x) = y$ where x is an input example (a vector) and y is the desired output (also known as supervisory signal). The model used in this type of learning describes the effect of one set of observations on the other set of observations. So, we can say that the user tries to find the connection between the sets of inputs and outputs. In nutshell, this algorithm analyses the training data and produces an inferred function which is called as a classifier (in case of discrete output) or a regression function (in case of continuous output). Also note that for a valid input object, the inferred function should predict correct output value.

Unsupervised learning involves all of the input data, x, and no corresponding output data, y, is available. The main objective is to model the distribution in the data in order to learn more about data. We define unsupervised learning as a type of learning with no correct answers and no teacher available for supervision. Algorithms are supposed to find the interesting structure present in the data thus figuring out the underlying structure. It enables users to learn larger and more complex problems as compared to supervised learning.

Unsupervised learning is put under two categories: -

1. **Clustering:** In this method, the inherent groupings in the data are discovered. The organization of unlabelled data into similar groups known as clusters. And the process of partitioning of a set of observations into subsets (or clusters) so that observation in the same cluster is similar is called as clustering. So, a cluster consists of data items which are similar in comparison to other clusters which contain dissimilar items. Please understand that the aim of unsupervised learning is to find clusters of similar inputs in the data without knowing that these data points belong to one class and those to different class. Rather the algorithm has to uncover similarities for itself. For example, there is a collection of 30,000 essays on voting process. These essays can be automatically grouped into small number on the basis of word frequency, page count, word limit etc.
2. **Association:** In this method, we discover a set of rules that describes large portions of data. For example, a doctor observes same set of symptoms in several patients suffering from some disease. Then based on his experience the doctor can conclude that the patient is suffering from the same disease.

Q.5. What is k-means Clustering technique? Explain giving its algorithm.

Ans. k-means is a simple unsupervised learning algorithm that solves the well-known clustering problems. The working of k-means is similar to that of a real-life situation in which we have observed that in a group of tourists with a few tourists guides who hold the umbrella up so that everybody can see them and follow them. On the other hand, in static k-means algorithm the data (i.e., the tourists) does not move rather only the tour guide (*s*) move. Analogous is the situation in k-means clustering.

Basic Principle of k-means : "Divide your data into *k* groups (you have to specify what '*k*' is) such that each data item is closer to the centre of its cluster than to the centre of any other cluster."

Explanation of k-means: We classify a given data-set into k number of clusters which is fixed in advance. Now the task is to define '*k*' centres (middle point) one for each cluster. But we do not know where their centres are. So, we need an algorithm that will find the middle points. The centre of a set of points is based on two parameters: -

a. **Distance Measure:** It measures the distance between a set of points. We may use Euclidean distance but other options are also available.

b. **Mean Average:** after we compute the distance measure (as stated above) we finally compute the central point of the set of data points which is the mean average.

Please note that this is valid in Euclidean space where everything is flat and easily measured. Now the need is to place cluster centres properly. We compute the mean of each cluster, μ_i (i) and position the cluster centre right there. Also note that this is similar to minimizing the Euclidean distance (*i.e.* sum-of-squares again) from each data point to the centre of cluster.

Now we would like to find out that which point belongs to which cluster. This is mandatory as it lets us know the position of cluster centres. It is crystal clear to associate closest point with the cluster centre. This might change as the algorithm iterates on. In the input space we start positioning the cluster centres randomly as we do not know where to put them exactly and further update their positions in accordance with the data. Now we start picking up the data points and find out which cluster, particular data point belongs to depending on the distance between each data point and all of the cluster centres and assigning it to cluster that is closest.

The purpose of the hidden layer is to summarize the data and compress it. The multidimensional data is to be reduced to either 2 or 3 dimensions only as then we can plot the graphs too. If we use the PYTHON LANGUAGE then note that layers and column indices are counted from zero while in R they are counted from one.

With auto-encoding neural networks we do learning one layer at a time.

For example, a model, m_1, say, has the following-

- 5 hidden layers
- 11 neurons (in middle layer)

It is trained on the raw data. Then that third hidden layer is extracted into a transformation, f1 with still 100 rows but only 11 columns. Model-2 (m_2) uses this f1 as its input and builds up a much simpler model, reducing 11 input nodes to 2 hidden nodes then back out to 11 output nodes. At the end, results are put in f_2. f_2 now has 2 columns but still 100 rows.

Algorithm : *k*-means clustering involves the following steps: -

Step-1: Randomly select '*c*' cluster centres.

Step-2: Compute the distance between each data point and cluster centres.

Step-3: Assign the data point to the cluster whose distance from the cluster centre is minimum in the value of cluster centres.

Step-4: Calculate the new cluster centre using the following formula:-

$$v = 1/\, c_i\, \Sigma\, (j = 1 \text{ to } c_i)\, x_i$$

where c_i represents the number of data points in the ith cluster.

Step-5: New cluster centres are computed.

Step-6: If no data point is reassigned then stop else repeat from step-3.

As we know that H_2O is software for machine learning and data analysis. H_2O algorithm has been developed keeping in mind clustering only. But clusters in H_2O have some limitations:-

a. Each H_2O node on the cluster must be of the same size. It implies that if the smallest machine in our cluster has 2GB free, then every node must be given 2GB even if some of them have 32GB.

b. You cannot add the machines once the cluster has started.

c. In case a machine dies then the whole of the cluster must be rebuilt. Please note that the whole cluster becomes unusable if a single node gets removed. In such a case, you cannot even export data or models from the left-over clusters.

d. Each node must run the same API version of h_2o.jar.

e. To reduce the network latency, the nodes should be physically close.

You can also give your cluster a name and specify this name when starting on each node. In H2O, the cluster can be created in two ways: -

1. **Flat-file:** A simple text file giving the IP address and port number of each node in the cluster. Note that you must prepare this file identically on each machine.
2. **Auto-discovery:** When you specify the network address then it searches through that subnet to find all nodes and join them together in a cluster. This is slower than the flat file.

Q.6. Give the Expectation Maximization (EM) Algorithm.

Ans. Many a times the presence of unobserved variables is observed as a problem of learning. In case of some variable that can be observed sometimes and cannot be observed at other times then the time when it was observed can be used to learn its values when it was not observed. So, EM is an algorithm for maximizing a likelihood function when some of the variables in your model are unobserved. A variable that is not directly observed is called as a latent variable/ hidden / unobserved variable / missing data.

Statement of EM algorithm: EM is applied where we are required to estimate a set of parameters θ that represents an underlying probability distribution, given only the observed portion of full data. In general, let $X = \{x_1, x_2, \ldots, x_m\}$ denote the observed data in a set of m independently drawn data items. Let $Z = \{z_1, \ldots, z_m\}$ mark the unobserved data in these same data items and let $Y = X \cup Z$; thus marks the full data.

The EM algorithm searches for the maximum likelihood hypothesis *h'* by seeking the *h'* that maximizes $E[\ln P(Y|h')]$, where,

$P(Y|h')$ is the likelihood of the full data *Y* given hypothesis *h'*

$\ln P(Y|h')$- maximizing logarithm value of this quantity further maximizes $P(Y|h')$ and

$E[\ln P(Y|h')]$ –expected value of full data is introduced as *Y* is a random variable.

We need to know that what is the probability distribution governing *Y*. In general, we will not know this distribution as it is determined by the parameters, θ, that is to be estimated. So, EM algorithm uses its current hypothesis, h, in place of θ to estimate the distribution governing, Y.

If we assume that θ = *h*, then, we define a function $Q(h'|h)$ as follows:-

$$Q(h'|h) = E[\ln P(Y|h') \mid h, X]$$

In general form of an EM algorithm, two steps are repeated until convergence:-

S1: Estimation (*E*) step: Calculate $Q(h'|h)$ using the current hypothesis, *h* and the observed data *X* to estimate the probability distribution over *Y*. So,

$$Q(h'|h) = E[\ln P(Y|h') \mid h, X]$$

S2: Maximization (*M*) step: Replace *h* by *h'* that maximizes this *Q* function-

$$H \leftarrow \underset{h'}{\operatorname{argmax}}\, Q(h' \mid h)$$

Please note that when the function, Q, is continuous, the EM algorithm converges to a fixed point of the probable function $P(Y|h')$. Also note that when this probable function has a single maximum, EM will converge to this global maximum probable estimate for *h'*.

Q.7. Write short notes on Mixture of Gaussians.

Ans. A very popular continuous probability distribution is Gaussian distribution / Normal Distribution. It is also called as a bell curve since it has a bell-shaped curve. The equation in one dimension is as follows:-

$$p(x) = \left(x_1 \right) \qquad \ldots\ldots(1)$$

where μ = mean

σ = standard deviation

Please note that it is useful because of its Central Limit Theorem which tells us that lots of random numbers will add up to something Gaussian.

In Gaussian Mixture Models (GMM), we assume that there are number of different classes. Each class comes from its own Gaussian distribution. And such type of data is known as multi-model data as there are number of modes or distribution for each particular class. We are unable to accommodate Gaussian to the data in totality as it does not appear to be Gaussian overall.

If we know the number of classes that are there in the data then we can put effort to estimate the parameters for that many number of Gaussians and that too all at the same time.

On the other hand, if we do not the number of classes then we can attempt for different numbers and finds out which one works best. Then the output for any specific data point which has already been an input to the algorithm will be the sum of the values expected by all of the 'M' Gaussians. That is,

$$f(x) = \Sigma\,(m = 1 \text{ to } M)\, \alpha_m\, \varphi(x; \mu_m, \Sigma_m) \qquad \ldots\ldots(2)$$

where $\varphi(x;\mu_m, \Sigma_m)$ = Gaussian function with mean μm and covariance matrix and the αm are the weights with the constraints *i.e.* $\Sigma\,(m = 1 \text{ to } M)\, \alpha_m = 1$.

The task is to choose the weights αm. The target is for Maximum likelihood solution. Note that likelihood refers to the conditional probability and Maximum Likelihood solution refers to maximizing the conditional probability.

Q.8. What is Factor Analysis and its applications?

Ans. Factor Analysis (FA) is a method for modelling observed variables and their covariance structure in terms of a smaller number of underlying unobservable/ latent factors. These 'factors' are typically observed as broad concepts or ideas that may describe an observed phenomenon. This method is quite comprehensive but is similar to principal components. Please understand that in factor analysis the observed variables are modelled as linear functions of the factors. On the other hand, principal components analysis (PCA) involves the creation of new variables that are linear combinations of the observed variables. But in both the methods, the dimensions of the data are reduced.

FA involves using of a data reduction tool to-

a. Remove redundancy from a set of correlated variables.

b. Represent correlated variables with a smaller set of derived variables.

c. Form factors that are independent of each other.

d. Two types of variables are used- latent variables (factors) and the observed variables.

Notations used:S ay, there is a vector X consisting of variables X's for each individual subject. Let Xi denote observable trait, i. This is the data of each subject and will be collected into a vector of traits.

That is,

$$X = \begin{pmatrix} x_1 \\ x_2 \\ x_3 \end{pmatrix} = \text{vector of traits}$$

This will be a random vector with a population mean. We assume that sampling of vector of traits X is done from a population with population mean vector:-

$$\mu = \begin{pmatrix} \mu_1 \\ \mu_2 \\ \mu_p \end{pmatrix} = \text{Population man vector}$$

Here, $E(X_i) = \mu_i$ denotes the population mean of variable *i*.

In general, consider 'm' unobservable common factors $f_2, f_2, \ldots\ldots f_m$.

The ith common factor is f_i. In general, m will be less than *p*.

The common factors will be collected into a vector only:-

$$F = \begin{pmatrix} f_1 \\ f_2 \\ f_p \end{pmatrix} = \text{Vector of common factors}$$

The Factor Model : Our factor model will be a collection of series of multiple regressions, predicting each of the observable variables, X_i from the values of the unobservable common factor, f_i. That is,

$$X_1 = \mu_1 + l_{11} f_1 + l_{12} f_2 + \ldots + l_{1m} f_m + \varepsilon_1$$

$$X_2 = \mu_2 + l_{21} f_1 + l_{22} f_2 + \ldots + l_{2m} f_m + \varepsilon_1$$

$$\vdots$$

$$\vdots$$

$$\vdots$$

$$X_P = \mu_P + l_{P1} f_1 + l_{P2} f_2 + \ldots + l_{pm} f_m + \varepsilon_p$$

Here, the variable means μ_1 through μ_P can be explained as the intercept terms for the multiple regression models. The regression coefficients l_{ij} (are the partial slopes) for all of these multiple regressions are called as factor loadings. The relationship of each variable to the underlying factor is expressed by factor loading. Here, l_{ij} = loading of the ith variable on the jth factor. These will be collected into a matrix as follows: -

$$L = \begin{pmatrix} l_{11} & l_{12} & \ldots\ldots l_{1m} \\ l_{21} & l_{22} & \ldots\ldots l_{2m} \\ \vdots & \vdots & \ldots\ldots\ldots \vdots \\ l_{p1} & l_{p2} & \ldots\ldots l_{pm} \end{pmatrix}$$

And that the errors, ε_i are called as the specific factors.

Here, ε_i = specific factor for variable *i*.

These specific factors are also collected in a vector:-

$$\varepsilon_i = \begin{pmatrix} \varepsilon_1 \\ \varepsilon_2 \\ \vdots \\ \varepsilon_p \end{pmatrix} = \text{Vector of specific vectors}$$

In nutshell, the basic model is like a regression model only. Each of our response variables *X* is to be predicted as a linear function of the unobserved common factors f_1, f_1 through f_m. Thus, our explanatory variables are f_1, f_2 through fm. Therefore, we conclude that we have m unobserved factors that control the variation among our data.

Generally, we can reduce this into a matrix notation as shown in this form below :-

$$X = \mu + Lf + \varepsilon$$

In general, we want m << *p*.

Assumptions of the model

***a.* Mean-**

1. The specific factors or random errors all have mean zero: $E(\varepsilon_i) = 0$; $i = 1,2,\ldots.p$.
2. The common factors, the f's also have a mean zero: E(fi) = 0; $i = 1,2,\ldots m$.
3. A consequence of these assumptions is that the mean response of the ith trait is μi. that is,

   $E(X_i) = \mu_i$

***b.* Variance-**

1. The common factors have variance one: var(f_i) =1,2,...m.
2. The variance of specific factor *i* is ψ_i : var(ε_i) = ψi ; $i = 1,2,\ldots p$. Here, ψ_i is called as the specific variance.

c. Correlation-

1. The common factors are uncorrelated with one another: cov(f_i, f_i) = 0 for *i* != *j*.
2. The specific factors are uncorrelated with one another: cov(ε_i , ε_i) = 0 for *i* != *j*.
3. The specific factors are uncorrelated with the common factors: cov((ε_i, ε_i) = cov; $i = 1,2,\ldots.p$; $j = 1,2,\ldots,m$.

To calculate the parameters these assumptions are necessary. An infinite number of equally well-fitted models with different values for the parameters may be obtained unless these suppositions are done. Also note that under this model, the variance for the ith observed variable is equal to the sum of the squared loadings for that variable and specific variance:-

The variance of trait is: $\sigma_i^2 = \text{var}(X_i) = \Sigma\ (j = 1 \text{ to } m)\ l^2_{ij} + \psi_i$

Where $\Sigma\ (j = 1 \text{ to } m)\ l^2_{ij}$ is called as the communality for variable, *i*. Please note that the larger is the communality, the better is the model performance for the ith variable.

The covariance between pairs of traits i and j is given by the formula-

$$\sigma_{ij} = \text{cov}(X_i, X_j) = \Sigma\ (k = 1 \text{ to } m)\ l_{ik}\ l_{jk}$$

The covariance between trait *i* and factor *j* is: cov $(X_i, f_i) = l_{ij}$

In matrix form, our model for the variance-covariance matrix is going to be expressed as shown below:-

$$\Sigma = LL' + \psi$$

This is the matrix of factor loadings times its transpose plus a diagonal matrix containing the specific variances.

Here ψ is as follows: -

$$\Psi 1 = \begin{pmatrix} \psi_1 & 0 & \cdots & 0 \\ 0 & \psi_2 & \cdots & 0 \\ \vdots & \vdots & & \vdots \\ 0 & 0 & \cdots & \psi_p \end{pmatrix}$$

Hence, a simplified model for the variance-covariance matrix is obtained. This is used for estimation.

Notes:

1. The model assumes that the data is a linear function of the common factors. But since the common factors are not observable, there is no amount of data that can be used to check for linearity.
2. The variance-covariance matrix is a symmetric matrix that is, the variance between variables *i* and *j* is the same thing as the variance between *j* and *i*. for this model-
$$\Sigma = LL' + \psi$$
3. The variance-covariance matrix is going to have $p\ (p + 1)/2$ unique elements of Σ that are approximated by mp factor loadings in the matrix L and p specific variances. Also understand that this means that there is going to be mp plus p parameters in this model of the variance-covariance matrix. Ideally, $(mp + p)$ is to be substantially smaller than $p\ (p + 1)/2$. However, if mp is too small, the $mp + p$ parameters may not be adequate to describe Σ. There may always be the case that perhaps this is not the right model. It may be the case that you cannot reduce the data to a linear combination of factors.
4. If we have more than one variable in our analysis, that is, if $p > 1$, the model is going to be inherently ambiguous. Say, T be any $(m * m)$ orthogonal matrix. Note that a matrix is said to be orthogonal if its inverse is equal to the transpose of the original matrix i.e.
$$T'T = TT' = 1$$
Hence, we can write our factor model in the matrix notation as follows:-
Please note that this does not change the calculation since the identity matrix times any matrix just gives back the original matrix. This results in an alternative factor model where the relationship between the new factor loadings and the original factor loadings is given by:-
$$L. = LT$$
And the relationship between the new common factors and the original common factors is:-
$$f. = T'f$$
This gives a model that fits equally well. Moreover, since there are an infinite number of orthogonal matrices then there is an infinite number of alternative models. This model, as it turns out, satisfies all of the assumptions that we have discussed earlier.
5. E (f.) =E(T'f) = T' E(f) = T'0 = 0 and
var(f.) = var(T'f) = T' var(f) T = T'IT = T'T = 1
6. Cov (f. , ε) = cov (T'f, ε) = T' cov(f, ε) = T'0 = 0

Thus, we can say that f. satisfies all of the assumptions and hence f. is an equally valid collection of common factors. So, there is a certain apparent ambiguity to these models.

However, it is the same ambiguity that we are going to exploit. This ambiguity is going to be used to justify the factor notation that will be used to derive more parsimonious description of data.

Applications of FA : The following are some of the applications of FA:-

1. **Identification of underlying factors:** It clusters variables into homogeneous sets, creates new variables/factors and allows us to gain insight to categories.
2. **Screening of Variables:** It identifies groupings to allow us to select one variable and is useful in regression/ recall collinearity applications of FA.
3. **Summary:** It allows us to describe many variables using few factors.
4. **Sampling of variables**: It helps us to select a small group of variables of representative variables from a larger set.
5. **Clustering of Object:** It helps us to put objects/people into categories depending on their factor scores.

Q.9. Explain Principal Component Analysis (PCA).

Ans. PCA refers to a mathematical procedure that tends to transform a number of possibly correlated variables into a small number of uncorrelated variables which are called as the principal components. The first PCA accounts for as much of the variability as possible in the data and the next following components takes into account possible remaining variability. Please understand that PCA is a technique used to focus on variation and figure out strong patterns in a dataset. The objective of PCA is to make data easy to explore and visualize.

Aim of PCA :

1. To discover or to reduce the dimensionality of the data set.
2. To identify new meaningful underlying variables.

Algorithm: Suppose that we have a random vector, X. That is,

$$X = \begin{pmatrix} X_1 \\ X_2 \\ \vdots \\ \vdots \\ X_p \end{pmatrix}$$

And with the population variance-covariance matrix as follows: -

$$\text{var}(X) = \begin{pmatrix} \sigma_1^2 & \sigma_{12} \ldots \sigma_{1p} \\ \sigma_{21} & \sigma_2^2 \ldots \sigma_{2p} \\ \vdots & \vdots & \vdots \\ \vdots & \vdots & \vdots \\ \sigma_{pl} & \sigma_{p2} \ldots \sigma_p^2 \end{pmatrix}$$

Now consider the following linear combinations:-

$$Y_1 = e_{11} X_1 + e_{12} X_2 + \ldots\ldots + e_{1p} X_p$$

$$Y_2 = e_{21} X_1 + e_{22} X_2 + \ldots\ldots + e_{2p} X_p$$

$$\vdots$$

$$\vdots$$

$$Y_p = e_{p1} X_1 + e_{p2} X_2 + \ldots\ldots + e_{pp} X_p$$

Each of these is just like a linear regression, predicting Y_i from $X_1, X_2, \ldots\ldots, X_p$. There is no intercept but $e_{i1}, e_{i2}, \ldots\ldots e_{ip}$ may be considered as the regression coefficients.

Also note that Yi is a function of our random data and hence it is also random. So, it has a population variance of-

$$\text{Var}(Y_i) = \Sigma(k = 1 \text{ to } p)\, \Sigma(l = 1 \text{ to } p)\, e_{ik}\, e_{il}\, \sigma_{kl} = e'_i \Sigma_{ei}$$

How to find 1st PCA, 2nd PCA and the ith PCA?

1. The 1st Principal Component *i.e.* PCA$_1$ means Y_1 and is computed as follows:-

   The 1st principal component is a linear combination of *x*-variables that has maximum variance (among all linear combinations). Thus, it accounts for as much possible variation in the data as possible. More specifically, we will define coefficients $e_{11}, e_{12}, \ldots.., e_{1p}$ for that component in such a way that its variance is maximized, subject to the constraint that the sum of the squared coefficients is equal to one. This constraint is required to obtain a unique answer.

   Formally, we select $e_{11}, e_{12}, \ldots.., e_{1p}$ that maximizes-V

   $$\text{ar}(Y_1) = \Sigma(k = 1 \text{ to } p)\, \Sigma(l = 1 \text{ to } p)\, e_{1k}\, e_{1l}\, \sigma_{kl} = e'_1 \Sigma_{e1}$$

   Subject to the constraints:-

   $$e'_1 e_1 = \Sigma\,(j = 1 \text{ to } p)\, e^2_{2j} = 1$$

2. The 2nd Principal Component *i.e.* PCA$_2$ means Y_2 and is computed as follows:-

   The 2nd principal component is a linear combination of x-variables that has maximum variance (among all linear combinations). Thus, it accounts for as much possible variation in the data as possible with the constraints that the correlation between the first and second component is 0. More specifically, we will define coefficients e11, e12, ...,

e1p for that component in such a way that its variance is maximized, subject to the constraint that the sum of the squared coefficients is equal to one. This constraint is required to obtain a unique answer.

Formally, we select $e_{21}, e_{22},....., e_{2P}$ that maximizes-

$$\text{var}(Y_2) = \Sigma(k = 1 \text{ to } p)\ \Sigma(l = 1 \text{ to } p)\ e_{2k}\, e_{2l}\, \sigma_{kl} = e'_2\, \Sigma_{e2}$$

Subject to the constraints:-

$$e'_2\, e_2 = \Sigma\ (j = 1 \text{ to } p)\ e^2{}_{2j} = 1$$

Please note that all subsequent PCAs have this same property *i.e.* they are linear combinations that account for as much of the remaining variation as possible and they are not correlated with the other PCAs. Also note that we will do it the same way for each and every additional component.

So, in general, the ith Principal Component *i.e.* PCA$_i$ means Y_i and is computed as follows:-

We select $e_{i1}, e_{i2},....., e_{ip}$ that maximizes-

$$\text{var}(Y_i) = \Sigma(k = 1 \text{ to } p)\ \Sigma(l = 1 \text{ to } p)\ e_{ik}\, e_{il}\, \sigma_{kl} = e'_i\, \Sigma_{ei}$$

This is subject to the constraints that the sums of squared coefficients add up to 1, along with the additional constraint that this new component will be uncorrelated with all the previously defined components. That is,

$$e'_i\, e_i = \Sigma\ (j = 1 \text{ to } p)\ e^2{}_{ij} = 1$$

How to find these coefficients e_{ij} for a principal component?

To solve these coefficients we use Eigen values and Eigen vectors of the variance-covariance matrix, Σ. Let λ_1 through λ_P represent the Eigen values of the variance-covariance matrix, Σ. These are ordered so that λ1 has the largest Eigen value and λ_P is the smallest. That is,

$$\lambda_1 \geq \lambda_2 \geq ..... \geq \lambda_P$$

Also say vectors e1 through ep *i.e.* ($e_1, e_1,..., e_P$) denote the corresponding Eigen vectors. Note that the elements for these Eigen vectors will be coefficients of our principal components.

The variance for the iit PC is equal to the ith Eigen value as follows:-

$$\text{var}(Y_i) = \text{var}(e_{i1} X_1 + e_{i2} X_2 + ... + e_{ip} X_p) = \lambda_i$$

Moreover, the principal components are uncorrelated with one another:-

$$\text{cov}(Y_i, Y_j) = 0$$

When we have correlations / multi-collinearity between the *x*-variables, the data may be more or less fall on a line or plane in a lower number of dimensions.

For example, consider a plot of two *x*-variables that have a nearly perfect correlation. The data points will fall close to a straight line. That line could be used as a new 1D axis to represent the variation among data points.

Let us define this now in terms of variance-covariance matrix, Σ, which is unknown. But we may estimate Σ by the sample variance-covariance matrix, Σ, which is given in the standard formula as follows:-

$$S = 1/(n-1)\ \Sigma\ (i = 1 \text{ to } n)\ (X_i - \bar{x})\ (X_i - \bar{x})'$$

Algorithm followed : We calculate the Eigen Values $\lambda_1', \lambda_2',......, \lambda_P'$ of the sample variance-covariance matrix, S, and the corresponding Eigen Vectors $e_1', e_2',......, e_P'$. Then we will define our estimated PCs using the Eigen Vectors as our coefficients:-

$$Y_1' = e_{11}' X_1 + e_{12}' X_2 + ... + e_{1p}' X_p$$

$$Y_2' = e_{21}' X_1 + e_{22}' X_2 + ... + e_{2p}' X_p$$

$$\vdots$$

$$\vdots$$

$$Y_p' = e_{P1}' X_1 + e_{p2}' X_2 + ... + e_{pp}' X_p$$

In general, we can retain only the first *k* principal component. But we need to balance two conflicting issues:-

1. To obtain the simplest possible interpretation, we want k to be as small as possible. If we can explain most of the variation just by 2 principal components then this would give us a much simpler description of data. The smaller is the K, the smaller amount of variation is explained by the first k component.
2. To avoid loss of information, we want the proportion of variation explained by the first principal components to be

large. That is, what we want is-

$$\frac{\lambda_1 + \lambda_2 + \ldots + \lambda_k}{\lambda_1 + \lambda_2 + \ldots + \lambda_p} = 1$$

So, we can say that all principal components are uncorrelated with one another.

Q.10. What is Independent Component Analysis (ICA)? Explain in detail. Also explain its variant.

Ans. A method for finding the underlying factors or components from multi-variate or multi-dimensional statistical data is called as Independent Component Analysis (ICA). This method is somewhat different. It is so because it uses both statistically independent and non-Gaussian.

For example, consider a scenario in which three people are speaking simultaneously in a room. There are 3 microphones that are present in different locations for the same. The microphones give us 3 recorded time signals which can be denoted by x1(t), x2(t) and x3(t) with x1, x2 and x3 referring to the amplitudes and t is basically the time index. Each of these recorded signals can be represented as a weighted sum of the speech signals produced by the three speakers which is denoted by $s_1(t)$, $s_2(t)$ and $s_3(t)$. In linear form we can represent it as follows:-

$$x_1(t) = a_{11}\, s_1\,(t) + a_{12}\, s_2\,(t) + a_{13}\, s_3\,(t)$$

$$x_2(t) = a_{21}\, s_1\,(t) + a_{22}\, s_2\,(t) + a_{23}\, s_3\,(t)$$

$$x_3(t) = a_{31}\, s_1\,(t) + a_{32}\, s_2\,(t) + a_{33}\, s_3\,(t)$$

where a_{ij} with j = 1...3, depend on the distances of the microphones from the speakers.

It is very innovative to estimate the original speech signals $s_1(t)$, $s_2(t)$ and $s_3(t)$ by making use of the recorded signals x_i (t). And this problem is known as a cocktail-party problem.

If we know the mixing parameter, aij value then we would have easily solved the linear equation by simply inverting the linear system. But the problem is that we neither have aij nor the $s_i(t)$. One of the ways of solving this problem is to use some information on the statistical properties of the signals, s_i (t). It is more than enough to assume that $s_1(t)$, $s_2(t)$ and $s_3(t)$ are statistically independent at each time instant, t. ICA can be used to estimate aij based on their information of their independence. This allows us to separate out the three original signals $s_1(t)$, $s_2(t)$ and $s_3(t)$ from their mixtures $x_1(t)$, $x_2(t)$ and $x_3(t)$. ICA was developed to deal with the variant forms of cocktail-party problem.

The Noise-free ICA Model : The ICA model is a generative model that means that it describes how the observed data are generated by a process of mixing the components, s_j.

To model ICA, the following points must be remembered:-

1. Use statistical latent variables in the system.
2. Use random variable, sk instead of time signal.
3. $X_j = a_{j1}s_1 + a_{j2}s_2 + \ldots + a_{jn}s_n$, for all jx = As
4. Task: Estimate A and S using only the observable random vector, x.
5. Assuming that number of Independent Components = number of observable mixtures and A is square and invertible, we can estimate A. Then we can calculate W= A^{-1} and thus s = Wx = A^{-1} x.

Limitations in ICA : The following are some of the limitations of ICA:-

1. The independent components are assumed statistically independent.
2. The independent components must have non-Gaussian distributions.
3. The joint density of unit variances, s_1 and s_2 is symmetric. So, it does not contain any information about the directions of the columns of the mixing matrix, A. So, A can't be estimated.
4. If only one Independent component is Gaussian then the estimation is still possible.

Ambiguities in ICA : The following are some of the ambiguities in ICA:-

1. It cannot determine the variances /energies of the independent components (ICs). Both s and A are unknowns and that any scalar multiple in one of the sources can always be cancelled by dividing the corresponding column of A by it. Also because of the fixed magnitudes of IC's assuming unit variance *i.e.* $E\{S_i^2\} = 1$.
2. It cannot determine the order of Independent components. The terms can be easily changed as both a and A are unknown, so, we call any IC as the first one.

How to centre the variables?

We can assume that both the mixture variables and the independent components have zero mean without any loss of generality. This assumption simplifies the theory and algorithms further. If the assumption of zero mean is not true, some pre-processing is done to make it hold. This is possible by centering the observable variables *i.e.* subtracting their sample mean. This means that the original mixtures, say x', are pre-processed by $x = x' - E\{x'\}$, before doing ICA. Thus, the independent components are also made zero mean because-

$$E\{s\} = A^{-1} E\{x\}$$

On the other hand, the mixing matrix remains intact after this pre-processing. So this can always be done without affecting the estimation of the mixing matrix. After estimating the mixing matrix and the independent components for the zero-mean data, the subtracted mean can be simply reconstructed by adding $E\{s\} = A^{-1} E\{x\}$to the zero-mean independent components.

Q.11. What is Latent Semantic Indexing (LSI)? Give its algorithm. Also list some of its advantages.

Ans. Latent Semantic Indexing (LSI) is a retrieval method that makes use of a mathematical technique called as Singular Value Decomposition (SVD) which in turn is used to figure out patterns in connection to terms and concepts included in unstructured collection of data. This process acts as an add-on to document indexing process. in addition to keeping track of keywords that are there in the document , this method analyzes the document entirely to find out which other document contains the same words. Please note that LSI considers documents to be semantically close if they have many words in common and semantically distant if few words are there in common. LSI algorithm is unable to understand the words as it does not know the meanings but still it is able to figure out the pattern that makes it look intelligent.

The LSI Algorithm :

Step-1: Convert each document in your index in a vector-form of word occurrences. Here,

Number of dimensions in vector = number of unique words in the entire document set.

Most document vectors will have large empty patches, some will be quite full. It is recommended that common words like 'this', 'him', 'the' etc. should be removed.

Step-2: Scale each vector so that every term reflects the frequency of its occurrence in context.

Step-3: Combine these column vectors into a large term-document matrix. Here, rows represent terms and columns represent document.

Step-4: Perform Singular Value Decomposition (SVD) on the term-document matrix. This will result in three matrices commonly called U, S and V. S, is a diagonal matrix of singular values for your document system. It is of use to us.

Step-5: Set all but the k-highest singular values to 0. K is a parameter that needs to be tuned based on your space. Very low values of k are very lossy and lands up with net poor results. But very high values of k do not change the results much from simple vector search. This gets a new matrix, S'.

Step-6: Recombine the terms to form the original matrix-

$$U * S' * V(t) = M'$$

Where (*t*) signifies transpose.

Step-7: Break this reduced rank term-document matrix back into column vectors. Associate these with their corresponding documents.

Step-8: Now you get the LSI i.e., Latent Semantic Index.

Advantages of LSI :

1. LSI is used to analyze the similarity between the bodies of the text. This can be used in dozens of ways, from finding related documents in a group to doing paragraph-wise LSI to find site summaries.
2. It can also be used to assist search in a smarter way of your document space.
3. To do document categorization.
4. You can take the inner product (dot product) of two of the LSI vectors and perform operations with that information. Sometimes you may do this operation on your unit LSI vectors, particularly when you are searching on a vector that is a search term. It will never have the magnitude that a full document would have.

Q.12. What is Spectral or Sub-space Clustering? Give its algorithm. Also define affinity.

Ans. It is one of the most modern and simple clustering algorithms. It can be solved efficiently by standard linear algebra software. Sometimes it is better than traditional k-means algorithm. Please understand that the objective of spectral clustering is to cluster connected data but not certainly compact or clustered within convex boundaries.

When we talk of compactness then k-means model is useful while when we talk of connectivity then spectral clustering is used.

Algorithm :

Step-1: Project your data into R^n.

Step-2: Define an Affinity matrix, A, using a Gaussian Kernel, K, or say just an adjacency matrix *i.e.* $A_{ij} = \delta_{ij}$.

Step-3: Construct the Laplacian Graph from A *i.e.* decide on a normalization.

Step-4: Solve an Eigen value problem such as Lv = λv or a Generalized Eigen Value problem *i.e.*, Lv = λDv.

Step-5: Select *k* Eigen Vectors $\{v_i, i=1, k\}$ corresponding to the *k*-lowest or highest Eigen values, to define a *k*-dimensional subspace Pt LP.

Step-6: Form clusters in this subspace using, say, k-means.

Metrics : A metric that computes the similarity or closeness of two points in space is called as an affinity. We either guess the metric or learn the metric. Now we will guess the metric. Please note that it is not the standard Euclidean metric. The next simplest one is Guassian Kernel.

Given 2 data points, x_i, x_j that is projected in R^n, we define an Affinity A_{ij} that is positive, symmetric and depends on the Euclidian distance $||x_i - x_j|$ between the data points:-

$$A_{ij} = \exp(-\alpha\, ||x_i - x_j||^2)$$

We might provide a hard cut-off *R* so that $A_{ij} = 0$ if $||x_i - x_j||^2 \geq R$ and in some applications we pre-multiply Aij with a feature Affinity Kernal. Just note that-

$A_{ij} = 1$ when the points are close in R^n and $A_{ij} \leftarrow 0$ if the points x_i, x_j are far apart. Please note that close data points are in the same cluster while data points in different clusters are far away. Also note that data points in the same cluster may also be far away in comparison to the points in different clusters.

Objective: Our task is now to transform the space so that when the 2 points x_i and x_j are close enough so that they are always in the same cluster and when they are far apart, they are in different clusters.

Many types of Laplacians (*L*) are given in the literature like Normalized, Generalized, Relaxed etc. they all share the degree matrix, *D*. We define a degree matrix as a diagonal matrix that measures the degree at each node as follows:-

$$D_{i,j} = \Sigma\,(j \text{ to } n)\; a_{i,j}$$

This is known as a local nearest neighbour mean-field average of the Affinity. *D* is a normalization factor for A so that the Cluster Affinities are balanced across different clusters.

Q.12. Explain the Hidden Markov Model.

Ans. A tool used for representing probability distributions over a sequence of observations is Hidden Markov Model (HMM). The observation is denoted at a particular instance time, *t*, by variable Y_t. As long as we can define a probability distribution, this symbol can vary from discrete alphabet to a real valued variable or to an integer. Here, we assume that 't' can be an integer valued time index as the observation are sampled at discrete equally spaced time intervals. This model assumes that the observation at time, *t*, was generated by the same process whose state Si is concealed or hidden from the observer. This model has two defining properties as follows:-

1. This process conforms the Markov Property *i.e.* given the value of S_{i-1}, the current state S_i is independent of all the states prior to *t*-1.

2. The outputs also conforms a Markov property in accordance to the states given S_i, Y_i is independent of the states and observation at other times indexes.

Markov properties signifies joint distribution of a sequence of states and observations. The factorization of joint distribution given in equation can be represented graphically as shown in figure 2.2:-

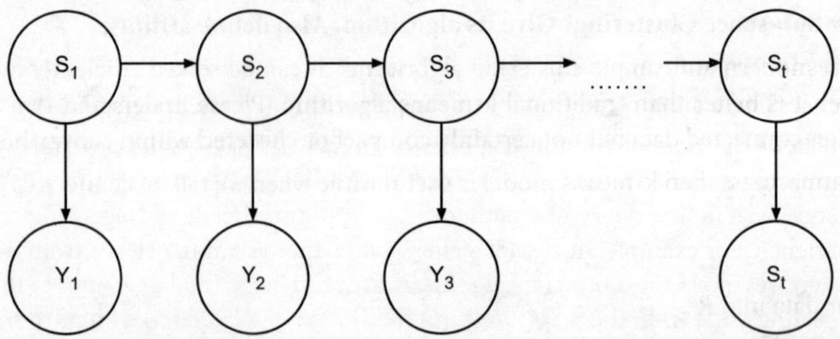

Figure 2.2: Bayesian Network specifying Conditional Independence relation for a Hidden Markov Model

Each variable is denoted by a node in the graph of figure 2.2. each node receives a directed graph from the nodes that is conditionally dependent on, in the factorization of joint distribution. It also assumes that hidden variable is discrete i.e. si can take on k values which will be denoted by the integers {1.....*k*}.

To define a probability distribution over sequences of observations:-

$P(S_i) =$ probability distribution over initial state.

$K X k =$ state transition matrix defining $P(S_i \mid S_{i-1})$

$P(Y_t \mid S_t) =$ Output Model.

Notes:

1. HMMs assume that the model is time invariant.
2. If the observables are in form of discrete symbols, taking one of *L* values, the *dp* model is represented by k X L emission matrix.
3. HMMs can be augmented to allow for input variables *i.e.* in such a way that there is an input dependent state transition probability. The system then steps ahead and models the conditional distribution of sequence of output distribution when you are provided with the input distributions.

Q.14. What are the goals and applications of Machine Learning?

Ans. Our objective is to devise such algorithms that does learning naturally without human interference. So, we can say that machine learning model can be considered in the form of programming by example. The following are some of the goals and applications of machine learning: -

1. To improve the image classification in apps like Google photos, deep learning is required.
2. To improve detection of malicious software, machine learning is used in anti-virus software.
3. Anti-spam software is trained better by machine learning. Identify e-mail messages as spam or non-spam and if it happens to be spam then penalize them
4. Tagging people in photos like Facebook does it. It shows whether a face is present or not in a photograph.
5. To diagnose patients' suffering from a particular disease or Not.
6. For speech recognition.
7. To predict a set of customers who will respond to a particular type of advertisement or promotion like Amazon recommends products especially for you.
8. To identify fraudulent credit card transactions.
9. When machine learning is applied to weather forecasting software it enhances quality of software by resulting in accurate predictions for instance whether it will rain today or not.
10. To categorize news articles to different categories of politics, sports, entertainments etc.

Q.15. What are the different aspects of developing a learning system, training experience, concept representation and function approximation?

Ans. There are three aspects of developing a learning system: -

1. Training Experience.
2. Concept Representation.

3. Function Approximation.

Let us study these one by one now.

I. Training Experience: There are three (3) attributes for the selection of the design-

   a. To make choice of the type of training experience from a set of experiences from which the system learns. The chosen training experience has a deep effect on learner's success or failure. Once the choice is made by the Performance System, the query of whether direct or indirect feedback regarding choices is provided by the training experience. For example, in case of a chess game, the system may learn from direct training (like board states, correct moves etc.) or indirect training (like move sequences, final outcomes of the games etc.). It has been found that learning done from the direct training feedback is easier than learning from indirect feedback.

   b. To what extent sequence of training examples is controlled by the learner. For example, for the selection of board states and correct move for each, the learner might require teacher's assistance. On the other hand, learner can use a different approach i.e., the board states that seems confusing to the learner might itself be proposed by the learner. A learner can have an entire control over both the conditions i.e., of the board states as well as of training classifications (indirect) as it does when it learns by playing against itself without the assistance of a teacher.

   c. How well it signifies the distribution of examples over which the final system's performance is measured. In chess game, the performance count metric, P_c is the number of games the system wins. The training experience, E_t, might not be fully illustrative of various situations over which it will be later on tested; if the games played against itself is only taken into account.

   Please note here that the most of the theory of machine learning is dependent on the assumption that distribution of training examples is identical to distribution of test examples.

   The training proceeds as follows. No external trainer will be present. Hence, the system gets trained by playing games against itself. This results in generation of lot of training data with time.

   Keep in mind these 3 points when viewing a complete design of the learning system.-

   1. Exact type of knowledge to be learned.
   2. How this target knowledge is represented.
   3. A learning means.

   How to choose the target function?

   The performance program will decide on what sort of knowledge will be learned and how will this program put it to use. For example, consider a chess program that can generate legal moves from any board state. The program needs to find out the best move, out of the large number of legal moves available. Now the type of function to be learned is a program or function that finds the best move from a lot of moves available for a particular board state.

II. **Concept Representation:** The learning task is narrowed down to the problem of finding an operational description of ideal target function, E, that is difficult to learn perfectly. Note that we expect learning algorithms to attain some approximation to the target function and thus the process of learning the target function is called as function approximation.

   For example, in chess problem-

   T_G is the task *i.e.*, to play chess.

   P_c is the percentage of games won against competitor.

   E is practising against itself.

   Target Function, *E*: Board → *R*

   So, Target Function Representation is-

$$E'(s) = w_0 + w_1b_1 + w_2b_2 + w_3b_3 + w_4b_4 + w_5b_5 + w_6b_5$$

   Note that the first three points relate to specification of learning task and last two items form design choices that are required for the implementation of the learning program.

III. **Function Approximation :** We need a set of training examples in order to learn target function, E', each describing a particular board states and training value *E* for *s*. Every training example is represented as an ordered pair of the form (*s*, E_{train} (*s*)). For example, consider the following training example that tells a board state in which red has won the game. Note that

$b_1 = 0$ = number of black pieces left for this target function value is E_{train} (s) + 100.

Q.16. What do you mean by 'Estimating Training Values'.

Ans. The only training information available to a learner, in accordance to the formulation of learning problem is whether the game was last won or lost. Also training instances are required so that particular board states can be given specific scores. In guessing the training values for intermediate board states there are some uncertainties associated.

Rules for estimating Training Values : To assign the training value of $E_{train}(s)$ for any intermediate board state (*s*) to be E' (successor(*b*)), where E' is the learner's current approximation to *E* and where successor (*s*) signifies the next board state following '*s*' for which it is again the program's turn to move *i.e.*, the board state following the program's move and the opponents response. This is known as a rule for estimating training values. It can be represented as follows:-

E_{train} (*s*) → *E*'(successor(*s*))

Please note here that we are using the estimates of the value of the successor (*s*) to estimate the value of board state (*s*). This will make sense if *E*' tends to be more accurate for board states closer to the games end. Also note that under certain situations the approach of iteratively estimating training values based on the estimates of successor state values can be proven to converge to perfect estimates of E_{train}.

The learning algorithm for choosing the weights, wi , to best fit the set of training examples {(s, Etrain (s))}. We mean to say the best fit to the training data. One general approach is to define the best hypothesis or a set of weights, which in turn minimizes the squared error, E, between the training values and the values predicted by the hypothesis E'. That is,

$$E' = \Sigma\,(s, E_{train\ (S)\ \varepsilon\ training\ examples}\ (E_{train}\ (s) - E'())^2$$

Thus, our objective is to seek the weights or equivalently *E*' that minimize *E* for the observed training examples.

Q.17. Explain Supervised and Unsupervised Learning with a CASE STUDY.

Ans. According to Simon Haykin, learning is the process by which free parameters of a neural network are adapted through a process of stimulation by the environment in which the network is embedded. The type of learning is determined by the manner in which the parameter changes take place." This process of learning involves three steps:-

S1: The neural network is stimulated by the environment (excitatory or inhibitory).

S2: The free parameters of the network like the synaptic weights and the biases, undergo a change as a result of this stimulation.

S3: The response of the neural network to the environment changes as a result of the change in its internal free parameters.

The process of learning involves two things: -

1. The Learning Paradigms, which determine the manner in which a neural network relates to the environment. Here a neural network represents a set of inter-connected neurons.
2. The Learning Law, which is a set of well-defined rules called as the learning algorithm. There is no unique algorithm. One law differs from the other in the manner in which weights and biases are adjusted.

Artificial neural networks can modify their behaviour in response to their environment. Given as a set of inputs with desired outputs, they self-adjust to produce consistent responses. Different types of training algorithms have been developed. Learning algorithms like ANNs, in general, can be presented in either differential-equation or difference-equation form.

A network is trained so that application of a set of inputs produces the desired set of outputs. Each such input is known as a vector. Training is accomplished by sequentially applying input vectors while adjusting network weights according to a predetermined procedure. During training, the network weighs gradually converge to values such that each input vector produces the desired output vector. Training algorithms are put under two categories- supervised and unsupervised.

Supervised Training: A type of training that needs the pairing of each input vector with a target vector showing the desired output. Together these are called as a **training pair.** A network is trained over a number of such training pairs. An input vector is applied, the output of the network is calculated and compared to the corresponding target vector and the difference (error) is fed back through the network and eights are changed according to an algorithm that tends to minimize the error. The vectors of the training set are applied sequentially and errors are calculated and weights adjusted for each vector until the error for the entire training set is at an acceptably low level.

The knowledge is represented in form of input-output examples called as the training data. The training data consists of pairs of input samples in form of a vector and the corresponding output, which happens to be the desired output. The teacher provides the desired output for a given input vector by virtue of inbuilt knowledge as shown in figure 2.3.

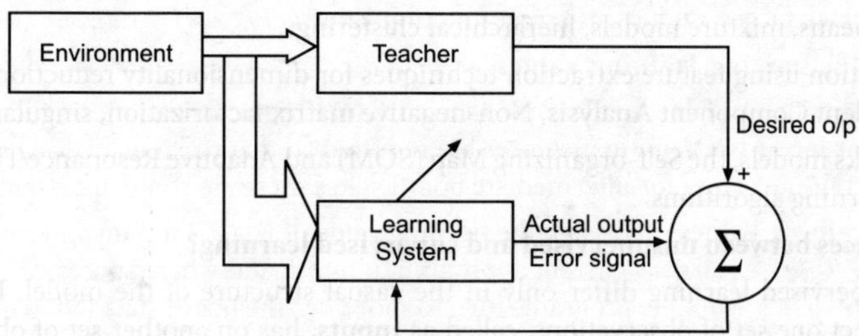

Figure 2.4: Supervised Learning

The network computes the output called as the actual output. The error signal is the difference between the desired output / response and the actual output/response.

Please understand that the network parameters like the synaptic weights and biases are adjusted by means of the learning law, under the influence of the error signal and the input vector. Also note that this is done iteratively until the actual response is close to the desired response. It is at this point that we can say that the network is trained. In nutshell, supervised learning involves the following steps:-

S1: Determine the type of training examples and form the training set. This is a set of input vector and the corresponding output vectors.

S2: The input vector must capture the features descriptive of the object. The number of features should not be too large but large enough to predict the output.

S3: Determine the learning law and train the network with the input training data.

S4: After the training is completed, the network is validated with a subset of the training set.

Please note that the mean Square error or the sum of squared errors over the training sample, defined as a function of the system parameters can be used as a performance measure for the system. Also note that for the system to improve the performance, the operating point must move towards a point of minimum error. Supervised learning is used in applications like pattern classification and function approximation.

Unsupervised Training: It is a more plausible model of learning in biological system. It was developed by Kohonen et. al. in 1984. It requires no target vector for the outputs. Hence no comparisons to pre-determined ideal responses can be made. The training set solely consists of input vectors. The training algorithm modifies the network weights to produce output vectors that are consistent. This means that both application of one of the training vectors or application of a vector that is similar to it, will produce the same pattern of outputs. **Please understand that the training process extracts the statistical properties of the training set and groups similar vectors into classes.** Applying a vector from a given class to the input will produce a specific output vector but there is no way to find out prior to training which specific output pattern will be produced by a given input vector class. Also note that the outputs of such a network must generally be transformed into a more comprehensible form following a training process. This is not difficult. It is so because it is simpler to identify the I/O relationships in a network.

In this type of learning, there is no teacher to see the process of learning. We deal with a class of problems to find out how data is organized. It is shown in figure 2.5.

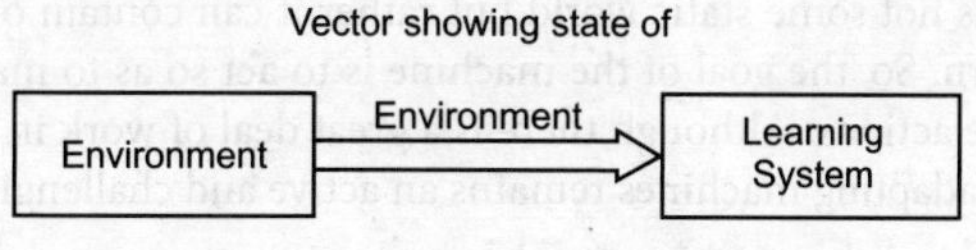

Fig. 2.5: Unsupervised Learning

In machine learning, unsupervised learning refers to the problem of trying to find hidden structure in unlabelled data. Because the examples given to the learner are unlabelled, there is no error or reward signal to evaluate a potential solution. Unsupervised learning is closely related to the problem of density estimation in statistics. However, unsupervised learning also covers many other techniques that seek to summarize and explain key features of the data. Many methods employed in unsupervised learning are based on data mining methods used to pre-process data. Unsupervised learning includes several approaches as listed below:-

- Clustering like k-means, mixture models, hierarchical clustering;
- Blind signal separation using feature extraction techniques for dimensionality reduction like Principal Component Analysis, Independent Component Analysis, Non-negative matrix factorization, singular value decomposition.

Among neural networks models, the Self-organizing Map (SOM) and Adaptive Resonance Theory (ART) are commonly used unsupervised learning algorithms.

Q.18. What are the differences between unsupervised and supervised learning?

Ans. Supervised and unsupervised learning differ only in the casual structure of the model. In supervised learning, the model defines the effect one set of observations, called as **inputs,** has on another set of observations, called **outputs.** His means that the inputs are assumed to be at the beginning and outputs at the end of the **causal chain.** The models can include mediating variables between the inputs and outputs. In unsupervised learning, all observations are assumed to be caused by latent variables. This means that the observations are assumed to be at the end of the causal chain. On the other hand, the models for supervised learning often leave the probability for inputs undefined. This model is not needed as long as the inputs are available but if some of the input values are missing then it is not possible to infer anything about the outputs. If the inputs are also modelled then missing inputs cause no problem since they can be considered latent variables as in unsupervised learning. With unsupervised learning it is possible to learn larger and more complex models than with supervised learning. This is so because in supervised learning one is trying to find the connection between two sets of observations. Please note that the difficulty of learning task increases exponentially in the number of steps between the two sets and that is why supervised learning cannot learn model with deep hierarchies. In unsupervised learning, learning can proceed hierarchically from the observations into ever more abstract levels of representation. Each additional hierarchy needs to learn only one step and therefore, the learning time increases linearly in the number of levels in the model hierarchy. Also note here that if the causal relation between the input and output observations is complex *i.e.* there is a large causal gap, it is often easier to bridge the gap using unsupervised learning instead of supervised learning. Instead of finding the casual pathway from the inputs to the outputs, one starts building the model upwards from both th sets of observations with the hope that in higher levels of abstractions the gap is easier to bridge. Note also that the input and output observations are in symmetrical positions in the model.

Consider a machine or a living organism which receives some sequences of inputs, x_1, x_2, x_3, ...x_t where x_t is the sensory input at time, *t*. This input, which we often call the data, could correspond to an image on the retina, the pixels in a camera or a sound waveform. It could also correspond to less obviously sensory data like words in a news story or the list of items in a mall. So, now four types of machine learning are possible:-

a. In supervised learning, the machine is also given a sequence of desired outputs as y_1, y_2, y_3.....yt and the goal of the machine is to learn to produce the correct output given a new input. The output could be a class label (in classification) or a real number (in regression).

b. In reinforcement learning, the machine interacts with its environment by producing actions a_1, a_2,.....a_n. these actions affect the state of the environment which in turn results in the machine receiving some scalar rewards or punishments, r_1, r_2....r_n. the goal of the machine is to learn to act in a way that maximizes the future rewards it receives or minimizes the punishments over its lifetime. Reinforcement learning is closely related to the fields of decision theory and control theory.

c. Another third type of machine learning is related to the game theory and it generalizes reinforcement learning. Here again the machine gets the inputs, produces actions and receives rewards. However, the environment that the machine interacts with is not some static world but rather it can contain other machines which can also sense, act, receive rewards and learn. So, the goal of the machine is to act so as to maximize rewards in light of the other machines current and future actions. Although there is a great deal of work in game theory for simple systems, the dynamic case with multiple adapting machines remains an active and challenging area of research.

d. Finally, in unsupervised learning, the machine simply receives inputs x_1, x_2, ..., but obtains neither supervised target outputs nor rewards from its environment. It may seem somewhat mysterious to imagine what the machine could possibly learn that it doesn't get any feedback from its environment. However, it is possible to develop a formal framework for unsupervised learning based on the notion that the machine's goal is to build representations of the input that can be used for decision making, predicting future inputs, efficiently communicating the inputs to another machine etc. in a sense, unsupervised learning can be thought of as finding patterns in the data above and beyond what would be considered pure unstructured noise.

Unsupervised algorithms can be compared to a three months old baby. As 3 months old child receives the same visual stimuli as a newborn infant but can make much more sense of them and can recognize various patterns and features of visual input data. These abilities are not acquired from an external teacher and illustrate that a significant amount of learning is accomplished by biological facts, the artificial neural network discussed in this chapter attempt to discover special features and patterns from the available data without using external help.

Our learning starts from birth only. Observe how a baby learns to recognize its mother. The first act of learning of baby is 'to recognize'. When a child is trained to recognize concepts by being provided with labels for each experienced instance then this is supervised learning. On the other hand, learning the features themselves is an example of unsupervised learning. In this the lower-level features are automatically grouped or clustered based on how similar they are across many observed instances. In computing terms, we may call these images i.e., collection of pixels. As a child sees many images of 'dogs' or 'cats', then those pixels that form 'legs' are automatically grouped or clustered together. So, now we can say that the child has learned a new concept of 'legs without any external supervision (or teacher) even though the baby does not know about "leg". Furthermore, this concept of 'leg' becomes a feature that takes a baby to the next higher level of learning.

Several types of learning do exist, like-

1. Learning how to parse sentences.
2. Learning to recognize whether a tweet is positive or negative.
3. Learning the topic, a particular web page is talking about or
4. Discovering the topics that are being discussed in a corpus of text.

In many cases, the machine needs to be trained using data labelled by humans like parsing or sentiment mining. These are the examples of supervised learning. On the other hand, topic discovery is an example of unsupervised learning wherein there is no pre-existing knowledge being provided by outside human intervention. Our computer observes a number of such instances. Its task is to learn the concepts from the training set so as to be able to recognize future instances.

A simple computer program for the above scenario of 'cat-dog' may choose to store all of the observed instances, just as Google stores web pages and also creating an index of features as Google indexes documents using the words they contain. Then when presented with a new instance, our program merely looks up its fast experience very fast, using binary searching.

Case 1: If an exact match is found, the new observation is given the same animal label as the old one it matches with.

Case 2: If no match is found, we might use the closest match, in terms of the number of features that match exactly or use a small number of close matches and choose the label that occurs most often amongst these. This is called as a k-nearest-neighbour (or KNN) classifier as it classifies the instances given to it. But please note that if the number of past observations is very large then the classification process may be slow.

Google also uses classifiers to filter spam, learn user preferences or to classify tweets as positive or negative. Also note that machine learning using classifiers is also at the heart of NLP wherein the computer is trained to parse sentences from a large corpora of human-parsed text.

Google Translate that does automated translation between different languages also uses machine learning heavily. Now the objective is to find out whether a new sentence is expressing positive or negative opinion and to learn how to do so from the past observations of sentences that have been labelled correctly by humans. Instead of size and sound, now our features are the occurrences of words in sentences.

Actually, learning from a small number of examples cannot be perfect so the accuracy with which a concept is learned also needs to be considered. Accuracy is usually measured in terms of the probability of the learned classifier making a mistake. Please note here that the larger the chance of a mistake, lower is the accuracy. Also note that the inverse of the mistake probability can be used a s a measure of accuracy.

Clustering *i.e.*, grouping items that are similar to each other is another basic technique of unsupervised learning. All that is needed is some way to compare two items.

Thus, we can say that machines can learn from examples, in case of supervised learning, such as for browsers versus surfers or dogs versus cats, a human-labelled set of training examples is needed. On the other hand, in unsupervised learning, machine learns from experiences as long as they can be clearly identified even if implicitly.

Web pages are mostly unstructured text. We know that text can be analysed using NLP techniques. And that,

NLP + Machine Learning techniques ⟶ allows machine to learn larger number of General Knowledge facts from such large corpus as the entire web.

Whole of our machine learning is based on first being able to distinguish objects along with some of the features describing them. On the other hand, computers derive this ability directly through our programming. The classifiers can distinguish between different classes of objects like cats from dogs, buyers from browsers etc. provided they have been trained suitably. Unsupervised rule learning can discover important features and frequently observed associations between features, there by learning some structure of the world. Latent learning techniques can also discover infrequent correlations between objects based on their features. Finally, the computer can learn facts from vast volumes of text available on the web.

In nutshell, the learning algorithm uses a large number of labelled instances to learn its model. Then the learned model is used to assign labels to future instances. This is supervised learning. On the other hand, in unsupervised learning, instances are grouped into clusters based on their mutual similarity. There are no labels but only clusters characterized by a set of similar features.

Q.19. Write an overview of classification.

Ans. In the field of machine learning, classification is the problem of finding out to which category a newly encountered observation belongs, based on the training dataset containing observations.

Before we discuss further, let us first of all define a multilayer perceptron and its training.

Multilayer Perceptron (MLP): It is a feed-forward ANN. It maps a set of input data to a set of output data. It consists of multiple layers of nodes represented in a directed graph with each layer being connected to the next layer completely. Apart from the input nodes, each node itself is a neuron or a processing element with a non-linear activation function. The activation function of a node in this context defines the output of that node given an input or set of inputs.

Activation Function: The problem to be considered here is that the jump should be in between firing and not firing to make it behave like neuron. So, we need an activation function that looks like a threshold function but it is differentiable so that gradient can be computed. If we look at the graph of the threshold function, it is similar to S-shaped functions whose mathematical form is called as a sigmoid function.

Error Function: The method that we ar using is called back-propagation error which depicts those errors are sent backward through the network. It is a type of gradient descent. In perceptron, the weights are changed so that the neurons were fired only when the targets indicate and they did not fire when the targets did not indicate. It was time to choose an error function, $E(t, o)$ and tried to make it as small as possible. Since there was only one set of weights available in the network, it was sufficient to train the same. We prepare to minimize the error so that neurons fire only when they should but on adding extra layers of weights it becomes difficult to arrange. Also, when trying to adapt the weights of MLP it is difficult to find out which weights caused the error. This could be any of the weights *i.e.*, the weights connecting inputs to the hidden layer or weights hidden layer to the output layer. We have so far used $E = t - o$ for the perceptron. Say, we have two errors-

1. The target is bigger than the output.
2. The output is bigger than the target.

Please understand that if these two errors are of same size, then we ass them the resultant zero which depicts that no error was made and is incorrect. To get this in line, we need to make all errors to have a same sign. To cope with this problem, the best way is to find the sum of squares error function. The sum of squares error function basically calculates the difference between target (t) and output (o) for each node, squares them and adds them all together. That is,

$$E(t, o) = ½ \, \Sigma \, l = 1 \text{ to } n \, (t_l - o_l)^2$$

Q.20. What are the steps involved in MLP in Practice?

Ans. Three steps are involved here: -

S1: Data Preparation.

S2: Training, Testing and Validation.

S3: Generalization and Overfitting.

Machine learning algorithms tend to learn from data. So, it is important that right data is fed for the problem to be solved. Please note that the more disciplined the data is handled, more consistent and better are the results.

Let us study these steps now.

S1: Data Preparation: It involves three sub-tasks-

1. **Select Data :** It involves the selection of subset of all available data that we will be dealing with. We need to take into consideration what data is needed to solve the problem that we are working on.
2. **Pre-process Data :** After you have selected the data, the next step is how you are going to use the data.
   Steps for data pre-processing: -
   1.1 Formatting: The data should be in a suitable format that you want to work on like the data may be in relational database and you want to use it as a text file.
   1.2 Cleaning: It is the removal or fixing of missing data.
   1.3 Sampling: It is better t take smaller representative sample of data instead of more selected data which results in shorter running times for algorithms and smaller computational and memory requirements.
3. **Transform Data :** The final step is to transform the processed data. The specific algorithms that you are using and the knowledge of the problem domain will influence this step and you will very likely have to revisit different transformations of your pre-processed data as you work on your problem. Three common data transformations are scaling, attribute decomposition and attribute aggregations. This step is also called as feature engineering. It involves-

a. **Scaling:** The pre-processed data may contain attributes with a mixtures of scales for various quantities like dollars, kgs and sales volume. Many machine learning methods like data attribute to have the same scale such as between 0 and for the smallest and the largest value for a given feature. Consider any scaling feature that you may need to perform.

b. **Decomposition:** There may be features that represent a complex concept that may be more useful to a machine learning method when split into the constituent parts. For example, a date that may have day and time components that in turn could split out further. Perhaps only the hour of the day is relevant to the problem being solved. Thus, consider what feature decompositions can be made performed.

c. **Aggregation:** There may be features that can be aggregated into a single feature that would be more meaningful to the problem you are trying to solve. For example, there may be data instance for each time a customer logged into a system that could be aggregated into a count for the number of logins allowing the additional instances to be discarded. You have to consider the type of feature aggregations to be performed.

Note: One can spend a lot of time engineering features from your data and it can be very beneficial for the algorithm performance. Start small and build on the skills you learn.

How data preparation is done in MLP?

Every machine learning algorithm is likely to learn more effectively if some pre-processing of the data inputs and targets is performed before the network is trained. In the case of Perceptron, if sigmoidal activation function is used then possible target values should be 0 and 1. In fact, the targets are scaled to lie between 0 and 1, no matter what sort of activation function is used for the output layer neurons. This helps in avoiding the weights to get too large values. The most common approach to scaling the data for MLP is to look at each data dimension independently and further make each dimension have a zero mean and unit variance in each dimension or simply to scale them so that maximum value is 1 and mi -nimum is -1. These scaling are basically data normalization (or standardization). In case of MLP, normalization is not mandatory but useful. In this, it is very easy to perform normalization by using in-built function mean( ) and var( ). But take care of which axis the mean and variance is to be computed. That is,

```
data = (data – data.mean (axix=0)) / data.var(axis=0)
targets = (targets – targets.mean(axis=0)) / targets.var(axis=0)
```

S2: Training, Testing and Validation : after mlp training is over, in next step we need to find out how well it performs. in case of trained network, the error can be computed by computing the sum of squares error between output and target. The next task is what data should be used to test the network. It is not intelligence to use the same data for training as well as testing. This is so because it would not tell us how well the network generalizes and whether or not overfitting has happened. Thus, we need to keep separate pairs in reserve for testset (input, target) which are not used for the training purpose. In this case, we have to adjust with the fact that the amount of data which is available for testing is reduced. It is more complex, scenario when we check how well the network is learning during training so that when to stop can be decided. Now to make such a decision we cannot use training data as we would not detect overfitting but we cannot use the testing data either as we are saving it for the final test.

So, a 3rd data set called as a validation set is required to validate the learning so far, in the field of statistics, it is called as cross validation.

The ratio of training to testing to validation data is-

50:25:25 if you have large amount of data and

60:20:20 if you have a lesser amount of data.

So, the input data set is split into three different sets-training set, testing set and validation set.

S3: Generalization and Overfitting : The ability of a machine to learn on being introduced with the sets of data during training so that when it is introduced to new and unseen examples, it can perform accurately is known as Generalization. To ensure that network generalizes well, we tend to use a neural network in order to generalize from the training examples to all possible inputs. Some troublesome situations also arise in both under training and over training the network. Every other weight can be changed in a neural network. Thus, degree of variability is quite high. This is certainly more than in variation than there is in the function we are learning. So, the care has to be taken if we are training for long. This implies that we will overfit the data which means that during the process we have also learnt about the noise and inaccuracies in the data along with the actual function. Overfitting makes the model quite complex by having too many parameters. By doing this it loses its generalization power which results in poor performance in new data.

Q.21. Explain Linear Discriminant Analysis (LDA). What are its limitations.

Ans. A linear discriminant method that is used in the field of statistics, pattern recognition and machine learning is Fisher's Linear Discriminant. It is used to find the linear combination of features that divides two or more classes of objects or events. The combination that comes out in the form of result may be used later as a linear classifier, in general, for dimensionality reduction before later classification. So, we can say that LDA is a supervised technique of feature extraction that is used to find a linear combination of the available features which separate the classes.

Applying LDA: The core objective is t decrease the dimension of the data in order to reduce the computational cost of classification. After applying the LDA to a dataset, the "new features" minimizes the dispersion between the samples of the same class and maximizes the dispersion between samples of different classes.

For example, say you have a dataset of players who practice different sports like may be cricket, basketball, soccer, Golf etc. imagine that the available features taken into consideration for these sports are height, weight and body mass index. Now when the instances are plotted, there might be some regions of intersection of two or more classes. So, when yu apply LDA to a data set, it will produce new features that might result in better separation of classes-lesser and smaller regions of intersection.

Limitations of LDA :

1. LDA can generate only C (number of classes) or a smaller number of features.
2. At times, one is dealing with datasets of 20 features, for example, and there are only 2 classes, so LDA have to be reduced to 2 axes. Such reductions usually result in loss of information that further results in low classification accuracy.

Q.22. What are the Probabilistic Models?

Ans. We discuss two types of models here: -

1. Generative Model.
2. Conditional Model.

I. A generative model is a model that generates observable data values randomly, usually provided with some hidden parameters. It states 'a joint probability distribution over observation and label sequences. As far as machine learning is concerned, these models are are used for either modelling data directly or as an intermediary phase to form a conditional probability density function. A conditional distribution can be derived from a generative model with the help of Bayes Rule. For example, Gaussian mixture model, Hidden Markov model, Naive Bayes, Restricted Boltzmann machine, generative adversial networks, probabilistic context-free Grammer etc.

II. Conditional models or discriminative models are used in machine learning for demonstrating the dependence of an unobserved variable 'y' on an observed variable 'x'. In terms of probability, this is prepared by modelling the conditional probability distribution P(y| x), which can be used for predicting from discriminative models, in contrast to generative models, that do not permit to generate samples from the joint distribution of x and y. For example, Logistic regression (a type of generalized linear regression used for predicting binary or categorical outputs—called as maximum entropy classifiers, Support Vector Machines, Boosting-a meta-algorithm, conditional random fields, linear regression, neural networks etc.

Tasks like classification and regression do not require joint distribution. In fact, conditional models can return excellent performance. Please understand that these generative models are more flexible than discriminative models in stating dependencies in complex learning tasks. Also note that most discriminative models are fundamentally supervised and cannot easily be stretched to unsupervised learning. Application decides whether to go for generative or conditional model.

Say, the input data is 'x' and the set of labels for x is 'y'. Then,

1. Generative model learns the joint probability distribution $p(x, y)$.
2. Discriminative model learns the conditional probability distribution $p(x \mid y)$ *i.e.* the 'probability of y given x'.

Q.23. Explain the Decision Trees in machine learning and deep learning.

Ans. In decision trees, we break the classification down into a set of choices about each feature starting at the root of the tree and progressing down to leaves where we receive the final classification decision. The data structure, tree, is very easy to understand and implement.

In this approach, we have handy, if-then-else rules which are useful for use in a production system. This type of algorithm has been applied successfully to a broad range of tasks from learning to diagnose medical cases to learning to assess credit risk of loan applicants.

Decision trees classify instances by sorting them down the tree from the root to some leaf nodes which provides the classification of the instance. Each node in the tree specifies a test of some attribute of the instance and each branch descending from that node corresponds to one of the possible values for this attribute. An instance is classified by starting at the root node of the tree, testing the attribute specified by this node then moving down the tree branch corresponding to the value of the attribute in the given example. This process is then repeated for the subtree rooted at the new node.

This method is very popular because we can turn into a set of logical disjunctions (if-then-else rules) that fit into program code easily.

Limitations of Decision Trees :

1. Instances are represented by attribute-value pairs.
2. Target function has discrete output values.
3. Disjunctive descriptions may be required.
4. Training data may contain errors.
5. Training data may contain missing attribute values.

This method of learning has been applied to problems like learning to classify medical patients on the basis of their disease, equipment breakdowns by their cause and loan applicants by their possibility of non-payment. Such problems, in which the task is to classify examples into one of a discrete set of possible categories, are often stated as classification problems.

For constructing a decision tree, the features that are required for the algorithm are as follows: -

1. The state of energy level.
2. The date of your nearest deadline.
3. Whether or not there is a party tonight.

Now the challenge is to construct a tree based on these features. Literature provides different types of decision tree algorithms that are based on the same principle but follow different approaches.

Principle: "The algorithm states that the algorithm built the tree in a greedy manner starting at the root and choosing the most informative feature (how the tree works) at each step".

ALGORITHM ID3 {by Quinlan} : This algorithm learns decision trees by constructing them in top-down fashion i.e. starts with the question "at the root of the tree, which attribute is to be tested?" In order to answer this question, each instance attribute is assessed using a statistical test to find out how well it classifies the training examples. The best

attribute is selected to be used as the test, as the root node of the tree. Then a successor of the root node is produced for each possible value of this attribute and the training examples are sorted to the suitable successor node *i.e.*, down the branch conforming to the example's value for this attribute. The complete process is then repeated using the training examples related with each descendant node to select the best attribute at test at that point in the tree. This practices a greedy search for an acceptable decision tree, in which the algorithm never backtracks to review earlier options.

Now the question is which attribute is the best classifier?

Selecting which attribute that is to be tested at each node in the tree is the basic factor that is to be considered in ID3 algorithm. We would like to make choice of the attribute that is most beneficial for the classifying examples.

What is a good quantitative measure of the value of an attribute?

A statistical property called as an information gain will compute how well a given attribute separates the training examples in accordance to their target classification. ID3 uses up this information gain measure to make a choice amongst the candidate attributes at each step while the tree grows.

ID3 (Examples, Target-attribute, Attributes) : (where, Examples are the training examples, Target-attribute is the attribute whose value is to be predicted by the tree and Attributes is a list of other attributes that may be tested by the learned decision tree)

(This algo returns a decision tree that correctly classifies the given Examples)

Step-1: Create a root node for the tree.

Step-2: If all Examples are positive, return the single-node tree Root, with label = +

Step-3: If all Examples are negative, return the single-node tree Root, with label = -

Step-4: If Attributes is empty, return the single-node tree Root with label = most common value of Target-attribute in Examples.

Step-5: Otherwise Begin

5.1 A ← the attribute from Attributes that best classifies Examples.

5.2 The decision attribute for Root ← A.

5.3 For each possible value, v_i, of A,

5.3.1 Add a new tree branch below Root, corresponding to the test A = v_i.

5.3.2 Let Example, sv_i be the subset of Examples that have value v_i for A.

5.3.3 If Example sv_i is empty

5.3.3.1 then below this new branch, add a leaf node with label = most common value of Target-attribute in Examples.

5.3.3.2 Else below this new branch add the subtree ID3 (Examples vi, Target-attribute, Attributes – (A))

Step-6: End

Step-7: Return Root

In nutshell, ID3 algorithm is dedicated to learning Boolean-valued functions. ID3 is a greedy algorithm that develops the tree in top-down fashion, at each node choosing the attribute that best classifies the local training examples. This process carries until the tree perfectly classifies the training examples or until all attributes have been taken into consideration.

Q.24. Write and explain K-nearest Neighbour Learning-distance weighted Nearest Neighbour Algorithm.

Ans. It is an instance-based method.

Principle: "This algorithm assumes that all instances relate to points in the n-dimensional space, Rn. The nearest neighbours of an instance are defined in terms of the standard Euclidean distance."

Let feature vector describe an arbitrary instance, x. The feature vector is-

$$< a_1 (x), a_2 (x),......a_n (x) >$$

Where $a_r (x)$ denotes the values of the rth attribute of instance, x. Then the distance between two instances, x_i and x_j is defined to be $d (x_i, x_j)$ and is calculated as follows:-

$$d (x_i, x_j) = \sqrt{\sum (r = 1 \text{ to } n)(a_r(x_i) - a_r(x_j))^2}$$

In nearest-neighbor learning, the target function may be either for discrete-valued or real-valued. Let us first of all study learning discrete valued target functions of the form-

f: R^n -> V where V is the finite set $\{v_1,......v_s\}$.

ALGORITHM k-nearest Neighbour { a discrete-valued target function }

Training algorithm: For each training example (x, f (x)), add the example to the list of training examples.

Classification algorithm: Given instance x_q is to be classified. Let $x_1......x_k$ denote the k-instances from training examples that are nearest to xq. Return

$f(x_q) \leftarrow \text{argmax} (v \,\varepsilon\, V) \ \Sigma \ (i=1 \text{ to } k) \ \delta(v, f(x_i))$

where $\delta (a, b) = 1$ if $a = b$ and where $\delta (a, b) = 0$ otherwise.

Explanation: The value f (x), given back by the algorithm as its approximation of $f(x_i)$ is just the most common value of f amongst the k training examples which are nearest to x.

If we choose $k = 1$, then the 1-nearest neighbour algorithm assigns the value $f(x_i)$ to $f(x_i)$ where x_i is the training instance which is nearest to x_i.

For larger values of k, the algorithm allots the most common value among the k-nearest training examples.

Figure 2.6 explains the working of the k-nearest neighbour algorithm for the case where the instances are basically points in a 2D space. Also the target function is in form of Boolean. The positive and negative training examples are depicted by "+" and "-" respectively. Please note that the 1-nearest neighbour algorithm classifies x, as a positive example in figure 2.6 whereas the 5-nearest neighbour algorithm classifies it as a negative example. Also note that k-nearest neighbour algorithm never forms a clear hypothesis regarding the target function, f. It just works out for the classification of each new query instance encountered as needed.

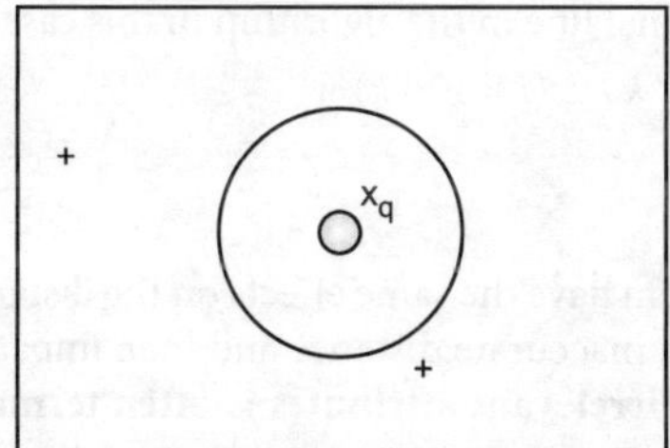

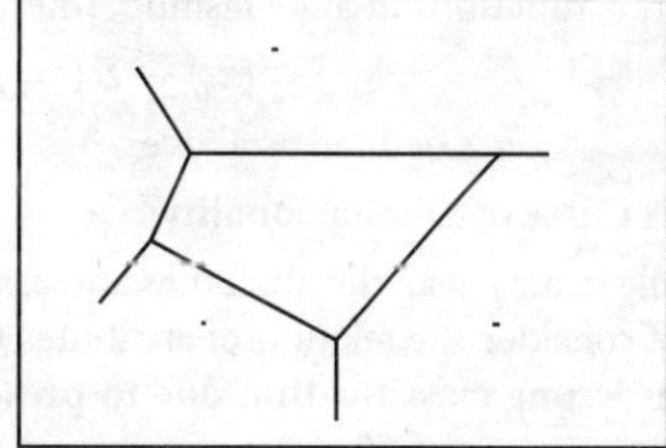

Figure 2.6: *k-Nearest Neighbour*

Explanation: A set of positive and negative training examples is shown on the left diagram of figure 2.6. The 1-nearest neighbour algorithm classifies x as positive whereas 5-nearest neighbour classifies it as negative. On the right- hand side of the figure 2.6, is the decision surface induced by the 1-nearest neighbour algorithm for a typical set of training examples. **Please note that the convex polygon surrounding each training example indicates the region of instance space closest to that point.** This means that the instances for which the 1-nearest neighbour algorithm will assign the classification belonging to that training example. On the right side of the figure 2.6, is shown a shape of the decision surface made by 1-nearest neighbour over the complete instance space. The decision surface is basically a grouping of convex polyhedral surrounding each of the training examples. For every training example, the polyhedron shows the set of query points whose classification will be completely decided by that training example. Also note that the query points that lie outside the polyhedron are closer to some other training example. And such a type of diagram is often called as the V**oronoi diagram of the** set of training examples. The k-nearest neighbour algorithm is easily adapted to approximating continuous-valued target functions. To accomplish this, we need the algorithm to calculate the mean value of k-nearest training examples rather than calculate their most common value. Practically speaking, to estimate a real-valued target function f: $R^n \rightarrow R$, we replace the final line of the above algorithm by: -

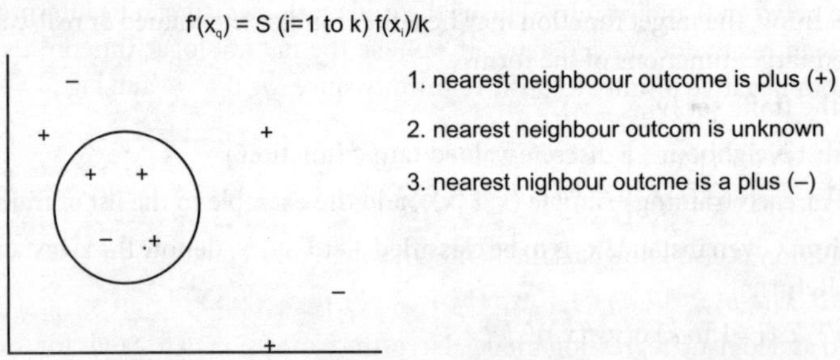

Figure 2.7: Accurate Estimate of Real-valued target Function

Q.25. Explain enhanced Distance weighted nearest-Neighbour Algorithm.

Ans. This algorithm is an enhancement of k-nearest algorithm.

Principle: Weigh the contribution of each of the k-neighbours depending on their distance to query point, x, awarding greater weight to closer neighbours.

For example, in the algorithm of k-nearest above, that approximates discrete-valued target functions, we might weight the support of each neighbour corresponding to the inverse square of its distance from xi. And this is done by interchanging the last line of the algorithm by:-

$$f(x_q) \leftarrow \text{argmax} \;(v \in V) \;\Sigma \;(i = 1 \text{ to } k) \;\; w_i \, \delta(v, f(x_i))$$

where $$w_i = 1 / d(x_q, x_i)^2$$

To consider the case where the query point, x, exactly matches one of the training instances, x_i and the denominator $d\,(x_q, x_i)^2$ is therefore zero, we assign $f(x_q)$ to be $f(x_i)$ in this particular case. We can distance-weight the instances for real-valued target functions in alike fashion, interchanging the final line in the algorithm in this case by-

$$f(x_q) \leftarrow \Sigma \;(i = 1 \text{ to } k) \; w_i f(x_i) \;/\; k \;/\; \Sigma \;(i = 1 \text{ to } k) \; w_i$$

where w_i is defined as above.

Q.26. Define what is Curse of Dimensionality?

Ans. Distance usually relates to all the attributes and assumes all of them have the same effects on the distance. The similarity metrics do not consider the relation of attributes which result in inaccurate distance and then impact on classification precision. **This wrong classification due to presence of many irrelevant attributes is often termed as the curse of dimensionality.**

For example, say each instance is described by 20 attributes out of which only 2 are relevant in determining the classification of the target function. In this case, instances that have identical values for the 2 relevant attributes may nevertheless be distant from one another in the 20-dimensional instance space.

Q.27. Give an introduction to Logistic Regression.

Ans. Logistics Regression was developed by statistician David Cox in 1958. Regression analysis needs always numeric data. When attributes are categorical, we have to change them to numeric values to apply regression analysis. For example, we can change the attribute gender, being male or female, to 0 and 1 respectively. This has no problem as far as the execution of the regression algorithm is concerned but certainly has problems with the interpretation of the output. If the output or dependent attribute is categorical, the numeric output from regression analysis may not make any sense. There are no restrictions on the output of a regression model. It can be any value from negative infinity to positive infinity. It is quite possible that we get a gender value of 0.5. So, the regression model of a categorical output is given by the expression: -

$$P(y = 1 \mid X) = b_0 + b_1 x_1 + b_2 x_2 + \ldots\ldots \qquad (1)$$

Where, $P(y = 1 \mid X)$ is the conditional probability of the output attribute, y being 1 given the values of the independent attributes, X. Here X represents a vector of independent variables x_1, x_2...... Because the value of probability lies within the range [0, 1], we can increase the range by considering the following ratio:-

$$\frac{P(y=1 \mid X)}{1-P(y=1 \mid X)}$$

This can have the value between 0 and infinity. This is the odds ratio, which can be interpreted as how often the class associated with y=1 is seen relative to other classes. If we take the natural logarithm of this odds ratio, we will get an unbounded function from negative infinity to positive infinity since log 0 = -∞ and log ∞ = + ∞. So, we can write:-

$$\text{In}\left[\frac{P(y=1|X)}{1-P(y=1|X)}\right] = b_0 + b_1 x_1 + b_2 x_2 + \ldots.. \quad (3)$$

Please note that this equation is also known as the logit. On solving the equation, we get: -

$$P(y = 1 \mid X) = \exp(b_0 + b_1 x_1 + b_2 x_2 + \ldots..) / 1 + \exp(b_0 + b_1 x_1 + b_2 x_2 + \ldots..) \quad (4)$$

This equation-4 is called as a logistic regression model. Here, the expression exp stands for the base of natural logarithm ($e = 2.7182$). If we plot this equation-4 then we will get an S-shaped curve as shown in figure 2.8.

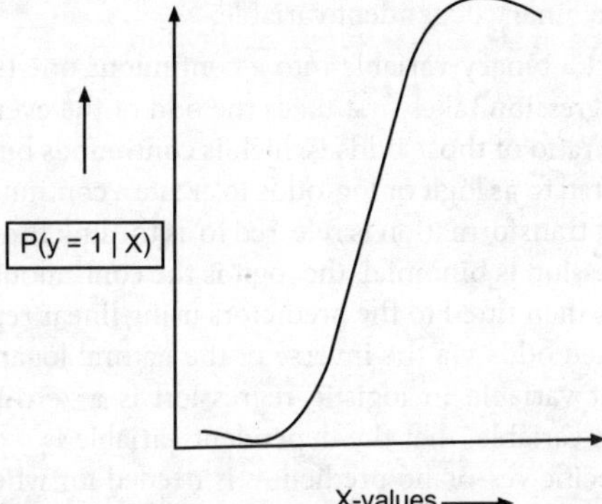

Fig. 2.8: *Graph of Logistic Regression Equatlon*

To find the coefficients b_0, b_1, b_2, ... of equation-4, we use iterative method. The purpose of the method is to minimize the sum of logarithms of conditional probabilities. **Please understand that the aim of the method is to minimize the sum of logarithms of the conditional probabilities. Also note that convergence occurs when this value is close to zero or it does not change from one iteration to the next.**

Cases with more than two categories are called as multinomial logistic regression. If the multiple categories are ordered then it is ordinal logistic regression. The binary logistic model is used to estimate the probability of a binary response based on one or more predictor or independent variables features. It is also called as **qualitative response or discrete choice model in economics field.** Logistic regression measures the relationship between the categorical dependent variable and one or more independent variables by estimating probabilities using a logistic function, which is the cumulative logistic distribution.

Applications : Logistic regression is used in various fields like machine learning, many medical fields and social sciences. For example, the Trauma and Injury Severity Score (TRISS), which is widely used to predict mortality in injured patients, was developed by Boyd et al. using Logistic regression only. It may be used to predict whether a patient has a given disease, based on observed characteristics of the patient.

Example 2, to predict whether an American voter will vote democratic or Republican, based on age, income, sex, race, previous votes etc.

Example 3, this technique can also be used in engineering field to predict the probability of failure of a given process, system or product.

Example 4, it is also used in marketing applications like prediction of a customer's propensity to purchase a product or halt a subscription etc.

Example 5, in economics, it can be used to predict the likelihood of a person's choosing to be in the labour force and a business application would be to predict the likelihood of a homeowner defaulting on a mortgage.

Example 6, conditional random fields that are an extension of logistic regression to sequential data, are used in NLP.

Logistic regression can be binomial, ordinal or multinomial. Binomial or binary logistic regression deals with situations in which the observed outcome for a dependent variable can have only two possible types like "win" or "loss". Multinomial logistic regression deals with situations where the outcome can have 3 or more possible types like disease A or disease B or disease C, that are not ordered. Ordinal logistic regression deals with dependent variables that are ordered. In binary logistic regression, the outcome is usually coded as "0" or "1", as his leads to the most straightforward interpretation. If a particular observed outcome for the dependent variable is the noteworthy possible outcome (referred to as a "success" or a "case") it is usually coded as "1" and the contrary outcome (referred to as a "failure" or a "noncase") as "0". Please note that this Logistic regression is used to predict the odds of being a case based on the values of the independent variables/ predictors. Also note that the odds are defined as the probability that a particular outcome is a case divided by the probability that it is a noncase.

Like other forms of Logistic regression analysis, Logistic regression makes use of one or more predictor variables that may be either continuous or categorical. However, unlike ordinary linear regression, logistic regression is used for predicting binary dependent variables rather than a continuous outcome. Given this difference, the assumptions of linear regression are violated. In particular, the residuals cannot be normally distributed. Also, linear regression may make non-sensical predictions for a binary dependent variable.

The aim is to find a way to convert a binary variable into a continuous one that can take on any real value (negative or positive). To do this, Logistic regression takes first takes the odd of the event happening for different levels of each independent variable then take the ratio of those odds (which is continuous but cannot be negative) and then takes the logarithm of that ratio. This is referred to as logit or log-odds to create a continuous criterion as a transformed version of the dependent variable. So, the logit transformation is referred to as the link function in Logistic regression although the dependent variable in logistic regression is binomial, the logit is the continuous criterion upon which linear regression is conducted. The logit of success is then fitted to the predictors using linear regression analysis. The predicted value of logit is converted back into predicted odds via the inverse of the natural logarithm, namely the exponential function. Although the observed dependent variable in logistic regression is a zero-or-one variable, the logistic regression estimates the odds as a continuous variable, that the dependent variable is a case. In some applications, the odds are all that are needed. In others, a specific yes-or-no prediction is needed for whether the dependent variable is or is not a case. This categorical prediction can be based on the computed odds of a success, with predicted odds above some chosen cut-off value being translated into a prediction of success.

Queries that can be answered here are like does body weight calorie intake, fat intake and age have an influence on heart attacks?

Assumptions made: -

1. The outcome must be discrete.
2. The dependent variable should be dichotomous in nature like 'present' or 'absent'.
3. There should be no outliers in the data which can be assessed by converting the continuous predictors to standardized or z-scores and remove values below -5 or above 5.
4. There should be no high inter-correlations or multi-collinearity among the predictors. This can be assessed by a correlation matrix among the predictors.
5. Tabachnick et al. suggest that as long as correlation coefficients among independent variables are less than 0.90 the assumption is met.
6. Standard linear regression requires the dependent variable to be of metric (interval or ratio) scale.
7. Logistic regression assumes that the dependent variable is a stochastic event. For instance, if we analyse a pesticide kill rate the outcome event is either killed or alive.
8. Since even the most resistant bug can only be either of these two states, logistic regression thinks in likelihoods of the bug getting killed. If the likelihood of killing the bug is > 0.5, it is assumed dead, if it is <0.5 then it is assumed alive.

Q.28. What is a Perceptron and Perceptron Learning Algorithm (PLA).

Ans. According to Minsky et al. a perceptron is defined as "A machine which learns from examples, to assign input samples (vectors) to different classes using a linear function of inputs". Simply stated, it is a neural network used for pattern classification. It consists of a single neuron with adjustable synaptic weights. It is also possible to expand the output layer of perceptron to include more than one neuron. So, they are also called as weighted networks. There are two types of perceptions as follows:-

a. Single layer perception.

b. Multi-layer perception.

Single layer perception: A single layer perceptron is shown in figure 2.9. It consists up of an input layer and an output layer with adjustable weights and a bias. It is used for classification of patterns that are linearly separable. The perception algorithm converges and positions the decision surface in the form of a hyper plane between the two classes. The limitation of this network is that it performs pattern classification with only two classes which are linearly separable. Please understand that the linearity and integrity learning makes the single layer perception network very simple. Also understand that the training in the perception continues till no error occurs.

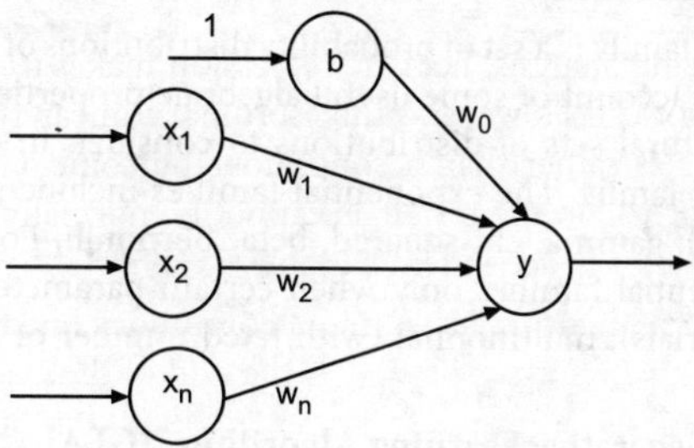

Fig. 2.9: Single Layer Perceptron

In this network, only the weights between the associator and the response unit are adjusted. The input layer consists of input neurons from $x_1, x_2, ..., x_n$. There always exists a common bias "1". The output is compared with this target, if any difference occurs, update weights else stop training process.

In machine learning, the perceptron is an algorithm for supervised learning of binary classifiers *i.e.*, functions that can decide whether an input represented by a vector of numbers, belongs to some specified class or not.

The Training Algorithm

Step-1: Initialize weights and bias to zero and set learning rate, α = 0 to 1.

Step-2: While stopping condition is false do step-3 to step-7.

Step-3: For each training pair s: t do step-4 to step-6.

Step-4: Set activation of input units-

$$x_i = s_j \text{ for } i = 1 \text{ to } n$$

Step-5: Determine the output unit response-

$$y_{in} = b + \Sigma\,(i = 1 \text{ to } n)\; x_i\, w_i$$

Where the activation function is-

$$y = f(y_{in}) = \begin{cases} = 1, \text{ if } y_{in} \geq \theta \\ = 0, \text{ if } y_{in} = -\theta \text{ to } \theta \\ = -1, \text{ if } y_{in} < -\theta \end{cases}$$

Step-6: Observe the match between the target and the output response. If they do not match, update the weights and bias. So,

$$\text{if } t \neq y \text{ and } x_i \neq 0$$

$$w_{i\,(new)} = w_{i\,(old)} + \alpha\, t x_i$$

$$b_{(new)} = b_{(old)} + \alpha_t$$

else

$$w_{i\,(new)} = w_{i\,(old)}$$

$$b_{(new)} = b_{(old)}$$

Step-7: Test for stopping condition based on weight changes.

Step-8: Only weights connecting active units, $x_i \neq 0$ are updated and weights are updated only for patterns that do not produce the correct value of *y*.

Notes:

1. Single layer perception can be implemented for AND, OR, NOT logic functions but cannot be used for EX-OR logic function.
2. The perception network for a single output class is extended for several output classes.
3. There are more number of output neurons or units.
4. The weight updated in this case is also based on the perception learning rule.

Q.29. Explain the concept of Exponential Family.

Ans. In probability field, an exponential family is a set of probability distributions of a certain form. this special form is chosen for mathematical convenience, on account of some useful algebraic properties as well as for generality, as exponential families are in a sense of very natural sets of distributions to consider. In 1935, Pitman et al. gave this concept of exponential families / exponential family. The exponential families include many of the most common distributions including the normal, exponential, gamma, chi-squared, beta, Bernoulli, Poisson, Inverse Wishart etc. A number of common distributions are exponential families only when certain parameters are considered fixed and known e.g., binomial (with fixed number of trials), multinomial (with fixed number of trials) and negative binomial (with fixed number of failures).

Q.30. Give the Generative Model and Generative Learning Algorithm (GLA).

Ans. A generative model is a model for randomly generating observable data values, typically given some hidden parameters. It specifies a joint probability distribution over observation and label sequences. Note that generative models are used in machine learning for either modelling data directly *i.e.*, modelling observations drawn from a probability density function, or as an intermediate step to form a conditional probability density function. A conditional distribution can be formed from a generative model through Baye's rule. Generative learning is a theory that involves the active integration of new ideas with the learners existing schemata. The main idea is that in order to learn with understanding, a learner has to construct meaning actively. According to Wittrock, learners construct meaning by actively building relationships between stimuli and their stored information such as knowledge and their experiences. This construction of semantic and distinctive idiosyncratic associations between stimuli and stored information is called as generation. So, we can say that Generative Learning is the process of constructing meaning through generating relationships and associations between stimuli and existing knowledge, beliefs and experiences.

Shannon in 1948, gave an example of in which a table of frequencies of English word pairs is used to generate a sentence beginning with "representing and speedily is an good"; which is not proper English but which will increasingly approximate it as the table is moved from word pairs to word triplets etc.

Q.31. Distinguish between the Generative Models v/s Discriminative Models.

Ans. A Generative model is a full probabilistic model of all variables while a discriminative model provides a model only for the target variables conditional on the observed variables for example, generative model can be used to simulate values of any variable in the model. On the other hand, discriminative model allows only the sampling of the target variables conditional on the observed quantities. Despite of the fact that descriptive model do not need to model the distribution of the observed variables, they cannot generally express more complex relationships between the observed and target variables. They do not necessarily perform better than generative models at classification and regression tasks. In modern applications, the two classes are complementary to each other.

Some examples of Generative models are:-

a. Gaussian mixture model.

b. Naive Baye's.

c. Context-free Grammar.

d. Hidden Markov Model.

e. Restricted Boltzman Machine.

f. Generative Adversial Networks.

Please note that if the observed data are truly samples from the generative model, then fitting parameters of the generative model to maximize the data likelihood is a common method. But since most of the statistical models are only approximations to the true distributions, if the model's application is to infer about a subset of variables conditional on known values of others, then it can be argued that the approximation makes more assumptions than are necessary to solve the problem at hand. In such cases, it can be more accurate to model the conditional density functions directly using a discriminative model. But the application-specific details will ultimately dictate which approach is most suitable in any particular case.

Generative model in context of Machine Learning : A generative algorithm models how the data was generated in order to categorize a signal. It answers to queries like 'based on my generation assumptions, which category is most likely to generate this signal? A discriminative algorithm does not care about how the data was generated; it simply categorizes a given signal.

Example: Say, the input data is x and the set of labels for x is y. A generative model learns the joint probability distribution $p(x, y)$ while a discriminative model learns the conditional probability distribution $p(y \mid x)$ *i.e.* the probability of y given x.

Discriminative algorithms try to learn $p(y \mid x)$ directly from the data and then tries to classify data. On the other hand, generative algorithms tries to learn $p(x, y)$ which can be transformed into $p(x \mid y)$ later to classify the data. One of the benefits of generative algorithms is that you can use $p(x, y)$ to generate new data similar to the existing data. On the other hand, discriminative algorithms generally give better performance in classification tasks.

Some examples of Discriminative models are: -

a. Logistic Regression.

b. Support Vector Machines.

c. Neural Networks.

d. Conditional Random Fields.

Q.32. Write short notes on Gaussian Discriminant Analysis.

Ans. Gaussian Discriminant Analysis (GDA) is a method for data classification commonly used when data can be approximated with a normal distribution.

The first step needs a training set *i.e.*, a bunch of data yet classified. These data are used to train your classifier and obtain a discriminant function that will tell you to which class a data has higher probability to belong. When you have your training set, you need to compute the mean and the standard deviation. These two variables allow us to compute normal distribution. Once you have computed the normal distribution for each class, to classify a data you will need to compute, for each one, the probability that the data belongs to. Note that the class with the highest probability will be chosen as the affinity class. GDA is a generative model for classification where the distribution of each class is modelled as a multivariate Gaussian. GDA is a generative learning algorithm. In this model, we will assume that $P(x \mid y)$ is distributed according to a multivariate normal distribution.

Note: We make stronger assumptions in GDA. If we do not know where the data comes from then the logistic regression analysis would be more robust. But if we know then GDA may perform better.

Q.33. Write the Naive Bayes and its Algorithm.

Ans. It is a supervised machine learning algorithm. It is often associated with NLP (Natural Language Processing) applications like spam recognition or sentiment analysis.

By the term 'naive' we mean "immature". A naive Bayes classifier is a simple probability-based algorithm. It uses Bayes theorem. It assumes that instances are independent of each other. They work very well in complex real world scenarios also. The naive Bayes algorithm offers a fast model building and scoring both for binary and multiclass situations for relatively low volumes of data. According to Hand et al., 2001, this algorithm makes predictions using Bayes theorem which includes evidence or prior knowledge in its prediction.

Tool like WEKA also uses this naive Bayes algorithm on the dataset provided to it. In WEKA, there is an option of naive Bayes classifier under 'bayes' subdirectory. Then in next step we keep the default settings of the Weka environment and the classifiers parameters. Next, we click on the Start button and the program executes and we will get the needed analysis. Thus, this model is used for analysis of the input dataset. Naive Bayes is a simple technique for constructing classifiers-models that assign class labels to problem instances that are represented as vectors of feature values. The class labels are drawn from some finite set.

Principle: "All Naive Bayes classifiers assume that the value of a particular feature is independent of the value of any other feature, given the class variable."

For example, a rectangle may be considered to be a whiteboard if it has a length, breadth and some thickness. A Naive Bayes classifier considers each of these features to contribute independently to the probability that this rectangle is a whiteboard, regardless of any possible correlations between the colour, its shape and its thickness.

Note that for some types of probability models, Naive Bayes classifiers can be trained very efficiently in a supervised learning setting. Practically, parameter estimation for Naive Bayes models uses the method of maximum likelihood. In other words, one can work with Naive Bayes model without accepting Bayesian methods.the advantage of this is that it requires only a small number of training data to estimate the parameters necessary for classification. As far as machine learning is concerned, Naive Bayes classifiers are a family of simple probabilistic classifiers based on applying Baye's theorem with strong independence assumptions between the features.

Naive Bayes classifiers have been studied extensively since 1950s. It forms the baseline for text categorization. With suitable pre-processing, it is competitive in this domain with more advanced methods including support vector machines. Also, it has some applications in automatic medical diagnosis. Naive Bayes classifiers are highly scalable, requiring a number of parameters linear in the number of variables (features/ predictors) in a learning problem. Also note that maximum-likelihood training can be done by evaluating a closed-form expression, which takes linear time rather than by expensive iterative approximation as used for many other types of classifiers.

Advantages of Naive Bayes Algorithm: -

1. The algorithm as well as its implementation process is simple. Calculations do not involve any numerical optimization, no matrix algebra and no calculus.
2. The algorithm is efficient to train and use. It can be easily updated with new data. This algorithm is similar to linear classifier and hence is fast too.
3. From one dataset we can estimate content features from messages without headers.
4. Unlabelled data can be used in parameter estimation for other applications. This algorithm performs well with smaller training sets.

Disadvantages of Naive Bayes Algorithm: -

1. The independence assumption is a very strong inference and untrue for most real-world problems.
2. The boundaries between classes have to be fine- tuned and not to be set analytically.
3. It is not very effective algorithm as it is simple.

Applications of Naive Bayes Algorithm: -

1. The classifiers used in text classification have higher success rate as compared to other algorithms. As a result, it is widely used in spam filtering i.e., identifying spam e-mail and sentiment analysis i.e. in social media analysis to identify positive and negative customer sentiments.
2. Naive Bayes classifier and collaborative filtering together builds a recommendation system that uses machine learning and data mining techniques to filter unseen information and predict whether a user would like a given resource or not.
3. It is an eager learning classifier and is thus fast. It could be used for making predictions in real-time too.
4. It can be used to do parameter estimation for any model application.
5. It can be used for document classification also.
6. In medical diagnosis field, it has been used for localization of primary tumour, thyroid diseases etc.

Q.34. What are Support Vector Machines (SVMs)? Explain in detail.

Ans. SVM belongs to the type of supervised learning methods used for classification and regression. SVM were developed by Vladimir Vapnik et al. in 1998 at UK. Statistical learning became important after its introduction.

Basic Idea: Construct a hyper plane that best separates classes. If this is not feasible in the input space then the goal is achieved in a higher dimensional space called as a **feature space,** reached by mapping the input vector through a non-linear function.

This mapping has a property that will linearly separate the data sets in the feature space. The hyper plane in the feature space will maximally separate the data set classes. The method is based on statistical learning theory and is successfully used in a number of applications like particle identification, face detection, text categorization. Technically speaking, it is mathematically intuitive, reproducible and does not have problems of local minima as the optimization function is convex and is robust to new classification data tasks.

In machine learning, SVMs or Support Vector Networks are supervised learning models with associated learning algorithms that analyse data used for classification and regression analysis. Given a set of training examples, each marked as belonging to one or the other of two categories, an SVM training algorithm builds a model that assigns new examples to one category or the other, making it a non-probabilistic binary linear classifier. An SVM model is a representation of the examples as points in space, mapped so that the examples of the separate categories are divided by a clear gap that is as wide as possible. Then new examples are mapped into that same space and predicted to belong to a category based on which side of the gap they fall. SVMs can also perform a non-linear classification using what is called the kernel trick i.e. implicitly mapping their inputs into high dimensional feature spaces. When data are not labelled, supervised learning is not possible and an unsupervised learning approach is required, which attempts to find natural clustering of the data to groups and then map new data to these formed groups. The clustering algorithm which provides an improvement to SVM is called support vector clustering. It is often used in industrial applications either when data are not labelled or when only some data are labelled as a pre-processing for a classification pass.

This is shown in figure 2.10.

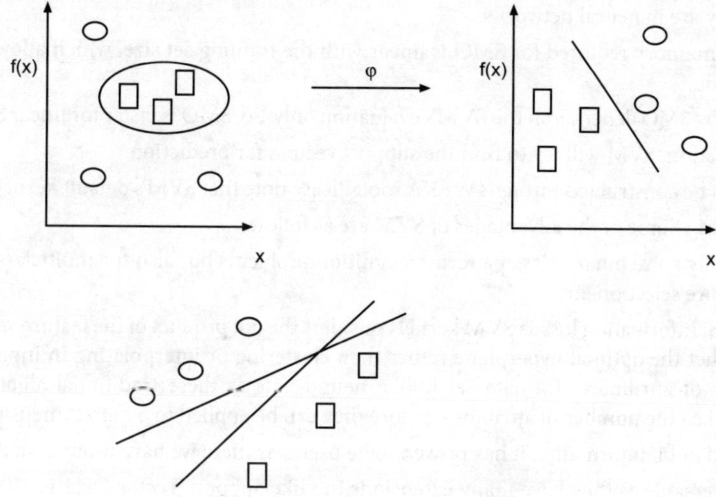

Fig. 2.10: Data sets and their Separation

The upper part of the figure 2.10 shows the mapping of the training data non-linearly into a higher dimensional feature space and constructs a hyperplane with maximum margins. The lower part of the figure 2.10 shows two potential hyperplanes that separate data sets. A hyperplane is a concept in geometry. Please note that hyperplane is a generalization of the concept of a plane which is used in SVM implementation for object separation. Also note that a hyperplane that separates the data points in the feature space with maximum distances among the classes in SVM is called as a maximum-margin hyperplane or optimal hyperplane. The data points on the outer margins/ outside ovals and the inner margins/ inside ovals that are on the boundary lines are called as support vectors.

Support vectors or SVs are transformed training patterns that are always placed at the optimal hyperplane in the feature space during SVM LEARNING. SVM is a statistical based learning algorithm that has been widely used by researchers in various fields like business, text categorization, pattern recognition and protein function prediction. Recently, researchers added a new dimension to SVM in cancer classification through its ability to deal with high dimensional data. SVM can handle any classification, clustering, regression and even novelty detection problems. The attractiveness of SVM algorithm lies in the fact that we do not have to consider all instances i.e., we can focus on the support vectors to do the analysis.

Algorithm: SVM : SVM architecture is analogous to neural network architecture. Like we have three layers of neural networks, similarly we have three phases of SVM-

a. Input or transformation phase,

b. Middle or Learning phase and

c. Output or function estimation phase.

Please note the following points here: -

1. Data extraction tool first collects the data about the object and feed these data as input.

2. Then these data are transformed into vectors in a new mathematical space called as a feature space.
3. SVM starts to find support vectors in the learning phase.
4. If data are not linearly separable, SVM calls non-linear kernel for transformation of the input data.
5. 'Kernel trick' can apply linear classification techniques to non-linear classification problems. Many types of kernels like linear, polynomial and radial bassis function can be followed by SVM.
6. After kernel transformation, SVM uses some optimization techniques (like sequential minimal optimization-SMO) to extract parameter values. Actually, training an SVM involves the solution of very large quadratic programming problem Also note that SVM breaks the large quadratic programming problems into a series of smaller problems and solves them analytically.
7. Large quadratic programming problems have only one minimum. So, SVMs do not suffer from finding local minima problems as they are in neural networks.
8. The amount of memory required for SMO is linear with the training set size, which allows it to handle very larger training sets also.
9. The time taken by SMO depends on the SVM's evaluation only. So, SMO is faster for linear SVMs and sparse datasets.
10. During optimization, SVM will try to find the support vectors for prediction.
11. SVM model can be constructed through WEKA tool. Please note that SVM's default kernel is polynomial in WEKA.

Advantages of SVM : Some of the advantages of SVM are as follows: -

1. They can not only solve binary class pattern recognition problems but also for multiclass classification, regression estimation, feature selection etc.
2. Lesser chances of information loss as SVM kernel considers the dot product of the feature vectors in high dimensional space to construct the optimal hyperplane rather than clustering or interpolating in input space. SVM can handle a large number of attributes of a data set unlike neural nets as these traditional algorithms need reduction of dimensionality i.e., the number of attributes, before they can be applied to a high dimensional problem.
3. Even in the field of bioinformatics, it has proven to be useful as there we have more than 20,000 attributes.
4. They are very versatile as they have many extensions too like Support Vector Decision Tree, neural network based SVM, fuzzy SVM etc.

Disadvantages of SVM : Some of the disadvantages of SVM are as follows: -

1. The best choice of kernel for a given problem is still an issue in research work.
2. Its speed and size during training and testing is still an issue. Training for very large datasets / millions of support vectors is still an unsolved problem.
3. It lacks efficiency in solving of multi-class problems. It is still an active research area.

Applications of SVM : Some of the applications of SVMs are listed below.

1. They have been used to study financial forecasting.
2. Spatial and temporal environmental data can be analysed to find patterns and trends using SVMs.
3. In field of biology also SVMs have proven to be very useful, particularly for remote homology detection.
4. They have been used for face expression classification.
5. They have been used for e-learning.
6. They have been used to control traffic congestion problems.

Q.35. What are Combining Classifiers?

Ans. When designing any pattern recognition systems, the objective is to achieve the best possible classification performance for the task in hand. So, different classification schemes are developed. Based on the results, one of the possible classifiers can be used as a final solution to the problem. **Please note here that although one of the designs would yield the best performance, the sets of patterns misclassified by the different classifiers would not necessarily overlap.** This suggested that different classifier designs potentially offered complementary information about the patterns to be classified which could be harnessed to improve the performance of the selected classifier. These observations motivated in combining of classifiers. One should not rely on single decision making scheme. In fact, all the designs or their subsets are used for decision making by combining their individual opinions. **Also note that it has been found that better results are achieved if classifiers are combined rather than single classifier.**

There are two reasons as to why should we combine classifiers-

a. Efficiency

b. Accuracy

Now to get efficiency, we can use multistage combination rules wherein objects are classified by a simple classifier using a small set of cheap features in combination with a reject option. Note that for more difficult objects, more complex procedures based on different features are used. Classifiers are useful when they are different. And this can be done by using different feature sets and different training sets. There are two types of classifier combinations: -

Case 1: All classifiers use the same representation of the input pattern. For example, a set of k-nearest neighbour classifiers, each using the same measurement vector but different classifier parameters.

Case 2: Each classifier uses its own representation of the input pattern i.e. the measurements extracted from the pattern are unique to each classifier.

Application of Combining Classifiers: Integrate physically different types of features. It is no longer possible to consider the computed aposteriori probabilities to be the estimates of the same functional value as the classification systems operate in different measurement spaces.

Q.36. How to evaluate Machine Learning Algorithms.

Ans. The standard approach followed is that we divide data into training set and testing sets, train method on training set and report results on the training set. But please understand that the testing set is not the same as the validation test.

Procedure to evaluate ML algorithm :

S1: Break all of the data into training/ testing sets.

S2: Break training set into training or validation set.

S3: Choose hyper-parameters using validation set.

S4: (optional step) Once we have selected the hyper-parameters, retrain using whole of the training set.

S5: Evaluate performance on the testing set.

Q.37. Write short notes on—

Ans. The classification error, Ei of an individual program, i, depends on the number of samples incorrectly classified (false positives and false negatives) and is computed by the formula:-

$$E_i = f / n * 100$$

where,

'*f*' is the number of sample cases incorrectly classified.

'*n*' is the total number of sample cases.

In supervised learning applications in machine learning and statistical learning theory, generalization error / out-of-sample error, is a measure of how accurately an algorithm is able to predict outcome values for previously unseen data. The evaluation of a learning algorithm may be sensitive to the sampling error because learning algorithms are evaluated on finite samples. So, the measurements of prediction error on the current data may not provide much information about the predictive ability on new data. Please note that this generalization error can be mitigated by avoiding overfitting in the learning algorithm. Also note that the performance of a machine learning algorithm is measured by plots of the generalization error values through the learning process, that are called as the learning curves.

SUMMARY

We have studied in this chapter that in machine learning instead of teaching a computer a massive list of rules to solve a problem, we give it a model with which it can evaluate examples. Also we give a small set of instructions to modify this model if it makes a mistake. We find that as the time passes by, w well suited model will be able to solve the problems in a batter and efficient way. The machine learning algorithm should be such that it tries to make the values of the parameters more and more accurate as it is exposed to more and more examples. But this is just a tip of an iceberg. Recently, scientists have developed the models that resemble the structures as used by a human brain. This involves deep learning only. .

MULTIPLE CHOICE QUESTIONS

1. Predicting the price of a house given its size is an example of-

(*a*) Supervised learning (*b*) Unsupervised learning
(*c*) Remote learning (*d*) None of the above

2. The inherent groupings in the data discovered is known as-

(*a*) Association (*b*) Clustering
(*c*) Classifying (*d*) None of the above

3. Discovering rules that describes large portions of data is called as-

(*a*) Association (*b*) Clustering
(*c*) Classifiers (*d*) None of the above

4. Conditional models are also known as-

(*a*) Demand models (*b*) Discriminative models
(*c*) Generative models (*d*) None of the above

5. Logistic regression is also named as-

(*a*) Login regression (*b*) Logit regression
(*c*) Logout regression (*d*) None of the above

6. Naive Bayes is an example of-

(*a*) Generative model (*b*) Discriminative model
(*c*) SVM (*d*) None of the above

7. A common task in machine learning is-

(*a*) Common data (*b*) Classifying data
(*c*) Global data (*d*) None of the above

8. The classification error, Ei of an individual program, i, depends on the number of samples incorrectly classified (false positives and false negatives) and is computed by the formula:-

(*a*) $E_i = f / n * 100$ (*b*) $E_i = f * n * 100$
(*c*) $E_i = f + n * 100$ (*d*) None of the above

9. PCA stands for-

(*a*) Peer Component Analysis (*b*) Principal Component Analysis
(*c*) Power Component Analysis (*d*) None of the above

10. Singular Value Decomposition is used in-

(*a*) Latent Semantic Indexing (*b*) Lateral Simple Indexing
(*c*) Lower Simple Indexing (*d*) None of the above

11. SVM stands for-

(*a*) Support Vector Machine (*b*) Simple Vector Machine
(*c*) Super Vector Machine (*d*) None of the above

12. A generalization of the concept of a plane which is used in SVM implementation for object separation is known as-

(*a*) Hyperplane (*b*) Airplane
(*c*) Aeroplane (*d*) None of the above

13. A model evaluation technique which is collection of methods used to examine the underlying constructs influence of the response of variables is-

(*a*) Factor Analysis (*b*) ICA
(*c*) PCA (*d*) Singular Value Composition

ANSWERS

1. (*a*)	**2.** (*b*)	**3.** (*b*)	**4.** (*b*)	**5.** (*b*)
6. (*a*)	**7.** (*b*)	**8.** (*a*)	**9.** (*b*)	**10.** (*a*)
11. (*a*)	**12.** (*a*)	**13.** (*a*)		

CONCEPTUAL SHORT QUESTIONS WITH ANSWERS

Q.1. What are the differences between data mining and machine learning?

Ans. Data mining is the process in which the unstructured data puts efforts to extract knowledge or unfamiliar interesting patterns. On the other hand, machine learning relates to the study, design and development of the algorithms that give systems the ability to learn without being clearly programmed.

Q.2. Give functions supervised and unsupervised learning.

Ans. Supervised learning involves-

a. Classifications.
b. Speech recognition.
c. Regression.
d. Predict time series.
e. Annotate strings.

On the other hand, unsupervised learning involves-

a. Finding the clusters of data.
b. Finding low dimensional representations of data.
c. Finding interesting coordinates and correlations.
d. Finding novel observations or cleaning databases.

Q.3. What is inductive machine learning?

Ans. Inductive machine learning covers the process of learning by examples where a system, from a set of perceived instances, tries to encourage a general rule.

Q.4. List at least five common machine learning algorithms.

Ans. Some of the popular ML algorithms are as follows:-

a. Decision Trees.
b. Neural Networks.
c. Probabilistic Networks.
d. Nearest Neighbour.
e. Support Vector Machines (SVM).

Q.5. Name different algorithm techniques in ML.

Ans. Different types of techniques in ML are as follows:-

a. Supervised learning.
b. Unsupervised learning.
c. Semi-supervised learning.
d. Reinforcement learning.
e. Transduction.
f. Learning to learn.

Q.6. Name three stages to build the models (or hypotheses) in machine learning.

Ans. Three stages to build the models in machine learning (ML) are as follows:-

a. Model building. *b.* Model testing.
c. Applying the model.

Q.7. What is the standard approach to supervised learning?

Ans. The standard approach to supervised learning is to break the data set of example into training set and the test set.

Q.8. Differentiate between 'training set' and 'test set'.

Ans. In different fields of data science like machine learning, a set of data is used to determine the potentially predictive relationship identified as training set. Training set is the example provided to the learner while test set is used to test the exactness of the hypotheses produced by the learner and it is the set of illustration weighed down from the learner. So, training sets are different from test sets.

Q.9. What are the different approaches of machine learning?

Ans. Different approaches of machine learning are as follows:-

a. Concept versus Classification Learning.

b. Symbolic versus Statistical Learning.

c. Inductive versus Analytical Learning.

Q.10. Define Overfitting during machine learning. Why it happens?

Ans. In ML, overfitting occurs when a statistical model defines a random error or noise rather than underlying relationship. When a model is extremely complex, overfitting is usually observed because of having too many parameters relating to the number of training data types. The model exihibits poor performance which has to be overfit. The risk of overfitting exists as the standards used for training the model is not the same as the standards used to judge the effectiveness of a model.

Q.11. How can overfitting be avoided?

Ans. BY means of loads of data, overfitting can be avoided. Overfitting happens when comparatively you have a small dataset and you make effort to learn from it. But if you have a small database and it is necessary to come with a model based on that then in such a scenario, cross validation method may be used. In this method, the dataset is divided into two segments, testing and training datasets. The testing dataset will only test the model while in training dataset, the data-points will come up with a model. In this method, a model is generally provided with a dataset of known data on which training data set is run and a dataset of unknown data against which the model is tested. The basic idea of cross validation is to define a dataset to test the model in the training phase.

Q.12. What is algorithm independent machine learning?

Ans. A type of machine learning in which mathematical foundations is independent of any particular classifier or learning algorithm is known as algorithm independent machine learning.

Q.13. Distinguish between AI and machine learning.

Ans. Designing and developing algorithms according to the behaviours based on empirical data is known as machine learning. On the other hand, artificial intelligence, in addition to machine learning, also covers other aspects like knowledge representation, natural language processing (NLP), planning, robotics etc.

Q.14. Define classifier as used in machine learning.

Ans. A classifier is a system that inputs a vector of discrete or continuous feature vales and outputs a single discrete value, the class.

Q.15. Where is pattern recognition used?

Ans. It is used in computer vision, speech recognition, data mining, statistics, information retrieval and bio-informatics.

Q.16. What is model selection in ML?

Ans. The process of selecting the models from different mathematical models that refer to the same data set is called as model selection. It is applied to the fields of statistics, machine learning and data mining.

Q.17. Name the method that is frequently used to prevent overfitting.

Ans. 'Isotonic Regression' is used to prevent overfiting when the data is sufficient.

Q.18. Why instance-based learning algorithm is sometimes also referred to as lazy-learning algorithm?

Ans. Instance-based learning algorithm is sometimes also referred to as lazy-learning algorithm because they delay the induction or generalization process until classification is performed.

Q.19. What are the 2 classification methods that SVM handle?

Ans. The two classification methods that SVM can handle are as follows:-

a. Combining binary classifiers.

b. Modifying binary to incorporate multiclass learning.

Q.20. For what purpose PCA and ICA are used?

Ans. PCA and ICA are used to extract features of data to reduce dimensions of data. They are important feature extraction techniques used for dimensionality reduction.

Q.21. What do you mean by dimension reduction?

Ans. It is the process of reducing the number of random variables under considerations and can be divided into feature selection and feature extraction.

Q.22. What are SVMs?

Ans. SVMs or Support Vector Machines are supervised learning algorithms that are used for classification and regression analysis.

Q.23. What are the different methods to solve sequential supervised learning problems?

Ans. The different methods to solve sequential supervised learning problems are:-

a. Sliding window methods.

b. Recurrent sliding windows.

c. Hidden Makov Models.

d. Maximum entropy Markov Models.

e. Conditional random fields.

f. Graph transformer networks.

Q.24. Name two techniques of ML. Give a very popular application of ML that you see everyday.

Ans. Genetic programming and inductive learning are the two methods of ML.

The recommendation engine implemented by major ecommerce websites uses machine learning (ML).

Q.25. How is KNN different from k-means clustering?

Ans. k-nearest neighbours is a supervised classification algorithm. On the other hand, k-means clustering is an unsupervised clustering algorithm. In order for k-nearest neighbours to work, labelled data is needed that we want to classify an unlabeled point. In case of k-means clustering only a set of unlabelled points and a threshold is required. The algorithm will take unlabelled points in consideration and slowly learn how to cluster them into groups by computing the mean of the distance between different points. In sutshell, KNN needs labelled points and is thus supervised learning while k-means doesn't need labelled points and is thus unsupervised learning.

Q.26. Why is "Naive" Bayes naive?

Ans. Even though it has practical applications, specially in text mining, Naive Bayes is still considered as Naive because the assumption that it makes becomes virtually impossible to be seen in real-life data. The conditional probability is computed as purely the product of the individual probabilities of different components. This denotes the absolute independence of features i.e. a condition that is probably never met in real life.

Q.27. Differentiate between a generative and discriminative model.

Ans. A generative model learns categories of data while a discriminative model merely learns the distinction between different categories of data. Discriminative models will leave behind generative models on the basis of classification tasks.

Q.28. Name at least three methods of reducing dimensionality.

Ans. The three methods of reducing dimensionality are as follows:-

a. Removing collinear features.

b. Performing PCA, ICA or other forms of algorithmic dimensionality reduction.

c. Combining features with feature engineering.

Q.29. What is the EM technique? How this algorithm works?

Ans. EM is an algorithm for maximizing a likelihood function when some of the variables in the model are unobserved i.e. when there are latent variables with you. To solve for our model parameters you need to know the distribution of your unobserved data but the distribution of your unobserved data is a function of your model parameters. EEM tries to get around this by guessing repeatedly about the distribution for the unobserved data then further estimating the model parameters by maximizing something that is lower bound on the actual likelihood function and repeating until convergence.

The EM algorithm starts with a guess for values of your model parameters as follows:-

The E-step: For each data point that has some missing values to solve for the distribution of the missing data, use your model equation, provided with your current guess of the model parameters and given the observed data. Please note that you are solving for a distribution for each missing value and not for the expected value. Also note that now we have available with us a distribution for each missing value, we can calculate the expectation of the likelihood function with respect to the unobserved variables. If our guess for the model parameter was correct, this expected likelihood will be the actual likelihood of our observed data. If the parameters were not correct, it will just be a lower bound.

The M-step: Now that we have got an expected likelihood function with no unobserved variables in it, maximize the function as you would in the fully observed case, to get a new estimate of your model parameters.

Repeat till convergence.

Q.30. What do you mean by curse of dimensionality?

Ans. The curse of dimensionality refers to the tendency of a state space to grow exponentially in its dimension i.e. in the number of state variables.

Q.31. What is H_2O? What is prcomp?

Ans. H_2O is software for machine learning and data analysis. PCA is named as prcomp in H_2O and R system.

Q.32. What is the principle of operation of the back-propagation algorithm?

Ans. Firstly, the inputs from the training data are propagated through the network to the output. Then the model outputs are compared with the actual outputs. The difference is the error. This error is then fed into the network backwards and connections weights are adjusted.

Q.33. Define the following:-

a. **Learning rate.**

b. **Momentum.**

Ans. a. **Learning rate:** A higher value of learning rate will make the algorithm converge more rapidly towards the desired values but it will reduce the stability of the algorithm.

b. **Momentum:** It is used to control oscillations in weights which could be caused by alternately signed error signals.

Q.34. WEKA tool may be used to construct neural network. Can it do the parameter value selection also for neural networks?

Ans. A neural network trains by repeated passes of the data. Each pass is called an epoch. With each epoch, the connecting weights are adjusted until a satisfactory level of performance is reached. We can ponder that if 50 epochs are good then 80 epochs should be better. But this argument does not hold with neural networks. With too many passes the network may over-train also. Please understand that a well trained neural network model would show similar performance levels with both test and training data. Also understand that keeping this in mind we can change the parameter values of the algorithm. We should not assume that default parameters are the best. We can change the parameters too. As the number of epochs increases we need more time for training. If we compare the outputs from the two different epochs, we can see the accuracy remains at the same level of 97.2%. that is why we say that higher the number of epochs has not improved the model performance. Just keep in mind that we should restrict ourselves to the lower number of epochs as it not only involves less computing time but also lowers the danger of over-fitting.

Q.35. Define the following terms:-

a. **Activation function.**

b. **Back-propagation learning.**

c. **Delta rule.**

d. **Epoch.**

e. **Feedforward neural networks.**

f. **Genetic algorithm.**

g. **Hyperplane.**

h. **Kernel.**

Ans. *a.* **Activation function:** A function that describes the output behaviours of a neuron in neural network.

b. **Back-propagation learning:** It is a form of supervised learning used to train mainly, feedforward neural networks, that works by making modifications in weights values, starting at the output layer and then moving backwards through the hidden layer.

c. **Delta Rule:** The delta rule changes the weight vector for a neural network in such a way that the error is reduced.

d. **Epoch:** It is one complete pass of the entire training set through the neural network. The learning process is repeated epoch-by-epoch until the averaged square error converges to a minimum value.

e. **Feedforward neural network:** It is a sort of ANN where connections between the units do not form a directed cycle.

f. **Genetic algorithm:** It is an adaptive heuristic search algorithm premised on the evolutionary ideas of natural selection theory.

g. **Hyperplane:** A plane (as in geometry) that is used to do object separation during SVM implementation.

h. **Kernel:** Linear, polynomial and rbf are some of the kernels of SVM that allows SVM to fit the maximum margin hyperplane in the transformed feature space.

Q.36. Tabulate the differences between supervised and unsupervised learning.

Ans. The following are the points of differences:-

Supervised Learning	Unsupervised Learning
It incorporates an external teacher so that each output unit is told what should be the desired response to that input signal.	Uses no external teacher.
Global error signals govern learning.	Local information is used for learning.
Uses pattern class information of each training pattern.	Adaptively clusters patterns to generate decision codes.
Paradigms are error correction learning, reinforcement learning and stochastic learning.	Paradigms are Hebbian learning and competitive learning.
Learning is usually off line. It means that learning and operation phases are different. In off-line learning, all of the given patterns are used together.	Learning is online. It means that the agent learns and operates at the same time. Here, the information in each new pattern is incorporated into the agent.
All learning data are stored and can be accessed repeatedly. So, we can see whether we are making progress in training or not.	Locality allows learning in real time. So, the progress cannot be monitored.
Inputs and outputs are defined.	Only inputs are defined.
Uses pattern class information of each training pattern.	Adaptively clusters patterns to generate decision class without any prior pattern class information.
Global error signal governs learning.	Local information/ rules are used for learning.
Learning is offline usually.	Locality allows synapses to learn in real-time.

Q.37. Explain different nets classes.

Ans. It is put under 2 main categories as follows:-

I. Unsupervised learning (i.e. without a teacher):

1. Feedback Nets:

a. Binary Adaptive Resonance Theory (ART1).

b. Analog adaptive Resonance Theory (ART2).

c. Discrete Hopfield (DH).

d. Continuous Hopfield (CH).

e. Discrete Bi-directional Associative Memory (BAM).

f. Temporal Associative Memory (TAM).

g. Adaptive Bi-directional Associative Memory (ABAM).

h. Kohonen Self-Organizing Map/ Topology Preserving Map (SOM/TPM).

i. Competitive learning.

2. **Feed-forward only Nets:**
   a. Learning Matrix (LM).
   b. Driver-reinforcement Learning (DR).
   c. Counter Propagation (CPN).

II. Supervised learning (i.e. with a teacher):

1. **Feedback Nets:**
   a. Boltzmann Machine. (BM).
   b. Mean Field Annealing (MFT).
   c. Recurrent Cascade Correlation (RCC).
   d. Learning Vector Quantization (LVQ).
   e. Back progpagation through time (BPTT).
   f. Real-time Recurrent Learning (RTRL).
2. **Feed-forward only Nets:**
   a. Perceptron.
   b. Adaline, Madaline.
   c. Backpropagation (BP).
   d. Cauchy Machine (CM).
   e. Artmap.
   f. Cascade Correlation (CasCor).

EXERCISE QUESTIONS

1. Define machine learning. Discuss the applications of Machine Learning.
2. Difference between training dataset and testing data set.
3. What are support vectors and margins?
4. Differences between supervised and unsupervised learning.
5. Explain Perceptron training algorithm for linear classification.
6. Explain PCA and ICA.
7. What are learning laws?

   [**Hint:** Learning laws provide a set of well-defined rules that determine how the network learns. The laws are as follows:-

   1. The learning algorithm/law must lead to convergence of weights.
   2. The learning time or training time should be small.
   3. The learning should make use of only the local information available. When the synaptic weight linking two neurons is changed, it should depend only on the states of these two units. In such a case, the learning process can be made parallel by changing weights parallel.
   4. Online training may be done wherein the weights are changed based on the inputs.
   5. Non-linear mapping between I/O pairs must be captured by the learning law.
   6. Pattern information storage capacity should be as large as possible for a given network.]
8. Explain delta rule of learning.
9. Explain convergence rule for learning.
10. Explain the back-propagation neural network principles.
11. Using WEKA tool, how will you construct a fully connected feed-forward ANN that has three input nodes, one output node and four internal nodes in the hidden layer?
12. Explain SVMs in detail.

3 Deep Feed Forward Networks

Q.1. Define networks with and without feedback.

Ans. There are two types of networks- with and without feedbacks. In networks with feedback, the output values can be traced back to the input values. On the other hand, in networks without feedback, for every input vector laid on the network, an output vector is calculated and this can be read from the output neurons. There is no feedback. So, only a forward flow of information is present. Such networks having this type of structure are called as **feed forward networks.** For example, Back Propagation Network.

Q.2. What do you mean by the "Training Neurons"?

Ans. Managing the weights in a neural network is a challenge today. We do this by the process called as training. During training, we show a neural network a large number of training examples. Then we iteratively modify the weights to minimize the errors that we make on the training examples. We should be intelligent when we pick our training sets. Researchers say that intelligently selecting the training examples is what needs to be pondered around.

Assume that we have a set of several training examples. We need to calculate what the neural networks will output on the ith training example. Please note that the objective is to train the neuron so that we select the optimal/ minimum weights possible. That is, the weights that minimize the errors we make on the training examples. We want to minimize errors we make on the training examples. Mathematically,

If we know that t(i) is the true answer for the ith training example and y(i) is the value calculated by the neural network then we want to reduce the value of the error function (E) as follows:-

$$E = \frac{1}{2} \Sigma i \, (t(i) - y(i))^2$$

Please note that this squared-error value is zero when our model makes a perfect prediction on every training example. Also note that closer is E to 0, the better is our model. So, our objective is to select our parameter vector, θ, so that E is as close as possible to 0 (zero).

We have a set of equations and a bunch/set of unknown weights, for each training example. This would automatically give an error of 0 (zero). This is **intelligent decision.** This is true as far as we have linear neurons but as we talk about non-linear neurons like sigmoidal, tanh neurons then we get complex equations and hence we need a better method to tackle the training process.

The training set is a set of examples that are randomly drawn from the dataset for the purpose of training the model. Training data is the data set on which you train the model. It can also be said that the data from which the model has learned the experiences. The test set is a set of examples drawn from the data set for the purpose of evaluating the performance of the model. This is kept separate from the training and tuning data and cannot be used in the training or tuning stages of the learning process. Doing this would only bias the model to the data and affect performance. Test data is the data which is used to check if the model has learnt good enough from the experiences it got in the trained data sets. In machine learning a set of data is used to determine the potentially predictive relationship called as the training set. Training set is an example provided to the learner. On the other hand, test set is used to test the exactness of the hypotheses produced by the learner and it is the set of illustrations weighed down from the learner. Hence, training sets are different from test set.

Q.3. Define the following terms:-

1. **Gradient Descent and Gradient-based Learning :** It has been observed that as the weights increase, so does the error. If we are discussing about a linear neuron with 2 inputs only and thus 2 weights only then we are actually working in a 2-dimensional plane where the dimensions correspond to the two weights. We define them as contours that correspond to these two weights. Please note here that contours correspond to the settings of two weights, w1 and w2 that evaluate to the same value of E. also note that the closer are the contours to each other, the steeper is the slope. It is observed that the direction of the steepest descent is always perpendicular to the contours. This direction is expressed in form of a vector called as the gradient.

This can be extended to non-linear neurons also and try to find out the weights that optimizes the error function. The purpose is to find the point of minimum error. This algorithm is known as gradient descent. This process is used to train individual neurons and hence the entire network.

2. **The Delta Rule :** The delta rule changes the weight vector for a neural network in such a way that the error is reduced. We need this rule to train our linear neuron. To find out, how to change each weight, we need to evaluate gradient which is the partial derivative of the error function with respect to each of the weights. It is also called as Widrow-Hoff rule. It controls the change in the synaptic weight with respect to the learning rate. **Please note that this rule is local in nature as the change in the synaptic weight depends only on the error of the neuron and the input to it.** The weight in the next iteration is also computed here. **Also note that the error correction learning rule is a closed-loop feed back system.** This is also a type of learning only and is known as error-correction learning. This rule is predecessor of the back propagation rule only. The total square error of the output computed by the net is minimized by a gradient descent method known as back propagation or generalized delta rule.
3. **The Rate of learning (η) :** Rate of learning is has a direct effect on change in synaptic weights. The back propagation algorithm is an approximation to the trajectory in weight space calculated by steepest descent method. **Please note that if we choose a small learning rate parameter, η, the trajectory will be smoother in the weight space but the rate of learning will be very slow. Also note that a large learning rate parameter, η, will result in large changes in the synaptic weights and the network may show oscillatory response and may become unstable.** We can even add a momentum constant as an improvement to this delta rule as its inclusion stabilizes the weights which tend to oscillate.
4. **The Backpropagation Algorithm :** It is a system method for training multi-layer ANNs. It is a multi-layer forward network using extended gradient-descent based delta learning rule that is commonly known as back propagation of errors rule. Back propagation of BP is an efficient method for changing the weights in a feed forward network with differentiable activation function units, to learn a training set of input-output examples. Hinton, Rumelhart et al. first introduced it in 1986. We do not know what the hidden layers may be doing but we can compute how fast the error changes as we change a hidden activity. So, we can find out how fast the error changes when we change the weight of an individual connection. Being a gradient descent method, it minimizes the total square error of the output computed by the net. The network is trained by the supervised learning method. The aim of this network is to train the network to achieve a balance between the ability to respond correctly to the input parameters that are used for training and the ability to provide good responses to the input that are similar. Each hidden unit can affect many output units.

The training algorithm for back propagation involves four steps:-

a. Initialization of weights.

b. Feed forward.

c. Back propagation of errors.

d. Updation of weights and biases.

Explanation: During the first step/stage, weights are initialized with some random values are assigned. During feed-forward stage, each input unit (x_i) receives an input signal and transmits this signal to each of the hidden units, z_i .... z_p. Then each hidden unit calculates the activation function and sends its signal z_j to each output unit. The output unit calculates the activation function from the response of the net for the given input pattern. During back propagation of errors, each output compares its computed activation, y_k with its target value, tk to determine the associated error for that pattern with that unit. Based on the error, the factor, δ_k (k =1,...,m) is computed and is used to distribute the error at the output unit, y_k back to all the units in the previous layer. Similarly, the factor δ_j (j =1,...,p) is computed for each hidden unit, z_j.

During the final step, the weight and biases are updated using the δ factor and activation.

Various parameters used in the training algorithm are:-

x: input training vector

x: (x_1, ...x_i,....,x_n)

t: (t_1.....t_k.....t_m)

δk : error at output unit, y_k

δj : error at hidden unit, z_j

α: learning rate

v_{oj} : bias on hidden unit j

z_j: hidden unit j

w_{ok} : bias on output unit k

y_k : output unit, k.

ALGORITHM: BACK PROPAGATION

S1: Initialize weights.

S2: If stopping conditions are false, do steps 3 to 10.

S3: For each training pair, do steps 4 to 9.

S4: Apply input, xi, and transmit these signals to the hidden units.

S5: Each hidden unit sums its weighted input signals and sends the signals to the output units.

S6: Each output unit sums its weighted input signals and applies its activation function to calculate the output signals.

S7: Each output unit receives a target pattern corresponding to an input pattern and error information is calculated.

S8: Each hidden unit sums its delta inputs. The error information is calculated.

S9 : Each output unit updates its bias and weights.

S10: Test the stopping condition based on minimum error.

Properties of back-propagation (BP)

Some of the main properties of BP are as follows:-

1. **Learning and NOT programming :** Any neural net can be converted into software like JAVA2 but at the level of neural network, the concepts are very different from conventional software.
2. **Generalization :** BP networks can generalize too. For example, the NETTalk network can pronounce words that it has not yet encountered. This is an essential property of intelligent systems that have to function in the real world. Please note that it implies that not every potential situation has to be predefined in the system. Generalization here means that, similar inputs leads to similar outputs. Also note that this is the reason as to why parity is not a good candidate problem for generalization. Like in XOR problem, change one bit in the input and the output has to change maximally say from 0 to 1.
3. **Noise and fault tolerance :** As we know that a network is noise and fault tolerant. The weights of NETTalk have been disturbed by adding random noise but the performance degradation was only gradual. Note that this property is not explicitly programmed into the model. It is the result of massive parallelism, in a sense, it comes for free.
4. **Re-learning :** The network shows fast re-learning. If the network is distorted to a particular performance level, it re-learns faster than a new network starting at the same performance level. So, despite of low performance, the network has retained something about its past.
5. **Emergent properties :** The consonant-vowel distinction that the nodes at the hidden layer pick-up has not been programmed into the system. Certain nodes can pick up these distinctions, which depends on how the examples are encoded. Secondly, since the net can pronounce words that it has not encountered, it has somehow learned the rules of English pronunciation. There are no rules in the network, only weights and activation levels. Note that it is these emergent properties that make the neural network not only attractive for applications but also to the researchers working in the field of deep learning.
6. **Universality :** According to Hornik et al. Machine language Programs are universal approximators. So we can say that with a 2-layer feed-forward network, every set of discrete function values can be represented or in a particular interval a continuous function can be approximated to any degree of accuracy. This is still a simplification but it is sufficient for our purposes. Please note that again there is a difference between what can be represented and what can be learned. Something that can be represented cannot be learned by BP algorithm. For example, BP might get stuck in local minima and we do not know whether the global minima will ever be reached. On one side, there are performance problems and on the other side, there are doubts whether supervised learning schemes like BP have a biological or psychological reality. Machine language Programs with BP have been tried on many different types of classification problems because:-
   a. They are universal function approximators,
   b. They are easy to use.

Most of these experiments remained in the prototype stage only. The entire knowledge in a NN is in the connection matrix. There are no explicit rules. But there are a number of steps to extract rules from NN especially for Self-Organizing Maps (SOMs).

Advantages of BP :

1. The mathematical formula can be applied to any network.
2. The computing time is less.
3. The batch update of weights is possible.

Disadvantages of BP :

1. More number of learning steps.
2. Many calculations are involved.
3. For complex problems, more time is required.
4. The network may get stuck.
5. Quite unstable too.

Applications of BP :

1. Optical Character Recognition (OCR).
2. Image and Data Compression.
3. Control systems.
4. Power systems.
5. Fault detection.
6. Non-linear simulation.
7. To train the multi-layer neural networks.

Q.4. What is Stochastic and Minibatch Gradient Descent?

Ans. We have already discussed about batch gradient descent. But the problem arises when our error surface tends to be more complex. So, to solve this problem we use stochastic and mini-batch gradient descent methods.

In Stochastic Gradient Descent (SGD), in each iteration, our error surface is estimated only with respect to a single example. Instead of single and static error surface, our error surface is dynamic now. The stochastic error surface fluctuates with respect to the batch error surface, thus enabling saddle point avoidance. As a result, descending on this stochastic surface significantly improves our ability to navigate flat regions.

The major drawback of this method is that looking at the error incurred, one example at a time may not be a good approximation of the error surface. So, gradient descent takes more time. To overcome this problem, we use mini-batch gradient descent method.

In Minibatch Gradient Descent method, at every iteration, we compute the error surface with respect to some subset of the total dataset instead of just a single example. This subset is called as a mini-batch. So, mini-batch size is another hyper-parameter just as we had learning rate earlier. Please note here that these mini-batches strike a balance between the efficiency of batch gradient descent and the local minima avoidance afforded by stochastic gradient descent. Also note that here instead of summing over all the examples in the dataset, we sum over the examples in the current mini-batch.

Q.5. What are Test Sets and Validation Sets, Overfitting -Phenomenon, Epoch, Training Data, Test Data?

Ans. As already discussed, a linear fit is always better than a polynomial of higher degree. But for complex problems, linear fit may not be possible. So, we never train our model on the entire dataset. Instead, we split up our data into two parts: -

a. A training set.

b. A test set.

Thus, now we can do better evaluation of our model by generalizing it. But please remember that if our test data is not well constructed then we cannot draw any meaningful results about our model. Also note that this may prompt us to reuse the training data for testing.

A complex model will perfectly fit our training dataset but it performs poorly if it a new data set. So, the complex model does not generalize well. This is known as overfitting. This phenomenon is very significant in case of deep learning where our neural networks have large number of layers consisting of many neurons. It has been observed that as the number of connections increases, so is our problem of overfitting increases. The same problem can be seen when we make our neural networks deep. So, a machine learning engineer has three trade-offs in hand: -

1. Overfitting and model complexity must be dealt with.
2. Both simple model and a complex model may not be the silver bullet.
3. It is very misleading if we evaluate the model using training data.
4. A stage is reached where instead of learning we start overfitting only.

Also note that deep learning takes the approach of solving complex problems with complex models and taking additional steps to prevent overfitting problem.

That is why we divide our training process into epochs. It is a single iteration over the entire data set. At the end of each epoch, we want to measure how well our model is generalizing. For this we use another validation set. At the end of each epoch, the validation set will tell us how the model does on data on the unseen data. Just remember that if the accuracy on the training set still increases and the accuracy on the validation set remains the same or decreases then it is a good sign to stop training as then otherwise, we would be overfitting.

In deep learning, however we also include this validation data along with training data and test data to prevent overfitting during the training process.

For example, if we have 70,000 rows of training data and we randomly select 10,000 rows to be test data then randomly select another 10000 from the remaining 60,000 rows to be my validation data, leaves us with 50,000 as my training data set.

We train our models with the training data and score it on the validation data. Then we change the models and score again on the validation data. This is also called as tweaking of the models. Finally, we choose our model and try to test it on the test set. It is shown in figure 3.1.

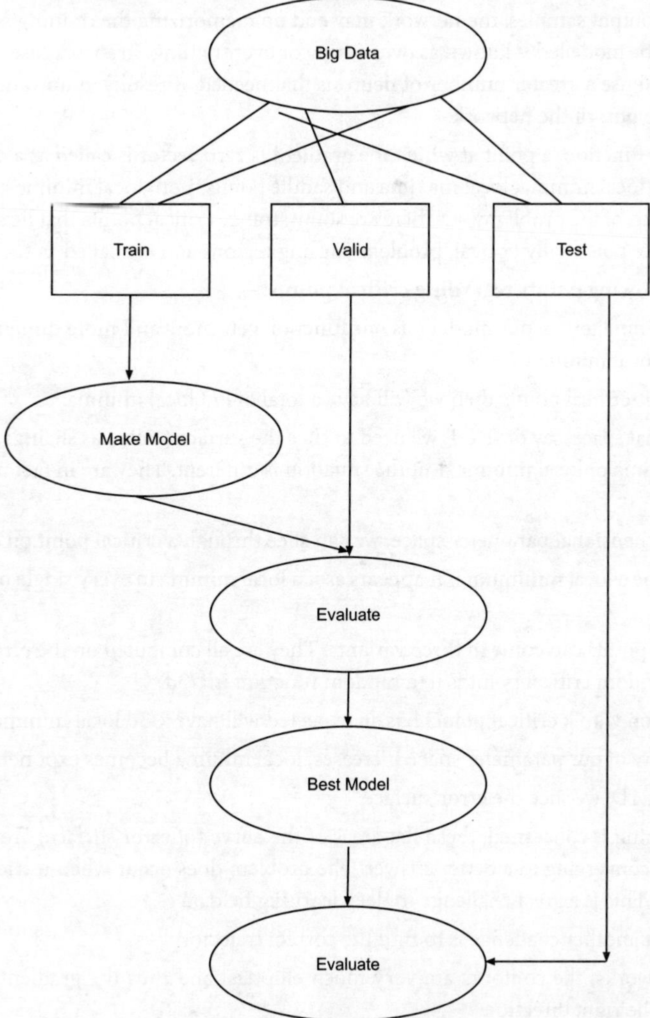

***Fig. 3.1:** Train, Valid and Test Data Sets*

The query is now how to split the data? There is no rule but unbalanced data is a problem with small datasets. This is so because we do not see any pattern in small data. When data is large/big then the law of big numbers tends to make sure that the data is evenly distributed. CASE TOOL like H_2O provides a split( ) function for the same.

Q.6. What is Hyperparameter Optimization? Also define critical points.

Ans. Several hyperparameters like learning rate, mini-batch size etc., have been dealt with in previous sections. But the need is to find a framework for how to find the optimal values for these hyperparameters. One method of finding the optimal parameters values is named as a grid search. In this method, we select a value for each hyperparameter from a finite set of options and batch size and train the model with every possible permutation of hyperparameter choices. The objective is to find out the accuracy of the model trained with the best set on the test set.

Critical Point : As studied earlier, in back propagation learning the network is trained with a number of input patterns. The training involves adaptation of the synaptic weights of a multilayer perceptron. For this we need to present the training patterns. **Please note that a network is said to generalize when the I/O mapping computed by the network is correct for the test data not used in the training. Also understand here that the learning process is considered to be a curve-fitting problem that involves some sort of interpolation.** By the term 'interpolation' we mean taking values outside the give range or near the range so as to fit the curve. And this process in which a neural network learns too many input-output samples, the network may end up memorizing the training set without trying to find the underlying function to be modelled is known as over-fitting or over training. In such a case, the network losses its ability to generalize. When you use a greater number of neurons that needed, it results in unwanted input domain due to the noise in the synaptic weights of the network.

Now given an arbitrary function, a point at which the gradient is zero vector is called as a critical point. Critical points are of various types like local minima, local maxima and saddle points. Both local minima and local maxima (discussed earlier) do not pose much of the problems but there are some strange critical points that lie somewhere in between. And these flat regions that are potentially critical, problem-causing regions and are called as saddle points.

Just remember the following points regarding critical points: -

1. As the number of parameters in our model / as our function gets more and more dimensions, the saddle points rise exponentially than local minima.
2. If we have a total of k-critical points then we will have a total of k/3 local minima.
3. In higher dimensional space, say of size'd', we need to slice the surface (called as slicing) then the critical points look like either local maxima or local minima. But the situation is different. They are in fact more complex and are called as saddle points.
4. In general, in a d-dimensional parameter space, we can slice through a critical point on d different axis.
5. A critical point can be a local minimum if it appears as if a local minima in every single one of the d one dimensional sub-spaces.
6. In 1D space, critical points can come in three variants. They are all computed on the error surface. It is found that a probability that a random critical point is in a random function is 1/3d.
7. So, a random function with k critical points has an expected will have k/3d local minima.
8. As the dimensionality of our parameter space increases, local minima becomes exponentially more rare.
9. In case of more than 1D, we slice the error surface.
10. As far as deep learning is concerned, these flat areas of the curve (of error surface) are an issue but finally they do not prevent it from converging to a better answer. The problem does occur when it tries to solve for a point where the gradient is zero. This is a great challenge in deep learning field.
11. In deep learning yet another challenge is to find the correct trajectory.
12. In case of deep networks, the contours are very much elliptical and thus the gradient can be as inaccurate as 90 degrees away from the right direction.

13. If contours are circular then we move ahead with a big step in the direction of the steepest descent because the gradient does not change the direction we move on. But this is not true in case of elliptical contours of deep networks.
14. We use simple derivation concept of mathematics here to find out how the gradient changes as we move on. That is, we can model this change of gradient with our derivatives.
15. We compile this entire information into a matrix form called as Hessian Matrix (H).
16. This matrix is said to be ill-conditioned when we describe an error surface when the gradient changes.
17. We can even take the 2nd derivative of the error function to find out the learning rate at each step that maximizes the reduction in the error function.

Q.7. Define the Learning Rate Adaptation.

Ans. The constant that is used in Artificial Neural Networks (ANNs) learning algorithms to affect the speed of learning is called as the learning rate.

One of the major challenges of training deep networks is to get the correct learning rate. This is so because it has a lot of impact on the network's performance. It has been observed that a learning rate that is too small does not learn quickly but a learning rate that is too large may have difficulty in converging as we approach the region of local minima. Modern deep network optimization provides a facility of learning rate adaption. We define the learning rate adaptation as the process of suitably modifying the optimal learning rate over the period of learning to get good convergence properties. Some of the learning rate algorithms are AdaGrad, RMSProp and Adam.

The deep learning practitioners must ponder on the point that their aim is not to build more and more advanced optimizers rather to discover the architectures that are simpler to train. They need not be busy on complex error surfaces only.

Q.8. With the help of a neat flowchart explain the Training Deep Learning Model.

Ans. The following are the steps followed to train and evaluate a deep learning model: -

S1: Define the Problem: It involves finding out the inputs, outputs and their vector representations. Say, we want t train a deep learning model to identify severe fever in a patient. Then our input will be the patient image that will be stored in form of a vector of pixel values. And the output will be the probability of it being viral, dengue or malaria.

S2: Building a Neural Network to solve it: The input layer will be of suitable size so as to accept the raw data from the image. And our output will be the type of the fever. Also, we will have to define the internal architecture of the network *i.e.*, the number of hidden layers, the connectives used etc.

S3: Train for an epoch: Now we want to collect a significant amount of data for training or modelling. Now we need the images of all with a uniform size.

S4: Divide this Data: Now we shuffle and divide this data as needed for training, validation and test sets.

S5: Train the model on the training set: We now train the model on our training set for an epoch at a time. At the end of each Epoch, we ensure that our error on the training set and validation set is decreasing. When one of this stops to improve, we terminate and check that our model performs well on the test data. If not, we need to design architecture again or check the data collected.

If our training set error stops improving, we need to do better by capturing the important features in our data.

If our validation set error stops improving, we need to take steps to prevent over-fitting/ over training.

But if we are satisfied with the performance of our model on the training data then we can measure its performance on the test data. If we are not satisfied, we need more data in our data set. This is so because the test set seems to consist of examples types that were not well represented in the training set. Else, we are to stop (finished).

This is shown in the flowchart of figure 3.2.

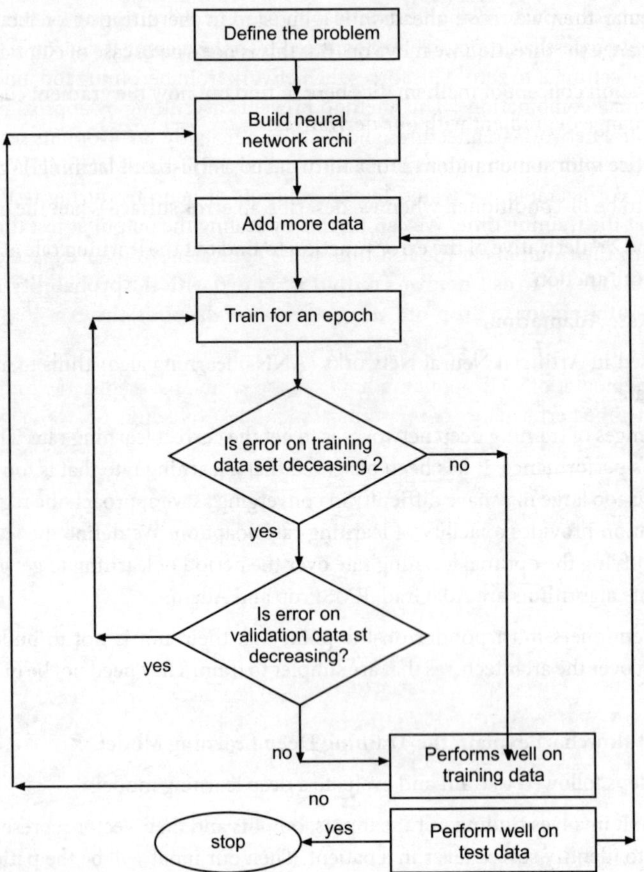

Fig. 3.2: Flowchart to Show Training and Evaluation of Deep Learning Model

Q.9. What all methods may be used for avoiding Overfitting in Deep Neural Networks?

Ans. Several methods have been proposed in the literature to prevent overfitting or overtraining. We discuss here some of them.

1. Regularization.
2. Dropout.

I. Regularization: In this method, we regularize the objective function. This is done by adding additional terms that penalize larger weights. Mathematically speaking, we modify the objective function so that it becomes-

$$\text{Error} + \lambda f(\theta)$$

Where $f(\theta)$ grows larger as the components of θ grow larger,

λ is the regularization strength, a new hyperparameter .

Please note that the value we choose for λ determines how much we want to prevent overfitting. That is,

a. $\lambda = 0$ means that we do not take any measures against the possibility of overfitting.

b. If λ is too large, then our model will prioritize keeping θ as small as possible.

The need is to find the parameter values that perform well on the training set we choose. So, selection of λ is very significant. We may even use brute-force method here.

Regularization method has been used in non-linear problems by the researchers. It is also of different types like L_2 regularization and L_1 regularization. Also note that during gradient descent update, using L_2 regularization means that every weight is decayed linearly to zero. That is why, this phenomenon is also known as weight decay.

II. **Dropout:** It is the most popular method used today to prevent overfitting or overtraining in deep neural networks. During the training process, a dropout is implemented by only keeping a neuron active with some probability, p (a hyperparameter) or setting it to zero. This forces the network from becoming too much dependent on any one of the neurons or their small combinations. This method prevents overfitting by approximately combining exponentially many different neural network architectures and that too efficiently. So, dropouts set each neuron in the network as inactive. This is done with some random probability during mini-batch training. Again, we need to consider some complexities here. For example, we would like the outputs of neurons during test time to be equivalent to their expected outputs at the training time. We can fix this by scaling the output at test time. For example, if p= 1/4 then neurons must 3/4th their outputs at the test time to be equivalent to their expected outputs at the training time. **Please note that this is easy to as a neuron's output is set to 0 with the probability 1-p. Also note that this means that if a neuron's output prior to drop-out was x, then after dropout, the expected output would be –**

$$E_{[output]} = px + (1 - p).0 = px \quad ....(1)$$

However, this implementation of dropout method is not very suitable as it needs scaling of neuron outputs at the test time. And that test-time performance is very critical to model evaluation. So, we suggest the use of inverted dropout method here. This is so because here scaling occurs at the training time instead of at test time. In this new method, any neuron whose activation has not been silenced has its output divided by *p* before the value is propagated to the next layer. So, with this modification we have:-

$$E_{[output]} = p.\,x/p + (1 - p).0 = x \quad ....(2)$$

So, we can avoid any random scaling neuronal output during the test time.

In nutshell, for deep learning, there are two methods:-

a. Regularization.

b. Drop connections when connecting one layer to the next.

Q.10. Define Reinforcement learning and Deep Reinforcement Learning.

Ans. The process of learning from the interaction with an environment from the consequences of action (rather than explicit teaching) is known as reinforcement learning.

Or

It is defined as the branch of machine learning that deals with learning via interactions and feedback. [Nicholas et al.]

In 2014, deep neural networks were applied to reinforcement learning.

The learning process includes an actor, an environment and a reward signal. The actor takes an action in the environment and gets points. The method in which an actor chooses the actions is known as a policy. Since the actor wants to maximize its points (rewards) so it must learn an optimal policy for environmental interactions. This is shown in figure 3.3.

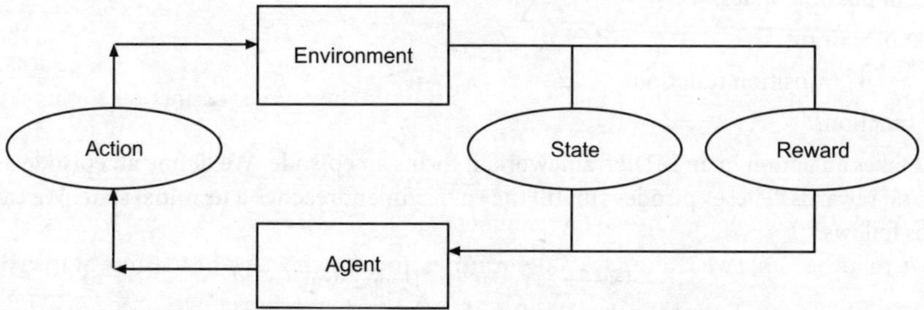

Figure 3.3: *Reinforced Learning Framework*

This type of learning is different from supervised or unsupervised learning as discussed earlier. Reinforcement learning is a general- purpose framework for creating intelligent agents. The agent learns to interact with that environment to maximize its total reward. This type of learning has been found to be very useful in applications like self-driving cars, robotics, game playing, air conditioner control, stock markets, autonomous helicopter, mobile network routing, factory control and efficient web page indexing.

In reinforcement learning framework we will provide our algorithms only a reward function that indicates to the learning agent when it is doing well and when it is doing poorly. For example, in a four-legged robot walking case, the reward function might give the robot positive rewards for moving forwards and negative rewards for either moving backwards or falling over. Then it will be the task of the learning algorithm to find out how to choose actions overtime so as to obtain large rewards.

Q.11. What do you understand by the Markov Decision Processes [MDP]?

Ans. The study of this type of reinforcement learning begins with Markov Decision Process (MDP) which provides the formalism in which reinforcement learning problems are usually posed.

Considering the reinforced learning framework of figure 3.3 we say that: -

a. **States:** These can refer to, for example, grid maps in robotics or like an open door and closed -door scenario.

b. **Actions:** A fixed set of actions like going north, south, east etc for a robot.

c. **Transition Probabilities:** It is defined as the probability of going from one state to another given an action. For instance, what is the probability of an open door if the action is open.

d. **Rewards:** These are used to guide the planning. For example, in case of a grid, we may like to go to a certain cell. The reward will be higher if we get closer. Like in case of a door example, an open door might give a high reward.

Please understand that once the MDP is defined, a policy can be learned by doing Value Iteration or Policy Iteration which calculates the expected reward for each of the states. Then the policy gives per state the best action to perform. Also note that MDP is useful when you want to have an efficient sequence of actions in which your actions can not always be 100% effective.

MDP provides a mathematical framework for modelling decisions making in situations where outcomes are partly random and partly under the control of a decision maker. MDPs are useful for studying a wide range of optimization problems that are solved using dynamic programming and reinforcement learning. In 1960, Ronald Howard published a book on Dynamic Programming and Markov Processes.

MDP is a discrete time stochastic control process. at each time step, the process is in some state, s, and the decision maker may choose any action, a, that is available in state, s. The process responds at the next time by randomly moving into a new state, s', and giving a decision maker a corresponding reward Ra (s, s').

Please note here that the probability that the process moves into its new state's is influenced by the chosen action only. This is given by the state transition function, Pa (s, s'). So, the next state s' depends on the current state, s, and the decision maker's action, a. But given s and a, it is conditionally independent of all previous states and actions. Just note here that the state transitions of an MDP process satisfies the Markov property. And MDPs are an extension of Markov chains. The difference is the addition of actions and rewards. Conversely, if only one action exists for each state (e.g. 'wait') and all rewards are the same (e.g. 'zero'), a Markov decision process reduces to a Markov chain.

A Markov decision process is defined:-

- S, a finite set of possible states.
- A, a finite set of actions.
- $P(r, s' |s, a)$, a state transition function.
- R, a reward function.

When an agent takes an action in an MDP framework, it forms an episode. We define an episode as a series of tuples of states, actions and rewards. These episodes run till the environment reaches a terminal state. We can show the variables in an episode as follows:-

$$(s_0, a_0, r_0), (s_1, a_1, r_1) ,........(s_n, a_n, r_n)$$

Objective: MDPs task is to find an optimal policy for our agent. We define policies as the ways in which our agent acts based on its current state. The aim is to find a policy to maximize the expected future return.

Q.12. What are BELLMAN Equations? Explain.

Ans. Richard Bellman, gave a dynamic programming equation known as BELLMAN equation. It is the necessary condition for optimality related to dynamic programming. It writes the value of a decision problem at a certain point in time in terms of the payoff from some initial choices and the value of the remaining decision problem that result from those initial choices. This breaks a dynamic optimization problem into simpler sub-problems. This is known as Principle of Optimality".

The Bellman equation was first applied to engineering control theory and to applied mathematics and in economic theory. The basic concepts of dynamic programming have been given in John Von Neumann and Oskar's theory of Games and Economic behaviour. It has been observed that any problem that can be solved using optimal control theory can also be solved by analysing a suitable Bellman equation. Bellman equation refers to the dynamic programming equation related to discrete-time optimization problems. In continuous-time optimization problems, the analogous equation is a partial differential equation which is usually called as the Hamilton-Jacobi-Bellman equation. Given a fixed policy, Π, its value function, VΠ, satisfies the Bellman equations:-

$$V^{\Pi}(s) = R(s) + \gamma \Sigma (s' \varepsilon S) P_{s\Pi(s)}(s') V^{\Pi}(s') \quad ......(3)$$

This expression shows that the expected sum of discounted rewards, $V^{\Pi}(s)$, for starting, s, consists of two terms-

a. Firstly, the immediate reward *R*(*s*) that we get right away simply for starting in state, *s*.

b. 2nd is the expected sum of future discounted rewards.

The 2nd term of the equation-3, shows the expected sum of discounted rewards for starting in state *s*', where *s*' is distributed according to $P_{s\Pi(s)}$, which is the distribution over where we will end up taking the first action in the MDP from state, *s*. So, the 2nd term gives the expected sum of discounted rewards obtained after the first step in the MDP.

These Bellman's equations can be used to efficiently solve V^{Π}. Specifically in a finite-state MDP ($|S| < \infty$), we can write down such equation for $V^{\Pi}(s)$ for every state, s. This gives us a set of |*S*| linear equations in |S| variables that can be then solved.

Q.13. Which policy is used more-Value Iteration or Policy Iteration? Explain.

Ans. Both value iteration and policy iteration are standard algorithms for solving MDPs. For small MDPs, policy iteration is often very fast and converges with very little iteration. On the other hand, for MDPs with large state spaces, solving for V^{Π} explicitly would involve solving a large system of linear equations and could be difficult. In these problems, value iteration may be preferred. This is the reason as to why practically, value iteration seems to be used more often than policy iteration.

Q.14. What is Linear Quadratic Regulation (LQR)?

Ans. The theory of optimal control is related to the operation of a dynamic system at a minimum cost. And the case where the system dynamics are described by a set of linear differential equations and the cost is described by a quadratic function is called as the LQ problem. One of the main results in the theory is that the solution is provided by the linear-quadratic regulator (LQR), a feedback controller whose equations are given here. LQR is an important part of the solution to the LQG (LINEAR QUADRATIC GAUSSIAN) PROBLEM. Like the LQR problem, the LQG problem is one of the most fundamental problems in control theory. The settings of a regulating controller governing either a machine or process like an airplane or chemical reactor, are found by using a mathematical algorithm that minimizes a cost function with weighting factors supplied by an engineer. The cost function is defined as the sum of the deviations of key measurements, desired altitude or process temperature, from their desired values. Thus, the algorithm finds those controller settings that minimize undesired deviations. The magnitude of the control action also may be included in the cost function.

The LQR algorithm reduces the amount of work done by the control system engineer to optimize the controller. However, the engineer still needs to specify the cost function parameters and compare the results with the specified design goals. Please note that this often means that the controller construction will be an iterative process in which an engineer judges the optimal controllers produced through simulation and then adjusts the parameters to produce a controller more consistent with the design goals.

The LQR algorithm is an automated way of finding an appropriate state-feedback controller. As such, it is not uncommon for control engineers to prefer alternative methods like full state feedback, also known as pole placement, wherein there is a clear relationship between the controller parameters and controller behaviour. Also note that difficulty in finding the right weighting factors limits the application of the LQR based controller synthesis.

Q.15. Compare Explore versus Exploit.

Ans. Consider a very famous mouse-maze problem. The mouse must either get the water or it may reach a poison container that is red in colour. Our agent must control the mouse to maximize reward. If the mouse gets water, it receives a reward of +1, if it reaches the poison container then it receives a reward of -10 and if the mouse gets the cheese, it receives a reward of +100. After receiving of the reward, the episode is over. Please note that the optimal policy involves the mouse successfully navigating to the cheese and eating it. The mouse may go left or right but the aim of mouse is to follow from its movements that if it goes left, it gets water and if it goes right it gets poison container. May be after 2 episodes the mouse may have found an optimal policy. It continues to follow its learned policy on subsequent episodes and gets the moderate reward. So, we can say that our agent uses a greedy method i.e. always it chooses a model's best action. Therefore, it gets struck in a policy that is a local maximum. To avoid this problem, our agent should deviate from the model's recommendation and take a suboptimal action in order to explore more of the environment. So, instead of taking the immediate right turn to exploit the environment to get water, our agent may choose a left turn and may enter into more dangerous areas in search of a more optimal policy. Also note here that too much of exploration and our agent fails to optimize any reward. Not enough exploration can result in our agent getting stuck in local minima. This balance of explore versus exploit is vital to learn a successful policy.

Q.16. Compare Policy versus Value Learning.

Ans. To maximize the rewards we have to teach an agent. And for this teaching there are 2 methods:-

a. Policy learning.

b. Value learning.

In policy learning, we directly learn a policy that maximizes reward.

In value learning, we are learning the value of every state and action (a pair).

For example, say you are trying to learn 'how to ride a bike'. Then a policy learning method would be to think about how pressing the right pedal would correct you, if you are falling on to the left. On the other hand, with a value learning approach, you would assign a score to different bike orientations and actions that you can take in those positions.

Q.17. Explain Q-Learning and Deep Q-Networks?

Ans. Q-learning comes under the catgory of reinforcement learning and is called as value learning. Here, instead of directly learning a policy, we will be learning the value of states and actions. It involves learning a function named as Q-function, that represents the quality of a state, action pair. We define Q-function as follows:-

"Q-function, $Q(s, a)$ is a function that calculates the maximum discounted future return when action, a, is performed in state, s".

Q-value represents our expected long-term rewards. Given that we are at a state and take an action. Then take every subsequent action perfectly to maximize expected future reward. Please understand that it is very difficult to know whether the action is good or not as you need to know how you are going to act in the future. Our future returns will depend on what our long-term methods are going to be. Also note here that in order to value a (state, action) pair you need to know all of the perfect subsequent actions. And to know the best actions, you need to have accurate values for a state and action.

Q-learning is an alternative Temporal Difference (TD) method. It learns action-value representation instead of utilities. $Q(a, s)$ denotes value of doing action, a, in state, s.

$$U(s) = \max Q(a, s)$$

A TD agent that learns a Q-function does not need a model for either learning or action selection. That is, it is model free.

Note: Q-learning agent learns optimal policy but much slower than ADP agent.

TD does not enforce consistency among values via a model.

According to Watkins and Dayan in 1992, the convergence results for Q-learning assumes a discrete time, finite-state system and requires the use of lookup-tables to represent Q-function. This is not suitable for the LQR domain where the states and actions are vectors of real numbers. We will use a parameterized representation of the Q-function and adjust the parameters through a learning process.

For instance, Jordan and Jacobs in 1990, Lin in 1992, used MLPs training using backpropagation to approximate the Q-function. **Please note that the function,** QU, **is a quadratic function of its** arguments, the state and control action but it is a linear function of the quadratic combinations from the vector $[z, u]$.

For example, if $x = [x_1, x_2]$ and $u = [u_1]$, then $QU(x, u)$ is a linear function of the vector $[x_{12}, x_{22}, u_{12}, x_1 x_2, x_1u_1, x_2u_1]$. This fact allows us to use Linear Recursive Least Squares (RLS) to implement Q-learning in the LQR domain.

We must relate the Q-values of past and future. This forms a new update rule i.e., we can update past Q-values to be based on future Q-values. This is useful as we know that there exists a Q-value that we know is correct i.e. the Q-value of the very last action before the episode is over. For this last state, we know that the next action resulted in the next reward. So we can perfectly set the Q-values for that state. Then we can use this update-rule to propagate that Q-value to the previous time step as follows:

$$Q'_j \to Q'_{j+1} \to Q'_{j+2} \to ....-->Q^*$$

And this process of updating of the Q-value is known as **value iteration.**

Our 1st Q-value may be wrong but it is fine as with the next iteration, we can update our Q-value via the correct one from the future. After 1st iteration, the last Q-value is accurate as it is just a reward from the last state and action before episode termination. Then we update our Q-value. This sets the 2nd to last Q-value. In next iteration, we can assure that the last two Q-values are correct and so on. Through this process of value iteration, we will be assured the convergence on the ultimate optimal Q-value.

There are two types of Q-learning as follows:-

a. Watkins Q-learning rule/ optimizing Q-learning as it learn the Q-function of the optimal policy directly.

b. The 2nd form of Q-learning tries to learn QU, the Q-function for some designated policy, U. U may or may not be the policy that is actually followed during training.

Bradtke et al. show in one of their papers that a linear RLS representation of the policy-based learning rule will converge to QU, for LQR problems.

Deep Q-Network (DQN) : DQN uses a deep neural network that takes an image (the state) in to estimate the Q-value for all possible actions. The aim is ti train our network to estimate the Q-function. We know that Q-learning is a value-learning algorithm. We are not learning a policy directly rather we are learning the values of each state, action pair. They may or may not be good.

Value iteration produces a mapping between state and action pairs with corresponding Q-values and we are constructing a table of these mappings called as Q-TABLE.

What will be the size of this Q-TABLE?

As studied, value iteration is an exhaustive process that requires a full traversal of the entire space of state, action pairs. In stochastic environments, the space of our Q-TABLE would even be larger and possibly infinite. With such a large space, it will be intractable for us to find all of the Q-vales for every state, action pair.

Note: If we approximate the Q-function then we need not perform an exhaustive and extensive search through all possible values of Q (Q-values) to learn a Q-function.

Deep Q Network is a Markov decision process that works on the Markov assumption. This assumption sates that "the next state (s_i + 1) depends only on the current state s_i and action a_i and not on any previous states or actions." This Markov assumption makes modelling decision processes simple and reliable too but at a loss of modelling power. DQN solves this problem by reusing the state history *i.e.*, DQN considers the past four game frames instead of using only one game frame. This makes DQN to utilize time-dependent information.

Two types of Q-networks are available in literature-

a. The prediction network.

b. The target Q-network.

It is observed in these two Q-networks that they have the same architecture definition as they are the same network with the target Q just having delayed parameter updates.

Limitations of DQN : It takes long to train. It does not work well on some games and needs re-training for every new game.

Deep Recurrent Q-Networks (DRQN) : Let us recall the Markov's assumption. It states that the next state relies only on the previous state and the action taken by the agent. Using this on DQN has some limitations like why should there be only 4 frames, why not 8 or 10 or 12? This is an imposed frames history parameter that limits the model's generality. For this purpose, we use DQRN.

DQRN uses a recurrent layer to transfer a latent knowledge of state from one time step to the next. Thus, the model itself can learn how many frames are informative that must be included in its state. DQRN has also been extended to include neural nets. The point to understand is that since DQRN deals with sequences of data, it can attend only certain parts of the sequence. And this ability to learn just parts of the image will improve performance as well as it provides model interpretability.

DQRN has been found to be better than DQN as far as the playing of certain games is concerned like DOOM, Atari games etc.

Q.18. Write short notes on POMDPS.

Ans. POMDPS stands for PARTIALLY OBSERVABLE MARKOV DECISION PROCESS. It is a generalization of a Markov decision process (MDP). A POMDP models an agent decision process in which it is assumed that the system dynamics are determined by an MDP but the agent cannot directly observer the underlying state. Instead, it must maintain a probability distribution over the set of possible states based on a set of observations and observation probabilities and the underlying MDP. A POMDP framework is general enough to model a variety of real-world sequential decision process. Applications like Robot navigation problems, machine maintenance and planning uncertainty are included here.

An exact solution to a POMDP yields the optimal action for each possible belief over the world states. The optimal action maximizes or minimizes the expected reward or cost of the agent over a possibly infinite horizon. The sequence of optimal actions is known as the optimal policy of the agent for interacting with its environment.

MDP assumes that the complete state of the world is visible to the agent. This is quite unrealistic. POMDPS models the information available to the agent by specifying a function from the hidden state to the observables. The goal now is to find a mapping from observations (not states) to actions. But the observations are not Markov because two different states might look the same, which invalidates all of the MDP solution techniques. The optimal solution to this problem is to construct a belief state MDP, where a belief state is a probability distribution over states.

Control theory is concerned with solving POMDPs. Practically speaking, control theory scientists make a strong assumption about the nature of the model (linear-Gaussian) and reward function (negative quadratic loss) in order to be able to make theoretical guarantees of optimality. Solving a generic discrete POMDP is wildly intractable. Finding tractable special cases like structured models is the current area of research today.

Limitations of POMDPs : They model the world in terms of a fixed size set of state variables, each of which can take on specific values, say true or false. These are called as propositional models.

Applications of POMDPs : POMDPs can be used to model real-life problems. It has been used in management of patients with ischemic heart disease, assistive technology for persons with dementia, the conservation of the critically endangered and difficult to detect Sumatran tigers and aircraft collision avoidance.

SUMMARY

We have studied the concept of reinforcement learning like MDPs, maximum rewards problem. Different approaches to deep reinforcement learning like policy gradients, deep-Q networks etc have also been studied in this chapter. Deep reinforcement learning is a step in this direction that has produced agents capable of mastering Atari games, driverless cars, robotics etc.

MULTIPLE CHOICE QUESTIONS

1. MDP stands for-

(*a*) Many Decision Problems

(*b*) Markov Decision Process

(*c*) Markov Dynamic Problem

(*a*) None of the above

2. A branch of machine learning that deals with learning with interaction and feedback is called as-

(*a*) Leaning by Example (*b*) Reinforcement Learning

(*c*) Deep Learning (*d*) None of the above

3. An application of reinforcement learning using deep networks is-

(*a*) DQN (*b*) AQN

(*c*) PQN (*d*) None of the above

4. Reinforcement learning involves-

(*a*) An actor (*b*) An environment

(c) A reward signal (*d*) All of the above

5. The ways in which our agent acts based on its current state is-

(*a*) Policy (*b*) Learning
(*c*) Testing (*d*) None of the above

6. Reinforcement learning is basically a-

(*a*) Trial and error process (*b*) Algorithmic process
(*c*) Dynamic process (*d*) None of the above

7. In which type of learning we learn the value of every (state+ action) pair-

(*a*) Policy learning (*b*) Value learning
(*c*) Machine learning (*d*) None of the above

8. Q-learning is put under-

(*a*) Policy learning (*b*) Value learning
(*c*) Machine learning (*d*) None of the above

9. The process of updating of the Q-value is known as-

(*a*) Policy iteration (*a*) Value iteration
(*c*) Research iteration (*d*) None of the above

10. DQN uses-

(*a*) Life history (*b*) State history
(*c*) Indian history (*d*) None of the above

11. Which of the following is a Q-network-

(*a*) The prediction network (*b*) The computer network
(*c*) LAN (*d*) None of the above

12. DQRN stands for-

(*a*) Deep Recurrent Q-Network (*b*) Direct Recursive Q-Network
(*c*) Prediction network (*d*) None of the above

13. Deep reinforcement learning has produced-

(*a*) Agents (*b*) Letters
(*c*) Messages (*d*) None of the above

ANSWERS

1. (*b*)	**2.** (*b*)	**3.** (*a*)	**4.** (*d*)	**5.** (*a*)
6. (*a*)	**7.** (*b*)	**8.** (*b*)	**9.** (*b*)	**10.** (*b*)
11. (*a*)	**12.** (*a*)	**13.** (*a*)		

CONCEPTUAL SHORT QUESTIONS WITH ANSWERS

Q.1. Distinguish between a perceptron and delta rule.

Ans. The following are the points of differences between the two:

A Perceptron	Delta Rule
It uses threshold unit.	It uses unthreshold linear unit.
It converges after a finite number of iterations.	It converges asymptotically toward a minimum error hypothesis.
Output hypothesis classifies training data perfectly.	Termination is not guaranteed.
Linear separability is mandatory.	Linear separability is not mandatory.

Q.2. List some applications of back propagation perceptrons.

Ans. The following are some of the applications:

1. Optical character recognition.
2. Data compression.
3. Image compression.
4. Load forecasting problems in power systems.
5. Speech synthesis.
6. Content problem.
7. Pattern recognition.
8. Fault detection problems.
9. Aircraft navigation.
10. Non-linear simulation

Q.3. Write a short note on SOMs.

Ans. SOMs stands for Self Organizing Feature Maps or Kohonen Network is a data visualization technique proposed by Kohonen, which provides a way of representing multidimensional data in much lower dimensional spaces. And this process of reducing the dimensionality of vectors is a data compression technique known as vector quantization. This technique creates a network that stores information in such a way that any topological relationships within the training set are maintained. So they are also called as topology-preserving maps. The topological structure property is observed in our brain and is not found in any other ANN except SOM. Please note that the self-organizing map as developed by Kohonen, groups the input data into clusters which are commonly used for unsupervised learning.

In SOM, there are '*m*' cluster units that are arranged in a 1D or 2d array, an input vector of n-tuples and a weight vector associated with the cluster unit. In self-organizing process, the cluster unit whose weight vector matches the input pattern closely is selected as a winner. The winning and the neighbouring unit update their weights. The neighbouring unit's weight vectors are not close to the input pattern but differ in some extent. That is why the connection weights do not multiply the signal sent from the input units to cluster units.

In SOM, all units in the neighbourhood that receive positive feedback from the winning unit participate in the learning process. Even if a neighbouring unit's weight is orthogonal to the input vector, its weight vector will still change in response to the input vector. This is required to maintain the order mapping.

Q.4. Differentiate between PCA and LDA.

Ans. The following are the points of differences:-

1. PCA does more of feature classification whereas LDA does data classification.
2. In PCA, the shape and the location of the original data sets changes when transformed to a different space. LDA does not change the location but only tries to provide more class separability and draw a decision region between the given classes. As such, LDA also helps in better understanding the distribution of the feature data.
3. PCA deals with unlabelled data and tries to maximize variance. PCA deals with unlabeled data and tries to maximize variance. PCA deals with unlabeled data and tries to maximize the discrimination between the classes.
4. If the discriminating information lies within the variances, then PCA works better than the LDA.
5. PCA is an unsupervised linear feature extraction method. LDA uses the category information associated with each pattern for extracting the most discriminatory features.

Q.5. List the three steps of PCA.

Ans. The summary of PCA steps is: -

1. Organize a data set as $m*n$ matrix, where m is the number of measurement types and n is the number of trials.
2. Subtract off the mean for each measurement type or row.
3. Calculate the Eigen vectors of the covariance.

Q.6. Define EBL. What are its advantages?

Ans. EBL extracts general rules from single examples by explaining the examples and generalizing the explanation. It provides a deductive method turning first-principles knowledge into useful, efficient and special purpose expertise. Some of its advantages are as follows:-

1. Training examples often contains irrelevant information. The domain theory allows the learner to select he relevant aspects of the training example.
2. EBL forms generalizations that are known to be relevant to specific goals that are logically guaranteed to be logically consistent with the domain theory.
3. By using domain knowledge, EBL allows learning from a single training instance.
4. Construction of an explanation allows the learner to hypothesize unstated relationships between its goals and its experiences.

Q.7. What do you mean by gap filling by EBL?

Ans. EBL or Explanation Based Learning makes up for small number of examples by using extensive domain knowledge. If the explanation is complete, then one can guarantee that the description is correct. But there are some problems as there might be instances where explanations may use reasoning steps that are not sound. When such gaps are found in the explanation, an EBL system may use abduction or induction to fill them.

Q.8. Why do we disparage the term Q-value?

Ans. Researchers in the field of reinforcement learning discuss about Q-values, Q-tables and Q-functions. Such usage almost always seems like jargon *i.e.* like apparently precise technical terms that are off-putting to new comers but really adds nothing. In this case, the Q-prefix means only that the values, tables or functions pertain to (state + action) pairs. In most of the cases, we give these functions different notations, all of which involve the letter, Q. The name Q-function appears to be technical but is in fact imprecise and undesirable.

Q.9. Which algorithm to use-actor critic method or Q-learning?

Ans. In 1980s, actor critic methods were very popular but in 1990s these were dominated by value-function methods like Q-learning and Sarsa. But Q-learning is instable with function approximation. So, it is not very useful for long run.

Q.10. Give some limitations of Multilayer perceptrons.

Ans. Limitations of multilayer perceptrons are as follows:-

1. It requires large number of iterations for learning that is unsuitable for real-time learning.
2. It gives no guaranteed solution.
3. They do not scale up well from small research systems to larger real systems.
4. It is very difficult to determine all of the weights and thresholds theoretically.
5. It is very difficult to decide which input pattern should be represented by hidden layer.

Q.11. What are the characteristics of delta learning rule?

Ans. The characteristics of delta learning rule are as follows:-

1. It uses output of activation function to generate error signal.
2. It can only be used with continuous activation functions.
3. It is a gradient based method *e.g.* the least mean square algorithm.
4. It can be generalized to multi-layer networks.
5. It gives continuous output so can be used for function approximation.

Q.12. Show how a multi-layered perceptron solves a non-linear separable class problem.

Ans. Logical XOR Function is as follows:-

X1	X2	Output (Y)
0	0	0
0	1	1
1	0	1
1	1	0

The output from a neuron is calculated as follows:-

$$Y = X_1 * W_1 + X_2 * W_2$$

In form of a graph, we can draw:-

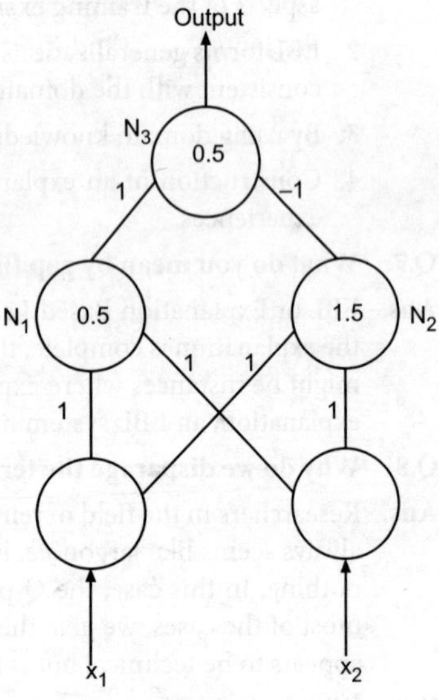

From this graph, the activations of output neuron can be formed:-

Neuron, N_1 uses the activation function-

$$O = f(\text{Net}) = \begin{cases} 1 \text{ if Net} \geq 0.5 \\ 0 \text{ if Net} < 0.5 \end{cases}$$

Neuron, N_2 uses the activation function-

$$O = f(\text{Net}) = \begin{cases} 1 \text{ if Net} \geq 1.5 \\ 0 \text{ if Net} < 1.5 \end{cases}$$

Neuron, N_3 uses the activation function-

$$O = f(\text{Net}) = \begin{cases} 1 \text{ if Net} \geq 0.5 \\ 0 \text{ if Net} < 0.5 \end{cases}$$

Now the network learns as follows:-

1. Output from neuron, N_1 is

   For input $X_1 = 0$ and $X_2 = 0$ and with threshold 0.5,

$$\begin{aligned} \text{Net} &= W_1 * X_1 + W_2 * X_2 \\ &= 1.X_1 + 1 * X_2 \\ &= 1 * 0 + 1 * 0 \\ &= 0 \end{aligned}$$

   So, $O = f(\text{Net}) = 0$ [as Net < 0.5]

2. Output from neuron, N_2 is

   For input $X_1 = 0$ and $X_1 = 0$ and with threshold 1.5,

$$\begin{aligned} \text{Net} &= W_1 * X_1 + W_2 * X_2 \\ &= 1.X_1 + 1 * X_2 \\ &= 1 * 0 + 1 * 0 \\ &= 0 \end{aligned}$$

   So, $O = f(\text{Net}) = 0$ [as Net < 0.5]

3. Output from neuron, N_3 is

   For input $X_1 = 0$ and $X_2 = 0$ and with threshold 0.5,

$$\begin{aligned} \text{Net} &= W_1 * X_1 + W_2 * X_2 \\ &= 1.X_1 \text{ (output from } N_1) + -1 * X_2 \text{ (output from } N_2) \\ &= 1 * 0 + -1 * 0 \\ &= 0 \end{aligned}$$

   So, $O = f(\text{Net}) = 0$ [as Net < 0.5]

(ii) Output from Neuron, N_1

For input $X_1 = 0$ and $X_2 = 1$ and with threshold 0.5,

$$\begin{aligned} \text{Net} &= W_1 * X_1 + W_2 * X_2 \\ &= 1.X_1 + 1 * X_2 \\ &= 1 * 0 + 1 * 1 \\ &= 1 \end{aligned}$$

So, $O = f(\text{Net}) = 1$ [as Net ≥ 0.5]

Output from neuron, N_2 is

For input $X_1 = 0$ and $X_2 = 1$ and with threshold 1.5,

$$\begin{aligned} \text{Net} &= W_1 * X_1 + W_2 * X_2 \\ &= 1.X_1 + 1 * X_2 \\ &= 1 * 0 + 1 * 1 \end{aligned}$$

$= 1$

So, $O = f(\text{Net}) = 0$ [as Net < 1.5]

Output from neuron, N_3 is

For input $X_1 = 0$ and $X_2 = 1$ and with threshold 0.5,

$$\text{Net} = W_1 * X_1 + W_2 * X_2$$
$$= 1.X_1 \text{ (output from } N_1) + -1 * X_2 \text{ (output from } N_2)$$
$$= 1 * 1 + -1 * 0$$
$$= 1$$

So, $O = f(\text{Net}) = 1$ [as Net ≥ 0.5]

(*iii*) Output from neuron N_1

For input $X_1 = 1$ and $X_2 = 0$ and with threshold 0.5,

$$\text{Net} = W_1 * X_1 + W_2 * X_2$$
$$= 1.X1 + 1 * X2$$
$$= 1 * 1 + 1 * 0$$
$$= 1$$

So, $O = f(\text{Net}) = 1$ [as Net ≥ 0.5]

Output from neuron, N_2 is

For input $X_1 = 1$ and $X_2 = 0$ and with threshold 1.5,

$$\text{Net} = W_1 * X_1 + W_2 * X_2$$
$$= 1.X_1 + 1 * X_2$$
$$= 1 * 1 + 1 * 0$$
$$= 1$$

So, $O = f(\text{Net}) = 0$ [as Net < 1.5]

Output from neuron, N_3 is

For input $X_1 = 1$ and $X_2 = 0$ and with threshold 0.5,

$$\text{Net} = W_1 * X_1 + W_2 * X_2$$
$$= 1.X_1 \text{ (output from } N_1) + -1 * X_2 \text{ (output from } N_2)$$
$$= 1 * 1 + -1 * 0$$
$$= 1$$

So, $O = f(\text{Net}) = 1$ [as Net ≥ 0.5]

Output from neuron, N_3 is

For input $X_1 = 1$ and $X_2 = 1$ and with threshold 0.5,

$$\text{Net} = W_1 * X_1 + W_2 * X_2$$
$$= 1.X_1 + 1 * X_2$$
$$= 1 * 1 + 1 * 1$$
$$= 2$$

So, $O = f(\text{Net}) = 1$ [as Net > 0.5]

Output from neuron, N_2 is

For input $X_1 = 1$ and $X_2 = 1$ and with threshold 1.5,

$$\text{Net} = W_1 * X_1 + W_2 * X_2$$
$$= 1.X_1 + 1 * X_2$$
$$= 1 * 1 + 1 * 1$$
$$= 2$$

So, $O = f(\text{Net}) = 1$ [as Net ≥ 1.5]

Output from neuron, N_3 is

For input $X_1 = 1$ and $X_2 = 1$ and with threshold 0.5,

$$\begin{aligned} \text{Net} &= W_1 * X_1 + W_2 * X_2 \\ &= 1.\, X_1 \text{ (output from } N_1) + -1 * X_2 \text{ (output from } N_2) \\ &= 1 * 1 + -1 * 1 = 1 - 1 \\ &= 0 \end{aligned}$$

So, $O = f(\text{Net}) = 0$ [as Net < 0.5]

Q.13. Define the following:-

a. **Pulling error signals.**

b. **Pushing error signals.**

Ans. *a.* **Pulling error signals:** The process of computing delta signals for each neuron in the previous layer by pulling the error signals from the current layer is called as pulling error signals.

b. **Pushing error signals:** The process of pushing the error signals from the current layer to the previous layer *i.e.* for each unit in the current layer, we update the related units in the previous layer.

Q.14. What is a confusion matrix or contingency table? What is its use?

Ans. In machine learning, a confusion matrix/contingency matrix is also known as an error matrix. It is a specific table layout that allows visualization of the performance of an algorithm, typically a supervised learning. The one in unsupervised learning is known as a matching matrix. Each column of the matrix represents the instances in a predicted class while each row represents the instances in an actual class or vice versa. Please note that the name stems from the fact that it makes it easy to see if the system is confusing two classes i.e. commonly mislabelling one as another. It is a special type of table with two dimensions-actual and predicted and identical set of classes in both the dimensions. So, each combination of dimension and class is a variable in the contingency table.

Q.15. Define the following terms:-

a. **Confusion matrix.**

b. **False positive rate.**

c. **True positive rate.**

Ans. *a.* **Confusion matrix:** A confusion matrix contains information about actual and predicted classifications done by a classification system. Performance of such systems is commonly evaluated using the data in the matrix. The following table shows the confusion matrix for a two class classifier. The entries in the confusion matrix have the following meaning in the context of our study:-

- *a* is the number of correct predictions that an instance is negative,
- *b* is the number of incorrect predictions that an instance is positive,
- *c* is the number of incorrect predictions that an instance is negative,
- *d* is the number of correct predictions that an instance is positive.

EXERCISE QUESTIONS

1. Explain *Q* learning.
2. Explain value function in the context of reinforcement learning.
3. Explain Hidden Markov Model in detail.
4. Explain the back propagation algorithm of Multilayer Neural Network. Also explain the factor influencing back propagation training.
5. Explain SOMs.
6. What is delta rule?

7. Distinguish between perceptron and delta rule.
8. Why self organizing neural net is called as the topology preserving maps?
9. Distinguish between classification and regression.
10. State 'Universal Approximation Theorem'.
11. Define curse of dimensionality.
12. Define overfitting / overtraining.
13. Define cross validation.
14. Explain how optimization is achieved in neural networks.
15. 'Q learning agent learns optimal policy but much slower than ADP agent'. Explain this statement.
16. Draw flowchart to explain --Training a Deep Learning Model.
17. Explain the following- Test Sets and Validation Sets, Overfitting Phenomenon,Epoch,Training Data, Test Data, Hyperparameter Optimization, Critical Point, Local Maxima, Saddle Points, Learning Rate Adaptation.
18. Explain the following:-
    a. Markov Decision Processes [MDP].
    b. BELLMAN Equations.
    c. Value Iteration and Policy Iteration.
    d. Linear Quadratic Regulation (LQR).
19. Draw a fully connected feedforward ANN that has three input nodes, one output node and four internal nodes in a hidden layer.
20. Explain how would you represent the ages of a group of people ranging from 20 to 50 years as input into an ANN.

4 Deep Learning Optimization

Q.1. What do you mean by optimization problem?

Ans. The purpose of any optimization problem is to either maximize or minimize the objective function with some constraints. Some of these problems can be solved using complex ANNs too. It is an art and science of allocating limited resources in a best possible way. **Pattern classification is a very common example of optimization.** Here, the objective is to classify or recognize a pattern. In machine learning, an optimizer is used to maximize the performance of a machine learning model iteratively. The parameters are adjusted till the error is minimized.

Q.2. Compare Learning versus Pure Optimization.

Ans. The main challenge in optimizing deep learning models is that we are compelled to use minimal local information to infer the global structure of the error surface. During training of deep networks, several challenges are observed like having complex error surfaces. The objective today is not to build a better optimizer rather it is to discover the architectures that are simple to train. Literature also describes the evolution of adaptive learning rate optimizers that tune the learning rate during the training process so as to get a better convergence.

Several hyperparameters like learning rate, mini-batch size etc., have been dealt with in previous sections. But the need is to find a framework for how to find the optimal values for these hyper-parameters. One method of finding the optimal parameters values is named as a **grid search.** In this method, we select a value for each hyperparameter from a finite set of options and batch size and train the model with every possible permutation of hyperparameter choices. The objective is to find out the accuracy of the model trained with the best set on the test set. This is pure optimization.

A MLP neural network trained by back propagation with 4026 input neurons and two hidden layers of 20 and 10 neurons each and with a single output neuron to say 'Yes' or 'No' was designed to classify the tissue data as cancerous or normal. A part of the available data i.e., 72 sets were used for training and 22 were kept for testing the network for generality. After training for 1000 iterations, the network predicted correctly on 91% of the test patterns.

Present day research is being done on the adaptation of neurocomputing, fuzzy logic and evolutionary search to overcome limitations found in the use of traditional optimization methods in problems of multi-disciplinary analysis and design. The challenges include reducing the high computational cost associated with repetitive analysis, adapting emergent optimization methods for large scale design problems involving a mix of continuous, discrete and integer variables.

On the other hand, learning is the process by which a free parameter of a neural network gets adapted through a process of simulation by the environment. And the set of rules defined for the solution of a learning problem is called as a learning algorithm.

According to Simon, "Learning denotes changes in the system that are adaptive in the sense that they enable the system to do the task or tasks drawn from the same population more efficiently and more effectively the next time." Learning may be supervised, unsupervised/ clustering, reinforcement learning and inductive learning. One of the simplest algorithms is decision tree learning. Explanation based learning extracts general rules from simple examples by explaining and generalizing them. Statistical learning includes data and hypothesis.

Learning may be done by complete data or hidden data. Let us differentiate between them.

Table-1: Differences between complete data and hidden data

Complete Data	Hidden Data
Parameters of the model can be estimated locally and independently.	Parameters cannot be estimated independently.
Local likelihood has a unique maximum.	There are many local maxima.
Closed-form solutions are obtained.	Closed-form solutions cannot be obtained.

Q.3. What are the challenges in Neural Network Optimization?

Ans. The main challenge in optimizing deep learning models is that we are compelled to use minimal local information to infer the global structure of the error surface. During training of deep networks, several challenges are observed like having complex error surfaces. The objective today is not to build a better optimizer rather it is to discover the architectures that are simple to train. Literature also describes the evolution of adaptive learning rate optimizers that tune the learning rate during the training process so as to get a better convergence.

Present day research is being done on the adaptation of neurocomputing, fuzzy logic and evolutionary search to overcome limitations found in the use of traditional optimization methods in problems of multi-disciplinary analysis and design. The challenges include reducing the high computational cost associated with repetitive analysis, adapting emergent optimization methods for large scale design problems involving a mix of continuous, discrete and integer variables.

Q.4. Explain 'Basic Optimization Algorithms'.

Ans. In 2011, Duchi et al. gave an algorithm named as AdaGrad that tries to adapt the global learning rate over time using an accumulation of the historical gradients. In this algorithm, we keep track of a learning rate for each parameter. This learning rate is inversely scaled with respect to the square root of the sum of squares (rms value) of all the parameter's historical gradients. In TensorFlow (a deep learning tool), it has been found that there is an inbuilt optimizer and that it allows us to easily utilize AdaGrad as a learning algorithm. Please note that the parameters with the largest gradients experience a rapid decrease in their learning rates while parameters with smaller gradients will observer only a small decrease in their learning rates. The final result is that AdaGrad compels better progress in a more gently sloped directions on the error surface.

Also AdaGrad has a drawback too. It causes a premature drop in learning rate. So, it does not perform well for some deep models.

AdaGrad works well for complex functions but it is not designed to navigate the complex error surfaces of deep networks. Also note that flat regions compel AdaGrad to decrease the learning rate before it reaches a minimum.

A solution to this is another algorithm- RMSProp. As RMSProp performs well with momentum, so it has been found to be better optimizer for deep neural networks. This algorithm was given by Geoffrey Hinton.

Yet another algorithm was proposed by Kingma et al. It is a combination of RMSProp and momentum. Here, we want to keep track of an exponentially weighted moving average of the gradient. We try to find the first moment of gradient, second moment of gradient and so on. Thse are our estimations. But here these estimations are biased relative to the real moments as we start by initializing both vectors to the zero vector. To remedy this bias, we derive the correction factor for both of the estimations. Recently, Adam has become very popular because of its corrective measure against the zero initialization bias, which happens to be a weakness of RMSProp, and its ability to combine the core concepts behind RMSProp with momentum more effectively. Also, Adam is robust to choices in hyperparameters, the only point is that the learning rate may need to be modified in certain cases from the default value of 0.001.

In nutshell, the adaptive learning rate optimizers evolve. They tune to the learning rate during the training process for better convergence.

Q.5. What do you mean by 'Parameter Initializations'?

Ans. A neural network trains by repeated passes of the data. Each pass is called as an epoch. With each epoch, the connecting weights are adjusted until a satisfactory level of performance is reached. We think that by increasing the number of epochs, the system will perform better. But this is not true with deep neural networks. It has been found that with several passes, the network gets overtrained and needs more computing time. This has been called as overfitting or overtraining.

We can change the parameter values of the algorithm. The default setting of hyperparameters may not always be good.

Several hyperparameters like learning rate, mini-batch size etc., have been dealt with in previous chapters. But the need is to find a framework for how to find the optimal values for these hyper-parameters. One method of finding the optimal parameters values is named as a grid search. In this method, we select a value for each hyperparameter from a finite set of options and batch size and train the model with every possible permutation of hyperparameter choices. The objective is to find out the accuracy of the model trained with the best set on the test set.

Q.6. Write short notes on Meta-algorithms.

Ans. The early stopping meta-algorithm for determining the best amount of time to train is discussed now. This meta-algorithm is a general strategy that works well with a variety of training algorithms. It gives ways of quantifying error on the validation set.

Let n be the number of steps between evaluations.

Let p be the "patience," the number of times to observe worsening validation set error before giving up.

Let θo be the initial parameters.

$\theta \leftarrow \theta o$

$i \leftarrow 0$

$j \leftarrow 0$

$v \leftarrow \infty$

$\theta \leftarrow \theta$

$i \leftarrow i$

while $j < p$ do

Update θ by running the training algorithm for n steps.

$i \leftarrow i + n$

$v \leftarrow$ ValidationSetError(θ)

if $v < v$ then

$j \leftarrow 0$

$\theta \leftarrow \theta$

$i \leftarrow i$

$v \leftarrow v$

else

$j \leftarrow j + 1$

end if

end while

Best parameters are θ and the best number of training steps is i.

This strategy is known as **early stopping.** It is probably the most commonly used form of regularization in deep learning. It is very popular as it is both effectiveness and its simplicity.

One way to think of early stopping is as a very efficient hyperparameter selection algorithm. So, the number of training steps is just another hyperparameter.

In the case of early stopping, we are controlling the effective capacity of the model by determining how many steps it can take to fit the training set. Most hyperparameters must be chosen using an expensive guess and check process, where we set a hyperparameter at the start of training, then run training for several steps to see its effect. The "training time" hyperparameter is unique in that by definition a single run of training tries out many values of the hyperparameter. The only significant cost to choosing this hyperparameter automatically via early stopping is running the validation set evaluation periodically during training. Ideally, this is done in parallel to the training process on a separate machine, separate CPU, or separate GPU from the main training process. If such resources are not available, then the

cost of these periodic evaluations may be reduced by using a validation set that is small compared to the training set or by evaluating the validation set error less frequently and obtaining a lower resolution estimate of the optimal training time.

An additional cost to early stopping is the need to maintain a copy of the best parameters. This cost is generally negligible, because it is acceptable to store these parameters in a slower and larger form of memory (for example, training in GPU memory, but storing the optimal parameters in host memory or on a disk drive). Since the best parameters are written to infrequently and never read during training, these occasional slow writes have little effect on the total training time.

Early stopping is a very unobtrusive form of regularization, in that it requires almost no change in the underlying training procedure, the objective function, or the set of allowable parameter values. Also note that this means that it is easy to use early stopping without damaging the learning dynamics. This is in contrast to weight decay, where one must be careful not to use too much weight decay and trap the network in a bad local minimum corresponding to a solution with pathologically small weights.

Early stopping may be used either alone or in conjunction with other regularization strategies. Even when using regularization strategies that modify the objective function to encourage better generalization, it is rare for the best generalization to occur at a local minimum of the training objective.

Early stopping requires a validation set, which means some training data is not fed to the model. To best exploit this extra data, one can perform extra training after the initial training with early stopping has completed.

SUMMARY

In this chapter, we have studied how learning is different from optimization. Optimization here refers to the optimization of deep learning networks. It also discusses about the best optimization algorithms and their parameters initializations. Also discussed is a meta-algorithm, namely early learning. In nutshell, the adaptive learning rate optimizers evolve. They tune to the learning rate during the training process for better convergence.

MULTIPLE CHOICE QUESTIONS

1. **Pattern classification is an example of-**
   (*a*) Classification (*b*) Optimization
   (*c*) Normalization (*d*) None of the above
2. **An optimizer aims to-**
   (*a*) Maximize the performance of machine learning model
   (*b*) Minimize the performance of machine learning model
   (*c*) Neutralize the performance of machine learning model
   (*d*) None of the above
3. **Which one of the following is a popular adaptive learning rate algorithm-**
   (*a*) AdaGrad (*b*) RMSProp
   (*c*) Adam (*d*) All of these
4. **Optimizers tune the learning rate during-**
   (*a*) Training (*b*) Generalizations
   (*c*) Specializations (*d*) None of the above
5. **Which of the following is a deep learning tool-**
   (*a*) TensorFlow (*b*) DataFlow
   (*c*) WtareFlow (*d*) None of the above

ANSWERS

1. (*b*) **2.** (*a*) **3.** (*d*) **4.** (*a*) **5.** (*a*)

CONCEPTUAL SHORT QUESTIONS WITH ANSWERS

Q.1. Are deep learning algorithms slower than other algorithms?

Ans. Yes, deep learning models take more CPU time than other algorithms. So, we have to keep our grid searches as precise as possible.

Q.2. What is early stopping? Explain.

Ans. A technique based on dividing data into three subsets. The first subset is the training set used for computing the gradient and updating the network weights and biases. The second subset is the validation set. When the validation error increases for a specified number of iterations, the training is stopped and the weights and biases at the minimum of the validation error are returned. The third subset is the test set. It is used to verify the network design.

Q.3. Define what is an Epoch?

Ans. A neural network trains by repeated passes of the data. Each pass is called as an epoch.

Q.4. 'Increasing the number of Epochs will make the system perform better'. Explain.

Ans. This is not true with deep neural networks. It has been found that with several passes, the network gets overtrained and needs more computing time. This has been called as overfitting or overtraining.

Q.5. What is grid search?

Ans. In grid search, we select a value for each hyperparameter from a finite set of options and batch size and train the model with every possible permutation of hyperparameter choices. The objective is to find out the accuracy of the model trained with the best set on the test set.

EXERCISE QUESTIONS

1. Define optimization and an optimizer.
2. Define an Epoch. What is its role during training?
3. What are meta-algorithms? Give an example to explain.
4. Write short notes on basic optimization algorithms.
5. Define the following:-
   a. Overfitting or overtraining.
   b. Grid Search.
   c. Hyperparameters.
   d. Early stopping.
   e. Training time.
   f. RMSProp.

5 Convolutional Neural Networks

Q.1. What are CNNs? Explain in terms of different layers?

Ans. A typical CNN consists up of many layers of hierarchy with some layers for feature representations or feature maps and others as a type of conventional neural networks for classification. It starts with 2 layers: -

a. Convolutional layers.

b. Subsampling layers.

The convolutional layers perform convolution operations with several filter maps of equal size. The subsampling layers reduce the sizes of the proceeding layers by averaging pixels within a small neighbourhood or by max-pooling.

The key parameters to be decided are weights between layers that are normally trained by standard backpropagation procedures and a gradient descent algorithm with mean squared-error as the loss function. Note that training deep CNN architectures can be unsupervised or supervised.

Inspired by the biological processes, CNN algorithms learn a hierarchical feature representation by utilizing strategies like local receptive fields where the size of each filter is normally small, shared weights-using the same weights to construct all of the feature maps at the same level reduces the number of parameters and subsampling to further reduce the dimensionality. Each filter bank can be trained with either supervised or unsupervised methods. A CNN is capable of learning good feature hierarchies automatically and providing some degree of translational and distortional invariances.

Q.2. What is Convolution? Also explain convolutional layers. Explain the convolution operation.

Ans. Consider the case of an image wherein the input to NN will be pixels. By looking at pixels, the first hidden layer units may learn to check for edges of various orientations, then the combining edges, the second hidden layer units can learn to check for combinations of edges like arcs, corners, line ends and then combining them in upper layers, the units can look for semi-circles, rectangles. Please note that this is an example of a hierarchical cone where features get more complex, abstract and fewer in numbers as we go up the network until we get to the classes. Such an architecture is called as convolutional neural network where the work of each hidden unit is considered to be a convolution of its input with its weight vector. The process of taking a filter and then multiplying it over the entire area of an input image is called as convolution.

The Convolutional Layer : It is also possible to further reduce the number of parameters by the process called as weight sharing. Like in case of visual recognition system, features like oriented edges may be present in different parts of the input space. So, instead of defining independent hidden units, learning different features in different parts of the input space, we can have copies of the same hidden units looking at different parts of the input space. This is shown in figure 5.1. During learning, we compute the gradients by taking different inputs and then we average these and make a single update. This implies a single parameter that defines the weight on multiple connections. As the update on a weight is based on gradients for several inputs, it is as if the training set is effectively multiplied.

In weight sharing, different units have connections to different inputs but share the same weight value (denoted by line type). Only one set of units is shown in figure 5.1. There should be multiple sets of units, each checking for different features.

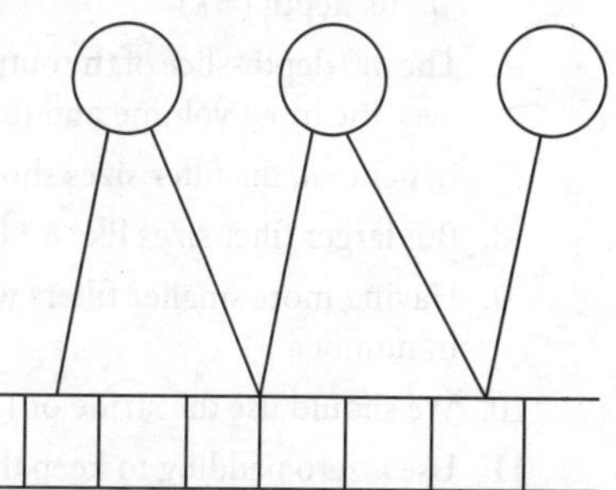

Fig. 5.1: Weight Sharing

The Convolution Operation : The process of taking a filter and then multiplying it over the entire area of an input image is called as convolution. Let us show this operation in terms of neurons in a network. In this schema, layers of neurons in a feed-forward neural net represent either the original image or a feature map. Filters represent combinations of connections that get replicated across the entirety of the input (as shown in figure 5.2). As shown in figure 5.2, connections in the same colour are restricted to always have the same weight. We can get this by initializing all the connections in a group with identical weights and by always averaging the weight updates of a group before applying them at the end of each of the iteration of backpropagation. Please note that the output layer is the feature map generated by this filter. Also note that a neuron in a feature map is activated if the filter contributing to its activity detected an appropriate feature at the corresponding position in the previous layer.

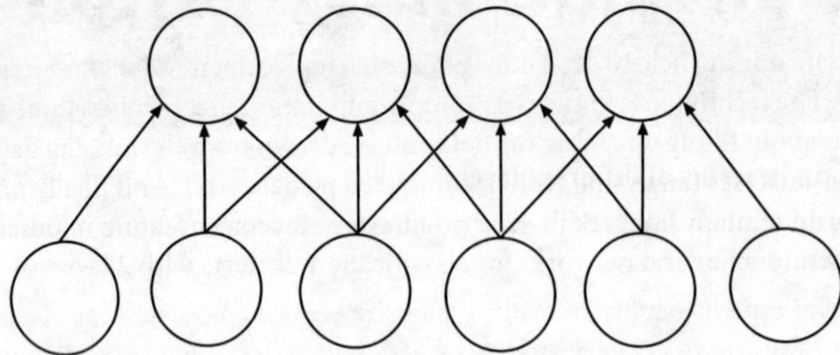

Fig. 5.2: Showing Filters and Feature Maps as Neurons in a Convolutional Layer

The point is that the feature maps must be able to operate over volumes and not just areas. Each cell in the input volume is a neuron. a local portion is multiplied with a filter, corresponding to the weights in the convolutional layer, to produce a neuron in a filter map in the following volumetric layers of neurons. **Please understand that a convolutional layer that consists of a set of filters, converts one volume of values into another volume of values.** The depth of the filter corresponds to the depth of the input volume. This is so that the filter can combine information from all the features that have been learned. **The depth of the output volume of a convolutional layer is equivalent to the number of filters in that layer as each filter produces its own slice.**

Please remember the following points regarding Convolutional Layer:-

1. A convolutional layer takes in an input volume.
2. This input volume has the following features- its width, its height, depth and zero padding.
3. This volume is processed by a total of k filters that represent the weights and connections in the convolutional network.
4. These filters have a number of hyperparameter as follows:-
   a. **Spatial extent (*e*):** It is equal to the filters height and width.
   b. **Stride (*s*):** The distance between consecutive applications of the filter on the input volume. If we use a stride of 1, we get the full convolution.
   c. **Bias (*b*):** A parameter learned like the values in the filter which is added to each component of the convolution.
5. This results in an output volume with the following features:-
   a. The function, f, which is applied to the incoming logit of each neuron in the output volume to determine its final volume.
   b. Its width;
   c. Its height;
   d. Its depth (= *k*)
6. The mth depth-slice of the output volume corresponds to the function, f, applied to the sum of the mth filter convoluted over the input volume and the bias, bm where $1 \le m \le k$.
7. In general, the filter sizes should be kept in smaller sizes like 3 * 3 or 5 * 5.
8. But larger filter sizes like 8 * 8 may be used at the first convolutional layer only.
9. Having more smaller filters will help us to achieve high representational power. Also, the parameters will be smaller in number.
10. We should use the stride of 1 to capture all useful information in the feature maps.
11. Use a zero padding to keep the output volume's height and width equivalent to the input volume's height and width.
12. Deep learning tool, TensorFlow, makes easier for us to perform a convolution on a mini-batch of input volumes. Also

note that we must choose and apply our choice of function, f, as it is not performed by the operation itself.

13. The basic idea is to match patterns (like a 5 * 5 patterns) as **sliding tiles**, all over your image. This is alternated with a shrink layer where the maximum pixel value is chosen from each non-overlapping 2 * 2 block. This gives a 12 * 12 output per pattern. Then we might repeat with a 3 * 3 pattern and another round of 2 * 2 shrinkage.

Q.3. What is Max Pooling?

Ans. Pooling has been used in data mining field to determine and assign replacement values for missing, invalid or inconsistent data that have failed edits. The technique is known as multiple imputation that involves three steps- imputation, analysis and pooling. Imputation is about filling up of missing data and are drawn from the missing data (we get m-complete data sets). Analysis results in m-analyses (analysing each of completed m-data sets). And finally pooling involves integration of these m-complete data sets into a final result. The point estimate from multiple imputations is the average of the estimate from each analysis.

The process of reducing the dimensionality of feature maps by breaking up each feature map into equally sized tiles and sharpening the located features to create a condensed feature map is known as max-pooling. Specifically, we create a cell for each tile, compute the maximum value in the tile and propagate this maximum value into the corresponding cell of the condensed feature map. So, we can say that max pooling significantly reduces parameters as we move up the network. A pooling layer will have 2 parameters:-

a. Its spatial extent (*e*),

b. Its stride (*s*).

Please note that only two major variations of the pooling layer are used as follows:-

a. Non-overlapping pooling layer with $e = 2$ and $s = 2$.

b. Overlapping pooling layer with $e = 3$ and $s = 2$.

Also note that max pooling is locally invariant. This means that even if the inputs shift around a little bit, the output of the max pooling layer stays constant. This has an application in visual algorithms also. Local invariance is a very useful property but we need to think more whether some feature is present or not rather than where it is exactly. But understand that compelling large amount of local invariance can destroy our networks ability to carry vital information. Also note that that is why we keep the spatial extent of our pooling layer smaller.

Another variant of max pooling has been given by Graham and is named as fractional max pooling. He used a pseudorandom number generator to generate tiling with non-integer lengths for pooling. This also prevents over-fitting or over-training.

Q.4. Explain with neat diagrams various Convolutional Network Architectures.

Ans. A typical CNN architecture is shown in figure 5.3.

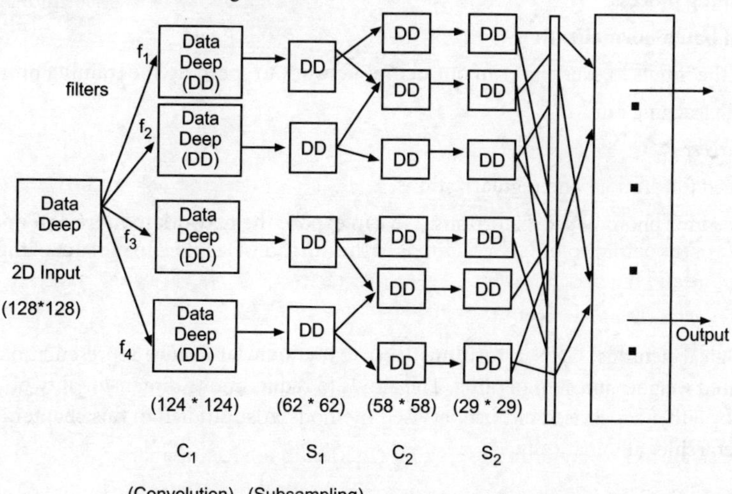

***Fig. 5.3:** A Convolutional Neural Net Architecture*

Explanation: The input is a 2D image. This image convolutes with four different filters, f_1 to f_4. This is followed by non-linear activation, to form the four feature maps in the second layer (C_1). These feature maps are then down-sampled by a factor of 2 to create the feature maps in layer, S_1. The sequence of convolution or non-linear activation or subsampling can be repeated many times. But at C_2 layer, we need 8 different filters (f_{11} to $f18_{18}$). The 1st, 3rd, 4th and 6th feature maps in layer C_2 are defined by one corresponding feature map in layer S1, each convoluting with a different filter. And the 2nd and 5th maps in layer C_2 are formed by two maps in S_1 convoluting with two different filters. The last layer is an output layer to form a fully connected 1D neural network *i.e.* the 2D outputs from the last subsampling later (S_2) will be concatenated into one long input vector with each neuron fully connected with all neurons in the next layer i.e. a hidden layer.

So, we find that the input is first convoluted with a set of filters (*C* layers). These 2D filtered data are called as feature maps. **Please note here that after a non-linear transformation, a subsampling is further performed to reduce the dimensionality (*S* layers).** The sequence of convolution and sampling can be repeated many times that is predetermined by the users. With local receptive fields, upper layer neurons extract some basic and complex visual features. Each convolutional layer consists of multiple feature maps that are constructed by convolving with inputs with different weight factors/ filters. So, the value of each unit in a feature map depends on a local receptive field in the previous layer and the filter. From figure 5.3, we observe that how a *2d* input of size 128 * 128 is reduced to 124 * 124 at C_1 which is further reduced to 62 * 62 at S1. By repeating this process again, we can further reduce the image to 58* 58 at layer C_2 and then to a 29 * 29 image at S_2.

The main factors to be decided are the weights between these layers and that these are trained by standard back-propagation algorithm as discussed earlier. Training deep CNN architectures can be unsupervised too.

Also note that as we build deeper networks, we reduce the number of pooling layers and instead stack multiple convolutional layers in tandem. This is better as pooling operations are inherently destructive only. So, stacking several convolutional layers before each pooling layer gives better representations. Practically speaking, deep convolutional networks may take significant amount of space. **The bottleneck is the memory capacity.** Many deep networks make a compromise by using strides and spatial extents at the 1st convolutional layer that reduces the amount of information that needs to propagate up the network.

Applications: CNN has been used to recognize handwritten digits. The feed-forward network was able to achieve an accuracy of 98.2% we can use Adam optimizer to train our network. The accuracy got further improved to 99.4%

Google scholars in 2015, gave another method of improving the training of feed-forward and CNNs by using a new technique named as batch normalization. During the process of training of weights of the network, the output distribution of the neurons in the bottom layer also starts to shift. This means that the top layer has to learn now both – the appropriate predictions as well as to modify itself to accommodate the shifts in the incoming distribution. This will slow down the training process.

But this process of batch normalization-

a. Will normalize the inputs to every layer in our neural network to speed up the training process.

b. Will increase the learning rate.

c. Acts as a regularizer.

d. Removes the need for dropout and regularizations.

e. Removes the need for photometric distortions. We can expose the network to more real images during the training process.

SUMMARY

As inspired by the biological neurons, CNN algorithms learn a hierarchical feature representation by using methods like local receptive fields, shared weights and subsampling. The aim is to reduce multi-dimensionality of data. We get a filter bank only that can be trained by either supervised or unsupervised methods. Also studied in this chapter is that CNN is capable of learning good feature hierarchies automatically.

MULTIPLE CHOICE QUESTIONS

1. **CNN stands for-**
   (*a*) Complex Neural Networks
   (*b*) Common Neural Nets
   (*c*) Convolutional Neural Networks
   (*d*) None of the above
2. **2D filtered data are called as-**
   (*a*) Feature maps (*b*) Political maps
   (*c*) Social maps (*d*) Google maps
3. **Training deep CNNs can be-**
   (*a*) Unsupervised (*b*) Supervised
   (*c*) Both (*a*) and (*b*) (*d*) None of the above.
4. **Convolution can be performed-**
   (*a*) By threads in parallel
   (*b*) By threads in sequence
   (*c*) By processes only
   (*d*) None of the above
5. **We can reduce the number of parameters by-**
   (*a*) Resource sharing
   (*b*) Weight sharing
   (*c*) Time sharing
   (*d*) None of the above
6. **Learning should follow-**
   (*a*) Early stopping (*b*) Late stopping
   (*c*) Normal stopping (*d*) None of the above
7. **The process of breaking each feature map into equally sized tiles is known as-**
   (*a*) Min pooling (*b*) Max pooling
   (*c*) Data pooling (*d*) Spooling
8. **Inherently pooling operations are-**
   (*a*) Constructive (*b*) Destructive
   (*c*) Objective (*d*) None of the above
9. **In fractional max pooling, we use-**
   (*a*) A clock (*b*) A monitor
   (*c*) A pseudorandom number generator (*d*) None of the above
10. **Before each pooling layer, we stack several-**
    (*a*) Hidden layers (*b*) Convolutional layers
    (*c*) Output layers (*d*) None of the above

ANSWERS

1. (*c*)	**2.** (*a*)	**3.** (*c*)	**4.** (*a*)	**5.** (*b*)
6. (*b*)	**7.** (*b*)	**8.** (*b*)	**9.** (*c*)	**10.** (*b*)

CONCEPTUAL SHORT QUESTIONS WITH ANSWERS

Q.1. Define cross validation.

Ans. It is defined as a re-sampling technique used to estimate a model's performance. It is always preferable if the number of examples in a data set is less than 1000.

Q.2. What is the optimal point of stopping training?

Ans. The optimal point of stopping training and the optimal number of hidden units depends on the process called as cross validation. Cross validation is the process of testing the network's performance on validation data that is not seen during training.

Q.3. What is max pooling?

Ans. The process of reducing the dimensionality of feature maps by breaking up each feature map into equally sized tiles and sharpening the located features to create a condensed feature map is known as max-pooling.

Q.4. Define a stride.

Ans. **Stride (*s*):** The distance between consecutive applications of the filter on the input volume. If we use a stride of 1, we get the full convolution.

Q.5. What are the advantages of batch normalization?

Ans. Batch normalization-

a. Will normalize the inputs to every layer in our neural network to speed up the training process.

b. Will increase the learning rate.

c. Acts as a regularizer.

d. Removes the need for dropout and regularizations.

e. Removes the need for photometric distortions. We can expose the network to more real images during the training process.

EXERCISE QUESTIONS

1. Define convolution.
2. Explain CNN architecture with a neat diagram.
3. What is max pooling in CNNs?
4. Explain any one method of convolution.
5. What is batch normalization? How is it done?
6. Explain the following:-
   a. The convolution layers.
   b. The convolution operation.
7. What is the role of filters and subsampling in CNN architectures?
8. Explain the hyperparameters of filters.
9. What is the role of a pseudorandom number generator?
10. Name some deep learning case tools that help in convolution.

6 Sequence Analysis

Q.1. Define sequence detection method.

Ans. A data mining method that helps us to understand which time-based sequences are usually encountered together in a domain is called as a sequence detection method. These frequent event sequences are very important elements.

Q.2. What is Variable –sized Inputs Analysis?

Ans. Everyday interactions that we make need is deep understanding of sequences of patterns that appears, say, in a newspaper, listening to radio etc. Similarly, to adjust variable-length inputs, we have to be a bit clever when designing deep learning models. Our feed-forward neural networks break when analysing sequences. If the sequence is the same size as the input layer, the model can perform as we expect it to be. It is also possible to deal with smaller inputs by padding zeros at the end of the input until its suitable length. **Also note that when the input size exceeds the size of the input layer, then this feed-forward network no longer works.** A popular method of tracing sequence-to-sequence of parts of speech (POS) is Neural N-Grams. A feed-forward neural network architecture is used to process a body of text. The aim is to convert an input sequence into a corresponding output sequence. We have to take a body of test all at once to predict the full sequence of POS tags. It is better to predict each POS tag one at a time by using a fixed-length subsequence. We use the subsequence starting from the word of interest and extending n-words into the past. This is neural n-gram method. In general, when we predict the POS tag for the ith word in the input, we will utilize the i-n+1st, i-n+2nd, ...,ith words as the input. This is also called as a **context window or sliding window** as here the context window is moved one word at a time, predicting the POS tag of rightmost word till we reach the end of the input. In order to process the entire text, we start at the beginning of the text and then proceed as explained above.

Q.3. Write features of Beam Search.

Ans. It is a variation of best-first search. Here, only n most promising states are kept for future consideration. It is efficient in terms of memory but it is possible to miss the solution due to early pruning of the tree. Please remember the following points regarding beam search-

1. It is like bfs in that it progresses level by level.
2. It moves downward only through the best, W nodes at each level by applying heuristics, the other nodes are ignored.
3. The number of nodes explored remains manageable even if there is a great deal of branching and the search is deep.
4. Whenever beam search is used, there are only W nodes under consideration at any depth rather than the exponentially explosive number of nodes as is done in bfs.
5. The width of the beam is fixed and whatever be the depth of the tree, the number of alternatives to be scanned is the product of the width of the beam and the depth.
6. Basic Principle- "Instead of greedily selecting the most probable prediction a each step, we maintain a beam of most likely hypothesis (up to a fixed beam size, b) for the sequence of first k actions and their associated probabilities".
7. Beam searching has two steps- expansion and pruning.
8. During the expansion step, we take each hypothesis and consider it as a possible input. Then we calculate the probability of each of possible hypothesis for the sequence of the first k+1 actions.
9. During the pruning step, we keep only the b hypothesis out of the total options with the largest probabilities.
10. Attempt has been made to bring closer the concept of beam searching to the process of training the network.
11. Andor et al. explains in his paper that global normalization provides a stronger guarantee and clear performance gains as compared to the local normalization.
12. In a locally normalized network, our network is tasked with selecting the best action given a configuration. The network gives as output a score that is normalized using a softmax layer. This is done to model a probability distribution over all possible actions. The loss function tries to compel the probability distribution to the ideal output.

13. In globally normalized networks, the interpretation of scores is somewhat different. Herein, we add up all of the scores for a hypothesis action sequence rather than putting the scores through a softmax to generate a per-action probability distribution. The problem here is that there is a large number of possible hypothesis sequences.
14. To cope with these problems, we use beam search, with a fixed beam size and reach the end of the sentence or the correct sequence of actions is no longer contained on the beam. Then we derive a loss function that tries to push the best action sequence as high as possible on the beam by maximizing its score relative to another hypothesis.

Q.4. What are Stateful Deep Learning Models?

Ans. Beam search and global normalization was used to get better solution for sequence analysis. But still this was useful for the scenarios where there was a one-to-one mapping between the elements in the input sequence to the elements in the output sequence. But sometimes the task is more complex, not just this.

For example, we may want a system model that can consume the entire text of input sequence at once and then conclude if the sentiment of the entire input was positive or negative.

Example2, we may want to develop a system model or an algorithm that consumes as input a complex image and generate a sentence, one word at a time, to describe that image (input).

Example 3, the task may be to translate the sentences from one language to another language, say from Hindi to English. In all these situations, there is no mapping direct between input tokens and output tokens.

An ideal model, for sequence analysis can store information in memory over longer periods of time, leading to coherent 'thought vector' that it can use to generate an answer. We want our model to maintain some sort of memory while reading the input sequences. As the process of reading continues, the model should be able to modify this memory bank and store the information that it observes. As the end of the input sequence is reached, this internal memory contains a 'thought' that shows the key pieces of information i.e. the meaning of the original input. then we should be able to use this thought vector to either produce a label for the original sequence or an output sequence like translation, summaries etc. But this is in contradiction to the concept studied earlier. Note that the feed-forward networks are inherently stateless. After it has been trained, the feed-forward network is a static structure. It cannot maintain memories between inputs as in sequential circuits. So, we now need the deep learning models that are stateful.

The standard deep neural network is a static classifier with input vectors having a fixed dimensionality. But many patterns recognition and information processing problems like speech recognition, machine translation, NLP, video processing and bio-information processing, need sequence recognition. In sequence recognition, also called as classification with structured I/O, the dimensionality of both inputs and outputs are variable. One method of solving this problem is through HMM. HMM is a tool to model the sequence data with variable length and is based on dynamic programming. Please note that by combining static classifiers and HMM, it is able to handle dynamic or sequential patterns. So, it is better to combine deep neural network and HMM to bridge the gap between the static and sequence pattern recognition. Networks like CNNs, RNNs have been applied to music with an error improvement of between 5% and 30% on a standard benchmark of four different datasets.

So, next we discuss some stateful models.

Q.5. What are Recurrent Neural Networks (RNN)? Explain with a neat diagram.

Ans. The networks in which in addition to feedforward connections, we also have self-connections or connections to the units in the previous layers are known as Recurrent Neural Networks (RNNs). They are also called as feedback networks. This recurrency acts as a short-term memory. So, the network now remembers what happened in the past. If we use a limited number of recurrent connections to a multilayer perceptron then it is called as a partially recurrent network. Thus, now we have combined the advantages of both non-linear approximation ability of the multilayer perceptron with the temporal representation ability of the recurrency. Such a network can be used to implement any of the three temporal association tasks. Please note that it is possible to have hidden units in the recurrent backward connections and these are known as context units. Also note that no formal results are known to determine how to choose the best architecture given a particular application.

The process that is used to convert an arbitrary recurrent network to an equivalent feedforward network is called as **unfolding in time.** It is used when the sequences have small maximum length. A separate unit and connection is created for copies at different times. The resulting network can be trained with backpropagation but with a constraint that all copies of each connection should remain identical.

Solution: As in weight sharing process explained earlier, the solution is to add/sum up the different weight changes in real time and change the weight by the average. Also note that this is known as backpropagation through time.

Problems: The problem with this approach is that of the memory requirement is the length of the sequence is large.

Another variant is real time recurrent learning algorithm to train recurrent networks without unfolding. It has a benefit that it can use sequences of any arbitrary length.

When connections are allowed both ways between a pair of units and also from a unit back to itself then it is called as a recurrent network. These networks do not settle down to a stable state even with a constant input. Symmetric connections $w_{ij} = w_{ji}$ ensures stable state. For example, Boltzman's machine is a symmetric machine.

A fully connected recurrent network is perhaps the simplest of neural network architectures. All units are connected to all other units and every unit is both an input and an output. Typically, a set of patterns is instantiated on all of the units, one at a time. As each pattern is instantiated the weights are modified. When a degraded version of one of the patterns is presented, the network attempts to reconstruct the pattern.

Recurrent networks are also useful in that they allow networks to process sequential information. Processing in recurrent networks depends on the state of the network at the last time step. Consequently, the response to the current input depends on previous inputs. Figure 6.1 shows a simple recurrent network.

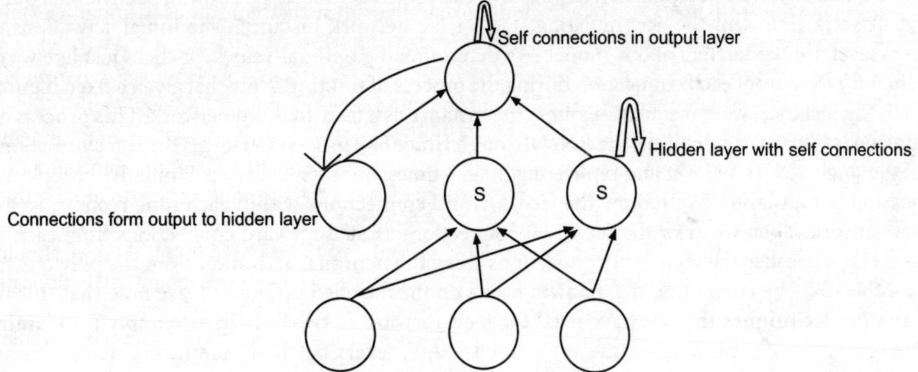

Fig. 6.1: *Simple Recurrent Network*

Figure 6.1 shows three types of recurrent connections:-

a. Self-connections in the hidden layer.

b. Self-connections in the output layer and

c. Connections from the output to the hidden layer.

Note that a combination of all these is also possible.

RNNs were introduced in 1980s. RNNs are different from feed-forward networks because they leverage a special type of neural layer known as recurrent layers that enable the network to maintain state between uses of the network.

Let us now study the neural architecture of a recurrent layer.

A recurrent layer contains recurrent connections *i.e.* the connections between neurons that are located in the same layer. Figure 6.2 shows recurrent layer and its connections.

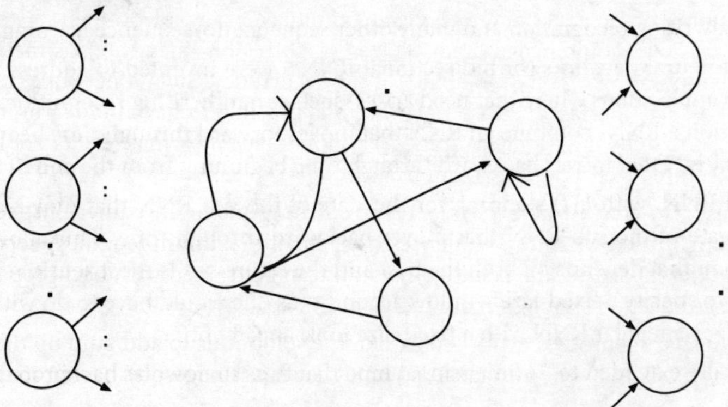

Fig. 6.2: *A Recurrent layer and Recurrent Connections*

From figure 6.2, it is observed that:-

a. All of the neurons have incoming connections emanating from all of the neurons of the previous layer.

b. All of the neurons have outgoing connections leading to all of the neurons to the subsequent layers.

Please note that however these are not the only connections that neurons of a recurrent layer have. Also note that unlike feed-forward layer, recurrent layers also have recurrent connections that propagate information between the neurons of the same layer. A fully connected recurrent layer has information flow from every neurons to every other neuron in its layer, including itself. Thus, we can say that a recurrent layer with r neurons has a total of r^2 recurrent connections.

Working of RNNs: Every time we want to process a new sequence, we create a fresh instance of our model. We can divide the life time of the network instance into discrete steps. At each time step, we feed the model the next element of the input. Feed-forward connections represent information flow from one neuron to another where the data being transferred is the computed neuronal activation from the current time step. However, recurrent connections represent information flow where the data is stored neuronal activation from the previous time step. Thus, the activations of the neurons in a recurrent network represent the accumulating state of the network instance. The initial activations of neurons in the recurrent layer are parameters of our model. We determine the optimal values for them just like we determine the optimal values for weights of each connection during the process of training. Note that given a fixed lifetime (say, *t* time-steps) of an RNN instance, we can actually express the instance as a feed-forward network. **This process of mapping or transformation is known as unrolling the RNN through time.** The process performs the transformation by taking the neurons of the single recurrent layer and replicating them t-times, once for each step. Similarly, we replicate the neurons of the input and output layers. We redraw the feed-forward connections within each time replica just as they were in the original network. Then we draw the recurrent connections as feed-forward connections from each step replica to the next. This is so because the recurrent connections carry the neuronal activation from the previous time step. Also we can train this RNN by computing the gradient based on the unrolled version. **Please note that this means that all backpropagation techniques that we have used for feed-forward networks will also apply for training RNNs.** But there lies an issue now. We use batch of training examples. After every batch of training examples, we must modify the weights based on the error derivatives that we computed.

In the unrolled network, we have sets of connections that all correspond to the same connection in the original RNN. But the error derivatives so calculated for these unrolled connections are not promised to be equal. To solve this issue, we average or sum up the error derivatives over all connections that belong to the same set. This permits us to use error derivative that considers all of the dynamics acting on the weight of a connection as we try to compel the network to construct an accurate output.

Q.6. What are Bidirectional RNNs? Give example to explain.

Ans. All of the recurrent networks we have considered up to now have a "causal" structure. This means that the state at time t only captures information from the past, $x(1), \ldots, x(t-1)$, and the present input $x(t)$. Some of the models we have discussed also allow information from past *y* values to affect the current state when the *y*-values are available. However, in many applications we want to output a prediction of $y(t)$ which may depend on the whole input sequence.

For example, in speech recognition, the correct interpretation of the current sound as a phoneme may depend on the next few phonemes because of co-articulation and potentially may even depend on the next few words because of the linguistic dependencies between nearby words.

This is also true of handwriting recognition and many other sequence-to-sequence learning tasks.

Bidirectional recurrent neural networks (or bidirectional RNNs) were invented to address that need. They have been extremely successful in applications where that need arises, such as handwriting recognition and bioinformatics. As the name suggests, bidirectional RNNs combine an RNN that moves forward through time beginning from the start of the sequence with another RNN that moves backward through time beginning from the end of the sequence.

A typical bidirectional RNN, with $h(t)$ standing for the state of the sub-RNN that moves forward through time and $g(t)$ standing for the state of the sub-RNN that moves backward through time. This allows the output units $o(t)$ to compute a representation that depends on both the past and the future but is most sensitive to the input values around time *t*, without having to specify a fixed-size window around t (as one would have to do with a feedforward network, a convolutional network, or a regular RNN with a fixed-size look-ahead buffer).

This idea can be naturally extended to 2-dimensional input, such as images, by having four RNNs, each one going in one of the four directions: up, down, left, right. At each point (i, j) of a 2-D grid, an output $O(i, j)$ could then compute a representation that would capture mostly local information but could also depend on long-range inputs, if the RNN is able to learn to carry that information.

Compared to a convolutional network, RNNs applied to images are typically more expensive but allow for long-range lateral interactions between features in the same feature map. Indeed, the forward propagation equations for such RNNs may be written in a form that shows they use a convolution that computes the bottom-up input to each layer, prior to the recurrent propagation across the feature map that incorporates the lateral interactions.

Q.7. Explain Deep Recurrent Networks.

Ans. In most of the RNNs the calculations can be decomposed into three blocks of parameters and associated transformations: -

1. from the input to the hidden state,
2. from the previous hidden state to the next hidden state, and
3. from the hidden state to the output.

When the network is unfolded, each of these corresponds to a shallow transformation. By a shallow transformation, we mean a transformation that would be represented by a single layer within a deep MLP. Typically, this is a transformation represented by a learned affine transformation followed by a fixed nonlinearity.

Graves et al. were the first to show a significant benefit of decomposing the state of an RNN into multiple layers. The lower layers in the hierarchy are playing a role in transforming the raw input into a representation that is more appropriate, at the higher levels of the hidden state.

Considerations of representational capacity are to allocate enough capacity in each of these three steps, but doing so by adding depth may hurt learning by making optimization difficult. In general, it is easier to optimize shallower architectures, and adding the extra depth makes the shortest path from a variable in time step t to a variable in time step $t + 1$ become longer.

For example, if an MLP with a single hidden layer is used for the state-to-state transition, we have doubled the length of the shortest path between variables in any two different time steps, compared with the ordinary RNN.

Q.8. What type of networks are named as Augmenting Recurrent Networks?

Ans. The best way to make a machine learning model generalize better is to train it on more data. Of course, in practice, the amount of data we have is limited. One method to solve this problem is to create fake data and add it to the training set.

For some machine learning tasks, it is reasonably straightforward to create new fake data. This approach is easiest for classification. A classifier needs to take a complicated, high dimensional input x and summarize it with a single category identity y.

This means that the main task facing a classifier is to be invariant to a wide variety of transformations. We can generate new (x, y) pairs easily just by transforming the x inputs in our training set. This approach is not as readily applicable to many other tasks.

For example, it is difficult to generate new fake data for a density estimation task unless we have already solved the density estimation problem.

Dataset augmentation has been a particularly effective technique for a specific classification problem: object recognition. Images are high dimensional and include an enormous variety of factors of variation, many of which can be easily simulated.

Operations like translating the training images a few pixels in each direction can often greatly improve generalization, even if the model has already been designed to be partially translation invariant by using the convolution and pooling techniques.

Many other operations such as rotating the image or scaling the image have also proven quite effective. One must be careful not to apply transformations that would change the correct class.

For example, optical character recognition tasks require recognizing the difference between 'b' and 'd' and the difference between '6' and '9', so horizontal flips and 180° rotations are not appropriate ways of augmenting datasets for these tasks.

There are also transformations that we would like our classifiers to be invariant to, but which are not easy to perform. For example, out-of-plane rotation can not be implemented as a simple geometric operation on the input pixels.

Dataset augmentation is effective for speech recognition tasks as well. Injecting noise in the input to a neural network can also be seen as a form of data augmentation. For many classifications and even some regression tasks, the task should still be possible to solve even if small random noise is added to the input. Neural networks prove not to be very robust to noise. One way to improve the robustness of neural networks is simply to train them with random noise applied to their inputs. Input noise injection is part of some unsupervised learning algorithms such as the denoising autoencoder. **Noise injection** also works when the noise is applied to the hidden units, which can be seen as doing dataset augmentation at multiple levels of abstraction.

When comparing machine learning benchmark results, it is important to take the effect of dataset augmentation into account. Often, hand-designed dataset augmentation schemes can dramatically reduce the generalization error of a machine learning technique.

To compare the performance of one machine learning algorithm to another, it is necessary to perform controlled experiments. When comparing machine learning algorithm, A and machine learning algorithm B, it is necessary to make sure that both algorithms were valuated using the same hand-designed dataset augmentation schemes. Suppose that algorithm A performs poorly with no dataset augmentation and algorithm B performs well when combined with numerous synthetic transformations of the input. In such a case it is likely the synthetic transformations caused the improved performance, rather than the use of machine learning algorithm B. Sometimes deciding whether an experiment has been properly controlled requires subjective judgment.

For example, machine learning algorithms that inject noise into the input are performing a form of dataset augmentation. Usually, operations that are generally applicable (such as adding Gaussian noise to the input) are considered part of the machine learning algorithm, while operations that are specific to one application domain (such as randomly cropping an image) are considered to be separate pre-processing steps.

Q.9. Explain Neural Turing Machines.

Ans. We have already studied in the previous section, how RNNs are useful for solving complex problems like machine translation. It is said that RNN architecture is a universal functional representer. This means that RNNs are Turing complete. This implies that given proper wiring and adequate parameters, an RNN can learn to solve any computable problem. This is analogous to the fact that any problem can be solved by an algorithmic method or by a Turing Machine concept.

Graves et al. in 2014, from Google DeepMind coined this term of Neural Turing Machines (NTMs). NTM according to them consists of a controller neural network *i.e.*, an RNN only, with an external memory that is similar to our brain's working memory.

Comparing NTM of figure 6.3 with our modern-day computer, we find that instead of RAM now we have an external memory, read/write heads instead of read/write buses and a controller of RNN instead of CPU. But the point of difference lies now in this point of reference. The controller learns its program in NTMs whereas CPU does not.

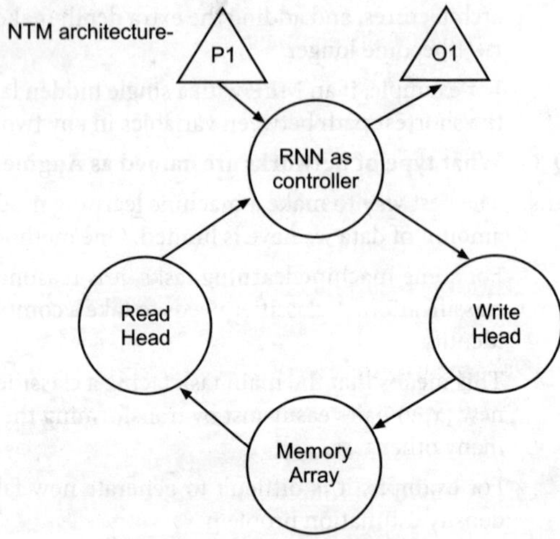

***Fig. 6.3:** NTM Architecture*

It is also possible to prune/ cut the search space as then we can further explore the potentials of RNNs. NTM can be used for doing reading comprehension tasks with gradient-based search (discussed earlier) only.

Limitations of NTMs :

1. NTMs do not ensure that no interference or overlap between written data would occur.
2. NTMs are unable to free and reuse memory locations.
3. Read and write operations may become asynchronous. This is so because they involve new data being written to new memory locations that are contiguous. So, read/write head may jump to wrong locations.

SUMMARY

In this chapter, we have seen how feed-forward networks fail when we do sequence analysis. This happens when the input exceeds the size of the input layer. Also we have seen in details the working and architectures of RNNs and NTMs.

MULTIPLE CHOICE QUESTIONS

1. During sequence processing, we make use of-

(*a*) Context window (*b*) Reference window

(*c*) MS WINDOWS (*d*) None of the above

2. Beam searching has two phases. One of them is expansion. The other phase is-

(*a*) Searching (*b*) Sorting

(*c*) Pruning (*d*) None of the above

3. Feed-forward networks are inherently-

(*a*) Stateful (*b*) Stateless

(*c*) Simple (*d*) None of the above

4. RNN stands for-

(*a*) Recurrent Neural Networks (*b*) Recursive Neural Networks

(*c*) Robust Neural Networks (*d*) None of the above

5. A special type of neural layer seen in RNNs is-

(*a*) Recurrent Layer (*b*) Transport Layer

(*c*) TCP/IP Layer (*d*) None of the above

6. RNNs are-

(*a*) NP complete (*b*) Turing complete

(*c*) Partially complete (*d*) None of the above

7. NTM stands for-

(*a*) Natural Turing Machine (*b*) Neural Turing Machine

(*c*) Natural Testing Machine (*d*) None of the above

8. A recurrent layer with r neurons has a total of –

(*a*) r^2 recurrent connections (*b*) $r/2r$ recurrent connections

(*c*) *r* recurrent connections (*d*) None of the above

9. One way to improve the robustness of neural networks is simply to train them with-

(*a*) Random noise applied to their inputs (*b*) Zero Noise at its inputs

(*c*) Maximum noise at its inputs (*d*) None of the above

10. A universal functional representer is-

(*a*) ATM (*b*) ATN

(*c*) RNN (*d*) None of the above

ANSWERS

1. (*a*)	**2.** (*c*)	**3.** (*b*)	**4.** (*a*)	**5.** (*a*)
6. (*b*)	**7.** (*b*)	**8.** (*a*)	**9.** (*a*)	**10.** (*c*)

CONCEPTUAL SHORT QUESTIONS WITH ANSWERS

Q.1. What is vanishing gradient phenomenon in RNNs?

Ans. It can be proved that a strong upper bound can be imposed on how much a change can be made in the input at time t-k that can impact the hidden state at time, t. As we know that the weights in our model are initialized to small values at the beginning of the training, the value of this derivative approaches zero as k increases. Thus, vanishing gradient problem arises. So, in this phenomenon, the gradient diminishes quickly when it is computed with respect to inputs several time steps into the past which limits our model's ability to learn long-term dependencies. This issue impacts the learning capabilities of RNNs.

Q.2. Which tool can be used to draw RNN models?

Ans. TensorFlow can be used to build RNN models.

Q.3. Write short note on 'Pipelines in Machine Learning'.

Ans. Pipeline used in training and hence in neural machine translation system is quite similar to most of the machine learning pipelines like gather data, prepare data, construct model, train the model, evaluate the model's performance and to train the model to get something fruitful.

Q.4. How will you do 'Engilsh to French' data sequencing?

Ans. If we want to translate to or from different languages, we will have to train a model from scratch with the new data. Then we pre-process our data into a format that can be easily used by our models during training and inference time. We may also do cleaning and tokenizing too at this step. We start with parsing of strings. A process called as tokenization. Our Engilsh or French sentence is now discretized. Then we do optimization. We use a concept called as bucketing here. It is a mechanism used basically in sequence-to-sequence tasks like machine translation that helps model efficiently handle sentences or phrases of different lengths. Finally, we reverse the source sequences.

Q.5. What is a differentiable neural computer? Who gave it?

Ans. Graves et al. in 2016, from DeepMind, introduced a new memory-augmented neural architecture called differentiable neural computer (DNC) that improves on NTMs. DNCs keep other data structures along with memory itself to keep track of the state of the memory.

EXERCISE QUESTIONS

1. Explain the role of context window.
2. Compare feed-forward and RNN networks.
3. Explain with diagrams RNN architecture and its working.
4. Explain the role of pipelining in ML.
5. What are NTMs? Explain their architecture and working.
6. What are the limitations of NTM? How are they overcome?
7. Write short note on DNCs.
8. What do you mean by unfolding in time?
9. What are bidirectional RNNs?
10. What do you mean by augmenting RNNs?

7 Practical Deep Learning

Q.1. Name some practical deep learning tools.

Ans. Several tools for analysis and design of deep neural networks have been developed and implemented by the researchers. Many more tools are in its infancy and yet a lot has to come. A very popular tool is H_2O software for machine learning and data analysis. It is an open source, easy to use, scalable to big data, well documented, on its 3rd version and supports different operating systems and languages. As far as machine learning is concerned, H_2O is not just a car rather a large truck for it!!!

Many industry giants are using H_2O for big data processing. More than 5000 companies are currently using H_2O. Unlike R and Python developers, H_2O is easy to use. It is scalable too. H_2O does not need clusters. It just compiles it to Java. There is no SVM algorithm. H_2O algorithms are still in its infancy stage but are somewhat faster.

Q.2. Write a short note on the TensorFlow Tool.

Ans. A tool or software that is used to build and train deep learning models is named as TensorFlow. It is an open-source software library. It was given by Google in 2015. It is used to design, build and train deep learning models.

Conventions used: TensorFlow is a Python library. The computations are shown by the users in form of a graph of data flows.

Where, Nodes = mathematical operations.

Edges = data that is communicated from one node to another.

Data in Tensor Flow is shown as tensors which are multidimensional arrays.

TensorFlow is used for deep learning, practically. We can think of deep neural networks as tensors and vice versa. If we show our deep neural networks like this gives us the advantage of making use of better speed-ups as available today. It also provides us cleaner and expressive ways of implementing models.

In TensorFlow, there are a number of libraries for developing deep neural networks. For example, Theano, Torch, Caffe, Neon and Keras. But we do not select these because-

a. Theano has an additional step of Graph Compilation that is time consuming when we set certain types of deep learning architectures.

b. TensorFlow has a much cleaner interface as compared to Theano.

c. Many classes of models can be expressed with lesser number of LOC.

d. TensorFlow was built with production in mind whereas Theano was designed by researcher purposes.

When we build a deep learning model in TensorFlow, certain variables are used to represent the parameters of the model.

Properties of TensorFlow variables : The three properties discussed below make TensorFlow useful for building machine learning models:-

1. Variables must be explicity initialized before a graph is used.
2. Gradient methods can be used to modify variables, iteration wise.
3. These variables can be stored on disk for later use too.

When we say that the size of the tensor is 200 * 300 then we mean that the weights connect a layer with 200 neurons to a layer with 300 neurons. Also TensorFlow provides certain operations like abstract transformations that are applied to tensors in the computation graph. Attributes of these operations may be specified at runtime also. Operations are also named just as we name variables in TensorFlow. **Also note that a TensorFlow program will interact with a computation graph using a session.** It is the TensorFlow session that actually builds an initial graph. It can also be used to initialize all variables and to run the computational graph. TensorFlow can be used to train our machine learning model. Actually, building complex models requires reusing and sharing of large data sets of variables that we want to instantiate together in one place.

TensorFlow permits us to use multiple computing devices also in order to build and train our models.

Q.3. How can Deep Learning be done with H_2O tool? Compare it with R language.

Ans. When we use H_2O all of the data is on cluster/ server and not on our client. This is done even when the client and cluster are on the same machine. So, whenever we want to train a model or make prediction, we have to get the data into the H_2O cluster. We need to split the data into training and test data so that overfitting or overtraining is prohibited.

In the nutshell, we are randomly choosing 80% of our data to train and then we will use our model on the remaining 20% to see its performance. The split is decided randomly for each row. The client has pointers that act as handlers to the actual data on the H_2O cluster. Our cluster is on local host. We can add machines to a cluster provided the total memory of the cluster is that much big that it can load and analyse billions of rows from a client. Next, we go in for deep learning. As far as Python is concerned, there are two steps here: -

a. Create an object for your machine learning algorithms and give parameters.

b. Tell it to train and the data sets to use.

When we do not specify any parameters to the constructor, we mean that the model is built with all defaults *i.e.*, with 2 hidden layers, each with 200 neurons and 10 epochs of training. Also note that it is easy to train on default settings.

Comparisons with R : In *R*, the machine learning is a single function call with parameters and training data being given at the same time.

In H_2O, the command was:-

$$m \leftarrow h_2o.deeplearning(x, y, train)$$

Just like data, the model is also stored on the H_2O cluster and '*m*' is a handle/pointer to it.

The command like-

```
h2o.mse (m) gives mean squared error (MSE)
```

Similarly, the command : h_2o.confusionMatrix (*m*) gives a confusion matrix on the training data set that you consider.

Also the command : $p \leftarrow h_2o$.predict(m, test) makes predictions using the model, *m*. Here, '*p*' is a handle to a frame on the H_2O server.

If the cluster is remote (far-off) or Big Data, then we also need to consider how much data is needed locally, how long will it take to download and will it fit on the machine or not.

Performance is different from prediction. In R, we use-

h_2o.performance(m, test) and in Python we could use-

m.model_performance(test).

This will give us a lot of statistics.

The name of the web interface that is part of H_2O is called as a Flow. It is another client written in CoffeScript (*a* javascript like scripting language). We can use this service to-

a. View data.

b. Upload data.

c. View models created by user at client side.

d. Create models easily.

e. View predictions and run them.

We need to import data when using the H_2O tool. You can select your files also. There are buttons to split the data into training sets and test frames or build a model.

Then click on 'train' option and then on 'Build Model'. From the algorithms, choose Deep Learning. A very large list of parameters also appears. You need to select only one as others are taken by default. They are considered to be good enough. Scroll down and click on 'Build Model' option. Now click on the View button.

Also, you can do full load-model-predict cycle in flow. From the model view, click on 'Predict' option. Or you can also choose Score from the main menu and then click on 'Predict' and choose a model. Then choose 'test data frame' and click on Predict button.

Another beauty here is that the Flow commands can be saved as scripts for future use. In R and Python you can do merging of data sets that Flow cannot do.

Flow can be useful if you want to use only *R* or Python. Please note that if you load data from R/Python, you can see it in Flow and if you load data in Flow, you can see it in R/Python. You can start a long running model from Python or R, then go over to Flow and get immediate feedback on how training is being done.

Q.4. How to install H_2O with R and H_2O with Python?

Ans. Start R. Type install.packages ("h_2o"). If you want to install H_2O in a way that it can be used by all of the users on that machine then run R as root and then type the command-

```
install.packages("h2o")
```

Then type-

```
library(h2o)
```

If everything goes Ok then type-

```
h2o.init ( )
```

This will use only a quarter of the system memory.

You can use-

```
h2o.shutdown
```

To shut down, start again to check what it does.

Let us see how to install H_2O with Python.

From the command line, we type-

```
pip install -U h2o
```

Start Python. Type the following

```
import h2o and then
h2o.init()
```

By default, H_2O instance is created that will be allowed to use all of your cores and will use 25% of your system memory. Also, you need to include two libraries-

```
import h2o
```

and

```
h2o.init( )
```

We get a complete script here. It downloads data, prepares it and creates a multi-layer neural net (deep learning).

SUMMARY

In the field of computer science use of CASE TOOLS have always been emphasized. Machine learning with deep learning is not far off. Tools like H_2O, TensorFlow are not far off as far as the design, implementation and analysis of neural networks is concerned. Tools make the job of deep engineer very simple, fast, efficient and effective. We have seen how to install H_2O for R and Python. Also studied in this chapter are the ways to import data, make models and make predictions in either R, Python or Flow.

MULTIPLE CHOICE QUESTIONS

1. A software that is used for machine learning and data analysis is-

(*a*) CO_2 (*b*) H_2O
(*c*) CH_4 (*d*) None of the above

2. H_2O has some code to call-

(*a*) Google Docs (*b*) Google Analytics
(*ac*) Google Drive (*d*) None of the above

3. TensorFlow is a library of-

(*a*) C (*b*) C++
(*c*) Python (*d*) ADA

4. **By splitting the data into training and test data , we avoid-**
   (*a*) Overlapping (*b*) Overfitting
   (*c*) Overlays (*d*) None of the above
5. **The command that gives a confusion matrix on the training data set that you consider is-**
   (*a*) h_2o.concocaveMatrix (m) (*b*) h_2o.commonMatrix (m)
   (*c*) h_2o.confusionMatrix (m) (*d*) None of the above
6. **The command h_2o.mse (m) gives**
   (*a*) Mean Squared Error (*b*) Middle Squared Error
   (*c*) Median Squared Error (*d*) None of the above
7. **The command used to shut down is-**
   (*a*) h_2o.shutdown (*b*) h_2o.close
   (*c*) h_2o.click (*d*) None of the above

ANSWERS

1. (*b*)	2. (*b*)	3. (*c*)	4. (*b*)	5. (*c*)
6. (*a*)	7. (*a*)			

CONCEPTUAL SHORT QUESTIONS WITH ANSWERS

Q.1. What is a confusion matrix?

Ans. A confusion matrix contains information about actual and predicted classifications done by a classification system. Performance of such systems is commonly evaluated using the data in the matrix. It is also called as an error matrix.

In the field of machine learning, it is a specific table layout that allows visualization of the performance of an algorithm, typically a supervised learning. In unsupervised learning it is called as a matching matrix, however. Each column of the matrix represents the instances in a predicted class while each row represents the instances in an actual class or vice versa. The name stems from the fact that it makes it easy to see if the system is confusing two classes.

Q.2. Distinguish between training dataset and testing dataset.

Ans. The training set is a set of examples that are randomly drawn from the dataset for the purposes of training the model. Training data is the data set on which you train the model or you can say the data from which the model has learned the experiences.

The test set is a set of examples drawn from the dataset for the purpose of evaluating the performance of the model. This cannot be used in training process.

EXERCISE QUESTIONS

1. Explain how Tensor tool helps in deep learning?
2. Why is H_2O a good tool for deep learning?
3. Explain some of the commands of TensorFlow and H_2O tool with their syntax and meaning.
4. How to install TensorFlow and H_20 tools?
5. Give some properties of TensorFlow variables.

8 Applications of Deep Learning

Q.1. Throw some light on where deep learning has been applied?

Ans. In today's world, deep learning has many applications. It is the current area of research too. During the past several years, the deep learning techniques have already been impacting a wide range of machine learning and AI. It has been applied in various fields like image processing, sounds, text and animations. Its success has been appreciated everywhere. The rapid increase in the field of deep learning has been appreciated by both academia and industry.

Q.2. What is shallow architecture? Also explain Large Scale Deep Learning.

Ans. In case of shallow architectures, only a few parameters are used to prevent overfitting. Deep learning has many benefits due to hidden layers of neurons large scale deep learning involves large volumes of data and large models. For large scale learning, many approaches have been proposed in the literature. Deng et al proposed a modified deep architecture called as Deep Stacking Network (DSN). It can be used parallel also. DSN has specialized neural networks called as modules with a single hidden layer. Thus, stacked modules with inputs composed of raw data vector and the outputs from the previous module form a DSN. Recently, a new deep architecture called as Tensor Deep Stacking Network (T-DSN) is implemented using CPU clusters for parallel processing. This has also led to Big Data Deep learning. Many deep learning frameworks make the use of GPUs *i.e.* Graphics Processors Units as they increase the power of computing. Gibbs et al. suggest the parallelization of both hidden and visible layers. This they achieve by splitting these hidden and visible layers into n machines. Some of the researchers have also stressed on the reusing of the large chunks of training examples.

The following table 8.1 shows some recent works in the field of large scale deep learning:-

Table-8.1: Recent Trends in Large-scale Deep Learning

Methods	Computing Power	No. of examples and parameters	Average running time
DBN	280 GPU, 1GB memory	1 million images and 100 million parameters	1 day (approx)
CNN	Two GTX 280 GPUs, 3GB memory	1.2 million high resolution images and 60 million parameters	5-6 days (approx.)
DisBelief	1000 CPUs	1.1 billion audio examples and 42 million model parameters	16 hours (approx.)
Sparse Autoencoder	1000 CPUs with 16,000 cores	10 million pixel images and 1 billion parameters	3 days (approx.)
COTS HPC	64 680 GPUs, each with 4GB memory	10 million images and 11 billion parameters	3 days (approx.)

It has been noticed that single CPU is not very practical for deep learning with large model. Deep learning is a big challenge for big data. The five Vs of big data are very significant here- Volume, Velocity, Veracity, Variety and Vulnerability of big data.

Q.3. How deep learning achieves the Computer Vision?

Ans.
1. A deep understanding of human vision is needed to develop better deep learning models for image related problems. To improve the image classification in apps like Google photos, deep learning is required.
2. It is difficult to teach a computer that an image is that of a face. Even traditional machine learning algorithms fail here. Now is needed a trade-off between traditional computer program and a machine learning technique.

3. In this trade-off, a program would choose the features (a lower dimensional representation of the same learning problem) while the machine learning algorithm would then use these new feature vectors to make classification decisions. The machine learning algorithm will then use these new feature vectors to make classification decisions. Also note that this feature extraction process will improve the signal-to-noise ratio as compared to older algorithms of image processing.
4. Jones et al. found that faces had certain patterns of light and dark patches that they could explore further. Like, there is a difference in the light intensity between the nose bridge and the eyes. The combined approach as explained in point no. 3 above, has proved to be very effective. Experimental results show that on a dataset of 130 images and 507 faces, the algorithm achieves a 91.4% detection rate with 50 false positives.
5. The basic goal of applying deep learning to computer vision is to remove the complex and limited process of feature selection.
6. One of the benchmarks in computer vision is ImageNet, that shows the power of deep learning.
7. An improvement on this was suggested in a deep learning architecture known as Convolutional Neural Network (CNN).

Q.4. What role does Speech Recognition plays in deep learning?

Ans. Speech recognition was one of the early applications of neural networks in CNNs or time delay neural neural networks. Both deep learning and representation learning had a strong impact in the field of speech recognition.

For example, MS (2002) has released a new version of their MAVIS-MICROSOFT AUDIO VIDEO INDEXING SERVICE, speech system based on deep learning.

The standard deep neural network is a static classifier with input vectors having a fixed dimensionality. But many pattern-recognition and information processing problems like speech recognition, machine translation, NLP, video processing and bio-information processing, need sequence recognition. In sequence recognition, also called as classification with structured I/O, the dimensionality of both inputs and outputs are variable. One method of solving this problem is through HMM (Hidden Markov Model). HMM is a tool to model the sequence data with variable length and is based on dynamic programming. Please note that by combining static classifiers and HMM, it is able to handle dynamic or sequential patterns. So, it is better to combine deep neural network and HMM to bridge the gap between the static and sequence pattern recognition. Networks like CNNs, RNNs have been applied to music with an error improvement of between 5% and 30% on a standard benchmark of four different datasets.

Q.5. Explain Natural Language Processing (NLP).

Ans. One of the areas of NLP is word embedding. In this application, the concept is that the symbolic data can be represented with distributed representation. It was first developed by Bengio et al. in 2003, in the context of statistical language modelling. And the learning of a distributed representation for each word is called as word embedding. Later in 2008, Collobert and Weston applied deep convolutional network to implement this idea. Deep learning has the transfer learning potential. Deep learning approaches are better in this way. They propose that the learned features from deep learning can be shared by all NLP tasks. They also defined a unified architecture for NLP that learns features related to many well known NLP tasks including part-of-speech the basic idea behind deep learning approach is different from the traditional NLP approach. Not only standard deep neural networks, RNNs have also been applied to NLP. RNN was also applied to parsing. RNN has been applied for sentiment analysis too.

Collobert et al. also proposed general deep NN architecture for NLP. It was trained in an end-to-end fashion. It states that-

1. The input sentence is processed by several layers of feature extraction.
2. The features in deep layers of the network are automatically trained by backpropagation to be relevant to the task.
3. In this structure, the first layer extracts features for each word.
4. The second layer extracts features from the sentence.
5. The following layers are classical NN layers.

Q.6. Give some other Applications of deep learning.

Ans. The study of deep learning is sub-field of machine learning which comes under Artificial Intelligence only. It is the current area of research. With the reinvigoration of neural networks (2000s), deep learning has resulted in modern machine learning. Industry giants like MS, Google, Facebook, Deloitte etc. have formed in-house deep learning teams for the same. Present day research papers in this field of deep learning are very rare, scattered and less supportive for deep learning. There seems to be a symbiotic association between Big Data and Deep Learning. The rise of data is exponential. So, the need is to go in for Big Data Analytics and Web Analytics. We define deep learning as a set of machine learning techniques that learn multiple levels of representations in deep architectures. A deep architecture is capable of learning feature representations from both the labelled data and unlabelled data available. We need to do deep learning from this sea of data. Several applications like speech recognition, collaborative filtering, computer vision, Robotics etc use deep learning. Companies giants like Apple, Google, Facebook, Amazon etc. who collect and analyze Big Data on daily basis, have now jumped to deep learning related projects only. Even IBM has used deep learning to make use of Big Data for their company's advantage.

Due to the big size of data, often called as data lakes, deep learning plays a pivotal role in providing big data predictive analytics solutions. Deep learning means a set of machine learning techniques that learn multiple levels of representations in deep architectures.

Deep learning is defined as the machine learning techniques that use supervised and/or unsupervised methods to automatically learn hierarchical representations in deep architectures for classification.

Deep learning is a subset of artificial intelligence field called as machine learning which is predicted on the basic idea of learning from example.

In machine learning, instead of teaching a computer a massive list of rules to solve the complex problem, we give it a model with which it can evaluate examples. Also, we give it a small set of instructions to modify the model when it makes a mistake. Please note that we have an expectation that as the time passes, a well-suited model would be able to solve the problem more accurately. For example, say our model is defined by a function $f(x, \theta)$. The input x is an example expressed in vector form. Like, if x were a gray-scale image, the vector's components would be pixel intensities at each position. The input θ is a vector of the parameters that our model uses. Also note now that it is our machine learning program that tries to perfect the values of these parameters as it is exposed to more and more examples. The conventional learning methods are shallow-structured learning architectures while deep learning is deep-hierarchical leveled learning architecture. It is based on the biological neurons within human brain. Several research domains like speech recognition, Natural Language Processing (NLP), collaborative filtering and computer vision. Big industry giants like Google, Apple and Facebook who work on sheer size of data lakes today have also given vital importance to Big Data Analytics and Web Data Analytics. Google applies deep learning algorithms to massive chunks of messy data obtained from Internet. IBMs brain-like computer uses techniques like deep learning to make available big data available for its betterment. Also note that as the data keeps increasing at an exponential rate, deep learning is playing a key role in providing in big data and web analytics. And that deep learning refers to a set of machine learning techniques that learn multiple levels of representations in deep architectures. Deep learning is the new name for neural networks. Deep learning algorithms have best performance as far as complex problems like pattern recognition are concerned. Practically speaking, even machine learning approaches find it difficult to solve. Theoretically, they can solve any problem. Several libraries also exist for neural nets or deep learning. But deep learning algorithms as an auto-encoder i.e unsupervised deep learning, several parameters and slower deep learning grids are some of the issues to be discussed in this book. These programs may need more hardware.

Big data is at the core of our society today. The need is to process yottabytes (a billion petabytes) of data. Traditional machine learning algorithms are not sufficient as they were designed for data that could be stored in memory. But today data is "big". So, algorithms that can learn from massive amount of data are required now. Large scale deep learning is still in its infancy.

Q.7. Explain "Deep Learning from High Volumes of Data".

Ans. The data pool available today is a major challenge for deep learning today. The sheer volume of data results in run – time complexity and model complexity. These data lakes often make it impossible to train a deep learning algorithm with a central processor and storage. Hence, distributed machines and parallel machines are preferred. In nutshell, in order to build the future deep learning system scalable to Big Data, we need to develop high performance computing infrastructure-based systems. Also, we need parallel learning algorithms now.

Another problem with these data lakes is that it results in data incompleteness and noisy labels. One of the features of deep learning algorithms is that they have the ability to use unlabelled data during training. So, the presence of large unlabelled data presents many chances for deep learning methods. Advanced deep learning methods are required to handle noisy big data.

Q.8. Explain "Deep Learning from High Variety of Data".

Ans. One advantage of deep learning is its ability of representational learning with either supervised or unsupervised methods or their combinations. Deep learning can integrate data from different sources. Deep learning can utilize heterogeneous sources for better system performance. In nutshell, deep learning seems to be well suited to integrate heterogeneous data with multiple modalities due to its capability of learning abstract representations.

Q.9. Explain "Deep Learning for High Velocity of Data".

Ans. Conventional neural networks have been used for online learning but still the progress is insufficient. Data is non-stationary i.e. it changes over time. Deep learning algorithm for big data is the ability to learn the data as a stream. So, deep online learning is yet to be explored.

SUMMARY

In nutshell, big data presents many challenges to deep learning including large scale, heterogeneity, noisy labels and non-stationary distribution etc. Both big data and deep learning have symbiotic relationships. Deep learning is the current area of Machine Learning research with the aim to move machine learning to Artificial Intelligence. Deep learning means learning multiple levels of representation and abstraction that help to make sense of data like images, sound and text. Several libraries do exist for developing deep models like Theano (a Python library).

Deep learning and Big Data are inter-related. Big data refers to the pools of data being generated every second while deep learning is an active research area in the field of machine learning. But as the data is growing at an exponential rate, deep learning is providing big data predictive analytical solutions. According to the report of National Security Agency (NSA), the Internet itself is processing 1,826 Petabytes of data per day. By 2020, the figure will reach 35 Trillion gigabytes. This leads to a remarkable paradigm shift in computer science literature towards data-driven discovery. Today machine learning techniques and newer software, hardware and computational power help in big data as well as web data analytics.

MULTIPLE CHOICE QUESTIONS

1. GPU stands for-

(*a*) Graphics Processors Units (*b*) Graphical Parallel Unit
(*C*) Global Processor Unit (*d*) None of the above

2. In which architecture, only a few parameters are used to prevent overfitting-

(*a*) Deep architecture (*b*) Shallow architecture
(*C*) Computer architecture (*d*) None of the above

3. MAVIS stands for-

(*a*) MICROSOFT AUDIO VIDEO INDEXING SOFTWARE
(*B*) MICROSOFT AUDIO VIDEO INDEXING SYSTEM
(*c*) MICROSOFT AUDIO VIDEO INDEXING SERVICE.
(*d*) None of the above

4. The learning of a distributed representation for each word is called as-

(*a*) Word embedding (*b*) OLE
(*c*) Machine learning (*d*) None of the above

5. Yottabytes refers to a-

(*a*) Billion petabytes of data
(*b*) Trillion petabytes of data
(*c*) Zetabytes of data
(*d*) None of the above

6. A set of machine learning techniques that learn multiple levels of representations in deep architectures-

(*a*) Shallow learning (*b*) Deep learning
(*c*) Recurrent learning (*d*) None of the above

7. One of the common applications of deep learning is-

(*a*) NLP (*b*) Data processing
(*c*) Language translation (*d*) None of the above

8. Several libraries do exist for developing deep models like

(*a*) Theano (a Python library) (*b*) Piano

(*c*) Diano (*d*) None of the above

9. One of the benchmarks in computer vision is-

(*a*) ImageNet (*b*) DataNet

(*c*) PaperNet (*d*) None of the above

10. Big data has a symbiotic relation with-

(*a*) Machine learning (*b*) Deep learning

(*c*) Training of data (*d*) None of the above

ANSWERS

1. (*a*)	**2.** (*b*)	**3.** (*c*)	**4.** (*a*)	**5.** (*a*)
6. (*b*)	**7.** (*a*)	**8.** (*a*)	**9.** (*a*)	**10.** (*b*)

CONCEPTUAL SHORT QUESTIONS WITH ANSWERS

Q.1. Define what is a stacked auto-encoder?

Ans. An auto-encoder is an artificial neural network that is used for efficient coding. The aim is to learn a compressed representation / encoding for a set of data. It means that it was being used for dimensionality reduction or data compression.

Q.2. What is transfer learning?

Ans. The ability of a learning algorithm to exploit commonalities between different learning tasks in order to share statistical strength and transfer knowledge across different tasks is known as transfer learning.

Q.3. Throw light on some of the recent works in the field of large scale deep learning.

Ans. The following table shows some recent works in the field of large scale deep learning:-

Methods	Computing Power	No. of examples and parameters	Average running time
DBN	280 GPU, 1GB memory	1 million images and 100 million parameters	1 day (approx)
CNN	Two GTX 280 GPUs, 3GB memory	1.2 million high resolution images and 60 million parameters	5-6 days (approx.)
DisBelief	1000 CPUs	1.1 billion audio examples and 42 million model parameters	16 hours (approx.)
Sparse Autoencoder	1000 CPUs with 16,000 cores	10 million pixel images and 1 billion parameters	3 days (appro.)
COTS HPC	64 680 GPUs, each with 4GB memory	10 million images and 11 billion parameters	3 days (appxrox.)

Q.4. Collobert et al. also proposed general deep NN architecture for NLP. It was trained in an end-to-end fashion. What does it state?

Ans. It states that-

1. The input sentence is processed by several layers of feature extraction.
2. The features in deep layers of the network are automatically trained by backpropagation to be relevant to the task.
3. In this structure, the first layer extracts features for each word.
4. The second layer extracts features from the sentence.
5. The following layers are classical NN layers.

Q.5. How are machine learning, AI and deep learning related to each other?

Ans. The study of deep learning is sub-field of machine learning which comes under Artificial Intelligence only. It is the current area of research. With the reinvigoration of neural networks (2000s), deep learning has resulted in modern machine learning. Industry giants like MS, Google, Facebook, Deloitte etc. have formed in-house deep learning teams for the same. Present day research papers in this field of deep learning are very rare, scattered and less supportive for deep learning. There seems to be a symbiotic association between Big Data and Deep Learning. The rise of data is exponential. So, the need is to go in for Big Data Analytics and Web Analytics. We define deep learning as a set of machine learning techniques that learn multiple levels of representations in deep architectures. A deep architecture is capable of learning feature representations from both the labelled data and unlabelled data available. We need to do deep learning from this sea of data. Several applications like speech recognition, collaborative filtering, computer vision, Robotics etc use deep learning. Companies giants like Apple, Google, Facebook, Amazon etc. who collect and analyze Big Data on daily basis, have now jumped to deep learning related projects only. Even IBM has used deep learning to make use of Big Data for their company's advantage.

Due to the big size of data, often called as data lakes, deep learning plays a pivotal role in providing big data predictive analytics solutions. Deep learning means a set of machine learning techniques that learn multiple levels of representations in deep architectures.

Deep learning is defined as the machine learning techniques that use supervised and/or unsupervised methods to automatically learn hierarchical representations in deep architectures for classification.

Deep learning is a subset of artificial intelligence field called as machine learning which is predicted on the basic idea of learning from example.

In machine learning, instead of teaching a computer a massive list of rules to solve the complex problem, we give it a model with which it can evaluate examples. Also we give it a small set of instructions to modify the model when it makes a mistake. Please note that we have an expectation that as the time passes, a well suited model would be able to solve the problem more accurately. For example, say our model is defined by a function f(x, θ). The input x is an example expressed in vector form. Like, if x were a gray-scale image, the vector's components would be pixel intensities at each position. The input θ is a vector of the parameters that our model uses. Also note now that it is our machine learning program that tries to perfect the values of these parameters as it is exposed to more and more examples. The conventional learning methods are shallow-structured learning architectures while deep learning is deep-hierarchical leveled learning architecture. It is based on the biological neurons within human brain. Several research domains like speech recognition, Natural Language Processing (NLP), collaborative filtering and computer vision. Big industry giants like Google, Apple and Facebook who work on sheer size of data lakes today have also given vital importance to Big Data Analytics and Web Data Analytics. Google applies deep learning algorithms to massive chunks of messy data obtained from Internet. IBMs brain-like computer uses techniques like deep learning to make available big data available for its betterment. Also note that as the data keeps increasing at an exponential rate, deep learning is playing a key role in providing in big data and web analytics. And that deep learning refers to a set of machine learning techniques that learn multiple levels of representations in deep architectures. Deep learning is the new name for neural networks. Deep learning algorithms have best performance as far as complex problems like pattern recognition are concerned. Practically speaking, even machine learning approaches find it difficult to solve. Theoretically, they can solve any problem. Several libraries also exist for neural nets or deep learning. But deep learning algorithms as an auto-encoder *i.e* unsupervised deep learning, several parameters and slower deep learning grids are some of the issues to be discussed in this book. These programs may need more hardware.

EXERCISE QUESTIONS

1. Explain DSN.
2. How is deep learning and big data related?
3. List some of the major applications of deep networks.
4. Explain the general deep NN architecture for NLP.
5. Explain the role of HMM.

9 Deep Learning Survey

Q.1. What are the challenges faced in unsupervised learning?

Ans. In the previous chapters, we have shown how to solve supervised learning problems—how to learn to map one vector to another, given enough examples of the mapping.

Not all problems we might want to solve fall into this category. We may wish to generate new examples, or determine how likely some point is, or handle missing values and take advantage of a large set of unlabelled examples or examples from related tasks.

A shortcoming of the current state of the art for industrial applications is that our learning algorithms require large amounts of supervised data to achieve good accuracy. In this part of the book, we discuss some of the speculative approaches to reducing the amount of labelled data necessary for existing models to work well and be applicable across a broader range of tasks. Accomplishing these goals usually requires some form of unsupervised or semi-supervised learning.

Many deep learning algorithms have been designed to tackle unsupervised learning problems, but none have truly solved the problem in the same way that deep learning has largely solved the supervised learning problem for a wide variety of tasks. In this part of the book, we describe the existing approaches to unsupervised learning and some of the popular thought about how we can make progress in this field.

A central cause of the difficulties with unsupervised learning is the high dimensionality of the random variables being modelled. This brings two different types of challenges-- a statistical challenge and a computational challenge. The statistical challenge regards generalization: the number of configurations we may want to distinguish can grow exponentially with the number of dimensions of interest, and this quickly becomes much larger than the number of examples one can possibly have (or use with bounded computational resources). The computational challenge associated with high-dimensional distributions arises because many algorithms for learning or using a trained model (especially those based on estimating an explicit probability function) involve intractable computations that grow exponentially with the number of dimensions.

Q.2. What is Representation Learning?

Ans. As we know that the larger is our input vector, the larger is our model. Also, we have discussed that larger model with large number of parameters are better but also, they are data hungry. Please understand that it implies that without large amount of training data, we will overfit or overtrain the model. Also note that CNNs help us to deal with the 'curse of dimensionality' by reducing the number of parameters in our models.

We have already discussed about Principal Component Analysis (PCA) as a traditional, classical method of dimensionality reduction. In 2006, Hinton et al. gave a paper on "Reducing the dimensionality of data with neural networks". It proposes to handle non-linear complexities of neural models unlike PCA. We define embeddings as low dimensional representations in an unsupervised way. And the process of improving the ability of the autoencoder to generate embeddings that are resistant to noise is known as denoising. The human ability for perception is resistant to noise.

Basic Principles of denoising: "We corrupt some fixed percentage of the pixels in the input image by setting them to zero".

The problem of Interpretability: Interpretability is the property of machine learning that measures how easy it is to inspect and explain its process and/or output. Deep learning models are not easy to interpret because of the non-linearities and large number of parameters that constitutes that model. This may be problematic here. Like if a machine learning model is predicting that a patient has or does not have Thyroid then the doctor will ask for the explanation to confirm the model's conclusion.

The auto : encoder produces a dense representation *i.e.* the representation of the original image is highly compresses. But we have many dimensions to work within the representation. So, the activations of the representation will join information from multiple features that are difficult to separate. The result is that as we add components or remove components, the output representation changes in unusual way.

In dimension reduction process, we have rich set of inputs that contain huge noise. In such a scenario, we want to extract this underlying information while ignoring the variations and noise that are external to this fundamental understanding of data. Sometimes we have input representations that say very little about the content that we are trying to capture. Here, the objective is not to extract information rather to gather information from context to build useful representations.

Q.3. What is Transfer Learning? Give examples to explain.

Ans. The ability of a learning algorithm to exploit commonalities between different learning tasks in order to share statistical strength and transfer knowledge across different tasks is called as transfer learning.

An approach related to supervised pretraining extends the idea to the context of transfer learning, pretrain a deep convolutional net with 8 layers of weights on a set of tasks (a subset of the 1000 ImageNet object categories) and then initialize a same-size network with the first k layers of the first net. Supervised pretraining for transfer learning is popular (Oquab et al., 2014) for use with convolutional networks pretrained on the ImageNet dataset.

Deep Learning Practitioners publish the parameters of these trained networks for this purpose, just like pre-trained word vectors are published for natural language tasks.

In transfer learning, the learner must perform two or more different tasks, but we assume that many of the factors that explain the variations in P1 are relevant to the variations that need to be captured for learning P2. This is typically understood in a supervised learning context, where the input is the same but the target may be of a different nature.

For example, we may learn about one set of visual categories, such as cats and dogs, in the first setting, then learn about a different set of visual categories, such as ants and wasps, in the second setting. If there is significantly more data in the first setting (sampled from P1), then that may help to learn representations that are useful to quickly generalize from only very few examples drawn from P2 . Many visual categories share low-level notions of edges and visual shapes, the effects of geometric changes, changes in lighting, etc.

In general, transfer learning, multi-task learning and domain adaptation can be achieved via representation learning when there exist features that are useful for the different settings or tasks, corresponding to underlying factors that appear in more than one setting.

However, sometimes, what is shared among the different tasks is not the semantics of the input but the semantics of the output.

For example, a speech recognition system needs to produce valid sentences at the output layer, but the earlier layers near the input may need to recognize very different versions of

the same phonemes or sub-phonemic vocalizations depending on which person is speaking. In cases like these, it makes more sense to share the upper layers (near the output) of the neural network, and have a task-specific pre-processing.

Q.4. Explain 'Exponential Gains from Depth'.

Ans. We have studied in previous chapters that multilayer perceptron are universal approximators and that some functions can be represented by exponentially smaller deep networks compared to shallow networks. This decrease in model size leads to improved statistical efficiency. In this section, we describe how similar results apply more generally to other kinds of models with distributed hidden representations.

Also, we saw an example of a generative model that learned about the explanatory factors underlying images of faces, including the person's gender and whether they are wearing glasses. The generative model that accomplished this task was based on a deep neural network. It would not be reasonable to expect a shallow network, such as a linear network, to learn the complicated relationship between these abstract explanatory factors and the pixels in the image. In this and other AI tasks, the factors that can be chosen almost independently in order to generate data are more likely to be very high-level and related in highly nonlinear ways to the input. This demands deep distributed representations, where the higher-level features (seen as functions of the input) or factors (seen as generative causes) are obtained through the composition of many nonlinearities.

It has been proven in many different settings that organizing computation through the composition of many nonlinearities and a hierarchy of reused features can give an exponential boost to statistical efficiency, on top of the exponential boost given by using a distributed representation. Many kinds of networks (e.g., Boolean gates, sum/products) with a single hidden layer can be shown to be universal approximators. A model family that is a universal approximator can approximate a large class of functions (including all continuous functions) up to any non-zero tolerance level, given enough hidden units. However, the required number of hidden units may be very large.

Theoretical results concerning the expressive power of deep architectures state that there are families of functions that can be represented efficiently by an architecture of depth k, but would require an exponential number of hidden units (with respect to the input size) with insufficient depth (depth 2 or depth $k - 1$).

Also, we saw that deterministic feedforward networks are universal approximators of functions. Many structured probabilistic models with a single hidden layer of latent variables, including restricted Boltzmann machines and deep belief networks, are universal approximators of probability distributions.

Q.5. What are the challenges of Unstructured Modelling?

Ans. The goal of deep learning is to scale machine learning to the kinds of challenges needed to solve artificial intelligence. This means being able to understand high dimensional data with rich structure.

For example, we would like AI algorithms to be able to understand natural images, audio waveforms representing speech, and documents containing multiple words and punctuation characters.

Classification algorithms can take an input from such a rich high-dimensional distribution and summarize it with a categorical label—what object is in a photo, what word is spoken in a recording, what topic a document is about. The process of classification discards most of the information in the input and produces a single output (or a probability distribution over values of that single output). The classifier is also often able to ignore many parts of the input. For example, when recognizing an object in a photo, it is usually possible to ignore the background of the photo.

It is possible to ask probabilistic models to do many other tasks. These tasks are often more expensive than classification. Some of them require producing multiple output values. Most require a complete understanding of the entire structure. A natural image is an image that might be captured by a camera in a reasonably ordinary environment, as opposed to a synthetically rendered image, a screenshot of a web page, etc.

Q.6. How to use graphs to explain model structure?

Ans. Structured probabilistic models use graphs (in the graph theory sense of "nodes" or "vertices" connected by edges) to represent interactions between random variables.

Each node represents a random variable. Each edge represents a direct interaction. These direct interactions imply other, indirect interactions, but only the direct interactions need to be explicitly modelled.

There is more than one way to describe the interactions in a probability distribution using a graph. In the following sections we describe some of the most popular and useful approaches. Graphical models can be largely divided into two categories: models based on directed acyclic graphs, and models based on undirected graphs.

I. **Directed Models :** One type of structured probabilistic model is the directed graphical model, otherwise known as the belief network or Bayesian network.

Directed graphical models are called "directed" because their edges are directed, that is, they point from one vertex to another. This direction is represented in the drawing with an arrow. The direction of the arrow indicates which variable's probability distribution is defined in terms of the others. Drawing an arrow from a to b means that we define the probability distribution over b via a conditional distribution, with a as one of the variables on the right side of the conditioning bar. In other words, the distribution over b depends on the value of a.

Suppose we represented time by discretizing time ranging from minute 0 to minute 10 into 6 second chunks. This would make t0 , t1 and t2 each be discrete variables with 100 possible values. If we attempted to represent p(t0, t1, t2) with a table, it would need to store 999,999 values (100 values of t0 × 100 values of t1 × 100 values of t2, minus 1, since the probability of one of the configurations is made redundant by the constraint that the sum of the probabilities be 1). If instead, we only make a table for each of the conditional probability distributions, then the distribution over t0 requires 99 values, the table defining t1 given t0 requires 9900 values, and so does the table defining t2 given t1. This comes to a total of 19,899 values. This means that using the directed graphical model reduced our number of parameters by a factor of more than 50!

In general, to model n discrete variables each having k values, the cost of the single table approach scales like O(kn). Now suppose we build a directed graphical model over these variables. If m is the maximum number of variables appearing (on either side of the conditioning bar) in a single conditional probability distribution, then the cost of the tables for the directed model scales like O (km). As long as we can design a model such that m << n, we get very dramatic savings.

In other words, so long as each variable has few parents in the graph, the distribution can be represented with very few parameters. Some restrictions on the graph structure, such as requiring it to be a tree, can also guarantee that operations like computing marginal or conditional distributions over subsets of variables are efficient.

It is important to realize what kinds of information can and cannot be encoded in the graph. The graph encodes only simplifying assumptions about which variables are conditionally independent from each other. It is also possible to make other kinds of simplifying assumptions.

II. Undirected Models : Directed graphical models give us one language for describing structured probabilistic models. Another popular language is that of undirected models, otherwise known as Markov Random Fields (MRFs) or Markov networks.

As their name implies, undirected models use graphs whose edges are undirected.

Directed models are most naturally applicable to situations where there is a clear reason to draw each arrow in one particular direction. Often these are situations where we understand the causality and the causality only flows in one direction. One such situation is the relay race example. Earlier runners affect the finishing times of later runners; later runners do not affect the finishing times of earlier runners.

Not all situations we might want to model have such a clear direction to their interactions. When the interactions seem to have no intrinsic direction, or to operate in both directions, it may be more appropriate to use an undirected model.

For example, consider a situation, suppose we want to model a distribution over three binary variables: whether or not you are sick, whether or not your co-worker is sick, and whether or not your roommate is sick. Assuming that your co-worker and your roommate do not know each other, it is very unlikely that one of them will give the other a disease such as a cold directly. This event can be seen as so rare that it is acceptable not to model it. However, it is reasonably likely that either of them could give you a cold, and that you could pass it on to the other. We can model the indirect transmission of a cold from your co-worker to your roommate by modelling the transmission of the cold from your co-worker to you and the transmission of the cold from you to your roommate.

In this case, it is just as easy for you to cause your roommate to get sick as it is for your roommate to make you sick, so there is not a clean, unidirectional narrative on which to base the model. This motivates using an undirected model.

As with directed models, if two nodes in an undirected model are connected by an edge, then the random variables corresponding to those nodes interact with each other directly. Unlike directed models, the edge in an undirected model has no arrow, and is not associated with a conditional probability distribution.

Q.7. Define Sampling.

Ans. Sampling is defined as the process of selecting a few representative instances from data in order to reduce the number of records to mine.

Graphical models also facilitate the task of drawing samples from a model.

One advantage of directed graphical models is that a simple and efficient

procedure called ancestral sampling can produce a sample from the joint distribution represented by the model.

The basic idea is to sort the variables x_i in the graph into a topological ordering, so that for all *i* and *j*, *j* is greater than i if xi is a parent of x_j. The variables can then be sampled in this order.

So long as each conditional distribution $p(\, x_i \mid P\ aG(x_i))$ is easy to sample from, then the whole model is easy to sample from. The topological sorting operation guarantees that we can read the conditional distributions and sample from them in order. Without the topological sorting, we might attempt to sample a variable before its parents are available.

For some graphs, more than one topological ordering is possible. Ancestral sampling may be used with any of these topological orderings.

Ancestral sampling is generally very fast (assuming sampling from each conditional is easy) and convenient.

One drawback to ancestral sampling is that it only applies to directed graphical models.

Another drawback is that it does not support every conditional sampling operation. When we wish to sample from a subset of the variables in a directed graphical model, given some other variables, we often require that all the conditioning variables come earlier than the variables to be sampled in the ordered graph.

In this case, we can sample from the local conditional probability distributions specified by the model distribution. Otherwise, the conditional distributions we need to sample from are the posterior distributions given the observed variables.

These posterior distributions are usually not explicitly specified and parametrized in the model. Inferring these posterior distributions can be costly. In models where this is the case, ancestral sampling is no longer efficient.

Ancestral sampling is applicable only to directed models only. We can sample from undirected models by converting them to directed models, but this often requires solving intractable inference problems (to determine the marginal distribution over the root nodes of the new directed graph) or requires introducing so many edges that the resulting directed model becomes intractable.

Sampling from an undirected model without first converting it to a directed model seems to require resolving cyclical dependencies. Every variable interacts with every other variable, so there is no clear beginning point for the sampling process. Unfortunately, drawing samples from an undirected graphical model is an expensive, multi-pass process. This simple approach is known as Gibbs sampling.

Suppose we have a graphical model over an n-dimensional vector of random variables x. We iteratively visit each variable x_i and draw a sample conditioned on all of the other variables, from p $(x_i \mid x{-}i)$. Due to the separation properties of the graphical model, we can equivalently condition on only the neighbors of x_i. Unfortunately, after we have made one pass through the graphical model and sampled all n variables, we still do not have a fair sample from $p(x)$. Instead, we must repeat the process and resample all n variables using the updated values of their neighbours.

Asymptotically, after many repetitions, this process converges to sampling from the correct distribution. It can be difficult to determine when the samples have reached a sufficiently accurate approximation of the desired distribution.

Q.8. Give some advantages of Structured Modelling

Ans. The main advantage of using structured probabilistic models is that they allow us to dramatically reduce the cost of representing probability distributions as well as learning and inference. Sampling is also accelerated in the case of directed models, while the situation can be complicated with undirected models. The main mechanism that allows all of these operations to use less runtime and memory is choosing to not model certain interactions. Graphical models convey information by leaving edges out. Note that anywhere there is not an edge, the model specifies the assumption that we do not need to model a direct interaction.

A less quantifiable benefit of using structured probabilistic models is that they allow us to explicitly separate representation of knowledge from learning of knowledge or inference given existing knowledge. This makes our models easier to develop and debug. We can design, analyse and evaluate learning algorithms and inference algorithms that are applicable to broad classes of graphs. We can design models that capture the relationships we believe are important in our data. Then we can combine these different algorithms and structures and obtain a Cartesian product of different possibilities. It would be much more difficult to design end-to-end algorithms for every possible situation.

Q.9. Explain the Deep Learning Approach to Structured Probabilistic Models.

Ans. Deep learning practitioners generally use the same basic computational tools as other machine learning practitioners who work with structured probabilistic models. However, in the context of deep learning, we usually make different design decisions about how to combine these tools, resulting in overall algorithms and models that have a very different flavour from more traditional graphical models.

Deep learning does not always involve these deep graphical models. In the context of graphical models, we can define the depth of a model in terms of the graphical model graph rather than the computational graph. Consider a latent variable hi as being at depth j if the shortest path from hi to an observed variable is j steps. We usually describe the depth of the model as being the greatest depth of any such hi. This kind of depth is different from the depth induced by the computational graph. Many generative models used for deep learning have no latent (hidden) variables or only one layer of latent (hidden) variables, but use deep computational graphs to define the conditional distributions within a model.

Deep learning essentially always makes use of the idea of distributed representations.

Even shallow models used for deep learning purposes always have a single, large layer of latent variables. Deep learning models typically have more latent variables than observed variables. Complicated nonlinear interactions between variables are accomplished via indirect connections that flow through multiple latent variables.

By contrast, traditional graphical models usually contain mostly variables that are at least occasionally observed, even if many of the variables are missing at random from some training examples. Traditional models mostly use higher-order terms and structure learning to capture complicated nonlinear interactions between variables. Latent variables are usually few in numbers.

The way that latent/hidden variables are designed also differs in deep learning. The deep learning practitioner typically does not intend for the latent variables to take on any specific semantics ahead of time. The training algorithm is free to invent the concepts it needs to model a particular dataset. The latent variables are usually not very easy for a human to interpret after the fact, though visualization techniques may allow some rough characterization of what they represent. When latent variables are used in the context of traditional graphical models, they are often designed with some specific semantics in mind like the topic of a document, the intelligence of a student, the disease causing a patient's symptoms, etc. These models are less able to scale to complex problems and are not reusable as deep models.

Another obvious difference is the kind of connectivity typically used in the deep learning approach. Deep graphical models typically have large groups of units that are all connected to other groups of units, so that the interactions between two groups may be described by a single matrix. Traditional graphical models have very few connections and the choice of connections for each variable may be individually designed. The design of the model structure is tightly linked with the choice of inference algorithm. Traditional approaches to graphical models typically aim to maintain the tractability of exact inference. When this constraint is too limiting, a popular approximate inference algorithm is used and is named as loopy belief propagation. Both of these approaches often work well with very sparsely connected graphs. By comparison, models used in deep learning tend to connect each visible unit vi to very many hidden units hj, so that h can provide a distributed representation of v_i.

Distributed representations have many advantages, but from the point of view of graphical models and computational complexity, distributed representations have the disadvantage of usually yielding graphs that are not sparse enough for the traditional techniques of exact inference and loopy belief propagation to be relevant. So, one of the most striking differences between the larger graphical model's community and the deep graphical models' community is that loopy belief propagation is almost never used for deep learning. Most deep models are instead designed to make Gibb's sampling or variational inference algorithms efficient. Also note that deep learning models contain a very large number of latent variables, making efficient numerical code essential.

Finally, the deep learning approach to graphical modelling is characterized by a marked tolerance of the unknown. Rather than simplifying the model until all quantities we might want can be computed exactly, we increase the power of the model until it is just barely possible to train or use. We often use models whose marginal distributions cannot be computed, and are satisfied simply to draw approximate samples from these models.

We often train models with an intractable objective function that we cannot even approximate in a reasonable amount of time, but we are still able to approximately train the model if we can efficiently obtain an estimate of the gradient of such a function. The deep learning approach is often to figure out what the minimum amount of information we absolutely need is, and then to figure out how to get a reasonable approximation of that information as quickly as possible.

Q.10. Write short notes on Deep Boltzmann Machines.

Ans. The learning is a stochastic learning. A neural net design that is based on this learning is called as Boltzmann learning. In this learning, the neurons constitute a recurrent structure and they work in binary form. This learning is characterized by an energy function, E, the value of which is determined by the particular states occupied by the individual neurons of the machine and is given by-

$$E = -1/2 \ \Sigma_i \Sigma_i \, w_{ij} \ x_j \, x_i \ (i \neq j)$$

Where x_i is the state of neuron *i* and w_{ij} is the weight from neuron *i* to neuron *j*.

The value $i \neq j$ means that none of these neurons in the machine has self-feedback. The operation of the machine is performed by choosing a neuron at random. The neurons of this learning process are divided into 2 types: -

a. Visible.

b. Hidden.

In visible neurons, there is an interface between the network and the environment in which it operates. But in hidden neurons, they operate independent of the environment. The visible neurons might be clamped onto specific states determined by the environment called as clamped condition. On the other hand, there is a free running condition, in which all neurons are allowed to operate freely.

A method of implementing the pre-training is through restricted Boltzmann machines (RBMS). It uses the learned restricted RBMs to try to regenerate the original input data. Please note here that the learned feature activations of one RBM are used as input data for training the next layer RBM in the stack. After pre-training, the RBMs are unrolled to create a deep network. Also note that the stacks of RBMs will create Deep Boltzmann Machines (DBM). Then use the pre-trained DBM to initialize a deep neural network and train with back propagation as the stacked auto-encoder. Boltzmann machine is based on a concept of annealing. The Boltzmann Machine is a stochastic machine comprising of stochastic neurons. A stochastic neuron resides in one of the two possible states in probabilistic manner. Synaptic connections are symmetric. The objective of Boltzmann Machine Learning is to produce a neural network that correctly models input patterns according to the Boltzmann distribution.

The states of the units used in Boltzmann machine are binary values with fixed weights. The weights represent constraints of the problem and the quantity is optimized. It consists of 2D array, a set of units and connection between the pair of units. Units in each row and column are fully interconnected and the weight on each interconnection is $-p$ and there is also a self -connection with weight, b, and the units are v_{ij}. It maximizes the consensus function: -

$$C = \Sigma_i [\Sigma_j w_{ij} x_i x_j]$$

Maximum consensus can be calculated by changing the units state-

$$\Delta c(i) = [1 - 2x_i] [w_{ij} + \Sigma_j w_{ij} x_j]$$

Where x_i is the current state.

And $$(1 - 2x_i) = \begin{cases} +1, \text{ if } x_i \text{ is ON} \\ -1, \text{ if } x_i \text{ is OFF} \end{cases}$$

The probability of the net accepting a change is state for unit x_i is-

$$A(i, t) = 1 / 1 + \exp [-\Delta e(i) / T]$$

To get maximum consensus, the parameter T is to be reduced.

The weights $-p$ are the penalties for violating the condition that almost one unit should be ON in each row and column b is self-connection weight or incentives or bonus to a unit to turn on without making more than one unit ON is a row or column. The net will function properly for $p > b$.

Steps in Boltzmann Machine:-

S1: The weights between vij is given by:-

$$W_{ij} = \begin{cases} -p, \text{ if } i = j \text{ or } j = 1, \text{ not both} \\ \text{b, otherwise} \end{cases}$$

S2: Initialize weights, control parameters and activation of units.

S3: While stopping condition, steps 3 to 9

S4: Choose integers i,j at random between 1 and n.

S5: Compare the change in consenses.

S6: Calculate the probability of acceptance of the changes.

S7: Reduce the control parameter T(new) = 0.95 T (old).

S8: Test for stopping condition based on temperature.

Applications of Boltzmann Learning :

1. It is used to solve the famous TSP (Travelling Salesman Problem).
2. It can be used to recall a stored pattern given the partial input. The partial unit is clamped to a suitable visible unit(*s*) and the network is annealed to reach equilibrium. The output state of the visible units at this stage corresponds to the pattern to be recalled. This is called as pattern completion because we get the desired pattern from a partial pattern.
3. Boltzmann Machine can be used for pattern association. During the training process, both the input and the output are given as a pair to visible units. So, I/O patterns are stored in the network. The input part is presented and clamped to the visible units. The steps of pattern completion are repeated to give the associated output vector.

   In nutshell, BM uses stochastic units. This can reduce the effect of false minima. To reduce error in recall, the weights are updated using the patterns and knowledge of their probabilities. The learning law involves only local computations and uses simulated annealing according to a schedule.

Q.11. What are 'Directed Generative Nets'.

Ans. Directed graphical models make a prominent class of graphical models. While directed graphical models have been very popular within the greater machine learning community, within the smaller deep learning community they have until roughly 2013 been overshadowed by undirected models such as the RBM.

We review some of the standard directed graphical models that have traditionally been associated with the deep learning community.

We have already described deep belief networks, which are a partially directed model. We have also already described sparse coding models, which can be thought of as shallow directed generative models. They are often used as feature learners in the context of deep learning, though they tend to perform poorly at sample generation and density estimation.

Sigmoid Belief Nets : As given by Neal in 1990, Sigmoid belief networks are a simple form of directed graphical model with a specific kind of conditional probability distribution. In general, we can think of a sigmoid belief network as having a vector of binary states s, with each element of the state influenced by its ancestors.

Generative models are used to visualize generative models for representing the process that we believe has created the data.

Differentiable Generator Nets : Many generative models are based on the idea of using a differentiable generator network.

The model transforms samples of latent variables z to samples x or to distributions over samples x using a differentiable function $g(z; \theta(g))$ which is typically represented by a neural network.

This model class includes variational autoencoders, which pair the generator net with an inference net, generative adversarial networks, which pair the generator network with a discriminator network, and techniques that train generator networks in isolation.

Generator networks are essentially just parametrized computational procedures for generating samples, where the architecture provides the family of possible distributions to sample from and the parameters select a distribution from within that family.

Q.12. What are Generative Stochastic Networks?

Ans. In probability theory, a stochastic process or random process is the counter part to a deterministic process. Error in pattern due to false minima can be reduced if initially the desired patterns are stored at the lowest energy minima of a network. This error can be reduced further by using suitable activation dynamics. It is possible to realistic a transition to a higher energy state from a lower energy state by using a stochastic update in each unit instead of the deterministic update of the output function as in Hopfield model.

In stochastic update, the activation value of a unit does not decide the next output state of the unit by directly using the output function, $f(x)$. Instead, the update is expressed in probabilistic terms. Please note that following points: -

1. If the activation value exceeds a threshold, then the probability of firing by the unit is greater than 0.5.
2. If the activation value is less than the threshold, then the probability of firing by the unit is less than 0.5.
3. The probability of firing of an activation value of x is given by:-

$$P(s = 1 \mid x) = 1/1 + e-(x - \theta) \mid T$$

The probability function is inversely proportional to the temperature, T. (see figure 9.1)

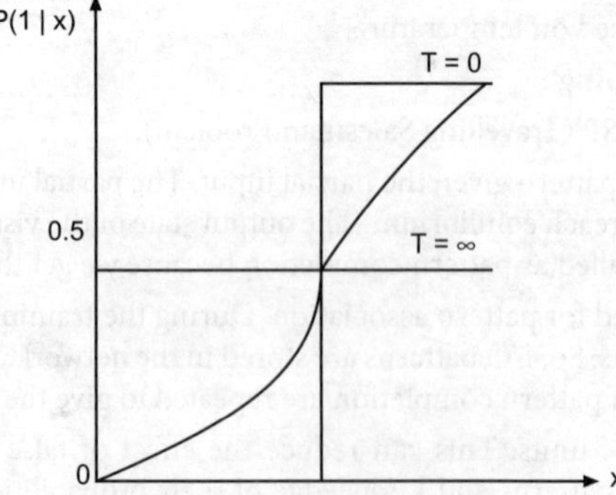

Fig. 9.1: The Probability Function

4. From figure 9.1, it is clear that at $T = 0$, the probability function is sharp. **As the temperature is** increase, the uncertainty in making the update increases and **network goes to a higher energy state.** At $T = \infty$, update of the unit does not depend on the activation value, x. The state of a unit changes randomly from 1 to 0 or vice versa.

5. Equilibrium of Stochastic Networks: A unit, i, is selected at random for updating:-

$$P(s_i = 1 \mid x_i) = 1/\ 1 + \exp(-x_i \mid T)$$

A network with dynamics is called as a stochastic network.

$$S_i = 1/\ 1 + \exp(-x_i \mid T)$$

This expression gives stationary or independent of time. This can be achieved by thermal equilibrium. Thermal averaging will give stability in stochastic networks.

6. The maximum number of stable states for a stochastic network is called as the capacity of the network. The capacity is different for different temperature shaded region and shows the existence of stable states *i.e.* stochastic network exhibits stable states for temperatures below critical temperature.
7. The operation involves monitoring the trajectory of the states of the feedback network and studying the features of the resulting random process in terms of probability distributions of states and the relation of these distributions with energy.

SUMMARY

In this chapter, we have seen how deep learning is the current filed of research. It has increasing ramifications everywhere today. Deep learning researchers have worked a lot on deep learning and are still working on it. Terms like deep learning, machine learning, machine intelligence and big data are all inter-related to deep learning. Deep learning is still in its infancy. Many more needs to be done.

MULTIPLE CHOICE QUESTIONS

1. **Low dimensional representations in an unsupervised way are called as-**

   (*a*) Embeddings (*b*) Data hidings
   (*c*) Dilation (*d*) None of the above

2. **The process of improving the ability of the autoencoder to generate embeddings that are resistant to noise is known as-**

   (*a*) Denoising (*b*) Deactivations
   (*c*) Denormalizations (*d*) None of the above

3. **The property of machine learning that measures how easy it is to inspect and explain its process and/or output is known as-**

   (*a*) Interpretability (*b*) Interoperability
   (*c*) Interdependence (*d*) None of the above

4. **The ability of a learning algorithm to exploit commonalities between different learning tasks in order to share statistical strength and transfer knowledge across different tasks is called as-**

   (*a*) Deep learning (*b*) Machine learning
   (*c*) Transfer learning (*d*) None of the above

5. **Multilayer perceptrons are-**

   (*a*) Universal standards (*b*) Universal approximators
   (*c*) Universal layers (*d*) None of the above

6. **Markov networks are-**

   (*a*) Undirected models (*b*) Directed models
   (*c*) Simple models (*d*) None of the above

7. **A neural net design that is based on this stochastic learning is called as-**

   (*a*) Boltzmann learning (*b*) Markov Learning
   (*c*) Learning by Example (*d*) None of the above

8. Boltzmann learning has been used to solve-

(*a*) TSP (Travelling Salesman Problem) (*b*) Water Jug Problem
(*c*) Barber's Problem (*d*) None of the above

9. A network with dynamics is called as a-

(*a*) Stochastic network (*b*) Parallel network
(*c*) Computer network (*d*) None of the above

10. The maximum number of stable states for a stochastic network is called as the-

(*a*) Coupling of the network (*b*) Capacity of the network
(*c*) Commonality of the network (*d*) None of the above

ANSWERS

1. (*a*)	**2.** (*a*)	**3.** (*a*)	**4.** (*c*)	**5.** (*b*)
6. (*a*)	**7.** (*a*)	**8.** (*a*)	**9.** (*a*)	**10.** (*b*)

CONCEPTUAL SHORT QUESTIONS WITH ANSWERS

Q.1. What is competitive learning rule?

Ans. The basic idea behind this rule is that there are a set of neurons that are similar in all aspects except for some randomly distributed synaptic weights. The output neurons of a neural network compete among themselves to become active. This rule is suitable for unsupervised network training. The winner neuron during competition is called as winner-takes-all neuron. The winner-takes-all or the competitive learning is used for learning statistical properties of inputs.

Q.2. What is out star learning rule?

Ans. Rule: "This rule is used to produce the desired response, t from the layer of n neurons". This type of learning is also called as Grossberg learning.

Q.3. What is Hebb's law?

Ans. Hebb's law states that :"If two neurons are activated simultaneously then the strength of the connection between them should be increased."

Q.4. Name the four stages of the training algorithm of back propagation.

Ans. It involves four stages:-

a. Initialization of weights.
b. Feed forward.
c. Back propagation of errors.
d. Updation of the weights and biases.

Q.5. State delta rule.

Ans. Rule: "The adjustment made to a synaptic weight of a neuron is proportional to the product of the error signal and the input signal of the synapse".

EXERCISE QUESTIONS

1. How is Boltzmann learning rule applied to the travelling salesman problem.
2. What do you mean by representation learning? Explain.
3. What is transfer learning?
4. Explain Deep Boltzmann Machines.
5. Write short notes on 'Equilibrium of Stochastic Networks'.
6. Explain how the stacks of RBMs will create Deep Boltzmann Machines?
7. Explain Deep Generative Models.
8. Explain Generative Stochastic Networks with the help of graphs.
9. What is Gibb's sampling?
10. What are the advantages of structural modelling?

10 Roses are Red, Violets are Blue, Deep Learning can Recognize Objects for you

10.1. INTRODUCTION

AI-as-a-Service is a new field today. Deep Learning is growing increasingly crowded with new frameworks. This bodes well for the end users as we observe the need of mature, capable and interpretable open source deep learning tools for the use cases spanning the technological landscape. Google is trying to show its expertise by developing ML-kit that supports TensorFlow and android market.

CNNs are regulated by the humans within some range. Deep learning is growing increasingly crowded with new frameworks. This bodes well for the end users as we observe the need of mature, capable and interpretable open source deep learning tools for the use cases spanning the technological landscape. Google is trying to show its expertise by developing ML-kit that supports TensorFlow and Android market (Hauert S, Zufferey *J*-C, Floreano *D*. Evolved, Sharma V, Kumar R, Zhang G, Yang K, Liu P, Feng X.). CNN is a neural network that uses identical replicas of the same neuron. This makes it possible for the network to learn the characteristics of a single neuron and then use it in a variety of different places (*T*. Bekmezci l, Sahingoz OK). To create a CNN, computers must be programmed to recognize an object. With CNNs you can use the same algorithms (as in NNs) but adapt them to different types of problems. So, we are now adapting the algorithm to recognize an object rather than doing a numerical calculation, as in NNs.

CNN use many types of identical copies of the same neuron. This makes it possible for the network to learn a neuron one time and then apply it in a number of different situations. This simplifies the overall learning process and lowers the chance of machine error. CNNs are made up of several different convolutional and sub-sampling layers all connected together. These layers are listed below in mathematical form:-

(A) Input Layer is represented by the formula-

$(m * n * r)$ picture where m = height of picture

n = width of picture

r = number of color channels

(B) convolutional or Input layer will have k-filters sized with the formula-

$$(n * n * q)$$

Where $n <$ dimensions of image $q <=$ image size.

Maps can then be sub-sampled with a mean of max. pooling that spreads out over a contiguous region using the formula-

$$(p * p)$$

Which is a value between 2 and 5 depending on size of the input.

(C) Beyond the convolutional layers, there could be any number of connected hidden layers.

(D) Each layer in the arrangement can change a single volume of activation through a differentiable function. All layers of CNN could be stacked to create a highly complex network. AI platform makes it easy for DL developers, data scientists and data engineers to take their DL projects from ideation to production and deployment, quickly and cost-effectively.

AI platform's integrated tool chain helps you build and run your own deep learning applications. AI platform supports Kubeflow, Google's open- source platform which lets you build portable ML pipelines that you can run on-premises or on Google cloud without significant code changes. And you will have access to cutting-edge Google AI techniques like TensorFlow, TPUs and TPX tools as you deploy your AI applications to productions.

Cloud storage or BigQuery may be used to store data. Then we can use the in-built data labelling service to label your training data by applying classification, object detection and entity extraction etc. for images, videos, audio and text. You can also import the labelled data to AutoML and train a model directly.

CNN = Train 1 neuron and apply it (or train) to all other neurons. The hallmark of human intelligence is the capacity to learn. It is no secret that creating the perfect product for the market is what all AI aims at. This can involve anything ranging from finding the target audience to the identification of consumer needs, the value proposition, product testing etc. businesses can harness the transformative capabilities of AI to this end, via audience segmentation, NLP etc.

Factually speaking, barely there is any industry today that has not been affected by AI and data analytics. AI has made a significant impact and garnered great results.

Gartner also predicts that by the year 2012, 70% of the organizations globally will integrate AI in the workplace in order to reap the concomitant benefits. There is no denying the fact that when applied in the most optimum manner, AI, ML, DL, big data can transform the medium-sized businesses to attain consistent business growth. DL algorithms mimic the cognitive capabilities of the human brain.

10.2. OBJECTIVE

Generic object detection/ object category detection/ generic object category detection/ object class detection is defined as follows-

"Given an image, determine whether or not there are instances of objects from the predefined categories and if present, to return the spatial location and extent of each instance."

The research community moves towards deeper scene understanding *i.e.* from image-level object classification to single object localization, to generic object detection and to pixelwise object segmentation. It is anticipated that the future challenges will be at the pixel level.

Data is the fuel for IT industry today. In this datasphere, research on these neuromorphic systems has gained momentum now-a-days. Deep learning is the final solution to everyday complex problems ranging from real-life to real-time applications.

Given an exceptionally rapid rate of progress, this paper attempts to track recent advances and summarize their achievements in order to gain a clearer picture of the current panorama in generic object detection. The objective of this paper is to use CNNs to make object detection more effective and efficient. The purpose of this article is to contribute a timely review and introduction of state-of-art deep learning techniques and their effectiveness and efficiencies for image/ object recognition.

10.3. BACKGROUND

The goal of object classification or object categorization is to assess the presence of objects from a given set of object classes in an image i.e. arranging one or more object class labels to a given image, determining the presence without the need of location.

The additional requirement to locate the instances in an image makes detection a more challenging task than classification.

After the object detection methods, a new technology has come that is known as generic object detection.

Deep learning algorithms mimic the cognitive capabilities of human brain.

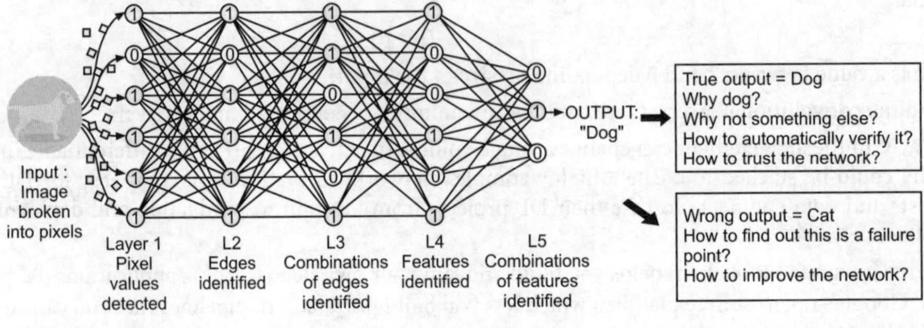

Fig. 10.1: Representation of Layers of Neural Networks

In figure-1, the input given is an animal. But input can be any object, may be plant, animal, human images etc. it is observed from figure-1 that-

- At layer-1, pixel values are detected.
- At layer-2, edges are identified.
- At layer-3, combinations of edges are identified.
- At layer-4, features are identified.
- At layer-5, combinations of features are identified. Also seen is that, layer-1 is in blue-color;

layer-2 is in pink-color; layer-3 is in red-color; layer-4 is in orange-color; layer-5 is in yellow-color.

Layer-5 gives as output i.e. the input-object is a 'dog' or a leaf or its disease, as the case may be. CNN can extract parameters of examined and translated data, rotation invariance, scaling, hence degree of effectiveness is higher for image recognition and analysis of speech. For the extraction of high- level features, we use the convolutional layer. Feature map is the result of outputs from the neuron. Sampling of non-overlapping areas for the equal size is done by the pooling layer. It also considers maximum or average for the output. Data dimensionality is reduced.

Generic object detection/ object category detection/ generic object category detection/ object class detection is defined as follows-

"Given an image, determine whether or not there are instances of objects from predefined categories and if present, to return the spatial location and extent of each instance."

The research community moves towards deeper scene understanding *i.e.* from image-level object classification to single object localization, to generic object detection and to pixelwise object segmentation. It is anticipated that future challenges will be at the pixel level.

The goal of object classification or object categorization is to assess the presence of objects from a given set of object classes in an image *i.e.* assigning one or more object class labels to a given image, determining the presence without the need of location.

In recent past years, deep learning systems have demonstrated remarkable success for a wide range of learning success for a wide range of learning tasks in multiple domains like computer vision, speech recognition and other pattern recognition- based application.

10.3.1 Challenges in Generic Object Detection

In recent past years, deep learning systems have demonstrated a remarkable success for a wide range of learning tasks in multiple domains like computer vision, speech recognition and other pattern recognition- based applications. The challenge is to show how the state-of-the-art deep learning techniques are effective and efficient in image/object recognition tasks.

10.3.2 High Quality and High Efficiency:

The idea is to develop a general-purpose algorithm that achieves two goals-

a. High quality / accuracy.

b. High efficiency.

High quality/ accuracy detection must accurately localize and recognize objects in images or video frames.

High efficiency requires that the entire detection task runs in real-time with acceptable memory and storage demands.

Challenges in detection accuracy stems from: -

a. The vast range of intra-class variations.

b. The huge number of object categories.

Note that these imaging condition variations are caused by environmental conditions that can have an impact on object's appearance like-

- Lightning (dawn, day, dusk, indoors).
- Physical location.
- Weather conditions.

- Cameras.
- Backgrounds.
- Illuminations.
- Occlusion.
- Viewing disturbances.

Also note that these conditions produce significant variations in object appearance like illumination, pose, scale, occlusion, clutter, shading, blur and motion.

Efficiency-related challenges includes the following-

- Due to mobiles, social media network has further increased the demands for analyzing visual data.
- Need to localize and recognize, computational complexity growing with the (possibly large) number of object categories and with the (possibly very large) number of locations and scales within a single image.
- Another challenge is that of scalability. A detector should beable to handle previously unseen objects, unknown situations and high data rates.
- As the number of images and the number of categories continue to grow, it may become impossible to annotate them manually, forcing a reliance on weakly supervised strategies.
- The successes of deep detectors rely heavily on vast training data and large networks with millions or even billions of parameters.
- Availability of GPUs (= CPU s + ALUs) with very high computational capability and large-scale detection datasets play a key role in their success.
- Larger datasets have allowed researchers to target more realistic and complex problems from images with large intra-class variations and inter-class similarities.
- The research community has started moving towards the challenging goal of building general purpose object detection systems whose ability to detect many object categories matches that of humans.
- Despite of the remarkable progress of the past years, designing an accurate, robust, efficient detection and recognition system that approaches human-level performance on 104 – 105 categories is undoubtedly an unresolved problem.

10.3.3 More Challenges

Some more challenges may be added-

- Digitization artifacts.
- Noise corruption.
- Poor resolution.
- Filtering distortions.

In addition to intraclass variations, the large number of object categories, of the order of 104 – 105 , demands greater discrimination power from the detector to distinguish between different interclass variations.

10.3.4 Security

One very challenging part in DCNNs is that they have shown serious vulnerability to attacks.

10.3.5 Datasets

The datasets have played a key role throughout the history of object recognition research. Access to large number of images on the Internet makes it possible to build comprehensive datasets for generic object detection, four datasets are very popular-

- PASCAL VOC (Everingham et. al 2010. 2015)
- ImageNet (Deng et. al 2009)
- OpenImages (Kuznetsova et. al 2018)
- MS COCO (Lin et. al 2014)

These four datasets form the backbone of their respective detection challenges. Data do not give up their secrets easily. They must be tortured to confess.

10.3.6 Detection Algorithm Performance

There are three criteria for evaluating the performance of detection algorithms-

- Detection speed in Frames/sec (FPS),
- Precision,
- Recall.

The most commonly used metric is- "Average Precision (AP)" that is derived from precision and recall. It is computed for each object category separately. To compare the performance over all object categories, the mean AP (m AP) averaged over all object categories is adopted as the final measure of performance.

10.3.7 Object Detection Frameworks

As the number of windows is large and grows quadratically with the number of image pixels, so the need to search over multiple scales and aspect ratios further increases the search space. Hence, the design of efficient and effective detection frameworks to reduce this computational cost is another challenge.

10.3.8 RCNNs Challenges

Girshick et. al (2014,2016) were among the first to explore CNNs for generic object detection and developed RCNN. RCNN provide high object detection quality. But it is expensive in terms of disk space and time because CNN features need to be extracted from each object proposal in each image, posing great challenges for large scale detection, particularly with deep networks. Here, testing is slow as CNN features are extracted per object proposal in each test image, without shared computation. So, a number of improved detection frameworks like SPPNet, Fast RCNN, Faster RCNN etc. have been proposed.

10.3.9 Open World Challenges

Working in an open world is also a challenge. It involves-

a. Being robust to any number of environment changes.

b. Being able to evolve or adapt.

The ultimate goal is to develop object detection capable of accurately and efficiently recognizing and localizing instances in thousands or more object categories in open world scenes.

10.3.10 Object Detection in other Modalities:

- Most detectors are based on still 2D images.
- Object detection in other modalities can be highly relevant in domains like-
    - o Autonomous vehicles.
    - o Unmanned aerial vehicles.
    - o Robotics.

These modalities raise new challenges in effectively using depth, video and point clouds.

10.4. PROPOSED WORK

Deep learning is a hyponym in relation to "machine learning", which in turn is a hyponym in relation to artificial intelligence. Datasets have played a key role throughout the history of object recognition research. Access to large number of images on the Internet makes it possible to build comprehensive datasets. For generic object detection, there are four famous datasets-

- PASCAL VOC (Everingham et al. 2010, 2015)
- ImageNet (Deng et al. 2009)

- OpenImages (Kuznetsova et al 2018)
- MS COCO (Lin et al 2014)

The four datasets given earlier form the backbone of their respective detection challenges. The number of windows is large and grows quadratically with the number of image pixels. The need to search over multiple scales and aspect ratios further increases the search space. So, the design of efficient and effective detection frameworks plays a key role in reducing this computational cost. Commonly used methods include cascading, sharing feature computation and reducing per-window computation. Object proposals/ region proposals/detection proposals are a set of candidate regions or bounding boxes in an image that may potentially contain an object.

Several popular CNN architectures used in Generic Object Detection includes-

☐ AlexNet
☐ ZFNet
☐ VGGNet
☐ GoogleNet
☐ Inception Series
☐ Resnet
☐ DenseNet
☐ SENet

The trend in architecture evolution is for greater depth like-

☐ AlexNet has 8 layers.
☐ VGGNet has 16 layers.
☐ ResNet and DenseNet has more than 100 layers.

Huang et al. (2017) proposed DenseNets. These are built from "dense blocks" connecting each layer to every other layer in a feedforward fashion, leading to compelling advantages such as parameter efficiency, implicit deep supervision and feature reuse. In these nets, individual layers receive additional supervision from other layers through the shorter connections. Pre-trained CNNs without fine-tuning were explored for object classification and detection by Aggarwal at al. (2014). They showed that detection accuracies are different for features extracted from different layers. For example, AlexNet pretrained on ImageNet, FC6, FC7, Pool5 are in descending order of detection accuracy. In other words, fine-tuning a pre- trained network can increase detection performance significantly.

Redmon et al. (2016) proposed YOLO detector of objects. YOLO is You Only Look Once. It directly predicts using a small set of candidate regions. In 2019 Redmon et al. also introduced YOLO9000 that can detect over 9000 objecr categories in real-time by proposing a joint optimization method to train simultaneously on an ImageNet classification dataset and a COCO detection dataset, with WordTree to combine data from multiple sources. But it had some drawbacks like slowness in training, introduction of extra hyperparameters and causing huge imbalance between positive and negative examples.

An object can be located at any position and scale in an image. During the heyday of handcrafted feature descriptors, the most successful methods for object detection used sliding window techniques. However, the number of windows is huge, growing with the number of pixels in an image and the need to search at multiple scales and aspect ratios further increases the search space. It is too expensive to apply complex classifiers. Sliding window- based detection, requires classifying around 104- 105 windows per image. The number of windows grows significantly to 106- 107windows per image when considering multiple scales and aspect ratios. But there are some characteristics that are expected out of detection proposals as follows-

1. High recall, which can be achieved with only a few proposals.
2. Accurate localization such that the proposals match the object bounding boxes as accurately as possible.
3. Low computational cost.

There are many other issues to be considered-

☐ Data Augmentation.
☐ Novel Training Strategies.
☐ Reducing Localization Error.
☐ Class Imbalance Handling.
☐ Combinations of backbone models.
☐ Multiple detection frameworks.

- ☐ Incorporating information from other related tasks.
- ☐ Methods for reducing localization error.
- ☐ Handling huge imbalance between positive and negative samples.
- ☐ Mining of hard negative samples.
- ☐ Improving loss functions.

Trivial data augmentation refers to perturbing an image by transformations that leave the underlying category unchanged like cropping, flipping, rotating, scaling, translating, color perturbations and adding noise. This helps in reducing overfitting and improving generalization. It can be used at training as well as at the test time or both. But it has a limitation that the time required for training increases significantly.

The variations of real-world images is a key challenge in object recognition. The variations include lightning, pose, deformations, background clutter, occlusions, blur, resolution, noise and camera distortions. Large variations of object scale, particularly those of small objects, pose a greater challenge. Some methods used here are as follows-

1. Using image pyramids.
2. Using features from convolutional layers of different resolutions.
3. Using dilated convolutions *i.e.* to maintain high resolution feature maps.
4. Up-scaling *i.e.* high-resolution networks can be developed.

Despite recent advances, the detection accuracy for small objects is still much lower than that of larger ones. Detection proposals significantly reduce search spaces. Future detection proposals will have to improve in repeatedly, recall, localization accuracy and speed.

In this decade of "Big Data", we need a new paradigm- Data Intensive Science, to deal with Exabyte data scale in many modern social, economic and scientific areas. We define sparsifying as the process in which the input image is sparsified, represented in a sparsified form, before the classification task should greatly reduce the leaning problem. This is because sparsity enforces a hidden layer to learn a "code dictionary" that minimizes reconstruction error while restricting the number of code-words required for reconstruction. Note that-

1. When you sparsify your input image, it needs to be reconstructed. For this reconstruction, a "code-dictionary" is also used.
2. If we impose a sparsity constraint on the hidden neurons neglecting weak ones with very small activation, then an autoencoder will discover important structures in data, even if the number of hidden units is large.

Training stacked layers allows a deep network to learn a good representation in a greedy layer-wise fashion instead of trying to train the whole network from a random initialization of weights. Most intriguing results were shown recently by 'MS deep residual networks' with hundreds of layers and millions of parameters.

The process of selecting of optimal hyperparameters for network models involves the following steps-

Step-1: Choose an optimal number of Principal Components (PCs) for the best input data recovering by our autoencoder. We suppose the upper boundary of the number of PCs as 250 to prevent the model from an extra growing complexity.

Step-2 (Test-1): Then, we calculate the dependence of the autoencoder loss function for different number of neurons in the bottle-neck layer. It is shown below in fig. 10.2.

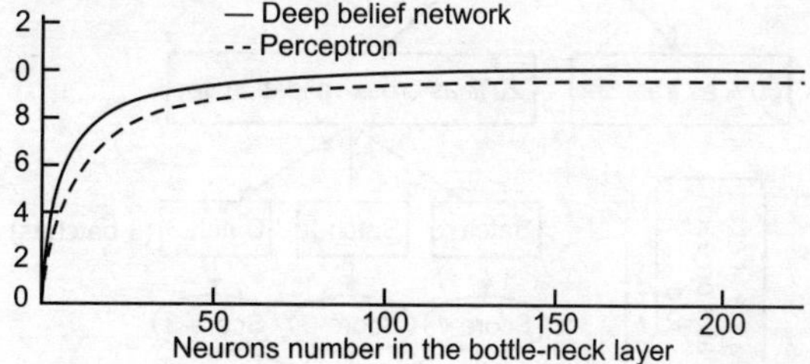

***Fig. 10.2:** Accuracy dependence on no. of neurons*

From the graph of fig-1, kit is observed that-

η DBN > η perceptron
(many layers) (1-layer)

Also it is observed that the acceptable number of the principal components begines from 60 components.

Step-3 (Test-2): Next, we calculate how many epoch numbers are needed to train the network with the different number of PCs. It is shown in fig. 10.3.

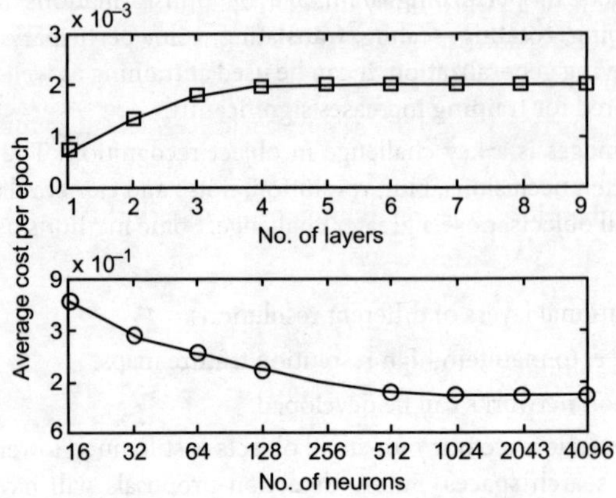

***Fig. 10.3:** Epochs versus No. of Neurons in bottleneck layer*

It is observed (from fig-2) that-

Epoch no. α 1/ (no. of bottlenech neurons)

i.e., epoch number is inversely proportional to the number of bottleneck neurons. This is because of insufficient number of neurons for the input data reconstruction. Note that the curve stabilizes around 512 neurons. From test-1 and test-2, we find that the optimal no. of PCs lies between 50 and 200.

The leraning rate *(s) i.e.*, the time needed to train neural network also depends on the no. of neurons in the bottleneck layer.

G. Ososkov et al. apply a grid search cross-validation method for tuning model parameters. They spli it as shown in fig. 3. Now after fitting the estimator on a parameter grid, we choose parameters to maximize the cross-validation score, for which the network classification efficiency is selected. For the beginning we need to choose the number of the hidden layers in our deep classifiers. The point is that we have to determine an optimal combination of hidden neurons per layer. It is hard to determine which combination of hidden neurons is better. Some of the observations made are as follows:-

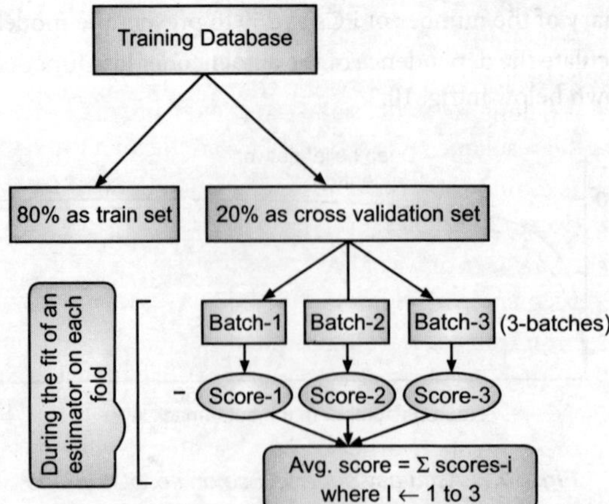

1. Deep learning techniques give 100% classification efficiency on the faces database and 93-98% efficiency on the handwritten digits datasets.
2. Deep Belief Networks can make better predictions in the case of digits, even than the human can.
3. Generally, real image examples are not so clean as they have a lot of noise.
4. A denoising procedure takes noisy data as input abd outputs this data, wheere the noise is removed.
5. A Neural Network has to be trained to clear from the noise by minimizing the sum of square errors between the output image (produced by feed forward noisy image through the network) and the clear image thar noisy image refers to. In fact, such a denoising autoencoder network learns how to clear images from noise.

The main efforts to deal with deep learning networks are spent to-

a. Optimize structures of those networks and their components, as activation functions.

b. Weights.

c. Procedures of minimizing their loss function to improve their performance.

Hence, we have to make a pecial study to find optimal numbers of layers and hidden neurons, to choose most suitable activation functions and weight normalization in order to improve performance of all used neural networks and speed-up their learning time. Also we observe the remarkable feature of deep autoencoders as their ability for denoising images after being trained on an image-set corrupted in a special way.

A Convolutional Neural Network (CNN) is a deep learning algorithm which can take in an input image, assign importance (learnable weights and biases) to various aspects/objects in the image and be able to diffrentiate one from the other.

The objective of convolutional operation os to extract the high-level features such as edges, from the input image. ConvNets is one exmaple of a CNN network. In this net-

- The first ConvLayer is responsible for capturing the 'low level features' such as edges, colors, gradient orientation etc.
- With more addded layers, the architecture adapts to the high- level features as well, giving us a network which has the wholesome understanding of images in the dataset, similar to how we would.
- A fully -connected layer is a cheap way of learning non-linear combinations of the high-level features as represented by the output of the convolutional layer. So, a fully- connetced layer is learning a non-linear functions in that space.
- Now that we have converted our input image into a suitable form for our Multi-level perceptron, we shall flatten the image into a column vector.
- This flattened output is fed to a feed-forward neural network and backpropagation applied to every iteration of training.
- Over a series of epochs, the model is able to distinguish between dominating and certain low-level features in images and classify them using the 'Software Classification' technique.

After decades of exploration and analysis, essential propertiues of various objects (input) have been revealed for a deep understanding of the mechanism for production, propagation and perception (PPP).

Due to the property of parameter sharing in CNNs, the kernels are shared by all pixel areas of the input. Pooiling layers are introduced to reduce over-fitting problems caused by high dimensional inputs.note that the weights and the bias are shared by the neurons belonging to the same layer. The 'softmax operator' is commonly used output layer for classification tasks, of which the resultant vectors present a classification probability distribution summing to 1.

For training a CNN, the goal is to minimize the objective function defined for the task. With an suitable optimizer, the best fitting set of parameters (weights and bias terms) can be solved.

Yann Le Cun quotes that- "If intelligence was a cake, unsupervised learning would be the cake, supervised learning would be the icing and reinforcement learning would be the carry."

Current resaecrh also focusses on transfer learning. A good way to explain transfer learning is to look at the student-teacher relationship. A teacher offers a course after gathering detail knowledge regarding the subject. The informaion will be conveyed through a series of lectures over time. This can be considered that the teacher (expert) is transferring information (knowledge) to the students (learner). Deep learning is anlogous to this scenario. In deep learning too, a network is trained with a big amount of data and during the training, the model learns the weights and bias. These weights can be transferred to other networks for testing or retraining a similar new model. The network can start with pre-trained weights instead of training from scratch, *i.e.*

Teacher (expert) ←→ Deep learning

Information (knowledge) ←-→ big data

Studenst (learner) ←-> model (learner)

A pretrained model is a model which is already trained on the same domains as the intended domain. For example, for an image recognition task an Inception model already trained on ImageNet can be downloaded. Then the inception model can be used for a different recognition task and instead of training it from scratch the weights can be left as is with some laerned features. This method of training is useful when there is lack of sample data. Several pre-trained models are available like VGG, ResNet ans InceptionNet on different datasets, in the model zoo.

Why to use pre-trained models?

1. It requires a lot of expensive computation power to train big models on big datasets.
2. It can take upto multiple weeks to train big models.

Training new models with pre-trained weights can speed up convergence as well as help the network generalization.

How to use pre-trained models?

We need to consider the following criterions with respective application domains and size of the dataset when using the pre-trained weights as shown in table- .

Table-1: Criterion to consider for transfer learning

	New small dataset	New dataset but large
Pre-trained model on similar but new dataset.	Freeze weights and train linear classifier from top-level features.	Fine-tune all the layers (pre-train) for faster convergence and better generalization.
Pre-trained model on different but new dataset.	Freeze weights and train linear classifier from top-level features.	Fine-tune all the layers (pre-train) for faster convergence speed.

Working with inferences : Researchers working specifically on inference applications look into optimization approaches that includes model compression. Model compression is important in the realm of mobile devices or special purpose hardware because it makes models more energy efficient as well as faster.

Myths about Deep Learning :

Myth: You need a million of labelled samples for training a deep learning model.

Answer: The answer is "yes" but in most cases'; the transfer learning approach is used to train deep learning approaches without having large amounts of label data.

Some of the important points to remember regarding deep learning are as follows: -

1. It is possible to learn useful representations from both labeled data as well as unlabeled data.
2. Transfer learning can help learned representation from the related task.
3. We can take a trained network for a different domain which can be adapted for any other domain for the target task.
4. Recently researchers have been training and testing with deeper abd wider networks to achieve even better classification accuracy to achieve human or beyond human-level recognition accuracy in some cases.
5. while the size of the neural networks is increasing, it becomes more powerful and provides better classification accuracy. However, the storage consumption, memory bandwidth and computational costs are increasing exponentially.
6. On the other hand, these types of massive scale implementation with large number of network parameters is NOTY suitable for low power implementation, unmanned aerial vehicle (UAV), different medical devices, low mwmory system such as mobile devices, FPGA etc.
7. Much research is going on to develop better network structures or networks with lower consumption cost, less number of parameters for low power and low memory system without lowering classification accuracy.

There are two ways of designing efficient deep network architectures-

1st approach: is to optimize the internal operational cost with an efficient network structure.

2nd approach: a network with low precision operations or a hardware efficient network.

The internal operations and parameters of a network structure can be reduced by using low dimensional convolutional filters for convolution layers.

Benefits of this approach-

1. The convolutional with rectification operations makes the decision more discriminative.
2. The main benefit of this approach is to reduce the number of computation parameters drastically.

For *e.g.*1 if one layer has (5 * 5) dimensional filters which can be replaced with two (3*3) dimensional filters (without pooling layer in between them) for better feature learning.

e.g. 2 three (3 * 3) dimensional filters can be used as a replacement of (7 * 7) dimensional filters.

Note that the benefits of using lower dimensional filter is that assuming both the present convolutional layer has C channels,

For 3 layers for (3 * 3) filter, the total number of parameters are weights = 3 * (3 * 3 * C * C) = 27C2 weights.

Whereas in case of (7 * 7) filters, the total number of parameters are = (7 * 7 * C * C) = 49C2 , which is almost double compared to the three (3 * 3) filter parameters.

Strategies to optimize the network architecture to design efficient deep learning models:-

Strategy-1: Replace (3 * 3) filters with (1 * 1) filters.

Reason: Main reason to use lower dimensional filter to reduce the overall number of parameters. By replacing (3 * 3) filters with (1 * 1) can be reduced, (9 * number of parameters) i.e. 9 times number of parameters.

Strategy-2: Decrease the number of input channels to (3 * 3) filters.

For a layer, the size of the output feature maps are calculated which is related to the network parameters using-

$$(N - F) / S + 1$$

Where N = input map's size F = Filter size

S = strides

Also note that to reduce the number of parameters, it is not only enough to reduce the size of filters but also it requires to control the number of input channels or feature dimension.

Strategy-3: Down-sample late in the network so that convolutional layers have activation maps.

The outputs of present convolutional layers can be at least (1 * 1) of often larger than (1 * 1). The output width and height can be controlled by some criterions:-

a. The size of the input sample (*e.g.* 256 * 256)

b. Choosing the post down sample layer.

- ☐ Pooling layers such as average or max pooling layers are also used.
- ☐ There is an alternative sub-sampling layer with conmvolutional (3 *3) filters and stride =2.
- ☐ If mots of earlier layers have larger stride, then most of layers
- ☐ On the other hand, if most of the layers have a stride of 1 and the stride larger than one applied in the end of the network, then many layers of'network will have large activation maps.
- ☐ Larger activation maps (due to delayed down sampling) can lead to higher classification accuracy.
- ☐ Recent literature states that deep learning based representation learning involves a hierarchy of features or concepts, where the high-level concepts can be defined from the low-level ones and vice versa.
- ☐ CNN architecture consists of a combination of 3-types of layers-

Convolution → max pooling → classification.

- ☐ There are two types of layers in CNNs—convolutional and max pooling layers. Note that the even numbered layers are for convolutions and odd nubered layers are for max-pooilng operations.
- ☐ The output nodes of the convolutional and max-pooling layers are grouped into a 2D plane called as feature mapping.
- ☐ Each node of the convolutional layer extracts the features from the input images by convolution operations on the input nodes.
- ☐ Higher-level features are derived from features propagated from lower-level layers.
- ☐ As the features propagate to the highest layer or level, the dimensions of features are reduced depending on the size of kernel for the convolutional and max-pooling operations respectively.
- ☐ However, the number of feature maps usually increased for representing bettwer features of the input images for ensuring classification accuracy.

- ☐ The output of the last layer of the CNN are used as the input to a fully connected network which is called as classification layer.
- ☐ Feed-forward neural networks have been used as the classification layer as they have better performance.
- ☐ In the classification layer, the desired number of features are selected as inputs with respect to the dimension of the weight matrix of the final neural network.
- ☐ However, the fully connected layers are expensive in terms of network or learning parameters.
- ☐ Now-a-days there are several new techniques including average pooling and global average pooling that are used as an alternative of fully -connected networks.
- ☐ The score of the respective class is calculated in the top classification layer using a soft-max layer.
- ☐ The number of computational parameters is an important metric to measure the com[lexity of a deep learning model.

- The sixe of the output feature maps can be calculated by the formula-

$$M = (N - F) / S + 1$$

Where N = dimensions of the input feature maps,

F = dimensions of the filters or the receptive field,

M = dimensions of output feature maps,

S = stride length.

- A convolutional operation to ensure that the input and output feature map have the same dimensions is called as padding. The amount of padding depends on the size of the kernel.
- The number of rows and columns for padding can be found by the formula-

$$P = (F - 1) / 2$$

Where P = amount of oadding,

F = dimensions of the kernels.

- The number of parameters, Parml , of the l-th layer is given by the formula-

$$Parm_l = (F * F * FM_{l-1}) * FM_l$$

If bias is also added with the weights then the above equation can be modified as follows-

$$Parm_l = (F * (F + 1) * FM_{l-1}) * FM_l$$

Where,

The total number of parameters of l-th layer can be represented with P_l ,

Total number of output feature maps = FM_l

Total number of input feature maps/ channels = FM_{l-1}

For example, Assume that the l-th layer has-

FM_{l-1} = 32 input feature maps FM_l= 64 output feature maps Filter size, F = 5

Therefore, total number of parameters with bias for this layer is-

$$Param_l = (5 * 5 * 33) * 64 = 528{,}000$$

- The amount of memory (Meml) needs for the operations of the l-th layer can be given by the formuls-

$$Mem_l = (N_l * N_l * FM_l)$$

- Popular CNN architecture are as follows-
  - ☐ LeNet (1998)
  - ☐ AlexNet (2012)
  - ☐ ZFNET / Clarifai (2013)
  - ☐ Nin
  - ☐ VGGNET (2014)
  - ☐ DenseNet
  - ☐ FractalNet(2016)
- Let us now discuss about CapsuleNet.

- CNNs have a limitation that it does not take into account special relationships, perspective, size and orientation, of features.
- For example, A CNN which also contains the likelihood with properties of features (like size, perspective, orientation of image etc. can detect face efficiently with distinct information. This special types of neurons are called as capsules. The capsule network consists of several layers of capsule nodes.the first version of capsule network (CapsNet) consisted of 3-layers of capsule nodes in an encoding unit.
- For example, this architecture for MNIST (28 * 28) images, the 256, (9 * 9) kernels are applied with a stride = 1. So, the output is-

$$M = (N - F) / S + 1$$
$$= (28 - 9)/1 + 1$$
$$= 20 \text{ with 256 feature maps.}$$

Then, the outputs aare fed to the primary capsule layer which is a modofied convolution layer that generates an 8D vector instead of a scalar.

In 1st convolutional layer, (9 * 9) kernels are applied with a stride of 2, the output dimension is-

$$= ((20 - 9) / 2 + 1 = 6$$

The primary capsules are used, (8 * 32) kernels which generates= (32 * 8 * 6 * 6) *i.e.* 32 groups for 8 neurons with (6 * 6) size.

- As the capsule contains the weighted sum of features from the previous layer, so this approach is capable of detecting overlapped features which is important for segmentation and detection tasks.
- In traditional CNN, we use a 'single cost' function to evaluate the overall error which propagates backward during training. On the other hand, in capsule network, if the weight between two neurons is zero then the activation of a neuron is not propagated from that neuron. The signal is routed with respect to the feature parameters rather than a one size fits all cost function in iterative dynamic routing agreement.
- This new CNN architecture provides the state-of-the-art accuracy for handwritten digits recognition on MNIST dataset.
- Reinforcement learning (RL) is a technique for what to do and how-to match a situation.
- RL is defined not by characterizing learning methods but by characterizing a learning problem.
- According to the learning strategy, RL technique is learned through observation. For observing the environment, the promising DL techniques include CNN, RNN, LSTM, and GRU, are used depending upon the observation space.
- As DL techniques encode data efficiently, so the following step of action is performed more accurately.
- According to the action, the agent receives an appropriate reward respectively.
- As a result, the entire RL approach becomes more efficient to learn and interact in the environment with better performance.

Q-Learning :

- There are some basic methods that are considered to know for working with Deep Reinforcement Learning (DRL).
- RL learning approach has a function that calculates the Quality of State-action combinations which is called as Q-Learning (Q-function) *i.e.*

$$Q : S * A \dashrightarrow R$$

The *Q*-function which is learned from the observation states, *S*, action of states, *A* abd reward, *R*. this is an iterative approach to update the values.

- Q-learning is defined as a model-free reinforcement learning approach which is used to find an optimal action-selection policy for any given (finite) Markov Decision Process (MDP). MDP is a mathematical framework for modeling decision using state, action and rewards.
- Q-learning only needs to know about the states available and what are the possible actions in each state.

Machine Learning v/s Deep Learning : Machine learning involves a 2-step process—training and inference.

PHASE-1: During training, a ML algorithm processes dataset and chooses the function that best matches the patterns in the data.

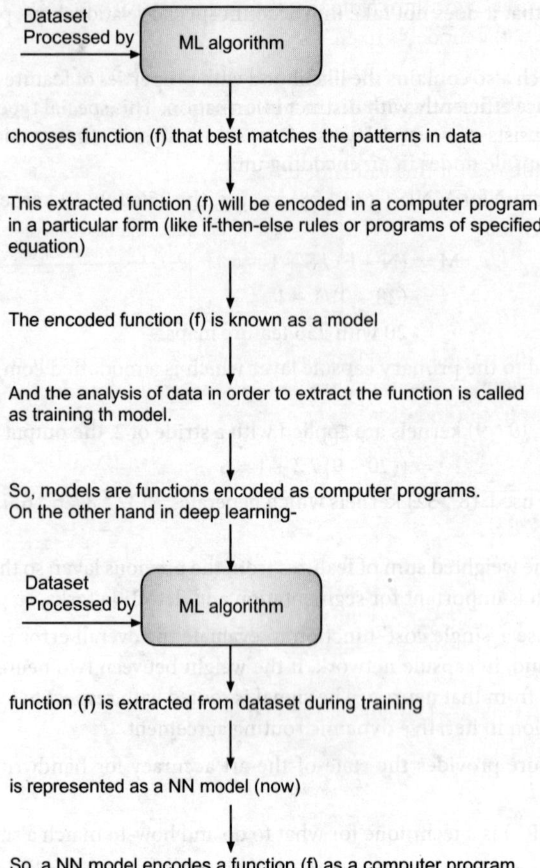

a. The standard process used to train a NN is to begin training with a NN where the parameters of the network are randomly initialized.

b. This randomly initialized network will be very inaccurate in terms of its ability to match the relationship between the various input values and target outputs for the examples in the dataset.

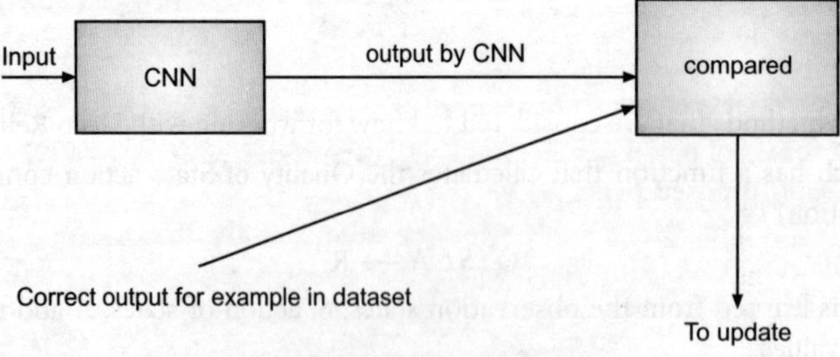

c. The training process then proceeds by iterating through the examples in the dataset. For each example, presenting the input values to the network and then using the difference between the output returned by the network and the correct output for the example listed in the dataset to update the network's parameters so that it matches the data more closely.

network parameters, so that it matches the data more closely.

Once the ML algorithm has found a function (f) that is sufficiently accurate (in terms of the outputs it generates matching the correct outputs listed in the dataset) for the problem we are trying to solve, the training process is completed and the final model is returned by the algorithm. Note that this is tha point at which the learning in machine learning stops. Once the training has finished, the model is fixed.

Training ------gives → model

PHASE-II: During inference, the model is applied to new examples in dataset *i.e.* examples for which we do not known the correct output value. That is,

New examplesto generate estimates for this value for us.

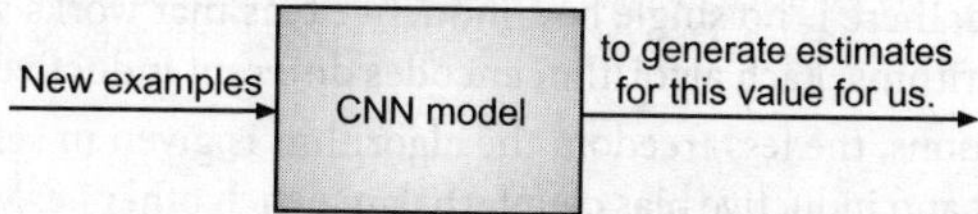

Most of the work in ML is focussed on how to train accurate models i.e. extracting an accurate finction from data.note that the skills and methods required to deploy a trained ML model into production, in order to do inference on new examples at scale, are different from those that a typical data scientist will possess.

Why is extracting a function from data useful?

The reason is that once a function has been extracted from a dataset, it can be applied to unseen data. And the values returned by the function in response to these new inputs can provide insight into the correct decisions for these new problems (*i.e.* it can be used for inference). In nutshell,

From dataset --→function extracted (*f*) ---applied to → unseen data --→ values are returned by *f* ---by inference → correct decisions made.

Recall that a function is simply a deterministic mapping from inputs to outputs. Some variety also exists within the set of functions-

- Spam filtering is a function that takes an email as input and returns a value that classifies the email as spam or NOT.
- Face recognition is a function that takes an image as input and returns a labeling of pixels in the image that demarcataes the face in the image.
- Gene prediction is a function that takes a genomic DNA sequence as input abd returns the regions of the DNA that encode a gene.
- Speech recognition is a function that takes an audio speech signal as input and returns a textual transcription of the speech.
- Machine translation is a function that takes a sentence in one language as inputr and returns the translation of that sentence in another language.

It is because the solutions to so many problems across so many domains can be framed as functions that machine learning has become so important in recent years.

Why is ML difficult?

1. Most datasets will include noise in the data. So, searching for a function that matches the data exactly is not necessarily the best strategy to follow, as it is equivalent to learning the noise.
2. It is often the case that the set of possible functions is larger than the set of examples in the dataset. **Please note that this means that ML is an ill-posed problem *i.e.* the information given** in the problem is not sufficient to find a single best solution; instead multiple possible solutions will match the data. One possible strategy to solve an ill-posed problem is to collect more data (more examples) in the hope that the new examples will help us to discriminate between the correct underlying function and the remaining alternatives.
3. This strategy is not feasible because the extra data is not available or is too expensive to collect. Instead, ML algorithms overcome the ill-posed nature of the ML task by supplementing the information provided by the data with a set of assumptions about the characteristics of the best functions and use these assumptions to influence the process used by the algorithm that selects the best function (or model). These assumptions are known as the inductive bias of the algorithm because in logic a process that infers a general rule from a set of specific examples is known as inductive reasoning.

For example, if all swans that you have seen in your life are white, you might induce from these examples, a general rule that 'All swans are white'. This concept of inductive reasoning relates to ML because a ML algorithm induces (or extracts) a general rule (a function) from a set of specific examples (the datasets).

Therefore, ML algorithms uses two sources of information to select the best function-

a. One is the dataset.

b. Other is the inductive bias. It is the assumptions that bias the algorithm to prefer some functions over others, irrespective of the patterns in the dataset. The inductive bias of a ML algorithm can be understood as providing the algorithm with a perspective on a dataset.

However, in this real world, there is no single best inductive bias that works well for all datasets. That is why, there are so many different ML algorithms. Each algorithm encodes different inductive bias. Rule is-

"The stronger the assumptions, the less freedom the algorithm is given in selecting a function that fits the patterns in the dataset." Hence, dataset and inductive bias counterbalance each other i.e. ML algorithms that have a strong inductive bias pay less attention to the dataset when selecting a function.

For *e.g.* if a ML algorithm is coded to prefer a very simple function. No matter how complex the patterns in the data, then it has a very strong inductive bias.

Like, $y = mx + c$ is the equation of a straight line. Now, we can use the equation of a line as a template structure to define a function. This equation of the line is a very simple type of mathematical function.

Therefore, ML algorithms that use the equation of a line as the template structure for the functions they fit to a dataset make the assumption that the model they generate should encode a simple linear mapping from input to output.

This assumption is an example of an inductive bias. It is, in fact, an example of a strong inductive bias, as no matter how complex (or non-linear) the patterns in the data are the algorithm will be restricted (or biased) to fit a linear model to it.

Two problems arise if we choose a ML algorithm with a wrong bias-

I. If the inductive bias of a ML algorithm is too strong: In this case, the algorithm will ignore important information in the data and the returned function will not capture the nuances of the true patterns in the data. In other words, the returned function will be too simple for the domain and the outputs it generates will not be accurate. This outcome is known as the function underfitting the data.

II. If the inductive bias of a ML algorithm is too weak: Then, the algorithm is allowed too much freedom to find a function that closely fits the data. In this case, the returned function is likely to be too complex for the domain. The function is likely to fit the noise in the sample of data that was supplied to the algorithm during training. Fitting to the noise in the training data will reduce the function's ability to generalize to new data (data that is not in the training sample). This outcome is known as overfitting the data.

Conclusions: Finding a ML algorithm that balances data and inductive bias appropriately for a given domain is the key to learning a function that neither underfits or overfits the data and that generalizes successfully in that domain i.e. that is accurate at inference or processing new examples that were not in the training data.

NNs have a relatively weak inductive bias. As a result, generally, the danger with DL is that the NN model will overfit rather than underfit the data. It is because NNs pay so much attention to the data that they are best suited to contexts where there are very large datasets. The larger the dataset, the more information the data provides and therefore it becomes more sensible to pay more attention to the data.

One of the most important factors driving the emergence of DL over the last decade has been the emergence of Big Data. The massive datasets that have become available through online social platforms and the proliferation of sensors have combined to provide the data necessary to train NN models to support new applications in a range of domains. That is why, Facebook's face recognition software, DeepFace, was trained on a dataset of four million facial images.

Ingredients of Machine Learning : Three main ingredients in Machine Learning are as follows-

1. Data (a set of historical examples).
2. A set of functions that the algorithm will search through to find the best match with the data.
3. Some measure of fitness that can be used to evaluate how well each candidate function matches the data.

Note that languages like Python, tools like Keras, TensorFlow etc. provide us in-built functions that help us to get best fit model. Also measure of fitness is a function.

An easy way to access a GPU VM is to use Colaboratory or Colab that is free. The Colab notebook is opned by the user

and then it runs a free Google VM dedicated to you and is named as Colab Runtime. By default,the Runtime is CPU-only, but you can change this by going to Runtime→"Change runtime type", selecting GPU in the "Hardware accelerator" drop-down menu, then clicking Save. Note that if you run multiple Colab notebooks using the same runtime type, they will use the same Colab Runtime. So, if one writes to a file, the others will be able to read that file. Colab is intended for interactive use. Please do not use Colaboratory for cryptocurrency mining. The web interface will automatically disconnect from the colab runtime, say, after 30 minutes. In fact, it is a fabulous tool to run tests easily and get quick results.

By default, TensorFlow automatically grabs all RAM in all available GPUs the first time you run a computation. It does this to limit GPU RAM fragmentation. Please note that this means that if you try to start a second TensorFlow program or any program that needs GPU, it will quickly run out of RAM.

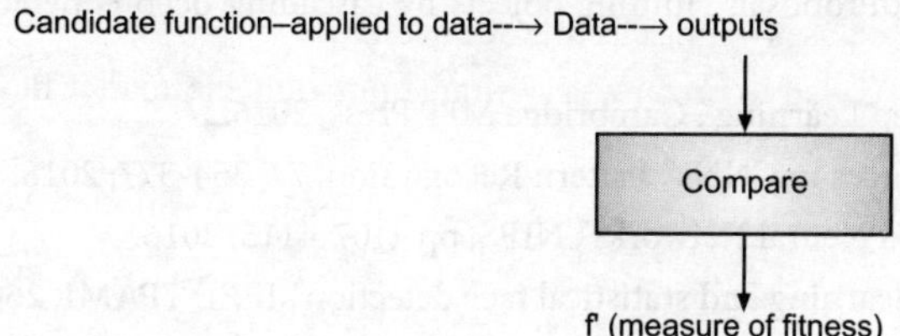

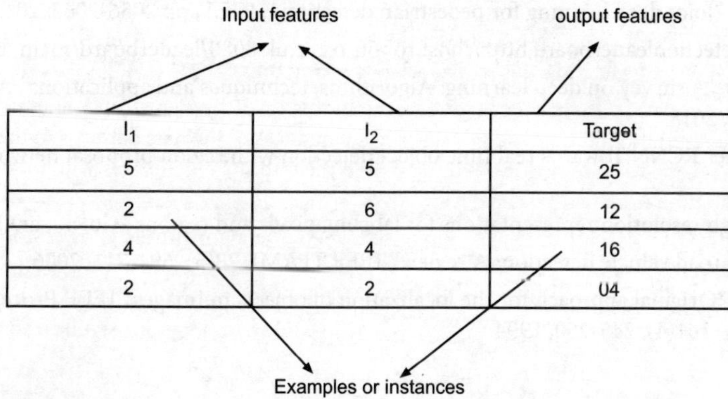

I_1	I_2	Target
5	5	25
2	6	12
4	4	16
2	2	04

In table-1, we have the following statistics-

- Multiplication will score 4/5
- Addition will score ¼
- Division and subtraction will score 0/4 So, we see numbers are multiplying to get target result.

10.6. REFERENCES

[1] Yukihiro Nomura, Issei Sato et al, "Development of training environment for deep learning with medical images on supercomputer system based on asynchronous parallel Bayesian optimization", The Journal of Supercomputing, springer, Jan. 2020.

[2] Raouf Boutaba, Mohammad A. Salahuddin et al, "A comprehensive survey on machine learning for networking: evolution, applications and research opportunities", Journal of Internet Services and Applications, SpringerOpen, 2019.

[3] Agarwal P, et al, "Analyzing the performance of multilayer neural networks for object detection", ECCV, pp 329-344, 2014.

[4] Alexe B. et al, "What is an object?", CVPR, pp 73-80, 2010.

[5] Cheng Y et al, "Model compression and acceleration for deep neural networks: The Principles, Progress and Challenges", IEEE Signal Processing Magazine, 35(1), 126-136, 2018.

[6] Dong X et. al, "Few-example object detection with model communication", IEEE Transactions on Pattern Analysis and Machine Intelligence, 41(7), 1641-1654, 2018.

[7] Erhan D et. al, "Scalable object detection using deep neural networks", CVPR, pp 2147-2154, 2014.

[8] Feichtenhofer C. Pinz A & Zisserman A, "Detect to track and track to detect, ICCV, pp 918-927, 2017.

[9] FeiFei L et. al ,"One shot learning of object categories", IEEE TPAMI, 28(4), 594-611.

[10] Fischler M et. al, "The representation and matching of pictorial structures", IEEE Transactions on Computers, 100(1), 67-92, 1973.

[11] Geronimo D et. al, "Survey of pedestrian detection for advanced driver assistance systems", IEEE TPAMI, 32(7), 1239-1258, 2010.

[12] Ghodrati A et. al, "DeepProposal: Hunting objects by cascading deep convolutional layers", ICCV, pp2578-2586, 2015.

[13] Goodfellow I et. al, "Deep Learning", Cambridge MIT Press, 2016.

[14] Gu J et. al, "Recent advances in CNNs", Pattern Recognition, 77, 354-377, 2018.

[15] Hubara I et al, "Binarized Neural Networks", NIPS, pp 4107-4115, 2016.

[16] Li S Z et al, "Floatboost learning and statistical face detection", IEEE TPAMI, 26(9), pp1112-1123, 2004.

[17] LoyC et. al, "WIDER face and pedestrian challenge 2018: Methods and results", arXiv: 1902.06854, 2019.

[18] Ma J et. al, "Arbitrary oriented scene text detection via rotation proposals", IEEE TMM, 20(11), 3111-3122, 2018.

[19] Ouyang W et. al, "Joint deep learning for pedestrian detection ", ICCV, pp 2056-2063, 2013.

[20] PASCAL VOC detectionleaderboard,http://host.robots.ox.ac.uk:8080/leaderboard/main_bootstrap .php.

[21] Pouyanfar S et. al, "A survey on deep learning: Algorithms, techniques and applications", ACM Computing Surveys, 51(5), 92:1-92:36, 2018.

[22] Ren S et. al, "Faster RCNN:Towards real time object detection with region proposal networks", IEEE TPAMI, 39(6), 1137-1149, 2017.

[23] Sun K. et. al, "High resolution representations for labeling pixels and regions", CoRR., arXiv:1904.04514, 2019.

[24] Sun Z. et. al, "On road vehicle detection: A review", IEEE TPAMI, 28(5), 694-711, 2006.

[25] Vaillant R, et. al, "Original approach for the localization of objects in images", IEEE Proceedings Vision, Image and Signal Processing, 141(4), 245-250, 1994.

UNIT-IV

DATA SCIENCE

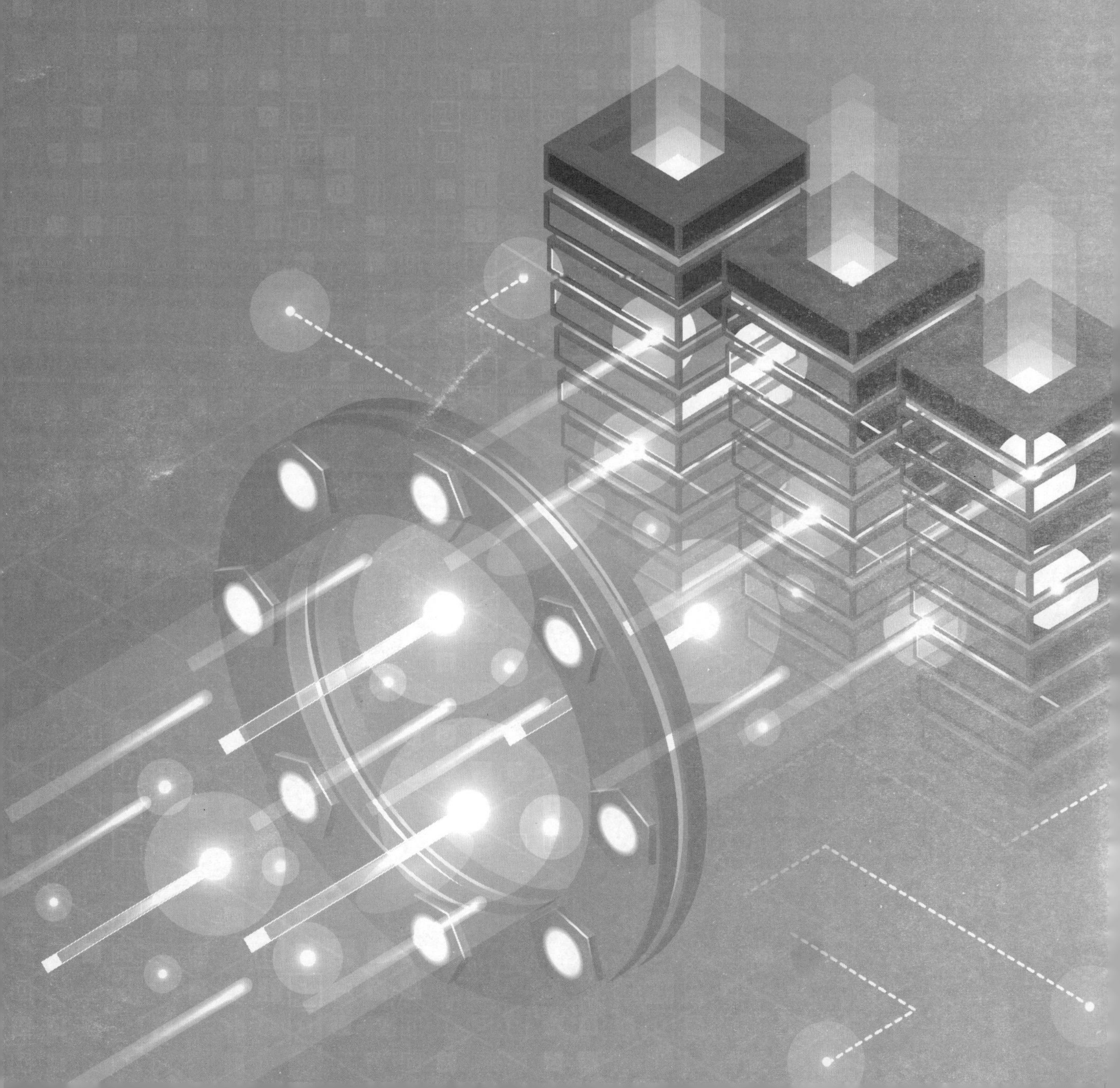

DATA SCIENCE

Q.1. What is data science? What are the steps followed in data science?

Ans. The science of understanding data using processes, tools and techniques that help in the decision-making process is known as data science. It involves the following steps: -

Step-1: Get data from the various sources available.

Step-2: Generate research question from data.

Step-3: Identify variables present in data. Identify the important variables or variables to be analyzed as such.

Step-4: Generate hypothesis.

Step-5: Analyze data using graph data like histogram.

Step-6: Fit a model from the analyzed data.

Step-7: Accept or reject the hypothesis.

Step-8: Answer to the research question is found.

Q.2. What are the five V's of big data?

Ans. There are 5 V's on the basis of which we measure big data-

- **Volume :** it involves zettabytes of data.
- **Variety :** it means the different forms and types of data.
- **Veracity :** it refers to the difficulty to trace data (predictions).
- **Velocity :** it means the speed at which the data is being generated.
- **Vulnerability :** it refers to the ease with which this big data can be hacked.

Another V that is being discussed now is Value of data. Data value can vary drastically if the data is handled differently.

Q.3. What is customer segmentation? Give an example to explain.

Ans. It is a common technique used to identify segments of customers that behave similarly with regard to their interaction with the business. For example, airlines and hotels are interested in segmenting customers into business travelers and non-business travelers or domestic versus international passengers. The advantage of doing this is the ability to increase marketing efficiency. Clustering techniques like k-means are common techniques for accomplishing customer segmentation. As data deluge is found today so organizations are able to apply new data inputs to customer segmentation algorithms, apply the clustering algorithms on larger datasets and improve overall accuracy.

Q.4. What is predictive maintenance?

Ans. The objective behind the predictive maintenance is that the failure rate patterns of various types of equipment are predictable. If we can predict when a piece of hardware will fail accurately and replace that component before it fails, we can achieve much higher levels of operational efficiency.

Q.5. Are there any Hadoop tools for data science?

Ans. Data scientist's job includes data acquisition, data quality analysis, cleaning of data, scripting, statistical computing, distributed computing and visualization. Some of the Hadoop tools for data sciences include Apache Sqoop, Apache Flume, Apache Hive, Apache Pig, Apache Spark.

Q.6. Write short notes on Apache Spark.

Ans. Apache Spark is a new framework for distributed, in-memory data processing. It supports interactive data processing for Scala or Python and is very efficient for pre-processing of data. The main abstraction is that of a resilient distributed dataset (RDD) on which different relational operators like SELECT, JOIN, GROUP BY etc. can be applied. On the top of this abstraction is a better abstraction called as DataFrame to make slicing and dicing of data simpler. Spark SQL supports both traditional SQL queries and the DataFrames API that provides a programmatic API for faster processing of relational algebra for larger datasets. Spark MLib provides a machine learning library that is integrated with the Spark toolset. Spark GraphX provides a library for graphs and graph-parallel computations on top of Spark with a support for common algorithms like PageRank algorithm. Another vital component of spark is Spark Streaming that is used for building scalable fault tolerant streaming applications and has the capability to process data in slices. That is,

Input data stream → Spark Streaming → Spark Engine → batches of processed data. This is known as Spark Streaning. Note that RDD was traditional while Spark streaming is a discretized stream on which then processing can be done.

Q.7. Name some Java ML packages.

Ans. WEKA : a collection of ML algorithms in Java for data mining tasks.

Vowpal Wabbit : is a Java-based fast ML library developed by Yahoo.

OpenNLP, CoreNLP and Mallet are Java : based packages for NLP.

Q.8. List down some of the features of Hadoop that makes it useful for a data scientist.

Ans. Some of the features of Hadoop are as follows: -

1. It provides cost-effective fault tolerant storage.
2. It supports multi-language tooling.
3. It provides robust scheduling and resource management.
4. It provides multiple levels of distributed system abstractions.
5. It provides scalable creation and execution of models.

Q.9. Name some data ingestion tools.

Ans. Apache NiFi, Apache Atlas are some data ingestion tool sets.

Q.10. What is data munging?

Ans. Data munging involves two activities—identifying data quality problems and transforming raw data into a feature matrix and this is called as feature engineering.

Q.11. List some data quality features?

Ans. The features of data quality include -

a. **Completeness:** It refers to having all parts of the data. No missing data is allowed.

b. **Validity:** It refers to the fact that the data values are correct, actual and legal.

c. **Consistency:** It refers to the data values should be represented in the same manner (uniformity of data).

d. **Timeliness:** It refers to not having a stale (old) data. Like if we have some person's address and that the person has changed his house, so the data is not timely.

e. **Accuracy:** It refers to the preciseness of data. Like the age of the customer might be 47 whereas our data reads it 49.

Q.12. What are the tasks on which ML practitioners will often focus on?

Ans. The core objective of ML is to automatically identify or learn the patterns in the data. Machine learning practitioners will focus on these tasks-

a. **Predictive modeling :** Learn a function given a set of examples, often called as the training set. Of the target variable for learning is categorical in nature then the problem is called as classification problem like classifying an email as spam or not-spam. If the target variable is numerical, then the problem is called as regression like predicting the price of a house given features like number of rooms, area of house etc.

b. **Clustering:** Identify natural grouping or clusters of observations that are similar to each other.

c. **Anomaly detection:** To identify observations that are anomalous if compared to normality.

d. **Recommender systems:** To predict the user preferences for product or item given historical preference data from other users.

e. **Market basket analysis:** To identify patterns of associations between items that co-occur in the same observation. This technique is also called as association rules.

Q.13. Name some tools for ML.

Ans. 1. Many R machine learning packages like caret, e1071, rpart, C50, randomForest, gbm, clust, glmnet, neuralnet, arules etc.

2. Python's scikit-learn package.
3. java libraries for ML like WEKA, RapidMiner.
4. Vowpal Wabbit- a C++ bsed ML library.

Q.14. Name some open-source tools and some closed source tools for distributed ML.

Ans. Open-source tools: Apache Mahout, Apache Flink ML, Conjecture and ML-ease.

Closed-source tools: SAS, Microsoft ML.

Q.15. Define the following: -

***a.* Descriptive analytics.** ***b.* Diagnostic analytics.**

***c.* Predictive analytics.** ***d.* Prescriptive analytics.**

Ans. Let us define these terms one by one.

***a.* Descriptive analytics:** It refers to the description of the data and deriving meaningful inference from the past data with pattern recognition and data visualization methods. actually, it answers the question "What has happened?".

***b.* Diagnostic analytics:** It is an extension of descriptive analytics which asks the question- "Why it happened?". It explores the reasons for occurrence and analyzes the underlying reasons for such occurrences.

***c.* Predictive analytics:** It consists of model building involving prediction of future trends using forecasting and simulation. Actually, it answers the question- "What will happen?".

***d.* Prescriptive analytics:** It involves prescribing some viable alternative action plan about the future.

Q.16. What are the steps of the machine learning process?

Ans. The following steps are followed in a learning process-

Step-1: Divide the input data into training dataset and testing dataset.

Step-2: Develop a ML model by training it using a subset of input data i.e., training dataset.

Step-3: Test the model by predicting using the remaining subset of data i.e., testing dataset.

Step-4: Compute the model performance measures on the test dataset to check accuracy.

Step-5: If the accuracy is higher than the acceptable level, the model is deployed in real-world scenario to perform prediction task.

Step-6: if the accuracy is lower than the acceptable level, the model is trained multiple times using different input features.

Q.17. It is desired to implement a decision tree using some programming language like R, Python etc. what are the steps that you will follow for the same.

Ans. The following steps may be followed: -

Step-1: Install the packages.

Step-2: Load the dataset. *e.g.* churn ←read.csv(file.choose( ), header = TRUE)

Step-3: Understand the data *i.e.*, structure the dataset. *e.g.* str(churn)

Step-4: Pre-processing the data *i.e.* remove outliers and blank values.

Step-5: Splitting the data into training and testing data. Data are split into training and test datasets.

Step-6: Setting the control parameters for the decision tree.

Step-7: Building the decision tree.

Step-8: Plotting the decision tree.

Step-9: Pruning the decision tree. The process of cutting down the excess branches in order to give accurate results is known as pruning.

Step-10: Predicting using the train data.

Step-11: Predicting using the test data.

Q.18. What are the steps that you will follow for implementing random forest?

Ans. The following steps may be followed: -

Step-1: Install the packages.

Step-2: Load the dataset.

Step-3: Understand the data i.e., structure the dataset.

Step-4: Pre-processing the data i.e., remove outliers and blank values.

Step-5: Splitting the data into training and testing data. Data are split into training and test datasets.

Step-6: Setting the control parameters for the random forest.

Step-7: Tuning the random forest.

Step-8: Variable importance plot.

Step-9: Predicting using the train data.

Step-10: Predicting using the test data.

Q.19. Define what is Out of Bag error rate?

Ans. It is a metric used to measure the prediction accuracy of the random forest. Please note that the lesser is the error rate, the better is the model.

Q.20. Time series data consists of four important components that should be analyzed before model building. Name and define them.

Ans. The four components of time series analysis are as follows-

1. **Trend:** It shows either an upward or downward movement showing growth or decline.
2. **Seasonality:** It refers to the fixed cycles shown in time series data that happens regularly in consecutive time intervals. It is periodic pattern in data.
3. **Cyclical component:** It refers to the business cycles that happen over a longer period of time like 15-20 years. Like recession at longer time periods.
4. **Irregularity/ noise:** It refers to the events happening in a short span of time that could not be controlled. These irregularities can cause a sudden spike or a sudden dip in demand. This is also known as error or noise in the data. Like corona pandemic in a country leading to a huge loss in sales.

Note: The time series data are decomposed to identify the components like trend and seasonality in the data decomposition helps in identifying unusual observations.

Q.21. Define the following terms: -

a. **ARIMA.**

b. **Deseasonalization.**

c. **Differencing.**

d. **Exponential smoothing model.**

e. **Residuals.**

Ans. Let us define these terms one by one: -

a. **ARIMA:** It stands for Autoregressive Integrated Moving Average. These algorithms are used to build models using time series data for predicting future values in the series.

b. **Deseasonalization:** The process of removing the seasonal effect in the data is called as deseasonalization.

c. **Differencing:** The process of taking the difference of the consecutive terms in order to make data stationary is called as differencing.

d. **Exponential smoothing model:** It assigns weights to the data and minimizes the random variation. The weights are assigned in the decreasing order of the past observations. The weights are reduced further exponentially for the older observations.

e. **Residuals:** Residuals in time series model are the differences between the observations and the corresponding predicted values.

Q.22. Distinguish between non-stationary and stationary time series.

Ans. Non-Stationary time series is the time series in which the mean, variance and auto correlation values change over time. On the other hand, Stationary time series is one whose properties do not depend on the time at which the series is observed. Here, the basic measures like mean, variance and autocorrelation of the data remains constant.

Q.23. Define multi-collinearity.

Ans. When the correlation between the independent variables is high, there exists multi-collinearity between the variables.

Q.24. It is observed that a model gives 90% accuracy. Can we adopt that model just for this accuracy parameter?

Ans. The answer is no. Please note that if the prediction of positive cases is more important then, the 'sensitivity value' needs to be taken into consideration and if the prediction of negative cases is more important then, the 'specificity value' needs to be taken into consideration. Also note that if the concerned value is low, even if the accuracy is 90%, the model would still not be adapted.

Q.25. When is a value considered an outlier?

Ans. A value is considered as an outlier if it is below $Q_1 - 1.5 * IQR$ or above $Q_3 + 1.5 * IQR$ where $IQR = (Q_3 - Q_1)$ where Q_1 is the first quartile and Q_3 is the 3rd quartile and IQR is the Interquartile Range.

Q.26. In clustering, what are the different linkage methods?

Ans. The following linkage methods are used: -

1. **Single linkage:** The shortest distance between the points in the cluster is considered.
2. **Average linkage:** The average distance between the points in the cluster is considered.
3. **Centroid linkage:** The distance between the centroids of the two clusters is taken into consideration.
4. **Ward's linkage:** The variance within the cluster is considered for comparison of the distance between the clusters.

Q.27. How can we decide on the number of factors in PCA?

Ans. The number of factors can be found out by eigen values. Note that this eigen value indicates the variance of the variables. Eigen values are the measure to find out how well the factor represents the summary of the variables. They help identify the number of factors that could be used for analysis. As per Kaiser's paper, the number of eigen values of more than 1 should be the number of factors.

Q.28. Differentiate between classification and regression.

Ans. The following table lists the differences-

Classification	Regression
1. It predicts classes.	1. It predicts quantity.
2. It can be evaluated using accuracy.	2. It can be evaluated using Root-Mean-Square-Error (RMSE).
3. Discrete class label is the output.	3. Continuous quantity is the output.

But there is a similarity between the two that both try to make prediction based on input values.

Q.28. What is GINI index?

Ans. The GINI index is the cost function used to evaluate splits in the dataset. It gives the measure of impurity. How effective is the split of data based on features can be easily determined by this Gini index? A Gini score of 0 is ideal expected result while one having half-half probability is not preferred.

Q.29. Which other measure can be used with decision tree, other than Gini?

Ans. Entropy is another measure that can be used with decision tree.

Q.30. Differentiate between Random Forest and Decision tree.

Ans. The following table differentiates between the two-

Decision Tree	Random Forest
1. It is a sub-part of Random Forest.	1. It consists of lots of decision trees.
2. Overfitting can occur.	2. Overfitting is avoided.
3. Faster.	3. Slower.
4. Easy to interpret.	4. Difficult to interpret.

Q.31. What is Bootstrap sample?

Ans. it is used to estimate the distribution. A sample is taken with replacement from an observed data set and is called as a bootstrap sample.

Q.32. Define the following: -

a. **Selection bias.**

b. **Resampling.**

c. **Tail.**

d. **Degree of Freedom.**

Ans. Let us define these terms now-

a. **Selection bias:** It is the bias introduced by the selection of individuals, groups or data for analysis in such a way that proper randomization is not achieved. This ensures that the sample obtained is not representative of the population intended to be analyzed.

b. **Resampling:** It combines shuffling and bootstrapping.

c. **Tail:** It is the portion of frequency distribution where extreme values are observed at a very low frequency.

d. **Tail:** It is the portion of frequency distribution where extreme values are observed at a very low frequency.

e. **Degree of Freedom:** It indicates how much value from the given samples are supposed to vary to give the required result.

Q.33. What is a frozenset in Python?

Ans. It gives immutability to the set i.e., nothing can be modified.

Q.34. How is diamond problem resolved in Python?

Ans. Diamond problem occurs whenever child class inherits same method with different body from two different parents. In case of Python, it is resolved by order in which parent is inherited. Please note here that the parent which is inherited first is given more importance.

Q.35. Differentiate between static methods and class methods.

Ans. The following table differentiates between the two-

Static method	Class method
1. It needs no specific parameters though static function can be parameterized.t	1. It takes cls as the first parameter. Cls represents the class on which the method is created.
2. It cannot modify class state.	2. It can modify and access the class state.
3. It is created by using @staticmethod annotation.	3. It is created by @classmethod annotation.
4. It is used to create utilities.	4. It is used to create factories.
5. No such feature.	5. It is a descriptor, wrapping a function and can call the resulting object on a class.
6. It is a self-contained code.	6. Code access is till the Class level.

Q.35. What are Generators? Give an example.

Ans. They are used to save memory as they store only some values in memory at a time rather than storing entire dataset in memory. They are invoked using the next function. For example, if we want to process the entire file having million of records, generator function would bring only one record at a time in the memory.

Q.36. Define a decorator function.

Ans. It allows performing wrapper around a function. It acts as an interceptor which allows performing pre-processing and post-processing.

Q.37. What is anaconda? What is its job?

Ans. Anaconda is easy-to-use distribution which comes bundled up with lot of modules used in the data science world. It provides a packaged environment to get started easily. It also manages dependencies.

Q.38. What is a Jupyter notebook?

Ans. It is a web application that allows you to create and share documents that contains- Python code, visualizations and explanatory text of code.

Q.39. What is pickling and unpickling in Python?

Ans. The process of converting from Python format to intermediate string formats which can be then stored on a file is known as pickling. On the other hand, the process of bringing or loading the stored Python objects back into memory is known as unpickling.

Q.40. How Python supports database connections? Give an example to explain.

Ans. Python supports connection to database with Dp-Api modules. The mechanism to query remains the same but difference lies in the classes to be imported to suit various databases. To connect to database like MYSQL, the following code may be used-

```
    import mysql.connector//connector for Mysql
    mydb = mysql.connector.connect (
        host = "localhost", //details of database
        port = 3306,
        user = "root",
        passwd = "root",
        database = 'pymsql'
    )
To fetch the data from the database table, we write-
    mycursor = mydb.cursor( ) //create a cursor to execute query
    sql = "SELECT * FROM emp ORDER BY sal DESC"
    mycursor.execute(sql);//SQL is executed
    myresult= mycursor.fetchall( ) //result of query is fetched and stored
          //in myresult variable.
  //looping through resultset to print data row or tuple by tuple
    for x in myresult:
    print(x)
```

Q.41. What is meta programming? Give some examples.

Ans. A programming technique in which the program itself is treated as data. Such languages do not have knowledge of itself and can change or manipulate itself during run-time.

For example, adding attribute and method to a class, creating inheritance chain, creating dynamic constructor or linking constructor etc.

Q.42. What is broadcast? Explain the rules of broadcasting.

Ans. The ability of numpy to treat arrays with different dimensions or shape in a uniform way is known as broadcasting. We can do broradcasting with the help of broadcast method.

Example,

```
import numpy as np
x = np.array([[1], [2], [3]])
```

```
y = np.array([4, 5, 6])
b = np.broadcast(y, x) //will repeat each element of y wrt. X
for t in b:
print (t)
```

OUTPUT:

(4, 1)
(5, 1)
(6, 1)
(4, 2)
(5, 2)
(6, 2)
(4, 3)
(5, 3)
(6, 3)

Rules of broadcasting: -

1. Whenever two arrays have different dimensions, the shape of the one with fewer dimensions is adjusted by padding with ones on its leading (left) side.
2. If there is a difference in the shape of two arrays, it does not match in any dimension, then dimension is stretched to match the other shape for that array with shape one.
3. An error is raised in case the dimension and sizes disagree and neither is equal to 1.

Q.43. Write the program statements to save numpy data from memory to flat file.

Ans. Numpy data can be stored in npy format files which are custom serialized or they can be stored in text file. The following statements can do this-

```
import numpy as np
a = np.array([1,2,3,4,5])
np.save('outfile', a)//  saves numpy data in outfile.npy file
b = np.load('outfile.npy') // loads data from npy file into memory
print (b)
np.savetxt('out.txt', a) //saves data in text file format
b = np.loadtxt('out.txt')// loads data from text file format to numpy in
memory
print (b)
```

Q.44. Distinguish between 'where' and 'extract' in numpy.

Ans. Both where and extract are used to match data based on the conditions.

where:

where sample:

```
import numpy as np
x = np.arange(9.) .reshape(3, 3)
print (x)
y = np.where(x > 3)  //find out the index where value is greater than 3
print (x[y])  //prints value corresponding to condition.
```

Output: [4, 5, 6, 7, 8.]

Extract: It specifies data and the corresponding condition.

```
x = np.arange (9.) .reshape(3, 3)
condition = np.mod(x, 2) == 0
print (condition)
```

```
print (np.extract(condition, x))    //applies above created condition on
dataset
```

Q.45. In numpy, what is the usage of ndenumerate?

Ans. ndenumerate returns the coordinates and corresponding values in the coordinates.

A = np.array([[11, 22], [33, 43]])
for index, x in np.ndenumerate(a):
print (index, x)

Outputs:

(0, 0) 11
(0, 1) 22
(1, 0) 33
(1, 1) 43

Q.46. Is it possible to draw a histogram using numpy?

Ans. Let us write a program to understand it.

```
import numpy as np
// creates histogram based on values and ranges given by bins
hist, be = np.histogram([1, 1, 2, 2, 2, 2, 3], bins = range(5))
print (hist)
print (be)
```

OUTPUTS:

Range	Bin	Count
0-1	0	1
1-2	1	2
2-3	2	4
3-4	3	1

Explanation: The print(be) method prints bin while hist prints the count.

Q.47. What is Pandas? How data is represented in Pandas?

Ans. Pandas is a 3rd party module which helps in easier representation of data in memory to perform analysis. Pandas help in faster representation and processing of data.

Data representation in Pandas: In Pandas, data representation is similar to an Excel sheet that consists of row and columns. Columns in Pandas are known as series. Collection of series is called as data frame. So, we can say that data frame is the unit of representation of data which is collection of various series. Row index is also known as index and each column is known as series.

Q.48. Write programs to-

***a.* Create series in Pandas.**

***b.* Create Data Frame in Pandas.**

Ans. *a.* To create Series, we write a program as follows-

```
import pandas as pd
data = pd.Series([0.25, 0.5, 0.75, 1.0]) //series is created using pd.Series
print (data)
print (data.values) // print values stored in series
print (data.index) // prints index associated with each series
```

c. To create Data Frame, we write a program as follows- Data frame can be created directly from dictionary or it can also be created by combining various series.

```
import pandas as pd
```

```
country_population = {'India': 1400000,
                                          'China': 3987654,
                                             'UK': 8500000}
population = pd.Series(country_population) //creates population series from //
country_population dictionary
//now let us create another series based on area
country_land = {'India': '35000 hectares',
                          'China': '67000 hectares',
                            'UK': '67000 hectares'}
area = pd.Series(country_land) // creates an area series from country_land
//now create a data frame with these 2 series
df = pd.Dataframe ({'Population': population, 'SpaceOccupied': area})
print (df)
```

Q.49. How are the missing values represented in the data frame?

Ans. The following lines of code can do it-

import pandas as pd

// data frame generated by using 2 dictionaries with some non-common keys resulting in NA

missing = pd.DataFrame([{'a' : 1, 'b' :2}, {'b': 3, 'c': 4}])

print (missing)

OUTPUT:

	a	b	c
0	1	2	NaN
1	NaN	3	4

Here, missing values are represented as NaN.

Q.50. How can Pandas create indexes?

Ans. Indexes can be created using pd.Index function. Indexes support intersection and union.

```
indA = pd.Index([1, 3, 5, 7, 9])
indB = pd.Index([2, 3, 5, 7, 11])
print (indA & indB)// & stands for intersection
print (indA | indB)// | stands for OR
```

Q.51. Define reindexing.

Ans. Reindexing allows us to modify the index of one data frame by keeping the other data frame as reference. It can also be achieved by passing index and corresponding columns.

Q.52. Explain bfill and ffill.

Ans. While reindexing, NaN can be introduced. Bfill and ffill are used to handle NaN.

Q.53. Name some of the iterations as provided in Pandas data frame.

Ans. The following are the data frames-

a. iteritems( ): to iterate over the (key, value) pairs.

b. iterrows( ): to iterate over the rows as (index, series) pairs.

c. itertuples( ): to iterate over the rows as namedtuples.

Q.54. Can we perform sorting in Pandas?

Ans. Yes, Pandas supports sorting.

sort_index: allows sorting on index(row) or column wise.

sort_values: allows sorting on values.

Q.55. Can Pandas do slicing?

Ans. Pandas supports the following slicing: -

```
.loc( ) label used.
.iloc( ) integer based.
.ix( ) both label and integer based.
```

Q.56. It is possible to override default reload option in Pandas?

Ans. Yes, as follows-

pd.set_option("display.max_rows", 80) //set max. rows to be displayed

pd.set_option("display.max_columns", 30) //set max. cols to be displayed

Q.57. Explain the rolling function and expanding function in Pandas.

Ans. Rolling function allows us to define window size and perform various operations w.r.t. the window. Expanding function is an alternative to rolling statistics. It yields the value of the statistic with all the data available up to that point in time.

Q.58. Explain different merge functions with respect to the data frames.

Ans. Data frame in Pandas support merge operations in which two related data from diverse data frames can be brought in single view.

For example, consider the following left and right data frame: -

Left data frame:

	FirstName	Id	Subj-id
0	Ripudaman	11	Sub1
1	Harupdesh	2	Sub2
2	Rajan	33	Sub4
3	Sajan	44	Sub6
4	Raman	55	Sub5

Right data frame:

	LastName	Id	Subj-id
0	Singh	11	Sub1
1	Uppal	2	Sub4
2	Kumar	3	Sub3
3	Mathew	4	Sub6

Then, if we write-

print('id merge', pd.merge (left, right, on ='id'))

Please note here that the records matching by id on both data frames would be returned. That is, the output will be-

Id	Merge	FirstName	Id2	subj-id-x	LastName	subject-id-y
0	Ripudaman	11	Sub1	Singh	Sub1	
1	Rajan	2	Sub2	Uppal	Sub4	

Also note that in left merge, all data from left side will come and only those matching from right would come. That is,

If we write-

print ('left', pd.merge(left, right, on='id', how = 'left'))

Here, 'left' indicates everything from left.

So, after left merge we get: -

Left	FirstName	Id	Subj-id-x	LastName	Subj-id-y
0	Ripudaman	11	Sub1	Singh	Sub1
1	Harupdesh	2	Sub2	Uppal	Sub4
2	Rajan	33	Sub4	NaN	NaN

3	Sajan	44	Sub6	NaN	NaN
4	Raman	55	Sub5	NaN	NaN

Note: NaN can be introduced.

Right Merge operation:

In right merge, everything from right side comes and only matching in left would come else it would come as NaN.

```
print('right', pd.merge(left, right, on = 'id', how='right'))
```

Outer Merge operation: In outer merge, data from both left and right would come.

```
print('outer', pd.merge(left, right, on = 'subj-id', how='outer'))
```

Q.59. Give the usage of concat method.

Ans. Concat method allows combining two different data frames either at row-level or at column-level.

Consider the following left and right data frame-

Left data frame:

	FirstName	Id	Subj-id
1	Ripudaman	11	Sub1
2	Harupdesh	2	Sub2
3	Rajan	33	Sub4
4	Sajan	44	Sub6
5	Raman	55	Sub5

Right data frame:

	LastName	Id	Subj-id
1	Singh	11	Sub1
2	Uppal	2	Sub4
3	Kumar	3	Sub3
4	Mathew	4	Sub6

Then for concatenation we may write-

print(pd.concat([left, right])) will return-

	FirstName	Id	Subj-id
0	Ripudaman	11	Sub1
1	Harupdesh	2	Sub2
2	Rajan	33	Sub4
3	Sajan	44	Sub6
4	Raman	55	Sub5
0	Singh	11	Sub1
1	Uppal	2	Sub4
2	Kumar	3	Sub3
3	Mathew	4	Sub6

print(pd.concat([left, right], axis=1)) will return-

	Name	Id	Subj-id	Name	Id	Subj-id
0	Ripudaman	11	Sub1	Singh	11	Sub1
1	Harupdesh	2	Sub2	Uppal	2	Sub4
2	Rajan	33	Sub4	Kumar	3	Sub3
3	Sajan	44	Sub6	Mathew	4	Sub6
4	Raman	55	Sub5	NaN	NaN	NaN

Q.60. How Pandas handles date and time?

Ans. Pandas provides date range with the help of two functions-

```
date_range and bdate_range.
```

Periods and frequency can be specified as attribute to the ranges. Like,

```
start = pd.datetime (2022,1,1)
end = pd.datetime (2021, 2, 2)
print (pd.bdate_range(start, end)) //prints periods
```

and

```
print (pd.bdate_range('1/2/2022', periods = 3, freq = 'M' )) //prints freq.
```

Q.61. Which all file formats Pandas supports?

Ans. Pandas supports text, binary, SQL and remote data sources. Data may be in form of csv (comma separated values), HTML, MS EXCEL, GOOGLE BIG QUERY, STATA, Feather Format etc.

Q.62. Can you print a histogram using Pandas?

Ans. Pandas provides Series( ) function for the same. Using series.value_counts( ) functions we can easily generate the value and its corresponding count, as follows: -

```
import panadas as pd
import numpy as np
s = pd.series([1, 1, 10, 200, 10, 20, 30, 40])
print (s);
print(s.value_counts( ))
```

Outputs:

S

0	1
1	1
2	10
3	200
4	10
5	20
6	30
7	40

Histogram

Value count

10	2
1	2
20	1
30	1
40	1
200	1

Q.63. What is Scipy library for?

Ans. Scipy library is used for scientific computation. It is a collection of components and provides ecosystem for scientific computing. SymPy is used for symbolic mathematics and computer algebra, scikit-image is used for image processing, scikit-learn is used for machine learning.

Q.64. Explain how to-

***a.* Implement logistic regression in Python.**

b. **Implement decision tree in Python.**

c. **Random Forest in Python.**

d. **SVM in Python.**

e. **KNN in Python.**

f. **K-means in Python.**

Ans. Let us see this one by one.

a. **Logistic regression in Python** : sklearn.linear_model contains LogisticRegression that can be used to represent logistic regression. This can be achieved as follows: -

```
import sklearn.linear_model as sklm
logmodel = sklm.LogisRgression( )
logmodel.fit(features,   label)   //make   model   with   the   help   of
trained data,
  //features  and  label  represent  data  and  corresponding  labels
used for training the model.
y_pred  =  logmodel.predict  (X_test)     predict  using  the  above
created and //enhanced model with test data.
```

b. **Decision tree in Python-** sklearn.tree module contains DecisionTreeClassifier that can be used for classification. This can be achieved as follows: -

```
import sklearn.tree as slt
model  slt.DecisionTreeClassifier( )
model.fit   (features,   label)   //fit   the   model   using   features
and label
```

where

```
//features   represents   data   and   labels   represents   labels
generated used for training.
y_pred = model.predict(X_test)
```

c. **Random Forest in Python** : sklearn.ensemble module contains RandomForestClassifier that can be used for Random Forest generation. This can be achieved as follows: -

```
import sklearn.ensemble as ske
model   =   ske.RandomForestClassifier(n_estimators   =   50)   //   n_
estimators
// indicates no. of trees in random forest.
Model.fit(features, label)
y_pred = clf.predict(X_test)
```

Note that for regression type, we will use RandomForestRegressor instead of Random Forest Classifier.

d. SVM in Python : SVM stands for Support Vector Machine. Sklearn.svm module contains SVC which is used for svm.

SVM for linear model code is-

```
import sklearn.svm as svm
model    =    svm.SVC(kernel    =    'linear')    //indicates    linearly
separable approach
model.fit (features, label)
y_pred = clf.predict(X_test)
```

Similarly, SVM for non-linear/ polynomial mode code is-

```
import sklearn.svm as svm
model = svm.SVC(kernel = 'poly', degree = 9) //value of
kernel to poly and
//degree indicates that this svm supports polynomial approach.
model.fit (features, label)
y_pred = clf.predict(X_test)
```

Note: Linear, poly, sigmoid and guassian are supported by svm in Python.

e. **KNN in Python** : Sklearn.neighbors mocule contains KNeighborsClassifier that can be used for classification. The code is as follows: -

```
import sklearn.neighbors as sn
model = sn.KNeighborsClassifier(n_neighbors = 3) //n_
neighbors stands for
//number of neighbors used for classification.
model.fit(features, label)
```

f. **K-means in Python** : It is possible to implement k-means with the help of sklearn.cluster module that contains KMeans. The code is-

```
import sklearn.cluster as skc
kmeans = skc.KMeans (n_clusters = 35) // n_clusters stands for
number of clusters
model = kmeans.fit(X)
labels = model.predict(X)
centroids = model.cluster_centers //cluster centers can also be
determined.
```

Q.65. How will you select k in KNN algorithm?

Ans. The value of k depends on the dataset. Please note that a very small value of k implies noise can have a bigger influence on the result. Also note that a very large value of k implies more calculations that can be time and memory consuming. Odd classes are preferred and k = sqrt(NoOfElements).

Q.66. Define underfitting and overfitting.

Ans. **Underfitting:** It is a situation in which model does not perform well on the training data and testing data.

Overfitting: It is the situation where the model gives good results with the training data but does not give good results with the testing data.

Q.67. Scaling can be done in two ways- normalization and standardization. What is the difference between them?

Ans. Normalization means using the minimum and maximum values while standardization uses mean and standard deviation.

Q.68. What is the main difference between supervised, unsupervised and semi-supervised learning set?

Ans. Supervised learning set = {(sample[acquisition], class [expert])}

Unsupervised learning set = unlabeled samples

Semi-supervised learning set = some labeled samples + many unlabeled samples

Q.69. Define an oracle.

Ans. Active learners are allowed to dynamically pose queries during the training process, usually in form of unlabeled data instances to be labeled by what is called as an oracle.

Q.70. Distinguish between supervised and unsupervised learning.

Ans. The following table distinguishes between the two-

Supervised Learning	Unsupervised Learning
1. It uses known and labelled input data.	1. It uses unknown input data.
2. Input variables and output variables will be given.	2. Only input data will be given.
3. It is very complex in computation.	3. It has less computational complexity.
4. It uses offline analysis.	4. It uses real-time analysis of data.
5. Number of classes are known.	5. Number of classes are not known.
6. It gives accurate and reliable results.	6. It uses moderate accurate results.
7. It is used in image and speech recognition, forecasting, financial analysis, ANN training, SVM decision trees etc.	7. It is used to pre-process the text during exploratory analysis or to pre-train supervised learning algorithms.
8. It is also known as associative learning, in which the network is trained by providing it with input and matching output patterns.	8. It is also known as self-organization, in which an output unit is trained to respond to clusters of patterns within the input.
9. It requires pairing of each input vector with a target vector representing the desired output.	9. It is employed in self-organizing neural networks.
10. During the training session, an input vector is applied to the network and it results in an output vector. This response is then compared with the target response.	10. During training, the neural network receives input patterns and organizes these patterns into categories. When new input pattern is applied, then neural network provides an output response indicating the class to which the input patterns belong.
1. If the actual response differs from the target response, the network will generate an error signal.	11. If a class cannot be found for the input pattern, a new class is generated.
12. The error minimization in this type of training requires a supervisor or a teacher. These input-output pairs can be provided by an external teacher or by the system which contains neural network.	12. It does not require a teacher. It requires certain guidelines to form groups. Grouping can be done based on color, shape and any other property of the object.
13. These methods are used to perform non-linear mapping in pattern classification networks, pattern association networks and multi-layer neural networks.	13. It is useful for data compression and clustering.
14. It generates a global model and a local model.	14. Here, a system is supposed to discover statistically salient features of the input population.

Q.71. Define dendrogram.

Ans. A tree structure that is commonly used to represent the process of hierarchical clustering. It shows how objects are grouped together step by step.

Q.72. Explain what is the use of Colaboratory?

Ans. A simpler method to access a GPU VM is to use Colaboratory or Colab. It is free. You have to just go to https://colab.research.google.com/ and create a new Python 3 notebook. This will create a Jupyter notebook on your Google Drive. Colab's GUI is similar to Jupyter's GUI.

Q.73. How to handle missing data in machine learning?

Ans. Some of the ways of handling missing data in problem: -

1. Remove features which contain missing values.
2. Remove rows containing missing values.
3. Replace missing values with significant data. For numerical attributes we can replace missing values by-
   - Mean of the feature values.

- Median of the feature values.
- Zero.

While for the categorical attributes, we can create a new category "default" for each missing data point and do the analysis.

Q.74. What is data visualization? Name some popular packages in Python that help us to visualize the data.

Ans. Data visualization is graphical representation of the data. It is easier to understand the result by charts and graphs rather than reading tables or thousands of lines of raw data. Data scientist use this as a tool to build a story around the data.

Some popular packages in Python to visualize the data are: -

✓ Matplotlib ✓ Seaborn
✓ Ggplot ✓ Geoplotlib
✓ Bokeh ✓ plotly

Q.75. Differentiate between Data Science and Machine Learning.

Ans. The following table differentiates between the two-

Data Science	Machine Learning
1. It is concerned with deciphering and identifying hidden patterns or valuable insights in data that may be used to make more informed business choices in the future.	1. It is the branch of data science that allows a computer to learn data from data by observing patterns in the data and making decisions without being explicitly programmed.
2. It is used to extract insights from data.	2. To make predictions and to categorize the results for fresh data points, it is necessary to use this function.
3. In data science, the main steps involved to create a model include extraction of data, cleaning of data, various tools like Tableau, Micro Strategy etc. to analyze essential patterns that are involved, making a workable model by using algorithms like supervised learning, unsupervised learning etc. evaluating and deploying the model.	3. In machine learning, the steps involved to create a ML model includes collecting the data, visualizing the data, using different ML models like Logical Regression, Bayesian Classifiers, Random Forest etc., training the dataset, evaluating the dataset and parameter tuning.
4. A good data scientist must be knowledgeable of big data technologies like Hadoop, Hive, Pig and programming in Python, R or Scala.	4. Computer science basics, programming languages like Python, R, statistics and probability ideas etc. are required for a ML Engineer to become successful.
5. It can deal with different types of data *i.e.*, raw, structured and unstructured data.	5. ML relies on structured data to perform its functions.
6. Data scientist spend most of their time and effort in data management, data cleaning and identifying the patterns in the data.	6. ML Engineers spend most of their time and effort in dealing with complications that arise during the implementation of algorithms.
7. Data science is data processing that covers not just algorithms and statistics but also the actual processing of the data.	7. It is concerned mainly with algorithm statistics.
8. For example, Netflix makes use of Data Science technologies. Pokeman Go is a game that is built using data science and virtual reality.	8. For example, Facebook makes use of ML technologies. Pinterest is a platform where users upload their content, uses ML to provide user with better and accurate results.
9. Logistic companies like DHL, FedEx uses data science to optimize the delivery process by calculating the suited time to deliver, best route to deliver that is cost optimized.	9. Twitter uses ML algorithm to make a decision about displaying tweets on the timeline of users.

Q.76. Differentiate between data science and data analytics.

Ans.

Data Science	Data Analytics
Data science involves the task of transforming data by using different technical analysis methods to extract meaningful insights using which a data analyst can apply to their businesses.	It deals with checking the existing hypothesis and information. It answers questions for a better and effective business-related decision-making process.
It drives innovation by answering questions that build connections and answers for futuristic problems. It focuses on predictive modeling.	It focuses on getting present meaning from existing historical context.
It is a broad subject that makes use of various mathematical and scientific tools and algorithms for solving complex problems.	It can be considered as a specific field dealing with specific concentrated problems using fewer tools of statistics and visualization.

Q.77. What do you mean by imbalanced data?

Ans. Data is said to be highly imbalanced it its is distributed unequally across different categories. These datasets result in an error and in inaccuracy of the model.

Q.78. Suppose there is a dataset having variables with missing values of more than 25%, how will you deal with such a dataset?

Ans. It depends on the size of the dataset. Hence, two cases arise here: -

Case-1: If datasets are small, then the missing values are substituted with the mean or average of the remaining data. In Pandas, this can be done using-

```
mean = df.mean( )
```

where df represents the pandas dataframe representing the dataset;

```
mean( ) calculates the mean of data.
```

To substitute the missing values with the calculated mean, we can use df.fillna(mean).

Case-2: If datasets are large, then the rows with missing values can be removed and the remaining data can be used for data prediction.

Q.79. Define Cross-Validation.

Ans. It is a statistical technique used for improving a model's performance. The model, in this method, is trained and tested with rotation using different samples of the training dataset to ensure that the model performs well for unknown data. The training data will be split into various groups and the model is run and validated against these groups in rotation. It uses techniques like K-Fold method, Leave-p-out method, Leave-one-out method and Holdout method.

Q.80. Data analysis cannot be done on big data as it involves larger datasets. Then, how it is managed?

Ans. The process of sampling is used in such cases of larger datasets. It implies to take some data samples that represents a whole population and then perform analysis on it. The data sample so chosen should be such that it truly represents the entire dataset. It should be a healthy representative. Two types of sampling can be done-

a. **Probability sampling method:** like clustered sampling, random sampling etc.

b. **Non-probability sampling method:** like quota sampling, snowball sampling etc.

Q.81. What will be the future of ML and AI in 2022?

Ans. In 2022, ML and AI will become the part of standard software product development lifecycle. Better case tools will also emerge for management of their development, deployment and monitoring. In 2022, we expect-

✓ On Device AI.
✓ Sustainable AI.
✓ Synthetic AI.
✓ No code/ Low Code AI.
✓ Mission critical AI.
✓ Explainable AI.
✓ Regulation in AI.

Q.82. What is boosting? On which principle does it work? Given the following dataset, how will you apply AdaBoost Algrothm?

Ans. In 1997, Freund and Schapire gave boosting as an ensemble modeling technique. It was very popular technique to tackle binary classification problems. Please note that these algorithms improve the prediction power by converting a number of weak learners to strong learners.

Principle: "We build a model on the training dataset, then a second model is built to rectify the errors present in the first model. this procedure is continued till the errors are minimized and the data set is predicted correctly".

For example, consider the Titanic dataset. Suppose you built a decision tree algorithm on this dataset. From there you get an accuracy of 90%. After this you apply a different algorithm and check the accuracy and it comes out to be 80% for KNN and 75% for linear regression. Note here that the accuracy differs when we built a different model on the same dataset. Also note that if we use combinations of all these algorithms for making final predictions then we will get more accurate results, if we take the average of all of the results from these models. This will also increase the prediction power. Boosting algorithms work in a similar way. It combines multiple models (weak learners) to reach the final output (strong learners).

There are 3 types of boosting algorithms, namely: -

a. AdaBoost algorithm.

b. Gradient descent algorithm.

c. Xtreme gradient descent algorithm.

AdaBoost (or Adaptive Boosting) is a technique in ML used as an Ensemble method.

What is ensemble? Figure below shows ensemble methode with all its predecessors.

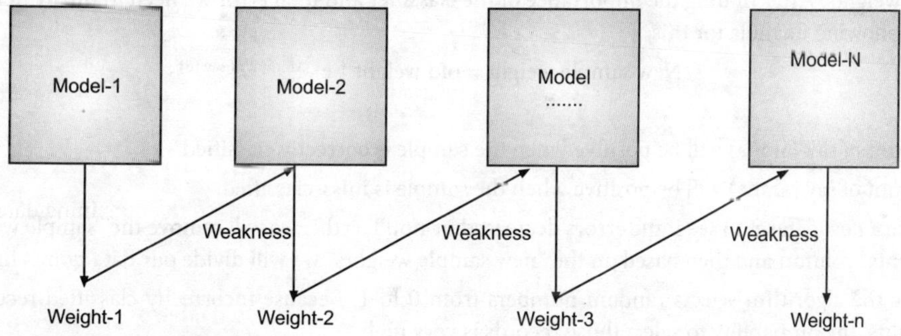

The most commonly used algorithm is the decision tree with one level *i.e.*, decision trees with only 1 split. These trees are also known as Decision Stumps.

Algorithm: This algorithm builds a model and gives equal weights to all of the data points. Then it assigns higher weights to points that are wrongly classified. Now all the points that have higher weights are given more importance in the next model. it will keep training models till a lower error is received.

Working (AdaBoost Algorithm):

Step-1: Assign weights to data points in the dataset. Say, if we have 5 data points then the sample weights will be 1/5. The formula used to compute the sample weight is-

$$w(x_i, y_i) = 1 / N, \qquad i = 1, 2, \ldots\ldots n$$

where '*N*' is the total number of datapoints.

Step-2: We will now create a decision stump for each of the features and then calculate the Gini Index of each tree. The tree with the lowest Gini index will be our first stump.

Step-3: Next, we compute the "Amount of Say" or "Importance" or "Influence" for this classifier in classifying the datapoints. The formula used is as follows: -

$$\tfrac{1}{2} \log [(1 - \text{Total Error}) / \text{Total Error}]$$

Please note that this total error is nothing else but the summation of all of the sample weights of misclassified data points.

e.g. say in our dataset there is 1 wrong output. Hence, total error will be 1/5 and alpha (performance of the stump) will be computed as follows: -

Performance of the stump = ½ loge [(1 – Total Error) / Total Error]

Or α = ½ loge [(1-1/5) / (1/5)]

= ½ loge (0.8/0.2)

= ½ loge (4)

= ½ * (1.38) = 0.69

Note:

1. Total error will always be between 0 and 1. 0 indicates perfect stump and 1 indicates horrible stump.
2. If there is no misclassification then we have no error i.e., Total Error = 0. Hence, the amount of alpha will be a large number.
3. When the classifier predicts half right and half wrong then the Total Error = 0.5 and the importance of the classifier will be 0.
4. If all of the samples have been incorrectly classified then, the error will be very high (1 approx.). hence, our alpha value will be a negative integer.

Step-4: We have calculated the Total Error and Performance of the Stump as we need to update the weights because if the same weights are applied to the next model, then the output received will be the sane as what was received in the first model. Also note that the wrong predictions will be given more weight while the correct prediction weights will be decreased. Now when we build our next model after updating the weights, more preference will be given to the points with higher weights. After finding the importance of the classifier and total error we need to finally update the weights. We use the following formula for this: -

New sample weight = old weight * $e^{\pm \text{ Amount of say } (\alpha)}$

Notes:

1. The amount of say (alpha) will be positive when the sample is correctly classified.
2. The amount of say (alpha) will be positive when the sample is miss-classified.

Step-5: Make a new dataset to see if the errors decreased or not. For this we will remove the "sample weights" and "new sample weights" column and then based on the "new sample weights" we will divide our data points into buckets.

Step-6: Now the algorithm selects random numbers from 0 to 1. Because incorrectly classified records have higher sample weights, the probability to select those records is very high.

Step-7: This forms our new dataset. we need to repeat all of the above steps, that is,

1. Assign equal weights to all datapoints.
2. Find the stump that does the best job classifying the new collection of samples by finding their Gini Index and selecting the one with the lowest Gini index.
3. Calculate the "Amount of Say" and "Total Error" to update the previous sample weights.
4. Normalize the new sample weights.
5. Iterate through these steps until a low training error is achieved.

Assume that with respect to our dataset we have constructed three decision trees in a sequential manner. If we send our text data now, it will pass through all of the decision trees. Finally, we will see which class has the majority and based on that we will do predictions for our test dataset.

Q.83. What is Regularization in ML? what are its different types?

Ans. Regularization is an approach to address overfitting in ML. Overfitted model fails to generalize estimations on test data. When the underlying model to be learned is low bias/ high variance or when we have a small amount of data, the estimated model is prone to overfitting. Also, regularization reduces the variance of the model.

Types of regularizations-

1. Modify the loss function.

2. Modify data sampling: It includes data augmentation i.e., create more data from available data by randomly cropping, dilating, rotating, adding a small amount of noise etc. K-fold cross-validation means to divide the data into k groups. tTrain on (k–1) groups and test on 1 group. Try all k possible combinations.
3. Change training approach: It involves-

a. **Injecting noise:** Add random noise to the weights when they are being learned. It pushes the model to be relatively insensitive to small variations in weights, hence regularization.

b. **Dropout:** In neural networks, connections between consecutive layers are randomly dropped based on a drop-out ratio and the remaining network is trained in the current iteration. In the next iteration, another set of random connections are dropped.

Q.84. Compare the differences between AI, Machine Learning and Deep Learning.

Ans.

Artificial Intelligence (AI)	Machine Learning (ML)	Deep Learning (DL)
AI represents simulated intelligence in machines.	ML is the practice of getting machines to make decisions without being programmed.	DL is the process of using Artificial Neural Networks to solve complex problems.
It originated in 1950s.	It originated in 1960s.	It originated in 1970s.
AI is subset of Data Science.	ML is a subset of AI and Data Science.	DL is subset of ML, AI and Data Science.
Aim is to built machines that are capable of thinking like humans.	Aim is to make machines learn through data so that they can solve problems.	Aim is to build neural networks that automatically discover patterns for feature detection.

Q.85. What is the need of deep learning?

Ans. Several types of ML algorithms exist. But a data scientist gravitates towards deep learning algorithms. Different types of neural networks in deep learning like CNN, ANN etc. are changing the way in we interact with the world. These NNs are at the core of the deep learning revolution, powering applications like unmanned aerial vehicles, self-driving cars, speech recognition etc.

Q.86. How will you copy the data within an array or a subarray in NumPy?

Ans. It is achieved with the help of copy( ) method. The code is-

```
x2_sub_copy = x2[:2, :2].copy( )
print(x2_sub_copy)
```

Q.87. How is NumPy array slicing different from Python list slicing? Give examples and explain.

Ans. In Python list slicing, slices will be copies. But in NumPy, array slices return views rather than copies of the array data. For example, Consider a 2D array-

```
[[12  5  3  8]
 [7   6  5  5]
 [1   6  3  4]]
```

Let us extract 2*2 subarray from this-

```
x2_sub = x2[:2, :2]
print(x2_sub)
```

outputs:

```
[[12  5]
 [7   6]]
```

Now we can modify this subarray also-

```
x2_sub[0, 0] = 99
print(x2_sub)
```

Outputs:

```
[[99  5  3  8]
 [7   6  5  5]
 [1   6  3  4]]
```

Note here that as we modify the subarray, the original array is also changed. This default behavior is very useful. Also note that this means that when we are working on large datasets then we can access and process pieces of datasets without the need to copy the underlying data buffer.

Q.88. Explain the concept of reshaping of an array? Give examples to explain.

Ans. Reshaping is done with the help of reshape( ) method. For example, say if we want to put the numbers 1 to 9 in a (3*3) grid, we may write: -

```
grid = np.arange(1, 10).reshape((3, 3))
print(grid)
```

Outputs:

```
[[1  2  3]
 [4  5  6]
 [7  8  9]]
```

Please note that for this to work, the size of the initial array must match the size of the reshaped array. Also note that if possible, the reshape( ) method will use a no-copy view of the initial array but with non-contiguous memory buffers this is not always possible.

Another application of reshaping is the process of conversion of a 1D array into a 2D row or column matrix. For example,

```
x = np.array([4, 5, 6])
x.reshape((1, 3))#row vector formed using reshape( ) i.e. 1 row and# 3 columns
```

Outputs:

```
array([[4, 5, 6]])
```

But if we write-

```
x.reshape((3, 1))
```

Outputs:

```
array([[1],        #now 3 rows and 1 column are formed.
[2],
[3]])
```

Q.89. What is array concatenation in NumPy?

Ans. The process of joining of two arrays in NumPy is called as concatenation. This is achieved with the help of methods like np.concatenate, np.vstack and np.hstack.

For example,

```
#lets see how np.concatenate works on 2 arrays, x and y.
x = np.array([4, 5, 6])
y = np.array([7, 8, 9])
np.concatenate([x, y])
```

Outputs:

```
array([4, 5, 6, 7, 8, 9])
```

Also, we can concatenate more than two arrays. Say, the third array is z.

That is,

```
z = [88  86  88]
print(np.concatenate([x, y, z])
```

Outputs:

array([4, 5, 6, 7, 8, 9, 88, 86, 88])

Similarly, we can perform these operations on 2D arrays. But for arrays with mixed dimensions, we can use np.vstack (vertical stack) and np.hstack (horizontal stack) functions as follows: -

```
np. vstack([x, grid])       #vertically stack the arrays
np.hstack([grid, y])        #horizontally stack the arrays
```

Also, np.dstack will stack arrays along the third axis.

Q.90. Define what is splitting of arrays in NumPy?

Ans. It is the reverse process of concatenation (discussed above). It is implemented by the functions: -

```
np.split, np.hsplit and np.vsplit
```

For example,

x =[1, 2, 3, 4, 5, 6, 7, 8] # say array is x

x1, x2, x3 = np.split(x, [3, 5])

print(x1, x2, x3)

this will split the array, x, as follows: -

[1 2 3] [4 5] [6 7 8]

Please note here that N split points lead to N+1 subarrays. In this example, 2 split points are there i.e., at index 3 and at 5 splitting was done. So, we got 2+1 = 3 arrays.

Similarly, np.hsplit and np.vsplit are same.

Q.91. Name some Numpy's universal functions.

Ans. NumPy's universal functions (or ufunc) are used to make computations faster. ufunc are of 2 types: -

- unary ufunc.
- binary ufunc.

Unary ufunc of NumPy make use of Python's native arithmetic operators like addition, subtraction, multiplication and division. The following table lists them-

Operator	Equivalent ufunc	Examples
+	np.add	Addition like 2 + 3 = 5.
-	np.subtract	Subtraction like 5 – 3 = 2
-	np.negative	Unary negation like -5
*	np.multiply	Multiplication like 5 * 3 = 15
/	np.divide	Division like 5/2 = 2.5
//	np.floor_divide	Floor division like 3 // 2 = 1
**	np.power	Exponentiation like 3 **2 = 9
%	np.mod	Modulus/remainder like 4 % 3 = 1.

For example,

$$\text{Say, array } x = [2 \quad 4 \quad 6 \quad 8]$$

So,

$$x + 3 = [5 \quad 7 \quad 9 \quad 11]$$
$$x - 3 = [-1 \quad 1 \quad 3 \quad 5]$$
$$x * 2 = [4 \quad 8 \quad 12 \quad 16]$$
$$x / 2 = [1 \quad 2 \quad 3 \quad 4]$$
$$x // 3 = [0 \quad 1 \quad 2 \quad 2]$$

Also, we can do negation and exponentiation and mod (%) operations as follows: -

```
print("-x =", -x)
print("x ** 2=", x ** 2)
print("x % 2=", x % 2)
```

Outputs:

```
-x = [-2  -4  -6  -8]
x ** 2 = [4  16  36  64]
x % 2 = [0  0  0  0]
```

We can also write ufunc as follows: -

```
np.add(x,1)
```

It will output:

```
[3  5  7  9]
```

Q.92. How can NumPy find the absolute values?

Ans. NumPy understands Python's inbuilt arithmetic operators. It also understands Python's in-built absolute value function as follows: -

For example,

```
x = np.array([3  -2  -1  5  6])
abs(x)
```

Outputs:

```
array([3  2  1  5  6])
```

Also note that the corresponding NumPy ufunc is np.absolute or np.abs.

For example,

```
np.absolute(x)
```

Outputs:

```
array([3  2  1  5  6])
```

and

```
np.abs(x)
```

Outputs:

```
array([3  2  1  5  6])
```

What is the use of ufunc here?

This ufunc can also handle complex data in which the absolute value returns the magnitude:

```
x = np.array([1-2j, 3-5j, 6+7j, 0+7j])
np.abs(x)
```

Q.93. What is fancy indexing?

Ans. Passing an array of indices to access multiple array elements at once is known as fancy indexing.

For example,

```
import numpy as np
rand= np.random.RandomState(42)
x = rand.randint(100, size = 10)
print (x)
[x[2], x[5], x[1]] # to access three different elements
```

Outputs:

```
[51  92  14  71  60  20  82  86  74  74]
[14  20  92]
```

Also, it is possible to pass a single list or array of indices to obtain the same result:

```
ind = [2, 5, 1]
x[ind]
```

Outputs:

array ([14, 20, 92])

Please note that with fancy indexing, the shape of the result reflects the shape of the index arrays rather than the shape of the array being indexed. Also note that fancy indexing works in multiple dimensions too.

For example,

```
X = np.arrange(12).reshape((3, 4))
X
```

Outputs:

```
array    ([[0,  1,  2,  3],
           [4,  5,  6,  7],
          [8,  9,  10,  11]])
```

Here, the first index refers to the row no. and second to the column no.

```
row = np.array([0, 1, 2])
col = np.array([2,1, 3])
X[row, col]
```

Outputs:

array ([2, 5, 11])

Note here that the first value in the result is X[0, 2], the second is X[1, 1] and the third is X[2, 3]. Also note that the pairing indices in fancy indexing follows all of the broadcasting rules.

Note: With fancy indexing the return value reflects the broadcasted shape of indices rather than the shape of the array being indexed.

Q.94. Why is sorting faster in NumPy?

Ans. Although Python has inbuilt sorting functions to work with lists yet sorting in NumPy is faster as NumPy's np.sort function turns out to be much more efficient and useful. By default, np.sort uses quick sort algorithm with a time complexity of O(n log n).

For example,

```
x = np.array([5,  4,  1,  2,  3])
np.sort(x)
```

Outputs:

array([1, 2, 3, 4, 5])

if you want to sort the array in-place then you can instead use sort method of arrays as follows: -

```
x.sort()
print(x)
```

Outputs:

[1 2 3 4 5]

Q.95. How to return the indices of the sorted elements?

Ans. A related function is argsort( ).

For example,

```
x = np.array([5,  4,  1,  2,  3])
i = np.argsort(x)
print (i)
```

Outputs:

[2 3 4 1 0]

That is, the first element of this result gives the index of the smallest element, the second value gives the index of the second smallest and so on.

Q.96. In Numpy, can we sort along specific row or a column?

Ans. Yes, in NumPy we can sort along a specific row or a column of a multi-dimensional array. It uses the axis argument.

For example,

```
rand = np.random.RandomState(42)
X = rand.randint(0, 10, (4, 6))
print (X)
```

Outputs:

```
[[6 3 7 4 6 9]
 [2 6 7 4 3 7]
 [7 2 5 4 1 7]
 [5 1 4 0 9 5]]
```

```
# sort each column of X
np.sort(X, axis = 0)
```

Outputs:

```
array ([[2, 1, 4, 0, 1, 5],
        [5, 2, 5, 4, 3, 7],
        [6, 3, 7, 4, 6, 7],
        [7, 6, 7, 4, 9, 9]])
```

Similarly, we can sort each row of X as follows: -

```
# sort each row of X
np.sort(X, axis = 1)
```

Outputs:

```
array ([[3, 4, 6, 6, 7, 9],
        [2, 3, 4, 6, 7, 7],
        [1, 2, 4, 5, 7, 7],
        [0, 1, 4, 5, 5, 9]])
```

Please note that it treats each row or column as an independent array. Also note that any relationships between the row or column values will be lost.

Q.97. Explain how k-nearest neighbors be located and drawn using NumPy?

Ans. We can use argsort( ) function along multiple axis to find the nearest neighbors of each point in a set.

Step-1: First of all. we create a random set of 10 points on a two-dimensional plane. Using standard method, we will arrange these in a (10 * 2) array as follows: -

X = rand.rand(10, 2)

To get an idea of how these points looks like, we scatter plot them as follows: -

```
%matplotlib inline
import matplotlib.pyplot as plt
import seaborn;
seaborn.set( )# plot styling
plt.scatter (X[:, 0], X[:, 1], s = 100);
```

Step-2: Next, we calculate the distance between each pair of points. Please remember that the squared-distance between two points is the sum of the squared differences in each dimension using broadcasting method. We can compute the matrix of square distances in a single LOC also-

```
dist_sq = np.sum((X[:, np.newaxis, :] - X[np.newaxis, :, :]) ** 2,
axis = -1)
```

with pairwise square-distances converted, we can now use np.argsort( ) to sort along each row. Then, the left-most columns will give the indices of the nearest neighbors, as follows: -

```
nearest = np.argsort(dist_sq, axis = 1)
print(nearest)
```

Outputs:

```
[[0 3 9 7 1 4 2 5 6 8]
[1 4 7 9 3 6 8 5 0 2]
[2 1 4 6 3 0 8 9 7 5]
[3 9 7 0 1 4 5 8 6 2]
[4 1 8 5 6 7 9 3 0 2]
[5 8 6 4 1 7 9 3 2 0]
[6 8 5 4 1 7 9 3 2 0]
[7 9 3 1 4 0 5 8 6 2]
[8 5 6 4 1 7 9 3 2 0]
[9 7 3 0 1 4 5 8 6 2]]
```

Please note here that the first column gives the numbers 0 through 9 in order This is because of the fact that each point's closest neighbor is itself as we expected it to be.

Step-3: As we are interested in the nearest k neighbors, what we have to do is to partition each row so that the smallest $(k + 1)$ squared distances come first, with larger distances filling the remaining positions of the array. And this can be done with the help of np.argpartition function as follows: -

$K = 2$

nearest_partition = np.argpartition(dist_sq, K + 1, axis)

Step-4: To visualize thus network of neighbors, we rapidly plot the points along with lines representing the connections from each point to its two nearest neighbors, as follows: -

```
plt.scatter(X[:, 0], X[:, 1], s = 100)
#draw lines from each point to its two nearest neighbors
K = 2
for i in range(X.shape[0]);
 for j in nearest_partition[i, :k+1]:
# plot a line from X[i] to X[j]
# use some zip magic to make it happen:
plt.plot(*zip(X[j], X[i], color = 'black')
```

When you run this code, you will observe that each point has lines drawn to its two nearest neighbors. Also note that it may look quite strange if some points have more than two lines coming out of them. Note that this is due to the fact that if a point A is one of the two nearest neighbors of point B, then this does not necessarily imply that point B is one of the two nearest neighbors of point A.

The advantage of this approach is that we can easily compute the neighbors among 100 or 1,000,000 points in any number of dimensions and the code would be same.

Step-5: When we do very large nearest-neighbor searches, there are tree-based and some approximate algorithms that can scale as O(n log n) or better also.

Q.98. What is Data Science? What are its applications?

Ans. Data Science is a field that involves a combined study of scientific methods, mathematics, statistics and coding to develop a system. such a system extracts meaningful insights from data. Data Science helps to create intelligent systems. Such systems are capable of taking independent decisions. They are based on old and new datasets (i.e., the collection of the same type or related data) available. Data Scientists develop ML algorithms using their knowledge in various domains to produce AI systems that bring out hidden information when applied to data. They use wide range of tools like Python, R, Tableau, GitHub, Apache Spark, Hadoop and SQL and many more to accomplish this. These languages support various packages like NumPy, Pandas etc. for example, companies like Amazon, Facebook, LinkedIn, Prime Video use recommendation systems for their members. A recommendation engine is a set of algorithms that keeps track of the user behavior on a website and based on that, makes suggestions for products/ entities/ people that the user might be interested in.

Applications of Data Sciences :

1. **Fraud Detection:** Currently, banks are using intelligent systems to track transactions made by credit card holders. This helps them in detecting fraudulent activities, thereby labelling customers or transactions as fraudulent or genuine. Banks use smart systems for insurance and accounting also. They analyze the investment patterns of customers and suggest offers and more investments. As unexpected change in data patterns can often be a sign of something going wrong or possible fraud.

2. **Healthcare:** There is an immense impact of data science on healthcare industry too. Different industries in healthcare that use data science are: -

   a. Genetics and Genomics.

   b. Predictive Modeling for Diagnosis.

   Genetics and Genomics: Data Science helps find biological connections between genetics, risk of diseases and drug response. An intelligent model applies statistical techniques to genomic sequences, following scientists to understand the complexities of genetic structures in detail. Genetic risk prediction is a giant leap towards more personalized healthcare.

   Predictive Modeling: It helps to predict the outcome of a diagnosis given the previous data of the patients. Hence, it provides helpful insights to doctors and medical practitioners. You can imagine a system predicting how well a person will respond to medicine by simply collecting and analyzing data based on his past health.

3. Internet Searches: Data Science is evolving Internet searches. All of the search engines like Google, Bing, AOL etc., use data science algorithms to bring out results for the searched query. All of this is done in a fraction of seconds.

4. **E-commerce:** One of the basic industries that will benefit from data sciences is retail and e-commerce. It is used not just for forecasting sales of goods and services but also for predicting trends. In addition, these intelligent systems identify a potential customer base while optimizing price structures for a particular section of customers. And the process of applying data science to the feedback provided by the customers is known as sentiment analysis. The targeted advertising is another branch of e-commerce that focuses on the digital marketing spectrum. Data science algorithms track user's past searches and surfing the Internet to display ad banners on different websites.

5. **Manufacturing:** Data science helps manufacturing industries to develop autonomous systems that help to promote production to new levels. Smart systems for industries have enabled companies to predict problems and find solutions. Data science also helps industries to monitor product quality, costs, hours etc.

6. **Transport:** Data Science has been most powerful in developing intelligent vehicles like self-driving cars / driverless cars. Data Science has also made smart systems that monitors routes and share details with the drivers in real-time. For example, if the route is congested then the system will suggest an alternate route. They also monitor the fuel consumption patterns, vehicle routes etc. note that these intelligent models continuously inspect driving environments for drivers. The goal is to provide safe environments. Data sciences has also impacted air transport industry. Airlines also use smart systems to predict flight arrivals, flight delays, monitor customer behavior, best route etc.

Q.99. Explain the following and their roles-

a. **Data scientists.** *b.* **Data analysts.**

c. **Data engineers.** *d.* **Business Analysts.**

Ans. *a.* **Data Scientists:** They look for the problem areas, examine the current trends and predict the future ones. Knowledge in mathematics, statistics and computer science helps data scientists to develop actionable plans for organizations after studying a huge amount of data—structured or unstructured big data.

b. **Data Analyst:** They analyze the data and examine the trends. They work on specific problems and analyze structured data, their knowledge in mathematics, statistics and computer science helps them to create AI models.

c. **Data Engineers (or Architects):** They are the creators of the database in an organization. Their job is to oversee data handling at all the levels including classification. Note that we can say that they are the managers of large amount of data in an organization. they work with other data professionals to build a robust database that gives meaningful and insightful information. So, they are basically software engineers with high-level coding capabilities.

d. **Business Analysts (or Business Intelligence Analysts):** They are the subsets of data analysts. They are more focused on the impact of data on the business or the market. They tell their organization how to strategize a project. Knowledge in business administration is an added advantage for them.

Q.100. Name some online and offline data collection sources.

Ans. Some online data collection sources are as follows: -

- Digital records of the organization.
- Government portals.
- Websites like Kaggle.
- Many statistical websites.

Offline sources of data are surveys, observations and interviews.

Q.101. What is cohort analysis?

Ans. cohort means that group of people with shared characteristic. It compares data related to groups and cohorts. For example, the data professional can create a date-wise cohort of patients when they visit a dentist. Then, he can study the visiting trends of cohorts from different periods in time to find out whether the quality of the average acquired patient is increasing or decreasing over time.

Q.102. Name some most commonly used visual representation tools.

Ans. MS EXCEL, R, Google Chart, Tableau, Qlik Infogram, MS power BI.

Q.103. What is PCA?

Ans. It is an analysis method to convert correlated variables into a smaller number of uncorrelated variables.

Q.104. Python is loosely typed language. What does that mean?

Ans. No data types, no semicolons, no curly braces make it loosely typed language.

Q.105. Write a Python program to print the following triangle-

```
*

* *

* * *

* * * *?
```

Ans. This can be done in Python just in 2 lines of code-

```
for i in range (0, 6):
print("*" * i)
```

Q.106. How will you print this triangle of stars in Python-

```
  *
 * * *
* * * * *
```

Ans. The following program can do this-

```
For i in range (0, 10):
print(' ' * (10 - i) + '*' * (2 * i + 1))
```

That is, we print (10 – i), concatenate with '*' and then 2i + 1 as odd number of *'s are required *i.e.*, 1, 3, 5, 7.

Q.107. Can you suggest some source of dataset?

Ans. https://archive.ics.uci.edu/ml/datasets.html

Q.108. Name some Python IDEs.

Ans. Spyder, PyCharm are some examples of Python IDE.

Q.109. Which data structure is used by Pandas?

Ans. Pandas is a popular Python package for data science. It uses DataFrame as the main data structure that maintains the flexibility of the Pandas library. We define DtataFrame as a 2D structure that represents data in a tabular form with rows and columns. Various arithmetic operations can be performed on these DataFrames. It resembles to that of a spreadsheet or a table in the database. This DataFrame can be created in many ways and from various inputs like lists, dictionary, series and NumPy arrays.

Q.110. How do you create DataFrame in Pandas?

Ans. As we know that DataFrames are very helpful in data munging. It can be created from scratch as Empty or Basic DataFrame. Pandas uses DataFrame method to create an empty DataFrame. The code for this is-

```
import pandas as pd
df = pd.DataFrame( )
print (df)
```

Outputs:

```
Empty DataFrame
Columns: [ ]
Index: [ ]
```

In this code, we are not assigning any value or anything. We just create a fundamental frame.

Q.111. Throw some light on-

a. **Creating data frames from lists.**

b. **Creating data frames from dictionary.**

c. **Creating data frames from series.**

Ans. *a.* Using lists- DataFrames can be created from lists having a single value or from those having more than one value.

```
import pandas as pd
data = [11, 22, 33, 44, 55]
df = pd.DataFrame (data)
print (df)
```

Outputs:

```
   0
0  11
1  22
2  33
3  44
4  55
>>>
```

In this code, we mention "data" clearly and it is represented with list. The DataFrame will be defined by "df" and get the data through with the help of list. In that case, we need to say exactly "data" to the list then only you will get the output with the index taken automatically else if you do not assign the "data" to the list or take some other variable like "m" to the list, you can get the output like a list. You can get the output like a list.

If you have more than one column then columns should be named as follows: -

```
import pandas as pd
content = [[0, 'Sun']. [1, 'Mon'], [2, Tues']]
```

```
df = pd.DataFrame (content, columns = ['Number', 'Dateof Week']]
print (df)
```

Outputs:

	Number	DateofWeek
0	0	Sun
1	1	Mon
2	2	Tues
3	3	Wed
4	4	Thu
5	5	Fi
6	6	Sat

Ans. ***b.*** **From Dictionary:** DataFrames can be created when a list of dictionaries is passed as input data. By default, the keys in the dictionary are used as column heading. Series of Dictionaries is assigned and agreed as input of data to build a DataFrame. The dictionary keys are evasion occupied with column names.

Example,

```
import pandas as pd
data = [{'x' : 5, 'y' : 6) , {'x' : 5, 'y' : 6, 'z' : 7}]
df = pd.DataFrame (data)
print (df)
```

Outputs:

	a	b	c
0	1	2	NaN
1	5	6	7.0

c. **From Series** : DataFrames can be created from a series as input. Dictionary of series can be assigned to create a DataFrame. The output of a catalog is exceptional of all the series index passes.

Example,

```
import pandas as pd
d = {'one' : pd.Series ([5, 6, 7], index = ['row1', 'row2', 'row3']),
{'two' : pd.Series ([5, 6, 7,8], index = ['row1', 'row2', 'row3', 'row4'])}]),
df = pd.DataFrame (d)
df
```

Outputs:

One:

Row1 5

Row2 6

Row3 7

Dtype: int 64

Two:

Row1 5

Row2 6

Row3 7

Row4 8

Dtype: int 64

Also note that the dimensions of the DataFrame can be found by the shape option-

```
df = pd.DataFrame(np.array([[1, 2, 3], [4, 5, 6]]))
print(df.shape)
```

Output: (2, 3)

But the len() function, in combination with index property, will only give information on the height of the DataFrame. That is,

```
df = pd.DataFrame(np.array([[1, 2, 3], [4, 5, 6]]))
print(len(df.index))
```

Output: 2

Q.112. What is a Panel? Give its syntax. How to create a Panel?

Ans. A panel is used for 3D ampoule of data. The work panel data comes from econometrics and is partly answerable for the title Pandas: pan(el)-da(ta)-s. the Pandas will be supported as 3 axes are included to give little semantic definition to explain the actions through panel data. They are as follows: -

1. **Major_axis:** Represented by index or rows for each DataFrame.
2. **Minor_axis:** Represented by columns for each DataFrame.
3. **Items:** relates the DataFrame confined inside.

Syntax (for Panel Creation):

```
pandas.Panel(data, items, major_axis, minor_axis, dtype, copy)
```

where,

data: data collects from different areas like ndarray, series, map, lists, dict, constants and other DataFrame

```
Items: axis = axis = 0
major_axis = axis = 1
minor_axis = axis = 2
```

dtype: data type of column.

copy: copying data by default will be False

How to create a Panel?

A panel can be built using different methods i.e., from ndarrays, dict of DataFrames.

```
import pandas as pd
import numpy as np
data = np.random.rand(3, 5, 7)
p = pd.panel(data)
p
```

Outputs:

```
<class 'pandas.core.panel.Panel'>
Dimensions: 3 (items) * 5 (major_axis) * 7 (minor_axis)
     Items exist: 0 to 2
 Major_axis axis: 0 to 4
 Minor_axis axis: 0 to 6
```

Q.113. What is the use of dropna() function in Pandas? Give an example to explain.

Ans. If we want to remove the missing values from the dataset, then we use dropna() function. It takes axis argument. By default, axix = 0 *i.e.*, along a row which means that if any value within a row is NaN then the whole row is excluded.

For example,

```
import pandas as pd
import numpy as np
```

```
df = pd.DataFrame(np.random.randn(5, 3), index = ['a', 'c'],
columns = (['one', 'two', 'three'])
df = df.reindex(['a', 'b' , 'c'])
        print df.dropna( )
```

Inputs:

	one	two	three
a	-0.7788	0.3456	0.9876
b	NaN	NaN	NaN
c	5.567	3.1417	-2.3345

Outpus:

	one	two	three
a	-0.7788	0.3456	0.9876
c	5.567	3.1417	-2.3345

That is, with axis = 0 *i.e.*, along a row, drop all NaN values.

Similarly, we write axis = 1, then it will be done column-wise.

Q.114. Distinguish between data smoothing and outlier detection of noisy data.

Ans. Data smoothing refers to techniques that eliminate unwanted noise or behaviors in data. On the other hand, outlier detection identifies data points that are significantly different from the rest. Smoothing of data can be sone by three methods- binning method, regression and outlier analysis.

Binning method: It smooths a sorted data value by consulting its 'neighbors' i.e., the values around it. The sorted values are distributed into a number of bins. Note that this is also known as local smoothing because binning methods consult a neighborhood of values. Also, we can smooth the data by using median binning method.

Smoothing by Regression: Regression can also be used for data smoothing which is a technique that conforms data values to a function. Like linear regression helps in finding the best line to fit two attributes or variables so that one attribute can be used to predict values of the other variable.

Outlier Analysis: Outliers may be detected by clustering where similar values are organized into groups or clusters. Note that the values that lie outside the set of clusters may be considered outliers.

Q.115. Define the following data preprocessing methods-

a. **Data cleaning.**

b. **Data integration.**

c. **Data transformation.**

d. **Data reduction.**

Ans. *a.* **Data cleaning:** It is the process of removing noise and correcting inconsistencies in the data.

b. **Data integration:** It involves merging of data from different sources.

c. **Data transformation/ normalization:** It is the process of organizing database to remove redundancy.

d. **Data reduction:** It is the process of reducing data size by eliminating redundant features.

Q.116. Distinguish between syntactic transformations and semantic transformations.

Ans. Syntactic Transformation are those transformations that can be done by applying a formula or a program on the input values like Celsius temperature to Fahrenheit.

On the other hand, transformation that require finding the mappings between the input and output values in a repository of data are known as semantic transformations. Like changing date format from mm-dd to dd-mm.

Q.117. Define data reduction or dimensionality reduction.

Ans. Dimensionality reduction means deriving new features from the old ones. This is done by applying transforms to the dataset which change the axes/ coordinate system of the graph by moving and rotating them. This can be written as a matrix that we apply to the data. This enables us to combine features and identify useful data. One such technique is PCA *i.e.*, Principal Component Analysis. PCA is a useful statistical technique. It is used for finding patterns in in high dimensional data.

Q.118. What is the need of Pandas when Python is already there?

Ans. It has been observed that Python is great for munging data and preparing data while Pandas is good for data analysis and modeling. Pandas provides fast, flexible and better data structures to make working with labeled data better and better. It allows for complex hierarchical data structures to be accessed using Pandas functions in a better way. Please note that you can merge and join datasets as well as convert many types of data into the ubiquitous Pandas data objects known as DataFrames. Also note that Pandas is based on NumPy and shares the speed of the Python library. Pandas DataFrames are used to store data in rectangular grids. A DataFrame can contain other DataFrames, a 1D series of data, a NumPy tensor and dictionaries for tensors and matrices.

Q.119. What is the purpose of MatPlotLib?

Ans. It is a library that adds the missing data visualization functions to Python. It provides Python, an object-oriented API for embedded plots into applications using general purpose GUI interfaces. Matplotlib provides a procedural version called as PyLab.

Q.120. Can you install NumPy and Pandas on Raspberry Pi?

Ans. The following commands may be used: -

sudo apt-get install python3-numpy

sudo apt-get install python3-pandas

Q.121. Explain the data structures used by Pandas.

Ans. Two basic data structures in Pandas are Series and DataFrame. Series is 1D and DataFrame is 2D. for doing feature engineering, Pandas has a lot of inbuilt functions that can be applied directly of Series and DataFrames.

Q.122. How will you install Pandas?

Ans. We can do it with the use of pip command-

pip install pandas

Pandas comes with default Anaconda package. After its installation is complete, we firstly import it. Also, we can check for Pandas version as follows: -

```
import pandas
print pandas._version_
```

This command will print the version of Pandas that is installed in your system.

How to read csv file?

The following command can do this-

csv_file = pandas.read_csv(filename)

SUMMARY

Data is omnipresent and has become a buzzword today. It is limitless and ranges from your wardrobe to space stations. Data when processed becomes information, information when processed becomes knowledge and in knowledge lies the power. Data science is like nutrition to AI. According to Tim Berners-Lee, "Data is a precious thing and will last longer than the systems themselves".

Different skills are required to shift to AI and its subset data science. Job opportunities in this field of data science are mushrooming at a large scale.

MULTIPLE CHOICE QUESTIONS

1. **Select the command that will create a list-**

   (*a*) list1 = list( ) (*b*) list1 = [ ]

   (*c*) list1 = list([1, 2, 3]) (*d*) All of the above

2. **Give the output of list("hello")-**

   (*a*) ['h', 'e', 'l', 'l', 'o'] (*b*) ['hello']

   (*c*) ['llo'] (*d*) ['olleh']

3. **Say, list1 is [2445, 133, 12454, 123] then, max(list1) is-**

   (*a*) 2445 (*b*) 133

   (*c*) 12454 (*d*) 123

4. **Say, list1 is [1, 5, 9] then sum(list1) is-**
(*a*) 1 (*b*) 9
(*c*) 15 (*d*) Error

5. **Give the output-**
>>>list1 = [11, 2, 23]
>>>list2 = [11, 2, 2]
>>>list1 < list2
(*a*) True (*b*) False
(*c*) Error (*d*) None

6. **Give the output-**
numb = [1, 2, 3, 4]
numb.append([5, 6, 7, 8])
print(len(numbers))
(*a*) 4 (*b*) 5
(*c*) 8 (*d*) 12

7. **Say, list is [2, 33, 222, 14, 25]. What will be list[-1]?**
(*a*) Error (*b*) None
(*c*) 25 (*d*) 2

8. **Give the output of the following code snippet-**
>>>list("a#b#c#d".split('#'))
(*a*) ['a', 'b', 'c', 'd'] (*b*) ['a b c d']
(*c*) ['a#b#c#d'] (*d*) ['abcd']

9. **Give the output-**
>>>t = [1, 2, 3, 4]
>>>t[1:3]
(*a*) [1, 2] (*b*) [1, 2, 4]
(*c*) [2, 4] (*d*) [2, 4, 3]

10. **Give the output-**
>>>t = [1, 2]
>>>2 * t
(*a*) [1, 2, 1, 2] (*b*) [1, 1, 2, 2]
c) (1, 1, 2, 2) (*d*) None of the above

11. **If a = [1, 2, 3, 4] then a[1: -1] is-**
(*a*) Error, no tuple slicing possible (*b*) [2, 3]
(*c*) (2, 3, 4) (*d*) (2, 3)

12. **Give the output-**
>>>a = [2, 3, 4]
>>>sum(a, 3)
(*a*) Too many arguments for sum( ) method
(*b*) The method sum( ) does not exist for tuples
(*c*) 12
(*d*) 9

13. **Is the following code correct?**
>>>a, b, c = 1, 2, 3
>>>a, b, c
(*a*) Yes, [1, 2, 3] is the output (*b*) No, invalid syntax
(*c*) Yes, [1, 2, 3] is printed (*d*) 1 is printed

14. Which of the following statements will create an empty set?

(*a*) {} (*b*) set( )

(*c*) [] (*d*) ()

15. Give the output of following code-

>>>a = {1, 2, 3, 4}

>>>b = {4, 3, 2, 1}

>>> a == b

(*a*) True (*b*) False

16. Which of these is not true about frozen set?

(*a*) Mutable data type

(*b*) Allows duplicate values

(*c*) Data type with unordered values

(*d*) Immutable data type

17. Give the output-

>>>a = {1, 2, 3}

>>>b = a.add(4)

>>>b

(*a*) None (*b*) {1, 2, 3, 4}

(*c*) {1, 2, 3} (*d*) Nothing is printed

18. Give the output-

s = set( )

type(s)

(*a*) <'set'> (*b*) <class 'set'>

(*c*) set (*d*) class set

19. What is the output of the code snippet-

z = set('abc$de')

'a' in z

(*a*) True (*b*) False

(*c*) No output (*d*) Error

20. The _______________ functions removes the first element of a set and the last element of a list.

(*a*) remove (*b*) pop

(*c*) discard (*d*) dispose

21. Which of the following statements creates a dictionary?

(*a*) d = { } (*b*) d = {"john" :40, "peter":45}

(*c*) d = {40: "john", 45: "peter"} (*d*) All of the above.

22. From the code given below, pick out the keys-

d = {"john": 40, "peter": 45}

(*a*) "john", 40, 45 and "peter" (*b*) "john" and "peter"

(*c*) 40 and 45 (*d*) d = (40: "john", 45: "peter")

23. Give the output-

>>>a = {1:"A", 2: "B", 3: "C"}

>>>del a

(*a*) method del does not exist for the dictionary

(*b*) del deletes the values in the dictionary

(*c*) del deletes the entire dictionary

(*d*) del deletes the keys in the dictionary

24. Give the output-
test = {1: 'A', 2: 'B', 3:'C'}
test = { }
print(len(test))

(*a*) 0 (*b*) None
(*c*) 3 (*d*) An exception is thrown

25. How many elements are in m?
m = [[x, y] for x in range (0, 4) for y in range (0, 4)]

(*a*) 8 (*b*) 12
(*c*) 16 (*d*) 32

26. Which of the following software is needed to install ML packages-

(*a*) Miniconda (*b*) Anaconda
(*c*) Conda (*d*) None of the above.

27. Which of the following statement is correct to install numpy package-

(*a*) Miniconda install numpy
(*b*) Conda install numpy
(*c*) Activate install numpy
(*d*) None of the above

28. Choose the correct statement-

(*a*) NumPy's main object is a homogeneous multidimensional array
(*b*) In NumPy, dimensions are called as axes
(*c*) NumPy's array class is called ndarray
(*d*) All of the above

29. Which of the following is used for ML in Python?

(*a*) scikit-learn (*b*) seaborn-learn
(*c*) stats-learn (*d*) None of the above

30. Which of the following function provides unsupervised prediction-

(*a*) cl_forecast (*b*) cl_nowcast
(*c*) cl_present (*d*) None of the above

31. The command used to install NumPy in Ubuntu is-

(*a*) sudo apt-get install python-numpy (*b*) apt-get install python-n
(*c*) install numpy (*d*) None of the above

32. What are the packages that belong to ML-

(*a*) NumPy and SciPy (*b*) SymPy and Pandas
(*c*) Matplotlib (*d*) All of the above

ANSWERS

1. (*d*)	**2.** (*a*)	**3.** (*c*)	**4.** (*c*)	**5.** (*b*)
6. (*b*)	**7.** (*c*)	**8.** (*a*)	**9.** (*c*)	**10.** (*a*)
11. (*d*)	**12.** (*c*)	**13.** (*c*)	**14.** (*b*)	**15.** (*a*)
16. (*a*)	**17.** (*d*)	**18.** (*b*)	**19.** (*a*)	**20.** (*b*)
21. (*d*)	**22.** (*b*)	**23.** (*c*)	**24.** (*a*)	**25.** (*c*)
26. (*a*)	**27.** (*b*)	**28.** (*d*)	**29.** (*a*)	**30.** (*d*)
31. (*a*)	**32.** (*d*)			

EXERCISE QUESTIONS

1. With the help of a neat diagram, explain the steps involved in data science.
2. What are the different types of variations?
3. Explain the fit of a model.
4. What is overfitting and underfitting?
5. What is NumPy? How will you install NumPy?
6. What is slicing in NumPy?
7. Explain Boolean indexing.
8. Perform matrix addition and multiplication in NumPy.
9. What is broadcasting? Explain the rules of broadcasting.
10. What is Pandas?
11. How to create series and data frames?
12. Define reindexing.
13. Explain bfill and ffill.
14. Explain merge functions w.r.t. data frame.
15. Explain rolling function.
16. Explain concat method with examples.
17. How will you print a histogram in Pandas?
18. How to select k in KNN algorithm?
19. Does MS Excel have any support for statistics?
20. What are the differences between AI, ML and DL?
21. Can you apply the data science process model for a restaurant?
22. Visit a Grocery mall near you. Perform the following-
    a. Identify the different data points available to them.
    b. Identify the types of analytics possible in this grocery store.
    c. What are the data available in the store for descriptive analytics?
    d. What kind of prediction would the grocery store need to do?
23. Write short notes on R and its IDE RStudio.
24. A five-star hotel wants to create a database of their customers who book rooms on a daily basis. The data are given in the following table-

Cust_Name	Room_Type	Length_of_stay	Meals_Selection	Type_of_Visit
Gaurav	Standard	5 days	Non-veg	Personal
Hansen	Premium	3 days	Veg	Business
Sandeep	Suite	2 days	Veg	Business
Rahul	Standard	6 days	Non-veg	Personal

    a. Create a data frame in Python using the data.
    b. Assign row index as C1, C2, C3, C4 and C5.
    c. Select 3 columns Cust_Name, Room_Type, Length_of_stay to send it to reception.

d. Add a new column Cab_Services with data yes, no, yes, yes using the insert command.

e. Drop a row C4 from the dataset.

f. Sort the data frame by Length_of_stay.

g. Group the data by the type of visit and the room.

25. Visit the Cowin site of Govt. of India www.cowin.gov.in. create a database using Python containing data about the latest vaccine (covaxin, or covishield) given to the people in a particular area. The database should contain the following columns: -

Vaccine_Name Approval_Agency No_of_Doses_given Successful

26. Consider the dataset from the following link:

https://www.kaggle.com/uciml/autompg-dataset

The attributes are as follows: -

- Fixed acidity.
- Volatile acidity
- Density.
- pH
- alcohol
- sugar

Answer the following queries: -

a. Load the dataset.

b. Identify the dimensions, structure and summary of dataset.

c. Plot the histogram/ bar plot for the variables.

d. Check if the dataset has any "na" values.

e. Standardize the continuous variables.

27. Net profit (in crores) for five different banks is as follows. Develop a 3D pie chart in Python for the data-

Bank	Net Profit (in crores)
India Bulls	1500
Axis Bank	600
Kotak Mahindra	930
PNB	555
Canara Bank	800

28. Identify the type of machine learning algorithm that you will apply in the scenarios given below: -

a. Studying the molecular structure of organic compounds.

b. Using Natural Language Processing (NLP) to do sentiment analysis.

c. Sales of Maruti car in the company.

d. Whether student will get campus placement or NOT?

e. Plant disease classifier.

29. Visit www.amazon.in website for ecommerce. Browse through its webpages and analyze the website in terms of its navigations. Make a list of features that will help customers to search for required products. Which ML algorithm can be used or is being used by them to increase the customer's experience?

30. Visit a coffee shop near your home. Identify the type of ML algorithm that can be used to understand the order in which the customers place order for coffee.

31. Visit a hotel booking website like expedia.com. download the recent customer reviews and do sentiment analysis. Provide the sentiments of the customers about the hotel, whether it is positive or negative. Give your comments too.

GLOSSARY

1. **Adaline:** It is an abbreviation for a linear neuron (ADAptiveLINear Element).
2. **Adaptation:** A training method that proceeds through the specified sequence of inputs, calculating the output, error and network adjustment for each input vector in the sequence as the inputs are presented.
3. **Adaptive Learning Rate:** A learning rate that is adjusted according to an algorithm during training to minimize the training time.
4. **Backtracking Search:** A linear search routine that begins with a step multiplier of 1 and then backtracks until an acceptable reduction in the performance is obtained.
5. **Batch:** A matrix of input or target vectors applied to the network simultaneously.
6. **Bayesian framework:** Assumes that the weights and biases of the network are random variables with specified distributions.
7. **Bias:** A neuron parameter that is summed up with the neuron's weighted inputs and passed through the neuron's transfer function to generate the neuron's output.
8. **Bias vector:** A column vector of bias values for a layer of neurons.
9. **Cascade Forward Network:** A layered network in which each layer only receives inputs from the previous layers.
10. **Classification:** An association of an input vector with a particular target vector.
11. **Competitive Learning:** The unsupervised training of a competitive layer with the instar rule or Kohonen rule. Individual neurons learn to become feature detectors.
12. **Conjugate Gradient Algorithm:** In the conjugate gradient algorithm, a search is performed along the conjugate directions which produces generally faster convergence than a search along the steepest descent directions.
13. **Connection:** A one-way link between neurons in a network.
14. **Connection Strength:** The strength of a link between two neurons in a network. It is also called as weight.
15. **Cycle:** A single presentation of an input vector, calculation of output and new weights and biases.
16. **Dead Neurons:** A competitive layer neuron that never won any competition during training.
17. **Delta Rule:** A learning rule used to train single layer linear networks.
18. **Distance:** The distance between neurons that is computed from their positions with a distance function.
19. **Early Stopping:** A technique based on dividing the data into three subsets. The first subset is the training set used for computing the gradient and updating the network weights and biases. The second subset is the validation set. When the validation error increases for a specified number of iterations, the training is stopped and the weights and the biases at the minimum of the validation error are returned. The third sbset is the test set. It is used to verify the network design.
20. **Epoch:** The presentation of the set of training vectors to a network and the calculation of new weights and biases. The training vectors may be represented one at a time or all together in a batch.
21. **Error Jumping:** A sudden increase in a networks sum-squared error during training. This happens due to large learning rate.
22. **Error Ratio:** A training parameter used with adaptive learning rate and momentum training of back propagation networks.
23. **Function Approximation:** The task performed by a network trained to respond to inputs with an approximation of a desired function.

24. **Global Minimum:** The lowest value of a function over the entire range of its input parameters.
25. **Gradient Descent:** The process of making changes to the weights and biases where the changes are proportional to the derivatives of the network error with respect to those weights and biases. This is done to minimize network error. This is done to find the global minimum of error for a network.
26. **Hard limit transfer function:** A transfer that maps inputs greater-than or equal to 0 or 1 and all other values to 0.
27. **Hebb learning rule:** It is the first proposed learning rule for neurons. Weights are adjusted proportional to the product of the outputs of pre and post –weight neurons.
28. **Home Neuron:** A neuron at the center of a neighbourhood.
29. **Learning:** The process by which weights and biases are adjusted to achieve some desired network behaviour.
30. **Local Minimum:** The minimum of a function over a limited range of input values. A local minimum may not be the global minimum.
31. **Mean Square Error Function:** The performance function that calculates the average squared error between the network outputs and the target outputs.
32. **Momentum:** A technique used to make it less likely for a backpropagation networks to get caught in a shallow minima.
33. **Outstar Learning Rule:** A learning rule that trains a neuron's output weight vector to take on the values of the current output vector of the post-weight layer.
34. **Overfitting:** A situation in which the error on training set is driven to a very small value but when new data is presented to the network, the error is large.
35. **Pass:** Each traverse through all of the training input and target vectors.
36. **Pattern Recognition:** The task performed by a network trained to respond when an input vector close to a learned vector is presented. The network recognizes the input as one of the original target vectors.
37. **Perceptron:** A single layer network with a hard-limit transfer function.
38. **Performance:** The behaviour of a network.
39. **Pre-processing:** To perform some transformation of the input or target data before it is presented to the neural network.
40. **Post-processing:** It converts normalized outputs back into the same units that were used for the original targets.
41. **Principal Component Analysis (PCA):** To orthogonalize the components of network input vectors. It also reduces the dimensions of the input vectors by eliminating redundant components.
42. **Resilient Back Propagation:** A training algorithm that eliminates the harmful effect of having a small slope at the extreme ends of the sigmoid squashing transfer functions.
43. **Sigmoid: Monotonic S** : shaped mapping numbers in the interval, to a finite interval such as (-1, +1) or (0, 1).
44. **Sum squared error:** The sum of squared differences between the network targets and the actual outputs for a given input vector or set of vectors.
45. **Update:** To make changes in weights and biases.
46. **Validation Vectors:** A set of input vectors that is used to monitor training progress so as to keep the network from overtraining/overfitting.
47. **Weight Matrix:** A matrix containing connection strengths from a layer's inputs to its neurons.
48. **Widrow** : Hoff Learning Rule: A learning rule used to train single layer linear networks. It is also called as Delta rule.

APPENDIX-B: MODEL QUESTION PAPERS

1. What is a neural network? Explain its need.
2. Differentiate between single layer and multi-layer neural networks.
3. Describe the working of the single layer perceptron neural network.
4. Which type of activation function is used:-
   a. In single layer perceptron network.
   b. In multilayer perceptron network.
5. Write different steps in backpropagation algorithm.
6. Distinguish between feedback and feed-forward neural networks.
7. Draw and explain Boltzmann machine in detail.
8. Explain unsupervised learning neural networks.
9. Distinguish between supervised and unsupervised learning.
10. Explain PCA in detail.
11. Describe SOMs.
12. What are SVMs? Discuss their characteristics.
13. What is reinforcement learning? How does the passive reinforcement learning differ from active reinforcement learning?
14. Define direct utility estimation.
15. Define curse of dimensionality.
16. How is big data and deep learning related?
17. What do you mean by deep neural networks?
18. Illustrate decision trees learning technique with a suitable example.
19. Write a short note on Naive Bayes model of statistical learning.
20. What is clustering? Explain k-mean clustering technique.
21. Compare weights and bias.
22. Write a short note on learning rate.
23. Which factor improves the performance of bias?
24. If the net input to an output neuron is 0.64, calculate its output when the activation function is-
   a. Binary sigmoidal.
   b. Bipolar sigmoidal.
   [**Hint:** Net input to the neuron = 0.64
   a. For binary sigmoidal activation function,
   $Y = \text{f(netinput)} = 1/\ (1+ e^{-0.64}) = 0.6548$
   b. For bipolar sigmoidal actiovation function,
   $Y = \text{f(netinput)} = 2/\ (1+ e^{-0.64}) = 0.3095$
25. Differentiate between local minima and global minima.
26. Explain RNNs.
27. What is a confusion matrix?
28. Write short note on Learning Vector Quantization (LVQ).

29. Describe the basic structure of a biological neuron. How this model has been adapted in ANNs like Pitts model or Perceptron model.
30. Differentiate between classification and recognition.
31. Construct a feed forward network with 3 neurons in input layer 2 in hidden layer and 2 in output layer. Explain the concept of input vector, connection matrix and activation functions.
32. Explain how a neural network can be trained using back propagation? Derive equation for weight modification in a multi-layer perception model. What role is played by learning rate and momentum?
33. What is delta learning rule?
34. What is overfitting?
35. Explain the term 'fully connected'.
36. What is beam search? Write its algorithm
37. Explain convergence rule for learning.
38. What is feature mapping?
39. Define generalization. On what factors does it depends?
40. Define cross validation.
41. Explain early stopping.
42. Explain regularization.
43. How can overtraining or overfitting be avoided?
44. Compare RBN network with MLP.
45. What is machine learning? Give an overview of ML with a suitable diagram.
46. How is training data set different from testing dataset.
47. What are hard margin SVM and soft margin SVM?
48. Explain ML approach to Knowledge Acquisition.
49. What are the main goals of ML.
50. Explain the three step data preparation process in ML.
51. Explain LDA.
52. Distinguish between generative model and conditional model.
53. Explain k-nearest neighbour learning.
54. What is inductive machine learning?
55. Explain EM algorithm.
56. What is LSI? Write its algorithm.
57. Explain MDPs.
58. Write short notes on- 'Bellman Equation and LQR'.
59. Explain Q-Learning for LQR.
60. Write a note on POMDPS.
61. What is Reinforcement learning? Who gave it? How does it relate to Neuro-dynamic programming? Is RL useful in operations research field? Is it related to Neuroscience?
62. Explain the jargon of Q-values, Q-tables and Q-functions.
63. What is contingency table? How is it useful?
64. What are context units in RNNs? Define unfolding in time and back propagation through time. What are Real-time recurrent learning?
65. Is classification a supervised way of learning. Explain.
66. Explain Q-learning.
67. Explain the value function in context of reinforcement learning.
68. Distinguish between shallow learning and deep learning architectures.
69. What are deep belief networks?
70. With a neat sketch explain CNN architecture.
71. Explain the term large scale deep learning.

72. Explain the relation between deep learning and the five V's of Big Data.
73. What is an auto-encoder?
74. Explain deep Boltzmann machines.
75. Why is deep learning vital? Explain transfer learning.
76. Discuss in details the applications of deep learning and their architectures.
77. What is word embedding? Where is it used?
78. Explain deep neural network architecture, layerwise.
79. Explain noise robustness.
80. Explain the term 'Dropout'.
81. Explain the following:-
    a. Bidirectional RNNs.
    b. Deep Recurrent Networks.
    c. Recursive Neural Networks.
82. Explain the deep learning approach to structured probabilistic models.
83. Discuss about H_2O tool used in deep learning. What are the minimum requirements for its installation?
84. Explain the role of TensorFlow tool in deep learning.
85. Explain the following:-
    a. Deep Neural Networks
    b. Deep Machine Learning
    c. Deep Web Intelligence
    d. Deep Big Data
    e. Deep Machine Intelligence.
86. What is maxpooling?
87. What is sequence analysis? Give some examples from real-life.
88. Explain Neural Turing Machines and their architectures?
89. What are differentiable neural computers? Explain.
90. List down the applications of deep neural networks.
91. Explain Capacity, Overfitting and Underfitting.
92. Explain the model for sequence analysis.
93. Explain the 3-tier architecture for feed-forward neural network.
94. What is Gradient Descent?
95. How the complete dataset is divided during training?
96. Define an Epoch.
97. What are hyperparameters of a model?
98. With a flowchart, explain the workflow for training a deep learning model.
99. What is regularization? Explain mathematically.
100. What are the advantages of TensorFlow.
101. How do you optimize deep learning models.
102. Explain critical points and saddle points.
103. What is momentum based optimization?
104. What is an ImageNet challenge?
105. What is batch normalization?
106. Distinguish between local normalized network and global normalized network.
107. What are vanishing gradients?
108. What are machine learning pipelines?
109. RNNs are Turing complete. Explain.
110. What is deep reinforcement learning? Explain rewards, action and action terms related to it.
111. What is Q-learning and Deep Q-learning?

REFERENCES

[1] http://sciencemag.org/content/293/5539/2425.

[2] Ethem Alpaydin, "Introduction to Machine Learning", Third Edition, PHI learning.

[3] Rajiv Chopra, "Web Engineering", First Edition, PHI learning.

[4] Nikhil Buduma, "Fundamentals of Deep Learning", O' Reilly, Delhi.

[5] Cloud Computing: An Introduction by Dr. Rajiv Chopra (Mercury Learning and Information USA, 2018 ; listed in Library Catalogue, USA).

[6] E. Crego et al., "Big Data and Deep Learning", Business Online, 2013.

[7] G. Hinton, "A Practical Guide to Training Restricted Boltzmann Machines", Department of Computer Science, Univ. Toronto, Canada, 2010.

[8] Rajiv Chopra, "Testing Web Applications: The state of art and future trends", First Edition, Cambridge International Science Publishing, UK.

[9] K. Uma Rao, " AI and Neural Networks", First Impression, Pearson Education, 2011.

[10] Rajiv Chopra, "Artificial Intelligence", Reprint 2020, S. Chand & company.

[11] Rajiv Chopra, "Machine Learning", 2nd Edition, 2020 Khanna Publishing.

[12] Rajiv Chopra, "Deep Learning", 2nd Edition, 2020 Khanna publishing.

[13] Rajiv Chopra, "Advancd IoT", 1st Edition, 2020, Saddle Publishers.